Walker's Manual
of
Unlisted Stocks

Walker's Manual of Unlisted Stocks

Published by:

Walker's Manual, LLC
3650 Mt. Diablo Blvd., Suite 240
Lafayette, California 94549-9957

Copyright © 1996 by Walker's Manual, LLC

First Printing 1996

Printed in the United States of America

ISBN 0-9652088-9-3

Dedicated to

the contribution made by many

of the companies in this book

to the growth and transformation of

America

through their business achievements.

Building America

Our first edition of *Walker's Manual of Unlisted Stocks* includes historical vignettes about eight of the companies in our book who are nearing or have exceeded their first century in age. We hope you will enjoy reading about these made-in-America success stories.

Table of Contents

Preface

In the summer of 1995, I stumbled upon the financial statements of two companies not listed on any of the stock exchanges: **Alaska Power & Telephone** and **American River Holdings**. This excited me. Both were above average performers and yet neither company was covered in any of the informational investment publications or databases. In addition to my own research, I asked three astute investors to see what they could find. They all returned empty-handed and curious.

As I increased my research efforts more of these companies appeared. I like to refer to them as the *friendly* unlisted companies. They include **Bozzuto's**, **Decker Manufacturing Corporation**, **The Fisher Companies**, and **Robroy Industries**. Again, they were all strong performers with no accessible public information. Most of the companies profiled in this book fall into the friendly category.

Thinking to myself that this information isn't all that difficult to locate, I wondered why someone hadn't already compiled it. The real challenge emerged when I discovered the *secretive* unlisted companies. These include public companies that for a variety of reasons would like to be considered private and do not want public exposure. **Rand McNally** told me they were private, but within ten minutes and a call to my stockbroker, I became a shareholder.

The universe of unlisted companies includes many secretive ones. The response of the company's representative when asked for a copy of the annual report is a good clue. Most public companies are delighted that you are expressing interest and promptly oblige with information. But when the representative begins quizzing you as to who you are and why you want the information, and then states that only shareholders are entitled to financial information, you know you have found a secretive company. When you tell this person that you are not a shareholder but would like to consider buying some shares, you receive a very abrupt rebuff. These companies may be excellent investment opportunities, but require more effort on your part in order to understand their merits.

For example, advertisements in *The Sheboygan Press* and *The Commercial Appeal* resulted in reports obtained for **Kohler Co.** and **Anderson-Tully Company**, respectively. Both of these companies trade for in excess of $100,000 per share (don't worry, those prices are the exceptions, not the rule). Existing shareholders, feeling deprived of an active market, also volunteered reports on such companies as **Kentucky River Coal**, **Carolina Mills**, **Case Pomeroy**, **Hershey Creamery**, **A.D. Makepeace**, and **Union Pump**.

Peter Lynch, in his book *One Up on Wall Street*, recommends doing your own research to find undiscovered companies, companies with little or no institutional ownership, or simple companies that appear dull or mundane but have price/earnings ratios that make them attractive investment candidates, and I concur. Bank stocks are a good example. Seldom can you buy stock in a great company at six or seven times earnings and at a price as low as fifty percent of book value. Don't look for these in the *Wall Street Journal*. Approximately five hundred banks are followed by the financial community. But there are sixteen thousand banks, most of them publicly owned. **Bremen Bancorp** of St. Louis trades only when shares become available. I am number twenty-four on that waiting list. The last trade made was in October 1995 at $50 per share, a time when book value was about $92 a share and the return on equity for the year was in excess of twenty percent. I would happily pay $92 a share, but in this case there is no free market. Pity the selling shareholders who will only get $50 a share. About seventy of these unlisted bank stocks are included in this book.

Local companies offer some of the best investment opportunities. **Ben & Jerry's** is an example of a once unlisted company that raised a little money locally with the intent of preparing a registered offering and exchange listing at a later date. **Real Goods Trading Company**, now traded on the Pacific Stock Exchange, is a newer vintage of the once local company. Companies you may not know about because they are still very local are **Portland Brewing** and **Calyx & Corolla**. Local investment clubs have a great opportunity to track down and follow these emerging companies.

At the midpoint of this project, I obtained a copy of the preface that H.D. Walker used in 1909 to initially introduce *Walker's Manual*. For the first time, I realized that I was doing the same thing as he was near the turn of the century. His task of finding information on companies not available elsewhere must have seemed insurmountable then. Remember, it was a time of little government regulation, minimal accounting standards, no copy or fax machines and no e-mail. I am fortunate in having all of these modern conveniences, but I wonder if I had it any easier in obtaining a good portion of this book's data. To honor Mr. Walker, I conclude by reproducing his original preface, which seems as applicable today as when he wrote it eighty-seven years ago:

> *Walker's Manual of California Securities* has been compiled at the request of a number of bankers, brokers, and investors, with a view to giving reliable information annually regarding the various securities dealt in The Stock and Bond Exchange, San Francisco, and also some of the leading issues which are dealt in unofficially.

> Considerable difficulty has been experienced in obtaining information from some corporations. In such cases every effort has been made to secure reliable information from other sources. It is believed that the benefits of the publication given through this source will be so manifest before the publication of the next annual number, that official statements will be given in all cases.

> Next year's edition of *Walker's Manual* will contain the details of a number of corporations not included in the present number, and also new features. Suggestions as to improvements will be appreciated. - H. D. Walker, 1909

Harry K. Eisenberg, 1996

Acknowledgments

My wife Cindy and I were devastated when on February 7, 1994, our friend Bob Walsh died both suddenly and unexpectedly at the age of forty-six. Bob had been a successful entrepreneur in several fields. He established a publishing business only three years prior to his death and had succeeded in making two separate publications profitable. His plans were to turn around a third book called *Walker's Manual of Western Corporations* as well. This business reference manual was regarded at that time as a dinosaur and was completely outdated compared to its competition. Unfortunately, we will never know what Bob's plans for the book were.

Beth Walsh, his wife, made the decision to continue Bob's business and to begin a new career as a publisher. This decision was made with courage and determination at a time of unequaled pain and personal loss for Beth and her four children, ages 6, 8, 9 and 11. We would like to extend our first acknowledgment to Beth for her unbroken spirit as well as her devotion to her children.

The coming together of unique and diverse individuals to achieve a mutual objective is the beginning of a partnership experience. Ours was also an adventure as we united to develop a new and evolving product. Karen L. Johnston, Walter R. Sikes and I shared in the creation and birth of *Walker's Manual of Unlisted Stocks*. Our process has included a physically arduous twelve plus hours per day, seven days per week production schedule, the mental concentration required for the design and production process, the joy of creation, the spirit of camaraderie and the success of teamwork. I could not have had better partners.

Cindy Eisenberg, my loving and caring wife, was supportive to all of us and, in addition, has left her own significant mark on this book. She edited our text, shared insights and made herself available for any assignment. Most importantly, the short historical vignettes that we have included were authored by her. The companies she wrote about actually participated in the building of America, its culture and our lives. A recurring theme is that each of these successful companies honor the contributions of their employees and celebrate the rewarding combination of human spirit and entrepreneurial challenge. We wish to thank and acknowledge the companies and/or their shareholders who have provided us with the historical information that Cindy used in preparing her summaries: Finch, Pruyn & Co., Hershey Creamery, Keller Manufacturing, Kohler Co., Louisville Bedding, Rand McNally, Stonecutter Mills and Troy Mills.

My special thanks to Drew Field, author of *Take Your Company Public* and renowned expert on direct public offerings, for his patient counsel and constant encouragement.

We would not have published this book without clearly understanding securities laws, rules and regulations. We appreciate all of the advice we received from Donald C. Reinke of the Oakland law firm of Pezzola & Reinke, Mike Jacobson of the Palo Alto office of Cooley, Godward, Tatum, Castro & Huddleson, the San Francisco law offices of Richard D. Silberman, Curtis W. Berner of the San Francisco firm of Buell & Berner, the San Francisco offices of Joel Wallock, and Lee A. Trucker of the San Francisco firm of Trucker & Huss. The technical competence and accessibility of these individuals deserves the highest accolade.

One of the delights of this project has been making new friends, and I have made many. One individual in particular has had a great impact throughout our development process. To appreciate his contribution, you first must understand that many of the included securities are unknown to the investing public. Only a handful of investors around the country follow these stocks. There is a giant among them; namely Ed McLaughlin. Ed is the modern day father of this specialty: dealing with hard-to-find securities and even harder-to-find information. He developed an interest in these securities while on Wall Street and has been a very successful investor for his own account. Ed has also paved the way for many of the people who have since become significant players in this field. He unselfishly shares his knowledge and experiences and lays out a map for the rest of us to follow. A collector of 19th century art, antiques and fine French wines, Ed is also a collector of fine stocks. His collection would impress any connoisseur. Thank you Ed. We could not have done it without you.

Walker's Manual of Unlisted Stocks

Introduction

This first edition of *Walker's Manual of Unlisted Stocks* is being published in response to a growing demand on the part of investors and the financial community for information on companies traded in the over-the-counter market or those traded only through private transactions. Information on the majority of these companies is not readily available and when available it is usually not complete enough for investment analysis.

The proliferation of information available for companies traded on the major stock exchanges and the monitoring of most of these companies by institutional investors and the financial press has caused many respected investment experts to recommend that investors try to find these entities before they become well known. According to experts, early discovery may allow for investment before share prices are affected by institutional investing activity or the financial press. Another factor is that after companies start trading on major exchanges and reporting their earnings quarterly, they may become focused on short-term rather than long-term results and their long-term performance may suffer.

Listed vs. Unlisted Securities

Those companies whose securities are listed and traded on the major exchanges such as the New York Stock Exchange (NYSE), The American Stock Exchange (AMEX), and the National Association of Securities Dealers Automated Quotation System (NASDAQ) can differ from those that are traded through market makers (firms that facilitate trading in unlisted securities) or through private transactions. Companies listed on the major exchanges are generally, but not always, larger and usually have more shareholders. Listed companies must meet a number of criteria regarding:

- Asset base
- Number of shares publicly traded
- Total market value of the shares traded

Companies trading through market makers or private transactions are less concerned with the above. These companies may not want their shares listed for other reasons, including:

- Substantial listing fees
- Securities and Exchange Commission (SEC) quarterly and annual filing requirements
- Exposure to public review and comment on management's decisions
- Interference by outside investors and related reporting requirements

However, if management's primary responsibility is to maximize shareholder value, then a company should *insure that there is a market for its shares*. Viable markets provide shareholders with the ability to realize an investment's value. Many times management loses sight of the fact that the shareholders are the owners. Making sure there is a market for desired stock transactions should be an objective of management.

Trading in Unlisted Securities

Most people think that *publicly traded* refers to companies listed on the NYSE, AMEX or NASDAQ. Trading in these markets is easy. Daily share prices are listed in most papers and up to the minute information on the latest trades and prices is available via online services. An investor simply has to contact a brokerage firm, tell a representative the name, price and quantity of the desired purchase and the transaction can be executed immediately. These markets are very efficient, with hundreds of millions of shares being bought and sold each day.

Buying and selling unlisted securities is not always as straightforward. The first step involved is usually the same; the investor communicates with a brokerage firm regarding the security to be purchased. If the security is unlisted, the broker will review the Pink Sheets, the OTC Bulletin Board or the National Quotation Bureau's Stock Summary to determine which market maker handles the company. The broker contacts the company's market maker to determine the shares' offering price. If the price is acceptable to the buyer, the transaction is completed. Market makers use the Pink Sheets and also the OTC Bulletin Board (which provides online information) to list information on the companies in which they maintain a market.

What Does Publicly Traded Mean?

When a company's securities are offered for public sale by the company or its shareholders, the securities qualify as being *publicly traded*. The number of shares offered, the capital raised, and the offering's geographic dispersion all impact regulatory reporting. Many types of public offerings exist, all with varying filing requirements.

For instance, companies issuing shares with a total market value of less than $5,000,000 to a limited number of investors all of whom reside within the state where the company does business, may be exempt from annual federal reporting requirements. Companies qualifying for this exemption, however, are generally required to provide potential shareholders with certain information prior to their purchase of shares and, in some cases, annually thereafter. A bank serving a single metropolitan area, as an example, may raise adequate capital without relinquishing its exemption from regulatory filing requirements. **American River Holdings**, a bank featured in this book, raised $3.3 million in 1983 via such a public stock offering. This allowed it to become a viable competitor in its market. With forty-eight consecutive profitable quarters and performance ratios which rank high according to industry standards, the bank has been a success. On the other hand, a larger bank serving the needs of an entire state might find it difficult to raise enough capital in a stock offering and still stay below the reporting exemption threshold.

Once shares have been issued and trading is taking place, regardless of the type of offering, they are considered *publicly traded* whether there are ten or ten thousand shareholders and irrespective of whether the trading takes place on the NYSE or via the Pink Sheets.

Other Markets

In addition to the major markets and the over-the-counter market, several other markets exist for securities trading. The Philadelphia, Chicago, Boston and Pacific Stock Exchanges are available for listings. Many U.S. companies also list on the Vancouver, Montreal and Toronto Stock Exchanges in Canada. Each of these has its own listing requirements.

Other unique markets exist. Featured in this book, for example, are several public limited partnerships whose securities are traded by the Chicago Partnership Board (CPB). The CPB provides a secondary market for limited partnership interests and facilitates trading in more than 1,200 limited partnerships with an estimated market value of over $15 billion. One of these, **Aircraft Income Partners L.P.**, raised $193 million in 1988 for the purpose of acquiring aircraft and leasing them to the airline industry. The ownership units of this limited partnership were trading at 80% of their underlying net asset value at December 31, 1995.

Investment Considerations

The limited exposure to the investing public of most companies profiled in this book has resulted in a limited or *thin* market for their securities. Investments in these companies may not be as liquid as those in companies traded on the major exchanges and should be viewed as long-term in nature. Actually, many investment advisors would argue that most equity investments should be viewed as long-term. In evaluating the companies profiled in this book, some items to be considered include:

Performance - Several performance statistics are included for each of the profiled companies, such as return on average assets, return on average equity, compounded growth rates (total revenues, net earnings and earnings per share), and return on total revenues (profit margin). Questions that the investor might ask include:

- Is there earnings growth?
- Are the company's earnings comparable to similar size companies?
- What industry norms apply?

Financial Strength - The financial position of the company should be analyzed:

- How does the company's current ratio and debt/equity ratio compare to the industry?
- What is the cash position of the company?
- Have any assets, such as real estate, appreciated above book value?

Products and Markets - Review the nature of the company's business and its future prospects:

- Does the company have a unique product?
- Is there a market niche?
- What is their competitive advantage?

Ownership - Understand the makeup of the profiled company's ownership:

- How many shareholders are there and how many shares are outstanding?
- Is there significant *insider* ownership (i.e., owners that can influence business decisions)?
- Is the company buying back its own shares?

Both the company's financial performance and strength should be reflected in its market price per share. Key ratios to review in this regard are the price/earnings ratio and the price/book value percentage. After answering all of the above questions and comparing the results of these ratios to industry standards, you can make a determination as to the share's price.

Following the presentation of the 500 profiled companies, we include indices that rank the companies by market capitalization, price/earnings ratio, price/book value percentage, compounded growth rates and total revenues. These will give you a quick way to see how the companies compare and to evaluate possible investment opportunities.

After completing your analysis, you may conclude that more information is necessary before you make an investment decision. The firm making a market in the company's stock may be able to provide additional data. The company itself, of course, is the best source of information. Contact details are included for each company as well as its market maker or broker dealer.

The information contained in this book has been obtained from company reports and documents. In most cases the financial information has been audited by the company's independent auditors and/or is a part of a required filing with a governmental agency. While we take significant measures to insure that the information which we present is objective and accurate, Walker's Manual, LLC does not take any responsibility for its underlying accuracy or reliability. The inclusion of companies in this book is not an endorsement of their investment desirability.

Certain of the principals of Walker's Manual, LLC have, in some cases, ownership positions in the profiled companies. In all cases, the principals' combined investment represents less than one percent of the outstanding shares.

Our objective is to bring our readers information on companies that is unavailable elsewhere. We will continue our search for new material to include in future editions of our book.

Company Profiles

The company profiles contained in this book all follow the same format. Individual financial information, ratios and statistical presentation may differ as the appropriate measurement criteria changes from industry to industry. A descriptive review of a sample profiled company follows:

General Corporate Information

Sample Company Name
2300 Falling Springs Road • Sauget, IL 62206-1102 • Telephone (314)353-5800
Company Description
This section lists Company name, address and phone number. Readers interested in contacting the profiled company for more information should use this address. A brief description of the Company's business follows. Industry, principal products, markets, operating locations, subsidiary information, where and when incorporated is noted here. Other information deemed to be helpful in understanding the profiled Company is also included.

Per Share Information

	09/30/95	09/30/94	09/30/93	09/30/92
Per Share Information				
Stock Price	23.00	17.50	12.50	11.50
Earnings Per Share	5.50	6.26	1.93	1.63
Price / Earnings Ratio	4.18	2.80	6.48	7.06
Book Value Per Share	30.98	26.24	20.50	18.97
Price / Book Value %	74.24	66.69	60.98	60.62
Dividends Per Share	0.75	0.52	0.40	0.40

Stock Price - The average bid/ask price for the Company's stock at the end of the year or period presented. Amounts are adjusted retroactively for stock splits and dividends.

Earnings Per Share - Net income after all items divided by average shares outstanding for the period.

Price/Earnings Ratio - This ratio results from dividing the stock price by earnings per share. The ratio is expressed as a multiple; a price/earnings (p/e) of 7.25 means that the shares are trading at 7.25 times earnings.

Book Value Per Share - Total stockholders' equity divided by total shares outstanding at the end of the period.

Price/Book Value % - The percentage relationship between the stock price and the book value per share.

Dividends Per Share - Dividends for the period expressed on a per share basis.

Annual Financial Data (Four years of data are displayed)

Annual Financial Data				
Operating Results (000's)				
Total Revenues	26,820.0	21,334.0	12,945.0	12,744.0
Costs & Expenses	-23,150.0	-17,901.0	-11,878.0	-11,786.0
Income Before Taxes and Other	3,556.0	3,401.0	1,051.0	936.0
Other Items	-502.0	-336.0	-106.0	-167.0
Income Tax	-1,414.0	-1,199.0	-369.0	-282.0
Net Income	1,640.0	1,866.0	576.0	487.0
Cash Flow From Operations	2,393.0	3,995.0	705.0	1,369.0
Balance Sheet (000's)				
Cash & Equivalents	1,368.0	2,576.0	1,238.0	1,420.0
Total Current Assets	9,550.0	8,384.0	6,148.0	5,459.0
Fixed Assets, Net	5,036.0	4,506.0	3,481.0	3,258.0
Total Assets	14,998.0	13,511.0	9,767.0	8,900.0
Total Current Liabilities	2,352.0	2,032.0	1,327.0	1,126.0
Long-Term Debt	N.A.	726.0	58.0	109.0
Stockholders' Equity	9,239.0	7,824.0	6,115.0	5,658.0
Performance & Financial Condition				
Return on Total Revenues %	6.11	8.75	4.45	3.82
Return on Avg Stockholders' Equity %	19.22	26.77	9.79	8.88
Return on Average Assets %	11.51	16.03	6.17	5.58
Current Ratio	4.06	4.13	4.63	4.85
Debt / Equity %	N.A.	9.28	0.95	1.93

Operating Results

Total Revenues	The Company's total sales and revenues.
Costs & Expenses	All costs and expenses for the period.
Income Before Taxes & Other	Total income less all costs & expenses and before minority interest, accounting changes and extraordinary items.
Other Items	Includes minority shareholders' interest in the earnings of a subsidiary, extraordinary items and the cumulative effect of accounting changes. If considered significant, these items will be discussed in Comments.
Income Tax	The total amount of income taxes for the period.
Net Income	Income net of income taxes, extraordinary items and minority interests; used to compute earnings per share.
Cash Flow From Operations	Cash flow generated from operations during the period. This is obtained from the Company's statements of cash flows, which are not presented.

Balance Sheet

Cash & Equivalents	Cash and all items immediately convertible into cash at the end of the year.
Total Current Assets	Those assets which are available to use in the Company's operations during the current fiscal year.
Fixed Assets, Net	The Company's investment in property, plant and equipment.
Total Assets	The sum of all assets at the balance sheet date.
Total Current Liabilities	Those liabilities at the balance sheet date that the Company must satisfy during the current fiscal year.
Long Term Debt	Obligations such as bonds, notes and capital lease obligations, as of the end of the year, which are due more than one year from the balance sheet date.
Stockholders' Equity	The amount by which total assets exceed total liabilities.

Performance and Financial Condition

Three performance measures are calculated for each year presented. These are the Company's Net Income as a percentage of: (1) Total Revenues, (2) Average Stockholders' Equity, and (3) Average Assets.

Two financial condition measures are also presented:

Current Ratio	The ratio of current assets to current liabilities.
Debt/Equity %	Measures debt as a % of equity.

Compound Growth %'s

Compound Growth %'s	EPS %	49.99	Net Income %	49.89	Total Revenues %	28.15

The Company's compound growth rate, expressed in terms of earnings per share, net income, and total revenues is calculated for the years presented.

Comments

Comments
This segment is used to describe and discuss items, transactions or other events affecting the balance sheet or operating results which are significant or help the reader to better understand the Company's operations.

Officers and Ownership Information

Officers	Position	Ownership Information	09/30/95
Christian B. Peper, Jr.	Chairman	Number of Shares Outstanding	298,225
Earl J. Bewig	President, COO	Market Capitalization	$ 6,859,175
Robert H. Schnellbacher	Secretary	Frequency Of Dividends	Quarterly
Robert N. Stewart	Treasurer	Number of Shareholders	212
Gregory D. Fore	VP - Sales		

A listing of the corporate officers along with their positions is presented. Ownership information includes market capitalization which is equal to the stock price multiplied by the year-end shares outstanding. Other ownership information such as year-end shares outstanding and number of shareholders is self explanatory.

Other Information

Other Information						
Transfer Agent	KeyCorp Shareholder Services, Inc.			Where Listed	OTC-BB
Auditor	Kerber, Eck & Braeckel			Symbol	STLO
Market Maker	Burns, Pauli & Co., Inc.	Telephone	(800)325-3373	SIC Code	3320
Broker Dealer	Regular stockbroker			Employees	75

This section contains general corporate information such as number of employees and service providers such as auditors and stock transfer agents. The Company's stock symbol, market maker and broker dealer for stock transactions are also identified. Where Listed abbreviations include the following:

BE.......	Boston Exchange	OTC-PS ..	Over the Counter - Pink Sheets
CE.......	Chicago Exchange	PHL.....	Philadelphia Exchange
CPB	Chicago Partnership Board	PSE	Pacific Stock Exchange
MSE	Montreal Exchange	TSE	Toronto Stock Exchange
OTC-BB..	Over the Counter - Bulletin Board	VSE.....	Vancouver Stock Exhange

Walker's Manual
of
Unlisted Stocks

1st edition

Published by Walker's Manual, LLC
1996

AFA Protective Systems, Inc.

155 Michael Drive • Syosset, NY 11791 • Telephone (516)496-2322 • Fax (516)496-2848

Company Description

Originally founded in 1873, AFA has provided 123 years of uninterrupted central station alarm service to its customers. The Company has also proudly paid dividends to its shareholders for 107 consecutive years. The major portion of the Company's revenue consists of the recurring annual service fees paid by customers for inspection and maintenance services, primarily in the New York City, Long Island, Boston, and North Brunswick areas. The Company also monitors about 12,000 locations for 150 alarm dealers who do not have their own central stations.

	12/31/95	12/31/94	12/31/93	12/31/92
Per Share Information				
Stock Price	117.50	95.00	92.00	80.00
Earnings Per Share	6.70	7.44	8.14	6.29
Price / Earnings Ratio	17.54	12.77	11.30	12.72
Book Value Per Share	68.28	64.02	58.55	52.05
Price / Book Value %	172.09	148.39	157.13	153.70
Dividends Per Share	1.80	1.60	1.60	1.55
Annual Financial Data				
Operating Results (000's)				
Total Revenues	27,817.8	25,913.5	25,262.8	24,321.4
Costs & Expenses	-25,437.1	-23,197.4	-22,266.0	-22,011.3
Income Before Taxes and Other	2,380.7	2,716.1	2,996.8	2,310.1
Other Items	n.a.	n.a.	n.a.	-21.2
Income Tax	-1,042.0	-1,213.0	-1,343.0	-1,007.0
Net Income	1,338.7	1,503.1	1,653.8	1,281.9
Cash Flow From Operations	3,633.6	3,936.6	4,131.5	3,689.9
Balance Sheet (000's)				
Cash & Equivalents	4,564.8	6,446.9	5,466.2	4,850.8
Total Current Assets	10,455.1	10,154.9	9,596.9	8,848.9
Fixed Assets, Net	12,337.7	11,750.8	12,215.1	11,419.7
Total Assets	28,487.3	26,742.4	25,656.0	23,723.7
Total Current Liabilities	3,880.1	3,712.8	4,287.0	3,323.0
Long-Term Debt	2,013.6	754.8	n.a.	n.a.
Stockholders' Equity	13,527.9	12,917.9	11,894.6	10,587.2
Performance & Financial Condition				
Return on Total Revenues %	4.81	5.80	6.55	5.27
Return on Avg Stockholders' Equity %	10.12	12.12	14.71	12.67
Return on Average Assets %	4.85	5.74	6.70	5.57
Current Ratio	2.69	2.74	2.24	2.66
Debt / Equity %	14.89	5.84	n.a.	n.a.

Compound Growth %'s	EPS %	2.13	Net Income %	1.46	Total Revenues %	4.58

Comments

In late 1994, the Company acquired two companies with combined revenues of about $1.2 million. This accounted for more than half of the 1995 revenue increase. A restructuring of operations was started in 1995 whereby there will be a consolidation in receiving alarm signals at four separate locations to one location. Management believes that passage of the Telecommunications Act will create opportunities for the Company, particularly in the area of additional acquisitions. The balance sheet is strong and should be able to support these activities.

Officers	**Position**	**Ownership Information**	**12/31/95**
Philip Kleinman	CEO, President	Number of Shares Outstanding	198,129
Robert D. Kleinman	Exec VP, Secretary	Market Capitalization	$ 23,280,158
Raymond S. Greenberger	Treasurer	Frequency Of Dividends	Quarterly
Richard D. Kleinman	Vice President, COO	Number of Shareholders	Under 500
Bruce Thomason	Vice President		

Other Information

Transfer Agent	Mellon Securities Trust Company			Where Listed	OTC-BB
Auditor	Edward Isaacs & Company			Symbol	AFAP
Market Maker	Carr Securities Corporation	Telephone	(800)221-2243	SIC Code	7382
Broker Dealer	Regular Stockbroker			Employees	n.a.

AM Communications, Inc.

1900 AM Drive • Quakertown, PA 18951-9004 • Telephone (215)536-1354 • Fax (215)536-1475

Company Description

The Company is a supplier of network status and performance monitoring systems for hybrid fiber/coaxial telecommunications networks. Products are sold directly to cable system operators and through OEM's, including AT&T, General Instrument, Philips and Hewlett-Packard. The Company was incorporated in Delaware in 1974.

	04/01/95	04/02/94	04/03/93	03/28/92
Per Share Information				
Stock Price	2.19	0.32	0.19	0.13
Earnings Per Share	0.02	0.02	-0.03	-0.04
Price / Earnings Ratio	109.50	16.00	n.a.	n.a.
Book Value Per Share	0.01	-0.02	-0.25	-0.23
Price / Book Value %	21,900.00	n.a.	n.a.	n.a.
Dividends Per Share	n.a.	n.a.	n.a.	n.a.
Annual Financial Data				
Operating Results (000's)				
Total Revenues	5,290.0	3,906.0	2,875.0	2,050.0
Costs & Expenses	-5,339.0	-3,461.0	-3,375.0	-2,775.0
Income Before Taxes and Other	-49.0	445.0	-500.0	-725.0
Other Items	n.a.	n.a.	n.a.	n.a.
Income Tax	816.0	-62.0	n.a.	n.a.
Net Income	767.0	383.0	-500.0	-725.0
Cash Flow From Operations	217.0	413.0	-74.0	-385.0
Balance Sheet (000's)				
Cash & Equivalents	454.0	190.0	224.0	127.0
Total Current Assets	2,896.0	2,262.0	1,876.0	1,764.0
Fixed Assets, Net	194.0	150.0	122.0	224.0
Total Assets	4,181.0	2,690.0	2,213.0	2,231.0
Total Current Liabilities	1,363.0	686.0	850.0	781.0
Long-Term Debt	n.a.	n.a.	6,271.0	5,858.0
Stockholders' Equity	2,818.0	2,004.0	-4,908.0	-4,408.0
Performance & Financial Condition				
Return on Total Revenues %	14.50	9.81	-17.39	-35.37
Return on Avg Stockholders' Equity %	31.81	n.a.	n.a.	n.a.
Return on Average Assets %	22.33	15.62	-22.50	n.a.
Current Ratio	2.12	3.30	2.21	2.26
Debt / Equity %	n.a.	n.a.	n.a.	n.a.

Compound Growth %'s	EPS %	n.a.	Net Income %	100.26	Total Revenues %	37.16

Comments

Included in Stockholder's Equity for fiscal years 1995 and 1994, is convertible redeemable preferred stock of $2.6 million resulting from the conversion, during 1994, of the existing debt to the major stockholder. During April and May 1995, warrants to purchase 5,848,570 shares of the Company's common stock were excercised with proceeds of approximately $1.8 million. Net operating loss carryforwards available through 1999 to 2008 total $24.6 million. The Company had sales of $5.4 million and a net loss of $1.0 million for the nine months ended December 30, 1995.

Officers	Position	Ownership Information	04/01/95
Henry I. Boreen	Chairman, CEO	Number of Shares Outstanding	24,564,391
Keith D. Schneck	President, CFO	Market Capitalization	$ 53,796,016
Michael L. Quelly	Exec VP	Frequency Of Dividends	n.a.
Patricia A. Eynon	Secretary	Number of Shareholders	1,090
David L. DeLane	Vice President		

Other Information

Transfer Agent	Continental Stock Transfer & Trust Co.			Where Listed	OTC-BB
Auditor	Deloitte & Touche LLP			Symbol	AMCI
Market Maker	Paragon Capital Corporation	Telephone	(800)521-8877	SIC Code	3663
Broker Dealer	Regular Stockbroker			Employees	67

AMCOR Capital Corporation

52300 Enterprise Way • Coachella, CA 92236 • Telephone (619)398-9520 • Fax (619)398-9530

Company Description

The Company's primary business is agriculture and includes the operations of a wholly-owned subsidiary, ACI Farms, Inc. The Company's principal agribusiness operations involve the production and processing of table grapes and dates. The operations are located in the Coachella Valley of southern California. Land planning and development activities are located in southern California and Texas. Some of the agribusiness and land properties managed by the Company are owned by limited partnerships for which the Company or its affiliates are general partners. The Company was incorporated in Delaware in 1988. During 1988, pursuant to a plan of reorganization, the Company acquired 100% of the common stock of AMCOR Capital, Inc., in exchange for 6,591,271 shares of the Company's common stock. AMCOR Capital, Inc. was formed in 1986 as a holding company to consolidate the business of several entities engaged in agriculture and venture capital activities and was dissolved in 1994. Officers and directors owned approximately 40% of the Company's outstanding shares at August 31, 1995.

	08/31/95	08/31/94	11/30/93	11/30/92
Per Share Information				
Stock Price	0.90	0.69	0.25	0.25
Earnings Per Share	0.10	0.05	n.a.	-0.23
Price / Earnings Ratio	9.00	13.80	n.a.	n.a.
Book Value Per Share	0.44	0.39	0.31	0.33
Price / Book Value %	204.55	176.92	80.65	75.76
Dividends Per Share	n.a.	n.a.	n.a.	n.a.
Annual Financial Data				
Operating Results (000's)				
Total Revenues	11,721.8	7,993.8	8,858.8	5,866.6
Costs & Expenses	-10,536.2	-7,274.0	-9,409.3	-8,388.4
Income Before Taxes and Other	1,185.6	719.8	-740.1	-3,032.8
Other Items	n.a.	n.a.	697.4	n.a.
Income Tax	-12.3	-81.6	-2.4	577.1
Net Income	1,173.3	638.2	-45.1	-2,455.7
Cash Flow From Operations	3,124.9	34.9	-3,337.8	2,452.8
Balance Sheet (000's)				
Cash & Equivalents	1,809.3	384.0	309.6	3.1
Total Current Assets	9,510.7	4,622.7	2,399.6	6,891.1
Fixed Assets, Net	10,475.2	9,621.0	3,486.6	14,385.9
Total Assets	21,707.4	21,456.1	17,573.5	29,918.9
Total Current Liabilities	5,455.1	3,257.0	3,197.1	8,162.3
Long-Term Debt	5,544.9	6,847.4	7,079.7	14,842.9
Stockholders' Equity	10,707.4	9,826.9	3,627.7	3,808.7
Performance & Financial Condition				
Return on Total Revenues %	10.01	7.98	-0.51	-41.86
Return on Avg Stockholders' Equity %	11.43	9.49	-1.21	-55.95
Return on Average Assets %	5.44	3.27	-0.19	n.a.
Current Ratio	1.74	1.42	0.75	0.84
Debt / Equity %	51.79	69.68	195.16	389.71

Compound Growth %'s	EPS %	100.00	Net Income %	83.84	Total Revenues %	25.95

Comments

The Company changed its fiscal year end from November 30, to August 31, effective in the year beginning September 1, 1994. Comparability of the financial statements may be affected by the difference in the length of the two periods included.

Officers	Position	Ownership Information	08/31/95
Fred H. Behrens	Chairman, CEO	Number of Shares Outstanding	10,331,288
Robert A. Wright	President, COO	Market Capitalization	$ 9,298,159
Graceann Johnsen	Secretary	Frequency Of Dividends	Irregular
Barry Goverman	Vice President	Number of Shareholders	1,211
Marlene Tapie	Vice President		

Other Information

Transfer Agent	American Stock Transfer & Trust Company			Where Listed	OTC-BB
Auditor	Kelly & Company			Symbol	APTO
Market Maker	Alpine Securities Corporation	Telephone	(800)274-5588	SIC Code	0179
Broker Dealer	Regular Stockbroker			Employees	2100

ATS Money Systems, Inc.

25 Rockwood Place • Englewood, NJ 07631 • Telephone (201)894-1700 • Fax (201)894-0958

Company Description

The Company is engaged in the development, sale and service of currency counting systems and equipment for department and chain stores' cash transactions and for the commercial vaults of banks and communications systems primarily used by chain stores. The Company was formed in 1979 as a subsidiary of a Swiss company. It was acquired in 1986, and merged into an existing public company that was previously incorporated in the State of Nevada.

	12/31/95	12/31/94	12/31/93	12/31/92
Per Share Information				
Stock Price	1.10	0.78	0.69	0.09
Earnings Per Share	0.06	0.06	0.18	0.01
Price / Earnings Ratio	18.33	13.00	3.83	9.00
Book Value Per Share	0.35	0.29	0.22	0.04
Price / Book Value %	314.29	268.97	313.64	225.00
Dividends Per Share	n.a.	n.a.	n.a.	n.a.
Annual Financial Data				
Operating Results (000's)				
Total Revenues	8,438.7	5,758.5	5,469.7	3,404.1
Costs & Expenses	-7,881.2	-5,384.7	-4,434.0	-3,322.6
Income Before Taxes and Other	557.5	373.9	1,035.8	81.5
Other Items	n.a.	n.a.	n.a.	23.6
Income Tax	-187.9	-13.8	n.a.	-23.6
Net Income	369.7	360.0	1,035.8	81.5
Cash Flow From Operations	-58.8	942.7	488.4	478.8
Balance Sheet (000's)				
Cash & Equivalents	164.5	527.4	139.3	361.5
Total Current Assets	2,418.4	2,109.1	1,556.5	1,028.3
Fixed Assets, Net	84.6	70.7	23.9	27.3
Total Assets	3,199.7	2,732.3	1,964.8	1,300.0
Total Current Liabilities	937.1	815.3	683.4	836.9
Long-Term Debt	246.0	274.4	n.a.	217.5
Stockholders' Equity	2,016.6	1,642.6	1,281.4	245.5
Performance & Financial Condition				
Return on Total Revenues %	4.38	6.25	18.94	2.39
Return on Avg Stockholders' Equity %	20.20	24.63	135.67	39.78
Return on Average Assets %	12.46	15.33	63.45	6.28
Current Ratio	2.58	2.59	2.28	1.23
Debt / Equity %	12.20	16.71	n.a.	88.58

Compound Growth %'s	EPS %	81.71	Net Income %	65.55	Total Revenues %	35.34

Comments

Sales to three major customers made up approximately 60% of total revenues for 1995, 1994, and 1993. As of March 15, 1996, officers and directors as a group, owned 63.4% of the Company's outstanding shares.

Officers	Position	Ownership Information	12/31/95
Gerard F. Murphy	President, CEO	Number of Shares Outstanding	5,735,794
James H. Halpin	Exec VP	Market Capitalization	$ 6,309,373
Joseph M. Burke	VP - Finance	Frequency Of Dividends	n.a.
Michael M. Smith	Treasurer	Number of Shareholders	426
Ray T. Riley	Vice President		

Other Information

				Where Listed	OTC-BB
Transfer Agent	American Stock Transfer & Trust Company			Symbol	ATSDM
Auditor	Deloitte & Touche LLP			SIC Code	3578
Market Maker	Paragon Capital Corporation	Telephone	(800)345-0505	Employees	49
Broker Dealer	Regular Stockbroker				

AVCOM International, Inc.

P.O. Box 1243 • Sedona, AZ 86339 • Telephone (520)282-1982 • Fax (520)282-9428

Company Description

The Company develops resort properties for timeshare sales, finances ownership interests in the properties and manages the operations of the resort properties and their related homeowners' associations. The principal properties are located in Sedona, Arizona and South Lake Tahoe, California. The Company was formed in 1993 as American Vacation Company, Inc. for the purpose of acquiring and operating the businesses of Villashare Partners Limited Partnership and All Seasons Development, Inc. The Company changed its name in September, 1993.

	09/30/95	12/31/94	12/31/93	12/31/92
Per Share Information				
Stock Price	2.70	3.12	2.00	1.50
Earnings Per Share	0.22	0.16	0.05	0.33
Price / Earnings Ratio	12.27	19.50	40.00	4.55
Book Value Per Share	1.15	0.74	0.55	0.43
Price / Book Value %	234.78	421.62	363.64	348.84
Dividends Per Share	n.a.	n.a.	n.a.	n.a.
Annual Financial Data				
Operating Results (000's)				
Total Revenues	26,737.0	25,597.0	15,435.0	9,648.0
Costs & Expenses	-24,527.0	-23,981.0	-13,252.0	-8,261.0
Income Before Taxes and Other	2,210.0	1,616.0	2,183.0	1,387.0
Other Items	n.a.	n.a.	n.a.	n.a.
Income Tax	-936.0	-695.0	-1,970.0	-12.0
Net Income	1,274.0	921.0	213.0	1,375.0
Cash Flow From Operations	3,101.0	291.0	2,907.0	-1,552.0
Balance Sheet (000's)				
Cash & Equivalents	486.0	1,026.0	589.0	n.a.
Total Current Assets	486.0	1,026.0	589.0	n.a.
Fixed Assets, Net	1,852.0	1,906.0	335.0	n.a.
Total Assets	31,380.0	20,852.0	8,459.0	n.a.
Total Current Liabilities	3,672.0	1,914.0	742.0	n.a.
Long-Term Debt	18,540.0	12,582.0	3,281.0	n.a.
Stockholders' Equity	5,673.0	3,415.0	2,514.0	n.a.
Performance & Financial Condition				
Return on Total Revenues %	4.76	3.60	1.38	14.25
Return on Avg Stockholders' Equity %	28.04	31.07	n.a.	143.98
Return on Average Assets %	4.88	6.28	n.a.	n.a.
Current Ratio	0.13	0.54	0.79	n.a.
Debt / Equity %	326.81	368.43	130.51	n.a.

Compound Growth %'s	EPS % 15.87	Net Income % 7.30	Total Revenues % 55.10

Comments

Inside ownership accounts for 56% of shares. There are no institutional owners. The Company benefits from an industry that is gaining increasing popularity. Glaser Capital estimates 1996 earnings to be $.50 per share. 1995 results are for the nine months ended September 30, 1995. Compounded growth rates are based on annualized results for 1995. Actual results may differ.

Officers	Position	Ownership Information	09/30/95
Robert M. Eckenroth	Senior VP, CFO	Number of Shares Outstanding	4,952,636
Bob Maxwell	Other	Market Capitalization	$ 13,372,117
		Frequency Of Dividends	n.a.
		Number of Shareholders	Under 500

Other Information

Transfer Agent	Fidelity Transfer Co., Salt Lake City	Where Listed	OTC-BB
Auditor	Ernst & Young LLP	Symbol	AVMI
Market Maker	Fahnestock & Co., Inc.	Telephone (800)223-3012	SIC Code	6550
Broker Dealer	Regular Stockbroker	Employees	260

Acacia Research Corporation

12 South Raymond Avenue • Pasadena, CA 91105 • Telephone (818)449-6431 • Fax (818)449-7189

Company Description

The Company invests in and develops emerging or start-up businesses that they believe have a potential for success. The Company provides formation capital and management expertise to a new business or affiliate, then raises capital through a private placement to further advance the affiliate until it has matured to a point where it can become a free-standing corporation. An investee, Whitewing Labs, was established by the Company, went public in 1995, and is now traded on the Nasdaq Stock Market. The Company was incorporated in California on January 25, 1993, and had stock offerings in 1995, 1994 and 1993, in which it raised $1.0 million, $672,000, and $1.7 millon, respectively.

	12/31/95	12/31/94	12/31/93
Per Share Information			
Stock Price	8.50	n.a.	n.a.
Earnings Per Share	0.81	-0.35	-0.44
Price / Earnings Ratio	10.49	n.a.	n.a.
Book Value Per Share	2.23	0.27	0.45
Price / Book Value %	381.17	n.a.	n.a.
Dividends Per Share	n.a.	n.a.	n.a.
Annual Financial Data			
Operating Results (000's)			
Total Revenues	3,517.7	37.5	8.2
Costs & Expenses	-1,399.0	-722.9	-596.3
Income Before Taxes and Other	2,118.7	-824.4	-866.1
Other Items	0.5	n.a.	n.a.
Income Tax	-55.8	-3.5	-1.5
Net Income	2,063.4	-828.0	-867.6
Cash Flow From Operations	1,940.9	-695.6	-514.2
Balance Sheet (000's)			
Cash & Equivalents	788.6	361.0	474.8
Total Current Assets	2,915.3	748.4	638.9
Fixed Assets, Net	63.6	28.7	37.3
Total Assets	4,463.2	779.2	685.2
Total Current Liabilities	353.8	349.6	33.3
Long-Term Debt	n.a.	n.a.	n.a.
Stockholders' Equity	4,094.4	427.0	650.5
Performance & Financial Condition			
Return on Total Revenues %	58.66	n.a.	n.a.
Return on Avg Stockholders' Equity %	91.27	-153.70	n.a.
Return on Average Assets %	78.72	-113.08	n.a.
Current Ratio	8.24	2.14	19.21
Debt / Equity %	n.a.	n.a.	n.a.

Compound Growth %'s	EPS % n.a.	Net Income % n.a.	Total Revenues % 1969.31

Comments

The Company was formed in January 1993, and had no significant operating results prior to the year ended December 31, 1995. The first period displayed is for the eleven months ended December 31, 1993. Prior to the Company's stock issuance and SEC filing in 1995, there was no market for its' stock. Acccordingly, no price related information is presented.

Officers	Position	Ownership Information	12/31/95
R. Bruce Stewart	President, CEO	Number of Shares Outstanding	1,837,672
Paul R. Ryan	Vice President	Market Capitalization	$ 15,620,212
Brooke P. Anderson	Vice President	Frequency Of Dividends	n.a.
Kathryn King-Van Wie	Vice President, Secretary	Number of Shareholders	400

Other Information				
Transfer Agent	U.S. Stock Transfer Corporation		Where Listed	OTC-BB
Auditor	Finocchiaro & Co.		Symbol	ACRI
Market Maker	Koonce Securities, Inc.	Telephone (800)368-2802	SIC Code	7372
Broker Dealer	Regular Stockbroker		Employees	5

Accuhealth, Inc.

1575 Bronx River Ave. • Bronx, NY 10460 • Telephone (718)518-9511 • Fax (718)824-2432

Company Description

The Company is a home health care company and provides a variety of medical services to critically ill home-bound patients. The Company also delivers home care equipment and provides pharmaceutical supplies and management services to residential care facilities serving the critically ill. Services are provided to patients throughout the states of New York, New Jersey and Connecticut. A new management team assumed responsibility for the Company in 1994. Also during 1995, an investment group invested $2.65 million in exchange for 1,325,000 shares of the Company's convertible preferred stock. Officers and directors owned approximately 41% of the outstanding shares at June 30, 1995.

	03/31/95	03/31/94
Per Share Information		
Stock Price	3.25	n.a.
Earnings Per Share	0.24	n.a.
Price / Earnings Ratio	13.54	n.a.
Book Value Per Share	1.30	n.a.
Price / Book Value %	250.00	n.a.
Dividends Per Share	n.a.	n.a.
Annual Financial Data		
Operating Results (000's)		
Total Revenues	15,468.4	15,380.0
Costs & Expenses	-15,806.6	-16,329.1
Income Before Taxes and Other	676.1	-1,403.1
Other Items	-325.6	-1,187.1
Income Tax	n.a.	44.5
Net Income	350.6	-2,545.7
Cash Flow From Operations	-2,034.9	-336.1
Balance Sheet (000's)		
Cash & Equivalents	147.3	28.7
Total Current Assets	4,519.2	5,465.2
Fixed Assets, Net	2,640.6	2,299.0
Total Assets	7,294.9	7,823.5
Total Current Liabilities	4,582.5	6,655.7
Long-Term Debt	694.6	1,586.4
Stockholders' Equity	2,017.8	-418.6
Performance & Financial Condition		
Return on Total Revenues %	2.27	n.a.
Return on Avg Stockholders' Equity %	43.84	n.a.
Return on Average Assets %	4.64	n.a.
Current Ratio	0.99	n.a.
Debt / Equity %	34.42	n.a.

Compound Growth %'s	EPS %	n.a.	Net Income %	n.a.	Total Revenues %	0.57

Comments

The Company discontinued its retail drugstore operations resulting in a charge to operations of $278,000 and $1,187,000 for the years ended March 31, 1995 and 1994. The Company is continuing its efforts to reduce costs and expenses through productivity improvements and cost containment initiatives. Years prior to fiscal 1993/1994, are not presented due to the changes in management, operational and ownership structure making them non-comparable.

Officers	**Position**	**Ownership Information**	**03/31/95**
Glenn C. Davis	President, CEO	Number of Shares Outstanding	1,550,000
Gary S. LaPorta	CFO, Secretary	Market Capitalization	$ 5,037,500
		Frequency Of Dividends	n.a.
		Number of Shareholders	49

Other Information

Transfer Agent	North American Transfer Company			Where Listed	OTC-BB
Auditor	Ernst & Young LLP			Symbol	AHLT
Market Maker	Herzog, Heine, Geduld, Inc.	Telephone	(800)221-3600	SIC Code	8082
Broker Dealer	Regular Stockbroker			Employees	96

Adrian Steel Company

906 James Street • Adrian, MI 49221-3914 • Telephone (517)265-6194 • Fax (517)265-3016

Company Description

The Company and its subsidiaries are in the steel fabrication business with sales primarily to the automobile industry. Sales to three customers account for 40% of total sales. The Company was formed and began operations in 1953 and went public in 1961. However, it has been buying and continues to buy back stock as it becomes available.

	09/30/95	09/30/94	09/30/93	09/30/92
Per Share Information				
Stock Price	172.52	165.00	165.00	110.00
Earnings Per Share	16.58	14.71	13.08	10.08
Price / Earnings Ratio	10.41	11.22	12.61	10.91
Book Value Per Share	114.59	104.22	100.11	96.89
Price / Book Value %	150.55	158.32	164.82	113.53
Dividends Per Share	8.00	7.00	7.00	3.00
Annual Financial Data				
Operating Results (000's)				
Total Revenues	45,947.2	33,394.6	30,673.4	22,493.6
Costs & Expenses	-40,991.4	-29,036.8	-26,727.1	-19,476.8
Income Before Taxes and Other	4,845.0	4,357.8	3,946.4	3,016.8
Other Items	n.a.	n.a.	n.a.	n.a.
Income Tax	-1,502.7	-1,293.0	-1,166.0	-850.0
Net Income	3,342.3	3,064.8	2,780.4	2,166.8
Cash Flow From Operations	1,815.1	2,178.1	2,973.6	2,061.1
Balance Sheet (000's)				
Cash & Equivalents	2,153.2	2,463.0	2,889.5	2,200.5
Total Current Assets	14,220.0	10,739.5	9,461.9	7,742.6
Fixed Assets, Net	5,625.8	4,473.4	3,672.7	2,165.5
Total Assets	28,366.0	25,535.1	24,992.6	21,965.3
Total Current Liabilities	4,882.3	3,904.9	3,691.4	1,395.9
Long-Term Debt	92.0	191.2	n.a.	n.a.
Stockholders' Equity	23,081.9	21,324.9	21,269.2	20,517.4
Performance & Financial Condition				
Return on Total Revenues %	7.27	9.18	9.06	9.63
Return on Avg Stockholders' Equity %	15.05	14.39	13.31	10.78
Return on Average Assets %	12.40	12.13	11.84	10.06
Current Ratio	2.91	2.75	2.56	5.55
Debt / Equity %	0.40	0.90	n.a.	n.a.

Compound Growth %'s	EPS %	18.04	Net Income %	15.54	Total Revenues %	26.88

Comments

The Company classifies its holdings in marketable securities as non-current assets. These holdings amounted to $7.2 million, $9.1 million, $11.5 million and $11.8 million for the years 1995, 1994, 1993 and 1992, respectively. The gradual decline is due to substantial investments in property and equipment and the ongoing stock repurchase program.

Officers	Position	Ownership Information	09/30/95
Harley J. Westfall	President, Treasurer	Number of Shares Outstanding	201,434
Harold E. Stieg	Secretary	Market Capitalization	$ 34,751,394
Lynford R. Baugh	VP - Sales	Frequency Of Dividends	Quarterly
Joseph E. Emens	Other	Number of Shareholders	Under 500

Other Information

Transfer Agent	American Stock Transfer & Trust Company			Where Listed	OTC-BB
Auditor	Curtis Bailey Exelby & Sposito			Symbol	ADST
Market Maker	Roney & Co.	Telephone	(800)321-2038	SIC Code	3312
Broker Dealer	Regular Stockbroker			Employees	130

Ainslie Corporation

531 Pond Street • Braintree, MA 02185 • Telephone (617)848-0850 • Fax (617)843-2584

Company Description

The Company manufactures microwave antennas and related products used primarily in the defense industries. There is a wide range between bid and ask prices and not many transactions occur. It is also difficult to get any information from the Company. The Company bought back shares in 1992, 1993, and 1994 for $3.50 per share.

	07/31/95	07/31/94	07/31/93	07/31/92
Per Share Information				
Stock Price	10.25	4.50	3.50	3.50
Earnings Per Share	2.05	1.63	0.33	-3.10
Price / Earnings Ratio	5.00	2.76	10.61	n.a.
Book Value Per Share	26.53	24.48	22.83	22.37
Price / Book Value %	38.64	18.38	15.33	15.65
Dividends Per Share	n.a.	n.a.	n.a.	n.a.
Annual Financial Data				
Operating Results (000's)				
Total Revenues	7,987.0	8,940.4	7,782.5	6,396.5
Costs & Expenses	-7,614.5	-8,662.6	-7,721.8	-7,154.7
Income Before Taxes and Other	372.5	277.8	60.7	-758.2
Other Items	n.a.	n.a.	n.a.	n.a.
Income Tax	-123.2	-80.1	-20.6	379.6
Net Income	249.3	197.7	40.1	-378.6
Cash Flow From Operations	n.a.	n.a.	n.a.	n.a.
Balance Sheet (000's)				
Cash & Equivalents	604.9	892.0	454.1	918.3
Total Current Assets	3,404.1	2,996.5	2,519.7	2,722.6
Fixed Assets, Net	393.0	359.9	468.9	647.1
Total Assets	3,890.0	3,440.2	3,064.8	3,437.6
Total Current Liabilities	544.1	298.2	291.5	671.8
Long-Term Debt	120.8	170.8	n.a.	n.a.
Stockholders' Equity	3,219.8	2,970.6	2,773.3	2,737.2
Performance & Financial Condition				
Return on Total Revenues %	3.12	2.21	0.52	-5.92
Return on Avg Stockholders' Equity %	8.05	6.88	1.46	n.a.
Return on Average Assets %	6.80	6.08	1.23	n.a.
Current Ratio	6.26	10.05	8.64	4.05
Debt / Equity %	3.75	5.75	n.a.	n.a.

Compound Growth %'s	EPS %	149.24	Net Income %	149.35	Total Revenues %	7.68

Comments

The Company appears to be having an excellent recovery from its 1992 performance and certainly has plenty of cash and T-bills ($2,129,901, or $17.55 per share) to invest in the right opportunities. Compounded earnings growth rates can be misleading because of the loss in 1992 and the relatively low income in 1993.

Officers	Position	Ownership Information	07/31/95
Janice Mather	Other	Number of Shares Outstanding	121,361
		Market Capitalization	$ 1,243,950
		Frequency Of Dividends	n.a.
		Number of Shareholders	Under 500

Other Information

Transfer Agent	First National Bank of Boston			Where Listed	OTC-BB
Auditor	Bernard J. McDonald, Jr.			Symbol	ANSE
Market Maker	S.J. Wolfe & Co.	Telephone	(800)262-2244	SIC Code	3699
Broker Dealer	Regular Stockbroker			Employees	100

Aircraft Income Partners, L.P.

411 West Putnam Avenue • Greenwich, CT 06830 • Telephone (203)862-7000 • Fax (203)862-7388

Company Description

The Partnership is in the business of owning and leasing aircraft and aircraft parts. As of December 31, 1995, there were 14 aircraft remaining, of the 16 originally purchased, and all were on lease. The Partnership was formed in 1988. Through a public offering, it sold 385,800 units and raised $197.9 million. Integrated Resources, Inc., the original general partner was replaced by Presidio Capital Corp. upon the bankrupcy of the former. The officers indicated are those of Presidio Capital Corp.

	12/31/95	12/31/94	12/31/93	12/31/92
Per Unit Information				
Price Per Unit	78.90	98.00	103.00	158.00
Earnings Per Unit	3.49	1.32	-24.04	-2.46
Price / Earnings Ratio	22.61	74.24	n.a.	n.a.
Book Value Per Unit	157.37	185.87	215.56	274.10
Price / Book Value %	50.14	52.73	47.78	57.64
Distributions Per Unit	32.00	31.00	34.50	43.75
Cash Flow Per Unit	35.01	37.66	36.83	49.78
Annual Financial Data				
Operating Results (000's)				
Total Revenues	13,374.2	13,755.5	16,227.5	21,342.5
Costs & Expenses	-11,877.4	-13,190.6	-26,513.6	-21,495.0
Operating Income	1,496.8	564.9	-10,306.1	-1,053.4
Other Items	n.a.	n.a.	n.a.	n.a.
Net Income	1,496.8	564.9	-10,306.1	-1,053.4
Cash Flow From Operations	13,508.7	14,530.5	14,209.1	19,206.9
Balance Sheet (000's)				
Cash & Equivalents	7,448.5	6,350.2	5,872.8	8,006.9
Total Current Assets	9,685.8	8,802.0	7,846.6	10,540.1
Investments In Aircraft	41,868.9	52,663.4	64,614.1	87,727.3
Total Assets	52,365.6	63,596.7	76,240.0	101,811.4
Total Current Liabilities	3,648.5	3,315.7	4,037.6	5,409.0
Long-Term Debt	n.a.	n.a.	n.a.	n.a.
Partners' Capital	46,034.8	58,255.6	70,979.5	96,074.8
Performance & Financial Condition				
Return on Total Revenues %	11.19	4.11	-63.51	-4.94
Return on Average Partners' Capital %	n.a.	n.a.	n.a.	n.a.
Return on Average Assets %	2.58	0.81	-11.58	-0.94
Current Ratio	2.65	2.65	1.94	1.95
Debt / Equity %	n.a.	n.a.	n.a.	n.a.

Compound Growth %'s	EPU %	164.39	Net Income %	164.96	Total Revenues %	-14.43

Comments

Compounded growth rates are affected by the decline in depreciation expense. Operating cash flow is actually declining primarily due to the gradual reduction of the number of aircraft. Four aircraft will come off-lease during 1996, followed by 5, 4, and 1 in 1997, 1998, and 1999, respectively. The aircraft leasing industry is highly competitive. New or extended leases will be impacted by air traffic demands as well as the type of aircraft. Sales of the aircraft and their residual values are also affected.

Officers	Position	Ownership Information	12/31/95
Douglas J. Lambert	President, CFO	Number of Shares Outstanding	385,805
Diane M. Deagan	Senior VP	Market Capitalization	$ 30,440,015
Robert Holtz	Vice President, Director	Frequency Of Distributions	n.a.
Mark Plaumann	Vice President, Director	Number of Partners	15,100
Jill F. Schiaparelli	Vice President		

Other Information

Transfer Agent	Company Office			Where Listed	Order Matching Only
Auditor	Hays & Company			Symbol	n.a.
Market Maker	None			SIC Code	7359
Broker Dealer	Chicago Partnership Board	Tel/Ext	(800)272-6273 · 690	Employees	None

Alaska Northwest Properties, Inc.

P. O. Box 68934 • Seattle, WA 98168 • Telephone (206)433-0750 • Fax (206)246-4559

Company Description

The principal business of the Company is real estate investment and operations. The Company holds for investment purposes several parcels of undeveloped land in Alaska, as well as the State of Washington. The primary operating properties include a facility at the Fairbanks International Airport, a condominium in Hawaii and lodging facilities in Washington State. The Company intends to continue its attempt to sell existing properties and to look for opportunities to acquire additional properties that will provide attractive long-term investment returns. During 1979, the Company was spun off from its parent, Alaska Airlines, Inc. and in 1980, the shares of the Company were distributed to the shareholders of Alaska Airlines.

	12/31/95	12/31/94	12/31/93	12/31/92
Per Share Information				
Stock Price	237.50	282.00	185.00	150.00
Earnings Per Share	-3.39	-11.28	-6.83	-13.01
Price / Earnings Ratio	n.a.	n.a.	n.a.	n.a.
Book Value Per Share	322.52	324.42	339.39	347.78
Price / Book Value %	73.64	86.92	54.51	43.13
Dividends Per Share	n.a.	n.a.	1.00	2.00
Annual Financial Data				
Operating Results (000's)				
Total Revenues	521.5	388.0	597.2	548.5
Costs & Expenses	-619.7	-712.0	-792.6	-917.8
Income Before Taxes and Other	-98.2	-324.0	-195.4	-369.3
Other Items	n.a.	n.a.	n.a.	n.a.
Income Tax	n.a.	n.a.	n.a.	n.a.
Net Income	-98.2	-324.0	-195.4	-369.3
Cash Flow From Operations	-191.7	-147.6	-111.7	-155.3
Balance Sheet (000's)				
Cash & Equivalents	147.8	111.2	198.3	n.a.
Total Current Assets	453.9	551.7	747.4	817.8
Fixed Assets, Net	813.1	863.7	957.3	2,862.2
Total Assets	9,754.3	9,699.2	10,012.9	10,252.4
Total Current Liabilities	261.4	100.4	50.8	80.4
Long-Term Debt	111.7	160.8	226.1	228.9
Stockholders' Equity	9,381.2	9,438.0	9,736.0	9,943.2
Performance & Financial Condition				
Return on Total Revenues %	-18.83	-83.49	-32.72	-67.34
Return on Avg Stockholders' Equity %	-1.04	-3.38	-1.99	-3.65
Return on Average Assets %	-1.01	-3.29	-1.93	-3.54
Current Ratio	1.74	5.49	14.70	10.17
Debt / Equity %	1.19	1.70	2.32	2.30

Compound Growth %'s	EPS % n.a.	Net Income % n.a.	Total Revenues % -1.67

Comments

Included in Other Assets are Land held for Investment of $7,015,000 and Notes Receivable resulting from property sales of $1,368,000. In addition to Property and Equipment these are the key assets of the Company. The disposition of these assets will ultimately play an important role in the overall success of the Company.

Officers	Position	Ownership Information	12/31/95
Ronald F. Cosgrave	Chairman	Number of Shares Outstanding	29,087
Michael W. Shimasaki	President, Treasurer	Market Capitalization	$ 6,908,163
Michael K. Chung	Vice President, Secretary	Frequency Of Dividends	n.a.
		Number of Shareholders	724

Other Information

Transfer Agent	Company Office			Where Listed	OTC-BB
Auditor	BDO Seidman, LLP			Symbol	ANWP
Market Maker	Martin Nelson & Co., Inc.	Telephone	(206)682-6261	SIC Code	6512
Broker Dealer	Regular Stockbroker			Employees	8

Alaska Power & Telephone Company

191 Otto Street • Port Townsend, WA 98368 • Telephone (360)385-1733 • Fax (360)385-5177

Company Description

The Company supplies electric and telephone service to communities in eastern Alaska. Formed in 1957, it has ben adding service to a broader territory on an ongoing basis. New communities have been added for seven consecutive years. It is subject to regulation by the State and federal public utility commissions. The Company has an employee stock ownership plan covering virtually all employees. The Plan owns 299,570 shares of stock which is about 35% of the Company.

	12/31/95	12/31/94	12/31/93	12/31/92
Per Share Information				
Stock Price	19.00	15.25	13.00	11.00
Earnings Per Share	2.02	1.95	1.72	1.51
Price / Earnings Ratio	9.41	7.82	7.56	7.28
Book Value Per Share	12.63	11.11	9.62	8.52
Price / Book Value %	150.44	137.26	135.14	129.11
Dividends Per Share	0.85	0.48	0.44	0.36
Annual Financial Data				
Operating Results (000's)				
Total Revenues	11,895.6	10,641.0	10,031.2	8,650.2
Costs & Expenses	-8,982.8	-7,862.9	-7,832.2	-6,735.1
Income Before Taxes and Other	2,912.8	2,778.0	2,199.0	1,915.1
Other Items	n.a.	n.a.	n.a.	n.a.
Income Tax	-983.5	-964.3	-660.3	-636.7
Net Income	1,929.3	1,813.7	1,538.7	1,278.4
Cash Flow From Operations	3,350.8	3,526.4	3,337.0	2,630.4
Balance Sheet (000's)				
Cash & Equivalents	793.7	443.9	234.6	262.1
Total Current Assets	3,603.0	2,670.0	2,626.4	2,200.0
Fixed Assets, Net	28,911.7	21,366.2	13,924.6	12,189.5
Total Assets	34,733.1	25,322.2	18,729.4	16,105.7
Total Current Liabilities	2,199.0	1,930.0	1,863.1	1,506.5
Long-Term Debt	17,613.8	10,676.8	6,609.3	6,351.5
Stockholders' Equity	11,885.5	10,094.8	8,091.1	6,189.7
Performance & Financial Condition				
Return on Total Revenues %	16.22	17.04	15.34	14.78
Return on Avg Stockholders' Equity %	17.56	19.95	21.55	23.11
Return on Average Assets %	6.43	8.23	8.83	8.80
Current Ratio	1.64	1.38	1.41	1.46
Debt / Equity %	148.20	105.77	81.69	102.61

Compound Growth %'s	EPS %	10.19	Net Income %	14.70	Total Revenues %	11.20

Comments

During 1995, Northway Power & Light, Inc. was acquired for 11,000 shares of Company stock and $450,000 cash. Customers in Northway and Northway Village will now be served by A P & T. Strong growth, dedicated employees and an increasing dividend make this a particularly interesting company to follow.

Officers	Position	Ownership Information	12/31/95
Robert S. Grimm	President	Number of Shares Outstanding	937,016
Vernon Neitzer	Senior VP	Market Capitalization	$ 17,803,304
Howard Garner	Treasurer, VP - Finance	Frequency Of Dividends	Quarterly
Michael Garrett	Controller	Number of Shareholders	Under 500

Other Information

Transfer Agent	Marilou R. Sullivan, 800-982-0136			Where Listed	OTC-BB
Auditor	Ernst & Young LLP			Symbol	APTL
Market Maker	S.J. Wolfe & Co.	Telephone	(513)223-1256	SIC Code	4910
Broker Dealer	Regular Stockbroker			Employees	80

Alden Lee Company, Inc.

845 Oak Grove Avenue, Ste. 100 • Menlo Park, CA 94025 • Telephone (415)324-5000 • Fax (415)324-5001

Company Description

The Company intends to produce and market a line of fine hardwood furniture for musicians, including wooden music stands, sheet music cabinets, performers' benches and instrument stands. Operations are expected to commence in 1996. The Company is the successor to Early Music Stands, a proprietorship operated by Richard and Anne Lee between 1974 and 1982. The Lees contributed certain properties to the Company in exchange for stock. The Company raised $275,000 in a Reg. D offering followed by a fully subscribed intrastate offering which raised $2,650,000.

	12/31/95	06/30/95	06/30/94
Per Share Information			
Stock Price	2.00	2.00	0.50
Earnings Per Share	n.a.	-0.01	n.a.
Price / Earnings Ratio	n.a.	n.a.	n.a.
Book Value Per Share	0.62	0.18	0.09
Price / Book Value %	310.00	1,111.10	555.56
Dividends Per Share	n.a.	n.a.	n.a.
Annual Financial Data			
Operating Results (000's)			
Total Revenues	n.a.	10.8	0.9
Costs & Expenses	n.a.	-65.5	-14.7
Income Before Taxes and Other	n.a.	-54.7	-13.8
Other Items	n.a.	n.a.	n.a.
Income Tax	n.a.	-0.8	-0.8
Net Income	n.a.	-55.5	-14.6
Cash Flow From Operations	n.a.	-233.3	-14.0
Balance Sheet (000's)			
Cash & Equivalents	1,856.9	306.2	234.5
Total Current Assets	1,981.9	306.2	234.5
Fixed Assets, Net	48.8	19.2	11.8
Total Assets	2,483.2	730.9	334.2
Total Current Liabilities	17.3	28.3	8.8
Long-Term Debt	n.a.	n.a.	n.a.
Stockholders' Equity	2,465.9	702.6	325.4
Performance & Financial Condition			
Return on Total Revenues %	n.a.	-511.69	n.a.
Return on Avg Stockholders' Equity %	n.a.	n.a.	n.a.
Return on Average Assets %	n.a.	n.a.	n.a.
Current Ratio	143.54	10.81	26.65
Debt / Equity %	n.a.	n.a.	n.a.

Compound Growth %'s	EPS %	n.a.	Net Income %	n.a.	Total Revenues %	n.a.

Comments

The six month period ended December 31, 1995 is unaudited. The Company is still in a start-up phase. Management states that plans are on schedule with the first catalog to be mailed during the third week of July. Manufacturing of product started since in early 1996. None of the originally issued shares have been offered for sale through May 31, 1996.

Officers	Position	Ownership Information	12/31/95
Richard J. Lee	President	Number of Shares Outstanding	3,984,300
Dean Abercrombie	COO	Market Capitalization	$ 7,968,600
Jeffrey W. Gardiner	CFO	Frequency Of Dividends	n.a.
Richard A. Denholtz	VP - Sales	Number of Shareholders	Under 500

Other Information

Transfer Agent	Company Office			Where Listed	Order Matching Only
Auditor	Frank, Rimerman & Co.			Symbol	n.a.
Market Maker	None			SIC Code	2490
Broker Dealer	Ted Prescott	Tel/Ext	(707)468-8646	Employees	n.a.

All For A Dollar, Inc.

3664 Main Street • Springfield, MA 01107 • Telephone (413)733-1203 • Fax (413)785-5696

Company Description

The Company operates 116 retail close-out stores. Almost all items or packages of items for sale are priced at $1.00. The stores offer a constantly changing variety of national brand names and generic products. As a result of recurring losses and limited cash availability, the Company filed for bankruptcy protection in June of 1994. While operating under bankruptcy protection the Company closed 50 of its stores, reorganized its operations and obtained outside financing. In June of 1995, a plan of reorganization was approved and the Company emerged from bankruptcy.

	12/30/95	12/31/94	01/01/94	01/02/93
Per Share Information				
Stock Price	0.70	0.73	2.38	10.25
Earnings Per Share	1.19	-1.78	-0.18	0.45
Price / Earnings Ratio	0.59	n.a.	n.a.	22.78
Book Value Per Share	1.85	0.66	2.43	2.70
Price / Book Value %	37.84	110.61	97.94	379.63
Dividends Per Share	n.a.	n.a.	n.a.	n.a.
Annual Financial Data				
Operating Results (000's)				
Total Revenues	47,345.4	55,177.9	69,021.0	58,509.8
Costs & Expenses	-48,239.8	-59,730.1	-70,885.2	-53,701.8
Income Before Taxes and Other	-894.4	-4,552.2	-1,864.2	4,808.0
Other Items	6,579.1	-8,027.4	n.a.	n.a.
Income Tax	2,585.0	220.3	610.0	-1,563.1
Net Income	8,269.7	-12,359.3	-1,254.2	3,245.0
Cash Flow From Operations	-2,742.1	2,944.0	-677.8	-5,781.2
Balance Sheet (000's)				
Cash & Equivalents	2,586.7	4,687.4	1,442.3	1,565.8
Total Current Assets	16,104.9	17,180.8	19,447.4	19,096.7
Fixed Assets, Net	1,938.2	2,969.5	5,764.6	5,777.0
Total Assets	20,242.1	20,438.9	25,677.6	25,337.0
Total Current Liabilities	6,225.9	15,874.9	8,534.9	6,263.3
Long-Term Debt	1,182.5	n.a.	219.4	311.1
Stockholders' Equity	12,833.7	4,564.0	16,923.3	18,762.6
Performance & Financial Condition				
Return on Total Revenues %	17.47	-22.40	-1.82	5.55
Return on Avg Stockholders' Equity %	95.07	-115.04	-7.03	29.57
Return on Average Assets %	40.66	-53.60	-4.92	17.95
Current Ratio	2.59	1.08	2.28	3.05
Debt / Equity %	9.21	n.a.	1.30	1.66

Compound Growth %'s	EPS %	38.29	Net Income %	36.59	Total Revenues %	-6.81

Comments

Income for the year ended December 30, 1995, includes $6.6 million of debt forgiveness and the loss for 1994, includes $8.0 million of costs related to the reorganization. Officers and directors, as a group, owned 38.7% of the Company's outstanding shares at December 30, 1995.

Officers	Position	Ownership Information	12/30/95
V. Martin Effron	Chairman	Number of Shares Outstanding	6,950,190
Roger A. Slate	President, CEO	Market Capitalization	$ 4,865,133
Donald A. Molta	Vice President, CFO	Frequency Of Dividends	n.a.
Richard P. Crowley	Vice President, Secretary	Number of Shareholders	284

Other Information

Transfer Agent	Boston EquiServe			Where Listed	OTC-BB
Auditor	Mottle McGrath Braney & Flynn			Symbol	AFAD
Market Maker	Troster Singer Corporation	Telephone	(800)222-0890	SIC Code	5331
Broker Dealer	Regular Stockbroker			Employees	991

Alleghany Pharmacal Corporation

277 Northern Boulevard • Great Neck, NY 11022 • Telephone (516)466-0660 • Fax (516)482-1525

Company Description

The Company distributes hair care products to wholesalers, retailers, chain and beauty supply stores. The Company also receives royalty income from the sub-licensing of product rights.

	06/30/95	06/30/94	06/30/93	06/30/92
Per Share Information				
Stock Price	1.75	1.25	1.50	0.87
Earnings Per Share	0.56	0.35	0.65	0.20
Price / Earnings Ratio	3.13	3.57	2.31	4.35
Book Value Per Share	2.47	1.77	1.23	0.58
Price / Book Value %	70.85	70.62	121.95	150.00
Dividends Per Share	n.a.	n.a.	n.a.	n.a.
Annual Financial Data				
Operating Results (000's)				
Total Revenues	14,433.0	8,111.6	8,203.8	8,987.3
Costs & Expenses	-13,840.1	-7,293.8	-8,148.3	-8,392.6
Income Before Taxes and Other	593.0	817.7	55.5	594.6
Other Items	n.a.	n.a.	n.a.	n.a.
Income Tax	2.4	-440.5	638.6	-385.3
Net Income	595.4	377.2	694.1	209.4
Cash Flow From Operations	325.6	357.7	-826.6	505.2
Balance Sheet (000's)				
Cash & Equivalents	276.3	499.2	167.2	884.4
Total Current Assets	7,814.7	3,677.1	2,967.7	3,504.9
Fixed Assets, Net	27.8	31.2	39.9	54.2
Total Assets	10,187.8	4,244.8	3,573.4	4,247.4
Total Current Liabilities	6,533.9	2,343.5	2,106.4	2,175.5
Long-Term Debt	947.9	n.a.	n.a.	310.0
Stockholders' Equity	2,641.1	1,895.6	1,316.1	622.0
Performance & Financial Condition				
Return on Total Revenues %	4.13	4.65	8.46	2.33
Return on Avg Stockholders' Equity %	26.25	23.49	71.63	40.47
Return on Average Assets %	8.25	9.65	17.75	5.44
Current Ratio	1.20	1.57	1.41	1.61
Debt / Equity %	35.89	n.a.	n.a.	49.84

Compound Growth %'s	EPS %	40.95	Net Income %	41.68	Total Revenues %	17.11

Comments

Royalty income is lower in 1995 because of the completion of the Heaven Sent sub-license in 1994. Howvever, overall revenue jumped 78% during fiscal 1995. In August, 1994, the Company acquired the inventory, trade names and customer lists of the Lustrasilk product line from the Gillette Company. 1993 results benefitted from the nonrecurring reversal of a deferred tax liability. Earnings before tax and this nonrecurring item were $55,492, or $.05 per share.

Officers	Position	Ownership Information	06/30/95
David Geller	President	Number of Shares Outstanding	1,070,055
Arthur Gutowitz	CFO	Market Capitalization	$ 1,872,596
		Frequency Of Dividends	n.a.
		Number of Shareholders	Under 500

Other Information

Transfer Agent	Continental Stock Transfer & Trust Co.			Where Listed	OTC-BB
Auditor	KPMG Peat Marwick LLP			Symbol	ALGY
Market Maker	Carr Securities Corporation	Telephone	(800)221-2243	SIC Code	5120
Broker Dealer	Regular Stockbroker			Employees	30

Allstar Inns, Inc.

200 E. Carrillo St., Ste. 300 • Santa Barbara, CA 93101 • Telephone (805)687-3383 • Fax (805)730-3369

Company Description

The Company was formed in Delaware in 1992, to assume the business and operations of a limited partnership. The Company's primary business is to own and receive rental income from the ecomomy motels it owns and leases. At December 31, 1995, the Company owned or leased 72 motels with a total of 7,641 rooms. In 1992, the Company reached an agreement with a "Motel 6" operator to manage the motels through 2011. The agreement resulted in unfavorable results and was terminated in 1995, and replaced with a triple net, 15 year term, master lease agreement with the same operator. The lease agreement has a purchase option through 1998, to purchase the motels for $40 million plus the assumption of their related indebtedness and has certain other provisions.

	12/31/95	12/31/94	12/31/93	12/31/92
Per Share Information				
Stock Price	24.50	2.69	7.00	0.33
Earnings Per Share	-0.77	-6.63	-8.17	-26.46
Price / Earnings Ratio	n.a.	n.a.	n.a.	n.a.
Book Value Per Share	-55.32	-54.82	-48.19	-40.01
Price / Book Value %	n.a.	n.a.	n.a.	n.a.
Dividends Per Share	2.00	n.a.	n.a.	3.75
Annual Financial Data				
Operating Results (000's)				
Total Revenues	52,424.0	56,842.0	52,034.0	41,058.0
Costs & Expenses	-60,173.0	-63,101.0	-59,755.0	-65,351.0
Income Before Taxes and Other	-7,749.0	-6,259.0	-7,721.0	-24,293.0
Other Items	n.a.	n.a.	n.a.	n.a.
Income Tax	7,012.0	-2.0	n.a.	n.a.
Net Income	-737.0	-6,261.0	-7,721.0	-24,293.0
Cash Flow From Operations	-12,854.0	9,855.0	2,531.0	n.a.
Balance Sheet (000's)				
Cash & Equivalents	13,518.0	20,320.0	n.a.	n.a.
Total Current Assets	15,653.0	24,966.0	n.a.	n.a.
Fixed Assets, Net	136,232.0	145,614.0	n.a.	n.a.
Total Assets	160,290.0	174,048.0	n.a.	n.a.
Total Current Liabilities	10,204.0	28,299.0	n.a.	n.a.
Long-Term Debt	204,556.0	197,533.0	n.a.	n.a.
Stockholders' Equity	-54,470.0	-51,784.0	n.a.	n.a.
Performance & Financial Condition				
Return on Total Revenues %	-1.41	-11.01	-14.84	n.a.
Return on Avg Stockholders' Equity %	n.a.	n.a.	n.a.	n.a.
Return on Average Assets %	-0.44	n.a.	n.a.	n.a.
Current Ratio	1.53	0.88	n.a.	n.a.
Debt / Equity %	n.a.	n.a.	n.a.	n.a.

Compound Growth %'s	EPS % n.a.	Net Income % n.a.	Total Revenues % 8.49

Comments

One look at the operating results is enough to understand why the arrangements prior to 1995 were not satisfactory to the Company. The operating results under the new agreement will look a lot different, primarily lease revenue, interest costs, depreciation and some administration expenses. Investors must like the new arrangements also, given the ten-fold increase in share price since 1994. Balance sheet information prior to 1994, was not available. With this Company, it is the future and not the past that is worth looking at.

Officers	Position	Ownership Information	12/31/95
Daniel R. Shaughnessy	Chairman, CEO	Number of Shares Outstanding	984,710
Edward A. Paul	Vice President	Market Capitalization	$ 24,125,395
Edward J. Gallagher	Other	Frequency Of Dividends	Irregular
		Number of Shareholders	692

Other Information

Transfer Agent	Chemical Mellon Shareholder Services		Where Listed	OTC-BB
Auditor	Ernst & Young LLP		Symbol	ALST
Market Maker	Wien Securities Corp.	Telephone (800)624-0050	SIC Code	7011
Broker Dealer	Regular Stockbroker		Employees	6

Alpha Pro Tech, Ltd.

60 Centurian Drive, Ste. 112 • Markham, Ontario L3R 9R2 Canada • Telephone (905)479-0654 • Fax (905)479-9732

Company Description

The Company manufactures and markets infection control, wound care and disposable apparel products for the medical, dental, and clean room environment market. The Company's main manufacturing facilities are located in Utah, Wisconsin and Mexico. The Company was incorporated in British Columbia, Canada in 1983 and reincorporated in the State of Delaware in 1994.

	12/31/95	12/31/94	12/31/93	12/31/92
Per Share Information				
Stock Price	1.75	1.08	0.91	3.63
Earnings Per Share	-0.31	-0.05	-0.22	-0.06
Price / Earnings Ratio	n.a.	n.a.	n.a.	n.a.
Book Value Per Share	0.15	0.38	0.41	0.40
Price / Book Value %	1,166.70	284.21	221.95	907.50
Dividends Per Share	n.a.	n.a.	n.a.	n.a.
Annual Financial Data				
Operating Results (000's)				
Total Revenues	13,041.0	11,966.0	9,439.0	8,130.0
Costs & Expenses	-14,085.0	-12,909.0	-11,826.0	-8,657.0
Income Before Taxes and Other	-5,966.0	-943.0	-2,546.0	-527.0
Other Items	-5.0	n.a.	n.a.	n.a.
Income Tax	n.a.	285.0	-80.0	-48.0
Net Income	-5,971.0	-658.0	-2,626.0	-575.0
Cash Flow From Operations	-480.0	-1,015.0	-1,143.0	-897.0
Balance Sheet (000's)				
Cash & Equivalents	344.0	340.0	440.0	1,081.0
Total Current Assets	4,860.0	4,715.0	2,749.0	4,126.0
Fixed Assets, Net	1,350.0	1,076.0	905.0	821.0
Total Assets	6,410.0	11,192.0	9,578.0	11,100.0
Total Current Liabilities	3,166.0	3,879.0	2,885.0	4,847.0
Long-Term Debt	226.0	1,154.0	110.0	474.0
Stockholders' Equity	3,004.0	6,159.0	6,415.0	5,600.0
Performance & Financial Condition				
Return on Total Revenues %	-45.79	-5.50	-27.82	-7.07
Return on Avg Stockholders' Equity %	-130.33	-10.47	-43.71	-18.21
Return on Average Assets %	-67.84	-6.34	-25.40	-9.40
Current Ratio	1.54	1.22	0.95	0.85
Debt / Equity %	7.52	18.74	1.71	8.46

Compound Growth %'s	EPS % n.a.	Net Income % n.a.	Total Revenues % 17.06

Comments

The 1995 loss includes a writeoff of $4,922,000 related to goodwill associated with a corporate acquisition in 1992. Intangibles remaining at December 31, 1995, total $165,000. During April 1996, the Company announced an exclusive three-year distribution agreement with Chicopee, Inc. that could total more than $26 million in sales.

Officers	Position	Ownership Information	12/31/95
Alexander W. Millar	President	Number of Shares Outstanding	19,911,130
Sheldon Hoffman	CEO	Market Capitalization	$ 34,844,478
lloyd Hoffman	Vice President	Frequency Of Dividends	n.a.
Dan Schaefer	Vice President	Number of Shareholders	625

Other Information				
Transfer Agent	American Stock Transfer & Trust Company		Where Listed	OTC-BB
Auditor	Price Waterhouse LLP		Symbol	APTD
Market Maker	Allen & Company, Inc.	Telephone (800)221-2246	SIC Code	3841
Broker Dealer	Regular Stockbroker		Employees	383

Amador, Bank of

P.O. Box 908 • Jackson, CA 95642-0908 • Telephone (209)223-2320 • Fax (209)223-4746

Company Description

The Bank, which was opened in 1983, serves Amador County, California, and the surrounding areas, from its central office in Jackson and from branch offices located in the communities of Buckhorn and Ione. Timber, recreation/tourism and agriculture are the predominant industries. The Bank's business has been derived primarily from the consumer, professional and agricultural communities.

	12/31/95	12/31/94	12/31/93	12/31/92
Per Share Information				
Stock Price	8.31	6.50	6.25	6.75
Earnings Per Share	0.89	0.72	0.63	0.54
Price / Earnings Ratio	9.34	9.03	9.92	12.50
Book Value Per Share	6.05	5.52	5.12	4.69
Price / Book Value %	137.36	117.75	122.07	143.92
Dividends Per Share	0.36	0.31	0.22	0.15
Annual Financial Data				
Operating Results (000's)				
Net Interest Income	3,893.9	3,480.2	3,036.7	2,695.4
Loan Loss Provision	-138.0	-102.5	-46.6	-57.5
Non-Interest Income	372.8	317.8	415.0	435.0
Non-Interest Expense	-2,269.4	-2,226.6	-2,105.2	-1,922.9
Income Before Taxes and Other	1,859.3	1,468.9	1,299.8	1,150.0
Other Items	n.a.	n.a.	n.a.	n.a.
Income Tax	-705.0	-544.0	-467.0	-433.0
Net Income	1,154.3	924.9	832.8	717.0
Balance Sheet (000's)				
Cash & Securities	19,695.1	17,173.4	23,911.4	n.a.
Loans, Net	46,439.5	37,295.4	36,664.5	n.a.
Fixed Assets, Net	522.3	260.8	376.4	n.a.
Total Assets	67,567.1	55,498.1	61,634.4	n.a.
Deposits	59,311.0	48,136.1	54,778.6	n.a.
Stockholders' Equity	7,915.8	7,122.1	6,596.9	n.a.
Performance & Financial Condition				
Net Interest Margin	n.a.	n.a.	n.a.	n.a.
Return on Avg Stockholders' Equity %	15.35	13.48	13.17	n.a.
Return on Average Assets %	1.88	1.58	1.40	n.a.
Equity to Assets %	11.72	12.83	10.70	n.a.
Reserve as a % of Non-Performing Loans	67.98	907.90	1110.82	n.a.

Compound Growth %'s	EPS %	18.12	Net Income %	17.21	Net Interest Income %	13.05

Comments

The loan portfolio at December 31, 1995, was construction, mortgage and commercial loans of 38%, 35% and 23%, respectively. During 1995, the Bank acquired the assets, totalling $6.3 million, of the Ione branch of U.S. Bank. This Bank of Amador is recording excellent returns on both equity and assets.

Officers	Position	Ownership Information	12/31/95
Larry Standing	President, CEO	Number of Shares Outstanding	1,308,138
Thomas L. Walker	Senior VP, CFO	Market Capitalization	$ 10,870,627
Richard J. Roy	Senior VP	Frequency Of Dividends	Semi-Annual
Gareth Abel	Secretary	Number of Shareholders	n.a.
Barbara Matranga	Vice President		

Other Information				
Transfer Agent	U.S. Stock Transfer Corp.		Where Listed	OTC-BB
Auditor	Perry-Smith & Co.		Symbol	BNKA
Market Maker	Hoefer & Arnett, Inc.	Telephone (415)362-7160	SIC Code	6020
Broker Dealer	Regular Stockbroker		Employees	46

Amelco Corporation

19208 S. Vermont Avenue • Gardena, CA 90248 • Telephone (310)327-3070 • Fax (310)538-3417

Company Description

The Company was organized in 1967, to become the parent of existing operating companies. Through its subsidiaries, the Company engages in specialty construction work, primarily electrical and mechanical construction. Work is generally performed under fixed-price contracts and is undertaken by the Company alone, with subcontractors or in partnership with other contractors. Construction operations are conducted in the western continental U.S., Hawaii and Guam.

	09/30/95	09/30/94	09/30/93	09/30/92
Per Share Information				
Stock Price	2.50	2.75	3.13	3.38
Earnings Per Share	0.70	0.56	0.63	0.48
Price / Earnings Ratio	3.57	4.91	4.97	7.04
Book Value Per Share	10.23	9.63	9.22	8.84
Price / Book Value %	24.44	28.56	33.95	38.24
Dividends Per Share	0.10	0.15	0.25	0.15
Annual Financial Data				
Operating Results (000's)				
Total Revenues	126,611.0	114,504.0	95,882.0	91,195.0
Costs & Expenses	-124,803.0	-113,021.0	-94,212.0	-89,824.0
Income Before Taxes and Other	1,706.0	1,380.0	1,517.0	1,234.0
Other Items	n.a.	-31.0	20.0	1.0
Income Tax	-691.0	-545.0	-627.0	-535.0
Net Income	1,015.0	804.0	910.0	700.0
Cash Flow From Operations	899.0	-125.0	914.0	269.0
Balance Sheet (000's)				
Cash & Equivalents	3,863.0	2,690.0	3,406.0	1,679.0
Total Current Assets	38,126.0	35,441.0	24,185.0	22,936.0
Fixed Assets, Net	1,772.0	1,797.0	1,882.0	1,785.0
Total Assets	43,629.0	40,789.0	29,659.0	28,221.0
Total Current Liabilities	26,965.0	24,890.0	14,297.0	15,390.0
Long-Term Debt	1,863.0	1,911.0	1,956.0	n.a.
Stockholders' Equity	14,767.0	13,896.0	13,309.0	12,760.0
Performance & Financial Condition				
Return on Total Revenues %	0.80	0.70	0.95	0.77
Return on Avg Stockholders' Equity %	7.08	5.91	6.98	5.59
Return on Average Assets %	2.40	2.28	3.14	2.36
Current Ratio	1.41	1.42	1.69	1.49
Debt / Equity %	12.62	13.75	14.70	n.a.

Compound Growth %'s	EPS %	13.40	Net Income %	13.19	Total Revenues %	11.56

Comments

For the three months ended December 31, 1995, the Company had revenues of $27.5 million and net income of $187,000 ($.13 per share) as compared to $31.4 million and $308,000 ($.21 per share) for the same period in 1994. At September 30, 1995, the Company had a backlog of future construction work of $87.7 million.

Officers	Position	Ownership Information	09/30/95
Samuel M. Angelich	President, CEO	Number of Shares Outstanding	1,443,542
Mark S. Angelich	Exec VP	Market Capitalization	$ 3,608,855
Patrick T. Miike	VP - Finance, Treasurer	Frequency Of Dividends	Annual
John M. Carmack	Secretary	Number of Shareholders	315

Other Information

Transfer Agent	U.S. Stock Transfer Corporation	Where Listed	OTC-BB
Auditor	KPMG Peat Marwick LLP	Symbol	AMLC
Market Maker	Abel-Behnke Corp. Honolulu	SIC Code	1731
Broker Dealer	Regular Stockbroker	Employees	526

American Atlantic Company

900 E. Eighth Avenue, Ste. 107 • King of Prussia, PA 19406 • Telephone (610)337-8160 • Fax (610)337-8166

Company Description

The Company, formerly known as American Dredging Company, is in the process of liquidating. The dredging business constituted virtually all of the Company's revenue and expenses prior to 1993. The preferred stock of the Company was liquidated in 1994.

	12/31/94	12/31/93
Per Share Information		
Stock Price	7.75	7.50
Earnings Per Share	2.38	4.12
Price / Earnings Ratio	3.26	1.82
Book Value Per Share	7.99	6.32
Price / Book Value %	97.00	118.67
Dividends Per Share	n.a.	n.a.
Annual Financial Data		
Operating Results (000's)		
Total Revenues	420.8	516.0
Costs & Expenses	-425.1	-252.2
Income Before Taxes and Other	-4.4	263.8
Other Items	1,761.3	3,558.5
Income Tax	n.a.	n.a.
Net Income	1,757.0	3,822.3
Cash Flow From Operations	4,185.6	1,280.8
Balance Sheet (000's)		
Cash & Equivalents	3,689.2	12,116.9
Total Current Assets	3,969.3	15,951.7
Fixed Assets, Net	2,852.2	2,852.2
Total Assets	6,821.5	18,804.0
Total Current Liabilities	641.0	1,767.1
Long-Term Debt	n.a.	n.a.
Stockholders' Equity	6,180.6	17,036.9
Performance & Financial Condition		
Return on Total Revenues %	417.56	740.75
Return on Avg Stockholders' Equity %	15.13	23.89
Return on Average Assets %	13.71	22.22
Current Ratio	6.19	9.03
Debt / Equity %	n.a.	n.a.

Compound Growth %'s	EPS %	-42.23	Net Income %	-54.03	Total Revenues %	-18.46

Comments

1994 and 1993 results include income from discontinued operation of $1.8 million and $3.5 million, respectively. 1993 book value per share was restated to reflect the 1994 redemption of preferred stock. The remaining 617 acre property in an industrial complex in Logan Township, New Jersey, is being offered for sale at an asking price of $8 million. The 1995 annual report will be available in June.

Officers	Position	Ownership Information	12/31/94
Christopher H. Browne	Chairman	Number of Shares Outstanding	773,758
		Market Capitalization	$ 5,996,625
		Frequency Of Dividends	n.a.
		Number of Shareholders	Under 500

Other Information

Transfer Agent	Company Office			Where Listed	OTC-BB
Auditor	Price Waterhouse LLP			Symbol	AMRL
Market Maker	Herzog, Heine, Geduld, Inc.	Telephone	(800)221-3600	SIC Code	6790
Broker Dealer	Regular Stockbroker			Employees	2

American Bancorp, Inc.

P.O. Box 1579 • Opelousas, LA 70570 • Telephone (318)948-3056 • Fax (318)942-1134

Company Description

American Bancorp, Inc. is a one-bank holding company whose sole subsidiary is American Bank and Trust Company, a commercial bank whose general business is providing banking services to the Opelousas, Louisiana area with six banking locations.

	12/31/95	12/31/94	12/31/93	12/31/92
Per Share Information				
Stock Price	22.50	22.50	22.50	25.00
Earnings Per Share	8.03	8.02	6.04	6.75
Price / Earnings Ratio	2.80	2.81	3.73	3.70
Book Value Per Share	56.55	48.49	41.12	35.58
Price / Book Value %	39.79	46.40	54.72	70.26
Dividends Per Share	0.85	0.65	0.50	n.a.
Annual Financial Data				
Operating Results (000's)				
Net Interest Income	3,064.6	2,567.1	2,442.4	2,450.1
Loan Loss Provision	n.a.	-12.0	-36.0	-36.0
Non-Interest Income	677.4	693.5	600.8	600.9
Non-Interest Expense	-2,328.7	-2,342.5	-2,268.2	-2,190.2
Income Before Taxes and Other	1,413.2	906.1	738.9	824.8
Other Items	n.a.	n.a.	n.a.	n.a.
Income Tax	-449.8	56.4	-14.4	-15.4
Net Income	963.5	962.5	724.5	809.4
Balance Sheet (000's)				
Cash & Securities	34,223.3	35,943.8	23,075.4	25,832.8
Loans, Net	26,390.2	27,053.0	26,432.5	25,257.0
Fixed Assets, Net	1,435.4	1,375.1	1,500.2	1,380.8
Total Assets	63,070.3	65,140.9	51,746.2	53,382.2
Deposits	55,654.7	59,230.2	46,676.3	48,996.7
Stockholders' Equity	6,785.5	5,818.3	4,934.5	4,270.0
Performance & Financial Condition				
Net Interest Margin	5.79	5.09	5.02	5.23
Return on Avg Stockholders' Equity %	15.29	17.90	15.74	20.94
Return on Average Assets %	1.50	1.65	1.38	1.53
Equity to Assets %	10.76	8.93	9.54	8.00
Reserve as a % of Non-Performing Loans	505.10	421.37	176.59	292.97

Compound Growth %'s	EPS %	5.96	Net Income %	5.98	Net Interest Income %	7.74

Comments

Although growth rates are low, the Bank has exceptional returns on total assets and equity. The stock trades infrequently and the Company does not maintain a list of potential buyers. They will match you up with a seller if you happen to call when one is around. Share price information was provided by the Company based on their knowledge of specific transactions. The last shares to trade, as we went to press, were in May, 1996, at $22.50 per share.

Officers	Position	Ownership Information	12/31/95
Salvador L. Diesi, Sr.	Chairman, President	Number of Shares Outstanding	120,000
Ronald J. Lashute	CEO, Exec VP	Market Capitalization	$ 2,700,000
Walter J. Champagne, Jr.	Senior VP	Frequency Of Dividends	Annual
Joan T. Muller	Vice President, CFO	Number of Shareholders	572
Charlene Louviere	Vice President		

Other Information

Transfer Agent	Company Office			Where Listed	Order Matching Only
Auditor	Broussard, Poche, Lewis & Breaux			Symbol	n.a.
Market Maker	Company Office	Telephone	(318)543-2383	SIC Code	6020
Broker Dealer	None			Employees	46

American Consolidated Laboratories, Inc.

6416 Parkland Drive • Sarasota, FL 34243 • Telephone (941)753-0383 • Fax (941)755-5432

Company Description

The Company manufactures contact lenses. The focus has changed from full-line manufacture of soft and hard lenses to rigid gas permeable lenses and specialty soft lenses only, emphasizing multifocal lenses for the aging population. The Company also distributes soft lenses produced by all manufacturers. Formed in Florida in 1985 as Salvatori Opthalmics, the Company's name was changed in 1994. A venture capital group, Tullis-Dickerson Capital Focus LP, owns approximately 64% of the Company's common stock.

	12/31/95	12/31/94	12/31/93	12/31/92
Per Share Information				
Stock Price	1.31	0.69	0.11	0.91
Earnings Per Share	-0.51	0.07	0.07	-0.99
Price / Earnings Ratio	n.a.	9.86	1.57	n.a.
Book Value Per Share	0.02	0.46	0.26	0.19
Price / Book Value %	6,550.00	150.00	42.31	478.95
Dividends Per Share	n.a.	n.a.	n.a.	n.a.
Annual Financial Data				
Operating Results (000's)				
Total Revenues	9,003.2	4,166.5	4,017.6	4,595.2
Costs & Expenses	-10,992.9	-4,062.2	-3,938.0	-5,246.9
Income Before Taxes and Other	-2,094.4	104.2	79.6	-1,078.8
Other Items	n.a.	n.a.	n.a.	n.a.
Income Tax	n.a.	n.a.	n.a.	n.a.
Net Income	-2,094.4	104.2	79.6	-1,078.8
Cash Flow From Operations	-456.6	420.7	144.4	-506.7
Balance Sheet (000's)				
Cash & Equivalents	37.8	320.9	200.4	113.5
Total Current Assets	1,772.7	2,216.2	875.7	986.8
Fixed Assets, Net	621.5	572.2	636.7	813.2
Total Assets	3,841.6	4,381.3	1,904.8	2,247.8
Total Current Liabilities	2,663.0	2,234.5	528.3	890.1
Long-Term Debt	1,050.6	332.5	1,015.1	1,080.6
Stockholders' Equity	69.7	1,753.4	300.1	218.3
Performance & Financial Condition				
Return on Total Revenues %	-23.26	2.50	1.98	-23.48
Return on Avg Stockholders' Equity %	-229.77	10.15	30.73	-155.17
Return on Average Assets %	-50.94	3.32	3.84	-41.53
Current Ratio	0.67	0.99	1.66	1.11
Debt / Equity %	1506.80	18.96	338.26	494.93

Compound Growth %'s	EPS % n.a.	Net Income % n.a.	Total Revenues % 25.13

Comments

Sales increased 118% in 1995, due primarily to the acquisition of two companies involved in the manufacture and distribution of contact lenses. The net loss in 1995, is primarily due to increased administrative costs.

Officers	Position	Ownership Information	12/31/95
Grady A. Deal	President, COO	Number of Shares Outstanding	4,436,927
Wayne U. Smith	CEO, Chairman	Market Capitalization	$ 5,812,374
Edward J. Pocilujko	CFO	Frequency Of Dividends	n.a.
Anthony L. Salvatori	Secretary	Number of Shareholders	1,000

Other Information

Transfer Agent	American Stock Transfer & Trust Company			Where Listed	OTC-BB
Auditor	Deloitte & Touche LLP			Symbol	EYES
Market Maker	Herzog, Heine, Geduld, Inc.	Telephone	(800)221-3600	SIC Code	3851
Broker Dealer	Regular Stockbroker			Employees	109

American Consumers, Inc.

P.O. Box 2328 • Fort Oglethorpe, GA 30742 • Telephone (706)861-3347 • Fax (706)861-3364

Company Description

The Company is engaged in the operation of a chain of retail grocery stores in Tennessee, Alabama and Georgia. The stores are operated under the name of "Shop-Rite Supermarket". The Company was incorporated in Georgia in 1968.

	06/03/95	05/28/94	05/29/93	05/30/92
Per Share Information				
Stock Price	0.50	n.a.	n.a.	n.a.
Earnings Per Share	0.18	0.25	0.03	0.19
Price / Earnings Ratio	2.78	n.a.	n.a.	n.a.
Book Value Per Share	2.52	2.39	2.17	2.14
Price / Book Value %	19.84	n.a.	n.a.	n.a.
Dividends Per Share	0.08	0.04	n.a.	0.08
Annual Financial Data				
Operating Results (000's)				
Total Revenues	28,834.9	28,541.6	30,153.4	31,521.6
Costs & Expenses	-22,895.8	-22,727.1	-24,399.3	-25,536.7
Income Before Taxes and Other	287.0	384.9	37.1	270.3
Other Items	n.a.	n.a.	n.a.	n.a.
Income Tax	-114.9	-146.2	-4.3	-93.6
Net Income	172.1	238.7	32.8	176.7
Cash Flow From Operations	22.6	704.1	101.4	476.1
Balance Sheet (000's)				
Cash & Equivalents	416.5	420.5	420.5	353.2
Total Current Assets	2,859.8	3,034.1	2,696.8	2,801.5
Fixed Assets, Net	837.4	750.5	827.3	919.4
Total Assets	3,736.6	3,808.1	3,560.2	3,768.3
Total Current Liabilities	1,208.3	1,350.3	1,293.3	1,513.0
Long-Term Debt	n.a.	n.a.	n.a.	n.a.
Stockholders' Equity	2,333.8	2,251.1	2,053.0	2,020.2
Performance & Financial Condition				
Return on Total Revenues %	0.60	0.84	0.11	0.56
Return on Avg Stockholders' Equity %	7.51	11.09	1.61	8.98
Return on Average Assets %	4.56	6.48	0.89	4.87
Current Ratio	2.37	2.25	2.09	1.85
Debt / Equity %	n.a.	n.a.	n.a.	n.a.

Compound Growth %'s	EPS %	-1.79	Net Income %	-0.87	Total Revenues %	-2.93

Comments

The Company operates on a 52/53 week year. During the two years ended June 3, 1995, the Company repurchased a total of 17,391 shares of its common stock from unaffiliated shareholders. Prior to 1995, there was very limited trading in the Company's stock with no published quotations. The Company had sales of $14.5 million and net income of $69,000 for the 26 weeks ended December 2, 1995, as compared to $13.9 million and $97,000 for the same period in 1994.

Officers	Position	Ownership Information	06/03/95
Michael A. Richardson	President, CEO	Number of Shares Outstanding	927,444
Paul R. Cook	Exec VP, Treasurer	Market Capitalization	$ 463,722
Reba S. Southern	Secretary	Frequency Of Dividends	Quarterly
James E. Floyd	Vice President	Number of Shareholders	951
Virgil Bishop	Vice President		

Other Information				
Transfer Agent	Company Office		Where Listed	OTC-PS
Auditor	Hazlett, Lewis A & Bieter PLLC		Symbol	n.a.
Market Maker	Carr Securities Corporation	Telephone (800)221-2243	SIC Code	5410
Broker Dealer	Regular Stockbroker		Employees	194

American Electromedics Corp.

13 Columbia Drive, Suite 18 • Amherst, NH 03031 • Telephone (603)880-6300 • Fax (603)880-8977

Company Description

The Company manufactures and sells medical testing equipment. Products include devices designed for audiological testing purposes: tympanometers, which are used to detect disease of the middle ear, and audiometers, which use sound at descending decibel levels to screen for hearing loss.

	07/29/95	07/30/94	07/31/93	08/01/92
Per Share Information				
Stock Price	0.43	0.27	0.31	0.09
Earnings Per Share	0.02	0.01	0.05	-0.06
Price / Earnings Ratio	21.50	27.00	6.20	n.a.
Book Value Per Share	0.10	0.08	0.08	0.02
Price / Book Value %	430.00	337.50	387.50	450.00
Dividends Per Share	n.a.	n.a.	n.a.	n.a.
Annual Financial Data				
Operating Results (000's)				
Total Revenues	2,456.0	1,967.0	2,358.0	1,638.0
Costs & Expenses	-2,272.0	-1,902.0	-2,155.0	-1,989.0
Income Before Taxes and Other	184.0	61.0	203.0	-421.0
Other Items	n.a.	n.a.	378.0	n.a.
Income Tax	-12.0	-4.0	-182.0	n.a.
Net Income	172.0	57.0	399.0	-421.0
Cash Flow From Operations	19.0	49.0	398.0	38.0
Balance Sheet (000's)				
Cash & Equivalents	505.0	265.0	234.0	104.0
Total Current Assets	1,232.0	609.0	717.0	644.0
Fixed Assets, Net	51.0	49.0	54.0	66.0
Total Assets	1,513.0	899.0	1,023.0	981.0
Total Current Liabilities	317.0	124.0	315.0	691.0
Long-Term Debt	n.a.	4.0	4.0	111.0
Stockholders' Equity	1,196.0	771.0	704.0	179.0
Performance & Financial Condition				
Return on Total Revenues %	7.00	2.90	16.92	-25.70
Return on Avg Stockholders' Equity %	17.49	7.73	90.37	-125.30
Return on Average Assets %	14.26	5.93	39.82	-36.82
Current Ratio	3.89	4.91	2.28	0.93
Debt / Equity %	n.a.	0.52	0.57	62.01

Compound Growth %'s	EPS % -36.75	Net Income % -34.34	Total Revenues % 14.46

Comments

Included as Other Items in the 1993 operating results is income of $378,000 relating to debt restructuring. As of October 24, 1995, officers and directors, as a group, owned 23.4% of the Company's outstanding common stock. For the six months ended January 27, 1996, the Company had sales of $1.5 million and net income of $224,000 ($.02 per share) as compared to $1.1 million and $135,000 ($.01 per share) for the same period in the prior fiscal year.

Officers	Position	Ownership Information	07/29/95
Noel A. Wren	President, CEO	Number of Shares Outstanding	11,718,333
Michael T. Pieniazek	CFO	Market Capitalization	$ 5,038,883
		Frequency Of Dividends	n.a.
		Number of Shareholders	110

Other Information

Transfer Agent	American Stock Transfer & Trust Company		Where Listed	OTC-BB
Auditor	Ernst & Young LLP		Symbol	AECO
Market Maker	Fahnestock & Co., Inc.	Telephone (800)253-6825	SIC Code	3845
Broker Dealer	Regular Stockbroker		Employees	11

American Industrial Loan Association

3420 Holland Road, Ste. 107 • Virginia Beach, VA 23450-2179 • Telephone (804)430-1400 • Fax (804)430-1978

Company Description

The Company is primarily engaged in wholesale loan originations and sales of noncomforming residential mortgages. Business is conducted in the states of Georgia, Virginia, North Carolina, South Carolina, and Florida and the District of Columbia. The Company was incorporated in 1952. Its most recent stock offering was 225,000 shares at $6.25 per share in 1992. During 1994, the Company repurchased 3,000 shares at $8.17 per share.

	12/31/94	12/31/93	12/31/92
Per Share Information			
Stock Price	8.00	10.50	n.a.
Earnings Per Share	0.79	1.70	1.53
Price / Earnings Ratio	10.13	6.18	n.a.
Book Value Per Share	8.94	8.46	n.a.
Price / Book Value %	89.49	124.11	n.a.
Dividends Per Share	0.32	0.31	n.a.
Annual Financial Data			
Operating Results (000's)			
Total Revenues	5,540.0	6,206.6	6,518.5
Costs & Expenses	-4,682.3	-4,369.1	-5,052.1
Income Before Taxes and Other	857.7	1,837.4	1,466.4
Other Items	3.0	n.a.	n.a.
Income Tax	-360.0	-760.7	-584.0
Net Income	500.7	1,076.7	882.4
Cash Flow From Operations	-518.6	6,539.2	-1,940.6
Balance Sheet (000's)			
Cash & Equivalents	405.5	1,398.5	n.a.
Total Current Assets	405.5	1,398.5	n.a.
Fixed Assets, Net	1,036.3	999.1	n.a.
Total Assets	23,109.4	21,662.9	n.a.
Total Current Liabilities	278.2	40.9	n.a.
Long-Term Debt	n.a.	n.a.	n.a.
Stockholders' Equity	5,644.6	5,371.6	n.a.
Performance & Financial Condition			
Return on Total Revenues %	9.04	17.35	13.54
Return on Avg Stockholders' Equity %	9.09	n.a.	n.a.
Return on Average Assets %	2.24	n.a.	n.a.
Current Ratio	1.46	34.18	n.a.
Debt / Equity %	n.a.	n.a.	n.a.

Compound Growth %'s	EPS %	-28.14	Net Income %	-24.68	Total Revenues %	-7.81

Comments

In 1994, the Company acquired an 11% interest in a joint venture which originates nonconforming residential mortgages at retail locations. This venture produced $392,639 of income for the Company in 1994, nearly half of total pre-tax income. It would have been a dismal without that boost. We were anxiously awaiting 1995 results when we went to press.

Officers	Position	Ownership Information	12/31/94
Allen D. Wykle	President, CEO	Number of Shares Outstanding	631,680
Neil W. Phelan	Senior VP, COO	Market Capitalization	$ 5,053,440
Stanley W. Broaddus	Vice President	Frequency Of Dividends	Quarterly
		Number of Shareholders	Under 500

Other Information					
Transfer Agent	Registrar & Transfer Company			Where Listed	OTC-BB
Auditor	Ernst & Young LLP			Symbol	AILY
Market Maker	Anderson & Strudwick, Inc.	Telephone	(800)827-2515	SIC Code	6090
Broker Dealer	Regular Stockbroker			Employees	n.a.

American Public Life Insurance Company

P.O. Box 925 • Jackson, MS 39205-0925 • Telephone (601)936-6600 • Fax (601)939-0655

Company Description

The Company offers a diversified line of insurance products including cancer, general health, disability and dental. The Company is licensed and operates in 21 states. There was a 1 for 20 reverse split in 1986.

	12/31/95	12/31/94	12/31/93	12/31/92
Per Share Information				
Stock Price	145.00	101.00	95.00	95.00
Earnings Per Share	8.03	12.70	30.01	23.96
Price / Earnings Ratio	18.06	7.95	3.17	3.96
Book Value Per Share	180.34	170.09	152.59	130.56
Price / Book Value %	80.40	59.38	62.26	72.76
Dividends Per Share	4.70	4.70	5.16	n.a.
Annual Financial Data				
Operating Results (000's)				
Total Revenues	28,096.3	26,656.0	23,766.3	22,567.3
Costs & Expenses	-27,533.7	-25,605.0	-21,436.9	-20,665.0
Income Before Taxes and Other	562.6	1,051.0	2,329.5	1,902.3
Other Items	n.a.	n.a.	n.a.	n.a.
Income Tax	-131.6	-313.2	-585.3	-509.8
Net Income	431.1	737.9	1,744.2	1,392.5
Cash Flow From Operations	n.a.	n.a.	n.a.	n.a.
Balance Sheet (000's)				
Cash & Equivalents	312.6	1,801.7	4,288.6	4,312.5
Total Current Assets	312.6	1,801.7	4,288.6	4,312.5
Fixed Assets, Net	2,773.5	n.a.	n.a.	n.a.
Total Assets	38,273.7	37,489.0	35,845.7	33,582.6
Total Current Liabilities	n.a.	n.a.	n.a.	n.a.
Long-Term Debt	n.a.	n.a.	n.a.	n.a.
Stockholders' Equity	9,682.7	9,885.3	8,867.7	7,587.4
Performance & Financial Condition				
Return on Total Revenues %	1.53	2.77	7.34	6.17
Return on Avg Stockholders' Equity %	4.41	7.87	21.20	20.26
Return on Average Assets %	1.14	2.01	5.02	4.31
Current Ratio	n.a.	n.a.	n.a.	n.a.
Debt / Equity %	n.a.	n.a.	n.a.	n.a.

Compound Growth %'s	EPS % -30.54	Net Income % -32.35	Total Revenues % 7.58

Comments

New management has taken the helm during 1995, and is in the process of re-evaluating all administrative functions as well as market definition, focus and new product development. The Company continues to diversify its product lines and is less dependent on cancer insurance. This insurance accounted for 39.2% of revenue in 1995, down from 62.5% in 1992. There is no indication that the financial results have been audited.

Officers	Position	Ownership Information	12/31/95
Ralph B. Plummer	President, CEO	Number of Shares Outstanding	53,691
Edwin R. Pearce	Exec VP	Market Capitalization	$ 7,785,195
Frank K. Junkin, Jr.	Senior VP	Frequency Of Dividends	Quarterly
Joseph C. Hartley, Jr.	Senior VP, Secretary	Number of Shareholders	Under 500
Alison James, Jr.	Vice President		

Other Information

Transfer Agent	First National Bank of Jackson (MS)		Where Listed	OTC-BB
Auditor	Not indicated		Symbol	APUB
Market Maker	Morgan Keegan & Company, Inc.	Telephone (800)238-7533	SIC Code	6311
Broker Dealer	Regular Stockbroker		Employees	75

American River Holdings

1545 River Park Dr., Suite 107 • Sacramento, CA 95815 • Telephone (916)565-6100 • Fax (916)641-1262

Company Description

American River Holdings is the parent company of American River Bank. The Bank is a regional bank with four branches serving the greater Sacramento, California area. The Bank offers business and personal checking accounts; residential, commercial and consumer lending; various investment products; cash management and other services. The Bank was formed in 1983 and has had 48 consecutive quarters of earnings through December 31, 1995. A private placement in 1983 raised $3,554,000.

	12/31/95	12/31/94	12/31/93	12/31/92
Per Share Information				
Stock Price	11.25	8.35	8.00	7.25
Earnings Per Share	1.54	1.17	0.89	0.76
Price / Earnings Ratio	7.31	7.14	8.99	9.54
Book Value Per Share	10.73	9.19	8.59	7.94
Price / Book Value %	104.85	90.86	93.13	91.31
Dividends Per Share	0.26	0.25	0.25	0.50
Annual Financial Data				
Operating Results (000's)				
Net Interest Income	7,195.0	6,234.0	3,537.0	3,233.0
Loan Loss Provision	-420.0	-300.0	-241.0	-205.0
Non-Interest Income	1,272.0	1,000.0	1,325.0	741.0
Non-Interest Expense	-5,249.0	-4,906.0	-3,202.0	-2,532.0
Income Before Taxes and Other	2,798.0	2,028.0	1,419.0	1,237.0
Other Items	n.a.	n.a.	52.0	n.a.
Income Tax	-1,153.0	-833.0	-571.0	-477.0
Net Income	1,645.0	1,195.0	900.0	760.0
Balance Sheet (000's)				
Cash & Securities	34,085.0	26,704.0	23,253.0	15,234.0
Loans, Net	90,986.0	82,570.0	74,763.0	50,064.0
Fixed Assets, Net	787.0	857.0	815.0	492.0
Total Assets	134,496.0	120,181.0	111,869.0	75,261.0
Deposits	122,233.0	109,528.0	102,468.0	66,747.0
Stockholders' Equity	11,455.0	9,820.0	8,656.0	8,007.0
Performance & Financial Condition				
Net Interest Margin	n.a.	n.a.	n.a.	n.a.
Return on Avg Stockholders' Equity %	15.46	12.94	10.80	9.67
Return on Average Assets %	1.29	1.03	0.96	1.15
Equity to Assets %	8.52	8.17	7.74	10.64
Reserve as a % of Non-Performing Loans	239.76	370.74	5254.17	n.a.

Compound Growth %'s	EPS %	26.54	Net Income %	29.36	Net Interest Income %	30.56

Comments

The Bank seems to benefit from the winning combination of a strong local economy and housing market, good management and satisfied customers. A recent annual survey showed 99% overall client satisfaction. The Bank does an excellent job in keeping investors informed with interesting quarterly reports as well as the detailed annual which, among other items, discloses the overall shareholder return including appreciation and dividends. It was 37% in 1995.

Officers	Position	Ownership Information	12/31/95
William L. Young	President, CEO	Number of Shares Outstanding	1,068,000
David T. Taber	President, CEO	Market Capitalization	$ 12,015,000
Ralph J. Sabin	Senior VP	Frequency Of Dividends	Semi-Annual
Mitchell A. Derenzo	Senior VP	Number of Shareholders	400

Other Information

Transfer Agent	U.S. Stock Transfer Corporation			Where Listed	OTC-BB
Auditor	Perry-Smith & Co.			Symbol	AMRB
Market Maker	Hoefer & Arnett, Inc.	Telephone	(800)346-5544	SIC Code	6020
Broker Dealer	Regular Stockbroker			Employees	74

Americold Corporation

7007 S.W. Cardinal Lane, Ste125 • Portland, OR 97224-7140 • Telephone (503)624-8585 • Fax (503)598-8610

Company Description

The Company operates a nationwide network of 51 owned or leased refrigerated warehouse facilities in 15 states. There are also two unrelated businesses: a limestone quarry and a transportation broker service. Net sales to H.J. Heinz, its largest customer, were $45.5 million in 1995 comprising 23.2% of total sales.

	02/28/95	02/28/94	02/28/93
Per Share Information			
Stock Price	10.00	3.50	3.50
Earnings Per Share	-1.80	-16.00	-1.24
Price / Earnings Ratio	n.a.	n.a.	n.a.
Book Value Per Share	-21.10	-20.51	-5.19
Price / Book Value %	n.a.	n.a.	n.a.
Dividends Per Share	n.a.	n.a.	n.a.
Annual Financial Data			
Operating Results (000's)			
Total Revenues	234,783.0	200,324.0	196,742.0
Costs & Expenses	-222,716.0	-211,297.0	-201,264.0
Income Before Taxes and Other	10,791.0	-12,222.0	-5,695.0
Other Items	n.a.	-66,082.0	n.a.
Income Tax	-5,227.0	1,183.0	-2,455.0
Net Income	5,564.0	-77,121.0	-8,150.0
Cash Flow From Operations	12,684.0	18,476.0	17,700.0
Balance Sheet (000's)			
Cash & Equivalents	33,163.0	3,892.0	2,449.0
Total Current Assets	61,992.0	34,836.0	28,625.0
Fixed Assets, Net	367,248.0	375,772.0	359,629.0
Total Assets	544,595.0	528,703.0	490,151.0
Total Current Liabilities	76,910.0	42,293.0	44,681.0
Long-Term Debt	442,912.0	467,337.0	443,003.0
Stockholders' Equity	-91,958.0	-97,229.0	-20,402.0
Performance & Financial Condition			
Return on Total Revenues %	2.37	-38.50	-4.14
Return on Avg Stockholders' Equity %	n.a.	n.a.	n.a.
Return on Average Assets %	1.04	-15.14	n.a.
Current Ratio	0.81	0.82	0.64
Debt / Equity %	n.a.	n.a.	n.a.

Compound Growth %'s	EPS %	n.a.	Net Income %	n.a.	Total Revenues %	9.24

Comments

1994 results reflect $66 million of nonrecurring charges, or $13.61 per share. The largest change resulted from the adoption of GAAP for the reporting of income taxes, approximately $62 million. All three years had substantial cash flow from operations.

Officers	Position	Ownership Information	02/28/95
Ronald H. Dykehouse	President, CEO	Number of Shares Outstanding	4,860,934
Joel M. Smith	Senior VP, CFO	Market Capitalization	$ 48,609,340
John P. Lenevue	Senior VP	Frequency Of Dividends	n.a.
Stanley F. Sena	Senior VP	Number of Shareholders	84
Lon V. Lenevue	Secretary, Treasurer		

Other Information				
Transfer Agent	Company Office		Where Listed	Order Matching Only
Auditor	KPMG Peat Marwick LLP		Symbol	n.a.
Market Maker	Dabney/Resnick Inc.	Telephone (310)246-3700	SIC Code	4222
Broker Dealer	None		Employees	1889

Ames National Corporation

Post Office Box 846 • Ames, IA 50010 • Telephone (515)232-6251 • Fax (515)232-5778

Company Description

Ames National Corporation was established in 1978 as a bank holding company of First National Bank of Ames, Iowa. State Bank & Trust Co. became a subsidiary in 1983, followed by Boone Bank & Trust Co. in 1992 and Randall-Story State Bank at the beginning of 1995. These four banks serve eight central Iowa communities through eleven banking offices.

	12/31/95	12/31/94	12/31/93	12/31/92
Per Share Information				
Stock Price	98.00	92.00	80.00	64.00
Earnings Per Share	7.93	9.89	9.75	8.32
Price / Earnings Ratio	12.36	9.30	8.21	7.69
Book Value Per Share	78.87	67.02	63.20	56.53
Price / Book Value %	124.26	137.27	126.58	113.21
Dividends Per Share	4.00	3.60	3.25	2.95
Annual Financial Data				
Operating Results (000's)				
Net Interest Income	15,644.7	15,290.8	16,297.1	14,537.8
Loan Loss Provision	-21.2	-210.0	-929.7	-537.3
Non-Interest Income	3,074.7	2,730.5	2,784.0	2,705.2
Non-Interest Expense	-8,395.8	-7,740.6	-8,252.3	-7,709.4
Income Before Taxes and Other	10,302.4	10,070.8	9,899.0	8,996.3
Other Items	n.a.	n.a.	n.a.	n.a.
Income Tax	-3,219.7	-2,924.3	-2,887.9	-3,034.3
Net Income	7,082.7	7,146.5	7,011.1	5,962.0
Balance Sheet (000's)				
Cash & Securities	239,690.6	209,027.5	233,467.2	227,331.6
Loans, Net	216,181.1	176,226.2	157,468.8	142,587.8
Fixed Assets, Net	4,960.8	3,150.0	2,645.9	2,393.7
Total Assets	468,569.4	395,248.5	400,355.9	379,429.8
Deposits	390,628.3	337,608.9	349,310.4	330,211.6
Stockholders' Equity	61,776.6	48,407.1	45,506.5	40,518.0
Performance & Financial Condition				
Net Interest Margin	n.a.	n.a.	n.a.	n.a.
Return on Avg Stockholders' Equity %	12.86	15.22	16.30	15.46
Return on Average Assets %	1.64	1.80	1.80	1.74
Equity to Assets %	13.18	12.25	11.37	10.68
Reserve as a % of Non-Performing Loans	731.15	1512.20	n.a.	358.78

Compound Growth %'s	EPS %	-1.59	Net Income %	5.91	Net Interest Income %	2.48

Comments

The financial statements of Randall-Story State Bank are not included prior to the year of its acquisition. The loan portfolio is made up primarily of real estate mortgages, commercial and agricultural loans, representing 67%, 15% and 9% of total loans, respectively. The Company benefitted from two consecutive strong years in agriculture. Despite the decline in earnings, the Company is still doing extremely well by industry standards. First National Bank of Ames was incorporated in 1939.

Officers	Position	Ownership Information	12/31/95
Robert W. Stafford	Chairman, CEO	Number of Shares Outstanding	783,246
Daniel L. Krieger	Exec VP	Market Capitalization	$ 76,758,108
Edward C. Jacobson	Vice President, Treasurer	Frequency Of Dividends	Quarterly
		Number of Shareholders	365

Other Information				
Transfer Agent	Company Office		Where Listed	OTC-BB
Auditor	McGladry & Polard		Symbol	ATLO
Market Maker	Monroe Securities, Inc.	Telephone (800)766-5560	SIC Code	6020
Broker Dealer	Regular Stockbroker		Employees	156

Anchor Financial Corporation

2002 Oak Street, P.O. Box 242 • Myrtle Beach, SC 29578 • Telephone (803)946-3105 • Fax (803)946-3169

Company Description

Anchor Financial Corporation is a multi-bank company which, through its principal subsidiaries, The Anchor Bank and The Anchor Bank of North Carolina, offers standard banking services to individuals and small to medium-sized businesses. The subisidiaries have seventeen offices located along the coast of South Carolina and North Carolina. In 1995, the Company formed an investment subsidiary, Anchor Capital Corporation, to offer non-traditional banking services such as mutual funds, annuities and other securities.

	12/31/95	12/31/94	12/31/93	12/31/92
Per Share Information				
Stock Price	19.25	13.88	12.50	8.19
Earnings Per Share	1.39	1.38	0.96	0.69
Price / Earnings Ratio	13.85	10.06	13.02	11.87
Book Value Per Share	11.23	9.75	9.23	103.10
Price / Book Value %	171.42	142.36	135.43	7.94
Dividends Per Share	0.36	0.32	0.30	0.30
Annual Financial Data				
Operating Results (000's)				
Net Interest Income	16,671.3	14,259.3	12,060.2	9,979.1
Loan Loss Provision	-596.0	-940.1	-521.5	-586.5
Non-Interest Income	2,976.5	4,432.8	3,349.7	2,724.9
Non-Interest Expense	-13,559.6	-12,367.7	-11,152.6	-9,401.7
Income Before Taxes and Other	5,492.3	5,384.2	3,735.9	2,715.8
Other Items	n.a.	n.a.	49.5	2.0
Income Tax	-1,953.4	-1,879.6	-1,366.6	-971.2
Net Income	3,538.9	3,504.6	2,418.8	1,746.5
Balance Sheet (000's)				
Cash & Securities	104,061.9	99,016.8	86,931.4	57,787.2
Loans, Net	282,057.9	233,975.3	200,625.6	185,038.2
Fixed Assets, Net	13,866.6	11,666.5	11,285.4	10,739.1
Total Assets	407,506.4	351,867.0	304,334.4	259,787.4
Deposits	353,875.8	308,208.4	271,758.6	232,230.6
Stockholders' Equity	28,542.0	24,774.6	23,216.6	21,629.3
Performance & Financial Condition				
Net Interest Margin	n.a.	n.a.	n.a.	n.a.
Return on Avg Stockholders' Equity %	13.28	14.61	10.79	8.29
Return on Average Assets %	0.93	1.07	0.86	0.72
Equity to Assets %	7.00	7.04	7.63	8.33
Reserve as a % of Non-Performing Loans	1666.10	638.27	805.32	353.19

Compound Growth %'s	EPS %	26.30	Net Income %	26.54	Net Interest Income %	18.66

Comments

1994 results include a nonrecurring, before-tax gain of $1.7 million related to the sale of stock that had not had a known value. Had this gain not occurred, the earnings trend would have been more consistent. During 1995 there was a 2 for 1 stock split. Information presented in this report has been restated to reflect this split.

Officers	Position	Ownership Information	12/31/95
Steven L. Chryst	President, CEO	Number of Shares Outstanding	2,540,985
Robert E. Coffee	Exec VP	Market Capitalization	$ 48,913,961
Robert E. Durant, III	Exec VP	Frequency Of Dividends	n.a.
Tommy E. Looper	CFO, Secretary	Number of Shareholders	1,807

Other Information

Transfer Agent	Company Office			Where Listed	OTC-BB
Auditor	Price Waterhouse LLP			Symbol	AFCJ
Market Maker	Interstate/Johnson Lane Corp.	Telephone	(800)541-1977	SIC Code	6020
Broker Dealer	Regular Stockbroker			Employees	5

Anderson-Tully Company

P.O. Box 28 • Memphis, TN 38101 • Telephone (901)576-1400 • Fax (901)526-8842

Company Description

The Company is in the wood and wood products business and has substantial timberland and timber resources. It also generates miscellaneous revenues from its properties. Prior to 1988, there were 1,200 shares of stock issued to 180 stockholders of record. In 1988 the shareholders approved a reverse split of 1 for 20 thereby decreasing the number of shares issued to about 659. Fractional shares were issued at that time. The purpose of the split was explained by the Company as to help prevent the Company from being required to report to the SEC.

	07/31/95	07/31/94	07/31/93	07/31/92
Per Share Information				
Stock Price	170,000.00	122,100.00	111,111.00	n.a.
Earnings Per Share	12,935.32	9,913.84	8,312.45	2,048.99
Price / Earnings Ratio	13.14	12.32	13.37	n.a.
Book Value Per Share	58,579.83	51,283.30	46,171.44	42,104.42
Price / Book Value %	290.20	238.09	240.65	n.a.
Dividends Per Share	5,250.00	4,750.00	4,175.00	3,525.00
Annual Financial Data				
Operating Results (000's)				
Total Revenues	84,224.3	80,423.8	75,636.3	66,921.8
Costs & Expenses	-72,726.3	-71,888.0	-68,105.4	-64,713.2
Income Before Taxes and Other	11,498.0	8,535.9	7,530.8	1,733.6
Other Items	n.a.	n.a.	n.a.	n.a.
Income Tax	-3,969.6	-2,766.0	-2,693.0	-537.0
Net Income	7,528.4	5,769.9	4,837.8	1,196.6
Cash Flow From Operations	10,033.8	9,429.5	11,985.5	5,603.8
Balance Sheet (000's)				
Cash & Equivalents	415.2	1,254.4	1,316.1	536.9
Total Current Assets	20,081.6	17,460.4	16,548.3	16,257.3
Fixed Assets, Net	32,998.4	20,736.9	17,586.4	16,194.0
Total Assets	68,911.9	52,400.4	47,099.9	45,595.8
Total Current Liabilities	8,115.9	6,584.6	9,740.8	7,151.2
Long-Term Debt	26,702.5	14,179.0	8,207.3	12,558.3
Stockholders' Equity	34,093.5	29,846.9	26,871.8	24,589.0
Performance & Financial Condition				
Return on Total Revenues %	8.94	7.17	6.40	1.79
Return on Avg Stockholders' Equity %	23.55	20.35	18.80	4.78
Return on Average Assets %	12.41	11.60	10.44	2.66
Current Ratio	2.47	2.65	1.70	2.27
Debt / Equity %	78.32	47.51	30.54	51.07

Compound Growth %'s	EPS %	84.82	Net Income %	84.61	Total Revenues %	7.97

Comments

The Company is strong financially but remains secretive about their plans. This was evidenced by a shareholder's failed suit and proxy fight in 1990 seeking to have management make more information available to shareholders as well as specifically attempting to maximize shareholder value.

Officers	Position	Ownership Information	07/31/95
John M. Tully	President	Number of Shares Outstanding	582
Mary Ann Sandidge	Secretary	Market Capitalization	$ 98,940,000
		Frequency Of Dividends	Quarterly
		Number of Shareholders	Under 500

Other Information						
Transfer Agent	Company Office				Where Listed	OTC-BB
Auditor	Deloitte & Touche LLP				Symbol	ANTY
Market Maker	Martin Nelson & Co., Inc.	Telephone	(206)938-5783		SIC Code	2490
Broker Dealer	Standard Investment	Tel/Ext	(888)783-4688	Jack	Employees	873

Annie's Homegrown, Inc.

200 Gate Five Road, Suite 211 • Sausalito, CA 94965 • Telephone (415)332-2322 • Fax (415)332-4932

Company Description

The Company sells premium macaroni and cheese food products to the natural food and grocery business, mainly in the Northeast and West Coast markets. In May, 1995, the Company acquired a 50% interest in Pasta Products, Inc., a new company intending to produce and market a line of premium organic pasta products. The Company was formed in 1989. The Company is just completing its first public offering of 600,000 shares at $6 per share. The proceeds will be used for national expansion and working capital.

	12/31/94	12/31/93
Per Share Information		
Stock Price	0.80	0.80
Earnings Per Share	0.01	0.03
Price / Earnings Ratio	80.00	26.67
Book Value Per Share	0.04	-0.01
Price / Book Value %	2,000.00	n.a.
Dividends Per Share	n.a.	n.a.
Annual Financial Data		
Operating Results (000's)		
Total Revenues	3,070.6	1,760.6
Costs & Expenses	-3,044.4	-1,636.8
Income Before Taxes and Other	26.2	123.8
Other Items	n.a.	n.a.
Income Tax	-2.3	-2.0
Net Income	23.9	121.8
Cash Flow From Operations	-79.9	76.3
Balance Sheet (000's)		
Cash & Equivalents	2.4	4.7
Total Current Assets	808.8	483.2
Fixed Assets, Net	23.2	7.9
Total Assets	833.3	491.1
Total Current Liabilities	682.2	512.3
Long-Term Debt	n.a.	n.a.
Stockholders' Equity	151.1	-21.1
Performance & Financial Condition		
Return on Total Revenues %	0.78	6.92
Return on Avg Stockholders' Equity %	36.74	n.a.
Return on Average Assets %	3.61	n.a.
Current Ratio	1.19	0.94
Debt / Equity %	n.a.	n.a.

Compound Growth %'s	EPS %	-66.67	Net Income %	-80.39	Total Revenues %	74.40

Comments

The Company is not releasing the 1995 financials until filings with the SEC are complete. First quarter revenues were $1.2 million, up 52% from the same period in the preceding year. Compound earnings and earnings per share growth rates are misleading because they are calculated on only two years of data. The financial statements of the Company will look considerably different once they complete their stock offering.

Officers	Position	Ownership Information	12/31/94
Andrew Martin	Chairman, CEO	Number of Shares Outstanding	4,013,906
Neil Raiff	COO, Treasurer	Market Capitalization	$ 3,211,125
Paul Nardone	Exec VP	Frequency Of Dividends	n.a.
Celinda Shannon	Secretary	Number of Shareholders	Under 500

Other Information

Transfer Agent	Company Office			Where Listed	Order Matching Only
Auditor	KPMG Peat Marwick LLP			Symbol	n.a.
Market Maker	Company Office	Telephone	(415)332-2322	SIC Code	2098
Broker Dealer	None			Employees	n.a.

Arrow-Magnolia International, Inc.

2646 Rodney Lane • Dallas, TX 75229 • Telephone (214)247-7111 • Fax (214)484-2896

Company Description

The Company manufactures and distributes approximately 400 speciality chemical products for use in cleaning and maintaining equipment and for general maintenance and sanitation. The products are sold throughout the U.S., Canada and other countries to a variety of customers in the aircraft, construction, and telecommunications industries. These industries accounted for approximately 40% of the Company's sales in 1995. The Company was incorporated in the State of Texas in 1937.

	12/31/95	12/31/94	12/31/93	12/31/92
Per Share Information				
Stock Price	4.50	1.00	n.a.	n.a.
Earnings Per Share	0.61	0.33	0.28	0.14
Price / Earnings Ratio	7.38	3.03	n.a.	n.a.
Book Value Per Share	1.90	1.32	0.87	0.58
Price / Book Value %	236.84	75.76	n.a.	n.a.
Dividends Per Share	n.a.	n.a.	n.a.	n.a.
Annual Financial Data				
Operating Results (000's)				
Total Revenues	8,420.5	6,697.7	6,268.7	6,676.9
Costs & Expenses	-7,353.8	-6,112.0	-5,972.5	-6,404.9
Income Before Taxes and Other	1,066.7	585.8	296.3	156.8
Other Items	n.a.	n.a.	125.5	49.2
Income Tax	-387.6	-224.7	-112.3	-49.2
Net Income	679.1	361.1	309.5	156.8
Cash Flow From Operations	427.2	453.8	535.2	347.2
Balance Sheet (000's)				
Cash & Equivalents	761.4	856.9	517.4	247.0
Total Current Assets	3,588.0	2,453.3	1,910.9	1,872.8
Fixed Assets, Net	371.3	400.4	479.4	511.0
Total Assets	4,135.7	3,036.0	2,596.0	2,609.0
Total Current Liabilities	892.0	662.5	465.8	1,431.7
Long-Term Debt	790.0	690.0	444.0	527.3
Stockholders' Equity	2,202.9	1,322.2	961.2	650.0
Performance & Financial Condition				
Return on Total Revenues %	8.06	5.39	4.94	2.35
Return on Avg Stockholders' Equity %	38.53	31.63	38.42	27.49
Return on Average Assets %	18.94	12.82	11.89	5.91
Current Ratio	4.02	3.70	4.10	1.31
Debt / Equity %	35.86	52.18	46.20	81.12

Compound Growth %'s	EPS %	63.33	Net Income %	62.99	Total Revenues %	8.04

Comments

Prior to 1994, there was no active market in the Company's stock and no reliable price quotes. As of December 31, 1995, officers and directors, as a group, owned 71.9% of the Company's outstanding common stock. Subsequent to year end, the Company announced intentions to be listed on the Nasdaq Stock Market. If they are listed and maintain their listing status we will, unfortunately, miss them in next years edition. The Company's stock was recently quoted at $7.00 per share. The 55% increase in stock price, since year end, may be an indication of the power of a little publicity.

Officers	Position	Ownership Information	12/31/95
Morris Schwiff	Chairman, President	Number of Shares Outstanding	1,157,600
Mark I. Kenner	Exec VP	Market Capitalization	$ 5,209,200
Fred Kenner	Secretary, Treasurer	Frequency Of Dividends	n.a.
		Number of Shareholders	400

Other Information

Transfer Agent	KeyCorp Shareholder Services, Inc.		Where Listed	OTC-BB
Auditor	KPMG Peat Marwick LLP		Symbol	ARWM
Market Maker	Carr Securities Corporation	Telephone (800)221-2243	SIC Code	2890
Broker Dealer	Regular Stockbroker		Employees	100

Artesian Resources Corporation

664 Churchmans Road • Newark, DE 19702 • Telephone (302)456-6900 • Fax (302)453-6957

Company Description

The Company, founded in 1905, operates as a water utility providing water to over 56,000 customers in New Castle County, Delaware. Operating revenues have increased as a result of growth in the service area and rate increases. Water sales to single and multi-family residences make up approximately 75% of water revenues which comprise approximately 91% of operating revenue.

	12/31/95	12/31/94	12/31/93	12/31/92
Per Share Information				
Stock Price	14.50	14.75	10.63	9.50
Earnings Per Share	1.06	1.34	1.50	0.63
Price / Earnings Ratio	13.68	11.01	7.09	15.08
Book Value Per Share	14.84	14.48	13.78	12.62
Price / Book Value %	97.71	101.86	77.14	75.28
Dividends Per Share	0.63	0.60	0.30	0.05
Annual Financial Data				
Operating Results (000's)				
Total Revenues	22,863.4	21,068.0	20,354.1	18,231.0
Costs & Expenses	-20,665.0	-18,568.9	-18,036.9	-16,996.3
Income Before Taxes and Other	1,998.9	2,449.3	2,289.0	1,130.1
Other Items	n.a.	n.a.	250.9	n.a.
Income Tax	-791.4	-963.5	-914.1	-364.1
Net Income	1,207.4	1,485.8	1,625.8	766.0
Cash Flow From Operations	3,056.6	4,595.5	3,371.4	1,994.2
Balance Sheet (000's)				
Cash & Equivalents	149.7	229.7	1,112.2	34.8
Total Current Assets	4,920.9	4,319.6	5,285.9	3,493.8
Fixed Assets, Net	83,160.4	73,237.9	66,787.4	64,518.2
Total Assets	96,841.2	87,453.2	81,926.8	76,482.5
Total Current Liabilities	21,846.5	7,335.4	4,081.4	9,762.5
Long-Term Debt	17,558.3	24,653.2	24,677.5	17,812.4
Stockholders' Equity	16,640.1	16,119.5	15,240.1	13,954.4
Performance & Financial Condition				
Return on Total Revenues %	5.28	7.05	7.99	4.20
Return on Avg Stockholders' Equity %	7.37	9.48	11.14	6.45
Return on Average Assets %	1.31	1.75	2.05	1.02
Current Ratio	0.23	0.59	1.30	0.36
Debt / Equity %	105.52	152.94	161.93	127.65

Compound Growth %'s	EPS %	18.94	Net Income %	16.38	Total Revenues %	7.84

Comments

The Company, at December 31, 1995, had $1.2 million of preferred stock, of which $973,000 is mandatorily redeemable. Preferred stock dividends have been deducted in determining net income per share during each of the years presented.

Officers	Position	Ownership Information	12/31/95
Dian C. Taylor	CEO, President	Number of Shares Outstanding	1,037,494
Peter N. Johnson	Senior VP, COO	Market Capitalization	$ 15,043,663
David B. Spacht	Vice President, CFO	Frequency Of Dividends	Quarterly
Joseph A. DiNunzio	Vice President, Secretary	Number of Shareholders	758
Keith A. Hausknecht	Other		

Other Information			
Transfer Agent	Chemical Mellon Shareholder Services	Where Listed	OTC-BB
Auditor	KPMG Peat Marwick LLP	Symbol	ARTN
Market Maker	Wheat, First Securities, Inc.	Telephone (800)446-1016	SIC Code	4941
Broker Dealer	Regular Stockbroker	Employees	160

Ash Grove Cement Company

8900 Indian Creek Parkway • Overland Park, KS 66225 • Telephone (913)451-8900 • Fax (913)451-8324

Company Description

The Company operates eight cement manufacturing plants throughout the Midstates and Northwest. Products include ready-mixed concrete, aggregates and package materials. The Company is also involved in real estate development.

	12/31/95	12/31/94	12/31/93
Per Share Information			
Stock Price	112.00	68.00	61.00
Earnings Per Share	12.67	10.33	2.97
Price / Earnings Ratio	8.84	6.58	20.54
Book Value Per Share	85.11	73.57	64.11
Price / Book Value %	131.59	92.43	95.15
Dividends Per Share	1.40	1.20	1.00
Annual Financial Data			
Operating Results (000's)			
Total Revenues	407,745.3	370,848.1	314,102.1
Costs & Expenses	-326,131.0	-301,441.5	-270,704.3
Income Before Taxes and Other	79,986.5	66,383.9	42,395.6
Other Items	-1,030.6	-1,337.8	-14,802.9
Income Tax	-28,563.0	-23,937.8	-15,759.0
Net Income	50,392.9	41,108.3	11,833.8
Cash Flow From Operations	64,610.5	65,749.6	56,530.0
Balance Sheet (000's)			
Cash & Equivalents	30,425.5	10,006.3	8,395.2
Total Current Assets	133,240.0	102,586.0	92,411.9
Fixed Assets, Net	312,698.3	310,047.7	320,206.1
Total Assets	532,918.3	499,888.2	448,187.9
Total Current Liabilities	42,043.3	40,495.1	34,355.9
Long-Term Debt	70,750.1	86,626.1	73,542.8
Stockholders' Equity	338,524.4	292,641.1	255,288.1
Performance & Financial Condition			
Return on Total Revenues %	12.36	11.08	3.77
Return on Avg Stockholders' Equity %	15.97	15.00	4.70
Return on Average Assets %	9.76	8.67	n.a.
Current Ratio	3.17	2.53	2.69
Debt / Equity %	20.90	29.60	28.81

Compound Growth %'s	EPS %	106.54	Net Income %	106.36	Total Revenues %	13.94

Comments

The Company operated near capacity in 1995 and is proceeding with major expansion programs. The cash position is strong. Growth in 1995 was 22.6% over the previous year and another strong year is forecast. Management remains very confident about the future. Compounded growth in earnings percentages are only based on three years of data.

Officers	Position	Ownership Information	12/31/95
James P. Sunderland	Chairman	Number of Shares Outstanding	3,977,635
George M. Wells	President	Market Capitalization	$ 445,495,120
John H. Ross III	Exec VP	Frequency Of Dividends	Quarterly
George J. McCausland	Treasurer, Controller	Number of Shareholders	Under 500

Other Information					
Transfer Agent	Company Office			Where Listed	OTC-PS
Auditor	KPMG Peat Marwick LLP			Symbol	ASHG
Market Maker	George K. Baum & Company	Telephone	(800)821-7570	SIC Code	3240
Broker Dealer	Standard Investment	Tel/Ext	(888)783-4688 Jack	Employees	1800

Atlas Environmental, Inc.

150 S. Pine Island Rd, Ste 100 • Plantation, FL 33324 • Telephone (305)370-9011 • Fax (954)370-9405

Company Description

The Company provides soil decontamination and truck services, excavation and restoration of petroleum-contaminated sites, petroleum storage tank removal and general trucking services. The Company also recycles construction and demolition debris. Currently operating only in Florida, the Company intends to expand in the Southeast and eventually throughout the nation. Incorporated in Florida in 1994, the Company was formed to raise capital through a public offering and then acquire privately held businesses.

	12/31/95	12/31/94	12/31/93
Per Share Information			
Stock Price	8.75	6.50	1.19
Earnings Per Share	-0.94	-0.03	-0.27
Price / Earnings Ratio	n.a.	n.a.	n.a.
Book Value Per Share	-0.36	0.37	-0.27
Price / Book Value %	n.a.	1,756.80	n.a.
Dividends Per Share	n.a.	n.a.	n.a.
Annual Financial Data			
Operating Results (000's)			
Total Revenues	9,416.8	3,485.5	1,189.4
Costs & Expenses	-12,119.8	-3,334.9	-1,868.1
Income Before Taxes and Other	-2,703.0	-23.3	-678.7
Other Items	n.a.	n.a.	n.a.
Income Tax	168.6	30.0	n.a.
Net Income	-2,534.4	6.7	-678.7
Cash Flow From Operations	-1,504.3	-200.3	-402.2
Balance Sheet (000's)			
Cash & Equivalents	467.9	700.5	129.7
Total Current Assets	2,529.5	1,909.6	129.7
Fixed Assets, Net	9,963.3	9,867.1	n.a.
Total Assets	17,305.7	16,032.3	129.7
Total Current Liabilities	5,822.5	2,551.3	0.2
Long-Term Debt	5,121.0	4,443.4	n.a.
Stockholders' Equity	6,362.1	8,860.5	129.6
Performance & Financial Condition			
Return on Total Revenues %	-26.91	0.19	-57.07
Return on Avg Stockholders' Equity %	-33.30	0.15	n.a.
Return on Average Assets %	-15.20	0.08	n.a.
Current Ratio	0.43	0.75	686.47
Debt / Equity %	80.49	50.15	n.a.

Compound Growth %'s	EPS % n.a.	Net Income % n.a.	Total Revenues % 181.38

Comments

The Company acquired two soil decontamination companies during 1994, and completed the acquisition of six demolition and waste management companies in January, 1996. The total purchase price for the six companies was approximately $28.7 million, paid for with a combination of cash, notes and newly issued shares of the Company's common stock. To finance the 1996 transaction, the Company secured $30 million in new credit facilities.

Officers	Position	Ownership Information	12/31/95
Gary R. Kabot	CEO, President	Number of Shares Outstanding	3,437,000
T. Alec Rigby	Exec VP, Secretary	Market Capitalization	$ 30,073,750
		Frequency Of Dividends	n.a.
		Number of Shareholders	450

Other Information			
Transfer Agent	Corporate Stock Transfer, Inc.	Where Listed	OTC-BB
Auditor	Ernst & Young LLP	Symbol	ATEV
Market Maker	Alpine Securities Corporation	Telephone (800)521-5588 SIC Code	4959
Broker Dealer	Regular Stockbroker	Employees	340

Audio Communications Network, Inc.

1000 Legion Place, Ste. 1515 • Orlando, FL 32801 • Telephone (407)649-8877 • Fax (407)649-8873

Company Description

The Company owns and operates MUZAK franchises, which provide background music programming and ancillary services to customers located in Baltimore, Maryland; Kansas City and St. Louis Missouri; Fresno, California; and Jacksonville, Florida. In addition, other sound, video, and communication system products and services are provided.

	12/31/95	12/31/94	12/31/93	12/31/92
Per Share Information				
Stock Price	1.57	1.19	1.25	0.69
Earnings Per Share	0.27	0.15	0.08	0.09
Price / Earnings Ratio	5.81	7.93	15.63	7.67
Book Value Per Share	1.24	0.97	0.54	0.43
Price / Book Value %	126.61	122.68	231.48	160.47
Dividends Per Share	n.a.	n.a.	n.a.	n.a.
Annual Financial Data				
Operating Results (000's)				
Total Revenues	7,690.4	7,019.0	5,534.6	5,216.1
Costs & Expenses	-7,023.8	-6,669.3	-5,380.1	-5,041.0
Income Before Taxes and Other	666.6	349.7	154.5	175.1
Other Items	n.a.	n.a.	n.a.	63.2
Income Tax	-57.5	-37.7	-12.7	-85.9
Net Income	609.1	312.0	141.8	152.5
Cash Flow From Operations	624.5	902.2	871.6	1,065.3
Balance Sheet (000's)				
Cash & Equivalents	590.1	509.1	363.3	554.9
Total Current Assets	1,503.2	1,373.8	1,118.4	1,057.9
Fixed Assets, Net	3,358.2	2,896.5	2,032.3	1,813.1
Total Assets	8,411.1	8,241.6	5,604.0	6,121.1
Total Current Liabilities	1,484.9	1,651.1	1,146.4	1,040.5
Long-Term Debt	4,089.0	4,366.8	3,472.1	4,217.2
Stockholders' Equity	2,787.2	2,161.0	907.5	716.1
Performance & Financial Condition				
Return on Total Revenues %	7.92	4.45	2.56	2.92
Return on Avg Stockholders' Equity %	24.62	20.34	17.46	24.07
Return on Average Assets %	7.32	4.51	2.42	2.69
Current Ratio	1.01	0.83	0.98	1.02
Debt / Equity %	146.71	202.07	382.60	588.88

Compound Growth %'s	EPS %	44.22	Net Income %	58.68	Total Revenues %	13.82

Comments

The Company has grown profitably by expanding existing business and acquiring other companies with similar operations. In 1994, the Company acquired a MUZAK franchise in California for 528,474 shares of the Company's common stock and in January 1996, it acquired a MUZAK franchise in northern Florida for $5.8 million, financed with a bank loan.

Officers	Position	Ownership Information	12/31/95
A.J. Schell	President, CEO	Number of Shares Outstanding	2,243,821
Doris K. Krummenacker	Secretary, Treasurer	Market Capitalization	$ 3,522,799
Mary Flemmings	Vice President	Frequency Of Dividends	n.a.
Frank Crooks	Vice President	Number of Shareholders	618
Mike Regan	Vice President		

Other Information				
Transfer Agent	Chemical Mellon Shareholder Services		Where Listed	OTC-BB
Auditor	Deloitte & Touche LLP		Symbol	AUCM
Market Maker	Gruntal & Co., Incorporated	Telephone (212)943-6418	SIC Code	7389
Broker Dealer	Regular Stockbroker		Employees	56

Auric Corporation

470 Frelinghuysen Avenue • Newark, NJ 07114 • Telephone (201)242-4110 • Fax (201)242-4110

Company Description

The Company manufactures and sells chemical products for the metal finishing industry in general and for electronic manufacturers in particular. An employee stock ownership plan owns approximately 30% of the Company's shares. Per share amounts have been computed using average shares outstanding rather than year end balances.

	09/30/95	09/30/94	09/30/93	09/30/92
Per Share Information				
Stock Price	39.25	24.62	15.00	9.25
Earnings Per Share	6.26	2.73	4.01	4.82
Price / Earnings Ratio	6.27	9.02	3.74	1.92
Book Value Per Share	32.65	26.54	22.38	17.75
Price / Book Value %	120.21	92.77	67.02	52.11
Dividends Per Share	n.a.	n.a.	n.a.	n.a.
Annual Financial Data				
Operating Results (000's)				
Total Revenues	29,994.7	22,872.7	21,149.9	20,915.5
Costs & Expenses	-25,385.3	-19,900.0	-18,229.2	-17,409.1
Income Before Taxes and Other	4,212.4	1,630.8	2,616.3	3,116.1
Other Items	n.a.	n.a.	n.a.	n.a.
Income Tax	-1,744.3	-603.2	-1,015.3	-1,214.5
Net Income	2,468.1	1,027.6	1,601.0	1,901.6
Cash Flow From Operations	4,565.9	1,251.0	1,446.6	2,416.1
Balance Sheet (000's)				
Cash & Equivalents	4,424.3	1,641.3	2,708.1	2,523.5
Total Current Assets	13,519.2	11,423.6	10,086.8	8,927.9
Fixed Assets, Net	5,076.4	3,800.0	2,790.8	2,366.5
Total Assets	19,061.1	15,613.3	13,219.1	11,614.3
Total Current Liabilities	4,887.9	4,076.0	2,618.8	2,775.2
Long-Term Debt	328.7	395.5	326.1	1,660.8
Stockholders' Equity	12,873.7	9,989.9	8,936.3	7,001.3
Performance & Financial Condition				
Return on Total Revenues %	8.23	4.49	7.57	9.09
Return on Avg Stockholders' Equity %	21.59	10.86	20.09	32.29
Return on Average Assets %	14.24	7.13	12.89	17.63
Current Ratio	2.77	2.80	3.85	3.22
Debt / Equity %	2.55	3.96	3.65	23.72

Compound Growth %'s	EPS %	9.10	Net Income %	9.08	Total Revenues %	12.77

Comments

1994 results include a nonrecurring charge of $1 million in connection with the buyout of a distributor. Construction of a chemical manufacturing plant in Malaysia started in 1995.

Officers	Position	Ownership Information	09/30/95
Maurice Bick	President	Number of Shares Outstanding	394,259
Leo Kosowsky	Vice President, Secretary	Market Capitalization	$ 15,474,666
		Frequency Of Dividends	n.a.
		Number of Shareholders	Under 500

Other Information

Transfer Agent	Midlantic National Bank		Where Listed	OTC-BB
Auditor	J.H. Cohn & Company		Symbol	AURP
Market Maker	S.J. Wolfe & Co.	Telephone (800)262-2244	SIC Code	2810
Broker Dealer	Regular Stockbroker		Employees	n.a.

Auto-Graphics, Inc.

3201 Temple Avenue • Pomona, CA 91768-3200 • Telephone (909)595-7204 • Fax (909)595-3506

Company Description

The Company provides software products and processing services to information and database publishers. These products and services are used to create, maintain and distribute information databases through printed and/or electronic products such as CD-ROM and Internet/Web software systems. The Company was incorporated in California in 1960.

	12/31/95	12/31/94	12/31/93	12/31/92
Per Share Information				
Stock Price	1.88	1.36	2.00	2.63
Earnings Per Share	0.16	0.12	0.10	0.02
Price / Earnings Ratio	11.75	11.33	20.00	131.50
Book Value Per Share	2.16	1.99	1.87	1.77
Price / Book Value %	87.04	68.34	106.95	148.59
Dividends Per Share	n.a.	n.a.	n.a.	n.a.
Annual Financial Data				
Operating Results (000's)				
Total Revenues	9,612.9	9,219.8	9,759.3	9,362.5
Costs & Expenses	-9,254.8	-8,925.6	-9,524.8	-9,295.9
Income Before Taxes and Other	358.2	294.2	234.5	44.6
Other Items	n.a.	n.a.	n.a.	n.a.
Income Tax	-164.0	-136.0	-102.0	-17.0
Net Income	194.2	158.2	132.5	27.6
Cash Flow From Operations	1,622.9	880.9	1,816.0	1,011.5
Balance Sheet (000's)				
Cash & Equivalents	106.5	80.9	63.1	52.5
Total Current Assets	2,547.8	2,603.0	2,279.4	2,706.5
Fixed Assets, Net	3,929.3	3,307.0	3,279.7	3,623.4
Total Assets	6,687.7	6,106.1	5,840.9	6,636.6
Total Current Liabilities	1,746.1	1,372.1	1,392.8	2,192.0
Long-Term Debt	1,905.9	1,695.9	1,591.9	1,749.9
Stockholders' Equity	2,441.8	2,550.7	2,440.9	2,313.0
Performance & Financial Condition				
Return on Total Revenues %	2.02	1.72	1.36	0.29
Return on Avg Stockholders' Equity %	7.78	6.34	5.57	1.20
Return on Average Assets %	3.04	2.65	2.12	0.40
Current Ratio	1.46	1.90	1.64	1.23
Debt / Equity %	78.05	66.49	65.22	75.65

Compound Growth %'s	EPS %	100.00	Net Income %	91.73	Total Revenues %	0.88

Comments

During the year ended December 31, 1995, the Company invested approximately $1.6 million in capital improvements and repurchased 149,600 shares of its common stock, for a total of $303,094. Approximately 890,000 (79%) of the Company's common stock was owned by officers or directors at December 31, 1995.

Officers	Position	Ownership Information	12/31/95
Robert S. Cope	President, CEO	Number of Shares Outstanding	1,130,478
Paul R. Cope	Vice President	Market Capitalization	$ 2,125,299
William J. Kliss	Vice President	Frequency Of Dividends	n.a.
Daniel E. Luebben	Vice President, CFO	Number of Shareholders	265

Other Information				
Transfer Agent	First Interstate Bank		Where Listed	OTC-BB
Auditor	Ernst & Young LLP		Symbol	AUGR
Market Maker	Carr Securities Corporation	Telephone (800)221-2243	SIC Code	7375
Broker Dealer	Regular Stockbroker		Employees	115

© 1996 Walker's Manual, LLC   All rights reserved.   No part of this information may be reproduced without written permission.   (510) 283-9993

Avesis Incorporated

100 West Clarendon, Suite 2300 • Phoenix, AZ 85013 • Telephone (602)241-3400 • Fax (602)240-9100

Company Description

The Company markets and administers dental, vision, hearing and chiropractic discount programs. These programs are designed to enable members, who are enrolled through various sponsoring organizations such as insurance carriers, corporations, associations and unions, to realize savings on purchases of products and services through Company organized networks of providers. The Company's discount programs are also designed to reduce the cost to sponsors of providing benefits to members. The Company was incorporated in the state of Delaware in 1978.

	05/31/95	05/31/94	05/31/93	05/31/92
Per Share Information				
Stock Price	1.19	0.94	0.50	0.38
Earnings Per Share	0.02	-0.12	-0.29	-0.32
Price / Earnings Ratio	59.50	n.a.	n.a.	n.a.
Book Value Per Share	0.21	0.09	0.12	0.59
Price / Book Value %	566.67	1,044.40	416.67	64.41
Dividends Per Share	n.a.	n.a.	n.a.	n.a.
Annual Financial Data				
Operating Results (000's)				
Total Revenues	6,529.1	4,523.3	3,656.0	4,233.8
Costs & Expenses	-6,023.7	-4,657.8	-4,332.2	-5,375.2
Income Before Taxes and Other	505.4	-134.6	-676.2	-1,141.4
Other Items	n.a.	n.a.	n.a.	294.3
Income Tax	n.a.	n.a.	n.a.	n.a.
Net Income	505.4	-134.6	-676.2	-847.1
Cash Flow From Operations	408.3	-149.0	-809.7	-1,616.2
Balance Sheet (000's)				
Cash & Equivalents	815.6	347.7	569.8	2,082.1
Total Current Assets	1,242.5	647.5	1,025.4	2,692.1
Fixed Assets, Net	353.8	157.9	228.3	325.8
Total Assets	1,839.4	1,195.8	1,649.8	3,264.8
Total Current Liabilities	495.0	417.8	636.5	776.6
Long-Term Debt	412.3	409.6	454.7	291.6
Stockholders' Equity	859.6	354.1	488.7	2,071.2
Performance & Financial Condition				
Return on Total Revenues %	7.74	-2.97	-18.50	-20.01
Return on Avg Stockholders' Equity %	83.28	-31.93	-52.83	-32.34
Return on Average Assets %	33.30	-9.46	-27.52	-19.12
Current Ratio	2.51	1.55	1.61	3.47
Debt / Equity %	47.96	115.67	93.05	14.08

Compound Growth %'s	EPS % n.a.	Net Income % n.a.	Total Revenues %	15.53

Comments

The Company has net operating loss carryforwards of $7,083,000, expiring between 1999 and 2009, to offset against future taxable income. Long-term debt consists of notes payable to stockholders of $160,000 and convertible debt of $252,000.

Officers	Position	Ownership Information	05/31/95
Frank C. Cappadora	President	Number of Shares Outstanding	4,075,420
Mark L. Smith	CFO, Secretary	Market Capitalization	$ 4,849,750
		Frequency Of Dividends	n.a.
		Number of Shareholders	170

Other Information

Transfer Agent	Continental Stock Transfer & Trust Co.		Where Listed	OTC-BB
Auditor	KPMG Peat Marwick LLP		Symbol	AVSS
Market Maker	Carr Securities Corporation	Telephone (800)221-2243	SIC Code	8099
Broker Dealer	Regular Stockbroker		Employees	43

Avoca, Incorporated

P.O. Box 61260 • New Orleans, LA 70161 • Telephone (504)552-4720 • Fax (504)586-3613

Company Description

The Company owns and manages approximately 16,000 acres, comprising virtually all of Avoca Island, located about 90 miles west of New Orleans. The island is rural and undeveloped except for the exploration and development of its oil and gas reserves. The Company is largely a passive royalty company which derives most of its income from royalties, bonuses and rentals under oil and gas leases covering the island's acreage. The Company was incorporated in the State of Louisana in 1931.

	12/31/95	12/31/94	12/31/93	12/31/92
Per Share Information				
Stock Price	6.13	6.44	5.75	6.63
Earnings Per Share	0.19	0.21	0.21	0.20
Price / Earnings Ratio	32.26	30.67	27.38	33.15
Book Value Per Share	2.55	2.51	2.46	2.36
Price / Book Value %	240.39	256.57	233.74	280.93
Dividends Per Share	0.15	0.15	0.11	0.18
Annual Financial Data				
Operating Results (000's)				
Total Revenues	289.9	403.5	307.3	420.0
Costs & Expenses	-174.0	-161.9	-181.9	-203.4
Income Before Taxes and Other	115.9	241.6	125.4	216.6
Other Items	69.6	n.a.	73.4	n.a.
Income Tax	-28.6	-69.7	-24.6	-52.0
Net Income	157.0	171.9	174.2	164.6
Cash Flow From Operations	34.4	147.4	76.5	172.0
Balance Sheet (000's)				
Cash & Equivalents	204.7	15.0	1,090.8	51.7
Total Current Assets	1,521.1	2,175.2	2,116.2	2,016.2
Fixed Assets, Net	78.3	72.7	23.8	24.7
Total Assets	2,321.9	2,247.9	2,140.0	2,040.9
Total Current Liabilities	186.9	137.8	75.2	82.8
Long-Term Debt	n.a.	n.a.	n.a.	n.a.
Stockholders' Equity	2,120.6	2,088.2	2,040.9	1,958.0
Performance & Financial Condition				
Return on Total Revenues %	54.15	42.61	56.70	39.18
Return on Avg Stockholders' Equity %	7.46	8.33	8.71	8.44
Return on Average Assets %	6.87	7.84	8.33	8.12
Current Ratio	8.14	15.78	28.14	24.34
Debt / Equity %	n.a.	n.a.	n.a.	n.a.

Compound Growth %'s	EPS %	-1.70	Net Income %	-1.56	Total Revenues %	-11.62

Comments

Revenues fluctuate primarily as a result of production related to the oil and gas leases on the Company's property. The Company is encouraging its lessees to further develop the property's resources.

Officers	Position	Ownership Information	12/31/95
Edward B. Grimball	President, Exec VP	Number of Shares Outstanding	830,500
M. Cleland Powell, III	Treasurer, Secretary	Market Capitalization	$ 5,090,965
		Frequency Of Dividends	Semi-Annual
		Number of Shareholders	848

Other Information				
Transfer Agent	Company Office		Where Listed	OTC-BB
Auditor	Ernst & Young LLP		Symbol	AVOC
Market Maker	Howard, Weil et. al.	Telephone (504)582-2612	SIC Code	6792
Broker Dealer	Regular Stockbroker		Employees	n.a.

© 1996 Walker's Manual, LLC   All rights reserved.   No part of this information may be reproduced without written permission.   (510) 283-9993

B.B. Walker Company

414 East Dixie Drive • Asheboro, NC 27203-1167 • Telephone (910)625-1380 • Fax (910)625-8258

Company Description

The Company manufacturers and distributes men's and women's footwear. The Company's products consist of high quality, medium-priced western and work/outdoor boots and shoes. A majority of the Company's sales are under trademarked brands. Private label footwear manufactured for large retailers and other manufacturers amounted to 19.1% of sales for the year ended October 28, 1995. The Company also operates three retail stores. The Company was incorporated in North Carolina in 1952. A substantial portion of the Company's common stock is owned by employees through participation in an ESOP and by many employees individually. As of October 28, 1995, the ESOP owned 25.7% of the outstanding shares. Per share amounts reflect a three-for-two stock split in 1994.

	10/28/95	10/29/94	10/30/93	10/31/92
Per Share Information				
Stock Price	2.00	7.00	6.75	2.88
Earnings Per Share	-0.72	0.26	1.12	1.02
Price / Earnings Ratio	n.a.	26.92	6.03	2.82
Book Value Per Share	4.91	5.56	5.47	4.89
Price / Book Value %	40.73	125.90	123.40	58.90
Dividends Per Share	n.a.	0.07	0.10	n.a.
Annual Financial Data				
Operating Results (000's)				
Total Revenues	43,453.0	51,148.0	55,777.0	47,956.0
Costs & Expenses	-45,321.0	-50,336.0	-52,722.0	-46,173.0
Income Before Taxes and Other	-1,868.0	812.0	3,055.0	1,783.0
Other Items	-2.0	-2.0	-2.0	475.0
Income Tax	626.0	-336.0	-1,160.0	-579.0
Net Income	-1,244.0	474.0	1,893.0	1,679.0
Cash Flow From Operations	-1,918.0	-1,366.0	738.0	1,809.0
Balance Sheet (000's)				
Cash & Equivalents	1.0	1.0	1.0	1.0
Total Current Assets	30,898.0	30,264.0	27,727.0	25,099.0
Fixed Assets, Net	2,968.0	3,593.0	2,148.0	1,985.0
Total Assets	34,377.0	34,016.0	30,028.0	27,234.0
Total Current Liabilities	21,533.0	20,510.0	17,357.0	16,253.0
Long-Term Debt	4,257.0	3,692.0	3,189.0	3,290.0
Stockholders' Equity	8,553.0	9,780.0	9,447.0	7,649.0
Performance & Financial Condition				
Return on Total Revenues %	-2.86	0.93	3.39	3.50
Return on Avg Stockholders' Equity %	-13.57	4.93	22.15	24.59
Return on Average Assets %	-3.64	1.48	6.61	6.16
Current Ratio	1.43	1.48	1.60	1.54
Debt / Equity %	49.77	37.75	33.76	43.01

Compound Growth %'s	EPS %	n.a.	Net Income %	n.a.	Total Revenues %	-3.23

Comments

Included in current liabilities are borrowings of $14 million at October 31, 1995. These borrowings provide for working capital needs and are secured by inventory and receivables. To address the loss in 1995, the Company has undertaken plans to reduce its cost structure and pursue new markets for its products.

Officers	Position	Ownership Information	10/28/95
Kent T. Anderson	Chairman, CEO	Number of Shares Outstanding	1,726,535
French P. Humphries	Exec VP	Market Capitalization	$ 3,453,070
William C. Massie	Exec VP	Frequency Of Dividends	Irregular
Dorothy W. Craven	Secretary	Number of Shareholders	1,229
Rich S. Rich	Other		

Other Information				
Transfer Agent	Company Office		Where Listed	OTC-PS
Auditor	Price Waterhouse LLP		Symbol	n.a.
Market Maker	Scott & Stringfellow, Inc.	Telephone (800)446-7074	SIC Code	3140
Broker Dealer	Regular Stockbroker		Employees	637

BWC Financial Corp.

1400 Civic Drive • Walnut Creek, CA 94596 • Telephone (510)932-5353 • Fax (510)932-6628

Company Description

BWC Financial Corp. has two subsidiaries; Bank of Walnut Creek and BWC Real Estate. The Bank operates five branches in several communities in the fast-growing East Bay area of the San Francisco Bay area in California. The Company is engaged principally in making loans to small and middle-market businesses and middle-income individuals. BWC Real Estate owns a 51% joint venture interest in a company that originates and places long-term financing for real estate mortgages. The Bank was formed in 1982.

	12/31/95	12/31/94	12/31/93	12/31/92
Per Share Information				
Stock Price	16.75	14.06	9.38	9.50
Earnings Per Share	1.64	1.21	0.91	0.87
Price / Earnings Ratio	10.21	11.62	10.31	10.92
Book Value Per Share	15.91	15.22	14.21	13.13
Price / Book Value %	105.28	92.38	66.01	72.35
Dividends Per Share	n.a.	n.a.	n.a.	n.a.
Annual Financial Data				
Operating Results (000's)				
Net Interest Income	8,081.0	7,126.0	6,125.0	5,440.0
Loan Loss Provision	-330.0	-255.0	-120.0	n.a.
Non-Interest Income	1,136.0	651.0	616.0	828.0
Non-Interest Expense	-6,444.0	-5,867.0	-5,397.0	-4,942.0
Income Before Taxes and Other	2,443.0	1,655.0	1,224.0	1,326.0
Other Items	n.a.	n.a.	n.a.	n.a.
Income Tax	-823.0	-481.0	-377.0	-516.0
Net Income	1,620.0	1,174.0	847.0	810.0
Balance Sheet (000's)				
Cash & Securities	47,088.0	43,624.0	32,100.0	33,303.0
Loans, Net	99,776.0	86,411.0	80,916.0	71,733.0
Fixed Assets, Net	1,475.0	993.0	935.0	n.a.
Total Assets	150,597.0	133,144.0	115,417.0	108,510.0
Deposits	134,601.0	119,972.0	103,166.0	96,901.0
Stockholders' Equity	14,893.0	12,643.0	11,814.0	11,035.0
Performance & Financial Condition				
Net Interest Margin	6.63	6.34	6.13	6.11
Return on Avg Stockholders' Equity %	11.77	9.60	7.41	7.64
Return on Average Assets %	1.14	0.94	0.76	0.78
Equity to Assets %	9.89	9.50	10.24	10.17
Reserve as a % of Non-Performing Loans	804.21	273.86	187.81	317.55

Compound Growth %'s	EPS %	23.53	Net Income %	25.99	Net Interest Income %	14.10

Comments

The slow down in the California economy failed to dent the consistency of Bank of Walnut Creek. Management also reported that 1995 was the first year of profitability for BMC Real Estate. Expansion plans will follow the population and business growth along the 680 Corridor (Interstate Highway 680). Management is very optimistic about 1996. Officers and directors, as a group, own 38% of the outstanding shares.

Officers	Position	Ownership Information	12/31/95
James L. Ryan	Chairman, CEO	Number of Shares Outstanding	935,907
Tom J. Mantor	President, COO	Market Capitalization	$ 15,676,442
Leland E. Wines	Exec VP, CFO	Frequency Of Dividends	Irregular
Andrea L. Head	Senior VP	Number of Shareholders	511
Robert W. McDoulett	Senior VP		

Other Information

Transfer Agent	First Interstate Bank, Corp Trust Dept		Where Listed	OTC-PS
Auditor	Arthur Andersen LLP		Symbol	BWCF
Market Maker	Sutro & Company, Inc.	Telephone (800)227-4422	SIC Code	6020
Broker Dealer	Regular Stockbroker		Employees	70

Balcor Current Income Fund 85

Balcor Plaza, 4849 Golf Road • Skokie, IL 60077 • Telephone (847)677-2900

Company Description

Operations consist exclusively of operating five income producing properties including one mall, two apartment complexes, and two self-storage warehouses. The Company was formed as a limited partnership in 1985 and raised $57 million for the purpose of acquiring five real property investments. Equity Resource Find-XVII, an unrelated party, made a tender offer in early 1996 and acquired a 2% limited partner interest.

	12/31/95	12/31/94	12/31/93	12/31/92
Per Unit Information				
Price Per Unit	315.00	211.00	181.58	109.00
Earnings Per Unit	-16.93	-128.17	-18.65	-96.26
Price / Earnings Ratio	n.a.	n.a.	n.a.	n.a.
Book Value Per Unit	327.57	356.81	484.98	503.63
Price / Book Value %	96.16	59.14	37.44	21.64
Distributions Per Unit	12.31	n.a.	n.a.	n.a.
Cash Flow Per Unit	11.10	n.a.	19.08	0.34
Annual Financial Data				
Operating Results (000's)				
Total Revenues	10,007.3	10,366.1	10,016.6	9,112.1
Costs & Expenses	-10,443.8	-11,055.2	-11,092.1	-11,261.7
Operating Income	-436.5	-7,389.1	-1,075.4	-5,549.6
Other Items	-539.5	n.a.	n.a.	560.0
Net Income	-976.0	-7,389.1	-1,075.4	-4,989.6
Cash Flow From Operations	633.7	1,458.0	1,089.2	19.2
Balance Sheet (000's)				
Cash & Equivalents	5,475.5	2,872.5	1,121.4	128.5
Total Current Assets	5,668.5	3,265.4	1,280.0	369.3
Investments In	n.a.	n.a.	n.a.	n.a.
Total Assets	52,642.5	50,448.4	57,538.0	59,087.1
Total Current Liabilities	107.9	160.3	152.5	554.2
Long-Term Debt	33,824.5	29,854.1	29,561.0	29,657.2
Partners' Capital	18,452.3	20,130.9	27,519.9	28,595.4
Performance & Financial Condition				
Return on Total Revenues %	-9.75	-71.28	-10.74	-54.76
Return on Average Partners' Capital %	-5.06	-31.01	-3.83	n.a.
Return on Average Assets %	-1.89	-13.69	-1.84	-8.19
Current Ratio	52.54	20.37	8.39	0.67
Debt / Equity %	183.31	148.30	107.42	103.71

Compound Growth %'s	EPU %	n.a.	Net Income %	n.a.	Total Revenues %	3.17

Comments

Although the original agreements state that proceeds from sale or refinance can be used to acquire additional properties, management has indicated that it may very well liquidate the partnership. Property sales will depend on general market conditions and other factors. Management believes that it may be the appropriate time to dispose of the apartment complexes because of conditions now favorable to sellers of such properties.

Officers	Position	Ownership Information	12/31/95
Thomas E. Meador	President, CEO	Number of Shares Outstanding	57,074
Alexander J. Darragh	Senior VP	Market Capitalization	$ 17,978,310
Josette V. Goldberg	Senior VP	Frequency Of Distributions	n.a.
Brian D. Parker	CFO, Treasurer	Number of Partners	n.a.

Other Information							
Transfer Agent	Company Office				Where Listed	Order Matching Only
Auditor	Coopers & Lybrand LLP				Symbol	n.a.
Market Maker	None				SIC Code	6500
Broker Dealer	Chicago Partnership Board	Tel/Ext	(800)272-6273	690	Employees	None

Barnstable Holding Co., Inc.

47 Old Yarmouth Road • Hyannis, MA 02601-0326 • Telephone (508)775-0063 • Fax (508)790-1313

Company Description

The Company provides water service to residential and business customers in the Hyannis area of Massachusetts through its subsidiary, Barnstable Water Company, of which it owns 95.5%. There are 20 registered shareholders of the Company. Shares recently traded at $100. Direct contact with the Company may be a way to access the existing owners.

	12/31/94	12/31/93
Per Share Information		
Stock Price	100.00	100.00
Earnings Per Share	204.10	265.26
Price / Earnings Ratio	0.49	0.38
Book Value Per Share	2,255.64	2,106.54
Price / Book Value %	4.43	4.75
Dividends Per Share	55.00	n.a.
Annual Financial Data		
Operating Results (000's)		
Total Revenues	1,900.1	1,876.0
Costs & Expenses	-1,449.3	-1,530.0
Income Before Taxes and Other	253.3	153.0
Other Items	-12.2	86.9
Income Tax	-94.9	-50.0
Net Income	146.1	189.9
Cash Flow From Operations	188.8	297.3
Balance Sheet (000's)		
Cash & Equivalents	138.0	114.6
Total Current Assets	987.4	869.5
Fixed Assets, Net	4,919.0	4,965.6
Total Assets	6,127.2	5,979.8
Total Current Liabilities	390.1	336.1
Long-Term Debt	2,000.0	2,000.0
Stockholders' Equity	1,615.0	1,508.3
Performance & Financial Condition		
Return on Total Revenues %	7.69	10.12
Return on Avg Stockholders' Equity %	9.36	13.44
Return on Average Assets %	2.41	3.24
Current Ratio	2.53	2.59
Debt / Equity %	123.84	132.60

Compound Growth %'s	EPS %	-23.06	Net Income %	-23.06	Total Revenues %	1.28

Comments

1993 results include a one-time benefit for adopting GAAP for the accounting of income taxes in the amount of $103,539, or $144.61 per share. 1995 reports were not yet available. Although it might appear that a lot of value has accumulated in the Company, there is a problem in terms of doing anything with it. Since the original funding was made in part by a local municipality, Massachusettes law might require that some or all of the assets be paid to the government upon liquidation. Are there any cleaver attorneys in the house?

Officers	Position	Ownership Information	12/31/94
Richard Wadsworth	President, CEO	Number of Shares Outstanding	716
		Market Capitalization	$ 71,600
		Frequency Of Dividends	Quarterly
		Number of Shareholders	Under 500

Other Information

Transfer Agent	Company Office			Where Listed	Order Matching Only
Auditor	Ernst & Young LLP			Symbol	n.a.
Market Maker	None - Company Office	Telephone	(508)775-0063	SIC Code	4941
Broker Dealer	None			Employees	9

Batterymarch Trust

125 High Street • Boston, MA 02110-2704

Company Description

The Trust is a Massachusetts business trust whose primary activities have been investment in marketable securities, real estate partnerships, and oil and gas operating properties. The Trust was formed as a result of the 1987 liquidation of Federal Power & Light Co. & American Electric Share Co.

	12/31/95	12/31/94	12/31/93
Per Share Information			
Stock Price	260.00	225.00	260.00
Earnings Per Share	54.75	47.64	5.78
Price / Earnings Ratio	4.75	4.72	44.98
Book Value Per Share	331.47	289.72	255.06
Price / Book Value %	78.44	77.66	101.94
Dividends Per Share	13.00	13.00	13.00
Annual Financial Data			
Operating Results (000's)			
Total Revenues	4,573.3	124.6	707.8
Costs & Expenses	-243.6	-237.3	-268.6
Income Before Taxes and Other	4,329.6	-112.7	439.2
Other Items	n.a.	2,415.7	n.a.
Income Tax	-1,545.0	120.0	-145.0
Net Income	2,784.6	2,423.1	294.2
Cash Flow From Operations	n.a.	344.2	226.2
Balance Sheet (000's)			
Cash & Equivalents	3.5	3.0	2.3
Total Current Assets	17,894.5	14,544.5	11,436.1
Fixed Assets, Net	n.a.	n.a.	n.a.
Total Assets	18,944.5	15,691.4	13,125.0
Total Current Liabilities	186.8	277.2	146.7
Long-Term Debt	n.a.	n.a.	n.a.
Stockholders' Equity	16,858.7	14,735.2	12,978.3
Performance & Financial Condition			
Return on Total Revenues %	60.89	1943.99	41.57
Return on Avg Stockholders' Equity %	17.63	17.49	2.21
Return on Average Assets %	16.08	16.82	2.15
Current Ratio	95.78	52.47	77.94
Debt / Equity %	n.a.	n.a.	n.a.

Compound Growth %'s	EPS %	207.77	Net Income %	207.65	Total Revenues %	154.19

Comments

1994 results include a one-time benefit of $2.4 million, or $47.50 per share, for adopting GAAP for the recording of certain investments. None of the years reported have comparable income statement results, but balance sheets are comparable for 1995 and 1994. Compound growth rates may be distorted because of low revenue and income in 1993.

Officers	Position	Ownership Information	12/31/95
Kingsley Durant	President	Number of Shares Outstanding	50,860
William Spears, Jr.	Director	Market Capitalization	$ 13,223,600
Lindsey Hooper, Jr.	Director	Frequency Of Dividends	n.a.
Robert Goodrow	Director	Number of Shareholders	Under 500
Carol Payton	Director		

Other Information				
Transfer Agent	Company Office		Where Listed	OTC-BB
Auditor	Michael K. Schaefer		Symbol	BTYM
Market Maker	Gruntal & Co., Incorporated	Telephone (800)223-7632	SIC Code	6790
Broker Dealer	Regular Stockbroker		Employees	n.a.

Bay Area Bancshares

900 Veterans Boulevard • Redwood City, CA 94063 • Telephone (415)367-1600 • Fax (415)365-3954

Company Description

The Company is a one bank holding company of Bay Area Bank, a full service commercial bank serving the communities of Redwood City and San Carlos, California. The Bank concentrates its lending activities in three areas: short-term real estate loans, business loans, and construction loans which, at December 31, 1995, accounted for 46%, 29% and 18% of all loans, respectively. The short-term real estate loans have the particular emphasis of providing loans to small and medium-sized businesses. The Bank was founded in 1979.

	12/31/95	12/31/94	12/31/93	12/31/92
Per Share Information				
Stock Price	11.63	7.19	5.88	4.00
Earnings Per Share	1.31	1.09	1.02	0.91
Price / Earnings Ratio	8.88	6.60	5.76	4.40
Book Value Per Share	9.82	8.70	7.92	7.14
Price / Book Value %	118.43	82.64	74.24	56.02
Dividends Per Share	0.29	0.23	0.20	0.20
Annual Financial Data				
Operating Results (000's)				
Net Interest Income	5,284.0	4,773.0	4,549.0	4,295.4
Loan Loss Provision	-210.0	-300.0	-420.0	-450.0
Non-Interest Income	2,532.0	1,833.0	692.0	312.0
Non-Interest Expense	-5,556.0	-4,722.0	-3,375.0	-2,984.4
Income Before Taxes and Other	2,050.0	1,584.0	1,446.0	1,173.0
Other Items	n.a.	n.a.	n.a.	n.a.
Income Tax	-839.0	-637.0	-586.0	-472.0
Net Income	1,211.0	947.0	860.0	701.0
Balance Sheet (000's)				
Cash & Securities	31,423.0	24,825.0	21,594.3	18,639.2
Loans, Net	59,209.0	52,017.0	54,973.3	52,430.7
Fixed Assets, Net	948.0	1,023.0	167.7	77.0
Total Assets	93,815.0	79,537.0	78,718.6	73,651.6
Deposits	83,979.0	72,014.0	71,981.7	67,728.3
Stockholders' Equity	8,078.0	6,971.0	6,204.0	5,410.2
Performance & Financial Condition				
Net Interest Margin	n.a.	n.a.	n.a.	n.a.
Return on Avg Stockholders' Equity %	16.09	14.38	14.81	13.65
Return on Average Assets %	1.40	1.20	1.13	0.98
Equity to Assets %	8.61	8.76	7.88	7.35
Reserve as a % of Non-Performing Loans	322.55	752.50	162.33	206.41

Compound Growth %'s	EPS % 12.91	Net Income % 19.99	Net Interest Income % 7.15

Comments

Management attributes the recent growth to a 16.6% increase in deposits over 1994 and net loan growth of 14.6%. The recently created mortgage department has not had a significant impact but is now in full operation with its own set of goals. With great returns on both equity and assets, it is no wonder that the officers and directors, as a group, own 37% of shares outstanding.

Officers	Position	Ownership Information	12/31/95
Robert R. Haight	President, CEO	Number of Shares Outstanding	821,829
John O. Brooks	Exec VP, COO	Market Capitalization	$ 9,557,871
Frank M. Bartaldo, Jr.	Exec VP	Frequency Of Dividends	Quarterly
Peter J. Altieri	Senior VP	Number of Shareholders	380
Anthony J. Gould	Senior VP, CFO		

Other Information

Transfer Agent	U.S. Stock Transfer Corporation			Where Listed	OTC-BB
Auditor	Ernst & Young LLP			Symbol	BYAR
Market Maker	Van Kasper & Company	Telephone	(800)652-1747	SIC Code	6020
Broker Dealer	Regular Stockbroker			Employees	46

Beaver Coal Company, Ltd.

668 Public Ledger Bldg. • Philadelphia, PA 19106 • Telephone (215)923-3641 • Fax (215)923-5535

Company Description

The Company holds fee and mineral rights to approximately 40,000 acres of coal bearing lands and additionally holds approximately 9,800 acres without coal rights in Raleigh County, West Virginia. Timber and surface rental income comprises two-thirds of revenue. Pursuant to the liquidation of Beaver Coal corporation in 1967, cash and coal lands were contributed in the formation of this partnership. This entity will continue until October 31, 2009, unless terminated before then.

	12/31/94	12/31/93	12/31/92
Per Unit Information			
Price Per Unit	316.00	275.00	272.50
Earnings Per Unit	35.42	33.98	21.94
Price / Earnings Ratio	8.92	8.09	12.42
Book Value Per Unit	108.31	108.31	108.31
Price / Book Value %	291.76	253.90	251.59
Distributions Per Unit	35.00	33.50	22.50
Cash Flow Per Unit	34.86	32.12	22.88
Annual Financial Data			
Operating Results (000's)			
Total Revenues	1,354.7	1,274.0	953.3
Costs & Expenses	-473.4	-428.6	-406.5
Operating Income	881.2	845.3	546.8
Other Items	n.a.	n.a.	n.a.
Net Income	881.2	845.3	546.8
Cash Flow From Operations	867.3	799.2	569.3
Balance Sheet (000's)			
Cash & Equivalents	184.1	175.1	136.8
Total Current Assets	184.1	175.1	136.8
Investments In Coal lands	2,490.9	2,491.2	2,485.4
Total Assets	2,759.1	2,748.7	2,706.0
Total Current Liabilities	33.8	n.a.	n.a.
Long-Term Debt	n.a.	n.a.	n.a.
Partners' Capital	2,725.2	2,716.3	2,706.0
Performance & Financial Condition			
Return on Total Revenues %	65.05	66.36	57.36
Return on Average Partners' Capital %	32.39	31.18	n.a.
Return on Average Assets %	32.00	30.99	19.95
Current Ratio	5.44	n.a.	n.a.
Debt / Equity %	n.a.	n.a.	n.a.

Compound Growth %'s	EPU %	27.06	Net Income %	26.94	Total Revenues %	19.21

Comments

Small sales of land indicate substantial appreciation not reflected on the books. The real value of a partnership interest is not apparent. Cash flow is consistent. The 1995 report was not yet issued when we went to press.

Officers	Position	Ownership Information	12/31/94
Paul M. Ingersoll	President	Number of Shares Outstanding	24,878
A.J. Drexel Paul, Jr.	Vice President, Secretary	Market Capitalization	$ 7,861,448
David R. Wilmerding, Jr.	Vice President, Treasurer	Frequency Of Distributions	Quarterly
R. Woodrow Duba	General Manager	Number of Partners	Under 500

Other Information				
Transfer Agent	Company Office		Where Listed	OTC-BB
Auditor	Price Waterhouse LLP		Symbol	BVERS
Market Maker	Herzog, Heine, Geduld, Inc.	Telephone (800)221-3600	SIC Code	1200
Broker Dealer	Pink sheet specialist		Employees	10

Bell National Corporation

4209 Vineland Rd., Ste. J-1 • Orlando, FL 32811 • Telephone (407)849-0290 • Fax (407)849-0625

Company Description

Through its subsidiary, Payne Fabrics, Inc., the Company designs and distributes decorative drapery and upholstery fabrics. The Company's other subsidiaries are inactive. Officers and directors as a group owned 28.8% of the Company's common shares on March 8, 1996. The Company was incorporated in California in 1958. Its' principal subsidiary, Bell Savings & Loan, filed for bankruptcy protection in 1987 and ownership was assumed by a receiver. In 1990, the Company acquired 100% of the common stock of Payne Fabrics, Inc., which had been in business since 1865.

	12/31/95	12/31/94	12/31/93	12/31/92
Per Share Information				
Stock Price	0.13	0.25	0.21	0.06
Earnings Per Share	0.01	0.06	0.04	0.01
Price / Earnings Ratio	13.00	4.17	5.25	6.00
Book Value Per Share	0.30	0.29	0.23	0.19
Price / Book Value %	43.33	86.21	91.30	31.58
Dividends Per Share	n.a.	n.a.	n.a.	n.a.
Annual Financial Data				
Operating Results (000's)				
Total Revenues	13,653.0	13,877.0	14,107.0	14,018.0
Costs & Expenses	-13,531.0	-13,510.0	-13,884.0	-13,982.0
Income Before Taxes and Other	77.0	323.0	212.0	36.0
Other Items	n.a.	143.0	n.a.	n.a.
Income Tax	-29.0	-146.0	-14.0	-11.0
Net Income	48.0	320.0	198.0	25.0
Cash Flow From Operations	1,737.0	1,043.0	1,772.0	1,000.0
Balance Sheet (000's)				
Cash & Equivalents	n.a.	n.a.	n.a.	n.a.
Total Current Assets	5,279.0	5,671.0	5,152.0	4,868.0
Fixed Assets, Net	212.0	199.0	255.0	346.0
Total Assets	7,910.0	7,505.0	7,298.0	7,596.0
Total Current Liabilities	3,134.0	2,742.0	3,632.0	2,948.0
Long-Term Debt	2,645.0	2,627.0	2,250.0	3,430.0
Stockholders' Equity	1,574.0	1,526.0	1,203.0	1,005.0
Performance & Financial Condition				
Return on Total Revenues %	0.35	2.31	1.40	0.18
Return on Avg Stockholders' Equity %	3.10	23.45	17.93	2.52
Return on Average Assets %	0.62	4.32	2.66	0.33
Current Ratio	1.68	2.07	1.42	1.65
Debt / Equity %	168.04	172.15	187.03	341.29

Compound Growth %'s	EPS %	n.a.	Net Income %	24.29	Total Revenues %	-0.88

Comments

At December 31, 1995, the Company had net operating loss carryforwards of approximately $115.0 million which expire through the year 2010. These may be limited, however, based on a final ruling as to whether or not an ownership change took place in the past.

Officers	Position	Ownership Information	12/31/95
Alexander M. Milley	Chairman, Secretary	Number of Shares Outstanding	5,283,114
Robert C. Shaw	President, Treasurer	Market Capitalization	$ 686,805
Thomas R. Druggish	CFO	Frequency Of Dividends	n.a.
		Number of Shareholders	1,075

Other Information				
Transfer Agent	Continental Stock Transfer & Trust Co.		Where Listed	OTC-BB
Auditor	Ernst & Young LLP		Symbol	BLBN
Market Maker	Carr Securities Corporation	Telephone (800)221-2243	SIC Code	2200
Broker Dealer	Regular Stockbroker		Employees	89

Belle Isle Net Profit Units

P.O. Box 2009 • Amarillo, TX 79189-2009 • Telephone (806)378-1000 • Fax (806)378-8614

Company Description

The Trust is an entity with no existing activities. Arrangements have been made whereby the unit holders receive their share of royalty payments made to the Trust. Under the terms of a 1964 agreement, Pioneer Natural Gas Company purchased certain property interests from Belle Isle Corporation, subject to specified net profits payments. In 1986, Mesa Limited Partnership, now Mesa Inc., acquired Pioneer Natural Gas Company and, accordingly, the obligations under the agreement.

	12/31/95	12/31/94	12/31/93
Per Share Information			
Stock Price	2.12	3.00	3.00
Earnings Per Share	0.48	0.82	0.57
Price / Earnings Ratio	4.42	3.66	5.26
Book Value Per Share	n.a.	n.a.	n.a.
Price / Book Value %	n.a.	n.a.	n.a.
Dividends Per Share	0.48	0.82	0.57
Annual Financial Data			
Operating Results (000's)			
Total Revenues	446.9	762.4	525.8
Costs & Expenses	n.a.	n.a.	n.a.
Income Before Taxes and Other	446.9	762.4	525.8
Other Items	n.a.	n.a.	n.a.
Income Tax	n.a.	n.a.	n.a.
Net Income	446.9	762.4	525.8
Cash Flow From Operations	n.a.	n.a.	n.a.
Balance Sheet (000's)			
Cash & Equivalents	n.a.	n.a.	n.a.
Total Current Assets	n.a.	n.a.	n.a.
Fixed Assets, Net	n.a.	n.a.	n.a.
Total Assets	n.a.	n.a.	n.a.
Total Current Liabilities	n.a.	n.a.	n.a.
Long-Term Debt	n.a.	n.a.	n.a.
Stockholders' Equity	n.a.	n.a.	n.a.
Performance & Financial Condition			
Return on Total Revenues %	100.00	100.00	100.00
Return on Avg Stockholders' Equity %	n.a.	n.a.	n.a.
Return on Average Assets %	n.a.	n.a.	n.a.
Current Ratio	n.a.	n.a.	n.a.
Debt / Equity %	n.a.	n.a.	n.a.

Compound Growth %'s	EPS %	-8.23	Net Income %	-7.82	Total Revenues %	-7.82

Comments

There is no valuation of the remaining royalty interests. Royalty payments will only cease when less than $250,000 of royalties are earned for two consecutive years. Proved oil and gas reserves are estimated each year. The pattern has been that each year also has a positive revision to the estimated reserve which replenishes it from each year's extraction.

Officers	Position	Ownership Information	12/31/95
Not Available		Number of Shares Outstanding	925,000
		Market Capitalization	$ 1,961,000
		Frequency Of Dividends	Quarterly
		Number of Shareholders	Under 500

Other Information

Transfer Agent	American Stock Transfer & Trust Company			Where Listed	OTC-BB
Auditor	Arthur Andersen LLP			Symbol	BISLU
Market Maker	H.G. Wellington & Co. Inc.	Telephone	(212)732-6800	SIC Code	6733
Broker Dealer	Regular Stockbroker			Employees	None

Benjamin Moore & Co.

51 Chestnut Ridge Road • Montvale, NJ 07645-1862 • Telephone (201)573-9600 • Fax (201)573-9046

Company Description

The Company formulates, manufactures and sells a broad line of coatings consisting of paints, stains and clear finishes for use by the general public, painting contractors and industrial and commercial users. The Company operates in both the United States and international markets. The Company also has its own retail stores in certain markets. The Company was founded in 1883. It is subject to the Securities and Exchange Act of 1934 and, accordingly, files annually with the SEC.

	12/31/95	12/31/94	12/31/93	12/31/92
Per Share Information				
Stock Price	71.50	70.50	64.00	55.00
Earnings Per Share	3.19	4.29	3.66	3.66
Price / Earnings Ratio	22.41	16.43	17.49	15.03
Book Value Per Share	25.99	25.30	23.28	22.06
Price / Book Value %	275.11	278.66	274.91	249.32
Dividends Per Share	1.80	1.78	1.68	1.65
Annual Financial Data				
Operating Results (000's)				
Total Revenues	564,211.4	547,063.6	512,700.1	484,851.9
Costs & Expenses	-509,764.3	-476,344.7	-451,749.1	-424,453.0
Income Before Taxes and Other	52,800.0	70,366.2	60,950.9	60,399.0
Other Items	210.7	-626.0	-543.0	-573.6
Income Tax	-22,554.6	-28,417.7	-23,897.1	-23,518.0
Net Income	30,456.1	41,322.4	36,510.9	36,307.3
Cash Flow From Operations	19,978.3	48,300.5	32,281.8	39,972.0
Balance Sheet (000's)				
Cash & Equivalents	11,232.3	3,435.1	5,011.5	5,000.0
Total Current Assets	207,284.4	192,185.1	185,197.8	181,118.0
Fixed Assets, Net	78,360.8	74,268.5	60,269.7	60,000.0
Total Assets	330,155.3	304,087.8	276,040.1	263,610.0
Total Current Liabilities	85,487.0	65,479.3	51,996.0	48,537.0
Long-Term Debt	3,968.1	5,005.5	6,477.2	7,825.0
Stockholders' Equity	227,660.8	221,538.4	209,760.3	199,054.0
Performance & Financial Condition				
Return on Total Revenues %	5.40	7.55	7.12	7.49
Return on Avg Stockholders' Equity %	13.56	19.16	17.86	18.49
Return on Average Assets %	9.60	14.25	13.53	13.99
Current Ratio	2.42	2.94	3.56	n.a.
Debt / Equity %	1.74	2.26	3.09	n.a.

Compound Growth %'s	EPS %	-4.48	Net Income %	-5.69	Total Revenues %	5.18

Comments

Although 1995 results were below expectations, the Company maintains a strong balance sheet with little long term debt. It also paid more than $10 million for stock repurchases in each of the last four years. Some would interpret this, as well as their unfriendliness to inquiring investors, as an indication that they are planning to become private.

Officers	Position	Ownership Information	12/31/95
Richard Roob	Chairman	Number of Shares Outstanding	9,467,893
Maurice C. Workman	President	Market Capitalization	$ 676,954,350
Benjamin M. Belcher, Jr.	Exec VP	Frequency Of Dividends	Quarterly
Yvan Dupuy	Senior VP	Number of Shareholders	1,775
William J. Fritz	VP - Finance, Treasurer		

Other Information				
Transfer Agent	Company Office		Where Listed	OTC-PS
Auditor	Deloitte & Touche LLP		Symbol	MBEN
Market Maker	Ernst & Company	Telephone (800)845-4330	SIC Code	2851
Broker Dealer	Pink sheet specialist		Employees	2000

Benthos, Inc.

49 Edgerton Drive • North Falmouth, MA 02556-2826 • Telephone (508)563-1000 • Fax (508)563-6444

Company Description

The Company designs, manufactures, sells and services oceanographic and robotic equipment for underwater exploration, research and defense, and electronic inspection equipment for the automated assessment of the seal integrity of consumer food, beverage, pharmaceutical and chemical containers. President Samuel O. Raymond founded the Company in 1962 and took it public in 1969. During 1995, the Company repurchased 72,786 shares for $3 per share. The Board of Directors cumulatively owns 35.8% of the Company.

	09/30/95	09/30/94	09/30/93	09/30/92
Per Share Information				
Stock Price	4.75	2.62	3.75	3.00
Earnings Per Share	0.18	0.24	0.41	0.24
Price / Earnings Ratio	26.39	10.92	9.15	12.50
Book Value Per Share	4.55	4.72	4.38	4.08
Price / Book Value %	104.40	55.51	85.62	73.53
Dividends Per Share	n.a.	n.a.	n.a.	n.a.
Annual Financial Data				
Operating Results (000's)				
Total Revenues	8,014.4	9,505.9	10,638.6	10,400.1
Costs & Expenses	-7,766.6	-9,233.9	-10,096.4	-10,070.5
Income Before Taxes and Other	247.8	272.0	542.2	329.6
Other Items	n.a.	n.a.	n.a.	n.a.
Income Tax	-86.0	-67.0	-175.0	-121.0
Net Income	161.8	205.0	367.2	208.6
Cash Flow From Operations	147.7	642.1	854.8	253.1
Balance Sheet (000's)				
Cash & Equivalents	17.5	189.6	49.4	49.9
Total Current Assets	4,666.9	4,384.6	4,434.8	4,007.2
Fixed Assets, Net	1,493.4	1,533.6	1,637.1	1,479.2
Total Assets	6,384.1	6,120.4	6,192.2	5,730.0
Total Current Liabilities	1,462.1	1,105.7	1,352.7	1,257.5
Long-Term Debt	868.7	902.7	932.5	938.8
Stockholders' Equity	4,053.4	4,112.0	3,907.0	3,533.6
Performance & Financial Condition				
Return on Total Revenues %	2.02	2.16	3.45	2.01
Return on Avg Stockholders' Equity %	3.96	5.11	9.87	6.11
Return on Average Assets %	2.59	3.33	6.16	3.62
Current Ratio	3.19	3.97	3.28	3.19
Debt / Equity %	21.43	21.95	23.87	26.57

Compound Growth %'s	EPS %	-9.14	Net Income %	-8.12	Total Revenues %	-8.32

Comments

Growth has stalled since 1993 because of a number of factors including reductions in defense funding and offshore oil exploration. The Company is expending significant effort in new products and the advancement of its container inspection division.

Officers	Position	Ownership Information	09/30/95
Samuel O. Raymond	Chairman	Number of Shares Outstanding	890,111
Lawrence W. Gray	President, CEO	Market Capitalization	$ 4,228,027
J. Luke Sabella	Treasurer, CFO	Frequency Of Dividends	n.a.
Peter Zentz	Other	Number of Shareholders	Under 500

Other Information

Transfer Agent	American Stock Transfer & Trust Company			Where Listed	OTC-BB
Auditor	Arthur Andersen LLP			Symbol	BTHS
Market Maker	H.C. Wainwright & Co., Inc.	Telephone	(800)225-6790	SIC Code	5049
Broker Dealer	Regular Stockbroker			Employees	63

Berlin City Bank, The

9 Main Street • Berlin, NH 03570 • Telephone (603)752-1171 • Fax (603)752-4620

Company Description

The Berlin City Bank is a community bank offering standard banking services through its six branches located in northern New Hampshire. The industries dominant in the area are forest products and recreation.

	12/31/95	12/31/94	12/31/93	12/31/92
Per Share Information				
Stock Price	270.00	217.00	175.00	155.00
Earnings Per Share	36.67	33.57	30.69	24.56
Price / Earnings Ratio	7.36	6.46	5.70	6.31
Book Value Per Share	311.34	243.17	251.58	235.11
Price / Book Value %	86.72	89.24	69.56	65.93
Dividends Per Share	6.60	6.30	6.00	5.00
Annual Financial Data				
Operating Results (000's)				
Net Interest Income	9,684.0	9,049.0	7,660.0	7,575.0
Loan Loss Provision	-540.0	-540.0	-795.0	-920.0
Non-Interest Income	584.0	702.0	1,164.0	688.0
Non-Interest Expense	-6,146.0	-5,931.0	-5,104.0	-5,289.0
Income Before Taxes and Other	3,582.0	3,280.0	2,925.0	2,054.0
Other Items	n.a.	n.a.	n.a.	n.a.
Income Tax	-1,261.0	-1,155.0	-982.0	-499.0
Net Income	2,321.0	2,125.0	1,943.0	1,555.0
Balance Sheet (000's)				
Cash & Securities	95,005.0	92,624.0	86,376.0	78,932.0
Loans, Net	134,025.0	130,435.0	118,899.0	120,967.0
Fixed Assets, Net	4,620.0	4,758.0	4,065.0	4,402.0
Total Assets	240,594.0	236,278.0	214,033.0	208,680.0
Deposits	213,775.0	213,003.0	186,830.0	189,915.0
Stockholders' Equity	19,708.0	15,393.0	15,925.0	14,883.0
Performance & Financial Condition				
Net Interest Margin	n.a.	4.24	3.88	n.a.
Return on Avg Stockholders' Equity %	13.22	13.57	12.61	10.92
Return on Average Assets %	0.97	0.94	0.92	0.77
Equity to Assets %	8.19	6.51	7.44	7.13
Reserve as a % of Non-Performing Loans	122.84	91.28	92.86	52.50

Compound Growth %'s	EPS %	14.30	Net Income %	14.28	Net Interest Income %	8.53

Comments

The loan portfolio is heavily concentrated in real estate loans, comprising 84% of the total loans outstanding. However, in 1995, the bank gained the capability of originating residential mortgages for sale directly to the secondary market. This allows for a greater ability to offer a variety of mortgages and to generate fee income.

Officers	Position	Ownership Information	12/31/95
William J. Woodward	President, CEO	Number of Shares Outstanding	63,301
Paul G. Campagna	Senior VP, Senior Loan Officer	Market Capitalization	$ 17,091,270
John H. Stratton	Senior VP	Frequency Of Dividends	Annual
David J. O'Commor	CFO, Treasurer	Number of Shareholders	1,400
James M. O'Donnell	Vice President, Controller		

Other Information				
Transfer Agent	The First National Bank of Boston		Where Listed	OTC-BB
Auditor	KPMG Peat Marwick LLP		Symbol	BCNB
Market Maker	First Albany Corporation	Telephone (800)541-5061	SIC Code	6020
Broker Dealer	Regular Stockbroker		Employees	107

Best Lock Corporation

P.O. Box 50444 • Indianapolis, IN 46250 • Telephone (317)849-2250 • Fax (317)595-7626

Company Description

The principal business of the Company is the manufacture, distribution and sale of access control products and services, including locks and lock components. The Company specializes in providing locking systems for commercial end-users, including institutional, industrial and government facilities. The Company was incorporated in the state of Delaware in 1928. The Company has two non-operating parent companies. Its immediate parent, Best Universal Lock Co. (Universal), owns 79% of the Company's common stock. Frank E. Best, Inc., in turn, owns 83% of Universal.

	12/31/95	12/31/94	12/31/93	12/31/92
Per Share Information				
Stock Price	390.00	385.00	370.00	355.00
Earnings Per Share	-33.88	16.83	13.73	18.73
Price / Earnings Ratio	n.a.	22.88	26.95	18.95
Book Value Per Share	208.38	312.61	370.00	362.00
Price / Book Value %	187.16	123.16	100.00	98.07
Dividends Per Share	5.41	5.40	5.00	4.90
Annual Financial Data				
Operating Results (000's)				
Total Revenues	118,546.5	104,669.0	98,731.2	85,094.5
Costs & Expenses	-124,620.8	-101,891.1	-96,700.0	-81,192.8
Income Before Taxes and Other	-6,563.9	2,403.4	2,031.2	3,901.7
Other Items	n.a.	n.a.	n.a.	n.a.
Income Tax	2,359.4	-195.3	-881.7	-1,443.4
Net Income	-4,204.5	2,208.2	1,149.5	2,458.3
Cash Flow From Operations	1,376.0	11,053.6	5,391.9	1,600.6
Balance Sheet (000's)				
Cash & Equivalents	1,348.9	4,792.1	1,602.5	1,595.9
Total Current Assets	33,502.8	37,364.7	33,092.5	31,666.9
Fixed Assets, Net	30,871.6	30,137.1	30,789.3	30,179.1
Total Assets	69,016.9	71,003.4	64,217.0	62,259.9
Total Current Liabilities	16,546.2	14,339.7	8,517.0	7,396.3
Long-Term Debt	15,197.1	n.a.	n.a.	n.a.
Stockholders' Equity	31,282.3	49,949.4	48,559.7	47,509.6
Performance & Financial Condition				
Return on Total Revenues %	-3.55	2.11	1.16	2.89
Return on Avg Stockholders' Equity %	-10.35	4.48	2.39	5.26
Return on Average Assets %	-6.01	3.27	1.82	3.98
Current Ratio	2.02	2.61	3.89	4.28
Debt / Equity %	48.58	n.a.	n.a.	n.a.

Compound Growth %'s	EPS % n.a.	Net Income % n.a.	Total Revenues % 11.69

Comments

The Company experienced record sales in 1995. However, several factors occurred during the year resulting in the Company posting a significant loss. The Company recorded a $3.1 million charge for anticipated closing costs associated with a restructuring plan to reduce operating costs. Professional fees were higher than in 1994 by $3.0 million, attributable to the implementation of new computer software. Product costs increased disproportionally to sales as a result of necessary adjustments to product inventories of $4.9 million.

Officers	Position	Ownership Information	12/31/95
Walter E. Best	Chairman, President	Number of Shares Outstanding	121,653
Russell C. Best	CEO	Market Capitalization	$ 47,444,670
Roger E. Beaverson	Treasurer, Secretary	Frequency Of Dividends	Annual
Gregg A. Dykstra	Vice President	Number of Shareholders	215
Richard E. Best	Vice President		

Other Information			
Transfer Agent	Company Office	Where Listed	OTC-BB
Auditor	Arthur Andersen LLP	Symbol	BLOC
Market Maker	Martin Nelson & Co., Inc.	Telephone (206)682-6261	SIC Code	3429
Broker Dealer	Regular Stockbroker	Employees	1195

Biddeford and Saco Water Company

181 Elm Street • Biddeford, ME 04005-2351 • Telephone (207)282-1543 • Fax (207)282-1544

Company Description

The Company provides water to individuals, businesses and government agencies in Biddeford, Saco, Old Orchard Beach, Scarborough, Old Orchard Beach, Pine Port, Kennebunk, Kennebunkport and Wells Water District, all in Maine.

	12/31/95	12/31/94	12/31/93	12/31/92
Per Share Information				
Stock Price	46.50	44.00	42.00	40.50
Earnings Per Share	3.74	3.54	3.63	3.58
Price / Earnings Ratio	12.43	12.43	11.57	11.31
Book Value Per Share	46.44	50.57	50.04	49.40
Price / Book Value %	100.13	87.01	83.93	81.98
Dividends Per Share	3.00	3.00	3.00	3.00
Annual Financial Data				
Operating Results (000's)				
Total Revenues	3,201.2	3,100.2	2,943.9	2,894.4
Costs & Expenses	-2,543.6	-2,734.1	-2,562.9	-2,556.3
Income Before Taxes and Other	657.1	366.1	381.0	338.1
Other Items	n.a.	n.a.	-17.5	n.a.
Income Tax	-260.8	-25.0	-13.0	7.0
Net Income	396.3	341.1	350.5	345.1
Cash Flow From Operations	894.9	688.6	648.6	896.5
Balance Sheet (000's)				
Cash & Equivalents	79.0	261.8	504.0	21.2
Total Current Assets	872.6	1,162.6	1,312.1	729.3
Fixed Assets, Net	12,361.3	11,921.9	11,636.2	11,301.7
Total Assets	13,496.2	13,331.7	13,149.8	12,355.0
Total Current Liabilities	531.3	435.9	349.1	812.6
Long-Term Debt	4,275.0	4,325.0	4,375.0	3,045.0
Stockholders' Equity	4,927.5	4,878.2	4,826.5	4,765.4
Performance & Financial Condition				
Return on Total Revenues %	12.38	11.00	11.90	11.92
Return on Avg Stockholders' Equity %	8.08	7.03	7.31	7.28
Return on Average Assets %	2.95	2.58	2.75	2.79
Current Ratio	1.64	2.67	3.76	0.90
Debt / Equity %	86.76	88.66	90.65	63.90

Compound Growth %'s	EPS %	1.47	Net Income %	4.72	Total Revenues %	3.42

Comments

Rates for water are regulated by the Maine Public Utilities Commission which granted the Company an 8.3% increase in May, 1994. This is partly responsible for the rise in 1995 revenues. Management seems pleased with their 16% improvement to the bottom line. This is happening at a time when the Company has an obligation to be involved in considerable street reconstruction in many of the communities served.

Officers	Position	Ownership Information	12/31/95
Harry M. Wooster	Chairman	Number of Shares Outstanding	106,104
Clifford S. Mansfield, Jr.	President, Treasurer	Market Capitalization	$ 4,933,836
Roger N. Parker, Sr.	Vice President	Frequency Of Dividends	Annual
John W L. White	Senior Clerk	Number of Shareholders	Under 500

Other Information

Transfer Agent	Company Office		Where Listed	OTC-BB
Auditor	Berry, Dunn, McNeil & Parker		Symbol	BIDS
Market Maker	Gruntal & Co., Incorporated	Telephone (800)225-8520	SIC Code	4940
Broker Dealer	Regular Stockbroker		Employees	28

Big Sky Transportation Co.

1601 Aviation Place • Billings, MT 59105 • Telephone (406)245-9449

Company Description

The Company does business as Big Sky Airlines and operates as a small regional commuter air carrier, primarily providing scheduled passenger, freight, express package and charter services. Most service is provided to nine communities in Montana. Seven of these communities are served under contract with the U.S. Department of Transportation under the Essential Air Service (EAS) program. The Company filed for bankrupcy in 1989 and emerged in 1992.

	06/30/95	06/30/94	06/30/93
Per Share Information			
Stock Price	0.22	0.20	0.23
Earnings Per Share	0.01	0.01	0.02
Price / Earnings Ratio	22.00	20.00	11.50
Book Value Per Share	0.14	0.13	0.12
Price / Book Value %	157.14	153.85	191.67
Dividends Per Share	n.a.	n.a.	n.a.
Annual Financial Data			
Operating Results (000's)			
Total Revenues	5,184.6	5,001.1	5,373.0
Costs & Expenses	-5,109.2	-4,865.0	-5,185.4
Income Before Taxes and Other	67.7	135.4	187.6
Other Items	n.a.	n.a.	n.a.
Income Tax	-30.9	-59.1	-81.0
Net Income	36.8	76.3	106.6
Cash Flow From Operations	112.2	292.2	261.1
Balance Sheet (000's)			
Cash & Equivalents	408.5	570.0	713.3
Total Current Assets	1,482.3	1,770.5	1,841.6
Fixed Assets, Net	895.4	847.7	424.4
Total Assets	2,414.6	2,711.8	2,443.7
Total Current Liabilities	824.4	1,032.6	1,002.1
Long-Term Debt	518.9	668.7	802.9
Stockholders' Equity	768.2	715.0	638.7
Performance & Financial Condition			
Return on Total Revenues %	0.71	1.53	1.98
Return on Avg Stockholders' Equity %	4.97	11.27	18.21
Return on Average Assets %	1.44	2.96	4.44
Current Ratio	1.80	1.71	1.84
Debt / Equity %	67.55	93.51	125.70

Compound Growth %'s	EPS %	-29.29	Net Income %	-41.23	Total Revenues %	-1.77

Comments

The Company has posted profits for all five years since emerging from bankrupcy. While results are not stellar, a gradual improvement is being made which may allow the Company to more actively pursue a list of possibilities. We have not included many penny stocks in this book because of long term patience required of an investor. However, this management gets credit for trying to make things work.

Officers	Position	Ownership Information	06/30/95
Terry D. Marshall	President, CEO	Number of Shares Outstanding	5,307,314
Craig Denney	Exec VP	Market Capitalization	$ 1,167,609
Jon Marchi	Treasurer	Frequency Of Dividends	n.a.
Jane Southworth	General Manager	Number of Shareholders	n.a.
Jack K. Daniels	Other		

Other Information			
Transfer Agent	Continental Stock Transfer & Trust Co.	Where Listed	PSE
Auditor	KPMG Peat Marwick, LLP	Symbol	BSA
Market Maker	Carr Securities Corporation	Telephone (800)221-2243	SIC Code	4510
Broker Dealer	Regular Stockbroker	Employees	77

Biloxi Marsh Lands Corporation

835 Union St., 2nd floor • New Orleans, LA 70112-1401 • Telephone (504)544-7237 • Fax (504)679-5237

Company Description

The Company collects rents, mineral royalties and other income related to its ownership of 88,101 acres of marsh lands in St. Bernard Parish, located 20 miles from New Orleans. There is also a portfolio of marketable securities.

	12/31/95	12/31/94
Per Share Information		
Stock Price	5.00	5.00
Earnings Per Share	0.01	0.01
Price / Earnings Ratio	500.00	500.00
Book Value Per Share	2.42	2.41
Price / Book Value %	206.61	207.47
Dividends Per Share	n.a.	n.a.
Annual Financial Data		
Operating Results (000's)		
Total Revenues	110.6	131.7
Costs & Expenses	-131.4	-158.7
Income Before Taxes and Other	-20.8	-27.0
Other Items	n.a.	n.a.
Income Tax	24.8	34.5
Net Income	4.0	7.6
Cash Flow From Operations	175.2	-80.7
Balance Sheet (000's)		
Cash & Equivalents	319.6	64.3
Total Current Assets	1,401.6	1,390.9
Fixed Assets, Net	n.a.	n.a.
Total Assets	1,676.6	1,672.6
Total Current Liabilities	n.a.	n.a.
Long-Term Debt	n.a.	n.a.
Stockholders' Equity	1,676.6	1,672.6
Performance & Financial Condition		
Return on Total Revenues %	3.65	5.74
Return on Avg Stockholders' Equity %	0.24	n.a.
Return on Average Assets %	0.24	n.a.
Current Ratio	n.a.	n.a.
Debt / Equity %	n.a.	n.a.

Compound Growth %'s	EPS % n.a.	Net Income % -46.54	Total Revenues % -15.99

Comments

Estimates of proven reserves are not available. The Company won a lawsuit which was upheld by the Louisiana Supreme Court in 1995 and, accordingly, amounts held in escrow since the dispute began are expected to be released, in part, to the Company. It is believed that the ultimate value of the property will be dependent on oil and gas exploration which has been at minimal levels in recent years. Not reflected in the balance sheet is the appreciation in the marketable securities of $1,006,000 and $513,000 at the end of 1995 and 1994, respectively. Compound growth rates are based on only two years of data.

Officers	Position	Ownership Information	12/31/95
William Ogden	Chairman	Number of Shares Outstanding	693,104
Sharlton B. Ogden II	President, CEO	Market Capitalization	$ 3,465,520
		Frequency Of Dividends	n.a.
		Number of Shareholders	Under 500

Other Information

Transfer Agent	Company Office		Where Listed	OTC-BB
Auditor	George W. Hill, CPA		Symbol	BLMC
Market Maker	Paine Webber Incorporated	Telephone (212)713-3766	SIC Code	6790
Broker Dealer	Pink sheet specialist		Employees	1

Biochem International Inc.

W238 N1650 Rockwood Drive • Waukesha, WI 53188-1199 • Telephone (414)542-3100 • Fax (414)523-4313

Company Description

The Company is a designer and manufacturer of patient monitoring equipment. The Company's products are used to monitor respiration, gases, blood pressure and related cardiovascular/pulmonary functions. The Company was incorporated in 1976 in order to acquire from the Medical Systems Business Division of General Electric Company, certain assets, patents and technology associated with its blood gas chemistry business. The acquisition was completed in 1978. At June 30, 1995, officers and directors owned 83% of the outstanding common stock.

	06/30/95	06/30/94	06/30/93	06/30/92
Per Share Information				
Stock Price	4.31	3.06	0.31	0.31
Earnings Per Share	0.32	0.56	0.14	0.08
Price / Earnings Ratio	13.47	5.46	2.21	3.88
Book Value Per Share	0.77	0.45	-0.12	-1.06
Price / Book Value %	559.74	680.00	n.a.	n.a.
Dividends Per Share	n.a.	n.a.	n.a.	n.a.
Annual Financial Data				
Operating Results (000's)				
Total Revenues	25,207.3	17,972.0	12,895.9	10,046.5
Costs & Expenses	-18,472.7	-14,468.4	-11,041.3	-8,973.0
Income Before Taxes and Other	6,734.6	3,503.6	1,854.6	1,073.5
Other Items	n.a.	5,196.6	n.a.	n.a.
Income Tax	-2,474.8	-1,308.8	-46.2	-11.9
Net Income	4,259.8	7,391.4	1,808.4	1,061.6
Cash Flow From Operations	6,230.6	2,853.7	1,068.0	989.7
Balance Sheet (000's)				
Cash & Equivalents	2,628.4	1,756.6	40.3	26.3
Total Current Assets	10,579.9	10,062.5	4,746.9	3,202.8
Fixed Assets, Net	1,437.7	431.2	345.0	285.5
Total Assets	12,304.9	12,767.1	5,093.8	3,489.1
Total Current Liabilities	2,191.5	6,916.1	2,693.8	2,948.8
Long-Term Debt	n.a.	n.a.	3,948.4	5,897.2
Stockholders' Equity	10,113.3	5,851.0	-1,548.4	-5,356.8
Performance & Financial Condition				
Return on Total Revenues %	16.90	41.13	14.02	10.57
Return on Avg Stockholders' Equity %	53.37	343.58	n.a.	n.a.
Return on Average Assets %	33.98	82.77	42.14	34.19
Current Ratio	4.83	1.45	1.76	1.09
Debt / Equity %	n.a.	n.a.	n.a.	n.a.

Compound Growth %'s	EPS %	58.74	Net Income %	58.91	Total Revenues %	35.88

Comments

At June 30, 1995, the Company had remaining operating loss carryforwards available for income tax purposes of approximately $4,739,500. Export sales, principally to the Far East, Central and South America and Western Europe, were $11,736,000 in 1995.

Officers	Position	Ownership Information	06/30/95
Frank A. Katarow	President, COO	Number of Shares Outstanding	13,083,284
David H. Sanders	CEO, Treasurer	Market Capitalization	$ 56,388,954
Keith R. Harper	Senior VP	Frequency Of Dividends	n.a.
Ann M. Johnson	Vice President	Number of Shareholders	800
Robert H. Wesel	VP - Sales		

Other Information

Transfer Agent	First Bank, Milwaukee			Where Listed	OTC-BB
Auditor	Coopers & Lybrand LLP			Symbol	BCHM
Market Maker	Robert W. Baird & Co.	Telephone	(800)562-2288	SIC Code	3845
Broker Dealer	Regular Stockbroker			Employees	105

Bismarck Hotel Company

171 West Randolph Street • Chicago, IL 60601 • Telephone (312)236-0123 • Fax (312)236-3177

Company Description

The Company owns and operates a 500 room hotel located on The Loop in downtown Chicago and an adjacent office building. The hotel is 102 years old and, although it had been restored to much of its original grandeur, is reportedly in need of some additional work. American Mart Corporation, Chicago, acquired a 80.7% interest in the Company decades ago.

	06/30/95	06/30/94
Per Share Information		
Stock Price	35.00	45.00
Earnings Per Share	-40.34	-27.32
Price / Earnings Ratio	n.a.	n.a.
Book Value Per Share	-102.24	-61.90
Price / Book Value %	n.a.	n.a.
Dividends Per Share	n.a.	n.a.
Annual Financial Data		
Operating Results (000's)		
Total Revenues	11,604.0	10,240.0
Costs & Expenses	-14,323.4	-12,060.5
Income Before Taxes and Other	-2,719.4	-1,820.5
Other Items	n.a.	n.a.
Income Tax	1,006.0	660.0
Net Income	-1,713.4	-1,160.5
Cash Flow From Operations	-2,011.2	-671.6
Balance Sheet (000's)		
Cash & Equivalents	n.a.	205.2
Total Current Assets	1,888.2	1,710.7
Fixed Assets, Net	4,012.5	3,587.4
Total Assets	5,900.6	5,298.1
Total Current Liabilities	10,204.0	7,869.4
Long-Term Debt	n.a.	n.a.
Stockholders' Equity	-4,342.3	-2,629.0
Performance & Financial Condition		
Return on Total Revenues %	-14.77	-11.33
Return on Avg Stockholders' Equity %	49.15	n.a.
Return on Average Assets %	-30.60	n.a.
Current Ratio	0.19	0.22
Debt / Equity %	n.a.	n.a.

Compound Growth %'s	EPS %	n.a.	Net Income %	n.a.	Total Revenues %	13.32

Comments

Although the Company currently shows an operating loss, one would have to factor in the potential value of this historic property in any analysis. Current deficits are being funded by American Mart Corporation. The carrying value of the hotel and adjacent property was $4 million at June 30, 1995. The stock trades infrequently.

Officers	Position	Ownership Information	06/30/95
William Wirtz	Chairman, CEO	Number of Shares Outstanding	42,472
		Market Capitalization	$ 1,486,520
		Frequency Of Dividends	n.a.
		Number of Shareholders	Under 500

Other Information

Transfer Agent	First Trust of Illinois, N.A.			Where Listed	OTC-PS
Auditor	Kupferberg, Goldberg & Neimark			Symbol	BSMK
Market Maker	Chicago Corporation, The	Telephone	(800)621-1674	SIC Code	7000
Broker Dealer	Pink sheet specialist			Employees	n.a.

Blue Diamond Coal Company

P.O. Box 59015 • Knoxville, TN 37950-9015 • Telephone (423)588-8511 • Fax (423)584-5080

Company Description

The Company is in the business of leasing coal properties and the purchasing, processing and selling of bituminous coal. Most of the Company's operations are located in Kentucky. Beginning in 1991, and lasting until April, 1995, the Company was operating under protection of the bankruptcy court. In January and May, 1993, pursuant to a plan of reorganization, 30% of the then outstanding common shares were issued to creditors as partial payment for their claims and 30% to an equity investor for cash. The Company was incorporated in Delaware in 1922.

	03/31/95	03/31/94	03/31/93	03/31/92
Per Share Information				
Stock Price	14.25	13.00	7.75	9.00
Earnings Per Share	3.97	-30.38	1.67	-28.71
Price / Earnings Ratio	3.59	n.a.	4.64	n.a.
Book Value Per Share	26.80	22.80	53.09	113.85
Price / Book Value %	53.17	57.02	14.60	7.91
Dividends Per Share	n.a.	n.a.	n.a.	n.a.
Annual Financial Data				
Operating Results (000's)				
Total Revenues	77,253.6	69,276.5	65,029.2	67,681.3
Costs & Expenses	-73,540.5	-63,824.3	-64,094.1	-78,420.4
Income Before Taxes and Other	3,713.1	5,452.2	935.1	-10,739.1
Other Items	n.a.	-31,891.1	571.0	n.a.
Income Tax	n.a.	-1,970.4	-655.1	n.a.
Net Income	3,713.1	-28,409.3	851.0	-10,739.1
Cash Flow From Operations	4,724.0	9,601.1	7,793.3	2,934.4
Balance Sheet (000's)				
Cash & Equivalents	694.8	1,453.6	496.5	1,902.5
Total Current Assets	12,002.5	10,121.8	10,536.2	10,442.8
Fixed Assets, Net	72,211.9	74,439.8	75,870.5	77,245.3
Total Assets	86,053.7	86,817.9	89,055.2	94,246.2
Total Current Liabilities	12,011.6	10,648.2	9,789.0	32,297.2
Long-Term Debt	17,204.1	21,100.0	24,383.4	130.0
Stockholders' Equity	25,067.3	21,322.4	49,659.2	42,588.6
Performance & Financial Condition				
Return on Total Revenues %	4.81	-41.01	1.31	-15.87
Return on Avg Stockholders' Equity %	16.01	-80.05	1.84	-22.39
Return on Average Assets %	4.30	-32.31	0.93	-10.48
Current Ratio	1.00	0.95	1.08	0.32
Debt / Equity %	68.63	98.96	49.10	0.31

Compound Growth %'s	EPS %	54.18	Net Income %	108.89	Total Revenues %	4.51

Comments

During the year ended March 31, 1994, the Company accrued a liability for coal miners retiree health care of $26.6 million which is included as a charge to income and reflected in Other Items. For the nine months ended December 31, 1995, the Company had total revenues of $65.8 million and net income of $3.9 million ($4.12 per share) as compared to $59.0 million and $3.4 milllion ($3.68 per share) for the same period in 1994. At December 29, 1995, the Company's stock was quoted at an average bid/ask price of $23.25 per share.

Officers	Position	Ownership Information	03/31/95
Ted B. Helms	President	Number of Shares Outstanding	935,220
William S. Lyon III	Treasurer	Market Capitalization	$ 13,326,885
K. Roger Foster	Vice President, Secretary	Frequency Of Dividends	n.a.
John E. Way, Jr.	Vice President	Number of Shareholders	500

Other Information

Transfer Agent	Company Office		Where Listed	OTC-BB
Auditor	Coulter & Justus PC		Symbol	BLDC
Market Maker	Carr Securities Corporation	Telephone (800)221-2243	SIC Code	1221
Broker Dealer	Regular Stockbroker		Employees	51

Blue Fish Clothing, Inc.

No. 3 Sixth Street • Frenchtown, NJ 08825 • Telephone (908)996-7333

Company Description

The Company is a designer, manufacturer, wholesaler and retailer of specially block-printed merchandise sold to upscale department and specialty stores and through three Company-owned stores. The Company has an attractive product brochure which you can obtain by calling (908)996-7333. The Company completed their initial public offering and the stock began trading on May 14, 1996. 800,000 shares were offered at $5 per share. The proceeds will be used for retail store expansion, management information systems and working capital.

	06/30/95	12/31/94	12/31/93
Per Share Information			
Stock Price	n.a.	n.a.	n.a.
Earnings Per Share	n.a.	0.13	n.a.
Price / Earnings Ratio	n.a.	n.a.	n.a.
Book Value Per Share	n.a.	0.24	n.a.
Price / Book Value %	n.a.	n.a.	n.a.
Dividends Per Share	n.a.	n.a.	n.a.
Annual Financial Data			
Operating Results (000's)			
Total Revenues	4,207.0	7,651.7	5,212.1
Costs & Expenses	-4,018.2	-6,800.2	-4,916.4
Income Before Taxes and Other	188.8	851.5	295.7
Other Items	n.a.	n.a.	n.a.
Income Tax	-78.7	-355.1	-123.3
Net Income	110.1	496.4	172.4
Cash Flow From Operations	-142.9	350.6	86.6
Balance Sheet (000's)			
Cash & Equivalents	233.7	348.7	n.a.
Total Current Assets	3,135.3	2,623.8	n.a.
Fixed Assets, Net	634.6	586.9	n.a.
Total Assets	3,887.8	3,345.7	n.a.
Total Current Liabilities	3,076.6	2,205.8	n.a.
Long-Term Debt	200.9	239.4	n.a.
Stockholders' Equity	610.3	900.6	n.a.
Performance & Financial Condition			
Return on Total Revenues %	2.62	6.49	n.a.
Return on Avg Stockholders' Equity %	14.57	n.a.	n.a.
Return on Average Assets %	3.04	n.a.	n.a.
Current Ratio	n.a.	1.19	n.a.
Debt / Equity %	n.a.	26.58	n.a.

Compound Growth %'s	EPS %	n.a.	Net Income %	n.a.	Total Revenues %	n.a.

Comments

1995 results are for the six month period ended June 30, 1995. The historical financial results did not provide for income taxes because it was an S corporation. Those statements were adjusted to reflect income taxes that would be payable had it been a regular corporation to make it consistent with future reporting upon completion of the public offering. The financial statements issued after completion of the public offering will look considerably different from those of the past. Compounded growth rates were not computed because of noncomparable data.

Officers	Position	Ownership Information	06/30/95
Jennifer Barclay	Chairman, President	Number of Shares Outstanding	n.a.
Marc Wallach	CEO	Market Capitalization	n.a.
Sally Brunkus	COO	Frequency Of Dividends	n.a.
Cameron Waite	CFO, Treasurer	Number of Shareholders	Under 500

Other Information			
Transfer Agent	U.S. Stock Transfer Corporation	Where Listed	CE
Auditor	Arthur Andersen LLP	Symbol	BLF
Market Maker	None	SIC Code	2300
Broker Dealer	Regular Stockbroker	Employees	n.a.

Blue Ridge Real Estate Company

P.O. Box 707 • Blakeslee, PA 18610-0707 • Telephone (717)443-8433 • Fax (717)443-8479

Company Description

This entity is represented by two companies with similar ownership: Blue Ridge Real Estate Company and Big Boulder Corporation. The Companies operate two ski resorts in the Pocono Mountains of northeastern Pennsylvania. The Companies have large landholdings with future development and sales potential; permits for 800 homesites and a golf course are in place. Officers and directors of the Companies own approximately 33% of the outstanding common stock.

	05/31/95	05/31/94	05/31/93	05/31/92
Per Share Information				
Stock Price	5.38	5.88	6.38	6.38
Earnings Per Share	-0.21	-0.08	0.06	0.08
Price / Earnings Ratio	n.a.	n.a.	106.33	79.75
Book Value Per Share	4.78	5.05	5.14	5.10
Price / Book Value %	112.55	116.44	124.12	125.10
Dividends Per Share	n.a.	n.a.	n.a.	n.a.
Annual Financial Data				
Operating Results (000's)				
Total Revenues	12,327.4	13,529.8	13,493.8	13,823.5
Costs & Expenses	-13,036.0	-13,813.2	-13,369.0	-13,468.3
Income Before Taxes and Other	-708.6	-283.4	124.9	355.2
Other Items	n.a.	8.4	n.a.	n.a.
Income Tax	272.8	111.2	5.4	-174.8
Net Income	-435.8	-163.9	130.2	180.4
Cash Flow From Operations	1,660.2	2,076.5	1,463.3	2,955.1
Balance Sheet (000's)				
Cash & Equivalents	2,085.3	2,888.6	3,015.1	2,601.8
Total Current Assets	2,879.7	3,599.4	3,542.1	3,217.0
Fixed Assets, Net	20,733.5	21,578.5	22,615.7	22,780.3
Total Assets	23,663.7	25,232.8	26,190.0	26,037.0
Total Current Liabilities	2,090.3	1,863.7	1,925.2	5,146.3
Long-Term Debt	9,578.0	10,051.5	10,571.0	6,883.5
Stockholders' Equity	9,570.2	10,615.8	10,905.1	10,915.6
Performance & Financial Condition				
Return on Total Revenues %	-3.53	-1.21	0.96	1.31
Return on Avg Stockholders' Equity %	-4.32	-1.52	1.19	n.a.
Return on Average Assets %	-1.78	-0.64	0.50	n.a.
Current Ratio	1.38	1.93	1.84	0.63
Debt / Equity %	100.08	94.68	96.94	63.06

Compound Growth %'s	EPS % n.a.	Net Income % n.a.	Total Revenues % -3.75

Comments

The Companies have contribution and net operating loss carryovers totaling approximately $2.2 million available to offset future taxable income. Ownership units are traded representing concurrent ownership in the same number of shares in each company. During 1993, 1994 and 1995 the Companies repurchased 97,000 shares of their combined common shares.

Officers	Position	Ownership Information	05/31/95
Michael J. Flynn	Chairman	Number of Shares Outstanding	2,004,014
Gary A. Smith	President	Market Capitalization	$ 10,781,595
Lois K. McCurdy	Secretary	Frequency Of Dividends	n.a.
R. Bruce Reiner	Controller	Number of Shareholders	855
Cynthia G. Derolf	Other		

Other Information				
Transfer Agent	First Valley Bank		Where Listed	OTC-BB
Auditor	Coopers & Lybrand LLP		Symbol	BLRGZ
Market Maker	Robotti & Eng, Incorporated	Telephone (212)986-4800	SIC Code	6979
Broker Dealer	Regular Stockbroker		Employees	69

Bollinger Industries, Inc.

222 W. Airport Freeway • Irving, TX 75062 • Telephone (214)445-0386 • Fax (214)438-8471

Company Description

Bollinger is a leading domestic supplier of consumer fitness accessory products and safety products. The Company markets, primarily to mass retailers, a complete line of more than 290 fitness accessory products. In addition, the Company manufactures and sells a wide variety of sports medicine and safety products with both preventive and rehabilitative applications. Officers and directors, as a group, owned 64.9% of the Company's outstanding shares on September 21,1995. The Company was reincorporated in Delaware during 1993.

	03/31/95	03/31/94	03/31/93	03/31/92
Per Share Information				
Stock Price	11.75	10.25	10.93	n.a.
Earnings Per Share	0.02	0.59	0.45	0.37
Price / Earnings Ratio	587.50	17.37	24.29	n.a.
Book Value Per Share	5.52	5.40	1.85	1.35
Price / Book Value %	212.86	189.81	590.81	n.a.
Dividends Per Share	n.a.	n.a.	n.a.	n.a.
Annual Financial Data				
Operating Results (000's)				
Total Revenues	73,159.3	45,217.5	32,894.5	17,972.4
Costs & Expenses	-72,963.2	-41,286.1	-30,089.5	-16,894.7
Income Before Taxes and Other	149.3	3,931.4	2,805.0	1,056.2
Other Items	n.a.	-725.1	-534.1	-58.0
Income Tax	-80.0	-1,403.6	-1,080.5	-7.5
Net Income	69.3	1,802.8	1,190.4	990.7
Cash Flow From Operations	-19,592.0	-8,449.1	-3,602.7	-1,570.1
Balance Sheet (000's)				
Cash & Equivalents	116.5	26.5	n.a.	n.a.
Total Current Assets	50,398.0	25,699.8	19,021.7	10,632.0
Fixed Assets, Net	2,365.0	1,106.7	875.6	800.0
Total Assets	55,422.4	27,631.9	20,662.7	12,058.0
Total Current Liabilities	34,673.0	7,662.0	15,538.0	8,037.1
Long-Term Debt	223.3	500.0	690.0	842.0
Stockholders' Equity	20,467.4	19,397.6	4,369.2	3,178.9
Performance & Financial Condition				
Return on Total Revenues %	0.09	3.99	3.62	5.51
Return on Avg Stockholders' Equity %	0.35	15.17	31.54	36.92
Return on Average Assets %	0.17	7.47	7.28	9.88
Current Ratio	1.45	3.35	1.22	1.32
Debt / Equity %	1.09	2.58	15.79	26.49

Compound Growth %'s	EPS % -62.19	Net Income % -58.80	Total Revenues % 59.67

Comments

During 1993, the Company completed an initial public offering of common stock with the issuance of 1.2 million shares at $12.50 per share. Net proceeds of approximately $13.1 million were used to repay existing debt and increase working capital.

Officers	Position	Ownership Information	03/31/95
Glenn D. Bollinger	Chairman, CEO	Number of Shares Outstanding	3,708,090
Bobby D. Bollinger	President	Market Capitalization	$ 43,570,058
Ron C. Bollinger	Exec VP	Frequency Of Dividends	n.a.
James A. Burgin	Exec VP	Number of Shareholders	54
Stephen P. Richman	Senior VP, CFO		

Other Information

Transfer Agent	Chemical Mellon Shareholder Services			Where Listed	OTC-PS
Auditor	King Burns and Company, P.C.			Symbol	DPBT
Market Maker	Robotti & Eng, Incorporated	Telephone	(212)986-4800	SIC Code	5091
Broker Dealer	Regular Stockbroker			Employees	700

Bolt Technology Corporation

Four Duke Place • Norwalk, CT 06854 • Telephone (203)853-0700 • Fax (203)854-9601

Company Description

The Company is engaged in developing, manufacturing, leasing and selling geophysical equipment and providing geophysical data acquisition services for use in the exploration of oil and gas. As a group, officers and directors owned 20.1% of the Company's outstanding stock on October 6, 1995. The Company was incorporated in 1961 in Connecticut.

	06/30/95	06/30/94	06/30/93	06/30/92
Per Share Information				
Stock Price	1.03	0.41	0.75	0.50
Earnings Per Share	0.38	0.17	0.12	0.07
Price / Earnings Ratio	2.71	2.41	6.25	7.14
Book Value Per Share	0.74	0.40	0.19	0.04
Price / Book Value %	139.19	102.50	394.74	1,250.00
Dividends Per Share	n.a.	n.a.	n.a.	n.a.
Annual Financial Data				
Operating Results (000's)				
Total Revenues	7,707.0	6,743.0	7,786.0	5,707.0
Costs & Expenses	-6,754.0	-5,914.0	-7,066.0	-5,305.0
Income Before Taxes and Other	953.0	829.0	720.0	402.0
Other Items	n.a.	234.0	244.0	137.0
Income Tax	1,000.0	n.a.	-244.0	-137.0
Net Income	1,953.0	1,063.0	720.0	402.0
Cash Flow From Operations	536.0	1,368.0	299.0	100.0
Balance Sheet (000's)				
Cash & Equivalents	59.0	60.0	359.0	58.0
Total Current Assets	4,150.0	2,916.0	3,849.0	2,737.0
Fixed Assets, Net	131.0	97.0	132.0	412.0
Total Assets	4,922.0	3,049.0	4,006.0	3,168.0
Total Current Liabilities	1,260.0	1,043.0	3,076.0	2,988.0
Long-Term Debt	n.a.	n.a.	n.a.	n.a.
Stockholders' Equity	3,662.0	2,006.0	930.0	180.0
Performance & Financial Condition				
Return on Total Revenues %	25.34	15.76	9.25	7.04
Return on Avg Stockholders' Equity %	68.91	72.41	129.73	n.a.
Return on Average Assets %	49.00	30.13	20.07	12.66
Current Ratio	3.29	2.80	1.25	0.92
Debt / Equity %	n.a.	n.a.	n.a.	n.a.

Compound Growth %'s	EPS %	75.75	Net Income %	69.37	Total Revenues %	10.53

Comments

During the three years ended June 30, 1995, an average of 65% of the Company's revenues were generated from foreign sales and service. In 1995, sales to Schlumberger, Ltd. and Petroleum Geo. Services accounted for 38% and 14% of total revenue. The Company has net operating loss carry-forwards of $18,011,000 resulting primarily from disposed of unprofitable operations.

Officers	Position	Ownership Information	06/30/95
Raymond M. Soto	President, CEO	Number of Shares Outstanding	4,971,431
Joseph Mayerick, Jr.	Senior VP	Market Capitalization	$ 5,120,574
Alan Levy	VP - Finance, Secretary	Frequency Of Dividends	n.a.
		Number of Shareholders	492

Other Information				
Transfer Agent	Mellon Securities Trust Company		Where Listed	OTC-BB
Auditor	Deloitte & Touche LLP		Symbol	BOLT
Market Maker	Herzog, Heine, Geduld, Inc.	Telephone (800)221-3600	SIC Code	1382
Broker Dealer	Regular Stockbroker		Employees	42

Bonal International, Inc.

21178 Bridge Street • Southfield, MI 48034 • Telephone (810)353-2041 • Fax (810)353-2028

Company Description

The Company is engaged in the design, development and manufacturing of metal stress-relieving equipment including the Meta-Lax products. The Company was incorporated in 1990 as a successor to Sport Connection, Inc. which had acquired Bonal Technologies, Inc. in a reverse acquisition. There was a 1 for 10 reverse stock split in 1992 and, accordingly, per share amounts were adjusted to be consistent.

	03/31/95	03/31/94	03/31/93	03/31/92
Per Share Information				
Stock Price	0.87	1.25	0.75	0.25
Earnings Per Share	0.21	-0.10	0.12	-0.02
Price / Earnings Ratio	4.14	n.a.	6.25	n.a.
Book Value Per Share	0.48	0.27	0.38	0.25
Price / Book Value %	181.25	462.96	197.37	100.00
Dividends Per Share	n.a.	n.a.	n.a.	n.a.
Annual Financial Data				
Operating Results (000's)				
Total Revenues	1,817.0	1,198.8	1,520.0	1,068.1
Costs & Expenses	-1,640.6	-1,283.7	-1,338.3	-1,086.6
Income Before Taxes and Other	176.3	-85.3	102.3	-18.5
Other Items	n.a.	n.a.	n.a.	n.a.
Income Tax	-5.1	n.a.	n.a.	n.a.
Net Income	171.1	-85.3	102.3	-18.5
Cash Flow From Operations	104.4	44.4	85.4	-13.3
Balance Sheet (000's)				
Cash & Equivalents	100.1	71.9	56.6	32.2
Total Current Assets	635.7	461.0	559.6	338.5
Fixed Assets, Net	71.2	71.7	83.9	56.8
Total Assets	706.9	532.7	643.5	395.4
Total Current Liabilities	263.7	234.7	252.3	185.6
Long-Term Debt	n.a.	n.a.	n.a.	n.a.
Stockholders' Equity	396.4	225.2	310.5	208.2
Performance & Financial Condition				
Return on Total Revenues %	9.42	-7.12	6.73	-1.73
Return on Avg Stockholders' Equity %	55.06	-31.84	39.44	-9.49
Return on Average Assets %	27.61	-14.50	19.70	-3.69
Current Ratio	2.41	1.96	2.22	1.82
Debt / Equity %	n.a.	n.a.	n.a.	n.a.

Compound Growth %'s	EPS %	32.29	Net Income %	29.34	Total Revenues %	19.37

Comments

Management attributes the recent surge in revenue to a number of factors including an excellent performance of the internal sales staff, intensified marketing efforts, and an increasingly receptive and motivated market for Meta-Lax stress relieving equipment.

Officers	Position	Ownership Information	03/31/95
A. George Hebel, III	Chairman, President	Number of Shares Outstanding	827,961
Paul Y. Hebel	Secretary	Market Capitalization	$ 720,326
Brian F. York	Treasurer	Frequency Of Dividends	n.a.
Thomas E. Hebel	Vice President	Number of Shareholders	115

Other Information					
Transfer Agent	OTC Stock Transfer, Inc., Salt Lake City			Where Listed	OTC-BB
Auditor	Deloitte & Touche LLP			Symbol	BONL
Market Maker	Olsen Payne & Company	Telephone	(800)453-5321	SIC Code	3600
Broker Dealer	Regular Stockbroker			Employees	20

Boonton Electronics Corporation

25 Eastmans Road • Parsippany, NJ 07054-0465 • Telephone (201)386-9696 • Fax (201)386-9191

Company Description

The Company designs and produces electronic testing and measuring instruments including power meters, voltmeters and modulation meters. The equipment is marketed throughout the world to commercial and government customers in the electronics industry. During September, 1993, the Company and its subsidiaries filed petitions in bankruptcy court for court approved reorganizations. During November, 1994, the plans of reorganization were approved. The success of the reorganization was due to the sale of an appreciated piece of real estate and the termination of an overfunded employee pension plan.

	09/30/95	09/30/94	09/30/93
Per Share Information			
Stock Price	2.59	0.53	2.50
Earnings Per Share	0.17	1.01	-4.64
Price / Earnings Ratio	15.24	0.52	n.a.
Book Value Per Share	1.99	1.84	n.a.
Price / Book Value %	130.15	28.80	301.20
Dividends Per Share	n.a.	n.a.	n.a.
Annual Financial Data			
Operating Results (000's)			
Total Revenues	6,859.0	6,807.0	6,662.9
Costs & Expenses	-6,718.4	-6,580.0	-13,197.3
Income Before Taxes and Other	-82.5	-216.6	-6,682.0
Other Items	n.a.	1,487.6	n.a.
Income Tax	316.3	36.4	660.6
Net Income	233.8	1,307.3	-6,021.4
Cash Flow From Operations	35.7	160.9	765.4
Balance Sheet (000's)			
Cash & Equivalents	146.6	132.1	n.a.
Total Current Assets	2,732.9	2,633.9	n.a.
Fixed Assets, Net	102.2	56.8	n.a.
Total Assets	4,089.0	3,750.5	n.a.
Total Current Liabilities	905.2	996.5	n.a.
Long-Term Debt	516.3	365.3	n.a.
Stockholders' Equity	2,667.5	2,388.7	n.a.
Performance & Financial Condition			
Return on Total Revenues %	3.41	19.21	-90.37
Return on Avg Stockholders' Equity %	9.25	n.a.	n.a.
Return on Average Assets %	5.97	n.a.	n.a.
Current Ratio	3.02	2.64	n.a.
Debt / Equity %	19.35	15.29	n.a.

Compound Growth %'s	EPS %	-83.17	Net Income %	-82.11	Total Revenues %	1.46

Comments

Significant items in 1994 net income include, debt forgiveness of $1.5 million, a net gain on the sale of assets of $806,000 and $290,000 of reorganization expenses, all a result of the plan of reorganization. In February, 1996, the Company entered into an agreement with a French company for it to acquire, in two stages, a significant ownership interest in the Company. In March, 1996, the French company acquired 180,300 shares of stock held in the Company's treasury for $563,438. The French company has until July, 1996 to exercise its option to buy another 523,700 shares at $3.125 per share.

Officers	Position	Ownership Information	09/30/95
Holmes Bailey	President, CEO	Number of Shares Outstanding	1,341,785
John E. Titterton	VP - Finance, Secretary	Market Capitalization	$ 3,475,223
		Frequency Of Dividends	n.a.
		Number of Shareholders	709

Other Information				
Transfer Agent	First Fidelity Bancorporation		Where Listed	OTC-BB
Auditor	I. Weismann Associates		Symbol	BOON
Market Maker	Hill, Thompson, Magid & Co.Inc	Telephone (800)631-3083	SIC Code	3825
Broker Dealer	Regular Stockbroker		Employees	56

Borel Bank and Trust Company

160 Bovet Road • San Mateo, CA 94402 • Telephone (415)378-3700 • Fax (415)378-3774

Company Description

Borel Bank & Trust Company is a one branch community bank, primarily servicing businesses in the upper-class communities of San Mateo and Hillborough in the San Francisco Bay area. The Bank was incorporated in 1979 and began operations in 1980.

	12/31/95	12/31/94	12/31/93	12/31/92
Per Share Information				
Stock Price	16.50	11.88	9.00	15.00
Earnings Per Share	1.85	1.35	1.11	0.68
Price / Earnings Ratio	8.92	8.80	8.11	22.06
Book Value Per Share	14.85	14.62	14.46	13.41
Price / Book Value %	111.11	81.26	62.24	111.86
Dividends Per Share	1.00	0.60	0.30	1.00
Annual Financial Data				
Operating Results (000's)				
Net Interest Income	9,939.6	8,479.4	7,735.4	7,617.3
Loan Loss Provision	-425.0	-380.0	-540.0	-2,130.0
Non-Interest Income	2,131.1	2,085.3	2,283.7	2,000.0
Non-Interest Expense	-7,671.0	-7,346.2	-7,194.8	-6,108.1
Income Before Taxes and Other	3,974.6	2,838.5	2,284.3	1,379.2
Other Items	n.a.	n.a.	n.a.	n.a.
Income Tax	-1,665.6	-1,180.4	-926.4	-532.9
Net Income	2,309.0	1,658.0	1,357.9	846.3
Balance Sheet (000's)				
Cash & Securities	74,115.9	68,573.3	55,320.9	49,455.2
Loans, Net	94,632.2	90,061.8	96,803.6	111,485.8
Fixed Assets, Net	1,394.9	1,536.4	1,012.6	1,128.8
Total Assets	177,199.8	169,205.8	159,739.0	168,313.0
Deposits	156,746.4	151,395.0	142,315.8	151,721.2
Stockholders' Equity	18,379.0	16,264.3	16,022.5	14,860.5
Performance & Financial Condition				
Net Interest Margin	6.40	5.60	5.26	5.09
Return on Avg Stockholders' Equity %	13.33	10.27	8.79	5.67
Return on Average Assets %	1.33	1.01	0.83	0.51
Equity to Assets %	10.37	9.61	10.03	8.83
Reserve as a % of Non-Performing Loans	168.94	149.90	58.51	52.18

Compound Growth %'s	EPS %	39.60	Net Income %	39.73	Net Interest Income %	9.28

Comments

The Bank primarily makes commercial loans, representing 74% of total loans. In 1995, an independent study by a marketing firm disclosed that 97% of respondents indicated that they were either satisfied or extremely satisfied with the Bank's services. The Bank participates in an international exercise and has hosted two young bankers from the Soviet Republic of Georgia as part of an internship program.

Officers	Position	Ownership Information	12/31/95
Harold A. Fick	President, CEO	Number of Shares Outstanding	1,238,004
Ronald G. Fick	Exec VP, Secretary	Market Capitalization	$ 20,427,066
William W. Abraham	Senior VP, Senior Loan Officer	Frequency Of Dividends	Irregular
Carol J. Olson	Senior VP, Other	Number of Shareholders	638
Emanuela M. Allgood	Senior VP, CFO		

Other Information				
Transfer Agent	First Interstate Bank		Where Listed	OTC-BB
Auditor	KPMG Peat Marwick LLP		Symbol	BLCA
Market Maker	Hoefer & Arnett, Inc.	Telephone (415)362-7111	SIC Code	6020
Broker Dealer	Regular Stockbroker		Employees	70

Boston Sand & Gravel Co.

169 Portland Street • Boston, MA 02102 • Telephone (617)227-9000 • Fax (617)523-7947

Company Description

The Company's principal business activities consist of the production and sale of ready-mixed concrete, sand, gravel and quarry materials. Most of these materials are used on local construction projects. The Company was established at the turn of the century and went public in 1929.

	12/31/95	12/31/94	12/31/93	12/31/92
Per Share Information				
Stock Price	155.00	144.00	119.00	94.00
Earnings Per Share	16.47	32.20	21.69	5.42
Price / Earnings Ratio	9.41	4.47	5.49	17.34
Book Value Per Share	259.10	246.49	217.20	198.01
Price / Book Value %	59.82	58.42	54.79	47.47
Dividends Per Share	1.50	2.50	1.00	1.00
Annual Financial Data				
Operating Results (000's)				
Total Revenues	50,869.7	67,227.6	60,472.5	46,016.2
Costs & Expenses	-47,122.0	-59,377.5	-56,294.6	-44,351.7
Income Before Taxes and Other	3,329.1	7,393.2	3,888.6	1,208.2
Other Items	n.a.	n.a.	442.0	n.a.
Income Tax	-1,020.0	-2,879.0	-1,290.0	-449.0
Net Income	2,309.1	4,514.2	3,040.6	759.2
Cash Flow From Operations	7,217.6	8,383.6	3,227.7	-1,089.9
Balance Sheet (000's)				
Cash & Equivalents	6,369.6	4,122.0	1,160.5	1,698.2
Total Current Assets	18,514.8	19,300.5	15,876.5	14,158.0
Fixed Assets, Net	15,694.0	15,997.6	17,466.8	17,701.2
Total Assets	44,244.5	45,608.2	43,770.9	41,185.0
Total Current Liabilities	5,142.6	7,272.0	8,469.1	7,410.9
Long-Term Debt	560.1	681.2	787.3	3,000.8
Stockholders' Equity	36,309.8	34,552.1	30,446.5	27,756.3
Performance & Financial Condition				
Return on Total Revenues %	4.54	6.71	5.03	1.65
Return on Avg Stockholders' Equity %	6.52	13.89	10.45	2.74
Return on Average Assets %	5.14	10.10	7.16	1.79
Current Ratio	3.60	2.65	1.87	1.91
Debt / Equity %	1.54	1.97	2.59	10.81

Compound Growth %'s	EPS %	44.84	Net Income %	44.89	Total Revenues %	3.40

Comments

1995 was a disappointing year for management after the record pace of 1994. Most of the decline in revenues can be linked to construction activity in and around Company facilities. The financial statement remains very strong. Sand and gravel lands and land held for investment is approximately $7 million on a cost basis.

Officers	Position	Ownership Information	12/31/95
Dean M. Boylan, Jr.	President	Number of Shares Outstanding	140,137
Mary C. Moran	CFO	Market Capitalization	$ 21,721,235
Jeanne-Marie Boylan	Vice President, Treasurer	Frequency Of Dividends	Quarterly
David B. McNeil	VP - Sales	Number of Shareholders	Under 500

Other Information					
Transfer Agent	Bank of Boston			Where Listed	OTC-BB
Auditor	Ernst & Young			Symbol	BSND
Market Maker	Gruntal & Co., Incorporated	Telephone	(800)225-8520	SIC Code	3273
Broker Dealer	Standard Investment	Tel/Ext	(888)783-4688 Jack	Employees	150

Boswell (J.G.) Company

101 West Walnut Street • Pasadena, CA 91103 • Telephone (818)583-3000 • Fax (818)583-3090

Company Description

The Company generates approximately 94% of its revenue from the production, processing and marketing of farm commodities, primarily cotton and cottonseed products. Domestic cotton operations are in California. The Company has an Australian subsidiary which maintains its cotton operations in the state of New South Wales. The Company also owns and operates two real estate development projects.

	06/30/95	06/30/94	06/30/93	06/30/92
Per Share Information				
Stock Price	1,217.50	1,125.00	1,100.00	1,100.00
Earnings Per Share	64.99	63.99	9.97	84.85
Price / Earnings Ratio	18.73	17.58	110.33	12.96
Book Value Per Share	1,268.34	1,248.88	1,174.55	1,233.60
Price / Book Value %	95.99	90.08	93.65	89.17
Dividends Per Share	35.00	27.50	25.00	50.00
Annual Financial Data				
Operating Results (000's)				
Total Revenues	224,232.0	250,490.0	240,632.0	231,282.0
Costs & Expenses	-207,351.0	-233,476.0	-239,968.0	-203,861.0
Income Before Taxes and Other	16,881.0	17,014.0	1,761.0	27,244.0
Other Items	n.a.	n.a.	n.a.	n.a.
Income Tax	-3,730.0	-3,994.0	278.0	-9,745.0
Net Income	13,151.0	13,020.0	2,039.0	17,499.0
Cash Flow From Operations	-1,832.0	47,063.0	31,346.0	67,012.0
Balance Sheet (000's)				
Cash & Equivalents	526.0	18,475.0	100,000.0	100,000.0
Total Current Assets	111,231.0	125,942.0	100,000.0	100,000.0
Fixed Assets, Net	256,679.0	211,486.0	200,000.0	205,000.0
Total Assets	524,042.0	460,386.0	458,700.0	510,025.0
Total Current Liabilities	80,849.0	64,714.0	60,217.0	89,416.0
Long-Term Debt	157,121.0	126,467.0	147,839.0	143,421.0
Stockholders' Equity	256,568.0	253,039.0	239,282.0	253,677.0
Performance & Financial Condition				
Return on Total Revenues %	5.86	5.20	0.85	7.57
Return on Avg Stockholders' Equity %	5.16	5.29	0.83	6.94
Return on Average Assets %	2.67	2.83	0.42	3.29
Current Ratio	1.38	1.95	1.66	1.12
Debt / Equity %	61.24	49.98	61.78	56.54

Compound Growth %'s	EPS %	-8.50	Net Income %	-9.08	Total Revenues %	-1.03

Comments

During 1995, the Company acquired an additional 26,000 acres of farmland, significant water rights and related processing facilities. Accessible water has always been a problem for the Company. There is reportedly a large potential for appreciation of the properties held if the water problem can be solved.

Officers	Position	Ownership Information	06/30/95
Not Available		Number of Shares Outstanding	202,286
		Market Capitalization	$ 246,283,205
		Frequency Of Dividends	Quarterly
		Number of Shareholders	Under 500

Other Information

Transfer Agent	Company Office			Where Listed	OTC-PS
Auditor	Ernst & Young LLP			Symbol	BWEL
Market Maker	Advest, Inc.	Telephone	(212)238-4400	SIC Code	0720
Broker Dealer	Regular Stockbroker			Employees	40

Bovar Inc.

4 Manning Close N.E. • Calgary, Alberta Canada • Telephone (403)235-8329 • Fax (403)248-3306

Company Description

The Company is a leading environmental and waste management company, operating North America's only fully intergrated waste management facility. Their expertise also includes engineered products for environmental applications and process control, and environmental consulting and technical services. In 1992, the original preferred shareholders converted their shares into voting and non-voting common shares. Additional shares were issued in 1994 for $12.5 million Canadian.

	12/31/95	12/31/94	12/31/93	12/31/92
Per Share Information				
Stock Price	1.20	1.05	1.25	0.90
Earnings Per Share	0.13	0.09	0.01	0.01
Price / Earnings Ratio	9.23	11.67	125.00	90.00
Book Value Per Share	0.47	0.35	0.05	0.05
Price / Book Value %	255.32	300.00	2,500.00	1,800.00
Dividends Per Share	n.a.	n.a.	n.a.	n.a.
Annual Financial Data				
Operating Results (000's)				
Total Revenues	98,304.0	80,536.0	50,396.0	48,786.0
Costs & Expenses	-87,440.0	-73,561.0	-49,690.0	-48,013.0
Income Before Taxes and Other	10,864.0	6,975.0	706.0	773.0
Other Items	n.a.	n.a.	-586.0	n.a.
Income Tax	-40.0	76.0	-184.0	n.a.
Net Income	10,824.0	7,051.0	-64.0	773.0
Cash Flow From Operations	19,439.0	11,556.0	4,096.0	n.a.
Balance Sheet (000's)				
Cash & Equivalents	17,891.0	2,585.0	2,006.0	668.0
Total Current Assets	53,725.0	29,009.0	23,701.0	23,968.0
Fixed Assets, Net	84,952.0	96,956.0	97,955.0	56,876.0
Total Assets	142,530.0	129,537.0	121,656.0	80,844.0
Total Current Liabilities	33,373.0	27,966.0	31,099.0	34,711.0
Long-Term Debt	70,621.0	73,095.0	87,390.0	43,022.0
Stockholders' Equity	38,536.0	28,476.0	3,167.0	3,111.0
Performance & Financial Condition				
Return on Total Revenues %	11.01	8.76	-0.13	1.58
Return on Avg Stockholders' Equity %	32.30	44.57	-2.04	-17.29
Return on Average Assets %	7.96	5.61	-0.06	1.04
Current Ratio	1.61	1.04	0.76	0.69
Debt / Equity %	183.26	256.69	2759.40	1382.90

Compound Growth %'s	EPS %	135.13	Net Income %	141.03	Total Revenues %	26.31

Comments

All amounts are stated in Canadian dollars. Management believes strong growth will continue because of their products, technology and international growth. Although waste management remains an important core business, the Company expects the other divisions to play increasingly significant roles in future revenue growth. 1993 results include a nonrecurring expense of $586,000 in connection with a discontinued operation. First quarter 1996 results were flat.

Officers	Position	Ownership Information	12/31/95
Monty L. Davis	President, CEO	Number of Shares Outstanding	81,232,801
E.J. W. Adkins	Treasurer	Market Capitalization	$ 97,479,361
Daryl W. Ferko	Vice President, CFO	Frequency Of Dividends	n.a.
Franklin T. Bailey	Vice President, Secretary	Number of Shareholders	Under 500
Donald G. Colley	VP - Sales		

Other Information

Transfer Agent	Montreal Trust Co of Canada			Where Listed	TSE
Auditor	Price Waterhouse			Symbol	BVR
Market Maker	Gilford Securities	Telephone	(212)886-6400	SIC Code	4940
Broker Dealer	Regular Stockbroker			Employees	485

Bowles Fluidics Corporation

6625 Dobbin Road • Columbia, MD 21045 • Telephone (410)381-0400 • Fax (410)381-2718

Company Description

The Company is the leading designer, manufacturer and supplier of windshield and rear window washer nozzles for passenger cars and light trucks in North America. Defroster nozzles for trucks are also manufactured and sold. The Company has had 15 years of increases in total revenues. The Company was incorporated in the State of Maryland in 1961.

	10/28/95	10/29/94	10/30/93	10/31/92
Per Share Information				
Stock Price	0.91	0.57	0.75	0.29
Earnings Per Share	0.11	0.11	0.07	0.06
Price / Earnings Ratio	8.27	5.18	10.71	4.83
Book Value Per Share	0.45	0.32	0.18	0.10
Price / Book Value %	202.22	178.13	416.67	290.00
Dividends Per Share	n.a.	n.a.	n.a.	n.a.
Annual Financial Data				
Operating Results (000's)				
Total Revenues	17,071.5	15,142.3	12,335.3	10,014.3
Costs & Expenses	-14,138.7	-12,735.8	-11,041.3	-8,954.2
Income Before Taxes and Other	2,932.8	2,406.5	1,294.0	1,040.6
Other Items	n.a.	n.a.	n.a.	n.a.
Income Tax	-1,148.9	-679.5	-218.0	n.a.
Net Income	1,783.9	1,727.0	1,076.0	1,040.6
Cash Flow From Operations	851.2	2,632.6	1,860.6	1,263.4
Balance Sheet (000's)				
Cash & Equivalents	677.0	1,557.2	652.2	445.8
Total Current Assets	6,324.2	5,814.9	3,873.5	2,917.1
Fixed Assets, Net	2,821.8	2,500.3	2,148.3	1,717.2
Total Assets	9,292.4	8,478.2	6,231.1	4,880.5
Total Current Liabilities	2,027.8	2,688.0	2,082.3	1,601.3
Long-Term Debt	202.8	512.8	584.6	1,028.3
Stockholders' Equity	6,629.9	4,907.7	3,246.6	2,242.2
Performance & Financial Condition				
Return on Total Revenues %	10.45	11.41	8.72	10.39
Return on Avg Stockholders' Equity %	30.92	42.36	39.21	63.29
Return on Average Assets %	20.08	23.48	19.37	22.36
Current Ratio	3.12	2.16	1.86	1.82
Debt / Equity %	3.06	10.45	18.01	45.86

Compound Growth %'s	EPS %	22.39	Net Income %	19.68	Total Revenues %	19.46

Comments

The Company has 933,080 shares of $1 par value, 8% convertible preferred stock outstanding. Preferred stock dividends totaling $74,648 per year have been deducted from net income in calculating earnings per share. For the three months ended January 27, 1996, sales amounted to $4.6 million and net income was $393,000 ($.02 per share) as compared to $4.2 million and $453,000 (.03 per share) for the same period in the previous fiscal year.

Officers	Position	Ownership Information	10/28/95
William Ewing, Jr.	Chairman	Number of Shares Outstanding	12,610,011
Ronald D. Stouffer	President, CEO	Market Capitalization	$ 11,475,110
Melvyn J. Clough	Vice President	Frequency Of Dividends	n.a.
Richard W. Hess	Vice President	Number of Shareholders	442
Julian Lazrus	Other		

Other Information

Transfer Agent	Chemical Mellon Shareholder Services			Where Listed	CE
Auditor	Coopers & Lybrand LLP			Symbol	BOWE
Market Maker	Paragon Capital Corporation	Telephone	(800)345-0505	SIC Code	3714
Broker Dealer	Regular Stockbroker			Employees	223

Bozzuto's Incorporated

275 Schoolhouse Road • Cheshire, CT 06410-1241 • Telephone (203)272-3511 • Fax (203)250-7955

Company Description

The Company is engaged in the wholesale distribution of food products and certain non-food, household and personal items to independent retail supermarket and convenience store operators in Long Island, southeastern New York, northern New Jersey and southern New England. The Company also owns and operates retail supermarkets. The Company was formed in 1945.

	09/30/95	09/30/94	09/30/93	09/30/92
Per Share Information				
Stock Price	28.25	20.75	16.00	10.00
Earnings Per Share	2.73	3.68	3.49	3.12
Price / Earnings Ratio	10.35	0.64	4.58	3.21
Book Value Per Share	27.78	25.83	23.09	20.50
Price / Book Value %	101.69	80.33	69.29	48.78
Dividends Per Share	0.40	0.40	0.40	0.40
Annual Financial Data				
Operating Results (000's)				
Total Revenues	372,438.0	346,219.9	319,641.1	290,000.2
Costs & Expenses	-369,653.2	-342,861.0	-316,467.7	-287,274.0
Income Before Taxes and Other	2,784.8	3,358.9	3,173.4	2,726.3
Other Items	-57.2	0.5	n.a.	n.a.
Income Tax	-1,289.3	-1,417.7	-1,332.9	-1,080.2
Net Income	1,438.3	1,941.7	1,840.5	1,646.0
Cash Flow From Operations	5,168.0	4,609.8	2,503.0	1,063.0
Balance Sheet (000's)				
Cash & Equivalents	773.4	1,544.3	1,304.5	n.a.
Total Current Assets	32,006.1	32,052.2	29,106.0	n.a.
Fixed Assets, Net	7,207.0	7,338.8	7,472.8	n.a.
Total Assets	46,584.4	45,348.2	41,875.7	n.a.
Total Current Liabilities	20,589.7	17,501.2	14,069.2	n.a.
Long-Term Debt	7,663.2	10,800.5	12,615.8	n.a.
Stockholders' Equity	17,523.9	16,296.4	14,565.7	n.a.
Performance & Financial Condition				
Return on Total Revenues %	0.39	0.56	0.58	0.57
Return on Avg Stockholders' Equity %	8.51	12.58	n.a.	13.47
Return on Average Assets %	3.13	4.45	n.a.	n.a.
Current Ratio	1.55	1.83	2.07	n.a.
Debt / Equity %	43.73	66.28	86.61	n.a.

Compound Growth %'s	EPS %	-4.35	Net Income %	-4.40	Total Revenues %	8.70

Comments

A new state-of-the-art distribution center was completed in 1995. Retail stores increased from 2 at the end of 1993 to 8 by the end of 1995. Preopening expenses may account for some of the lackluster performance in earnings.

Officers	Position	Ownership Information	09/30/95
Adam J. Bozzuto	Chairman	Number of Shares Outstanding	630,828
Michael A. Bozzuto	President, Treasurer	Market Capitalization	$ 17,820,891
Thomas A. Zatina	Exec VP, COO	Frequency Of Dividends	Quarterly
Jayne A. Bozzuto	Vice President	Number of Shareholders	Under 500
Robert H. Wood	Vice President		

Other Information			
Transfer Agent	First National Bank of Boston	Where Listed	OTC-BB
Auditor	Daniel J. Bartz	Symbol	BOZZ
Market Maker	Macallaster Pitfield MacKay	Telephone (212)422-9250 SIC Code	5140
Broker Dealer	Regular Stockbroker	Employees	450

Brake Headquarters U.S.A., Inc.

33-16 Woodside Avenue • Long Island City, NY 11101 • Telephone (718)779-4800 • Fax (718)898-6913

Company Description

The Company distributes brake system and other "undercar" parts for virtually all makes and models of domestic and foreign passenger cars and light trucks from model year 1976 to the present. The Company operates its distribution business from distribution centers in New York State, Illinois and Oregon. The Company was originally incorporated in Deleware in 1988, and through a series of name changes and corporate transactions took on the name of Brake Headquarters in 1995.

	12/31/95	12/31/94	12/31/93	12/31/92
Per Share Information				
Stock Price	4.35	5.31	45.30	30.60
Earnings Per Share	-0.06	-0.92	n.a.	0.05
Price / Earnings Ratio	n.a.	n.a.	n.a.	612.00
Book Value Per Share	1.13	1.38	1.03	0.89
Price / Book Value %	384.96	384.78	4,398.10	3,438.20
Dividends Per Share	n.a.	n.a.	n.a.	n.a.
Annual Financial Data				
Operating Results (000's)				
Total Revenues	30,466.5	25,082.2	17,720.5	13,720.0
Costs & Expenses	-30,423.6	-26,656.1	-17,661.8	-13,328.0
Income Before Taxes and Other	-205.1	-1,573.9	58.6	392.0
Other Items	n.a.	n.a.	n.a.	-65.7
Income Tax	26.0	-395.0	-17.5	-156.0
Net Income	-179.1	-1,968.9	41.2	170.3
Cash Flow From Operations	-2,705.0	-2,076.2	-1,762.5	-667.5
Balance Sheet (000's)				
Cash & Equivalents	17.9	12.0	35.2	15.8
Total Current Assets	14,298.9	11,302.0	9,703.3	7,792.9
Fixed Assets, Net	921.1	324.8	207.0	129.7
Total Assets	15,496.3	11,937.1	10,189.9	8,070.8
Total Current Liabilities	11,010.0	7,595.7	7,879.9	5,815.8
Long-Term Debt	630.5	216.5	133.9	80.1
Stockholders' Equity	3,855.8	4,125.0	2,176.1	2,174.9
Performance & Financial Condition				
Return on Total Revenues %	-0.59	-7.85	0.23	1.24
Return on Avg Stockholders' Equity %	-4.49	-62.49	1.89	10.93
Return on Average Assets %	-1.31	-17.80	0.45	2.41
Current Ratio	1.30	1.49	1.23	1.34
Debt / Equity %	16.35	5.25	6.15	3.68

Compound Growth %'s	EPS %	n.a.	Net Income %	n.a.	Total Revenues %	30.46

Comments

Per share amounts have been adjusted to give effect to stock splits in 1995 and 1993. As of April 26, 1996, officers and directors, as a group, owned 79% of the Company's outstanding common stock.

Officers	Position	Ownership Information	12/31/95
Joseph Ende	President, CEO	Number of Shares Outstanding	3,416,197
Mark J. Ruskin	CFO	Market Capitalization	$ 14,860,457
Sandra Ende	Secretary	Frequency Of Dividends	n.a.
Scott Osias	VP - Sales	Number of Shareholders	531

Other Information			
Transfer Agent	Continental Stock Transfer & Trust Co.	Where Listed	OTC-BB
Auditor	Deloitte & Touche LLP	Symbol	BHQU
Market Maker	Hill, Thompson, Magid & Co.Inc	Telephone (800)631-3083	SIC Code	5013
Broker Dealer	Regular Stockbroker	Employees	111

Bresler & Reiner, Inc.

401 M Street S.W. • Washington D.C., CA 20024 • Telephone (202)488-8800 • Fax (202)488-8084

Company Description

The Company has two principal activities, residential land development and construction and rental property ownership and management. The Company holds for sale or development several partially developed residential tracts of land within the greater Washington, D.C. area. The Company also owns and manages apartments, offices, a motel and a hotel. The Company was included in the Washington Post's 1996 "The Post 200", a listing of the top 100 public companies in the Washington area.

	12/31/95	12/31/94	12/31/93	12/31/92
Per Share Information				
Stock Price	10.25	10.50	n.a.	n.a.
Earnings Per Share	2.18	1.20	-1.81	-0.70
Price / Earnings Ratio	4.70	8.75	n.a.	n.a.
Book Value Per Share	20.76	18.41	19.02	19.02
Price / Book Value %	49.37	57.03	n.a.	n.a.
Dividends Per Share	n.a.	n.a.	n.a.	n.a.
Annual Financial Data				
Operating Results (000's)				
Total Revenues	33,824.0	39,563.0	31,683.0	34,086.0
Costs & Expenses	-26,302.0	-46,033.0	-45,414.0	-38,812.0
Income Before Taxes and Other	7,522.0	-6,470.0	-13,731.0	-4,726.0
Other Items	1,705.0	7,538.0	3,293.0	2,916.0
Income Tax	-3,087.0	2,336.0	5,305.0	-163.0
Net Income	6,140.0	3,404.0	-5,133.0	-1,973.0
Cash Flow From Operations	7,214.0	7,575.0	9,547.0	7,305.0
Balance Sheet (000's)				
Cash & Equivalents	10,921.0	7,200.0	6,287.0	7,102.0
Total Current Assets	11,912.0	9,933.0	31,395.0	39,909.0
Fixed Assets, Net	38,018.0	40,337.0	42,948.0	34,419.0
Total Assets	101,395.0	103,401.0	151,681.0	165,196.0
Total Current Liabilities	3,562.0	4,229.0	11,327.0	19,725.0
Long-Term Debt	34,229.0	42,495.0	91,336.0	91,177.0
Stockholders' Equity	57,969.0	52,214.0	48,813.0	53,946.0
Performance & Financial Condition				
Return on Total Revenues %	18.15	8.60	-16.20	-5.79
Return on Avg Stockholders' Equity %	11.15	6.74	-9.99	-3.59
Return on Average Assets %	6.00	2.67	-3.24	-1.16
Current Ratio	3.34	2.35	2.77	2.02
Debt / Equity %	59.05	81.39	187.11	169.02

Compound Growth %'s	EPS %	81.67	Net Income %	80.38	Total Revenues %	-0.26

Comments

In an effort to eliminate underperforming properties, the Company has allowed certain properties it owned to be foreclosed and renegotiated the debt terms on others. As a result of these transactions, the Company charged to operations over the years 1992 through 1995, a loss on real estate of $32.9 million and recognized income from debt elimination (included in Other Items) totaling $12.5 million for the same period. The Company also wrote down its equity investment in real estate ventures by a total of $17.5 million in 1992 and 1993. There was little activity in the Company's stock and no price quotations until the second quarter of 1994.

Officers	Position	Ownership Information	12/31/95
Charles S. Bresler	Chairman, CEO	Number of Shares Outstanding	2,792,653
Burton J. Reiner	President	Market Capitalization	$ 28,624,693
Edwin Horowitz	Secretary	Frequency Of Dividends	n.a.
William L. Oshinsky	Treasurer	Number of Shareholders	168

Other Information				
Transfer Agent	Continental Stock Transfer & Trust Co.		Where Listed	OTC-BB
Auditor	Arthur Andersen LLP		Symbol	BRER
Market Maker	Herzog, Heine, Geduld, Inc.	Telephone (212)962-0300	SIC Code	6513
Broker Dealer	Regular Stockbroker		Employees	137

Broadway Bancshares Inc.

1177 N.E. Loop 410 • San Antonio, TX 78209 • Telephone (210)283-6500 • Fax (210)283-6545

Company Description

The Company is a bank holding company for Broadway National Bank (BNB), Eisenhower National Bank (ENB) and Broadway Brokerage Services, Inc. Both banks are headquartered in San Antonio, Texas. BNB's customer concentration consists of residents of south Texas while ENB's customers are principally military personnel. Both grant commercial, consumer and real estate loans.

	12/31/95	12/31/94	12/31/93	12/31/92
Per Share Information				
Stock Price	44.00	40.50	36.00	24.51
Earnings Per Share	5.72	5.58	6.30	4.78
Price / Earnings Ratio	7.69	7.26	5.71	5.13
Book Value Per Share	43.84	35.36	33.40	27.61
Price / Book Value %	100.36	114.54	107.78	88.77
Dividends Per Share	0.60	0.44	0.45	0.22
Annual Financial Data				
Operating Results (000's)				
Net Interest Income	34,256.0	35,150.0	36,102.0	32,008.0
Loan Loss Provision	-734.0	-38.0	170.0	-368.0
Non-Interest Income	13,453.0	11,257.0	11,333.0	11,018.0
Non-Interest Expense	-28,144.0	-27,894.0	-26,456.0	-27,225.0
Income Before Taxes and Other	18,831.0	18,475.0	21,149.0	15,433.0
Other Items	n.a.	n.a.	-324.0	n.a.
Income Tax	-6,501.0	-6,445.0	-7,290.0	-5,218.0
Net Income	12,330.0	12,030.0	13,535.0	10,215.0
Balance Sheet (000's)				
Cash & Securities	530,219.0	540,810.0	550,875.0	520,716.0
Loans, Net	259,129.0	242,272.0	229,851.0	208,452.0
Fixed Assets, Net	16,945.0	14,292.0	11,734.0	10,866.0
Total Assets	814,585.0	809,032.0	800,592.0	755,943.0
Deposits	714,024.0	729,129.0	724,948.0	687,755.0
Stockholders' Equity	94,769.0	76,258.0	72,029.0	59,292.0
Performance & Financial Condition				
Net Interest Margin	n.a.	n.a.	n.a.	n.a.
Return on Avg Stockholders' Equity %	14.42	16.23	20.61	18.80
Return on Average Assets %	1.52	1.49	1.74	1.45
Equity to Assets %	11.63	9.43	9.00	7.84
Reserve as a % of Non-Performing Loans	213.65	1081.39	283.65	184.53

Compound Growth %'s	EPS %	6.17	Net Income %	6.47	Net Interest Income %	2.29

Comments

The Company sold its' mortgage service operation during 1995 as well as some nonoperational assets. It also announced plans to sell all student loans to Sallie Mae as they are originated. Expansion continues with smaller branch banks at key locations. ENB is in the process of opening a branch at Goodfellow Air Force Base and is bidding on another military location in Texas. No one can complain about the numbers. Return on assets and equity rank high among all banks.

Officers	Position	Ownership Information	12/31/95
Charles E. Cheever, Jr.	President	Number of Shares Outstanding	2,161,896
Gregory W. Crane	Exec VP, Secretary	Market Capitalization	$ 95,123,424
Karl Knobelsdorf	Vice President	Frequency Of Dividends	n.a.
Gary Woytasczyk	Vice President, Treasurer	Number of Shareholders	220
Elizabeth A. Mead	Vice President, Senior Loan Officer		

Other Information				
Transfer Agent	Company Office		Where Listed	Order Matching Only
Auditor	KPMG Peat Marwick LLP		Symbol	n.a.
Market Maker	Rauscher, Pierce, Refsnes,Inc.	Telephone (210)225-6611	SIC Code	6020
Broker Dealer	Regular stockbroker		Employees	381

Broughton Foods Company

P.O. Box 656 • Marietta, OH 45750 • Telephone (614)373-4121 • Fax (614)373-2861

Company Description

The Company is primarily in the business of producing dairy and dairy-related food products for wholesale and retail distribution. The Company was first organized in 1933. Members of the founding Broughton family are still very involved in management of the business. The Company has increased its treasury stock over the last several years with purchases that were greater than sales.

	12/31/95	12/31/94	12/31/93	12/31/92
Per Share Information				
Stock Price	42.00	35.00	33.00	24.00
Earnings Per Share	-2.83	5.13	5.57	3.26
Price / Earnings Ratio	n.a.	6.82	5.92	7.36
Book Value Per Share	56.29	58.61	53.19	45.65
Price / Book Value %	74.61	59.72	62.04	52.57
Dividends Per Share	0.75	0.80	0.80	0.80
Annual Financial Data				
Operating Results (000's)				
Total Revenues	72,384.5	73,624.3	68,231.0	66,044.9
Costs & Expenses	-72,949.1	-72,467.6	-66,860.3	-65,245.8
Income Before Taxes and Other	-564.6	1,156.7	1,370.7	799.1
Other Items	n.a.	n.a.	n.a.	n.a.
Income Tax	184.8	-432.5	-558.4	-326.4
Net Income	-379.8	724.2	812.3	472.7
Cash Flow From Operations	-216.2	1,650.1	1,120.3	1,131.0
Balance Sheet (000's)				
Cash & Equivalents	161.2	956.5	596.7	968.1
Total Current Assets	10,145.9	10,056.0	9,722.2	9,175.0
Fixed Assets, Net	5,790.8	5,247.9	5,663.0	5,515.2
Total Assets	16,204.0	15,574.7	15,663.2	14,971.9
Total Current Liabilities	6,479.7	5,239.0	5,589.7	6,445.6
Long-Term Debt	1,862.5	1,524.0	1,769.7	958.7
Stockholders' Equity	7,359.9	8,243.1	7,757.2	7,078.3
Performance & Financial Condition				
Return on Total Revenues %	-0.52	0.98	1.19	0.72
Return on Avg Stockholders' Equity %	-4.87	9.05	10.95	6.87
Return on Average Assets %	-2.39	4.64	5.30	3.34
Current Ratio	1.57	1.92	1.74	1.42
Debt / Equity %	25.31	18.49	22.81	13.54

Compound Growth %'s	EPS % n.a.	Net Income % n.a.	Total Revenues % 3.10

Comments

Management attributes the 1995 loss to unusually competitive markets with the erratic behavior of butterfat costs, which nearly doubled during the year before falling back in December. Samuel R. Cook, chairman and CEO, announced his retirement in November, 1995. R.M. Collier succeeds him at the helm. Management is streamlining operations by eliminating marginal divisions. Food division capacity is at maximum and additional expansion is being studied. The food division, according to management, represents the greatest opportunity for future growth.

Officers	Position	Ownership Information	12/31/95
Rodney M. Collier	President, CEO	Number of Shares Outstanding	130,172
George W. Broughton	Exec VP	Market Capitalization	$ 5,467,224
John R. Broughton	Treasurer	Frequency Of Dividends	Quarterly
Samuel R. Lipscomb	Vice President	Number of Shareholders	Under 500
Gary R. Cowell	VP - Manufacturing		

Other Information				
Transfer Agent	BancOhio National Bank, Columbus, Ohio		Where Listed	OTC-BB
Auditor	Coopers & Lybrand LLP		Symbol	BRGHB
Market Maker	Carr Securities Corporation	Telephone (800)221-2243	SIC Code	2020
Broker Dealer	Pink sheet specialist		Employees	200

Bryan Steam Corporation

11 South Meridian #13 • Indianapolis, IN 46204 • Telephone (317)473-6651 • Fax (317)473-3074

Company Description

The Company manufactures and sells oil, gas and electrically fired boilers, commercial water heaters and swimming pool heaters. The Company also manufactures and sells a limited number of storage tanks and other equipment for use in connection with boilers. Most boilers are sold directly to contractors for installation in new apartment, commercial, industrial and institutional buildings. The Company was incorporated in New Mexico in 1918.

	06/30/95	06/30/94	06/30/93	06/30/92
Per Share Information				
Stock Price	46.00	40.50	30.00	23.00
Earnings Per Share	4.85	3.74	5.56	3.25
Price / Earnings Ratio	9.48	10.83	5.40	7.08
Book Value Per Share	63.82	60.28	58.84	54.97
Price / Book Value %	72.08	67.19	50.99	41.84
Dividends Per Share	1.30	1.30	0.95	0.85
Annual Financial Data				
Operating Results (000's)				
Total Revenues	17,727.6	17,179.3	16,416.0	16,226.1
Costs & Expenses	-13,913.9	-13,708.0	-12,503.7	-13,188.3
Income Before Taxes and Other	1,475.6	1,125.1	1,578.4	911.6
Other Items	n.a.	n.a.	n.a.	n.a.
Income Tax	-548.5	-409.7	-513.1	-285.8
Net Income	927.1	715.4	1,065.3	625.8
Cash Flow From Operations	1,008.1	1,000.0	2,152.6	1,024.8
Balance Sheet (000's)				
Cash & Equivalents	2,192.9	360.2	751.6	319.4
Total Current Assets	11,545.6	9,928.2	9,875.2	9,485.6
Fixed Assets, Net	3,524.4	3,293.4	2,984.9	2,876.7
Total Assets	15,090.7	13,247.4	12,906.3	12,429.1
Total Current Liabilities	1,751.2	1,408.5	1,491.3	1,586.2
Long-Term Debt	800.0	n.a.	n.a.	n.a.
Stockholders' Equity	12,208.0	11,530.8	11,254.5	10,577.0
Performance & Financial Condition				
Return on Total Revenues %	5.23	4.16	6.49	3.86
Return on Avg Stockholders' Equity %	7.81	6.28	9.76	6.05
Return on Average Assets %	6.54	5.47	8.41	5.17
Current Ratio	6.59	7.05	6.62	5.98
Debt / Equity %	6.55	n.a.	n.a.	n.a.

Compound Growth %'s	EPS %	14.28	Net Income %	14.00	Total Revenues %	2.99

Comments

At June 30, 1995, there was a backlog of sales orders of approximately $4,600,000. The Company formed a new subsidiary during 1995, Wendland Manufacturing Co., which acquired all of the tank manufacturing assets of a Texas corporation for $1,115,000 subsequent to the balance sheet date. Sales and net income for the six months ended December 31, 1995, amounted to $12.11 million and $738,000 ($3.86 per share) as compared to $9.5 million and $441,000 ($2.30 per share) for the same period in 1994.

Officers	Position	Ownership Information	06/30/95
Harold V. Koch	Chairman	Number of Shares Outstanding	191,284
Albert J. Bishop	President	Market Capitalization	$ 8,799,064
Kurt J. Krauskopf	Secretary	Frequency Of Dividends	Annual
Paul D. Donaldson	Treasurer	Number of Shareholders	996
H. Jesse McVay	Vice President		

Other Information				
Transfer Agent	Company Office		Where Listed	OTC-BB
Auditor	M.S. Cassen & Co.		Symbol	BSTM
Market Maker	Chicago Corporation, The	Telephone (312)855-7664	SIC Code	3443
Broker Dealer	Regular Stockbroker		Employees	180

Buck Hill Falls Company

P.O. Box 426 • Buck Hill Falls, PA 18323 • Telephone (717)595-7511 • Fax (717)595-9426

Company Description

The Company provides a variety of services to the residents of Buck Hill Falls, Pennsylvania. These services include providing recreational facilities, water and sewage services and miscellaneous maintenance services. In addition, certain of the Company's recreational facilities are made available to the general public. The Company was incorporated in Pennyslvania in 1901.

	10/31/95	10/31/94	10/31/93	10/31/92
Per Share Information				
Stock Price	29.50	20.00	12.50	10.50
Earnings Per Share	-1.21	0.74	1.35	0.99
Price / Earnings Ratio	n.a.	27.03	9.26	10.61
Book Value Per Share	12.25	13.45	12.70	11.36
Price / Book Value %	240.82	148.70	98.43	92.43
Dividends Per Share	n.a.	n.a.	n.a.	n.a.
Annual Financial Data				
Operating Results (000's)				
Total Revenues	2,218.1	2,203.5	2,048.5	2,086.1
Costs & Expenses	-2,306.9	-2,135.1	-1,914.6	-1,941.4
Income Before Taxes and Other	-88.7	68.4	99.5	144.6
Other Items	n.a.	21.6	33.8	138.0
Income Tax	n.a.	-35.3	-33.8	-209.6
Net Income	-88.7	54.7	99.5	73.0
Cash Flow From Operations	-106.4	239.5	203.5	238.9
Balance Sheet (000's)				
Cash & Equivalents	31.5	20.2	13.4	4.0
Total Current Assets	307.1	219.0	180.4	205.4
Fixed Assets, Net	2,756.4	2,761.8	2,234.0	2,008.4
Total Assets	3,149.9	3,104.0	2,536.5	2,299.9
Total Current Liabilities	1,079.3	1,192.9	1,002.6	1,288.0
Long-Term Debt	1,096.2	815.9	498.5	89.0
Stockholders' Equity	900.5	989.3	934.6	835.1
Performance & Financial Condition				
Return on Total Revenues %	-4.00	2.48	4.86	3.50
Return on Avg Stockholders' Equity %	-9.39	5.68	11.24	9.14
Return on Average Assets %	-2.84	1.94	4.11	3.12
Current Ratio	0.28	0.18	0.18	0.16
Debt / Equity %	121.73	82.48	53.34	10.66

Compound Growth %'s	EPS %	n.a.	Net Income %	n.a.	Total Revenues %	2.07

Comments

Management believes that revisions in the Company's operating requirements, including rate increases for services provided and the water rate increase implemented in 1995, will return the Company to profitability.

Officers	Position	Ownership Information	10/31/95
David B. Ottaway	Chairman, CEO	Number of Shares Outstanding	73,537
George J. Byron	President, COO	Market Capitalization	$ 2,169,342
Grace M. Godshalk	Vice President, Secretary	Frequency Of Dividends	n.a.
Patricia J. Rauch	Vice President, Treasurer	Number of Shareholders	509
Carl R. Benasutti	General Manager		

Other Information

Transfer Agent	Chemical Mellon Shareholder Services			Where Listed	OTC-BB
Auditor	Parente, Randolph et. al.			Symbol	BUHF
Market Maker	Robotti & Eng, Incorporated	Telephone	(212)986-4800	SIC Code	6500
Broker Dealer	Regular Stockbroker			Employees	17

Buffalo Valley Telephone Company

20 South Second Street • Lewisburg, PA 17837 • Telephone (717)523-1211 • Fax (717)524-0459

Company Description

The Company is an independent local exchange carrier which provides local telephone service to Union and Northumberland Counties in central Pennsylvania. It was founded in 1904. In 1995, Conestoga Enterprises, Inc. made an offer to acquire all shares for consideration valued between $65 and $70 per share, depending on whether the seller wanted cash, stock of the acquirer, or a preferred stock. The vote to approve the transaction was to be made on May 22, 1996.

	12/31/95	12/31/94	12/31/93
Per Share Information			
Stock Price	64.50	48.00	46.50
Earnings Per Share	2.50	3.04	2.78
Price / Earnings Ratio	25.80	15.79	16.73
Book Value Per Share	22.23	21.48	20.09
Price / Book Value %	290.15	223.46	231.46
Dividends Per Share	1.80	1.68	1.60
Annual Financial Data			
Operating Results (000's)			
Total Revenues	11,725.5	11,654.9	10,669.7
Costs & Expenses	-6,614.2	-6,693.5	-6,010.4
Income Before Taxes and Other	3,915.6	4,443.7	4,180.1
Other Items	n.a.	n.a.	n.a.
Income Tax	-1,648.8	-1,694.7	-1,667.4
Net Income	2,266.8	2,749.0	2,512.7
Cash Flow From Operations	4,113.5	4,508.1	4,446.6
Balance Sheet (000's)			
Cash & Equivalents	2,330.2	4,491.2	5,377.9
Total Current Assets	7,382.5	9,721.4	10,230.1
Fixed Assets, Net	16,021.4	16,324.6	15,351.1
Total Assets	26,715.5	29,240.4	29,033.4
Total Current Liabilities	1,359.4	3,825.4	4,629.9
Long-Term Debt	1,404.0	1,485.0	1,566.0
Stockholders' Equity	19,984.7	19,988.4	18,662.5
Performance & Financial Condition			
Return on Total Revenues %	19.33	23.59	23.55
Return on Avg Stockholders' Equity %	11.34	14.22	13.92
Return on Average Assets %	8.10	9.43	8.52
Current Ratio	5.43	2.54	2.21
Debt / Equity %	7.03	7.43	8.39

Compound Growth %'s	EPS %	-5.17	Net Income %	-5.02	Total Revenues %	4.83

Comments

1995 results include $624,994 of nonrecurring merger expenses, or $.70 per share. Although it may be too late to own an interest in this company, we thought it would be interesting to present it anyway. It is an example of a small regulated company, and there are a number in this book, that trades at a reasonable price, pays a dividend, gradually appreciates in value and then BINGO, gets acquired.

Officers	Position	Ownership Information	12/31/95
James G. Apple	Chairman	Number of Shares Outstanding	899,154
F. Ellis Harley	Senior VP	Market Capitalization	$ 57,995,433
Dennis J. Reed	Treasurer	Frequency Of Dividends	Quarterly
David E. Lynn	Vice President, Secretary	Number of Shareholders	Under 500

Other Information				
Transfer Agent	Company Office		Where Listed	OTC-BB
Auditor	William R. Maslo		Symbol	BUFF
Market Maker	Chicago Corporation, The	Telephone (800)621-1674	SIC Code	4810
Broker Dealer	Regular Stockbroker		Employees	50

Bulova Corporation

One Bulova Avenue • Woodside, NY 11377-7874 • Telephone (718)204-3300 • Fax (718)204-3546

Company Description

The Company, which is 97% owned by Loews Corporation, distributes and sells watches, clocks and timepiece parts for consumer use. The principal watch brands are Bulova, Caravelle, Accutron and Sportstime. Bulova's principal markets are the U.S. and Canada, which have accounted for 87% and 13%, respectively, of sales.

	12/31/95	12/31/94	12/31/93	12/31/92
Per Share Information				
Stock Price	4.13	3.25	4.00	4.44
Earnings Per Share	0.57	0.18	0.54	-2.87
Price / Earnings Ratio	7.25	18.06	7.41	n.a.
Book Value Per Share	14.23	13.68	13.94	13.46
Price / Book Value %	29.02	23.76	28.69	32.99
Dividends Per Share	n.a.	n.a.	n.a.	n.a.
Annual Financial Data				
Operating Results (000's)				
Total Revenues	109,223.0	100,046.0	101,303.0	98,841.0
Costs & Expenses	-102,309.0	-98,683.0	-98,174.0	-100,476.0
Income Before Taxes and Other	6,756.0	783.0	1,708.0	-3,193.0
Other Items	363.0	302.0	603.0	-11,847.0
Income Tax	-4,487.0	-251.0	203.0	1,851.0
Net Income	2,632.0	834.0	2,514.0	-13,189.0
Cash Flow From Operations	528.0	-3,931.0	10,272.0	7,858.0
Balance Sheet (000's)				
Cash & Equivalents	5,963.0	3,857.0	5,639.0	6,287.0
Total Current Assets	104,758.0	121,276.0	120,230.0	138,895.0
Fixed Assets, Net	12,260.0	12,750.0	13,072.0	27,270.0
Total Assets	134,127.0	151,035.0	149,865.0	183,268.0
Total Current Liabilities	17,748.0	18,240.0	22,190.0	39,032.0
Long-Term Debt	n.a.	19,200.0	16,600.0	35,275.0
Stockholders' Equity	65,463.0	62,930.0	64,101.0	61,893.0
Performance & Financial Condition				
Return on Total Revenues %	2.41	0.83	2.48	-13.34
Return on Avg Stockholders' Equity %	4.10	1.31	3.99	-19.12
Return on Average Assets %	1.85	0.55	1.51	-7.75
Current Ratio	5.90	6.65	5.42	3.56
Debt / Equity %	n.a.	30.51	25.90	56.99

Compound Growth %'s	EPS %	2.74	Net Income %	2.32	Total Revenues %	3.39

Comments

In January, 1995, the Company sold its industrial and defense products segment for $20.8 million in cash. The Company applied $18.0 million to repay the entire debt owed to its parent. Also, during 1995, the Company collected $10.6 million from its parent relating to a tax audit adjustment from the examination of the parent's tax returns for 1984 through 1990. In 1992, the Company implemented the new accounting requirement requiring the accrual of post-retirement benefits other than pensions. The cumulative effect of this change was to reduce net income in 1992, by $25.6 million.

Officers	Position	Ownership Information	12/31/95
Herbert C. Hofmann	President, CEO	Number of Shares Outstanding	4,599,000
Paul S. Sayegh	COO	Market Capitalization	$ 18,993,870
Warren J. Neitzel	Secretary	Frequency Of Dividends	n.a.
John T. O'Reilly	Controller	Number of Shareholders	1,500

Other Information

Transfer Agent	Registrar & Transfer Company		Where Listed	OTC-BB
Auditor	Deloitte & Touche LLP		Symbol	BULV
Market Maker	Carr Securities Corporation	Telephone (800)221-2243	SIC Code	3873
Broker Dealer	Regular Stockbroker		Employees	430

Burke-Parsons-Bowlby Corporation

P.O. Box 231 • Ripley, WV 25271 • Telephone (304)372-2211 • Fax (304)372-1211

Company Description

The Company is a producer of wood products of various kinds, primarily pressure-treated heavy timbers for industrial, construction, railroad, mining, highway, farm, and general use. It operates four treatment plants located in West Virginia, Virginia, Kentucky and Pennsylvania. The Company was incorporated in West Virginia in 1955. 37% of the Company's 794,323 shares are owned by an Employee Stock Ownership Plan.

	03/31/95	03/31/94	03/31/93	03/31/92
Per Share Information				
Stock Price	7.50	6.00	4.75	2.62
Earnings Per Share	1.71	1.19	0.50	-0.01
Price / Earnings Ratio	4.39	5.04	9.50	n.a.
Book Value Per Share	10.81	9.31	6.30	5.75
Price / Book Value %	69.38	64.45	75.40	45.57
Dividends Per Share	0.14	0.14	0.11	0.04
Annual Financial Data				
Operating Results (000's)				
Total Revenues	52,132.9	43,699.8	34,405.1	35,135.5
Costs & Expenses	-49,916.5	-42,377.4	-33,586.7	-35,569.2
Income Before Taxes and Other	2,216.4	1,322.3	818.4	-433.7
Other Items	n.a.	n.a.	n.a.	341.1
Income Tax	-901.4	-437.6	-329.8	86.6
Net Income	1,315.0	884.8	488.6	-6.0
Cash Flow From Operations	-532.8	-3,826.8	1,212.5	5,229.3
Balance Sheet (000's)				
Cash & Equivalents	97.2	170.5	124.9	59.2
Total Current Assets	22,013.8	18,836.8	13,044.5	13,046.9
Fixed Assets, Net	4,549.9	3,707.4	3,602.5	3,734.8
Total Assets	27,018.7	22,960.1	16,981.6	17,079.2
Total Current Liabilities	14,178.5	10,828.9	8,007.3	7,955.9
Long-Term Debt	3,913.5	4,762.4	2,568.8	3,206.1
Stockholders' Equity	8,586.0	7,169.2	6,213.5	5,670.9
Performance & Financial Condition				
Return on Total Revenues %	2.52	2.02	1.42	-0.02
Return on Avg Stockholders' Equity %	16.69	13.22	8.22	-0.11
Return on Average Assets %	5.26	4.43	2.87	-0.04
Current Ratio	1.55	1.74	1.63	1.64
Debt / Equity %	45.58	66.43	41.34	56.54

Compound Growth %'s	EPS %	84.93	Net Income %	64.06	Total Revenues %	14.06

Comments

The Company has demonstrated strong growth during the last two years and is increasing capacity at two of its facilities. Early 1996 results are similar to 1995 and management remains optimistic. 1992 results benefit from a nonrecurring insurance windfall of $341,080 which offset most of an operating loss. Compound growth rates may be misleading because of the loss in 1992.

Officers	Position	Ownership Information	03/31/95
Richard E. Bowlby	Chairman, President	Number of Shares Outstanding	794,323
R. Floyd Bowlby	Secretary	Market Capitalization	$ 5,957,423
Robert L. DeHart	Treasurer, Controller	Frequency Of Dividends	Quarterly
Richard E. Bowlby, Jr.	Vice President	Number of Shareholders	Under 500
Norman C. Hildreth	VP - Manufacturing		

Other Information				
Transfer Agent	The Huntington National Bank VW		Where Listed	OTC-BB
Auditor	Simpson & Osborne		Symbol	BPAB
Market Maker	Koonce Securities, Inc.	Telephone (800)368-2802	SIC Code	2490
Broker Dealer	Regular Stockbroker		Employees	720

Burnham Corporation

P.O. Box 3205 • Lancaster, PA 17604-3205 • Telephone (717)293-5800 • Fax (717)293-5816

Company Description

The Company is a producer of boilers and related heating equipment for residential, commercial and industrial applications and also a distributor of a broad range of residential boilers, radiators and light commercial boilers to plumbing and heating wholesale distributors. There was a two-for-one split in 1995. All numbers reflect the effect of this transaction. The Company has also approved a stock repurchase plan.

	12/31/95	12/31/94	12/31/93	12/31/92
Per Share Information				
Stock Price	25.12	27.75	23.50	20.00
Earnings Per Share	3.37	3.17	3.30	2.63
Price / Earnings Ratio	7.45	8.75	7.12	7.60
Book Value Per Share	25.71	23.65	21.68	19.50
Price / Book Value %	97.71	117.34	108.39	102.56
Dividends Per Share	1.32	1.20	2.20	19.50
Annual Financial Data				
Operating Results (000's)				
Total Revenues	148,730.0	143,837.0	128,494.0	124,816.0
Costs & Expenses	-136,396.0	-132,386.0	-117,945.0	-114,748.0
Income Before Taxes and Other	12,334.0	11,451.0	10,549.0	9,398.0
Other Items	n.a.	n.a.	854.0	183.0
Income Tax	-4,706.0	-4,291.0	-3,999.0	-3,579.0
Net Income	7,628.0	7,160.0	7,404.0	6,002.0
Cash Flow From Operations	6,984.0	5,698.0	8,040.0	10,983.0
Balance Sheet (000's)				
Cash & Equivalents	2,725.0	8,142.0	12,292.0	16,948.0
Total Current Assets	48,603.0	53,278.0	52,963.0	57,517.0
Fixed Assets, Net	45,057.0	35,480.0	32,304.0	21,710.0
Total Assets	95,759.0	90,524.0	86,759.0	80,902.0
Total Current Liabilities	22,219.0	21,114.0	19,539.0	17,840.0
Long-Term Debt	5,218.0	8,252.0	11,307.0	11,763.0
Stockholders' Equity	58,641.0	53,796.0	49,119.0	44,222.0
Performance & Financial Condition				
Return on Total Revenues %	5.13	4.98	5.76	4.81
Return on Avg Stockholders' Equity %	13.57	13.91	15.86	14.02
Return on Average Assets %	8.19	8.08	8.83	7.78
Current Ratio	2.19	2.52	2.71	3.22
Debt / Equity %	8.90	15.34	23.02	26.60

Compound Growth %'s	EPS %	8.62	Net Income %	8.32	Total Revenues %	6.02

Comments

The last few years, except for 1995, have marked a revival in growth. 1993 results include a nonrecurring benefit of $854,000, $.76 cents per share, for adopting an accounting change. 1992 results also include several nonrecurring items.

Officers	Position	Ownership Information	12/31/95
John B. Dodge	Chairman	Number of Shares Outstanding	2,260,163
Albert Morrison, III	President, CEO	Market Capitalization	$ 56,775,295
Ronald L. Griffith	Senior VP, CFO	Frequency Of Dividends	Quarterly
Donald E. Sweigart	Senior VP	Number of Shareholders	Under 500
Shaun D. McMeans	Controller		

Other Information

Transfer Agent	First Union National Bank of NC			Where Listed	OTC-PS
Auditor	Arthur Andersen LLP			Symbol	BURCA
Market Maker	Chicago Corporation, The	Telephone	(312)855-7664	SIC Code	3430
Broker Dealer	Regular Stockbroker			Employees	400

CBR Brewing Company, Inc.

433 N Camden Dr, Suite 1200 • Beverly Hills, CA 90210 • Telephone (310)274-5172 • Fax (310)274-6403

Company Description

The Company manages and controls all of the production and sale of Pabst Blue Ribbon beer in the People's Republic of China. The Company was incorporated in Florida in 1988. Through a 100% owned subsidiary, the Company acquired, in October of 1994, a 60% interest in the Zhaoqing Brewery located in China and changed its name to CBR Brewing.

	09/30/95	12/31/94
Per Share Information		
Stock Price	2.57	2.57
Earnings Per Share	0.33	0.05
Price / Earnings Ratio	7.79	51.40
Book Value Per Share	1.95	1.59
Price / Book Value %	131.79	161.64
Dividends Per Share	n.a.	n.a.
Annual Financial Data		
Operating Results (000's)		
Total Revenues	45,965.0	1,493.2
Costs & Expenses	-44,955.3	-1,152.7
Income Before Taxes and Other	1,009.7	-8.2
Other Items	1,864.3	447.6
Income Tax	-241.0	n.a.
Net Income	2,633.0	439.5
Cash Flow From Operations	14,336.6	-706.4
Balance Sheet (000's)		
Cash & Equivalents	13,771.8	875.5
Total Current Assets	37,211.0	3,143.3
Fixed Assets, Net	20,346.0	13,297.8
Total Assets	84,905.0	42,266.2
Total Current Liabilities	41,258.8	7,991.9
Long-Term Debt	15,862.2	12,167.4
Stockholders' Equity	15,615.0	12,751.6
Performance & Financial Condition		
Return on Total Revenues %	5.73	29.43
Return on Avg Stockholders' Equity %	18.56	n.a.
Return on Average Assets %	4.14	n.a.
Current Ratio	0.90	0.39
Debt / Equity %	101.58	95.42

Compound Growth %'s	EPS %	560.00	Net Income %	499.10	Total Revenues %	2978.19

Comments

Prior to October, 1994, when it acquired a 60% interest in Zhaoqing Brewery, the Company had no operations and there was no trading activity in its' stock. The results of operations and balance sheets presented above are for December 31, 1994, and the two months then ended, and as of September 30,1995, and the nine months then ended. The annual report and financial statements for the year ended December 31, 1995, are not yet available. As of September 15, 1995, officers and directors, as a group, owned 90% of the Company's outstanding common stock.

Officers	Position	Ownership Information	12/31/94
John Z. Li	President	Number of Shares Outstanding	8,000,013
Ge Ming	CFO	Market Capitalization	$ 20,560,033
Niu Z. Hang	Vice President, COO	Frequency Of Dividends	n.a.
Liu Y. Zhong	General Manager, Chairman	Number of Shareholders	26
Wong L. Tak	Other		

Other Information				
Transfer Agent	Interwest Transfer Co., Inc.		Where Listed	OTC-BB
Auditor	Ernst & Young		Symbol	BLUE
Market Maker	Paragon Capital Corporation	Telephone (800)521-8877	SIC Code	2082
Broker Dealer	Regular Stockbroker		Employees	1341

CMP Industries, Inc.

P.O. Box 350 • Albany, NY 12201 • Telephone (518)434-3147 • Fax (518)434-1288

Company Description

The Company manufactures certain products for use by dental laboratories and also supplies them with products manufactured elsewhere.

	05/31/95	05/31/94	05/31/93	05/31/92
Per Share Information				
Stock Price	37.75	25.00	35.00	20.00
Earnings Per Share	4.43	5.59	4.79	3.48
Price / Earnings Ratio	8.52	4.47	7.31	5.75
Book Value Per Share	50.81	47.71	42.20	37.97
Price / Book Value %	74.30	52.40	82.94	52.67
Dividends Per Share	0.88	0.60	0.60	0.60
Annual Financial Data				
Operating Results (000's)				
Total Revenues	8,699.2	8,089.7	8,313.1	8,167.8
Costs & Expenses	-7,886.9	-7,356.8	-7,460.1	-7,678.5
Income Before Taxes and Other	720.8	715.7	662.2	452.8
Other Items	n.a.	128.7	n.a.	n.a.
Income Tax	-221.3	-204.3	-112.0	-52.4
Net Income	499.6	640.0	550.2	400.3
Cash Flow From Operations	459.5	829.5	457.8	1,323.6
Balance Sheet (000's)				
Cash & Equivalents	811.4	1,247.5	764.6	688.9
Total Current Assets	5,511.4	5,106.8	5,011.2	4,651.3
Fixed Assets, Net	889.4	840.2	772.6	620.1
Total Assets	7,076.5	6,715.9	6,714.0	6,097.3
Total Current Liabilities	802.2	787.0	955.7	870.6
Long-Term Debt	n.a.	n.a.	n.a.	n.a.
Stockholders' Equity	5,736.4	5,367.7	4,840.9	4,362.9
Performance & Financial Condition				
Return on Total Revenues %	5.74	7.91	6.62	4.90
Return on Avg Stockholders' Equity %	9.00	12.54	11.96	9.54
Return on Average Assets %	7.24	9.53	8.59	6.46
Current Ratio	6.87	6.49	5.24	5.34
Debt / Equity %	n.a.	n.a.	n.a.	n.a.

Compound Growth %'s	EPS %	8.38	Net Income %	7.66	Total Revenues %	2.12

Comments

The Company has not shown any growth although management has sought possible acquisitions during recent years. Having found no interested sellers, the Board initiated a stock buy-back program and raised the dividend. 1994 results reflect a nonrecurring benefit of $128,722, or $1.12 per share, arising from the adoption of GAAP for the reporting of income taxes.

Officers	Position	Ownership Information	05/31/95
William J. Regan	President, CEO	Number of Shares Outstanding	112,896
Charles B. Buchanan	Secretary	Market Capitalization	$ 4,261,824
Edward J. Civiok, Jr.	Treasurer	Frequency Of Dividends	n.a.
		Number of Shareholders	Under 500

Other Information

Transfer Agent	Company Office			Where Listed	OTC-BB
Auditor	KPMG Peat Marwick LLP			Symbol	CMPN
Market Maker	Hill, Thompson, Magid & Co.Inc	Telephone	(800)631-3083	SIC Code	3843
Broker Dealer	Regular Stockbroker			Employees	60

CSM Environmental Systems, Inc.

2333 Morris Avenue, Suite C-4 • Union, NJ 07083 • Telephone (908)688-1177 • Fax (908)688-1045

Company Description

The Company is engaged in engineering, designing, fabricating, selling, installing and servicing special purpose electro-mechanical process equipment for industrial applications, including catalytic air pollution abatement systems for the movement, tempering and purification of air from industrial sources. The Company had a 1 for 100 reverse split in late 1995 for the stated purpose of eliminating filings with the SEC and for "cleaning up CSM's stockholder lists". No fractional shares were issued and anyone with less than 100 shares was required to be completely redeemed.

	09/30/95	12/31/94	12/31/93	12/31/92
Per Share Information				
Stock Price	2.69	2.37	1.43	1.62
Earnings Per Share	0.01	0.08	0.11	-0.54
Price / Earnings Ratio	269.00	29.63	13.00	n.a.
Book Value Per Share	1.20	1.19	1.11	1.00
Price / Book Value %	224.17	199.16	128.83	162.00
Dividends Per Share	n.a.	n.a.	n.a.	n.a.
Annual Financial Data				
Operating Results (000's)				
Total Revenues	7,966.2	6,331.8	5,049.0	7,678.0
Costs & Expenses	-7,951.0	-6,169.9	-5,094.0	-8,255.0
Income Before Taxes and Other	15.2	161.9	-45.0	-577.0
Other Items	n.a.	n.a.	n.a.	n.a.
Income Tax	-5.0	-90.0	143.0	96.0
Net Income	10.2	71.9	98.0	-481.0
Cash Flow From Operations	-29.8	-13.9	-96.0	-628.0
Balance Sheet (000's)				
Cash & Equivalents	102.7	622.5	646.0	76.0
Total Current Assets	2,702.2	4,093.7	2,982.0	3,031.0
Fixed Assets, Net	146.1	97.1	182.0	238.0
Total Assets	3,030.3	4,374.6	3,293.0	3,398.0
Total Current Liabilities	1,788.9	3,156.3	1,886.0	2,174.0
Long-Term Debt	12.8	n.a.	97.0	12.0
Stockholders' Equity	1,059.1	1,048.9	977.0	879.0
Performance & Financial Condition				
Return on Total Revenues %	0.17	1.14	1.94	-6.26
Return on Avg Stockholders' Equity %	0.97	7.10	10.56	n.a.
Return on Average Assets %	0.28	1.87	2.93	n.a.
Current Ratio	1.51	1.30	1.58	1.39
Debt / Equity %	1.21	n.a.	9.93	1.37

Compound Growth %'s	EPS %	-69.85	Net Income %	-67.70	Total Revenues %	1.24

Comments

In early 1995, the Company reported a doubling of new order bookings and a number of other favorable developments. On April 17, 1996, however, it was announced that the Company will no longer be issuing annual reports. Officers and directors owned 76% of the Company before the reverse split. 1995 results were obtainable only for the nine months ended September 30, 1995, and are shown above, with the exception that revenues are annualized so as to produce meaningful revenue growth percentages.

Officers	Position	Ownership Information	09/30/95
William J. Brennan	Chairman	Number of Shares Outstanding	883,058
Thomas G. Otchy	President, CEO	Market Capitalization	$ 2,375,426
Thomas J. Smith	Exec VP	Frequency Of Dividends	n.a.
Donald E. Ciccolella	VP - Sales	Number of Shareholders	Under 500
Kathy V. Jovine	Controller		

Other Information				
Transfer Agent	Company Office		Where Listed	OTC-BB
Auditor	Ernst & Young LLP		Symbol	CSMS
Market Maker	Fahnestock & Co., Inc.	Telephone (800)223-3012	SIC Code	7389
Broker Dealer	Regular Stockbroker		Employees	50

CT Communications, Inc.

68 Cabarrrus Ave. East • Concord, NC 28025 • Telephone (704)788-0244 • Fax (704)788-6322

Company Description

The Company and its subsidiaries operate entirely in the communications industry and provide local and long distance services primarily to customers who are residents of Cabarrus, Stanly and Rowan counties in North Carolina. Revenue is generated mostly through local, access and toll service charges. The Company was organized in 1993 as a result of a corporate reorganization whereby two existing telephone companies each became wholly owned subsidiaries of the Company. Three other subsidiaries were formed in 1994 and 1995 which are in the business of cellular telephone and wireless communication services.

	12/31/95	12/31/94	12/31/93	12/31/92
Per Share Information				
Stock Price	321.00	285.00	150.00	180.00
Earnings Per Share	26.22	16.77	15.98	15.54
Price / Earnings Ratio	12.24	16.99	9.39	11.58
Book Value Per Share	148.22	131.03	121.12	112.86
Price / Book Value %	216.57	217.51	123.84	159.49
Dividends Per Share	8.10	7.92	7.76	7.49
Annual Financial Data				
Operating Results (000's)				
Total Revenues	56,018.8	50,427.4	43,281.3	40,150.1
Costs & Expenses	-38,802.6	-39,057.8	-31,811.4	-28,220.2
Income Before Taxes and Other	19,777.4	13,033.3	12,241.1	12,095.6
Other Items	-93.1	-93.9	-93.6	-95.3
Income Tax	-6,760.6	-4,688.9	-4,282.2	-4,355.5
Net Income	12,923.6	8,250.4	7,865.3	7,644.8
Cash Flow From Operations	20,335.7	24,071.4	16,271.8	17,071.6
Balance Sheet (000's)				
Cash & Equivalents	4,751.2	8,346.2	2,661.2	2,613.1
Total Current Assets	18,926.0	21,994.0	14,760.4	11,861.0
Fixed Assets, Net	57,975.7	53,840.4	56,102.1	58,859.9
Total Assets	107,765.5	99,886.6	91,938.4	87,171.3
Total Current Liabilities	12,697.6	13,578.9	7,060.5	6,371.5
Long-Term Debt	4,074.0	4,714.0	6,331.0	6,469.0
Stockholders' Equity	76,272.7	66,150.5	61,294.6	57,222.7
Performance & Financial Condition				
Return on Total Revenues %	23.07	16.36	18.17	19.04
Return on Avg Stockholders' Equity %	18.15	12.95	13.27	13.84
Return on Average Assets %	12.45	8.60	8.78	8.96
Current Ratio	1.49	1.62	2.09	1.86
Debt / Equity %	5.34	7.13	10.33	11.30

Compound Growth %'s	EPS %	19.05	Net Income %	19.13	Total Revenues %	11.74

Comments

The Company has investments totaling $33.6 million at December 31, 1995, which consist of equity ownership in affiliated companies and state, county and municipal securities. The Company's equity in the earnings of its affiliates amounted to $2.2 million for 1995.

Officers	Position	Ownership Information	12/31/95
L.D. Coltrane, III	Chairman	Number of Shares Outstanding	494,340
Michael R. Coltrane	President, CEO	Market Capitalization	$ 158,683,140
Jerry H. McClellan	Exec VP, General Manager	Frequency Of Dividends	Quarterly
Thomas A. Norman	Senior VP	Number of Shareholders	1,375
Nicholas L. Kottyan	Senior VP		

Other Information

Transfer Agent	Company Office		Where Listed	OTC-PS
Auditor	KPMG Peat Marwick LLP		Symbol	CNOT
Market Maker	Legg Mason Wood Walker, Inc.	Telephone (212)428-4949	SIC Code	4813
Broker Dealer	Regular Stockbroker		Employees	296

CUSA Technologies, Inc.

986 W. Atherton Drive • Salt Lake City, UT 84123 • Telephone (801)263-1840 • Fax (801)265-3222

Company Description

The Company is a full service provider of integrated computer systems including hardware, software, installation, training, software support and hardware maintenance, to the financial industry, the healthcare industry, and the equipment rental industry. The Company was incorporated as Mountain Surgical Centers, Inc. in the State of Nevada during 1986. The Company entered the software market in June 1994, through a series of nine acquisitions.

	06/30/95	06/30/94
Per Share Information		
Stock Price	3.00	1.35
Earnings Per Share	0.08	-0.03
Price / Earnings Ratio	37.50	n.a.
Book Value Per Share	0.89	0.40
Price / Book Value %	337.08	337.50
Dividends Per Share	n.a.	n.a.
Annual Financial Data		
Operating Results (000's)		
Total Revenues	32,621.1	3,102.2
Costs & Expenses	-31,058.2	-3,212.2
Income Before Taxes and Other	1,562.9	-109.9
Other Items	n.a.	n.a.
Income Tax	-786.9	25.8
Net Income	776.0	-84.1
Cash Flow From Operations	1,799.8	158.1
Balance Sheet (000's)		
Cash & Equivalents	818.9	379.1
Total Current Assets	7,522.9	1,839.3
Fixed Assets, Net	4,105.2	3,160.2
Total Assets	29,118.9	12,043.4
Total Current Liabilities	15,019.1	5,395.5
Long-Term Debt	3,223.8	1,765.8
Stockholders' Equity	9,921.0	4,235.4
Performance & Financial Condition		
Return on Total Revenues %	2.38	-2.71
Return on Avg Stockholders' Equity %	10.96	n.a.
Return on Average Assets %	3.77	n.a.
Current Ratio	0.50	0.34
Debt / Equity %	32.49	41.69

Compound Growth %'s	EPS % n.a.	Net Income % n.a.	Total Revenues %	951.54

Comments

Virtually all of the Company's operations for the year ended June 30, 1995, result from acquisitions completed from June, 1994 through June, 1995. For the six months ended December 31, 1995, the Company had sales of $23.8 million, net earnings of $248,000 ($.02 per share) as compared to $13.2 million and $576,000 ($.09 per share) for the same period in 1994. Total assets at December 31, 1995, were $33.0 million and the Company's common stock was trading at approximately $6.20 per share.

Officers	Position	Ownership Information	06/30/95
Richard N. Beckstrand	Chairman, CEO	Number of Shares Outstanding	8,509,516
David J. Rank	President, COO	Market Capitalization	$ 25,528,548
Debbie Sanich	Secretary	Frequency Of Dividends	n.a.
L. James Jensen, Jr.	Treasurer	Number of Shareholders	264
L. Bruce Ford	Vice President		

Other Information				
Transfer Agent	Interwest Transfer Co., Inc.		Where Listed	OTC-BB
Auditor	Grant Thorton LLP		Symbol	CSAT
Market Maker	Wilson-Davis & Co., Inc.	Telephone (801)532-1313	SIC Code	7370
Broker Dealer	Regular Stockbroker		Employees	412

Cable Link, Inc.

280 Cozzins Street • Columbus, OH 43215-2379 • Telephone (614)221-3131 • Fax (614)222-0581

Company Description

The Company sells new and refurbished cable TV equipment in addition to repairing equipment for cable companies within the U.S. and various international markets. Their single leased facility is located in Columbus, Ohio. The Company began business in 1983 as a sole proprietorship and was incorporated in 1987. In 1992, the Company sold 28,000 shares in a private placement. This was followed by two placements in 1993 totalling 122,000 shares at $7 per share. There was a 2 for 1 stock split in 1994 and another small private placement.

	12/31/95	12/31/94	12/31/93	12/31/92
Per Share Information				
Stock Price	1.62	3.25	4.00	n.a.
Earnings Per Share	-0.43	0.12	0.24	n.a.
Price / Earnings Ratio	n.a.	27.08	16.67	n.a.
Book Value Per Share	0.86	1.29	0.95	n.a.
Price / Book Value %	188.37	251.94	421.05	n.a.
Dividends Per Share	n.a.	n.a.	n.a.	n.a.
Annual Financial Data				
Operating Results (000's)				
Total Revenues	7,650.4	8,736.3	6,139.6	4,483.4
Costs & Expenses	-7,999.3	-8,313.3	-5,999.1	-4,666.6
Income Before Taxes and Other	-360.1	184.8	140.5	-183.2
Other Items	n.a.	n.a.	n.a.	n.a.
Income Tax	68.9	-103.0	n.a.	n.a.
Net Income	-291.2	81.7	140.5	-183.2
Cash Flow From Operations	-198.1	-309.3	-550.6	-151.8
Balance Sheet (000's)				
Cash & Equivalents	149.8	27.0	35.2	3.0
Total Current Assets	2,471.6	2,227.1	1,487.1	924.2
Fixed Assets, Net	539.0	393.0	265.9	180.7
Total Assets	3,053.6	2,652.4	1,761.5	1,104.9
Total Current Liabilities	2,365.2	1,744.4	1,138.3	1,346.5
Long-Term Debt	2.0	12.0	15.7	21.5
Stockholders' Equity	586.0	877.2	607.5	-263.1
Performance & Financial Condition				
Return on Total Revenues %	-3.81	0.94	2.29	-4.09
Return on Avg Stockholders' Equity %	-39.80	11.01	81.61	398.28
Return on Average Assets %	-10.21	3.70	9.81	-17.35
Current Ratio	1.04	1.28	1.31	0.69
Debt / Equity %	0.34	1.37	2.59	n.a.

Compound Growth %'s	EPS %	n.a.	Net Income %	n.a.	Total Revenues %	19.50

Comments

The Company replaced and added senior management in 1994 and 1995 as well as improving systems and upgrading production equipment and capacity. A significant stock price increase in early 1996 may be attributable to first quarter results which showed a 52% increase in revenue and a profit per share of $.29 as compared to a loss of $.13 in the same period of the prior year. 1992 results are unaudited.

Officers	Position	Ownership Information	12/31/95
Bob Binsky	Chairman, CEO	Number of Shares Outstanding	681,812
Brenda Thompson	President	Market Capitalization	$ 1,104,535
Anthony Matteo	COO	Frequency Of Dividends	n.a.
Tom Osborn	Senior VP	Number of Shareholders	Under 500
Michael Allen	Senior VP		

Other Information

Transfer Agent	Fifth Third Bank, Cincinatti		Where Listed	OTC-BB
Auditor	Coopers & Lybrand LLP		Symbol	CBLK
Market Maker	Wien Securities Corp.	Telephone (800)624-0050	SIC Code	4840
Broker Dealer	Regular Stockbroker		Employees	100

Cagy Industries, Inc.

P.O. Box 1109 • Columbus, MS 39703 • Telephone (601)329-7710 • Fax (601)329-7705

Company Description

The Company is a Delaware corporation organized for the purpose of serving as a holding company for railroad service companies. It currently operates three railroads in the states of Mississippi, Alabama, Georgia, and Tennessee.

	12/31/95	12/31/94	12/31/93	12/31/92
Per Share Information				
Stock Price	3.38	2.63	1.25	1.25
Earnings Per Share	0.04	0.48	0.21	0.27
Price / Earnings Ratio	84.50	5.48	5.95	4.63
Book Value Per Share	4.53	4.53	4.11	3.89
Price / Book Value %	74.61	58.06	30.41	32.13
Dividends Per Share	n.a.	n.a.	n.a.	n.a.
Annual Financial Data				
Operating Results (000's)				
Total Revenues	6,288.1	6,086.3	6,450.4	6,384.0
Costs & Expenses	-6,315.9	-5,493.4	-6,087.2	-5,887.0
Income Before Taxes and Other	-27.8	592.8	363.2	497.0
Other Items	5.6	-16.3	23.2	1.0
Income Tax	69.1	-16.2	-145.0	-186.0
Net Income	46.9	560.3	241.4	312.0
Cash Flow From Operations	668.8	727.9	1,068.1	n.a.
Balance Sheet (000's)				
Cash & Equivalents	768.7	1,189.3	1,198.0	651.1
Total Current Assets	4,190.7	3,649.2	3,815.9	2,679.0
Fixed Assets, Net	11,206.1	11,574.8	15,196.6	14,874.0
Total Assets	17,053.2	17,206.9	20,400.7	18,794.0
Total Current Liabilities	2,499.1	2,364.5	3,025.7	2,162.0
Long-Term Debt	3,531.6	3,337.3	6,054.2	5,555.0
Stockholders' Equity	5,413.8	5,348.9	4,765.6	4,524.0
Performance & Financial Condition				
Return on Total Revenues %	0.75	9.21	3.74	4.89
Return on Avg Stockholders' Equity %	0.87	11.08	5.20	7.14
Return on Average Assets %	0.27	2.98	1.23	1.65
Current Ratio	1.68	1.54	1.26	1.24
Debt / Equity %	65.23	62.39	127.04	122.79

Compound Growth %'s	EPS %	-47.09	Net Income %	-46.82	Total Revenues %	-0.50

Comments

For the year ended December 31, 1995, four major shippers accounted for over 50% of total operating revenue for the Company's main railroad. Expected expenditures for 1996 include about $2.6 million for rail line and maintenance and $850,000 for the purchase of railcars and locomotives. Officers and directors, as a group, held about 61% of the Company's stock at May 24, 1996.

Officers	Position	Ownership Information	12/31/95
Roger D. Bell	President, CEO	Number of Shares Outstanding	1,195,472
H. Lynn Gibson	Exec VP, CFO	Market Capitalization	$ 4,040,695
Shelia M. Cain	Secretary	Frequency Of Dividends	n.a.
Milton C. Neyman	Treasurer, Controller	Number of Shareholders	380

Other Information				
Transfer Agent	Company Office		Where Listed	OTC-BB
Auditor	T.E. Lott & Company		Symbol	CAGY
Market Maker	Carr Securities Corporation	Telephone (800)221-2243	SIC Code	4013
Broker Dealer	Regular Stockbroker		Employees	64

California Almond Investors I

2245 Challenger Way, Ste. 100 • Santa Rosa, CA 95407-5422 • Telephone (707)579-3742 • Fax (707)579-3996

Company Description

The Partnership acquired and is currently farming almond orchards. The ultimate objective is to sell these orchards and liquidate the Partnership. The Partnership was organized as a limited partnership in 1986. Vintech Almond Advisors, Inc. is the managing partner and its sole shareholder is Mr. Donald D. Bade. On formation, $6 million was raised and the proceeds were used to acquire almond orchards.

	12/31/95	12/31/94	12/31/93
Per Unit Information			
Price Per Unit	250.00	140.38	140.00
Earnings Per Unit	20.22	29.53	32.95
Price / Earnings Ratio	12.36	4.75	4.25
Book Value Per Unit	356.79	355.44	344.78
Price / Book Value %	70.07	39.49	40.61
Distributions Per Unit	18.88	18.88	18.88
Cash Flow Per Unit	90.42	53.35	33.18
Annual Financial Data			
Operating Results (000's)			
Total Revenues	1,591.0	1,646.7	1,676.4
Costs & Expenses	-1,346.7	-1,289.9	-1,278.4
Operating Income	244.3	356.7	398.0
Other Items	n.a.	n.a.	n.a.
Net Income	244.3	356.7	398.0
Cash Flow From Operations	1,092.1	644.4	400.8
Balance Sheet (000's)			
Cash & Equivalents	1,069.5	698.9	328.3
Total Current Assets	2,216.6	1,883.5	1,496.5
Investments In Orchards	2,706.7	2,986.9	3,245.3
Total Assets	4,923.2	4,870.4	4,741.8
Total Current Liabilities	181.6	121.0	97.1
Long-Term Debt	432.0	456.0	480.0
Partners' Capital	4,309.7	4,293.4	4,164.7
Performance & Financial Condition			
Return on Total Revenues %	15.35	21.66	23.74
Return on Average Partners' Capital %	n.a.	n.a.	n.a.
Return on Average Assets %	4.99	7.42	n.a.
Current Ratio	12.21	15.56	15.41
Debt / Equity %	10.02	10.62	11.53

Compound Growth %'s	EPU %	-21.66	Net Income %	-21.66	Total Revenues %	-2.58

Comments

There are six separate ranches all located in the central or south/central San Joaquin Valley of California. The current price of a unit is still below the original investment although recent bidding action has shown considerable interest and a price rise. A careful inspection of these properties would be most useful.

Officers	Position	Ownership Information	12/31/95
David A. Bade	CEO	Number of Shares Outstanding	12,079
		Market Capitalization	$ 3,019,750
		Frequency Of Distributions	Quarterly
		Number of Partners	n.a.

Other Information

Transfer Agent	Company Office				Where Listed	Order Matching Only
Auditor	Moss Adams LLP				Symbol	n.a.
Market Maker	None				SIC Code	0179
Broker Dealer	Chicago Partnership Board	Tel/Ext	(800)272-6273	690	Employees	n.a.

California Orchard Company

P.O. Box O • King City, CA 93930 • Telephone (408)385-3858 • Fax (408)385-5909

Company Description

The Company is primarily engaged in leasing ground to tenants for vegetable row crop production.

	12/31/95	12/31/94	12/31/93	12/31/92
Per Share Information				
Stock Price	62.00	62.00	50.00	50.00
Earnings Per Share	4.06	4.18	6.47	5.07
Price / Earnings Ratio	15.27	14.83	7.73	9.86
Book Value Per Share	35.70	35.64	37.85	37.38
Price / Book Value %	173.67	173.96	132.10	133.76
Dividends Per Share	4.00	4.00	6.00	4.00
Annual Financial Data				
Operating Results (000's)				
Total Revenues	946.0	923.0	993.7	931.0
Costs & Expenses	-829.8	-802.3	-790.4	-780.9
Income Before Taxes and Other	116.2	120.7	203.3	150.1
Other Items	n.a.	n.a.	n.a.	1.6
Income Tax	-35.2	-37.3	-74.2	-50.5
Net Income	81.0	83.4	129.1	101.2
Cash Flow From Operations	238.8	-4.8	262.8	62.7
Balance Sheet (000's)				
Cash & Equivalents	351.1	194.2	284.1	169.0
Total Current Assets	402.0	356.4	366.9	310.0
Fixed Assets, Net	482.3	515.5	546.2	534.6
Total Assets	884.3	871.9	913.0	844.6
Total Current Liabilities	163.4	151.9	199.8	90.2
Long-Term Debt	n.a.	n.a.	n.a.	n.a.
Stockholders' Equity	712.6	711.4	707.9	746.2
Performance & Financial Condition				
Return on Total Revenues %	8.56	9.03	13.00	10.87
Return on Avg Stockholders' Equity %	11.38	11.75	17.76	13.76
Return on Average Assets %	9.23	9.34	14.69	11.83
Current Ratio	2.46	2.35	1.84	3.44
Debt / Equity %	n.a.	n.a.	n.a.	n.a.

Compound Growth %'s	EPS %	-7.14	Net Income %	-7.15	Total Revenues %	0.54

Comments

An investigation of the value of the underlying farm properties might indicate whether or not this is an investment worth seeking. Cash flow is very consistent.

Officers	Position	Ownership Information	12/31/95
Alan M. Teague	President	Number of Shares Outstanding	19,962
Gregory H. Smith	Secretary	Market Capitalization	$ 1,237,644
Lawrence J. Porter	Treasurer, General Manager	Frequency Of Dividends	Annual
C.J. Hurst, Jr.	Vice President	Number of Shareholders	Under 500

Other Information

Transfer Agent	Company Office			Where Listed	OTC-BB
Auditor	Hayashi & Wayland			Symbol	CAOX
Market Maker	Robotti & Eng, Incorporated	Telephone	(212)986-4800	SIC Code	6510
Broker Dealer	Standard Investment	Tel/Ext	(888)783-4688 Jack	Employees	14

California-Michigan Land and Water Company

3725 East Mountain View Avenue • Pasadena, CA 91107 • Telephone (408)385-3858 • Fax (408)385-5909

Company Description

The primary business, conducted by it's subsidiary East Pasadena Water Company, is the sale and distribution of water to residential and commercial consumers. These operations include production, storage and distribution of water. The Company is also engaged in real estate investment activities. Shares trade infrequently. The best way to acquire shares is to deal with a broker who specializes in thinly traded pink sheet stocks. However, the National Quotation Bureau price of $39 is not correct. Plan on spending a higher price if you are interested. A reliable source estimated a trading range between $400 and $600 per share.

	12/31/94	12/31/93
Per Share Information		
Stock Price	600.00	600.00
Earnings Per Share	-5.51	89.10
Price / Earnings Ratio	n.a.	6.73
Book Value Per Share	1,201.60	1,313.02
Price / Book Value %	49.93	45.70
Dividends Per Share	8.91	9.75
Annual Financial Data		
Operating Results (000's)		
Total Revenues	1,381.8	1,278.6
Costs & Expenses	-1,197.6	-973.2
Income Before Taxes and Other	184.2	305.4
Other Items	-131.6	-3.9
Income Tax	-64.6	-108.0
Net Income	-12.0	193.4
Cash Flow From Operations	222.0	383.6
Balance Sheet (000's)		
Cash & Equivalents	654.5	446.8
Total Current Assets	1,015.9	1,199.5
Fixed Assets, Net	2,494.7	2,755.3
Total Assets	4,347.8	4,748.1
Total Current Liabilities	406.3	400.4
Long-Term Debt	656.9	851.8
Stockholders' Equity	1,946.5	1,998.8
Performance & Financial Condition		
Return on Total Revenues %	-0.87	15.13
Return on Avg Stockholders' Equity %	-0.61	10.11
Return on Average Assets %	-0.26	4.30
Current Ratio	2.50	3.00
Debt / Equity %	33.75	42.61

Compound Growth %'s	EPS % n.a.	Net Income % n.a.	Total Revenues % 8.07

Comments

The Company constructed two new reservoirs and filed with regulatory agencies for a 21% water rate increase. 1994 results include a one-time charge of $131,605, or $60.62 per share, due to a change in depreciation methods. 1995 financial statements were released in June, 1996, but were not available when we went to press.

Officers	Position	Ownership Information	12/31/94
Anton C. Garnier	President	Number of Shares Outstanding	2,171
Shirley King	Vice President, COO	Market Capitalization	$ 1,302,600
		Frequency Of Dividends	Annual
		Number of Shareholders	Under 500

Other Information

Transfer Agent	Company Office			Where Listed	OTC-PS
Auditor	Horsfall, Murphy & Pindroh			Symbol	CMLW
Market Maker	Legg Mason Wood Walker, Inc.	Telephone	(212)428-4949	SIC Code	4940
Broker Dealer	Pink sheet specialist			Employees	11

Call Now, Inc.

P.O. Box 531399 • Miami Shores, FL 33153 • Telephone (305)751-5115 • Fax (305)751-7761

Company Description

The Company is a holding company which pursues acquisitions primarily in the communications industry. Presently, the Company is in the business of providing alternative access to long distance telephone service through a wholly owned subsidiary in southern Florida. The Company, organized in Florida in 1990, has gone through several name changes and the acquisition and disposal of several businesses. As a result of these corporate transactions, the Company realized a gain of approximately $4.2 million in 1994.

	12/31/95	12/31/94	12/31/93	06/30/93
Per Share Information				
Stock Price	1.50	1.13	3.63	2.13
Earnings Per Share	-0.09	0.56	-0.05	-0.03
Price / Earnings Ratio	n.a.	2.02	n.a.	n.a.
Book Value Per Share	1.00	0.72	0.02	0.02
Price / Book Value %	150.00	156.94	18,150.00	10,650.00
Dividends Per Share	n.a.	n.a.	n.a.	n.a.
Annual Financial Data				
Operating Results (000's)				
Total Revenues	1,376.3	1,492.8	54.3	498.0
Costs & Expenses	-2,395.4	-2,830.5	-257.2	-534.6
Income Before Taxes and Other	-1,019.1	-1,337.7	-202.9	-36.6
Other Items	n.a.	4,240.8	n.a.	n.a.
Income Tax	377.8	685.0	-35.4	-93.4
Net Income	-641.2	3,588.1	-238.2	-130.0
Cash Flow From Operations	-553.6	905.2	-93.6	-57.8
Balance Sheet (000's)				
Cash & Equivalents	241.3	n.a.	78.7	34.7
Total Current Assets	12,979.5	9,079.6	129.3	34.7
Fixed Assets, Net	79.9	108.7	86.7	100.0
Total Assets	13,573.7	9,455.2	261.0	176.7
Total Current Liabilities	6,352.0	4,162.0	88.8	17.5
Long-Term Debt	11.1	28.4	n.a.	n.a.
Stockholders' Equity	7,210.6	5,264.9	172.2	159.2
Performance & Financial Condition				
Return on Total Revenues %	-46.59	240.36	-438.60	-26.11
Return on Avg Stockholders' Equity %	-10.28	131.99	-143.77	n.a.
Return on Average Assets %	-5.57	73.86	-108.88	n.a.
Current Ratio	2.04	2.18	1.46	1.99
Debt / Equity %	0.15	0.54	n.a.	n.a.

Compound Growth %'s	EPS % n.a.	Net Income % n.a.	Total Revenues % 40.33

Comments

As a result of the various acquisitions and disposals and the fact that the Company changed its year end from June 30 to December 31 in 1993, it is very difficult to analyze this company on historic operations. A better measure would be to look at growth in assets and equity over the period. As of January 10, 1996, officers and directors, as a group, owned 54% of the Company's outstanding shares.

Officers	Position	Ownership Information	12/31/95
William M. Allen	President	Number of Shares Outstanding	7,243,700
Susan Lurvey	Secretary	Market Capitalization	$ 10,865,550
Alan R. Niederhoffer	Vice President	Frequency Of Dividends	n.a.
		Number of Shareholders	333

Other Information

Transfer Agent	Interwest Transfer Co., Inc.		Where Listed	OTC-BB
Auditor	BDO Seidman LLP		Symbol	CNOW
Market Maker	Barron Chase Securities, Inc.	Telephone (800)937-4466	SIC Code	4813
Broker Dealer	Regular Stockbroker		Employees	4

Capital Directions, Inc.

P.O. Box 130 • Mason, MI 48854-0130 • Telephone (517)676-0500 • Fax (517)676-0528

Company Description

Capital Directions, Inc., a one-bank holding company, commenced operations in 1988. The Company has two wholly-owned subsidiaries, Mason State Bank and Monex Financial Services, Inc. Mason State Bank operates predominantly in Central Michigan as an independent commercial bank and provides standard banking services. Monex Financial Services is a broker-dealer investment company offering a broad range of financial services.

	12/31/95	12/31/94	12/31/93	12/31/92
Per Share Information				
Stock Price	31.50	24.63	22.75	19.50
Earnings Per Share	3.53	3.13	2.92	2.81
Price / Earnings Ratio	8.92	7.87	7.79	6.94
Book Value Per Share	28.89	25.72	24.34	22.27
Price / Book Value %	109.03	95.76	93.47	87.56
Dividends Per Share	1.04	1.00	1.00	1.00
Annual Financial Data				
Operating Results (000's)				
Net Interest Income	3,299.0	3,127.0	3,073.0	3,240.0
Loan Loss Provision	-193.0	-25.0	-63.0	-234.0
Non-Interest Income	1,046.0	735.0	848.0	745.0
Non-Interest Expense	-2,714.0	-2,580.0	-2,703.0	-2,616.0
Income Before Taxes and Other	1,438.0	1,257.0	1,155.0	1,135.0
Other Items	n.a.	n.a.	n.a.	n.a.
Income Tax	-388.0	-327.0	-286.0	-300.0
Net Income	1,050.0	930.0	869.0	835.0
Balance Sheet (000's)				
Cash & Securities	25,466.0	21,369.0	25,377.0	28,113.0
Loans, Net	48,689.0	50,550.0	47,245.0	47,126.0
Fixed Assets, Net	649.0	803.0	895.0	648.0
Total Assets	77,835.0	76,112.0	76,027.0	78,188.0
Deposits	66,208.0	66,880.0	67,698.0	70,557.0
Stockholders' Equity	8,594.0	7,648.0	7,239.0	6,624.0
Performance & Financial Condition				
Net Interest Margin	4.94	4.79	4.53	4.68
Return on Avg Stockholders' Equity %	12.93	12.49	12.54	13.14
Return on Average Assets %	1.36	1.22	1.13	1.06
Equity to Assets %	11.04	10.05	9.52	8.47
Reserve as a % of Non-Performing Loans	n.a.	341.38	302.40	1825.00

Compound Growth %'s	EPS %	7.90	Net Income %	7.94	Net Interest Income %	0.60

Comments

The Bank declared a 2 for 1 stock split in 1994. Accordingly, all per share information has been restated for comparability. In late 1995, Terry Shultis retired as president and CEO. Timothy Gaylord was the executive vice president before taking charge. Monex Financial Services had its first full year of operations in 1995 and four other community banks have signed on to be served by them.

Officers	Position	Ownership Information	12/31/95
Douglas W. Dancer	Chairman	Number of Shares Outstanding	297,428
Timothy P. Gaylord	President, CEO	Market Capitalization	$ 9,368,982
George A. Sullivan	Secretary	Frequency Of Dividends	Quarterly
Robert G. Kennedy	Treasurer	Number of Shareholders	425
Gerald Ambrose	Other		

Other Information

Transfer Agent	American Stock Transfer & Trust Company		Where Listed	OTC-BB
Auditor	Crowe, Chizek and Company LLP		Symbol	CTDN
Market Maker	Roney & Co.	Telephone (800)321-2038	SIC Code	6020
Broker Dealer	Regular Stockbroker		Employees	40

Capital Properties, Inc.

One Hospital Trust Plaza • Providence, RI 02903 • Telephone (401)331-0100 • Fax (401)331-2965

Company Description

The Company's business consists of the leasing of certain of its real estate interests in downtown Providence, Rhode Island, the operation of other downtown Providence properties, and the leasing of its petroleum storage terminal facilities in East Providence. Through its wholly-owned subsidiary, the Company also leases outdoor advertising locations along interstate and primary highways. The Company was organized under the laws of Rhode Island in 1983.

	12/31/95	12/31/94	12/31/93	12/31/92
Per Share Information				
Stock Price	8.50	7.31	7.88	7.13
Earnings Per Share	0.08	0.19	-0.63	-0.05
Price / Earnings Ratio	106.25	38.47	n.a.	n.a.
Book Value Per Share	13.35	13.57	13.77	14.77
Price / Book Value %	63.67	53.87	57.23	48.27
Dividends Per Share	0.30	0.40	0.32	0.15
Annual Financial Data				
Operating Results (000's)				
Total Revenues	3,020.0	2,832.0	2,709.0	2,594.0
Costs & Expenses	-2,859.0	-2,493.0	-2,390.0	-2,516.0
Income Before Taxes and Other	161.0	339.0	319.0	78.0
Other Items	n.a.	n.a.	-866.0	n.a.
Income Tax	-83.0	-146.0	-89.0	-132.0
Net Income	78.0	193.0	-636.0	-54.0
Cash Flow From Operations	167.0	436.0	540.0	394.0
Balance Sheet (000's)				
Cash & Equivalents	767.0	757.0	813.0	800.0
Total Current Assets	1,175.0	1,175.0	1,330.0	1,326.0
Fixed Assets, Net	9,376.0	9,793.0	10,151.0	9,924.0
Total Assets	15,444.0	17,803.0	18,669.0	19,342.0
Total Current Liabilities	536.0	648.0	610.0	4,122.0
Long-Term Debt	n.a.	2,053.0	2,627.0	n.a.
Stockholders' Equity	13,345.0	13,567.0	13,774.0	14,807.0
Performance & Financial Condition				
Return on Total Revenues %	2.58	6.81	-23.48	-2.08
Return on Avg Stockholders' Equity %	0.58	1.41	-4.45	-0.36
Return on Average Assets %	0.47	1.06	-3.35	-0.28
Current Ratio	2.19	1.81	2.18	0.32
Debt / Equity %	n.a.	15.13	19.07	n.a.

Compound Growth %'s	EPS %	-57.89	Net Income %	-59.59	Total Revenues %	5.20

Comments

The Company's primary source of revenue is the leasing and renting of its properties. The Company has development plans for a number of its properties and is exploring development opportunities on others. The ultimate development of these properties may have a significant positive financial impact on the future financial condition of the Company.

Officers	Position	Ownership Information	12/31/95
Barbara J. Dreyer	President, Treasurer	Number of Shares Outstanding	1,000,000
Edwin G. Torrance	Secretary	Market Capitalization	$ 8,500,000
Linda Eder	Vice President	Frequency Of Dividends	Quarterly
		Number of Shareholders	507

Other Information			
Transfer Agent	Fleet National Bank	Where Listed	BE
Auditor	Lefkowitz, Garfinkel et. al.	Symbol	CPI
Market Maker	Herzog, Heine, Geduld, Inc.	Telephone (800)221-3600	SIC Code	6510
Broker Dealer	Regular Stockbroker	Employees	4

Carc, Inc.

500 Downs Loop • Clemson, SC 29631 • Telephone (864)654-1155 • Fax (864)654-1191

Company Description

CARC operates a retirement community which includes apartment buildings, a health care center and recreational and social facilities.

	03/31/95	03/31/94	03/31/93	03/31/92
Per Share Information				
Stock Price	5.00	n.a.	n.a.	n.a.
Earnings Per Share	0.42	0.41	0.34	-0.15
Price / Earnings Ratio	11.90	n.a.	n.a.	n.a.
Book Value Per Share	2.44	2.03	1.62	1.43
Price / Book Value %	204.92	n.a.	n.a.	n.a.
Dividends Per Share	n.a.	n.a.	n.a.	n.a.
Annual Financial Data				
Operating Results (000's)				
Total Revenues	3,031.4	2,988.4	3,006.3	2,729.0
Costs & Expenses	-2,806.1	-2,764.9	-2,815.1	-2,807.3
Income Before Taxes and Other	223.0	219.2	182.2	-79.3
Other Items	n.a.	n.a.	n.a.	n.a.
Income Tax	n.a.	n.a.	n.a.	n.a.
Net Income	223.0	219.2	182.2	-79.3
Cash Flow From Operations	530.5	373.1	421.1	170.2
Balance Sheet (000's)				
Cash & Equivalents	221.6	187.0	459.0	45.9
Total Current Assets	520.7	462.1	615.7	187.6
Fixed Assets, Net	4,099.6	4,233.4	4,394.5	4,509.1
Total Assets	4,946.3	5,047.9	5,217.5	5,123.6
Total Current Liabilities	402.2	330.1	190.3	194.1
Long-Term Debt	3,145.5	3,527.3	4,062.5	4,245.0
Stockholders' Equity	1,308.9	1,085.9	866.7	684.5
Performance & Financial Condition				
Return on Total Revenues %	7.36	7.33	6.06	-2.91
Return on Avg Stockholders' Equity %	18.62	22.45	23.49	-10.95
Return on Average Assets %	4.46	4.27	3.52	-1.51
Current Ratio	1.29	1.40	3.23	0.97
Debt / Equity %	240.32	324.83	468.72	620.13

Compound Growth %'s	EPS %	11.14	Net Income %	10.63	Total Revenues %	3.56

Comments

The Company has net operating loss and investment tax credit carryforwards of $1,426,118 and $16,982. The Company has shown three consecutive years of net profit after several years of losses. The Company acts as its own stock transfer agent and order matcher for stock transactions. While no published price quotes were available, the Company indicated that trades, when made, were generally at $5.00 per share.

Officers	Position	Ownership Information	03/31/95
Anita M. Davis	CEO	Number of Shares Outstanding	536,000
Hazel C. Poe	Secretary	Market Capitalization	$ 2,680,000
		Frequency Of Dividends	n.a.
		Number of Shareholders	536

Other Information

Transfer Agent	Company Office		Where Listed	Order Matching Only
Auditor	Crisp Hughes & Co. LLP		Symbol	n.a.
Market Maker	None-Company Office		SIC Code	8052
Broker Dealer	None		Employees	75

Carco Electronics

195 Constitution Drive • Menlo Park, CA 94025 • Telephone (415)321-8174 • Fax (415)321-1890

Company Description

The Company designs, manufactures, and markets precision, servo-controlled systems including flight motion simulators, precision rate tables, microwave boresight measuring systems, and target positioners. The Company was incorporated in 1961. There are two classes of stock but only class A trades. Class B is held by the founder for voting control purposes.

	09/30/95	09/30/94	09/30/93	09/30/92
Per Share Information				
Stock Price	7.50	5.00	6.25	7.50
Earnings Per Share	-0.57	0.09	0.32	0.08
Price / Earnings Ratio	n.a.	55.56	19.53	93.75
Book Value Per Share	9.20	9.78	9.69	9.47
Price / Book Value %	81.52	51.12	64.50	79.20
Dividends Per Share	n.a.	n.a.	0.06	0.12
Annual Financial Data				
Operating Results (000's)				
Total Revenues	5,582.8	6,549.2	9,649.6	8,824.6
Costs & Expenses	-5,891.2	-6,467.5	-9,434.0	-8,779.6
Income Before Taxes and Other	-308.3	81.7	215.6	45.0
Other Items	n.a.	-22.5	n.a.	n.a.
Income Tax	77.8	-23.3	-88.0	-12.3
Net Income	-230.6	35.9	127.6	32.7
Cash Flow From Operations	-1,096.8	2,577.7	-1,289.3	496.3
Balance Sheet (000's)				
Cash & Equivalents	700.9	1,852.8	48.3	612.5
Total Current Assets	3,970.9	4,211.5	5,077.3	5,189.7
Fixed Assets, Net	241.7	282.1	384.6	469.0
Total Assets	4,225.2	4,506.2	5,477.2	5,673.2
Total Current Liabilities	490.2	540.6	1,585.5	1,884.9
Long-Term Debt	n.a.	n.a.	n.a.	n.a.
Stockholders' Equity	3,697.0	3,927.6	3,891.7	3,788.2
Performance & Financial Condition				
Return on Total Revenues %	-4.13	0.55	1.32	0.37
Return on Avg Stockholders' Equity %	-6.05	0.92	3.32	0.86
Return on Average Assets %	-5.28	0.72	2.29	0.59
Current Ratio	8.10	7.79	3.20	2.75
Debt / Equity %	n.a.	n.a.	n.a.	n.a.

Compound Growth %'s	EPS % n.a.	Net Income % n.a.	Total Revenues % -14.15

Comments

Although there have been consecutive drops in sales, the Company now reports a record backlog of more than double the previous year with additional orders in negotiation. The balance sheet remains very strong with no long term debt and a current ratio of over 8 to 1. At the end of May, 1996, the Company reported six-month results. Sales increased 69% over the comparable period in 1995 and income was $.06 per share as compared to a loss of $.41 per share.

Officers	Position	Ownership Information	09/30/95
John M. Carter	President, CEO	Number of Shares Outstanding	401,710
William R. Meckfessel	CFO, Treasurer	Market Capitalization	$ 3,012,825
Hugh D. Carter	VP - Manufacturing	Frequency Of Dividends	Annual
Rudy L. Schneider	VP - Research	Number of Shareholders	Under 500

Other Information

Transfer Agent	Company Office		Where Listed	OTC-PS
Auditor	KPMG Peat Marwick LLP		Symbol	CAROA
Market Maker	Seidler Companies, Inc., The	Telephone (800)421-0164	SIC Code	3500
Broker Dealer	Regular Stockbroker		Employees	61

Cardiac Control Systems, Inc.

3 Commerce Boulevard • Palm Coast, FL 32164 • Telephone (904)445-5450 • Fax (904)445-7226

Company Description

The Company designs, develops, manufactures, and markets implantable cardiac pacemaker systems. Principal products are implantable pacemakers, connecting electrode leads and devices used for programming and monitoring the pacemaker systems. The Company was incorporated in Delaware in 1980. A private placement of convertible debentures was completed in December, 1995, raising $2.9 million.

	03/31/95	03/31/94	03/31/93	03/31/92
Per Share Information				
Stock Price	2.75	2.19	2.63	0.63
Earnings Per Share	0.79	-0.87	-1.24	-1.48
Price / Earnings Ratio	3.48	n.a.	n.a.	n.a.
Book Value Per Share	-0.49	-2.23	-1.37	-0.84
Price / Book Value %	n.a.	n.a.	n.a.	n.a.
Dividends Per Share	n.a.	n.a.	n.a.	n.a.
Annual Financial Data				
Operating Results (000's)				
Total Revenues	5,743.5	4,456.8	4,919.4	4,073.5
Costs & Expenses	-6,025.3	-5,503.5	-6,281.9	-5,483.2
Income Before Taxes and Other	-281.8	-1,046.7	-1,362.5	-1,409.7
Other Items	1,656.8	n.a.	n.a.	n.a.
Income Tax	n.a.	n.a.	n.a.	n.a.
Net Income	1,375.0	-1,046.7	-1,362.5	-1,409.7
Cash Flow From Operations	-2,047.0	84.0	-300.7	-445.2
Balance Sheet (000's)				
Cash & Equivalents	667.5	106.2	127.1	119.0
Total Current Assets	3,923.9	2,112.1	2,488.9	2,185.0
Fixed Assets, Net	1,410.3	1,260.6	1,289.2	1,364.1
Total Assets	5,797.9	3,381.3	3,786.0	3,561.6
Total Current Liabilities	1,478.6	4,981.6	2,877.2	4,102.4
Long-Term Debt	4,289.1	172.4	2,562.6	197.2
Stockholders' Equity	-659.8	-2,690.2	-1,653.9	-838.0
Performance & Financial Condition				
Return on Total Revenues %	23.94	-23.48	-27.70	-34.61
Return on Avg Stockholders' Equity %	n.a.	n.a.	n.a.	n.a.
Return on Average Assets %	29.96	-29.21	-37.09	-37.97
Current Ratio	2.65	0.42	0.87	0.53
Debt / Equity %	n.a.	n.a.	n.a.	n.a.

Compound Growth %'s	EPS %	n.a.	Net Income %	n.a.	Total Revenues %	12.13

Comments

Included in income for the year ended March 31,1995, under Other Items, is $1.6 million forgiveness of debt relating to the restructuring of the Company's financing arrangements. In 1994, the Company effected a 1 for 7 reverse stock split; per share amounts have been adjusted accordingly. Officers and directors, as a group, owned 30.7% of the Company's outstanding common stock at May 31, 1995.

Officers	Position	Ownership Information	03/31/95
Bart C. Gutekunst	Chairman	Number of Shares Outstanding	1,342,819
Alan J. Rabin	CEO	Market Capitalization	$ 3,692,752
Robert R. Brownlee	Exec VP, Secretary	Frequency Of Dividends	n.a.
Terry McMahon	Vice President	Number of Shareholders	628
Robert S. Miller	VP - Sales		

Other Information				
Transfer Agent	Trust Company Bank		Where Listed	OTC-BB
Auditor	BDO Seidman LLP		Symbol	CDCS
Market Maker	Frankel (WM.V.) & Co., Inc.	Telephone (800)631-3091	SIC Code	3845
Broker Dealer	Regular Stockbroker		Employees	73

Cardinal Bancorp, Inc.

140 East Main Street, POBox327 • Everett, PA 15537-0327 • Telephone (814)652-2131 • Fax (814)652-9338

Company Description

Cardinal Bancorp, Inc., is the bank holding company of First American National Bank of Pennsylvania which has five full-service offices in south central Pennsylvania in the communities of Everett, Bedford, Breezewood, Altoona/Hollidaysburg and Woodbury. It has been serving the area since 1902.

	12/31/95	12/31/94	12/31/93	12/31/92
Per Share Information				
Stock Price	33.31	32.00	29.00	26.00
Earnings Per Share	3.51	3.36	2.12	-1.26
Price / Earnings Ratio	9.49	9.52	13.68	n.a.
Book Value Per Share	29.96	24.49	24.35	22.59
Price / Book Value %	111.18	130.67	119.10	115.10
Dividends Per Share	0.60	1.10	0.45	0.60
Annual Financial Data				
Operating Results (000's)				
Net Interest Income	5,243.4	4,713.9	4,368.4	4,911.7
Loan Loss Provision	n.a.	300.0	-125.0	-2,470.0
Non-Interest Income	475.9	456.8	529.2	929.8
Non-Interest Expense	-3,714.1	-3,487.2	-3,509.5	-4,155.3
Income Before Taxes and Other	2,005.2	1,983.4	1,263.1	-783.9
Other Items	n.a.	n.a.	60.0	n.a.
Income Tax	-265.5	-318.3	-273.0	161.4
Net Income	1,739.7	1,665.1	1,050.1	-622.5
Balance Sheet (000's)				
Cash & Securities	59,245.3	48,401.0	53,471.9	44,972.4
Loans, Net	60,267.8	59,351.3	62,918.2	69,018.4
Fixed Assets, Net	2,871.4	2,101.9	2,171.0	2,274.1
Total Assets	124,472.0	112,606.2	121,221.8	118,932.6
Deposits	108,796.2	99,650.1	108,589.9	107,172.6
Stockholders' Equity	14,829.4	12,123.2	12,052.5	11,180.9
Performance & Financial Condition				
Net Interest Margin	4.81	4.45	4.06	n.a.
Return on Avg Stockholders' Equity %	12.91	13.78	9.04	-5.35
Return on Average Assets %	1.47	1.42	0.87	-0.51
Equity to Assets %	11.91	10.77	9.94	9.40
Reserve as a % of Non-Performing Loans	102.62	240.61	203.64	177.74

Compound Growth %'s	EPS %	28.67	Net Income %	28.71	Net Interest Income %	2.20

Comments

The Bank maintains a diversified loan portfolio consisting of real estate mortgages, consumer loans, and commercial and agricultural loans, representing 23%, 35% and 42% of total loans, respectively. After a significant operating loss in 1992, present CEO Jim Bexley was hired to head a turnaround. He not only succeeded but also managed to achieve outstanding returns on both assets and equity in 1994 and 1995. Earnings and earnings per share growth rates only reflect three years because of the loss in 1992. Most shareholders reside in Bedford County, Pennsylvania.

Officers	Position	Ownership Information	12/31/95
James B. Bexley	President, CEO	Number of Shares Outstanding	495,000
Ted J. Chwatek	Senior VP, Senior Loan Officer	Market Capitalization	$ 16,488,450
Merle W. Helsel	Senior VP, CFO	Frequency Of Dividends	Quarterly
Bonnie K. Redinger	Head Cashier	Number of Shareholders	483
Robert F. Lafferty	Other		

Other Information

				Where Listed	OTC-BB
Transfer Agent	Company Office			Symbol	CADL
Auditor	S.R. Snodgrass, A.C.			SIC Code	6020
Market Maker	Legg Mason Wood Walker, Inc.	Telephone	(212)428-4949	Employees	77
Broker Dealer	Regular Stockbroker				

Carolina First BancShares, Inc.

402 East Main St. P.O. Box 657 • Lincolnton, NC 28092 • Telephone (704)732-2222 • Fax (704)734-6238

Company Description

Carolina First BancShares, Inc. is a bank holding company, formed in June, 1989, which owns all of the outstanding common stock of Lincoln Bank of North Carolina and Cabarrus Bank of North Carolina. Lincoln Bank operates in the Charlotte, North Carolina area and Cabarrus Bank serves Cabarrus County, North Carolina. The principal business of the banks include retail and commercial banking and mortgage lending.

	12/31/95	12/31/94	12/31/93	12/31/92
Per Share Information				
Stock Price	24.93	18.38	15.08	10.60
Earnings Per Share	2.61	2.29	1.78	1.02
Price / Earnings Ratio	9.55	8.03	8.47	10.39
Book Value Per Share	19.06	16.23	14.70	13.23
Price / Book Value %	130.80	113.25	102.59	80.12
Dividends Per Share	0.45	0.41	0.40	n.a.
Annual Financial Data				
Operating Results (000's)				
Net Interest Income	15,460.2	13,745.9	12,189.8	11,069.9
Loan Loss Provision	-710.2	-667.3	-821.4	-794.0
Non-Interest Income	4,174.4	3,710.9	3,308.9	3,099.6
Non-Interest Expense	-12,640.6	-11,871.6	-11,040.7	-10,011.2
Income Before Taxes and Other	6,283.8	4,917.8	3,636.6	3,364.3
Other Items	n.a.	n.a.	n.a.	-300.6
Income Tax	-2,154.1	-1,548.0	-1,017.4	-1,585.4
Net Income	4,129.7	3,369.9	2,619.2	1,478.4
Balance Sheet (000's)				
Cash & Securities	99,765.9	81,321.2	91,481.7	82,437.8
Loans, Net	253,589.4	220,840.9	195,353.8	171,556.4
Fixed Assets, Net	8,572.0	8,174.1	8,548.4	8,059.3
Total Assets	369,833.4	318,605.0	301,258.6	268,676.4
Deposits	335,602.7	292,621.3	277,898.5	246,675.6
Stockholders' Equity	31,123.0	23,888.8	21,615.0	19,419.8
Performance & Financial Condition				
Net Interest Margin	5.02	4.94	4.74	4.54
Return on Avg Stockholders' Equity %	15.01	14.81	12.77	7.92
Return on Average Assets %	1.20	1.09	0.92	1.10
Equity to Assets %	8.42	7.50	7.17	7.23
Reserve as a % of Non-Performing Loans	441.93	535.28	331.19	212.19

Compound Growth %'s	EPS %	36.78	Net Income %	40.84	Net Interest Income %	11.78

Comments

The Bank's loan portfolio consists primarily of real estate mortgages, commercial and consumer loans, representing 66%, 13% and 12% of total loans, respectively. Management credits a strong Carolina economy together with a series of well executed marketing programs for the excellent results. However, we have noted that each of the four years presented were strong, indicating that the top brass deserve credit as well. Lincoln Bank was named the "Best Bank in North Carolina" by Money Magazine (June, 1995).

Officers	Position	Ownership Information	12/31/95
D. Mark Boyd	Chairman, CEO	Number of Shares Outstanding	1,632,458
James E. Burt, III	President	Market Capitalization	$ 40,697,178
Jan H. Hollar	Treasurer, Secretary	Frequency Of Dividends	Quarterly
James A. Atkinson, III	Vice President	Number of Shareholders	3,300
James H. Mauney, II	Vice President		

Other Information				
Transfer Agent	Wachovia Bank of North Carolina		Where Listed	OTC-PS
Auditor	KPMG Peat Marwick LLP		Symbol	CAFP
Market Maker	Interstate/Johnson Lane Corp.	Telephone (800)929-0175	SIC Code	6020
Broker Dealer	Regular Stockbroker		Employees	200

Carolina Mills Inc.

618 Carolina Avenue • Maiden, NC 28650 • Telephone (704)428-9911 • Fax (704)428-2335

Company Description

The Company has several divisions; weaving, finishing, yarn manufacturing, yarn sales, and furniture manufacture and sales. The Company has been in existence for more than 65 years. Revenue has not shown any growth since 1987 although it has had a profit and paid a dividend in each of the ten years from 1985 through 1994.

	10/01/94	10/02/93	09/30/92
Per Share Information			
Stock Price	20.50	20.50	19.50
Earnings Per Share	1.24	1.61	2.47
Price / Earnings Ratio	16.53	12.73	7.89
Book Value Per Share	21.67	21.43	20.81
Price / Book Value %	94.60	95.66	93.70
Dividends Per Share	1.00	1.00	1.00
Annual Financial Data			
Operating Results (000's)			
Total Revenues	190,281.7	200,452.6	203,725.7
Costs & Expenses	-183,646.1	-190,699.1	-187,986.3
Income Before Taxes and Other	6,635.6	9,753.5	15,739.5
Other Items	n.a.	n.a.	n.a.
Income Tax	-1,780.3	-3,425.0	-6,139.0
Net Income	4,855.3	6,328.5	9,600.5
Cash Flow From Operations	n.a.	n.a.	n.a.
Balance Sheet (000's)			
Cash & Equivalents	805.3	1,091.1	n.a.
Total Current Assets	58,183.6	56,913.8	n.a.
Fixed Assets, Net	56,303.4	54,697.2	n.a.
Total Assets	115,955.0	116,305.0	n.a.
Total Current Liabilities	18,813.7	19,466.4	n.a.
Long-Term Debt	626.2	835.0	n.a.
Stockholders' Equity	84,217.5	84,153.8	n.a.
Performance & Financial Condition			
Return on Total Revenues %	2.55	3.16	4.71
Return on Avg Stockholders' Equity %	5.77	7.61	12.15
Return on Average Assets %	4.18	5.50	8.35
Current Ratio	3.09	2.92	n.a.
Debt / Equity %	0.74	0.99	n.a.

Compound Growth %'s	EPS %	-29.15	Net Income %	-28.89	Total Revenues %	-3.36

Comments

The Company refused to send us the 1995 shareholders' report. We have been told that this even happens with shareholders from time to time. Furthermore, no auditor's opinion or even an indication of an audit are provided. And to top matters off, neither the traditional statement of cash flows nor financial statement footnotes are offered. This puts in perspective some of the reasons we have a Securities and Exchange Commission. If this was an SEC reporting company, which may happen if it ever has more than 500 shareholders, it would be required to provide full disclosure. At December 31, 1995, the stock price was bid $21.25 and ask $24.75.

Officers	Position	Ownership Information	10/01/94
Edward P. Schrum	President, Treasurer	Number of Shares Outstanding	3,885,825
Thomas P. Pruitt, Jr.	Vice President	Market Capitalization	$ 79,659,413
Stephen G. Dobbins, Jr.	Vice President	Frequency Of Dividends	Quarterly
George A. Moretz	Vice President	Number of Shareholders	Under 500
Kenneth C. Isaac	Vice President		

Other Information

Transfer Agent	Company Office			Where Listed	OTC-BB
Auditor	Not indicated			Symbol	CMLL
Market Maker	Interstate/Johnson Lane Corp.	Telephone	(800)438-4134	SIC Code	2200
Broker Dealer	Regular Stockbroker			Employees	2220

Case, Pomeroy & Company, Inc.

529 Fifth Avenue • New York, NY 10017-4608 • Telephone (212)867-2211 • Fax (212)682-2353

Company Description

The Company operates in the mining, oil and gas, investment and real estate industries. Mining revenues are from the sale of gold dore. Oil and gas revenue is from the sale of crude oil and natural gas within the contiguous U.S. and the Gulf of Mexico. The Company is involved in numerous joint ventures and participations. In 1986, a class B stock was created. Class A has a 25% greater dividend. Class B has 10 times the voting power, a right to convert to class A at any time, and equal liquidation preferences.

	06/30/95	06/30/94	06/30/93	06/30/92
Per Share Information				
Stock Price	1,237.50	1,140.00	1,350.00	1,350.00
Earnings Per Share	90.69	95.40	58.93	-22.59
Price / Earnings Ratio	13.65	11.95	22.91	n.a.
Book Value Per Share	862.20	792.83	711.51	690.22
Price / Book Value %	143.53	143.79	189.74	195.59
Dividends Per Share	21.75	13.75	5.50	26.50
Annual Financial Data				
Operating Results (000's)				
Total Revenues	62,541.0	68,533.0	53,044.3	38,658.0
Costs & Expenses	-42,352.0	-43,026.0	-38,979.8	-42,249.9
Income Before Taxes and Other	19,465.0	20,457.0	12,371.5	-6,383.0
Other Items	n.a.	311.0	n.a.	n.a.
Income Tax	-4,570.0	-5,018.0	-2,550.0	2,835.5
Net Income	14,895.0	15,750.0	9,821.5	-3,547.5
Cash Flow From Operations	14,192.0	19,075.0	12,454.4	6,277.7
Balance Sheet (000's)				
Cash & Equivalents	43,703.0	27,363.0	15,427.4	16,935.7
Total Current Assets	60,183.0	68,374.0	46,364.8	44,267.4
Fixed Assets, Net	73,571.0	57,345.0	62,404.2	48,521.5
Total Assets	182,491.0	155,966.0	141,435.0	124,719.3
Total Current Liabilities	7,330.0	5,982.0	5,041.4	4,196.2
Long-Term Debt	27,607.0	12,977.0	13,060.8	n.a.
Stockholders' Equity	141,674.0	131,112.0	118,658.9	115,167.9
Performance & Financial Condition				
Return on Total Revenues %	23.82	22.98	18.52	-9.18
Return on Avg Stockholders' Equity %	10.92	12.61	8.40	-3.04
Return on Average Assets %	8.80	10.59	7.38	-2.67
Current Ratio	8.21	11.43	9.20	10.55
Debt / Equity %	19.49	9.90	11.01	n.a.

Compound Growth %'s	EPS %	24.05	Net Income %	23.15	Total Revenues %	17.39

Comments

1995 results include a nonrecurring charge of $1.2 million related to the start-up costs of a four-year joint exploration program in the western Gulf of Mexico. Valuation is the key to understanding the investment merits of this stock. The Company currently owns working interests in 106,383 gross producing acres located offshore of Texas and Louisiana and onshore in those same states plus New Mexico and Wyoming. The Company's real estate interests include shopping centers, residential developments and undeveloped land.

Officers	Position	Ownership Information	06/30/95
Roger H. Clark, Jr.	President, CEO	Number of Shares Outstanding	162,012
Adele R. Wailand	Vice President, Secretary	Market Capitalization	$ 200,489,850
Felix M. Lista	Vice President, Treasurer	Frequency Of Dividends	Quarterly
Douglas B. Keith, III	Vice President	Number of Shareholders	Under 500
Paul R. Totilo	Controller		

Other Information

Transfer Agent	The Bank of New York			Where Listed	OTC-PS
Auditor	Arthur Andersen LLP			Symbol	CASP
Market Maker	Ragen MacKenzie Incorporated	Telephone	(206)343-5000	SIC Code	1041
Broker Dealer	Standard Investment	Tel/Ext	(800)746-5743 Jack	Employees	n.a.

Cass County Iron Company

215 East 48th Street • New York, NY 10017 • Telephone (212)753-1902

Company Description

The Company holds investments and certain mineral properties for lease and exploration and continues to search for new opportunities primarily in the development of natural resources. The Company was incorporated in 1974 as a result of a spin-off of certain assets of East Texas Iron Company.

	09/30/95	09/30/94
Per Share Information		
Stock Price	175.00	175.00
Earnings Per Share	21.12	20.29
Price / Earnings Ratio	8.29	8.62
Book Value Per Share	222.08	212.51
Price / Book Value %	78.80	82.35
Dividends Per Share	5.00	5.00
Annual Financial Data		
Operating Results (000's)		
Total Revenues	193.3	171.7
Costs & Expenses	-61.4	-56.9
Income Before Taxes and Other	131.9	114.8
Other Items	n.a.	n.a.
Income Tax	-37.5	-28.0
Net Income	94.4	86.8
Cash Flow From Operations	38.8	-46.3
Balance Sheet (000's)		
Cash & Equivalents	252.4	138.6
Total Current Assets	1,274.6	1,050.7
Fixed Assets, Net	7.6	7.8
Total Assets	1,282.1	1,058.5
Total Current Liabilities	10.1	4.0
Long-Term Debt	n.a.	n.a.
Stockholders' Equity	1,092.5	917.8
Performance & Financial Condition		
Return on Total Revenues %	48.85	50.56
Return on Avg Stockholders' Equity %	9.39	n.a.
Return on Average Assets %	8.07	n.a.
Current Ratio	126.82	263.92
Debt / Equity %	n.a.	n.a.

Compound Growth %'s	EPS %	4.09	Net Income %	8.77	Total Revenues %	12.57

Comments

Substantial income comes from assets that have small carrying values. The real value of these assets would be a key in valuing the common stock of the Company.

Officers	Position	Ownership Information	09/30/95
J. Paul Barringer	Chairman	Number of Shares Outstanding	4,919
Dyer S. Wadsworth	President, Treasurer	Market Capitalization	$ 860,825
Lewin B. Barringer	Secretary	Frequency Of Dividends	Annual
Beverley B. Wadsworth	Vice President	Number of Shareholders	Under 500

Other Information

Transfer Agent	Company Office			Where Listed	OTC-PS
Auditor	James Matthews, CPA			Symbol	CIRN
Market Maker	A.G. Edwards & Sons, Inc.	Telephone	(800)325-8197	SIC Code	6790
Broker Dealer	Pink sheet specialist			Employees	1

Central Bancorporation

Post Office Box 3026 • Wenatchee, WA 98807 • Telephone (509)663-0733 • Fax (509)664-2276

Company Description

Central Bancorporation is a bank holding company for two wholly owned bank subsidiaries, Central Washington Bank and North Central Washington Bank. Together, the two banks provide standard banking services at ten branch offices throughout the State of Washington.

	12/31/95	12/31/94	12/31/93	12/31/92
Per Share Information				
Stock Price	21.50	20.94	20.00	16.00
Earnings Per Share	2.46	1.70	1.77	1.72
Price / Earnings Ratio	8.74	12.32	11.30	9.30
Book Value Per Share	15.63	13.41	12.78	11.62
Price / Book Value %	137.56	156.15	156.49	137.69
Dividends Per Share	0.60	0.60	0.55	0.47
Annual Financial Data				
Operating Results (000's)				
Net Interest Income	9,409.0	8,115.0	6,225.0	5,637.0
Loan Loss Provision	-120.0	n.a.	n.a.	n.a.
Non-Interest Income	2,295.0	1,457.0	1,633.0	1,639.0
Non-Interest Expense	-7,769.0	-6,943.0	-5,295.0	-4,772.0
Income Before Taxes and Other	3,815.0	2,629.0	2,563.0	2,504.0
Other Items	n.a.	n.a.	n.a.	n.a.
Income Tax	-1,260.0	-864.0	-749.0	-763.0
Net Income	2,555.0	1,765.0	1,814.0	1,741.0
Balance Sheet (000's)				
Cash & Securities	62,949.0	65,811.0	53,833.0	51,089.0
Loans, Net	131,099.0	120,483.0	76,374.0	73,668.0
Fixed Assets, Net	6,074.0	6,437.0	5,068.0	4,841.0
Total Assets	203,412.0	195,660.0	136,601.0	131,031.0
Deposits	179,913.0	175,190.0	117,065.0	116,195.0
Stockholders' Equity	15,853.0	13,398.0	12,619.0	11,201.0
Performance & Financial Condition				
Net Interest Margin	5.22	5.23	5.20	5.05
Return on Avg Stockholders' Equity %	17.47	13.57	15.23	16.49
Return on Average Assets %	1.28	1.06	1.36	1.58
Equity to Assets %	7.79	6.85	9.24	8.55
Reserve as a % of Non-Performing Loans	787.28	322.44	426.57	611.25

Compound Growth %'s	EPS %	12.67	Net Income %	13.64	Net Interest Income %	18.62

Comments

During January 1996, the banks entered into an agreement and plan of mergers with InterWest Bancorp, Inc., Oak Harbor, Washington and InterWest's subsidiary, InterWest Savings Bank. According to the agreement, Central Bancorp's common stock will be exchanged for shares of InterWest common stock pursuant to a specified exchange ratio. The transaction was still pending when we went to press.

Officers	Position	Ownership Information	12/31/95
Don Wm. Telford	Chairman	Number of Shares Outstanding	1,014,565
Gary M. Boylard	President, CEO	Market Capitalization	$ 21,813,148
Larry Carlson	Secretary	Frequency Of Dividends	Quarterly
Joseph E. Riordan	Treasurer	Number of Shareholders	334
Lonnie DeCamp	Other		

Other Information

Transfer Agent	Company Office			Where Listed	OTC-BB
Auditor	Deloitte & Touche LLP			Symbol	CBWA
Market Maker	Piper Jaffray Inc.	Telephone	(800)328-7488	SIC Code	6020
Broker Dealer	Regular Stockbroker			Employees	148

Central Coal & Coke Corporation

127 W.10th Street, Ste. 666 • Kansas City, MO 64105 • Telephone (816)842-2430 • Fax (816)471-8676

Company Description

The primary business of the Company is the leasing of its interests in real property to others for the exploration and the extraction of coal, oil and gas and for surface use. The Company's property interests consist of whole or part interests in approximately 64,000 acres of real property located in Arkansas, Louisiana, Texas, Kansas, Oklahoma and Missouri. Through a subsidiary, the Company began a fast food bagel and delicatessen business during 1993. Three locations existed at December 31, 1995 with plans for more openings in 1996. The Company was formed in 1936 and incorporated in the State of Delaware.

	12/31/95	12/31/94	12/31/93	12/31/92
Per Share Information				
Stock Price	30.00	27.50	26.00	26.00
Earnings Per Share	2.22	1.26	1.22	1.31
Price / Earnings Ratio	13.51	21.83	21.31	19.85
Book Value Per Share	29.16	28.58	28.17	27.95
Price / Book Value %	102.88	96.22	92.30	93.02
Dividends Per Share	1.85	1.00	1.00	1.31
Annual Financial Data				
Operating Results (000's)				
Total Revenues	2,560.4	1,558.8	1,316.4	1,008.1
Costs & Expenses	-1,377.1	-767.8	-474.7	-249.1
Income Before Taxes and Other	1,183.2	791.0	841.7	759.0
Other Items	n.a.	n.a.	-20.0	n.a.
Income Tax	-352.6	-321.6	-367.7	-269.3
Net Income	830.7	469.4	454.0	489.7
Cash Flow From Operations	542.5	285.5	347.2	407.1
Balance Sheet (000's)				
Cash & Equivalents	755.4	1,589.0	1,729.5	6,638.7
Total Current Assets	9,198.4	7,907.8	8,224.6	7,601.0
Fixed Assets, Net	n.a.	n.a.	1,168.4	1,233.6
Total Assets	11,181.5	10,741.7	10,691.1	10,583.1
Total Current Liabilities	244.1	57.0	71.3	53.5
Long-Term Debt	n.a.	n.a.	n.a.	n.a.
Stockholders' Equity	10,899.3	10,684.6	10,609.8	10,529.6
Performance & Financial Condition				
Return on Total Revenues %	32.44	30.11	34.49	48.58
Return on Avg Stockholders' Equity %	7.70	4.41	4.30	4.63
Return on Average Assets %	7.58	4.38	4.27	4.59
Current Ratio	37.69	138.64	115.34	142.13
Debt / Equity %	n.a.	n.a.	n.a.	n.a.

Compound Growth %'s	EPS %	19.22	Net Income %	19.26	Total Revenues %	36.44

Comments

Other Assets consist of equity and government agency securities ($577,000 and $1,607,000 in 1995 and 1994), net coal deposits, mineral rights, surface lands, equipment and leasehold improvements ($1,406,000 and $1,226,000 in 1995 and 1994). Coal deposits, mineral rights and surface lands were acquired from a trustee in bankruptcy and are recorded at the valuations placed on them by the receivers in bankruptcy in 1931.

Officers	Position	Ownership Information	12/31/95
Beekman Winthrop	President	Number of Shares Outstanding	373,830
S.M. Riddle	Secretary	Market Capitalization	$ 11,214,900
Leonard Noah	Vice President, Treasurer	Frequency Of Dividends	Quarterly
Gary J. Pennington	General Manager	Number of Shareholders	530
Ernest N. Yarnevich, Jr.	Other		

Other Information

Transfer Agent	UMB Bank			Where Listed	OTC-BB
Auditor	KPMG Peat Marwick LLP			Symbol	CCCK
Market Maker	Chicago Corporation, The	Telephone	(312)855-7664	SIC Code	6792
Broker Dealer	Regular Stockbroker			Employees	89

Central Coast Bancorp

301 Main Street • Salinas, CA 93901 • Telephone (408)422-6642 • Fax (408)422-2037

Company Description

Central Coast Bancorp was organized in 1994 to act as the bank holding company of Bank of Salinas which had been operating since 1983. The Bank has two branches in Salinas and King City, California and offers a wide range of bank services to individuals, merchants, small and medium-sized businesses, professionals and agribusiness enterprises.

	12/31/95	12/31/94	12/31/93	12/31/92
Per Share Information				
Stock Price	16.13	12.61	9.74	9.96
Earnings Per Share	1.61	1.15	1.06	0.86
Price / Earnings Ratio	10.02	10.97	9.19	11.58
Book Value Per Share	11.73	9.98	8.74	7.64
Price / Book Value %	137.51	126.35	111.44	130.37
Dividends Per Share	n.a.	n.a.	n.a.	n.a.
Annual Financial Data				
Operating Results (000's)				
Net Interest Income	14,957.0	12,867.0	10,746.0	9,537.0
Loan Loss Provision	-545.0	-1,535.0	-605.0	-707.0
Non-Interest Income	738.0	729.0	776.0	784.0
Non-Interest Expense	-8,288.0	-7,256.0	-6,652.0	-5,836.0
Income Before Taxes and Other	6,862.0	4,805.0	4,265.0	3,778.0
Other Items	n.a.	n.a.	n.a.	n.a.
Income Tax	-2,974.0	-2,045.0	-1,760.0	-1,556.0
Net Income	3,888.0	2,760.0	2,505.0	2,222.0
Balance Sheet (000's)				
Cash & Securities	146,088.0	113,635.0	77,687.0	62,561.0
Loans, Net	161,780.0	159,228.0	158,950.0	147,816.0
Fixed Assets, Net	728.0	855.0	661.0	546.0
Total Assets	313,533.0	278,295.0	240,349.0	213,138.0
Deposits	286,488.0	255,346.0	220,428.0	195,932.0
Stockholders' Equity	25,986.0	22,064.0	19,221.0	16,548.0
Performance & Financial Condition				
Net Interest Margin	5.60	5.50	5.00	n.a.
Return on Avg Stockholders' Equity %	16.18	13.37	14.01	14.46
Return on Average Assets %	1.31	1.06	1.10	1.13
Equity to Assets %	8.29	7.93	8.00	7.76
Reserve as a % of Non-Performing Loans	482.91	144.04	86.18	2365.88

Compound Growth %'s	EPS %	23.25	Net Income %	20.50	Net Interest Income %	16.18

Comments

The Bank has had stock dividends in each of the last four years. Per share amounts have been retated for consistency. In December, 1995, the Company signed a definitive agreement to acquire Cypress Coast Bank whereby Cypress would become a subsidiary of the Company and continue to operate from its branches in Seaside and Marina, California. Shareholders of Cypress will receive common stock of the Company based upon a conversion ratio. Cypress has total assets of $43.7 million from which it makes commercial and real estate loans representing 40% and 57% of total loans, respectively. Officers and directors own 29% of total shares outstanding.

Officers	Position	Ownership Information	12/31/95
Nick Ventimiglia	President, CEO	Number of Shares Outstanding	2,214,630
John F. McCarthy	Exec VP, COO	Market Capitalization	$ 35,721,982
Esther Kiefer-Miyamoto	Senior VP, Controller	Frequency Of Dividends	Irregular
Thomas A. Sa	CFO, Secretary	Number of Shareholders	886

Other Information

Transfer Agent	Chemical Mellon Shareholder Services			Where Listed	OTC-PS
Auditor	Deloitte & Touche LLP			Symbol	BSLI
Market Maker	Dean Witter	Telephone	(212)524-3790	SIC Code	6020
Broker Dealer	Regular Stockbroker			Employees	127

Central Investment Corporation

10560 Ashview Place, Ste.250 • Cincinnati, OH 45242-0670 • Telephone (513)563-4700 • Fax (513)563-5912

Company Description

The Company's principal business consists of the bottling and distribution of soft drinks to supermarkets, mass merchandisers, convenience stores and other customers, either directly or through vending machines in certain northern Ohio and southern Florida franchised territories.

	09/30/95	09/30/94	09/30/93	09/30/92
Per Share Information				
Stock Price	310.83	310.00	300.00	261.88
Earnings Per Share	32.76	32.29	51.42	46.49
Price / Earnings Ratio	9.49	9.60	5.83	5.63
Book Value Per Share	491.98	476.73	459.44	415.20
Price / Book Value %	63.18	65.03	65.30	63.07
Dividends Per Share	17.50	15.00	10.00	35.00
Annual Financial Data				
Operating Results (000's)				
Total Revenues	164,792.3	157,924.7	148,502.3	139,762.7
Costs & Expenses	-158,245.6	-148,431.2	-138,196.4	-129,928.1
Income Before Taxes and Other	6,546.7	7,115.8	10,305.9	9,834.7
Other Items	n.a.	n.a.	n.a.	n.a.
Income Tax	-2,464.0	-3,091.2	-3,896.7	-3,931.6
Net Income	4,082.7	4,024.6	6,409.2	5,903.0
Cash Flow From Operations	10,335.7	11,397.3	7,513.4	12,394.8
Balance Sheet (000's)				
Cash & Equivalents	5,089.2	7,588.2	6,269.1	5,035.5
Total Current Assets	36,310.9	36,453.2	34,417.7	35,294.0
Fixed Assets, Net	34,936.6	34,017.2	31,036.1	26,822.9
Total Assets	80,562.5	79,173.8	74,640.7	69,429.4
Total Current Liabilities	8,532.6	8,742.2	7,732.9	7,897.4
Long-Term Debt	5,701.5	6,481.6	5,314.9	3,943.7
Stockholders' Equity	61,321.4	59,419.9	57,264.9	52,718.9
Performance & Financial Condition				
Return on Total Revenues %	2.48	2.55	4.32	4.22
Return on Avg Stockholders' Equity %	6.76	6.90	11.65	11.73
Return on Average Assets %	5.11	5.23	8.90	8.76
Current Ratio	4.26	4.17	4.45	4.47
Debt / Equity %	9.30	10.91	9.28	7.48

Compound Growth %'s	EPS %	-11.01	Net Income %	-11.57	Total Revenues %	5.64

Comments

1994 results include a nonrecurring expense of $2,377,758, or $1.91 per share. Cash flow is very significant. A key question is how the Company will reinvest its available cash and if that will restore return on equity to historical levels.

Officers	Position	Ownership Information	09/30/95
Keven E. Shell	Vice President, Treasurer	Number of Shares Outstanding	124,640
		Market Capitalization	$ 38,741,851
		Frequency Of Dividends	Quarterly
		Number of Shareholders	Under 500

Other Information

Transfer Agent	Star Bank, Cincinnati, OH			Where Listed	OTC-BB
Auditor	J.D. Cloud & Co. PLL			Symbol	COHI
Market Maker	Chicago Corporation, The	Telephone	(312)855-7664	SIC Code	2086
Broker Dealer	Regular Stockbroker			Employees	25

Central Sierra Bank

P.O. Box 729 • San Andreas, CA 95249 • Telephone (209)754-3000 • Fax (209)754-3709

Company Description

Central Sierra Bank is a California State chartered bank which commenced operations in 1981. The Bank's operations have been designed to meet the banking needs of individuals and small to medium size businesses in the central Sierra area of California through its six branches.

	12/31/95	12/31/94	12/31/93	12/31/92
Per Share Information				
Stock Price	10.13	8.00	8.50	7.50
Earnings Per Share	1.41	1.23	1.07	1.00
Price / Earnings Ratio	7.18	6.50	7.94	7.50
Book Value Per Share	9.61	8.89	8.21	7.50
Price / Book Value %	105.41	89.99	103.53	100.00
Dividends Per Share	0.69	0.54	0.54	0.54
Annual Financial Data				
Operating Results (000's)				
Net Interest Income	4,565.9	4,695.8	4,383.8	4,285.5
Loan Loss Provision	-102.5	-135.0	-204.7	-200.8
Non-Interest Income	741.7	731.2	814.1	749.7
Non-Interest Expense	-3,403.8	-3,733.7	-3,649.1	-3,579.0
Income Before Taxes and Other	1,801.4	1,558.3	1,344.1	1,255.4
Other Items	n.a.	n.a.	n.a.	n.a.
Income Tax	-737.2	-631.1	-535.6	-498.2
Net Income	1,064.2	927.2	808.5	757.2
Balance Sheet (000's)				
Cash & Securities	35,104.7	26,485.5	25,813.9	28,770.0
Loans, Net	47,556.7	46,129.2	49,015.1	48,534.7
Fixed Assets, Net	1,950.3	1,778.1	1,917.4	2,187.2
Total Assets	86,020.7	75,797.2	77,685.7	80,185.1
Deposits	77,870.1	68,642.1	70,974.2	73,903.0
Stockholders' Equity	7,260.1	6,717.0	6,197.6	5,661.0
Performance & Financial Condition				
Net Interest Margin	n.a.	n.a.	n.a.	n.a.
Return on Avg Stockholders' Equity %	15.23	14.36	13.64	13.88
Return on Average Assets %	1.32	1.21	1.02	1.05
Equity to Assets %	8.44	8.86	7.98	7.06
Reserve as a % of Non-Performing Loans	77.12	120.85	75.22	n.a.

Compound Growth %'s	EPS %	12.13	Net Income %	12.01	Net Interest Income %	2.14

Comments

Real estate loans, excluding agriculture, comprise 81.2% of all loans. Approximately 71% of the entire loan portfolio was either on a floating rate basis and/or maturities of twelve months or less. Although their numbers look strong, management reports that the last several years were difficult ones. They look forward to 1996 which shows signs of significant new real estate development and other attractions to its service area.

Officers	Position	Ownership Information	12/31/95
Clarence E. Hartley	Chairman, CEO	Number of Shares Outstanding	755,257
David L. Redman	Exec VP	Market Capitalization	$ 7,650,753
David C. Vietmeier	Vice President, Head Cashier	Frequency Of Dividends	Quarterly
		Number of Shareholders	n.a.

Other Information			
Transfer Agent	Company Office	Where Listed	BE
Auditor	Arthur Andersen LLP	Symbol	CESR
Market Maker	Hoefer & Arnett, Inc.	Telephone (415)362-7160	SIC Code	6020
Broker Dealer	Regular Stockbroker	Employees	68

Central Steel and Wire Company

3000 W. 51st Street • Chicago, IL 60632-2198 • Telephone (312)471-3800 • Fax (800)232-9279

Company Description

The Company distributes, from its service centers, processed and unprocessed ferrous and non-ferrous metals in many forms purchased from producing mills or specialty mills. The Company carries about 21,000 separate inventory items in plants located in Chicago, Detroit, Cincinnati and Milwaukee. Central Steel & Wire Company was founded on 1908.

	12/31/95	12/31/94	12/31/93	12/31/92
Per Share Information				
Stock Price	585.00	587.50	600.00	590.00
Earnings Per Share	61.26	49.56	19.58	-21.86
Price / Earnings Ratio	9.55	11.85	30.64	n.a.
Book Value Per Share	498.70	478.32	468.53	471.43
Price / Book Value %	117.30	122.83	128.06	125.15
Dividends Per Share	40.00	40.00	22.00	22.00
Annual Financial Data				
Operating Results (000's)				
Total Revenues	628,700.0	596,400.0	504,200.0	460,700.0
Costs & Expenses	-599,000.0	-572,500.0	-494,800.0	-456,900.0
Income Before Taxes and Other	29,700.0	23,900.0	9,400.0	3,800.0
Other Items	n.a.	n.a.	n.a.	-8,600.0
Income Tax	-12,300.0	-9,700.0	-3,800.0	-1,500.0
Net Income	17,400.0	14,200.0	5,600.0	-6,300.0
Cash Flow From Operations	39,300.0	10,700.0	18,400.0	-9,000.0
Balance Sheet (000's)				
Cash & Equivalents	54,400.0	33,000.0	44,500.0	40,300.0
Total Current Assets	197,100.0	206,600.0	168,200.0	155,500.0
Fixed Assets, Net	34,200.0	34,900.0	29,100.0	25,800.0
Total Assets	238,400.0	248,200.0	203,700.0	187,400.0
Total Current Liabilities	80,400.0	95,300.0	54,500.0	37,800.0
Long-Term Debt	n.a.	n.a.	n.a.	n.a.
Stockholders' Equity	141,100.0	136,800.0	134,000.0	135,300.0
Performance & Financial Condition				
Return on Total Revenues %	2.77	2.38	1.11	-1.37
Return on Avg Stockholders' Equity %	12.52	10.49	4.16	-4.45
Return on Average Assets %	7.15	6.28	2.86	-3.30
Current Ratio	2.45	2.17	3.09	4.11
Debt / Equity %	n.a.	n.a.	n.a.	n.a.

Compound Growth %'s	EPS %	76.88	Net Income %	76.27	Total Revenues %	10.92

Comments

On January 4, 1996, president and chief executive officer James R. Lowenstine died. He is deeply missed by his family, friends, community and the Company to which he dedicated more than 50 years of service. Mr. Lowenstine's shares will be retained by a perpetual charitable trust. Management intends for the Company to remain independent which is consistent with Mr. Lowenstine's wishes. Management reports that all plants are in excellent condition. There has been no long term debt for the last 16 years.

Officers	Position	Ownership Information	12/31/95
Frank A. Troike	Chairman, CEO	Number of Shares Outstanding	283,000
Alfred G. Jensen	President	Market Capitalization	$ 165,555,000
John M. Tiernan	Exec VP	Frequency Of Dividends	Quarterly
Edward J. Kentra	Senior VP	Number of Shareholders	300
Michael X. Cronin	Vice President, Secretary		

Other Information					
Transfer Agent	First Chicago Trust Co. of NY			Where Listed	OTC-BB
Auditor	KPMG Peat Marwick LLP			Symbol	CSTW
Market Maker	Herzog, Heine, Geduld, Inc.	Telephone	(800)523-4936	SIC Code	5051
Broker Dealer	Standard Investment	Tel/Ext	(888)783-4688 Jack	Employees	1400

Century Realty Trust

320 N. Meridian St., Ste. 419 • Indianapolis, MN 46204 • Telephone (317)632-5467 • Fax (317)685-1588

Company Description

The principal business of the Trust, is the ownership of income producing properties, which consist of nine apartment complexes, two restaurants, two commercial properties, and various parcels of undeveloped land. The trust has elected to be treated as a real estate investment trust and, as such, distributes substantially all its income and pays only state income tax. The Trust is incorporated and does business in the State of Indiana.

	12/31/95	12/31/94	12/31/93	12/31/92
Per Share Information				
Stock Price	8.82	8.81	8.00	6.50
Earnings Per Share	0.60	0.52	1.66	0.68
Price / Earnings Ratio	14.70	16.94	4.82	9.56
Book Value Per Share	5.84	5.91	6.32	4.99
Price / Book Value %	151.03	149.07	126.58	130.26
Dividends Per Share	0.78	0.75	0.77	0.75
Annual Financial Data				
Operating Results (000's)				
Total Revenues	7,761.5	6,043.7	5,237.4	3,461.3
Costs & Expenses	-6,798.0	-5,225.0	-3,076.9	-2,550.6
Income Before Taxes and Other	963.5	818.7	2,160.5	910.7
Other Items	n.a.	n.a.	n.a.	n.a.
Income Tax	-131.1	-115.7	-74.1	-58.0
Net Income	832.4	703.0	2,086.4	852.7
Cash Flow From Operations	1,887.5	1,440.5	1,407.4	1,377.1
Balance Sheet (000's)				
Cash & Equivalents	483.9	255.7	557.1	287.3
Total Current Assets	793.7	420.7	932.0	409.8
Fixed Assets, Net	29,101.4	22,896.2	17,164.9	6,711.9
Total Assets	30,762.1	24,180.7	18,877.1	7,827.1
Total Current Liabilities	2,103.7	1,068.5	907.9	832.1
Long-Term Debt	19,748.1	14,606.8	10,014.2	780.0
Stockholders' Equity	8,485.5	8,158.8	7,676.8	6,215.0
Performance & Financial Condition				
Return on Total Revenues %	10.72	11.63	39.84	24.63
Return on Avg Stockholders' Equity %	10.00	8.88	30.04	13.70
Return on Average Assets %	3.03	3.27	15.63	10.77
Current Ratio	0.38	0.39	1.03	0.49
Debt / Equity %	232.73	179.03	130.45	12.55

Compound Growth %'s	EPS %	-4.09	Net Income %	-0.80	Total Revenues %	30.89

Comments

The Trust continues to grow in terms of total assets and total revenues. Included in Total Revenues for 1993, is a gain on the disposal of real estate of $1.3 million. As of December 31, 1995, the occupancy rate in apartment properties owned by the Trust was 96%.

Officers	Position	Ownership Information	12/31/95
King R. Traub	President	Number of Shares Outstanding	1,451,939
John I. Bradshaw, Jr.	Exec VP, Secretary	Market Capitalization	$ 12,806,102
John A. Wallace	Treasurer	Frequency Of Dividends	Semi-Annual
		Number of Shareholders	3,700

Other Information

Transfer Agent	Company Office			Where Listed	OTC-BB
Auditor	Ernst & Young LLP			Symbol	CRLTS
Market Maker	First Manhattan Co.	Telephone	(212)756-3411	SIC Code	6510
Broker Dealer	Regular Stockbroker			Employees	35

Chambersburg Engineering Company

150 Derbyshire Street • Chambersburg, PA 17201-0802 • Telephone (717)264-7151 • Fax (717)267-2201

Company Description

The Company engineers and manufactures a line of heavy capital equipment used to shape or form ferrous and non-ferrous metals by impaction. The Company was formed in 1897 and went public in the 1920's. In 1994, the Company entered into a joint venture agreement with a foreign manufacturer of forging equipment. The venture had no operations in 1994 or 1995.

	12/31/95	12/31/94	12/31/93	12/31/92
Per Share Information				
Stock Price	25.00	22.00	22.00	22.00
Earnings Per Share	36.83	0.58	-1.83	-8.59
Price / Earnings Ratio	0.68	37.93	n.a.	n.a.
Book Value Per Share	60.72	24.14	23.56	25.39
Price / Book Value %	41.17	91.14	93.38	86.65
Dividends Per Share	0.25	n.a.	n.a.	n.a.
Annual Financial Data				
Operating Results (000's)				
Total Revenues	6,291.8	3,996.0	4,772.5	5,824.6
Costs & Expenses	-5,054.9	-3,947.6	-4,387.8	-5,681.0
Income Before Taxes and Other	1,237.0	31.2	326.4	-160.5
Other Items	n.a.	n.a.	-371.6	n.a.
Income Tax	482.4	-4.1	-40.0	1.1
Net Income	1,719.4	27.1	-85.2	-159.5
Cash Flow From Operations	1,142.4	543.5	343.7	377.9
Balance Sheet (000's)				
Cash & Equivalents	1,355.2	457.4	82.6	12.3
Total Current Assets	4,298.7	2,629.8	1,793.1	2,721.3
Fixed Assets, Net	281.4	243.8	224.4	279.2
Total Assets	4,697.4	2,898.7	2,042.5	3,025.5
Total Current Liabilities	1,862.6	1,746.2	824.9	1,628.8
Long-Term Debt	n.a.	25.3	117.6	211.4
Stockholders' Equity	2,834.8	1,127.1	1,100.0	1,185.3
Performance & Financial Condition				
Return on Total Revenues %	27.33	0.68	-1.79	-2.74
Return on Avg Stockholders' Equity %	86.79	2.43	-7.46	n.a.
Return on Average Assets %	45.27	1.10	-3.36	n.a.
Current Ratio	2.31	1.51	2.17	1.67
Debt / Equity %	n.a.	2.25	10.69	17.84

Compound Growth %'s	EPS %	6250.00	Net Income %	6251.81	Total Revenues %	2.61

Comments

1993 and 1992 results included nonrecurring expenses related to discontinued operations of $371,620 and $241,352, or $7.98 and $5.18 per share, respectively. The rebound of revenue and earnings is attributable to a revival of activity in the impression die forging industry. Back orders for new state-of-the-art machinery as well as for parts for older machinery are at record levels. Compound growth rates are misleading because of losses in 1992 and 1993 and a relatively low income in 1994.

Officers	Position	Ownership Information	12/31/95
Eugene C. Clarke	Chairman	Number of Shares Outstanding	46,684
Samuel C. Clarke	President	Market Capitalization	$ 1,167,100
Erma M. Fleming	Secretary	Frequency Of Dividends	Annual
George A. Davis	Treasurer	Number of Shareholders	Under 500

Other Information			
Transfer Agent	Company Office	Where Listed	OTC-PS
Auditor	Mathieson Aitken Jemison	Symbol	CEGR
Market Maker	Carr Securities Corporation	Telephone (800)221-2243	SIC Code	3540
Broker Dealer	Regular Stockbroker	Employees	55

Charter National Bancorp, Inc.

P.O.Box 400 • Taylor, MI 48180 • Telephone (313)285-1900 • Fax (313)285-1339

Company Description

Charter National Bancorp, Inc. is a bank holding company for its wholly owned subsidiary, Charter National Bank. The Bank offers standard banking services through eight offices in Wayne County, Michigan.

	12/31/95	12/31/94	12/31/93	12/31/92
Per Share Information				
Stock Price	40.50	34.06	32.37	30.00
Earnings Per Share	6.92	5.65	4.28	5.04
Price / Earnings Ratio	5.85	6.03	7.56	5.95
Book Value Per Share	56.16	49.06	48.47	45.54
Price / Book Value %	72.12	69.43	66.78	65.88
Dividends Per Share	3.00	2.50	1.75	1.50
Annual Financial Data				
Operating Results (000's)				
Net Interest Income	9,343.0	8,627.0	7,533.0	7,135.0
Loan Loss Provision	-220.0	-225.0	-100.0	-150.0
Non-Interest Income	2,359.0	1,939.0	1,682.0	2,215.0
Non-Interest Expense	-7,706.0	-7,385.0	-6,869.0	-6,688.0
Income Before Taxes and Other	3,776.0	2,956.0	2,246.0	2,512.0
Other Items	n.a.	n.a.	n.a.	n.a.
Income Tax	-1,311.0	-936.0	-710.0	-701.0
Net Income	2,465.0	2,020.0	1,536.0	1,811.0
Balance Sheet (000's)				
Cash & Securities	96,069.0	74,044.0	57,349.0	60,629.0
Loans, Net	115,838.0	106,052.0	108,015.0	105,122.0
Fixed Assets, Net	4,805.0	3,922.0	2,732.0	2,787.0
Total Assets	219,997.0	186,792.0	170,490.0	171,515.0
Deposits	189,081.0	166,741.0	150,573.0	151,970.0
Stockholders' Equity	20,005.0	17,481.0	17,410.0	16,360.0
Performance & Financial Condition				
Net Interest Margin	n.a.	n.a.	n.a.	n.a.
Return on Avg Stockholders' Equity %	13.15	11.58	9.10	11.52
Return on Average Assets %	1.21	1.13	0.90	1.06
Equity to Assets %	9.09	9.36	10.21	9.54
Reserve as a % of Non-Performing Loans	736.84	n.a.	1969.33	281.20

Compound Growth %'s	EPS %	11.15	Net Income %	10.82	Net Interest Income %	9.40

Comments

The loan portfolio of the Bank consists of commercial, real estate, home equity and installment loans, representing 60%, 17%, 16% and 7% of total loans, respectively. The Bank opened its eighth office during 1995. Although the Bank has experienced declines in earnings in both 1990 and 1993, the returns on assets and equity have all been favorable. The Bank was originally opened in 1933 with $165,000 of capital and a handful of employees. It has been profitable in every year of its existence.

Officers	Position	Ownership Information	12/31/95
Charles A. Brethen, Jr.	Chairman	Number of Shares Outstanding	356,236
Robert M. Taylor	President, CEO	Market Capitalization	$ 14,427,558
Paul R. Krueger	Exec VP, Secretary	Frequency Of Dividends	Quarterly
Richard S. Metzger	Senior VP	Number of Shareholders	n.a.
Alan L. Anderson	Treasurer		

Other Information				
Transfer Agent	Company Office		Where Listed	OTC-BB
Auditor	Plante & Moran, LLP		Symbol	CNAT
Market Maker	McDonald & Company Securities	Telephone (216)443-2350	SIC Code	6020
Broker Dealer	Regular Stockbroker		Employees	136

Cherokee Equity Corporation

3022 Vanderbilt Place • Nashville, TN 37212 • Telephone (615)327-4089 • Fax (615)327-4626

Company Description

The Company has two major lines of business: a marine terminal, located in Nashville, Tennessee, and real estate operations located in Tennessee, Mississippi and Kentucky. The marine terminal provides loading, unloading, storage and barge towing services. The Company was spun-off to shareholders of Cherokee Insurance Co. in 1968.

	12/31/95	12/31/94	12/31/93	12/31/92
Per Share Information				
Stock Price	19.50	18.00	18.00	18.00
Earnings Per Share	2.07	2.12	4.05	0.83
Price / Earnings Ratio	9.42	8.49	4.44	21.69
Book Value Per Share	52.19	39.36	41.76	24.64
Price / Book Value %	37.36	45.73	43.10	73.05
Dividends Per Share	n.a.	n.a.	n.a.	n.a.
Annual Financial Data				
Operating Results (000's)				
Total Revenues	5,707.3	5,584.9	3,816.0	4,660.4
Costs & Expenses	-4,730.0	-4,501.8	-3,244.2	-4,413.9
Income Before Taxes and Other	977.3	1,083.1	571.8	246.5
Other Items	117.1	69.1	1,045.8	0.7
Income Tax	-354.8	-397.1	-168.7	53.6
Net Income	739.6	755.2	1,448.9	300.8
Cash Flow From Operations	1,093.7	1,450.2	935.6	646.1
Balance Sheet (000's)				
Cash & Equivalents	325.2	1,358.6	813.6	286.5
Total Current Assets	15,329.7	10,241.8	11,252.7	3,704.3
Fixed Assets, Net	11,159.1	10,733.7	6,310.5	6,737.7
Total Assets	34,395.8	26,793.2	21,642.0	13,679.2
Total Current Liabilities	6,759.1	2,577.5	2,956.5	607.6
Long-Term Debt	7,977.5	9,242.6	2,349.9	2,636.3
Stockholders' Equity	19,243.1	14,687.8	14,924.4	8,892.2
Performance & Financial Condition				
Return on Total Revenues %	12.96	13.52	37.97	6.46
Return on Avg Stockholders' Equity %	4.36	5.10	12.17	3.43
Return on Average Assets %	2.42	3.12	8.20	2.51
Current Ratio	2.27	3.97	3.81	6.10
Debt / Equity %	41.46	62.93	15.75	29.65

Compound Growth %'s	EPS %	35.61	Net Income %	34.96	Total Revenues %	6.99

Comments

1993 results include a nonrecurring benefit of $1 million due to the adoption of GAAP for the reporting of income taxes. The per share price may look attractive as compared to book value, but the earnings performance appears weak. The true value may be in the underlying assets, particularly the real estate.

Officers	Position	Ownership Information	12/31/95
David K. Wilson	Chairman	Number of Shares Outstanding	356,764
William M. Wilson	President	Market Capitalization	$ 6,956,898
Wilma T. Ward	Secretary	Frequency Of Dividends	n.a.
James R. Sweeney	Treasurer	Number of Shareholders	Under 500
Frank M. Farris, Jr.	Vice President		

Other Information

Transfer Agent	Company Office			Where Listed	OTC-BB
Auditor	Byrd, Proctor & Mills, PC			Symbol	CQTY
Market Maker	Robotti & Eng, Incorporated	Telephone	(212)986-4800	SIC Code	4499
Broker Dealer	Standard Investment	Tel/Ext	(800)746-5743 Jack	Employees	10

Chesapeake Investors, Inc.

11785 Beltsville Dr. Ste. 1600 • Beltsville, MD 20705-3121 • Telephone (301)572-7800 • Fax (301)572-4797

Company Description

The Company is a diversified, closed-end management investment company with a portfolio consisting of tax exempt municipal bonds.

	09/30/95	09/30/94	09/30/93	09/30/92
Per Share Information				
Stock Price	3.12	4.00	4.00	3.00
Earnings Per Share	0.31	-0.06	0.38	0.36
Price / Earnings Ratio	10.06	n.a.	10.53	8.33
Book Value Per Share	4.19	4.16	4.49	4.42
Price / Book Value %	74.46	96.15	89.09	67.87
Dividends Per Share	0.28	0.29	0.30	0.32
Annual Financial Data				
Operating Results (000's)				
Total Revenues	1,294.4	1,229.7	1,570.7	1,522.2
Costs & Expenses	-117.7	-119.8	-117.1	-121.1
Income Before Taxes and Other	1,176.7	-99.7	1,453.7	1,401.2
Other Items	n.a.	n.a.	n.a.	n.a.
Income Tax	n.a.	n.a.	n.a.	n.a.
Net Income	1,176.7	-99.7	1,453.7	1,401.2
Cash Flow From Operations	1,176.7	-99.7	1,453.7	1,401.2
Balance Sheet (000's)				
Cash & Equivalents	n.a.	n.a.	n.a.	n.a.
Total Current Assets	n.a.	n.a.	n.a.	n.a.
Fixed Assets, Net	n.a.	n.a.	n.a.	n.a.
Total Assets	15,884.1	15,774.8	17,013.5	16,727.8
Total Current Liabilities	24.0	22.5	35.8	21.7
Long-Term Debt	n.a.	n.a.	n.a.	n.a.
Stockholders' Equity	15,860.1	15,752.4	16,977.8	16,706.2
Performance & Financial Condition				
Return on Total Revenues %	90.91	-8.11	92.55	92.05
Return on Avg Stockholders' Equity %	7.44	-0.61	8.63	8.44
Return on Average Assets %	7.43	-0.61	8.62	8.42
Current Ratio	n.a.	n.a.	n.a.	n.a.
Debt / Equity %	n.a.	n.a.	n.a.	n.a.

Compound Growth %'s	EPS %	-4.86	Net Income %	-5.65	Total Revenues %	-5.26

Comments

Buying this stock at a discount from the current valuation of the bond portfolio should result in a higher tax free yield than could be obtained by a direct purchase of similar bonds.

Officers	Position	Ownership Information	09/30/95
Albert W. Turner	Chairman	Number of Shares Outstanding	3,783,960
Warren W. Pearce, Jr.	President	Market Capitalization	$ 11,805,955
Herdon G. Kilby	Secretary, Treasurer	Frequency Of Dividends	Quarterly
		Number of Shareholders	Under 500

Other Information

Transfer Agent	Registrar & Transfer Company, NJ		Where Listed	OTC-BB
Auditor	Stoy, Malone & Company, PC		Symbol	CPVI
Market Maker	Mayer & Schweitzer, Inc.	Telephone (800)631-3094	SIC Code	6799
Broker Dealer	Regular Stockbroker		Employees	2

Chillicothe Telephone Company

68 E. Main Street • Chillicothe, OH 45601-2503 • Telephone (614)772-8244 • Fax (614)775-5151

Company Description

The Company provides basic local service, network access and various other telephone company services to customers in seven states. It celebrated 100 years in business in 1995. Alltel Corporation (NYSE) acquired a 20% interest in 1990. The Company is now reorganizing under a new parent company named Horizon Telcom, Inc.

	12/31/95	12/31/94	12/31/93	12/31/92
Per Share Information				
Stock Price	277.00	250.00	232.00	162.00
Earnings Per Share	33.24	30.18	33.88	35.47
Price / Earnings Ratio	8.33	8.28	6.85	4.57
Book Value Per Share	295.10	279.93	266.49	249.61
Price / Book Value %	93.87	89.31	87.06	64.90
Dividends Per Share	17.40	17.40	17.00	16.00
Annual Financial Data				
Operating Results (000's)				
Total Revenues	34,700.8	30,675.2	25,811.8	25,119.1
Costs & Expenses	-27,698.3	-24,079.7	-17,415.5	-16,238.2
Income Before Taxes and Other	6,953.0	6,311.0	7,113.9	7,296.7
Other Items	n.a.	n.a.	n.a.	n.a.
Income Tax	-3,638.6	-3,301.8	-3,735.2	-3,759.3
Net Income	3,314.4	3,009.3	3,378.7	3,537.3
Cash Flow From Operations	7,976.8	4,835.8	6,562.0	6,617.2
Balance Sheet (000's)				
Cash & Equivalents	1,213.3	802.4	2,184.2	1,110.1
Total Current Assets	9,326.8	9,850.5	8,540.3	7,236.9
Fixed Assets, Net	40,628.6	38,381.9	36,495.6	34,667.6
Total Assets	54,161.0	51,985.8	48,509.8	44,730.8
Total Current Liabilities	7,714.2	7,757.7	5,649.6	7,660.8
Long-Term Debt	10,300.0	10,400.0	10,100.0	5,943.8
Stockholders' Equity	29,429.4	27,850.2	26,576.1	24,892.8
Performance & Financial Condition				
Return on Total Revenues %	9.55	9.81	13.09	14.08
Return on Avg Stockholders' Equity %	11.57	11.06	13.13	14.79
Return on Average Assets %	6.24	5.99	7.25	7.76
Current Ratio	1.21	1.27	1.51	0.94
Debt / Equity %	35.00	37.34	38.00	23.88

Compound Growth %'s	EPS %	-2.14	Net Income %	-2.15	Total Revenues %	11.37

Comments

The Company aggressively expands new product lines. The operator services department grew 35% in 1994. 1995 and 1996 displays a major commitment to the new wireless (PCS) market. The annual report reveals a company dedicated to its community, employees and shareholders.

Officers	Position	Ownership Information	12/31/95
Robert McKell	Chairman	Number of Shares Outstanding	99,726
Thomas McKell	President	Market Capitalization	$ 27,624,102
Gary L. Seitz	COO	Frequency Of Dividends	Quarterly
Jack E. Thompson	Secretary, Treasurer	Number of Shareholders	315

Other Information

Transfer Agent	Company Office			Where Listed	OTC-BB
Auditor	Arthur Andersen & Co LLP			Symbol	CHIL
Market Maker	A.G. Edwards & Sons, Inc.	Telephone	(800)325-8197	SIC Code	4810
Broker Dealer	Regular Stockbroker			Employees	263

Christian Brothers, Inc.

P.O. Box C • Warroad, MN 56763-1003 • Telephone (218)386-1111 • Fax (218)386-2067

Company Description

The Company is engaged in the manufacturing and distribution of hockey sticks and related products primarily to the Canadian and U.S. markets. In 1994, the Company introduced a new line of inline sticks, blades and balls as well as their own line of protective equipment for both inline and ice hockey. The Company has been repurchasing small amounts of its shares every year.

	12/31/95	12/31/94	12/31/93	12/31/92
Per Share Information				
Stock Price	13.50	15.00	13.00	9.00
Earnings Per Share	-0.37	-0.76	1.07	2.74
Price / Earnings Ratio	n.a.	n.a.	12.15	3.28
Book Value Per Share	11.70	12.07	12.92	11.90
Price / Book Value %	115.38	124.28	100.62	75.63
Dividends Per Share	n.a.	n.a.	n.a.	n.a.
Annual Financial Data				
Operating Results (000's)				
Total Revenues	5,721.6	5,651.9	5,989.5	7,179.2
Costs & Expenses	-5,853.8	-5,980.0	-5,678.9	-6,183.2
Income Before Taxes and Other	-140.7	-328.1	310.6	996.1
Other Items	n.a.	n.a.	n.a.	n.a.
Income Tax	59.4	160.0	-68.1	-373.4
Net Income	-81.3	-168.1	242.5	622.7
Cash Flow From Operations	301.2	-400.6	162.1	618.4
Balance Sheet (000's)				
Cash & Equivalents	106.2	165.5	216.2	126.4
Total Current Assets	3,276.8	3,639.9	3,589.2	3,371.0
Fixed Assets, Net	508.0	580.2	585.1	586.3
Total Assets	4,106.1	4,550.2	4,359.5	4,179.4
Total Current Liabilities	1,537.3	1,867.6	1,441.4	1,486.2
Long-Term Debt	n.a.	n.a.	n.a.	n.a.
Stockholders' Equity	2,568.9	2,682.6	2,908.6	2,693.3
Performance & Financial Condition				
Return on Total Revenues %	-1.42	-2.97	4.05	8.67
Return on Avg Stockholders' Equity %	-3.10	-6.01	8.66	25.84
Return on Average Assets %	-1.88	-3.77	5.68	15.09
Current Ratio	2.13	1.95	2.49	2.27
Debt / Equity %	n.a.	n.a.	n.a.	n.a.

Compound Growth %'s	EPS % n.a.	Net Income % n.a.	Total Revenues % -7.29

Comments

Declining sales in recent years are in part attributable to the weak Canadian dollar. 1994 results were particularly bad, in part because of an inventory writedown. Credit lines require the personal guarantees of the principal officers. However, there is no long term debt and the current ratio is not showing any strain. Early bookings indicate strong first year sales of the new protective equipment products, according to management.

Officers	Position	Ownership Information	12/31/95
Harold O. Bakke, Jr.	President	Number of Shares Outstanding	219,615
Dick L. Johnson	Secretary	Market Capitalization	$ 2,964,803
Roger A. Christian	Treasurer	Frequency Of Dividends	Irregular
William D. Christian	Vice President	Number of Shareholders	Under 500

Other Information				
Transfer Agent	American Bank, St. Paul, MN		Where Listed	OTC-PS
Auditor	Brady, Martz & Associates, PC		Symbol	CHBI
Market Maker	Folger Nolan Fleming Douglas	Telephone (800)326-3633	SIC Code	3940
Broker Dealer	Regular Stockbroker		Employees	65

Chromaline Corporation

4832 Grand Avenue • Duluth, MN 55807-2743 • Telephone (218)628-2217 • Fax (218)628-3245

Company Description

The Company develops and manufactures high quality photochemical imaging systems for sale primarily to a wide range of printers and decorators of surfaces. Applications include circuit boards, fine china, billboards, glassware and textiles. The Company started in 1952 as a screen printer of precision graphics. It went public in 1961. The Company has bought back 11% of its stock over recent years.

	12/31/95	12/31/94	12/31/93	12/31/92
Per Share Information				
Stock Price	6.81	5.50	2.87	2.81
Earnings Per Share	0.65	0.43	0.13	0.16
Price / Earnings Ratio	10.48	12.79	22.08	17.56
Book Value Per Share	3.34	2.70	2.27	2.00
Price / Book Value %	203.89	203.70	126.43	140.50
Dividends Per Share	n.a.	n.a.	n.a.	2.13
Annual Financial Data				
Operating Results (000's)				
Total Revenues	7,583.8	6,515.7	4,994.1	4,672.5
Costs & Expenses	-6,787.7	-5,998.5	-4,902.8	-4,445.2
Income Before Taxes and Other	796.1	517.2	91.2	227.3
Other Items	n.a.	n.a.	35.0	n.a.
Income Tax	-296.0	-186.0	-23.0	-99.0
Net Income	500.1	331.2	103.2	128.3
Cash Flow From Operations	452.6	410.3	99.0	154.2
Balance Sheet (000's)				
Cash & Equivalents	132.4	64.1	113.0	56.0
Total Current Assets	2,358.1	1,952.3	1,627.4	1,281.9
Fixed Assets, Net	879.1	768.5	801.9	776.3
Total Assets	3,277.2	2,760.8	2,461.4	2,058.2
Total Current Liabilities	691.7	683.4	688.0	353.9
Long-Term Debt	n.a.	n.a.	21.4	36.8
Stockholders' Equity	2,585.4	2,077.3	1,752.0	1,667.6
Performance & Financial Condition				
Return on Total Revenues %	6.59	5.08	2.07	2.75
Return on Avg Stockholders' Equity %	21.45	17.30	6.04	7.81
Return on Average Assets %	16.57	12.68	4.57	6.43
Current Ratio	3.41	2.86	2.37	3.62
Debt / Equity %	n.a.	n.a.	1.22	2.20

Compound Growth %'s	EPS %	59.56	Net Income %	57.38	Total Revenues %	17.52

Comments

Sales have grown from $1.5 million in 1986 to $7.6 million in 1995, a compounded growth rate of 19.75 %. Management has aggressively set their course on a five year plan.

Officers	Position	Ownership Information	12/31/95
William C. Ulland	Chairman	Number of Shares Outstanding	773,377
Thomas L. Erickson	President, CEO	Market Capitalization	$ 5,266,697
Richard G. Bourman	CFO	Frequency Of Dividends	n.a.
Claude Piquet	VP - Manufacturing	Number of Shareholders	Under 500
Toshifumi Komatsu	VP - Research		

Other Information

Transfer Agent	Norwest Bank Duluth, N.A.			Where Listed	OTC-PS
Auditor	McGladrey & Pullen, LLP			Symbol	CMLH
Market Maker	Adkins Securities, Inc.	Telephone	(800)443-8103	SIC Code	2759
Broker Dealer	Regular Stockbroker			Employees	62

Cimetrix Incorporated

2222 South 950 East • Provo, UT 84606 • Telephone (201)344-7000 • Fax (801)344-7077

Company Description

The Company is engaged in the development, production, and sale of computer software and hardware for manufacturing automation. Products are targeted for current users of automation devices seeking alternative methods to lower the cost of automation and improve production efficiency. Since its incorporation in 1989, the Company has incurred operating losses. These losses have been financed by several stock offerings, the latest in 1995, when the Company sold 1 million of its common shares at a price of $4.00 per share raising $4.0 million. Recently the Company engaged an investment banking firm to explore the possibility of establishing strategic and/or financial relationships which may include the sale or merger of the Company.

	12/31/95	12/31/94	12/31/93	12/31/92
Per Share Information				
Stock Price	7.31	4.13	n.a.	n.a.
Earnings Per Share	-0.16	-0.08	-0.07	-0.05
Price / Earnings Ratio	n.a.	n.a.	n.a.	n.a.
Book Value Per Share	0.49	0.25	-0.03	-0.02
Price / Book Value %	1,491.80	1,652.00	n.a.	n.a.
Dividends Per Share	n.a.	n.a.	n.a.	n.a.
Annual Financial Data				
Operating Results (000's)				
Total Revenues	836.9	530.9	1,141.6	331.9
Costs & Expenses	-3,580.0	-1,961.3	-2,212.0	-1,213.1
Income Before Taxes and Other	-2,743.1	-1,433.1	-1,073.9	-881.2
Other Items	198.8	288.1	n.a.	n.a.
Income Tax	n.a.	n.a.	-0.1	-0.1
Net Income	-2,544.2	-1,145.1	-1,074.0	-881.3
Cash Flow From Operations	-2,944.4	-1,817.2	-775.6	-855.2
Balance Sheet (000's)				
Cash & Equivalents	2,345.5	3,365.2	0.8	8.7
Total Current Assets	3,267.8	3,835.1	229.9	68.7
Fixed Assets, Net	1,732.2	1,271.0	118.2	150.8
Total Assets	9,722.1	5,632.0	351.5	222.8
Total Current Liabilities	337.6	1,451.2	853.4	479.1
Long-Term Debt	271.7	n.a.	33.4	40.6
Stockholders' Equity	9,070.6	3,613.3	-535.3	-296.9
Performance & Financial Condition				
Return on Total Revenues %	-304.00	-215.68	-94.08	-265.50
Return on Avg Stockholders' Equity %	-40.12	-74.40	n.a.	n.a.
Return on Average Assets %	-33.14	-38.27	-373.99	-348.68
Current Ratio	9.68	2.64	0.27	0.14
Debt / Equity %	3.00	n.a.	n.a.	n.a.

Compound Growth %'s	EPS % n.a.	Net Income % n.a.	Total Revenues %	36.11

Comments

As of March 25, 1996, the Company had 18,771,428 shares of its common stock outstanding. The closing quotation on that day was $11.50 per share resulting in a market capitalization of $216.0 million. On that same date officers and directors, as a group, owned 53.6% of the Company's outstanding shares. Prior to the quarter ended December 31,1994, there was no public trading in the Company's stock.

Officers	Position	Ownership Information	12/31/95
Paul A. Bilzerian	President	Number of Shares Outstanding	18,456,103
Steven K. Sorenson	Exec VP	Market Capitalization	$ 134,914,113
Kitt R. Finlinson	CFO, Treasurer	Frequency Of Dividends	n.a.
Robert H. Reback	Vice President	Number of Shareholders	1,200
Xuguang Wang	Vice President		

Other Information

Transfer Agent	First Security Bank of Utah			Where Listed	OTC-BB
Auditor	Pritchett, Siler & Hardy PC			Symbol	CMXX
Market Maker	Alpine Securities Corporation	Telephone	(800)274-5588	SIC Code	7372
Broker Dealer	Regular Stockbroker			Employees	33

Citizens Growth Properties

188 East Capitol Street • Jackson, MS 39225-2728 • Telephone (601)948-4091 • Fax (601)949-4077

Company Description

The Company holds marketable securities and a 34.55% interest in a resort development in Highlands, North Carolina known as Golf Properties, Inc. The officers of the Company oversee these investments without the need for active management. The Company is buying back shares as they become available and acquired 17,300 and 12,100 shares in 1994 and 1993, respectively.

	01/31/95	01/31/94	01/31/93	01/31/92
Per Share Information				
Stock Price	5.75	4.50	2.75	n.a.
Earnings Per Share	0.31	0.36	-0.69	n.a.
Price / Earnings Ratio	18.55	12.50	n.a.	n.a.
Book Value Per Share	9.66	7.92	7.98	n.a.
Price / Book Value %	59.52	56.82	34.46	n.a.
Dividends Per Share	n.a.	n.a.	1.00	n.a.
Annual Financial Data				
Operating Results (000's)				
Total Revenues	129.0	143.0	290.0	n.a.
Costs & Expenses	-56.0	-68.0	-75.0	n.a.
Income Before Taxes and Other	73.0	75.0	215.0	n.a.
Other Items	n.a.	n.a.	n.a.	n.a.
Income Tax	1.0	15.0	4.0	n.a.
Net Income	74.0	90.0	219.0	n.a.
Cash Flow From Operations	-33.0	-26.0	-32.0	n.a.
Balance Sheet (000's)				
Cash & Equivalents	40.0	264.0	142.0	n.a.
Total Current Assets	1,844.0	1,346.0	1,123.0	n.a.
Fixed Assets, Net	n.a.	n.a.	n.a.	n.a.
Total Assets	2,232.0	1,973.0	2,090.0	n.a.
Total Current Liabilities	16.0	18.0	24.0	n.a.
Long-Term Debt	n.a.	n.a.	n.a.	n.a.
Stockholders' Equity	2,216.0	1,955.0	2,066.0	n.a.
Performance & Financial Condition				
Return on Total Revenues %	57.36	62.94	75.52	n.a.
Return on Avg Stockholders' Equity %	3.55	4.48	10.21	n.a.
Return on Average Assets %	3.52	4.43	10.11	n.a.
Current Ratio	115.25	74.78	46.79	n.a.
Debt / Equity %	n.a.	n.a.	n.a.	n.a.

Compound Growth %'s	EPS % -13.89	Net Income % -41.87	Total Revenues % -33.30

Comments

The joint venture interest is on the balance sheet at $388,000 and produced income of $76,000 in the year ended January, 1995. There is no estimate of current value available. The January, 1996, results are not available until July, 1996.

Officers	Position	Ownership Information	01/31/95
David R. Bell	Chairman	Number of Shares Outstanding	229,392
Brent D. Baird	President, CEO	Market Capitalization	$ 1,319,004
David Fowler	Vice President	Frequency Of Dividends	n.a.
Susan Egger	Vice President, Treasurer	Number of Shareholders	Under 500

Other Information

Transfer Agent	Society National Bank			Where Listed	OTC-BB
Auditor	Ernst & Young			Symbol	CITGS
Market Maker	Carr Securities Corporation	Telephone	(800)221-2243	SIC Code	6790
Broker Dealer	Regular Stockbroker			Employees	None

Citizens' Electric Company

1775 Industrial Boulevard • Lewisburg, PA 17837 • Telephone (717)524-2231 • Fax (717)634-2680

Company Description

The Company provides electrial service in the area in and around Lewisburg, Pennylvania, through production and redistribution of purchased power. The Company takes pride in having been a private investor utility since 1911.

	12/31/95	12/31/94	12/31/93	12/31/92
Per Share Information				
Stock Price	26.00	26.00	25.75	22.00
Earnings Per Share	3.45	3.39	3.41	3.36
Price / Earnings Ratio	7.54	7.67	7.55	6.55
Book Value Per Share	38.62	35.80	33.56	31.74
Price / Book Value %	67.32	72.63	76.73	69.31
Dividends Per Share	1.68	1.64	1.60	1.56
Annual Financial Data				
Operating Results (000's)				
Total Revenues	9,253.6	9,162.6	9,377.5	9,431.4
Costs & Expenses	-8,494.8	-8,396.7	-8,616.2	-8,661.0
Income Before Taxes and Other	746.9	753.7	751.4	757.5
Other Items	n.a.	n.a.	n.a.	n.a.
Income Tax	-271.3	-286.2	-280.6	-293.7
Net Income	475.6	467.5	470.7	463.8
Cash Flow From Operations	n.a.	n.a.	n.a.	n.a.
Balance Sheet (000's)				
Cash & Equivalents	1,173.5	1,216.6	1,196.7	1,105.2
Total Current Assets	1,959.9	1,899.9	1,879.3	1,828.2
Fixed Assets, Net	4,907.2	4,701.3	4,609.7	4,400.1
Total Assets	7,705.3	7,215.1	6,955.5	6,684.4
Total Current Liabilities	1,516.3	1,323.1	1,438.3	1,430.5
Long-Term Debt	141.5	171.0	200.6	230.1
Stockholders' Equity	5,312.6	4,937.7	4,628.0	4,378.0
Performance & Financial Condition				
Return on Total Revenues %	5.14	5.10	5.02	4.92
Return on Avg Stockholders' Equity %	9.28	9.77	10.45	10.90
Return on Average Assets %	6.38	6.60	6.90	7.11
Current Ratio	1.29	1.44	1.31	1.28
Debt / Equity %	2.66	3.46	4.33	5.26

Compound Growth %'s	EPS %	0.89	Net Income %	0.84	Total Revenues %	-0.63

Comments

The Company is a consistent performer. The audit report is available only at the Company's office. The 1995 shareholder's letter indicates that the Company was named as a potentially responsible party for a site declared contaminated by the EPA. The Company has not completed its assessment of the exposure to loss, if any.

Officers	Position	Ownership Information	12/31/95
Eric L. Brouse	President	Number of Shares Outstanding	137,922
Graham C. Showalter	Secretary	Market Capitalization	$ 3,585,972
Bonnie L. Shadle	Vice President, Treasurer	Frequency Of Dividends	Quarterly
Eric W. Winslow	Vice President	Number of Shareholders	Under 500
Kathy A. Zechman	Other		

Other Information				
Transfer Agent	Company Office		Where Listed	OTC-BB
Auditor	Not indicated		Symbol	CZEL
Market Maker	Legg Mason Wood Walker, Inc.	Telephone (212)428-4949	SIC Code	4910
Broker Dealer	Regular Stockbroker		Employees	15

Clayton & Lambert Manufacturing Company

3813 W. Highway 146 • Buckner, KY 40010 • Telephone (502)222-1411 • Fax (502)222-1415

Company Description

The Company manufactures steel panels for in-ground swimming pools as well as parts for steel storage structures. Of the 199,905 original shares issued, most at the time of the public offering in 1949, the Company has reacquired 138,284 shares.

	12/31/94
Per Share Information	
Stock Price	8.00
Earnings Per Share	-0.71
Price / Earnings Ratio	n.a.
Book Value Per Share	7.54
Price / Book Value %	106.10
Dividends Per Share	n.a.
Annual Financial Data	
Operating Results (000's)	
Total Revenues	2,179.3
Costs & Expenses	-2,222.9
Income Before Taxes and Other	-43.6
Other Items	n.a.
Income Tax	n.a.
Net Income	-43.6
Cash Flow From Operations	26.1
Balance Sheet (000's)	
Cash & Equivalents	89.5
Total Current Assets	336.2
Fixed Assets, Net	186.6
Total Assets	522.8
Total Current Liabilities	58.4
Long-Term Debt	n.a.
Stockholders' Equity	464.4
Performance & Financial Condition	
Return on Total Revenues %	-2.00
Return on Avg Stockholders' Equity %	n.a.
Return on Average Assets %	n.a.
Current Ratio	5.75
Debt / Equity %	n.a.

Compound Growth %'s	EPS % n.a.	Net Income % n.a.	Total Revenues % n.a.

Comments

The financial report was compiled by Ernst & Young LLP. It was not audited. The facilities are nearly fully depreciated. In fact, the rental of a warehouse produced $257,355 of revenue in 1994. This would suggest asset values not reflected on the books. However, we do not have information as to the earnings trend at this time.

Officers	Position	Ownership Information	12/31/94
Charles F. Lambert	President, Treasurer	Number of Shares Outstanding	61,621
Neil R. Kinley	Senior VP	Market Capitalization	$ 492,968
Charles F. Lambert, III	Secretary	Frequency Of Dividends	n.a.
John W. Lambert	Director	Number of Shareholders	Under 500
Shirley J. Costigan	Director		

Other Information				
Transfer Agent	Company Office		Where Listed	OTC-BB
Auditor	Ernst & Young LLP		Symbol	CLLA
Market Maker	Carr Securities Corporation	Telephone (800)221-2243	SIC Code	3462
Broker Dealer	Pink sheet specialist		Employees	14

Cloverleaf Kennel Club

P.O. Box 88 • Loveland, CO 80539-0088 • Telephone (970)667-6211 • Fax (970)667-9106

Company Description

The Company is the owner and operator of a state licensed greyhound race track located in Loveland, Colorado, at the intersection of Interstate 25 and Highway 34.

	09/30/95	09/30/94	09/30/93	09/30/92
Per Share Information				
Stock Price	4.00	2.00	3.00	3.87
Earnings Per Share	0.46	0.36	0.36	0.56
Price / Earnings Ratio	8.70	5.56	8.33	6.91
Book Value Per Share	1.71	1.24	1.22	1.60
Price / Book Value %	233.92	161.29	245.90	241.88
Dividends Per Share	n.a.	0.34	0.74	1.25
Annual Financial Data				
Operating Results (000's)				
Total Revenues	43,556.6	38,358.8	42,339.3	46,505.7
Costs & Expenses	-42,980.7	-37,910.2	-41,889.5	-45,806.8
Income Before Taxes and Other	575.9	448.5	449.8	699.0
Other Items	n.a.	n.a.	n.a.	n.a.
Income Tax	-214.2	-166.8	-167.3	-261.0
Net Income	361.8	281.8	282.5	438.0
Cash Flow From Operations	481.8	267.7	346.5	547.9
Balance Sheet (000's)				
Cash & Equivalents	951.6	585.8	603.8	949.3
Total Current Assets	1,052.9	639.8	661.6	1,012.6
Fixed Assets, Net	448.2	408.3	491.4	486.4
Total Assets	1,501.1	1,048.1	1,153.0	1,499.0
Total Current Liabilities	166.5	75.3	195.4	243.9
Long-Term Debt	n.a.	n.a.	n.a.	n.a.
Stockholders' Equity	1,334.5	972.8	957.6	1,255.2
Performance & Financial Condition				
Return on Total Revenues %	0.83	0.73	0.67	0.94
Return on Avg Stockholders' Equity %	31.36	29.19	25.53	n.a.
Return on Average Assets %	28.38	25.60	21.30	n.a.
Current Ratio	6.32	8.50	3.39	4.15
Debt / Equity %	n.a.	n.a.	n.a.	n.a.

Compound Growth %'s	EPS %	-6.35	Net Income %	-6.17	Total Revenues %	-2.16

Comments

Operating income is in a decline because of increased competition in both the entertainment dollar and the gaming industry overall. The Company is liquid and the underlying property is of an unknown value.

Officers	Position	Ownership Information	09/30/95
David Scherer	President	Number of Shares Outstanding	782,124
Joseph Pardi	Secretary	Market Capitalization	$ 3,128,496
Alyce Donahue	Treasurer	Frequency Of Dividends	Annual
Luther F. Hess	Vice President	Number of Shareholders	Under 500

Other Information			
Transfer Agent	Corporate Stock Transfer, Inc., Denver	Where Listed	BE
Auditor	Brock, Watkins and Schommer	Symbol	CLVFA
Market Maker	Folger Nolan Fleming Douglas	Telephone (800)326-3633	SIC Code	7948
Broker Dealer	Regular Stockbroker	Employees	150

Coal Creek Mining and Manufacturing Company

800 S. Gay Street, Ste. 1706 • Knoxville, TN 37929-1706 • Telephone (423)435-7158

Company Description

The Company receives royalties from coal mined on its properties in Tennessee and has various other revenues from timber sales, gas and oil royalties, and investments. The Company also owns a 50.2% interest in Tennessee Energy Pipe and Storage Company, a transporter of natural gas to distributors.

	12/31/95	12/31/94	12/31/93	12/31/92
Per Share Information				
Stock Price	99.50	113.50	95.00	93.50
Earnings Per Share	7.67	5.96	8.15	13.48
Price / Earnings Ratio	12.97	19.04	11.66	6.94
Book Value Per Share	46.04	45.04	45.34	43.19
Price / Book Value %	216.12	252.00	209.53	216.49
Dividends Per Share	6.00	6.00	6.00	6.45
Annual Financial Data				
Operating Results (000's)				
Total Revenues	2,607.4	2,495.2	2,429.3	3,500.4
Costs & Expenses	-931.5	-938.2	-853.4	-825.9
Income Before Taxes and Other	1,567.0	1,115.7	1,541.9	2,663.2
Other Items	n.a.	n.a.	n.a.	n.a.
Income Tax	-610.6	-369.6	-521.4	-974.0
Net Income	956.5	746.1	1,020.5	1,689.2
Cash Flow From Operations	720.3	803.7	450.4	543.8
Balance Sheet (000's)				
Cash & Equivalents	1,120.3	364.7	195.6	201.0
Total Current Assets	2,082.7	1,634.0	1,710.4	2,497.6
Fixed Assets, Net	2,330.3	2,398.6	2,371.7	2,387.0
Total Assets	7,993.5	8,104.8	8,347.1	8,434.8
Total Current Liabilities	190.6	125.1	112.1	278.1
Long-Term Debt	n.a.	n.a.	n.a.	n.a.
Stockholders' Equity	5,699.0	5,643.4	5,680.3	5,411.5
Performance & Financial Condition				
Return on Total Revenues %	36.68	29.90	42.01	48.26
Return on Avg Stockholders' Equity %	16.87	13.18	18.40	n.a.
Return on Average Assets %	11.88	9.07	12.16	n.a.
Current Ratio	10.93	13.06	15.26	8.98
Debt / Equity %	n.a.	n.a.	n.a.	n.a.

Compound Growth %'s	EPS %	-17.14	Net Income %	-17.27	Total Revenues %	-9.35

Comments

The decline in coal mining in the Appalachia region has had an impact on the Company, although the development of new mines continues. The Company is buying back stock, an action which it considers to be in the best interest of its shareholders.

Officers	Position	Ownership Information	12/31/95
Lewis S. Howard	President	Number of Shares Outstanding	123,783
Fred W. Wyatt	Exec VP	Market Capitalization	$ 12,316,409
Laura F. Martin	Secretary, Treasurer	Frequency Of Dividends	Quarterly
McGhee T. Gilpin	Vice President	Number of Shareholders	Under 500

Other Information

					Where Listed	OTC-BB
Transfer Agent	Company Office				Symbol	CCRK
Auditor	Cherry, Bekaert & Holland, LLP				SIC Code	1200
Market Maker	Forbes, Walsh, Kelly & Co, Inc	Telephone	(800)221-3747		Employees	n.a.
Broker Dealer	Standard Investment	Tel/Ext	(888)783-4688	Jack		

Cochrane Furniture Company, Inc.

P.O. box 220 • Lincolnton, NC 28093-0220 • Telephone (704)732-1151 • Fax (800)232-3307

Company Description

The Company manufactures case goods and upholstered furniture for sale to retail stores primarily located in the U.S. The Company's employee stock ownership plan owns 71,962 shares of stock, or 15.4% of the Company.

	04/01/95	04/02/94	04/03/93	03/28/92
Per Share Information				
Stock Price	13.00	11.50	9.50	12.50
Earnings Per Share	0.05	-3.89	2.87	0.12
Price / Earnings Ratio	260.00	n.a.	3.31	104.17
Book Value Per Share	24.71	24.47	25.73	22.57
Price / Book Value %	52.61	47.00	36.92	55.38
Dividends Per Share	n.a.	0.07	0.07	n.a.
Annual Financial Data				
Operating Results (000's)				
Total Revenues	77,310.4	69,568.0	68,685.6	57,485.8
Costs & Expenses	-77,162.0	-73,045.4	-66,800.7	-57,417.7
Income Before Taxes and Other	148.4	-3,477.5	1,884.9	68.1
Other Items	n.a.	n.a.	285.8	n.a.
Income Tax	-123.0	1,664.1	-812.4	-11.2
Net Income	25.4	-1,813.3	1,358.2	56.9
Cash Flow From Operations	-2,405.4	2,652.1	1,042.5	748.1
Balance Sheet (000's)				
Cash & Equivalents	1.5	0.8	0.6	n.a.
Total Current Assets	27,369.3	20,522.5	20,534.4	17,555.0
Fixed Assets, Net	15,248.1	12,518.7	13,804.8	14,257.0
Total Assets	45,350.4	33,879.8	35,685.5	33,142.7
Total Current Liabilities	21,442.4	12,920.0	11,506.7	8,959.2
Long-Term Debt	10,288.2	7,234.9	10,863.5	12,104.2
Stockholders' Equity	11,515.1	11,406.3	11,996.3	10,800.9
Performance & Financial Condition				
Return on Total Revenues %	0.03	-2.61	1.98	0.10
Return on Avg Stockholders' Equity %	0.22	-15.50	11.92	0.53
Return on Average Assets %	0.06	-5.21	3.95	0.17
Current Ratio	1.28	1.59	1.78	1.96
Debt / Equity %	89.34	63.43	90.56	112.07

Compound Growth %'s	EPS %	-25.31	Net Income %	-23.63	Total Revenues %	10.38

Comments

1994 was a difficult year for a number of reasons including the implementation of a major rstructuring program. The current ratio has been deteriorating over recent years which may account for the switch off LIFO in 1994. Management recognizes the need to reduce costs, re-engineer manufacturing operations, introduce new products and take better advantage of plant capacity.

Officers	Position	Ownership Information	04/01/95
T E. Cochrane	Chairman	Number of Shares Outstanding	465,971
Jerry W. Cochrane	President	Market Capitalization	$ 6,057,623
Bruce R. Cochrane	Exec VP	Frequency Of Dividends	Semi-Annual
Grover S. Elliott	CFO, Secretary	Number of Shareholders	Under 500

Other Information

Transfer Agent	First Citizens Bank, Raleigh, NC				Where Listed	OTC-BB
Auditor	McGladrey & Pullen, LLP				Symbol	CFUR
Market Maker	Scott & Stringfellow, Inc.	Telephone	(800)446-7074		SIC Code	2512
Broker Dealer	Standard Investment	Tel/Ext	(888)783-4688	Jack	Employees	1200

Columbia Water Company

220 Locust Street • Columbia, PA 17512 • Telephone (717)684-2188 • Fax (713)694-4566

Company Description

The Company provides water service to residential and business customers in Columbia, Pennsylvania and surrounding communities. Nothing has changed much since the Company first went public. Only 25,200 shares are issued and outstanding.

	12/31/94	12/31/93	12/31/92
Per Share Information			
Stock Price	80.00	74.00	70.00
Earnings Per Share	12.99	8.50	9.45
Price / Earnings Ratio	6.16	8.71	7.41
Book Value Per Share	129.83	119.24	113.14
Price / Book Value %	61.62	62.06	61.87
Dividends Per Share	2.40	2.40	2.40
Annual Financial Data			
Operating Results (000's)			
Total Revenues	2,258.1	1,944.7	1,809.5
Costs & Expenses	-1,712.0	-1,648.1	-1,378.2
Income Before Taxes and Other	543.9	294.2	429.1
Other Items	n.a.	n.a.	n.a.
Income Tax	-216.5	-80.2	-190.9
Net Income	327.5	214.1	238.2
Cash Flow From Operations	649.7	538.4	-415.4
Balance Sheet (000's)			
Cash & Equivalents	560.3	737.1	464.4
Total Current Assets	1,213.5	1,337.0	1,066.2
Fixed Assets, Net	11,525.1	10,746.1	10,788.7
Total Assets	13,045.5	12,557.6	11,894.3
Total Current Liabilities	1,279.7	1,182.3	1,210.3
Long-Term Debt	4,479.2	4,749.3	4,500.2
Stockholders' Equity	3,271.8	3,004.8	2,851.2
Performance & Financial Condition			
Return on Total Revenues %	14.50	11.01	13.16
Return on Avg Stockholders' Equity %	10.43	7.31	n.a.
Return on Average Assets %	2.56	1.75	n.a.
Current Ratio	0.95	1.13	0.88
Debt / Equity %	136.90	158.06	157.83

Compound Growth %'s	EPS %	17.24	Net Income %	17.25	Total Revenues %	11.71

Comments

The Company continues to expand its service area and also serves new developments within existing service areas. It has generally had a steady growth in revenue over the last 15 years, averaging 9%.

Officers	Position	Ownership Information	12/31/94
Donald H. Nikolaus	President	Number of Shares Outstanding	25,200
John F. Hinkle, Jr.	Secretary, Treasurer	Market Capitalization	$ 2,016,000
Philip H. Glatfelter II	Vice President	Frequency Of Dividends	Annual
Charles E. Gohn	General Manager	Number of Shareholders	Under 500

Other Information

Transfer Agent	Company Office		Where Listed	OTC-PS
Auditor	Sager, Swisher and Company		Symbol	n.a.
Market Maker	Chicago Corporation, The	Telephone (312)855-7664	SIC Code	4940
Broker Dealer	Pink sheet specialist		Employees	13

Columbian Rope Company

145 Towery Street • Guntown, MS 38849 • Telephone (601)348-2241 • Fax (601)348-5749

Company Description

The Company manufactures traditional rope and cords as well as a variety of specialty products including technically advanced ropes. Monorail, a subsidiary, develops and exports new car wash systems. PlymKraft, another subsidiary, produces monofilament and film cable fiber.

	12/31/94	12/31/93
Per Share Information		
Stock Price	2.12	1.25
Earnings Per Share	29.42	9.19
Price / Earnings Ratio	0.07	0.14
Book Value Per Share	71.93	44.50
Price / Book Value %	2.95	2.81
Dividends Per Share	n.a.	n.a.
Annual Financial Data		
Operating Results (000's)		
Total Revenues	21,565.4	18,328.3
Costs & Expenses	-20,353.8	-17,873.6
Income Before Taxes and Other	1,114.2	339.6
Other Items	-475.1	n.a.
Income Tax	448.4	n.a.
Net Income	1,087.6	339.6
Cash Flow From Operations	912.5	930.1
Balance Sheet (000's)		
Cash & Equivalents	755.1	436.8
Total Current Assets	6,993.2	5,971.1
Fixed Assets, Net	1,523.9	1,371.1
Total Assets	9,522.0	7,809.9
Total Current Liabilities	2,695.9	1,846.3
Long-Term Debt	2,870.0	3,447.5
Stockholders' Equity	2,658.5	1,644.9
Performance & Financial Condition		
Return on Total Revenues %	5.04	1.85
Return on Avg Stockholders' Equity %	50.54	22.81
Return on Average Assets %	12.55	4.47
Current Ratio	2.59	3.23
Debt / Equity %	107.95	209.59

Compound Growth %'s	EPS %	220.13	Net Income %	220.26	Total Revenues %	17.66

Comments

The Company does not report calendar year results until June and therefore, results were too late for publication. 1995 revenues were expected to decline because 1994 had nonrecurring specialty contracts with the federal government. 1994 results also included nonrecurring items related to income taxes and the reporting of postretirement benefits. Net Income before these items was $1.1 million. The Company seems to have recovered from difficult financial times. As recently as 1988, the Company had a debt/equity ratio of 23.5 to 1 and was classified as a problem loan by their bank. The stock prices indicated are no longer. However, we have first hand information on a trade at $8 per share in February, 1996. Compounded growth rates may be misleading because there are only two years of data.

Officers	Position	Ownership Information	12/31/94
Michael M. Chapman	Chairman	Number of Shares Outstanding	36,962
		Market Capitalization	$ 78,359
		Frequency Of Dividends	n.a.
		Number of Shareholders	Under 500

Other Information

Transfer Agent	Company Office				Where Listed	OTC-PS
Auditor	Nail McKinney Tate & Robinson				Symbol	CRPE
Market Maker	Seidler Companies, Inc., The	Telephone	(800)421-0164		SIC Code	2298
Broker Dealer	Standard Investment	Tel/Ext	(888)783-4688	Jack	Employees	94

Commercial Bancshares Incorporated

118 S. Sandusky Ave. P.O.Box90 • Upper Sandusky, OH 43351 • Telephone (419)294-5781 • Fax (419)294-2350

Company Description

Commercial Bancshares, Inc. is a bank-holding company of Commercial Savings Bank which is engaged in commercial and retail banking in Upper Sandusky, Ohio, and neighboring communities.

	12/31/95	12/31/94	12/31/93	12/31/92
Per Share Information				
Stock Price	58.00	50.00	44.75	41.75
Earnings Per Share	6.07	5.24	5.23	4.41
Price / Earnings Ratio	9.56	9.54	8.56	9.47
Book Value Per Share	50.69	41.40	43.55	40.32
Price / Book Value %	114.42	120.77	102.76	103.55
Dividends Per Share	2.00	2.00	2.00	2.00
Annual Financial Data				
Operating Results (000's)				
Net Interest Income	6,381.0	6,264.6	5,629.1	4,469.2
Loan Loss Provision	-100.0	-234.7	-51.3	-50.0
Non-Interest Income	1,045.1	728.2	956.0	969.2
Non-Interest Expense	-5,076.9	-4,810.1	-4,652.6	-3,834.8
Income Before Taxes and Other	2,249.2	1,948.0	1,881.2	1,553.6
Other Items	n.a.	n.a.	n.a.	n.a.
Income Tax	-561.7	-489.5	-428.0	-328.1
Net Income	1,687.5	1,458.5	1,453.2	1,225.5
Balance Sheet (000's)				
Cash & Securities	60,731.7	59,211.4	50,862.0	63,919.5
Loans, Net	97,515.9	94,168.9	99,693.9	79,434.8
Fixed Assets, Net	3,895.8	3,465.4	3,416.2	3,285.5
Total Assets	166,296.2	160,720.9	158,324.3	148,597.2
Deposits	151,622.2	148,706.5	144,853.1	136,267.6
Stockholders' Equity	14,095.7	11,512.4	12,110.7	11,213.7
Performance & Financial Condition				
Net Interest Margin	n.a.	n.a.	n.a.	n.a.
Return on Avg Stockholders' Equity %	13.18	12.35	12.46	11.27
Return on Average Assets %	1.03	0.91	0.95	0.92
Equity to Assets %	8.48	7.16	7.65	7.55
Reserve as a % of Non-Performing Loans	388.26	546.29	n.a.	n.a.

Compound Growth %'s	EPS %	11.24	Net Income %	11.25	Net Interest Income %	12.60

Comments

Commercial loans and real estate mortgages comprise 55% and 25%, respectively, of the total loan portfolio. Loans related to the agriculture industry represent 11% of all loans. The Company has a history of stock splits and stock dividends, occurring 8 times since 1973, and has declared a 25% stock dividend in early 1996.

Officers	Position	Ownership Information	12/31/95
Richard Sheaffer	Chairman	Number of Shares Outstanding	278,089
Raymond E. Graves	President, CEO	Market Capitalization	$ 16,129,162
James A. Deer	Secretary, Treasurer	Frequency Of Dividends	Semi-Annual
Philip W. Kinley	Vice President	Number of Shareholders	1,300

Other Information

Transfer Agent	Company Office		Where Listed	OTC-PS
Auditor	Crowe, Chizek and Company LLP		Symbol	n.a.
Market Maker	The Ohio Company	Telephone (419)243-2291	SIC Code	6020
Broker Dealer	Regular Stockbroker		Employees	110

Community Bank of South Florida, Inc.

28801 S.W. 157th Avenue • Homestead, FL 33033 • Telephone (305)245-2211 • Fax (309)245-2997

Company Description

Community Bank of South Florida, Inc. is a one bank holding company whose wholly-owned subsidiary, Community Bank of Homestead, offers standard banking services through its seven banking locations. The Bank also has three subsidiaries: Community Investment Services, Inc., Combank Mortgage Company and Community Leasing,Inc., all operating in Homestead, Florida. The Bank was founded in 1973.

	12/31/95	12/31/94	12/31/93	12/31/92
Per Share Information				
Stock Price	26.50	22.00	20.87	18.75
Earnings Per Share	3.39	3.05	3.77	2.41
Price / Earnings Ratio	7.82	7.21	5.54	7.78
Book Value Per Share	26.46	22.10	21.08	17.85
Price / Book Value %	100.15	99.55	99.00	105.04
Dividends Per Share	0.55	0.55	0.62	0.37
Annual Financial Data				
Operating Results (000's)				
Net Interest Income	12,319.0	12,176.0	13,230.6	10,990.7
Loan Loss Provision	-550.0	-450.0	-1,150.0	-600.0
Non-Interest Income	4,298.0	3,165.0	4,682.7	3,927.6
Non-Interest Expense	-11,090.0	-10,582.0	-11,593.8	-11,091.5
Income Before Taxes and Other	4,977.0	4,309.0	5,169.5	3,226.8
Other Items	n.a.	n.a.	n.a.	n.a.
Income Tax	-1,641.0	-1,320.0	-1,534.3	-899.6
Net Income	3,336.0	2,989.0	3,635.2	2,327.2
Balance Sheet (000's)				
Cash & Securities	71,673.0	75,605.0	95,412.9	213,000.0
Loans, Net	139,960.0	126,652.0	121,667.7	104,810.6
Fixed Assets, Net	6,795.0	7,286.0	6,984.2	5,690.4
Total Assets	221,704.0	214,653.0	228,813.9	330,307.6
Deposits	183,905.0	179,910.0	202,058.0	309,728.1
Stockholders' Equity	26,036.0	21,744.0	20,492.1	17,212.8
Performance & Financial Condition				
Net Interest Margin	n.a.	n.a.	n.a.	n.a.
Return on Avg Stockholders' Equity %	13.96	14.15	19.28	14.28
Return on Average Assets %	1.53	1.35	1.30	0.90
Equity to Assets %	11.74	10.13	8.96	5.21
Reserve as a % of Non-Performing Loans	91.75	87.24	50.36	38.86

Compound Growth %'s	EPS %	12.05	Net Income %	12.75	Net Interest Income %	3.88

Comments

The Bank had a 2 for 1 stock split during 1994. All share and per share information has been restated to reflect this split. Real estate loans account for approximately 65% of total loans with commercial and industrial loans representing an additional 28%. The Bank continued to show good results despite a slowdown in both agriculture and tourism, the area's primary industries. Furthermore, there was the post-storm economic cycle of Hurricane Andrew which management now believes has bottomed with new economic growth beginning. 1992 assets were inflated because of the deposit of insurance monies as a result of the Hurricane.

Officers	Position	Ownership Information	12/31/95
Robert L. Epling	President, CEO	Number of Shares Outstanding	984,088
Eric S. Johnson	Exec VP	Market Capitalization	$ 26,078,332
Daniel D. Braun	Exec VP	Frequency Of Dividends	Semi-Annual
Daniel P. Lipe	Controller	Number of Shareholders	450
James C. Hagood	Head Cashier		

Other Information			
Transfer Agent	Sun Trust Bank, Atlanta, GA	Where Listed	Order Matching Only
Auditor	Deloitte & Touche LLP	Symbol	n.a.
Market Maker	Communmity Investment Services	SIC Code	6020
Broker Dealer	Regular Stockbroker	Employees	150

Community Bank, The (NC)

P.O. Box 1368 • Pilot Mountain, NC 27041 • Telephone (910)368-5334 • Fax (910)368-2269

Company Description

The Community Bank was incorporated and began operations in 1987, and is engaged in commercial banking in Surry County, North Carolina and the surrounding communities. During 1994, the bank established and became a 25% owner in an independent mortgage company, Community Mortgage Corporation of North Carolina.

		12/31/95	12/31/94	12/31/93	12/31/92
Per Share Information					
	Stock Price	12.00	10.50	7.00	6.25
	Earnings Per Share	1.56	1.04	0.57	0.27
	Price / Earnings Ratio	7.69	10.10	12.28	23.15
	Book Value Per Share	9.12	7.56	6.70	6.28
	Price / Book Value %	131.58	138.89	104.48	99.52
	Dividends Per Share	n.a.	0.17	0.15	n.a.
Annual Financial Data					
Operating Results (000's)					
	Net Interest Income	4,058.9	3,588.8	2,975.7	2,797.5
	Loan Loss Provision	-115.0	-50.0	-340.0	-884.6
	Non-Interest Income	701.9	649.6	502.0	463.9
	Non-Interest Expense	-2,789.2	-2,867.3	-2,664.8	-2,153.2
	Income Before Taxes and Other	1,856.6	1,321.0	472.9	223.6
	Other Items	n.a.	n.a.	n.a.	37.9
	Income Tax	-553.1	-459.3	n.a.	-37.9
	Net Income	1,303.4	861.7	472.9	223.6
Balance Sheet (000's)					
	Cash & Securities	35,527.5	28,320.2	28,362.1	25,516.0
	Loans, Net	59,565.5	47,453.6	39,205.7	35,399.9
	Fixed Assets, Net	2,539.7	1,803.0	1,897.2	1,922.0
	Total Assets	99,848.1	78,887.5	70,888.7	64,083.5
	Deposits	90,983.9	68,948.3	61,545.4	58,464.3
	Stockholders' Equity	7,610.4	6,305.6	5,574.5	5,226.4
Performance & Financial Condition					
	Net Interest Margin	5.15	5.20	4.94	4.90
	Return on Avg Stockholders' Equity %	18.73	14.51	8.76	4.37
	Return on Average Assets %	1.46	1.15	0.70	0.35
	Equity to Assets %	7.62	7.99	7.86	8.16
	Reserve as a % of Non-Performing Loans	8538.04	783.70	6853.72	464.62

Compound Growth %'s	EPS % 79.44	Net Income % 79.97	Net Interest Income % 13.21

Comments

Management attributes the good operating results to strong loan growth, good expense control and reduced credit losses, along with a modest contribution from other operating revenue. There is no established trading market for the stock of the bank. Community Mortgage Corporation has not yet produced a profit. However, significant staffing and operational changes were made during 1995 in an effort to improve the possibility of profitable operations.

Officers	Position	Ownership Information	12/31/95
James O. Frye	President, CEO	Number of Shares Outstanding	834,185
Merle B. Andrews	Exec VP, CFO	Market Capitalization	$ 10,010,220
Fred E. Venable	Secretary	Frequency Of Dividends	Irregular
Donna S. Marion	Vice President	Number of Shareholders	1,412
Billy Van Coe	Vice President		

Other Information				
Transfer Agent	Company Office		Where Listed	Order Matching Only
Auditor	Coopers & Lybrand LLP		Symbol	n.a.
Market Maker	None - Company Office	Telephone (919)368-5334	SIC Code	6020
Broker Dealer	None		Employees	59

Community Service Communications, Inc.

33 Main Street • Winthrop, ME 04364-0400 • Telephone (207)377-9911 • Fax (207)377-9969

Company Description

The Company is a holding company whose subsidiaries are engaged in telecommunications activities in both regulated and deregulated environments. The Company's primary business is its local telephone exchange serving all or portions of 15 Maine communities. A subsidiary that sold equipment as well as network services for both intra-state and inter-state toll carriers was sold in 1994. The Company was established in 1988 as a result of consolidations, merger absorption and reorganizations of telecommunications enterprises dating as far back as 1888.

	12/31/95	12/31/94	12/31/93	12/31/92
Per Share Information				
Stock Price	110.00	95.00	90.00	85.00
Earnings Per Share	14.86	20.79	12.10	10.64
Price / Earnings Ratio	7.40	4.57	7.44	7.99
Book Value Per Share	115.60	109.50	96.42	91.65
Price / Book Value %	95.16	86.76	93.34	92.74
Dividends Per Share	8.76	7.71	7.33	6.55
Annual Financial Data				
Operating Results (000's)				
Total Revenues	6,130.6	6,204.2	9,272.0	8,861.7
Costs & Expenses	-4,725.9	-4,400.3	-8,250.9	-7,978.2
Income Before Taxes and Other	1,404.6	1,804.0	1,021.1	883.6
Other Items	-73.8	37.0	n.a.	n.a.
Income Tax	-457.5	-618.8	-309.8	-258.0
Net Income	873.4	1,222.2	711.3	625.6
Cash Flow From Operations	2,062.3	2,549.3	2,152.8	2,210.5
Balance Sheet (000's)				
Cash & Equivalents	900.2	400.7	65.1	541.8
Total Current Assets	3,120.2	2,527.9	2,700.6	3,295.3
Fixed Assets, Net	9,038.7	9,230.1	9,525.9	9,157.4
Total Assets	12,586.4	12,190.7	12,248.4	12,480.9
Total Current Liabilities	1,741.8	1,302.0	3,557.1	3,362.4
Long-Term Debt	2,797.4	3,142.7	1,813.3	2,308.5
Stockholders' Equity	6,795.3	6,436.8	5,667.9	5,387.4
Performance & Financial Condition				
Return on Total Revenues %	14.25	19.70	7.67	7.06
Return on Avg Stockholders' Equity %	13.20	20.19	12.87	11.88
Return on Average Assets %	7.05	10.00	5.75	4.90
Current Ratio	1.79	1.94	0.76	0.98
Debt / Equity %	41.17	48.82	31.99	42.85

Compound Growth %'s	EPS %	11.78	Net Income %	11.77	Total Revenues %	-11.56

Comments

Results of the last three years were affected by the discontinuance of certain operations in the per share amounts of $(1.25), $ .63, and $(6.69), for 1995, 1994 and 1993, respectively. On May 17, 1996, the president announced that the Board of Directors had rejected an offer to purchase the Company. The offer was $200 per share, which was the same price the potential acquiring group paid in a private transaction for 3,533 shares. The Board concluded that the offer very substantially understates the value of the Company.

Officers	Position	Ownership Information	12/31/95
John W. Connor	President, Secretary	Number of Shares Outstanding	58,782
Leland C. Davis	Vice President	Market Capitalization	$ 6,466,020
Normand J. Savard	Vice President	Frequency Of Dividends	Quarterly
Mark H. Blake	Vice President, Treasurer	Number of Shareholders	Under 500

Other Information			
Transfer Agent	Company Office	Where Listed	OTC-BB
Auditor	Berry, Dunn, McNeil & Parker	Symbol	CMYS
Market Maker	Chicago Corporation, The	Telephone (312)855-7664	SIC Code	4810
Broker Dealer	Regular Stockbroker	Employees	45

Components Specialties, Inc.

1172 Route 109 • Lindenhurst, NY 11757-0624 • Telephone (516)957-8700 • Fax (516)957-9142

Company Description

The Company sells and distributes electronic equipment manufactured by other companies, including commercial sound equipment, paging systems, sound accessories, intercoms and more. Most of the products are imported from the Far East and sold under recognized tradenames.

	03/31/95	03/31/94	03/31/93	03/31/92
Per Share Information				
Stock Price	2.62	1.75	1.25	1.25
Earnings Per Share	0.58	0.27	0.09	0.07
Price / Earnings Ratio	4.52	6.48	13.89	17.86
Book Value Per Share	3.37	3.17	2.52	2.43
Price / Book Value %	77.74	55.21	49.60	51.44
Dividends Per Share	n.a.	n.a.	n.a.	n.a.
Annual Financial Data				
Operating Results (000's)				
Total Revenues	9,443.2	6,806.8	5,503.6	4,645.1
Costs & Expenses	-9,036.8	-6,618.1	-5,439.3	-4,604.9
Income Before Taxes and Other	406.4	188.7	64.3	40.2
Other Items	n.a.	n.a.	n.a.	n.a.
Income Tax	-184.4	-83.7	-31.0	-11.9
Net Income	222.0	105.0	33.3	28.3
Cash Flow From Operations	-134.4	269.2	-241.4	464.3
Balance Sheet (000's)				
Cash & Equivalents	133.2	143.1	181.5	153.9
Total Current Assets	3,086.5	2,938.0	2,583.1	2,115.7
Fixed Assets, Net	127.9	144.5	135.4	106.0
Total Assets	3,244.5	3,108.3	2,744.0	2,248.3
Total Current Liabilities	1,751.2	1,826.2	1,586.2	1,171.7
Long-Term Debt	n.a.	n.a.	n.a.	n.a.
Stockholders' Equity	1,293.4	1,071.5	966.5	933.2
Performance & Financial Condition				
Return on Total Revenues %	2.35	1.54	0.60	0.61
Return on Avg Stockholders' Equity %	18.77	10.30	3.50	3.09
Return on Average Assets %	6.99	3.59	1.33	1.18
Current Ratio	1.76	1.61	1.63	1.81
Debt / Equity %	n.a.	n.a.	n.a.	n.a.

Compound Growth %'s	EPS %	102.35	Net Income %	98.62	Total Revenues %	26.68

Comments

A good selection of products including the new Pro-Video line (surveillance equipment), has propelled the Company to new heights. Management remains optimistic. 1996 results were not available when we went to press but could be obtained directly from the Company.

Officers	Position	Ownership Information	03/31/95
Louis W. Keller	President, Treasurer	Number of Shares Outstanding	383,240
Todd I. Keller	Exec VP	Market Capitalization	$ 1,004,089
Rhonda Mutterperl	Secretary	Frequency Of Dividends	n.a.
		Number of Shareholders	Under 500

Other Information			
Transfer Agent	American Stock Transfer & Trust Company	Where Listed	OTC-BB
Auditor	Marden, Harrison & Kreuter	Symbol	CSPC
Market Maker	M. Rimson & Co., Inc. Telephone (800)207-3195	SIC Code	5060
Broker Dealer	Regular Stockbroker	Employees	25

CompuDyne Corporation

120 Union Street • Willimantic, CT 06226 • Telephone (203)456-4187 • Fax (203)456-1187

Company Description

The Company is an engineering services firm providing turn-key systems and a variety of services to both government and industry. Products include physical security appllctions and telemetry and satellite command and control systems. The Company was incorporated in Pennsylvania in 1952.

	12/31/95	12/31/94	12/31/93	12/31/92
Per Share Information				
Stock Price	1.38	2.75	2.00	0.19
Earnings Per Share	-0.40	0.99	0.12	0.15
Price / Earnings Ratio	n.a.	2.78	16.67	1.27
Book Value Per Share	-0.30	n.a.	-1.17	-1.43
Price / Book Value %	n.a.	n.a.	n.a.	n.a.
Dividends Per Share	n.a.	n.a.	n.a.	n.a.
Annual Financial Data				
Operating Results (000's)				
Total Revenues	10,308.0	11,368.0	9,571.0	9,330.0
Costs & Expenses	-10,365.0	-9,274.0	-9,292.0	-9,208.0
Income Before Taxes and Other	-265.0	2,094.0	270.0	122.0
Other Items	-453.0	-337.0	-50.0	79.0
Income Tax	55.0	-29.0	-17.0	n.a.
Net Income	-663.0	1,728.0	203.0	201.0
Cash Flow From Operations	-478.0	1,208.0	803.0	-424.0
Balance Sheet (000's)				
Cash & Equivalents	n.a.	176.0	298.0	283.0
Total Current Assets	3,241.0	2,092.0	2,314.0	2,603.0
Fixed Assets, Net	588.0	7.0	40.0	42.0
Total Assets	5,033.0	2,114.0	2,377.0	2,652.0
Total Current Liabilities	2,536.0	1,682.0	2,858.0	3,062.0
Long-Term Debt	470.0	n.a.	1,050.0	1,201.0
Stockholders' Equity	1,367.0	n.a.	-1,736.0	-1,939.0
Performance & Financial Condition				
Return on Total Revenues %	-6.43	15.20	2.12	2.15
Return on Avg Stockholders' Equity %	n.a.	n.a.	n.a.	n.a.
Return on Average Assets %	-18.55	76.95	8.07	6.91
Current Ratio	1.28	1.24	0.81	0.85
Debt / Equity %	34.38	n.a.	n.a.	n.a.

Compound Growth %'s	EPS % n.a.	Net Income % n.a.	Total Revenues % 3.38

Comments

In order to address unprofitable operations, the Company, in 1995, increased R&D spending to speed up the development of several new products, made management changes, and added a subsidiary by acquiring all the stock of MicroAssembly Systems, Inc., in exchange for $1.9 million of its convertible preferred stock. In conjunction with the restructuring, the Company disposed of an operating division. Sales to the federal government were 86%, 90%, and 84%, for 1995, 1994 and 1993. At March 27, 1996, officers and directors, as a group, owned 55.9% of the Company's common stock and 100% of its preferred stock.

Officers	Position	Ownership Information	12/31/95
Martin A. Roenigk	President, CEO	Number of Shares Outstanding	1,749,622
Philip M. Blackmon	Exec VP	Market Capitalization	$ 2,414,478
		Frequency Of Dividends	n.a.
		Number of Shareholders	2,011

Other Information

Transfer Agent	1st National Bank of Maryland			Where Listed	OTC-BB
Auditor	Deloitte & Touche LLP			Symbol	CDCY
Market Maker	Troster Singer Corporation	Telephone	(800)222-0890	SIC Code	3812
Broker Dealer	Regular Stockbroker			Employees	118

Computer Integration, Corp.

7900 Glades Road • Boca Raton, FL 33434 • Telephone (407)482-6678 • Fax (407)483-5638

Company Description

The Company, organized in 1992, is a reseller of microcomputers, workstations and related products to large and medium-sized corporations, federal, state and local government entities and colleges. The Company is also one of the largest resellers of computer products made by Hewlett-Packard and, in fiscal 1995, sales of these products accounted for 69% of the Company's sales. The Company markets its products directly to end-user customers through a total of 37 offices in 27 states.

	06/30/95	06/30/94	06/30/93
Per Share Information			
Stock Price	n.a.	n.a.	n.a.
Earnings Per Share	0.18	0.02	0.01
Price / Earnings Ratio	n.a.	n.a.	n.a.
Book Value Per Share	1.03	0.47	0.49
Price / Book Value %	n.a.	n.a.	n.a.
Dividends Per Share	n.a.	n.a.	n.a.
Annual Financial Data			
Operating Results (000's)			
Total Revenues	209,225.8	103,786.3	27,134.2
Costs & Expenses	-206,422.4	-102,529.5	-26,718.0
Income Before Taxes and Other	2,001.5	351.6	275.6
Other Items	-202.3	-5.5	-93.0
Income Tax	-868.6	-265.2	-125.4
Net Income	930.6	81.0	57.2
Cash Flow From Operations	-2,369.5	-3,519.1	-3,708.3
Balance Sheet (000's)			
Cash & Equivalents	797.7	909.8	n.a.
Total Current Assets	44,567.7	26,165.2	20,857.6
Fixed Assets, Net	1,693.7	1,100.9	1,000.0
Total Assets	54,754.6	29,784.8	24,457.0
Total Current Liabilities	35,345.8	21,551.5	14,291.6
Long-Term Debt	12,507.8	5,453.2	7,582.0
Stockholders' Equity	6,590.8	2,780.1	2,583.4
Performance & Financial Condition			
Return on Total Revenues %	0.44	0.08	0.21
Return on Avg Stockholders' Equity %	19.86	3.02	n.a.
Return on Average Assets %	2.20	0.30	n.a.
Current Ratio	1.26	1.21	1.46
Debt / Equity %	189.78	196.15	293.49

Compound Growth %'s	EPS %	324.26	Net Income %	303.20	Total Revenues %	177.68

Comments

In July, 1995, the Company acquired all of the assets and liabilities of Cedar Computer Center, Inc. for $18.0 million in cash, notes and common stock. For the six months ended December 31, 1995, the Company had sales of $232.7 million and net income of $2.1 million, as compared to $97.8 million and $647,000, for the same period in 1994. Since the Company was organized in 1992, there have been no quotes for the stock. Discussions with the Company indicate that they intend to initiate trading in the Company's shares in the near future. A phone call to the Company may provide opportunity.

Officers	Position	Ownership Information	06/30/95
Ronald G. Farrell	Chairman, CEO	Number of Shares Outstanding	6,400,000
John F. Chiste	CFO	Market Capitalization	n.a.
		Frequency Of Dividends	n.a.
		Number of Shareholders	154

Other Information

Transfer Agent	Continental Stock Transfer & Trust Co.	Where Listed	Order Matching Only
Auditor	Ernst & Young LLP	Symbol	n.a.
Market Maker	None-Company Office	SIC Code	7373
Broker Dealer	None	Employees	455

Computer Services, Inc.

1301 Broadway • Paducah, KY 42002-0060 • Telephone (502)442-7361 • Fax (502)442-7361

Company Description

The Company provides data processing services, supplies, equipment, forms and maintenance to financial institutions in the central United States. The Company was incorporated in 1965. Shares were split 2 for 1 in 1995 All per share amounts have been adjusted accordingly.

	02/28/95	02/28/94	02/28/93	02/28/92
Per Share Information				
Stock Price	30.00	35.00	21.00	12.50
Earnings Per Share	1.64	1.62	1.47	1.22
Price / Earnings Ratio	18.29	21.60	14.29	10.25
Book Value Per Share	10.72	9.38	8.09	6.84
Price / Book Value %	279.85	373.13	259.58	182.75
Dividends Per Share	0.35	0.31	0.27	0.24
Annual Financial Data				
Operating Results (000's)				
Total Revenues	36,222.5	36,104.2	28,787.6	19,377.5
Costs & Expenses	-30,286.0	-30,465.8	-23,694.0	-15,264.5
Income Before Taxes and Other	5,936.5	5,638.3	5,093.6	4,113.0
Other Items	n.a.	n.a.	n.a.	n.a.
Income Tax	-2,431.0	-2,198.0	-2,006.0	-1,578.0
Net Income	3,505.5	3,440.3	3,087.6	2,535.0
Cash Flow From Operations	7,871.6	5,708.9	4,176.0	4,179.4
Balance Sheet (000's)				
Cash & Equivalents	7,231.3	5,556.5	5,978.6	7,099.4
Total Current Assets	12,300.3	11,073.6	11,644.7	9,954.1
Fixed Assets, Net	10,436.7	9,933.7	9,990.8	5,455.1
Total Assets	25,784.8	23,334.5	22,944.0	15,622.0
Total Current Liabilities	2,975.3	3,154.1	5,652.3	894.0
Long-Term Debt	n.a.	n.a.	n.a.	n.a.
Stockholders' Equity	22,117.3	19,333.7	16,361.9	13,825.6
Performance & Financial Condition				
Return on Total Revenues %	9.68	9.53	10.73	13.08
Return on Avg Stockholders' Equity %	16.91	19.28	20.46	19.80
Return on Average Assets %	14.27	14.87	16.01	14.08
Current Ratio	4.13	3.51	2.06	11.13
Debt / Equity %	n.a.	n.a.	n.a.	n.a.

Compound Growth %'s	EPS %	10.36	Net Income %	11.41	Total Revenues %	23.19

Comments

Loaded with cash in a non-capital intensive industry, will the Company continue to grow at its historic pace? A new facility was completed in 1995. The 1996 annual report can be obtained directly from the Company as it was not available at press time.

Officers	Position	Ownership Information	02/28/95
John A. Williams	Chairman, CEO	Number of Shares Outstanding	2,062,732
Steven A. Powless	President, COO	Market Capitalization	$ 61,881,960
Ann T. Carney	Vice President, Secretary	Frequency Of Dividends	n.a.
		Number of Shareholders	Under 500

Other Information				
Transfer Agent	Company Office		Where Listed	OTC-PS
Auditor	Crowe, Chizek and Company		Symbol	n.a.
Market Maker	J.J.B. Hilliard, W.L.Lyons,Inc	Telephone (800)627-3557	SIC Code	7370
Broker Dealer	Regular Stockbroker		Employees	376

ConBraCo Industries, Inc.

P.O. Box 247 • Matthews, NC 28106-0247 • Telephone (704)847-9191 • Fax (704)786-8111

Company Description

The Company is a manufacturer of boiler trimmings, bronze and stainless steel water gauges and pop safety and relief valves. Manufacturing facilities are in North and South Carolina and the Company sells most of its products to wholesale distributors throughout the United States and in many foreign countries. These distributors sell to end-users which include the industrial, chemical, pulp and paper and other processing industries. The Company also invests in real estate.

	12/31/95	12/31/94
Per Share Information		
Stock Price	677.50	495.00
Earnings Per Share	35.26	40.66
Price / Earnings Ratio	19.21	12.17
Book Value Per Share	385.38	355.13
Price / Book Value %	175.80	139.39
Dividends Per Share	1.75	1.50
Annual Financial Data		
Operating Results (000's)		
Total Revenues	162,633.2	152,108.9
Costs & Expenses	-145,536.1	-131,347.8
Income Before Taxes and Other	17,097.2	20,442.9
Other Items	n.a.	n.a.
Income Tax	-6,412.9	-7,692.6
Net Income	10,684.3	12,750.3
Cash Flow From Operations	4,533.4	19,486.2
Balance Sheet (000's)		
Cash & Equivalents	2,042.2	1,438.7
Total Current Assets	77,949.3	60,199.1
Fixed Assets, Net	56,470.7	53,130.0
Total Assets	149,854.0	127,198.5
Total Current Liabilities	23,241.7	8,632.1
Long-Term Debt	9,862.5	7,400.0
Stockholders' Equity	115,559.8	109,923.3
Performance & Financial Condition		
Return on Total Revenues %	6.57	8.38
Return on Avg Stockholders' Equity %	9.48	n.a.
Return on Average Assets %	7.71	n.a.
Current Ratio	3.35	6.97
Debt / Equity %	8.53	6.73

Compound Growth %'s	EPS %	-13.28	Net Income %	-16.20	Total Revenues %	6.92

Comments

The Company acquired 9,666 and 6,214 shares of its own stock during 1995 and 1994, respectively. $10 million of real estate investments are carried at cost with no indication of value. The balance sheet shows a favorable current ratio and little debt.

Officers	Position	Ownership Information	12/31/95
Carl Mosack	President	Number of Shares Outstanding	299,860
Everett Lowery	CFO	Market Capitalization	$ 203,155,150
		Frequency Of Dividends	Quarterly
		Number of Shareholders	Under 500

Other Information

Transfer Agent	Company Office			Where Listed	OTC-BB
Auditor	Dixon, Odom & Co. LLP			Symbol	CNIN
Market Maker	Roney & Co.	Telephone	(800)321-2038	SIC Code	5085
Broker Dealer	Regular Stockbroker			Employees	400

Congress Rotisserie, Inc.

10 Columbus Boulevard • Hartford, CT 06106-2511 • Telephone (203)549-2211 • Fax (203)549-2213

Company Description

The Company owns and franchises a quality take-out and dine-in restaurant concept featuring rotisserie roasted chicken, made-to-order sandwiches and entree salads. The owned restaurants are in West Hartford and Hartford, Connecticut. There are five franchised locations. The Company completed its initial public offering of 125,000 shares in January, 1994.

	06/30/95	06/30/94	06/30/93
Per Share Information			
Stock Price	4.00	8.56	n.a.
Earnings Per Share	0.05	0.06	0.04
Price / Earnings Ratio	80.00	142.67	n.a.
Book Value Per Share	1.71	1.27	n.a.
Price / Book Value %	233.92	674.02	n.a.
Dividends Per Share	n.a.	n.a.	n.a.
Annual Financial Data			
Operating Results (000's)			
Total Revenues	1,851.8	1,587.4	1,449.5
Costs & Expenses	-1,786.2	-1,530.2	-1,419.0
Income Before Taxes and Other	65.6	57.2	30.5
Other Items	n.a.	n.a.	n.a.
Income Tax	-30.7	-14.0	-8.2
Net Income	34.9	43.2	22.4
Cash Flow From Operations	-27.2	-39.0	63.9
Balance Sheet (000's)			
Cash & Equivalents	463.8	725.0	77.3
Total Current Assets	870.3	857.7	107.2
Fixed Assets, Net	113.1	76.3	87.9
Total Assets	1,107.0	1,039.3	208.1
Total Current Liabilities	87.0	48.8	85.9
Long-Term Debt	36.2	41.6	46.4
Stockholders' Equity	983.8	948.9	75.7
Performance & Financial Condition			
Return on Total Revenues %	1.88	2.72	1.54
Return on Avg Stockholders' Equity %	3.61	8.43	n.a.
Return on Average Assets %	3.25	6.93	n.a.
Current Ratio	10.01	17.57	1.25
Debt / Equity %	3.68	4.38	61.30

Compound Growth %'s	EPS %	11.80	Net Income %	24.83	Total Revenues %	13.03

Comments

A new Company-owned location opened in February, 1996. A series of new menu items were also introduced in an effort to stimulate sales.

Officers	Position	Ownership Information	06/30/95
Louis J. Miazga	Chairman, President	Number of Shares Outstanding	782,124
Wayne Garrett	COO	Market Capitalization	$ 3,128,496
Dorothy Waskiewicz	Vice President, Secretary	Frequency Of Dividends	n.a.
		Number of Shareholders	Under 500

Other Information

Transfer Agent	Registrar & Transfer Company			Where Listed	OTC-BB
Auditor	Urso, Kosovsky & Pratesi			Symbol	CONGA
Market Maker	Coburn & Meredith, Inc.	Telephone	(203)522-7171	SIC Code	5812
Broker Dealer	Regular Stockbroker			Employees	n.a.

Connohio, Inc.

1031 Ellicott Square • Buffalo, NY 14203 • Telephone (716)852-6858 • Fax (716)852-0694

Company Description

The Company is involved in a variety of energy providing activites for residents and businesses in the states of Connecticut and New York. It also is involved in a joint exploration and development program to develop oil and gas reserves. In addition, the Company owns 11.9% of Medina Power Company, a cogeneration plant in western New York.

	12/31/95	12/31/94	12/31/93	12/31/92
Per Share Information				
Stock Price	6.00	6.00	7.50	7.50
Earnings Per Share	-0.81	-0.77	-1.25	-1.14
Price / Earnings Ratio	n.a.	n.a.	n.a.	n.a.
Book Value Per Share	6.19	7.20	7.98	9.78
Price / Book Value %	96.93	83.33	93.98	76.69
Dividends Per Share	0.20	0.25	0.30	0.30
Annual Financial Data				
Operating Results (000's)				
Total Revenues	3,411.7	3,172.1	3,668.0	3,103.2
Costs & Expenses	-3,403.4	-3,591.5	-3,745.2	-3,345.7
Income Before Taxes and Other	-260.3	-880.8	-270.4	-242.6
Other Items	n.a.	538.8	n.a.	n.a.
Income Tax	84.4	174.5	-3.6	-7.6
Net Income	-175.9	-167.5	-274.0	-250.1
Cash Flow From Operations	-97.9	-199.3	-215.8	n.a.
Balance Sheet (000's)				
Cash & Equivalents	92.2	98.8	100.5	n.a.
Total Current Assets	484.5	486.3	558.7	688.9
Fixed Assets, Net	951.6	968.2	1,027.1	1,199.9
Total Assets	2,846.7	3,153.4	3,022.6	3,587.8
Total Current Liabilities	1,423.6	1,506.5	1,150.6	1,370.4
Long-Term Debt	n.a.	n.a.	n.a.	2.8
Stockholders' Equity	1,423.1	1,646.9	1,872.0	2,214.5
Performance & Financial Condition				
Return on Total Revenues %	-5.15	-5.28	-7.47	-8.06
Return on Avg Stockholders' Equity %	-11.46	-9.52	-13.41	-10.53
Return on Average Assets %	-5.86	-5.42	-8.29	-7.57
Current Ratio	0.34	0.32	0.49	0.50
Debt / Equity %	n.a.	n.a.	n.a.	0.13

Compound Growth %'s	EPS % -10.77	Net Income % -11.08	Total Revenues %	3.21

Comments

We assumed that the preferred stock would not be converted in our per share calculations. 1994 results include a nonrecurring benefit of $538,800 in connection with the adoption of GAAP for the reporting of income taxes. Marketable securities are recorded at cost but are valued at more than $2 million above cost, or approximately $10 per share. If the Company can stabilize itself after years of losses, it could make an interesting investment.

Officers	Position	Ownership Information	12/31/95
Jack A. Keenan	President, CEO	Number of Shares Outstanding	219,491
Majorie E. Hutz	Secretary	Market Capitalization	$ 1,316,946
Richard M. Hilliker	Treasurer	Frequency Of Dividends	Quarterly
John A. Macey	Vice President	Number of Shareholders	Under 500
William G. Griffin	General Manager		

Other Information

Transfer Agent	National City Bank, Cleveland, OH		Where Listed	OTC-BB
Auditor	Courtney, Fink & Forbes		Symbol	CNNO
Market Maker	Robotti & Eng, Incorporated	Telephone (212)986-4800	SIC Code	4930
Broker Dealer	Regular Stockbroker		Employees	n.a.

Continental Health Affiliates, Inc.

910 Sylvan Avenue • Englewood Cliffs, NJ 07632 • Telephone (201)567-4600 • Fax (201)567-1072

Company Description

The Company provides a variety of non-hospital based health care services to patients. At June 30, 1995, the Company was operating or managing eight nursing homes with approximately 1,175 beds. On October 31, 1995, the Company concluded a $46.0 million financing to purchase four facilities which the Company had previously leased or managed. The Company was incorporated in 1981. In 1993, the Company issued 13,884 shares of preferred stock as part of an exchange with holders of its bonds. The 5% cumulative preferred stock has a liquidation preference of $100 per share and is exchangeable into the common stock of the Company's subsidiary, subject to certain provisions.

	06/30/95	12/31/94	12/31/93	12/31/92
Per Share Information				
Stock Price	1.38	1.00	0.75	1.00
Earnings Per Share	-0.08	0.04	0.33	0.71
Price / Earnings Ratio	n.a.	25.00	2.27	1.41
Book Value Per Share	-0.17	-0.18	-0.17	-1.01
Price / Book Value %	n.a.	n.a.	n.a.	n.a.
Dividends Per Share	n.a.	n.a.	n.a.	n.a.
Annual Financial Data				
Operating Results (000's)				
Total Revenues	28,724.0	54,378.0	61,270.0	60,364.0
Costs & Expenses	-29,648.0	-55,295.0	-59,623.0	-58,546.0
Income Before Taxes and Other	-915.0	-1,423.0	17.0	3,434.0
Other Items	353.0	1,433.0	1,327.0	1,858.0
Income Tax	n.a.	341.0	385.0	-1,750.0
Net Income	-562.0	351.0	1,729.0	3,542.0
Cash Flow From Operations	-149.0	-750.0	435.0	834.0
Balance Sheet (000's)				
Cash & Equivalents	546.0	1,161.0	3,527.0	4,436.0
Total Current Assets	10,435.0	11,117.0	13,527.0	12,946.0
Fixed Assets, Net	9,934.0	9,903.0	30,728.0	31,482.0
Total Assets	29,675.0	30,485.0	46,194.0	46,700.0
Total Current Liabilities	16,495.0	15,509.0	27,113.0	43,760.0
Long-Term Debt	10,766.0	10,806.0	13,298.0	3,832.0
Stockholders' Equity	32.0	628.0	113.0	-7,760.0
Performance & Financial Condition				
Return on Total Revenues %	-1.96	0.65	2.82	5.87
Return on Avg Stockholders' Equity %	-170.30	94.74	n.a.	n.a.
Return on Average Assets %	-1.87	0.92	3.72	7.68
Current Ratio	0.63	0.72	0.50	0.30
Debt / Equity %	n.a.	1720.70	n.a.	n.a.

Compound Growth %'s	EPS % n.a.	Net Income % n.a.	Total Revenues % -21.93

Comments

The Company changed it's year end from December 31, to June 30, during 1995. The statement of operations for June 30, 1995, is for six months, and is not comparable to those of prior years. For the six months ended December 31, 1995, the Company had revenues of $33.6 million and net income of $341,000 as compared to $27.3 million and a loss of $576,000 for the same period in 1994.

Officers	Position	Ownership Information	06/30/95
Jack Rosen	President, CEO	Number of Shares Outstanding	7,830,059
Richard S. Gordon	Exec VP	Market Capitalization	$ 10,805,481
Israel Ingberman	Treasurer, Secretary	Frequency Of Dividends	n.a.
Benjamin Geizhals	Vice President	Number of Shareholders	390
Joseph Rosen	Vice President		

Other Information

Transfer Agent	American Stock Transfer & Trust Company		Where Listed	OTC-BB
Auditor	KPMG Peat Marwick LLP		Symbol	CTHL
Market Maker	Ernst & Company	Telephone (212)898-6330	SIC Code	8082
Broker Dealer	Regular Stockbroker		Employees	1129

Continental Resources, Inc.

175 Middlesex Turnpike • Bedford, MA 01730-9137 • Telephone (617)275-0850 • Fax (617)275-6563

Company Description

The Company's principal business activities are the sale, rental and servicing of electronic instruments and computer equipment. They also produce, configure, test, maintain and service complete lines of high quality computer and test equipment products. The Company also owns a 49% interest in Wall Industries, Inc., a manufacturer of power supplies and converters. The Company was formed in 1962 and went public in 1970. Shares are hard to come by and require patience. In fact, we expect the availability of these shares to disappear shortly after publication of this book.

	12/31/95	12/31/94	12/31/93	12/31/92
Per Share Information				
Stock Price	65.00	60.00	n.a.	n.a.
Earnings Per Share	22.67	1.38	-5.51	7.60
Price / Earnings Ratio	2.87	43.48	n.a.	n.a.
Book Value Per Share	186.62	163.95	n.a.	n.a.
Price / Book Value %	34.83	36.60	n.a.	n.a.
Dividends Per Share	n.a.	n.a.	n.a.	n.a.
Annual Financial Data				
Operating Results (000's)				
Total Revenues	107,740.7	58,441.2	53,534.9	57,933.0
Costs & Expenses	-105,203.5	-58,326.3	-54,008.5	-57,518.6
Income Before Taxes and Other	2,537.2	114.9	-473.6	414.4
Other Items	n.a.	n.a.	n.a.	280.0
Income Tax	-1,040.8	-23.5	110.0	-192.9
Net Income	1,496.4	91.4	-363.6	501.5
Cash Flow From Operations	14,294.6	4,688.9	n.a.	n.a.
Balance Sheet (000's)				
Cash & Equivalents	940.5	736.2	n.a.	n.a.
Total Current Assets	18,129.9	18,143.1	n.a.	n.a.
Fixed Assets, Net	18,506.6	17,794.9	n.a.	n.a.
Total Assets	37,939.5	37,288.4	n.a.	n.a.
Total Current Liabilities	15,452.0	20,077.5	n.a.	n.a.
Long-Term Debt	9,352.0	5,416.0	n.a.	n.a.
Stockholders' Equity	12,320.0	10,823.6	n.a.	n.a.
Performance & Financial Condition				
Return on Total Revenues %	1.39	0.16	-0.68	0.87
Return on Avg Stockholders' Equity %	12.93	n.a.	n.a.	n.a.
Return on Average Assets %	3.98	n.a.	n.a.	n.a.
Current Ratio	1.17	0.90	n.a.	n.a.
Debt / Equity %	75.91	50.04	n.a.	n.a.

Compound Growth %'s	EPS %	43.95	Net Income %	43.97	Total Revenues %	22.98

Comments

Management expects strong growth in all divisions to continue. Wall Industries was ranked by World Trade Magazine to be in the top 100 fastest growing, high-tech global manufacturers. 1995 results were excellent and place the Company in a stronger financial position for expansion.

Officers	Position	Ownership Information	12/31/95
James F. McCann, Sr.	Chairman	Number of Shares Outstanding	66,018
James F. Cann, Jr.	President	Market Capitalization	$ 4,291,170
James M. Bunt	VP - Finance	Frequency Of Dividends	n.a.
Joseph P. Tyrrell	CFO	Number of Shareholders	Under 500
Kevin McCann	Vice President		

Other Information				
Transfer Agent	State Street Bank		Where Listed	OTC-BB
Auditor	G.T. Reilly & Company		Symbol	CTLR
Market Maker	Chicago Corporation, The	Telephone (800)621-1674	SIC Code	3600
Broker Dealer	Pink sheet specialist		Employees	n.a.

Cornet Stores

411 South Arroyo Parkway • Pasadena, CA 91109-0847 • Telephone (818)796-5123 • Fax (818)796-8635

Company Description

The Company operates a chain of variety stores doing business primarily in the western United States and develops and leases property to others primarily for retail use. In conjunction with the settlement of a shareholders' suit, the Company has agreed to contract its retail operations and sell its properties over a period of time with the adoption of a complete plan of liquidation by January 31, 2001.

	05/31/95	05/31/94
Per Share Information		
Stock Price	5.12	4.00
Earnings Per Share	-0.40	-2.50
Price / Earnings Ratio	n.a.	n.a.
Book Value Per Share	14.13	14.52
Price / Book Value %	36.23	27.55
Dividends Per Share	n.a.	n.a.
Annual Financial Data		
Operating Results (000's)		
Total Revenues	28,419.7	28,060.7
Costs & Expenses	-29,193.3	-31,015.5
Income Before Taxes and Other	-773.6	-6,279.0
Other Items	n.a.	395.5
Income Tax	210.1	2,329.9
Net Income	-563.5	-3,553.5
Cash Flow From Operations	864.5	1,183.6
Balance Sheet (000's)		
Cash & Equivalents	5,783.5	1,511.3
Total Current Assets	14,048.4	15,230.5
Fixed Assets, Net	11,991.7	14,509.4
Total Assets	31,766.9	33,507.6
Total Current Liabilities	7,004.4	7,943.4
Long-Term Debt	2,807.3	3,155.7
Stockholders' Equity	20,074.0	20,637.9
Performance & Financial Condition		
Return on Total Revenues %	-1.98	-12.66
Return on Avg Stockholders' Equity %	-2.77	n.a.
Return on Average Assets %	-1.73	n.a.
Current Ratio	2.01	1.92
Debt / Equity %	13.98	15.29

Compound Growth %'s	EPS % n.a.	Net Income % n.a.	Total Revenues % 1.28

Comments

1994 results include a $3.3 million expense related to the shareholders' suit. As the Company has started the process of contracting (15 stores were closed in 1995), the real question becomes how much of book value will be preserved in the process and ultimately paid to the shareholders.

Officers	Position	Ownership Information	05/31/95
Joe Cornet	President	Number of Shares Outstanding	1,420,538
		Market Capitalization	$ 7,273,155
		Frequency Of Dividends	n.a.
		Number of Shareholders	Under 500

Other Information

Transfer Agent	Bank of America, San Francisco, CA		Where Listed	OTC-BB
Auditor	Maginnis, Knechtel & McIntyre		Symbol	CIUS
Market Maker	Hill, Thompson, Magid & Co.Inc	Telephone (800)631-3083	SIC Code	5331
Broker Dealer	Regular Stockbroker		Employees	250

Corning Natural Gas Corporation

330 West William Street • Corning, NY 14830 • Telephone (607)936-3755 • Fax (607)962-2844

Company Description

The Company is a gas distribution company providing natural gas to its customers in the southern part of New York State. The Company's service area encompasses about 415 square miles with a population of over 56,000. A subsidiary, Corning Natural Gas Appliance Company sells, rents and services residential and commercial appliances. The Company has three major gas customers which, for the year ended December 31, 1995, accounted for 18% of total revenues.

	12/31/95	12/31/94	12/31/93	12/31/92
Per Share Information				
Stock Price	23.50	24.50	24.50	16.25
Earnings Per Share	1.35	1.43	1.26	1.10
Price / Earnings Ratio	17.41	17.13	19.44	14.77
Book Value Per Share	11.09	10.98	10.78	10.73
Price / Book Value %	211.90	223.13	227.27	151.44
Dividends Per Share	1.25	1.23	1.21	1.20
Annual Financial Data				
Operating Results (000's)				
Total Revenues	18,697.4	18,727.5	20,061.6	15,839.7
Costs & Expenses	-17,834.5	-17,858.1	-19,232.3	-15,195.9
Income Before Taxes and Other	862.9	869.4	829.3	643.8
Other Items	n.a.	n.a.	n.a.	n.a.
Income Tax	-242.1	-212.9	-250.5	-136.1
Net Income	620.7	656.5	578.8	507.7
Cash Flow From Operations	1,817.4	601.4	1,169.7	-794.4
Balance Sheet (000's)				
Cash & Equivalents	142.9	183.1	203.8	239.6
Total Current Assets	3,891.3	4,064.5	4,828.7	3,881.4
Fixed Assets, Net	14,157.0	13,499.0	13,223.9	13,082.1
Total Assets	21,812.7	22,439.4	22,428.1	19,383.9
Total Current Liabilities	7,039.6	7,033.7	6,747.8	6,605.5
Long-Term Debt	6,300.0	6,400.0	6,500.0	6,600.0
Stockholders' Equity	5,099.0	5,051.0	4,958.0	4,933.6
Performance & Financial Condition				
Return on Total Revenues %	3.32	3.51	2.88	3.21
Return on Avg Stockholders' Equity %	12.23	13.12	11.70	10.33
Return on Average Assets %	2.81	2.93	2.77	2.59
Current Ratio	0.55	0.58	0.72	0.59
Debt / Equity %	123.55	126.71	131.10	133.78

Compound Growth %'s	EPS %	7.06	Net Income %	6.93	Total Revenues %	5.68

Comments

The Company's wholly-owned subsidiary, Corning Natural Gas Appliance Corp., accounted for between 32% to 41% of the Company's net income during the four years ended December 31, 1995.

Officers	Position	Ownership Information	12/31/95
Thomas K. Barry	President, CEO	Number of Shares Outstanding	460,000
Kenneth J. Robinson	Exec VP	Market Capitalization	$ 10,810,000
Edgar F. Lewis	Senior VP	Frequency Of Dividends	Quarterly
Gary K. Earley	Treasurer	Number of Shareholders	406
Thomas S. Roye	Vice President		

Other Information					
Transfer Agent	Company Office			Where Listed	OTC-BB
Auditor	KPMG Peat Marwick LLP			Symbol	CNNG
Market Maker	Monroe Securities, Inc.	Telephone	(800)766-5560	SIC Code	4923
Broker Dealer	Josephthal Lyon & Ross, Inc.	Tel/Ext	(214)907-4060	Employees	72

Country-Wide Insurance Company

90 Washington Street • New York, NY 10006-2214 • Telephone (212)514-7000 • Fax (212)514-7292

Company Description

The Company is a New York domiciled property and casualty insurance company licensed in New York and New Jersey. Its major lines of business are auto liability and auto physical damage. The Company was formed in 1963. On June 23, 1995, the Company offered to buy back all outstanding shares at $10 per share. An appraisal was prepared to justify the offer price. It is reported that a number of the shareholders were offended by the Company action. One such shareholder claims the value is $50 per share.

	12/31/94	12/31/93	12/31/92
Per Share Information			
Stock Price	14.00	7.75	5.75
Earnings Per Share	9.67	6.98	3.40
Price / Earnings Ratio	1.45	1.11	1.69
Book Value Per Share	44.13	38.67	30.92
Price / Book Value %	31.72	20.04	18.60
Dividends Per Share	1.55	0.85	0.60
Annual Financial Data			
Operating Results (000's)			
Total Revenues	37,167.0	29,164.4	28,591.2
Costs & Expenses	-33,342.8	-26,668.3	-26,658.5
Income Before Taxes and Other	3,824.2	2,496.1	1,767.4
Other Items	n.a.	n.a.	n.a.
Income Tax	-1,107.0	-534.6	-811.3
Net Income	2,717.2	1,961.5	956.1
Cash Flow From Operations	2,932.4	2,796.0	4,392.4
Balance Sheet (000's)			
Cash & Equivalents	742.6	201.9	1,536.7
Total Current Assets	50,160.1	48,416.0	46,121.7
Fixed Assets, Net	n.a.	n.a.	n.a.
Total Assets	59,505.9	57,354.3	55,986.2
Total Current Liabilities	47,101.9	46,487.5	47,294.7
Long-Term Debt	n.a.	n.a.	n.a.
Stockholders' Equity	12,404.1	10,866.8	8,691.5
Performance & Financial Condition			
Return on Total Revenues %	7.31	6.73	3.34
Return on Avg Stockholders' Equity %	23.35	20.06	11.45
Return on Average Assets %	4.65	3.46	1.78
Current Ratio	1.06	1.04	0.98
Debt / Equity %	n.a.	n.a.	n.a.

Compound Growth %'s	EPS % 68.65	Net Income % 68.58	Total Revenues % 14.02

Comments

1995 results had not been released at the time we went to press. We would like to know what you think? Which party has done a better job in valuing the stock, the Company at $10 or the disgruntled shareholder at $50. Earnings have been on a steady rise. In 1994, the Company earned $9.67 per share. Book value at year end was $44.13. The compounded growth rate in earnings over the 2 year period ending in 1994 was 68% in earnings and 14% in revenues. You make the call.

Officers	Position	Ownership Information	12/31/94
Raymond Cheven	President	Number of Shares Outstanding	281,054
Michael D. Jaffe	Exec VP, Treasurer	Market Capitalization	$ 3,934,756
Barbara A. Cheven	Vice President	Frequency Of Dividends	Quarterly
Walter J. Convery	Vice President	Number of Shareholders	Under 500
Myles M. Saposnick	Vice President		

Other Information				
Transfer Agent	Company Office		Where Listed	OTC-PS
Auditor	Israeloff, Trattner & Co.		Symbol	CWID
Market Maker	Legg Mason Wood Walker, Inc.	Telephone (212)428-4949	SIC Code	6400
Broker Dealer	Pink sheet specialist		Employees	n.a.

Cowles Media Company

329 Portland Avenue • Minneapolis, MN 55415-1112 • Telephone (612)673-7100 • Fax (612)673-7020

Company Description

The Company is a newspaper, magazine, and information services company headquartered in Minneapolis. Publications include the Star Tribune, the Scottsdale Progress, Cowles Magazines and Cowles Business Media. Business began in 1935 when John Cowles acquired and began to build The Minneapolis Star. In 1993 the shares split 6 for 1. Per share amounts have been adjusted accordingly.

	04/01/95	04/02/94	04/03/93	03/28/92
Per Share Information				
Stock Price	23.50	23.50	23.00	18.75
Earnings Per Share	1.61	1.40	1.09	0.75
Price / Earnings Ratio	14.60	16.79	21.10	25.00
Book Value Per Share	3.49	2.21	10.62	0.37
Price / Book Value %	673.35	1,063.40	216.57	5,067.60
Dividends Per Share	0.56	0.52	0.49	0.47
Annual Financial Data				
Operating Results (000's)				
Total Revenues	455,657.0	360,079.0	337,647.0	308,011.0
Costs & Expenses	-415,994.0	-326,907.0	-308,928.0	-290,542.0
Income Before Taxes and Other	39,663.0	33,172.0	28,719.0	17,469.0
Other Items	n.a.	n.a.	-1,336.0	n.a.
Income Tax	-17,164.0	-13,744.0	-12,344.0	-7,238.0
Net Income	22,499.0	19,428.0	15,039.0	10,231.0
Cash Flow From Operations	32,926.0	38,945.0	37,873.0	34,833.0
Balance Sheet (000's)				
Cash & Equivalents	2,759.0	34,711.0	30,506.0	19,239.0
Total Current Assets	78,808.0	87,855.0	68,899.0	57,249.0
Fixed Assets, Net	114,710.0	104,546.0	110,518.0	116,246.0
Total Assets	314,221.0	279,169.0	246,365.0	237,640.0
Total Current Liabilities	142,281.0	113,525.0	108,507.0	103,589.0
Long-Term Debt	90,031.0	91,034.0	83,840.0	90,787.0
Stockholders' Equity	48,510.0	30,483.0	14,652.0	5,073.0
Performance & Financial Condition				
Return on Total Revenues %	4.94	5.40	4.45	3.32
Return on Avg Stockholders' Equity %	56.96	86.09	152.49	375.59
Return on Average Assets %	7.58	7.39	6.21	4.28
Current Ratio	0.55	0.77	0.63	0.55
Debt / Equity %	185.59	298.64	572.21	1789.60

Compound Growth %'s	EPS %	29.00	Net Income %	30.04	Total Revenues %	13.94

Comments

Growth appears fueled by management's diversification beyond the core newspaper business through acquisitions and internal innovation. Current liabilities include unearned income on subscriptions paid in advance which distorts some of the traditional ratios.

Officers	Position	Ownership Information	04/01/95
David C. Cox	President, CEO	Number of Shares Outstanding	13,884,536
James A. Alcott	Vice President	Market Capitalization	$ 326,286,596
Pamela J. Sveinson	Vice President	Frequency Of Dividends	Quarterly
James J. Viera	Vice President, CFO	Number of Shareholders	Under 500

Other Information

Transfer Agent	Sherburne & Coughlin, Ltd.			Where Listed	OTC-PS
Auditor	KPMG Peat Marwick LLP			Symbol	n.a.
Market Maker	Piper Jaffray Inc.	Telephone	(800)328-7488	SIC Code	2700
Broker Dealer	Regular Stockbroker			Employees	n.a.

Crowley Maritime Corporation

155 Grand Avenue • Oakland, CA 94612 • Telephone (510)251-7500 • Fax (510)251-7788

Company Description

The Company was founded in the San Francisco Bay Area in 1892. It now has two primary operating divisions. Crowley American Transport, Inc. conducts liner and common carrier shipping operations and is the third largest American shipping company. Crowley Marine Services, Inc. provides worldwide contract and specialized marine transportation services.

	12/31/95	12/31/94	12/31/93	12/31/92
Per Share Information				
Stock Price	1,000.00	825.00	900.00	700.00
Earnings Per Share	142.27	48.45	80.48	64.56
Price / Earnings Ratio	7.03	17.03	11.18	10.84
Book Value Per Share	1,336.03	1,168.80	1,123.72	1,047.03
Price / Book Value %	74.85	70.59	80.09	66.86
Dividends Per Share	n.a.	n.a.	n.a.	n.a.
Annual Financial Data				
Operating Results (000's)				
Total Revenues	1,111,158.0	1,100,004.0	1,074,777.0	1,076,527.0
Costs & Expenses	-1,067,811.0	-1,072,438.0	-1,041,793.0	-1,040,270.0
Income Before Taxes and Other	42,904.0	27,103.0	31,848.0	36,257.0
Other Items	n.a.	n.a.	n.a.	n.a.
Income Tax	-21,100.0	-16,900.0	-16,800.0	-20,800.0
Net Income	21,804.0	10,203.0	15,048.0	15,457.0
Cash Flow From Operations	53,172.0	51,275.0	39,484.0	n.a.
Balance Sheet (000's)				
Cash & Equivalents	54,356.0	44,648.0	27,974.0	n.a.
Total Current Assets	263,981.0	253,465.0	217,321.0	230,850.0
Fixed Assets, Net	306,799.0	317,469.0	341,477.0	341,534.0
Total Assets	607,980.0	607,397.0	602,934.0	624,553.0
Total Current Liabilities	214,797.0	219,586.0	213,225.0	243,735.0
Long-Term Debt	132,786.0	143,660.0	160,629.0	157,583.0
Stockholders' Equity	221,075.0	217,184.0	211,611.0	207,105.0
Performance & Financial Condition				
Return on Total Revenues %	1.96	0.93	1.40	1.44
Return on Avg Stockholders' Equity %	9.95	4.76	7.19	7.34
Return on Average Assets %	3.59	1.69	2.45	2.60
Current Ratio	1.23	1.15	1.02	0.95
Debt / Equity %	60.06	66.15	75.91	76.09

Compound Growth %'s	EPS %	30.13	Net Income %	12.15	Total Revenues %	1.06

Comments

Thomas B. Crowley, Sr. ran the Company until the day he died in July of 1994. He is deeply missed by his family, friends, community and the company to which he devoted 60 years of service. Fortunately, Thomas B. Crowley, Jr. was well prepared for the day he would assume the top job at this $1 billion giant of American industry. Long-term strategic planning and a new overall management system is sharpening Crowley's vision for the next 100 years.

Officers	Position	Ownership Information	12/31/95
Thomas B. Crowley, Jr.	Chairman, CEO	Number of Shares Outstanding	133,025
William A. Pennella	Exec VP	Market Capitalization	$ 133,025,000
Richard M. Oster	Senior VP, CFO	Frequency Of Dividends	n.a.
Scott G. Skillman	Senior VP	Number of Shareholders	Under 500
Tana G. Shipman	Secretary		

Other Information

Transfer Agent	Company Office			Where Listed		OTC-BB
Auditor	Deloitte & Touche LLP			Symbol		CWLM
Market Maker	Seidler Companies, Inc., The	Telephone	(800)421-0164	SIC Code		4492
Broker Dealer	Standard Investment	Tel/Ext	(888)783-4688	Jack	Employees	5000

Crown City Plating Co.

4350 Temple City Boulevard • El Monte, CA 91731-1010 • Telephone (818)444-9291 • Fax (818)448-6915

Company Description

The Company provides metal-finishing and plastics-finishing to component parts used by companies such as Apple Computer, General Motors, Ford, General Electric and Gillette. Production is at a state-of-the-art facility in California. The Company was organized in 1911. The original family still manages the business, now in the fourth generation with Robert L. Coombes, Jr. as President. The Company has an employee stock ownership plan, (ESOP), for the benefit of all full-time employees.

	03/31/95	03/31/94	03/31/93	03/31/92
Per Share Information				
Stock Price	5.25	5.25	4.50	4.00
Earnings Per Share	1.47	1.63	1.11	-1.15
Price / Earnings Ratio	3.57	3.22	4.05	n.a.
Book Value Per Share	17.04	15.70	14.76	13.57
Price / Book Value %	30.81	33.44	30.49	29.48
Dividends Per Share	0.40	0.15	n.a.	n.a.
Annual Financial Data				
Operating Results (000's)				
Total Revenues	23,927.3	22,792.7	22,176.7	20,720.7
Costs & Expenses	-23,124.5	-21,795.2	-21,953.4	-21,197.1
Income Before Taxes and Other	712.9	897.5	223.4	-476.5
Other Items	n.a.	n.a.	n.a.	n.a.
Income Tax	-185.0	-312.0	177.2	61.0
Net Income	527.9	585.5	400.6	-415.5
Cash Flow From Operations	n.a.	n.a.	n.a.	n.a.
Balance Sheet (000's)				
Cash & Equivalents	n.a.	n.a.	n.a.	n.a.
Total Current Assets	5,979.9	7,760.7	7,235.0	6,679.7
Fixed Assets, Net	3,466.6	3,591.1	3,888.4	4,495.9
Total Assets	9,597.4	11,622.2	11,405.5	11,432.2
Total Current Liabilities	2,802.4	4,179.7	4,605.4	4,554.1
Long-Term Debt	n.a.	n.a.	n.a.	n.a.
Stockholders' Equity	6,120.6	5,639.1	5,324.4	4,901.4
Performance & Financial Condition				
Return on Total Revenues %	2.21	2.57	n.a.	-2.01
Return on Avg Stockholders' Equity %	8.98	10.68	7.83	-8.04
Return on Average Assets %	4.98	5.09	3.51	-3.59
Current Ratio	2.13	1.86	n.a.	1.47
Debt / Equity %	n.a.	n.a.	n.a.	n.a.

Compound Growth %'s	EPS %	15.08	Net Income %	14.80	Total Revenues %	4.91

Comments

Management projected fiscal year 1996 to be a difficult year because of the loss of volume associated with the Ford Ranger wheel ornament job but expects the volume will be replaced in fiscal 1997. The financial information we received was not accompanied by an audit report. The Company has an annual appraisal of the stock for purposes of supporting the price used in transactions with the ESOP. It was reported to us by an outside source that the last valuation was at $30 per share.

Officers	Position	Ownership Information	03/31/95
Robert L. Coombes	Chairman, CEO	Number of Shares Outstanding	359,090
Robert L. Coombes, Jr.	President	Market Capitalization	$ 1,885,223
Thomas A. Gardner	CFO	Frequency Of Dividends	Annual
John A. Dom	VP - Sales	Number of Shareholders	Under 500
Brooke Fix	VP - Sales		

Other Information

Transfer Agent	Chemical Mellon Shareholder Services			Where Listed	OTC-BB
Auditor	n.a.			Symbol	CCPG
Market Maker	Seidler Companies, Inc., The	Telephone	(800)421-0164	SIC Code	3471
Broker Dealer	Regular Stockbroker			Employees	320

Crystal Mountain, Inc.

One Crystal Mountain Blvd. • Crystal Mountain, WA 98022 • Telephone (360)825-3865 • Fax (360)825-6261

Company Description

The Company owns and operates a ski resort in the Cascade Mountains of Washington State. The resort is the largest ski area in the state comprising over 4,300 acres and is rated as one of the top resorts in the pacific Northwest with summer activities as well. The Company was incorporated in 1955 and began operations in 1962.

	09/30/95	09/30/94	09/30/93	09/30/92
Per Share Information				
Stock Price	325.00	350.00	285.00	250.00
Earnings Per Share	-16.03	-8.75	20.72	5.80
Price / Earnings Ratio	n.a.	n.a.	13.75	43.10
Book Value Per Share	98.00	115.00	130.29	109.58
Price / Book Value %	331.63	304.35	218.74	228.14
Dividends Per Share	n.a.	n.a.	n.a.	n.a.
Annual Financial Data				
Operating Results (000's)				
Total Revenues	9,272.0	8,889.0	9,643.0	8,176.0
Costs & Expenses	-9,765.0	-9,128.0	-9,249.0	-8,107.0
Income Before Taxes and Other	-493.0	-239.0	394.0	69.0
Other Items	n.a.	n.a.	n.a.	n.a.
Income Tax	55.0	n.a.	-10.0	90.0
Net Income	-438.0	-239.0	384.0	159.0
Cash Flow From Operations	1,145.0	129.0	1,562.6	1,057.8
Balance Sheet (000's)				
Cash & Equivalents	154.0	148.0	150.2	96.4
Total Current Assets	591.0	538.0	531.5	501.9
Fixed Assets, Net	8,089.0	8,109.0	8,639.4	8,261.6
Total Assets	8,826.0	8,844.0	9,187.6	8,787.0
Total Current Liabilities	1,684.0	1,305.0	1,296.4	1,119.9
Long-Term Debt	4,442.0	4,346.0	4,260.0	4,600.0
Stockholders' Equity	2,700.0	3,138.0	3,559.7	2,993.5
Performance & Financial Condition				
Return on Total Revenues %	-4.72	-2.69	3.98	1.94
Return on Avg Stockholders' Equity %	-15.01	-7.14	11.72	5.45
Return on Average Assets %	-4.96	-2.65	4.27	1.76
Current Ratio	0.35	0.41	0.41	0.45
Debt / Equity %	164.52	138.50	119.67	153.66

Compound Growth %'s	EPS % n.a.	Net Income % n.a.	Total Revenues %	4.28

Comments

The success of ski resorts is very dependent on variations in the weather. The 1993/94 ski season in Washington State was poor and, accordingly, the Company's operations suffered. In an effort to smooth this erratic performance, the Company has focused efforts on year-round recreational activities.

Officers	Position	Ownership Information	09/30/95
Robert E. Carlson	Chairman	Number of Shares Outstanding	27,319
Thomas F. Leonard	President	Market Capitalization	$ 8,878,675
Lawrence E. Hard	Secretary	Frequency Of Dividends	n.a.
Delight S. Mahalko	Treasurer	Number of Shareholders	n.a.
Peter G. Gillis	Vice President		

Other Information

Transfer Agent	Company Office	Where Listed	OTC-BB
Auditor	Moss Adams LLP	Symbol	CRTLA
Market Maker	Martin Nelson & Co., Inc.	Telephone (800)543-3332	SIC Code	7011
Broker Dealer	Regular Stockbroker	Employees	740

DHB Capital Group Inc.

11 Old Westbury Road • Old Westbury, NY 11568 • Telephone (516)997-1155 • Fax (516)997-1144

Company Description

The Company, through several subsidiaries acquired since 1992, manufactures and distributes ballistic-resistant equipment, apparel and related products used by police and other law-enforcement and security personnel and protective athletic apparel and equipment. Other business includes a majority interest in a development stage telecommunications company and since March 1996, a 100% interest in an orthopedic products company. The Company was initially incorporated in New york in 1992, then reincorporated in Delaware in 1995. A private placement of 1,955,000 shares in 1995 raised $3.9 milion and one in 1994, of 387,000 shares, raised $875,000. The Company's stock was first traded in September, 1993.

	12/31/95	12/31/94	12/31/93	12/31/92
Per Share Information				
Stock Price	4.00	3.51	5.00	n.a.
Earnings Per Share	0.02	-0.01	0.02	-0.04
Price / Earnings Ratio	200.00	n.a.	250.00	n.a.
Book Value Per Share	0.86	0.62	0.68	-0.04
Price / Book Value %	465.12	566.13	735.29	n.a.
Dividends Per Share	n.a.	n.a.	n.a.	n.a.
Annual Financial Data				
Operating Results (000's)				
Total Revenues	15,519.0	9,103.5	7,292.7	816.9
Costs & Expenses	-14,442.0	-8,937.2	-7,054.3	-842.2
Income Before Taxes and Other	827.1	-546.3	238.4	-298.1
Other Items	n.a.	91.7	n.a.	n.a.
Income Tax	-517.3	379.4	-7.6	n.a.
Net Income	309.8	-75.2	230.8	-298.1
Cash Flow From Operations	-742.4	-1,039.3	-758.4	-40.4
Balance Sheet (000's)				
Cash & Equivalents	475.1	407.4	1,880.3	132.4
Total Current Assets	14,189.2	8,743.8	5,940.3	2,568.5
Fixed Assets, Net	1,077.1	659.0	479.8	283.0
Total Assets	19,555.9	11,675.5	6,871.2	3,359.7
Total Current Liabilities	7,688.6	3,355.6	1,924.4	1,049.8
Long-Term Debt	n.a.	n.a.	n.a.	2,600.0
Stockholders' Equity	11,867.3	7,180.0	4,946.8	-290.1
Performance & Financial Condition				
Return on Total Revenues %	2.00	-0.83	3.16	-36.49
Return on Avg Stockholders' Equity %	3.25	-1.24	9.91	n.a.
Return on Average Assets %	1.98	-0.81	4.51	-17.74
Current Ratio	1.85	2.61	3.09	2.45
Debt / Equity %	n.a.	n.a.	n.a.	n.a.

Compound Growth %'s	EPS %	n.a.	Net Income %	15.86	Total Revenues %	166.83

Comments

At December 31, 1995, the Company had investments in marketable securities of $1.8 million and nonmarketable securities of $3.3 million. For the three months ended March 31, 1996, the Company reported sales of $7.0 milllion and income before taxes of $706,000, as compared to $2.7 million and $42,000 for the same period in 1995.

Officers	Position	Ownership Information	12/31/95
Douglas T. Burns	President	Number of Shares Outstanding	13,841,326
David H. Brooks	CEO	Market Capitalization	$ 55,365,304
Mary Kreidell	Secretary, Treasurer	Frequency Of Dividends	n.a.
		Number of Shareholders	800

Other Information			
Transfer Agent	American Stock Transfer & Trust Company	Where Listed	BE
Auditor	Capraro, Centofranchi, et. al.	Symbol	DHB
Market Maker	Frankel (WM.V.) & Co., Inc. Telephone (800)631-3091	SIC Code	3842
Broker Dealer	Regular Stockbroker	Employees	271

DK Investors Inc.

333 Seventh Avenue, Third Fl. • New York, NY 10001-4509 • Telephone (212)239-7979 • Fax (212)239-7978

Company Description

The Company is registered under the Investment Company Act of 1940 as a diversified, closed-end, management investment company. Its investment portfolio consists of municipal bonds.

	12/31/95	12/31/94
Per Share Information		
Stock Price	10.37	11.75
Earnings Per Share	0.08	1.04
Price / Earnings Ratio	129.63	11.30
Book Value Per Share	13.04	13.35
Price / Book Value %	79.52	88.01
Dividends Per Share	0.78	0.73
Annual Financial Data		
Operating Results (000's)		
Total Revenues	1,389.7	261.4
Costs & Expenses	-167.0	-167.7
Income Before Taxes and Other	1,222.7	93.6
Other Items	n.a.	n.a.
Income Tax	n.a.	n.a.
Net Income	1,222.7	93.6
Cash Flow From Operations	842.6	915.1
Balance Sheet (000's)		
Cash & Equivalents	28.9	42.4
Total Current Assets	16,516.6	16,035.9
Fixed Assets, Net	n.a.	n.a.
Total Assets	16,516.6	16,035.9
Total Current Liabilities	819.4	703.1
Long-Term Debt	n.a.	n.a.
Stockholders' Equity	15,697.2	15,332.8
Performance & Financial Condition		
Return on Total Revenues %	87.99	35.82
Return on Avg Stockholders' Equity %	7.88	n.a.
Return on Average Assets %	7.51	n.a.
Current Ratio	20.16	22.81
Debt / Equity %	n.a.	n.a.

Compound Growth %'s	EPS %	-92.31	Net Income %	1205.88	Total Revenues %	431.69

Comments

Expenses of administering and managing this portfolio approximate 1.06% of average net assets. Noteworthy is that the tax-free yield is quite favorable since the stock sells below book value. Compounded net income and earnings per share growth is distorted because only two years are presented and they include changes in asset valuations.

Officers	Position	Ownership Information	12/31/95
Gene Nadler	President	Number of Shares Outstanding	1,175,664
Thomas B. Schulhof	Secretary	Market Capitalization	$ 12,191,636
Glenn O. Thornhill, Sr.	Treasurer	Frequency Of Dividends	Quarterly
Ann Nadler	Vice President	Number of Shareholders	Under 500

Other Information

Transfer Agent	American Stock Transfer & Trust Company			Where Listed	OTC-BB
Auditor	Cummings & Carroll, PC			Symbol	DKII
Market Maker	Pennsylvania Merchant Group	Telephone	(800)762-8624	SIC Code	6790
Broker Dealer	Regular Stockbroker			Employees	1

Daedalus Enterprises, Inc.

300 Parkland Plaza • Parkland, DE 48106 • Telephone (313)769-5649 • Fax (313)769-0429

Company Description

The Company manufactures products for and performs development projects in the field of remote sensing. Principal products are airborne imaging systems used to acquire optical radiation data from objects on the earth's surface and in the atsmosphere. A principal application of the Company's products is the measurement of environmental parameters in support of pollution control programs and environmental impact studies. The Company was incorporated in the state of Delaware in 1968.

	07/31/95	07/31/94	07/31/93	07/31/92
Per Share Information				
Stock Price	2.25	3.63	5.25	6.50
Earnings Per Share	-0.70	-1.28	0.78	0.70
Price / Earnings Ratio	n.a.	n.a.	6.73	9.29
Book Value Per Share	4.64	5.53	6.96	6.24
Price / Book Value %	48.49	65.64	75.43	104.17
Dividends Per Share	0.17	0.15	0.13	0.11
Annual Financial Data				
Operating Results (000's)				
Total Revenues	3,624.4	2,453.1	6,305.2	6,001.0
Costs & Expenses	-4,161.1	-3,434.1	-5,671.8	-5,401.0
Income Before Taxes and Other	-536.8	-981.0	633.4	600.0
Other Items	n.a.	22.2	n.a.	n.a.
Income Tax	175.0	328.0	-179.0	-172.0
Net Income	-361.8	-630.8	454.4	428.0
Cash Flow From Operations	-403.9	-520.5	304.4	1,121.6
Balance Sheet (000's)				
Cash & Equivalents	76.8	163.2	918.0	1,212.2
Total Current Assets	2,341.8	2,395.8	2,959.6	4,122.4
Fixed Assets, Net	1,409.5	1,445.8	1,519.0	1,451.6
Total Assets	3,930.4	4,041.2	4,761.1	5,761.8
Total Current Liabilities	1,540.3	833.7	815.8	2,278.0
Long-Term Debt	n.a.	278.4	313.9	351.8
Stockholders' Equity	2,390.1	2,830.1	3,516.4	3,094.0
Performance & Financial Condition				
Return on Total Revenues %	-9.98	-25.71	7.21	7.13
Return on Avg Stockholders' Equity %	-13.86	-19.88	13.75	14.19
Return on Average Assets %	-9.08	-14.33	8.64	8.82
Current Ratio	1.52	2.87	3.63	1.81
Debt / Equity %	n.a.	9.84	8.93	11.37

Compound Growth %'s	EPS % n.a.	Net Income % n.a.	Total Revenues % -15.47

Comments

In the year ended July 31, 1995, approximately 62% of the Company's revenues were from business in Europe. The Company had three customers who, accumulatively, accounted for 91%, 88% and 85% of total revenue for 1995, 1994 and 1993, respectively.

Officers	Position	Ownership Information	07/31/95
Thomas R. Ory	President, CEO	Number of Shares Outstanding	514,913
Vincent J. Killewald	VP - Finance, Treasurer	Market Capitalization	$ 1,158,554
Charles G. Stanich	VP - Research, COO	Frequency Of Dividends	Irregular
		Number of Shareholders	200

Other Information

Transfer Agent	Chemical Mellon Shareholder Services		Where Listed	OTC-BB
Auditor	Deloitte & Touche LLP		Symbol	DDEI
Market Maker	Wachtel & Co., Inc.	Telephone (202)898-1018	SIC Code	3829
Broker Dealer	Regular Stockbroker		Employees	25

Dale System, Inc.

1101 Stewart Avenue • Garden City, NY 11530-3301 • Telephone (516)794-2800 • Fax (516)542-1063

Company Description

The Company is in the business of providing security services to business and industry.   The Company was incorporated in 1935 under the laws of Connecticut.

	05/31/95	05/31/94	05/31/93	05/31/92
Per Share Information				
Stock Price	1.00	0.87	0.69	0.50
Earnings Per Share	-0.67	0.01	-0.01	0.08
Price / Earnings Ratio	n.a.	87.00	n.a.	6.25
Book Value Per Share	0.97	1.64	1.63	1.63
Price / Book Value %	103.09	53.05	42.33	30.67
Dividends Per Share	n.a.	n.a.	n.a.	n.a.
Annual Financial Data				
Operating Results (000's)				
Total Revenues	5,939.1	6,294.1	6,898.5	6,703.4
Costs & Expenses	-6,129.0	-6,288.2	-6,894.2	-6,645.4
Income Before Taxes and Other	-193.1	5.8	1.7	44.9
Other Items	n.a.	n.a.	n.a.	n.a.
Income Tax	34.1	-3.9	-4.0	-13.1
Net Income	-159.0	1.9	-2.3	31.8
Cash Flow From Operations	-132.9	44.3	45.2	-172.1
Balance Sheet (000's)				
Cash & Equivalents	3.2	31.2	33.6	36.5
Total Current Assets	1,110.3	1,008.1	1,266.4	1,315.4
Fixed Assets, Net	159.1	90.4	112.1	115.2
Total Assets	1,580.4	1,388.1	1,611.8	1,617.4
Total Current Liabilities	932.7	621.4	841.0	845.1
Long-Term Debt	321.1	300.8	382.1	305.9
Stockholders' Equity	231.5	390.6	388.7	391.1
Performance & Financial Condition				
Return on Total Revenues %	-2.68	0.03	-0.03	0.47
Return on Avg Stockholders' Equity %	-51.13	0.49	-0.60	8.47
Return on Average Assets %	-10.72	0.13	-0.14	2.14
Current Ratio	1.19	1.62	1.51	1.56
Debt / Equity %	138.73	77.00	98.31	78.22

Compound Growth %'s	EPS % n.a.	Net Income % n.a.	Total Revenues % -3.95

Comments

Revenues declined despite an escalating avalanche of crimes against business. Management claims it has sharpened its focus to capitalize on a record demand for service. Unfortunately, no details were provided.

Officers	Position	Ownership Information	05/31/95
Harvey M. Yaffe	President	Number of Shares Outstanding	238,550
Alan Lowell	Treasurer, Secretary	Market Capitalization	$ 238,550
Anthony Sorrentino, Jr.	Vice President	Frequency Of Dividends	n.a.
		Number of Shareholders	Under 500

Other Information				
Transfer Agent	Trust Company of New Jersey		Where Listed	OTC-BB
Auditor	Goldstein Karlewicz Goldstein		Symbol	DALE
Market Maker	S.J. Wolfe & Co.	Telephone (800)262-2244	SIC Code	7382
Broker Dealer	Regular Stockbroker		Employees	n.a.

Damariscotta Bankshares, Inc.

25 Main St. P.O. Box 999 • Damariscotta, ME 04543-0999 • Telephone (207)563-8121 • Fax (207)563-8345

Company Description

Damariscotta Bankshares, Inc. is the holding company for its wholly owned subsidiary, Damariscotta Bank & Trust Company. The subsidiary is a single bank which accepts deposits and makes residential, consumer and small commercial loans in the mid-coastal region of Maine. The Bank was organized in 1972.

	12/31/95	12/31/94	12/31/93	12/31/92
Per Share Information				
Stock Price	20.00	11.25	9.50	8.62
Earnings Per Share	2.03	1.75	1.64	1.60
Price / Earnings Ratio	9.85	6.43	5.79	5.39
Book Value Per Share	16.36	14.24	7.50	11.58
Price / Book Value %	122.25	79.00	126.67	74.44
Dividends Per Share	0.25	0.20	0.19	0.17
Annual Financial Data				
Operating Results (000's)				
Net Interest Income	2,764.5	2,485.9	2,309.1	2,104.9
Loan Loss Provision	-84.0	-30.0	-30.0	-20.0
Non-Interest Income	368.4	225.0	532.7	260.1
Non-Interest Expense	-2,007.6	-1,755.6	-2,039.8	-1,516.0
Income Before Taxes and Other	1,041.3	925.4	772.0	829.0
Other Items	n.a.	n.a.	n.a.	n.a.
Income Tax	-278.0	-278.0	-172.3	-250.0
Net Income	763.3	647.4	599.6	579.0
Balance Sheet (000's)				
Cash & Securities	24,681.9	21,336.7	20,422.9	22,642.6
Loans, Net	36,807.1	32,585.2	30,735.7	28,761.7
Fixed Assets, Net	1,356.6	1,340.6	1,416.4	1,395.1
Total Assets	64,504.0	56,748.6	53,961.2	54,128.1
Deposits	57,440.0	50,452.0	48,370.7	48,288.6
Stockholders' Equity	6,145.0	5,288.8	4,780.3	4,207.7
Performance & Financial Condition				
Net Interest Margin	n.a.	n.a.	n.a.	n.a.
Return on Avg Stockholders' Equity %	13.35	12.86	13.34	12.99
Return on Average Assets %	1.26	1.17	1.11	1.07
Equity to Assets %	9.53	9.32	8.86	7.77
Reserve as a % of Non-Performing Loans	168.60	195.89	269.15	n.a.

Compound Growth %'s	EPS %	8.26	Net Income %	9.65	Net Interest Income %	9.51

Comments

During 1995, the Bank declared a four for one stock split for the purpose of increasing the liquidity of the stock and making it more affordable. All references to shares and earnings per share have been restated to reflect the split. "Community Banking at its Best" is the phrase that they use as a corporate objective. So far they have done well.

Officers	Position	Ownership Information	12/31/95
Walter C. Gallant, Jr.	Chairman	Number of Shares Outstanding	375,696
William H. Dunlavey	President, CEO	Market Capitalization	$ 7,513,920
Thomas F. Finn, Jr.	Exec VP, Senior Loan Officer	Frequency Of Dividends	Irregular
Scott D. Conant	Vice President, Treasurer	Number of Shareholders	400
Robert H. Reny	Other		

Other Information			
Transfer Agent	Company Office	Where Listed	Order Matching Only
Auditor	Chester M. Kearney	Symbol	n.a.
Market Maker	None - Company Office	SIC Code	6020
Broker Dealer	None	Employees	40

Damson Birtcher Realty Income Fund II

P.O. Box 30009 • Laguna Niguel, CA 92607-0009 • Telephone (714)643-7490 • Fax (714)643-7504

Company Description

The Partnership owns and leases office buildings, research and development facilities, shopping centers and other commercial and industrial properties. These properties are not located in the same geographic area. The Partnership was formed in 1985 as a limited partnership. It raised more than $52 million in a private placement at that time. The general partner is Birtcher/Liquidity Properties who, through its affiliates, provides ongoing management.

	12/31/95	12/31/94	12/31/93	12/31/92
Per Unit Information				
Price Per Unit	355.00	345.00	202.00	81.00
Earnings Per Unit	-10.82	8.78	10.38	-63.57
Price / Earnings Ratio	n.a.	39.29	19.46	n.a.
Book Value Per Unit	543.70	589.24	609.40	623.88
Price / Book Value %	65.29	58.55	33.15	12.98
Distributions Per Unit	34.76	31.35	22.27	31.85
Cash Flow Per Unit	37.00	34.93	25.35	29.38
Annual Financial Data				
Operating Results (000's)				
Total Revenues	3,905.0	4,834.0	4,338.0	4,224.0
Costs & Expenses	-3,773.0	-3,772.0	-3,792.0	-3,751.0
Operating Income	-575.0	462.0	546.0	-3,377.0
Other Items	n.a.	n.a.	n.a.	n.a.
Net Income	-575.0	462.0	546.0	-3,377.0
Cash Flow From Operations	1,946.0	1,837.0	1,333.0	1,545.0
Balance Sheet (000's)				
Cash & Equivalents	1,055.0	1,058.0	1,000.0	1,047.0
Total Current Assets	1,855.0	1,818.0	1,557.0	1,485.0
Investments In Partnership	3,892.0	4,817.0	4,922.0	5,095.0
Total Assets	29,134.0	31,496.0	32,737.0	33,483.0
Total Current Liabilities	712.0	653.0	690.0	799.0
Long-Term Debt	n.a.	n.a.	n.a.	n.a.
Partners' Capital	28,422.0	30,843.0	32,047.0	32,684.0
Performance & Financial Condition				
Return on Total Revenues %	-14.72	9.56	12.59	-79.95
Return on Average Partners' Capital %	n.a.	n.a.	n.a.	n.a.
Return on Average Assets %	-1.90	1.44	1.65	-9.38
Current Ratio	2.61	2.78	2.26	1.86
Debt / Equity %	n.a.	n.a.	n.a.	n.a.

Compound Growth %'s	EPU % n.a.	Net Income % n.a.	Total Revenues %	-2.58

Comments

The Partnership has decided to sell the properties and liquidate the partnership as soon as is practical. It desires to achieve a reasonable price for the properties while not waiting for a theoretical top dollar. Management reports that independent appraisal estimates a value of about $612 per unit. The officers listed are officers of the two general partners to the partnership.

Officers	Position	Ownership Information	12/31/95
Richard G. Wollack	Chairman	Number of Shares Outstanding	52,588
Brent R. Donaldson	President	Market Capitalization	$ 18,668,740
Deborah M. Richard	CFO	Frequency Of Distributions	Quarterly
Ronald E. Birtcher	Other	Number of Partners	n.a.
Arthur B. Birtcher	Other		

Other Information						
Transfer Agent	Company Office				Where Listed	Order Matching Only
Auditor	KPMG Peat Marwick LLP				Symbol	n.a.
Market Maker	None				SIC Code	6512
Broker Dealer	Chicago Partnership Board	Tel/Ext	(800)272-6273	690	Employees	None

Danbury Industrial Corporation

57 North Street, Ste 407 • Danbury, CT 06810 • Telephone (203)743-0306 • Fax (203)744-0915

Company Description

The Company owns, in whole or in part, five commercial buildings in Commerce Park, in Danbury, Connecticut. The Company was organized in 1918 as a community development corporation for the purpose of attracting industry to the greater Danbury area through commercial development. At inception, it raised capital to acquire land for industrial sites.

	07/31/95	07/31/94	07/31/93	07/31/92
Per Share Information				
Stock Price	101.00	100.00	65.00	65.00
Earnings Per Share	1.57	-0.78	14.30	15.95
Price / Earnings Ratio	64.33	n.a.	4.55	4.08
Book Value Per Share	200.08	201.50	203.50	191.31
Price / Book Value %	50.48	49.63	31.94	33.98
Dividends Per Share	3.00	3.00	3.00	3.00
Annual Financial Data				
Operating Results (000's)				
Total Revenues	895.1	795.2	980.0	977.2
Costs & Expenses	-808.7	-796.9	-645.3	-593.5
Income Before Taxes and Other	27.6	-9.3	334.7	383.7
Other Items	n.a.	n.a.	n.a.	n.a.
Income Tax	-6.3	-1.3	-139.3	-164.8
Net Income	21.3	-10.6	195.4	218.8
Cash Flow From Operations	350.3	-11.1	380.7	572.9
Balance Sheet (000's)				
Cash & Equivalents	146.7	139.7	351.8	493.4
Total Current Assets	189.4	261.5	409.4	527.5
Fixed Assets, Net	4,831.6	4,538.4	3,935.5	3,700.2
Total Assets	5,151.2	4,953.2	4,519.3	4,401.9
Total Current Liabilities	330.4	413.0	268.4	203.5
Long-Term Debt	2,072.3	1,804.8	1,462.8	1,570.0
Stockholders' Equity	2,716.0	2,735.4	2,775.6	2,615.6
Performance & Financial Condition				
Return on Total Revenues %	2.38	-1.33	19.94	22.40
Return on Avg Stockholders' Equity %	0.78	-0.38	7.25	n.a.
Return on Average Assets %	0.42	-0.22	4.38	n.a.
Current Ratio	0.57	0.63	1.53	2.59
Debt / Equity %	76.30	65.98	52.70	60.02

Compound Growth %'s	EPS %	-53.83	Net Income %	-54.02	Total Revenues %	-2.88

Comments

Management has a difficult time in maximizing shareholder value in view of the original goal of helping a community. President Wrinn is respected for the way he handles this difficult position. Perhaps they should reorganize as a nonprofit land trust and redeem those shareholders more interested in making a buck.

Officers	Position	Ownership Information	07/31/95
Ricard F. Gretsch, Sr.	Chairman	Number of Shares Outstanding	13,575
Charles E. Wrinn	President	Market Capitalization	$ 1,371,075
James C. Driscoll, III	Secretary	Frequency Of Dividends	Annual
Anthony M. Rizzo	Treasurer	Number of Shareholders	Under 500
John D. Dolan	Vice President		

Other Information				
Transfer Agent	Registrar & Transfer Company		Where Listed	OTC-BB
Auditor	Seward and Monde		Symbol	DBRI
Market Maker	Legg Mason Wood Walker, Inc.	Telephone (212)428-4949	SIC Code	6510
Broker Dealer	Regular Stockbroker		Employees	2

Datamark Holding, Inc.

348 E. Winchester St., Ste 220 • Salt Lake City, UT 84107 • Telephone (801)268-2202 • Fax (801)268-2292

Company Description

The Company provides highly targeted direct mail advertising for its clients. Services offered are being expanded to include an advertiser funded, online network. The Company uses sophisticated consumer profiling techiques to target advertising to the persons most likely to purchase the specific product or service being offered.

	06/30/95	06/30/94	06/30/93	06/30/92
Per Share Information				
Stock Price	3.63	n.a.	n.a.	n.a.
Earnings Per Share	-0.06	0.01	0.01	n.a.
Price / Earnings Ratio	n.a.	n.a.	n.a.	n.a.
Book Value Per Share	0.18	0.11	0.08	0.07
Price / Book Value %	2,016.70	n.a.	n.a.	n.a.
Dividends Per Share	n.a.	n.a.	n.a.	n.a.
Annual Financial Data				
Operating Results (000's)				
Total Revenues	3,447.1	3,023.2	2,518.0	2,878.0
Costs & Expenses	-3,714.5	-2,931.6	-2,446.2	-2,866.7
Income Before Taxes and Other	-267.4	91.6	71.7	11.4
Other Items	n.a.	n.a.	n.a.	n.a.
Income Tax	3.1	-28.6	-18.4	-10.2
Net Income	-264.3	63.0	53.3	1.2
Cash Flow From Operations	-85.1	84.2	178.5	n.a.
Balance Sheet (000's)				
Cash & Equivalents	39.0	89.7	103.4	51.9
Total Current Assets	1,327.0	711.5	667.9	829.5
Fixed Assets, Net	219.8	169.8	43.1	54.1
Total Assets	1,556.6	884.5	711.0	883.7
Total Current Liabilities	532.9	361.0	87.2	243.4
Long-Term Debt	25.3	47.2	127.6	139.7
Stockholders' Equity	998.4	476.2	496.2	500.5
Performance & Financial Condition				
Return on Total Revenues %	-7.67	2.08	2.12	0.04
Return on Avg Stockholders' Equity %	-35.84	12.96	10.70	0.24
Return on Average Assets %	-21.65	7.90	6.69	0.15
Current Ratio	2.49	1.97	7.66	3.41
Debt / Equity %	2.54	9.92	25.71	27.91

Compound Growth %'s	EPS %	n.a.	Net Income %	n.a.	Total Revenues %	6.20

Comments

Prior to 1995, there was no public market for the securities of the Company and, therefore, no stock price quotations are presented. As of September 30, 1995, officers and directors, as a group, owned 76.7% of the Company's outstanding common stock. For the six months ended December 31,1995, the Company had sales of $2.0 million and a net loss of $511,000 as compared to $1.7 million and $26,000 for the same period in 1994.

Officers	Position	Ownership Information	06/30/95
Arthur Benjamin	President	Number of Shares Outstanding	5,539,953
Chad L. Evans	CEO	Market Capitalization	$ 20,110,029
James Bowers	Secretary, Treasurer	Frequency Of Dividends	n.a.
		Number of Shareholders	834

Other Information			
Transfer Agent	OTC Stock Transfer, Inc.	Where Listed	OTC-BB
Auditor	Hansen, Barnett & Maxwell PC	Symbol	DTAM
Market Maker	Alpine Securities Corporation	Telephone (800)521-5588	SIC Code	7331
Broker Dealer	Regular Stockbroker	Employees	32

Davey Tree Expert Co.

1500 N. Mantua Street • Kent, OH 44240-5193 • Telephone (216)673-9511 • Fax (330)673-9843

Company Description

The Company is in the business of providing horticultural services to a variety of residential, corporate, institutional and government customers. Services include care for trees, shrubs and other plant life and includes landscaping. The Company was incorporated in 1909 (the same year as the first edition of Walker's Manual). Since 1979, the Company has offered to buy stock from any selling shareholder. In 1995, it acquired 165,027 shares for $4,083,000. In 1991, the Company adopted a plan restricting transfer of Company shares without the selling shareholder first giving the employee stock ownership plan the right to purchase those shares.

	12/31/95	12/31/94	12/31/93
Per Share Information			
Stock Price	27.12	24.38	29.63
Earnings Per Share	2.55	1.68	2.33
Price / Earnings Ratio	9.71	16.00	11.48
Book Value Per Share	19.33	17.89	16.93
Price / Book Value %	128.04	150.25	158.00
Dividends Per Share	0.48	0.52	0.55
Annual Financial Data			
Operating Results (000's)			
Total Revenues	230,101.0	209,961.0	218,645.0
Costs & Expenses	-219,754.0	-202,946.0	-208,537.0
Income Before Taxes and Other	10,347.0	6,865.0	10,057.0
Other Items	n.a.	n.a.	n.a.
Income Tax	-3,974.0	-2,826.0	-4,001.0
Net Income	6,373.0	4,039.0	6,056.0
Cash Flow From Operations	21,192.0	16,205.0	18,102.0
Balance Sheet (000's)			
Cash & Equivalents	1,470.0	973.0	1,022.0
Total Current Assets	43,007.0	37,885.0	35,320.0
Fixed Assets, Net	54,136.0	54,424.0	59,464.0
Total Assets	104,452.0	99,779.0	99,780.0
Total Current Liabilities	30,514.0	25,302.0	21,861.0
Long-Term Debt	17,049.0	21,124.0	26,778.0
Stockholders' Equity	46,530.0	44,531.0	44,058.0
Performance & Financial Condition			
Return on Total Revenues %	2.77	1.92	2.77
Return on Avg Stockholders' Equity %	14.00	9.12	14.35
Return on Average Assets %	6.24	4.05	6.29
Current Ratio	1.41	1.50	1.62
Debt / Equity %	36.64	47.44	60.78

Compound Growth %'s	EPS %	4.61	Net Income %	2.58	Total Revenues %	2.59

Comments

The restrictions placed on the trading of the stock will dampen most investor interest even though operating cash flow per share is outstanding. Operating cash flows per share for 1995, 1994 and 1993 were $8.80, $6.51 and $6.95, respectively. The Company valuations per share (independently prepared) were $27.12, $24.38 and $29.63, respectively.

Officers	Position	Ownership Information	12/31/95
R. Douglas Cowan	President, CEO	Number of Shares Outstanding	2,406,769
David E. Adante	Exec VP, CFO	Market Capitalization	$ 59,567,533
Karl J. Warnke	Exec VP	Frequency Of Dividends	Quarterly
Rosemary T. Nicholas	Secretary	Number of Shareholders	1,632
Bradley L. Comport	Controller		

Other Information				
Transfer Agent	Company Office		Where Listed	OTC-PS
Auditor	Deloitte & Touche LLP		Symbol	n.a.
Market Maker	Hill, Thompson. Magid & Co.Inc	Telephone (800)631-3083	SIC Code	0783
Broker Dealer			Employees	5800

Decker Manufacturing Corporation

703 North Clark Street • Albion, MI 49224-1455 • Telephone (517)629-3955 • Fax (517)629-3535

Company Description

The Company is in the business of manufacturing cold headed industrial fasteners and pipe plugs. Approximately two-thirds of its product are sold to a customer base which is either directly or indirectly engaged in the manufacture of automobiles. The Company was organized in 1927.

	12/31/95	12/31/94	12/31/93	12/31/92
Per Share Information				
Stock Price	39.75	40.25	28.75	21.50
Earnings Per Share	4.28	3.56	3.54	2.53
Price / Earnings Ratio	9.29	11.31	8.12	8.50
Book Value Per Share	27.75	26.37	25.51	24.28
Price / Book Value %	143.24	152.64	112.70	88.55
Dividends Per Share	2.90	2.70	2.45	2.25
Annual Financial Data				
Operating Results (000's)				
Total Revenues	22,199.9	21,456.7	19,967.8	17,787.1
Costs & Expenses	-18,223.2	-18,147.5	-16,253.7	-15,020.1
Income Before Taxes and Other	3,976.8	3,309.2	3,714.1	2,767.0
Other Items	n.a.	n.a.	n.a.	n.a.
Income Tax	-1,262.1	-1,052.3	-1,468.9	-1,158.0
Net Income	2,714.6	2,256.9	2,245.1	1,609.0
Cash Flow From Operations	1,935.4	3,116.9	3,016.9	2,349.4
Balance Sheet (000's)				
Cash & Equivalents	2,286.7	2,229.1	n.a.	n.a.
Total Current Assets	16,161.1	15,445.3	14,232.6	12,851.4
Fixed Assets, Net	3,401.2	3,517.0	3,838.2	4,090.3
Total Assets	19,731.1	19,172.0	18,270.8	17,141.7
Total Current Liabilities	1,737.1	2,046.7	1,752.9	1,378.6
Long-Term Debt	n.a.	n.a.	n.a.	n.a.
Stockholders' Equity	17,591.1	16,715.0	16,169.8	15,392.6
Performance & Financial Condition				
Return on Total Revenues %	12.23	10.52	11.24	9.05
Return on Avg Stockholders' Equity %	15.83	13.73	14.23	10.51
Return on Average Assets %	13.96	12.06	12.68	9.43
Current Ratio	9.30	7.55	8.12	9.32
Debt / Equity %	n.a.	n.a.	n.a.	n.a.

Compound Growth %'s	EPS %	19.15	Net Income %	19.05	Total Revenues %	7.67

Comments

The Company notes 57 consecutive years of profitability. We also observe a solid consistency when looking at the last 10 years and quick assets almost equal to shareholders' equity. The Company has in excess of $6 million in marketable securities as part of a 9.3 to 1 current ratio.

Officers	Position	Ownership Information	12/31/95
Henry R. Konkle	Chairman, CEO	Number of Shares Outstanding	633,958
Bernard L. Konkle l	President, General Manager	Market Capitalization	$ 25,199,831
Terrence B. DeWeerd	Secretary, Treasurer	Frequency Of Dividends	Quarterly
Steven M. Konkle	Vice President	Number of Shareholders	Under 500
Bernard L. Konkle ll	Vice President		

Other Information

Transfer Agent	Manufacturers Bank, NA Detroit			Where Listed	OTC-BB
Auditor	Foote and Lloyd			Symbol	DMCO
Market Maker	Seidler Companies, Inc., The	Telephone	(800)421-0164	SIC Code	3499
Broker Dealer	Pink sheet specialist			Employees	140

Del Paint Corporation

3105 East Reno Avenue • Oklahoma City, OK 73117-6615 • Telephone (405)672-1431 • Fax (405)672-0804

Company Description

The Company manufactures and distributes architectural paint and industrial coatings. Products are distributed through retail outlets, outside sales personnel and independent dealers. The Company was organized in Oklahoma in 1963.

	03/31/95	03/31/94	03/31/93	03/31/92
Per Share Information				
Stock Price	0.22	0.22	n.a.	n.a.
Earnings Per Share	0.44	-0.22	-0.13	-0.06
Price / Earnings Ratio	0.50	n.a.	n.a.	n.a.
Book Value Per Share	0.28	-0.19	-0.17	-0.03
Price / Book Value %	78.57	n.a.	n.a.	n.a.
Dividends Per Share	n.a.	n.a.	n.a.	n.a.
Annual Financial Data				
Operating Results (000's)				
Total Revenues	2,776.9	2,358.9	2,345.5	2,768.9
Costs & Expenses	-2,676.1	-2,765.3	-2,595.6	-2,845.4
Income Before Taxes and Other	99.5	-406.3	-250.1	-100.0
Other Items	803.2	n.a.	n.a.	n.a.
Income Tax	44.4	n.a.	n.a.	n.a.
Net Income	947.2	-406.3	-250.1	-100.0
Cash Flow From Operations	70.8	99.0	210.0	39.3
Balance Sheet (000's)				
Cash & Equivalents	160.1	43.1	17.7	44.7
Total Current Assets	808.2	509.2	739.7	1,445.8
Fixed Assets, Net	307.7	355.3	431.7	497.9
Total Assets	2,068.9	973.0	1,316.1	2,102.5
Total Current Liabilities	678.9	658.1	536.6	989.4
Long-Term Debt	235.5	166.9	222.9	310.3
Stockholders' Equity	633.2	-393.9	-286.0	-43.3
Performance & Financial Condition				
Return on Total Revenues %	34.11	-17.22	-10.66	-3.61
Return on Avg Stockholders' Equity %	791.59	n.a.	n.a.	-51.12
Return on Average Assets %	62.28	-35.50	-14.63	-4.63
Current Ratio	1.19	0.77	1.38	1.46
Debt / Equity %	37.20	n.a.	n.a.	n.a.

Compound Growth %'s	EPS % n.a.	Net Income % n.a.	Total Revenues %	0.10

Comments

Net income for the year ended March 31, 1995, includes $803,000 relating to the cumulative effect of changes in accounting for income taxes. The Company has net operating loss carryforwards of approximately $2.3 million, available through 2003. For the nine months ended December 31, 1995, the Company had sales of $2.6 million and net income of $45,000 ($.02 per share) as compared to $1.9 million and $26,000 ($.01 per share), for the same period in 1994. Stock transactions have been sporadic and the Company has been acting as its own order matcher. Stock prices for 1995 and 1994 are Company estimates.

Officers	Position	Ownership Information	03/31/95
Dan S. Howie	President	Number of Shares Outstanding	2,231,152
Bob Crawley	Secretary, Treasurer	Market Capitalization	$ 490,853
Sean Childers	Vice President	Frequency Of Dividends	n.a.
		Number of Shareholders	162

Other Information				
Transfer Agent	Liberty Bank & Trust Company		Where Listed	Order Matching Only
Auditor	R.J. Towe		Symbol	n.a.
Market Maker	None-Company Office	Telephone (405)672-1431	SIC Code	2851
Broker Dealer	None		Employees	40

Delaware Bancshares, Inc.

P.O.Box 389 • Walton, NY 13586-0389 • Telephone (607)865-4126 • Fax (607)865-6530

Company Description

Delaware Bancshares, Inc. provides a full range of banking services to individual and small business customers through its wholly owned subsidiary, The National Bank of Delaware County in New York.

	12/31/95	12/31/94	12/31/93	12/31/92
Per Share Information				
Stock Price	40.50	40.18	43.00	42.00
Earnings Per Share	3.82	3.88	3.60	3.30
Price / Earnings Ratio	10.60	10.36	11.94	12.73
Book Value Per Share	33.06	29.70	27.54	27.52
Price / Book Value %	122.50	135.29	156.14	152.62
Dividends Per Share	1.30	1.20	1.07	1.08
Annual Financial Data				
Operating Results (000's)				
Net Interest Income	4,875.0	4,997.0	4,844.0	4,522.0
Loan Loss Provision	-15.0	n.a.	-105.0	-112.0
Non-Interest Income	259.0	242.0	300.0	269.0
Non-Interest Expense	-2,501.0	-2,593.0	-2,552.0	-2,403.0
Income Before Taxes and Other	2,618.0	2,646.0	2,487.0	2,276.0
Other Items	n.a.	n.a.	n.a.	n.a.
Income Tax	-746.0	-744.0	-723.0	-661.0
Net Income	1,872.0	1,902.0	1,764.0	1,615.0
Balance Sheet (000's)				
Cash & Securities	59,118.0	57,058.0	56,012.0	53,931.0
Loans, Net	43,476.0	44,655.0	44,938.0	47,429.0
Fixed Assets, Net	1,630.0	1,416.0	1,350.0	1,404.0
Total Assets	105,996.0	105,051.0	104,081.0	104,571.0
Deposits	88,849.0	89,713.0	89,926.0	91,626.0
Stockholders' Equity	16,201.0	14,554.0	13,493.0	12,254.0
Performance & Financial Condition				
Net Interest Margin	n.a.	n.a.	n.a.	n.a.
Return on Avg Stockholders' Equity %	12.17	13.56	13.70	13.82
Return on Average Assets %	1.77	1.82	1.69	1.57
Equity to Assets %	15.28	13.85	12.96	11.72
Reserve as a % of Non-Performing Loans	34.96	n.a.	n.a.	n.a.

Compound Growth %'s	EPS %	5.00	Net Income %	5.05	Net Interest Income %	2.54

Comments

Real estate mortgages make up over 86% of the Bank's loan portfolio. In addition, the Bank makes loans to farmers, commercial loans and installment loans to individuals. Return on average assets places the Bank at the top of its peer group. Although growth is not impressive, the consistency in performance should make the shareholders happy. The Bank was established in 1891.

Officers	Position	Ownership Information	12/31/95
Dale A. Carlson	President	Number of Shares Outstanding	489,979
Marian S. Budine	Secretary	Market Capitalization	$ 19,844,150
Patrick R. Galloway	Treasurer	Frequency Of Dividends	Quarterly
James R. Carey	Other	Number of Shareholders	480
Lois R. Hodge	Other		

Other Information				
Transfer Agent	Company Office		Where Listed	OTC-BB
Auditor	Dannible & McKee, LLP		Symbol	NABD
Market Maker	Ryan, Beck & Co.	Telephone (800)325-7926	SIC Code	6020
Broker Dealer	Regular Stockbroker		Employees	30

Denver and Ephrata Telephone and Telegraph Co.

130 East Main Street • Ephrata, PA 17522-2739 • Telephone (717)733-4101 • Fax (717)733-7461

Company Description

The Company furnishes telephone service to a population of almost 100,000 in an area of approximately 227 square miles in southeastern Pennsylvania. Revenues are derived from local and long distance access and network services, directory advertising and the sale and installation of communications equipment. The Company was founded in 1911 in the state of Pennsylvania.

	12/31/95	12/31/94	12/31/93	12/31/92
Per Share Information				
Stock Price	73.25	66.00	52.25	33.00
Earnings Per Share	1.76	1.71	1.78	1.21
Price / Earnings Ratio	41.62	38.60	29.35	27.27
Book Value Per Share	18.18	17.18	16.28	15.35
Price / Book Value %	402.92	384.17	320.95	214.98
Dividends Per Share	1.09	1.04	0.98	0.89
Annual Financial Data				
Operating Results (000's)				
Total Revenues	40,810.9	36,735.9	32,470.3	29,358.4
Costs & Expenses	-34,810.6	-31,933.4	-27,826.7	-25,908.7
Income Before Taxes and Other	5,576.2	5,519.7	5,242.2	3,633.0
Other Items	n.a.	n.a.	n.a.	n.a.
Income Tax	-2,166.4	-2,203.2	-1,795.8	-1,265.0
Net Income	3,409.7	3,316.5	3,446.4	2,367.9
Cash Flow From Operations	13,532.4	8,148.6	10,218.5	7,951.9
Balance Sheet (000's)				
Cash & Equivalents	50.9	139.6	386.8	4,000.2
Total Current Assets	10,307.6	11,031.7	7,659.6	10,091.2
Fixed Assets, Net	66,265.0	65,856.2	66,053.7	52,923.2
Total Assets	88,521.3	85,174.6	78,246.5	66,337.1
Total Current Liabilities	17,051.4	15,428.3	11,394.8	5,889.2
Long-Term Debt	26,137.5	26,512.3	26,269.5	21,064.0
Stockholders' Equity	36,097.0	34,201.1	32,438.5	30,676.8
Performance & Financial Condition				
Return on Total Revenues %	8.35	9.03	10.61	8.07
Return on Avg Stockholders' Equity %	9.70	9.95	10.92	7.56
Return on Average Assets %	3.93	4.06	4.77	3.75
Current Ratio	0.60	0.72	0.67	1.71
Debt / Equity %	72.41	77.52	80.98	68.66

Compound Growth %'s	EPS %	13.30	Net Income %	12.92	Total Revenues %	11.60

Comments

Included in assets are investments in affiliated companies totaling $8.2 million. $5.2 million of this amount represents a 16% interest in a holding company which has a controlling interest in a Hungarian telephone company serving approximately 42,000 telephone access lines.

Officers	Position	Ownership Information	12/31/95
Anne B. Sweigart	President, CEO	Number of Shares Outstanding	1,905,859
Robert M. Lauman	Exec VP, COO	Market Capitalization	$ 139,604,172
G. William Ruhl	Senior VP	Frequency Of Dividends	Quarterly
W. Garth Sprecher	Secretary	Number of Shareholders	845
Thomas E. Morell	Treasurer, CFO		

Other Information

Transfer Agent	Company Office			Where Listed	OTC-BB
Auditor	Coopers & Lybrand			Symbol	DETT
Market Maker	F.J. Morrissey & Co., Inc.	Telephone	(800)842-8928	SIC Code	4813
Broker Dealer	Regular Stockbroker			Employees	276

Detroit Legal News Company

2001 W. Lafayette • Detroit, MI 48216 • Telephone (313)961-3949 • Fax (313)961-7817

Company Description

The Company's primary business is producing and selling sheetfeed commercial printing (d.b.a. Inland Press). In addition, the Company publishes The Detroit Legal News, a daily legal newspaper. During 1994, the Company redeemed 578 of its shares for $80 per share.

	12/31/95	12/31/94	12/31/93	12/31/92
Per Share Information				
Stock Price	80.00	80.00	61.00	53.00
Earnings Per Share	10.04	12.89	12.89	9.77
Price / Earnings Ratio	7.97	6.21	4.73	5.42
Book Value Per Share	126.18	118.29	107.35	104.10
Price / Book Value %	63.40	67.63	56.82	50.91
Dividends Per Share	2.15	2.40	1.73	1.80
Annual Financial Data				
Operating Results (000's)				
Total Revenues	13,060.4	12,678.3	11,723.3	13,985.2
Costs & Expenses	-12,459.5	-11,921.9	-11,491.8	-13,411.2
Income Before Taxes and Other	600.9	756.5	231.6	574.0
Other Items	n.a.	n.a.	n.a.	n.a.
Income Tax	-216.0	-261.0	-76.0	-194.0
Net Income	384.9	495.5	155.6	380.0
Cash Flow From Operations	525.4	1,173.2	661.2	722.0
Balance Sheet (000's)				
Cash & Equivalents	1,349.7	1,403.5	679.2	334.5
Total Current Assets	3,989.6	4,006.4	3,355.7	3,098.8
Fixed Assets, Net	2,513.2	2,581.9	2,648.5	3,011.8
Total Assets	6,607.9	6,716.9	6,243.3	6,291.4
Total Current Liabilities	1,107.7	1,454.1	1,216.8	1,271.3
Long-Term Debt	400.0	500.0	600.0	700.0
Stockholders' Equity	4,836.3	4,533.8	4,176.5	4,089.0
Performance & Financial Condition				
Return on Total Revenues %	2.95	3.91	1.33	2.72
Return on Avg Stockholders' Equity %	8.22	11.38	3.76	9.66
Return on Average Assets %	5.78	7.65	2.48	5.78
Current Ratio	3.60	2.76	2.76	2.44
Debt / Equity %	8.27	11.03	14.37	17.12

Compound Growth %'s	EPS %	0.91	Net Income %	0.43	Total Revenues %	-2.25

Comments

The Company is strong financially and produces excellent cash flow per share. Balance sheet assets may be undervalued. Long-term corporate plans are not known.

Officers	Position	Ownership Information	12/31/95
Bradley M. Thompson	Chairman, President	Number of Shares Outstanding	38,329
Fred W. Freeman	Secretary	Market Capitalization	$ 3,066,320
		Frequency Of Dividends	Quarterly
		Number of Shareholders	Under 500

Other Information					
Transfer Agent	Company Office			Where Listed	OTC-BB
Auditor	KPMG Peat Marwick LLP			Symbol	DTRL
Market Maker	Roney & Co.	Telephone	(800)521-1196	SIC Code	2750
Broker Dealer	Pink sheet specialist			Employees	100

Discus Acquisition Corporation

333 South Seventh St. • Minneapolis, MN 55402 • Telephone (612)305-0339 • Fax (612)371-9651

Company Description

On December 18, 1995, the Company completed the acquisition of Peerless Chain Company, Inc. (Peerless) for $23.7 million. Peerless manufactures and sells a varied line of traction products, all types of hardware and industrial chain and wire form products. Sales for Peerless for the year ended December 31, 1995, amounted to $42 million with net income of $1.0 million. Prior to the acquisition of Peerless, the Company had no operating business since early 1994, when it sold its nine Fuddruckers restaurants. The Company was incorporated in Minnesota in 1983. In January, 1996, the Company issued 1.26 million shares of its common stock at $1.10 per share, raising a total of $1.4 million.

	12/31/95	12/25/94
Per Share Information		
Stock Price	1.39	1.00
Earnings Per Share	-0.08	0.73
Price / Earnings Ratio	n.a.	1.37
Book Value Per Share	1.02	1.03
Price / Book Value %	136.27	97.09
Dividends Per Share	n.a.	n.a.
Annual Financial Data		
Operating Results (000's)		
Total Revenues	1,535.0	2,333.0
Costs & Expenses	-1,707.0	-225.0
Income Before Taxes and Other	-172.0	1,718.0
Other Items	n.a.	n.a.
Income Tax	-30.0	n.a.
Net Income	-202.0	1,718.0
Cash Flow From Operations	571.0	4,888.0
Balance Sheet (000's)		
Cash & Equivalents	108.0	2,608.0
Total Current Assets	20,355.0	2,608.0
Fixed Assets, Net	12,586.0	61.0
Total Assets	39,497.0	2,669.0
Total Current Liabilities	18,563.0	190.0
Long-Term Debt	7,767.0	43.0
Stockholders' Equity	5,094.0	2,436.0
Performance & Financial Condition		
Return on Total Revenues %	-13.16	73.64
Return on Avg Stockholders' Equity %	-5.37	55.15
Return on Average Assets %	-0.96	55.15
Current Ratio	1.10	13.73
Debt / Equity %	152.47	1.77

Compound Growth %'s	EPS % n.a.	Net Income % n.a.	Total Revenues % -34.20

Comments

The Company recognized a gain of $2.3 million in 1994, resulting from the sale of its nine restaurants for approximately $5.5 million. The results do not include the results of Peerless because the acquisition was late in 1995. However, if they were included the Company's sales (and earnings per share) would have been $42 million ($.16 per share), in 1995, and $43 million ($.18 per share), in 1994.

Officers	Position	Ownership Information	12/31/95
Harry W. Spell	Chairman	Number of Shares Outstanding	4,971,174
Jan C. van Osnabrugge	President	Market Capitalization	$ 6,909,932
William H. Spell	CEO	Frequency Of Dividends	n.a.
Robert E. Deter	CFO	Number of Shareholders	388
Bruce A. Richard	Secretary		

Other Information					
Transfer Agent	Norwest Bank Minnesota			Where Listed	OTC-BB
Auditor	Coopers & Lybrand LLP			Symbol	DISC
Market Maker	Paragon Capital Corp.	Telephone	(212)785-4700	SIC Code	3499
Broker Dealer	Principal Financial	Tel/Ext	(612)229-7025	Employees	335

Dover Investments Corporation

350 California St., Ste. 1650 • San Francisco, CA 94104 • Telephone (415)951-0200 • Fax (415)951-8905

Company Description

The Company, formerly known as Homestead Financial Corporation, is in the business of developing and building single family homes in Northern California. Incorporated in the state of Delaware, the Company previously owned all of the stock of Homestead Savings, a federal S&L. In 1992, the Resolution Trust Company took over Homestead. The Company retains no interest in Homestead. A quasi-reorganization, effective January 1, 1993, resulted in the elimination of an accumulated deficit of $16 million, primarily relating to the Company's ownership of Homestead. The Company has Class A and Class B common stock which have similar rights and generally trade at the same price.

	12/31/95	12/31/94	12/31/93	12/31/92
Per Share Information				
Stock Price	6.63	2.38	0.50	0.05
Earnings Per Share	0.42	0.22	0.32	-0.80
Price / Earnings Ratio	15.79	10.82	1.56	n.a.
Book Value Per Share	19.72	13.70	10.51	9.87
Price / Book Value %	33.62	17.37	4.76	0.51
Dividends Per Share	n.a.	n.a.	n.a.	n.a.
Annual Financial Data				
Operating Results (000's)				
Total Revenues	5,312.0	9,344.0	9,872.0	158.0
Costs & Expenses	-4,609.0	-8,728.0	-8,947.0	-899.0
Income Before Taxes and Other	700.0	616.0	850.0	-741.0
Other Items	n.a.	n.a.	-3.0	-121.0
Income Tax	-248.0	-368.0	-489.0	-1.0
Net Income	452.0	248.0	358.0	-863.0
Cash Flow From Operations	-3,449.0	-796.0	1,813.0	-5,063.0
Balance Sheet (000's)				
Cash & Equivalents	639.0	381.0	1,667.0	1,362.0
Total Current Assets	4,202.0	4,072.0	4,167.0	1,462.0
Fixed Assets, Net	22,745.0	22,231.0	21,280.0	20,499.0
Total Assets	28,120.0	29,818.0	27,558.0	23,049.0
Total Current Liabilities	466.0	3,806.0	4,369.0	1,468.0
Long-Term Debt	8,020.0	10,400.0	11,342.0	10,450.0
Stockholders' Equity	19,583.0	15,315.0	11,847.0	11,131.0
Performance & Financial Condition				
Return on Total Revenues %	8.51	2.65	3.63	-546.20
Return on Avg Stockholders' Equity %	2.59	1.83	3.12	-7.46
Return on Average Assets %	1.56	0.86	1.41	-3.80
Current Ratio	9.02	1.07	0.95	1.00
Debt / Equity %	40.95	67.91	95.74	93.88

Compound Growth %'s	EPS %	14.56	Net Income %	12.36	Total Revenues %	222.75

Comments

During 1995, the Company received $4.0 million from the Internal Revenue Service as a result of examinations of its consolidated tax returns for the years 1985 through 1990. Additionally, the Company has been allowed a loss carryforward from 1990 of $37.9 million. During 1995, the Company repurchased 134,860 shares of its common stock for approximately $673,000.

Officers	Position	Ownership Information	12/31/95
Lawrence Weissberg	President, CEO	Number of Shares Outstanding	992,896
Michael Raddie	CFO	Market Capitalization	$ 6,582,900
		Frequency Of Dividends	n.a.
		Number of Shareholders	777

Other Information				
Transfer Agent	Chemical Trust Company of California		Where Listed	OTC-BB
Auditor	Grant Thornton		Symbol	DOVR
Market Maker	Troster Singer Corporation	Telephone (800)222-0890	SIC Code	1531
Broker Dealer	Regular Stockbroker		Employees	4

Du Art Film Laboratories, Inc.

245 West 55th Street • New York, NY 10019-5202 • Telephone (212)757-4580 • Fax (212)333-7647

Company Description

The Company is engaged in the business of motion picture, sound and video processing and the operation of a majority-owned television property in Puerto Rico.

	12/31/95	12/31/94	12/25/93
Per Share Information			
Stock Price	66.00	61.00	55.12
Earnings Per Share	8.83	4.98	6.24
Price / Earnings Ratio	7.47	12.25	8.83
Book Value Per Share	80.75	60.02	56.04
Price / Book Value %	81.73	101.63	98.36
Dividends Per Share	n.a.	n.a.	n.a.
Annual Financial Data			
Operating Results (000's)			
Total Revenues	22,592.4	20,050.7	18,504.6
Costs & Expenses	-18,962.5	-17,501.3	-16,670.2
Income Before Taxes and Other	3,188.0	1,934.0	1,593.5
Other Items	-346.9	n.a.	58.5
Income Tax	-1,500.0	-1,178.8	-709.3
Net Income	1,341.2	755.2	942.7
Cash Flow From Operations	2,704.5	3,488.0	1,454.4
Balance Sheet (000's)			
Cash & Equivalents	1,429.3	2,011.7	535.6
Total Current Assets	9,663.1	8,417.6	7,283.9
Fixed Assets, Net	7,587.6	6,887.4	7,081.8
Total Assets	17,851.9	16,247.0	15,188.0
Total Current Liabilities	1,887.8	2,125.4	1,645.8
Long-Term Debt	n.a.	n.a.	187.5
Stockholders' Equity	12,303.3	10,932.8	10,165.2
Performance & Financial Condition			
Return on Total Revenues %	5.94	3.77	5.09
Return on Avg Stockholders' Equity %	11.54	7.16	9.72
Return on Average Assets %	7.87	4.80	6.33
Current Ratio	5.12	3.96	4.43
Debt / Equity %	n.a.	n.a.	1.84

Compound Growth %'s	EPS %	18.96	Net Income %	19.28	Total Revenues %	10.49

Comments

Management reports that substantial equipment and facility expenditures will be incurred in 1996 and remains cautiously optimistic about the year. 1994 results were negatively impacted by a loss of $545,383 resulting from the sale of long term government bonds. The Company has since adopted a policy of investing excess funds in instruments with maturities of two years or less. There is no long term debt and the Company maintains an excellent current ratio.

Officers	Position	Ownership Information	12/31/95
Irwin W. Young	Chairman	Number of Shares Outstanding	152,371
Robert M. Smith	President	Market Capitalization	$ 10,056,486
Linda Young	Exec VP	Frequency Of Dividends	n.a.
Carmine J. Donigi	Senior VP	Number of Shareholders	Under 500
Stewart Deitch	CFO, Treasurer		

Other Information				
Transfer Agent	Registrar & Transfer Company		Where Listed	OTC-BB
Auditor	Ernst & Young LLP		Symbol	DAFL
Market Maker	Carr Securities Corporation	Telephone (800)221-2243	SIC Code	7810
Broker Dealer	Regular Stockbroker		Employees	40

EMC Corporation

300 York Avenue • Saint Paul, MN 55101-4082 • Telephone (612)771-1555 • Fax (612)771-5629

Company Description

The Company develops, manufactures and distributes educational materials and provides media manufacturing, recording, packaging and fulfillment services to a broad range of customers nationwide. There have been no stock offerings or registrations since the original incorporation in 1954. In 1994 the shares were split 20 for 1. All per share amounts have been adjusted accordingly.

	12/31/95	12/31/94	12/31/93	12/31/92
Per Share Information				
Stock Price	16.50	10.00	6.00	3.50
Earnings Per Share	1.05	0.97	0.73	0.45
Price / Earnings Ratio	15.71	10.31	8.22	7.78
Book Value Per Share	5.41	4.55	3.76	3.19
Price / Book Value %	304.99	219.78	159.57	109.72
Dividends Per Share	0.18	0.17	0.15	0.10
Annual Financial Data				
Operating Results (000's)				
Total Revenues	29,574.6	27,549.6	22,842.4	19,123.4
Costs & Expenses	-26,075.9	-24,229.8	-20,145.2	-16,771.0
Income Before Taxes and Other	3,498.8	3,319.8	2,133.6	1,645.4
Other Items	n.a.	n.a.	220.0	n.a.
Income Tax	-1,236.5	-1,224.0	-774.0	-668.0
Net Income	2,262.3	2,095.8	1,579.6	977.4
Cash Flow From Operations	3,101.1	3,942.1	4,039.8	3,612.4
Balance Sheet (000's)				
Cash & Equivalents	627.7	2,189.6	934.1	1,107.1
Total Current Assets	10,789.8	11,375.7	8,626.7	8,593.0
Fixed Assets, Net	3,026.9	3,047.9	3,074.9	2,928.8
Total Assets	18,867.3	17,962.7	15,800.7	15,835.1
Total Current Liabilities	4,876.8	5,138.2	4,122.4	3,590.0
Long-Term Debt	1,972.9	2,636.3	3,224.7	3,784.3
Stockholders' Equity	11,702.5	9,840.2	8,134.7	6,938.0
Performance & Financial Condition				
Return on Total Revenues %	7.65	7.61	6.92	5.11
Return on Avg Stockholders' Equity %	21.00	23.32	20.96	14.90
Return on Average Assets %	12.29	12.41	9.99	7.21
Current Ratio	2.21	2.21	2.09	2.39
Debt / Equity %	16.86	26.79	39.64	54.54

Compound Growth %'s	EPS %	32.64	Net Income %	32.28	Total Revenues %	15.64

Comments

Consistent growth and new product lines combined with no institutional following make this an interesting company to follow.

Officers	Position	Ownership Information	12/31/95
David E. Feinberg	Chairman, CEO	Number of Shares Outstanding	2,161,740
Paul Winter	President, Treasurer	Market Capitalization	$ 35,668,710
Wolfgang S. Kraft	Vice President	Frequency Of Dividends	Annual
Robert F. O'Reilly	Vice President	Number of Shareholders	109
Richard T. Stevens	Vice President		

Other Information

Transfer Agent	First Trust, N.A., St. Paul			Where Listed	OTC-BB
Auditor	Coopers & Lybrand LLP			Symbol	EMCM
Market Maker	Dain Bosworth Incorporated	Telephone	(800)285-4964	SIC Code	2740
Broker Dealer	Regular Stockbroker			Employees	211

Ellensburg Telephone Company

305 North Ruby • Ellensburg, WA 98926-0308 • Telephone (509)925-1425 • Fax (509)962-8540

Company Description

The Company provides local and long distance telephone services to the communities that surround and include Ellensburg and Yakima in the state of Washington. The Company formed a new subsidiary in early 1995, Elltel Wireless, Inc., which will provide personal communication services in the wireless field.

	12/31/95	12/31/94	12/31/93	12/31/92
Per Share Information				
Stock Price	56.00	51.50	49.25	47.00
Earnings Per Share	5.27	4.52	4.31	4.65
Price / Earnings Ratio	10.63	11.39	11.43	10.11
Book Value Per Share	43.50	40.83	38.91	35.14
Price / Book Value %	128.74	126.13	126.57	133.75
Dividends Per Share	2.60	2.60	2.60	2.60
Annual Financial Data				
Operating Results (000's)				
Total Revenues	13,742.6	12,513.3	11,533.6	12,047.5
Costs & Expenses	-8,605.7	-8,023.6	-7,289.8	-7,419.4
Income Before Taxes and Other	5,136.9	4,489.7	4,243.8	4,620.0
Other Items	n.a.	n.a.	n.a.	n.a.
Income Tax	-1,523.1	-1,395.0	-1,289.0	-1,432.1
Net Income	3,613.8	3,094.7	2,954.8	3,187.9
Cash Flow From Operations	6,544.5	6,358.2	5,996.9	5,934.4
Balance Sheet (000's)				
Cash & Equivalents	1,048.8	743.7	29.4	380.7
Total Current Assets	5,079.5	5,086.4	6,092.4	6,542.3
Fixed Assets, Net	28,474.6	28,369.6	27,383.6	25,000.5
Total Assets	37,619.4	35,813.3	35,646.2	33,317.2
Total Current Liabilities	1,858.9	1,854.1	2,985.2	1,350.0
Long-Term Debt	133.3	266.5	369.3	1,098.0
Stockholders' Equity	29,804.7	27,972.3	26,659.1	25,485.6
Performance & Financial Condition				
Return on Total Revenues %	26.30	24.73	25.62	26.46
Return on Avg Stockholders' Equity %	12.51	11.33	11.33	12.86
Return on Average Assets %	9.84	8.66	8.57	9.82
Current Ratio	2.73	2.74	2.04	4.85
Debt / Equity %	0.45	0.95	1.39	4.31

Compound Growth %'s	EPS %	4.26	Net Income %	4.27	Total Revenues %	4.49

Comments

The Company's balance sheet shows available capital and no debt which should enable it to pursue a number of growth opportunities and technological advancements.

Officers	Position	Ownership Information	12/31/95
G F. Kachlein III	President, Chairman of the Board	Number of Shares Outstanding	685,158
		Market Capitalization	$ 38,368,624
		Frequency Of Dividends	Quarterly
		Number of Shareholders	Under 500

Other Information

Transfer Agent	Company Office			Where Listed	OTC-BB
Auditor	Moss-Adams			Symbol	ELEN
Market Maker	Ragen MacKenzie Incorporated	Telephone	(206)343-5000	SIC Code	4810
Broker Dealer	Regular Stockbroker			Employees	n.a.

Emergent Group, Inc.

15 South Main St., Ste. 750 • Greenville, SC 29606 • Telephone (864)235-8056 • Fax (864)271-8374

Company Description

The Company is a diversified financial services company which originates, services and sells residential mortgage loans, small business loans, and pre-owned automobile loans. The Company also manages two equity investment funds which have a total of $27.1 million in assets. During 1995, the Company made an equity investment of $1.0 million in one of the funds. 1995 management fee income related to these funds amounted to $570,000.

	12/31/95	12/31/94	12/31/93	12/31/92
Per Share Information				
Stock Price	5.25	1.10	0.63	0.42
Earnings Per Share	0.10	0.35	0.18	0.08
Price / Earnings Ratio	52.50	3.14	3.50	5.25
Book Value Per Share	1.55	0.97	0.74	0.60
Price / Book Value %	338.71	113.40	85.14	70.00
Dividends Per Share	n.a.	n.a.	n.a.	n.a.
Annual Financial Data				
Operating Results (000's)				
Net Interest Income	7,112.0	5,024.0	2,910.0	2,309.0
Loan Loss Provision	-2,480.0	-2,510.0	-686.0	-349.0
Non-Interest Income	10,639.0	7,292.0	4,063.0	4,015.0
Non-Interest Expense	-10,419.0	-7,359.0	-5,624.0	-5,821.0
Income Before Taxes and Other	4,852.0	2,447.0	663.0	154.0
Other Items	-4,005.0	500.0	348.0	379.0
Income Tax	-190.0	-609.0	186.0	-95.0
Net Income	657.0	2,338.0	1,197.0	438.0
Balance Sheet (000's)				
Cash & Securities	1,560.0	875.0	5,907.0	5,235.0
Loans, Net	129,225.0	95,809.0	62,482.0	56,405.0
Fixed Assets, Net	3,370.0	2,062.0	5,561.0	3,970.0
Total Assets	144,931.0	109,448.0	90,663.0	73,208.0
Long Term Debt	129,950.0	95,015.0	79,611.0	66,577.0
Stockholders' Equity	9,885.0	9,700.0	7,362.0	5,057.0
Performance & Financial Condition				
Return on Avg Stockholders' Equity %	6.71	27.41	19.28	9.04
Return on Average Assets %	0.52	2.34	1.46	0.67
Equity to Assets %	6.82	8.86	8.12	6.91

Compound Growth %'s	EPS %	7.72	Net Income %	14.47	Net Interest Income %	45.50

Comments

In connection with the Company's strategic plan to focus on financial services, it divested itself of the apparel and transportation segments. The financial impact of this was a charge to net income of $3.9 million in 1995, and an increase to net income of $546,000 and $260,000 in 1994 and 1993, respectively. The Company has two classes of common stock which are combined for all share and per share calculations. On March 1, 1996, the Company filed a registration statement with the SEC for an offering of up to approximately 3.3 million shares of common stock. Expected proceeds of approximately $2.4 million are to be used to repay company debt and the balance used for general corporate purposes.

Officers	Position	Ownership Information	12/31/95
John M. Sterling, Jr.	President, CEO	Number of Shares Outstanding	6,397,474
Keith B. Giddens	Exec VP, COO	Market Capitalization	$ 33,586,739
Kevin J. Mast	Treasurer	Frequency Of Dividends	n.a.
Robert S. Davis	Vice President, CFO	Number of Shareholders	1,296

Other Information			
Transfer Agent	First Union Bank of N.C.	Where Listed	OTC-BB
Auditor	Elliott, Davis & Co. LLP	Symbol	EGER
Market Maker	Herzog, Heine, Geduld, Inc.	Telephone (800)221-3600	SIC Code	6141
Broker Dealer	Regular Stockbroker	Employees	143

Empire Gas Corporation

1700 South Jefferson Street • Lebanon, MO 65536 • Telephone (417)532-3103 • Fax (417)532-8529

Company Description

The Company is in the business of retail distribution of propane gas. During the fiscal year ended June 30,1995, the Company sold approximately 86.7 million gallons of propane to approximately 112,000 customers in 21 states. The Company also sells related gas-burning appliances and equipment and rents storage tanks to customers. The Company has been operating since 1963.

	06/30/95	06/30/94	06/30/93	06/30/92
Per Share Information				
Stock Price	3.00	3.00	3.00	3.50
Earnings Per Share	-5.53	2.23	0.16	-0.06
Price / Earnings Ratio	n.a.	1.35	18.75	n.a.
Book Value Per Share	-23.38	-17.87	2.48	-0.07
Price / Book Value %	n.a.	n.a.	120.97	n.a.
Dividends Per Share	n.a.	n.a.	n.a.	n.a.
Annual Financial Data				
Operating Results (000's)				
Total Revenues	74,640.0	124,552.0	128,401.0	112,080.0
Costs & Expenses	-82,153.0	-121,578.0	-122,224.0	-111,493.0
Income Before Taxes and Other	-13,326.0	-840.0	4,268.0	-1,184.0
Other Items	n.a.	32,315.0	n.a.	n.a.
Income Tax	4,600.0	-350.0	-2,040.0	-290.0
Net Income	-8,726.0	31,125.0	2,228.0	-1,474.0
Cash Flow From Operations	1,427.0	12,918.0	6,241.0	10,000.0
Balance Sheet (000's)				
Cash & Equivalents	821.0	2,927.0	362.0	209.0
Total Current Assets	14,516.0	17,064.0	18,557.0	15,287.0
Fixed Assets, Net	71,106.0	67,273.0	109,680.0	99,128.0
Total Assets	105,128.0	104,644.0	148,020.0	127,455.0
Total Current Liabilities	12,880.0	10,751.0	13,597.0	29,211.0
Long-Term Debt	115,143.0	105,320.0	74,068.0	62,368.0
Stockholders' Equity	-36,946.0	-28,220.0	25,913.0	6,268.0
Performance & Financial Condition				
Return on Total Revenues %	-11.69	24.99	1.74	-1.32
Return on Avg Stockholders' Equity %	n.a.	n.a.	13.85	n.a.
Return on Average Assets %	-8.32	24.64	1.62	-1.14
Current Ratio	1.13	1.59	1.36	0.52
Debt / Equity %	n.a.	n.a.	285.83	995.02

Compound Growth %'s	EPS % n.a.	Net Income % n.a.	Total Revenues % -12.67

Comments

During 1994, a number of significant ownership and corporate restructuring events took place, resulting in a $31.1 million increase in income from the transfer of certain assets to departing shareholders in exchange for subsidiary stock, the issuance of debentures in the amount of $127.2 million and a reduction in stockholder's equity of $84.0 million. The result of these transactions is the ownership by one individual of 95.5% of a Company that is much different from what it was. While no active market appears to exist for the Company's stock, published bid quotations of $3.00 per share have been recorded for the past three years and several market makers handle the trades.

Officers	Position	Ownership Information	06/30/95
Paul S. Lindsey, Jr.	President, CEO	Number of Shares Outstanding	1,579,957
Mark Castaneda	VP - Finance	Market Capitalization	$ 4,739,871
Valeria Schall	Secretary, Vice President	Frequency Of Dividends	n.a.
Kristin L. Lindsey	Vice President	Number of Shareholders	9
Willis D. Green	Controller		

Other Information				
Transfer Agent	First Trust N.A.		Where Listed	OTC-PS
Auditor	Baird, Kurtz & Dobson		Symbol	EGCS
Market Maker	Allen & Company, Inc.	Telephone (800)221-2246	SIC Code	5984
Broker Dealer	Regular Stockbroker		Employees	600

Equisure Financial Network Inc.

510 Main Street East • North Bay, Ontario P1B 1B8 Canada • Telephone (705)476-5010 • Fax (705)472-3625

Company Description

The Company holds equity investments in a number of companies which operate as general insurance brokers. The Company provides financing and network services to the companies. Approximately 28 offices deliver full service general and life insurance products to about 90,000 clients. The Company was incorporated in 1987 and merged with a publicly listed company in 1992. The Company issued convertible preferred shares as well as convertible debentures in 1995.

	12/31/95	12/31/94	12/31/93	12/31/92
Per Share Information				
Stock Price	3.60	1.70	1.15	1.15
Earnings Per Share	0.09	0.02	0.02	0.05
Price / Earnings Ratio	40.00	85.00	57.50	n.a.
Book Value Per Share	1.99	0.52	0.22	0.36
Price / Book Value %	180.90	326.92	522.73	n.a.
Dividends Per Share	n.a.	n.a.	n.a.	n.a.
Annual Financial Data				
Operating Results (000's)				
Total Revenues	6,311.2	952.6	708.6	913.5
Costs & Expenses	-5,301.2	-775.1	-572.8	-606.9
Income Before Taxes and Other	1,010.0	177.6	135.8	247.5
Other Items	n.a.	n.a.	n.a.	n.a.
Income Tax	-443.9	-64.3	-57.4	-111.0
Net Income	566.1	113.3	78.5	136.5
Cash Flow From Operations	832.6	-285.2	213.4	-189.1
Balance Sheet (000's)				
Cash & Equivalents	3,103.7	125.7	230.9	94.3
Total Current Assets	13,809.1	2,464.7	1,139.4	506.8
Fixed Assets, Net	2,196.4	139.0	78.6	65.8
Total Assets	30,869.8	7,822.1	4,557.0	3,639.4
Total Current Liabilities	5,257.0	151.5	359.4	561.9
Long-Term Debt	7,154.0	4,943.5	1,608.3	1,591.0
Stockholders' Equity	17,367.4	2,702.5	2,589.2	1,486.6
Performance & Financial Condition				
Return on Total Revenues %	8.97	11.89	11.07	n.a.
Return on Avg Stockholders' Equity %	5.64	4.28	3.85	n.a.
Return on Average Assets %	2.93	1.83	1.91	n.a.
Current Ratio	2.63	16.26	3.17	n.a.
Debt / Equity %	41.19	182.92	62.12	n.a.

Compound Growth %'s	EPS %	21.64	Net Income %	60.66	Total Revenues %	90.46

Comments

Continued growth is planned through both the acquisition of additional brokerage firms as well as the addition of new product lines to be provided to the entire existing network.

Officers	Position	Ownership Information	12/31/95
George R. Hutchison	CEO, President	Number of Shares Outstanding	8,739,457
Hal S. Beatty,C.A.	CFO	Market Capitalization	$ 31,462,045
Neil G. Forth	Secretary, Treasurer	Frequency Of Dividends	n.a.
		Number of Shareholders	Under 500

Other Information			
Transfer Agent	The R-M Trust Company, Toronto, Ontario	Where Listed	TSE
Auditor	B.D.O. Dunwoody	Symbol	EFN
Market Maker	None	SIC Code	6400
Broker Dealer	Regular Stockbroker	Employees	125

Erie Family Life Insurance Company

100 Erie Insurance Pl. • Erie, PA 16530 • Telephone (814)870-2000 • Fax (800)533-5144

Company Description

The Company is engaged in the business of underwriting and selling nonparticipating individual and group life insurance policies, including universal life and annuity products. The Company markets its products through independent agents in eleven states. A majority of of the Company's business is written in Pennsylvania, Ohio, Maryland and Virginia. The Company waas incorporated in Pennsylvania in 1967.

	12/31/95	12/31/94	12/31/93	12/31/92
Per Share Information				
Stock Price	59.00	52.50	53.00	38.00
Earnings Per Share	5.68	5.34	5.57	5.05
Price / Earnings Ratio	10.39	9.83	9.52	7.52
Book Value Per Share	40.92	28.84	28.49	23.95
Price / Book Value %	144.18	182.04	186.03	158.66
Dividends Per Share	1.36	1.20	1.10	1.00
Annual Financial Data				
Operating Results (000's)				
Total Revenues	78,350.0	66,768.8	64,787.1	58,523.3
Costs & Expenses	-51,946.1	-40,289.3	-36,910.8	-33,181.8
Income Before Taxes and Other	26,403.9	26,479.5	27,876.3	25,341.5
Other Items	n.a.	n.a.	-567.6	n.a.
Income Tax	-8,522.3	-9,649.8	-9,772.0	-9,446.9
Net Income	17,881.6	16,829.7	17,536.6	15,894.6
Cash Flow From Operations	8,297.4	12,805.7	5,270.7	3,201.0
Balance Sheet (000's)				
Cash & Equivalents	34,847.3	6,559.2	14,800.8	7,819.9
Total Current Assets	47,113.2	17,822.1	24,341.5	16,496.4
Total Assets	673,794.2	528,632.1	455,135.6	376,485.3
Total Current Liabilities	4,421.1	4,324.8	4,318.3	5,865.2
Long-Term Debt	n.a.	n.a.	n.a.	n.a.
Stockholders' Equity	128,905.4	90,855.6	89,744.9	75,427.3
Performance & Financial Condition				
Return on Total Revenues %	22.82	25.21	27.07	27.16
Return on Avg Stockholders' Equity %	16.27	18.64	21.23	22.90
Return on Average Assets %	2.97	3.42	4.22	4.72
Current Ratio	10.66	4.12	5.64	2.81
Debt / Equity %	n.a.	n.a.	n.a.	n.a.

Compound Growth %'s	EPS %	4.00	Net Income %	4.00	Total Revenues %	10.21

Comments

Total insurance in force at December 31, 1995, totaled $9.6 billion resulting from 185,000 policies. Policy liabilities, at December 31, 1995, total $501.9 million and include $451.3 million of annuity and universal life deposits and $48.8 million of future life policy benefits. At March 31, 1995, the Company was owned by Erie Indemnity Company, 21.6%, Erie Insurance Exchange, 52.2%, and officers and directors, as a group, 6.4%.

Officers	Position	Ownership Information	12/31/95
Stephen A. Milne	President, CEO	Number of Shares Outstanding	3,150,000
Thomas M. Sider	Exec VP, CFO	Market Capitalization	$ 185,850,000
Jan R. Van Gorder	Exec VP, Secretary	Frequency Of Dividends	Annual
John J. Brinling	Exec VP	Number of Shareholders	1,145
Douglas F. Ziegler	Senior VP, Treasurer		

Other Information

Transfer Agent	Company Office			Where Listed	OTC-BB
Auditor	Brown Schwab Berqquist & Co.			Symbol	ERIF
Market Maker	Advest, Inc.	Telephone	(800)998-9834	SIC Code	6311
Broker Dealer	Regular Stockbroker			Employees	79

Esco Transportation Co.

3925 Old Galveston Road • Houston, TX 77017 • Telephone (713)644-0265 • Fax (713)644-9892

Company Description

The Company is primarily a short haul contractor of freight for major shipping companies. The Company was incorporated as Power Oil Company in 1916. Until December 1993, the Company was primarily in the business of exploration, production and sale of crude oil and natural gas. The Company acquired Esco Transportation, Inc. in December of 1993, and changed its name to Esco Transportation Co. Oil and gas are now an immaterial portion of the Company's business.

	12/31/95	12/31/94	12/31/93	12/31/92
Per Share Information				
Stock Price	1.03	2.25	1.19	n.a.
Earnings Per Share	0.07	0.05	0.06	-0.01
Price / Earnings Ratio	14.71	45.00	19.83	n.a.
Book Value Per Share	0.51	0.43	0.39	0.11
Price / Book Value %	201.96	523.26	305.13	n.a.
Dividends Per Share	n.a.	n.a.	n.a.	n.a.
Annual Financial Data				
Operating Results (000's)				
Total Revenues	8,296.2	6,443.3	5,397.3	110.6
Costs & Expenses	-8,220.3	-6,379.9	-5,331.0	-120.5
Income Before Taxes and Other	75.9	63.4	66.3	-9.8
Other Items	n.a.	n.a.	n.a.	n.a.
Income Tax	n.a.	-12.5	n.a.	n.a.
Net Income	75.9	50.8	66.3	-9.8
Cash Flow From Operations	-91.1	247.0	-280.5	7.6
Balance Sheet (000's)				
Cash & Equivalents	12.4	93.1	7.3	3.3
Total Current Assets	839.0	603.9	650.6	177.9
Fixed Assets, Net	932.7	375.7	242.5	128.3
Total Assets	1,861.3	1,062.4	893.1	306.2
Total Current Liabilities	721.5	411.5	471.8	44.1
Long-Term Debt	585.6	182.7	n.a.	n.a.
Stockholders' Equity	554.1	468.2	421.4	262.1
Performance & Financial Condition				
Return on Total Revenues %	0.92	1.23	0.79	-8.89
Return on Avg Stockholders' Equity %	14.86	11.43	19.41	-5.21
Return on Average Assets %	5.20	5.20	11.06	-4.47
Current Ratio	1.16	1.47	1.38	4.03
Debt / Equity %	105.68	39.03	n.a.	n.a.

Compound Growth %'s	EPS %	8.01	Net Income %	7.01	Total Revenues %	321.68

Comments

As of December 31, 1995, officers and directors, as a group, owned 82% of the outstanding common stock of the Company. Two customers accounted for 40% of revenues during 1995, and four customers made up 80% in 1994.

Officers	Position	Ownership Information	12/31/95
Edwis L. Selph	Chairman	Number of Shares Outstanding	1,092,676
Frederick Doutel, Jr.	Secretary	Market Capitalization	$ 1,125,456
Edwis L. Selph, Jr.	Vice President	Frequency Of Dividends	n.a.
		Number of Shareholders	129

Other Information

Transfer Agent	Company Office			Where Listed	OTC-BB
Auditor	Hein & Associates LLP			Symbol	ESCO
Market Maker	Carr Securities Corporation	Telephone	(800)221-2243	SIC Code	1311
Broker Dealer	Regular Stockbroker			Employees	30

Exolon-Esk Company

1000 East Niagara Street • Tonawanda, NY 14150 • Telephone (716)693-4550 • Fax (716)693-6607

Company Description

The Company is in the business of manufacturing and selling products which are used principally for abrasive, refractory and metallurgical applications. The primary products are fused aluminum oxide and silicon carbide. The Company's production facilities are located in Illinois, New York and Canada. The Company also has operations in Norway conducted through a joint venture of which the Company owns 50%. The Exolon Company was founded in 1914 and reincorporated as a Delaware corporation in 1976. In 1984, as a result of a merger with the ESK Corporation, the Company was renamed. In conjunction with this merger, the Company issued all the shares of its Class A common stock and all the shares of its Series B preferred stock to Wacker Chemical Corp. In 1995, Wacker Chemical Corp. transferred all of its stock in the Company to Wacker Chemicals, Inc., a wholly owned subsidiary of Wacker Chemie GmbH.

	12/31/95	12/31/94	12/31/93	12/31/92
Per Share Information				
Stock Price	20.32	17.25	20.50	18.50
Earnings Per Share	3.44	1.42	0.03	1.39
Price / Earnings Ratio	5.91	12.15	683.33	13.31
Book Value Per Share	21.00	17.28	16.41	16.45
Price / Book Value %	96.76	99.83	124.92	112.46
Dividends Per Share	n.a.	n.a.	n.a.	n.a.
Annual Financial Data				
Operating Results (000's)				
Total Revenues	68,592.0	59,494.0	58,225.0	58,387.0
Costs & Expenses	-62,512.0	-56,142.0	-55,989.0	-55,505.0
Income Before Taxes and Other	6,857.0	1,942.0	1,918.0	2,236.0
Other Items	n.a.	n.a.	-1,173.0	n.a.
Income Tax	-2,893.0	-426.0	-712.0	-923.0
Net Income	3,964.0	1,516.0	33.0	1,313.0
Cash Flow From Operations	3,539.0	4,176.0	2,197.0	3,507.0
Balance Sheet (000's)				
Cash & Equivalents	440.0	467.0	113.0	126.0
Total Current Assets	29,395.0	25,441.0	25,434.0	23,937.0
Fixed Assets, Net	15,193.0	15,395.0	16,591.0	17,643.0
Total Assets	50,215.0	45,309.0	45,834.0	45,925.0
Total Current Liabilities	7,981.0	7,387.0	8,660.0	8,021.0
Long-Term Debt	15,350.0	14,900.0	16,900.0	18,691.0
Stockholders' Equity	22,298.0	18,628.0	16,770.0	16,813.0
Performance & Financial Condition				
Return on Total Revenues %	5.78	2.55	0.06	2.25
Return on Avg Stockholders' Equity %	19.37	8.57	0.20	7.93
Return on Average Assets %	8.30	3.33	0.07	2.81
Current Ratio	3.68	3.44	2.94	2.98
Debt / Equity %	68.84	79.99	100.78	111.17

Compound Growth %'s	EPS %	35.26	Net Income %	44.53	Total Revenues %	5.52

Comments

The Company has two classes of common stock and two series of convertible preferred stock. Each of the classes and series has equal dividend, preference, conversion and voting rights.

Officers	Position	Ownership Information	12/31/95
J. Fred Silver	President, CEO	Number of Shares Outstanding	481,995
James A. Bernardoni	VP - Finance	Market Capitalization	$ 9,794,138
Kersi Dordi	Vice President	Frequency Of Dividends	n.a.
Armand Ladage	Vice President	Number of Shareholders	178
John L. Redshaw	Vice President		

Other Information

Transfer Agent	State Street Bank & Trust			Where Listed	BE
Auditor	Ernst & Young LLP			Symbol	EXOL
Market Maker	Hill, Thompson, Magid & Co.Inc	Telephone	(800)631-3083	SIC Code	3290
Broker Dealer	Regular Stockbroker			Employees	267

Fairbanco Holding Company, Inc.

P.O. Box 37 • Fairburn, GA 30213 • Telephone (770)964-1551 • Fax (770)964-6076

Company Description

Fairbanco Holding Company, Inc. is a holding company for its subsidiary, Fairburn Banking Company, which provides community banking services in the Fairburn, Georgia area. The Company has been operating for over 100 years, since 1891.

	12/31/95	12/31/94	12/31/93	12/31/92
Per Share Information				
Stock Price	62.00	55.00	60.00	53.50
Earnings Per Share	11.64	10.44	7.26	7.31
Price / Earnings Ratio	5.33	5.27	8.26	7.32
Book Value Per Share	77.09	62.09	72.40	64.05
Price / Book Value %	80.43	88.58	82.87	83.53
Dividends Per Share	2.00	1.50	n.a.	n.a.
Annual Financial Data				
Operating Results (000's)				
Net Interest Income	3,901.7	3,427.5	2,997.1	2,744.4
Loan Loss Provision	n.a.	n.a.	n.a.	n.a.
Non-Interest Income	575.1	668.2	596.1	1,051.6
Non-Interest Expense	-3,085.3	-2,992.7	-2,827.7	-3,108.1
Income Before Taxes and Other	1,391.5	1,103.0	765.5	687.9
Other Items	n.a.	n.a.	n.a.	n.a.
Income Tax	-473.0	-278.9	-193.0	-119.0
Net Income	918.5	824.1	572.5	568.9
Balance Sheet (000's)				
Cash & Securities	35,652.3	37,214.6	39,346.5	42,396.6
Loans, Net	39,915.3	34,332.2	28,725.3	24,250.2
Fixed Assets, Net	863.5	836.1	939.3	842.9
Total Assets	77,313.4	73,454.5	70,269.2	68,960.4
Deposits	69,534.6	67,038.3	63,974.1	63,129.2
Stockholders' Equity	6,082.9	4,899.1	5,712.5	4,983.4
Performance & Financial Condition				
Net Interest Margin	n.a.	n.a.	n.a.	n.a.
Return on Avg Stockholders' Equity %	16.73	15.53	10.71	12.23
Return on Average Assets %	1.22	1.15	0.82	0.92
Equity to Assets %	7.87	6.67	8.13	7.23
Reserve as a % of Non-Performing Loans	n.a.	n.a.	n.a.	n.a.

Compound Growth %'s	EPS %	16.77	Net Income %	17.31	Net Interest Income %	12.44

Comments

The last public quote on the Company's stock was in 1990. Since then, all sales of stock have been conducted privately between individuals. However the Company did issue new shares in 1992 and 1993 for $53.50 and $60.00, respectively. There is currently nobody making a market in the Company's stock.

Officers	Position	Ownership Information	12/31/95
Robert W. Fuller, Jr.	President	Number of Shares Outstanding	78,902
Nina H. Ray	Exec VP	Market Capitalization	$ 4,891,924
Howard V. Turner, Jr.	Senior VP	Frequency Of Dividends	Annual
Douglas F. Fields	Vice President	Number of Shareholders	112

Other Information

Transfer Agent	Company Office		Where Listed	n.a.
Auditor	Grantland Davis, CPA		Symbol	n.a.
Market Maker	None - Company Office	Telephone (770)964-1551	SIC Code	6020
Broker Dealer	Pink sheet specialist		Employees	38

Fairmount Chemical Co., Inc.

117 Blanchard Street • Newark, NJ 07105 • Telephone (201)344-5790 • Fax (201)690-5298

Company Description

The Company Manufactures and sells chemicals, principally for use in the imaging, plastics, and pharmaceutical industries. Also, hydrazine-based products are manufactured and sold to a variety of users in different industries. The Company was incorporated in New Jersey in 1938.

	12/31/95	12/31/94	12/31/93	12/31/92
Per Share Information				
Stock Price	0.23	0.18	0.05	0.05
Earnings Per Share	0.03	0.02	n.a.	-0.25
Price / Earnings Ratio	7.67	9.00	n.a.	n.a.
Book Value Per Share	0.14	0.10	0.06	0.07
Price / Book Value %	164.29	180.00	83.33	71.43
Dividends Per Share	n.a.	n.a.	n.a.	n.a.
Annual Financial Data				
Operating Results (000's)				
Total Revenues	12,403.0	11,379.2	10,072.6	8,967.8
Costs & Expenses	-12,024.3	-11,142.9	-10,101.8	-10,702.7
Income Before Taxes and Other	378.7	236.3	-29.2	-1,736.4
Other Items	n.a.	n.a.	n.a.	n.a.
Income Tax	n.a.	n.a.	n.a.	-79.2
Net Income	378.7	236.3	-29.2	-1,815.6
Cash Flow From Operations	407.1	363.3	1,049.9	-363.9
Balance Sheet (000's)				
Cash & Equivalents	432.8	460.9	765.0	238.7
Total Current Assets	4,471.4	3,631.2	3,321.3	3,076.5
Fixed Assets, Net	5,163.6	5,029.1	5,171.6	5,700.5
Total Assets	9,635.7	8,661.0	8,493.6	8,777.7
Total Current Liabilities	1,161.2	800.0	837.4	960.8
Long-Term Debt	1,156.0	790.0	790.0	6,393.7
Stockholders' Equity	6,596.0	6,217.3	5,913.0	610.2
Performance & Financial Condition				
Return on Total Revenues %	3.05	2.08	-0.29	-20.25
Return on Avg Stockholders' Equity %	5.91	3.90	-0.90	n.a.
Return on Average Assets %	4.14	2.75	-0.34	n.a.
Current Ratio	3.85	4.54	3.97	3.20
Debt / Equity %	17.53	12.71	13.36	1047.80

Compound Growth %'s	EPS %	50.00	Net Income %	60.26	Total Revenues %	11.42

Comments

At December 31, 1995, the Estate of William E. Leistner (Leistner) owned 57.8% of the Company. During 1993, the Company converted $5.4 million of amounts owed Leistner to cumulative (when declared) convertible preferred stock. The preferred is convertible into the commmon on a one-for-one basis. Long-term debt at December 31, 1995, of $1.1 million plus accrued interest of $492,000 is due Leistner. The Company has net operating loss carryforwards of approximately $12.3 million which expire in 2006.

Officers	Position	Ownership Information	12/31/95
William Setzler	Chairman, President	Number of Shares Outstanding	8,292,866
Todd K. Walker	President, COO	Market Capitalization	$ 1,907,359
Sondra Jacoby	Secretary, Treasurer	Frequency Of Dividends	n.a.
Zaven S. Ariyan	Vice President	Number of Shareholders	294
Seymon Moshchitsky	Vice President		

Other Information				
Transfer Agent	Continental Stock Transfer & Trust Co.		Where Listed	OTC-BB
Auditor	KPMG Peat Marwick LLP		Symbol	FMTC
Market Maker	Herzog, Heine, Geduld, Inc.	Telephone (800)221-3600	SIC Code	2865
Broker Dealer	Regular Stockbroker		Employees	67

Fall River Gas Company

155 North Main Street • Fall River, MA 02722-0911 • Telephone (508)675-7811 • Fax (508)677-3242

Company Description

The Company sells, distributes, and transports natural gas through a pipeline system in the city of Fall River and the towns of Somerset, Swansea and Westport, Massachusetts. Customers served include over 45,000 residences, federal and state housing projects and commercial entities. The Company was organized as a Massachusetts corporation in 1880.

	09/30/95	09/30/94	09/30/93	09/30/92
Per Share Information				
Stock Price	24.50	25.00	18.25	17.63
Earnings Per Share	0.91	1.40	1.32	1.02
Price / Earnings Ratio	26.92	17.86	13.83	17.28
Book Value Per Share	7.26	7.31	6.89	6.53
Price / Book Value %	337.47	342.00	264.88	269.98
Dividends Per Share	0.96	0.98	0.97	0.92
Annual Financial Data				
Operating Results (000's)				
Total Revenues	45,190.5	49,145.8	45,509.3	36,606.3
Costs & Expenses	-43,102.9	-45,666.2	-42,175.0	-34,030.9
Income Before Taxes and Other	2,087.6	3,479.6	3,334.3	2,571.3
Other Items	n.a.	n.a.	n.a.	n.a.
Income Tax	-471.4	-988.5	-981.9	-751.4
Net Income	1,616.2	2,491.1	2,352.4	1,819.9
Cash Flow From Operations	5,507.2	6,783.6	-1,908.8	8,297.9
Balance Sheet (000's)				
Cash & Equivalents	315.3	360.8	356.3	206.3
Total Current Assets	9,934.3	12,150.2	12,292.1	5,751.3
Fixed Assets, Net	38,821.2	35,539.7	32,748.0	31,118.1
Total Assets	50,956.5	49,625.8	46,501.4	38,263.2
Total Current Liabilities	24,692.3	22,762.3	20,497.9	13,035.7
Long-Term Debt	6,500.0	7,380.0	7,560.0	7,680.0
Stockholders' Equity	12,921.0	13,014.1	12,268.0	11,633.8
Performance & Financial Condition				
Return on Total Revenues %	3.58	5.07	5.17	4.97
Return on Avg Stockholders' Equity %	12.46	19.71	19.68	16.15
Return on Average Assets %	3.21	5.18	5.55	4.70
Current Ratio	0.40	0.53	0.60	0.44
Debt / Equity %	50.31	56.71	61.62	66.01

Compound Growth %'s	EPS %	-3.73	Net Income %	-3.88	Total Revenues %	7.27

Comments

Included in revenues are earnings of a wholly owned subsidiary that rents heating appliances. Operations for the three months ended December 31, 1995, resulted in Net Income of $0.05 per share as compared to $0.15 for the same period in 1994. In 1992, the Company changed its year end from December 31 to September 30. Consequently, the nine month period ended September 30, 1992, is not comparable to the other years.

Officers	Position	Ownership Information	09/30/95
Bradford J. Faxon	Chairman, President	Number of Shares Outstanding	1,780,542
Peter H. Thanas	Senior VP, Treasurer	Market Capitalization	$ 43,623,279
John F. Fanning	Vice President	Frequency Of Dividends	Quarterly
		Number of Shareholders	866

Other Information			
Transfer Agent	State Street Bank	Where Listed	OTC-BB
Auditor	Arthur Andersen LLP	Symbol	FALL
Market Maker	Gruntal & Co., Incorporated	Telephone (212)344-2297	SIC Code	4924
Broker Dealer	Regular Stockbroker	Employees	175

Farm Fish, Inc.

P.O. Drawer 1292 • Jackson, MS 39215-1292 • Telephone (601)354-3801 • Fax (601)355-9134

Company Description

The Company is engaged in the hatching and growing of catfish on 1,750 acres of farmland in Mississippi. The catfish are raised until they reach marketable size. Then they are harvested and sold to processors for processing and sale to the public. The Company was incorporated in Mississippi in 1969. During 1984, through a private stock placement, Delta Industries, Inc. became an 80% owner of the Company.

	12/31/95	12/31/94	12/31/93	12/31/92
Per Share Information				
Stock Price	1.00	0.13	1.00	0.25
Earnings Per Share	0.18	0.21	0.16	0.10
Price / Earnings Ratio	5.56	0.62	6.25	2.50
Book Value Per Share	1.29	1.11	0.90	0.75
Price / Book Value %	77.52	11.71	111.11	33.33
Dividends Per Share	n.a.	n.a.	n.a.	n.a.
Annual Financial Data				
Operating Results (000's)				
Total Revenues	3,847.2	3,466.6	3,131.4	2,632.5
Costs & Expenses	-2,979.6	-2,534.4	-2,568.9	-2,338.9
Income Before Taxes and Other	763.7	903.5	562.4	293.5
Other Items	n.a.	n.a.	n.a.	n.a.
Income Tax	-280.6	-341.0	-137.0	-15.0
Net Income	483.1	562.4	425.4	278.5
Cash Flow From Operations	853.4	479.8	614.1	61.0
Balance Sheet (000's)				
Cash & Equivalents	22.2	96.9	82.7	105.3
Total Current Assets	3,954.1	3,963.7	3,446.5	3,297.7
Fixed Assets, Net	2,178.4	2,269.5	2,300.9	2,146.6
Total Assets	6,509.8	6,823.0	6,066.4	6,003.3
Total Current Liabilities	2,338.6	3,043.9	2,754.7	2,976.0
Long-Term Debt	570.0	670.0	770.0	1,020.0
Stockholders' Equity	3,478.3	2,995.1	2,432.7	2,007.3
Performance & Financial Condition				
Return on Total Revenues %	12.56	16.22	13.59	10.58
Return on Avg Stockholders' Equity %	14.93	20.72	19.16	14.91
Return on Average Assets %	7.25	8.73	7.05	4.72
Current Ratio	1.69	1.30	1.25	1.11
Debt / Equity %	16.39	22.37	31.65	50.82

Compound Growth %'s	EPS %	21.64	Net Income %	20.15	Total Revenues %	13.48

Comments

During 1995, 56% of the Company's production was sold to one processor, a cooperative in which the Company has an investment of $375,000. Included in liabilities are non-interest bearing advances of $2.1 million from Delta Industries.

Officers	Position	Ownership Information	12/31/95
Leland R. Speed	Chairman	Number of Shares Outstanding	2,688,605
Thomas R. Slough, Jr.	President	Market Capitalization	$ 2,688,605
Charles E. Horne	Treasurer, Secretary	Frequency Of Dividends	n.a.
David Robison	Vice President	Number of Shareholders	1,866

Other Information				
Transfer Agent	KeyCorp Shareholder Services, Inc.		Where Listed	OTC-BB
Auditor	Ernst & Young LLP		Symbol	FFIH
Market Maker	S.J. Wolfe & Co.	Telephone (800)262-2244	SIC Code	0200
Broker Dealer	Regular Stockbroker		Employees	22

Farmers National Bancorp, Inc.

121 West First Street • Geneseo, IL 61254 • Telephone (309)944-5361 • Fax (309)944-4897

Company Description

Farmers National Bancorp, Inc. is the parent company of The Farmers National Bank of Geneseo. The Bank provides standard banking services to predominantly small and middle market businesses and individuals in rural communities primarily in Henry County, Illinois.

	12/31/95	12/31/94	12/31/93	12/31/92
Per Share Information				
Stock Price	59.00	54.00	52.50	50.00
Earnings Per Share	7.00	6.50	6.33	6.01
Price / Earnings Ratio	8.43	8.31	8.29	8.32
Book Value Per Share	47.91	41.12	40.19	35.65
Price / Book Value %	123.15	131.32	130.63	140.25
Dividends Per Share	1.96	1.83	1.70	1.40
Annual Financial Data				
Operating Results (000's)				
Net Interest Income	6,156.4	6,115.0	5,903.2	5,703.9
Loan Loss Provision	n.a.	n.a.	101.2	n.a.
Non-Interest Income	957.8	1,072.8	917.9	959.2
Non-Interest Expense	-4,145.0	-4,110.5	-3,789.1	-3,652.0
Income Before Taxes and Other	2,969.2	3,077.3	3,133.1	3,011.1
Other Items	n.a.	n.a.	n.a.	n.a.
Income Tax	-696.0	-748.6	-828.6	-806.5
Net Income	2,273.2	2,328.7	2,304.6	2,204.6
Balance Sheet (000's)				
Cash & Securities	88,552.5	87,345.4	84,858.2	82,906.8
Loans, Net	89,293.2	84,213.3	79,432.5	72,470.8
Fixed Assets, Net	1,880.3	2,024.0	2,131.5	2,129.4
Total Assets	182,355.4	176,846.9	169,023.6	160,412.1
Deposits	160,522.6	152,923.3	146,343.5	142,705.4
Stockholders' Equity	14,769.0	14,649.1	14,524.7	13,073.9
Performance & Financial Condition				
Net Interest Margin	n.a.	n.a.	n.a.	n.a.
Return on Avg Stockholders' Equity %	15.45	15.96	16.70	18.03
Return on Average Assets %	1.27	1.35	1.40	1.39
Equity to Assets %	8.10	8.28	8.59	8.15
Reserve as a % of Non-Performing Loans	2049.80	911.37	575.60	406.03

Compound Growth %'s	EPS %	5.21	Net Income %	1.03	Net Interest Income %	2.58

Comments

The Bank is pursuing an aggressive common stock repurchase program in which 48,000 shares were repurchased in 1995. This accounted for the increase in earnings per share (actual earnings declined slightly). The loan portfolio is diversified with real estate mortgages representing 38%, agricultural loans 33% and commercial loans representing 18% of total loans. Although growth has not been impressive, the Bank continues to demonstrate excellent returns on assets and equity.

Officers	Position	Ownership Information	12/31/95
H. Willard Nelson	Chairman	Number of Shares Outstanding	308,249
Gaylon E. Martin	President	Market Capitalization	$ 18,186,691
Wayne A. Hulting	Secretary, Treasurer	Frequency Of Dividends	Quarterly
R. Timothy Harding	Other	Number of Shareholders	687

Other Information

Transfer Agent	Wiley Bros Inc., Nashville, TN			Where Listed	OTC-BB
Auditor	Clifton, Gunderson & Co.			Symbol	FRMY
Market Maker	Chicago Corporation, The	Telephone	(312)855-7664	SIC Code	6020
Broker Dealer	Regular Stockbroker			Employees	76

Fifty Associates

160 Federal Street • Boston, MA 02110-1702 • Telephone (617)330-9750 • Fax (617)443-9790

Company Description

This real estate investment trust owns and manages approximately 1.6 million square feet of primarily retail space. Shopping centers comprise the bulk of space with three centers in California, owned 50% by the Company, and one in Hawaii

	12/31/95	12/31/94	12/31/93
Per Share Information			
Stock Price	23.75	20.50	15.12
Earnings Per Share	2.66	5.63	1.69
Price / Earnings Ratio	8.93	3.64	8.95
Book Value Per Share	7.76	7.95	9.28
Price / Book Value %	306.06	257.86	162.93
Dividends Per Share	2.84	6.55	2.00
Annual Financial Data			
Operating Results (000's)			
Total Revenues	5,112.5	7,978.5	5,307.2
Costs & Expenses	-2,572.2	-3,005.0	-2,693.2
Income Before Taxes and Other	2,540.3	4,973.5	2,261.5
Other Items	n.a.	n.a.	n.a.
Income Tax	31.3	473.8	-624.0
Net Income	2,571.6	5,447.3	1,637.5
Cash Flow From Operations	2,845.6	5,208.4	3,100.4
Balance Sheet (000's)			
Cash & Equivalents	2,757.4	2,573.0	3,772.3
Total Current Assets	2,787.4	2,736.0	3,773.4
Fixed Assets, Net	4,494.0	4,740.7	4,995.5
Total Assets	8,333.5	8,471.3	9,439.6
Total Current Liabilities	357.7	356.7	268.6
Long-Term Debt	n.a.	n.a.	n.a.
Stockholders' Equity	7,514.8	7,660.6	8,547.0
Performance & Financial Condition			
Return on Total Revenues %	50.30	68.27	30.85
Return on Avg Stockholders' Equity %	33.89	67.22	18.84
Return on Average Assets %	30.61	60.83	17.24
Current Ratio	7.79	7.67	14.05
Debt / Equity %	n.a.	n.a.	n.a.

Compound Growth %'s	EPS %	25.46	Net Income %	25.32	Total Revenues %	-1.85

Comments

The Company has available cash and no debt. This puts it in the position of scouting for favorable opportunities.

Officers	Position	Ownership Information	12/31/95
Weston Howland, Jr.	Chairman	Number of Shares Outstanding	968,380
George M. Lovejoy, Jr.	President, Treasurer	Market Capitalization	$ 22,999,025
Frederick S. Moseley, III	Vice President	Frequency Of Dividends	Quarterly
		Number of Shareholders	Under 500

Other Information

Transfer Agent	Company Office			Where Listed	OTC-BB
Auditor	Arthur Andersen LLP			Symbol	FFTY
Market Maker	Gruntal & Co., Incorporated	Telephone	(800)223-7632	SIC Code	6510
Broker Dealer	Regular Stockbroker			Employees	2

This page left intentionally blank.

Finance Company of Pennsylvania

226 Walnut Street • Philadelphia, PA 19106

Company Description

The Company is a regulated open-end investment company under the Investment Company Act of 1940. Most of the assets are invested in common stocks and common stock mutual funds. There are also investments in U.S. Treasury notes. The Company was founded in 1871.

	12/31/95	12/31/94	12/31/93	12/31/92
Per Share Information				
Stock Price	665.00	637.50	650.00	578.00
Earnings Per Share	194.89	-54.67	35.33	56.10
Price / Earnings Ratio	3.27	n.a.	18.40	10.30
Book Value Per Share	736.90	568.74	646.40	633.16
Price / Book Value %	86.51	112.09	100.56	91.29
Dividends Per Share	26.73	22.99	22.09	20.89
Annual Financial Data				
Operating Results (000's)				
Total Revenues	12,304.5	1,659.8	7,482.8	3,575.2
Costs & Expenses	-347.3	-324.0	-311.8	-323.4
Income Before Taxes and Other	11,957.2	-3,168.4	7,171.0	3,251.9
Other Items	n.a.	n.a.	n.a.	n.a.
Income Tax	-499.4	n.a.	n.a.	n.a.
Net Income	11,457.9	-3,168.4	7,171.0	3,251.9
Cash Flow From Operations	11,457.9	-3,168.4	7,171.0	3,251.9
Balance Sheet (000's)				
Cash & Equivalents	12.6	n.a.	n.a.	n.a.
Total Current Assets	44,506.2	34,761.3	39,262.1	38,494.8
Fixed Assets, Net	n.a.	n.a.	n.a.	n.a.
Total Assets	44,509.3	34,761.3	39,262.1	38,494.8
Total Current Liabilities	1,802.4	1,800.0	1,800.0	1,800.0
Borrowings	n.a.	n.a.	n.a.	n.a.
Stockholders' Equity	42,706.9	32,961.3	37,462.1	36,694.8
Performance & Financial Condition				
Return on Total Revenues %	93.12	-190.89	95.83	90.95
Return on Avg Stockholders' Equity %	30.28	-9.00	19.34	9.12
Return on Average Assets %	28.91	-8.56	18.44	8.68
Current Ratio	24.69	n.a.	n.a.	n.a.
Debt / Equity %	n.a.	n.a.	n.a.	n.a.

Compound Growth %'s	EPS %	51.45	Net Income %	52.17	Total Revenues %	50.98

Comments

Annual portfolio turnover is usually between 5% and 10%. Annual ratios of expenses to average net assets range from 0.8% to 1.0%. Because this is an investment trust, compounded growth rates are not particularly valuable. The largest industry concentrations of investments were in banking, insurance and financial holding companies (41.17%), and manufacturing (18.76%).

Officers	Position	Ownership Information	12/31/95
Charles E. Mather III	President	Number of Shares Outstanding	57,955
Frank A. ood, Jr.	Secretary, Treasurer	Market Capitalization	$ 36,946,313
Doranne H. Case	Other	Frequency Of Dividends	Quarterly
Mary Ellen Christ	Other	Number of Shareholders	Under 500

Other Information

				Where Listed	OTC-BB
Transfer Agent	Company Office			Symbol	FCPA
Auditor	Deloitte & Touche LLP			SIC Code	6790
Market Maker	F.J. Morrissey & Co., Inc.	Telephone	(800)842-8928		
Broker Dealer	Standard Investment	Tel/Ext	(888)783-4688	Jack	Employees	2

Finch, Pruyn & Company, Incorporated

1 Glen Street • Glens Falls, NY 12801-2167 • Telephone (518)793-2541 • Fax (518)793-7364

Company Description

The Company is a manufacturer of high quality uncoated free-sheet printing paper sold throughout the United States. This gem of American business and history dates all the way back to 1865. This very sheet of paper is a product of Finch, Pruyn - their 50# Finch Opaque paper. Please enjoy reading a little about the Company's history on the opposite page.

	12/31/95	12/31/94	12/31/93	12/31/92
Per Share Information				
Stock Price	1,730.00	1,600.00	1,250.00	1,100.00
Earnings Per Share	599.26	263.72	344.99	282.89
Price / Earnings Ratio	2.89	6.07	3.62	3.89
Book Value Per Share	4,152.55	4,271.59	1,914.87	1,786.26
Price / Book Value %	41.66	37.46	65.28	61.58
Dividends Per Share	148.20	107.76	107.76	107.76
Annual Financial Data				
Operating Results (000's)				
Total Revenues	268,965.0	208,208.0	193,587.0	184,322.0
Costs & Expenses	-224,606.0	-191,108.0	-170,444.0	-168,871.0
Income Before Taxes and Other	44,359.0	17,100.0	23,143.0	15,451.0
Other Items	-1,136.0	n.a.	n.a.	3,209.0
Income Tax	-16,850.0	-5,229.0	-7,683.0	-5,940.0
Net Income	26,373.0	11,871.0	15,460.0	12,720.0
Cash Flow From Operations	51,911.0	25,010.0	28,694.0	25,158.0
Balance Sheet (000's)				
Cash & Equivalents	459.0	486.0	174.0	727.0
Total Current Assets	50,427.0	46,562.0	46,210.0	43,003.0
Fixed Assets, Net	228,734.0	202,740.0	194,722.0	184,372.0
Total Assets	295,380.0	265,392.0	254,938.0	238,913.0
Total Current Liabilities	38,981.0	26,552.0	26,988.0	25,666.0
Long-Term Debt	29,560.0	32,570.0	30,078.0	30,000.0
Stockholders' Equity	179,498.0	162,722.0	156,001.0	145,534.0
Performance & Financial Condition				
Return on Total Revenues %	9.81	5.70	7.99	6.90
Return on Avg Stockholders' Equity %	15.41	7.45	10.25	n.a.
Return on Average Assets %	9.41	4.56	6.26	n.a.
Current Ratio	1.29	1.75	1.71	1.68
Debt / Equity %	16.47	20.02	19.28	20.61

Compound Growth %'s	EPS %	28.43	Net Income %	27.51	Total Revenues %	13.42

Comments

Annual results are impacted by fluctuations of paper prices. The growth rate of the Company demonstrates their continued competitiveness. This stock doesn't have many sellers, but shares do trade.

Officers	Position	Ownership Information	12/31/95
Richard J. Carota	President, CEO	Number of Shares Outstanding	43,226
David P. Manny	Vice President, Secretary	Market Capitalization	$ 74,780,980
		Frequency Of Dividends	Quarterly
		Number of Shareholders	Under 500

Other Information

Transfer Agent	Company Office			Where Listed	OTC-PS
Auditor	Coopers & Lybrand			Symbol	FPCNB
Market Maker	Carr Securities Corporation	Telephone	(800)221-2243	SIC Code	2600
Broker Dealer	Standard Investment	Tel/Ext	(888)783-4688 Jack	Employees	1100

Paper

The mid-nineteenth century was a time of tremendous growth and expansion in the United States. In 1865, with the end of the Civil War, Americans looked once more towards building their futures. It was an ideal time for Jeremiah Finch, Daniel Finch and Samuel Pruyn to launch their business in building materials with the acquisition of a sawmill, a lumber business and lime and black marble quarries, all located on the Hudson River in Glens Falls, New York.

Cities along the Eastern seaboard initially provided a booming market for the Finch, Pruyn Company. Canal boats carried their products from Glens Falls as far south as New York City and returned with supplies for their logging camps back in the Adirondack Mountains. As the century drew to a close business was brisk, but the market for building materials was already moving westward, so Finch, Pruyn decided to refocus the Company. Paper seemed a logical progression, and they acquired their first machine for processing it in 1905. By 1911 they were producing newsprint, which would become their main product until after World War II.

When the time was right, Finch, Pruyn once again resolved to change direction and discontinued newsprint production just as it had ceased the lumber operation years before. The Company decided to concentrate on groundwood printing papers for magazines, books and business paper use. As their success continued, their product line evolved to include uncoated free sheet papers. All of these papers are used by the graphic arts as well as the commercial printing industries for a wide variety of printed products including college and professional textbooks, high-technology manuals and financial reports. *Walker's Manual of Unlisted Stocks* is proud to be printed on Finch, Pruyn paper.

Worth noting is that the Company always has been and remains deeply committed to preservation of the environment. They believe in working with nature to encourage new growth and natural reforestation. Their slow growing Adirondack forests are never clear-cut, but are selectively harvested leaving young trees to mature and plant life to feed the forest animals. The Company encourages recreational use of its forests as well and grants leases to various groups for this purpose.

Finch, Pruyn has made a point of changing with the times and continues to stay on top of trends. They are currently focusing on the high-quality segment of the paper market and are working towards becoming a self-sufficient company as well. These developments should contribute to a continuing success as they make their way into the twenty-first century.

Firecom, Inc.

39-27 59th Street • Woodside, NY 11377 • Telephone (718)899-6100 • Fax (718)899-1932

Company Description

The Company designs, manufactures, sells and services, safety and security systems for high-rise office buildings, hotels, apartment buildings and other large commercial buildings. The Company also sells life safety and other electronic building systems manufactured by other companies. The Company was incorporated in New York in 1978. On July 10, 1995, officers and directors, as a group, owned 52% of the Company's outstanding common stock.

	04/30/95	04/30/94	04/30/93	04/30/92
Per Share Information				
Stock Price	0.64	0.60	0.16	0.16
Earnings Per Share	0.30	0.23	0.14	n.a.
Price / Earnings Ratio	2.13	2.61	1.14	n.a.
Book Value Per Share	0.60	0.22	-0.09	-0.25
Price / Book Value %	106.67	272.73	n.a.	n.a.
Dividends Per Share	n.a.	n.a.	n.a.	n.a.
Annual Financial Data				
Operating Results (000's)				
Total Revenues	14,089.0	11,658.0	8,118.0	7,980.0
Costs & Expenses	-11,423.0	-10,500.0	-7,191.0	-7,220.0
Income Before Taxes and Other	2,666.0	1,150.0	923.0	38.0
Other Items	n.a.	n.a.	n.a.	-19.0
Income Tax	-775.0	400.0	-387.0	24.0
Net Income	1,891.0	1,550.0	536.0	43.0
Cash Flow From Operations	2,123.0	1,580.0	847.0	451.0
Balance Sheet (000's)				
Cash & Equivalents	1,704.0	690.0	909.0	642.0
Total Current Assets	6,551.0	5,663.0	4,006.0	3,866.0
Fixed Assets, Net	460.0	496.0	358.0	300.0
Total Assets	7,231.0	6,442.0	4,659.0	4,456.0
Total Current Liabilities	1,623.0	1,859.0	1,347.0	1,455.0
Long-Term Debt	1,029.0	2,030.0	2,309.0	2,814.0
Stockholders' Equity	4,444.0	2,553.0	1,003.0	187.0
Performance & Financial Condition				
Return on Total Revenues %	13.42	13.30	6.60	0.54
Return on Avg Stockholders' Equity %	54.05	87.18	90.08	n.a.
Return on Average Assets %	27.66	27.93	11.76	0.91
Current Ratio	4.04	3.05	2.97	2.66
Debt / Equity %	23.15	79.51	230.21	1504.80

Compound Growth %'s	EPS %	46.39	Net Income %	252.97	Total Revenues %	20.86

Comments

Included in equity is preferred stock with a total stated value of $1.4 million. In June, 1995, the Company entered into an agreement to repurchase 536,494 shares of its common stock for $.90 per share. In conjunction with this transaction the Company agreed to buy another 536,494 shares at the option of the same shareholders, at $1.10 per share. For the nine months ended January 31, 1996, the Company had total revenue of $11.0 million and net income of $1.0 million ($.17 per share) as compared to $10.6 million and net income of $1.4 million ($.21 per share) for the same period in fiscal year 1995.

Officers	Position	Ownership Information	04/30/95
Paul Mendez	Chairman, President	Number of Shares Outstanding	5,018,038
Howard L. Kogen	Exec VP	Market Capitalization	$ 3,211,544
Antoine P. Sayour	Senior VP	Frequency Of Dividends	n.a.
Richard K. Nelson	VP - Finance	Number of Shareholders	397

Other Information

Transfer Agent	American Stock Transfer & Trust Company		Where Listed	OTC-BB
Auditor	Rothstein, Kass & Co. PC		Symbol	FRCM
Market Maker	Paragon Capital Corporation	Telephone (800)521-8877	SIC Code	3669
Broker Dealer	Regular Stockbroker		Employees	112

Fireplace Manufacturers, Incorporated

2701 South Harbor Blvd. • Santa Ana, CA 92704 • Telephone (714)549-7782 • Fax (714)549-4723

Company Description

The Company is in the business of manufacturing and selling to distributors, factory-built, energy-efficient metal fireplace systems. Forty-eight models of fireplaces are produced, ranging in price from $345 to $3,200. The Company was incorporated in California in 1976.

	03/31/95	03/31/94	03/31/93	03/31/92
Per Share Information				
Stock Price	0.22	0.19	0.19	0.19
Earnings Per Share	0.13	0.01	0.01	0.01
Price / Earnings Ratio	1.69	19.00	19.00	19.00
Book Value Per Share	0.50	0.37	0.36	0.35
Price / Book Value %	44.00	51.35	52.78	54.29
Dividends Per Share	n.a.	n.a.	n.a.	n.a.
Annual Financial Data				
Operating Results (000's)				
Total Revenues	26,718.9	19,822.4	16,293.7	15,887.2
Costs & Expenses	-26,067.9	-19,720.2	-16,217.8	-15,810.4
Income Before Taxes and Other	651.0	102.2	75.9	76.8
Other Items	n.a.	n.a.	n.a.	n.a.
Income Tax	-194.0	-59.0	-39.0	-42.0
Net Income	457.0	43.2	36.9	34.8
Cash Flow From Operations	844.5	389.0	464.5	176.1
Balance Sheet (000's)				
Cash & Equivalents	117.3	114.8	23.4	23.8
Total Current Assets	6,572.0	4,303.2	3,563.7	3,310.4
Fixed Assets, Net	2,183.0	1,675.1	1,808.7	2,182.5
Total Assets	8,988.2	6,379.0	5,863.2	6,054.4
Total Current Liabilities	5,799.5	4,208.3	3,552.9	3,720.8
Long-Term Debt	997.6	731.6	861.3	1,019.7
Stockholders' Equity	1,780.1	1,323.1	1,279.9	1,243.0
Performance & Financial Condition				
Return on Total Revenues %	1.71	0.22	0.23	0.22
Return on Avg Stockholders' Equity %	29.45	3.32	2.93	2.83
Return on Average Assets %	5.95	0.71	0.62	0.54
Current Ratio	1.13	1.02	1.00	0.89
Debt / Equity %	56.04	55.29	67.30	82.04

Compound Growth %'s	EPS %	135.13	Net Income %	136.01	Total Revenues %	18.92

Comments

During the nine months ended December 31, 1995, the Company had sales of $22.4 million and net income of $77,000 ($.02 per share), as compared to $21.3 million and $475,000 ($.13 per share) for the same period in 1994. Officers and directors, as a group, owned 31.5% of the Company's outstanding common stock as of March 31, 1995.

Officers	Position	Ownership Information	03/31/95
Willard V. Harris, Jr.	Chairman	Number of Shares Outstanding	3,552,500
Willard P. Harris	President, CEO	Market Capitalization	$ 781,550
John D. Hornsby	Secretary, COO	Frequency Of Dividends	n.a.
		Number of Shareholders	956

Other Information				
Transfer Agent	Bank of New York		Where Listed	OTC-BB
Auditor	McGladrey & Pullen LLP		Symbol	FPMI
Market Maker	Drake Capital Secs., Inc.	Telephone (800)421-8504	SIC Code	5074
Broker Dealer	Regular Stockbroker		Employees	214

First Carolina Investors, Inc.

5224 Providence Country Club • Charlotte, NC 28277 • Telephone (704)846-1066 • Fax (704)846-6515

Company Description

The Company, organized in 1971 and incorporated in Delaware in 1987, was primarily a land development company through the end of 1994. As a result of its development activities being complete and significant marketable security holdings, the Company has become a non-diversified, closed-end management investment company in accordance with the Investment Company Act of 1940.

	12/31/95	12/31/94	12/31/93	12/31/92
Per Share Information				
Stock Price	31.75	27.50	24.25	17.88
Earnings Per Share	10.46	1.56	0.88	-0.19
Price / Earnings Ratio	3.04	17.63	27.56	n.a.
Book Value Per Share	43.93	31.19	29.79	16.17
Price / Book Value %	72.27	88.17	81.40	110.58
Dividends Per Share	0.60	0.33	0.25	n.a.
Annual Financial Data				
Operating Results (000's)				
Total Revenues	3,927.3	4,724.2	3,114.4	1,542.6
Costs & Expenses	-2,169.8	-2,025.0	-1,587.8	-1,867.7
Income Before Taxes and Other	1,757.5	2,699.2	1,526.6	-325.1
Other Items	10,302.3	n.a.	n.a.	-70.0
Income Tax	-487.0	-925.0	-500.0	170.0
Net Income	11,572.8	1,774.2	1,026.6	-225.1
Cash Flow From Operations	11,572.8	3,832.5	4,639.7	2,558.1
Balance Sheet (000's)				
Cash & Equivalents	1,342.2	3,090.0	286.1	299.2
Total Current Assets	68,681.2	44,472.3	46,186.9	22,209.0
Fixed Assets, Net	n.a.	n.a.	n.a.	n.a.
Total Assets	70,725.6	46,665.9	47,902.9	24,394.6
Total Current Liabilities	22,384.3	12,443.1	11,697.8	1,849.5
Long-Term Debt	n.a.	n.a.	2,400.0	3,500.0
Stockholders' Equity	48,305.5	34,104.6	33,528.1	18,895.3
Performance & Financial Condition				
Return on Total Revenues %	294.67	37.56	32.96	-14.59
Return on Avg Stockholders' Equity %	28.09	5.25	3.92	-1.15
Return on Average Assets %	19.72	3.75	2.84	-0.87
Current Ratio	3.07	3.57	3.95	12.01
Debt / Equity %	n.a.	n.a.	7.16	18.52

Compound Growth %'s	EPS %	244.77	Net Income %	235.75	Total Revenues %	36.55

Comments

Current Assets consist primarily of investments in securities and real estate at fair market value. Current Liabilities consist primarily of the deferred tax related to the unrealized appreciation on the Company's investments. Other Items, in 1995, represents the change in unrealized appreciation in investments. As an investment company, Stockholders' Equity is the equivalent of Net Asset Value. Per share amounts have been restated to reflect a 2 for 1 stock split in March, 1994. Assets and liabilities are stated at fair market value. The stock has traded, from time to time, at a substantial discount to book value.

Officers	Position	Ownership Information	12/31/95
Brent D. Baird	Chairman	Number of Shares Outstanding	1,099,646
H. Thomas Webb III	President	Market Capitalization	$ 34,913,761
James E. Traynor	Secretary, Treasurer	Frequency Of Dividends	Quarterly
Karen K. Sides	Other	Number of Shareholders	590

Other Information

Transfer Agent	Continental Stock Transfer & Trust Co.	Where Listed	BE
Auditor	KPMG Peat Marwick LLP	Symbol	FCAR
Market Maker	Interstate/Johnson Lane Corp.	SIC Code	6552
Broker Dealer	Regular Stockbroker	Employees	10

First International Bancorp

One Commercial Plaza • Hartford, CT 06103 • Telephone (860)727-0700 • Fax (860)525-2083

Company Description

First International Bancorp, Inc. is a holding company with two wholly-owned subsidiaries, First National Bank of Connecticut and First Regional Investcorp, Inc. Investcorp is a regional investment bank which is a registered broker\dealer. The results of Investcorp's operations are not material to the Company. The Bank was founded in 1955 and is committed to underwriting Small Business Administration guaranteed loans (SBA) to private companies and Export-Import Bank guaranteed loans to exporting companies. Standard banking services are also offered in Connecticut and, in addition, there are three representative offices in Boston and Springfield, MA, and Providence, RI.

	12/31/95	12/31/94	12/31/93	12/31/92
Per Share Information				
Stock Price	6.25	5.75	4.50	4.00
Earnings Per Share	1.23	0.67	0.20	0.07
Price / Earnings Ratio	5.08	8.58	22.50	57.14
Book Value Per Share	7.06	5.83	5.91	5.70
Price / Book Value %	88.53	98.63	76.14	70.18
Dividends Per Share	0.10	n.a.	n.a.	n.a.
Annual Financial Data				
Operating Results (000's)				
Net Interest Income	6,732.2	4,847.0	3,667.7	3,658.7
Loan Loss Provision	-1,237.5	-1,683.0	-2,224.8	-1,773.0
Non-Interest Income	4,153.7	3,608.4	3,574.5	2,026.0
Non-Interest Expense	-6,127.8	-5,129.4	-4,575.7	-3,755.7
Income Before Taxes and Other	3,520.6	1,642.9	441.8	155.9
Other Items	n.a.	n.a.	n.a.	9.0
Income Tax	-1,494.4	-583.0	-136.8	-57.0
Net Income	2,026.2	1,059.9	305.0	107.9
Balance Sheet (000's)				
Cash & Securities	21,681.4	21,565.0	31,348.0	37,305.7
Loans, Net	102,731.6	91,377.8	69,273.3	61,214.5
Fixed Assets, Net	1,270.3	1,213.2	1,329.7	1,533.9
Total Assets	141,222.5	125,609.2	109,735.0	105,662.9
Deposits	128,361.5	111,849.2	95,786.9	93,484.2
Stockholders' Equity	11,601.6	9,675.1	8,822.7	8,517.7
Performance & Financial Condition				
Net Interest Margin	n.a.	n.a.	n.a.	n.a.
Return on Avg Stockholders' Equity %	19.05	11.46	3.52	1.28
Return on Average Assets %	1.52	0.90	0.28	0.10
Equity to Assets %	8.22	7.70	8.04	8.06
Reserve as a % of Non-Performing Loans	158.93	89.06	188.60	n.a.

Compound Growth %'s	EPS % 159.98	Net Income % 165.78	Net Interest Income % 22.54

Comments

The Bank repurchased and retired 25,909 shares of its own stock during 1994 and 1995 at an average price of $5.86 per share. Directors, officers and their families are the majority owners of the Company. The Bank has obtained significant leverage by originating and selling, on a servicing-retained basis, the portion of loans guaranteed under the various government programs. In 1995, the portfolio of loans serviced grew by 56% while total balance sheet assets grew only 12%.

Officers	Position	Ownership Information	12/31/95
Brett N. Silvers	Chairman, President	Number of Shares Outstanding	1,643,779
William J. Anderson	Exec VP	Market Capitalization	$ 10,273,619
Brian J. Charlebois	Exec VP	Frequency Of Dividends	Irregular
Paul Pirrotta	Exec VP	Number of Shareholders	n.a.
Leslie A. Galbraith	Secretary, Treasurer		

Other Information			
Transfer Agent	Chemical Mellon Shareholder Services	Where Listed	OTC-PS
Auditor	Coopers & Lybrand LLP	Symbol	n.a.
Market Maker	Buell Securities Corpoation	Telephone (860)258-2300	SIC Code	6020
Broker Dealer	Regular Stockbroker	Employees	73

First National Bank Holding Company

P.O. Box 1159 • Longmont, CO 80502-1159 • Telephone (303)776-5800 • Fax (303)678-4168

Company Description

First National Bank Holding Company was formed in 1993 as the holding company for The First National Bank of Longmont, its sole subsidiary. The Bank serves the communities in and around Longmont, Colorado.

	12/31/95	12/31/94	12/31/93	12/31/92
Per Share Information				
Stock Price	211.00	180.00	128.00	124.00
Earnings Per Share	28.52	30.93	25.29	17.50
Price / Earnings Ratio	7.40	5.82	5.06	7.09
Book Value Per Share	208.35	181.08	162.79	142.31
Price / Book Value %	101.27	99.40	78.63	87.13
Dividends Per Share	6.00	9.00	4.00	4.00
Annual Financial Data				
Operating Results (000's)				
Net Interest Income	9,038.8	8,448.7	7,158.7	6,104.4
Loan Loss Provision	-240.0	n.a.	200.0	472.0
Non-Interest Income	1,170.0	1,774.7	1,496.0	1,246.8
Non-Interest Expense	-5,765.6	-5,601.9	-5,073.0	-5,300.6
Income Before Taxes and Other	4,203.3	4,621.4	3,781.8	2,522.6
Other Items	n.a.	n.a.	n.a.	n.a.
Income Tax	-1,351.0	-1,528.1	-1,252.3	-787.6
Net Income	2,852.3	3,093.3	2,529.5	1,735.0
Balance Sheet (000's)				
Cash & Securities	108,358.3	99,308.7	107,440.8	103,898.3
Loans, Net	94,721.9	80,380.8	64,455.0	56,546.7
Fixed Assets, Net	3,778.3	2,977.9	2,972.1	2,328.2
Total Assets	209,794.5	185,700.8	178,777.2	167,484.3
Deposits	189,697.6	166,201.9	161,896.0	152,713.5
Stockholders' Equity	19,316.7	18,095.7	16,352.5	14,231.4
Performance & Financial Condition				
Net Interest Margin	n.a.	n.a.	n.a.	n.a.
Return on Avg Stockholders' Equity %	15.25	17.96	16.54	12.79
Return on Average Assets %	1.44	1.70	1.46	1.03
Equity to Assets %	9.21	9.74	9.15	8.50
Reserve as a % of Non-Performing Loans	4.15	383.50	211.08	679.04

Compound Growth %'s	EPS %	17.68	Net Income %	18.02	Net Interest Income %	13.98

Comments

There is currently no market maker for the Company's stock. Any sales are negotiated between private parties. There is no indication that the financial statements have been audited. The Bank reports only $465,334 of nonperforming loans, less than 0.3% of assets. Return on equity and assets probably explain why the stock trades infrequently.

Officers	Position	Ownership Information	12/31/95
Richard L. Salberg	President	Number of Shares Outstanding	100,000
		Market Capitalization	$ 21,100,000
		Frequency Of Dividends	Irregular
		Number of Shareholders	237

Other Information

Transfer Agent	Company Office			Where Listed	Order Matching Only
Auditor	Not indicated			Symbol	n.a.
Market Maker	None - Company Office	Telephone	(303)776-5800	SIC Code	6020
Broker Dealer	Pink sheet specialist			Employees	95

First National Community Bank

102 East Drinker Street • Dunmore, PA 18512-2491 • Telephone (717)346-7667 • Fax (717)348-6454

Company Description

The Bank has six locations serving northeastern Pennsylvania by offering a range of commercial banking services to individuals and business. The Bank was established as a national banking association in 1910 as "The First National Bank of Dunmore". In 1988, the Bank changed its name to its current name.

	12/31/95	12/31/94	12/31/93	12/31/92
Per Share Information				
Stock Price	26.00	24.00	24.00	23.25
Earnings Per Share	3.68	3.36	2.84	2.16
Price / Earnings Ratio	7.07	7.14	8.45	10.76
Book Value Per Share	25.77	20.20	20.30	17.53
Price / Book Value %	100.89	118.81	118.23	132.63
Dividends Per Share	1.00	0.92	0.78	0.65
Annual Financial Data				
Operating Results (000's)				
Net Interest Income	11,286.5	9,882.3	8,577.7	7,558.6
Loan Loss Provision	-796.3	-700.0	-720.0	-1,005.0
Non-Interest Income	921.2	924.9	1,056.8	1,104.2
Non-Interest Expense	-7,097.4	-6,369.7	-5,879.9	-5,375.7
Income Before Taxes and Other	4,313.9	3,737.5	3,034.5	2,282.1
Other Items	n.a.	n.a.	n.a.	n.a.
Income Tax	-1,100.0	-887.8	-624.4	-448.7
Net Income	3,213.9	2,849.7	2,410.2	1,833.4
Balance Sheet (000's)				
Cash & Securities	81,145.0	68,758.2	65,807.6	51,761.8
Loans, Net	229,642.7	193,253.6	158,943.5	143,657.1
Fixed Assets, Net	3,470.0	3,099.2	3,049.0	2,447.8
Total Assets	318,025.5	269,678.7	229,846.1	201,356.3
Deposits	275,738.6	236,864.2	206,283.6	184,821.1
Stockholders' Equity	25,547.0	17,116.7	17,208.6	14,855.6
Performance & Financial Condition				
Net Interest Margin	4.19	4.48	4.58	4.37
Return on Avg Stockholders' Equity %	15.07	16.60	15.03	12.90
Return on Average Assets %	1.09	1.14	1.12	0.94
Equity to Assets %	8.03	6.35	7.49	7.38
Reserve as a % of Non-Performing Loans	162.81	94.50	75.96	45.99

Compound Growth %'s	EPS %	19.43	Net Income %	20.57	Net Interest Income %	14.30

Comments

During 1995, the bank offered and sold 144,000 shares of stock thereby increasing the number of outstanding shares to 991,504. Management believes that this increase in Tier 1 capital of $3.6 million will allow them to continue with the growth strategies that have paid off handsomely in the past. Commercial and financial loans account for approximately 52% of the bank's total loans, while real estate and installment loans account for the balance of total loans at 29% and 19%, respectively.

Officers	Position	Ownership Information	12/31/95
J. David Lombardi	President, CEO	Number of Shares Outstanding	991,504
Gerard A. Champi	Senior VP	Market Capitalization	$ 25,779,104
Stephen J. Kavulich	Senior VP	Frequency Of Dividends	Quarterly
William S. Lance	Senior VP	Number of Shareholders	886
Robert J. Mancuso	Senior VP, Head Cashier		

Other Information					
Transfer Agent	Company Office			Where Listed	OTC-BB
Auditor	Robert Rossi & Co.			Symbol	FNBP
Market Maker	Legg Mason Wood Walker, Inc.	Telephone	(800)346-4346	SIC Code	6020
Broker Dealer	Regular Stockbroker			Employees	145

First Real Estate Investment Trust of New Jersey

505 Main Street • Hackensack, NJ 07602 • Telephone (201)488-6400 • Fax (201)487-7881

Company Description

The Trust is an equity real estate investment trust (REIT), whose purpose is to acquire real estate for long-term investment. The Trust conducts its business in accordance with the requirements of the IRS Code regarding REIT's. Accordingly, the Trust distributes substantially all of its earnings to its shareholders and does not pay income tax. The Trust was formed in 1961 in the state of New Jersey. There was an additional stock offering in 1988.

	10/31/95	10/31/94	10/31/93	10/31/92
Per Share Information				
Stock Price	22.25	23.00	23.88	24.50
Earnings Per Share	1.79	1.53	1.47	1.56
Price / Earnings Ratio	12.43	15.03	16.24	15.71
Book Value Per Share	12.82	13.56	13.65	13.74
Price / Book Value %	173.56	169.62	174.95	178.31
Dividends Per Share	2.53	1.62	1.56	1.77
Annual Financial Data				
Operating Results (000's)				
Total Revenues	13,250.0	11,162.0	9,948.0	8,465.0
Costs & Expenses	-9,592.0	-8,235.0	-7,268.0	-5,899.0
Income Before Taxes and Other	2,915.0	2,468.0	2,303.0	2,447.0
Other Items	-123.0	-76.0	n.a.	n.a.
Income Tax	-6.0	-9.0	-8.0	-9.0
Net Income	2,786.0	2,383.0	2,295.0	2,438.0
Cash Flow From Operations	4,120.0	3,740.0	3,448.0	3,278.0
Balance Sheet (000's)				
Cash & Equivalents	533.0	238.0	928.0	570.0
Total Current Assets	1,692.0	1,164.0	1,625.0	2,117.0
Fixed Assets, Net	62,548.0	63,390.0	48,857.0	47,947.0
Total Assets	65,535.0	65,613.0	51,356.0	50,064.0
Total Current Liabilities	1,515.0	344.0	243.0	1,073.0
Long-Term Debt	39,767.0	39,447.0	28,883.0	27,561.0
Stockholders' Equity	19,989.0	21,148.0	21,292.0	21,430.0
Performance & Financial Condition				
Return on Total Revenues %	21.03	21.35	23.07	28.80
Return on Avg Stockholders' Equity %	13.54	11.23	10.74	11.29
Return on Average Assets %	4.25	4.07	4.53	6.16
Current Ratio	1.12	3.38	6.69	1.97
Debt / Equity %	198.94	186.53	135.65	128.61

Compound Growth %'s	EPS %	4.69	Net Income %	4.55	Total Revenues %	16.11

Comments

Fixed Assets includes 15 properties comprised of apartment buildings, shopping centers, commercial property and unimproved land. Most of the properties are located in affluent areas of northern New Jersey. A number of the properties that the Trust still owns were acquired between 1961 and 1969.

Officers	Position	Ownership Information	10/31/95
Robert S. Hekemian	Chairman	Number of Shares Outstanding	1,559,788
Donald W. Barney	President	Market Capitalization	$ 34,705,283
John B. Voskian, M.D.	Secretary	Frequency Of Dividends	Quarterly
William R. DeLorenzo, Jr.	Treasurer	Number of Shareholders	406

Other Information				
Transfer Agent	Registrar & Transfer Company		Where Listed	OTC-BB
Auditor	J.H. Cohn & Company		Symbol	FREVS
Market Maker	Janney Montgomery Scott, Inc.	Telephone (201)488-8500	SIC Code	6510
Broker Dealer	Regular Stockbroker		Employees	n.a.

First of Michigan Capital Corporation

100 Renaissance Center, 26th • Detroit, MI 48243 • Telephone (313)259-2600 • Fax (313)259-7853

Company Description

The Company's principal subsidiary is First of Michigan Corp. (FoM), founded in 1933. FoM is a securities broker-dealer registered in all fifty states with a total of 33 offices. FoM also acts as an investment banker involved in the underwriting and distribution of securities. FoM has approximately 160,000 active accounts. At December 31, 1995, officers and directors, as a group, owned approximately 41.8% of the outstanding shares.

	09/29/95	09/30/94	09/24/93	09/25/92
Per Share Information				
Stock Price	9.50	13.63	13.63	12.50
Earnings Per Share	0.04	0.35	1.16	1.81
Price / Earnings Ratio	237.50	38.94	11.75	6.91
Book Value Per Share	10.59	10.80	11.70	10.78
Price / Book Value %	89.71	126.20	116.50	115.96
Dividends Per Share	0.18	0.16	0.36	1.15
Annual Financial Data				
Operating Results (000's)				
Total Revenues	62,864.9	61,196.5	63,029.6	59,879.0
Costs & Expenses	-62,471.8	-59,728.6	-57,809.1	-52,624.1
Income Before Taxes and Other	393.1	1,467.9	5,220.5	7,255.0
Other Items	n.a.	n.a.	n.a.	n.a.
Income Tax	-285.0	-425.0	-1,820.0	-2,550.0
Net Income	108.1	1,042.9	3,400.5	4,705.0
Cash Flow From Operations	-830.4	-12,764.2	-6,231.7	n.a.
Balance Sheet (000's)				
Cash & Equivalents	2,995.5	2,612.5	2,276.9	1,669.4
Total Current Assets	99,285.2	87,514.2	73,232.0	56,187.4
Fixed Assets, Net	2,828.9	2,597.2	897.0	942.5
Total Assets	110,457.5	103,768.0	86,506.3	67,958.7
Total Current Liabilities	49,946.1	44,891.0	43,753.9	37,588.0
Long-Term Debt	30,726.6	27,750.0	12,000.0	2,500.0
Stockholders' Equity	29,784.8	31,127.0	30,752.4	27,870.7
Performance & Financial Condition				
Return on Total Revenues %	0.17	1.70	5.40	7.86
Return on Avg Stockholders' Equity %	0.35	3.37	11.60	17.45
Return on Average Assets %	0.10	1.10	4.40	7.58
Current Ratio	1.99	1.95	1.67	1.49
Debt / Equity %	103.16	89.15	39.02	8.97

Compound Growth %'s	EPS %	-71.94	Net Income %	-71.57	Total Revenues %	1.64

Comments

For the year ended September 30, 1995, commissions made up approximately 54% and investment banking and principal transactions made up approximately 24% of total revenues.

Officers	Position	Ownership Information	09/29/95
Steve Gasper, Jr.	President, CEO	Number of Shares Outstanding	2,811,442
Conrad W. Koski	Exec VP, Treasurer	Market Capitalization	$ 26,708,699
John S. Albright	Senior VP	Frequency Of Dividends	Quarterly
Urban A. MacDonald	Senior VP	Number of Shareholders	327
Charles R. Roberts	Senior VP		

Other Information			
Transfer Agent	Boston Financial Data Services	Where Listed	CE
Auditor	Ernst & Young LLP	Symbol	FMG
Market Maker	n.a.	SIC Code	6211
Broker Dealer	Regular Stockbroker	Employees	236

Fisher Companies Inc.

600 University Street, Ste1525 • Seattle, WA 98101-3185 • Telephone (206)624-2752 • Fax (206)224-6769

Company Description

The Company, through its operating subsidiaries, is engaged in television and radio broadcasting, flour milling for the bakery, mix and food service industries, proprietary real estate development and the management and licensing of grain handling and tempering technology. The Company was founded in 1910. There was a 4 for 1 stock split in 1995. All per share amounts have been adjusted accordingly.

	12/31/95	12/31/94	12/31/93	12/31/92
Per Share Information				
Stock Price	76.25	61.50	40.00	43.75
Earnings Per Share	5.32	3.95	2.89	2.26
Price / Earnings Ratio	14.33	15.57	13.84	19.36
Book Value Per Share	47.75	40.03	25.32	23.70
Price / Book Value %	159.69	85.14	80.86	184.60
Dividends Per Share	1.52	1.34	1.26	1.26
Annual Financial Data				
Operating Results (000's)				
Total Revenues	220,365.9	184,112.1	169,996.8	161,190.3
Costs & Expenses	-185,801.5	-156,537.8	-151,823.9	-147,382.5
Income Before Taxes and Other	34,564.4	27,574.3	18,172.9	13,807.9
Other Items	n.a.	-1,305.1	n.a.	n.a.
Income Tax	-11,881.0	-9,422.0	-5,830.0	-4,187.0
Net Income	22,683.4	16,847.1	12,342.9	9,620.9
Cash Flow From Operations	29,232.1	19,555.1	18,969.0	16,140.1
Balance Sheet (000's)				
Cash & Equivalents	19,489.1	2,161.6	1,356.0	21,837.1
Total Current Assets	84,946.8	74,918.6	75,820.6	72,194.0
Fixed Assets, Net	134,033.7	131,200.8	121,783.6	96,769.4
Total Assets	353,035.1	308,072.2	211,000.2	179,850.6
Total Current Liabilities	35,202.8	27,691.3	26,831.3	27,407.3
Long-Term Debt	58,109.9	64,314.9	59,573.0	37,508.3
Stockholders' Equity	203,681.3	170,751.1	107,996.1	101,070.8
Performance & Financial Condition				
Return on Total Revenues %	10.29	9.15	7.26	5.97
Return on Avg Stockholders' Equity %	12.12	12.09	11.81	9.72
Return on Average Assets %	6.86	6.49	6.32	5.19
Current Ratio	2.41	2.71	2.83	2.63
Debt / Equity %	28.53	37.67	55.16	37.11

Compound Growth %'s	EPS %	33.03	Net Income %	33.10	Total Revenues %	10.99

Comments

The Company's growth rate has accelerated in recent years. Marketable securities of $106 million, that are classified as noncurrent assets, add to an already strong balance sheet. Management has an extensive agenda and a string of recent successes.

Officers	Position	Ownership Information	12/31/95
W W. Krippaehne, Jr.	President, CEO	Number of Shares Outstanding	4,265,172
David D. Hillard	CFO, Secretary	Market Capitalization	$ 325,219,365
G O. Fisher	Vice President, Treasurer	Frequency Of Dividends	Quarterly
Glen P. Christofferson	Controller	Number of Shareholders	480

Other Information

Transfer Agent	Company Office			Where Listed	OTC-BB
Auditor	Price Waterhouse LLP			Symbol	FSCI
Market Maker	Martin Nelson & Co., Inc.	Telephone	(206)682-6261	SIC Code	4830
Broker Dealer	Regular Stockbroker			Employees	970

Florafax International, Inc.

8075 20th Street • Vero Beach, FL 32966 • Telephone (407)563-0263 • Fax (407)563-9958

Company Description

The Company is principally (82% of net revenues) in the business of generating floral orders and providing floral order placement services to retail florists. In addition, the Company is a third party processor of credit cards. The Company was incorporated in Delaware in 1970. In 1991, the Company formed a subsidiary to provide credit card processing services to both floral and nonfloral businesses and a second subsidiary to generate additional orders for its member florists.

	08/31/95	08/31/94	08/31/93	08/31/92
Per Share Information				
Stock Price	0.50	0.19	0.22	0.17
Earnings Per Share	0.12	-0.06	-0.08	-0.45
Price / Earnings Ratio	4.17	n.a.	n.a.	n.a.
Book Value Per Share	-0.30	-0.46	-0.40	-0.36
Price / Book Value %	n.a.	n.a.	n.a.	n.a.
Dividends Per Share	n.a.	n.a.	n.a.	n.a.
Annual Financial Data				
Operating Results (000's)				
Total Revenues	7,046.0	7,093.0	7,164.0	7,041.0
Costs & Expenses	-6,094.0	-7,073.0	-7,412.0	-9,734.0
Income Before Taxes and Other	707.0	-311.0	-248.0	-2,317.0
Other Items	n.a.	n.a.	-153.0	n.a.
Income Tax	n.a.	n.a.	n.a.	n.a.
Net Income	707.0	-311.0	-401.0	-2,317.0
Cash Flow From Operations	2,406.0	595.0	849.0	-877.0
Balance Sheet (000's)				
Cash & Equivalents	1,972.0	558.0	186.0	343.0
Total Current Assets	4,117.0	2,847.0	2,610.0	3,128.0
Fixed Assets, Net	369.0	626.0	622.0	955.0
Total Assets	6,852.0	5,946.0	5,257.0	6,253.0
Total Current Liabilities	5,515.0	5,259.0	4,270.0	4,982.0
Long-Term Debt	3,034.0	3,142.0	3,007.0	3,026.0
Stockholders' Equity	-1,756.0	-2,515.0	-2,209.0	-1,843.0
Performance & Financial Condition				
Return on Total Revenues %	10.03	-4.38	-5.60	-32.91
Return on Avg Stockholders' Equity %	n.a.	n.a.	n.a.	n.a.
Return on Average Assets %	11.05	-5.55	-6.97	-32.71
Current Ratio	0.75	0.54	0.61	0.63
Debt / Equity %	n.a.	n.a.	n.a.	n.a.

Compound Growth %'s	EPS % n.a.	Net Income % n.a.	Total Revenues % 0.02

Comments

During 1995, the most profitable year for the Company since 1983, the Company granted 245,000 shares of common stock to certain of its employees and marketing consultants. For the six months ended February 29, 1996, the Company had revenues of $4.0 million and net income of $743,000 ($.11 per share), as compared to $3.5 million and $276,000 ($.05 per share) for the same period in the prior fiscal year.

Officers	Position	Ownership Information	08/31/95
James H. West	President, CFO	Number of Shares Outstanding	5,770,874
Andrew W. Williams	CEO, Chairman	Market Capitalization	$ 2,885,437
Kelly S. McMakin	Treasurer, Secretary	Frequency Of Dividends	n.a.
		Number of Shareholders	2,200

Other Information

Transfer Agent	Mellon Securities Trust Company		Where Listed	OTC-BB
Auditor	Ernst & Young LLC		Symbol	FIIF
Market Maker	Frankel (WM.V.) & Co., Inc.	Telephone (800)631-3091	SIC Code	7389
Broker Dealer	Regular Stockbroker		Employees	124

Foremost Industries, Inc.

460 Grand Boulevard • Westbury, NY 11590 • Telephone (516)334-6800

Company Description

The Company's principal business activity is commercial refrigeration and air conditioning maintenance and installation, primarily in the metropolitan New York City area. Approximately 50% of revenues are derived from sales to a limited number of customers.

	12/31/93	12/31/92
Per Share Information		
Stock Price	0.82	0.37
Earnings Per Share	0.34	0.54
Price / Earnings Ratio	2.41	0.69
Book Value Per Share	3.64	3.30
Price / Book Value %	22.53	11.21
Dividends Per Share	n.a.	n.a.
Annual Financial Data		
Operating Results (000's)		
Total Revenues	11,433.4	9,193.3
Costs & Expenses	-11,043.5	-8,875.8
Income Before Taxes and Other	332.5	317.5
Other Items	n.a.	n.a.
Income Tax	-155.4	-38.3
Net Income	177.1	279.2
Cash Flow From Operations	-265.7	721.0
Balance Sheet (000's)		
Cash & Equivalents	361.4	232.8
Total Current Assets	3,301.3	2,554.4
Fixed Assets, Net	117.0	113.8
Total Assets	4,209.2	3,329.3
Total Current Liabilities	2,333.5	1,623.2
Long-Term Debt	n.a.	n.a.
Stockholders' Equity	1,875.7	1,698.6
Performance & Financial Condition		
Return on Total Revenues %	1.55	3.04
Return on Avg Stockholders' Equity %	9.91	17.91
Return on Average Assets %	4.70	8.08
Current Ratio	1.41	1.57
Debt / Equity %	n.a.	n.a.

Compound Growth %'s	EPS %	-37.04	Net Income %	-36.56	Total Revenues %	24.37

Comments

Compound statistics are only based on two years of data. We were unable to obtain more current information on the Company. This penny stock is worthy of further investigation because it is an established company with more than $10 million in revenue.

Officers	Position	Ownership Information	12/31/93
Seymour Fiance	President, Chairman of the Board	Number of Shares Outstanding	515,228
Flamin Pinnola	Secretary, Treasurer	Market Capitalization	$ 422,487
Charles Mehlich	Director	Frequency Of Dividends	n.a.
Alvin Katz	Director	Number of Shareholders	Under 500
Robert Uttal	Director		

Other Information

Transfer Agent	Continental Stock Transfer & Trust Co.			Where Listed	OTC-PS
Auditor	Edward Isaacs & Company			Symbol	FODT
Market Maker	Carr Securities Corporation	Telephone	(800)477-2750	SIC Code	4960
Broker Dealer	Regular stockbroker			Employees	n.a.

Franklin Credit Management Corp

Six Harrison Street • New York, NY 10013 • Telephone (212)925-8745 • Fax (212)225-8760

Company Description

The Company, incorporated in Delaware in 1990, is a consumer finance company, and was formed to acquire loans and notes from mortgage and finance companies, the RTC and the FDIC at discounted prices. It then proceeds to collect the amounts due.

	12/31/95	12/31/94	12/31/93	12/31/92
Per Share Information				
Stock Price	2.25	1.00	0.19	n.a.
Earnings Per Share	0.02	0.05	0.80	n.a.
Price / Earnings Ratio	112.50	20.00	0.24	n.a.
Book Value Per Share	0.59	0.48	0.30	n.a.
Price / Book Value %	381.36	208.33	63.33	n.a.
Dividends Per Share	n.a.	n.a.	n.a.	n.a.
Annual Financial Data				
Operating Results (000's)				
Net Interest Income	6,176.3	4,655.4	3,207.2	1,822.3
Loan Loss Provision	-1,090.5	-701.1	-329.4	-222.3
Non-Interest Income	320.4	554.1	443.2	611.0
Non-Interest Expense	-5,049.8	-3,718.0	-2,789.0	-969.3
Income Before Taxes and Other	356.4	790.4	532.0	1,241.7
Other Items	-54.8	694.5	3,017.1	-820.6
Income Tax	-176.9	-1,242.6	n.a.	n.a.
Net Income	124.7	242.3	3,549.1	421.0
Balance Sheet (000's)				
Cash & Securities	1,952.9	1,063.6	953.9	698.8
Loans, Net	66,996.1	42,734.0	16,032.8	5,666.6
Fixed Assets, Net	4,484.1	385.3	477.4	93.8
Total Assets	77,931.1	48,546.3	19,456.9	7,296.5
Stockholders' Equity	3,254.7	2,495.4	1,414.1	480.7
Performance & Financial Condition				
Return on Avg Stockholders' Equity %	4.34	12.40	374.61	n.a.
Return on Average Assets %	0.20	0.71	26.53	n.a.
Equity to Assets %	4.18	5.14	7.27	6.59

Compound Growth %'s	EPS % -84.19	Net Income % -33.34	Net Interest Income % 50.21

Comments

The 1993 financial statements have been restated to reflect the pooling-of-interests merger, in 1994, of the Company and Miramar Resources, Inc. The 1992 results are for the former Franklin only. Comparable earnings per share and stock price are not determinable for 1992. Income for 1994 includes $760,000 of litigation proceeds. As of December 31, 1995, officers and directors and directors, as a group, controlled 74% of the outstanding common stock of the Company.

Officers	Position	Ownership Information	12/31/95
Thomas J. Axon	President	Number of Shares Outstanding	5,503,896
Frank B. Evans	Vice President, CFO	Market Capitalization	$ 12,383,766
Harvey R. Hirschfeld	Vice President	Frequency Of Dividends	n.a.
		Number of Shareholders	2,382

Other Information

Transfer Agent	American Securities Transfer, Inc.			Where Listed	OTC-BB
Auditor	McGladrey & Pullen			Symbol	FCMC
Market Maker	Herzog, Heine, Geduld, Inc.	Telephone	(800)966-7022	SIC Code	6153
Broker Dealer	Regular Stockbroker			Employees	30

GNB Financial Services, Inc.

P.O.Box 159 • Gratz, PA 17030 • Telephone (717)365-3181 • Fax (717)365-3902

Company Description

GNB Financial Services, Inc. is an independent bank servicing the communities surrounding Gratz, Pennsylvania. The Bank was formed in 1934 and shares were distributed in connection with the reorganization of Gratz National Bank in 1986.

	12/31/95	12/31/94	12/31/93	12/31/92
Per Share Information				
Stock Price	34.63	30.00	27.50	18.00
Earnings Per Share	3.01	2.83	2.27	2.17
Price / Earnings Ratio	11.50	10.60	12.11	8.29
Book Value Per Share	25.28	21.85	20.08	18.20
Price / Book Value %	136.99	137.30	136.95	98.90
Dividends Per Share	0.62	0.55	0.46	0.37
Annual Financial Data				
Operating Results (000's)				
Net Interest Income	1,657.0	1,609.2	1,506.3	1,426.6
Loan Loss Provision	n.a.	n.a.	-55.0	-55.0
Non-Interest Income	58.9	46.5	39.7	39.3
Non-Interest Expense	-820.5	-825.7	-813.2	-742.0
Income Before Taxes and Other	895.4	830.0	677.8	668.9
Other Items	n.a.	n.a.	n.a.	n.a.
Income Tax	-294.3	-263.4	-223.8	-221.0
Net Income	601.2	566.6	454.0	447.9
Balance Sheet (000's)				
Cash & Securities	17,077.6	15,087.8	16,573.3	14,513.9
Loans, Net	21,974.6	19,893.8	18,061.6	17,094.8
Fixed Assets, Net	218.3	222.5	234.7	185.4
Total Assets	39,671.0	35,664.6	35,186.2	32,150.7
Deposits	34,343.8	30,360.2	30,995.3	28,343.7
Stockholders' Equity	5,056.5	4,369.1	4,015.1	3,640.8
Performance & Financial Condition				
Net Interest Margin	n.a.	n.a.	n.a.	n.a.
Return on Avg Stockholders' Equity %	12.76	13.52	11.86	12.94
Return on Average Assets %	1.60	1.60	1.35	1.42
Equity to Assets %	12.75	12.25	11.41	11.32
Reserve as a % of Non-Performing Loans	n.a.	n.a.	n.a.	n.a.

Compound Growth %'s	EPS %	11.52	Net Income %	10.31	Net Interest Income %	5.12

Comments

The Bank is planning to open a second branch office late in 1996. The shares were split 2 for 1 in 1993 and an additional 1 share for each 4 shares in 1995. All per share amounts were adjusted for consistency. This small bank continues to show excellent returns and will be interesting to watch as is starts to be more active in expansion.

Officers	Position	Ownership Information	12/31/95
John T. Pfeiffer, III	Chairman	Number of Shares Outstanding	200,000
Ted R. Bonwit, Jr.	President	Market Capitalization	$ 6,926,000
Carl H. Klinger	Secretary	Frequency Of Dividends	Quarterly
Charles H. Masser	Treasurer	Number of Shareholders	300
Carlos D. Koppenhaver	Vice President		

Other Information

Transfer Agent	Company Office		Where Listed	OTC-BB
Auditor	KPMG Peat Marwick		Symbol	GNBF
Market Maker	Janney Montgomery Scott, Inc.	Telephone (212)425-5673	SIC Code	6020
Broker Dealer	Regular Stockbroker		Employees	12

Garden City Company

10 Lake Circle • Colorado Springs, CO 80906-0064 • Telephone (719)633-7733 • Fax (719)471-6181

Company Description

The Company owns 27,500 acres of farm land in southwest Kansas which it rents to tenant farmers on a crop share basis. Wheat, milo, corn and soybeans are the primary crops. In addition, the Company receives oil and gas royalties from approximately 100 wells maintained by third parties on their property. 22,000 acres are under irrigation and were appraised in 1990 by the Federal Land Bank at $850 per acre. 80% of the Company is owned by the El Pomar Foundation which was established by Spencer Penrose.

	02/28/96	02/28/95	02/28/94	02/28/93
Per Share Information				
Stock Price	323.00	264.00	260.25	260.00
Earnings Per Share	38.04	42.34	40.50	28.62
Price / Earnings Ratio	8.49	6.24	6.43	9.08
Book Value Per Share	311.62	294.21	260.88	254.38
Price / Book Value %	103.65	63.60	70.71	72.45
Dividends Per Share	35.00	40.00	34.00	27.00
Annual Financial Data				
Operating Results (000's)				
Total Revenues	3,685.8	3,831.8	3,618.6	2,961.2
Costs & Expenses	1,963.0	-1,956.3	-1,743.2	-1,679.2
Income Before Taxes and Other	1,722.9	1,875.5	1,875.5	1,282.0
Other Items	n.a.	n.a.	n.a.	n.a.
Income Tax	562.9	-590.8	-646.6	-413.7
Net Income	1,160.0	1,284.7	1,228.8	868.3
Cash Flow From Operations	1,555.0	1,375.1	874.0	1,686.8
Balance Sheet (000's)				
Cash & Equivalents	236.4	214.7	282.4	340.7
Total Current Assets	5,741.4	4,802.6	3,146.1	2,568.5
Fixed Assets, Net	3,927.4	4,047.2	4,221.6	4,391.3
Total Assets	10,957.8	10,019.1	8,429.7	8,244.5
Total Current Liabilities	1,192.8	871.9	251.1	233.7
Long-Term Debt	n.a.	n.a.	n.a.	n.a.
Stockholders' Equity	9,549.0	8,927.3	7,915.8	7,718.7
Performance & Financial Condition				
Return on Total Revenues %	31.47	33.53	33.96	29.32
Return on Avg Stockholders' Equity %	12.56	15.25	15.72	11.28
Return on Average Assets %	11.06	13.93	14.74	10.72
Current Ratio	4.81	5.51	12.53	10.99
Debt / Equity %	n.a.	n.a.	n.a.	n.a.

Compound Growth %'s	EPS %	9.95	Net Income %	10.14	Total Revenues %	4.52

Comments

1995 was a difficult farming year because of the occurrence of several weather related events. However, prices for wheat, corn, milo and soybeans were at record levels. In the oil division, there was a net gain of six new wells during the fiscal year. Gas production was up but prices were lower. The Company continues to accumulate cash and marketable securities. Shares are scarce but do trade.

Officers	Position	Ownership Information	02/28/96
William J. Hybl	President	Number of Shares Outstanding	30,643
R. Thayer Tutt, Jr.	Exec VP	Market Capitalization	$ 9,897,689
Robert J. Hilbert	Secretary, Treasurer	Frequency Of Dividends	Quarterly
David A. Brenn	General Manager	Number of Shareholders	71
Ronald Conway	Other		

Other Information						
Transfer Agent	Company Office			Where Listed		OTC-PS
Auditor	Lewis, Hooper & Dick, LLC			Symbol		GCTY
Market Maker	Herzog, Heine, Geduld, Inc.	Telephone	(800)221-3600	SIC Code		6500
Broker Dealer	Standard Investment	Tel/Ext	(888)783-4688	Jack	Employees	12

Gateway Energy Corporation

10842 Old Mill Road, Ste. 5 • Omaha, NE 68154 • Telephone (402)330-8268 • Fax (402)330-7738

Company Description

The Company purchases, develops, owns, and operates natural gas gathering pipeline facilities on the Gulf Coast and in the states of Texas, New Mexico, Oklahoma and Louisiana. In addition, the Company operates a local natural gas distribution company in Oklahoma and conducts limited oil and gas exploration and production activities. In fiscal year 1994/95, sales to four customers accounted for over 50% of revenues.

	11/30/95	02/28/95	02/28/94	02/28/93
Per Share Information				
Stock Price	0.50	0.52	0.38	0.30
Earnings Per Share	-0.06	-0.03	-0.01	-0.01
Price / Earnings Ratio	n.a.	n.a.	n.a.	n.a.
Book Value Per Share	0.17	0.14	-0.01	-0.03
Price / Book Value %	294.12	371.43	n.a.	n.a.
Dividends Per Share	n.a.	n.a.	n.a.	n.a.
Annual Financial Data				
Operating Results (000's)				
Total Revenues	8,460.0	8,172.2	8,383.4	2,928.9
Costs & Expenses	-8,210.7	-7,568.3	-8,163.3	-2,921.0
Income Before Taxes and Other	249.3	603.9	220.1	7.9
Other Items	83.2	18.0	n.a.	2.3
Income Tax	-31.9	-46.6	-4.0	-2.3
Net Income	300.6	575.3	216.1	7.9
Cash Flow From Operations	65.9	460.0	542.5	-140.8
Balance Sheet (000's)				
Cash & Equivalents	361.8	337.9	532.4	38.2
Total Current Assets	4,068.8	3,419.9	1,595.4	1,446.5
Fixed Assets, Net	11,353.5	9,956.0	2,469.1	1,260.5
Total Assets	16,392.0	14,656.3	5,231.1	2,737.0
Total Current Liabilities	2,942.7	2,709.8	1,342.0	1,488.7
Long-Term Debt	152.6	191.2	n.a.	n.a.
Stockholders' Equity	4,446.1	3,483.3	2,650.1	1,248.1
Performance & Financial Condition				
Return on Total Revenues %	3.55	7.04	2.58	0.27
Return on Avg Stockholders' Equity %	7.58	18.76	11.09	1.66
Return on Average Assets %	1.94	5.79	5.42	0.58
Current Ratio	1.38	1.26	1.19	0.97
Debt / Equity %	3.43	5.49	n.a.	n.a.

Compound Growth %'s	EPS % n.a.	Net Income % n.a.	Total Revenues % 42.41

Comments

Information for the year ended February 29, 1996, is not yet available. Information as of November 30, 1995, is for the nine months then ended and, therefore, is not comparable to the preceding years. The Company has several series of preferred stock outstanding with varying terms, conditions and preferences. Income per share amounts have been adjusted for preferred stock dividends. However, book value per share amounts could be affected by a number of indeterminable factors. In December, 1995, the Company acquired eight separate gathering systems off the coast of Texas for $710,000.

Officers	Position	Ownership Information	11/30/95
Larry J. Horbach	President, CEO	Number of Shares Outstanding	26,136,081
Charles A. Holtgraves	Secretary	Market Capitalization	$ 13,068,041
Neil A. Fortkamp	Vice President, Treasurer	Frequency Of Dividends	n.a.
Donald L. Anderson	Vice President	Number of Shareholders	3,500
Roger E. Pfeifer	Controller		

Other Information

Transfer Agent	American Stock Transfer & Trust Company		Where Listed	OTC-BB
Auditor	Grant Thornton LLP		Symbol	GECO
Market Maker	Carr Securities Corp.	Telephone (800)221-2243	SIC Code	4922
Broker Dealer	Regular Stockbroker		Employees	13

Genetic Laboratories Wound Care, Inc.

2726 Patton Road • St. Paul, MN 55113 • Telephone (612)633-0805 • Fax (612)633-3188

Company Description

The Company manufactures and markets wound care products, primarily adhesive backed wound closure strips, elastic net dressings for wounds, nasogastric tube fastners, and urinary catheter fasteners . The Company was incorporated in Minnesota in 1988.

	05/31/95	05/31/94	05/31/93	05/31/92
Per Share Information				
Stock Price	1.19	0.50	0.50	0.44
Earnings Per Share	0.06	0.05	0.02	0.05
Price / Earnings Ratio	19.83	10.00	25.00	8.80
Book Value Per Share	0.38	0.32	0.27	0.25
Price / Book Value %	313.16	156.25	185.19	176.00
Dividends Per Share	n.a.	n.a.	n.a.	n.a.
Annual Financial Data				
Operating Results (000's)				
Total Revenues	2,217.9	2,092.6	1,981.2	1,904.5
Costs & Expenses	-2,018.5	-1,934.5	-1,913.9	-1,781.8
Income Before Taxes and Other	199.4	158.1	67.3	122.7
Other Items	n.a.	n.a.	n.a.	20.8
Income Tax	-65.6	-49.5	-22.6	-37.8
Net Income	133.8	108.6	44.7	105.7
Cash Flow From Operations	47.9	207.1	33.1	60.1
Balance Sheet (000's)				
Cash & Equivalents	295.8	259.2	77.9	54.5
Total Current Assets	1,042.4	811.1	687.2	708.0
Fixed Assets, Net	31.6	36.9	34.5	47.5
Total Assets	1,086.0	865.5	745.0	782.1
Total Current Liabilities	208.0	121.3	109.4	186.8
Long-Term Debt	n.a.	n.a.	n.a.	8.1
Stockholders' Equity	878.0	744.2	635.6	587.3
Performance & Financial Condition				
Return on Total Revenues %	6.03	5.19	2.26	5.55
Return on Avg Stockholders' Equity %	16.49	15.74	7.31	19.77
Return on Average Assets %	13.71	13.49	5.85	14.74
Current Ratio	5.01	6.69	6.28	3.79
Debt / Equity %	n.a.	n.a.	n.a.	1.38

Compound Growth %'s	EPS %	6.27	Net Income %	8.17	Total Revenues %	5.21

Comments

Approximately 30% of the Company's sales are to two customers. For the nine months ended February 29, 1996, the Company's sales and net income were $1,814,000 and $140,000 ($.05 per share) as compared to $1,665,000 and $118,000 ($.05 per share) for the same period in the prior fiscal year.

Officers	Position	Ownership Information	05/31/95
H. James Thompson	President, COO	Number of Shares Outstanding	2,326,100
Arthur A. Beisang	CEO	Market Capitalization	$ 2,768,059
Robert A. Ersek	Secretary	Frequency Of Dividends	n.a.
		Number of Shareholders	1,100

Other Information			
Transfer Agent	American Stock Transfer & Trust Company	Where Listed	OTC-BB
Auditor	McGladrey & Pullen LLP	Symbol	GELW
Market Maker	R.J. Steichen & Co.	Telephone (800)328-8217	SIC Code	5047
Broker Dealer	Regular Stockbroker	Employees	13

George Risk Industries, Inc.

802 South Elm • Kimball, NE 69145-1599 • Telephone (308)235-4645 • Fax (308)235-2554

Company Description

The Company is engaged in the design, manufacture, and sale of computer keyboards, push button switches, and burgular alarm components and systems. Security alarm products comprise more than 90% of revenues. Officers, directors and the Company's employee fund, as a group, own approximately 42% of the outstanding shares of the Company's common stock. The Company was incorporated in the State of Colorado in 1967.

	04/30/95	04/30/94	04/30/93	04/30/92
Per Share Information				
Stock Price	0.70	0.70	0.25	n.a.
Earnings Per Share	0.18	0.11	0.12	0.05
Price / Earnings Ratio	3.89	6.36	2.08	n.a.
Book Value Per Share	0.66	0.48	0.38	0.23
Price / Book Value %	106.06	145.83	65.79	n.a.
Dividends Per Share	n.a.	n.a.	n.a.	n.a.
Annual Financial Data				
Operating Results (000's)				
Total Revenues	9,769.0	7,878.0	7,065.0	5,777.0
Costs & Expenses	-7,699.0	-6,691.0	-5,658.0	-5,186.0
Income Before Taxes and Other	1,989.0	1,187.0	1,407.0	591.0
Other Items	n.a.	n.a.	-38.0	-12.0
Income Tax	-760.0	-441.0	-566.0	-222.0
Net Income	1,229.0	746.0	803.0	357.0
Cash Flow From Operations	1,041.0	65.0	974.0	408.0
Balance Sheet (000's)				
Cash & Equivalents	479.0	292.0	672.0	450.3
Total Current Assets	4,666.0	3,591.0	3,470.0	2,303.4
Fixed Assets, Net	598.0	520.0	467.0	309.3
Total Assets	5,277.0	4,120.0	3,946.0	2,612.7
Total Current Liabilities	493.0	570.0	1,028.0	471.5
Long-Term Debt	n.a.	n.a.	n.a.	n.a.
Stockholders' Equity	4,754.0	3,494.0	2,834.0	1,900.3
Performance & Financial Condition				
Return on Total Revenues %	12.58	9.47	11.37	6.18
Return on Avg Stockholders' Equity %	29.80	23.58	33.92	20.74
Return on Average Assets %	26.16	18.50	24.49	15.16
Current Ratio	9.46	6.30	3.38	4.89
Debt / Equity %	n.a.	n.a.	n.a.	n.a.

Compound Growth %'s	EPS %	53.26	Net Income %	50.99	Total Revenues %	19.14

Comments

In July, 1995, the Company purchased from a shareholder 725,000 shares of its common stock for $544,000. The selling shareholder reserved a repurchase option. At December 31, 1995, the Company had 12,850 shares of $20 stated value, convertible preferred stock outstanding and included in Stockholder's Equity. For the nine months ended January 31, 1996, the Company had sales of $7.0 million and Net Income of $882,000 ($.14 per share) as compared to $7.2 million and $845,000 ($.12 per share) for the same period in the prior year.

Officers	Position	Ownership Information	04/30/95
Ken R. Risk	Chairman, President	Number of Shares Outstanding	6,798,397
Mary Ann Brothers	Exec VP	Market Capitalization	$ 4,758,878
Eileen M. Risk	Secretary, Treasurer	Frequency Of Dividends	n.a.
		Number of Shareholders	2,000

Other Information			
Transfer Agent	Company Office	Where Listed	OTC-BB
Auditor	Mason Reynolds West LLC	Symbol	RISKA
Market Maker	Castle Securities Corp.	Telephone (516)867-0848	SIC Code	3577
Broker Dealer	Regular Stockbroker	Employees	225

Glengate Apparel, Inc.

207 Sheffield Street • Mountainside, NJ 07092 • Telephone (908)518-0006 • Fax (908)518-0450

Company Description

The Company designs, contracts to have made, and markets mens' golf apparel under the Glengate label. The Company was formed November, 1993, and completed an offering of its common stock and redeemable warrants for total gross proceeds of $2.5 million in August, 1994. The warrants are subject to cancellation or redemption through August, 1995. In July, 1995, the Company received $288,400 for 144,200 shares of common stock as a result of a private placement.

	09/30/95	09/30/94
Per Share Information		
Stock Price	2.06	1.00
Earnings Per Share	-0.25	-0.10
Price / Earnings Ratio	n.a.	n.a.
Book Value Per Share	0.19	0.32
Price / Book Value %	1,084.20	312.50
Dividends Per Share	n.a.	n.a.
Annual Financial Data		
Operating Results (000's)		
Total Revenues	3,330.3	11.8
Costs & Expenses	-4,755.8	-410.0
Income Before Taxes and Other	-1,425.5	-398.2
Other Items	n.a.	n.a.
Income Tax	n.a.	n.a.
Net Income	-1,425.5	-398.2
Cash Flow From Operations	-3,076.7	-385.8
Balance Sheet (000's)		
Cash & Equivalents	10.0	1,812.7
Total Current Assets	1,900.7	2,098.2
Fixed Assets, Net	218.5	3.7
Total Assets	2,135.2	2,110.4
Total Current Liabilities	907.6	286.7
Long-Term Debt	32.5	70.2
Stockholders' Equity	1,195.0	1,753.4
Performance & Financial Condition		
Return on Total Revenues %	-42.80	n.a.
Return on Avg Stockholders' Equity %	-96.70	n.a.
Return on Average Assets %	-67.15	n.a.
Current Ratio	2.09	7.32
Debt / Equity %	2.72	4.01

Compound Growth %'s	EPS %	n.a.	Net Income %	n.a.	Total Revenues %	n.a.

Comments

The Company's operations during the periods presented are not necessarily indicative of future results as the Company was primarily involved in developmental activities. Future success, however, is dependent on customer acceptance and adequate financing.

Officers	Position	Ownership Information	09/30/95
George J. Gatesy	Chairman, President	Number of Shares Outstanding	6,284,600
Norman Britman	Treasurer, Secretary	Market Capitalization	$ 12,946,276
		Frequency Of Dividends	n.a.
		Number of Shareholders	450

Other Information

Transfer Agent	Continental Stock Transfer & Trust Co.		Where Listed	OTC-BB
Auditor	BDO Seidman		Symbol	GLNN
Market Maker	Herzog, Heine, Geduld, Inc.	Telephone (800)221-3600	SIC Code	2329
Broker Dealer	Regular Stockbroker		Employees	11

Gloucester Bank & Trust Company

P.O. Box 30 • Gloucester, MA 01930 • Telephone (508)281-6270 • Fax (508)283-5072

Company Description

Gloucester Bank and Trust Company is a state chartered bank which was incorporated in 1987 and is headquartered in Gloucester, Massachusetts. The Bank is engaged principally in making real estate, consumer and small business loans.

	12/31/95	12/31/94	12/31/93	12/31/92
Per Share Information				
Stock Price	56.50	35.00	27.50	27.00
Earnings Per Share	8.67	6.06	2.64	-1.05
Price / Earnings Ratio	6.52	5.78	10.42	n.a.
Book Value Per Share	63.47	56.70	53.63	50.99
Price / Book Value %	89.02	61.73	51.28	52.95
Dividends Per Share	4.00	2.00	n.a.	n.a.
Annual Financial Data				
Operating Results (000's)				
Net Interest Income	4,203.0	3,574.0	3,266.0	3,112.0
Loan Loss Provision	n.a.	190.0	-525.0	-1,025.0
Non-Interest Income	670.0	626.0	706.0	633.0
Non-Interest Expense	-3,115.0	-3,164.0	-2,962.0	-2,880.0
Income Before Taxes and Other	1,758.0	1,226.0	485.0	-160.0
Other Items	n.a.	n.a.	20.0	n.a.
Income Tax	-733.0	-510.0	-193.0	36.0
Net Income	1,025.0	716.0	312.0	-124.0
Balance Sheet (000's)				
Cash & Securities	38,718.0	30,940.0	28,011.0	23,477.0
Loans, Net	55,033.0	50,789.0	49,442.0	53,367.0
Fixed Assets, Net	2,744.0	2,534.0	2,476.0	2,647.0
Total Assets	99,242.0	87,246.0	82,023.0	81,258.0
Deposits	85,163.0	74,201.0	69,343.0	74,844.0
Stockholders' Equity	7,501.0	6,701.0	6,339.0	6,027.0
Performance & Financial Condition				
Net Interest Margin	n.a.	n.a.	n.a.	n.a.
Return on Avg Stockholders' Equity %	14.43	10.98	5.05	-2.04
Return on Average Assets %	1.10	0.85	0.38	-0.15
Equity to Assets %	7.56	7.68	7.73	7.42
Reserve as a % of Non-Performing Loans	106.54	129.53	125.85	69.50

Compound Growth %'s	EPS %	81.22	Net Income %	81.25	Net Interest Income %	10.54

Comments

Commercial and residential real estate loans account for approximately 73% of total loans. Compound earnings and earnings per share growth are distorted because of lower than average performance in the base years. The Bank experienced difficult times because of the local economy and appears to have completely recovered. In late 1995, the Bank began performing data processing services for another bank and sees this service as becoming an important source of non-interest income in the years ahead.

Officers	Position	Ownership Information	12/31/95
David L. Marsh	President, CEO	Number of Shares Outstanding	118,189
Stephen R. Parkhurst	Exec VP	Market Capitalization	$ 6,677,679
Richard J. Edelstein	Senior VP	Frequency Of Dividends	Quarterly
Kevin W. Nunes	Vice President, Treasurer	Number of Shareholders	340
Doreen A. Gallagher	Vice President		

Other Information

Transfer Agent	Boston EquiServe		Where Listed	OTC-BB
Auditor	Shatswell, MacLeod & Co, P.C.		Symbol	GBTR
Market Maker	Moors & Cabot Inc.	Telephone (617)426-7320	SIC Code	6020
Broker Dealer	Regular Stockbroker		Employees	35

Goddard Industries, Inc.

705 Plantation Street • Worcester, MA 01605 • Telephone (508)852-2435 • Fax (508)852-2443

Company Description

Through one of its subsidiaries the Company designs and manufactures cryogenic gate, globe and check valves and control devices required for the handling of liquefied natural gas, liquid oxygen and other liquefied gases. The Company's other subsidiary imports brass, stainless steel and plastic plumbing products and valves for the gas and housing industry. The Company was organized in Massachusetts in 1959.

	09/30/95	09/30/94	10/02/93	10/03/92
Per Share Information				
Stock Price	0.44	0.22	0.25	0.22
Earnings Per Share	0.21	0.06	0.11	0.13
Price / Earnings Ratio	2.10	3.67	2.27	1.69
Book Value Per Share	1.30	1.09	1.04	0.93
Price / Book Value %	33.85	20.18	24.04	23.66
Dividends Per Share	n.a.	n.a.	n.a.	n.a.
Annual Financial Data				
Operating Results (000's)				
Total Revenues	6,818.1	5,048.1	5,388.5	5,363.5
Costs & Expenses	-6,109.0	-4,861.0	-4,975.9	-4,922.2
Income Before Taxes and Other	709.1	187.1	412.6	441.3
Other Items	n.a.	n.a.	-33.9	n.a.
Income Tax	-279.0	-69.0	-158.0	-179.0
Net Income	430.1	118.1	220.7	262.3
Cash Flow From Operations	405.9	-244.1	363.7	279.1
Balance Sheet (000's)				
Cash & Equivalents	74.9	62.6	119.6	64.5
Total Current Assets	4,038.7	3,526.2	2,793.0	2,689.8
Fixed Assets, Net	950.7	1,021.0	1,019.6	861.1
Total Assets	5,150.5	4,691.0	3,933.2	3,715.6
Total Current Liabilities	894.1	735.4	506.6	595.3
Long-Term Debt	1,092.5	1,259.8	917.9	891.0
Stockholders' Equity	2,650.9	2,220.8	2,101.8	1,880.1
Performance & Financial Condition				
Return on Total Revenues %	6.31	2.34	4.10	4.89
Return on Avg Stockholders' Equity %	17.66	5.47	11.09	15.19
Return on Average Assets %	8.74	2.74	5.77	7.20
Current Ratio	4.52	4.80	5.51	4.52
Debt / Equity %	41.21	56.73	43.67	47.39

Compound Growth %'s	EPS %	17.33	Net Income %	17.92	Total Revenues %	8.33

Comments

In fiscal 1995, sales to two customers accounted for 38% of total sales. The Company has been named as a potentially responsible party in two environmental matters, the outcomes of which are uncertain. Accordingly, the Company has made no provision for any potential liability that may result from their resolution.

Officers	Position	Ownership Information	09/30/95
Saul I. Reck	President, Treasurer	Number of Shares Outstanding	2,032,804
Lucy J. Rybacki	Treasurer	Market Capitalization	$ 894,434
Donald R. Nelson	Vice President	Frequency Of Dividends	n.a.
Joel M. Reck	Other	Number of Shareholders	938

Other Information

Transfer Agent	American Stock Transfer & Trust Company		Where Listed	OTC-PS
Auditor	Greenberg, Rosenblatt et al		Symbol	GODD
Market Maker	Carr Securities Corporation	Telephone (800)221-2243	SIC Code	3494
Broker Dealer	Regular Stockbroker		Employees	38

Golden Cycle Gold Corporation

2340 Robinson St., Ste. 209 • Colorado Springs, CO 80904 • Telephone (719)471-9013 • Fax (719)520-1442

Company Description

The Company was formed for the purpose of acquiring and developing mining properties located in the Cripple Creek Mining District of Colorado. The primary business of the Company is its participation, as a 33% interest holder, in the Cripple Creek & Victor Gold Mining Company, a joint venture with Pikes Peak Mining Company. The Company was incorporated in Colorado in 1972.

	12/31/95	12/31/94	12/31/93	12/31/92
Per Share Information				
Stock Price	8.38	7.68	8.20	7.38
Earnings Per Share	n.a.	-0.12	-0.06	-0.90
Price / Earnings Ratio	n.a.	n.a.	n.a.	n.a.
Book Value Per Share	0.33	0.32	43.00	0.45
Price / Book Value %	2,539.40	2,400.00	19.07	1,640.00
Dividends Per Share	n.a.	n.a.	n.a.	n.a.
Annual Financial Data				
Operating Results (000's)				
Total Revenues	273.1	274.2	272.1	24.4
Costs & Expenses	-270.8	-456.6	-361.9	-1,424.3
Income Before Taxes and Other	2.3	-182.4	-89.7	-1,399.9
Other Items	n.a.	n.a.	n.a.	n.a.
Income Tax	n.a.	n.a.	n.a.	n.a.
Net Income	2.3	-182.4	-89.7	-1,399.9
Cash Flow From Operations	5.0	-151.7	-83.6	-404.1
Balance Sheet (000's)				
Cash & Equivalents	9.8	517.4	5.9	25.7
Total Current Assets	364.5	844.9	476.0	488.4
Fixed Assets, Net	7.0	11.1	24.7	20.6
Total Assets	548.4	1,032.9	693.5	701.9
Total Current Liabilities	14.1	515.0	13.2	11.9
Long-Term Debt	n.a.	n.a.	n.a.	n.a.
Stockholders' Equity	514.3	497.9	680.3	689.9
Performance & Financial Condition				
Return on Total Revenues %	0.84	-66.52	-32.98	n.a.
Return on Avg Stockholders' Equity %	0.45	-30.96	-13.10	-100.83
Return on Average Assets %	0.29	-21.13	-12.86	-99.96
Current Ratio	25.93	1.64	36.00	40.97
Debt / Equity %	n.a.	n.a.	n.a.	n.a.

Compound Growth %'s	EPS %	n.a.	Net Income %	n.a.	Total Revenues %	123.61

Comments

The joint venture, in which the Company has a 33% interest, has total assets of $164.3 million, venturers' equity of $8.5 million and losses during 1995, 1994, and 1993, of $3.7 million, $9.4 million and $8.5 million, respectively. As a result of previously reducing the carrying value of its investment to zero, the Company has not recorded its share of these losses since 1993. Revenues presented represent distributions from the joint venture.

Officers	Position	Ownership Information	12/31/95
Alan P. Ploesser	Chairman	Number of Shares Outstanding	1,573,050
Birl W. Worley, Jr.	President, CEO	Market Capitalization	$ 13,182,159
R. Herbert Hampton	VP - Finance, Secretary	Frequency Of Dividends	n.a.
		Number of Shareholders	1,263

Other Information

Transfer Agent	American Stock Transfer & Trust Company	Where Listed	PSE
Auditor	KPMG Peat Marwick LLP	Symbol	GCC
Market Maker	n.a.	SIC Code	1041
Broker Dealer	Regular Stockbroker	Employees	3

Goodheart-Willcox Company, Inc., (The)

123 Taft Drive • South Holland, IL 60473-2089 • Telephone (708)333-7200 • Fax (708)333-9130

Company Description

The Company publishes textbooks on trade, family and consumer sciences, technology and vocational subjects. Activities include the search for authors, acquisition of manuscripts, and the design and marketing of the books. Printing and binding of the Company's books are done by outside contractors. At May 1, 1995, officers and directors, as a group, owned 64% of the Company's outstanding shares. The Company was incorporated in Illinois in 1949.

	04/30/95	04/30/94	04/30/93	04/30/92
Per Share Information				
Stock Price	20.50	18.50	17.00	19.50
Earnings Per Share	2.70	1.81	1.63	1.25
Price / Earnings Ratio	7.59	10.22	10.43	15.60
Book Value Per Share	12.26	11.45	10.11	10.32
Price / Book Value %	167.21	161.57	168.15	188.95
Dividends Per Share	0.80	0.70	0.60	0.60
Annual Financial Data				
Operating Results (000's)				
Total Revenues	14,968.0	12,742.0	11,983.0	11,235.0
Costs & Expenses	-11,644.0	-10,260.0	-10,061.0	-9,766.0
Income Before Taxes and Other	3,324.0	2,307.0	1,920.0	1,469.0
Other Items	n.a.	n.a.	n.a.	n.a.
Income Tax	-1,307.0	-950.0	-700.0	-529.0
Net Income	2,017.0	1,357.0	1,220.0	940.0
Cash Flow From Operations	3,505.0	2,091.0	2,227.0	1,557.0
Balance Sheet (000's)				
Cash & Equivalents	7,460.0	5,570.0	4,481.0	3,074.0
Total Current Assets	10,859.0	9,142.0	8,233.0	6,913.0
Fixed Assets, Net	683.0	702.0	671.0	703.0
Total Assets	13,192.0	11,136.0	10,385.0	9,261.0
Total Current Liabilities	2,272.0	1,638.0	1,741.0	1,399.0
Long-Term Debt	n.a.	n.a.	n.a.	n.a.
Stockholders' Equity	7,169.0	6,697.0	5,914.0	6,035.0
Performance & Financial Condition				
Return on Total Revenues %	13.48	10.65	10.18	8.37
Return on Avg Stockholders' Equity %	29.09	21.52	20.42	16.57
Return on Average Assets %	16.58	12.61	12.42	10.34
Current Ratio	4.78	5.58	4.73	4.94
Debt / Equity %	n.a.	n.a.	n.a.	n.a.

Compound Growth %'s	EPS %	29.27	Net Income %	28.98	Total Revenues %	10.03

Comments

The terms of an agreement with a principal officer/shareholder of the Company requires that the Company purchase approximately 163,000 shares of the Company's stock owned by him upon his death. The estimated redemption value of these shares at April 30, 1995 is $3.6 million and is included in liabilities. Sales for the six months ended October 31, 1995, totaled $9.5 million with Net Income of $1.6 million ($2.15 per share) as compared to $10.3 million and $2.2 million ($2.95 per share) for the same period in 1994.

Officers	Position	Ownership Information	04/30/95
John F. Flanagan	President, CEO	Number of Shares Outstanding	584,700
Dick G. Snyder	Secretary	Market Capitalization	$ 11,986,350
Donald A. Massucci	Vice President, Treasurer	Frequency Of Dividends	Semi-Annual
		Number of Shareholders	145

Other Information

Transfer Agent	First National Bank of Chicago			Where Listed	OTC-BB
Auditor	Grant Thornton LLP			Symbol	GWOX
Market Maker	Chicago Corporation, The	Telephone	(312)855-7664	SIC Code	2731
Broker Dealer	Regular Stockbroker			Employees	60

Grange National Banc Corp.

101 East Main Street • Laceyville, PA 18623 • Telephone (717)869-1522 • Fax (717)869-2498

Company Description

Grange National Banc Corp. and its subsidiary, the Grange National Bank of Wyoming County, provide banking and trust services to customers primarily in northeastern Pennsylvania. The Bank just opened its seventh office in March, 1996.

	12/31/95	12/31/94	12/31/93	12/31/92
Per Share Information				
Stock Price	30.00	26.50	21.07	20.00
Earnings Per Share	3.41	3.42	3.30	2.96
Price / Earnings Ratio	8.80	7.75	6.38	6.76
Book Value Per Share	27.30	23.85	21.14	18.17
Price / Book Value %	109.89	111.11	99.67	110.07
Dividends Per Share	0.47	0.42	0.33	0.33
Annual Financial Data				
Operating Results (000's)				
Net Interest Income	3,740.8	3,202.9	2,850.1	2,485.4
Loan Loss Provision	-115.0	-87.0	-120.0	-97.5
Non-Interest Income	393.2	315.7	298.4	235.8
Non-Interest Expense	-2,321.9	-1,901.0	-1,776.2	-1,506.3
Income Before Taxes and Other	1,697.1	1,530.5	1,252.3	1,117.4
Other Items	n.a.	n.a.	n.a.	n.a.
Income Tax	-518.0	-485.0	-387.0	-340.0
Net Income	1,179.1	1,045.5	865.3	777.4
Balance Sheet (000's)				
Cash & Securities	36,173.8	27,020.4	26,351.6	22,292.7
Loans, Net	52,005.5	46,253.9	40,590.0	37,395.5
Fixed Assets, Net	2,236.4	2,201.1	2,127.8	1,920.3
Total Assets	91,622.0	76,305.3	69,860.1	62,223.1
Deposits	79,865.6	67,013.7	62,832.4	55,908.8
Stockholders' Equity	9,522.3	8,243.0	5,544.1	4,766.3
Performance & Financial Condition				
Net Interest Margin	n.a.	n.a.	n.a.	n.a.
Return on Avg Stockholders' Equity %	13.27	15.17	16.78	17.59
Return on Average Assets %	1.40	1.43	1.31	1.39
Equity to Assets %	10.39	10.80	7.94	7.66
Reserve as a % of Non-Performing Loans	341.23	380.47	97.06	270.93

Compound Growth %'s	EPS %	4.83	Net Income %	14.89	Net Interest Income %	14.60

Comments

All share and per share amounts have been restated to give effect to a 3 for 1 stock split which occured in 1994. The 1995 dividend was partially a stock dividend. Real estate loans account for 65% of total loans and commercial loans account for an additional 19%. The Company has maintained outstanding return ratios despite the 1994 public offering, which raised approximately $2 million. (Oftentimes it is difficult to move a capital infusion into fully productive use.) Management continues to have ambitious growth plans. The Bank was established in 1907.

Officers	Position	Ownership Information	12/31/95
Robert C. Wheeler	Chairman	Number of Shares Outstanding	348,774
Thomas A. McCullough	President	Market Capitalization	$ 10,463,220
Sally A. Steele	Secretary	Frequency Of Dividends	Semi-Annual
Melvin E. Milner	Vice President	Number of Shareholders	720
Phillip O. Farr	Controller		

Other Information

Transfer Agent	Company Office			Where Listed	OTC-PS
Auditor	Daniel Kenia, P.C.			Symbol	GRGN
Market Maker	Hooper Soliday & Company, Inc.	Telephone	(717)560-3000	SIC Code	6020
Broker Dealer	Regular Stockbroker			Employees	55

Great Lakes Realty Corp.

28900 Schoolcraft • Livonia, MI 48150 • Telephone (313)425-4870 • Fax (313)425-4874

Company Description

The Company owns and operates bowling alleys. Sometime after an initial stock offering in 1960, it lost interest in being a public company and now disclaims that fact to anyone who calls. The Company changed its name from Great Lakes Recreation Co., but is still referred to as such in the pink sheets. One more bowling alley was acquired in 1995.

	05/31/95	05/31/94	05/31/92
Per Share Information			
Stock Price	23.00	21.50	18.00
Earnings Per Share	1.33	0.32	-8.89
Price / Earnings Ratio	17.29	67.19	n.a.
Book Value Per Share	n.a.	n.a.	20.74
Price / Book Value %	n.a.	n.a.	86.79
Dividends Per Share	n.a.	n.a.	n.a.
Annual Financial Data			
Operating Results (000's)			
Total Revenues	4,011.7	3,540.9	3,666.8
Costs & Expenses	-3,889.3	-3,507.9	-4,130.4
Income Before Taxes and Other	122.5	30.1	-773.7
Other Items	n.a.	n.a.	n.a.
Income Tax	-45.3	-11.8	259.3
Net Income	77.1	18.3	-514.4
Cash Flow From Operations	358.2	268.9	93.3
Balance Sheet (000's)			
Cash & Equivalents	n.a.	n.a.	366.6
Total Current Assets	n.a.	n.a.	1,047.7
Fixed Assets, Net	n.a.	n.a.	2,035.1
Total Assets	n.a.	n.a.	3,626.3
Total Current Liabilities	n.a.	n.a.	420.2
Long-Term Debt	n.a.	n.a.	1,627.1
Stockholders' Equity	n.a.	n.a.	1,200.1
Performance & Financial Condition			
Return on Total Revenues %	1.92	0.52	-14.03
Return on Avg Stockholders' Equity %	n.a.	n.a.	n.a.
Return on Average Assets %	n.a.	n.a.	n.a.
Current Ratio	n.a.	n.a.	2.49
Debt / Equity %	n.a.	n.a.	135.58

Compound Growth %'s	EPS %	315.63	Net Income %	320.82	Total Revenues %	3.04

Comments

The last full financial statement issued was in 1992. We assume that shares outstanding are the same as in 1992, although the Company was buying back its stock at that time. The 1995 and 1994 results are not audited. The property is substantially depreciated and it would be interesting to ascertain its real value. We believe this may explain the wide range between bid and ask prices. Compound earnings and earnings per share growth are distorted because only two years were available for the calculation.

Officers	Position		Ownership Information	05/31/95
Kenneth H. Kubit	President, CEO		Number of Shares Outstanding	57,862
			Market Capitalization	$ 1,330,826
			Frequency Of Dividends	n.a.
			Number of Shareholders	Under 500

Other Information							
Transfer Agent	Bankers Trust Co., New York, NY				Where Listed		OTC-BB
Auditor	None indicated				Symbol		GLRC
Market Maker	Monroe Securities, Inc.	Telephone	(800)766-5560		SIC Code		7930
Broker Dealer	Standard Investment	Tel/Ext	(888)783-4688	Jack	Employees		120

Guaranty Corporation

P.O. Box 2231 • Baton Rouge, LA 70821-2231 • Telephone (504)383-0355 • Fax (504)343-0047

Company Description

The Company, through its subsidiaries, operates in the following businesses: life insurance, mortgage banking, radio broadcast, real estate development, and consumer finance. The largest single block of shares recently offered was 181 shares by the Balfour family in late 1995. Offers in the $8,000 to $10,000 per share range were received and the final outcome is not certain.

	12/31/94	12/31/93	12/31/92
Per Share Information			
Stock Price	8,000.00	5,000.00	4,000.00
Earnings Per Share	1,917.60	1,499.21	48.69
Price / Earnings Ratio	4.17	3.34	82.15
Book Value Per Share	11,942.15	13,669.57	12,176.60
Price / Book Value %	66.99	36.58	32.85
Dividends Per Share	n.a.	n.a.	n.a.
Annual Financial Data			
Operating Results (000's)			
Total Revenues	24,659.0	24,506.0	21,171.0
Costs & Expenses	-21,760.0	-21,956.0	-21,140.0
Income Before Taxes and Other	2,899.0	2,550.0	31.0
Other Items	n.a.	n.a.	n.a.
Income Tax	-477.0	-658.0	32.0
Net Income	2,422.0	1,892.0	63.0
Cash Flow From Operations	-638.0	1,055.0	39,760.0
Balance Sheet (000's)			
Cash & Equivalents	3,648.0	1,831.0	8,775.0
Total Current Assets	145,366.0	1,831.0	9,028.0
Fixed Assets, Net	2,966.0	2,801.0	2,809.0
Total Assets	201,068.0	208,616.0	206,508.0
Total Current Liabilities	1,731.0	2,100.0	2,803.0
Long-Term Debt	1,898.0	1,100.0	112.0
Stockholders' Equity	15,071.0	17,251.0	15,379.0
Performance & Financial Condition			
Return on Total Revenues %	9.82	7.72	0.30
Return on Avg Stockholders' Equity %	14.99	11.60	0.41
Return on Average Assets %	1.18	0.91	0.03
Current Ratio	83.98	0.87	3.22
Debt / Equity %	12.59	6.38	0.73

Compound Growth %'s	EPS %	527.57	Net Income %	520.04	Total Revenues %	7.92

Comments

Most of the increased profits over the last couple years have been generated from investment transactions in the life insurance company. However, 1993 results include a nonrecurring benefit of $1.1 million from adopting GAAP in the reporting of income taxes. Pearl Broadcasting, Inc. was acquired in October, 1993. 1995 results were not available when we went to press. A serious investor should have a total understanding of corporate businesses and assets in order to arrive at a true value of the shares. Trades are infrequent. Compound growth rates in earnings and earnings per share may be distorted because of low earnings in 1992, the base year for the calculation.

Officers	Position	Ownership Information	12/31/94
George A. Foster, Jr.	Chairman, CEO	Number of Shares Outstanding	1,262
Janet D. Baldwin	Secretary	Market Capitalization	$ 10,096,000
		Frequency Of Dividends	n.a.
		Number of Shareholders	Under 500

Other Information

Transfer Agent	Company Office				Where Listed	OTC-PS
Auditor	Postlethwaite & Netterville				Symbol	n.a.
Market Maker	Paine Webber Incorporated	Telephone	(212)713-3766		SIC Code	6300
Broker Dealer	Standard Investment	Tel/Ext	(888)783-4688	Jack	Employees	n.a.

HIA, Inc.

4275 • Forest Street, CO 80216 • Telephone (303)394-6040 • Fax (303)394-2667

Company Description

The Company is a holding company with all of its business conducted through its wholly-owned subsidiary, CPS Distributors,Inc. (CPS). The Company distributes turf irrigation equipment and commercial, industrial and residential well pumps and related equipment on a wholesale basis. CPS is a 90-year-old company based in Denver, Colorado, serving five states in the Rocky Mountain region. The Company was incorporated in Colorado in 1974.

	11/30/95	11/30/94	11/30/93	11/30/92
Per Share Information				
Stock Price	0.18	0.25	0.25	0.02
Earnings Per Share	0.03	0.04	0.01	0.03
Price / Earnings Ratio	6.00	6.25	25.00	0.67
Book Value Per Share	0.19	0.16	0.13	0.11
Price / Book Value %	94.74	156.25	192.31	18.18
Dividends Per Share	n.a.	n.a.	n.a.	n.a.
Annual Financial Data				
Operating Results (000's)				
Total Revenues	14,528.7	13,322.3	9,912.5	9,175.1
Costs & Expenses	-13,890.1	-12,732.8	-9,763.8	-9,191.2
Income Before Taxes and Other	638.6	589.5	148.6	-16.1
Other Items	n.a.	97.1	34.7	400.3
Income Tax	-285.1	-216.7	-43.9	n.a.
Net Income	353.5	469.9	139.4	384.2
Cash Flow From Operations	-182.2	419.7	529.6	172.8
Balance Sheet (000's)				
Cash & Equivalents	115.1	17.7	8.9	16.8
Total Current Assets	3,426.8	2,749.3	2,193.2	2,401.4
Fixed Assets, Net	128.7	103.1	163.5	204.4
Total Assets	3,627.9	2,960.9	2,442.8	2,698.4
Total Current Liabilities	1,589.4	1,041.4	739.6	992.6
Long-Term Debt	n.a.	5.0	45.5	218.2
Stockholders' Equity	2,038.5	1,914.4	1,639.9	1,437.0
Performance & Financial Condition				
Return on Total Revenues %	2.43	3.53	1.41	4.19
Return on Avg Stockholders' Equity %	17.89	26.44	9.06	30.52
Return on Average Assets %	10.73	17.39	5.42	13.07
Current Ratio	2.16	2.64	2.97	2.42
Debt / Equity %	n.a.	0.26	2.78	15.18

Compound Growth %'s	EPS %	n.a.	Net Income %	-2.73	Total Revenues %	16.56

Comments

During 1995 and 1994, the Company acquired, from officers and other stockholders, a total of 3,218,501 shares of its common stock at prices ranging from $.14 to $.18 per share. During these same years officers excercised options, at a price of $.14 to $.18 per share, and received shares in lieu of compensation, totaling 697,749 shares. At November 30, 1995, officers and directors, as a group, owned 49.9% of the outstanding shares.

Officers	Position	Ownership Information	11/30/95
R. Thomas Dalbey	President, Treasurer	Number of Shares Outstanding	10,489,394
Alan C. Bergold	Exec VP, Secretary	Market Capitalization	$ 1,888,091
		Frequency Of Dividends	n.a.
		Number of Shareholders	2,000

Other Information			
Transfer Agent	American Securities Transfer, Inc.	Where Listed	OTC-BB
Auditor	Mitchell, Finley & Co.	Symbol	HIAI
Market Maker	Paragon Capital Corporation	Telephone (212)785-4700	SIC Code	5083
Broker Dealer	Regular Stockbroker	Employees	56

Hamburg Industries, Inc.

218 Pine Street • Hamburg, PA 19526-0027 • Telephone (610)562-3031 • Fax (610)562-0209

Company Description

The Company manufactures brooms, brushes, mops and handles. In 1995, a full line of equipment was added to manufacture a full line of institutional brushes. On January 1, 1996 the name was changed from Hamburg Broom Works, which had been the name of the Company since it was founded in 1894. The Company was formed in 1894. There was a 2.5 to 1 split in 1987.

	12/31/95	12/31/94	12/31/93
Per Share Information			
Stock Price	4.50	4.25	5.06
Earnings Per Share	0.04	0.18	0.25
Price / Earnings Ratio	112.50	23.61	20.24
Book Value Per Share	3.92	3.88	3.92
Price / Book Value %	114.80	109.54	129.08
Dividends Per Share	n.a.	0.21	0.19
Annual Financial Data			
Operating Results (000's)			
Total Revenues	2,659.4	2,780.7	2,590.0
Costs & Expenses	-2,650.0	-2,739.4	-2,517.7
Income Before Taxes and Other	9.4	41.3	72.3
Other Items	n.a.	n.a.	n.a.
Income Tax	-1.6	-4.7	-22.0
Net Income	7.7	36.5	50.3
Cash Flow From Operations	-52.8	156.5	41.9
Balance Sheet (000's)			
Cash & Equivalents	77.0	55.8	59.1
Total Current Assets	834.6	658.2	808.7
Fixed Assets, Net	482.4	320.1	292.3
Total Assets	1,338.2	998.9	1,103.8
Total Current Liabilities	529.3	201.2	302.2
Long-Term Debt	n.a.	n.a.	n.a.
Stockholders' Equity	802.9	791.1	798.4
Performance & Financial Condition			
Return on Total Revenues %	0.29	1.31	1.94
Return on Avg Stockholders' Equity %	0.97	4.59	6.34
Return on Average Assets %	0.66	3.47	4.90
Current Ratio	1.58	3.27	2.68
Debt / Equity %	n.a.	n.a.	n.a.

Compound Growth %'s	EPS %	-60.00	Net Income %	-60.77	Total Revenues %	1.33

Comments

Management has recognized the need to expand and has introduced a full line of institutional mops and dust mop handles, metal threaded handles, and wet mop handles. This both allows for greater sales opportunities and makes the Company a more viable supplier. Management believes that the North American Free Trade Agreement was a major detriment to the U.S. broom industry, but has forged ahead with a long term growth plan. Sales for the first quarter of 1996 were reported at $777,665 compared to $653,853 for the prior year.

Officers	Position	Ownership Information	12/31/95
William Bierlin, Jr.	Chairman	Number of Shares Outstanding	204,845
Richard E. Stiller	President, CEO	Market Capitalization	$ 921,803
William L. Bast	Secretary, Treasurer	Frequency Of Dividends	Quarterly
June A. Kline	Other	Number of Shareholders	Under 500
Grace A. Vinglinsky	Other		

Other Information

Transfer Agent	Midatlantic Bank, N.A., Edison, NJ		Where Listed	OTC-PS
Auditor	Beard & Company, Inc.		Symbol	HBBWB
Market Maker	Carr Securities Corporation	Telephone (800)221-2243	SIC Code	3991
Broker Dealer	Regular Stockbroker		Employees	24

Hammett (J.L.) Co.

P.O. Box 545 • Braintree, MA 02184 • Telephone (617)848-1000 • Fax (617)356-5021

Company Description

The Company is a direct mail retailer of educational products that include virtually every item and accessory used by children in classrooms or at home. The Holden family continues to own most of the 114,000 shares outstanding and a number of family members are active in the business. There is also an employee stock ownership plan for all nonunion employees.

	12/31/93	12/31/92
Per Share Information		
Stock Price	50.00	40.00
Earnings Per Share	7.09	-1.83
Price / Earnings Ratio	7.05	n.a.
Book Value Per Share	114.82	109.07
Price / Book Value %	43.55	36.67
Dividends Per Share	1.50	1.50
Annual Financial Data		
Operating Results (000's)		
Total Revenues	77,126.2	71,756.6
Costs & Expenses	-76,067.0	-70,757.0
Income Before Taxes and Other	1,059.2	-439.9
Other Items	135.7	n.a.
Income Tax	-369.4	244.6
Net Income	825.5	-195.3
Cash Flow From Operations	825.5	27.9
Balance Sheet (000's)		
Cash & Equivalents	481.8	345.6
Total Current Assets	19,248.8	17,925.5
Fixed Assets, Net	7,924.8	9,580.5
Total Assets	30,337.6	28,519.9
Total Current Liabilities	11,869.1	9,885.6
Long-Term Debt	4,078.8	4,828.8
Stockholders' Equity	13,095.7	12,506.9
Performance & Financial Condition		
Return on Total Revenues %	1.07	-0.27
Return on Avg Stockholders' Equity %	6.45	n.a.
Return on Average Assets %	2.81	n.a.
Current Ratio	1.62	1.81
Debt / Equity %	31.15	38.61

Compound Growth %'s	EPS %	n.a.	Net Income %	n.a.	Total Revenues %	7.48

Comments

We were not able to obtain the 1995 or 1994 statements. 1993 results include a nonrecurring benefit of $135,700, or $1.19 per share, because of an accounting change. The Company's products can be reviewed at their internet site (info@Hammett.com).

Officers	Position	Ownership Information	12/31/93
Richmond Y. Holden, Jr.	President, CEO	Number of Shares Outstanding	114,054
Eugene R. Grant	Treasurer	Market Capitalization	$ 5,702,700
Dick Krause	Vice President	Frequency Of Dividends	Quarterly
Jeff Holden	VP - Sales	Number of Shareholders	Under 500
Dave Shepard	Other		

Other Information

Transfer Agent	Company Office				Where Listed	OTC-BB
Auditor	Not available				Symbol	HAMT
Market Maker	Monroe Securities, Inc.	Telephone	(800)766-5560		SIC Code	5961
Broker Dealer	Standard Investment	Tel/Ext	(888)783-4688	Jack	Employees	n.a.

Harriet & Henderson Yarns, Inc.

1724 Graham Avenue • Henderson, NC 27536-0789 • Telephone (919)430-5000 • Fax (919)430-5101

Company Description

The Company operates principally as a manufacturer of cotton, blended and synthetic yarns sold primarily to apparel and hosiery manufacturers located in the southeastern U.S. The Company celebrated its 100th anniversary in 1995. It has been repurchasing its common shares and has retired 5,110 shares over the last four years.

	01/31/96	01/31/95	01/31/94	01/31/93
Per Share Information				
Stock Price	300.00	300.00	145.00	145.00
Earnings Per Share	-65.71	-56.31	40.43	149.32
Price / Earnings Ratio	n.a.	n.a.	3.59	0.97
Book Value Per Share	490.96	557.33	607.66	580.57
Price / Book Value %	61.10	53.83	23.86	24.98
Dividends Per Share	1.00	3.75	14.50	15.00
Annual Financial Data				
Operating Results (000's)				
Total Revenues	203,669.3	195,829.9	190,552.0	224,749.8
Costs & Expenses	217,210.6	-207,617.1	-181,654.2	-187,171.6
Income Before Taxes and Other	-13,541.3	-11,787.2	8,980.4	36,956.3
Other Items	n.a.	n.a.	n.a.	-2,186.9
Income Tax	5,000.3	4,425.9	-3,547.3	-14,647.7
Net Income	-8,541.0	-7,361.2	5,433.1	20,121.8
Cash Flow From Operations	4,745.8	2,496.9	18,297.5	40,262.0
Balance Sheet (000's)				
Cash & Equivalents	1,234.0	2,837.4	20,121.1	16,554.2
Total Current Assets	43,923.4	44,751.3	57,170.9	52,751.2
Fixed Assets, Net	98,733.6	74,613.7	66,010.5	74,209.3
Total Assets	150,840.7	131,739.9	134,336.7	134,905.7
Total Current Liabilities	8,760.8	28,296.3	14,701.3	17,675.1
Long-Term Debt	65,000.0	14,890.0	23,638.4	26,276.9
Stockholders' Equity	63,779.1	72,508.7	81,637.9	78,207.8
Performance & Financial Condition				
Return on Total Revenues %	-4.19	-3.76	2.85	8.95
Return on Avg Stockholders' Equity %	-12.53	-9.55	6.80	29.09
Return on Average Assets %	-6.05	-5.53	4.04	15.50
Current Ratio	5.01	3.89	3.89	2.98
Debt / Equity %	101.91	28.96	28.96	33.60

Compound Growth %'s	EPS % n.a.	Net Income % n.a.	Total Revenues % -3.70

Comments

$37 million was invested in a new plant and equipment in 1995. Poor results are blamed on extreme weakness in the retail market for apparel. Despite the losses of the last two years, each year still resulted in positive cash flow from operations. The new bank debt carries certain restrictions as to dividends and further stock repurchases.

Officers	Position	Ownership Information	01/31/96
Marshall Y. Cooper, Jr.	Chairman, President	Number of Shares Outstanding	129,908
Thomas R. Allen	VP - Finance, Treasurer	Market Capitalization	$ 38,972,400
Virginia L. Cook	Secretary	Frequency Of Dividends	Quarterly
Samuel W. Brummitt	VP - Manufacturing	Number of Shareholders	Under 500
C. Gary Walker	VP - Sales		

Other Information

Transfer Agent	Company Office				Where Listed	OTC-BB
Auditor	McGladrey & Pullen				Symbol	HHYN
Market Maker	Hill, Thompson, Magid & Co.Inc	Telephone	(800)631-3083		SIC Code	2280
Broker Dealer	Standard Investment	Tel/Ext	(888)783-4688	Jack	Employees	1300

Hartcourt Companies, Inc. (The)

20022 State Road • Cerritos, CA 90703 • Telephone (310)403-1126 • Fax (310)403-1130

Company Description

The Company is an emerging company that designs, produces and assembles high quality pens and other writing instruments in state-of-the-art factories in China and California. Products are intended for sale in the U.S., China and Eastern Europe. The Company was formed in 1993, and began limited operations and sales in November, 1994. Operations in China are through a venture with a local provincial government, which owns 40% and the Company which owns 60%. Two other production ventures are anticipated: another joint venture in China with China's largest pen manufacturer who would own 45% and the Company would own 55% and also a joint venture in Slovakia where the Company would be a 51% owner.

	12/31/94	12/31/93
Per Share Information		
Stock Price	3.50	n.a.
Earnings Per Share	-0.02	-0.01
Price / Earnings Ratio	n.a.	n.a.
Book Value Per Share	0.13	-0.04
Price / Book Value %	2,692.30	n.a.
Dividends Per Share	n.a.	n.a.
Annual Financial Data		
Operating Results (000's)		
Total Revenues	75.6	4.0
Costs & Expenses	-386.4	-175.2
Income Before Taxes and Other	-310.8	-171.2
Other Items	n.a.	n.a.
Income Tax	n.a.	n.a.
Net Income	-310.8	-171.2
Cash Flow From Operations	-5.8	-908.7
Balance Sheet (000's)		
Cash & Equivalents	196.6	254.2
Total Current Assets	1,425.6	1,170.5
Fixed Assets, Net	6,425.1	1,290.7
Total Assets	9,183.2	2,621.3
Total Current Liabilities	3,689.8	1,023.8
Long-Term Debt	981.9	221.0
Stockholders' Equity	2,049.5	-88.2
Performance & Financial Condition		
Return on Total Revenues %	-411.03	n.a.
Return on Avg Stockholders' Equity %	-31.69	n.a.
Return on Average Assets %	-5.27	n.a.
Current Ratio	0.39	1.14
Debt / Equity %	47.91	n.a.

Compound Growth %'s	EPS % n.a.	Net Income % n.a.	Total Revenues %	1796.96

Comments

The Company's 1995 financial statements were not available at the time of publication. At December 31, 1995, the Company's common stock was selling at an average bid/ask price of $5.75. In February, 1996, the Company announced the acquisition of YAFA Pen Company which had sales of $2.4 million in 1995.

Officers	Position	Ownership Information	12/31/94
Alan V. Phan	Chairman, President	Number of Shares Outstanding	16,127,500
Frederic Cohn	Secretary	Market Capitalization	$ 56,446,250
James Beattie	Vice President	Frequency Of Dividends	n.a.
Gary Wilmoth	Vice President	Number of Shareholders	158
Frances Fesuk	Vice President		

Other Information

Transfer Agent	I, Data			Where Listed	OTC-BB
Auditor	BDO Seidman			Symbol	HRCT
Market Maker	Alpine Securities Corporation	Telephone	(800)521-5588	SIC Code	3951
Broker Dealer	Regular Stockbroker			Employees	153

Hayward Industries, Inc.

900 Fairmount Avenue • Elizabeth, NY 07207 • Telephone (908)351-5400 • Fax (908)351-2189

Company Description

The Company is a leading manufacturer of residential swimming pool and spa products, and industrial flow control products. For all years presented, swimming pool and spa products account for approximately 80% of total Company sales.

	12/31/94	12/31/93	12/31/92
Per Share Information			
Stock Price	84.40	70.00	70.00
Earnings Per Share	14.17	11.60	11.22
Price / Earnings Ratio	5.96	6.03	6.24
Book Value Per Share	95.28	83.60	76.79
Price / Book Value %	88.58	83.73	91.16
Dividends Per Share	3.00	3.00	3.00
Annual Financial Data			
Operating Results (000's)			
Total Revenues	203,740.0	178,073.0	179,617.0
Costs & Expenses	-173,682.0	-152,133.0	-153,329.0
Income Before Taxes and Other	25,054.0	20,678.0	20,123.0
Other Items	n.a.	n.a.	n.a.
Income Tax	-9,712.0	-8,201.0	-8,197.0
Net Income	15,342.0	12,477.0	11,926.0
Cash Flow From Operations	16,687.0	13,101.0	22,160.0
Balance Sheet (000's)			
Cash & Equivalents	3,553.0	10,266.0	15,836.0
Total Current Assets	75,707.0	65,206.0	65,146.0
Fixed Assets, Net	63,094.0	58,179.0	60,014.0
Total Assets	168,554.0	153,981.0	156,148.0
Total Current Liabilities	33,812.0	24,608.0	26,395.0
Long-Term Debt	26,222.0	34,724.0	43,373.0
Stockholders' Equity	103,281.0	90,367.0	81,654.0
Performance & Financial Condition			
Return on Total Revenues %	7.53	7.01	6.64
Return on Avg Stockholders' Equity %	15.85	14.51	15.37
Return on Average Assets %	9.51	8.05	76.69
Current Ratio	2.24	2.65	2.47
Debt / Equity %	25.39	38.43	53.12

Compound Growth %'s	EPS %	12.38	Net Income %	13.42	Total Revenues %	6.50

Comments

The Company doesn't release 1995 results until June. Therefore the results are not possible to include. The Company recently completed a new manufacturing, warehouse and distribution facility in Clemmons, North Carolina . The Company has demonstrated good growth and is beginning to expand in foreign markets as well.

Officers	Position	Ownership Information	12/31/94
Oscar Davis	Chairman	Number of Shares Outstanding	1,083,961
Anthony T. Castor III	President, CEO	Market Capitalization	$ 91,486,308
Edward C. Teter	Vice President	Frequency Of Dividends	Quarterly
		Number of Shareholders	Under 500

Other Information			
Transfer Agent	Chemical Mellon Shareholder Services	Where Listed	OTC-BB
Auditor	Grant Thornton LLP	Symbol	HWRI
Market Maker	Herzog, Heine, Geduld, Inc. Telephone (800)221-3600	SIC Code	3949
Broker Dealer	Regular Stockbroker	Employees	500

Health Insurance Company of Vermont, Inc.

One Roosevelt Highway • Colchester, VT 05446 • Telephone (802)655-5500

Company Description

The Company was incorporated in the state of Vermont in 1961 as an accident and health insurance company. The Company markets guaranteed renewable disability income insurance which is written on an individual basis. All business is produced by licensed insurance agents who have broker contracts with the Company. The Company is licensed to write insurance in all states except Alaska, Iowa, New York and Wisconsin.

	12/31/95	12/31/94	12/31/93	12/31/92
Per Share Information				
Stock Price	12.25	10.38	8.50	7.50
Earnings Per Share	0.35	0.74	1.44	1.36
Price / Earnings Ratio	35.00	14.03	5.90	5.51
Book Value Per Share	15.85	15.01	14.67	13.23
Price / Book Value %	77.29	69.15	57.94	56.69
Dividends Per Share	n.a.	n.a.	n.a.	n.a.
Annual Financial Data				
Operating Results (000's)				
Total Revenues	7,062.4	6,475.9	5,645.5	5,447.3
Costs & Expenses	-6,832.9	-6,003.6	-4,826.3	-4,585.1
Income Before Taxes and Other	229.5	472.3	819.2	862.2
Other Items	n.a.	n.a.	n.a.	n.a.
Income Tax	-39.0	-79.8	-62.9	-148.3
Net Income	190.5	392.4	756.3	713.9
Cash Flow From Operations	884.4	794.9	1,263.3	1,262.1
Balance Sheet (000's)				
Cash & Equivalents	1,072.8	248.5	68.1	147.3
Total Current Assets	3,569.0	2,166.0	2,478.5	672.4
Fixed Assets, Net	620.2	656.4	682.6	496.9
Total Assets	21,137.8	19,067.1	18,126.2	16,644.3
Total Current Liabilities	452.3	316.5	359.9	412.7
Long-Term Debt	n.a.	n.a.	n.a.	n.a.
Stockholders' Equity	8,720.0	7,845.2	7,669.7	6,913.4
Performance & Financial Condition				
Return on Total Revenues %	2.70	6.06	13.40	13.11
Return on Avg Stockholders' Equity %	2.30	5.06	10.37	10.88
Return on Average Assets %	0.95	2.11	4.35	4.76
Current Ratio	7.89	6.84	6.89	1.63
Debt / Equity %	n.a.	n.a.	n.a.	n.a.

Compound Growth %'s	EPS %	-36.39	Net Income %	-35.62	Total Revenues %	9.04

Comments

The Company's primary assets and liabilities are investments and policy liabilities. At December 31, 1995, investments totaled $12.7 million, and consisted almost entirely of government bonds. Policy liabilities at December 31, 1995, totaled $11.8 million, consisting primarily of future policy benefits and claims. In March, 1996, the Company entered into a merger agreement with Penn Treaty American Corporation whereby the Company would become a wholly owned subsidiary. The proposed acquisition price is $20 per share, consisting of $4.00 in cash and $16.00 in Penn Treaty stock. The merger is expected to be consumated in July, 1996. After the announcement the Company's stock was quoted at $17.75 per share.

Officers	Position	Ownership Information	12/31/95
John W. Mahoney	President	Number of Shares Outstanding	549,095
James L. Fraser	Secretary	Market Capitalization	$ 6,726,414
David W. Lesperance	Vice President, Treasurer	Frequency Of Dividends	n.a.
Anne M. Brosseau	Vice President	Number of Shareholders	510
James R. Foster	Vice President		

Other Information

Transfer Agent	Chittenden Trust Company			Where Listed	OTC-BB
Auditor	Coopers & Lybrand LLP			Symbol	HIVT
Market Maker	Black & Company, Inc.	Telephone	(800)423-2124	SIC Code	6321
Broker Dealer	Regular Stockbroker			Employees	35

Health International, Inc.

1840 Century Park East, Ste770 • Los Angeles, CA 90067 • Telephone (310)551-1840 • Fax (310)277-1809

Company Description

The Company is a national health advisory service organization which provides utilization review services, including a second surgical opinion program, and a hospital case management program to employers throughout the United States.

	09/30/95	09/30/94	09/30/93	09/30/92
Per Share Information				
Stock Price	4.75	1.75	2.75	2.25
Earnings Per Share	0.08	0.22	0.04	0.06
Price / Earnings Ratio	59.38	7.95	68.75	37.50
Book Value Per Share	0.62	0.54	0.31	-0.13
Price / Book Value %	766.13	324.07	887.10	n.a.
Dividends Per Share	n.a.	n.a.	n.a.	n.a.
Annual Financial Data				
Operating Results (000's)				
Total Revenues	7,639.9	7,006.5	4,509.1	3,936.8
Costs & Expenses	-7,383.0	-6,287.3	-4,387.5	-3,784.7
Income Before Taxes and Other	256.9	719.2	121.6	152.1
Other Items	n.a.	n.a.	36.3	51.7
Income Tax	-29.8	-68.0	-52.6	-65.9
Net Income	227.1	651.2	105.3	137.9
Cash Flow From Operations	1,252.9	736.2	313.2	234.8
Balance Sheet (000's)				
Cash & Equivalents	1,585.6	878.5	106.0	107.4
Total Current Assets	1,819.7	1,470.4	714.8	639.5
Fixed Assets, Net	1,594.5	935.5	951.2	530.3
Total Assets	3,466.8	2,444.9	1,691.3	1,207.5
Total Current Liabilities	1,148.9	664.8	515.7	389.4
Long-Term Debt	n.a.	n.a.	n.a.	n.a.
Stockholders' Equity	1,701.7	1,468.6	814.9	676.6
Performance & Financial Condition				
Return on Total Revenues %	2.97	9.29	2.33	3.50
Return on Avg Stockholders' Equity %	14.33	57.03	14.12	n.a.
Return on Average Assets %	7.68	31.49	7.26	13.79
Current Ratio	1.58	2.21	1.39	1.64
Debt / Equity %	n.a.	n.a.	n.a.	n.a.

Compound Growth %'s	EPS %	10.06	Net Income %	18.07	Total Revenues %	24.73

Comments

The first quarter ended December 31, 1995, shows revenue of $2,956,905 (earnings per share $.12) as compared to $1,817,251 (earnings per share $.05) in the comparable quarter last year.

Officers	Position	Ownership Information	09/30/95
Donald K. Kelly, M.D.	Chairman, CEO	Number of Shares Outstanding	2,756,267
		Market Capitalization	$ 13,092,268
		Frequency Of Dividends	n.a.
		Number of Shareholders	Under 500

Other Information

Transfer Agent	Chemical Mellon Shareholder Services		Where Listed	OTC-BB
Auditor	Arthur Andersen LLP		Symbol	HTHN
Market Maker	Wilson-Davis & Co., Inc.	Telephone (800)453-5735	SIC Code	8090
Broker Dealer	Regular Stockbroker		Employees	130

Heartland Group of Companies, Inc.

6230 Busch Blvd., Ste. 201 • Columbus, OH 43229-1863 • Telephone (614)848-5100 • Fax (614)848-8949

Company Description

The Company was organized in 1990 for the purpose of investing in financial services companies as well as trading and investing in independent bank stocks. Through three subsidiaries, the Company acts as an interstate broker dealer specializing in bank stocks, is an investment advisor providing money management services to its customers and is a NASD registered broker-dealer providing porfolio management and brokerage services.

	02/29/96	02/28/95	02/28/94	02/28/93
Per Share Information				
Stock Price	2.82	2.75	n.a.	n.a.
Earnings Per Share	0.08	-0.03	-0.11	0.01
Price / Earnings Ratio	35.25	n.a.	n.a.	n.a.
Book Value Per Share	1.00	0.85	0.69	0.69
Price / Book Value %	282.00	323.53	n.a.	n.a.
Dividends Per Share	n.a.	n.a.	n.a.	n.a.
Annual Financial Data				
Operating Results (000's)				
Total Revenues	2,589.0	1,774.3	1,063.7	2,540.4
Costs & Expenses	1,951.0	-2,009.9	-1,725.3	-2,451.5
Income Before Taxes and Other	638.0	-235.6	-661.6	88.9
Other Items	n.a.	n.a.	n.a.	n.a.
Income Tax	n.a.	n.a.	n.a.	-10.0
Net Income	638.0	-235.6	-661.6	78.9
Cash Flow From Operations	1,771.1	-2,594.3	-2,000.0	n.a.
Balance Sheet (000's)				
Cash & Equivalents	405.3	267.8	157.9	197.4
Total Current Assets	6,123.3	7,187.7	4,615.5	6,572.3
Fixed Assets, Net	86.6	137.0	143.2	216.9
Total Assets	8,114.2	9,817.4	7,256.8	7,956.7
Total Current Liabilities	273.0	1,995.7	2,531.6	3,425.6
Long-Term Debt	n.a.	654.1	n.a.	470.8
Stockholders' Equity	7,841.2	7,167.5	4,725.2	4,060.2
Performance & Financial Condition				
Return on Total Revenues %	24.64	-13.28	-62.20	3.11
Return on Avg Stockholders' Equity %	8.50	-3.96	-15.06	n.a.
Return on Average Assets %	7.12	-2.76	-8.70	n.a.
Current Ratio	22.43	3.60	1.82	1.92
Debt / Equity %	n.a.	9.13	n.a.	11.60

Compound Growth %'s	EPS %	100.00	Net Income %	100.72	Total Revenues %	0.63

Comments

Included in Current Assets are marketable equity securities of $5.6 million, comprised of $3.5 million of equities traded on national markets and $2.1 million of equities not traded on national markets, but with ascertainable market values. The Company has two classes of common stock outstanding, Class A and Class B. Only the Class A shares are traded. As of March 31, 1996, directors and officers, as a group, owned approximately 15.7% of the Company's outstanding Class A stock. There was no public trading in the Company's stock prior to 1995. The Company has net operating loss carryforwards of approximately $3.5 million which expire in 2002.

Officers	Position	Ownership Information	02/29/96
Michael E. Guirlinger	President, Treasurer	Number of Shares Outstanding	7,811,677
Michael J. McKenzie	Exec VP	Market Capitalization	$ 22,028,929
Jeffrey C. Barton	CFO	Frequency Of Dividends	n.a.
Sandra L. Quinn	Vice President, Secretary	Number of Shareholders	870

Other Information

Transfer Agent	Harris Trust & Savings Bank			Where Listed	OTC-BB
Auditor	Price Waterhouse LLP			Symbol	HGRC
Market Maker	Tradetech Securities LP	Telephone	(800)211-1250	SIC Code	6211
Broker Dealer	Regular Stockbroker			Employees	8

This page left intentionally blank.

Henry County Plywood Corporation

P.O. Box 406 • Ridgeway, VA 24148-0406 • Telephone (540)956-3121 • Fax (540)956-4742

Company Description

The Company manufactures and sells custom wood parts primarily for use in the furniture and marine industries. It has two major customers in the furniture industry whose combined purchases represent 40% of total sales volume. The Company was founded in 1948 in Virginia.

	06/02/95	05/27/94	05/28/93	05/29/92
Per Share Information				
Stock Price	3.25	2.50	2.50	3.00
Earnings Per Share	-0.23	0.22	-0.07	0.08
Price / Earnings Ratio	n.a.	11.36	n.a.	37.50
Book Value Per Share	6.15	6.43	6.20	6.26
Price / Book Value %	52.85	38.88	40.32	47.92
Dividends Per Share	0.12	0.04	0.03	0.60
Annual Financial Data				
Operating Results (000's)				
Total Revenues	8,171.3	8,533.5	6,858.2	6,736.7
Costs & Expenses	-8,307.2	-8,248.1	-6,879.6	-6,693.6
Income Before Taxes and Other	-147.9	237.7	-38.1	36.3
Other Items	n.a.	-66.4	n.a.	n.a.
Income Tax	62.9	-84.7	9.7	-5.6
Net Income	-85.0	86.5	-28.4	30.7
Cash Flow From Operations	-7.2	501.7	-69.8	233.6
Balance Sheet (000's)				
Cash & Equivalents	136.6	68.1	22.8	201.7
Total Current Assets	1,914.4	1,662.3	1,610.3	1,508.3
Fixed Assets, Net	1,555.5	1,666.8	1,630.7	1,611.9
Total Assets	3,609.7	3,454.2	3,355.7	3,225.2
Total Current Liabilities	1,151.9	742.2	783.3	701.1
Long-Term Debt	128.2	197.8	107.7	n.a.
Stockholders' Equity	2,294.4	2,457.2	2,396.8	2,446.6
Performance & Financial Condition				
Return on Total Revenues %	-1.04	1.01	-0.41	0.46
Return on Avg Stockholders' Equity %	-3.58	3.57	-1.17	1.26
Return on Average Assets %	-2.41	2.54	-0.86	0.95
Current Ratio	1.66	2.24	2.06	2.15
Debt / Equity %	5.59	8.05	4.50	n.a.

Compound Growth %'s	EPS % n.a.	Net Income % n.a.	Total Revenues % 6.65

Comments

The Company has thus far survived an industry shake up although competition remains strong. There is only a small amount of long-term debt outstanding.

Officers	Position	Ownership Information	06/02/95
Edward M. Gravely	Chairman, President	Number of Shares Outstanding	372,941
G. W. Whitmore	Vice President, Secretary	Market Capitalization	$ 1,212,058
J M. Cassady	VP - Sales	Frequency Of Dividends	Quarterly
		Number of Shareholders	176

Other Information

Transfer Agent	Company Office		Where Listed	OTC-BB
Auditor	Fulp and Associates		Symbol	HRYC
Market Maker	Carr Securities Corporation	Telephone (800)221-2243	SIC Code	2439
Broker Dealer	Regular Stockbroker		Employees	146

Hershey Creamery Company

P.O.Box 1821 • Harrisburg, PA 17105 • Telephone (717)238-8134 • Fax (717)233-7195

Company Description

The Company manufactures, distributes, and sells ice cream products from its facilitities in Pennsylvania. Distribution is throughout the northeastern sector of the United States. The Company was founded in 1894. Please enjoy the brief history displayed on the opposite page.

	12/31/95	12/31/94	12/31/93	12/31/92
Per Share Information				
Stock Price	1,772.50	1,825.00	n.a.	1,500.00
Earnings Per Share	148.91	112.59	n.a.	114.81
Price / Earnings Ratio	11.90	16.21	n.a.	13.07
Book Value Per Share	1,519.12	1,375.56	n.a.	1,130.23
Price / Book Value %	116.68	132.67	n.a.	132.72
Dividends Per Share	9.90	9.40	n.a.	8.40
Annual Financial Data				
Operating Results (000's)				
Total Revenues	74,166.1	69,219.1	n.a.	63,669.5
Costs & Expenses	-65,778.8	-62,474.5	n.a.	-56,654.8
Income Before Taxes and Other	8,387.3	6,744.6	n.a.	7,014.7
Other Items	n.a.	n.a.	n.a.	n.a.
Income Tax	-2,941.5	-2,627.0	n.a.	-2,816.0
Net Income	5,445.8	4,117.6	n.a.	4,198.7
Cash Flow From Operations	9,301.4	7,607.1	n.a.	7,595.4
Balance Sheet (000's)				
Cash & Equivalents	1,717.9	2,255.6	n.a.	3,577.8
Total Current Assets	31,222.1	29,914.5	n.a.	13,030.4
Fixed Assets, Net	29,975.3	25,725.4	n.a.	22,945.3
Total Assets	61,242.4	55,660.2	n.a.	46,618.3
Total Current Liabilities	2,157.0	1,932.4	n.a.	1,737.8
Long-Term Debt	n.a.	n.a.	n.a.	n.a.
Stockholders' Equity	55,555.8	50,306.8	n.a.	41,333.6
Performance & Financial Condition				
Return on Total Revenues %	7.34	5.95	n.a.	6.59
Return on Avg Stockholders' Equity %	10.29	n.a.	n.a.	n.a.
Return on Average Assets %	9.32	n.a.	n.a.	n.a.
Current Ratio	14.47	15.48	n.a.	7.50
Debt / Equity %	n.a.	n.a.	n.a.	n.a.

Compound Growth %'s	EPS %	9.06	Net Income %	9.06	Total Revenues %	5.22

Comments

1995 results were excellent, especially when there was earlier concern about the requirement to disclose fat content on all packaging. The Company continues to maintain a large investment in marketable securities ($23.3 million at December 31, 1995), although there have been no indications of specific expansion plans.

Officers	Position	Ownership Information	12/31/95
George H. Holder	Chairman	Number of Shares Outstanding	36,571
George Hugh Holder	President	Market Capitalization	$ 64,822,098
Virginia H. Westfall	Treasurer	Frequency Of Dividends	Quarterly
William S. Holder	Vice President, Secretary	Number of Shareholders	Under 500
Thomas J. Ryan, III	Vice President		

Other Information				
Transfer Agent	Company Office		Where Listed	OTC-BB
Auditor	KPMG Peat Marwick LLP		Symbol	HRCR
Market Maker	Folger Nolan Fleming Douglas	Telephone (800)326-3633	SIC Code	2024
Broker Dealer			Employees	450

Ice Cream

For any of you who grew up in the Harrisburg, Pennsylvania area within the last century, reference to Hershey's Ice Cream must bring back fond memories. Perhaps you savored a Hershey's Ice Cream cone at the local ice cream parlor after a hot walk home from school, or enjoyed some on your birthday. While your childhood memories go back perhaps a few decades, Hershey Creamery Company's long and prosperous history begins way back in 1894.

That was when four Hershey brothers, who owned and operated a small dairy, began making ice cream. Hershey's Ice Cream was born. Decades later, a merger with the Meyer Dairy Company of Bethlehem, Pennsylvania brought the Holder family into the picture, and ever since, either a Holder or a Hershey has been at the helm of the Company.

In the beginning and to this day their primary concern has been to manufacture and distribute quality ice cream with the best possible methods. Especially in the early days, the distribution (i.e. refrigeration) part was tough to handle. In those days brine was used to freeze ice cream into three and five gallon metal cans. More brine than ice cream was carried on the original wagons and deliverymen spent more time keeping the brine box than actually delivering ice cream. All of this changed, however, with the advent of the refrigeration truck. Hershey takes great pride in its current fleet of trucks which includes state-of-the-art refrigeration systems and is the envy of the ice cream industry.

Of course, they have a lot more to deliver these days. Unlike the early years, when the company was smaller and the demand for various ice cream forms and flavors ran to vanilla, chocolate or strawberry only, today's menu has expanded to include fifty-eight flavors, ice cream bars, premium, super-premium, no-fat, reduced-fat and no-sugar-added ice creams, fat-free ices, sherbet and even low-fat yogurt. Hershey markets them all with flourish, and has a history of making their product affordable without sacrificing quality. Back in the 1930's, their "15 cents a pint" campaign shocked the industry (how could they make any money?) but was undoubtedly a big hit with kids of all ages.

After 102 years, Hershey has expanded well beyond the Harrisburg area. It now operates in seventeen states throughout the northeastern United States and is moving into the South and the Midwest. They have plans to add a new production facility before the end of the decade and it is their hope at that time to expand across the country. The Holder family considers it to be "a reasonable dream" to shoot for the next one hundred years with even greater profitability than the first. With their sound business practices not to mention their experience, undoubtedly they will realize that dream.

Hilliard Corporation

100 West Fourth Street • Elmira, NY 14902-1504 • Telephone (607)733-7121 • Fax (607)733-3009

Company Description

The Company is a specialty applications engineering company that manufactures a broad line of motion control products, oil filtration and reclamation equipment, gas turbine starters and plate and frame filter presses, with manufacturing facilities in New York and South Carolina. The Company was founded in 1905 and incorporated in 1925.

	12/31/95	12/31/94
Per Share Information		
Stock Price	118.00	116.00
Earnings Per Share	44.92	-31.25
Price / Earnings Ratio	2.63	n.a.
Book Value Per Share	222.84	183.62
Price / Book Value %	52.95	63.17
Dividends Per Share	5.70	5.00
Annual Financial Data		
Operating Results (000's)		
Total Revenues	28,861.5	23,427.8
Costs & Expenses	-24,911.9	-20,904.1
Income Before Taxes and Other	3,544.6	2,198.8
Other Items	n.a.	-2,896.0
Income Tax	-1,306.0	-859.4
Net Income	2,238.6	-1,556.6
Cash Flow From Operations	2,381.0	952.1
Balance Sheet (000's)		
Cash & Equivalents	699.4	970.8
Total Current Assets	10,571.1	9,706.0
Fixed Assets, Net	6,427.0	5,017.2
Total Assets	19,179.8	16,849.5
Total Current Liabilities	2,653.6	2,623.1
Long-Term Debt	n.a.	n.a.
Stockholders' Equity	11,105.9	9,151.4
Performance & Financial Condition		
Return on Total Revenues %	7.76	-6.64
Return on Avg Stockholders' Equity %	22.10	n.a.
Return on Average Assets %	12.43	n.a.
Current Ratio	3.98	3.70
Debt / Equity %	n.a.	n.a.

Compound Growth %'s	EPS % n.a.	Net Income % n.a.	Total Revenues % 23.19

Comments

The 1995 growth rate of 23.2% is noted. Unfortunately we were unable to obtain earlier financial statements. The balance sheet is strong and has no long term debt. 1994 earnings reflect a $2.9 million charge to record postretirement benefits under GAAP. EPS without this charge would have been $26.88.

Officers	Position	Ownership Information	12/31/95
Nelson Mooers van den Blink	Chairman, CEO	Number of Shares Outstanding	49,838
Gerald F. Schichtel	President, COO	Market Capitalization	$ 5,880,884
		Frequency Of Dividends	n.a.
		Number of Shareholders	Under 500

Other Information						
Transfer Agent	Company Office				Where Listed	OTC-BB
Auditor	Mengel, Metzger, Barr & Co.LLP				Symbol	HLRD
Market Maker	Tweedy Browne Company L.P.	Telephone	(212)916-0606		SIC Code	3599
Broker Dealer	Standard Investment	Tel/Ext	(888)783-4688	Jack	Employees	250

Homasote Company

P.O. Box 7240 • West Trenton, NJ 08628-0240 • Telephone (609)883-3300 • Fax (609)530-1584

Company Description

The Company manufactures and sells insulated wood fibre board and foam products for industrial customers. The Company's primary basic raw material is wastepaper. Most of the Company's products are used in the building industry with 77% of sales atributed to this industry and 23% derived from industrial manufacturers. The Company was founded in the same year as Walker's Manual, 1909.

	12/31/95	12/31/94	12/31/93	12/31/92
Per Share Information				
Stock Price	20.50	15.32	15.44	15.25
Earnings Per Share	2.05	3.06	-4.28	0.77
Price / Earnings Ratio	10.00	5.01	n.a.	19.81
Book Value Per Share	22.32	20.72	17.94	22.41
Price / Book Value %	91.85	73.94	86.06	68.05
Dividends Per Share	0.58	0.50	0.50	0.05
Annual Financial Data				
Operating Results (000's)				
Total Revenues	25,733.5	25,792.1	23,903.7	23,586.0
Costs & Expenses	-24,421.6	-23,801.7	-23,099.3	-23,029.2
Income Before Taxes and Other	1,311.9	1,990.5	804.4	556.7
Other Items	n.a.	n.a.	-2,299.7	n.a.
Income Tax	-525.8	-763.3	-328.7	-216.0
Net Income	786.1	1,227.2	-1,824.0	340.7
Cash Flow From Operations	440.2	2,222.4	1,812.3	965.4
Balance Sheet (000's)				
Cash & Equivalents	2,329.0	3,385.6	2,061.8	1,766.7
Total Current Assets	8,425.6	9,045.6	7,368.5	7,582.0
Fixed Assets, Net	5,695.1	5,341.8	5,631.7	5,857.6
Total Assets	15,303.0	15,501.0	14,253.6	13,808.8
Total Current Liabilities	1,921.9	1,942.7	1,113.7	2,208.0
Long-Term Debt	n.a.	775.0	932.2	1,123.6
Stockholders' Equity	8,424.8	8,100.0	7,389.9	9,832.3
Performance & Financial Condition				
Return on Total Revenues %	3.05	4.76	-7.63	1.44
Return on Avg Stockholders' Equity %	9.51	15.85	-21.18	3.50
Return on Average Assets %	5.10	8.25	-13.00	2.50
Current Ratio	4.38	4.66	6.62	3.43
Debt / Equity %	n.a.	9.57	12.61	11.43

Compound Growth %'s	EPS %	38.60	Net Income %	32.13	Total Revenues %	2.95

Comments

The net loss in 1993, includes the cumulative effect of changes in accounting principles in the amount of $2.3 million relating to the accrual of employee postretirement benefits. The Company has been repurchasing its outstanding common and, during the four years presented, repurchased a total of 70,390 shares at a cost of $1.1 million.

Officers	Position	Ownership Information	12/31/95
Irving Flicker	Chairman, CEO	Number of Shares Outstanding	377,451
Warren L. Flicker	President, COO	Market Capitalization	$ 7,737,746
Joseph A. Bronsard	President	Frequency Of Dividends	Quarterly
Cindy Adler	Secretary	Number of Shareholders	304
Neil F. Bacon	Treasurer, CFO		

Other Information			
Transfer Agent	Registrar & Transfer Company	Where Listed	PHL
Auditor	KPMG Peat Marwick LLP	Symbol	HMST
Market Maker	n.a.	SIC Code	2400
Broker Dealer	Regular Stockbroker	Employees	212

Hosoi Garden Mortuary, Inc.

30 North Kukui Street • Honolulu, HI 96817 • Telephone (808)538-3877 • Fax (808)533-4981

Company Description

The Company is engaged in the funeral and mortuary business in Honolulu, Hawaii. The Company also owns 50% of Garden Life Plan, Ltd. which sells pre-need funeral service contracts. The Company principally serves persons of Japanese ancestry who follow a particular and special order of worship in accordance with their religious beliefs. The Company was incorporated in Hawaii in 1957, as the successor to a business founded in 1900.

	05/31/95	05/31/94	05/31/93	05/31/92
Per Share Information				
Stock Price	5.00	4.38	4.75	3.50
Earnings Per Share	0.21	0.26	0.14	0.14
Price / Earnings Ratio	23.81	16.85	33.93	25.00
Book Value Per Share	2.50	2.32	2.14	2.04
Price / Book Value %	200.00	188.79	221.96	171.57
Dividends Per Share	0.05	0.04	0.04	0.03
Annual Financial Data				
Operating Results (000's)				
Total Revenues	2,691.0	2,970.7	2,329.9	2,043.9
Costs & Expenses	-2,503.0	-2,547.7	-2,323.0	-1,959.2
Income Before Taxes and Other	187.9	423.0	6.8	84.7
Other Items	268.9	224.1	252.6	228.6
Income Tax	-65.9	-155.4	11.9	-37.4
Net Income	391.0	491.7	271.4	276.0
Cash Flow From Operations	589.9	175.0	238.8	-137.4
Balance Sheet (000's)				
Cash & Equivalents	938.7	606.1	572.2	740.5
Total Current Assets	2,267.7	2,366.5	1,655.6	2,460.1
Fixed Assets, Net	1,554.5	1,621.8	1,616.2	968.1
Total Assets	5,080.9	4,844.3	4,475.4	4,385.4
Total Current Liabilities	432.5	480.3	314.2	385.6
Long-Term Debt	n.a.	n.a.	n.a.	n.a.
Stockholders' Equity	4,603.6	4,304.2	4,071.9	3,914.5
Performance & Financial Condition				
Return on Total Revenues %	14.53	16.55	11.65	13.50
Return on Avg Stockholders' Equity %	8.78	11.74	6.80	7.20
Return on Average Assets %	7.88	10.55	6.13	6.44
Current Ratio	5.24	4.93	5.27	6.38
Debt / Equity %	n.a.	n.a.	n.a.	n.a.

Compound Growth %'s	EPS %	14.47	Net Income %	12.31	Total Revenues %	9.60

Comments

As of May 31, 1995, officers and directors, as a group, owned approximately 27% of the Company's common stock. The Company has been reacquiring its stock regularly. For the nine months ended February 29, 1996, revenues were $2.0 million and Net Income was $368,000 ($.20 per share), as compared to $1.9 million and $335,000 ($.18 per share), for the same period in the prior fiscal year.

Officers	Position	Ownership Information	05/31/95
Clifford Hosoi	President	Number of Shares Outstanding	1,839,410
Elaine Nakamura	Secretary	Market Capitalization	$ 9,197,050
Keith Numazu	Treasurer	Frequency Of Dividends	Annual
Anne T. Tamori	Vice President	Number of Shareholders	1,752
David Fujishige	Vice President		

Other Information

Transfer Agent	Hawaiian Trust Company Ltd.			Where Listed	OTC-BB
Auditor	Endo & Company			Symbol	HGMI
Market Maker	Chicago Corporation, The	Telephone	(800)621-1674	SIC Code	7261
Broker Dealer	Regular Stockbroker			Employees	29

Houlihan's Restaurant Group, Inc.

Two Brush Creek Blvd. • Kansas City, MO 64112 • Telephone (816)756-2200 • Fax (816)561-2842

Company Description

The Company and its subsidiaries operate full service casual restaurants in 25 states. At December 25, 1995, it operated 98 restaurants including 61 Houlihan's, 28 Darryl's, and 9 others. As of that date the Company also franchised 18 Houlihan's in seven states and Puerto Rico. The Company, a Delaware corporation formed in 1968, is the successor to a business founded in Kansas City, Missouri, in 1962. In 1991, the Company filed a bankruptcy petition and in 1992 had satisfied the conditions of a plan of reorganization. As a result of the reorganization, a new reporting entity was created and the assets and liabilities were restated at their fair market values. The Company's 1992 financials reflect these adjustments.

	12/25/95	12/26/94	12/27/93	12/28/92
Per Share Information				
Stock Price	5.82	8.34	7.82	n.a.
Earnings Per Share	0.43	0.30	0.30	2.55
Price / Earnings Ratio	13.53	19.40	26.07	n.a.
Book Value Per Share	7.00	6.59	6.30	6.00
Price / Book Value %	83.14	88.32	124.13	n.a.
Dividends Per Share	n.a.	n.a.	n.a.	n.a.
Annual Financial Data				
Operating Results (000's)				
Total Revenues	267,622.0	259,367.0	257,225.0	266,532.0
Costs & Expenses	-254,178.0	-248,983.0	-245,878.0	-262,392.0
Income Before Taxes and Other	8,181.0	5,858.0	6,995.0	-6,709.0
Other Items	n.a.	n.a.	n.a.	31,031.0
Income Tax	-3,916.0	-2,900.0	-4,026.0	1,173.0
Net Income	4,265.0	2,958.0	2,969.0	25,495.0
Cash Flow From Operations	19,370.0	14,097.0	29,337.0	5,319.0
Balance Sheet (000's)				
Cash & Equivalents	10,314.0	10,310.0	24,380.0	8,791.0
Total Current Assets	18,570.0	18,135.0	31,611.0	14,491.0
Fixed Assets, Net	104,521.0	102,843.0	98,444.0	104,453.0
Total Assets	191,016.0	192,508.0	204,235.0	197,301.0
Total Current Liabilities	34,064.0	30,405.0	39,241.0	23,438.0
Long-Term Debt	72,779.0	83,376.0	89,997.0	100,140.0
Stockholders' Equity	70,192.0	65,927.0	62,969.0	60,000.0
Performance & Financial Condition				
Return on Total Revenues %	1.59	1.14	1.15	-2.08
Return on Avg Stockholders' Equity %	6.27	4.59	4.83	121.26
Return on Average Assets %	2.22	1.49	1.48	11.78
Current Ratio	0.55	0.60	0.81	0.62
Debt / Equity %	103.69	126.47	142.92	166.90

Compound Growth %'s	EPS %	-44.75	Net Income %	-44.90	Total Revenues %	0.14

Comments

The Company reports fiscal year results of operations based on 52 or 53 week periods. Substantially all of Other Assets represents the excess of reorganization value over identifiable assets, resulting from the "fresh start reporting" implemented in 1992. This asset is being amortized and charged to income over 20 years. A gain of $31.0 million was recognized in 1992, as a result of the discharge of prepetition liabilities. No reliable stock price quotes were available for 1992.

Officers	Position	Ownership Information	12/25/95
Frederick R. Hipp	President, CEO	Number of Shares Outstanding	9,998,012
William W. Moreton	Exec VP, CFO	Market Capitalization	$ 58,188,430
Henry C. Miller	Senior VP	Frequency Of Dividends	n.a.
Andrew C. Gunkler	Senior VP	Number of Shareholders	50
Mark T. Walker	Vice President		

Other Information			
Transfer Agent	UMB Bank	Where Listed	BE
Auditor	Deloitte & Touche LLP	Symbol	HOUL
Market Maker	Donaldson, Lufkin & Jenrette	Telephone (415)249-2100	SIC Code	5812
Broker Dealer	Regular Stockbroker	Employees	8329

Hunter Manufacturing Corp.

P.O. Box 529 • Gurnee, IL 60031 • Telephone (847)855-9000 • Fax (800)323-8320

Company Description

The Company conducts its primary business through its wholly owned subsidiary, Tablecraft Products Co., Inc. Tablecraft is a national distributor of kitchen and tabletop supplies for restaurants. The Company went public in 1961, but has been regularly repurchasing shares in recent years.

	12/31/95	12/31/94	12/31/93
Per Share Information			
Stock Price	2.50	2.25	2.50
Earnings Per Share	1.75	2.21	0.78
Price / Earnings Ratio	1.43	1.02	3.21
Book Value Per Share	16.07	14.28	12.06
Price / Book Value %	15.56	15.76	20.73
Dividends Per Share	n.a.	n.a.	n.a.
Annual Financial Data			
Operating Results (000's)			
Total Revenues	12,187.5	11,487.0	10,830.5
Costs & Expenses	-11,310.0	-10,439.4	-10,387.8
Income Before Taxes and Other	876.3	1,047.5	441.8
Other Items	n.a.	n.a.	-38.0
Income Tax	-365.6	-402.3	-175.6
Net Income	510.8	645.3	228.3
Cash Flow From Operations	615.0	891.5	381.6
Balance Sheet (000's)			
Cash & Equivalents	n.a.	543.4	699.1
Total Current Assets	5,033.1	4,594.7	4,534.3
Fixed Assets, Net	810.6	811.7	876.3
Total Assets	5,888.1	5,444.8	5,410.6
Total Current Liabilities	1,183.0	1,286.7	1,897.8
Long-Term Debt	n.a.	n.a.	n.a.
Stockholders' Equity	4,680.0	4,158.0	3,512.8
Performance & Financial Condition			
Return on Total Revenues %	4.19	5.62	2.11
Return on Avg Stockholders' Equity %	11.56	16.82	6.72
Return on Average Assets %	9.01	11.89	4.57
Current Ratio	4.25	3.57	2.39
Debt / Equity %	n.a.	n.a.	n.a.

Compound Growth %'s	EPS %	49.79	Net Income %	49.59	Total Revenues %	6.08

Comments

1994 and 1993 results do not reflect positive prior period adjustments of $193,630 and $162,870, respectively. These are shown as increases to retained earnings without being reported on the income statement. It was reported to us that the Company has little competition in its marketplace. There is no long term debt and a very favorable current ratio is maintained. Compounded growth rates may be misleading because they are computed with only three years of data. However, sales in 1989 were $8,077,292. Therefore, the five year compound revenue growth rate from 1989 to 1994 is 7.25%. There is a buy-sell agreement among certain stockholders whereby the Company must purchase all of a deceased stockholder's stock at an agreed price. The Company has life insurance to fund such purchase.

Officers	Position	Ownership Information	12/31/95
Dalton Davis	President, CEO	Number of Shares Outstanding	291,281
		Market Capitalization	$ 728,203
		Frequency Of Dividends	Quarterly
		Number of Shareholders	Under 500

Other Information			
Transfer Agent	Chemical Mellon Shareholder Services	Where Listed	OTC-BB
Auditor	Klayman & Korman	Symbol	HUNM
Market Maker	Wachtel & Co., Inc. Telephone (202)898-1144	SIC Code	3089
Broker Dealer	Regular Stockbroker	Employees	50

Hydraulic Press Brick Company

705 Olive Street • St. Louis, MO 63101-2234 • Telephone (314)621-9306 • Fax (314)621-2795

Company Description

The Company is a producer and supplier of Haydite (a light weight aggregate produced from shale) which is used principally in the construction industry in components of walls, floors and structural elements. A significant portion is delivered to construction companies in the midwestern United States. Last year, 11% of sales were attributable to one customer. The Company was founded in 1928 and built its Cleveland plant the same year. In 1958, the Company purchased the Brooklyn, Indiana plant.

	09/30/95	09/30/94	09/30/93	09/30/92
Per Share Information				
Stock Price	15.87	8.25	6.37	5.00
Earnings Per Share	3.84	2.57	0.80	1.35
Price / Earnings Ratio	4.13	3.21	7.96	3.70
Book Value Per Share	20.07	16.78	14.53	13.92
Price / Book Value %	79.07	49.17	43.84	35.92
Dividends Per Share	0.55	0.32	0.20	0.20
Annual Financial Data				
Operating Results (000's)				
Total Revenues	9,993.0	8,674.0	7,262.0	7,444.0
Costs & Expenses	-8,147.0	-7,514.0	-6,871.0	-6,935.0
Income Before Taxes and Other	1,756.0	1,160.0	391.0	509.0
Other Items	n.a.	n.a.	n.a.	n.a.
Income Tax	-612.0	-394.0	-151.0	-130.0
Net Income	1,144.0	766.0	240.0	379.0
Cash Flow From Operations	1,107.0	1,429.0	712.0	988.0
Balance Sheet (000's)				
Cash & Equivalents	537.0	1,760.0	839.0	759.0
Total Current Assets	4,093.0	3,570.0	2,858.0	2,700.0
Fixed Assets, Net	3,188.0	2,475.0	2,429.0	2,252.0
Total Assets	7,293.0	6,047.0	5,323.0	5,030.0
Total Current Liabilities	1,045.0	844.0	761.0	709.0
Long-Term Debt	n.a.	6.0	58.0	109.0
Stockholders' Equity	5,978.0	4,998.0	4,331.0	4,151.0
Performance & Financial Condition				
Return on Total Revenues %	11.45	8.83	3.30	5.09
Return on Avg Stockholders' Equity %	20.85	16.42	5.66	9.50
Return on Average Assets %	17.15	13.47	4.64	7.71
Current Ratio	3.92	4.23	3.76	3.81
Debt / Equity %	n.a.	0.12	1.34	2.63

Compound Growth %'s	EPS %	41.69	Net Income %	44.52	Total Revenues %	10.31

Comments

Strong growth and balance sheet are noted. Management only reports its intention to make considerable capital improvements and replacements during the current year.

Officers	Position	Ownership Information	09/30/95
Christian B. Peper, Jr.	Chairman	Number of Shares Outstanding	297,938
W W. Allen, Jr.	President	Market Capitalization	$ 4,728,276
Donna Stewart	Secretary	Frequency Of Dividends	Quarterly
David Charlton	Treasurer	Number of Shareholders	Under 500
R N. Stewart	Vice President, Controller		

Other Information

Transfer Agent	KeyCorp Shareholder Services, Inc.			Where Listed	OTC-BB
Auditor	Kerber, Eck & Braeckel LLP			Symbol	HPRS
Market Maker	Burns, Pauli & Co., Inc.	Telephone	(800)325-3373	SIC Code	3251
Broker Dealer	Pink sheet specialist			Employees	100

Hytek Microsystems, Inc.

400 Hot Springs Road • Carson City, NV 89703 • Telephone (702)883-0820 • Fax (702)883-0827

Company Description

The Company designs, manufactures and sells custom and standard thick film hybrid microcircuits. Products manufactured by the Company are sold primarily to original equipment manufacturers serving the computer, telecommunications, military, medical, industrial electronics, and automatic test equipment markets. Approximately 88% of the Company's revenues are derived from products designed to meet a particular customers' need. The Company was incorporated in California in 1974.

	12/30/95	12/31/94	12/31/93	12/26/92
Per Share Information				
Stock Price	2.38	0.13	0.22	0.38
Earnings Per Share	0.18	n.a.	-0.09	0.05
Price / Earnings Ratio	13.22	n.a.	n.a.	7.60
Book Value Per Share	0.50	0.31	0.31	0.39
Price / Book Value %	476.00	41.94	70.97	97.44
Dividends Per Share	n.a.	n.a.	n.a.	n.a.
Annual Financial Data				
Operating Results (000's)				
Total Revenues	5,412.3	4,163.4	3,526.7	3,436.3
Costs & Expenses	-4,891.2	-4,161.4	-3,765.6	-3,293.3
Income Before Taxes and Other	521.0	2.0	-238.9	143.0
Other Items	n.a.	n.a.	n.a.	n.a.
Income Tax	n.a.	n.a.	n.a.	n.a.
Net Income	521.0	2.0	-238.9	143.0
Cash Flow From Operations	-250.9	181.1	-336.2	318.6
Balance Sheet (000's)				
Cash & Equivalents	93.0	383.6	215.4	593.0
Total Current Assets	2,544.2	1,380.9	1,522.2	1,358.5
Fixed Assets, Net	101.4	70.2	124.1	177.2
Total Assets	2,645.6	1,457.1	1,664.0	1,565.1
Total Current Liabilities	1,248.2	608.3	817.2	479.4
Long-Term Debt	n.a.	n.a.	n.a.	n.a.
Stockholders' Equity	1,397.4	848.8	846.8	1,085.8
Performance & Financial Condition				
Return on Total Revenues %	9.63	0.05	-6.78	4.16
Return on Avg Stockholders' Equity %	46.39	0.23	-24.73	14.10
Return on Average Assets %	25.40	0.13	-14.80	9.50
Current Ratio	2.04	2.27	1.86	2.83
Debt / Equity %	n.a.	n.a.	n.a.	n.a.

Compound Growth %'s	EPS % 53.26	Net Income % 53.88	Total Revenues % 16.35

Comments

During 1995, approximately 70% of the Company's revenues were from private sector programs. This differs significantly from 1994, when over 80% of revenues were derived from government related programs. Reductions in defense spending have reduced the amount of opportunities available. Reducing its reliance on government programs should have a positive long-term effect on the Company.

Officers	Position	Ownership Information	12/30/95
Charles S. Byrne	President, CEO	Number of Shares Outstanding	2,811,425
Jonathan B. Presnell	Vice President, General Manager	Market Capitalization	$ 6,691,192
		Frequency Of Dividends	n.a.
		Number of Shareholders	244

Other Information			
Transfer Agent	U.S. Stock Transfer Corporation	Where Listed	OTC-BB
Auditor	Ernst & Young LLP	Symbol	HTEK
Market Maker	Paragon Capital Corporation	Telephone (800)521-8877	SIC Code	3674
Broker Dealer	Regular Stockbroker	Employees	63

IEA Income Fund XI, L.P.

444 Market Street, 15th Floor • San Francisco, CA 94111 • Telephone (415)677-8990 • Fax (415)677-9196

Company Description

The Partnership owns and leases, through a leasing and management agent, marine dry cargo containers as well as marine refrigerated cargo containers. The Partnership was formed in 1990 as a limited partnership and raised $40 million during a private placement. Cronos Capital Corp. (CCC) is the general partner. The officers listed are officers and employees of CCC.

	12/31/95	12/31/94	12/31/93	12/31/92
Per Unit Information				
Price Per Unit	14.22	15.56	16.80	14.48
Earnings Per Unit	1.25	1.16	1.24	1.74
Price / Earnings Ratio	11.38	13.41	13.55	8.32
Book Value Per Unit	14.94	15.89	16.76	18.33
Price / Book Value %	95.18	97.92	100.24	79.00
Distributions Per Unit	2.22	2.04	2.23	2.29
Cash Flow Per Unit	2.66	2.29	2.57	2.92
Annual Financial Data				
Operating Results (000's)				
Total Revenues	5,065.4	4,913.9	5,014.9	6,042.6
Costs & Expenses	-2,307.4	-2,338.2	-2,328.4	-2,352.8
Operating Income	2,758.0	2,575.7	2,686.5	3,689.8
Other Items	n.a.	n.a.	n.a.	n.a.
Net Income	2,758.0	2,575.7	2,686.5	3,689.8
Cash Flow From Operations	5,329.0	4,573.5	5,129.6	5,847.6
Balance Sheet (000's)				
Cash & Equivalents	299.4	258.1	474.0	289.9
Total Current Assets	2,994.6	2,847.1	2,650.5	3,537.2
Investments In Containers	26,879.7	29,053.2	31,178.3	33,274.7
Total Assets	30,040.6	32,207.2	34,276.4	37,400.1
Total Current Liabilities	182.1	423.0	770.0	1,878.9
Long-Term Debt	n.a.	n.a.	n.a.	n.a.
Partners' Capital	29,858.5	31,784.2	33,506.4	35,521.2
Performance & Financial Condition				
Return on Total Revenues %	54.45	52.42	53.57	61.06
Return on Average Partners' Capital %	8.95	7.89	7.78	10.22
Return on Average Assets %	8.86	7.75	7.50	9.97
Current Ratio	16.44	6.73	3.44	1.88
Debt / Equity %	n.a.	n.a.	n.a.	n.a.

Compound Growth %'s	EPU %	-10.44	Net Income %	-9.25	Total Revenues %	-5.71

Comments

Cash flow and distributions have been consistent. The ultimate resale value and useful lives of the property may eventually produce a windfall if the property is well managed. The broker/dealer circulates a listing of units available for purchase to those on their mailing list. All potential buyers are simultaneously linked to an auction conference call at which a broker/dealer acts on your behalf in accordance with your instructions. You have the opportunity to raise the bid at any time.

Officers	Position	Ownership Information	12/31/95
Dennis J. Tietz	President, CEO	Number of Shares Outstanding	1,999,812
John Kallas	Treasurer, CFO	Market Capitalization	$ 28,437,327
Elinor Wexler	Vice President, Secretary	Frequency Of Distributions	Quarterly
John P. McDonald	VP - Sales	Number of Partners	3,288

Other Information						
Transfer Agent	Company Office				Where Listed	Order Matching Only
Auditor	Arthur Andersen LLP				Symbol	n.a.
Market Maker	None				SIC Code	4400
Broker Dealer	Chicago Partnership Board	Tel/Ext	(800)272-6273	690	Employees	n.a.

Image Systems Corporation

11595 K-Tel Drive • Hopkins, MN 55343 • Telephone (612)935-1171 • Fax (612)935-1386

Company Description

The Company designs, assembles and markets large, high resolution computer monitors. The sophisticated technology is targeted for medical, military, document imaging, air traffic control, simulation and other custom monitor markets. The Company was incorporated in Minnesota in 1988.

	04/30/95	04/30/94	04/30/93	04/30/92
Per Share Information				
Stock Price	2.81	2.19	2.44	1.28
Earnings Per Share	0.08	0.05	0.05	-0.05
Price / Earnings Ratio	35.13	43.80	48.80	n.a.
Book Value Per Share	0.36	0.28	0.23	0.18
Price / Book Value %	780.56	782.14	1,060.90	711.11
Dividends Per Share	n.a.	n.a.	n.a.	n.a.
Annual Financial Data				
Operating Results (000's)				
Total Revenues	5,026.9	4,023.3	3,039.7	1,466.3
Costs & Expenses	-4,456.7	-3,762.2	-2,830.8	-1,663.4
Income Before Taxes and Other	570.2	261.1	208.9	-197.0
Other Items	n.a.	n.a.	n.a.	n.a.
Income Tax	-208.0	-52.0	n.a.	n.a.
Net Income	362.2	209.1	208.9	-197.0
Cash Flow From Operations	74.3	14.6	-13.6	-477.6
Balance Sheet (000's)				
Cash & Equivalents	46.1	63.4	77.9	136.8
Total Current Assets	2,150.5	1,638.9	1,278.1	886.9
Fixed Assets, Net	146.8	124.9	102.0	44.0
Total Assets	2,297.2	1,763.8	1,380.1	930.9
Total Current Liabilities	719.9	545.4	361.2	150.5
Long-Term Debt	9.2	20.0	29.5	n.a.
Stockholders' Equity	1,568.2	1,198.5	989.4	780.5
Performance & Financial Condition				
Return on Total Revenues %	7.21	5.20	6.87	-13.44
Return on Avg Stockholders' Equity %	26.19	19.11	23.61	-24.41
Return on Average Assets %	17.84	13.30	18.08	-21.16
Current Ratio	2.99	3.01	3.54	5.89
Debt / Equity %	0.59	1.67	2.98	n.a.

Compound Growth %'s	EPS %	26.49	Net Income %	31.67	Total Revenues %	50.78

Comments

For the nine months ended January 31, 1996, the Company had total revenues of $5.1 million and net income of $544,000 ($.13 per share) as compared to $3.5 million and $177,000 ($.04 per share) for the same period in fiscal 1994/1995.

Officers	Position	Ownership Information	04/30/95
Dean Scheff	President	Number of Shares Outstanding	4,333,222
David Sorensen	COO	Market Capitalization	$ 12,176,354
Diana Scheff	Secretary	Frequency Of Dividends	n.a.
Marta S. Volbrecht	VP - Sales	Number of Shareholders	498
Laura Sorensen	General Manager		

Other Information

Transfer Agent	Securities Transfer Corporation		Where Listed	OTC-BB
Auditor	Arthur Andersen LLP		Symbol	IMGS
Market Maker	Paragon Capital Corporation	Telephone (800)521-8877	SIC Code	3577
Broker Dealer	Regular Stockbroker		Employees	33

Immudyne, Inc.

P.O. Box 51507 • Palo Alto, CA 94303-0707 • Telephone (415)949-3864 • Fax (415)949-3961

Company Description

The Company manufactures and markets certain natural water soluble immunostimulants for pharmaceutical, veterinary and agricultural use, based on their ability to stimulate and activate immune systems. The Company also produces a water insoluble skin revitalizing agent for cosmetic use. The Company was incorporated in 1986 and was in a developmental stage until 1990, at which time its main activity became producing and selling products.

	08/31/95	08/31/94	08/31/93	08/31/92
Per Share Information				
Stock Price	1.25	0.49	0.75	0.25
Earnings Per Share	0.15	0.01	0.04	-0.01
Price / Earnings Ratio	8.33	49.00	18.75	n.a.
Book Value Per Share	0.20	0.04	0.02	-0.04
Price / Book Value %	625.00	1,225.00	3,750.00	n.a.
Dividends Per Share	n.a.	n.a.	n.a.	n.a.
Annual Financial Data				
Operating Results (000's)				
Total Revenues	7,037.0	3,089.8	2,284.0	1,129.2
Costs & Expenses	-3,073.4	-3,218.7	-1,402.3	-1,067.2
Income Before Taxes and Other	3,734.1	-456.0	607.7	-151.8
Other Items	n.a.	n.a.	n.a.	n.a.
Income Tax	-1,061.1	154.3	n.a.	n.a.
Net Income	2,673.0	-301.7	607.7	-151.8
Cash Flow From Operations	-257.0	-338.7	232.9	-65.9
Balance Sheet (000's)				
Cash & Equivalents	154.3	373.0	219.3	3.8
Total Current Assets	1,238.8	778.2	710.1	144.3
Fixed Assets, Net	87.6	348.7	28.0	38.6
Total Assets	6,336.7	1,870.8	1,107.1	460.3
Total Current Liabilities	1,835.7	1,097.4	837.1	1,108.4
Long-Term Debt	n.a.	118.2	n.a.	n.a.
Stockholders' Equity	3,500.9	655.3	270.0	-648.0
Performance & Financial Condition				
Return on Total Revenues %	37.99	-9.76	26.60	-13.44
Return on Avg Stockholders' Equity %	128.63	-65.21	n.a.	n.a.
Return on Average Assets %	65.14	-20.26	77.54	-32.90
Current Ratio	0.67	0.71	0.85	0.13
Debt / Equity %	n.a.	18.04	n.a.	n.a.

Compound Growth %'s	EPS %	93.65	Net Income %	109.74	Total Revenues %	84.02

Comments

1995 results include a $4 million gain on the sale of a subsidiary's assets and licensing rights. A downpayment of $250,000 was received and the balance is reflected as a note receivable. The Company has had to defend its patents and has been successful in seven patent cases. 1995 results reflect income of $716,666 from the settlement of law suits.

Officers	Position	Ownership Information	08/31/95
James D. Wood	President, CEO	Number of Shares Outstanding	17,340,013
L. Melvin Cooper	VP - Finance, CFO	Market Capitalization	$ 21,675,016
Byron A. Donzis	Vice President	Frequency Of Dividends	n.a.
Martha H. Gibson	Vice President, Treasurer	Number of Shareholders	Under 500

Other Information				
Transfer Agent	The R-M Trust Company, Vancouver, B.C.		Where Listed	OTC-BB
Auditor	Snyder, MacAllister,Gonzales		Symbol	IMMD
Market Maker	Wien Securities Corp.	Telephone (800)624-0050	SIC Code	5122
Broker Dealer	Regular Stockbroker		Employees	20

Indiana Natural Gas Corporation

P.O. Box 450 • Paoli, IN 47454-0450 • Telephone (812)723-2151 • Fax (812)723-2188

Company Description

The Company distributes natural gas to residential, commercial and industrial customers in and around Paoli and Nashville, Indiana. In August, 1995, the Company offered to buy back up to 5,000 shares for $55 per share.

	08/31/95	08/31/94	08/31/93	08/31/92
Per Share Information				
Stock Price	55.00	27.00	27.00	27.00
Earnings Per Share	4.77	4.98	5.49	4.74
Price / Earnings Ratio	11.53	5.42	4.92	5.70
Book Value Per Share	61.38	57.06	42.24	38.01
Price / Book Value %	89.61	47.32	63.92	71.03
Dividends Per Share	1.60	1.60	1.25	1.20
Annual Financial Data				
Operating Results (000's)				
Total Revenues	4,930.6	6,346.8	5,258.4	3,839.2
Costs & Expenses	-4,219.0	-5,455.4	-4,420.4	-3,124.9
Income Before Taxes and Other	708.1	850.7	831.8	703.5
Other Items	n.a.	n.a.	n.a.	n.a.
Income Tax	-303.6	-428.1	-356.2	-292.4
Net Income	404.5	422.6	475.6	411.1
Cash Flow From Operations	1,024.0	1,335.5	977.0	131.0
Balance Sheet (000's)				
Cash & Equivalents	318.8	373.7	51.4	10.8
Total Current Assets	643.5	704.0	300.5	331.1
Fixed Assets, Net	5,189.4	4,534.2	4,220.4	3,683.8
Total Assets	5,854.3	5,279.2	4,601.2	4,112.5
Total Current Liabilities	1,316.1	1,078.1	734.7	625.7
Long-Term Debt	n.a.	n.a.	n.a.	n.a.
Stockholders' Equity	4,182.5	3,888.3	3,662.3	3,295.1
Performance & Financial Condition				
Return on Total Revenues %	8.20	6.66	9.04	10.71
Return on Avg Stockholders' Equity %	10.02	11.19	13.67	11.11
Return on Average Assets %	7.27	8.55	10.92	10.06
Current Ratio	0.49	0.65	0.41	0.53
Debt / Equity %	n.a.	n.a.	n.a.	n.a.

Compound Growth %'s	EPS %	0.21	Net Income %	-0.54	Total Revenues %	8.70

Comments

The Company grew from 4,439 customers in 1985 to 6,455 customers in 1995. This is partly attributable to expansion into new territories. There is no long term debt.

Officers	Position	Ownership Information	08/31/95
Not Available		Number of Shares Outstanding	68,141
		Market Capitalization	$ 3,747,755
		Frequency Of Dividends	Quarterly
		Number of Shareholders	Under 500

Other Information

Transfer Agent	American Fletcher Nat'l Bank & Trust Co.		Where Listed	OTC-BB
Auditor	London Witte Group LLP		Symbol	INNG
Market Maker	Smith, Moore & Co.	Telephone (314)421-5225	SIC Code	1320
Broker Dealer	Regular Stockbroker		Employees	18

Industrial Services of America, Inc.

7100 Grade Lane, Building 4 • Louisville, KY 40232 • Telephone (502)368-1661 • Fax (502)363-3756

Company Description

The Company is an integrated solid waste management company engaged in the business of retail and industrial waste management and waste handling equipment sales and service. Customers are located throughout the U.S. and Canada. The Company was incorporated in Florida in 1953.

	12/31/95	12/31/94	12/31/93	12/31/92
Per Share Information				
Stock Price	6.00	n.a.	n.a.	n.a.
Earnings Per Share	0.41	0.28	0.11	0.04
Price / Earnings Ratio	14.63	n.a.	n.a.	n.a.
Book Value Per Share	1.02	0.62	0.33	0.22
Price / Book Value %	588.24	n.a.	n.a.	n.a.
Dividends Per Share	n.a.	n.a.	n.a.	n.a.
Annual Financial Data				
Operating Results (000's)				
Total Revenues	30,604.1	23,998.8	23,390.0	3,570.8
Costs & Expenses	-29,266.4	-23,138.3	-22,995.8	-3,488.6
Income Before Taxes and Other	1,221.2	775.7	326.4	77.7
Other Items	n.a.	n.a.	9.1	18.3
Income Tax	-517.0	-286.3	-147.0	-28.0
Net Income	704.2	489.4	188.5	68.0
Cash Flow From Operations	1,351.0	125.1	663.9	799.4
Balance Sheet (000's)				
Cash & Equivalents	507.9	354.9	747.7	482.3
Total Current Assets	4,092.1	3,077.3	3,208.8	1,362.6
Fixed Assets, Net	1,961.4	941.3	541.0	315.9
Total Assets	6,209.4	4,093.4	3,869.9	1,841.3
Total Current Liabilities	4,007.3	2,993.9	3,262.2	1,443.8
Long-Term Debt	367.4	13.2	28.9	11.6
Stockholders' Equity	1,768.0	1,063.8	574.4	385.9
Performance & Financial Condition				
Return on Total Revenues %	2.30	2.04	0.81	1.90
Return on Avg Stockholders' Equity %	49.73	59.75	39.26	19.10
Return on Average Assets %	13.67	12.29	6.60	4.78
Current Ratio	1.02	1.03	0.98	0.94
Debt / Equity %	20.78	1.24	5.04	3.01

Compound Growth %'s	EPS %	117.22	Net Income %	117.98	Total Revenues %	104.65

Comments

Officers and directors, as a group, owned 66.6% of the Company's outstanding common stock on March 25, 1996. Prior to 1995, there was only limited trading in the Company's stock with no reliable price quotations.

Officers	Position	Ownership Information	12/31/95
Harry Kletter	President, CEO	Number of Shares Outstanding	1,729,600
Matthew Kletter	Secretary	Market Capitalization	$ 10,377,600
Roberta Kletter	Vice President	Frequency Of Dividends	n.a.
		Number of Shareholders	438

Other Information			
Transfer Agent	American Securities Transfer, Inc.	Where Listed	OTC-BB
Auditor	Mather, Hamilton & Co.	Symbol	IDSA
Market Maker	Heidtke & Company	Telephone (800)737-9777	SIC Code	4953
Broker Dealer	Regular Stockbroker	Employees	78

Information Analysis Incorporated

2222 Gallows Rd., Suite 300 • Dunn Loring, VA 22027 • Telephone (703)641-0955 • Fax (703)641-0206

Company Description

The activities of the Company and its subsidiary, DHD Systems, Inc., are primarily related to software applications development, hardware and software consulting services, software sales and support services. Software sales are limited to a few products for which the Company has a particular market niche. The Company has been engaged in various facets of the computer and information field since its incorporation in Virginia in 1979.

	12/31/95	12/31/94	12/31/93	12/31/92
Per Share Information				
Stock Price	4.00	4.00	4.75	4.75
Earnings Per Share	-0.15	-0.12	0.13	0.42
Price / Earnings Ratio	n.a.	n.a.	36.54	11.31
Book Value Per Share	4.13	4.29	4.41	4.29
Price / Book Value %	96.85	93.24	107.71	110.72
Dividends Per Share	n.a.	n.a.	n.a.	n.a.
Annual Financial Data				
Operating Results (000's)				
Total Revenues	15,704.5	16,704.9	15,621.0	13,898.4
Costs & Expenses	-15,805.1	-16,789.9	-15,584.2	-13,536.1
Income Before Taxes and Other	-100.6	-85.0	36.8	362.4
Other Items	n.a.	n.a.	48.8	n.a.
Income Tax	26.0	26.3	-16.5	-139.6
Net Income	-74.6	-58.7	69.1	222.8
Cash Flow From Operations	990.5	-144.0	n.a.	n.a.
Balance Sheet (000's)				
Cash & Equivalents	57.0	35.2	24.0	361.3
Total Current Assets	3,661.3	4,382.8	4,378.6	4,415.2
Fixed Assets, Net	344.1	462.3	496.6	332.1
Total Assets	4,173.1	4,899.6	4,885.2	4,757.3
Total Current Liabilities	2,162.4	2,712.1	2,553.4	2,398.1
Long-Term Debt	58.9	78.8	55.7	18.3
Stockholders' Equity	1,932.9	2,088.1	2,235.1	2,237.2
Performance & Financial Condition				
Return on Total Revenues %	-0.48	-0.35	0.44	1.60
Return on Avg Stockholders' Equity %	-3.71	-2.72	3.09	10.25
Return on Average Assets %	-1.65	-1.20	1.43	5.30
Current Ratio	1.69	1.62	1.71	1.84
Debt / Equity %	3.05	3.77	2.49	0.82

Compound Growth %'s	EPS % n.a.	Net Income % n.a.	Total Revenues % 4.16

Comments

In 1995, over 70% of the Company's revenue was attributed to government clients. In March 1996, the Company was informed that it lost the contract that accounted for over 50% of the Company's revenue in 1995. As of December 31, 1995, officers and directors, as a group, owned 58.2% of the Company's outstanding shares.

Officers	Position	Ownership Information	12/31/95
Sandor Rosenberg	Chairman, President	Number of Shares Outstanding	467,053
Richard S. DeRose	Exec VP	Market Capitalization	$ 1,868,212
Brian R. Moore	Treasurer	Frequency Of Dividends	n.a.
		Number of Shareholders	108

Other Information

Transfer Agent	American Stock Transfer & Trust Company	Where Listed	OTC-BB
Auditor	Rubino & McGeehin	Symbol	IAIC
Market Maker	Wachtel & Co., Inc.	SIC Code	7379
Broker Dealer	Regular Stockbroker	Employees	101

Telephone (202)898-1018

Inmark Enterprises, Inc.

One Plaza Road • Greenvale, NY 11548 • Telephone (516)625-3500 • Fax (516)625-3575

Company Description

The Company was formed in 1992, as Health Image Media, Inc. ("HIM") with an initial public offering of common stock and warrants totalling $6.0 million. In 1993, HIM discontinued and spun off its initial operations and began looking for an acquisition. During September, 1995, HIM completed a merger with Inmark Enterprises, Inc.("Inmark"), whereby Inmark became a wholly owned subsidiary and HIM changed its name to Inmark Enterprises, Inc. The Company currently is a marketing and sales promotion organization which develops and implements customized trade promotion programs. Officers and directors, as a group, owned 26.3% of the Company's outstanding common shares at June 28, 1995.

	03/31/95	03/31/94	03/31/93
Per Share Information			
Stock Price	0.93	3.38	n.a.
Earnings Per Share	-0.15	-0.93	n.a.
Price / Earnings Ratio	n.a.	n.a.	n.a.
Book Value Per Share	0.68	0.51	n.a.
Price / Book Value %	136.76	662.75	n.a.
Dividends Per Share	n.a.	n.a.	n.a.
Annual Financial Data			
Operating Results (000's)			
Total Revenues	50.3	96.0	86.2
Costs & Expenses	-341.2	-1,785.5	-61.0
Income Before Taxes and Other	-290.8	-1,689.5	25.2
Other Items	n.a.	-189.7	-3,116.8
Income Tax	n.a.	n.a.	n.a.
Net Income	-290.8	-1,879.2	-3,091.6
Cash Flow From Operations	-315.9	-589.0	-3,114.8
Balance Sheet (000's)			
Cash & Equivalents	125.8	68.2	n.a.
Total Current Assets	1,399.6	1,055.6	n.a.
Fixed Assets, Net	n.a.	n.a.	n.a.
Total Assets	1,399.6	1,055.6	n.a.
Total Current Liabilities	93.4	73.3	n.a.
Long-Term Debt	n.a.	n.a.	n.a.
Stockholders' Equity	1,306.2	982.3	n.a.
Performance & Financial Condition			
Return on Total Revenues %	-577.68	n.a.	n.a.
Return on Avg Stockholders' Equity %	-25.42	n.a.	n.a.
Return on Average Assets %	-23.69	n.a.	n.a.
Current Ratio	14.99	14.40	n.a.
Debt / Equity %	n.a.	n.a.	n.a.

Compound Growth %'s	EPS % n.a.	Net Income % n.a.	Total Revenues % -23.59

Comments

Included in Other Items are losses on discontinued operations totalling $3.8 million for the years ended March 31, 1994 and 1993. For the nine months ended December 31, 1995, the Company had sales of $11.1 million and Net Income of $242,000 ($.17 per share). The stock at the end of this period was quoted at an average bid/ask price of $1.87 per share.

Officers	Position	Ownership Information	03/31/95
John P. Benfield	President	Number of Shares Outstanding	1,927,145
Donald A. Bernard	Exec VP, CFO	Market Capitalization	$ 1,792,245
Paul Aershadian	Exec VP	Frequency Of Dividends	n.a.
Susan March	Vice President	Number of Shareholders	56

Other Information

Transfer Agent	American Stock Transfer & Trust Company		Where Listed	OTC-BB
Auditor	KPMG Peat Marwick LLP		Symbol	IMKE
Market Maker	Troster Singer Corporation	Telephone (800)222-0890	SIC Code	6799
Broker Dealer	Regular Stockbroker		Employees	26

Interactive Gaming & Communications Corp.

595 Skippack Pike, Ste. 100 • Blue Bell, PA 19422 • Telephone (215)540-8185 • Fax (215)540-8176

Company Description

The Company, through its subsidiary located in Antigua, West Indies, is in the business of accepting, processing, and managing wagers/bets on the outcome of domestic and international sporting events. The Company operates under a gaming license obtained from the government of Antigua. Revenue is derived primarily from the spread between the various odds offered on each event. Customers of the Company wagered $47.8 million and $48.2 million in 1995 and 1994.

	12/31/95	12/31/94
Per Share Information		
Stock Price	1.44	2.75
Earnings Per Share	0.02	0.03
Price / Earnings Ratio	72.00	91.67
Book Value Per Share	0.03	n.a.
Price / Book Value %	4,800.00	n.a.
Dividends Per Share	n.a.	n.a.
Annual Financial Data		
Operating Results (000's)		
Total Revenues	2,627.3	2,733.0
Costs & Expenses	-2,417.6	-2,433.5
Income Before Taxes and Other	209.7	299.5
Other Items	n.a.	n.a.
Income Tax	n.a.	n.a.
Net Income	209.7	299.5
Cash Flow From Operations	767.4	448.0
Balance Sheet (000's)		
Cash & Equivalents	667.8	450.8
Total Current Assets	1,275.9	605.5
Fixed Assets, Net	205.4	181.5
Total Assets	1,931.9	804.0
Total Current Liabilities	1,628.0	752.3
Long-Term Debt	n.a.	n.a.
Stockholders' Equity	303.9	51.7
Performance & Financial Condition		
Return on Total Revenues %	7.98	10.96
Return on Avg Stockholders' Equity %	117.93	n.a.
Return on Average Assets %	15.33	n.a.
Current Ratio	0.78	0.80
Debt / Equity %	n.a.	n.a.

Compound Growth %'s	EPS %	-33.33	Net Income %	-29.98	Total Revenues %	-3.87

Comments

The Company was formed in 1994, as the result of a reorganization of another previously formed, inactive business. There are no results to report prior to 1994. In May, 1995, the Company began work with a software developer to produce and market a "Virtual Casino", where customers could play classic casino games on their personal computers with the Company managing the wagering. You can keep tract of the Company's progress at http://www.gamblenet.com/bet/.

Officers	Position	Ownership Information	12/31/95
Michael F. Simone	President, CEO	Number of Shares Outstanding	10,942,566
Rina Moscariello	Vice President, Secretary	Market Capitalization	$ 15,757,295
		Frequency Of Dividends	n.a.
		Number of Shareholders	600

Other Information				
Transfer Agent	Company Office		Where Listed	OTC-BB
Auditor	Parente,Randolph et. al.		Symbol	SBET
Market Maker	Paragon Capital Corp.	Telephone (800)345-0505	SIC Code	7941
Broker Dealer	Regular Stockbroker		Employees	20

International American Homes, Inc.

4640 Forbes Boulevard • Lanham, MA 20706 • Telephone (301)306-5306

Company Description

The Company designs, builds, and sells single family homes, primarily in middle income communities of suburban areas in Washington D.C. and Tampa, Florida. In 1990, the Company filed a voluntary bankruptcy petition and on August 12, 1992, the court approved a plan of reorganization. The plan called for cash distributions to creditors of approximately $4.7 million (50% of annual future cash flows through 1998) and distribution of approximately two million shares of the Company's common stock. At March 31, 1995, all but $260,000 of the cash payment had been made and all but 113,000 of the shares issued.

	03/31/95	03/31/94	03/31/93	08/12/92
Per Share Information				
Stock Price	0.88	1.55	0.30	0.55
Earnings Per Share	0.40	0.40	0.36	23.59
Price / Earnings Ratio	2.20	3.88	0.83	0.02
Book Value Per Share	2.02	1.62	1.23	0.87
Price / Book Value %	43.56	95.68	24.39	63.22
Dividends Per Share	n.a.	n.a.	n.a.	n.a.
Annual Financial Data				
Operating Results (000's)				
Total Revenues	51,225.0	35,633.0	20,762.0	12,550.0
Costs & Expenses	-50,066.0	-34,677.0	-19,858.0	-12,802.0
Income Before Taxes and Other	1,159.0	956.0	904.0	-252.0
Other Items	n.a.	n.a.	n.a.	16,303.0
Income Tax	-72.0	124.0	65.0	18.0
Net Income	1,087.0	1,080.0	969.0	16,069.0
Cash Flow From Operations	-2,981.0	3,883.0	403.0	7,007.0
Balance Sheet (000's)				
Cash & Equivalents	1,481.0	1,821.0	2,068.0	1,250.0
Total Current Assets	18,922.0	13,429.0	11,810.0	10,496.0
Fixed Assets, Net	106.0	120.0	99.0	85.0
Total Assets	27,688.0	25,395.0	28,082.0	34,090.0
Total Current Liabilities	14,632.0	11,435.0	10,881.0	14,915.0
Long-Term Debt	n.a.	n.a.	n.a.	n.a.
Stockholders' Equity	5,511.0	4,424.0	3,344.0	2,375.0
Performance & Financial Condition				
Return on Total Revenues %	2.12	3.03	4.67	128.04
Return on Avg Stockholders' Equity %	21.88	27.81	33.89	n.a.
Return on Average Assets %	4.10	4.04	3.12	38.48
Current Ratio	1.29	1.17	1.09	0.70
Debt / Equity %	n.a.	n.a.	n.a.	n.a.

Compound Growth %'s	EPS %	-74.31	Net Income %	-59.25	Total Revenues %	59.81

Comments

In conjunction with the reorganization, the Company adopted fresh start reporting whereby all assets and liabilities were restated to reflect their fair value at August 12, 1992 (the first period presented is for the five months beginning Apri 1, 1992). The Company's inventory of real estate for sale and the related indebtedness are included in Current Assets and Current Liabilities. For the nine months ended December 31, 1995, the Company had revenues of $43.0 million and net income of $817,000 ($.30 per share) as compared to $38.5 million and $1.1 million ($.42 per share) for the same period in 1994.

Officers	Position	Ownership Information	03/31/95
Robert J. Suarez	Chairman, President	Number of Shares Outstanding	2,724,395
Michael P. Villa	Treasurer, CFO	Market Capitalization	$ 2,397,468
Robert I. Antle	Vice President, Secretary	Frequency Of Dividends	n.a.
		Number of Shareholders	2,790

Other Information

			Where Listed	OTC-BB
Transfer Agent	First Fidelity Bancorp.		Symbol	IAHM
Auditor	Arthur Andersen LLP		SIC Code	1531
Market Maker	Paragon Capital Corporation	Telephone (800)521-8877	Employees	58
Broker Dealer	Regular Stockbroker			

International Speedway Corporation

1801 W. Intl. Speedway Blvd. • Daytona Beach, FL 32114 • Telephone (904)254-2700 • Fax (904)257-0281

Company Description

The Company and its subsidiaries produce and conduct motor sport activities at Daytona International Speedway, Talladega Superspeedway, Darlington Raceway, Tucson Raceway Park and Watkins Glen International. The Company conducts the food, beverage and souvenir operations through its American Service Corp. subsidiary and produces and syndicates race and race-related radio broadcasts through MRN radio. Major events are sanctioned by the leading racing associations.

	08/31/95	08/31/94	08/31/93	08/31/92
Per Share Information				
Stock Price	176.00	96.50	98.00	70.00
Earnings Per Share	8.01	6.37	5.59	5.11
Price / Earnings Ratio	21.97	15.15	17.53	13.70
Book Value Per Share	37.18	29.83	24.18	19.10
Price / Book Value %	473.37	323.50	405.29	366.49
Dividends Per Share	0.70	0.60	0.50	0.40
Annual Financial Data				
Operating Results (000's)				
Total Revenues	83,893.0	70,112.0	59,937.0	53,479.0
Costs & Expenses	-54,476.0	-46,884.0	-39,635.0	-35,073.0
Income Before Taxes and Other	29,417.0	23,228.0	20,302.0	18,406.0
Other Items	n.a.	n.a.	288.0	n.a.
Income Tax	-11,054.0	-8,662.0	-7,827.0	-6,712.0
Net Income	18,363.0	14,566.0	12,763.0	11,694.0
Cash Flow From Operations	27,696.0	22,659.0	18,574.0	16,113.0
Balance Sheet (000's)				
Cash & Equivalents	7,871.0	5,227.0	6,123.0	3,630.0
Total Current Assets	44,895.0	31,363.0	32,717.0	29,016.0
Fixed Assets, Net	70,299.0	58,579.0	42,681.0	35,389.0
Total Assets	119,571.0	96,401.0	78,487.0	67,540.0
Total Current Liabilities	24,074.0	19,524.0	16,361.0	15,715.0
Long-Term Debt	n.a.	n.a.	n.a.	2,300.0
Stockholders' Equity	85,247.0	68,277.0	55,236.0	43,638.0
Performance & Financial Condition				
Return on Total Revenues %	21.89	20.78	21.29	21.87
Return on Avg Stockholders' Equity %	23.92	23.59	25.82	30.50
Return on Average Assets %	17.00	16.66	17.48	18.58
Current Ratio	1.86	1.61	2.00	1.85
Debt / Equity %	n.a.	n.a.	n.a.	5.27

Compound Growth %'s	EPS %	16.16	Net Income %	16.23	Total Revenues %	16.19

Comments

A high level of liquidity is maintained to address inherent weather and insurance risks. The Company continues to invest in the improvement and expansion of its facilities. Over $20 million of improvements are currently in progress at Daytona International Speedway. This Company's impressive results are reflective of the increasing popularity of motor sports and the Company's dominant market share. The France family controls over 60% of the Company's outstanding common stock.

Officers	Position	Ownership Information	08/31/95
William C. France	Chairman, CEO	Number of Shares Outstanding	2,293,065
James C. France	President	Market Capitalization	$ 403,579,440
James H. Foster	Exec VP	Frequency Of Dividends	Annual
H. Lee Combs	VP - Finance, CFO	Number of Shareholders	1,373
Lesa D. Kennedy	Secretary, Treasurer		

Other Information

Transfer Agent	Sun Trust Bank		Where Listed	OTC-BB
Auditor	Ernst & Young LLP		Symbol	ISWY
Market Maker	Herzog, Heine, Geduld, Inc.	Telephone (212)962-0300	SIC Code	7948
Broker Dealer	Regular Stockbroker		Employees	320

Investment Properties Associates

60 East 42nd Street • New York, NY 10165 • Telephone (212)687-6400 • Fax (212)687-6437

Company Description

The partnership owns fourteen office buildings, one loft building and two unimproved real properties in metropolitan areas of Illinois, New York, New Jersey and Texas. One of the office buildings is vacant. The properties have a total rentable area of approximately 5,423,000 square feet. Leasing the properties to tenants is the only activity of the partnership. The limited partnership was formed in New York in 1969.

	12/31/95	12/31/94	12/31/93	12/31/92
Per Unit Information				
Price Per Unit	35.88	49.50	47.50	56.00
Earnings Per Unit	5.84	5.43	6.61	6.21
Price / Earnings Ratio	6.14	9.12	7.19	9.02
Book Value Per Unit	19.60	20.54	21.08	21.15
Price / Book Value %	183.06	240.99	225.33	264.78
Distributions Per Unit	6.35	6.40	6.69	6.63
Cash Flow Per Unit	13.65	14.13	19.30	20.13
Annual Financial Data				
Operating Results (000's)				
Total Revenues	53,988.4	52,807.9	55,719.3	58,008.8
Costs & Expenses	-44,272.6	-43,722.1	-45,954.5	-48,267.2
Operating Income	9,331.3	8,702.5	9,369.9	8,949.5
Other Items	n.a.	n.a.	n.a.	2.5
Net Income	9,331.3	8,702.5	9,369.9	8,951.9
Cash Flow From Operations	11,190.6	11,590.6	15,826.7	16,503.8
Balance Sheet (000's)				
Cash & Equivalents	3,090.4	4,138.9	2,403.1	3,075.1
Total Current Assets	10,782.3	11,585.3	9,754.9	10,849.7
Investments In Real Properties	44,279.0	43,939.2	44,807.6	47,053.0
Total Assets	55,061.3	55,524.6	54,562.4	57,902.6
Total Current Liabilities	28,517.4	24,860.2	26,174.6	25,028.0
Long-Term Debt	61,363.3	64,408.7	60,330.8	63,224.1
Partners' Capital	-34,819.4	-33,744.3	-31,943.0	-30,349.5
Performance & Financial Condition				
Return on Total Revenues %	17.28	16.48	16.82	15.43
Return on Average Partners' Capital %	n.a.	n.a.	n.a.	n.a.
Return on Average Assets %	16.88	15.81	16.66	15.10
Current Ratio	0.38	0.47	0.37	0.43
Debt / Equity %	n.a.	n.a.	n.a.	n.a.

Compound Growth %'s	EPU %	-2.03	Net Income %	1.39	Total Revenues %	-2.37

Comments

The Partnership has three types of partners: general partners, special limited partners and limited partners, who share in the distributable net income of the Partnership at 1.5%, 48.5%, and 50%, respectively. The general partners and special limited partners owned directly or beneficially approximately 45% of the limited partnership participation units at December 31, 1995.

Officers	Position	Ownership Information	12/31/95
Harry B. Helmsley	President	Number of Shares Outstanding	820,000
Irving Schneider	Exec VP	Market Capitalization	$ 29,421,600
		Frequency Of Distributions	Annual
		Number of Partners	648

Other Information

Transfer Agent	American Stock Transfer & Trust Company			Where Listed	OTC-BB
Auditor	Ernst & Young LLP			Symbol	IVPA
Market Maker	Chicago Corporation, The	Telephone	(312)855-7664	SIC Code	6530
Broker Dealer	Regular Stockbroker			Employees	175

Investors Heritage Life Insurance Company

200 Capital Avenue • Frankfort, KY 40602 • Telephone (502)223-2361 • Fax (502)227-7205

Company Description

The Company sells and administers various insurance and annuity products including participating, non-participating, whole life, limited pay, universal life, annuity contracts, credit life, credit accident and health and group insurance policies. The principal markets are in Kentucky, Virginia, North Carolina, South Carolina, Ohio, Indiana, Florida, Tennessee, Illinois, Kansas, West Virginia and Texas. The Company was incorporated in Kentucky in 1960.

	12/31/95	12/31/94	12/31/93	12/31/92
Per Share Information				
Stock Price	26.75	27.00	26.00	27.00
Earnings Per Share	1.02	2.66	2.54	1.00
Price / Earnings Ratio	26.23	10.15	10.24	27.00
Book Value Per Share	42.93	34.13	37.05	35.07
Price / Book Value %	62.31	79.11	70.18	76.99
Dividends Per Share	0.76	0.74	0.72	0.72
Annual Financial Data				
Operating Results (000's)				
Total Revenues	44,076.4	46,804.2	45,426.0	45,569.7
Costs & Expenses	-14,742.5	-18,162.3	-20,208.7	-19,145.5
Income Before Taxes and Other	884.6	2,792.0	2,448.0	1,092.6
Other Items	n.a.	n.a.	182.0	n.a.
Income Tax	32.0	-391.0	-328.0	-178.0
Net Income	916.6	2,401.0	2,302.0	914.6
Cash Flow From Operations	11,999.4	10,313.0	5,772.6	7,733.0
Balance Sheet (000's)				
Cash & Equivalents	2,377.0	2,309.8	3,042.1	1,757.1
Total Current Assets	10,894.2	17,245.8	27,786.4	9,692.1
Fixed Assets, Net	1,823.8	1,921.7	2,130.9	2,253.0
Total Assets	210,489.9	194,262.0	201,196.6	173,885.1
Total Current Liabilities	6,369.1	3,243.0	7,760.5	8,999.8
Long-Term Debt	n.a.	n.a.	n.a.	n.a.
Stockholders' Equity	38,660.0	30,768.4	33,539.0	31,886.2
Performance & Financial Condition				
Return on Total Revenues %	2.08	5.13	5.07	2.01
Return on Avg Stockholders' Equity %	2.64	7.47	7.04	2.88
Return on Average Assets %	0.45	1.21	1.23	0.54
Current Ratio	1.71	5.32	3.58	1.08
Debt / Equity %	n.a.	n.a.	n.a.	n.a.

Compound Growth %'s	EPS %	0.66	Net Income %	0.07	Total Revenues %	-1.10

Comments

Kentucky Investors, Inc. is an investment holding company which owns 73% of the Company's outstanding stock. Policy liabilities total $165.5 million comprised primarily of benefit reserves of $155.2 million. Investments total $161.3 million, consisting of fixed maturities ($137.4 million), mortgage loans ($13.1 million), policy loans ($6.9 million), equity securities ($2.6 million) and other items amounting to $1.4 million.

Officers	Position	Ownership Information	12/31/95
Harry L. Waterfield II	President, CEO	Number of Shares Outstanding	900,623
Wilma Yeary	Secretary	Market Capitalization	$ 24,091,665
Jane S. Jackson	Secretary	Frequency Of Dividends	Annual
Jimmy R. McIver	Treasurer	Number of Shareholders	2,941
Robert M. Hardy, Jr.	Vice President		

Other Information				
Transfer Agent	Company Office		Where Listed	OTC-BB
Auditor	Ernst & Young LLP		Symbol	INLF
Market Maker	Hilliard, Lyons, Inc.	Telephone (800)627-3557	SIC Code	6311
Broker Dealer	Regular Stockbroker		Employees	119

Investors Insurance Holding Corp.

200 Schulz Drive • Red Bank, NJ 07701 • Telephone (908)224-0500 • Fax (908)741-2266

Company Description

The Company specializes in the "excess and surplus lines", or non-admitted, segment of the insurance industry with the majority of gross written premium generated from this market segment. The Company was incorporated as a holding company in 1977 and Investors Insurance Company of America became its wholly owned subsidiary. Carlisle Insurance Company and Special Risk Insurance Company were acquired in 1993.

	12/31/95	12/31/94	12/31/93	12/31/92
Per Share Information				
Stock Price	12.62	11.25	11.00	8.75
Earnings Per Share	-1.69	1.00	-0.72	2.96
Price / Earnings Ratio	n.a.	11.25	n.a.	2.96
Book Value Per Share	15.53	15.41	16.40	16.51
Price / Book Value %	81.26	73.00	67.07	53.00
Dividends Per Share	n.a.	n.a.	n.a.	n.a.
Annual Financial Data				
Operating Results (000's)				
Total Revenues	69,058.0	54,298.0	61,646.0	41,431.0
Costs & Expenses	-53,489.0	-37,248.0	-53,499.0	-22,681.0
Income Before Taxes and Other	-7,667.0	4,647.0	-3,570.0	5,029.0
Other Items	n.a.	n.a.	n.a.	5,938.0
Income Tax	2,525.0	-1,638.0	1,312.0	-1,622.0
Net Income	-5,142.0	3,009.0	-2,258.0	9,345.0
Cash Flow From Operations	14,673.0	6,178.0	15,755.0	6,993.0
Balance Sheet (000's)				
Cash & Equivalents	4,899.0	3,418.0	1,849.0	2,177.0
Total Current Assets	143,872.0	120,168.0	123,750.0	106,220.0
Fixed Assets, Net	n.a.	n.a.	n.a.	n.a.
Total Assets	221,590.0	190,575.0	197,088.0	177,444.0
Total Current Liabilities	36,721.0	29,089.0	25,787.0	22,586.0
Long-Term Debt	n.a.	n.a.	n.a.	n.a.
Stockholders' Equity	47,550.0	46,309.0	49,376.0	52,112.0
Performance & Financial Condition				
Return on Total Revenues %	-7.45	5.54	-3.66	22.56
Return on Avg Stockholders' Equity %	-10.96	6.29	-4.45	19.71
Return on Average Assets %	-2.50	1.55	-1.21	5.50
Current Ratio	3.92	4.13	4.80	4.70
Debt / Equity %	n.a.	n.a.	n.a.	n.a.

Compound Growth %'s	EPS % n.a.	Net Income % n.a.	Total Revenues %	18.57

Comments

Gross premiums written grew from $20 million in 1991 to $60 million in 1995, a growth rate in excess of 30%.

Officers	Position	Ownership Information	12/31/95
Jeremy D. Cooke	President, CEO	Number of Shares Outstanding	3,061,287
Edward J. Ryan, Jr.	Vice President, Controller	Market Capitalization	$ 38,633,442
Rodney R. Ayer	Vice President	Frequency Of Dividends	n.a.
Douglas A. Hillman	Vice President	Number of Shareholders	99

Other Information

Transfer Agent	Chemical Mellon Shareholder Services			Where Listed	OTC-BB
Auditor	Deloitte & Touche LLP			Symbol	IIHC
Market Maker	Robotti & Eng, Incorporated	Telephone	(212)986-4800	SIC Code	6330
Broker Dealer	Regular Stockbroker			Employees	54

Iowa First Bancshares Corp.

300 E. Second Street • Muscatine, IA 52761 • Telephone (319)263-4221 • Fax (319)262-4213

Company Description

Iowa First Bancshares Corp. is a bank holding company providing bank and bank related services through its subsidiaries, First National Bank of Muscatine and First National Bank in Fairfield, both in Iowa.

	12/31/95	12/31/94	12/31/93	12/31/92
Per Share Information				
Stock Price	50.00	39.00	34.00	23.25
Earnings Per Share	5.11	4.90	5.21	3.92
Price / Earnings Ratio	9.78	7.96	6.53	5.93
Book Value Per Share	40.27	35.79	32.93	28.43
Price / Book Value %	124.16	108.97	103.25	81.78
Dividends Per Share	1.60	1.35	1.15	0.85
Annual Financial Data				
Operating Results (000's)				
Net Interest Income	9,891.0	9,703.0	9,519.0	8,985.0
Loan Loss Provision	-45.0	-65.0	-56.0	-278.0
Non-Interest Income	1,576.0	1,682.0	1,699.0	1,682.0
Non-Interest Expense	-6,877.0	-7,141.0	-7,175.0	-6,998.0
Income Before Taxes and Other	4,545.0	4,179.0	3,987.0	3,391.0
Other Items	n.a.	n.a.	300.0	n.a.
Income Tax	-1,495.0	-1,304.0	-1,319.0	-1,141.0
Net Income	3,050.0	2,875.0	2,968.0	2,250.0
Balance Sheet (000's)				
Cash & Securities	96,391.0	84,507.0	95,423.0	103,975.0
Loans, Net	169,342.0	162,015.0	154,706.0	139,234.0
Fixed Assets, Net	4,342.0	4,545.0	4,759.0	4,954.0
Total Assets	272,830.0	253,800.0	257,403.0	251,097.0
Deposits	235,953.0	229,023.0	233,413.0	227,546.0
Stockholders' Equity	23,033.0	20,672.0	18,748.0	16,279.0
Performance & Financial Condition				
Net Interest Margin	4.28	4.22	4.19	4.20
Return on Avg Stockholders' Equity %	13.96	14.59	16.95	14.55
Return on Average Assets %	1.16	1.12	1.17	0.93
Equity to Assets %	8.44	8.15	7.28	6.48
Reserve as a % of Non-Performing Loans	232.29	181.47	144.40	159.23

Compound Growth %'s	EPS %	9.24	Net Income %	10.67	Net Interest Income %	3.25

Comments

The Company has an ongoing program of purchasing treasury shares. During 1995, 6,680 shares were repurchased. The Company's employee stock ownership plan owns 4.4% of outstanding shares. Total annual investment return (change in stock price plus dividends) for the past one, three and five-year periods has been 32%, 34%, and 31%, respectively.

Officers	Position	Ownership Information	12/31/95
George A. Shepley	President, CEO	Number of Shares Outstanding	571,921
Kim L. Bartling	Senior VP, CFO	Market Capitalization	$ 30,000,000
Patricia R. Thirtyacre	Secretary	Frequency Of Dividends	Semi-Annual
Sandra K. Roenfeldt	Other	Number of Shareholders	n.a.
Teresa A. Carter	Other		

Other Information

Transfer Agent	First National Bank of Muscatine		Where Listed	OTC-BB
Auditor	McGladrey & Pullen, LLP		Symbol	IFST
Market Maker	Chicago Corporation, The	Telephone (312)855-7664	SIC Code	6020
Broker Dealer	Pink sheet specialist		Employees	135

Irex Corporation

120 North Lime Street • Lancaster, PA 17602 • Telephone (717)397-3633 • Fax (717)399-5325

Company Description

The Company is primarily in the business of thermal insulation contracting and the direct sale of insulation and acoustical materials throughout the U.S. and Canada. In 1995, 55% of revenues were the result of the contracting business with 45% attributable to product sales. At March 6, 1996, officers and directors owned 18.3% of the Company's common stock. The Company was incorporated in Pennsylvania in 1969.

	12/31/95	12/31/94	12/31/93	12/31/92
Per Share Information				
Stock Price	18.63	14.00	17.50	23.50
Earnings Per Share	2.01	3.11	-3.36	1.03
Price / Earnings Ratio	9.27	4.50	n.a.	22.82
Book Value Per Share	25.59	23.14	19.94	23.35
Price / Book Value %	72.80	60.50	87.76	100.64
Dividends Per Share	n.a.	n.a.	n.a.	1.50
Annual Financial Data				
Operating Results (000's)				
Total Revenues	244,532.0	240,704.0	237,708.0	229,099.0
Costs & Expenses	-243,700.0	-236,763.0	-238,088.0	-227,285.0
Income Before Taxes and Other	832.0	3,941.0	-380.0	1,814.0
Other Items	1,377.0	n.a.	n.a.	n.a.
Income Tax	-431.0	-1,714.0	-9.0	-788.0
Net Income	1,778.0	2,227.0	-389.0	1,026.0
Cash Flow From Operations	-454.0	2,770.0	-2,937.0	5,724.0
Balance Sheet (000's)				
Cash & Equivalents	411.0	1,564.0	1,068.0	3,783.0
Total Current Assets	78,317.0	78,695.0	76,484.0	70,268.0
Fixed Assets, Net	3,199.0	3,481.0	4,107.0	4,677.0
Total Assets	81,635.0	82,560.0	81,483.0	76,606.0
Total Current Liabilities	48,518.0	47,043.0	45,544.0	37,618.0
Long-Term Debt	12,543.0	15,800.0	17,414.0	18,935.0
Stockholders' Equity	10,078.0	9,221.0	8,029.0	9,557.0
Performance & Financial Condition				
Return on Total Revenues %	0.73	0.93	-0.16	0.45
Return on Avg Stockholders' Equity %	18.43	25.82	-4.42	6.89
Return on Average Assets %	2.17	2.72	-0.49	13.42
Current Ratio	1.61	1.67	1.68	1.87
Debt / Equity %	124.46	171.35	216.89	198.13

Compound Growth %'s	EPS %	24.96	Net Income %	20.11	Total Revenues %	2.20

Comments

In 1995, the Company changed its method of measuring its potential liability for certain self-insured business risks and reflected the cumulative effect as an increase in 1995 Net Income. The $1.4 million related to this change is included in Other Items. Dividends on the Company's redeemable preferred stock ($980,000 per year) are deducted from Net Income to calculate Earnings Per Share.

Officers	Position	Ownership Information	12/31/95
W. Kirk Liddell	President, CEO	Number of Shares Outstanding	393,857
Donald M. Coffin	Vice President	Market Capitalization	$ 7,337,556
James E. Hipolit	Vice President	Frequency Of Dividends	Irregular
Jane E. Pinkerton	Vice President, Secretary	Number of Shareholders	340
Terry L. Troupe	Vice President, CFO		

Other Information					
Transfer Agent	Company Office			Where Listed	OTC-BB
Auditor	Arthur Andersen LLP			Symbol	IREX
Market Maker	F.J. Morrissey & Co., Inc.	Telephone	(800)842-8928	SIC Code	1742
Broker Dealer	A.G. Edwards & Sons	Tel/Ext	(800)325-8197	Employees	67

JMB Income Properties LTD X

900 North Michigan Avenue • Chicago, IL 60611 • Telephone (312)915-1987 • Fax (312)915-1362

Company Description

The Partnership holds (either directly or through joint ventures) equity interests in U.S. real estate. Business activities consist of rentals to a wide variety of commercial and retail companies and the sale or disposition of the properties. The Partnership expects an orderly liquidation of its remaining properties by the end of 1999. The officers listed are those of the general partner, JMB Realty Corporation.

	12/31/95	12/31/94	12/31/93	12/31/92
Per Unit Information				
Price Per Unit	175.00	456.00	226.00	334.50
Earnings Per Unit	4.45	387.40	30.40	-26.85
Price / Earnings Ratio	39.33	1.18	7.43	n.a.
Book Value Per Unit	308.04	769.60	398.19	389.78
Price / Book Value %	56.81	59.25	56.76	85.82
Distributions Per Unit	466.00	16.00	22.00	40.00
Cash Flow Per Unit	30.49	737.75	23.07	49.11
Annual Financial Data				
Operating Results (000's)				
Total Revenues	19,780.5	94,939.9	33,745.5	28,737.5
Costs & Expenses	-13,962.0	-27,989.7	-28,999.3	-28,190.0
Operating Income	-3,481.5	58,516.1	4,746.1	-4,196.7
Other Items	3,934.5	n.a.	n.a.	n.a.
Net Income	453.1	58,516.1	4,746.1	-4,196.7
Cash Flow From Operations	34,156.4	110,665.8	3,461.0	7,366.7
Balance Sheet (000's)				
Cash & Equivalents	21,431.9	84,486.5	1,061.3	n.a.
Total Current Assets	22,719.4	87,945.9	5,135.3	n.a.
Investments In Real Estate	33,405.6	81,231.2	133,558.7	n.a.
Total Assets	56,832.7	170,327.3	140,905.6	n.a.
Total Current Liabilities	1,816.4	53,748.6	33,629.9	n.a.
Long-Term Debt	7,890.3	n.a.	46,801.0	n.a.
Partners' Capital	47,109.6	116,558.8	60,442.8	n.a.
Performance & Financial Condition				
Return on Total Revenues %	2.29	61.63	14.06	-14.60
Return on Average Partners' Capital %	n.a.	n.a.	n.a.	n.a.
Return on Average Assets %	0.40	37.60	n.a.	n.a.
Current Ratio	12.51	1.64	0.15	n.a.
Debt / Equity %	16.75	n.a.	77.43	n.a.

Compound Growth %'s	EPU %	-61.74	Net Income %	-69.10	Total Revenues %	-11.71

Comments

The Partnership has sold properties over the last few years and has made distributions to the partners from cash arising from leasing as well as from the sales. 1995 and 1994 results include writedowns of asset value of $9.3 million and $8.4 million, respectively, and gains on the sale of assets of $3.8 million and $64.6 million, respectively. Because of the property writedowns and property sales, the compounded growth rates are not meaningful. Cash flow from operations and cash flow per unit include proceeds from the sale of properties.

Officers	Position	Ownership Information	12/31/95
Judd D. Malkin	Chairman	Number of Shares Outstanding	150,005
Neil G. Bluhm	President	Market Capitalization	$ 26,250,875
H. Rigel Barber	CEO	Frequency Of Distributions	Quarterly
Glenn E. Emig	COO	Number of Partners	14,815
Stuart C. Nathan	Exec VP		

Other Information

Transfer Agent	Company Office			Where Listed	Order Matching Only
Auditor	KPMG Peat Marwick LLP			Symbol	n.a.
Market Maker	None			SIC Code	6500
Broker Dealer	Chicago Partnership Board	Tel/Ext	(800)272-6273 690	Employees	None

Jamaica Water Supply Company

410 Lakeville Road • Lake Success, NY 11042-1101 • Telephone (516)327-4000 • Fax (516)327-4130

Company Description

The Company provides water utility service to a population of approximately 650,000 in southeastern Queens County and southwestern Nassau County on Long Island. Approximately 53% of its water supply is produced from its own wells and the remainder is purchased from the city of New York. The Company was founded in 1887 and is the largest investor-owned water utility in New York State.

	12/31/95	12/31/94	12/31/93	12/31/92
Per Share Information				
Stock Price	74.00	64.00	63.75	58.00
Earnings Per Share	14.77	11.08	4.62	10.43
Price / Earnings Ratio	5.01	5.78	13.80	5.56
Book Value Per Share	114.47	105.50	97.41	92.78
Price / Book Value %	64.65	60.66	65.45	62.51
Dividends Per Share	5.80	2.99	n.a.	2.05
Annual Financial Data				
Operating Results (000's)				
Total Revenues	63,547.0	63,156.0	65,010.0	58,722.0
Costs & Expenses	-49,829.0	-52,420.0	-53,175.0	-48,738.0
Income Before Taxes and Other	13,718.0	10,550.0	4,685.0	9,984.0
Other Items	n.a.	n.a.	n.a.	n.a.
Income Tax	-4,559.0	-3,539.0	-1,460.0	-3,290.0
Net Income	9,159.0	7,011.0	3,225.0	6,694.0
Cash Flow From Operations	15,863.0	3,985.0	15,338.0	12,111.0
Balance Sheet (000's)				
Cash & Equivalents	962.0	2,245.0	9,480.0	n.a.
Total Current Assets	13,499.0	16,992.0	22,836.0	20,000.0
Fixed Assets, Net	144,795.0	138,526.0	135,016.0	131,890.0
Total Assets	171,315.0	167,248.0	171,620.0	155,995.0
Total Current Liabilities	30,303.0	31,552.0	32,373.0	33,000.0
Long-Term Debt	28,486.0	28,985.0	33,984.0	39,300.0
Stockholders' Equity	72,619.0	67,812.0	63,515.0	61,960.0
Performance & Financial Condition				
Return on Total Revenues %	14.41	11.10	4.96	11.40
Return on Avg Stockholders' Equity %	13.04	10.68	5.14	11.25
Return on Average Assets %	5.41	4.14	1.97	4.47
Current Ratio	0.45	0.54	0.71	0.61
Debt / Equity %	39.23	42.74	53.51	63.43

Compound Growth %'s	EPS %	12.30	Net Income %	11.02	Total Revenues %	2.67

Comments

1993 Net Income was adversely affected by a one-time charge of $7 million in settlement of a rate rebate to customers for earlier years. EMCOR Group, Inc., the Company's largest shareholder, consented to an involuntary bankruptcy proceeding. In that regard, it has agreed to the sale of the assets of Jamaica Water Supply Company to the various water authorities in the Company's jurisdiction. Management did not comment on this seemingly very important event. It appears that the assets are being sold for a price substantially above book value, although there is no indication of the costs involved if the Company were to liquidate.

Officers	Position	Ownership Information	12/31/95
Hampton D. Graham, Jr.	Chairman, CEO	Number of Shares Outstanding	593,331
David E. Chardavoyne	President, COO	Market Capitalization	$ 43,906,494
Jeanette Clonan	Vice President	Frequency Of Dividends	Quarterly
Michael J. Tierney	Controller	Number of Shareholders	Under 500

Other Information				
Transfer Agent	Registrar & Transfer Company		Where Listed	OTC-BB
Auditor	Deloitte & Touche LLP		Symbol	JWTS
Market Maker	Wechsler & Co., Inc.	Telephone (914)242-6000	SIC Code	4940
Broker Dealer	Pink sheet specialist		Employees	239

Jetstream LP

3 World Financial Center, 29FL • New York, NY 10285 • Telephone (212)526-3237 • Fax (212)582-9696

Company Description

The Partnership acquired and is leasing used commercial aircraft. The fleet consists of six aircraft, all of which are currently on-lease. The Partnership was formed in 1987 and is required to dissolve no later than the year 2027. It may reinvest proceeds from the sale of aircraft up until 1998. After that time, such proceeds must be distributed to the partners. The officers listed are those of the general partners, CIS Aircraft Partners, Inc. and Jet Aircraft Leasing, Inc.

	12/31/95	12/31/94	12/31/93	12/31/92
Per Unit Information				
Price Per Unit	2.21	2.50	3.95	2.95
Earnings Per Unit	-0.03	-0.16	-3.62	0.14
Price / Earnings Ratio	n.a.	n.a.	n.a.	21.07
Book Value Per Unit	3.74	4.63	5.80	10.23
Price / Book Value %	59.09	54.00	68.10	28.84
Distributions Per Unit	0.86	1.00	0.91	1.65
Cash Flow Per Unit	0.87	1.29	0.81	1.33
Annual Financial Data				
Operating Results (000's)				
Total Revenues	5,052.5	5,193.3	7,262.1	7,853.6
Costs & Expenses	-5,669.2	-5,977.2	-6,872.9	-7,181.5
Operating Income	-616.7	-784.0	-17,876.9	672.1
Other Items	n.a.	n.a.	n.a.	n.a.
Net Income	-616.7	-784.0	-17,876.9	672.1
Cash Flow From Operations	4,282.2	6,301.1	3,980.0	6,516.6
Balance Sheet (000's)				
Cash & Equivalents	3,474.4	2,785.3	1,089.8	n.a.
Total Current Assets	3,536.9	2,786.2	1,153.9	5,000.0
Investments In Aircraft	14,885.0	20,109.5	25,684.0	44,511.4
Total Assets	18,936.4	23,457.5	29,886.8	55,477.0
Total Current Liabilities	1,303.4	1,427.9	1,982.8	2,409.0
Long-Term Debt	n.a.	n.a.	n.a.	n.a.
Partners' Capital	17,493.0	21,939.6	27,674.0	50,068.0
Performance & Financial Condition				
Return on Total Revenues %	-12.21	-15.10	-246.17	8.56
Return on Average Partners' Capital %	n.a.	n.a.	n.a.	n.a.
Return on Average Assets %	-2.91	-2.94	-41.88	1.12
Current Ratio	2.71	1.95	0.58	2.08
Debt / Equity %	n.a.	n.a.	n.a.	n.a.

Compound Growth %'s	EPU %	n.a.	Net Income %	n.a.	Total Revenues %	-13.67

Comments

1993 results include a write-down of the value of aircraft, amounting to $18.3 million. The industry remains very competitive, especially with the older Stage 2 aircraft which the Partnership owns. Two of the aircraft are on-lease to TWA on a month-to-month basis. Management believes it may be hard to release these aircraft if they are returned. The residual values are not readily available.

Officers	Position	Ownership Information	12/31/95
Thomas J. Prinzing	Chairman	Number of Shares Outstanding	4,895,005
Moshe Braver	President	Market Capitalization	$ 10,817,961
Susan E. Weatherwax	Secretary	Frequency Of Distributions	Quarterly
John Stanley	Vice President, CFO	Number of Partners	7,482
Frank J. Corcoran	Vice President, Treasurer		

Other Information

Transfer Agent	Company Office				Where Listed	Order Matching Only
Auditor	Arthur Andersen & Co. LLP				Symbol	n.a.
Market Maker	None				SIC Code	7359
Broker Dealer	Chicago Partnership Board	Tel/Ext	(800)272-6273	690	Employees	None

Justiss Oil Co., Inc.

1810 E. Oak Street • Jena, LA 71342-1385 • Telephone (318)992-4111 • Fax (318)992-7201

Company Description

The Company explores for and extracts oil and gas from its own properties and in conjunction with certain working interests. There is also a tank manufacturing division, farming division, and warehousing operations division. The Company has been operated as a family company since inception in 1946.

	11/30/95	11/30/94	11/30/93
Per Share Information			
Stock Price	43.00	41.00	37.00
Earnings Per Share	-0.28	3.48	8.14
Price / Earnings Ratio	n.a.	11.78	4.55
Book Value Per Share	63.67	64.95	55.33
Price / Book Value %	67.54	63.13	66.87
Dividends Per Share	1.00	1.00	1.00
Annual Financial Data			
Operating Results (000's)			
Total Revenues	42,495.3	51,621.2	62,633.5
Costs & Expenses	-42,567.5	-48,524.7	-54,833.6
Income Before Taxes and Other	-72.2	3,096.5	7,799.9
Other Items	n.a.	n.a.	n.a.
Income Tax	-117.1	-745.8	-2,296.0
Net Income	-189.3	2,350.7	5,503.8
Cash Flow From Operations	n.a.	n.a.	n.a.
Balance Sheet (000's)			
Cash & Equivalents	2,757.4	2,051.2	n.a.
Total Current Assets	16,148.2	22,328.4	n.a.
Fixed Assets, Net	24,281.2	23,705.7	n.a.
Total Assets	49,095.9	58,666.5	n.a.
Total Current Liabilities	5,893.2	14,214.4	n.a.
Long-Term Debt	16.5	n.a.	n.a.
Stockholders' Equity	43,044.1	43,909.5	n.a.
Performance & Financial Condition			
Return on Total Revenues %	-0.45	4.55	8.79
Return on Avg Stockholders' Equity %	-0.44	n.a.	n.a.
Return on Average Assets %	-0.35	n.a.	n.a.
Current Ratio	2.74	1.57	n.a.
Debt / Equity %	0.04	n.a.	n.a.

Compound Growth %'s	EPS %	n.a.	Net Income %	n.a.	Total Revenues %	-17.63

Comments

The decline in revenue and profits is mostly attributable to the low price received by the industry for natural gas in 1995 and the Company's decision to reduce U.S. production. To counter this decline, the Company has expanded to the international scene with a new operation in eastern Venezuela and has further plans.

Officers		Position	Ownership Information	11/30/95
J F. Justiss, Jr.		Chairman, Exec VP	Number of Shares Outstanding	676,044
J F. Justiss, III		COO	Market Capitalization	$ 29,069,892
W B. McCartney, Jr.		Exec VP	Frequency Of Dividends	n.a.
R L. Wood		Secretary, Treasurer	Number of Shareholders	Under 500
R L. Reiner		VP - Manufacturing		

Other Information					
Transfer Agent	Company Office			Where Listed	OTC-BB
Auditor	None indicated			Symbol	JSTS
Market Maker	Boenning & Scattergood Inc.	Telephone	(610)832-1212	SIC Code	1300
Broker Dealer	Regular Stockbroker			Employees	350

This page left intentionally blank.

Kansas Bankers Surety Company

611 Kansas Avenue • Topeka, KS 66601-1654 • Telephone (913)234-2631 • Fax (913)234-2917

Company Description

The Company provides surety to banks and is pursuing an orderly expansion into states that it has not previously served. The Company was founded in 1909. The stock was split 2 for 1 in 1994. All per share amounts have been adjusted for comparability.

	12/31/95	12/31/94	12/31/93	12/31/92
Per Share Information				
Stock Price	20.50	20.00	20.00	20.00
Earnings Per Share	1.88	2.09	2.03	2.01
Price / Earnings Ratio	10.90	9.57	9.85	9.95
Book Value Per Share	13.37	11.98	10.39	8.72
Price / Book Value %	153.33	166.94	192.49	229.36
Dividends Per Share	0.50	0.47	0.37	n.a.
Annual Financial Data				
Operating Results (000's)				
Total Revenues	20,359.1	20,982.5	22,603.0	24,603.3
Costs & Expenses	-11,768.6	-11,559.6	-12,961.2	-14,994.7
Income Before Taxes and Other	8,590.5	9,422.9	9,641.9	9,608.5
Other Items	n.a.	n.a.	n.a.	n.a.
Income Tax	-2,582.2	-2,743.5	-3,133.2	-3,180.5
Net Income	6,008.2	6,679.5	6,508.6	6,428.1
Cash Flow From Operations	7,195.4	6,465.2	6,563.9	n.a.
Balance Sheet (000's)				
Cash & Equivalents	1,039.7	860.1	2,672.2	2,292.3
Total Current Assets	66,780.6	55,285.5	50,879.1	45,919.5
Fixed Assets, Net	54.6	50.2	44.4	37.3
Total Assets	66,835.2	62,507.4	59,243.5	53,748.7
Total Current Liabilities	24,028.6	24,109.0	26,004.5	15,659.9
Long-Term Debt	n.a.	n.a.	n.a.	n.a.
Stockholders' Equity	42,806.6	38,398.4	33,238.9	27,930.3
Performance & Financial Condition				
Return on Total Revenues %	29.51	31.83	28.80	26.13
Return on Avg Stockholders' Equity %	14.80	18.65	21.28	25.47
Return on Average Assets %	9.29	10.97	11.52	12.55
Current Ratio	2.78	2.29	1.96	2.93
Debt / Equity %	n.a.	n.a.	n.a.	n.a.

Compound Growth %'s	EPS %	-2.20	Net Income %	-2.23	Total Revenues %	-6.12

Comments

Shareholder's equity of $42.8 million is well in excess of the $20 million statutory requirement. This should facilitate the expansion program.

Officers	Position	Ownership Information	12/31/95
Donald M. Towle	President	Number of Shares Outstanding	3,200,000
David E. Abendroth	Senior VP	Market Capitalization	$ 65,600,000
Sheila R. Watkins	Secretary	Frequency Of Dividends	n.a.
Anderson W. Chandler	Treasurer	Number of Shareholders	Under 500
Charles M. Towle	Vice President		

Other Information

Transfer Agent	Company Office			Where Listed	OTC-BB
Auditor	Berberich Trahan & Co., P.A.			Symbol	KSAS
Market Maker	Monroe Securities, Inc.	Telephone	(800)766-5560	SIC Code	6350
Broker Dealer	Regular Stockbroker			Employees	n.a.

Keller Manufacturing Company, Inc.

P.O. Box 8 • Corydon, IN 47112 • Telephone (812)738-2222 • Fax (812)738-7382

Company Description

The Company manufactures and sells quality solid wood furniture and is Harrison County's largest private employer. It has a 7,000 square foot showroom in Corydon, Indiana, and is visited by retailers around the world. Please enjoy our short summary of the history of the Company, on the opposite page.

	12/31/95	12/31/94	12/31/93	12/31/92
Per Share Information				
Stock Price	13.75	12.75	12.00	11.00
Earnings Per Share	2.07	1.49	0.89	0.83
Price / Earnings Ratio	6.64	8.56	13.48	13.25
Book Value Per Share	10.52	8.74	7.33	10.30
Price / Book Value %	130.70	145.88	163.71	106.80
Dividends Per Share	0.24	0.24	0.20	0.20
Annual Financial Data				
Operating Results (000's)				
Total Revenues	50,329.6	45,964.4	35,232.9	33,276.8
Costs & Expenses	-43,470.1	-40,945.7	-32,385.4	-30,588.1
Income Before Taxes and Other	6,859.6	5,018.7	2,847.5	2,688.7
Other Items	n.a.	n.a.	n.a.	n.a.
Income Tax	-2,794.8	-2,080.4	-1,108.1	-1,064.9
Net Income	4,064.8	2,938.3	1,739.4	1,623.8
Cash Flow From Operations	n.a.	n.a.	n.a.	n.a.
Balance Sheet (000's)				
Cash & Equivalents	1,900.6	620.0	125.6	508.7
Total Current Assets	19,710.8	16,387.7	15,082.9	13,678.8
Fixed Assets, Net	6,847.8	5,722.9	4,872.8	4,949.9
Total Assets	27,429.8	22,895.0	20,809.3	18,844.1
Total Current Liabilities	6,180.3	5,167.8	4,412.3	3,568.2
Long-Term Debt	n.a.	n.a.	848.1	1,459.3
Stockholders' Equity	20,625.1	17,222.5	14,341.1	13,381.2
Performance & Financial Condition				
Return on Total Revenues %	8.08	6.39	4.94	4.88
Return on Avg Stockholders' Equity %	21.48	18.62	12.55	12.99
Return on Average Assets %	16.15	13.45	8.77	8.78
Current Ratio	3.19	3.17	3.42	3.83
Debt / Equity %	n.a.	n.a.	5.91	10.91

Compound Growth %'s	EPS %	35.61	Net Income %	35.78	Total Revenues %	14.79

Comments

The Company has shown excellent growth over the last several years and has the financial strength to accommodate more. They will commence celebrating their 100th anniversary this year with a number of special promotions.

Officers	Position	Ownership Information	12/31/95
William H. Keller	Chairman	Number of Shares Outstanding	1,960,743
Robert Byrd	President, CEO	Market Capitalization	$ 26,960,216
Danny Utz	CFO	Frequency Of Dividends	Quarterly
		Number of Shareholders	Under 500

Other Information

Transfer Agent	Company Office		Where Listed	OTC-BB
Auditor	Deloitte & Touche LLP		Symbol	KMFC
Market Maker	JJB Hilliard, WL Lyons, Inc.	Telephone (800)627-3557	SIC Code	2510
Broker Dealer	Regular Stockbroker		Employees	680

Farm Wagons

The Keller Manufacturing Company has a long history that includes many successes as well as financial challenges. Their story begins with John L. Keller's immigration to the United States from Germany in 1846. Penniless upon arrival, he made his way from New York to his sister's home in Indiana, traveling in the company of a freed slave and working for food and lodging en route. Keller decided to remain in Harrison County and began to sell housewares as a country pack peddler. His business eventually developed into a store and in 1866, the business moved to its present location in Corydon, Indiana.

The manufacturing company started up in 1900 with the production of wagon spokes. By 1901 *Corydon* and *Keller* farm wagons were the Company's main products. The high quality of these wagons was recognized by International Harvester Company, who negotiated an agreement for Keller to produce wagons for them as well. With this and other successes, Keller's domestic and international markets grew during the 1920's. By 1929, sales of 12,615 wagons and farm truck parts produced record profits of $622,245.

But the prosperity of these years was fleeting indeed. Merely three years later, now mired in the Great Depression, Keller's customer base became virtually nonexistent and cash was depleted. Fortunately, International Harvester was able to come to the rescue with a $15,000 loan. Keller hung on.

By 1936 it was producing all of the wagons sold worldwide by International Harvester, but even as matters improved Keller was thinking ahead, anticipating the bleak prospects of the wagon business. With this in mind the Company launched its business in the manufacture of dining room furniture in 1943. Roller-coaster-like operating results were reported over the ensuing decade, but by 1953 profits were at record levels. In the ten years ending in 1955, Keller's sales had doubled to $2,000,000.

Plants were built in Virginia and Indiana so that manufacture could keep pace with customer demand. Eventually, Keller expanded production to include bedroom furniture and a product line made of cheaper lumber which is aimed at the price sensitive but quality conscious consumer was added as well. Sales have continued to grow and reached $50,000,000 in 1995, capping records set in each of the three preceding years.

The Company had plenty to celebrate in 1995, not the least of which was C.E.O. William H. Keller's fiftieth anniversary with the firm. A special edition rocking chair was created to honor Mr. Keller, and it has proven to have broad appeal with the company's customer base. Such a symbol of rest and relaxation commemorating years of hard work seems an interesting study in contrasts, but we bet that the people at Keller aren't the ones relaxing. Clearly they keep their corporate ear to the ground and are undoubtedly strategizing even now for their next hundred years.

Kentucky Investors, Inc.

200 Capital Avenue • Frankfort, KY 40602 • Telephone (502)223-2361 • Fax (502)227-7205

Company Description

The Company is the holding company of Investors Heritage Life Insurance Company (Investors Heritage), Investors Heritage Printing Company, and Investors Heritage Financial Services Group, Inc. Investors Heritage, which is featured elsewhere in this book, comprises 99% of the Company's operations. Investors Heritage sells and administers various insurance and annuity products including various types of life insurance, annuity contracts, credit accident and health and group insurance policies. The principal markets are in the south and southeast U.S.

	12/31/95	12/31/94	12/31/93	12/31/92
Per Share Information				
Stock Price	13.25	13.00	13.00	13.00
Earnings Per Share	0.71	1.97	1.55	0.65
Price / Earnings Ratio	18.66	6.60	8.39	20.00
Book Value Per Share	30.38	23.54	26.31	25.07
Price / Book Value %	43.61	55.23	49.41	51.85
Dividends Per Share	0.38	0.37	0.36	0.36
Annual Financial Data				
Operating Results (000's)				
Total Revenues	44,004.6	46,655.7	45,387.6	45,567.0
Costs & Expenses	-43,190.9	-44,039.4	-43,091.2	-44,596.6
Income Before Taxes and Other	813.8	2,616.3	2,296.4	970.5
Other Items	-239.8	-632.6	-681.6	-249.8
Income Tax	-19.0	-461.0	-422.0	-205.0
Net Income	554.9	1,522.7	1,192.8	515.6
Cash Flow From Operations	11,744.0	9,953.1	13,187.7	7,134.4
Balance Sheet (000's)				
Cash & Equivalents	2,417.4	2,336.7	3,067.7	1,790.4
Total Current Assets	12,935.1	17,273.3	27,812.2	9,725.6
Fixed Assets, Net	1,881.0	1,955.2	2,163.0	2,288.6
Total Assets	208,045.1	191,367.0	198,230.0	171,119.1
Total Current Liabilities	7,827.4	4,651.9	9,086.5	9,987.8
Long-Term Debt	n.a.	n.a.	n.a.	n.a.
Stockholders' Equity	24,641.5	18,357.4	20,306.2	19,422.5
Performance & Financial Condition				
Return on Total Revenues %	1.26	3.26	2.63	1.13
Return on Avg Stockholders' Equity %	2.58	7.88	6.00	3.43
Return on Average Assets %	0.28	0.78	0.65	0.31
Current Ratio	1.65	3.71	3.06	0.97
Debt / Equity %	n.a.	n.a.	n.a.	n.a.

Compound Growth %'s	EPS %	2.99	Net Income %	2.48	Total Revenues %	-1.16

Comments

The primary assets and liabilities of the Company are the investment portfolio and related policy liabilities of Investor Heritage. At December 31, 1995, policy liabilities total $165.5 million, comprised primarily of benefit reserves of $155.2 million. Investments total $161.4 million at December 31, 1995, consisting of fixed maturities of $137.4 million, mortgage loans of $13.1 million, policy loans of $6.9 million and equity securities and other of $4.0 million.

Officers	Position	Ownership Information	12/31/95
Harry Lee Waterfield II	President, CEO	Number of Shares Outstanding	811,128
Wilma Yeary	Secretary	Market Capitalization	$ 10,747,446
Jimmy R. McIver	Treasurer	Frequency Of Dividends	Annual
Howard L. Graham	Vice President	Number of Shareholders	2,593
Nancy W. Walton	Vice President		

Other Information				
Transfer Agent	Company Office		Where Listed	OTC-BB
Auditor	Ernst & Young LLP		Symbol	KINV
Market Maker	Hilliard, Lyons, Inc.	Telephone (800)627-3557	SIC Code	6311
Broker Dealer	Regular Stockbroker		Employees	119

Kentucky River Coal Corporation

200 West Vine Street, Ste. 8-K • Lexington, KY 40507 • Telephone (606)254-8498 • Fax (606)255-9362

Company Description

The Company is primarily engaged in leasing mineral reserves and, to a lesser degree, participating in partnerships and joint ventures which explore for and develop oil and gas properties. The majority of the Company's revenue-producing properties are located in eastern Kentucky. There are only 78,025 shares outstanding and the Company is purchasing shares that become available. However, shares can be acquired on the open market.

	12/31/95	12/31/94	12/31/93	12/31/92
Per Share Information				
Stock Price	2,700.00	3,175.00	3,125.00	3,000.00
Earnings Per Share	322.51	259.01	236.22	254.27
Price / Earnings Ratio	8.37	12.26	13.23	11.80
Book Value Per Share	1,208.54	1,056.55	1,037.57	981.83
Price / Book Value %	223.41	300.51	301.18	305.55
Dividends Per Share	200.00	195.00	170.00	260.00
Annual Financial Data				
Operating Results (000's)				
Total Revenues	46,428.0	36,848.0	36,981.0	38,594.0
Costs & Expenses	-6,812.0	-6,841.0	-7,987.0	-7,529.0
Income Before Taxes and Other	39,616.0	30,007.0	28,994.0	31,065.0
Other Items	n.a.	n.a.	n.a.	n.a.
Income Tax	-14,453.0	-10,320.0	-9,980.0	-10,533.0
Net Income	25,163.0	19,687.0	19,014.0	20,532.0
Cash Flow From Operations	14,736.0	13,513.0	20,080.0	25,677.0
Balance Sheet (000's)				
Cash & Equivalents	3,967.0	4,714.0	12,084.0	3,923.0
Total Current Assets	78,337.0	61,516.0	47,304.0	51,423.0
Fixed Assets, Net	11,490.0	12,462.0	13,180.0	13,153.0
Total Assets	102,282.0	85,979.0	85,179.0	81,752.0
Total Current Liabilities	568.0	1,242.0	808.0	2,576.0
Long-Term Debt	n.a.	n.a.	n.a.	n.a.
Stockholders' Equity	94,296.0	82,437.0	83,263.0	79,176.0
Performance & Financial Condition				
Return on Total Revenues %	54.20	53.43	51.42	53.20
Return on Avg Stockholders' Equity %	28.48	23.76	23.41	26.34
Return on Average Assets %	26.73	23.00	22.78	24.96
Current Ratio	137.92	49.53	58.54	19.96
Debt / Equity %	n.a.	n.a.	n.a.	n.a.

Compound Growth %'s	EPS %	8.25	Net Income %	7.01	Total Revenues %	6.35

Comments

Management states that "The main objective of the Company over the years has been to provide a stable and growing source of dividend income for the stockholders while utilizing retained earnings to build value for the future. The Company has always maintained a sound balance sheet and followed conservative accounting practices." We agree.

Officers	Position	Ownership Information	12/31/95
Catesby W. Clay	Chairman	Number of Shares Outstanding	78,025
James G. Kenan III	President, CEO	Market Capitalization	$ 210,667,500
Fred N. Parker	Secretary, Treasurer	Frequency Of Dividends	Quarterly
Gary I. Conley	Vice President	Number of Shareholders	Under 500

Other Information

Transfer Agent	Company Office		Where Listed	OTC-BB
Auditor	KPMG Peat Marwick LLP		Symbol	KRIV
Market Maker	Robotti & Eng, Incorporated	Telephone (212)986-4800	SIC Code	1200
Broker Dealer	Regular Stockbroker		Employees	10

Keweenaw Land Association, Limited

1801 East Cloverland Drive • Ironwood, MI 49938 • Telephone (906)932-3410 • Fax (906)932-5823

Company Description

The Company owns and harvests logs on 155,435 acres of forested property in the Upper Peninsula of Michigan. This wood is classified primarily as "northern hardwoods" types. Substantial revenue is also generated from land and mineral leases. The Company has been certified as "well managed" by Smartwood, a national program concerned with land mangement policy. Shares were split 2 for 1 in 1995. All per share amounts have been adjusted accordingly.

	12/31/95	12/31/94	12/31/93	12/31/92
Per Share Information				
Stock Price	37.00	36.25	30.00	25.75
Earnings Per Share	2.08	2.01	1.62	2.05
Price / Earnings Ratio	17.79	18.03	18.52	12.56
Book Value Per Share	17.32	17.03	15.57	14.69
Price / Book Value %	213.63	212.86	192.68	175.29
Dividends Per Share	0.80	0.80	0.80	0.80
Annual Financial Data				
Operating Results (000's)				
Total Revenues	6,027.4	5,177.4	4,341.2	3,705.7
Costs & Expenses	-3,506.9	-2,558.6	-2,463.5	-1,395.4
Income Before Taxes and Other	2,255.8	2,286.2	1,877.7	2,310.4
Other Items	n.a.	n.a.	n.a.	n.a.
Income Tax	-691.7	-720.3	-567.0	-705.0
Net Income	1,564.1	1,565.8	1,310.7	1,605.4
Cash Flow From Operations	1,509.8	1,232.8	1,214.8	712.6
Balance Sheet (000's)				
Cash & Equivalents	348.5	2,700.1	1,216.6	541.4
Total Current Assets	3,284.3	6,131.2	9,699.2	9,496.1
Fixed Assets, Net	8,226.9	5,141.9	801.8	544.5
Total Assets	14,336.7	13,740.2	12,593.4	11,951.1
Total Current Liabilities	494.1	319.5	407.9	420.2
Long-Term Debt	n.a.	n.a.	n.a.	40.3
Stockholders' Equity	13,405.4	13,183.6	12,170.9	11,485.7
Performance & Financial Condition				
Return on Total Revenues %	25.95	30.24	30.19	43.32
Return on Avg Stockholders' Equity %	11.77	12.35	11.08	14.97
Return on Average Assets %	11.14	11.89	10.68	14.73
Current Ratio	6.65	19.19	23.78	22.60
Debt / Equity %	n.a.	n.a.	n.a.	0.35

Compound Growth %'s	EPS %	0.49	Net Income %	-0.86	Total Revenues %	17.60

Comments

Adequate financial strengh is maintained for the purpose of property acquisitions. 30,000 acres of high-quality timberlands were acquired in 1994. Noncurrent assets are predominantly comprised of marketable securities.

Officers	Position	Ownership Information	12/31/95
David Ayer	Chairman	Number of Shares Outstanding	774,010
David E. McDonald	Secretary	Market Capitalization	$ 28,638,370
Alan W. Steege	General Manager	Frequency Of Dividends	Quarterly
Robert M. Davenport	Controller	Number of Shareholders	Under 500

Other Information				
Transfer Agent	Norwest Banks, South St. Paul, MN		Where Listed	OTC-BB
Auditor	Anderson, Tackman & Company		Symbol	KEWL
Market Maker	A.G. Edwards & Sons, Inc.	Telephone (314)289-3000	SIC Code	2410
Broker Dealer	Regular Stockbroker		Employees	17

Kiewit Royalty Trust

C/O First Bank NA • Omaha, NE 68102 • Telephone (402)348-6000 • Fax (402)348-6674

Company Description

The Trust was created in 1982 by Peter Kiewit Sons', Inc. and was organized to provide an efficient, orderly and practical means for the administration of income received from royalty and overriding royalty interests it owned in certain coal leases in Wyoming and Montana. The Trust has no officers or employees and is administered by a trustee, First Bank NA, who collects all income, pays expenses and distributes the remainder to the unit holders quarterly.

	12/31/95	12/31/94	12/31/93	12/31/92
Per Share Information				
Unit Price	6.25	5.63	5.00	4.63
Earnings Per Unit	0.60	0.62	0.66	0.56
Price / Earnings Ratio	10.42	9.08	7.58	8.27
Book Value Per Unit	0.01	0.01	0.01	0.01
Price / Book Value %	n.a.	n.a.	n.a.	n.a.
Distributions Per Unit	0.60	0.62	0.66	0.56
Annual Financial Data				
Operating Results (000's)				
Total Revenues	7,581.1	7,954.5	8,348.3	7,190.7
Costs & Expenses	-47.0	-63.7	-61.2	-72.4
Income Before Taxes and Other	7,534.1	7,890.8	8,287.1	7,118.3
Other Items	n.a.	n.a.	n.a.	n.a.
Income Tax	n.a.	n.a.	n.a.	n.a.
Net Income	7,534.1	7,890.8	8,287.1	7,118.3
Cash Flow From Operations	7,534.1	7,890.8	8,287.1	7,118.3
Balance Sheet (000's)				
Cash & Equivalents	162.0	398.6	383.0	618.2
Total Current Assets	258.9	507.4	512.4	750.5
Fixed Assets, Net	n.a.	n.a.	n.a.	n.a.
Total Assets	258.9	507.4	512.4	750.5
Total Current Liabilities	162.0	398.6	383.0	618.2
Long-Term Debt	n.a.	n.a.	n.a.	n.a.
Trust Equity	96.9	108.8	129.4	132.3
Performance & Financial Condition				
Return on Total Revenues %	99.38	99.20	99.27	98.99
Return on Avg Trust Equity %	7323.83	6624.86	6332.52	4165.82
Return on Average Assets %	1966.17	1547.43	1312.38	1022.67
Current Ratio	1.60	1.27	1.34	1.21
Debt / Equity %	n.a.	n.a.	n.a.	n.a.

Compound Growth %'s	EPU %	2.33	Net Income %	1.91	Total Revenues %	1.78

Comments

The Trust's operations and financial position clearly do not lend themselves to traditional analysis. However, based on the quoted unit prices and historical distributions, the units may be a worthwhile investment. Potential investors would, among other things, need to know the size of the coal reserves, the length of time left on the underlying coal leases, whether or not there are any renewal options and what the projected earnings of the royalty interests are for the future.

Officers	Position	Ownership Information	12/31/95
Susan Rosburg	Trust Officer, First Bank, N.A.	Number of Units Outstanding	12,633,432
		Market Capitalization	$ 78,958,950
		Frequency Of Distributions	Quarterly
		Number of Unit Holders	802

Other Information

Transfer Agent	First Bank N.A. Omaha			Where Listed	OTC-BB
Auditor	Coopers & Lybrand LLP			Symbol	KIRY
Market Maker	Legg Mason Wood Walker, Inc.	Telephone	(212)428-4949	SIC Code	6795
Broker Dealer	Regular Stockbroker			Employees	n.a.

King Kullen Grocery Co., Inc.

1194 Prospect Avenue • Westbury, NY 11590-2723 • Telephone (516)333-7100 • Fax (516)333-7929

Company Description

The Company operates a chain of 54 supermarkets in the counties of Queens, Nassau, and Suffolk, all in the New York. Store sizes range from 9000 to 43,800 square feet. It also owns its own grocery, meat and produce warehouses as well of a fleet of 15 tractors and 112 trailers. The Company owns two store locations and a 33 acre property in Westbury, New York, the site of its office and warehouse. The Company was formed in 1930 and went public in 1961 but is now buying back its shares. It reacquired between 30,000 and 60,000 shares in 1995. The Company also granted options to officers of the Company for 40,000 shares at an exercise price of $115 per share.

	09/30/95	10/01/94	10/02/93
Per Share Information			
Stock Price	84.50	68.00	68.00
Earnings Per Share	8.04	10.16	5.58
Price / Earnings Ratio	10.51	6.69	12.19
Book Value Per Share	101.99	109.19	99.96
Price / Book Value %	82.85	62.28	68.03
Dividends Per Share	0.50	0.50	0.50
Annual Financial Data			
Operating Results (000's)			
Total Revenues	702,780.0	723,372.0	702,279.0
Costs & Expenses	-698,455.0	-717,897.5	-699,145.0
Income Before Taxes and Other	4,325.0	5,474.5	3,134.0
Other Items	n.a.	283.5	n.a.
Income Tax	n.a.	n.a.	n.a.
Net Income	4,325.0	5,758.0	3,134.0
Cash Flow From Operations	13,801.0	14,797.0	11,089.0
Balance Sheet (000's)			
Cash & Equivalents	n.a.	n.a.	n.a.
Total Current Assets	58,901.0	61,175.0	60,506.0
Fixed Assets, Net	n.a.	n.a.	n.a.
Total Assets	157,152.0	155,179.0	149,701.0
Total Current Liabilities	57,131.0	56,839.0	57,510.0
Long-Term Debt	20,000.0	20,000.0	20,000.0
Stockholders' Equity	54,862.0	61,883.0	56,144.0
Performance & Financial Condition			
Return on Total Revenues %	0.62	0.80	0.45
Return on Avg Stockholders' Equity %	7.41	9.76	n.a.
Return on Average Assets %	2.77	3.78	n.a.
Current Ratio	1.03	1.08	1.05
Debt / Equity %	36.46	32.32	n.a.

Compound Growth %'s	EPS %	20.04	Net Income %	17.47	Total Revenues %	0.04

Comments

Only summary information is extracted from the financial statements for the report to shareholders. 1994 results include a nonrecurring benefit of $283,500, or $.50 per share, because of a change in accounting methods. The Company uses LIFO for calculating inventory. Had FIFO been used, the inventory would have been higher by $6.6 million, $6.2 million and $5.8 million in 1995, 1994 and 1993, respectively. Compounded growth rates are probably misleading because of a lower net income in 1993.

Officers	Position	Ownership Information	09/30/95
Bernard P. Kennedy	Secretary	Number of Shares Outstanding	537,935
Eugene C. Kennedy	Director	Market Capitalization	$ 45,455,508
Ronald E. Brackett	Director	Frequency Of Dividends	n.a.
Ronald Conklin	Director	Number of Shareholders	Under 500

Other Information

Transfer Agent	Chemical Bank, New York		Where Listed	OTC-BB
Auditor	Grant Thorton		Symbol	KKGR
Market Maker	Tweedy Browne Company L.P.	Telephone (212)916-0606	SIC Code	5410
Broker Dealer	Regular Stockbroker		Employees	4000

KnowledgeBroker, Inc.

13295 Mira Loma Road • Reno, NV 98511 • Telephone (800)829-4524 • Fax (213)258-3854

Company Description

The Company provides integrated information system "help desk" functions for Fortune 1000 companies throughout the U.S. and develops, sells and maintains informational databases for providing on-line computer hardware and software applications support. The Company operates HelpNet 800/900 Service, a live, 24-hour multi-vendor technical computer support bureau. The Company incorporated in California in March 1992.

	12/31/95	12/31/94	12/31/93
Per Share Information			
Stock Price	4.06	n.a.	n.a.
Earnings Per Share	-0.01	0.09	-0.06
Price / Earnings Ratio	n.a.	n.a.	n.a.
Book Value Per Share	0.06	0.07	-0.01
Price / Book Value %	6,766.70	n.a.	n.a.
Dividends Per Share	n.a.	n.a.	n.a.
Annual Financial Data			
Operating Results (000's)			
Total Revenues	1,974.8	2,558.1	517.8
Costs & Expenses	-2,557.7	-1,958.8	-681.9
Income Before Taxes and Other	-582.9	599.4	-164.1
Other Items	n.a.	n.a.	n.a.
Income Tax	513.0	-173.4	n.a.
Net Income	-69.9	425.9	-164.1
Cash Flow From Operations	-97.8	292.4	96.6
Balance Sheet (000's)			
Cash & Equivalents	131.7	328.8	115.3
Total Current Assets	1,028.0	804.2	240.5
Fixed Assets, Net	139.2	151.7	100.6
Total Assets	1,290.7	962.4	348.3
Total Current Liabilities	737.9	594.3	390.5
Long-Term Debt	n.a.	n.a.	7.4
Stockholders' Equity	552.8	354.0	-49.6
Performance & Financial Condition			
Return on Total Revenues %	-3.54	16.65	-31.68
Return on Avg Stockholders' Equity %	-15.41	279.90	n.a.
Return on Average Assets %	-6.20	64.99	n.a.
Current Ratio	1.39	1.35	0.62
Debt / Equity %	n.a.	n.a.	n.a.

Compound Growth %'s	EPS % n.a.	Net Income % n.a.	Total Revenues % 95.29

Comments

The Current ownership of the Company results from several transactions culminating with the merger of an existing corporation in May of 1995. As a result of these transactions, approximately 96% of the Company's stock is restricted from trading until May 1997. The remaining shares were not traded on any market before May of 1995.

Officers	Position	Ownership Information	12/31/95
Brad Stanley	President, CFO	Number of Shares Outstanding	9,267,947
James T. Alexander	Exec VP	Market Capitalization	$ 37,627,865
Kerry Hancock	General Manager	Frequency Of Dividends	n.a.
		Number of Shareholders	536

Other Information				
Transfer Agent	Securities Transfer Corporation		Where Listed	OTC-BB
Auditor	Hendrix, Sutton & Assoc LLP		Symbol	KBIZ
Market Maker	Alexander Securities, Inc.	Telephone (800)421-0258	SIC Code	7375
Broker Dealer	Regular Stockbroker		Employees	40

Kohler Co.

High Street • Kohler, WI 53044 • Telephone (414)457-4441 • Fax (414)457-1271

Company Description

The Company is an international manufacturer of plumbing products, furniture, engines and generators. These products are marketed through a wide variety of distribution channels. The Company also owns and operates a number of hospitality and real estate businesses in Kohler, Wisconsin. Shares were subject to a 1 for 20 reverse split in 1978. The stock usually trades by auction with only a handful of market makers and broker/dealers involved. Please enjoy a capsule of the history of this giant of American industry, displayed on the opposite page.

	12/31/94	12/31/93	12/31/92
Per Share Information			
Stock Price	90,000.00	80,000.00	75,000.00
Earnings Per Share	8,821.00	2,046.00	6,093.00
Price / Earnings Ratio	10.20	39.10	12.31
Book Value Per Share	79,479.51	71,238.71	70,344.54
Price / Book Value %	113.24	112.30	106.62
Dividends Per Share	850.00	600.00	600.00
Annual Financial Data			
Operating Results (000's)			
Total Revenues	1,771,959.2	1,542,113.8	1,472,470.4
Costs & Expenses	-1,636,366.0	-1,442,068.9	-1,391,157.6
Income Before Taxes and Other	113,674.6	80,111.6	78,927.0
Other Items	n.a.	-32,984.2	n.a.
Income Tax	-46,954.9	-31,648.2	-32,818.0
Net Income	66,719.7	15,479.2	46,109.0
Cash Flow From Operations	98,813.3	109,298.4	131,774.2
Balance Sheet (000's)			
Cash & Equivalents	32,955.1	46,252.3	16,009.5
Total Current Assets	583,531.2	540,686.5	482,936.7
Fixed Assets, Net	372,469.0	364,557.2	348,512.0
Total Assets	1,099,990.9	1,052,047.8	957,154.7
Total Current Liabilities	251,473.7	262,153.9	254,578.9
Long-Term Debt	132,208.9	140,601.1	104,901.0
Stockholders' Equity	601,183.3	538,992.1	532,156.5
Performance & Financial Condition			
Return on Total Revenues %	3.77	1.00	3.13
Return on Avg Stockholders' Equity %	11.70	2.89	8.99
Return on Average Assets %	6.20	1.54	4.78
Current Ratio	2.32	2.06	1.90
Debt / Equity %	21.99	26.09	19.71

Compound Growth %'s	EPS %	20.32	Net Income %	20.29	Total Revenues %	9.70

Comments

1993 results include a $33 million charge to change the method of accounting for postretirement benefits. Also in 1993, the Company acquired Sanijura SA, a French company. 1995 results were not available when we went to press, but we can give you an historical picture by going back further in reporting revenues and earnings. Revenues for 1991, 1990 and 1989 were $1.34 billion, $1.41 billion and $1.35 billion, respectively. Net income for the same years was $5.25 million, $20.16 million and $52.44 million, respectively. The 1991 results reflect $22.4 million of restructuring expenses.

Officers	Position	Ownership Information	12/31/94
Herbert V. Kohler, Jr.	Chairman, President	Number of Shares Outstanding	7,564
George R. Tiedens	Senior VP	Market Capitalization	$ 680,760,000
Richard A. Wells	VP - Finance	Frequency Of Dividends	Quarterly
William J. Drew	Secretary	Number of Shareholders	Under 500
Jeffrey P. Cheney	Treasurer		

Other Information

Transfer Agent	Company Office		Where Listed	OTC-PS
Auditor	Arthur Andersen LLP		Symbol	KHCO
Market Maker	Howe Barnes Investments, Inc.	Telephone (800)621-2364	SIC Code	3430
Broker Dealer	Standard Investment	Tel/Ext (888)783-4688 Jack	Employees	6000

The Kitchen Sink

How often have you returned from your travels around the world longing for your own commodious, well-equipped bathroom? Americans have John Michael Kohler to thank for these particular creature comforts of ours. When he immigrated from Austria to the United States in the late nineteenth century, Paris had only just constructed sewers and water lines in the decade between 1860-1870. Parisians may not have been enthusiastic about these new conveniences, but Kohler had the vision to embrace a new trend, and began to create bathtubs by applying enamel to cast-iron horse drinking troughs. As it turned out, many people appreciated a hot bath in 1874 as much as we do today, and so America's love affair with the bathroom was born.

Contemporary Americans have come to expect that the bathroom be a key component of their home and a showplace as well. Kohler continues to meet that expectation to this day with style, dominating the American bathroom fixture market and selling overseas in Europe and China. They were the first to manufacture fixtures in colors other than white, viewing their products as elements of furniture design suites. New York's Metropolitan Museum of Art must have agreed, for they put Kohler s innovation on display themselves.

This commitment to quality is undoubtedly one of the traits that helps enable Kohler Co. to stay way ahead of their closest competition, including American Standard, Crane Co., and Eljer Industries. Their 1994 earnings of $67 million on sales of $1.8 billion speak to their success. In addition to bathroom fixtures, Kohler also produces fine furniture, engines and generators and develops real estate. An impressive example of the latter enterprise is the resort complex in Kohler, Wisconsin, which includes the American Club Hotel, a tennis and sports club, a hunting preserve, a spa, a restaurant, shops and two Blackwolf Run golf courses designed by Pete Dye.

Design of the town of Kohler, Wisconsin as a whole was also taken under a Kohler's wing when, in 1917, Walter Kohler, the founder's son, hired the Olmstead Brothers to create a plan for a nurturing environment for Kohler employees. The family has remained committed to the town and remain personal residents themselves. Additional modernization was undertaken in 1977 when Herbert Kohler Jr. hired the Frank Lloyd Wright Foundation to plan for the future of Kohler.

After 122 years of operations, Kohler Co. remains largely privately held by family and employees and is managed by the fourth generation of the Kohler family, but potential estate tax issues could impact the fifth generation s ability to remain closely held. An exciting and forward-looking company, Kohler is definitely one to watch as it and we approach the twenty-first century.

Kopp Glass, Inc.

2108 Palmer Street • Pittsburgh, PA 15218-2516 • Telephone (412)271-0190 • Fax (412)271-4102

Company Description

The Company manufactures specialty industrial glass products. Major areas of industry concentration are interior and exterior aircraft lighting, airport lighting, and traffic control.

	12/31/92
Per Share Information	
Stock Price	8.00
Earnings Per Share	0.74
Price / Earnings Ratio	10.81
Book Value Per Share	21.20
Price / Book Value %	37.74
Dividends Per Share	1.00
Annual Financial Data	
Operating Results (000's)	
Total Revenues	8,264.5
Costs & Expenses	-7,824.0
Income Before Taxes and Other	420.5
Other Items	n.a.
Income Tax	-172.0
Net Income	248.5
Cash Flow From Operations	464.4
Balance Sheet (000's)	
Cash & Equivalents	1,203.8
Total Current Assets	5,153.3
Fixed Assets, Net	1,955.9
Total Assets	7,878.3
Total Current Liabilities	265.2
Long-Term Debt	n.a.
Stockholders' Equity	7,123.6
Performance & Financial Condition	
Return on Total Revenues %	3.01
Return on Avg Stockholders' Equity %	n.a.
Return on Average Assets %	n.a.
Current Ratio	19.43
Debt / Equity %	n.a.

Compound Growth %'s	EPS % n.a.	Net Income % n.a.	Total Revenues % n.a.

Comments

We could not obtain more recent information but decided to at least show 1992 results. In that year there was no debt and a 19 to 1 current ratio. Furthermore, inventory was calculated using the LIFO method.

Officers	Position	Ownership Information	12/31/92
Joe Pathwick	President, CEO	Number of Shares Outstanding	336,033
Terry Christy	Exec VP	Market Capitalization	$ 2,688,264
		Frequency Of Dividends	Quarterly
		Number of Shareholders	Under 500

Other Information

Transfer Agent	Company Office				Where Listed	OTC-BB
Auditor	D.G. Sisterson & Co.				Symbol	KOGL
Market Maker	Chicago Corporation, The	Telephone	(800)621-1674		SIC Code	3646
Broker Dealer	Standard Investment	Tel/Ext	(888)783-4688	Jack	Employees	n.a.

LAACO, Ltd.

431 West Seventh Street • Los Angeles, CA 90014-1601 • Telephone (213)625-2211 • Fax (213)689-1194

Company Description

The Company is a California limited partnership engaged in the ownership and operation of the Los Angeles Athletic Club, the California Yacht Club, and real estate investment and leasing operations. It also owns and operates 14 self storage facilities and approximately 1,600 acres of partially developed land in the Topanga Canyon area of Los Angeles County. Formed in 1978, the corporate structure was changed to that of a limited partnership in 1987. The entity is scheduled to be taxed as a corporation starting in 1998 unless the 10 year limitation is extended.

	12/31/95	12/31/94	12/31/93	12/31/92
Per Unit Information				
Price Per Unit	274.50	263.00	245.00	222.50
Earnings Per Unit	40.82	24.40	22.19	36.84
Price / Earnings Ratio	6.72	10.78	11.04	6.04
Book Value Per Unit	295.22	277.91	273.51	276.57
Price / Book Value %	92.98	94.63	89.58	80.45
Distributions Per Unit	23.50	20.00	25.25	20.00
Cash Flow Per Unit	41.93	32.48	48.82	18.29
Annual Financial Data				
Operating Results (000's)				
Total Revenues	26,790.0	23,959.0	23,110.0	24,105.0
Costs & Expenses	-19,610.0	-19,666.0	-20,303.0	-19,151.0
Operating Income	7,180.0	4,293.0	2,807.0	3,745.0
Other Items	n.a.	n.a.	1,096.0	2,735.0
Net Income	7,180.0	4,293.0	3,903.0	6,480.0
Cash Flow From Operations	7,375.0	5,713.0	8,588.0	3,217.0
Balance Sheet (000's)				
Cash & Equivalents	373.0	1,620.0	1,167.0	543.0
Total Current Assets	18,882.0	16,664.0	16,263.0	17,795.0
Investments In	n.a.	n.a.	n.a.	1,918.0
Total Assets	60,726.0	57,307.0	56,462.0	56,567.0
Total Current Liabilities	4,058.0	3,784.0	3,736.0	3,348.0
Long-Term Debt	3,221.0	3,276.0	3,347.0	3,417.0
Partners' Capital	51,931.0	48,885.0	48,110.0	48,649.0
Performance & Financial Condition				
Return on Total Revenues %	26.80	17.92	16.89	26.88
Return on Average Partners' Capital %	14.24	8.85	8.07	n.a.
Return on Average Assets %	12.17	7.55	6.91	12.19
Current Ratio	4.65	4.40	4.35	5.32
Debt / Equity %	6.20	n.a.	n.a.	n.a.

Compound Growth %'s	EPU %	3.48	Net Income %	3.48	Total Revenues %	3.58

Comments

The numbers reflect GAAP accounting on an historical cost basis. The tax basis of equity is higher by $8.6 million, or $49 per unit. The true fair market value is not readily known.

Officers	Position	Ownership Information	12/31/95
Karen L. Hathaway	President	Number of Shares Outstanding	175,907
John K. Hathaway	Senior VP	Market Capitalization	$ 48,286,472
Steven K. Hathaway	Senior VP	Frequency Of Distributions	Irregular
Richard T. LLewellyn	Senior VP	Number of Partners	Under 500
Jeffrey A. Sutton	Controller		

Other Information

					Where Listed	OTC-BB
Transfer Agent	Chemical Trust Company of California				Symbol	LACOZ
Auditor	Coopers & Lybrand LLP				SIC Code	7941
Market Maker	Gruntal & Co., Incorporated	Telephone	(617)728-2200		Employees	375
Broker Dealer	Standard Investment	Tel/Ext	(888)783-4688	Jack		

Labor Ready, Inc.

2156 Pacific Avenue • Tacoma, WA 98402 • Telephone (206)383-9101 • Fax (206)383-9311

Company Description

The Company, incorporated in Washington in 1985, provides temporary help primarily to construction, warehousing, landscaping and manufacturing businesses. The Company has developed a large pool of low to medium-skilled workers and processed over one million payroll checks written to 100,000 temporary laborers in 1995. The Company has more than 40,000 customers.

	12/31/95	12/31/94	12/31/93	12/31/92
Per Share Information				
Stock Price	15.75	5.84	2.38	0.04
Earnings Per Share	0.34	0.18	0.06	0.06
Price / Earnings Ratio	46.32	32.44	39.67	0.67
Book Value Per Share	1.31	0.42	0.26	0.09
Price / Book Value %	1,202.30	1,390.50	915.38	44.44
Dividends Per Share	n.a.	n.a.	n.a.	n.a.
Annual Financial Data				
Operating Results (000's)				
Total Revenues	94,361.6	38,950.7	15,658.8	8,424.1
Costs & Expenses	-91,148.1	-37,762.9	-15,405.9	-8,244.2
Income Before Taxes and Other	3,213.5	1,187.8	253.0	179.8
Other Items	n.a.	n.a.	47.8	n.a.
Income Tax	-1,151.7	-336.0	-31.8	-20.7
Net Income	2,061.8	851.8	269.0	159.1
Cash Flow From Operations	-3,708.0	-2,250.6	-449.9	-139.1
Balance Sheet (000's)				
Cash & Equivalents	5,359.1	604.0	229.3	398.2
Total Current Assets	20,215.6	7,571.6	2,313.3	1,454.0
Fixed Assets, Net	2,851.4	826.6	423.1	132.1
Total Assets	26,181.6	8,912.0	3,153.1	1,880.0
Total Current Liabilities	7,955.7	5,630.9	1,705.8	1,086.0
Long-Term Debt	9,694.6	319.3	730.3	577.0
Stockholders' Equity	8,531.3	2,961.9	669.9	217.0
Performance & Financial Condition				
Return on Total Revenues %	2.19	2.19	1.72	1.89
Return on Avg Stockholders' Equity %	35.88	46.91	60.66	45.00
Return on Average Assets %	11.75	14.12	10.69	12.73
Current Ratio	2.54	1.34	1.36	1.34
Debt / Equity %	113.63	10.78	109.03	265.90

Compound Growth %'s	EPS %	78.28	Net Income %	134.88	Total Revenues %	123.75

Comments

During the three years ended December 31, 1995, the Company had a number of stock transactions which included stock issued on the exercise of warrants and options, two private placements, stock issued on the conversion of debt and other stock issuances. As a result of these transactions, the number of shares outstanding increased by 3,354,231 and stockholders equity by $5.3 million. At March 20, 1996, officers and directors, as a group, owned 22.6% and 68.1% of the Company's outstanding common and preferred stock, respectively.

Officers	Position	Ownership Information	12/31/95
Glenn A. Welstad	President, CEO	Number of Shares Outstanding	5,879,133
Ralph E. Peterson	CFO	Market Capitalization	$ 92,596,345
Ronald Junck	Secretary	Frequency Of Dividends	n.a.
Robert J. Sullivan	Treasurer	Number of Shareholders	655
Thomas E. McChesney	Other		

Other Information			
Transfer Agent	TranSecurities, International, Inc.	Where Listed	OTC-BB
Auditor	BDO Seidman LLP	Symbol	LBOR
Market Maker	National Securities Corp.	Telephone (800)426-1613	SIC Code	7363
Broker Dealer	Regular Stockbroker		Employees	6450

Lady Baltimore Foods, Inc.

1601 Fairfax Trafficway • Kansas City, KS 66117 • Telephone (913)371-8300 • Fax (913)621-7217

Company Description

The Company and its subsidiaries operate primarily as institutional wholesalers of groceries, chemicals, and food service equipment and supplies. Sales are concentrated in the four state region of Kansas, Missouri, Oklahoma and Arkansas. There are no predominant customers. "Nugget" is a private label used for certain Company products.

	06/30/95	06/30/94	06/30/93	06/30/92
Per Share Information				
Stock Price	62.50	64.00	43.50	40.00
Earnings Per Share	5.41	6.25	6.27	5.31
Price / Earnings Ratio	11.55	10.24	6.94	7.53
Book Value Per Share	78.09	72.83	66.73	60.58
Price / Book Value %	80.04	87.88	65.19	66.03
Dividends Per Share	0.15	0.15	0.12	0.10
Annual Financial Data				
Operating Results (000's)				
Total Revenues	166,696.9	156,650.1	148,976.6	141,770.5
Costs & Expenses	-164,008.0	-153,579.2	-145,846.3	-138,981.5
Income Before Taxes and Other	2,688.9	3,070.9	3,130.3	2,758.2
Other Items	n.a.	n.a.	n.a.	-46.5
Income Tax	-979.5	-1,099.0	-1,150.1	-1,034.1
Net Income	1,709.4	1,971.8	1,980.2	1,677.6
Cash Flow From Operations	775.2	1,582.8	3,372.6	709.3
Balance Sheet (000's)				
Cash & Equivalents	2,819.6	3,809.8	3,983.5	2,456.2
Total Current Assets	25,859.7	25,257.9	23,311.7	21,530.3
Fixed Assets, Net	6,924.2	6,524.4	6,587.9	6,402.2
Total Assets	33,169.0	32,266.0	30,530.1	28,699.2
Total Current Liabilities	6,269.8	6,769.2	6,647.9	6,497.4
Long-Term Debt	572.5	930.4	1,305.8	1,650.4
Stockholders' Equity	24,657.0	22,995.0	21,070.5	19,128.2
Performance & Financial Condition				
Return on Total Revenues %	1.03	1.26	1.33	1.18
Return on Avg Stockholders' Equity %	7.17	8.95	9.85	9.16
Return on Average Assets %	5.22	6.28	6.69	5.95
Current Ratio	4.12	3.73	3.51	3.31
Debt / Equity %	2.32	4.05	6.20	8.63

Compound Growth %'s	EPS %	0.62	Net Income %	0.63	Total Revenues %	5.55

Comments

Inventories are stated at LIFO. On a FIFO basis, inventory would have been $1,238,612 higher at December 31, 1995.

Officers	Position	Ownership Information	06/30/95
Jack Baraban	Chairman	Number of Shares Outstanding	315,739
Melvin Cosner	President, CEO	Market Capitalization	$ 19,733,688
Alan Cosner	Secretary, Treasurer	Frequency Of Dividends	Quarterly
Francis J. Clifford	Vice President	Number of Shareholders	Under 500
Tom Miller	VP - Sales		

Other Information

Transfer Agent	Boatman's Trust Company, Kansas City			Where Listed	OTC-BB
Auditor	Mayer Hoffman McCann L.C.			Symbol	LDYBA
Market Maker	George K. Baum & Company	Telephone	(800)821-7570	SIC Code	5140
Broker Dealer	Regular Stockbroker			Employees	225

Lake Charles Naval Stores Co., Inc.

203 Carondelet Street, Ste.710 • New Orleans, LA 70130 • Telephone (504)561-8602 • Fax (504)561-8621

Company Description

The Company owns various parcels of land in Louisiana and Mississippi, principally used in harvesting timber, leasing oil and gas rights, and renting for recreational purposes.

	12/31/95	12/31/94
Per Share Information		
Stock Price	180.00	180.00
Earnings Per Share	221.68	27.33
Price / Earnings Ratio	0.81	6.59
Book Value Per Share	394.30	183.61
Price / Book Value %	45.65	98.03
Dividends Per Share	n.a.	n.a.
Annual Financial Data		
Operating Results (000's)		
Total Revenues	2,899.5	434.9
Costs & Expenses	-138.7	-101.9
Income Before Taxes and Other	2,760.8	333.0
Other Items	n.a.	n.a.
Income Tax	-1,025.9	-118.7
Net Income	1,734.9	214.2
Cash Flow From Operations	n.a.	n.a.
Balance Sheet (000's)		
Cash & Equivalents	100.1	5.3
Total Current Assets	1,272.7	936.7
Fixed Assets, Net	1,275.5	495.2
Total Assets	4,715.1	1,524.7
Total Current Liabilities	886.9	78.2
Long-Term Debt	n.a.	n.a.
Stockholders' Equity	3,085.8	1,439.1
Performance & Financial Condition		
Return on Total Revenues %	59.83	49.26
Return on Avg Stockholders' Equity %	76.68	n.a.
Return on Average Assets %	55.61	n.a.
Current Ratio	1.43	11.99
Debt / Equity %	n.a.	n.a.

Compound Growth %'s	EPS %	711.12	Net Income %	709.84	Total Revenues %	566.77

Comments

The Company reported that it exchanged 1,080 acres of 30 year old plantation timber that was ready to harvest for several pieces of property in Louisiana and Mississippi. Furthermore, it completed planting 351 open acres in the Indian Bayou tract in Calcasieu Parish as well as completing a number of other acquisitions. There is no indication that the financial statements are audited or that they are prepared under GAAP. Compounded growth rates may be misleading because they only reflect two years of data.

Officers	Position		Ownership Information	12/31/95
John F. White	President		Number of Shares Outstanding	7,826
			Market Capitalization	$ 1,408,680
			Frequency Of Dividends	n.a.
			Number of Shareholders	Under 500

Other Information

Transfer Agent	Company Office				Where Listed	OTC-PS
Auditor	Not indicated				Symbol	n.a.
Market Maker	None				SIC Code	6790
Broker Dealer	Standard Investment	Tel/Ext	(888)783-4688	Jack	Employees	1

Lakeland Bancorp, Inc.

250 Oakridge Road • Oak Ridge, NJ 07438 • Telephone (201)697-2000 • Fax (201)697-8385

Company Description

Lakeland Bancorp, Inc. is a holding company for its wholly owned subsidiary, Lakeland State Bank and the bank's wholly owned subsidiary, Lakeland Investment Corporation. The bank has 12 branch offices serving communities in northwestern New Jersey. During 1994, the Bank acquired a 9.9% interest in National Bank of Sussex County, a neighboring community bank with ten offices.

	12/31/95	12/31/94	12/31/93	12/31/92
Per Share Information				
Stock Price	18.25	13.94	12.12	10.50
Earnings Per Share	1.49	1.51	1.25	0.86
Price / Earnings Ratio	12.25	9.23	9.70	12.21
Book Value Per Share	9.87	8.12	7.18	5.61
Price / Book Value %	184.90	171.67	168.80	187.17
Dividends Per Share	0.49	0.38	0.31	0.26
Annual Financial Data				
Operating Results (000's)				
Net Interest Income	14,733.5	14,576.6	12,608.7	9,832.9
Loan Loss Provision	-128.7	-225.4	-694.8	-789.4
Non-Interest Income	1,982.7	1,912.4	1,832.2	1,703.8
Non-Interest Expense	-9,504.7	-9,257.7	-8,589.4	-7,389.8
Income Before Taxes and Other	7,082.9	7,006.0	5,156.8	3,357.6
Other Items	n.a.	n.a.	n.a.	n.a.
Income Tax	-2,286.7	-2,175.3	-1,509.2	-847.5
Net Income	4,796.2	4,830.7	3,647.6	2,510.1
Balance Sheet (000's)				
Cash & Securities	159,744.9	146,813.9	161,236.5	161,812.8
Loans, Net	187,812.1	172,196.8	145,957.1	118,999.9
Fixed Assets, Net	8,170.1	8,261.8	8,128.1	8,435.0
Total Assets	360,661.2	333,587.8	320,593.3	293,599.8
Deposits	327,941.9	307,121.3	297,300.8	272,903.2
Stockholders' Equity	32,039.8	26,161.0	23,069.2	17,341.4
Performance & Financial Condition				
Net Interest Margin	n.a.	n.a.	n.a.	n.a.
Return on Avg Stockholders' Equity %	16.48	19.62	18.05	15.24
Return on Average Assets %	1.38	1.48	1.19	1.01
Equity to Assets %	8.88	7.84	7.20	5.91
Reserve as a % of Non-Performing Loans	181.42	145.99	105.30	1150.23

Compound Growth %'s	EPS %	20.11	Net Income %	24.09	Net Interest Income %	14.43

Comments

The bank's loan portfolio is primarily in the residential real estate and commercial areas, representing 58% and 34% of total loans, respectively. There was a 2 for 1 stock split in 1995. All per share amounts have been adjusted accordingly. No explanation was provided for 1995's flat earnings. Return on assets and equity remained at impressive levels.

Officers	Position	Ownership Information	12/31/95
Robert B. Nicholson	Chairman	Number of Shares Outstanding	3,246,954
John W. Fredericks	President	Market Capitalization	$ 59,256,911
Arthur L. Zande	Exec VP, CEO	Frequency Of Dividends	Irregular
Bruce G. Bohuny	Secretary	Number of Shareholders	1,921
William J. Eckhardt	Vice President, Treasurer		

Other Information				
Transfer Agent	Atlantic National Bank in Edison		Where Listed	OTC-PS
Auditor	Radics & Co., LLC		Symbol	LLNW
Market Maker	Ryan, Beck & Co.	Telephone (800)325-7926	SIC Code	6020
Broker Dealer	Regular Stockbroker		Employees	167

Lamcor, Incorporated

Highway 169 North, P.O. Box 70 • Le Sueur, MN 56058 • Telephone (612)665-6658 • Fax (612)665-2870

Company Description

The Company is engaged in the business of laminating plastic and the manufacture of plastic pouches. Products are used primarily in the food, medical and industrial sectors with sales being made throughout the U.S. Many of the Company's products are used in the prepared food area where changing lifestyles dictate that meals be easily and safely stored and prepared. The Company was incorporated in Minnesota in 1986.

	09/30/95	09/30/94	09/30/93	09/30/92
Per Share Information				
Stock Price	3.38	1.56	0.75	0.75
Earnings Per Share	0.22	0.12	0.09	0.16
Price / Earnings Ratio	15.36	13.00	8.33	4.69
Book Value Per Share	1.35	1.06	0.92	0.84
Price / Book Value %	250.37	147.17	81.52	89.29
Dividends Per Share	n.a.	n.a.	n.a.	n.a.
Annual Financial Data				
Operating Results (000's)				
Total Revenues	7,163.8	4,826.6	3,694.4	3,194.6
Costs & Expenses	-6,578.9	-4,545.1	-3,506.3	-2,915.7
Income Before Taxes and Other	584.9	281.4	188.2	278.8
Other Items	n.a.	n.a.	n.a.	n.a.
Income Tax	-226.1	-104.5	-60.7	-86.5
Net Income	358.8	176.9	127.5	192.3
Cash Flow From Operations	413.1	-109.7	87.4	333.4
Balance Sheet (000's)				
Cash & Equivalents	62.9	6.2	89.2	128.7
Total Current Assets	2,122.7	1,878.9	1,187.0	1,080.8
Fixed Assets, Net	2,037.2	1,353.3	1,183.6	795.3
Total Assets	4,164.1	3,527.5	2,374.7	1,937.0
Total Current Liabilities	930.5	1,185.4	518.4	513.3
Long-Term Debt	1,277.8	837.8	589.6	316.0
Stockholders' Equity	1,809.9	1,407.3	1,211.8	1,074.6
Performance & Financial Condition				
Return on Total Revenues %	5.01	3.67	3.45	6.02
Return on Avg Stockholders' Equity %	22.30	13.51	11.15	19.78
Return on Average Assets %	9.33	5.99	5.91	10.65
Current Ratio	2.28	1.58	2.29	2.11
Debt / Equity %	70.60	59.53	48.65	29.41

Compound Growth %'s	EPS %	11.20	Net Income %	23.11	Total Revenues %	30.89

Comments

Sales and net income for the three months ended December 31, 1995, amounted to $1.8 million and $87,000 ($.05 per share), as compared to $1.7 million and $57,000 ($.04 per share), for the same period in 1994. A stabilization of raw material costs during 1995, with no significant increases seen for 1996, should position the Company well for the current year.

Officers	Position	Ownership Information	09/30/95
Toby N. Jensen	President	Number of Shares Outstanding	1,341,542
Leo W. Lund	Secretary	Market Capitalization	$ 4,534,412
		Frequency Of Dividends	n.a.
		Number of Shareholders	183

Other Information				
Transfer Agent	Corporate Stock Transfer, Inc.		Where Listed	OTC-BB
Auditor	House, Nezerka & Froelich		Symbol	LMOR
Market Maker	Paragon Capital Corporation	Telephone (800)345-0505	SIC Code	2671
Broker Dealer	Regular Stockbroker		Employees	42

Lancaster National Bank, The

P.O.Box 109 • Lancaster, NH 03584 • Telephone (603)788-4973 • Fax (603)788-2636

Company Description

The Lancaster National Bank is an independent bank serving the North Country communities of New Hampshire and Vermont. The Bank has been providing continuous service since 1881. The primary industries in the Bank's market area are wood products and tourism.

	12/31/95	12/31/94	12/31/93	12/31/92
Per Share Information				
Stock Price	44.50	40.00	35.00	30.00
Earnings Per Share	11.14	9.46	6.58	3.01
Price / Earnings Ratio	3.99	4.23	5.32	9.97
Book Value Per Share	77.96	68.14	60.08	53.31
Price / Book Value %	57.08	58.70	58.26	56.27
Dividends Per Share	1.80	1.40	1.10	0.85
Annual Financial Data				
Operating Results (000's)				
Net Interest Income	1,883.8	1,683.6	1,489.2	1,318.2
Loan Loss Provision	-36.1	-29.6	-60.6	-48.4
Non-Interest Income	93.5	93.2	81.2	74.4
Non-Interest Expense	-1,173.3	-1,107.1	-1,056.9	-1,092.6
Income Before Taxes and Other	767.9	640.0	452.9	251.5
Other Items	n.a.	n.a.	n.a.	n.a.
Income Tax	-266.6	-214.2	-156.7	-116.0
Net Income	501.3	425.8	296.2	135.5
Balance Sheet (000's)				
Cash & Securities	15,321.7	14,690.1	15,260.6	13,379.2
Loans, Net	21,483.8	23,017.6	22,539.2	22,563.1
Fixed Assets, Net	602.6	566.7	593.4	577.4
Total Assets	37,927.5	38,762.9	38,777.3	37,157.3
Deposits	34,250.5	35,543.0	35,947.6	34,553.4
Stockholders' Equity	3,508.1	3,066.3	2,703.5	2,398.8
Performance & Financial Condition				
Net Interest Margin	n.a.	n.a.	n.a.	n.a.
Return on Avg Stockholders' Equity %	15.25	14.76	11.61	5.88
Return on Average Assets %	1.31	1.10	0.78	0.36
Equity to Assets %	9.25	7.91	6.97	6.46
Reserve as a % of Non-Performing Loans	129.60	76.31	43.44	33.16

Compound Growth %'s	EPS %	54.68	Net Income %	54.64	Net Interest Income %	12.64

Comments

The bank's loan portfolio is heavily concentrated in residential real estate, representing 67% of total loans. Commercial real estate loans represent an additional 16%. The only significant concentration in loans, according to management, is to motels and bed and breakfast establishments, amounting to $1,074,614 at December 31, 1995. These loans equate to 31% of capital, but are considered by management to be of the highest quality. Although there are only 45,000 shares outstanding, 6,040 shares were traded during 1995.

Officers	Position	Ownership Information	12/31/95
Erling R. Roberts	Chairman	Number of Shares Outstanding	45,000
Lucius C. McIntire	President	Market Capitalization	$ 2,002,500
Jean R. Dion	COO	Frequency Of Dividends	Quarterly
J. Edward Perreault	Vice President	Number of Shareholders	110
James A. Seppala	Vice President, Head Cashier		

Other Information				
Transfer Agent	Company Office		Where Listed	OTC-PS
Auditor	Francis J. Dineen, CPA		Symbol	LNCE
Market Maker	Legg Mason Wood Walker, Inc.	Telephone (212)428-4949	SIC Code	6020
Broker Dealer	Pink sheet specialist		Employees	21

Lannett Company, Inc.

9000 State Road • Philadelphia, PA 19136 • Telephone (215)333-9000 • Fax (215)333-9004

Company Description

The Company manufactures and distributes pharmaceutical products sold under generic names, and has historically sold products under its trade or brand name. The Company also packages pharmaceutical products manufactured by other companies. In the 1991-1992 fiscal year, the Company suspended operations to upgrade and modernize the facilities.

	06/30/95	06/30/94	06/30/93	06/30/92
Per Share Information				
Stock Price	1.94	3.25	3.38	1.75
Earnings Per Share	0.03	-0.15	-0.33	-0.49
Price / Earnings Ratio	64.67	n.a.	n.a.	n.a.
Book Value Per Share	-0.78	-0.85	-0.75	-1.68
Price / Book Value %	n.a.	n.a.	n.a.	n.a.
Dividends Per Share	n.a.	n.a.	n.a.	n.a.
Annual Financial Data				
Operating Results (000's)				
Total Revenues	4,354.6	2,184.3	959.3	249.1
Costs & Expenses	-3,859.5	-2,941.3	-2,263.9	-2,443.2
Income Before Taxes and Other	351.1	-757.0	-1,645.3	-2,418.7
Other Items	n.a.	n.a.	n.a.	n.a.
Income Tax	-35.0	n.a.	n.a.	n.a.
Net Income	316.1	-757.0	-1,645.3	-2,418.7
Cash Flow From Operations	-16.1	-684.2	-1,395.4	-1,923.9
Balance Sheet (000's)				
Cash & Equivalents	39.0	133.6	221.7	200.0
Total Current Assets	1,113.0	757.9	485.9	311.7
Fixed Assets, Net	1,885.3	1,863.5	1,807.0	1,632.4
Total Assets	3,009.1	2,637.1	2,309.9	1,944.1
Total Current Liabilities	1,093.6	854.1	329.3	4,033.7
Long-Term Debt	5,956.3	6,207.4	5,715.5	n.a.
Stockholders' Equity	-4,040.8	-4,424.4	-3,734.8	-2,089.6
Performance & Financial Condition				
Return on Total Revenues %	7.26	-34.66	-171.50	-971.18
Return on Avg Stockholders' Equity %	n.a.	n.a.	n.a.	n.a.
Return on Average Assets %	11.20	-30.61	-77.35	-178.38
Current Ratio	1.02	0.89	1.48	0.08
Debt / Equity %	n.a.	n.a.	n.a.	n.a.

Compound Growth %'s	EPS % n.a.	Net Income % n.a.	Total Revenues % 159.55

Comments

Approximately $5.6 million of long-term debt at June 30, 1995, including a convertible debenture, is payable to the Company's Chairman. In accordance with the terms of the debt agreement, 8,000,000 shares of the Company's common stock are reserved for conversion. At February 15, 1996, officers and directors, as a group, owned approximately 27% of the Company's outstanding common stock.

Officers	Position	Ownership Information	06/30/95
William Farber	Chairman	Number of Shares Outstanding	5,206,128
Audrey Farber	Secretary, Treasurer	Market Capitalization	$ 10,099,888
Vlad Mikijanic	Vice President	Frequency Of Dividends	n.a.
		Number of Shareholders	554

Other Information			
Transfer Agent	Registrar & Transfer Company	Where Listed	OTC-PS
Auditor	Grant Thornton LLP	Symbol	LANN
Market Maker	Herzog, Heine, Geduld, Inc.	Telephone (800)221-3600	SIC Code	2834
Broker Dealer	Regular Stockbroker	Employees	30

Latshaw Enterprises, Inc.

2533 South West Street • Wichita, KS 67217 • Telephone (316)942-7266 • Fax (316)942-0518

Company Description

The Company, through its subsidiaries, manufactures and markets mechanical controls, cable devices, wire and screw machine parts, and precision injection molded and vacuum-formed plastic parts for use primarily by original equipment manufacturers. The Company also buys, or manufactures a limited number of consumer products for resale in the retail market. Sales to one customer accounted for 12% of sales in 1995, and sales to two customers accounted for 24% and 26% of sales in 1994 and 1993.

	10/28/95	10/29/94	10/30/93	10/31/92
Per Share Information				
Stock Price	7.50	8.00	5.25	4.25
Earnings Per Share	1.45	1.29	1.30	-0.15
Price / Earnings Ratio	5.17	6.20	4.04	n.a.
Book Value Per Share	23.09	20.53	18.18	13.98
Price / Book Value %	32.48	38.97	28.88	30.40
Dividends Per Share	n.a.	n.a.	n.a.	n.a.
Annual Financial Data				
Operating Results (000's)				
Total Revenues	41,277.0	38,463.0	31,619.0	26,825.0
Costs & Expenses	-39,143.0	-36,386.0	-29,573.0	-27,143.0
Income Before Taxes and Other	2,134.0	2,064.0	2,046.0	-318.0
Other Items	n.a.	n.a.	-681.0	124.0
Income Tax	-805.0	-871.0	-175.0	108.0
Net Income	1,329.0	1,193.0	1,190.0	-86.0
Cash Flow From Operations	1,676.0	1,938.0	710.0	1,566.0
Balance Sheet (000's)				
Cash & Equivalents	319.0	184.0	174.0	249.0
Total Current Assets	16,818.0	15,327.0	13,011.0	10,411.0
Fixed Assets, Net	7,075.0	6,411.0	5,843.0	4,680.0
Total Assets	24,648.0	21,964.0	19,066.0	15,631.0
Total Current Liabilities	7,827.0	6,900.0	5,379.0	4,258.0
Long-Term Debt	4,994.0	4,686.0	4,630.0	3,267.0
Stockholders' Equity	11,589.0	10,206.0	8,981.0	8,106.0
Performance & Financial Condition				
Return on Total Revenues %	3.22	3.10	3.76	-0.32
Return on Avg Stockholders' Equity %	12.20	12.44	13.93	-0.94
Return on Average Assets %	5.70	5.82	6.86	-0.46
Current Ratio	2.15	2.22	2.42	2.45
Debt / Equity %	43.09	45.91	51.55	40.30

Compound Growth %'s	EPS %	5.61	Net Income %	5.68	Total Revenues %	15.45

Comments

In September 1995, the Company acquired a company engaged in the manufacture and sale of injection molding products. The total purchase price of $1.2 million was primarily financed with a bank line of credit. Operations of this subsidiary have been included with those of the parent since September 1, 1995, the date of acquisition.

Officers	Position	Ownership Information	10/28/95
Michael E. Bukaty	President, COO	Number of Shares Outstanding	501,975
John Latshaw	CEO, Chairman of the Board	Market Capitalization	$ 3,764,813
David G. Carr	Senior VP, CFO	Frequency Of Dividends	n.a.
		Number of Shareholders	450

Other Information

			Where Listed	OTC-BB
Transfer Agent	United Missouri Bank		Symbol	LAEI
Auditor	Ernst & Young LLP		SIC Code	3625
Market Maker	Carr Securities Corporation	Telephone (800)221-2243	Employees	500
Broker Dealer	Regular Stockbroker			

Lexington Precision Corporation

767 Third Avenue • New York, NY 10017 • Telephone (212)319-4657 • Fax (212)319-4659

Company Description

The Company manufactures, to customer specifications, rubber and metal component parts used primarily by manufacturers of automobiles, industrial equipment, office equipment and computers, medical devices and home appliances. During 1995, 65.3% of the Company's sales were to the automobile industry. The Company was incorporated in the State of Delaware in 1966.

	12/31/95	12/31/94	12/31/93	12/31/92
Per Share Information				
Stock Price	3.13	2.00	n.a.	n.a.
Earnings Per Share	0.49	0.51	0.13	-1.11
Price / Earnings Ratio	6.39	3.92	n.a.	n.a.
Book Value Per Share	-1.18	-1.72	-2.38	-2.51
Price / Book Value %	n.a.	n.a.	n.a.	n.a.
Dividends Per Share	n.a.	n.a.	n.a.	n.a.
Annual Financial Data				
Operating Results (000's)				
Total Revenues	104,939.0	89,068.0	74,976.0	65,201.0
Costs & Expenses	-102,226.0	-86,702.0	-74,125.0	-69,378.0
Income Before Taxes and Other	2,713.0	2,366.0	851.0	-4,493.0
Other Items	n.a.	n.a.	n.a.	n.a.
Income Tax	-425.0	-34.0	n.a.	n.a.
Net Income	2,288.0	2,332.0	851.0	-4,493.0
Cash Flow From Operations	7,860.0	5,957.0	9,601.0	5,454.0
Balance Sheet (000's)				
Cash & Equivalents	118.0	79.0	33.0	32.0
Total Current Assets	24,478.0	22,752.0	15,715.0	14,257.0
Fixed Assets, Net	44,938.0	32,594.0	22,093.0	19,326.0
Total Assets	81,876.0	67,396.0	49,983.0	45,584.0
Total Current Liabilities	29,253.0	24,330.0	12,733.0	51,224.0
Long-Term Debt	56,033.0	49,627.0	46,273.0	3,795.0
Stockholders' Equity	-4,976.0	-7,215.0	-9,623.0	-10,170.0
Performance & Financial Condition				
Return on Total Revenues %	2.18	2.62	1.14	-6.89
Return on Avg Stockholders' Equity %	n.a.	n.a.	n.a.	n.a.
Return on Average Assets %	3.07	3.97	1.78	-9.31
Current Ratio	0.84	0.94	1.23	0.28
Debt / Equity %	n.a.	n.a.	n.a.	n.a.

Compound Growth %'s	EPS %	94.15	Net Income %	63.97	Total Revenues %	17.19

Comments

Included in assets at December 31, 1995, is unamortized goodwill of $9.7 million. Included in liabilities at December 31, 1995, is $555,000 of redeemable preferred stock. Dividends on the preferred stock are deducted when calculating earnings per share. At December 31,1995, the Company had net operating loss carryfowards for federal income tax purposes of $7.4 million that expire in the years 2004 through 2007. The Company is projecting sales of $110 to $120 million for 1996. During 1993 and 1992, there was little trading activity in the Company's shares and no reliable price information.

Officers	Position	Ownership Information	12/31/95
Michael A. Lubin	Chairman	Number of Shares Outstanding	4,228,036
Warren Delano	President	Market Capitalization	$ 13,233,753
Dennis J. Welhouse	Senior VP, CFO	Frequency Of Dividends	n.a.
Kenneth I. Greenstein	Secretary	Number of Shareholders	1,100

Other Information

Transfer Agent	KeyCorp Shareholder Services, Inc.			Where Listed	OTC-BB
Auditor	Ernst & Young LLP			Symbol	LEXP
Market Maker	McDonald & Company Securities	Telephone	(216)443-2350	SIC Code	3060
Broker Dealer	Regular Stockbroker			Employees	1131

Lexington Telephone Company

P.O. Box 808 • Lexington, NC 27293-0808 • Telephone (704)249-5781 • Fax (704)243-3026

Company Description

The Company provides telephone sales and services to the businesses and residents of Davidson County, North Carolina, and is regulated by state and federal commissions. The Company is celebrating its 100th year in 1996.

	12/31/94	12/31/93	12/31/92
Per Share Information			
Stock Price	210.00	175.00	160.00
Earnings Per Share	26.50	20.67	24.69
Price / Earnings Ratio	7.92	8.47	6.48
Book Value Per Share	198.44	181.60	172.44
Price / Book Value %	105.83	96.37	92.79
Dividends Per Share	9.80	8.65	7.80
Annual Financial Data			
Operating Results (000's)			
Total Revenues	21,819.1	19,721.4	19,920.7
Costs & Expenses	-15,126.8	-14,804.4	-13,866.1
Income Before Taxes and Other	6,136.5	4,917.0	6,015.5
Other Items	n.a.	n.a.	n.a.
Income Tax	-2,369.1	-1,938.5	-2,440.4
Net Income	3,767.4	2,978.5	3,575.1
Cash Flow From Operations	7,576.1	6,398.1	n.a.
Balance Sheet (000's)			
Cash & Equivalents	895.4	256.4	n.a.
Total Current Assets	4,360.0	3,474.7	n.a.
Fixed Assets, Net	36,716.7	33,606.4	n.a.
Total Assets	46,628.7	41,476.5	n.a.
Total Current Liabilities	4,562.4	4,668.8	n.a.
Long-Term Debt	4,265.0	1,815.0	n.a.
Stockholders' Equity	28,424.4	26,976.8	n.a.
Performance & Financial Condition			
Return on Total Revenues %	17.27	15.10	17.95
Return on Avg Stockholders' Equity %	13.60	11.36	13.63
Return on Average Assets %	8.55	7.64	n.a.
Current Ratio	0.96	0.74	n.a.
Debt / Equity %	15.00	6.73	n.a.

Compound Growth %'s	EPS %	3.60	Net Income %	2.65	Total Revenues %	4.66

Comments

The Company has investments in a number of emerging communications-related businesses, including Sprint Cellular, American Telecasting, Inc., Access/ON Multimedia Services, Inc. and others. The 1995 rsults were not available when we went to press. Compounded growth rates are based on only two years.

Officers	Position	Ownership Information	12/31/94
Richard G. Reese	Chairman, President	Number of Shares Outstanding	137,180
Meredith H. Mode	Secretary	Market Capitalization	$ 28,807,800
Charles D. Harris	Vice President, Treasurer	Frequency Of Dividends	Quarterly
B. Earl Hester, Jr.	Vice President	Number of Shareholders	Under 500
Royster M. Tucker, Jr.	Vice President		

Other Information				
Transfer Agent	Company Office		Where Listed	OTC-BB
Auditor	McGladrey & Pullen, LLP		Symbol	LENG
Market Maker	J.C. Bradford & Co.	Telephone (800)251-1740	SIC Code	4810
Broker Dealer	Regular Stockbroker		Employees	117

Life Insurance Company of Alabama

302 Broad Street • Gadsden, AL 35902 • Telephone (205)543-2022 • Fax (205)549-0070

Company Description

The Company underwrites life insurance policies. The Company was formed in 1952. It has two classes of stock: a $5 par voting common and a $1 par nonvoting class A. The dividend is always a percent of par value. There are 87,548 shares of voting common outstanding and 628,037 shares of class A outstanding We used a weighted average method for per share calculations and treated each share of $5 par as five shares of class A for total outstanding shares of 1,065,777.

	12/31/95	12/31/94	12/31/93	12/31/92
Per Share Information				
Stock Price	2.44	2.37	2.37	2.19
Earnings Per Share	0.71	0.18	0.41	0.40
Price / Earnings Ratio	3.44	13.17	5.78	5.48
Book Value Per Share	5.34	4.24	4.24	3.64
Price / Book Value %	45.69	55.90	55.90	60.16
Dividends Per Share	0.09	0.09	0.09	0.09
Annual Financial Data				
Operating Results (000's)				
Total Revenues	26,014.8	24,619.8	23,356.1	22,191.1
Costs & Expenses	-25,130.2	-24,300.8	-22,869.1	-21,759.8
Income Before Taxes and Other	849.2	283.7	444.9	431.3
Other Items	n.a.	n.a.	n.a.	n.a.
Income Tax	-90.0	-95.3	-7.2	n.a.
Net Income	759.2	188.4	437.7	431.3
Cash Flow From Operations	n.a.	n.a.	n.a.	n.a.
Balance Sheet (000's)				
Cash & Equivalents	632.5	2,985.4	1,972.8	2,035.8
Total Current Assets	2,031.6	4,096.6	3,247.3	3,067.4
Fixed Assets, Net	803.9	812.2	813.7	821.1
Total Assets	57,082.1	54,119.7	52,655.4	50,777.9
Total Current Liabilities	692.7	587.4	542.1	502.1
Long-Term Debt	n.a.	n.a.	n.a.	n.a.
Stockholders' Equity	5,693.6	4,517.1	4,514.0	3,877.7
Performance & Financial Condition				
Return on Total Revenues %	2.92	0.77	1.87	1.94
Return on Avg Stockholders' Equity %	14.87	4.17	10.43	11.94
Return on Average Assets %	1.37	0.35	0.85	0.87
Current Ratio	2.93	6.97	5.99	6.11
Debt / Equity %	n.a.	n.a.	n.a.	n.a.

Compound Growth %'s	EPS %	21.08	Net Income %	20.74	Total Revenues %	5.44

Comments

Noncurrent assets primarily consist of investments in bonds. Income taxes have been disproportionately low in 1992 and 1993 because of available net operating loss carryovers which have now been used. There is no indication whether or not the financial statements are audited.

Officers	Position	Ownership Information	12/31/95
Clarence W. Daugette, III	President	Number of Shares Outstanding	1,065,777
Robert W. Echols, Jr.	Exec VP, Secretary	Market Capitalization	$ 2,600,496
Raymond R. Renfrow, Jr.	Senior VP	Frequency Of Dividends	Annual
M. Lynn Lowe	Senior VP, Treasurer	Number of Shareholders	Under 500

Other Information

Transfer Agent	Company Office			Where Listed	OTC-BB
Auditor	Not indicated			Symbol	LINS
Market Maker	Morgan Keegan & Company, Inc.	Telephone	(800)238-7533	SIC Code	6310
Broker Dealer	Regular Stockbroker			Employees	75

Limco Del Mar, Ltd.

1141 Cummings Road • Santa Paula, CA 93060-9708 • Telephone (805)525-5541 • Fax (805)525-8211

Company Description

The Partnership is in the business of lemon and avocado farming on 211 acres of farmlands that it holds for eventual residential development. The property is located in Ventura, California. The partnership was formed in 1986. Limoneira Company, a general partner, owns appoximately 1% of the limited partner units.

	10/31/95	10/31/94	10/31/93	10/31/92
Per Unit Information				
Price Per Unit	9.00	7.00	9.00	9.00
Earnings Per Unit	1.56	1.26	0.51	0.36
Price / Earnings Ratio	5.77	5.56	17.65	25.00
Book Value Per Unit	5.62	4.61	3.40	2.91
Price / Book Value %	160.14	151.84	264.71	309.28
Distributions Per Unit	0.50	n.a.	n.a.	n.a.
Cash Flow Per Unit	1.75	1.38	0.62	0.46
Annual Financial Data				
Operating Results (000's)				
Total Revenues	1,115.2	764.5	512.8	506.9
Costs & Expenses	-567.5	-320.4	-335.0	-379.6
Operating Income	547.7	444.2	177.8	127.3
Other Items	n.a.	n.a.	n.a.	n.a.
Net Income	547.7	444.2	177.8	127.3
Cash Flow From Operations	614.0	485.6	218.7	160.1
Balance Sheet (000's)				
Cash & Equivalents	260.4	8.9	36.6	96.6
Total Current Assets	311.6	35.3	61.2	115.7
Investments In Farm property	1,793.1	1,792.2	1,672.0	1,588.8
Total Assets	2,261.8	2,151.8	2,057.0	2,010.4
Total Current Liabilities	17.3	1.7	1.2	7.7
Long-Term Debt	226.1	501.1	851.1	975.8
Partners' Capital	2,018.4	1,648.9	1,204.7	1,026.9
Performance & Financial Condition				
Return on Total Revenues %	49.11	58.10	34.68	25.11
Return on Average Partners' Capital %	n.a.	n.a.	n.a.	n.a.
Return on Average Assets %	24.82	21.11	8.74	6.36
Current Ratio	18.05	20.19	51.28	15.00
Debt / Equity %	11.20	30.39	70.65	95.03

Compound Growth %'s	EPU %	63.03	Net Income %	62.65	Total Revenues %	30.06

Comments

Cash arising from recent profitable years has been used to reduce bank debt and to make a distribution to partners. In November, 1995, a Ventura City initiative was passed by the voters which restricts zoning of the Company's properties to only agricultural usage until the year 2030 unless the zoning change is approved by the majority of Ventura City voters. As a result, previously capitalized development costs of $172,496 have been expensed. Compounded growth rates are misleading because of the annual fluctuations in agriculture.

Officers	Position	Ownership Information	10/31/95
J M. Dickenson	CEO	Number of Shares Outstanding	351,450
Volney H. Craig	Other	Market Capitalization	$ 3,163,050
Robert A. Hardison	Other	Frequency Of Distributions	n.a.
		Number of Partners	Under 500

Other Information

Transfer Agent	Company Office				Where Listed	OTC-BB
Auditor	Deloitte & Touche LLP				Symbol	LIDM
Market Maker	Seidler Companies, Inc., The	Telephone	(800)421-0164		SIC Code	0174
Broker Dealer	Standard Investment	Tel/Ext	(888)783-4688	Jack	Employees	None

Limoneira Company

1141 Cummings Road • Santa Paula, CA 93060-9708 • Telephone (805)525-5541 • Fax (805)525-8211

Company Description

The Company engages primarily in growing citrus, avocados and row crops, and picking, hauling and packing citrus. Products are marketed primarily through Sunkist Growers, Inc. and Calavo Growers of California. The Company was formed in 1894 and went public in 1915.

	10/31/93	10/31/92
Per Share Information		
Stock Price	24.00	24.00
Earnings Per Share	1.04	-0.77
Price / Earnings Ratio	23.08	n.a.
Book Value Per Share	22.71	22.07
Price / Book Value %	105.68	108.74
Dividends Per Share	0.39	1.26
Annual Financial Data		
Operating Results (000's)		
Total Revenues	10,014.6	6,562.2
Costs & Expenses	-8,690.5	-7,671.1
Income Before Taxes and Other	1,324.1	-1,108.9
Other Items	n.a.	n.a.
Income Tax	-484.1	483.8
Net Income	840.0	-625.1
Cash Flow From Operations	3,321.1	-3,112.7
Balance Sheet (000's)		
Cash & Equivalents	334.3	539.0
Total Current Assets	5,719.4	4,371.7
Fixed Assets, Net	19,595.2	17,352.6
Total Assets	26,723.4	23,995.2
Total Current Liabilities	4,227.6	2,125.2
Long-Term Debt	3,639.5	3,562.0
Stockholders' Equity	18,414.1	17,890.3
Performance & Financial Condition		
Return on Total Revenues %	8.39	-9.53
Return on Avg Stockholders' Equity %	4.63	-3.36
Return on Average Assets %	3.31	-2.57
Current Ratio	1.35	2.06
Debt / Equity %	19.76	19.91

Compound Growth %'s	EPS % n.a.	Net Income % n.a.	Total Revenues %	52.61

Comments

The Company owns approximately 3,075 acres of land acquired at various times over the last 100 years at an average cost of about $260 an acre. Substantial gains might be realized if the Company were to sell some of its real estate assets, although there has been no indication of such activity other than a small subdivision of beach front property. The compounded growth rate is probably misleading because only two years of data are available for the calculation. The 1995 and 1994 reports were not obtainable.

Officers	Position	Ownership Information	10/31/93
Alan M. Teague	Chairman	Number of Shares Outstanding	810,811
John M. Dickenson, III	President, CEO	Market Capitalization	$ 19,459,464
Alfonso A. Guilin	Exec VP	Frequency Of Dividends	Quarterly
Pierre Y. Tada	VP - Finance, CFO	Number of Shareholders	Under 500
T. Eugene Caulfield	VP - Sales		

Other Information

Transfer Agent	Company Office				Where Listed	OTC-BB
Auditor	Deloitte & Touche LLP				Symbol	LMNR
Market Maker	Robotti & Eng, Incorporated	Telephone	(212)986-4800		SIC Code	0174
Broker Dealer	Standard Investment	Tel/Ext	(888)783-4688	Jack	Employees	n.a.

Lipe-Rollway Corporation

P.O. Box 4827 • Syracuse, NY 13221 • Telephone (315)457-6211 • Fax (315)457-2263

Company Description

The Company manufactures and markets a broad range of radial thrust and straight cylindrical roller bearings and ball bearings. It also manufactures bar feed attachments for machine tools, vibratory brush feeder/orienters and conveyor systems. The Company was organized in 1882 and went public in 1941. It recently received a buyout offer which was expected to close in June, 1996.

	11/27/94	11/28/93
Per Share Information		
Stock Price	2.00	1.00
Earnings Per Share	0.01	-0.33
Price / Earnings Ratio	200.00	n.a.
Book Value Per Share	6.50	5.95
Price / Book Value %	30.77	16.81
Dividends Per Share	n.a.	n.a.
Annual Financial Data		
Operating Results (000's)		
Total Revenues	32,903.8	32,453.1
Costs & Expenses	-32,485.3	-32,451.1
Income Before Taxes and Other	418.5	2.0
Other Items	n.a.	n.a.
Income Tax	-317.0	-148.2
Net Income	101.6	-146.1
Cash Flow From Operations	-229.1	1,076.1
Balance Sheet (000's)		
Cash & Equivalents	59.7	9.3
Total Current Assets	19,419.6	15,944.4
Fixed Assets, Net	7,302.6	5,793.6
Total Assets	27,762.2	22,521.5
Total Current Liabilities	10,439.3	12,416.3
Long-Term Debt	10,165.4	3,702.7
Stockholders' Equity	4,948.7	4,535.4
Performance & Financial Condition		
Return on Total Revenues %	0.31	-0.45
Return on Avg Stockholders' Equity %	2.14	-2.95
Return on Average Assets %	0.40	-0.57
Current Ratio	1.86	1.28
Debt / Equity %	205.42	81.64

Compound Growth %'s	EPS %	n.a.	Net Income %	n.a.	Total Revenues %	1.39

Comments

The 1995 statements could not be released because of the pending buyout. However, we include this company because it is a good example of what often happens to over-the-counter stocks that trade at a price below book value. Lipe-Rollway more than quadrupled in price overnight. After the acquisition was announced, it traded at $9 per share.

Officers	Position	Ownership Information	11/27/94
H.Follett Hodgkins, Jr.	Chairman, CEO	Number of Shares Outstanding	761,898
Stephen M. Bregande	President, COO	Market Capitalization	$ 1,523,796
William J. Eames	CFO, Treasurer	Frequency Of Dividends	n.a.
Donald M. Mawhinney,Jr.	Secretary	Number of Shareholders	Under 500

Other Information

Transfer Agent	Key Bank of Central New York, Syracuse			Where Listed	OTC-BB
Auditor	Ernst & Young LLP			Symbol	LIPE
Market Maker	A.G. Edwards & Sons, Inc.	Telephone	(800)325-8197	SIC Code	3562
Broker Dealer	Regular Stockbroker			Employees	270

Logan Clay Products Company

P.O. Box 698 • Logan, OH 43138-0698 • Telephone (614)385-2184 • Fax (614)385-9336

Company Description

The Company's primary operation is a clay products manufacturing facility located in Logan, Ohio, but it also operates a gas pipeline and maintains working interests in oil and gas producing activities.

	11/30/95	11/30/94	11/30/93	11/30/92
Per Share Information				
Stock Price	20.75	25.50	20.50	20.50
Earnings Per Share	-0.04	0.45	-2.08	-1.52
Price / Earnings Ratio	n.a.	56.67	n.a.	n.a.
Book Value Per Share	45.13	43.34	41.41	43.78
Price / Book Value %	45.98	58.84	49.50	46.83
Dividends Per Share	0.10	n.a.	0.40	0.40
Annual Financial Data				
Operating Results (000's)				
Total Revenues	8,217.2	8,989.2	7,974.4	7,833.3
Costs & Expenses	-8,123.9	-8,761.9	-8,402.5	-8,101.3
Income Before Taxes and Other	11.3	132.2	-527.1	-353.2
Other Items	n.a.	n.a.	n.a.	n.a.
Income Tax	-18.6	-51.5	143.2	72.3
Net Income	-7.4	80.7	-383.9	-280.9
Cash Flow From Operations	336.1	675.2	259.7	488.1
Balance Sheet (000's)				
Cash & Equivalents	1,179.9	873.1	730.6	1,041.7
Total Current Assets	4,890.8	4,930.8	4,823.2	5,597.9
Fixed Assets, Net	2,545.1	2,495.8	2,546.8	2,430.8
Total Assets	8,100.2	8,524.2	8,759.8	9,418.3
Total Current Liabilities	538.9	510.1	342.9	429.8
Long-Term Debt	n.a.	n.a.	n.a.	n.a.
Stockholders' Equity	7,191.4	7,480.6	7,635.2	8,110.9
Performance & Financial Condition				
Return on Total Revenues %	-0.09	0.90	-4.81	-3.59
Return on Avg Stockholders' Equity %	-0.10	1.07	-4.88	-3.39
Return on Average Assets %	-0.09	0.93	-4.22	-2.99
Current Ratio	9.08	9.67	14.07	13.02
Debt / Equity %	n.a.	n.a.	n.a.	n.a.

Compound Growth %'s	EPS % n.a.	Net Income % n.a.	Total Revenues % 1.61

Comments

1995 results include a one time charge of $243,336 for the cost of pension plan curtailment. The Company has been using excess cash to repurchase shares and invest in other businesses including the construction and rental of a building for a Wendy's franchise.

Officers	Position	Ownership Information	11/30/95
Barton S. Holl	Chairman	Number of Shares Outstanding	159,359
Richard H. Holl	President, CEO	Market Capitalization	$ 3,306,699
Richard H. Brandt	Exec VP, COO	Frequency Of Dividends	Annual
		Number of Shareholders	Under 500

Other Information

Transfer Agent	Company Office		Where Listed	OTC-BB
Auditor	Robinson, Caltrider, Associates		Symbol	JGNC
Market Maker	Martin Nelson & Co., Inc.	Telephone (206)682-6261	SIC Code	3200
Broker Dealer	Regular Stockbroker		Employees	96

LogiMetrics, Inc.

121-03 Dupont Street • Plainview, NY 11803 • Telephone (516)349-1700 • Fax (516)349-8552

Company Description

The Company manufactures and sells travelling wave tube amplifiers and complete electronics systems used for communication, mapping, radar and other applications. The Company's products are used by the U.S. Government and foreign governments for both military and non-military purposes. When sold separately, the Company's amplifiers range in price from $12,500 to $395,000. The Company was incorporated in Delaware in 1968.

	06/30/95	06/30/94	06/30/93	06/30/92
Per Share Information				
Stock Price	0.63	0.63	0.63	0.63
Earnings Per Share	0.06	0.06	0.10	0.10
Price / Earnings Ratio	10.50	10.50	6.30	6.30
Book Value Per Share	0.93	1.08	0.90	0.93
Price / Book Value %	67.74	58.33	70.00	67.74
Dividends Per Share	n.a.	n.a.	n.a.	n.a.
Annual Financial Data				
Operating Results (000's)				
Total Revenues	8,905.6	6,899.2	8,065.3	8,329.5
Costs & Expenses	-8,677.3	-6,715.8	-7,760.1	-7,993.4
Income Before Taxes and Other	228.3	183.5	305.2	336.1
Other Items	n.a.	25.0	n.a.	n.a.
Income Tax	-70.5	-59.0	-83.4	-134.5
Net Income	157.8	149.5	221.8	201.6
Cash Flow From Operations	-210.9	-307.1	257.3	-137.9
Balance Sheet (000's)				
Cash & Equivalents	40.9	80.1	250.4	284.3
Total Current Assets	7,553.4	6,777.8	5,855.2	5,854.2
Fixed Assets, Net	379.6	466.9	544.7	494.4
Total Assets	7,979.2	7,299.7	6,463.2	6,419.6
Total Current Liabilities	2,715.6	4,604.9	3,806.5	3,895.7
Long-Term Debt	2,604.9	226.9	338.2	434.3
Stockholders' Equity	2,658.7	2,467.9	2,318.5	2,089.7
Performance & Financial Condition				
Return on Total Revenues %	1.77	2.17	2.75	2.42
Return on Avg Stockholders' Equity %	6.16	6.24	10.06	10.26
Return on Average Assets %	2.07	2.17	3.44	3.47
Current Ratio	2.78	1.47	1.54	1.50
Debt / Equity %	97.97	9.19	14.59	20.78

Compound Growth %'s	EPS %	-15.66	Net Income %	-7.84	Total Revenues %	2.25

Comments

Sales to agencies of the U.S. Government and to foreign governments during the year ended June 30, 1995, amounted to 29% and 48% of total sales, respectively. Trading in the Company's stock has been sporadic over the years presented with trades ranging from $.25 to $1.00. In July, 1995, the Company completed a private offering of convertible debentures and warrants which totaled $312,000. Sales and net income for the six months ended December 31, 1995, were $4.2 million and $657,000 ($.01 per share) as compared to $3.8 million and $501,000 ($.02 per share).

Officers	Position	Ownership Information	06/30/95
Murray H. Feigenbaum	President, CEO	Number of Shares Outstanding	2,860,602
Jerome Deutsch	Exec VP	Market Capitalization	$ 1,802,179
Steven D. Feigenbaum	Vice President	Frequency Of Dividends	n.a.
Barbara M. Divack	Vice President, Secretary	Number of Shareholders	443

Other Information

Transfer Agent	American Stock Transfer & Trust Company		Where Listed	OTC-PS
Auditor	Holtz, Rubenstein & Co., LLP		Symbol	DLUP
Market Maker	Carr Securities Corporation	Telephone (800)221-2243	SIC Code	3663
Broker Dealer	Regular Stockbroker		Employees	49

Louisville Bedding Company

10400 • Louisville, KY 40299-2510 • Telephone (502)491-3370 • Fax (502)493-7706

Company Description

The Company is engaged in the manufacture of textile home furnishings. Products include quilted mattress pads, pillows, pillow shams, dust ruffles and decorative home furnishings. The Company was incorporated in 1903 as the Louisville Pillow Company, successor to the business of a partnership organized in 1889. The present name was adopted in 1917. We prepared a brief historical vignette for your enjoyment, displayed on the following page.

	12/29/95	12/30/94	12/31/93	12/29/92
Per Share Information				
Stock Price	28.50	30.50	19.00	18.50
Earnings Per Share	3.47	6.14	4.05	1.78
Price / Earnings Ratio	8.21	4.97	4.69	10.39
Book Value Per Share	37.66	34.73	29.02	28.12
Price / Book Value %	75.68	87.82	65.47	65.79
Dividends Per Share	0.76	0.73	0.69	0.68
Annual Financial Data				
Operating Results (000's)				
Total Revenues	119,487.4	123,162.0	109,524.0	108,514.4
Costs & Expenses	-116,261.2	-117,318.9	-105,706.8	-106,460.6
Income Before Taxes and Other	3,226.2	5,843.0	3,817.2	2,053.8
Other Items	n.a.	n.a.	150.0	n.a.
Income Tax	-1,036.8	-2,027.0	-1,376.0	-860.1
Net Income	2,189.4	3,816.0	2,591.2	1,193.7
Cash Flow From Operations	7,715.5	563.4	2,511.1	1,686.4
Balance Sheet (000's)				
Cash & Equivalents	587.3	765.1	1,040.4	n.a.
Total Current Assets	33,996.1	40,309.8	33,246.1	30,362.0
Fixed Assets, Net	17,433.1	17,379.3	14,761.7	9,840.0
Total Assets	53,513.1	60,144.9	50,060.2	44,795.3
Total Current Liabilities	12,795.3	17,099.9	14,913.4	14,450.1
Long-Term Debt	17,472.6	20,396.2	15,216.3	11,637.0
Stockholders' Equity	22,186.8	21,246.9	17,647.8	17,208.3
Performance & Financial Condition				
Return on Total Revenues %	1.83	3.10	2.37	1.10
Return on Avg Stockholders' Equity %	10.08	19.62	14.87	7.12
Return on Average Assets %	3.85	6.93	5.46	2.87
Current Ratio	2.66	2.36	2.23	2.10
Debt / Equity %	78.75	96.00	86.22	67.62

Compound Growth %'s	EPS %	24.92	Net Income %	22.41	Total Revenues %	3.26

Comments

1995 was reported by management to be a very difficult year and included the relocation of the old, three-story manufacturing facility to a one story manufacturing and distribution facility. Only summary information was available for 1993 and 1992. Compounded earnings growth rates are misleading because of low profits in 1992, the base year. The Company reacquired 5% of its outstanding shares in 1995.

Officers	Position	Ownership Information	12/29/95
Harold C. Forrester, Sr.	Chairman	Number of Shares Outstanding	589,084
John M. Minihan	President, CEO	Market Capitalization	$ 16,788,894
Christian F. Rapp	Senior VP, CFO	Frequency Of Dividends	Quarterly
Dan J. Ricardson	VP - Manufacturing	Number of Shareholders	Under 500
Virginia L. Koernner	Controller		

Other Information

Transfer Agent	Company Office			Where Listed	OTC-BB
Auditor	KPMG Peat Marwick LLP			Symbol	LBED
Market Maker	Koonce Securities, Inc.	Telephone	(800)368-2802	SIC Code	2515
Broker Dealer	Standard Investment	Tel/Ext	(888)783-4688 Jack	Employees	800

Pillows & Mattresses

Seven years ago, in 1989, the Louisville Bedding Company proudly celebrated its centennial. There was indeed a great deal to celebrate. The Company, whose current sales of $120 million are backed by strong financial condition, has been in existence since before automobiles, radios or moving pictures were part of our landscape. It was born in an era of discovery, invention and expansion in America, when telephones were novelties and only forty-two states existed in the United States.

Situated as it is on the southern bank of the Ohio River, Louisville, Kentucky was in 1889 a major industrial and mercantile hub on the border between the north and south. The twentieth largest city in our nation, Louisville boasted the latest in modern conveniences and a pervasive spirit of enterprise. It was a perfect time, Samuel D. Cruse decided, to strike out on his own.

Mr. Cruse had gained early experience working for a mercantile company. He now began to manufacture mattresses and pillows himself by forming the Louisville Pillow and Mattress Company, which later became the Louisville Bedding Company. The business grew and by about 1900, wool as well as cotton comforters had been added to the company's product lines. In 1905 the Company, which now had an approximate value of $31,400, was sold to Milburn Kelly.

Over the next two decades Louisville Bedding Company's growth was impressive, with sales reaching $1,000,000 by 1923. Improvements during this time included the purchase of *auto trucks*, which began to replace the mules and wagons commonly used for deliveries in earlier years. The Company's prosperity was also reflected in its support of the war effort when, in 1917, it purchased $8,000 worth of Liberty Bonds. After the war, the Roaring Twenties saw America anxious to indulge in material comforts. The Company capitalized on this mood, advertising its wares with the slogan, "Invest in Rest".

By 1930, however, sales had mysteriously declined by over fifty percent. Good times vanished; in fact, the company stopped making *any* money. The Great Depression hit Louisville Bedding hard, and the company struggled simply to survive and keep its workers on the payroll. Their determination paid off. Employees later gratefully recalled that they always had a paycheck and that none were laid off. Not many companies can boast of an accomplishment of this magnitude.

Today, the Company has facilities located throughout Kentucky and in California. Sales showrooms exist in New York and Atlanta and all of their products are marketed internationally. The Company now has over 800 employees and a book value of $16,800,000. It is clear that Louisville Bedding Company has done much more than simply survive; it is a model for other would-be winners to follow.

M.H. Rhodes, Inc.

99 Thompson Road • Avon, CT 06001 • Telephone (860)673-3281 • Fax (860)673-8633

Company Description

The Company and its Canadian subsidiary manufacture mechanical and electrical timers. The Company, incorporated in Delaware, has been in business in the U.S. since 1930, and in Canada since 1960. Engineering during 1995, was focused on developing new timers to fill niche markets. Announcements are to be made in 1996.

	12/31/95	12/31/94	12/31/93	12/31/92
Per Share Information				
Stock Price	5.50	5.50	3.75	5.00
Earnings Per Share	-4.38	0.38	0.62	-3.23
Price / Earnings Ratio	n.a.	14.47	6.05	n.a.
Book Value Per Share	12.66	16.00	14.84	13.49
Price / Book Value %	43.44	34.38	25.27	37.06
Dividends Per Share	n.a.	n.a.	n.a.	n.a.
Annual Financial Data				
Operating Results (000's)				
Total Revenues	8,083.7	9,844.0	10,328.3	10,673.2
Costs & Expenses	-8,968.6	-9,771.5	-10,189.6	-11,338.6
Income Before Taxes and Other	-884.8	72.6	138.7	-665.4
Other Items	n.a.	n.a.	n.a.	n.a.
Income Tax	-10.6	6.8	-9.1	-13.0
Net Income	-895.5	79.4	129.5	-678.4
Cash Flow From Operations	370.6	2.9	82.8	315.4
Balance Sheet (000's)				
Cash & Equivalents	32.5	6.2	14.3	49.8
Total Current Assets	4,470.6	5,962.6	5,559.5	5,654.4
Fixed Assets, Net	844.3	995.1	1,086.0	1,300.2
Total Assets	5,347.0	6,998.3	6,709.1	7,000.0
Total Current Liabilities	2,384.7	2,380.5	2,520.7	4,097.0
Long-Term Debt	275.6	1,160.6	1,039.7	37.0
Stockholders' Equity	2,564.9	3,330.9	3,120.5	2,836.5
Performance & Financial Condition				
Return on Total Revenues %	-11.08	0.81	1.25	-6.36
Return on Avg Stockholders' Equity %	-30.38	2.46	4.35	-21.81
Return on Average Assets %	-14.51	1.16	1.89	-8.04
Current Ratio	1.87	2.50	2.21	1.38
Debt / Equity %	10.75	34.84	33.32	1.31

Compound Growth %'s	EPS % n.a.	Net Income % n.a.	Total Revenues %	-8.85

Comments

At December 31, 1995, the Company had a backlog of sale orders totaling $2.8 million. Officers and directors, as a group, owned 13.5% of the Company's outstanding common stock at March 27, 1996.

Officers	Position	Ownership Information	12/31/95
J. L. Morelli	President, Chairman	Number of Shares Outstanding	202,599
A. D. Springer	VP - Finance, Treasurer	Market Capitalization	$ 1,114,295
S. L. Vanasse	Secretary	Frequency Of Dividends	n.a.
H. B. Matles	Vice President	Number of Shareholders	667

Other Information

Transfer Agent	Mellon Shareholders Services, LLC		Where Listed	OTC-BB
Auditor	Riggs, Mahoney & Sabal		Symbol	RHMH
Market Maker	Chicago Corporation, The	Telephone (800)621-1674	SIC Code	3625
Broker Dealer	Regular Stockbroker		Employees	89

MLH Income Realty Partnership V

225 Liberty Street • New york, NY 10080-6112 • Telephone (212)236-4930 • Fax (212)236-1817

Company Description

The Partnership is a real estate investment company. It was formed in 1983 by the organizer selling 500,000 units in a public offering, thereby raising $500 million. The proceeds were used to acquire 20 properties in different cities, all within the United States. The officers listed are those of the general partner.

	09/30/95	09/30/94	09/30/93
Per Unit Information			
Price Per Unit	242.00	370.00	505.00
Earnings Per Unit	20.50	47.34	25.11
Price / Earnings Ratio	11.80	7.82	20.11
Book Value Per Unit	251.99	485.75	625.87
Price / Book Value %	96.04	76.17	80.69
Distributions Per Unit	254.27	187.45	48.90
Cash Flow Per Unit	246.22	212.27	48.54
Annual Financial Data			
Operating Results (000's)			
Total Revenues	49,451.0	74,501.0	46,837.0
Costs & Expenses	-23,601.0	-30,234.0	-31,108.0
Operating Income	12,621.0	33,572.0	14,636.0
Other Items	n.a.	n.a.	n.a.
Net Income	12,621.0	33,572.0	14,636.0
Cash Flow From Operations	129,394.0	111,555.0	25,511.0
Balance Sheet (000's)			
Cash & Equivalents	71,984.0	59,422.0	21,188.0
Total Current Assets	128,395.0	113,717.0	43,048.0
Investments In Real Estate	161,088.0	273,636.0	340,622.0
Total Assets	289,483.0	387,353.0	383,670.0
Total Current Liabilities	118,175.0	90,192.0	17,303.0
Long-Term Debt	n.a.	n.a.	n.a.
Partners' Capital	132,426.0	255,278.0	322,822.0
Performance & Financial Condition			
Return on Total Revenues %	25.52	45.06	31.25
Return on Average Partners' Capital %	n.a.	n.a.	n.a.
Return on Average Assets %	3.73	8.71	n.a.
Current Ratio	1.09	1.26	2.49
Debt / Equity %	n.a.	n.a.	n.a.

Compound Growth %'s	EPU %	-9.64	Net Income %	-7.14	Total Revenues %	2.75

Comments

The Partnership has sold 16 of the original properties and hopes to sell the balance in the short term. Future distributions will depend on proceeds from these sales as well as the rents collected prior to their sale. There is no debt. The properties that remain are all downtown office buildings. Cash flow from operations and cash flow per unit include proceeds from property sales.

Officers	Position	Ownership Information	09/30/95
D. Bruce Brunson	President, COO	Number of Shares Outstanding	525,529
George I. Wagner	Senior VP	Market Capitalization	$ 127,178,018
Michael A. Karmelin	Vice President, CFO	Frequency Of Distributions	Quarterly
Thomas J. Brown	Director	Number of Partners	80,362
Jack A. Cuneo	Director		

Other Information

Transfer Agent	Company office				Where Listed	Order Matching Only
Auditor	Deloitte & Touche LLP				Symbol	n.a.
Market Maker	None				SIC Code	6510
Broker Dealer	Chicago Partnership Board	Tel/Ext	(800)272-6273	690	Employees	None

Mahoning National Bancorp, Inc.

P.O.Box 479 • Youngstown, OH 44501 • Telephone (216)742-7000 • Fax (330)742-7091

Company Description

Mahoning National Bancorp, Inc. is a one bank holding company. The subsidiary, Mahoning National Bank of Youngstown, is an independent bank offering typical banking services through its 24 banking locations in the Mahoning-Shenango Valley, Ohio market area.

	12/31/95	12/31/94	12/31/93	12/31/92
Per Share Information				
Stock Price	34.50	30.00	20.00	16.50
Earnings Per Share	3.20	2.72	2.26	1.80
Price / Earnings Ratio	10.78	11.03	8.85	9.17
Book Value Per Share	22.11	19.06	17.70	16.14
Price / Book Value %	156.04	157.40	112.99	102.23
Dividends Per Share	0.93	0.79	0.69	0.62
Annual Financial Data				
Operating Results (000's)				
Net Interest Income	30,952.0	29,725.0	27,142.0	25,827.0
Loan Loss Provision	-1,900.0	-1,900.0	-2,405.0	-3,700.0
Non-Interest Income	6,038.0	5,495.0	5,139.0	5,097.0
Non-Interest Expense	-20,380.0	-20,642.0	-20,295.0	-19,340.0
Income Before Taxes and Other	14,710.0	12,678.0	9,581.0	7,884.0
Other Items	n.a.	n.a.	357.0	n.a.
Income Tax	-4,640.0	-4,118.0	-2,835.0	-2,220.0
Net Income	10,070.0	8,560.0	7,103.0	5,664.0
Balance Sheet (000's)				
Cash & Securities	243,618.0	269,746.0	269,256.0	273,675.0
Loans, Net	455,279.0	418,673.0	372,027.0	339,265.0
Fixed Assets, Net	9,502.0	7,565.0	7,207.0	6,393.0
Total Assets	720,135.0	707,874.0	657,468.0	626,544.0
Deposits	574,808.0	554,609.0	542,690.0	517,892.0
Stockholders' Equity	69,641.0	60,031.0	55,764.0	50,818.0
Performance & Financial Condition				
Net Interest Margin	4.68	4.76	4.73	4.74
Return on Avg Stockholders' Equity %	15.53	14.78	13.33	11.39
Return on Average Assets %	1.41	1.25	1.11	0.95
Equity to Assets %	9.67	8.48	8.48	8.11
Reserve as a % of Non-Performing Loans	316.92	n.a.	302.38	178.51

Compound Growth %'s	EPS %	21.14	Net Income %	21.14	Net Interest Income %	6.22

Comments

The Bank's loan portfolio is made up primarily of real estate mortgages, consumer, and commercial and industrial loans, making up 50%, 30% and 17% of total loans, respectively. There was a 2 for 1 stock split in 1994. All per share amounts have been adjusted for comparability. Non-accrual loans and loans over 90 days past due only amounted to 0.49% of total loans and are fully reserved. The Bank was formed in 1868 as the Youngstown Savings and Loan Association.

Officers	Position	Ownership Information	12/31/95
Gregory L. Ridler	President, CEO	Number of Shares Outstanding	3,150,000
Richard E. Davies	Secretary	Market Capitalization	$ 108,675,000
Norman E. Benden, Jr.	Treasurer	Frequency Of Dividends	Annual
Parker T. McHenry	Vice President	Number of Shareholders	1,470

Other Information			
Transfer Agent	Chemical Mellon Shareholder Services	Where Listed	OTC-BB
Auditor	Grant Thornton LLP	Symbol	MGNB
Market Maker	Butler, Wick & Co., Inc. Telephone (216)744-4351	SIC Code	6020
Broker Dealer	Regular Stockbroker	Employees	457

Makepeace (A.D.) Company

P.O. Box 151 • Wareham, MA 02571-0151 • Telephone (508)295-1000 • Fax (508)291-7453

Company Description

The Company grows cranberries and is a significant member of Ocean Spray Cranberries, Inc., which operates as a cooperative. In 1993, the Company issued a tender offer for 770 shares, approximately 10% of outstanding shares, at $5,000 per share. Only a small fraction of the offer was accepted.

	12/31/95	12/31/94	12/31/93	12/31/92
Per Share Information				
Stock Price	6,000.00	5,000.00	5,000.00	4,100.00
Earnings Per Share	431.32	396.31	510.94	486.82
Price / Earnings Ratio	13.91	12.62	9.79	8.42
Book Value Per Share	4,012.79	3,739.01	3,485.28	3,482.23
Price / Book Value %	149.52	133.73	143.46	117.74
Dividends Per Share	150.00	125.00	125.00	125.00
Annual Financial Data				
Operating Results (000's)				
Total Revenues	15,992.2	15,322.2	16,347.7	14,742.0
Costs & Expenses	-10,936.5	-10,641.6	-10,054.6	-8,580.3
Income Before Taxes and Other	5,055.7	4,680.6	6,293.1	5,879.9
Other Items	n.a.	n.a.	n.a.	n.a.
Income Tax	-2,026.5	-1,880.6	-2,641.4	-2,396.7
Net Income	3,029.1	2,800.0	3,651.7	3,483.2
Cash Flow From Operations	4,571.2	n.a.	n.a.	n.a.
Balance Sheet (000's)				
Cash & Equivalents	5,358.1	3,689.9	2,945.5	6,492.7
Total Current Assets	7,873.3	7,077.1	6,448.5	9,690.4
Fixed Assets, Net	15,622.2	14,779.9	14,728.9	14,461.6
Total Assets	35,544.1	33,129.3	32,224.8	35,609.8
Total Current Liabilities	5,265.3	1,616.9	2,005.6	2,746.7
Long-Term Debt	n.a.	2,931.4	3,202.6	3,470.0
Stockholders' Equity	28,181.8	26,416.1	24,909.3	24,916.0
Performance & Financial Condition				
Return on Total Revenues %	18.94	18.27	22.34	23.63
Return on Avg Stockholders' Equity %	11.10	10.91	14.66	15.84
Return on Average Assets %	8.82	8.57	10.77	11.27
Current Ratio	1.50	4.38	3.22	3.53
Debt / Equity %	n.a.	11.10	12.86	13.93

Compound Growth %'s	EPS %	-3.95	Net Income %	-4.55	Total Revenues %	2.75

Comments

The value of the underlying properties is not known. The Company did not retain an appraiser in connection with its tender offer. The financial statements are prepared on an income tax basis. A 2,400 acre property in Minnesota was purchased in 1995 and two 12-acre test bogs are now planted. The Company believes that this may result in better economics for future growth and in fulfilling the increasing needs of Ocean Spray.

Officers	Position	Ownership Information	12/31/95
Christopher Makepeace	President	Number of Shares Outstanding	7,023
Marshall C. Severance	Treasurer	Market Capitalization	$ 42,138,000
		Frequency Of Dividends	Quarterly
		Number of Shareholders	Under 500

Other Information

Transfer Agent	Company Office				Where Listed	OTC-BB
Auditor	Not indicated				Symbol	MAKE
Market Maker	T.R. Winston & Company, Inc.	Telephone	(908)234-9600		SIC Code	0171
Broker Dealer	Standard Investment	Tel/Ext	(888)783-4688	Jack	Employees	160

Market America, Inc.

7605-A Business Park Drive • Greensboro, NC 27409 • Telephone (910)605-0040 • Fax (910)605-0041

Company Description

The Company is a product brokerage and direct sales company using a proprietary marketing plan called binary marketing. The Company sells a variety of consumer home use products through a network of 30,000 independent distributors. The Company was formed originally in 1992 and merged with another company in 1993, via a reverse acquisition. Operations prior to 1993 were minimal. Trading in the Company's common stock began in 1994.

	04/30/95	04/30/94	04/30/93
Per Share Information			
Stock Price	2.19	1.41	n.a.
Earnings Per Share	0.04	0.01	n.a.
Price / Earnings Ratio	54.75	141.00	n.a.
Book Value Per Share	0.05	0.01	n.a.
Price / Book Value %	4,380.00	14,100.00	n.a.
Dividends Per Share	n.a.	n.a.	n.a.
Annual Financial Data			
Operating Results (000's)			
Total Revenues	19,615.6	9,391.9	1,321.9
Costs & Expenses	-18,287.0	-9,072.5	-1,368.7
Income Before Taxes and Other	1,328.6	319.5	-46.9
Other Items	n.a.	n.a.	n.a.
Income Tax	-533.8	-107.3	16.4
Net Income	794.8	212.2	-30.5
Cash Flow From Operations	2,129.2	870.5	-26.5
Balance Sheet (000's)			
Cash & Equivalents	2,830.0	807.9	50.8
Total Current Assets	3,285.8	1,000.7	124.4
Fixed Assets, Net	327.1	263.3	195.9
Total Assets	3,619.0	1,274.8	325.8
Total Current Liabilities	2,162.0	1,028.4	316.2
Long-Term Debt	128.3	24.6	n.a.
Stockholders' Equity	1,016.5	221.8	9.5
Performance & Financial Condition			
Return on Total Revenues %	4.05	2.26	-2.30
Return on Avg Stockholders' Equity %	128.37	183.49	n.a.
Return on Average Assets %	32.48	26.52	n.a.
Current Ratio	1.52	0.97	0.39
Debt / Equity %	12.62	11.09	n.a.

Compound Growth %'s	EPS %	300.00	Net Income %	274.52	Total Revenues %	285.22

Comments

For the six months ended October 31, 1995, the Company had sales of $17.6 million and Net Income of $1.8 million ($.08 per share) as compared to $9.0 million and $615,000 (.03 per share) for the same period in 1994.

Officers	Position	Ownership Information	04/30/95
James H. Ridinger	President, CEO	Number of Shares Outstanding	19,950,000
Dennis Franks	Exec VP	Market Capitalization	$ 43,690,500
Jerry Siciliano	Exec VP	Frequency Of Dividends	n.a.
Loren A. Ridinger	Secretary, Treasurer	Number of Shareholders	n.a.
Martin Weissman	Other		

Other Information				
Transfer Agent	TranSecurities, Inc.		Where Listed	OTC-BB
Auditor	Terrence J. Dunne, CPA		Symbol	MARK
Market Maker	Public Securities, Inc.	Telephone (800)888-2325	SIC Code	7319
Broker Dealer	Regular Stockbroker		Employees	64

Market Guide, Inc.

2001 Marcus Ave., Ste. So. 200 • Lake Success, NY 11042-1011 • Telephone (516)327-2400 • Fax (516)327-2420

Company Description

The Company acquires and publishes financial information on publicly traded companies and markets this information to the financial community. Information is primarily obtained from reports filed by the subject company with the Securities and Exchange Commission and annual reports to shareholders. The Company was incorporated in New York in 1983. In March of 1994, the Company issued 2,275,719 shares of restricted common stock, in a private placement, at a price of $.38 per share.

	02/28/95	02/28/94	02/28/93	02/29/92
Per Share Information				
Stock Price	0.68	0.35	0.11	0.16
Earnings Per Share	0.02	0.02	n.a.	0.01
Price / Earnings Ratio	34.00	17.50	n.a.	16.00
Book Value Per Share	0.11	0.04	0.02	0.02
Price / Book Value %	618.18	875.00	550.00	800.00
Dividends Per Share	n.a.	n.a.	n.a.	n.a.
Annual Financial Data				
Operating Results (000's)				
Total Revenues	2,688.0	2,001.1	1,614.5	1,244.9
Costs & Expenses	-2,332.7	-1,733.8	-1,559.2	-1,127.8
Income Before Taxes and Other	355.3	267.3	55.4	117.2
Other Items	n.a.	n.a.	n.a.	n.a.
Income Tax	-16.8	-19.1	-4.3	-11.6
Net Income	338.4	248.2	51.1	105.5
Cash Flow From Operations	119.9	395.0	157.5	176.1
Balance Sheet (000's)				
Cash & Equivalents	695.1	200.5	66.5	75.7
Total Current Assets	1,343.8	532.3	261.6	163.8
Fixed Assets, Net	426.8	136.9	78.5	100.7
Total Assets	2,603.1	1,230.8	931.3	885.3
Total Current Liabilities	576.9	625.9	586.4	576.1
Long-Term Debt	182.7	14.1	2.3	17.7
Stockholders' Equity	1,843.5	590.8	342.6	291.5
Performance & Financial Condition				
Return on Total Revenues %	12.59	12.40	3.16	8.48
Return on Avg Stockholders' Equity %	27.81	53.18	16.11	64.45
Return on Average Assets %	17.66	22.96	5.63	13.46
Current Ratio	2.33	0.85	0.45	0.28
Debt / Equity %	9.91	2.39	0.67	6.08

Compound Growth %'s	EPS %	25.99	Net Income %	47.47	Total Revenues %	29.25

Comments

The Company has a net operating loss carryforward of approximately $1.7 million which expires in fiscal years 2000 through 2003. For the nine months ended November 30, 1995, revenues were $2.9 million and Net Income was $352,000 ($.09 per share) as compared to $1.9 million and $229,000 ($.06 pershare) for the same period in 1994. The improvement in performance is reflected in the Company's stock price which at December 29, 1995, was at an average bid/ask price of $4.82. Officers and directors as a group, at February 28, 1995, owned 31.4% of the outstanding shares.

Officers	Position	Ownership Information	02/28/95
John D. Case	Chairman, Secretary	Number of Shares Outstanding	16,450,833
Homi M. Byramji	President, CEO	Market Capitalization	$ 11,186,566
		Frequency Of Dividends	n.a.
		Number of Shareholders	981

Other Information			
Transfer Agent	American Stock Transfer & Trust Company	Where Listed	OTC-BB
Auditor	Zerbo & McKiernan PC	Symbol	MARG
Market Maker	Herzog, Heine, Geduld, Inc. Telephone (800)221-3600	SIC Code	7380
Broker Dealer	Regular Stockbroker	Employees	43

Maui Land & Pineapple Company, Inc.

120 Kane Street • Kahului, HI 96732 • Telephone (808)877-3351 • Fax (808)871-0953

Company Description

The Company is both a land-holding and operating company with several wholly-owned subsidiaries, including Maui Pineapple Company, Ltd.("Pineapple") and Kapalua Land Company, Inc.("Kapalua"). The Company owns approximately 28,000 acres on the island of Maui. Pineapple is the sole supplier of private label canned pineapple products to U.S. supermarkets. Kapalua is the developer of a destination resort on Maui. The Company also owns and operates other significant commercial and residential property on Maui. The Company was organized in 1909 in the state of Hawaii.

	12/31/95	12/31/94	12/31/93	12/31/92
Per Share Information				
Stock Price	41.00	55.00	102.50	107.50
Earnings Per Share	-0.87	-2.18	-6.15	-0.70
Price / Earnings Ratio	n.a.	n.a.	n.a.	n.a.
Book Value Per Share	32.75	33.63	35.79	42.50
Price / Book Value %	125.19	163.54	286.39	252.94
Dividends Per Share	n.a.	n.a.	0.75	1.00
Annual Financial Data				
Operating Results (000's)				
Total Revenues	125,577.0	125,882.0	131,172.0	147,049.0
Costs & Expenses	-128,602.0	-132,620.0	-149,654.0	-138,446.0
Income Before Taxes and Other	-3,025.0	-6,738.0	-18,482.0	8,603.0
Other Items	n.a.	n.a.	n.a.	-7,673.0
Income Tax	1,466.0	2,829.0	7,423.0	-2,183.0
Net Income	-1,559.0	-3,909.0	-11,059.0	-1,253.0
Cash Flow From Operations	2,142.0	11,536.0	-2,360.0	-1,338.0
Balance Sheet (000's)				
Cash & Equivalents	166.0	2,269.0	1,223.0	993.0
Total Current Assets	36,554.0	40,960.0	49,460.0	45,933.0
Fixed Assets, Net	88,557.0	180,194.0	148,774.0	121,045.0
Total Assets	137,085.0	235,411.0	211,588.0	177,544.0
Total Current Liabilities	13,126.0	42,057.0	20,062.0	19,700.0
Long-Term Debt	36,227.0	99,180.0	96,108.0	60,569.0
Stockholders' Equity	58,870.0	60,429.0	64,321.0	76,187.0
Performance & Financial Condition				
Return on Total Revenues %	-1.24	-3.11	-8.43	-0.85
Return on Avg Stockholders' Equity %	-2.61	-6.27	-15.74	-1.62
Return on Average Assets %	-0.84	-1.75	-5.68	-0.73
Current Ratio	2.78	0.97	2.47	2.33
Debt / Equity %	61.54	164.13	149.42	79.50

Compound Growth %'s	EPS % n.a.	Net Income % n.a.	Total Revenues % -5.13

Comments

Most of the Company's land was acquired from 1911 to 1932 and is carried at cost. Operating Profit for 1995 includes pineapple operations ($3.6 million), resort operations ($7.3 million), and commercial and property operations ($3.6 million). Included in Other Items for 1992 is a charge of $7.6 million for accounting changes relating to inventory, income taxes and postretirement benefits. The large decrease in Fixed Assets and Debt in 1995, is due to a change in method of accounting for the Company's interest in a partnership.

Officers	Position	Ownership Information	12/31/95
Gary L. Gifford	President, CEO	Number of Shares Outstanding	1,797,125
Paul J. Meyer	Exec VP, Treasurer	Market Capitalization	$ 73,682,125
Douglas R. Schenk	Exec VP	Frequency Of Dividends	Irregular
Donald A. Young	Exec VP	Number of Shareholders	411
Adele H. Sumida	Secretary		

Other Information

Transfer Agent	Chemical Trust Company of California		Where Listed	OTC-BB
Auditor	Deloitte & Touche LLP		Symbol	MAUI
Market Maker	Martin Nelson & Co., Inc.	Telephone (206)682-6261	SIC Code	2033
Broker Dealer	Regular Stockbroker		Employees	2200

McIntosh Bancshares, Inc.

P.O.Box 3818 • Jackson, GA 30233 • Telephone (770)775-8300 • Fax (770)775-8325

Company Description

McIntosh Bancshares, Inc. is a one bank holding company. McIntosh State Bank is their wholly-owned subsidiary which offers standard banking services in the counties of Jackson and Butts, both in Georgia. In February of 1996, the Bank announced plans to acquire the Monticello branch of Bank South, Monticello, Georgia. Combined assets as of February would be over $125 million. Management says that the Monticello operation will be totally autonomous serving Monticello and Jasper County.

	12/31/95	12/31/94	12/31/93	12/31/92
Per Share Information				
Stock Price	50.00	45.45	37.19	33.83
Earnings Per Share	2.19	2.02	1.89	1.52
Price / Earnings Ratio	22.83	22.50	19.68	22.26
Book Value Per Share	17.56	15.20	13.59	11.81
Price / Book Value %	284.74	299.01	273.66	286.45
Dividends Per Share	0.15	0.15	0.15	0.15
Annual Financial Data				
Operating Results (000's)				
Net Interest Income	3,554.0	3,204.3	2,947.2	2,472.9
Loan Loss Provision	-196.0	-97.6	-96.7	-81.0
Non-Interest Income	635.0	550.0	519.5	523.0
Non-Interest Expense	-2,343.2	-2,135.1	-1,926.2	-1,815.7
Income Before Taxes and Other	1,649.9	1,521.6	1,443.8	1,099.2
Other Items	n.a.	n.a.	-11.0	n.a.
Income Tax	-430.1	-398.0	-385.5	-253.0
Net Income	1,219.8	1,123.6	1,047.3	846.1
Balance Sheet (000's)				
Cash & Securities	24,224.2	21,902.0	19,826.2	19,276.0
Loans, Net	52,050.6	45,039.1	42,024.6	37,901.1
Fixed Assets, Net	1,070.4	922.8	979.0	961.0
Total Assets	78,792.6	69,178.2	64,219.9	63,691.5
Deposits	68,505.2	60,367.9	56,197.2	56,618.9
Stockholders' Equity	9,762.4	8,449.8	7,556.3	6,567.9
Performance & Financial Condition				
Net Interest Margin	n.a.	n.a.	n.a.	n.a.
Return on Avg Stockholders' Equity %	13.40	14.04	14.83	13.71
Return on Average Assets %	1.65	1.68	1.64	1.38
Equity to Assets %	12.39	12.21	11.77	10.31
Reserve as a % of Non-Performing Loans	1612.94	2648.47	n.a.	n.a.

Compound Growth %'s	EPS %	12.94	Net Income %	12.97	Net Interest Income %	12.85

Comments

The Company has had a 10% stock dividend in each of the last four years. Per share amounts have been adjusted for comparability. Compounded growth rates are reasonable considering the excellent returns on assets and equity. The Board of Directors were having fun posing for their annual report picture, all dressed in a suit of a different color; nine different shades of dark blue. Now we know they are good bankers.

Officers	Position	Ownership Information	12/31/95
William H. Shapard, Sr.	Chairman	Number of Shares Outstanding	556,053
William K. Malone	CEO	Market Capitalization	$ 27,802,650
Peter J. Eley	Treasurer, Secretary	Frequency Of Dividends	Annual
William F. Grant	Vice President, Senior Loan Officer	Number of Shareholders	275
Dianne C. England	Vice President		

Other Information				
Transfer Agent	Mellon Securities Trust Company		Where Listed	Other
Auditor	Bricker & Melton, P.A.		Symbol	MITB
Market Maker	Contact Bank directly	Telephone (770)775-8300	SIC Code	6020
Broker Dealer	Regular Stockbroker		Employees	34

Meda, Inc.

15845 SW 72nd Street • Portland, OR 97224 • Telephone (503)639-1500 • Fax (503)968-4844

Company Description

The Company researches, develops, manufactures, and sells a wide variety of biological products which are used to test for and diagnose various conditions and illnesses. The Company acquired all of the stock of Prepared Media Laboratory, Inc.("PML") in December 1992, and does all of its business through PML. PML has been in the business since 1969. Over 38% of the Company's sales are exports to Canada.

	05/31/95	05/31/94	05/31/93	05/31/92
Per Share Information				
Stock Price	0.31	1.19	0.63	n.a.
Earnings Per Share	-1.00	n.a.	-0.12	0.01
Price / Earnings Ratio	n.a.	n.a.	n.a.	n.a.
Book Value Per Share	-0.40	0.60	0.60	0.86
Price / Book Value %	n.a.	198.33	105.00	n.a.
Dividends Per Share	n.a.	n.a.	n.a.	n.a.
Annual Financial Data				
Operating Results (000's)				
Total Revenues	15,319.8	13,921.5	11,832.4	10,284.0
Costs & Expenses	-16,732.8	-13,774.4	-11,861.5	-10,181.0
Income Before Taxes and Other	-1,648.1	129.9	-181.1	52.8
Other Items	n.a.	-12.0	n.a.	n.a.
Income Tax	35.2	-77.0	0.4	-39.3
Net Income	-1,612.9	40.9	-180.7	13.5
Cash Flow From Operations	140.1	-196.1	-468.9	128.5
Balance Sheet (000's)				
Cash & Equivalents	30.5	74.4	94.0	67.2
Total Current Assets	4,037.6	4,651.8	3,298.8	2,703.5
Fixed Assets, Net	1,615.3	1,559.4	1,214.6	998.7
Total Assets	5,763.1	6,360.1	4,639.3	3,878.6
Total Current Liabilities	5,339.7	2,695.1	1,672.0	2,252.8
Long-Term Debt	499.6	2,128.3	1,471.5	447.2
Stockholders' Equity	-76.2	1,536.7	1,495.8	1,178.5
Performance & Financial Condition				
Return on Total Revenues %	-10.53	0.38	-1.53	0.13
Return on Avg Stockholders' Equity %	-220.87	2.70	-13.52	n.a.
Return on Average Assets %	-26.61	0.74	-4.24	n.a.
Current Ratio	0.76	1.73	1.97	1.20
Debt / Equity %	n.a.	138.50	98.37	37.95

Compound Growth %'s	EPS % n.a.	Net Income % n.a.	Total Revenues % 14.21

Comments

In January 1995, the Company began a restructuring to stop the Company's losses and implemented changes to return the Company to profitability. For the nine months ended February 29, 1996, the Company had sales of $10.4 million and Net Income of $46,000, as compared to sales of $11.5 million and a net loss of $1.7 million for the same period in the prior year. The Company has tax loss carryforwards of approximately $1,500,000.

Officers	Position	Ownership Information	05/31/95
A. Ron Torland	Chairman, CEO	Number of Shares Outstanding	1,661,327
James N. Weider	CFO, Secretary	Market Capitalization	$ 515,011
		Frequency Of Dividends	n.a.
		Number of Shareholders	1,300

Other Information			
Transfer Agent	Mid-America Bank of Louisville	Where Listed	OTC-BB
Auditor	Deloitte & Touche LLP	Symbol	MDAN
Market Maker	Carr Securities Corporation	Telephone (800)221-2243	SIC Code	2835
Broker Dealer	Regular Stockbroker	Employees	185

Medical Advisory Systems, Inc.

8050 Southern Maryland Blvd. • Owings, MD 20736 • Telephone (310)855-8070 • Fax (410)257-2704

Company Description

The Company provides medical assistance products and services. Products and services include pharmaceuticals and medical supply kits sold to vessels operating in the maritime industry, 24-hour medical advice to ships at sea and 24-hour advice and services to the international travel industry. Services are provided from an operations center in Maryland. The Company was incorporated in Maryland in 1981.

	10/31/95	10/31/94	10/31/93	10/31/92
Per Share Information				
Stock Price	0.16	0.16	0.19	0.19
Earnings Per Share	0.07	0.15	0.07	0.21
Price / Earnings Ratio	2.29	1.07	2.71	0.90
Book Value Per Share	0.34	0.27	0.13	0.06
Price / Book Value %	47.06	59.26	146.15	316.67
Dividends Per Share	n.a.	n.a.	n.a.	n.a.
Annual Financial Data				
Operating Results (000's)				
Total Revenues	1,953.1	1,805.9	1,934.7	2,017.8
Costs & Expenses	-1,660.7	-1,621.7	-1,685.9	-1,785.3
Income Before Taxes and Other	292.4	184.2	248.8	232.5
Other Items	-13.2	363.3	94.4	634.9
Income Tax	-11.1	7.7	-94.4	-79.8
Net Income	268.1	555.2	248.8	787.6
Cash Flow From Operations	324.7	242.3	n.a.	n.a.
Balance Sheet (000's)				
Cash & Equivalents	402.8	280.7	763.7	684.2
Total Current Assets	869.2	745.3	1,178.8	1,245.3
Fixed Assets, Net	269.9	270.4	218.5	243.5
Total Assets	1,900.2	1,678.7	1,685.5	1,512.5
Total Current Liabilities	423.1	443.2	853.3	411.1
Long-Term Debt	146.8	186.4	349.7	867.7
Stockholders' Equity	1,305.8	1,037.7	482.5	233.7
Performance & Financial Condition				
Return on Total Revenues %	13.73	30.74	12.86	39.03
Return on Avg Stockholders' Equity %	22.88	73.05	69.48	n.a.
Return on Average Assets %	14.98	33.01	15.56	70.30
Current Ratio	2.05	1.68	1.38	3.03
Debt / Equity %	11.24	17.96	72.48	371.32

Compound Growth %'s	EPS %	-30.66	Net Income %	-30.17	Total Revenues %	-1.08

Comments

Included in Other Items for 1994 is $350,000 resulting from a change in accounting for income taxes, and in 1992, $428,000 resulting from a gain on disposal of discontinued operations. Revenues from two major customers accounted for 35% of sales for the year ended October 31, 1995. The Company has net operating loss carryforwards totaling approximately $2.4 million which expire through the year 2006. Officers and directors, as a group, held 55% of the Company's stock at February 1, 1996.

Officers	Position	Ownership Information	10/31/95
Ronald W. Pickett	President, Treasurer	Number of Shares Outstanding	3,816,933
Thomas M. Hall	CEO	Market Capitalization	$ 610,709
		Frequency Of Dividends	n.a.
		Number of Shareholders	278

Other Information			
Transfer Agent	American Securities Transfer, Inc.	Where Listed	OTC-BB
Auditor	Stefanou & Co.	Symbol	MEAS
Market Maker	Wachtel & Co., Inc.	Telephone (202)898-1018	SIC Code	8082
Broker Dealer	Regular Stockbroker	Employees	20

Megatech Corporation

555 Woburn Street • Tewksbury, MA 01876 • Telephone (508)937-9600 • Fax (508)453-9936

Company Description

The Company designs, develops, manufactures and distributes educational training programs and equipment for the study of energy, power and transportation. In recent years, the Company has focused on automotive training programs. The Company was incorporated in Massachusetts in 1970.

	12/31/95	12/31/94	12/31/93	12/31/92
Per Share Information				
Stock Price	3.25	2.13	0.09	0.04
Earnings Per Share	-0.02	0.05	0.03	0.01
Price / Earnings Ratio	n.a.	42.60	3.00	4.00
Book Value Per Share	0.19	0.21	0.14	0.10
Price / Book Value %	1,710.50	1,014.30	64.29	40.00
Dividends Per Share	n.a.	n.a.	n.a.	n.a.
Annual Financial Data				
Operating Results (000's)				
Total Revenues	2,825.0	4,052.9	2,648.2	2,286.2
Costs & Expenses	-2,876.3	-3,814.9	-2,523.5	-2,224.3
Income Before Taxes and Other	-56.6	236.0	123.4	36.6
Other Items	n.a.	n.a.	n.a.	6.5
Income Tax	-0.9	-32.9	-14.0	-11.5
Net Income	-57.5	203.0	109.4	31.6
Cash Flow From Operations	-26.7	15.4	331.9	-5.2
Balance Sheet (000's)				
Cash & Equivalents	55.6	189.1	208.5	179.0
Total Current Assets	922.8	1,163.4	915.7	1,124.1
Fixed Assets, Net	118.5	53.5	48.9	54.4
Total Assets	1,049.0	1,222.5	970.3	1,184.1
Total Current Liabilities	316.3	435.9	400.7	740.7
Long-Term Debt	1.2	8.7	75.3	58.6
Stockholders' Equity	731.5	777.8	494.3	384.9
Performance & Financial Condition				
Return on Total Revenues %	-2.04	5.01	4.13	1.38
Return on Avg Stockholders' Equity %	-7.62	31.92	24.88	8.57
Return on Average Assets %	-5.06	18.52	10.15	3.30
Current Ratio	2.92	2.67	2.29	1.52
Debt / Equity %	0.17	1.12	15.24	15.22

Compound Growth %'s	EPS % n.a.	Net Income % n.a.	Total Revenues % 7.31

Comments

Sales to Mexico accounted for 15%, 29%, and 45% of total sales for 1995, 1994, and 1993, respectively. The decrease in sales to Mexico was the major cause in the Company's poor performance in 1995. Officers and directors, as a group, owned 26.1% of the Company's outstanding stock as of April 1, 1996.

Officers	Position	Ownership Information	12/31/95
Vahan V. Basmajian	President, Treasurer	Number of Shares Outstanding	3,762,258
Bedros H. Dilsizian	Vice President	Market Capitalization	$ 12,227,339
Varant Z. Basmajian	VP - Sales	Frequency Of Dividends	n.a.
Dennis A. Humphrey	Senior Clerk	Number of Shareholders	839

Other Information

Transfer Agent	Company Office			Where Listed	OTC-BB
Auditor	Gordon, Harrington & Osborn PC			Symbol	MGTC
Market Maker	Carr Securities Corporation	Telephone	(800)221-2243	SIC Code	8299
Broker Dealer	Regular Stockbroker			Employees	21

Mendocino Brewing Company, Inc.

13351 South Highway 101 • Hopland, CA 95449 • Telephone (707)744-1015 • Fax (707)744-1910

Company Description

The Company produces domestic specialty beers and sells to distributors and other retailers. The Company's operations are located in Mendocino County, approximately 80 miles north of San Francisco. Distribution is primarily in Northern California, but it is also distributed in eight other western states. Production has been at capacity since 1988. Expansion is planned to increase capacity from 18,000 barrels per year to 50,000 barrels in 1996, and 200,000 barrels later. This expansion should help the Company keep up with the micro brewing industry which is growing at a 40% to 50% rate annually. The Company also has retail operations consisting of a brewpub and gift shop.

	12/31/95	12/31/94	12/31/93
Per Share Information			
Stock Price	7.56	6.00	n.a.
Earnings Per Share	0.08	0.08	n.a.
Price / Earnings Ratio	94.50	75.00	n.a.
Book Value Per Share	1.81	1.57	n.a.
Price / Book Value %	417.68	382.17	n.a.
Dividends Per Share	n.a.	n.a.	n.a.
Annual Financial Data			
Operating Results (000's)			
Total Revenues	3,714.1	3,552.1	3,389.4
Costs & Expenses	-3,387.5	-3,327.3	-3,168.7
Income Before Taxes and Other	326.6	224.8	220.7
Other Items	n.a.	n.a.	n.a.
Income Tax	-152.9	-71.5	-81.8
Net Income	173.7	153.3	138.9
Cash Flow From Operations	6.4	197.8	391.6
Balance Sheet (000's)			
Cash & Equivalents	1,696.1	2,900.8	296.0
Total Current Assets	2,473.8	3,422.0	757.0
Fixed Assets, Net	3,954.1	301.0	206.8
Total Assets	6,514.0	4,038.1	1,079.6
Total Current Liabilities	1,514.7	314.8	288.2
Long-Term Debt	554.9	n.a.	7.5
Stockholders' Equity	4,424.2	3,723.3	783.9
Performance & Financial Condition			
Return on Total Revenues %	4.68	4.31	4.10
Return on Avg Stockholders' Equity %	4.26	6.80	n.a.
Return on Average Assets %	3.29	5.99	n.a.
Current Ratio	1.63	10.87	2.63
Debt / Equity %	12.54	n.a.	0.96

Compound Growth %'s	EPS % n.a.	Net Income % 11.82	Total Revenues % 4.68

Comments

The Company was operated as a partnership from 1983 through 1993. After incorporation in 1994, the Company undertook a direct public offering of their stock, raising approximately $3.3 million (600,000 shares at an average of $5.52 per share) in the latter part of 1994 and the first part of 1995. In February, 1995, the Company was listed on the Pacific Stock exchange with an opening trade of $8.25. Included in stockholders' equity is preferred stock with a liquidation preference of $227,600. Officers and directors, as a group, owned 26.7% of the Company's outstanding common stock at March 29, 1996.

Officers	Position	Ownership Information	12/31/95
H. Michael Laybourn	CEO, President	Number of Shares Outstanding	2,322,222
Norman H. Franks	CFO, Treasurer	Market Capitalization	$ 17,555,998
Michael F. Lovett	Secretary	Frequency Of Dividends	n.a.
		Number of Shareholders	2,534

Other Information			
Transfer Agent	The First National Bank of Boston	Where Listed	PSE
Auditor	Moss Adams	Symbol	MBRP
Market Maker	None	SIC Code	2082
Broker Dealer	Regular Stockbroker	Employees	72

Merchants' National Properties, Inc.

708 Third Avenue • New York, NY 10017-4201 • Telephone (212)557-1400 • Fax (212)983-4532

Company Description

The Company owns and leases real estate to various commercial tenants and invests in various real estate ventures. The properties are located in the United States and Canada.

	12/31/94	12/31/93
Per Share Information		
Stock Price	135.00	135.00
Earnings Per Share	30.35	30.64
Price / Earnings Ratio	4.45	4.41
Book Value Per Share	411.30	325.83
Price / Book Value %	32.82	41.43
Dividends Per Share	15.00	20.00
Annual Financial Data		
Operating Results (000's)		
Total Revenues	5,755.6	5,719.7
Costs & Expenses	-170.0	-195.9
Income Before Taxes and Other	5,564.4	5,497.8
Other Items	n.a.	n.a.
Income Tax	-2,120.1	-1,995.6
Net Income	3,444.3	3,502.2
Cash Flow From Operations	1,807.0	-214.7
Balance Sheet (000's)		
Cash & Equivalents	1,437.4	1,482.9
Total Current Assets	7,102.1	8,675.5
Fixed Assets, Net	6,283.1	6,562.9
Total Assets	52,598.3	37,998.2
Total Current Liabilities	1,356.3	528.7
Long-Term Debt	n.a.	n.a.
Stockholders' Equity	46,597.0	36,979.2
Performance & Financial Condition		
Return on Total Revenues %	59.84	61.23
Return on Avg Stockholders' Equity %	8.24	9.62
Return on Average Assets %	7.60	9.47
Current Ratio	5.24	16.41
Debt / Equity %	n.a.	n.a.

Compound Growth %'s	EPS %	-0.95	Net Income %	-1.65	Total Revenues %	0.63

Comments

Stockholders' equity in the 1994 year was adjusted upward by approximately $8 million in order to adopt GAAP reporting of the fair market value of certain investments. The 1995 report was not yet available as we went to press.

Officers	Position	Ownership Information	12/31/94
Leonard Marx, Sr.	Chairman	Number of Shares Outstanding	113,291
		Market Capitalization	$ 15,294,285
		Frequency Of Dividends	Quarterly
		Number of Shareholders	Under 500

Other Information				
Transfer Agent	Company Office		Where Listed	OTC-BB
Auditor	Frank &Zimmerman & company LLP		Symbol	MNPP
Market Maker	Legg Mason Wood Walker, Inc.	Telephone (212)428-4949	SIC Code	6510
Broker Dealer	Regular stockbroker		Employees	3

Mercom, Inc.

105 Carnegie Center • Princeton, NJ 08540 • Telephone (609)734-3700 • Fax (609)951-8632

Company Description

The Company is a cable television operator with three cable systems in southern Michigan and one in Port St. Lucie, Florida. At December 31, 1995, the systems had 39,000 subscribers. The Company completed the issuance of 2,393,530 shares of common stock through a rights offering in August of 1995. Proceeds were used primarily to repay outstanding indebtedness.

	12/31/95	12/31/94	12/31/93	12/31/92
Per Share Information				
Stock Price	5.25	3.38	3.63	2.75
Earnings Per Share	0.16	-0.27	-0.10	-0.48
Price / Earnings Ratio	32.81	n.a.	n.a.	n.a.
Book Value Per Share	-0.92	-5.51	-5.24	-5.14
Price / Book Value %	n.a.	n.a.	n.a.	n.a.
Dividends Per Share	n.a.	n.a.	n.a.	n.a.
Annual Financial Data				
Operating Results (000's)				
Total Revenues	14,217.0	12,957.0	12,632.0	12,182.0
Costs & Expenses	-13,670.0	-12,952.0	-12,841.0	-13,326.0
Income Before Taxes and Other	547.0	-662.0	-219.0	-1,144.0
Other Items	n.a.	n.a.	n.a.	n.a.
Income Tax	2.0	4.0	-17.0	n.a.
Net Income	549.0	-658.0	-236.0	-1,144.0
Cash Flow From Operations	2,366.0	2,591.0	3,136.0	1,109.0
Balance Sheet (000's)				
Cash & Equivalents	2,033.0	96.0	989.0	376.0
Total Current Assets	2,590.0	697.0	1,310.0	571.0
Fixed Assets, Net	15,434.0	16,451.0	17,946.0	19,982.0
Total Assets	20,390.0	19,823.0	22,244.0	23,873.0
Total Current Liabilities	5,851.0	7,093.0	6,598.0	6,328.0
Long-Term Debt	18,930.0	25,926.0	28,184.0	29,847.0
Stockholders' Equity	-4,391.0	-13,196.0	-12,538.0	-12,302.0
Performance & Financial Condition				
Return on Total Revenues %	3.86	-5.08	-1.87	-9.39
Return on Avg Stockholders' Equity %	n.a.	n.a.	n.a.	n.a.
Return on Average Assets %	2.73	-3.13	-1.02	-4.53
Current Ratio	0.44	0.10	0.20	0.09
Debt / Equity %	n.a.	n.a.	n.a.	n.a.

Compound Growth %'s	EPS % n.a.	Net Income % n.a.	Total Revenues % 5.28

Comments

C-TEC Corporation owns approximately 62% of the outstanding stock of the Company. In November 1995, C-TEC engaged Merrill Lynch to assist with evaluating strategic options for enhancing shareholder value. In March 1996, C-TEC announced that it intends to spin-off its local telephone operations and other assets and then combine its domestic cable television operations, including the Company, with a third party.

Officers	Position	Ownership Information	12/31/95
David C. McCourt	Chairman, CEO	Number of Shares Outstanding	4,787,060
Michael J. Mahoney	President, COO	Market Capitalization	$ 25,132,065
Bruce C. Godfrey	Exec VP, CFO	Frequency Of Dividends	n.a.
Raymond B. Ostroski	Exec VP	Number of Shareholders	1,934
John D. Filipowicz	Secretary		

Other Information

Transfer Agent	Boston EquiServe		Where Listed	OTC-BB
Auditor	Coopers & Lybrand		Symbol	MEEO
Market Maker	Gabelli & Company, Inc.	Telephone (914)921-5153	SIC Code	4841
Broker Dealer	Regular Stockbroker		Employees	52

Meteor Industries, Inc.

216 Sixteenth Street, Ste.730 • Denver, CO 80202 • Telephone (303)572-1137 • Fax (303)572-1803

Company Description

The Company is a wholesale and retail distributor of petroleum products primarily in several western states. It also operates retail gasoline and convenience stores in New Mexico and Colorado. The Company was formed in December, 1992, and raised $1 million in equity capital in 1994 with a Reg. A offering. The Company is in the process of becoming a reporting company under the Securities Exchange Act of 1934.

	08/31/95	08/31/94
Per Share Information		
Stock Price	2.50	5.19
Earnings Per Share	0.12	0.02
Price / Earnings Ratio	20.83	259.50
Book Value Per Share	0.80	0.58
Price / Book Value %	312.50	894.83
Dividends Per Share	n.a.	n.a.
Annual Financial Data		
Operating Results (000's)		
Total Revenues	45,372.9	39,159.8
Costs & Expenses	-45,412.2	-39,169.0
Income Before Taxes and Other	-39.3	-9.2
Other Items	n.a.	n.a.
Income Tax	191.7	28.6
Net Income	152.3	19.4
Cash Flow From Operations	2,177.1	-702.3
Balance Sheet (000's)		
Cash & Equivalents	244.2	522.6
Total Current Assets	6,682.5	6,556.3
Fixed Assets, Net	5,767.7	4,561.7
Total Assets	14,581.3	12,255.6
Total Current Liabilities	6,950.6	5,606.1
Long-Term Debt	2,095.7	2,603.6
Stockholders' Equity	1,014.1	482.1
Performance & Financial Condition		
Return on Total Revenues %	0.34	0.05
Return on Avg Stockholders' Equity %	20.36	n.a.
Return on Average Assets %	1.14	n.a.
Current Ratio	0.96	1.17
Debt / Equity %	206.66	540.01

Compound Growth %'s	EPS %	500.00	Net Income %	686.48	Total Revenues %	15.87

Comments

Subsequent to the last financial statement, the Company issued 1,745,000 shares of common stock in exchange for all of the outstanding stock of Capco Resources, Inc. The shares issued represent 58% of shares outstanding and has shifted control to Capco Resources, Ltd., an Alberta corporation. The major assets acquired include a California environmental services firm, a $1.5 million promissory note, and an interest in a company that is involved in the development of a power plant in Pakistan. Compounded growth rates are misleading because only two years of data are used in the calculations.

Officers	Position	Ownership Information	08/31/95
Ilyas Chaudhary	Chairman, CEO	Number of Shares Outstanding	1,272,903
Edward J. Names	President, COO	Market Capitalization	$ 3,182,258
		Frequency Of Dividends	n.a.
		Number of Shareholders	Under 500

Other Information				
Transfer Agent	American Securities Transfer, Inc.		Where Listed	OTC-BB
Auditor	Squire & Woodward, P.C.		Symbol	METE
Market Maker	Sherwood Securities Corp.	Telephone (800)525-3499	SIC Code	5170
Broker Dealer	Regular Stockbroker		Employees	n.a.

Mexco Energy Corporation

214 W. Texas Avenue, Ste. 1101 • Midland, TX 79701 • Telephone (915)682-1119 • Fax (915)682-1123

Company Description

The Company is engaged in the acquisition, exploration and development of oil and gas properties, principally in Texas. The Company owns 100% of five producing oil wells which it operates and owns partial interests in an additional 301 producing wells located in the states of Texas, New Mexico and Oklahoma. At March 31, 1995, the Company held leasehold rights to 67,567 gross acres. The Company was organized in Colorado in 1972.

	03/31/95	03/31/94	03/31/93	03/31/92
Per Share Information				
Stock Price	2.00	1.38	0.75	0.63
Earnings Per Share	0.09	0.88	-0.01	0.01
Price / Earnings Ratio	22.22	1.57	n.a.	63.00
Book Value Per Share	1.57	1.48	0.61	0.61
Price / Book Value %	127.39	93.24	122.95	103.28
Dividends Per Share	n.a.	n.a.	n.a.	n.a.
Annual Financial Data				
Operating Results (000's)				
Total Revenues	573.9	1,579.9	352.7	316.7
Costs & Expenses	-459.1	-491.3	-361.7	-301.9
Income Before Taxes and Other	114.8	1,088.6	-9.0	14.9
Other Items	n.a.	n.a.	n.a.	2.2
Income Tax	-10.0	-59.9	n.a.	-2.2
Net Income	104.8	1,028.7	-9.0	14.9
Cash Flow From Operations	255.6	1,302.8	80.1	113.0
Balance Sheet (000's)				
Cash & Equivalents	221.0	739.5	10.4	190.9
Total Current Assets	303.4	823.3	64.3	239.3
Fixed Assets, Net	1,648.5	1,045.1	753.5	497.8
Total Assets	1,951.9	1,868.4	817.8	737.1
Total Current Liabilities	75.6	128.7	81.3	38.1
Long-Term Debt	n.a.	n.a.	25.5	n.a.
Stockholders' Equity	1,844.5	1,739.7	711.0	699.0
Performance & Financial Condition				
Return on Total Revenues %	18.27	65.11	-2.54	4.69
Return on Avg Stockholders' Equity %	5.85	83.95	-1.27	2.15
Return on Average Assets %	5.49	76.59	-1.15	2.08
Current Ratio	4.01	6.40	0.79	6.28
Debt / Equity %	n.a.	n.a.	3.59	n.a.

Compound Growth %'s	EPS %	108.01	Net Income %	91.76	Total Revenues %	21.91

Comments

Included in the operating results for the year ended March 31, 1994, are proceeds from the settlement of litigation in the amount of $1.2 milion. Revenues for the nine months ended December 31, 1995, were $323,000 and Net Income was $98,000 as compared to $211,000 and $41,000 for the same period in 1994. Officers and directors, as a group, owned 91.4% of the Company's stock at June 1, 1995.

Officers	Position	Ownership Information	03/31/95
Nicholas C. Taylor	President, Treasurer	Number of Shares Outstanding	1,173,229
Donna G. Yanko	Vice President	Market Capitalization	$ 2,346,458
		Frequency Of Dividends	n.a.
		Number of Shareholders	1,514

Other Information

Transfer Agent	American Securities Transfer, Inc.			Where Listed	OTC-BB
Auditor	Grant Thornton LLP			Symbol	MEXC
Market Maker	Carr Securities Corporation	Telephone	(800)221-2243	SIC Code	1311
Broker Dealer	Regular Stockbroker			Employees	2

Michigan Rivet Corporation

13201 Stephens Road • Warren, MI 48089-2092 • Telephone (810)754-5100 • Fax (810)754-2750

Company Description

The Company and its subsidiary manufacture highly specialized fasteners, nuts, washers and components, primarily for automotive manufacturers and their suppliers. As of December 31, 1995, officers and directors, as a group, owned approximately 48% of the Company's outstanding common stock. The Company was incorporated in Michigan in 1969.

	10/31/95	10/31/94	10/31/93	10/31/92
Per Share Information				
Stock Price	3.25	2.00	3.00	3.75
Earnings Per Share	2.55	0.07	-1.20	-0.55
Price / Earnings Ratio	1.27	28.57	n.a.	n.a.
Book Value Per Share	11.51	9.19	9.12	10.32
Price / Book Value %	28.24	21.76	32.89	36.34
Dividends Per Share	0.24	n.a.	n.a.	n.a.
Annual Financial Data				
Operating Results (000's)				
Total Revenues	40,352.2	38,375.2	33,057.4	31,364.2
Costs & Expenses	-38,546.5	-38,486.0	-34,124.9	-32,016.8
Income Before Taxes and Other	1,805.7	-110.8	-1,067.5	-652.6
Other Items	n.a.	n.a.	n.a.	190.0
Income Tax	-175.8	155.0	300.0	110.0
Net Income	1,629.9	44.2	-767.5	-352.6
Cash Flow From Operations	3,861.3	1,329.9	526.9	456.9
Balance Sheet (000's)				
Cash & Equivalents	110.7	638.3	201.6	367.7
Total Current Assets	11,328.4	12,854.3	10,599.4	10,794.1
Fixed Assets, Net	8,821.1	8,815.1	9,380.2	9,250.6
Total Assets	20,654.8	21,736.3	20,041.9	20,102.3
Total Current Liabilities	6,114.5	9,548.5	13,074.5	7,813.7
Long-Term Debt	4,436.8	4,379.6	571.0	4,779.6
Stockholders' Equity	7,346.4	5,866.1	5,821.8	6,589.4
Performance & Financial Condition				
Return on Total Revenues %	4.04	0.12	-2.32	-1.12
Return on Avg Stockholders' Equity %	24.67	0.76	-12.37	-5.21
Return on Average Assets %	7.69	0.21	-3.82	-1.69
Current Ratio	1.85	1.35	0.81	1.38
Debt / Equity %	60.39	74.66	9.81	72.53

Compound Growth %'s   EPS % 3542.86   Net Income % 3583.77   Total Revenues % 8.76

Comments

As a result of implementing the new accounting standard requiring the accrual of postretirement employee benefits other than pensions, the Company charged against income $1.1 million and $1.4 million in FY 1995 and FY 1994, respectively. In FY 1995, the Company realized proceeds of $1.2 million from an insurance policy on a former president of the Company who passed away during the year. The net gain of $1.1 million is included in revenues. Compound earnings and earnings per share have been distorted because of this gain.

Officers	Position	Ownership Information	10/31/95
Dorothy E. Knuppenburg	Chairman	Number of Shares Outstanding	638,525
William B. Stade	President	Market Capitalization	$ 2,075,206
William P. Lianos	Exec VP, Treasurer	Frequency Of Dividends	Irregular
Clark V. Stevens	Secretary	Number of Shareholders	315

Other Information			
Transfer Agent	Bank of Boston	Where Listed	OTC-PS
Auditor	Plante & Moran	Symbol	n.a.
Market Maker	Carr Securities Corporation	Telephone (800)221-2243	SIC Code	3452
Broker Dealer	Regular Stockbroker	Employees	283

Micropac Industries, Inc.

905 E. Walnut Street • Garland, TX 75040 • Telephone (214)272-3571 • Fax (214)494-2281

Company Description

The Company Manufactures and sells various types of hybrid microcircuits and optoelectronic components and assemblies. Products are used as components in a broad range of military and industrial systems, including aircraft instrumentation and navigation systems, power supplies, electronic controls, computers and medical devices. The Company was incorporated in the State of Delaware in 1969. Shares owned by the Company's officers and directors comprised 31.3% of the outstanding stock at November 30,1995.

	11/30/95	11/30/94	11/30/93	11/30/92
Per Share Information				
Stock Price	1.00	0.58	0.63	0.63
Earnings Per Share	0.12	0.07	0.17	0.06
Price / Earnings Ratio	8.33	8.29	3.71	10.50
Book Value Per Share	1.40	1.28	1.21	1.03
Price / Book Value %	71.43	45.31	52.07	61.17
Dividends Per Share	n.a.	n.a.	n.a.	n.a.
Annual Financial Data				
Operating Results (000's)				
Total Revenues	11,445.0	9,365.0	10,575.0	9,101.0
Costs & Expenses	-10,720.0	-8,946.0	-9,558.0	-8,739.0
Income Before Taxes and Other	725.0	419.0	1,017.0	362.0
Other Items	n.a.	n.a.	n.a.	n.a.
Income Tax	-282.0	-172.0	-387.0	-137.0
Net Income	443.0	247.0	630.0	225.0
Cash Flow From Operations	10.0	662.0	n.a.	n.a.
Balance Sheet (000's)				
Cash & Equivalents	213.0	264.0	567.0	68.0
Total Current Assets	5,723.0	4,862.0	4,420.0	4,440.0
Fixed Assets, Net	1,180.0	1,015.0	1,041.0	1,065.0
Total Assets	6,903.0	5,877.0	5,461.0	5,505.0
Total Current Liabilities	1,660.0	1,068.0	997.0	1,682.0
Long-Term Debt	n.a.	n.a.	n.a.	n.a.
Stockholders' Equity	5,068.0	4,625.0	4,378.0	3,748.0
Performance & Financial Condition				
Return on Total Revenues %	3.87	2.64	5.96	2.47
Return on Avg Stockholders' Equity %	9.14	5.49	15.51	6.19
Return on Average Assets %	6.93	4.36	11.49	4.10
Current Ratio	3.45	4.55	4.43	2.64
Debt / Equity %	n.a.	n.a.	n.a.	n.a.

Compound Growth %'s	EPS %	25.99	Net Income %	25.34	Total Revenues %	7.94

Comments

Sales to the U.S. Government amounted to 72% and 85% of sales for the years ended Novembver 30, 1995 and 1994, respectively.

Officers	Position	Ownership Information	11/30/95
Nicholas Nadolsky	Chairman, CEO	Number of Shares Outstanding	3,627,151
Connie Wood	Vice President	Market Capitalization	$ 3,627,151
Richard Schlueter	VP - Sales	Frequency Of Dividends	n.a.
		Number of Shareholders	645

Other Information

Transfer Agent	Chemical Mellon Shareholder Services			Where Listed	OTC-BB
Auditor	Arthur Andersen LLP			Symbol	MPAD
Market Maker	Paragon Capital Corporation	Telephone	(800)345-0505	SIC Code	3674
Broker Dealer	Regular Stockbroker			Employees	169

Mid Valley Bank

P.O.Box 580 • Red Bluff, CA 96080 • Telephone (916)527-7614 • Fax (916)527-8657

Company Description

Mid Valley Bank is a state chartered community bank serving the very northern part of northern California with three branches, as well as a loan production office and an expertise in manufactured housing. The Bank was founded in 1975 with local capital and eight employees.

	12/31/95	12/31/94	12/31/93	12/31/92
Per Share Information				
Stock Price	8.25	6.25	4.17	3.16
Earnings Per Share	1.16	0.89	0.90	0.95
Price / Earnings Ratio	7.11	7.02	4.63	3.33
Book Value Per Share	8.62	7.43	6.51	7.00
Price / Book Value %	95.71	84.12	64.06	45.14
Dividends Per Share	n.a.	n.a.	n.a.	n.a.
Annual Financial Data				
Operating Results (000's)				
Net Interest Income	4,127.2	3,596.7	3,046.8	2,756.8
Loan Loss Provision	-132.0	-36.0	-69.0	-180.0
Non-Interest Income	873.4	514.2	465.3	395.4
Non-Interest Expense	-3,253.5	-2,847.9	-2,385.6	-2,062.5
Income Before Taxes and Other	1,615.1	1,226.9	1,057.5	909.7
Other Items	n.a.	n.a.	n.a.	175.0
Income Tax	-540.0	-416.0	-304.0	-296.0
Net Income	1,075.1	810.9	753.5	788.7
Balance Sheet (000's)				
Cash & Securities	26,395.1	23,810.5	19,867.2	20,339.5
Loans, Net	50,457.8	43,865.2	40,361.6	36,434.7
Fixed Assets, Net	1,833.8	1,505.3	1,425.1	1,119.2
Total Assets	80,277.3	70,624.9	62,380.4	58,599.6
Deposits	72,420.4	64,364.6	56,989.1	53,976.7
Stockholders' Equity	7,215.6	5,838.8	5,024.1	4,271.4
Performance & Financial Condition				
Net Interest Margin	n.a.	n.a.	n.a.	n.a.
Return on Avg Stockholders' Equity %	16.47	14.93	16.21	20.83
Return on Average Assets %	1.42	1.22	1.25	1.48
Equity to Assets %	8.99	8.27	8.05	7.29
Reserve as a % of Non-Performing Loans	1503.63	283.01	430.07	398.61

Compound Growth %'s	EPS %	6.88	Net Income %	10.88	Net Interest Income %	14.40

Comments

The Bank declared 20% stock dividends in 1992, 1993 and 1994, and had a two-for-one stock split in 1995. References to the number of shares and per share data have been restated to be comparable. Real estate loans and commercial loans represent 53% and 34% of total loans, respectively. An investment of $150 in this bank in 1986 is worth $825 as of the end of 1995.

Officers	Position	Ownership Information	12/31/95
John B. Dickerson	President, CEO	Number of Shares Outstanding	837,328
Michael C. Mayer	Senior VP, Sr Loan Officer	Market Capitalization	$ 6,907,956
Joan M. Blocker	Vice President	Frequency Of Dividends	Irregular
Vicky Reilly	Vice President	Number of Shareholders	351
Rodney M. Wiessner	Vice President, CFO		

Other Information

Transfer Agent	U.S. Stock Transfer Corporation		Where Listed	OTC-PS
Auditor	Perry-Smith & Co.		Symbol	MIVB
Market Maker	Hoefer & Arnett, Inc.	Telephone (800)346-5544	SIC Code	6020
Broker Dealer	Regular Stockbroker		Employees	61

Mid-Plains Telephone, Inc.

1912 Parmenter Street • Middleton, WI 53562-0070 • Telephone (608)831-1000 • Fax (608)836-8060

Company Description

The Company provides telephone and data services for the communities of Middleton, Cross Plains and the west side of Madison, Wisconsin. The Company also provides business systems, installation and service to a base of customers throughout southern Wisconsisn and northern Illinois. The Company was incorporaated in the State of Wisconsin in 1901.

	12/31/95	12/31/94	12/31/93	12/31/92
Per Share Information				
Stock Price	40.00	35.00	30.50	25.38
Earnings Per Share	1.73	1.47	1.47	1.38
Price / Earnings Ratio	23.12	23.81	20.75	18.39
Book Value Per Share	9.95	9.28	8.53	7.76
Price / Book Value %	402.01	377.16	357.56	327.06
Dividends Per Share	1.12	0.86	0.78	0.86
Annual Financial Data				
Operating Results (000's)				
Total Revenues	24,605.0	21,478.0	19,052.0	18,075.0
Costs & Expenses	-18,114.0	-16,874.0	-14,619.0	-13,833.0
Income Before Taxes and Other	5,534.0	4,604.0	4,433.0	4,242.0
Other Items	n.a.	n.a.	n.a.	n.a.
Income Tax	-2,109.0	-1,715.0	-1,551.0	-1,562.0
Net Income	3,425.0	2,889.0	2,882.0	2,680.0
Cash Flow From Operations	6,923.0	6,116.0	5,271.0	4,673.0
Balance Sheet (000's)				
Cash & Equivalents	560.0	186.0	1,606.0	765.0
Total Current Assets	5,920.0	5,291.0	6,283.0	4,960.0
Fixed Assets, Net	29,535.0	25,658.0	23,826.0	22,551.0
Total Assets	40,714.0	33,889.0	33,676.0	31,079.0
Total Current Liabilities	8,998.0	8,126.0	5,946.0	4,776.0
Long-Term Debt	7,597.0	3,574.0	6,955.0	7,756.0
Stockholders' Equity	19,722.0	18,232.0	16,766.0	15,158.0
Performance & Financial Condition				
Return on Total Revenues %	13.92	13.45	15.13	14.83
Return on Avg Stockholders' Equity %	18.05	16.51	18.06	18.00
Return on Average Assets %	9.18	8.55	8.90	9.00
Current Ratio	0.66	0.65	1.06	1.04
Debt / Equity %	38.52	19.60	41.48	51.17

Compound Growth %'s	EPS %	7.83	Net Income %	8.52	Total Revenues %	10.83

Comments

Telephone operations contributed 74%, and system sales and service 26%, to total revenues in 1995. The total return on the Company's common stock over the past ten years amounted to 767% more than double that of the S&P 500.

Officers	Position	Ownership Information	12/31/95
Dean W. Voeks	President	Number of Shares Outstanding	1,982,960
Daniel J. Stein	Exec VP	Market Capitalization	$ 79,318,400
Fredrick E. Urben	VP - Finance, Secretary	Frequency Of Dividends	Quarterly
Howard G. Hopeman	Vice President, CFO	Number of Shareholders	2,281

Other Information

Transfer Agent	Company Office			Where Listed	OTC-BB
Auditor	Kiesling Assoc. LLP			Symbol	MPLN
Market Maker	Gabelli & Company, Inc.	Telephone	(914)921-5154	SIC Code	4813
Broker Dealer	Regular Stockbroker			Employees	159

Mid-State Raceway, Inc.

P.O. Box 860 • Vernon, NY 13476-0860 • Telephone (315)829-2201 • Fax (315)829-2931

Company Description

The Company operates a harness racing track known as "Vernon Downs" located in Vernon, New York. The racing facility has been maintained and modernized regularly, can accomodate approximately 14,000 patrons and has stables for 1,000 horses. The number of racing days has ranged from 337 to 155 during the four years ended March 31, 1995. The Company is incorporated in the State of New York; operations began in 1953.

	03/31/95	03/31/94	03/31/93	03/31/92
Per Share Information				
Stock Price	19.00	19.25	17.25	17.25
Earnings Per Share	-2.68	-1.65	0.04	0.55
Price / Earnings Ratio	n.a.	n.a.	431.25	31.36
Book Value Per Share	11.47	14.17	16.01	16.64
Price / Book Value %	165.65	135.85	107.75	103.67
Dividends Per Share	n.a.	0.20	0.65	0.80
Annual Financial Data				
Operating Results (000's)				
Total Revenues	7,880.4	7,508.5	7,878.7	8,222.4
Costs & Expenses	-8,563.8	-8,020.6	-7,887.7	-8,068.0
Income Before Taxes and Other	-683.4	-512.1	-8.9	154.4
Other Items	n.a.	-100.0	n.a.	n.a.
Income Tax	11.8	199.9	19.7	-16.2
Net Income	-671.6	-412.2	10.8	138.2
Cash Flow From Operations	-359.1	-42.9	50.3	639.2
Balance Sheet (000's)				
Cash & Equivalents	619.7	326.2	n.a.	n.a.
Total Current Assets	1,582.7	1,808.2	2,562.2	2,239.4
Fixed Assets, Net	2,018.0	2,125.3	1,776.5	1,776.1
Total Assets	4,422.3	5,162.4	5,490.2	5,849.9
Total Current Liabilities	520.2	582.4	390.0	511.8
Long-Term Debt	n.a.	n.a.	n.a.	n.a.
Stockholders' Equity	2,871.3	3,548.7	4,011.0	4,187.8
Performance & Financial Condition				
Return on Total Revenues %	-8.52	-5.49	0.14	1.68
Return on Avg Stockholders' Equity %	-20.92	-10.91	0.26	3.26
Return on Average Assets %	-14.01	-7.74	0.19	2.35
Current Ratio	3.04	3.10	6.57	4.38
Debt / Equity %	n.a.	n.a.	n.a.	n.a.

Compound Growth %'s	EPS %	n.a.	Net Income %	n.a.	Total Revenues %	-1.41

Comments

During 1995, the Company increased the authorized number of shares to 10 million from 612,000 and decreased par value from $1.00 per share to $.10 per share. Revenue for the six months ended September 30, 1995, the most current reporting available, was $5.6 million with a net loss of $134,000 ($.54 per share) as compared to revenue of $6.0 million and a loss of $892,000 ($3.56 per share) for the same period in 1994.

Officers	Position	Ownership Information	03/31/95
Frank O. White, Jr.	President, CEO	Number of Shares Outstanding	250,386
Thomas P. Hegeman	Treasurer	Market Capitalization	$ 4,757,334
James J. Moran	Vice President, Secretary	Frequency Of Dividends	Irregular
		Number of Shareholders	555

Other Information			
Transfer Agent	Company Office	Where Listed	OTC-BB
Auditor	Coopers Lybrand LLP	Symbol	MRWY
Market Maker	Chicago Corporation, The	Telephone (800)621-1674	SIC Code	7948
Broker Dealer	Regular Stockbroker	Employees	283

Midland Bancorporation, Inc.

80 East Ridgewood Avenue • Paramus, NJ 07652 • Telephone (201)265-3162

Company Description

The Bank provides a full range of banking services to individual and corporate customers through thirteen offices in northern New Jersey. These offices are located primarily in affluent areas of Bergen County. Shares were issued in July, 1985, in accordance with the reorganization of Midland Bank & Trust Co.

	12/31/95	12/31/94	12/31/93	12/31/92
Per Share Information				
Stock Price	276.00	229.00	176.50	75.00
Earnings Per Share	34.99	29.16	22.45	13.80
Price / Earnings Ratio	7.89	7.85	7.86	5.43
Book Value Per Share	257.40	222.85	219.80	203.85
Price / Book Value %	107.23	102.76	80.30	36.79
Dividends Per Share	13.00	12.00	6.50	5.00
Annual Financial Data				
Operating Results (000's)				
Net Interest Income	19,187.0	18,135.0	16,116.0	15,857.0
Loan Loss Provision	-500.0	-787.0	-1,036.0	-2,345.0
Non-Interest Income	2,934.0	2,979.0	3,379.0	2,822.0
Non-Interest Expense	-14,520.0	-14,487.0	-14,502.0	-13,880.0
Income Before Taxes and Other	7,101.0	5,840.0	3,957.0	2,454.0
Other Items	n.a.	n.a.	151.0	n.a.
Income Tax	-2,664.0	-2,137.0	-1,256.0	-701.0
Net Income	4,437.0	3,703.0	2,852.0	1,753.0
Balance Sheet (000's)				
Cash & Securities	157,094.0	150,166.0	179,735.0	155,727.0
Loans, Net	254,344.0	238,180.0	214,801.0	208,537.0
Fixed Assets, Net	7,659.0	7,765.0	8,221.0	5,133.0
Total Assets	424,092.0	401,730.0	407,961.0	375,135.0
Deposits	388,260.0	370,235.0	377,303.0	346,453.0
Stockholders' Equity	32,372.0	28,279.0	27,920.0	25,894.0
Performance & Financial Condition				
Net Interest Margin	n.a.	n.a.	n.a.	n.a.
Return on Avg Stockholders' Equity %	14.63	13.18	10.60	6.92
Return on Average Assets %	1.07	0.91	0.73	0.48
Equity to Assets %	7.63	7.04	6.84	6.90
Reserve as a % of Non-Performing Loans	181.40	226.69	115.67	58.69

Compound Growth %'s	EPS %	36.36	Net Income %	36.28	Net Interest Income %	6.56

Comments

Commercial loans comprise 59% of loans outstanding. Real estate mortgage loans and installment debt account for 23% and 18% of all loans, respectively. A recent customer survey revealed that over 90% of consumer account customers were satisfied with the Bank's services and would recommend them to others. Performance results have been trending up in each year since 1992. The growth rate has been strong. Returns on equity and assets were very good the last two years. Management claims that it is prepared for a new wave of growth.

Officers	Position	Ownership Information	12/31/95
Walter H. Jones III	Chairman	Number of Shares Outstanding	125,743
Robert M. Meyer	President, CEO	Market Capitalization	$ 34,705,068
Sharon A. Martin	Vice President	Frequency Of Dividends	Quarterly
Patricia K. Davino	Vice President	Number of Shareholders	251

Other Information				
Transfer Agent	The First National Bank of Boston		Where Listed	OTC-BB
Auditor	KPMG Peat Marwick LLP		Symbol	MDLB
Market Maker	Robotti & Eng, Incorporated	Telephone (212)986-4800	SIC Code	6020
Broker Dealer	Regular Stockbroker		Employees	195

Million Dollar Saloon, Inc.

6848 Greenville Avenue • Dallas, TX 75231 • Telephone (214)691-6757 • Fax (214)691-6788

Company Description

The Company owns and operates an adult entertainment nightclub named The Million Dollar Saloon. It is also in the business of owning and managing income producing real estate. The Company is the result of a merger in 1995 between an inactive Nevada corporation, which became the successor, and several Texas corporations with similar ownership.

	12/31/95	12/31/94
Per Share Information		
Stock Price	3.38	n.a.
Earnings Per Share	0.04	0.02
Price / Earnings Ratio	84.50	n.a.
Book Value Per Share	0.51	0.54
Price / Book Value %	662.75	n.a.
Dividends Per Share	n.a.	n.a.
Annual Financial Data		
Operating Results (000's)		
Total Revenues	3,270.6	2,988.0
Costs & Expenses	-3,120.6	-2,821.6
Income Before Taxes and Other	149.9	70.8
Other Items	115.8	n.a.
Income Tax	-52.0	0.8
Net Income	213.7	71.6
Cash Flow From Operations	167.2	211.4
Balance Sheet (000's)		
Cash & Equivalents	133.4	123.1
Total Current Assets	235.1	174.8
Fixed Assets, Net	2,250.2	2,276.8
Total Assets	3,532.0	3,322.3
Total Current Liabilities	267.4	466.8
Long-Term Debt	623.2	45.1
Stockholders' Equity	2,551.1	2,738.6
Performance & Financial Condition		
Return on Total Revenues %	6.53	2.40
Return on Avg Stockholders' Equity %	8.08	n.a.
Return on Average Assets %	6.23	n.a.
Current Ratio	0.88	0.37
Debt / Equity %	24.43	1.65

Compound Growth %'s	EPS %	100.00	Net Income %	198.46	Total Revenues %	9.46

Comments

The financial information presented represents the consolidated activities of the merged companies for the most recent two year period. The stock of the new company began trading in January of 1996.

Officers	Position	Ownership Information	12/31/95
Nina Furrh	Chairman, President	Number of Shares Outstanding	4,999,991
Bjorn Heyerdahl	CEO	Market Capitalization	$ 16,899,970
Dewanna Ross	Secretary	Frequency Of Dividends	n.a.
		Number of Shareholders	300

Other Information

Transfer Agent	Securities Transfer Corporation		Where Listed	OTC-BB
Auditor	S.W. Hatfield & Assoc.		Symbol	MLDS
Market Maker	J. Alexander Securities, Inc.	Telephone (800)421-0258	SIC Code	7999
Broker Dealer	Regular Stockbroker		Employees	200

Mills Music Trust

140 Broadway • New York, NY 10015 • Telephone (212)658-6014 • Fax (212)658-6425

Company Description

The Trust was created in 1964 for the purpose of acquiring the rights to receive payment for a deferred contingent purchase price obligation payable to Mills Music, Inc. The payments are determined quarterly and are based on a formula which considers gross royalty income paid to composers, authors and others for the 25,000 titles contained in the "Old Mills Catalogue" of musical compositions. All of the income, less minimal administrative expenses, is distributed. The Trust was created when 277,712 units of beneficial interest were sold to the holders of outstanding common stock of Utilities & Industries Corporation.

	12/31/95	12/31/94	12/31/93	12/31/92
Per Share Information				
Stock Price	40.00	34.00	36.00	32.50
Earnings Per Share	4.42	4.57	3.75	3.28
Price / Earnings Ratio	9.05	7.44	9.60	9.91
Book Value Per Share	n.a.	n.a.	n.a.	n.a.
Price / Book Value %	n.a.	n.a.	n.a.	n.a.
Dividends Per Share	4.42	4.57	3.75	3.28
Annual Financial Data				
Operating Results (000's)				
Total Revenues	1,268.4	1,308.1	1,065.5	942.3
Costs & Expenses	-42.0	-38.6	-23.1	-30.8
Income Before Taxes and Other	1,226.4	1,269.5	1,042.4	911.5
Other Items	n.a.	n.a.	n.a.	n.a.
Income Tax	n.a.	n.a.	n.a.	n.a.
Net Income	1,226.4	1,269.5	1,042.4	911.5
Cash Flow From Operations	1,226.4	1,269.5	1,042.4	911.5
Balance Sheet (000's)				
Cash & Equivalents	0.0	0.8	0.8	0.8
Total Current Assets	0.0	0.8	0.8	0.8
Fixed Assets, Net	n.a.	n.a.	n.a.	n.a.
Total Assets	0.0	0.8	0.8	0.8
Total Current Liabilities	n.a.	n.a.	n.a.	n.a.
Long-Term Debt	n.a.	n.a.	n.a.	n.a.
Stockholders' Equity	0.0	0.8	0.8	0.8
Performance & Financial Condition				
Return on Total Revenues %	96.69	97.05	97.83	96.73
Return on Avg Stockholders' Equity %	n.a.	n.a.	n.a.	n.a.
Return on Average Assets %	n.a.	n.a.	n.a.	n.a.
Current Ratio	n.a.	n.a.	n.a.	n.a.
Debt / Equity %	n.a.	n.a.	n.a.	n.a.

Compound Growth %'s	EPS %	10.45	Net Income %	10.40	Total Revenues %	10.41

Comments

Statements of cash receipts and disbursements are the only financial statements prepared. There is no book value per unit because cumulative distributions exceed the initial investment in the trust. The Trust's receipts are derived from copyrights established prior to 1964 and as such, they fluctuate based upon public interest in the nostalgia appeal of older songs.

Officers	Position		Ownership Information	12/31/95
Bernard D. Fischman	Other		Number of Shares Outstanding	277,712
Bank Marine Midland	Other		Market Capitalization	$ 11,108,480
			Frequency Of Dividends	Quarterly
			Number of Shareholders	321

Other Information

Transfer Agent	Marine Midland Bank N.A.		Where Listed	OTC-BB
Auditor	KPMG Peat Marwick		Symbol	MMTRS
Market Maker	Carr Securities Corporation	Telephone (800)221-2243	SIC Code	6790
Broker Dealer	Regular Stockbroker		Employees	n.a.

Mod U Kraf Homes, Inc.

822 Pell Avenue • Rocky Mount, VA 24151 • Telephone (540)483-0291 • Fax (540)483-2228

Company Description

The Company manufactures and sells sectionalized custom single family homes of its own design. The Company also manufactures a commercial line of products consisting of multi-family and diversified speciality structures. The single family homes range in price from $55,000 to $2,250,000. Products are sold to home builders, developers and realtors in Virginia, Maryland, West Virginia and North Carolina. The Company was incorporated in Virginia in 1971.

	12/31/95	12/31/94	12/31/93	12/31/92
Per Share Information				
Stock Price	4.00	4.88	3.39	2.28
Earnings Per Share	0.46	0.38	0.66	0.31
Price / Earnings Ratio	8.70	12.84	5.14	7.35
Book Value Per Share	5.55	5.25	4.99	4.42
Price / Book Value %	72.07	92.95	67.94	51.58
Dividends Per Share	0.12	0.12	0.10	0.10
Annual Financial Data				
Operating Results (000's)				
Total Revenues	9,275.5	9,481.7	8,050.3	7,092.7
Costs & Expenses	-8,541.0	-8,811.9	-7,522.2	-6,551.1
Income Before Taxes and Other	607.5	555.0	342.8	431.3
Other Items	n.a.	n.a.	342.2	n.a.
Income Tax	-228.7	-246.8	-147.7	-178.5
Net Income	378.8	308.2	537.3	252.8
Cash Flow From Operations	273.0	883.0	166.6	538.8
Balance Sheet (000's)				
Cash & Equivalents	1,426.7	1,226.7	1,110.5	986.6
Total Current Assets	4,498.1	4,591.5	4,128.7	3,923.3
Fixed Assets, Net	2,245.6	897.8	911.4	791.5
Total Assets	7,845.5	6,329.5	5,883.2	5,241.4
Total Current Liabilities	897.8	863.2	568.7	550.3
Long-Term Debt	2,365.3	1,195.3	1,253.5	1,074.6
Stockholders' Equity	4,582.4	4,271.0	4,061.0	3,616.4
Performance & Financial Condition				
Return on Total Revenues %	4.08	3.25	6.67	3.56
Return on Avg Stockholders' Equity %	8.56	7.40	14.00	7.16
Return on Average Assets %	5.34	5.05	9.66	5.02
Current Ratio	5.01	5.32	7.26	7.13
Debt / Equity %	51.62	27.99	30.87	29.72

Compound Growth %'s	EPS %	14.06	Net Income %	14.43	Total Revenues %	9.36

Comments

On March 27, 1996, officers and directors, as a group, owned approximately 48% of the outstanding shares of the Company's common stock. Included as a benefit to income is $342,000 (Other Items) during 1993, from the accrual of postretirement benefits in accordance with new accounting standards.

Officers	Position	Ownership Information	12/31/95
Dale H. Powell	Chairman, President	Number of Shares Outstanding	825,649
Jeffrey L. Boudreaux	CFO	Market Capitalization	$ 3,302,596
Edwin J. Campbell	Vice President, Secretary	Frequency Of Dividends	Quarterly
		Number of Shareholders	438

Other Information

Transfer Agent	First Union Bank		Where Listed	OTC-BB
Auditor	Brown, Edwards & Company		Symbol	MODU
Market Maker	Koonce Securities, Inc.	Telephone (800)368-2803	SIC Code	2452
Broker Dealer	Regular Stockbroker		Employees	90

Momed Holding Co.

8630 • St. Louis, MO 63124 • Telephone (314)872-8000 • Fax (314)872-8785

Company Description

The primary business of the Company is selling and issuing policies of medical professional liability insurance to eligible physicians, dentists, professional partnerships and corporations whose members are physicians licensed to practice and who are practicing in the states of Missouri and Kansas and also to Certified Registered Nurse Anesthetists. The Company has been in business since 1978 and is incorporated in the state of Missouri.

	12/31/95	12/31/94	12/31/93	12/31/92
Per Share Information				
Stock Price	2.50	2.59	2.08	2.25
Earnings Per Share	6.07	2.55	-0.62	1.96
Price / Earnings Ratio	0.41	1.02	n.a.	1.15
Book Value Per Share	25.31	14.63	15.10	15.73
Price / Book Value %	9.88	17.70	13.77	14.30
Dividends Per Share	n.a.	n.a.	n.a.	n.a.
Annual Financial Data				
Operating Results (000's)				
Total Revenues	16,686.8	14,855.7	14,953.9	15,009.2
Costs & Expenses	-13,416.2	-12,613.8	-17,049.0	-13,688.3
Income Before Taxes and Other	3,270.6	2,241.9	-2,095.1	1,320.9
Other Items	n.a.	n.a.	900.0	n.a.
Income Tax	806.4	-528.8	776.6	-2.0
Net Income	4,077.0	1,713.1	-418.5	1,319.0
Cash Flow From Operations	987.4	1,932.8	8,715.3	1,965.5
Balance Sheet (000's)				
Cash & Equivalents	89.9	343.6	272.0	330.1
Total Current Assets	6,062.8	8,450.7	8,442.6	2,733.5
Fixed Assets, Net	851.4	889.7	878.9	891.9
Total Assets	81,275.2	77,523.9	77,596.4	61,053.6
Total Current Liabilities	1,509.4	1,177.4	1,082.1	8,895.1
Long-Term Debt	n.a.	n.a.	n.a.	n.a.
Stockholders' Equity	17,014.9	9,838.7	10,148.4	10,573.1
Performance & Financial Condition				
Return on Total Revenues %	24.43	11.53	-2.80	8.79
Return on Avg Stockholders' Equity %	30.36	17.14	-4.04	13.36
Return on Average Assets %	5.13	2.21	-0.60	2.22
Current Ratio	4.02	7.18	7.80	0.31
Debt / Equity %	n.a.	n.a.	n.a.	n.a.

Compound Growth %'s	EPS %	45.76	Net Income %	45.67	Total Revenues %	3.59

Comments

Insurance premiums and investment income represent approximately 70% and 30% of total revenue in 1995, respectively. Investments represent approximately 88% of the Company's total assets and loss reserves approximately 86% of total liabilities, at December 31, 1995. Officers and directors, as a group, owned 30.4% of the Company's common stock at December 31, 1995. During February 1996, the Company signed a letter of intent to become acquired by MAIC Holdings, Inc. As we go to press the transaction has not yet been consumated.

Officers	Position	Ownership Information	12/31/95
Richard V. Bradley	President, CEO	Number of Shares Outstanding	672,054
Kriete Hollrah	Exec VP	Market Capitalization	$ 1,680,135
Garth S. Russell	CFO	Frequency Of Dividends	n.a.
James M. Stokes	Treasurer, Secretary	Number of Shareholders	272
Russell L. Oldham	Vice President		

Other Information				
Transfer Agent	Boatman's Trust Co.		Where Listed	OTC-PS
Auditor	KPMG Peat Marwick LLP		Symbol	MOMHA
Market Maker	Burns, Pauli & Co., Inc.	Telephone (800)325-3373	SIC Code	6351
Broker Dealer	Regular Stockbroker		Employees	20

Monarch Cement Company (The)

P.O. Box 1000 • Humboldt, KS 66748-1000 • Telephone (316)473-2222 • Fax (316)473-2447

Company Description

The Company manufactures and sells portland cement, the basic material used in the production of ready-mixed concrete used in highway, bridge and building construction, where strength and durability are primary requirements. The Company is also in the ready-mixed concrete, concrete products and sundry building materials business. Products are distributed in the states of Kansas, Iowa, Nebraska, Missouri, Arkansas and Oklahoma. The Company has been in business since 1908. During 1994, a stock split was effected whereby one share of Class B Capital Stock was issued for each outstanding share of Capital Stock. Class B Capital Stock has voting rights of ten votes per share, restricted transferability and is convertible into the Capital Stock on a share-for-share basis. Per share amounts have been restated to reflect this transaction.

	12/31/95	12/31/94	12/31/93	12/31/92
Per Share Information				
Stock Price	12.63	12.50	7.88	7.19
Earnings Per Share	1.81	0.94	-0.02	0.74
Price / Earnings Ratio	6.98	13.30	n.a.	9.72
Book Value Per Share	9.68	8.11	7.68	8.05
Price / Book Value %	130.48	154.13	102.60	89.32
Dividends Per Share	0.46	0.46	0.40	0.40
Annual Financial Data				
Operating Results (000's)				
Total Revenues	81,666.8	73,645.7	66,118.3	58,721.1
Costs & Expenses	-69,374.8	-67,694.5	-59,579.3	-53,821.1
Income Before Taxes and Other	12,073.5	6,373.4	7,406.9	4,900.0
Other Items	n.a.	n.a.	-5,080.0	n.a.
Income Tax	-4,400.0	-2,375.0	-2,415.0	-1,700.0
Net Income	7,673.5	3,998.4	-88.1	3,200.0
Cash Flow From Operations	10,355.3	8,195.9	7,309.1	5,546.4
Balance Sheet (000's)				
Cash & Equivalents	5,071.3	3,668.8	1,665.9	1,042.2
Total Current Assets	31,732.5	26,523.0	28,569.1	23,019.3
Fixed Assets, Net	22,517.8	20,988.2	17,191.0	17,716.0
Total Assets	59,782.8	52,522.0	49,862.8	42,993.3
Total Current Liabilities	6,638.3	6,703.8	6,316.7	5,181.8
Long-Term Debt	n.a.	n.a.	n.a.	n.a.
Stockholders' Equity	41,023.8	34,398.4	32,546.7	34,098.0
Performance & Financial Condition				
Return on Total Revenues %	9.40	5.43	-0.13	5.45
Return on Avg Stockholders' Equity %	20.35	11.95	-0.26	9.52
Return on Average Assets %	13.67	7.81	-0.19	7.55
Current Ratio	4.78	3.96	4.52	4.44
Debt / Equity %	n.a.	n.a.	n.a.	n.a.

Compound Growth %'s	EPS %	6.70	Net Income %	33.85	Total Revenues %	11.62

Comments

During 1995, a capital improvement program was completed at the Company's cement plant allowing for increased production at a reduced cost per ton. Net Income for 1993 includes an expense of $5.5 million (Other Items) related to the implementation of the new accounting standard requiring accrual of postretirement employee benefits.

Officers	Position	Ownership Information	12/31/95
Jack R. Callahan	President	Number of Shares Outstanding	4,239,290
Walter H. Wulf	Exec VP	Market Capitalization	$ 53,542,233
Karl Callaway	Secretary	Frequency Of Dividends	Annual
B;yron K. Radcliff	Treasurer	Number of Shareholders	700
Robert M. Kissick	Vice President		

Other Information

Transfer Agent	Company Office			Where Listed	OTC-BB
Auditor	Arthur Andersen			Symbol	MCEM
Market Maker	Fahnestock & Co., Inc.	Telephone	(212)422-7813	SIC Code	3270
Broker Dealer	Regular Stockbroker			Employees	555

Monroe Title Insurance Corporation

47 West Main Street • Rochester, NY 14614-1499 • Telephone (716)232-2070 • Fax (716)232-4988

Company Description

The Company issues title insurance and renders abstracts of title throughout New York State. There was a 4 for 1 stock split in 1994. All per share amounts were adjusted accordingly.

	12/31/95	12/31/94	12/31/93
Per Share Information			
Stock Price	9.12	11.50	7.50
Earnings Per Share	0.53	0.91	2.14
Price / Earnings Ratio	17.21	12.64	3.50
Book Value Per Share	9.92	8.82	8.87
Price / Book Value %	91.94	130.39	84.55
Dividends Per Share	0.22	0.60	1.09
Annual Financial Data			
Operating Results (000's)			
Total Revenues	13,436.3	17,407.6	19,782.5
Costs & Expenses	-12,869.3	-15,575.6	-16,648.2
Income Before Taxes and Other	567.1	1,832.1	3,134.2
Other Items	n.a.	-420.0	300.0
Income Tax	-1.0	-440.0	-866.0
Net Income	566.1	972.1	2,568.2
Cash Flow From Operations	-509.7	-508.0	2,358.4
Balance Sheet (000's)			
Cash & Equivalents	8.3	10.7	109.5
Total Current Assets	15,649.2	15,241.7	18,294.1
Fixed Assets, Net	1,944.5	2,064.9	2,139.6
Total Assets	20,581.2	20,155.7	24,902.4
Total Current Liabilities	2,836.8	2,787.0	5,211.0
Long-Term Debt	97.6	190.2	489.1
Stockholders' Equity	11,905.3	10,578.6	10,642.0
Performance & Financial Condition			
Return on Total Revenues %	4.21	5.58	12.98
Return on Avg Stockholders' Equity %	5.04	9.16	n.a.
Return on Average Assets %	2.78	4.31	n.a.
Current Ratio	5.52	5.47	3.51
Debt / Equity %	0.82	1.80	4.60

Compound Growth %'s	EPS % -50.23	Net Income % -53.05	Total Revenues % -17.59

Comments

1994 results included a $420,000 charge under GAAP to record postretirement health care benefits. 1993 results include a $300,000 benefit under GAAP to adjust tax liabilities. Both are reflected as Other Items.

Officers	Position	Ownership Information	12/31/95
Thomas A. Podsiadlo	VP - Finance	Number of Shares Outstanding	1,200,000
		Market Capitalization	$ 10,944,000
		Frequency Of Dividends	Quarterly
		Number of Shareholders	Under 500

Other Information

Transfer Agent	Company Office		Where Listed	OTC-BB
Auditor	Arthur Andersen LLP		Symbol	MTTL
Market Maker	Pennsylvania Merchant Group	Telephone (800)762-8624	SIC Code	6540
Broker Dealer	Regular Stockbroker		Employees	300

Mortgage Oil Company

1545 Wilshire Boulevard • Los Angeles, CA 90017-4501 • Telephone (213)482-2742 • Fax (213)483-2748

Company Description

The Company primarily invests in real estate partnerships, holds a number of marketable securities, and holds various oil, gas and mineral rights. The Company was spun-off on the liquidations of Mortgage Guarantee Company and Mortgage Service Co. in 1946 and 1949, respectively. The mineral rights which the Company owns trace back to the 1920's and 1930's which, at that time, were carved out of foreclosed farmlands throughout California's San Joaquin Valley.

	12/31/94	12/31/93	12/31/92
Per Share Information			
Stock Price	23.00	27.00	24.00
Earnings Per Share	0.92	1.26	0.72
Price / Earnings Ratio	25.00	21.43	33.33
Book Value Per Share	29.42	29.70	29.16
Price / Book Value %	78.18	90.91	82.30
Dividends Per Share	1.26	0.72	2.00
Annual Financial Data			
Operating Results (000's)			
Total Revenues	104.4	124.4	92.5
Costs & Expenses	-57.3	-54.5	-61.1
Income Before Taxes and Other	47.2	69.9	31.4
Other Items	n.a.	n.a.	n.a.
Income Tax	-9.4	-17.6	-1.7
Net Income	37.7	52.3	29.7
Cash Flow From Operations	6.8	-69.2	-14.8
Balance Sheet (000's)			
Cash & Equivalents	0.8	54.7	6.5
Total Current Assets	384.3	595.4	589.3
Fixed Assets, Net	n.a.	n.a.	n.a.
Total Assets	1,218.2	1,250.3	1,220.2
Total Current Liabilities	1.1	5.7	7.1
Long-Term Debt	n.a.	n.a.	n.a.
Stockholders' Equity	1,207.1	1,234.6	1,212.2
Performance & Financial Condition			
Return on Total Revenues %	36.12	42.02	32.15
Return on Avg Stockholders' Equity %	3.09	4.27	n.a.
Return on Average Assets %	3.06	4.23	n.a.
Current Ratio	358.19	104.26	83.51
Debt / Equity %	n.a.	n.a.	n.a.

Compound Growth %'s	EPS %	13.04	Net Income %	12.62	Total Revenues %	6.26

Comments

The oil, gas and mineral rights are carried on the balance sheet as $2.00. This accounting dates back to the formation and spin-off of the Company in the 1940's. 1995 financial reports are not available until August, 1996.

Officers	Position	Ownership Information	12/31/94
Morgan Adams, Jr.	President	Number of Shares Outstanding	41,030
David V. Adams	Secretary, Treasurer	Market Capitalization	$ 943,690
		Frequency Of Dividends	Annual
		Number of Shareholders	Under 500

Other Information

Transfer Agent	Company Office			Where Listed	OTC-BB
Auditor	Oberlies & Pearson, Inc.			Symbol	MGAG
Market Maker	Seidler Companies, Inc., The	Telephone	(800)421-0164	SIC Code	6790
Broker Dealer	Regular Stockbroker			Employees	1

Moyco Technologies, Inc.

200 Commerce Drive • Montgomeryville, PA 18936 • Telephone (215)855-4300 • Fax (215)362-3809

Company Description

The Company manufactures and sells dental supplies such as waxes, abrasives, dental mirrors, medicaments, endodontic materials and equipment and other sundry dental items (approximately 62% of FY 1995 sales). The Company also manufactures and sells abrasive materials and polishing agents for commercial use (approximately 38% of FY 1995 sales). As of June 30, 1995, officers and directors, as a group, owned 77.4% of the Company's outstanding common stock. The Company was incorporated in Pennyslvania in 1968.

	06/30/95	06/30/94	06/30/93	06/30/92
Per Share Information				
Stock Price	2.10	2.00	2.00	0.28
Earnings Per Share	0.14	0.10	0.13	0.09
Price / Earnings Ratio	15.00	20.00	15.38	3.11
Book Value Per Share	1.05	0.92	0.82	0.69
Price / Book Value %	200.00	217.39	243.90	40.58
Dividends Per Share	n.a.	n.a.	n.a.	n.a.
Annual Financial Data				
Operating Results (000's)				
Total Revenues	11,880.2	10,031.3	11,237.2	9,031.7
Costs & Expenses	-10,460.7	-8,938.9	-10,200.8	-8,446.5
Income Before Taxes and Other	1,014.7	860.9	768.0	585.2
Other Items	n.a.	-60.2	n.a.	n.a.
Income Tax	-478.3	-408.8	-258.2	-234.4
Net Income	536.3	391.8	509.8	350.8
Cash Flow From Operations	864.3	497.8	509.3	-103.9
Balance Sheet (000's)				
Cash & Equivalents	1,097.3	1,447.6	1,140.8	1,193.1
Total Current Assets	6,512.5	5,971.1	5,491.0	5,829.6
Fixed Assets, Net	5,991.6	3,283.7	2,337.8	2,656.8
Total Assets	12,983.7	9,765.9	8,013.3	8,535.4
Total Current Liabilities	1,922.8	2,967.3	2,000.7	2,809.7
Long-Term Debt	6,735.5	3,046.2	2,734.4	2,959.5
Stockholders' Equity	4,150.6	3,613.0	3,219.3	2,707.4
Performance & Financial Condition				
Return on Total Revenues %	4.51	3.91	4.54	3.88
Return on Avg Stockholders' Equity %	13.82	11.47	17.20	14.03
Return on Average Assets %	4.71	4.41	6.16	5.56
Current Ratio	3.39	2.01	2.74	2.07
Debt / Equity %	162.28	84.31	84.94	109.31

Compound Growth %'s	EPS %	15.87	Net Income %	15.20	Total Revenues %	9.57

Comments

Sales for the six months ended December 31, 1995, amounted to $5.9 million and Net Income was $246,000 ($.06 per share) as compared to $5.7 million and $315,000 ($.08 per share) for the same period in 1994. At December 31, 1995, the Company's common stock was quoted at an average bid/ask price of $7.38 per share.

Officers	Position	Ownership Information	06/30/95
Marvin E. Sternberg	Chairman, President	Number of Shares Outstanding	3,938,915
William Woodhead	Secretary, Treasurer	Market Capitalization	$ 8,271,722
Jerome Lipkin	Vice President	Frequency Of Dividends	n.a.
		Number of Shareholders	701

Other Information				
Transfer Agent	First Pennsylvania Bank		Where Listed	OTC-BB
Auditor	Heffler, Radetich & Saitta		Symbol	MOYC
Market Maker	Morgan Keegan & Company, Inc.	Telephone (800)238-7533	SIC Code	3843
Broker Dealer	Regular Stockbroker		Employees	150

Mt. Carmel Public Utility Co.

316 Market Street • Mt. Carmel, IL 62863 • Telephone (618)262-5151

Company Description

The Company is the supplier of gas and electric power to the residents and businesses of Wabash County, Illinois. One major customer accounts for approximately 27% of revenues. The Company was incorporated in 1950.

	12/31/95	12/31/94
Per Share Information		
Stock Price	20.00	20.00
Earnings Per Share	0.04	-0.01
Price / Earnings Ratio	500.00	n.a.
Book Value Per Share	30.54	31.75
Price / Book Value %	65.49	62.99
Dividends Per Share	1.25	2.00
Annual Financial Data		
Operating Results (000's)		
Total Revenues	12,752.3	12,755.0
Costs & Expenses	-12,782.2	-12,844.0
Income Before Taxes and Other	-29.9	-97.0
Other Items	n.a.	n.a.
Income Tax	37.1	95.2
Net Income	7.2	-1.8
Cash Flow From Operations	1,020.4	1,000.0
Balance Sheet (000's)		
Cash & Equivalents	70.6	90.9
Total Current Assets	1,322.9	1,504.6
Fixed Assets, Net	10,564.6	10,428.6
Total Assets	11,916.7	12,034.7
Total Current Liabilities	2,277.6	1,828.3
Long-Term Debt	2,712.5	3,062.5
Stockholders' Equity	6,107.7	6,350.6
Performance & Financial Condition		
Return on Total Revenues %	0.06	-0.01
Return on Avg Stockholders' Equity %	0.12	-0.03
Return on Average Assets %	0.06	n.a.
Current Ratio	0.58	0.82
Debt / Equity %	44.41	48.22

Compound Growth %'s	EPS % n.a.	Net Income % n.a.	Total Revenues % -0.02

Comments

The Company has been named in a lawsuit by a neighboring utility provider which claims that the Company infringed upon its service territory in its sales to its major customer. We also note that the Company maintains life insurance on certain officers which is unusual for a public utility company.

Officers	Position	Ownership Information	12/31/95
Philip Barnhard IV	President	Number of Shares Outstanding	200,000
		Market Capitalization	$ 4,000,000
		Frequency Of Dividends	Annual
		Number of Shareholders	Under 500

Other Information

Transfer Agent	Company Office		Where Listed	OTC-BB
Auditor	Deloitte & Touche LLP		Symbol	MCPB
Market Maker	Chicago Corporation, The	Telephone (800)621-1674	SIC Code	4910
Broker Dealer	Pink sheet specialist		Employees	40

NCC Industries, Inc.

165 Main Street • Cortland, NY 13045 • Telephone (607)756-2841 • Fax (607)756-6607

Company Description

The Company designs, manufactures and sells womens undergarments. Sales are made to department, speciality, discount and chain stores throughout the United States. Much of the manufacturing process is performed overseas. In April, 1995, Maidenform Worldwide, Inc. (Maidenform) acquired approximately 92% of the Company's outstanding stock. The Company's Chairman and one of its Executive VP's own the majority of Maidenform's outstanding stock.

	12/31/95	12/31/94	12/31/93	12/31/92
Per Share Information				
Stock Price	9.00	7.88	7.13	4.31
Earnings Per Share	0.63	1.35	0.85	1.35
Price / Earnings Ratio	12.70	5.84	8.39	3.19
Book Value Per Share	8.87	8.22	6.89	6.07
Price / Book Value %	90.19	95.86	103.48	71.00
Dividends Per Share	n.a.	n.a.	n.a.	n.a.
Annual Financial Data				
Operating Results (000's)				
Total Revenues	125,987.3	128,042.4	110,597.8	106,607.4
Costs & Expenses	-122,183.5	-119,812.2	-105,531.4	-96,028.9
Income Before Taxes and Other	3,803.8	8,230.2	5,066.4	10,578.5
Other Items	n.a.	n.a.	n.a.	-884.4
Income Tax	-1,053.1	-2,329.2	-1,351.6	-3,481.3
Net Income	2,750.7	5,901.0	3,714.8	6,212.8
Cash Flow From Operations	19,764.9	15,415.4	-6,166.9	-1,020.2
Balance Sheet (000's)				
Cash & Equivalents	725.2	1,034.8	442.1	658.9
Total Current Assets	64,628.4	58,591.1	63,939.8	52,611.7
Fixed Assets, Net	10,155.6	11,186.3	11,557.5	9,714.0
Total Assets	75,368.7	71,588.0	76,664.6	62,561.7
Total Current Liabilities	32,955.6	23,442.3	33,029.9	22,864.9
Long-Term Debt	1,916.4	9,361.4	12,733.7	12,686.1
Stockholders' Equity	38,831.8	35,983.6	30,155.0	26,581.8
Performance & Financial Condition				
Return on Total Revenues %	2.18	4.61	3.36	5.83
Return on Avg Stockholders' Equity %	7.35	17.84	13.09	25.13
Return on Average Assets %	3.74	7.96	5.34	10.35
Current Ratio	1.96	2.50	1.94	2.30
Debt / Equity %	4.94	26.02	42.23	47.72

Compound Growth %'s	EPS %	-22.43	Net Income %	-23.78	Total Revenues %	5.73

Comments

Sales to Walmart, Penny's and Mervyn's accounted for 14%, 16%, and 11%, respectively, of total sales during 1995.

Officers	Position	Ownership Information	12/31/95
Elizabeth Coleman	Chairman, CEO	Number of Shares Outstanding	4,375,492
David Masket	President	Market Capitalization	$ 35,003,936
Ira Glazer	COO, Treasurer	Frequency Of Dividends	n.a.
Steven Masket	Exec VP, Secretary	Number of Shareholders	416
Frank Magrone	Exec VP		

Other Information				
Transfer Agent	Chemical Mellon Shareholder Services		Where Listed	OTC-BB
Auditor	Ernst & Young LLP		Symbol	NCCD
Market Maker	JA Glynn & Company	Telephone (800)966-4596	SIC Code	2342
Broker Dealer	Regular Stockbroker		Employees	1767

National Properties Corporation

4500 Merle Hay Road • Des Moines, IA 50310 • Telephone (515)278-1132 • Fax (515)278-1168

Company Description

The Company is in the business of developing commercial real estate for lease to tenants under net lease arrangements. At December 31, 1995, the Company had 38 properties located in Arizona, Georgia, Iowa, Kansas, Missouri, Nebraska, Oklahoma and Texas. The Company was incorporated in Texas in 1960.

	12/31/95	12/31/94	12/31/93	12/31/92
Per Share Information				
Stock Price	24.51	23.56	23.44	18.85
Earnings Per Share	1.97	1.96	1.68	1.52
Price / Earnings Ratio	12.44	12.02	13.95	12.40
Book Value Per Share	26.49	24.15	21.38	19.85
Price / Book Value %	92.53	97.56	109.64	94.96
Dividends Per Share	n.a.	0.18	0.17	0.16
Annual Financial Data				
Operating Results (000's)				
Total Revenues	3,334.9	3,234.6	2,882.2	2,624.0
Costs & Expenses	-1,406.3	-1,348.6	-1,155.3	-1,031.6
Income Before Taxes and Other	1,419.5	1,408.4	1,232.4	1,128.5
Other Items	n.a.	n.a.	n.a.	n.a.
Income Tax	-516.8	-503.2	-440.3	-395.7
Net Income	902.7	905.2	792.1	732.8
Cash Flow From Operations	1,367.1	1,629.8	1,522.7	1,359.9
Balance Sheet (000's)				
Cash & Equivalents	123.8	238.7	154.4	112.6
Total Current Assets	151.6	270.5	183.7	145.6
Fixed Assets, Net	17,394.3	17,681.9	16,351.7	13,995.7
Total Assets	19,117.6	19,599.6	17,411.6	15,031.2
Total Current Liabilities	1,563.1	1,442.8	1,166.1	1,158.7
Long-Term Debt	5,148.1	6,758.1	6,220.4	4,409.2
Stockholders' Equity	12,070.4	11,142.2	10,025.1	9,463.4
Performance & Financial Condition				
Return on Total Revenues %	27.07	27.99	27.48	27.93
Return on Avg Stockholders' Equity %	7.78	8.55	8.13	7.93
Return on Average Assets %	4.66	4.89	4.88	5.09
Current Ratio	0.10	0.19	0.16	0.16
Debt / Equity %	42.65	60.65	62.05	62.05

Compound Growth %'s	EPS %	9.03	Net Income %	7.20	Total Revenues %	8.32

Comments

Included in Total Assets in 1995 and 1994, are marketable securities of $1.5 million and $1.6 million, respectively. The Company has an ongoing stock repurchase program, subject to market prices. During the four years ended December 31, 1995, the Company repurchased a total of 32,443 shares of its outstanding common stock.

Officers	Position	Ownership Information	12/31/95
Raymond Di Paglia	President	Number of Shares Outstanding	455,655
Robert W. Guely	Vice President, CFO	Market Capitalization	$ 11,168,104
		Frequency Of Dividends	Irregular
		Number of Shareholders	882

Other Information			
Transfer Agent	Mellon Securities Trust Company	Where Listed	OTC-BB
Auditor	Northup, Haines et. al.	Symbol	NAPE
Market Maker	Carr Securities Corporation	Telephone (800)221-2243	SIC Code	6512
Broker Dealer	Regular Stockbroker	Employees	6

National Stock Yards Company

Exchange Building • National Stock Yards, IL 62071 • Telephone (618)274-6400 • Fax (618)274-6402

Company Description

The Company provides marketplaces on its land for the exchange of livestock in the greater St. Louis and Oklahoma City areas. The customer base consists of livestock suppliers who primarily distribute to meat packers and processors throughout the United States.

	12/31/95	12/31/94	12/31/93	12/31/92
Per Share Information				
Stock Price	69.50	53.00	39.00	20.00
Earnings Per Share	0.90	1.61	-0.38	9.23
Price / Earnings Ratio	77.22	32.92	n.a.	2.17
Book Value Per Share	240.28	239.38	237.77	238.15
Price / Book Value %	28.92	22.14	16.40	8.40
Dividends Per Share	n.a.	n.a.	n.a.	n.a.
Annual Financial Data				
Operating Results (000's)				
Total Revenues	4,811.6	5,036.1	5,101.1	5,077.5
Costs & Expenses	-4,756.3	-4,913.9	-5,115.7	-4,856.2
Income Before Taxes and Other	55.3	122.2	-14.5	-26.3
Other Items	n.a.	n.a.	n.a.	240.7
Income Tax	-16.0	-52.0	-2.0	188.0
Net Income	39.3	70.2	-16.5	402.4
Cash Flow From Operations	339.9	254.0	78.8	397.0
Balance Sheet (000's)				
Cash & Equivalents	434.2	337.6	397.2	473.2
Total Current Assets	673.8	574.0	650.7	661.2
Fixed Assets, Net	10,836.2	10,920.3	10,765.2	10,840.9
Total Assets	11,510.0	11,494.9	11,415.9	11,502.1
Total Current Liabilities	468.9	398.9	497.5	469.6
Long-Term Debt	136.8	155.4	n.a.	n.a.
Stockholders' Equity	10,479.3	10,440.0	10,369.8	10,386.3
Performance & Financial Condition				
Return on Total Revenues %	0.82	1.39	-0.32	7.93
Return on Avg Stockholders' Equity %	0.38	0.67	-0.16	3.95
Return on Average Assets %	0.34	0.61	-0.14	3.51
Current Ratio	1.44	1.44	1.31	1.41
Debt / Equity %	1.31	1.49	n.a.	n.a.

Compound Growth %'s	EPS % -53.97	Net Income % -53.94	Total Revenues % -1.78

Comments

1992 results include a one-time benefit of $240,672 to comply with GAAP for the reporting of income tax liabilities. Management reports a continuing decline in stock yard operations and has been investigating alternative uses of the Company's substantial real estate holdings. Average employee compensation is approximately $50,000.

Officers	Position	Ownership Information	12/31/95
Michael Bakwin	Chairman	Number of Shares Outstanding	43,612
George A. Hall	President	Market Capitalization	$ 3,031,034
Patrick Henry	Secretary, Treasurer	Frequency Of Dividends	Irregular
Kathryn Kueker	Other	Number of Shareholders	Under 500
Russell J. Porcelli	Other		

Other Information			
Transfer Agent	First National Bank of Chicago	Where Listed	OTC-BB
Auditor	Lopata Flegel Hoffman & Co.LLP	Symbol	NSYC
Market Maker	S.J. Wolfe & Co.	Telephone (800)262-2244	SIC Code	7389
Broker Dealer	Pink sheet specialist	Employees	40

National Union Bank of Kinderhook, The

One Hudson Street • Kinderhook, NY 12106 • Telephone (518)758-7101 • Fax (518)758-6963

Company Description

The Bank was established in 1853. The main office is in Kinderhook, New York and there is a branch in Valatie. Regular commercial and private banking services are provided. The loan portfolio consists of real estate, commercial and individual loans which comprise 61%, 25% and 14% of all loans, respectively.

	12/31/95	12/31/94	12/31/93	12/31/92
Per Share Information				
Stock Price	127.50	122.50	115.00	105.00
Earnings Per Share	12.00	10.43	8.90	8.90
Price / Earnings Ratio	10.63	11.74	12.92	11.80
Book Value Per Share	138.90	125.66	119.04	112.52
Price / Book Value %	91.79	97.49	96.61	93.32
Dividends Per Share	2.50	2.50	2.50	2.50
Annual Financial Data				
Operating Results (000's)				
Net Interest Income	2,120.4	2,027.3	1,858.2	1,879.7
Loan Loss Provision	-20.0	n.a.	-6.6	-6.6
Non-Interest Income	259.3	180.1	177.5	156.1
Non-Interest Expense	-1,444.6	-1,411.2	-1,351.5	-1,351.7
Income Before Taxes and Other	915.2	796.3	677.6	677.6
Other Items	n.a.	n.a.	n.a.	n.a.
Income Tax	-339.0	-295.6	-250.4	-250.4
Net Income	576.2	500.7	427.2	427.2
Balance Sheet (000's)				
Cash & Securities	30,525.0	30,497.4	32,453.0	28,823.0
Loans, Net	21,849.4	20,796.0	17,819.4	16,421.8
Fixed Assets, Net	426.2	452.7	482.2	393.9
Total Assets	53,657.3	52,862.7	51,636.9	48,483.7
Deposits	46,426.5	46,376.5	45,576.8	42,577.2
Stockholders' Equity	6,667.4	6,031.5	5,713.8	5,400.9
Performance & Financial Condition				
Net Interest Margin	n.a.	n.a.	n.a.	n.a.
Return on Avg Stockholders' Equity %	9.07	8.53	7.69	n.a.
Return on Average Assets %	1.08	0.96	0.85	n.a.
Equity to Assets %	12.43	11.41	11.07	11.14
Reserve as a % of Non-Performing Loans	82.92	383.53	137.07	307.69

Compound Growth %'s	EPS %	10.47	Net Income %	10.49	Net Interest Income %	4.10

Comments

The Bank's past due and nonaccrual loans increased to $455,000 in 1995, from $93,480 in the preceeding year. The return ratios have been inching up in recent years and return on assets exceeded 1% in 1995. The stock still trades slightly below book value. There is no indication that the numbers have been audited by an independent accounting firm.

Officers	Position	Ownership Information	12/31/95
Burns F. Barford, Jr.	Chairman, Vice President	Number of Shares Outstanding	48,000
Robert A. Sherwood	President, CEO	Market Capitalization	$ 6,120,000
Daniel R. Kline	COO, Head Cashier	Frequency Of Dividends	Quarterly
Frank J. Pidgeon	Other	Number of Shareholders	n.a.
Betty Ann Cristiano	Other		

Other Information			
Transfer Agent	Company Office	Where Listed	OTC-BB
Auditor	Not indicated	Symbol	NUBK
Market Maker	Legg Mason Wood Walker, Inc.	SIC Code	6020
Broker Dealer	Regular Stockbroker	Employees	25

Market Maker telephone: (212)428-4949

Naturade, Inc.

7110 East Jackson Street • Paramount, CA 90723 • Telephone (310)531-8120 • Fax (310)531-8170

Company Description

The Company manufactures and distributes health related products, including vitamins, nutritional supplements and skin and hair care products. Its products are sold primarily to distributors who resell to health and natural food stores. Approximately 17% of the Company's sales were made to foreign customers in fiscal year 1995. The Company was incorporated in Delaware in 1986 and acquired Naturade Products in 1989. Naturade was established in 1926.

	09/30/95	09/30/94	09/30/93	09/30/92
Per Share Information				
Stock Price	1.81	0.91	1.25	0.75
Earnings Per Share	0.14	0.18	0.01	-0.11
Price / Earnings Ratio	12.93	5.06	125.00	n.a.
Book Value Per Share	0.35	0.27	0.02	-0.02
Price / Book Value %	517.14	337.04	6,250.00	n.a.
Dividends Per Share	n.a.	n.a.	n.a.	n.a.
Annual Financial Data				
Operating Results (000's)				
Total Revenues	10,096.6	8,139.8	7,616.8	7,005.5
Costs & Expenses	-9,491.7	-7,752.2	-7,566.9	-7,449.9
Income Before Taxes and Other	336.8	387.6	49.9	-444.4
Other Items	n.a.	91.0	n.a.	136.4
Income Tax	58.3	29.0	-27.0	29.6
Net Income	395.1	507.6	22.9	-278.4
Cash Flow From Operations	90.6	496.6	176.7	12.1
Balance Sheet (000's)				
Cash & Equivalents	116.4	201.9	61.8	82.3
Total Current Assets	2,300.2	2,255.2	1,699.9	1,684.7
Fixed Assets, Net	2,182.5	110.4	119.4	148.0
Total Assets	4,820.8	2,564.6	2,093.2	2,048.8
Total Current Liabilities	1,367.5	1,602.8	1,632.2	1,507.5
Long-Term Debt	2,555.7	199.1	393.1	590.9
Stockholders' Equity	897.6	762.8	68.0	-49.6
Performance & Financial Condition				
Return on Total Revenues %	3.91	6.24	0.30	-3.97
Return on Avg Stockholders' Equity %	47.59	122.21	248.45	n.a.
Return on Average Assets %	10.70	21.80	1.10	-13.50
Current Ratio	1.68	1.41	1.04	1.12
Debt / Equity %	284.73	26.10	578.41	n.a.

Compound Growth %'s	EPS %	274.17	Net Income %	315.72	Total Revenues %	12.96

Comments

During 1995, the Company repurchased 440,411 shares of its common stock. In addition to common stock, the Company has two classes of warrants outstanding for the purchase of common stock at prices of $1.00 and $3.00 per share until December 31, 1996. For the years ended September 30, 1995, 1994, and 1993 the Company had sales to two customers amounting to 27%, 33% and 32%, respectively, of total sales. As of November 1, 1995, officers and directors, as a group, owned approximately 45% of the Company's outstanding common stock.

Officers	Position	Ownership Information	09/30/95
Allan Schulman	President, CEO	Number of Shares Outstanding	2,538,461
Matsuko Freeman	COO	Market Capitalization	$ 4,594,614
Michael Fernicola	Exec VP	Frequency Of Dividends	n.a.
Paul D. Shapnick	CFO, Secretary	Number of Shareholders	1,368
Richard Becker	VP - Sales		

Other Information

			Where Listed	OTC-BB
Transfer Agent	Registrar & Transfer Company		Symbol	NRDC
Auditor	McGladrey & Pullen LLP		SIC Code	2844
Market Maker	Baird, Patrick & Co	Telephone (800)221-5853	Employees	44
Broker Dealer	Regular Stockbroker			

Network Data Processing Corporation

200 Fifth Avenue, S.E. • Cedar Rapids, IA 52401-1810 • Telephone (319)398-1800 • Fax (319)398-1872

Company Description

The Company provides data processing services for the insurance industry throughout the United States, including computer software licensing agreements, system implementation and conversion, and repetitive and special processing. The Company was incorporated in 1956 to acquire a data processing business that began in 1916 as a consulting actuary firm by the name of Taylor & Taylor. It went public in 1969 and had a 1 for 100 reverse split in 1987.

	03/31/95	03/31/94	03/31/93	03/31/92
Per Share Information				
Stock Price	501.50	382.15	349.13	302.00
Earnings Per Share	123.81	-201.77	113.04	25.49
Price / Earnings Ratio	4.05	n.a.	3.09	11.85
Book Value Per Share	308.82	158.17	359.75	248.88
Price / Book Value %	162.39	241.61	97.05	121.34
Dividends Per Share	n.a.	n.a.	n.a.	n.a.
Annual Financial Data				
Operating Results (000's)				
Total Revenues	9,607.3	5,127.1	5,872.7	3,786.5
Costs & Expenses	-8,559.7	-6,750.3	-4,885.3	-3,623.3
Income Before Taxes and Other	1,047.6	-1,623.3	987.3	163.2
Other Items	n.a.	n.a.	n.a.	n.a.
Income Tax	-209.7	364.4	-328.6	-16.5
Net Income	837.9	-1,258.9	658.8	146.7
Cash Flow From Operations	1,259.7	377.0	873.6	785.4
Balance Sheet (000's)				
Cash & Equivalents	48.1	119.1	190.9	145.4
Total Current Assets	2,006.3	1,579.3	1,915.0	1,262.4
Fixed Assets, Net	679.3	807.3	749.2	769.3
Total Assets	5,913.0	5,658.4	5,718.3	3,842.1
Total Current Liabilities	2,756.8	3,310.2	2,063.9	1,032.9
Long-Term Debt	244.5	747.5	618.4	806.6
Stockholders' Equity	2,090.1	986.9	2,225.1	1,432.5
Performance & Financial Condition				
Return on Total Revenues %	8.72	-24.55	11.22	3.87
Return on Avg Stockholders' Equity %	54.47	-78.39	36.02	10.82
Return on Average Assets %	14.48	-22.13	13.78	3.96
Current Ratio	0.73	0.48	0.93	1.22
Debt / Equity %	11.70	75.75	27.79	56.31

Compound Growth %'s	EPS %	69.35	Net Income %	78.75	Total Revenues %	36.39

Comments

After a disappointing year in 1994, the Company rebounded with a sizzling year. Three-year compounded returns all look extremely favorable.

Officers	Position	Ownership Information	03/31/95
Howard F. Arner	CEO, President	Number of Shares Outstanding	6,768
		Market Capitalization	$ 3,394,152
		Frequency Of Dividends	n.a.
		Number of Shareholders	Under 500

Other Information

Transfer Agent	Norwest Bank Minneapolis, N.A.			Where Listed	OTC-BB
Auditor	McGladrey & Pullen, LLP			Symbol	NTDP
Market Maker	Bear, Stearns & Co. Inc.	Telephone	(800)247-7882	SIC Code	7374
Broker Dealer	Pink sheet specialist			Employees	90

Networks Electronic Corp.

9750 De Soto Avenue • Chatsworth, CA 91311 • Telephone (818)341-0440 • Fax (818)718-7133

Company Description

The Company designs, fabricates, assembles and sells high technology components for aerospace and U.S. Government defense contractors. Aerospace industry products are spherical, self-aligned, self-lubricating and specialized bearings. Other products include miniaturized devices such as switches, initiator-igniters for missile subsystems, thermal relay switches, and glass to metal seals used in the defense and aerospace industries. The Company was incorporated in California in 1953.

	06/30/95	06/30/94	06/30/93	06/30/92
Per Share Information				
Stock Price	0.34	0.19	0.94	2.69
Earnings Per Share	1.11	-0.50	-1.18	-0.16
Price / Earnings Ratio	0.31	n.a.	n.a.	n.a.
Book Value Per Share	-0.02	-1.18	-0.56	0.65
Price / Book Value %	n.a.	n.a.	n.a.	413.85
Dividends Per Share	n.a.	n.a.	n.a.	n.a.
Annual Financial Data				
Operating Results (000's)				
Total Revenues	4,711.1	2,873.4	4,629.2	6,623.5
Costs & Expenses	-3,200.5	-3,398.6	-5,671.5	-7,033.7
Income Before Taxes and Other	1,510.6	-798.7	-1,861.9	-410.2
Other Items	n.a.	n.a.	n.a.	n.a.
Income Tax	256.3	-0.8	-23.1	150.3
Net Income	1,766.9	-799.5	-1,885.0	-259.9
Cash Flow From Operations	-50.1	-359.6	901.1	196.0
Balance Sheet (000's)				
Cash & Equivalents	117.5	164.8	540.4	513.5
Total Current Assets	2,009.0	1,510.0	2,371.7	3,770.4
Fixed Assets, Net	918.2	1,093.2	1,310.5	1,562.5
Total Assets	3,175.4	2,603.2	3,682.1	5,484.0
Total Current Liabilities	881.2	2,514.1	4,544.2	4,429.8
Long-Term Debt	2,326.5	1,965.7	24.9	26.5
Stockholders' Equity	-32.3	-1,876.6	-887.0	991.2
Performance & Financial Condition				
Return on Total Revenues %	37.51	-27.83	-40.72	-3.92
Return on Avg Stockholders' Equity %	n.a.	n.a.	n.a.	-22.09
Return on Average Assets %	61.15	-25.44	-41.13	-4.39
Current Ratio	2.28	0.60	0.52	0.85
Debt / Equity %	n.a.	n.a.	n.a.	2.67

Compound Growth %'s	EPS % n.a.	Net Income % n.a.	Total Revenues % -10.74

Comments

Fiscal years 1993 and 1994 were difficult for the Company. The Company's founder passed away, the Company filed for bankruptcy protection and the Company's facilities were heavily damaged by the Northridge earthquake. The year ended June 30, 1995, was much improved. Working capital and operating results were positive, the Company was in compliance with its plan of reorganization and its auditors removed the going concern opinion in their audit report.

Officers	Position	Ownership Information	06/30/95
David Wachtel	CEO, President	Number of Shares Outstanding	1,596,221
Edwin J. Turner	Exec VP	Market Capitalization	$ 542,715
Mohammad Tabassi	Vice President	Frequency Of Dividends	n.a.
		Number of Shareholders	984

Other Information

Transfer Agent	First Interstate Bank			Where Listed	OTC-BB
Auditor	Hurley & Company			Symbol	NWRK
Market Maker	Paragon Capital Corporation	Telephone	(800)345-0505	SIC Code	3562
Broker Dealer	Regular Stockbroker			Employees	59

New Ulm Telecom, Inc.

400 Second Street North • New Ulm, MN 56073 • Telephone (507)354-4111 • Fax (507)354-1982

Company Description

The Company's principal business is the operation of local phone companies (seven subsidiaries) which provide local exchange telephone service and related access to the long distance network. At December 31, 1995, the Company provided telephone service to over 13,800 access lines in six Minnesota cities and one Iowa city and adjacent rural areas. The Company was incorporated in 1905 in the state of Minnesota.

	12/31/95	12/31/94	12/31/93	12/31/92
Per Share Information				
Stock Price	25.25	18.38	20.00	20.00
Earnings Per Share	3.90	3.68	3.66	2.98
Price / Earnings Ratio	6.47	4.99	5.46	6.71
Book Value Per Share	26.17	24.02	21.95	19.76
Price / Book Value %	96.48	76.52	91.12	101.21
Dividends Per Share	1.75	1.62	1.47	1.25
Annual Financial Data				
Operating Results (000's)				
Total Revenues	9,544.8	8,866.2	7,745.8	6,944.1
Costs & Expenses	-5,798.9	-5,326.6	-4,573.1	-4,097.0
Income Before Taxes and Other	3,745.9	3,539.6	3,172.6	2,820.6
Other Items	n.a.	n.a.	n.a.	n.a.
Income Tax	-1,491.1	-1,412.6	-1,057.9	-1,104.5
Net Income	2,254.8	2,127.0	2,114.8	1,716.2
Cash Flow From Operations	3,330.3	3,419.3	2,724.1	n.a.
Balance Sheet (000's)				
Cash & Equivalents	1,829.2	1,433.8	1,125.6	1,203.5
Total Current Assets	3,478.0	2,748.4	2,931.6	2,288.7
Fixed Assets, Net	12,370.6	12,108.3	12,377.5	10,245.6
Total Assets	22,021.5	20,976.2	21,309.1	15,236.0
Total Current Liabilities	949.5	821.8	1,574.8	1,428.0
Long-Term Debt	4,400.0	4,766.7	6,505.8	1,347.5
Stockholders' Equity	15,113.7	13,869.5	12,678.1	11,412.2
Performance & Financial Condition				
Return on Total Revenues %	23.62	23.99	27.30	24.71
Return on Avg Stockholders' Equity %	15.56	16.02	17.56	15.84
Return on Average Assets %	10.49	10.06	11.57	11.62
Current Ratio	3.66	3.34	1.86	1.60
Debt / Equity %	29.11	34.37	51.32	11.81

Compound Growth %'s	EPS %	9.38	Net Income %	9.53	Total Revenues %	11.19

Comments

The Company has been growing by acquiring interests in cellular phone companies, generally partnerships, and other telephone companies. The Company's most recent acquisition was that of Peoples Telephone Company in Iowa, for a total purchase price of approximately $3.9 million.

Officers	Position	Ownership Information	12/31/95
James Jensen	President	Number of Shares Outstanding	577,485
Bill Otis	Exec VP, COO	Market Capitalization	$ 14,581,496
Gary Nelson	Secretary	Frequency Of Dividends	Quarterly
Lavern Biebl	Treasurer	Number of Shareholders	864
Mark Retzlaff	Vice President		

Other Information			
Transfer Agent	Company Office	Where Listed	OTC-BB
Auditor	Olsen Thielen & Co.	Symbol	NULM
Market Maker	Legg Mason Wood Walker, Inc.	Telephone (212)428-4890	SIC Code	4813
Broker Dealer	Regular Stockbroker	Employees	42

New York and Harlem Railroad Company

One East Fourth Street • Cincinnati, OH 45202

Company Description

The Company owns land under Grand Central Station and various railroad tracks in the New York City area which are leased to the New York Metropolitan Transportation Authority (MTA). MTA has an option to purchase these properties which may be exercised up until the year 2019. The common stock is divided into two groups with differing rights. A preference goes to shares not held by American Premier Underwriters, Inc.,(APU), the insurance company that is a party to the various agreemnets.

	12/31/95	12/31/94
Per Share Information		
Stock Price	100.00	100.00
Earnings Per Share	7.99	4.25
Price / Earnings Ratio	12.52	23.53
Book Value Per Share	24.93	21.96
Price / Book Value %	401.12	455.37
Dividends Per Share	5.00	5.00
Annual Financial Data		
Operating Results (000's)		
Total Revenues	1,290.8	974.2
Costs & Expenses	-374.3	-372.0
Income Before Taxes and Other	546.4	-101.0
Other Items	n.a.	n.a.
Income Tax	n.a.	n.a.
Net Income	546.4	-101.0
Cash Flow From Operations	546.4	-101.0
Balance Sheet (000's)		
Cash & Equivalents	5,155.7	4,840.2
Total Current Assets	5,344.2	5,013.5
Fixed Assets, Net	154.7	154.7
Total Assets	14,885.4	15,622.3
Total Current Liabilities	168.6	422.8
Long-Term Debt	9,057.0	9,057.0
Stockholders' Equity	5,659.9	5,142.6
Performance & Financial Condition		
Return on Total Revenues %	42.33	-10.36
Return on Avg Stockholders' Equity %	10.12	n.a.
Return on Average Assets %	3.58	n.a.
Current Ratio	31.70	11.86
Debt / Equity %	160.02	176.12

Compound Growth %'s	EPS %	88.00	Net Income %	-30.44	Total Revenues %	-66.15

Comments

The financial statements are very difficult to interpret, primarily because of a $91 million receivable, without interest, that is not due until the year 2274, unless MTA exercises its purchase option. Since the present value of even this large sum is less than $1 million, we have decided to remove it from the balance sheet both as an asset and as shareholders equity. There is a lease which would be appropriate to examine by any serious investor. This may possibly reap benefits in the year 2019 or else be a good asset for the great-great-grandchildren's trust. Compound growth rates are misleading because only two years of information were obtainable. Earnings per share relate to the preferred common stock, shares not held by APU. There were earnings on these shares in 1994 even though there was a loss for the year.

Officers	Position	Ownership Information	12/31/95
James C. Kennedy	Secretary	Number of Shares Outstanding	173,121
		Market Capitalization	$ 17,312,100
		Frequency Of Dividends	Semi-Annual
		Number of Shareholders	Under 500

Other Information

Transfer Agent	Girard Bank, Philadelphia, PA			Where Listed	OTC-BB
Auditor	None indicated			Symbol	NYHA
Market Maker	Legg Mason Wood Walker, Inc.	Telephone	(212)428-4949	SIC Code	6510
Broker Dealer	Pink sheet specialist			Employees	n.a.

Nicholas Financial, Inc.

2454 McMullen Booth Road • Clearwater, FL 34619 • Telephone (813)726-0763 • Fax (813)726-2140

Company Description

The Company provides consumer loans and automobile loans for new cars, used cars and light trucks. Its software subsidiary, Nicholas Data Services, Inc., designs, develops, supports and sells accounting software to small businesses, primarily pest control companies. The Company was incorporated in Canada in 1985 and operates through two U.S. subsidiaries based in Florida. Substantially all of the Company's operations are in the United States.

	03/31/95	03/31/94	03/31/93	03/31/92
Per Share Information				
Stock Price	2.63	1.69	1.23	0.97
Earnings Per Share	0.08	0.05	0.02	0.01
Price / Earnings Ratio	32.88	33.80	61.50	97.00
Book Value Per Share	0.39	0.28	0.19	0.18
Price / Book Value %	674.36	603.57	647.37	538.89
Dividends Per Share	n.a.	n.a.	n.a.	n.a.
Annual Financial Data				
Operating Results (000's)				
Net Interest Income	2,619.6	1,489.2	735.5	390.8
Loan Loss Provision	-337.7	-299.2	-143.2	-68.3
Non-Interest Income	601.9	741.5	842.2	929.6
Non-Interest Expense	-2,038.9	-1,404.7	-1,240.0	-1,204.9
Income Before Taxes and Other	844.8	526.8	194.5	47.1
Other Items	n.a.	n.a.	n.a.	n.a.
Income Tax	-323.0	-209.9	-97.5	-19.8
Net Income	521.9	316.9	96.9	27.4
Balance Sheet (000's)				
Cash & Securities	283.3	276.8	563.0	115.5
Loans, Net	12,780.1	7,486.7	2,700.1	1,585.8
Fixed Assets, Net	186.6	177.5	105.2	66.4
Total Assets	13,784.9	8,422.3	3,855.8	2,148.7
Borrowings	10,326.9	6,088.9	2,189.9	800.0
Stockholders' Equity	2,187.7	1,516.9	1,019.5	733.0
Performance & Financial Condition				
Return on Avg Stockholders' Equity %	28.17	24.99	11.06	3.80
Return on Average Assets %	4.70	5.16	3.23	1.59
Equity to Assets %	15.87	18.01	26.44	34.11

Compound Growth %'s	EPS %	100.00	Net Income %	167.22	Net Interest Income %	88.55

Comments

All amounts presented are in U.S. dollars. In 1995, approximately 85% of the Company's revenues were related to its financing operations. Included in the Company's debt are notes payable and a line of credit used to finance loans made.

Officers	Position	Ownership Information	03/31/95
Peter L. Vosotas	President	Number of Shares Outstanding	5,774,539
Ralph T. Finkenbrink	VP - Finance	Market Capitalization	$ 15,187,038
Keith A. Bertholf	Vice President, Secretary	Frequency Of Dividends	n.a.
Michael J. Marika	Other	Number of Shareholders	438
Stephen Bragin	Other		

Other Information

Transfer Agent	Montreal Trust			Where Listed	OTC-BB
Auditor	Ernst & Young			Symbol	NCFNF
Market Maker	Fia Capital Group, Inc.	Telephone	(800)878-6256	SIC Code	6153
Broker Dealer	Regular Stockbroker			Employees	40

Nichols (J.C.) Company

310 Ward Parkway • Kansas City, MO 64112-2110 • Telephone (816)561-3456 • Fax (816)960-6211

Company Description

The Company owns and manages numerous retail properties, apartment buildings, office and industrial properties and a residential land development in the greater Kansas City area. The Company has recently settled various suits with former officers and directors and bought back outstanding shares that leaves the Company with 164,345 shares held in treasury and 60,655 shares outstanding. Barrett Brady took over as the new CEO and has installed new management.

	12/31/95	12/31/94	12/31/93	12/31/92
Per Share Information				
Stock Price	1,725.00	600.00	575.00	387.50
Earnings Per Share	-59.44	-76.82	2.83	20.11
Price / Earnings Ratio	n.a.	n.a.	203.18	19.27
Book Value Per Share	-605.47	-131.24	-175.80	-162.90
Price / Book Value %	n.a.	n.a.	n.a.	n.a.
Dividends Per Share	n.a.	10.00	10.00	10.00
Annual Financial Data				
Operating Results (000's)				
Total Revenues	99,305.0	93,802.0	96,204.0	112,554.0
Costs & Expenses	-115,803.0	-98,801.0	-96,178.0	-107,071.0
Income Before Taxes and Other	-16,498.0	-44,698.0	26.0	5,483.0
Other Items	n.a.	29,136.0	n.a.	n.a.
Income Tax	5,746.0	1,028.0	484.0	-1,820.0
Net Income	-10,752.0	-14,534.0	510.0	3,663.0
Cash Flow From Operations	22,017.0	5,339.0	18,736.0	20,450.0
Balance Sheet (000's)				
Cash & Equivalents	7,209.0	14,186.0	30,520.0	29,513.0
Total Current Assets	54,134.0	50,081.0	54,048.0	91,199.0
Fixed Assets, Net	229,524.0	245,192.0	239,008.0	255,758.0
Total Assets	328,695.0	351,712.0	362,112.0	410,897.0
Total Current Liabilities	32,571.0	19,490.0	19,139.0	24,085.0
Long-Term Debt	326,349.0	351,317.0	342,383.0	413,784.0
Stockholders' Equity	-36,725.0	-25,821.0	-31,568.0	-29,526.0
Performance & Financial Condition				
Return on Total Revenues %	-10.83	-15.49	0.53	3.25
Return on Avg Stockholders' Equity %	n.a.	n.a.	n.a.	n.a.
Return on Average Assets %	-3.16	-4.07	0.13	0.90
Current Ratio	1.66	2.57	2.82	3.79
Debt / Equity %	n.a.	n.a.	n.a.	n.a.

Compound Growth %'s	EPS %	n.a.	Net Income %	n.a.	Total Revenues %	-4.09

Comments

1995 results reflect a pre-tax charge related to the settlement of $19.5 million. Mr. Brady reports that the non-recurring items have not affected the core operations, which remain strong. Management is first to point out that "A real estate company, like J.C. Nichols, with many mature and valuable real estate holdings does not get credit for the substantial appreciation in its real estate assets under conventional accounting methods." If first quarter 1996 unaudited results are any indication, we are impressed. The Company reported $21 million in after tax earnings, $346.02 per share.

Officers	Position	Ownership Information	12/31/95
William H. Dunn, Sr.	Chairman	Number of Shares Outstanding	60,655
Brady Brady	President	Market Capitalization	$ 104,629,875
Brian G. Shanahan	Vice President	Frequency Of Dividends	Quarterly
Donnell J. Dixon	Vice President	Number of Shareholders	Under 500
Mark A. Peterson	Vice President, CFO		

Other Information

Transfer Agent	Company Office				Where Listed	OTC-BB
Auditor	KPMG Peat Marwick LLP				Symbol	NCJC
Market Maker	Dain Bosworth Incorporated	Telephone	(612)371-2811		SIC Code	6510
Broker Dealer	Standard Investment	Tel/Ext	(888)783-4688	Jack	Employees	350

North Carolina Railroad Company

234 Fayetteville Street Mall • Raleigh, NC 27601 • Telephone (919)829-7355 • Fax (919)829-7356

Company Description

The Company owns and leases approximately 317 miles of railroad lines running from Charlotte to Morehead City, North Carolina. The Company was incorporated in 1849. From 1856 to 1871, the Company conducted railroad operations. Since that time it has leased its property to others. Leases expired in 1994 and have been renegotiated.

	12/31/95	12/31/94	12/31/93	12/31/92
Per Share Information				
Stock Price	27.50	25.25	36.00	34.00
Earnings Per Share	2.07	0.03	-0.01	0.01
Price / Earnings Ratio	13.29	841.67	n.a.	3,400.00
Book Value Per Share	4.01	1.94	1.95	1.99
Price / Book Value %	685.79	1,301.60	1,846.20	1,708.50
Dividends Per Share	0.03	n.a.	0.03	0.03
Annual Financial Data				
Operating Results (000's)				
Total Revenues	15,132.6	851.1	777.8	773.4
Costs & Expenses	-988.6	-760.9	-694.9	-746.6
Income Before Taxes and Other	14,143.9	90.1	82.9	26.8
Other Items	n.a.	n.a.	-140.9	n.a.
Income Tax	-5,279.0	17.0	4.0	17.0
Net Income	8,864.9	107.1	-54.0	43.8
Cash Flow From Operations	13,847.8	194.3	-135.0	-49.0
Balance Sheet (000's)				
Cash & Equivalents	15,139.5	1,615.3	912.7	1,195.5
Total Current Assets	15,333.9	1,926.7	1,330.9	1,506.9
Fixed Assets, Net	7,790.8	7,792.8	7,799.3	7,803.5
Total Assets	24,480.3	10,084.8	9,640.0	9,803.7
Total Current Liabilities	6,084.7	549.5	56.3	161.4
Long-Term Debt	n.a.	n.a.	n.a.	n.a.
Stockholders' Equity	17,185.7	8,320.8	8,342.2	8,524.7
Performance & Financial Condition				
Return on Total Revenues %	58.58	12.59	-6.95	5.67
Return on Avg Stockholders' Equity %	69.51	1.29	-0.64	0.51
Return on Average Assets %	51.29	1.09	-0.56	0.44
Current Ratio	2.52	3.51	23.62	9.34
Debt / Equity %	n.a.	n.a.	n.a.	n.a.

Compound Growth %'s	EPS %	491.55	Net Income %	486.92	Total Revenues %	169.47

Comments

The new lease with Norfolk Southern provides a much improved cash flow and allows the Company the right to withdraw and develop properties that are not essential for railway operations. There is, however, a shareholder derivative action that challenges the approval of the lease. Compound growth rates are misleading because they reflect a nonrecurring change in lease revenues.

Officers	Position	Ownership Information	12/31/95
John F. McNair III	President	Number of Shares Outstanding	4,283,470
Scott M. Saylor	Exec VP	Market Capitalization	$ 117,795,425
John M. Alexander	Secretary	Frequency Of Dividends	Irregular
Lynn T. McConnell	Treasurer	Number of Shareholders	752
J. Melville Broughton, Jr.	Vice President		

Other Information			
Transfer Agent	First Citizens Bank & Trust, Raleigh, NC	Where Listed	OTC-BB
Auditor	Ernst & Young LLP	Symbol	NORA
Market Maker	Legg Mason Wood Walker, Inc. Telephone (212)428-4949	SIC Code	4011
Broker Dealer	Regular Stockbroker	Employees	3

North Coast Life Insurance Co.

1116 West Riverside Avenue • Spokane, WA 99210-1445 • Telephone (509)838-4235 • Fax (509)747-8569

Company Description

The Company writes a variety of life insurance and annuity products through 208 general agents, agents, and brokers who act as representatives. Business is conducted in 12 western states, although two-thirds of all revenue is generated in California. The Company was formed in 1964. Over one-half of the employees are shareholders. They, along with the officers and directors, own 68% of the common stock.

	12/31/95	12/31/94	12/31/93	12/31/92
Per Share Information				
Stock Price	5.00	5.00	5.00	n.a.
Earnings Per Share	3.60	1.82	-5.03	n.a.
Price / Earnings Ratio	1.39	2.75	n.a.	n.a.
Book Value Per Share	n.a.	n.a.	n.a.	n.a.
Price / Book Value %	n.a.	n.a.	n.a.	n.a.
Dividends Per Share	n.a.	n.a.	n.a.	n.a.
Annual Financial Data				
Operating Results (000's)				
Total Revenues	14,054.5	13,558.7	12,337.6	13,052.3
Costs & Expenses	-12,014.0	-11,863.8	-12,256.1	-12,846.2
Income Before Taxes and Other	1,353.4	862.0	-1,022.2	206.1
Other Items	n.a.	n.a.	n.a.	n.a.
Income Tax	n.a.	n.a.	n.a.	n.a.
Net Income	1,353.4	862.0	-1,022.2	206.1
Cash Flow From Operations	n.a.	n.a.	n.a.	n.a.
Balance Sheet (000's)				
Cash & Equivalents	538.5	52.1	7.6	n.a.
Total Current Assets	3,928.1	3,494.4	3,521.8	n.a.
Fixed Assets, Net	1,852.4	1,430.2	3,545.9	n.a.
Total Assets	71,573.4	68,102.0	66,468.6	n.a.
Total Current Liabilities	277.9	250.5	337.9	n.a.
Long-Term Debt	500.0	n.a.	n.a.	n.a.
Stockholders' Equity	4,036.9	2,849.0	3,084.1	n.a.
Performance & Financial Condition				
Return on Total Revenues %	9.63	6.36	-8.29	n.a.
Return on Avg Stockholders' Equity %	39.31	29.06	n.a.	n.a.
Return on Average Assets %	1.94	1.28	n.a.	n.a.
Current Ratio	14.14	13.95	10.42	n.a.
Debt / Equity %	12.39	n.a.	n.a.	n.a.

Compound Growth %'s	EPS %	n.a.	Net Income %	87.25	Total Revenues %	2.50

Comments

The financial statements are not presented in accordance with GAAP and therefore require insurance industry experience to interpret. The preferred stock, traded on NASDAQ, will probably be redeemed in a few years according to a Company official. Book value was not calculated because of insufficient information. We were told that it would be approximately $11 million, including the preferred, if GAAP accounting were used. Earnings per share are shown based upon the statutory accounting in the report and may be higher than GAAP reporting by 20% to 25%. The compounded growth in earnings rate is misleading because it represents a change only from 1994 to 1995.

Officers	Position	Ownership Information	12/31/95
C. Robert Ogden	President	Number of Shares Outstanding	275,106
Robert E. Blair	Senior VP	Market Capitalization	$ 1,375,530
Richard D. Hillier	Senior VP	Frequency Of Dividends	Quarterly
Clifford D. Kutsch	Secretary	Number of Shareholders	310
Gavin J. Cooley	Treasurer		

Other Information

Transfer Agent	Company Office			Where Listed	OTC-PS
Auditor	Coopers & Lybrand LLP			Symbol	n.a.
Market Maker	Martin Nelson & Co., Inc.	Telephone	(206)682-6261	SIC Code	6310
Broker Dealer	Regular Stockbroker			Employees	31

North Pittsburgh Systems, Inc.

4008 Gibsonia Road • Gibsonia, PA 15044-9311 • Telephone (412)443-9600 • Fax (412)443-9431

Company Description

The Company, organized in 1985, is the parent of North Pittsburg Telephone Company (NPTC) and PennTelecon, Inc. (PTI). NPTC has been providing telephone service since 1906, to a 287 square mile area in portions of four Western Pennsylvania counties. PTI sells, rents and services telecommunication equipment, message toll services and high capacity intercity facilities. Two other subsidiaries, formed in 1995, provide consulting, computer and internet access services.

	12/31/95	12/31/94	12/31/93	12/31/92
Per Share Information				
Stock Price	45.50	32.13	28.00	17.75
Earnings Per Share	1.42	1.32	1.22	1.07
Price / Earnings Ratio	32.04	24.34	22.95	16.59
Book Value Per Share	6.85	6.37	5.93	5.52
Price / Book Value %	664.23	504.40	472.18	321.56
Dividends Per Share	0.96	0.88	0.80	0.72
Annual Financial Data				
Operating Results (000's)				
Total Revenues	53,822.5	50,162.2	45,119.1	42,984.0
Costs & Expenses	-35,343.9	-33,373.0	-29,940.2	-29,609.6
Income Before Taxes and Other	17,740.9	16,789.2	14,620.9	13,374.4
Other Items	n.a.	n.a.	450.0	-18.0
Income Tax	-7,054.2	-6,884.8	-5,906.2	-5,292.7
Net Income	10,686.7	9,904.4	9,164.7	8,063.7
Cash Flow From Operations	18,429.8	17,403.6	17,726.4	16,088.5
Balance Sheet (000's)				
Cash & Equivalents	9,359.0	14,778.6	19,045.0	14,783.0
Total Current Assets	28,747.4	32,056.2	34,280.2	30,438.8
Fixed Assets, Net	58,616.4	50,994.1	47,645.9	47,206.7
Total Assets	96,156.1	91,577.9	88,771.2	84,573.6
Total Current Liabilities	10,944.6	9,388.4	9,498.4	7,059.3
Long-Term Debt	27,544.2	28,669.7	28,159.2	28,367.4
Stockholders' Equity	51,527.4	47,911.1	44,624.4	41,475.7
Performance & Financial Condition				
Return on Total Revenues %	19.86	19.74	20.31	18.76
Return on Avg Stockholders' Equity %	21.49	21.41	21.29	20.08
Return on Average Assets %	11.38	10.98	10.57	9.67
Current Ratio	2.63	3.41	3.61	4.31
Debt / Equity %	53.46	59.84	63.10	68.40

Compound Growth %'s	EPS %	9.89	Net Income %	9.84	Total Revenues %	7.78

Comments

The Company has been making significant improvements to its facilities. During the years 1991 through 1995, the Company made property additions of $51.3 million and retired property of approximately $20 million. The construction budget for 1996, is estimated to be $16 to $20 million. This aggressive rebuilding program should allow the Company to remain competitive in a very dynamic industry.

Officers	Position	Ownership Information	12/31/95
Charles E. Thomas	Chairman	Number of Shares Outstanding	7,520,000
Gerald A. Gorman	President	Market Capitalization	$ 342,160,000
Allen P. Kimble	Secretary, Treasurer	Frequency Of Dividends	Quarterly
Harry R. Brown	Vice President	Number of Shareholders	2,845
N. William Barthlow	Vice President, Secretary		

Other Information

Transfer Agent	Company Office			Where Listed	OTC-BB
Auditor	KPMG Peat Marwick LLP			Symbol	NORY
Market Maker	Hefren Tillotson, Inc.	Telephone	(412)434-0990	SIC Code	4813
Broker Dealer	Regular Stockbroker			Employees	288

North State National Bank

P.O. Box 3235 • Chico, CA 95927-3235 • Telephone (916)893-8861 • Fax (916)342-5136

Company Description

North State National Bank commenced operations in 1982 and provides banking services to the small business, professional, agricultural, and consumer markets in the Chico, California area. The Bank has one office.

		12/31/95	12/31/94	12/31/93	12/31/92
Per Share Information					
	Stock Price	6.25	5.50	4.63	3.50
	Earnings Per Share	0.78	0.65	0.48	0.44
	Price / Earnings Ratio	8.01	8.46	9.65	7.95
	Book Value Per Share	5.62	4.97	4.31	3.80
	Price / Book Value %	111.21	110.66	107.42	92.11
	Dividends Per Share	n.a.	n.a.	n.a.	n.a.
Annual Financial Data					
Operating Results (000's)					
	Net Interest Income	2,949.0	2,443.0	2,223.8	2,146.6
	Loan Loss Provision	15.0	85.0	n.a.	-248.2
	Non-Interest Income	376.0	376.8	386.2	391.7
	Non-Interest Expense	-2,242.4	-2,069.4	-2,150.0	-2,141.3
	Income Before Taxes and Other	1,097.6	835.4	459.9	148.8
	Other Items	n.a.	n.a.	n.a.	260.0
	Income Tax	-385.0	-241.0	-20.0	-12.8
	Net Income	712.6	594.4	439.9	396.0
Balance Sheet (000's)					
	Cash & Securities	38,687.1	33,166.4	27,767.6	22,076.1
	Loans, Net	29,400.2	28,074.2	25,433.0	29,167.4
	Fixed Assets, Net	1,747.7	1,908.4	1,899.3	1,808.9
	Total Assets	71,267.1	64,364.1	55,786.8	53,748.0
	Deposits	65,589.3	59,667.6	51,840.2	50,314.8
	Stockholders' Equity	5,105.6	4,295.1	3,726.3	3,286.4
Performance & Financial Condition					
	Net Interest Margin	4.91	4.86	5.08	4.09
	Return on Avg Stockholders' Equity %	15.16	14.82	12.55	12.82
	Return on Average Assets %	1.05	0.99	0.80	0.74
	Equity to Assets %	7.16	6.67	6.68	6.11
	Reserve as a % of Non-Performing Loans	477.78	216.84	127.21	100.92

Compound Growth %'s	EPS %	21.03	Net Income %	21.63	Net Interest Income %	11.17

Comments

The Bank's loan portfolio is heavily concentrated in commercial and agricultural loans and real estate mortgages, which represent 48% and 41% of total loans, respectively. In the 1980's, the Bank was under the supervision of the Office of the Controller of the Currency. It was released from those restraints and direct oversight in 1994. 1992 results include a nonrecurring benefit of $260,000 from adopting GAAP for the reporting of income taxes.

Officers	Position	Ownership Information	12/31/95
John A. Lucchesi	President, CEO	Number of Shares Outstanding	908,019
Randall A. Shell	Exec VP, Head Cashier	Market Capitalization	$ 5,675,119
Joe Drakulic	Senior VP	Frequency Of Dividends	Irregular
Gary Griswold	Senior VP	Number of Shareholders	n.a.
Calvin Foster	Controller		

Other Information					
Transfer Agent	Chemical Mellon Shareholder Services			Where Listed	OTC-BB
Auditor	Perry-Smith & Co			Symbol	NTSN
Market Maker	Paine Webber Incorporated	Telephone	(212)713-3766	SIC Code	6020
Broker Dealer	Regular Stockbroker			Employees	35

Northern Empire Bancshares

801 Fourth Street • Santa Rosa, CA 95404 • Telephone (707)579-2265 • Fax (707)579-5621

Company Description

Northern Empire Bancshares is a bank holding company whose only subsidiary is Sonoma National Bank. The Bank operates three branches in suburban communities in Sonoma County, California. The Bank makes commercial and real estate loans to customers who are predominantly small and middle-market businesses. It has been in business for 10 years.

	12/31/95	12/31/94	12/31/93	12/31/92
Per Share Information				
Stock Price	9.20	9.25	8.50	8.25
Earnings Per Share	1.27	1.03	0.99	0.83
Price / Earnings Ratio	7.24	8.98	8.59	9.94
Book Value Per Share	8.63	8.14	7.06	6.62
Price / Book Value %	106.60	113.64	120.40	124.62
Dividends Per Share	0.20	0.36	0.65	0.60
Annual Financial Data				
Operating Results (000's)				
Net Interest Income	7,565.0	6,119.0	5,183.0	4,945.0
Loan Loss Provision	-250.0	-280.0	-174.0	-355.0
Non-Interest Income	1,602.0	2,146.0	1,898.0	1,240.0
Non-Interest Expense	-5,859.0	-5,666.0	-4,857.0	-3,959.0
Income Before Taxes and Other	3,058.0	2,319.0	2,050.0	1,871.0
Other Items	n.a.	n.a.	51.0	n.a.
Income Tax	-1,338.0	-973.0	-802.0	-772.0
Net Income	1,720.0	1,346.0	1,299.0	1,099.0
Balance Sheet (000's)				
Cash & Securities	32,306.0	27,269.0	20,762.0	20,184.0
Loans, Net	129,587.0	90,116.0	81,632.0	73,122.0
Fixed Assets, Net	747.0	677.0	870.0	936.0
Total Assets	166,962.0	121,776.0	106,560.0	96,319.0
Deposits	154,221.0	111,083.0	97,332.0	87,784.0
Stockholders' Equity	11,982.0	10,199.0	8,897.0	8,309.0
Performance & Financial Condition				
Net Interest Margin	n.a.	n.a.	n.a.	n.a.
Return on Avg Stockholders' Equity %	15.51	14.10	15.10	13.99
Return on Average Assets %	1.19	1.18	1.28	1.17
Equity to Assets %	7.18	8.38	8.35	8.63
Reserve as a % of Non-Performing Loans	421.11	706.97	254.11	123.68

Compound Growth %'s	EPS %	15.23	Net Income %	16.10	Net Interest Income %	15.23

Comments

The original goal of becoming Sonoma County's premier independent community bank is largely achieved. The outstanding financial results reflect gains on sales of SBA guaranteed loans which represented approximately 17% and 57% of after tax income in 1995 and 1994, respectively. Sonoma County, an outstanding wine growing region, continues to attract business growth and an influx of people.

Officers	Position	Ownership Information	12/31/95
Deborah A. Meekins	President, CEO	Number of Shares Outstanding	1,388,355
David F. Titus	Exec VP, Senior Loan Officer	Market Capitalization	$ 12,772,866
JoAnn Barton	Senior VP	Frequency Of Dividends	Quarterly
Jane M. Baker	Senior VP, CFO	Number of Shareholders	341

Other Information			
Transfer Agent	Chemical Mellon Shareholder Services	Where Listed	OTC-BB
Auditor	Coopers & Lybrand, LLP	Symbol	NREB
Market Maker	Hoefer & Arnett, Inc.　　Telephone　(800)346-5544	SIC Code	6020
Broker Dealer	Regular Stockbroker	Employees	72

Northfield Precision Instrument Corporation

4400 Austin Boulevard • Island Park, Long Island, NY 11558-0550 • Telephone (516)431-1112 • Fax (516)431-1928

Company Description

The Company is in the business of manufacturing precision instruments. It was organized in 1953 and went public in 1959.

	12/31/94	12/31/93	12/31/92
Per Share Information			
Stock Price	7.00	7.00	7.00
Earnings Per Share	0.64	0.32	0.08
Price / Earnings Ratio	10.94	21.88	87.50
Book Value Per Share	9.49	9.65	9.76
Price / Book Value %	73.76	72.54	71.72
Dividends Per Share	0.80	0.40	0.75
Annual Financial Data			
Operating Results (000's)			
Total Revenues	2,876.1	2,858.3	2,646.6
Costs & Expenses	-2,642.2	-2,701.8	-2,624.6
Income Before Taxes and Other	233.9	156.4	22.0
Other Items	n.a.	n.a.	n.a.
Income Tax	-83.1	-80.6	-3.8
Net Income	150.7	75.9	18.2
Cash Flow From Operations	311.6	172.8	55.0
Balance Sheet (000's)			
Cash & Equivalents	717.8	651.0	640.8
Total Current Assets	2,159.1	2,165.1	2,127.3
Fixed Assets, Net	334.7	407.6	459.9
Total Assets	2,520.6	2,593.8	2,640.0
Total Current Liabilities	220.5	216.5	219.8
Long-Term Debt	42.6	86.7	119.4
Stockholders' Equity	2,223.0	2,259.7	2,285.7
Performance & Financial Condition			
Return on Total Revenues %	5.24	2.65	0.69
Return on Avg Stockholders' Equity %	6.72	3.34	0.77
Return on Average Assets %	5.89	2.90	0.69
Current Ratio	9.79	10.00	9.68
Debt / Equity %	1.92	3.84	5.22

Compound Growth %'s	EPS %	182.84	Net Income %	187.43	Total Revenues %	4.25

Comments

Compound growth rates can be misleading because of the low earnings in 1992. However, management believes that the improvement from 1993 to 1994 was attributable to cost cutting and operational efficiencies. 1995 results are released at the beginning of June, not in time for our press deadline. The Company acquired 538 shares of its stock in 1993 for approximately $15 per share which is higher than the quoted market price.

Officers	Position	Ownership Information	12/31/94
Timothy J. Steffen	President	Number of Shares Outstanding	234,237
Donald E. Freedman	Secretary, Treasurer	Market Capitalization	$ 1,639,659
Bernard Rourke	Director	Frequency Of Dividends	n.a.
		Number of Shareholders	Under 500

Other Information					
Transfer Agent	Continental Stock Transfer & Trust Co.			Where Listed	OTC-BB
Auditor	Frumkin & Lukin, P.C.			Symbol	NFPC
Market Maker	Carr Securities Corporation	Telephone	(800)221-2243	SIC Code	3800
Broker Dealer	Pink sheet specialist			Employees	n.a.

Northwest Bank & Trust Company

100 East Kimberly Road • Davenport, IA 52806 • Telephone (319)388-2511 • Fax (319)388-2658

Company Description

Northwest Bank & Trust Company is a state chartered bank in Iowa. The Bank is an independent commercial bank and has four offices, three of which are in Davenport and one in Bettendorf. These offices cover the entire Quad-City Metropolitan area consisting of the cities where the Bank is located as well as the primary cities of Rock Island and Moline, Illinois.

	12/31/95	12/31/94	12/31/93	12/31/92
Per Share Information				
Stock Price	28.50	20.50	19.50	18.75
Earnings Per Share	2.38	2.16	1.57	2.21
Price / Earnings Ratio	11.97	9.49	12.42	8.48
Book Value Per Share	19.37	19.17	18.96	18.95
Price / Book Value %	147.13	106.94	102.85	98.94
Dividends Per Share	2.18	1.95	1.56	1.72
Annual Financial Data				
Operating Results (000's)				
Net Interest Income	7,579.0	7,339.0	6,985.0	7,697.0
Loan Loss Provision	n.a.	-23.0	-76.0	-1,464.0
Non-Interest Income	1,701.0	1,740.0	2,213.0	5,745.0
Non-Interest Expense	-6,120.0	-6,194.0	-7,114.0	-9,016.0
Income Before Taxes and Other	3,160.0	2,862.0	2,008.0	2,962.0
Other Items	n.a.	n.a.	n.a.	n.a.
Income Tax	-1,139.0	-1,025.0	-677.0	-1,083.0
Net Income	2,021.0	1,837.0	1,331.0	1,879.0
Balance Sheet (000's)				
Cash & Securities	60,067.0	53,508.0	63,736.0	70,305.0
Loans, Net	87,007.0	87,746.0	86,338.0	80,538.0
Fixed Assets, Net	2,030.0	2,021.0	2,168.0	2,264.0
Total Assets	157,842.0	153,401.0	163,114.0	165,508.0
Deposits	132,472.0	126,066.0	135,644.0	137,630.0
Stockholders' Equity	16,463.0	16,295.0	16,115.0	16,110.0
Performance & Financial Condition				
Net Interest Margin	n.a.	n.a.	n.a.	n.a.
Return on Avg Stockholders' Equity %	12.34	11.34	8.26	11.82
Return on Average Assets %	1.30	1.16	0.81	1.12
Equity to Assets %	10.43	10.62	9.88	9.73
Reserve as a % of Non-Performing Loans	3083.33	257.90	412.01	115.09

Compound Growth %'s	EPS %	2.50	Net Income %	2.46	Net Interest Income %	-0.51

Comments

The Bank is 81% owned by Northwest Bank Holding Company, but the remaining stockholders are located throughout the country with a heavy concentration in the local market area. The Bank's loan portfolio is made up primarily of real estate mortgages which represent 70% of total loans. Commercial and financial loans represent an additional 18%. Management was optimistic at the beginning of 1995 and remains so in early 1996. The favorable results display themselves in return ratios rather than growth.

Officers	Position	Ownership Information	12/31/95
Bob Slavens	Chairman, CEO	Number of Shares Outstanding	850,000
James Slavens	President	Market Capitalization	$ 24,225,000
James DeBoeuf	COO, Head Cashier	Frequency Of Dividends	Semi-Annual
Roger Franke	Vice President, Sr Loan Officer	Number of Shareholders	1,100
Margo Hancock	Vice President		

Other Information

Transfer Agent	Company Office		Where Listed	OTC-BB
Auditor	McGladrey & Pullen, LLP		Symbol	NOTW
Market Maker	Piper Jaffray Inc.	Telephone (800)328-7488	SIC Code	6020
Broker Dealer	Regular Stockbroker		Employees	92

Oak Tree Medical Systems ,Inc.

16504 Stonehaven Road • Miami Lakes, FL 33014 • Telephone (305)822-8889 • Fax (305)823-5556

Company Description

The Company is principally engaged in providing medical and physical therapy care to patients under the direction of licensed physicians. Substantially all of the Company's operations are conducted in northeastern Florida. The Company was incorporated in Delaware in 1986. During the fiscal year ended May 31, 1993, the Company issued 656,250 shares of its common stock, netting proceeds of $5.0 million. Officers and directors, as a group, own approximately 47% of the outstanding common shares.

	05/31/95	05/31/94	05/31/93	05/31/92
Per Share Information				
Stock Price	3.00	0.18	0.06	0.06
Earnings Per Share	0.11	-0.19	-0.03	0.13
Price / Earnings Ratio	27.27	n.a.	n.a.	0.46
Book Value Per Share	2.50	3.80	3.99	-0.01
Price / Book Value %	120.00	4.74	1.50	n.a.
Dividends Per Share	n.a.	n.a.	n.a.	n.a.
Annual Financial Data				
Operating Results (000's)				
Total Revenues	2,652.9	n.a.	n.a.	89.3
Costs & Expenses	-2,264.9	-234.2	-15.1	-12.2
Income Before Taxes and Other	388.0	-234.2	-15.1	77.1
Other Items	n.a.	n.a.	n.a.	n.a.
Income Tax	-127.0	n.a.	n.a.	n.a.
Net Income	261.0	-234.2	-15.1	77.1
Cash Flow From Operations	-158.8	-224.9	-6.1	-5.9
Balance Sheet (000's)				
Cash & Equivalents	138.2	11.5	6.5	1.6
Total Current Assets	1,974.0	11.5	6.5	1.6
Fixed Assets, Net	333.7	n.a.	n.a.	n.a.
Total Assets	8,721.3	5,011.5	5,006.5	1.6
Total Current Liabilities	1,993.6	267.0	27.9	7.9
Long-Term Debt	n.a.	n.a.	n.a.	n.a.
Stockholders' Equity	5,128.4	4,744.5	4,978.7	-6.2
Performance & Financial Condition				
Return on Total Revenues %	9.84	n.a.	n.a.	86.29
Return on Avg Stockholders' Equity %	5.29	-4.82	-0.61	n.a.
Return on Average Assets %	3.80	-4.68	-0.60	1717.05
Current Ratio	0.99	0.04	0.23	0.21
Debt / Equity %	n.a.	n.a.	n.a.	n.a.

Compound Growth %'s	EPS %	-5.42	Net Income %	50.17	Total Revenues %	209.70

Comments

On May 31,1995, approximately 57% of the Company's assets were invested in gold ore reserves which were acquired in 1993. In June 1995, the Company exchanged its gold ore reserves for approximately a 30% interest in the outstanding shares of Accord Futronics Corporation. The Company believes that the $5.0 million valuation for their interest is appropriate.

Officers	Position	Ownership Information	05/31/95
Michael J. Gerber	President	Number of Shares Outstanding	2,046,969
Irwin B. Stack	COO, Secretary	Market Capitalization	$ 6,140,907
Henry Dubbin	Vice President	Frequency Of Dividends	n.a.
		Number of Shareholders	130

Other Information

Transfer Agent	Continental Stock Transfer & Trust Co.		Where Listed	OTC-BB
Auditor	Simon Krowitz Bolin & Assoc.		Symbol	MOAK
Market Maker	Fahnestock & Co., Inc.	Telephone (212)422-7813	SIC Code	8049
Broker Dealer	Regular Stockbroker		Employees	2

Oak Valley Community Bank

1250 North Third Avenue • Oakdale, CA 95361 • Telephone (209)848-2265 • Fax (209)848-1929

Company Description

Oak Valley Community Bank is an independent bank which began operations in 1991. The Bank's primary source of revenue is providing loans to customers who are predominantly small and middle-market businesses and middle-income individuals. The Bank operates one branch in Oakdale, California and a loan center in a neighboring community. Oakdale is located in the north central part of the San Joaquin Valley.

	12/31/95	12/31/94	12/31/93	12/31/92
Per Share Information				
Stock Price	10.25	10.00	10.00	10.00
Earnings Per Share	1.33	1.02	0.65	-0.72
Price / Earnings Ratio	7.71	9.80	15.38	n.a.
Book Value Per Share	10.59	9.21	8.22	7.23
Price / Book Value %	96.79	108.58	121.65	138.31
Dividends Per Share	n.a.	n.a.	n.a.	n.a.
Annual Financial Data				
Operating Results (000's)				
Net Interest Income	2,444.9	1,930.6	1,299.5	658.0
Loan Loss Provision	-68.0	-128.0	-80.0	-92.9
Non-Interest Income	142.6	85.5	68.3	95.6
Non-Interest Expense	-1,597.9	-1,447.9	-1,139.6	-914.7
Income Before Taxes and Other	921.6	440.1	148.1	-253.9
Other Items	n.a.	n.a.	103.0	n.a.
Income Tax	-348.2	-0.8	-0.8	-0.8
Net Income	573.4	439.3	250.3	-254.8
Balance Sheet (000's)				
Cash & Securities	12,319.0	9,833.8	8,745.5	6,609.0
Loans, Net	27,770.2	23,755.5	20,550.5	15,630.4
Fixed Assets, Net	360.0	375.5	407.6	405.9
Total Assets	41,271.2	34,562.9	30,150.7	22,903.7
Deposits	36,269.3	30,292.0	26,405.2	20,209.0
Stockholders' Equity	4,549.7	3,958.0	3,532.7	2,558.9
Performance & Financial Condition				
Net Interest Margin	n.a.	n.a.	n.a.	n.a.
Return on Avg Stockholders' Equity %	13.48	11.73	8.22	-9.48
Return on Average Assets %	1.51	1.36	0.94	-1.19
Equity to Assets %	11.02	11.45	11.72	11.17
Reserve as a % of Non-Performing Loans	n.a.	n.a.	n.a.	n.a.

Compound Growth %'s	EPS %	43.04	Net Income %	51.34	Net Interest Income %	54.88

Comments

The Bank's loan portfolio consists primarily of real estate mortgages and commercial loans which represent 51% and 36% of total loans, respectively. The Bank declared its first cash dividend in 1996 after having produced good results since the loss in 1992. 1993 results include a nonrecurring benefit of $103,000, or $.27 per share, from a change in accounting method. 1994 results are also not reliable for trend analysis because of a disproportunately low income tax provision. Because of these items and the loss in 1992, compound earnings and earnings per share growth rates are not particularly meaningful.

Officers	Position	Ownership Information	12/31/95
Ronald C. Martin	President, CEO	Number of Shares Outstanding	429,716
Ramon A. Esslinger	Exec VP, COO	Market Capitalization	$ 4,404,589
Virgil L. Thompson	Senior VP	Frequency Of Dividends	Irregular
Richard P. Brown	Vice President	Number of Shareholders	333
Janelle '. Scott	Vice President		

Other Information

Transfer Agent	U.S. Stock Transfer Corporation		Where Listed	Order Matching Only
Auditor	Grant Thornton		Symbol	n.a.
Market Maker	Hoefer & Arnett, Inc.	Telephone (800)346-5544	SIC Code	6020
Broker Dealer	Regular Stockbroker		Employees	32

Oakridge Energy, Inc.

4613 Jacksboro Highway • Wichita Falls, TX 76302 • Telephone (817)322-4772 • Fax (214)733-3048

Company Description

The Company is engaged in the exploration, development, production and sale of oil and gas, primarily in Texas, Mississippi, and Arkansas and to a lesser extent the exploration and development of coal and gravel in Colorado. In addition, the Company holds certain real estate in Colorado for investment. As a group, officers and directors owned 67.8% of the Company's outstanding common stock at May 19, 1995. The Company was formed in Texas in 1969.

	02/28/95	02/28/94	02/28/93	02/28/92
Per Share Information				
Stock Price	1.82	1.82	1.19	1.47
Earnings Per Share	-0.15	1.11	0.17	0.17
Price / Earnings Ratio	n.a.	1.64	7.00	8.65
Book Value Per Share	2.16	2.34	1.55	1.37
Price / Book Value %	84.26	77.78	76.77	107.30
Dividends Per Share	n.a.	0.25	n.a.	n.a.
Annual Financial Data				
Operating Results (000's)				
Total Revenues	721.3	19,367.3	5,251.6	5,550.7
Costs & Expenses	-1,679.2	-7,793.2	-3,773.1	-3,588.6
Income Before Taxes and Other	-1,035.3	11,574.1	1,478.5	1,954.0
Other Items	n.a.	118.8	472.0	531.5
Income Tax	211.2	-4,321.4	-582.8	-1,005.9
Net Income	-824.1	7,371.4	1,367.8	1,479.7
Cash Flow From Operations	-648.7	-3,892.1	1,143.5	1,651.4
Balance Sheet (000's)				
Cash & Equivalents	982.1	1,070.4	399.0	343.0
Total Current Assets	4,357.2	10,876.5	1,080.5	852.4
Fixed Assets, Net	3,247.9	3,283.2	12,194.6	12,871.3
Total Assets	12,815.2	15,035.3	14,493.5	14,567.8
Total Current Liabilities	1,004.0	1,037.1	1,605.1	927.0
Long-Term Debt	n.a.	n.a.	1,750.1	1,075.0
Stockholders' Equity	11,752.7	13,958.8	11,016.4	11,616.5
Performance & Financial Condition				
Return on Total Revenues %	-114.25	38.06	26.04	26.66
Return on Avg Stockholders' Equity %	-6.41	59.03	12.09	13.60
Return on Average Assets %	-5.92	49.93	9.41	10.23
Current Ratio	4.34	10.49	0.67	0.92
Debt / Equity %	n.a.	n.a.	15.89	9.25

Compound Growth %'s	EPS % n.a.	Net Income % n.a.	Total Revenues %	-49.35

Comments

During fiscal years 1994 and 1995, the Company repurchased approximately 1.7 million shares of its common stock at market prices ranging from $1.50 to $2.50 per share. Included in Total Revenues for the year ended February 28, 1994, is a gain on the disposition of oil and gas properties of $16.7 million. For the nine months ended November 30, 1995, the Company had total revenues of $338,000 and a net loss of $322,000 ($.06 per share) as compared to $257,000 and $668,000 ($.12 per share) for the same period in 1994.

Officers	Position	Ownership Information	02/28/95
Noel Pautsky	Chairman, President	Number of Shares Outstanding	5,444,202
Sandra Pautsky	Exec VP, Secretary	Market Capitalization	$ 9,908,448
Danny Croker	Vice President	Frequency Of Dividends	Irregular
		Number of Shareholders	674

Other Information

Transfer Agent	Stock Transfer Company of America			Where Listed	OTC-BB
Auditor	KPMG Peat Marwick LLP			Symbol	OKRG
Market Maker	Morgan Keegan & Company, Inc.	Telephone	(800)289-5019	SIC Code	1311
Broker Dealer	Regular Stockbroker			Employees	8

Ogden Telephone Company

21 West Avenue • Spencerport, NY 14559-1397 • Telephone (716)352-7200 • Fax (716)352-0232

Company Description

The Company provides local and toll telephone service to both residential and commercial customers in Spencerport and surrounding communities in New York.

	12/31/95	12/31/94	12/31/93	12/31/92
Per Share Information				
Stock Price	120.00	75.00	75.00	60.00
Earnings Per Share	10.00	8.80	7.82	4.83
Price / Earnings Ratio	12.00	8.52	9.59	12.42
Book Value Per Share	75.39	67.68	63.52	57.18
Price / Book Value %	159.17	110.82	118.07	104.93
Dividends Per Share	4.04	3.74	3.53	3.33
Annual Financial Data				
Operating Results (000's)				
Total Revenues	10,353.5	9,811.3	10,037.8	9,531.9
Costs & Expenses	-8,335.2	-8,019.6	-7,825.8	-8,538.8
Income Before Taxes and Other	2,018.3	1,791.7	2,212.0	993.1
Other Items	n.a.	n.a.	-437.2	n.a.
Income Tax	-636.2	-571.2	-686.3	-305.0
Net Income	1,382.1	1,220.5	1,088.5	688.2
Cash Flow From Operations	3,924.9	2,298.1	4,625.7	2,659.2
Balance Sheet (000's)				
Cash & Equivalents	387.8	717.0	191.6	n.a.
Total Current Assets	2,660.0	2,872.4	2,289.9	n.a.
Fixed Assets, Net	22,611.4	22,225.9	22,410.3	n.a.
Total Assets	27,680.2	27,737.1	27,214.3	n.a.
Total Current Liabilities	3,323.0	3,747.6	3,819.5	n.a.
Long-Term Debt	9,003.9	9,474.7	9,849.1	n.a.
Stockholders' Equity	10,680.8	9,819.8	9,087.2	n.a.
Performance & Financial Condition				
Return on Total Revenues %	13.35	12.44	10.84	7.22
Return on Avg Stockholders' Equity %	13.48	12.91	12.40	n.a.
Return on Average Assets %	4.99	4.44	4.03	n.a.
Current Ratio	0.80	0.77	0.60	n.a.
Debt / Equity %	84.30	96.49	108.38	n.a.

Compound Growth %'s	EPS %	27.45	Net Income %	26.17	Total Revenues %	2.79

Comments

1993 results include a one-time charge of $437,231 to adopt GAAP for the accounting of income taxes and pensions. Per share amounts reflect an assumed conversion of the convertible preferred stock. The 1995 report had not been issued by the time we went to press. Compounded growth rates can be misleading because they are based on only three years of data.

Officers	Position	Ownership Information	12/31/95
Philip T. Evans	President	Number of Shares Outstanding	134,316
Maxine B. Davison	CEO, Chairman of the Board	Market Capitalization	$ 16,117,920
Timothy J. Bancroft	VP - Finance	Frequency Of Dividends	Quarterly
Maureen L. Howard	Secretary, Treasurer	Number of Shareholders	Under 500
Richard M. Daly	Vice President		

Other Information

Transfer Agent	Company Office		Where Listed	OTC-BB
Auditor	Coopers & Lybrand LLP		Symbol	OGDT
Market Maker	Paine Webber Incorporated	Telephone (212)713-3766	SIC Code	4810
Broker Dealer	Pink sheet specialist		Employees	47

Ojai Oil Company

2161 Ventura Boulevard • Oxnard, CA 93030 • Telephone (805)988-0300 • Fax (805)485-1131

Company Description

The Company's operations include the production and sale of oil and gas, oil royalties, securities investments, and the operation of a car wash, self storage facilities and a mobile home park, most of which are located in southern California. The Company was formed in 1966. Dividends are both in cash and free car washes. Only shareholders of record, please.

	12/31/95	12/31/94	12/31/93
Per Share Information			
Stock Price	9.00	9.00	9.00
Earnings Per Share	0.98	0.40	0.83
Price / Earnings Ratio	9.18	22.50	10.84
Book Value Per Share	6.99	6.15	6.03
Price / Book Value %	128.76	146.34	149.25
Dividends Per Share	0.30	0.28	0.28
Annual Financial Data			
Operating Results (000's)			
Total Revenues	2,495.8	2,503.0	2,475.8
Costs & Expenses	-2,039.5	-2,315.6	-2,049.4
Income Before Taxes and Other	456.4	187.4	426.4
Other Items	n.a.	n.a.	n.a.
Income Tax	-159.0	-66.3	-172.3
Net Income	297.3	121.1	254.1
Cash Flow From Operations	-15.2	80.3	183.1
Balance Sheet (000's)			
Cash & Equivalents	93.2	90.7	62.1
Total Current Assets	1,112.4	698.0	634.1
Fixed Assets, Net	6,105.6	5,299.8	5,460.9
Total Assets	8,064.1	6,771.2	6,830.9
Total Current Liabilities	453.3	275.2	225.9
Long-Term Debt	5,056.4	4,225.1	4,402.6
Stockholders' Equity	2,126.1	1,870.0	1,834.1
Performance & Financial Condition			
Return on Total Revenues %	11.91	4.84	10.26
Return on Avg Stockholders' Equity %	14.88	6.54	n.a.
Return on Average Assets %	4.01	1.78	n.a.
Current Ratio	2.45	2.54	2.81
Debt / Equity %	237.82	225.93	240.04

Compound Growth %'s	EPS %	8.66	Net Income %	8.16	Total Revenues %	0.40

Comments

An earthquake was costly to 1994 results because of damage repair of approximately $200,000. In early 1996, the Company sold its car wash business and related office building and acquired an office building in the city of Ventura. This should help the Company in being identified more as a real estate company than a mini-conglomerate.

Officers	Position	Ownership Information	12/31/95
Theodore Off	President	Number of Shares Outstanding	304,318
Ann Dyer	VP - Finance	Market Capitalization	$ 2,738,862
C. Douglas Off	Secretary	Frequency Of Dividends	Irregular
Harry J. Edward	Vice President	Number of Shareholders	Under 500

Other Information				
Transfer Agent	Company Office		Where Listed	OTC-PS
Auditor	Lee, Sperling, Hisamune		Symbol	OJOC
Market Maker	Chicago Corporation, The	Telephone (312)855-7664	SIC Code	6700
Broker Dealer	Regular Stockbroker		Employees	8

Old Fashion Foods, Inc.

5521 Collins Boulevard, S.W. • Austell, GA 30001-3653 • Telephone (770)948-1177 • Fax (770)739-3254

Company Description

The Company is the largest independent vending machine company in Georgia, providing complete vending machine and buffet-style food service to major corporations, hospitals, and universities throughout metropolitan Atlanta and northwest Georgia. The Company started in 1965 as Old Fashion Sandwich Company. Three years later, it incorporated and changed its name. The Company has been buying back its outstanding shares.

	05/31/95	05/31/94	05/30/92
Per Share Information			
Stock Price	3.37	3.00	1.69
Earnings Per Share	0.23	-0.13	0.14
Price / Earnings Ratio	14.65	n.a.	12.07
Book Value Per Share	8.18	7.46	7.02
Price / Book Value %	41.20	40.21	24.07
Dividends Per Share	n.a.	n.a.	n.a.
Annual Financial Data			
Operating Results (000's)			
Total Revenues	14,977.1	14,845.8	18,848.8
Costs & Expenses	-14,492.7	-14,198.3	-18,619.5
Income Before Taxes and Other	484.4	647.5	227.8
Other Items	-67.6	-525.3	n.a.
Income Tax	-198.9	-252.4	-69.0
Net Income	217.9	-130.2	158.8
Cash Flow From Operations	1,153.1	339.3	1,450.0
Balance Sheet (000's)			
Cash & Equivalents	865.9	670.7	664.9
Total Current Assets	2,363.0	1,669.4	1,548.0
Fixed Assets, Net	4,953.7	5,161.9	10,065.6
Total Assets	9,760.9	10,186.5	13,654.8
Total Current Liabilities	1,151.2	1,399.6	2,448.5
Long-Term Debt	n.a.	229.9	2,247.3
Stockholders' Equity	7,230.8	7,304.9	7,695.4
Performance & Financial Condition			
Return on Total Revenues %	1.45	-0.88	0.84
Return on Avg Stockholders' Equity %	3.00	n.a.	n.a.
Return on Average Assets %	2.18	n.a.	n.a.
Current Ratio	2.05	1.19	0.63
Debt / Equity %	n.a.	3.15	29.20

Compound Growth %'s	EPS %	18.00	Net Income %	11.12	Total Revenues %	-7.38

Comments

1994 and 1995 results reflect losses of $67,584 and $525,345, respectively, in connection with the discontinuance and disposal of the restaurant business and its assets. Although smaller in revenue, the balance sheet is favorable with no long term debt. The Company has recently expanded into the coffee and water service market and should certainly benefit from the 1996 Summer Olympics. We were unable to obtain the 1993 financial statements.

Officers	Position	Ownership Information	05/31/95
Sheldon E. Smith	President	Number of Shares Outstanding	884,107
Jerry W. Seneker	Exec VP	Market Capitalization	$ 2,979,441
Joseph C. Hulsey	Senior VP	Frequency Of Dividends	n.a.
Tery C. Coker	Vice President	Number of Shareholders	Under 500
Billy D. Varner	Controller		

Other Information

Transfer Agent	American Stock Transfer & Trust Company			Where Listed	OTC-BB
Auditor	Ernst & Young LLP			Symbol	OFFI
Market Maker	Morgan Keegan & Company, Inc.	Telephone	(800)238-7533	SIC Code	5490
Broker Dealer	Regular Stockbroker			Employees	150

Olokele Sugar Company, Limited

P.O. Box 1826 • Honolulu, HI 96805 • Telephone (808)335-3133

Company Description

The Company was in the business of growing sugar cane. After substantial damage from Hurricane Iniki in 1992, the Company completed a sale of all sugar-producing assets. C. Brewer and Company owns approximately 87.8% of the Company. There is also a stock repurchase program in effect at $100 per share.

	12/25/94	12/26/93
Per Share Information		
Stock Price	100.00	75.00
Earnings Per Share	21.27	24.86
Price / Earnings Ratio	4.70	3.02
Book Value Per Share	182.62	162.62
Price / Book Value %	54.76	46.12
Dividends Per Share	3.35	1.40
Annual Financial Data		
Operating Results (000's)		
Total Revenues	2,239.4	10,462.0
Costs & Expenses	n.a.	n.a.
Income Before Taxes and Other	2,239.4	10,462.0
Other Items	1,789.2	-2,634.6
Income Tax	-789.5	-3,911.4
Net Income	3,239.1	3,916.0
Cash Flow From Operations	3,960.2	847.1
Balance Sheet (000's)		
Cash & Equivalents	6.6	0.5
Total Current Assets	34,475.2	29,283.9
Fixed Assets, Net	n.a.	8,399.7
Total Assets	37,775.7	37,689.2
Total Current Liabilities	7,083.0	5,357.7
Long-Term Debt	n.a.	n.a.
Stockholders' Equity	27,816.2	25,612.8
Performance & Financial Condition		
Return on Total Revenues %	144.64	37.43
Return on Avg Stockholders' Equity %	n.a.	n.a.
Return on Average Assets %	n.a.	n.a.
Current Ratio	4.87	5.47
Debt / Equity %	n.a.	n.a.

Compound Growth %'s	EPS %	n.a.	Net Income %	n.a.	Total Revenues %	n.a.

Comments

1994 results include a nonrecurring benefit of $1,789,195 from income from discontinued operations. 1993 results include several nonrecurring items which net to a benefit of $7,005,731. The Company may have some remaining liabilities related to employee benefit programs. 1995 results had not yet been released when we went to press. However, the primary asset is the amount receivable from C. Brewer and Company.

Officers	Position	Ownership Information	12/25/94
James S. Andrasick	Chairman, President	Number of Shares Outstanding	152,316
Kathleen F. Oshiro	Secretary	Market Capitalization	$ 15,231,600
Brad S. Baker	Treasurer	Frequency Of Dividends	Quarterly
Kent T. ucien	Vice President	Number of Shareholders	Under 500
Jon T. Iwatani	Other		

Other Information					
Transfer Agent	Company Office		Where Listed	OTC-BB
Auditor	Coopers & Lybrand LLP		Symbol	OLOK
Market Maker	Abel-Behnke Corp.	Telephone	(808)537-8500	SIC Code	6790
Broker Dealer	Regular Stockbroker		Employees	1

Ophthalmic Publishing Company

77 Wacker Drive, Suite 660 • Chicago, IL 60601 • Telephone (312)629-1690

Company Description

The Company is an Illinois corporation that was established in 1918. The principal business is publishing the American Journal of Ophthalmology. The Company also has substantial investments in marketable securities. Most Company shares are restricted in that shares cannot be transferred to other than the Company and the stock price is established by formula to be equal to the book value of the Company as of the end of the month prior to any transaction. There are also nonrestricted shares.

	12/31/95	12/31/94	12/31/93	12/31/92
Per Share Information				
Stock Price	1,540.54	1,245.73	n.a.	n.a.
Earnings Per Share	-18.37	30.42	66.07	103.44
Price / Earnings Ratio	n.a.	40.95	n.a.	n.a.
Book Value Per Share	1,540.54	1,245.73	n.a.	n.a.
Price / Book Value %	100.00	100.00	n.a.	n.a.
Dividends Per Share	26.00	26.00	n.a.	n.a.
Annual Financial Data				
Operating Results (000's)				
Total Revenues	2,045.6	2,011.5	2,010.4	2,111.8
Costs & Expenses	-2,001.4	-1,869.5	-1,743.8	-1,617.7
Income Before Taxes and Other	-102.9	126.5	266.5	494.1
Other Items	n.a.	n.a.	n.a.	n.a.
Income Tax	47.3	-34.6	-55.4	-149.2
Net Income	-55.5	92.0	211.2	345.0
Cash Flow From Operations	71.2	142.8	n.a.	n.a.
Balance Sheet (000's)				
Cash & Equivalents	254.3	130.2	n.a.	n.a.
Total Current Assets	429.7	298.1	n.a.	n.a.
Fixed Assets, Net	178.3	215.4	n.a.	n.a.
Total Assets	7,136.9	5,586.5	n.a.	n.a.
Total Current Liabilities	295.8	166.0	n.a.	n.a.
Long-Term Debt	n.a.	n.a.	n.a.	n.a.
Stockholders' Equity	4,657.0	3,765.9	n.a.	n.a.
Performance & Financial Condition				
Return on Total Revenues %	-2.72	4.57	n.a.	n.a.
Return on Avg Stockholders' Equity %	-1.32	n.a.	n.a.	n.a.
Return on Average Assets %	-0.87	n.a.	n.a.	n.a.
Current Ratio	1.45	1.80	n.a.	n.a.
Debt / Equity %	n.a.	n.a.	n.a.	n.a.

Compound Growth %'s	EPS % n.a.	Net Income % n.a.	Total Revenues % -1.06

Comments

Unrealized gains and losses on the security portfolio are reflected in book value but the changes do not flow through the income statement. The net gains in 1995 and 1994 were $1,552,855 and $1,834,000, respectively. There is little trading activity on this stock. It may be well suited for someone with a professional interest in the subject of ophthalmology.

Officers	Position	Ownership Information	12/31/95
Bruce E. Spivey, M.D.	President	Number of Shares Outstanding	3,023
June Ellen Groppi	COO	Market Capitalization	$ 4,657,052
Thomas M. Aaberg, M.D.	Vice President, Secretary	Frequency Of Dividends	n.a.
Richard M. Brubaker, M.D.	Vice President	Number of Shareholders	30
Bradley R. Straatsma, M.D.	Vice President		

Other Information

Transfer Agent	Company Office			Where Listed	Order Matching Only
Auditor	Martin & Martin			Symbol	n.a.
Market Maker	None			SIC Code	2720
Broker Dealer	Standard Investment	Tel/Ext	(888)783-4688 Jack	Employees	n.a.

Optical Specialties, Inc.

4281 Technology Drive • Fremont, CA 94538 • Telephone (510)490-6400 • Fax (510)490-1748

Company Description

The Company designs, manufactures and markets automated inspection and measurement systems used primarily by semiconductor manufacturers during the various stages of wafer fabrication. The Company's products are used in the engineering or during the high volume production of semiconductors and disk drives to improve yields and productivity through better process control.

	09/30/95	09/30/94	09/30/93	09/30/92
Per Share Information				
Stock Price	1.75	0.88	0.63	2.50
Earnings Per Share	-0.14	-0.54	-0.59	-4.70
Price / Earnings Ratio	n.a.	n.a.	n.a.	n.a.
Book Value Per Share	-1.92	-1.81	-1.20	-0.82
Price / Book Value %	n.a.	n.a.	n.a.	n.a.
Dividends Per Share	n.a.	n.a.	n.a.	n.a.
Annual Financial Data				
Operating Results (000's)				
Total Revenues	24,188.0	17,551.0	10,385.0	7,121.0
Costs & Expenses	-24,735.0	-19,444.0	-12,482.0	-184.0
Income Before Taxes and Other	-547.0	-1,893.0	-2,097.0	-4,786.0
Other Items	n.a.	n.a.	164.0	268.0
Income Tax	n.a.	n.a.	n.a.	n.a.
Net Income	-547.0	-1,893.0	-1,933.0	-4,518.0
Cash Flow From Operations	-1,305.0	-616.0	-3,852.0	-4,428.0
Balance Sheet (000's)				
Cash & Equivalents	344.0	989.0	72.0	404.0
Total Current Assets	12,503.0	7,054.0	7,069.0	6,599.0
Fixed Assets, Net	2,000.0	2,204.0	1,339.0	1,131.0
Total Assets	20,853.0	15,876.0	15,636.0	14,889.0
Total Current Liabilities	16,117.0	10,208.0	8,111.0	6,840.0
Long-Term Debt	1,850.0	3,825.0	4,875.0	4,700.0
Stockholders' Equity	2,386.0	1,343.0	2,150.0	2,849.0
Performance & Financial Condition				
Return on Total Revenues %	-2.26	-10.79	-18.61	-63.45
Return on Avg Stockholders' Equity %	-29.34	-108.39	-77.34	-403.57
Return on Average Assets %	-2.98	-12.01	-12.67	-46.80
Current Ratio	0.78	0.69	0.87	0.96
Debt / Equity %	77.54	284.81	226.74	164.97

Compound Growth %'s	EPS %	n.a.	Net Income %	n.a.	Total Revenues %	50.32

Comments

The Company has incurred substantial operating losses and has an accumulated deficit of over $25 million, at September 30, 1995. If the Company continues to incur losses in 1996, additional capital may be required. Management believes that should the Company require additional capital, it will be available in the form of additional investment from current or new shareholders. As of September 30, 1995, officers and directors, as a group, owned 54.2% of the Company's outstanding common stock. At September 30, 1995, there were two classes of preferred stock totaling approximately $8.1 million which were primarily owned by venture capitalists.

Officers	Position	Ownership Information	09/30/95
Jack R. Harris	President, CFO	Number of Shares Outstanding	2,973,532
John R. Dralla	Vice President	Market Capitalization	$ 5,203,681
Robert L. LoBianco	Vice President	Frequency Of Dividends	n.a.
Lawrence H. Lin	VP - Research	Number of Shareholders	750
Malcolm J. Knight	VP - Sales		

Other Information				
Transfer Agent	Chemical Mellon Shareholder Services		Where Listed	OTC-PS
Auditor	Deloitte & Touche LLP		Symbol	DOKF
Market Maker	Toluca Pacific Securities Corp	Telephone (800)284-8772	SIC Code	3829
Broker Dealer	Regular Stockbroker		Employees	129

Optimumcare Corporation

30011 Ivy Glenn Drive • Laguna Niguel, CA 92677 • Telephone (714)495-1100 • Fax (714)495-4316

Company Description

The Company develops health care facility based programs, managed by the Company, for the treatment of certain mental health disorders as well as programs for alcohol and drug abuse. The Company currently has 13 programs in six hospitals. The Company was incorporated in Delaware in 1987.

	12/31/95	12/31/94	12/31/93	12/31/92
Per Share Information				
Stock Price	1.28	0.82	0.43	0.19
Earnings Per Share	n.a.	0.09	0.07	0.03
Price / Earnings Ratio	n.a.	9.11	6.14	6.33
Book Value Per Share	0.31	0.30	0.21	0.14
Price / Book Value %	412.90	273.33	204.76	135.71
Dividends Per Share	n.a.	n.a.	n.a.	n.a.
Annual Financial Data				
Operating Results (000's)				
Total Revenues	6,035.9	5,604.8	3,826.8	2,314.6
Costs & Expenses	-6,033.0	-5,126.0	-3,459.5	-2,180.6
Income Before Taxes and Other	2.9	478.8	367.3	134.0
Other Items	n.a.	n.a.	n.a.	n.a.
Income Tax	-0.8	-13.8	-2.1	-7.0
Net Income	2.1	465.0	365.2	127.0
Cash Flow From Operations	159.6	-191.6	79.6	71.5
Balance Sheet (000's)				
Cash & Equivalents	170.9	36.7	302.6	256.3
Total Current Assets	1,739.1	1,699.8	1,287.9	904.1
Fixed Assets, Net	25.6	16.1	9.9	12.0
Total Assets	2,059.5	1,814.2	1,299.2	917.8
Total Current Liabilities	381.5	333.2	269.3	249.7
Long-Term Debt	166.0	n.a.	n.a.	n.a.
Stockholders' Equity	1,512.0	1,480.9	1,029.9	668.1
Performance & Financial Condition				
Return on Total Revenues %	0.03	8.30	9.54	5.49
Return on Avg Stockholders' Equity %	0.14	37.04	43.02	21.01
Return on Average Assets %	0.11	29.87	32.94	16.11
Current Ratio	4.56	5.10	4.78	3.62
Debt / Equity %	10.98	n.a.	n.a.	n.a.

Compound Growth %'s	EPS %	73.21	Net Income %	-74.65	Total Revenues %	37.64

Comments

The Company expects revenue to increase in 1996 as a result of an increased census under existing contracts and a larger number of programs operational for the entire year. As of March 31, 1996, officers and directors, as a group, owned 22% of the Company's outstanding shares of common stock.

Officers	Position	Ownership Information	12/31/95
Edward A. Johnson	President, Secretary	Number of Shares Outstanding	4,923,509
Michael S. Callison	Vice President	Market Capitalization	$ 6,302,092
		Frequency Of Dividends	n.a.
		Number of Shareholders	300

Other Information			
Transfer Agent	American Stock Transfer & Trust Company	Where Listed	OTC-BB
Auditor	Ernst & Young LLP	Symbol	OPMC
Market Maker	Paragon Capital Corporation	Telephone (800)521-8877	SIC Code	8060
Broker Dealer	Regular Stockbroker	Employees	121

Original Sixteen to One Mine, Inc.

527 Miners Street • Alleghany, CA 95910 • Telephone (916)287-3223

Company Description

The Company mines for gold on properties it owns or leases or on which it has claims. Company properties are in the Alleghany and French Gulch mining districts in the Sierra Nevada Mountains of Northern California. In addition to refined gold bullion sold to gold buyers and investors, the Company sells high-grade gold and quartz specimens and gold jewelry. The Company was incorporated in California in 1911 and has never been in bankruptcy, receivership or similar proceedings.

	12/31/95	12/31/94	12/31/93	12/31/92
Per Share Information				
Stock Price	4.31	3.88	4.50	1.38
Earnings Per Share	0.21	0.04	0.38	0.13
Price / Earnings Ratio	20.52	97.00	11.84	10.62
Book Value Per Share	0.86	0.69	0.65	0.27
Price / Book Value %	501.16	562.32	692.31	511.11
Dividends Per Share	0.05	n.a.	n.a.	n.a.
Annual Financial Data				
Operating Results (000's)				
Total Revenues	2,836.7	1,356.2	3,410.8	1,554.1
Costs & Expenses	-1,883.6	-1,213.6	-1,494.6	-1,079.1
Income Before Taxes and Other	953.1	142.7	1,916.1	463.1
Other Items	n.a.	n.a.	148.0	70.9
Income Tax	-221.0	15.0	-750.3	-92.4
Net Income	732.1	157.7	1,313.9	441.6
Cash Flow From Operations	571.1	628.1	272.3	130.5
Balance Sheet (000's)				
Cash & Equivalents	180.6	146.7	187.0	12.7
Total Current Assets	2,431.7	1,959.1	2,508.2	442.3
Fixed Assets, Net	1,621.1	1,201.8	439.8	486.0
Total Assets	4,087.1	3,200.9	2,993.7	979.8
Total Current Liabilities	1,036.5	767.7	718.2	51.5
Long-Term Debt	15.8	n.a.	n.a.	n.a.
Stockholders' Equity	3,034.8	2,433.2	2,275.5	928.3
Performance & Financial Condition				
Return on Total Revenues %	25.81	11.63	38.52	28.42
Return on Avg Stockholders' Equity %	26.78	6.70	82.02	63.54
Return on Average Assets %	20.09	5.09	66.13	58.60
Current Ratio	2.35	2.55	3.49	8.59
Debt / Equity %	0.52	n.a.	n.a.	n.a.

Compound Growth %'s	EPS %	17.33	Net Income %	18.36	Total Revenues %	22.21

Comments

The Company owns 412 acres of real property and has the mineral rights and limited surface rights to an additional 1300 acres. The Company's principal asset is gold bullion inventory which amounted to $2.2 million at December 31, 1995, based on the spot price of gold at $386.85 per ounce. Over 24,408 ounces of gold have been recovered from the Company's property since January 1992. While the vein system owned by the Company has produced over 1 million ounces and is a proven gold deposit, there are no assurances that this production will continue.

Officers	Position	Ownership Information	12/31/95
Michael M. Miller	President	Number of Shares Outstanding	3,513,062
Richard C. Sorlien	Secretary	Market Capitalization	$ 15,141,297
Charles I. Brown	Treasurer	Frequency Of Dividends	Irregular
Johan Raadsma	Vice President	Number of Shareholders	731
Leland O. Erdahl	Other		

Other Information			
Transfer Agent	Securities Registrar & Transfer	Where Listed	PSE
Auditor	Perry-Smith & Co.	Symbol	OAU
Market Maker	n.a.	SIC Code	1041
Broker Dealer	Regular Stockbroker	Employees	41

Orrstown Financial Services, Inc.

P.O.Box 250 • Shippensburg, PA 17257 • Telephone (717)532-6114 • Fax (717)532-4143

Company Description

Orrstown Financial Services, Inc.'s primary activity consists of owning and supervising its subsidiary, Orrstown Bank, which is engaged in providing bank and bank related services in south central Pennsylvania (principally Franklin and Cumberland Counties) through its five branches. During 1995, the Bank acquired the Spring Run branch of Valley Bank, including all deposits, which amounted to more than $12 million.

	12/31/95	12/31/94	12/31/93	12/31/92
Per Share Information				
Stock Price	30.00	27.00	23.00	25.00
Earnings Per Share	2.05	1.71	1.62	1.45
Price / Earnings Ratio	14.63	15.79	14.20	17.24
Book Value Per Share	15.34	12.95	12.95	11.49
Price / Book Value %	195.57	208.49	177.61	217.58
Dividends Per Share	0.62	0.54	0.50	0.45
Annual Financial Data				
Operating Results (000's)				
Net Interest Income	6,287.0	5,330.0	5,121.0	4,832.0
Loan Loss Provision	-270.0	-71.0	-121.0	-366.0
Non-Interest Income	935.0	860.0	602.0	693.0
Non-Interest Expense	-4,256.0	-3,964.0	-3,593.0	-3,369.0
Income Before Taxes and Other	2,696.0	2,155.0	2,009.0	1,790.0
Other Items	n.a.	n.a.	n.a.	n.a.
Income Tax	-742.0	-520.0	-525.0	-452.0
Net Income	1,954.0	1,635.0	1,484.0	1,338.0
Balance Sheet (000's)				
Cash & Securities	38,630.0	28,353.0	34,949.0	32,497.0
Loans, Net	101,424.0	89,639.0	74,449.0	69,865.0
Fixed Assets, Net	3,042.0	2,512.0	2,033.0	1,687.0
Total Assets	145,998.0	123,004.0	113,581.0	106,191.0
Deposits	127,330.0	106,365.0	98,582.0	94,231.0
Stockholders' Equity	14,633.0	12,353.0	11,597.0	10,583.0
Performance & Financial Condition				
Net Interest Margin	n.a.	n.a.	n.a.	n.a.
Return on Avg Stockholders' Equity %	14.48	13.65	13.38	12.93
Return on Average Assets %	1.45	1.38	1.35	1.31
Equity to Assets %	10.02	10.04	10.21	9.97
Reserve as a % of Non-Performing Loans	1085.61	4444.44	n.a.	133.42

Compound Growth %'s	EPS %	12.24	Net Income %	13.45	Net Interest Income %	9.17

Comments

Residential real estate loans account for approximately 73% of total loans. There was a 3 for 1 stock split in 1992. Earnings as a percentage of both assets and equity increased in each of the four years presented.

Officers	Position	Ownership Information	12/31/95
Kenneth R. Shoemaker	President, CEO	Number of Shares Outstanding	976,863
Stephen C. Oldt	Exec VP, COO	Market Capitalization	$ 29,305,890
Robert B. Russell	VP - Finance	Frequency Of Dividends	Quarterly
Philip E. Fague	Vice President	Number of Shareholders	1,422
Robert S. Nickey III	Vice President, Sr Loan Officer		

Other Information			
Transfer Agent	Company Office	Where Listed	OTC-BB
Auditor	Smith Elliott Kearns & Company	Symbol	ORRB
Market Maker	F.J. Morrissey & Co., Inc. Telephone (800)842-8928	SIC Code	6020
Broker Dealer	Regular Stockbroker	Employees	84

PAB Bankshares, Inc.

P.O.Box 3589 • Valdosta, GA 31604 • Telephone (912)242-7758 • Fax (912)241-2767

Company Description

PAB Bankshares, Inc. is a bank holding company headquartered in Valdosta, Georgia, which provides a broad array of financial services to consumer and commercial customers. It has three subsidiaries in south Georgia; The Park Avenue Bank, Farmers and Merchants Bank and First Federal Savings Bank. Each of these banks are encouraged to act autonomously to a large degree. The holding company was formed in 1982, but the individual banks have a combined 146 years of service in their respective communities.

	12/31/95	12/31/94	12/31/93	12/31/92
Per Share Information				
Stock Price	24.19	20.06	16.95	16.50
Earnings Per Share	2.14	1.70	1.44	1.30
Price / Earnings Ratio	11.30	11.80	11.77	12.69
Book Value Per Share	17.24	17.24	12.39	11.46
Price / Book Value %	313.75	116.36	136.80	143.98
Dividends Per Share	0.41	0.35	0.35	0.16
Annual Financial Data				
Operating Results (000's)				
Net Interest Income	10,291.1	7,111.0	5,825.7	5,280.8
Loan Loss Provision	-385.5	-330.0	-260.0	-467.0
Non-Interest Income	2,120.9	1,378.5	1,312.3	1,529.6
Non-Interest Expense	-7,580.7	-5,320.3	-4,715.7	-4,447.2
Income Before Taxes and Other	4,445.8	2,839.3	2,162.3	1,896.2
Other Items	n.a.	n.a.	n.a.	n.a.
Income Tax	-1,465.7	-894.1	-701.7	-578.9
Net Income	2,980.1	1,945.2	1,460.5	1,317.3
Balance Sheet (000's)				
Cash & Securities	82,954.2	47,790.2	49,783.8	42,588.9
Loans, Net	169,228.7	115,499.0	105,581.0	93,337.6
Fixed Assets, Net	6,517.7	4,249.1	4,123.5	3,838.7
Total Assets	267,088.3	172,898.8	163,290.6	143,160.6
Deposits	231,225.5	147,511.8	146,409.9	130,707.7
Stockholders' Equity	23,378.7	16,429.0	12,523.8	11,589.7
Performance & Financial Condition				
Net Interest Margin	4.53	4.64	4.23	4.32
Return on Avg Stockholders' Equity %	14.97	13.44	12.11	11.95
Return on Average Assets %	1.35	1.16	0.95	1.00
Equity to Assets %	8.75	9.50	7.67	8.10
Reserve as a % of Non-Performing Loans	1138.08	684.81	351.39	620.80

Compound Growth %'s	EPS %	18.07	Net Income %	31.27	Net Interest Income %	24.91

Comments

During 1995, the Company acquired all of the outstanding stock of First Federal Savings Bank of Bainbridge for the sum of $8,029,606, consisting of $3.9 million cash and 207,076 shares of additional Company stock valued at $20 per share. The purchase resulted in approximately $2.1 million of goodwill which is being amortized over 25 years. The Bank is concentrated in real estate mortgages which represent 66% of total loans. The remaining 34% is split between commercial, financial and agricultural loans at 13%, installment loans at 12% and other loans at 9%. The Bank facilitates trades in its' shares by putting buyers and sellers in contact with one another.

Officers	Position	Ownership Information	12/31/95
James L. Dewar, Sr.	Chairman	Number of Shares Outstanding	1,355,904
R. Bradford Burnette	President, CEO	Market Capitalization	$ 32,799,318
Nita Brantley	Secretary	Frequency Of Dividends	Annual
C. Lary Wilkinson	Vice President	Number of Shareholders	1,042

Other Information

Transfer Agent	Company Office		Where Listed	Order Matching Only
Auditor	Stewart, Fowler & Stalvey, PL		Symbol	n.a.
Market Maker	None-Company Office	Telephone (912)241-8051	SIC Code	6020
Broker Dealer	None		Employees	100

Pace Medical, Inc.

391 Totten Pond Road • Waltham, MA 02154 • Telephone (617)890-5656 • Fax (617)890-4894

Company Description

The Company is principally engaged in the design, manufacture and sale of single and dual-chamber temporary cardiac pacemakers, a dual-chamber pacing analyzer, heartwires, surgical and temporary pacemaker extension cables, and related accessories. The Company commenced operations in 1985 when the Company's founder and president acquired all the common stock of APC Medical Ltd. from its parent, American Pacemaker Corp. The Company was incorporated in Mssachusetts in January of 1986.

	12/31/95	12/31/94	12/31/93	12/31/92
Per Share Information				
Stock Price	1.00	0.63	0.69	3.00
Earnings Per Share	0.07	-0.02	-0.14	0.01
Price / Earnings Ratio	14.29	n.a.	n.a.	300.00
Book Value Per Share	0.41	0.34	0.36	0.50
Price / Book Value %	243.90	185.29	191.67	6,000.00
Dividends Per Share	n.a.	n.a.	n.a.	n.a.
Annual Financial Data				
Operating Results (000's)				
Total Revenues	1,784.9	1,246.1	701.8	1,478.7
Costs & Expenses	-1,538.1	-1,311.4	-1,164.6	-1,434.8
Income Before Taxes and Other	246.0	-65.3	-462.7	43.9
Other Items	n.a.	n.a.	n.a.	n.a.
Income Tax	n.a.	n.a.	n.a.	-2.5
Net Income	246.0	-65.3	-462.7	41.4
Cash Flow From Operations	-1.8	-184.5	-449.6	65.7
Balance Sheet (000's)				
Cash & Equivalents	772.0	781.1	964.8	1,422.3
Total Current Assets	1,706.3	1,494.9	1,506.5	1,959.3
Fixed Assets, Net	25.5	31.5	43.9	54.4
Total Assets	1,779.7	1,544.6	1,569.5	2,033.7
Total Current Liabilities	369.7	363.1	306.3	299.3
Long-Term Debt	n.a.	n.a.	n.a.	n.a.
Stockholders' Equity	1,395.3	1,152.2	1,219.2	1,675.8
Performance & Financial Condition				
Return on Total Revenues %	13.78	-5.24	-65.93	2.80
Return on Avg Stockholders' Equity %	19.31	-5.51	-31.97	3.59
Return on Average Assets %	14.80	-4.19	-25.68	2.71
Current Ratio	4.61	4.12	4.92	6.55
Debt / Equity %	n.a.	n.a.	n.a.	n.a.

Compound Growth %'s	EPS %	91.29	Net Income %	81.17	Total Revenues %	6.48

Comments

The Company has a wholly-owned subsidiary operating in the United Kingdom. Sales and net operating income of this subsidiary made up 35% and 47% of consolidated sales and operating income for 1995, respectively. Officers and directors, as a group, owned 36.5% of the Company's outstanding shares at March 22, 1996.

Officers	Position	Ownership Information	12/31/95
Ralph E. Hanson	President, CEO	Number of Shares Outstanding	3,380,850
Drusilla F. Hays	Vice President, Senior Clerk	Market Capitalization	$ 3,380,850
Anthony W. Bailey	Vice President, General Manager	Frequency Of Dividends	n.a.
		Number of Shareholders	350

Other Information			
Transfer Agent	American Stock Transfer & Trust Company	Where Listed	OTC-BB
Auditor	Deloitte & Touche LLP	Symbol	PMDL
Market Maker	Fechtor, Detwiler & Co., Inc. Telephone (800)225-6792	SIC Code	3845
Broker Dealer	Regular Stockbroker	Employees	12

Pacific Capital Bancorp

P.O.Box 1786 • Salinas, CA 93902-1786 • Telephone (408)757-4900 • Fax (408)757-6429

Company Description

Pacific Capital Bancorp is a bank holding company which was created in 1983 by a group of local businessmen. The First National Bank of central California, the Company's wholly owned subsidiary, commenced operations in 1984. The Bank is a full service commercial bank serving Monterey and Santa Cruz counties with five banking offices.

	12/31/95	12/31/94	12/31/93	12/31/92
Per Share Information				
Stock Price	22.22	18.70	15.75	14.41
Earnings Per Share	1.86	1.65	1.39	1.10
Price / Earnings Ratio	11.95	11.33	11.33	13.10
Book Value Per Share	16.50	15.65	15.23	14.80
Price / Book Value %	134.67	119.49	103.41	97.36
Dividends Per Share	0.53	0.40	0.30	n.a.
Annual Financial Data				
Operating Results (000's)				
Net Interest Income	18,816.0	16,971.0	15,082.0	14,298.0
Loan Loss Provision	-135.0	-100.0	-890.0	-925.0
Non-Interest Income	1,875.0	2,088.0	2,365.0	2,339.0
Non-Interest Expense	-12,342.0	-11,968.0	-11,691.0	-11,251.0
Income Before Taxes and Other	8,214.0	6,991.0	4,866.0	4,461.0
Other Items	n.a.	n.a.	549.0	n.a.
Income Tax	-3,180.0	-2,652.0	-1,727.0	-1,540.0
Net Income	5,034.0	4,339.0	3,688.0	2,921.0
Balance Sheet (000's)				
Cash & Securities	126,390.0	128,651.0	114,607.0	113,148.0
Loans, Net	212,823.0	200,643.0	180,925.0	181,392.0
Fixed Assets, Net	7,523.0	7,238.0	7,318.0	7,835.0
Total Assets	353,579.0	343,879.0	308,767.0	307,737.0
Deposits	307,819.0	303,229.0	271,773.0	272,940.0
Stockholders' Equity	42,976.0	38,750.0	35,432.0	32,787.0
Performance & Financial Condition				
Net Interest Margin	6.20	5.80	5.40	5.40
Return on Avg Stockholders' Equity %	12.32	11.70	10.81	9.34
Return on Average Assets %	1.44	1.33	1.20	0.98
Equity to Assets %	12.15	11.27	11.48	10.65
Reserve as a % of Non-Performing Loans	241.39	120.51	109.67	80.38

Compound Growth %'s	EPS %	19.14	Net Income %	19.89	Net Interest Income %	9.58

Comments

The loan portfolio consists primarily of real estate mortgages, commercial loans and real estate construction loans, representing 59%, 24% and 8% of total loans, respectively. In the last ten years, the Bank dipped below a return of 10% on equity only twice, 1992 and 1986. Both of these years still showed reasonable profits. There has been strong growth to go along with the fine returns. There have been 5% stock dividends in each of the four years presented. Per share amounts have been restated for consistency.

Officers	Position	Ownership Information	12/31/95
Stanley R. Haynes	Chairman	Number of Shares Outstanding	2,603,839
Clayton C. Larson	President	Market Capitalization	$ 57,857,303
D. Vernon Horton	CEO	Frequency Of Dividends	Quarterly
Dennis A. DeCius	Exec VP, CFO	Number of Shareholders	1,602

Other Information

Transfer Agent	1st Interstate Stock Transfer Admin.		Where Listed	OTC-BB
Auditor	KPMG Peat Marwick LLP		Symbol	PABN
Market Maker	Hoefer & Arnett, Inc.	Telephone (415)362-7160	SIC Code	6020
Broker Dealer	Regular Stockbroker		Employees	165

Pacific Northwest Development Corporation

9725 SW Beaverton-HillsdaleHwy • Beaverton, OR 97005-3364 • Telephone (503)626-9999 • Fax (503)646-5074

Company Description

The Company is involved in the development of real estate, brokerage of real estate mortgages and contracting and brokerage of real estate sales. Development projects are primarily located in the Portland, Willamette Valley and Bend-Redmond areas of Oregon. The Company went public in 1972.

	03/31/95	03/31/94	03/31/93	03/31/92
Per Share Information				
Stock Price	5.25	4.75	3.63	4.25
Earnings Per Share	0.57	1.13	0.16	0.38
Price / Earnings Ratio	9.21	4.20	22.69	11.18
Book Value Per Share	11.05	11.25	10.12	9.96
Price / Book Value %	47.51	42.22	35.87	42.67
Dividends Per Share	n.a.	n.a.	n.a.	n.a.
Annual Financial Data				
Operating Results (000's)				
Total Revenues	17,534.4	13,246.3	7,405.7	10,715.2
Costs & Expenses	-17,102.8	-12,440.1	-7,206.4	-10,371.2
Income Before Taxes and Other	431.6	806.1	199.3	344.0
Other Items	n.a.	n.a.	n.a.	n.a.
Income Tax	-169.7	-283.7	-126.8	-168.6
Net Income	261.8	522.4	72.5	175.4
Cash Flow From Operations	-863.2	-2,787.1	707.1	3,424.5
Balance Sheet (000's)				
Cash & Equivalents	831.4	1,150.6	2,197.7	721.7
Total Current Assets	7,792.0	10,264.3	12,711.8	15,228.5
Fixed Assets, Net	166.8	119.3	123.5	133.6
Total Assets	20,795.8	21,957.3	18,784.8	19,335.7
Total Current Liabilities	3,880.2	5,336.6	4,205.9	4,866.4
Long-Term Debt	9,046.6	9,244.7	8,881.7	9,134.3
Stockholders' Equity	5,528.3	5,194.4	4,672.0	4,599.5
Performance & Financial Condition				
Return on Total Revenues %	1.49	3.94	0.98	1.64
Return on Avg Stockholders' Equity %	4.88	10.59	1.56	3.89
Return on Average Assets %	1.22	2.56	0.38	0.69
Current Ratio	2.01	1.92	3.02	3.13
Debt / Equity %	163.64	177.97	190.11	198.60

Compound Growth %'s	EPS %	14.47	Net Income %	14.28	Total Revenues %	17.84

Comments

The sale of homes, the primary source of Company revenue, should show good results with a number of subdivision projects currently in progress, according to management. An investor should keep an eye on interest rates as well as the local economy.

Officers	Position	Ownership Information	03/31/95
O "Pete" M. Wilson	President	Number of Shares Outstanding	500,381
Vicki L. Stollberg	Secretary, Treasurer	Market Capitalization	$ 2,627,000
Joan M. Crew	Vice President	Frequency Of Dividends	n.a.
Michael H. Miller	Vice President	Number of Shareholders	160
Marvin C. Steadman	Vice President		

Other Information

Transfer Agent	First Interstate Bank, Los Angeles, CA			Where Listed	OTC-PS
Auditor	Moss Adams			Symbol	PNOD
Market Maker	Black and Company	Telephone	(503)248-9600	SIC Code	6530
Broker Dealer	Regular Stockbroker			Employees	18

PagePrompt USA

16810 Valley View Avenue • La Mirada, CA 90638 • Telephone (310)404-0444 • Fax (714)562-0662

Company Description

The Company is a provider of paging communications and telemessaging services. The primary service areas are northern and southern California and selected cities throughout the southwest and northwest United States. The Company went public in 1971. In March, 1996, an acquisition of Network One, a division of Pana Pacific, was made for Company stock.

	06/30/95	06/30/94	06/30/93
Per Share Information			
Stock Price	2.37	2.06	1.00
Earnings Per Share	-0.38	-0.03	-0.27
Price / Earnings Ratio	n.a.	n.a.	n.a.
Book Value Per Share	-0.20	-0.35	-0.61
Price / Book Value %	n.a.	n.a.	n.a.
Dividends Per Share	n.a.	n.a.	n.a.
Annual Financial Data			
Operating Results (000's)			
Total Revenues	4,702.5	5,169.7	3,161.8
Costs & Expenses	-6,428.8	-5,256.8	-3,965.3
Income Before Taxes and Other	-1,726.2	-87.1	-803.4
Other Items	n.a.	n.a.	n.a.
Income Tax	n.a.	n.a.	n.a.
Net Income	-1,726.2	-87.1	-803.4
Cash Flow From Operations	-113.8	479.6	-183.1
Balance Sheet (000's)			
Cash & Equivalents	400.8	86.4	n.a.
Total Current Assets	1,157.2	523.9	480.7
Fixed Assets, Net	818.1	847.3	843.6
Total Assets	2,074.0	1,507.3	1,522.8
Total Current Liabilities	2,738.8	1,456.0	1,424.2
Long-Term Debt	309.7	1,552.1	1,932.3
Stockholders' Equity	-974.6	-1,500.8	-1,833.7
Performance & Financial Condition			
Return on Total Revenues %	-36.71	-1.68	-25.41
Return on Avg Stockholders' Equity %	n.a.	n.a.	n.a.
Return on Average Assets %	-96.40	-5.75	-43.56
Current Ratio	0.42	0.36	0.34
Debt / Equity %	n.a.	n.a.	n.a.

Compound Growth %'s	EPS %	n.a.	Net Income %	n.a.	Total Revenues %	21.95

Comments

The auditors have issued "going concern opinions" in at least the last two years. Although plagued with a difficult financial condition, the Company has survived by raising additional capital and converting certain notes and accounts payable into stock.

Officers	Position	Ownership Information	06/30/95
Harry Brix	Chairman	Number of Shares Outstanding	4,923,652
Hal Linden	President, CEO	Market Capitalization	$ 11,669,055
William Topper	CFO	Frequency Of Dividends	n.a.
Herman Moore, Jr.	Secretary	Number of Shareholders	Under 500

Other Information

Transfer Agent	American Registrar and Transfer Company			Where Listed	OTC-BB
Auditor	Deloitte & Touche LLP			Symbol	PGSP
Market Maker	J. Alexander Securities, Inc.	Telephone	(800)421-0258	SIC Code	4890
Broker Dealer	Regular Stockbroker			Employees	54

Pan Smak Pizza Inc.

1106-750 W. Pender Street • Vancouver, B.C. V6C 2T8 Canada • Telephone (604)682-2325 • Fax (604)682-2397

Company Description

The Company operates a chain of pizza restaurants in the country of Poland under the "Pan Smak" name. There were 8 Company-owned stores at the end of fiscal 1995. There were also 7 restaurants operating under franchising agreements. The Company is 35% owned by institutional investors, the largest of which are foreign stock mutual funds.

	10/31/95	10/31/94
Per Share Information		
Stock Price	0.80	n.a.
Earnings Per Share	-0.08	-0.09
Price / Earnings Ratio	n.a.	n.a.
Book Value Per Share	0.29	0.08
Price / Book Value %	275.86	n.a.
Dividends Per Share	n.a.	n.a.
Annual Financial Data		
Operating Results (000's)		
Total Revenues	2,448.9	1,328.1
Costs & Expenses	-4,188.3	-2,827.6
Income Before Taxes and Other	-1,739.4	-1,510.6
Other Items	n.a.	n.a.
Income Tax	n.a.	n.a.
Net Income	-1,739.4	-1,510.6
Cash Flow From Operations	-1,635.2	-787.1
Balance Sheet (000's)		
Cash & Equivalents	791.4	254.4
Total Current Assets	5,639.2	590.3
Fixed Assets, Net	2,615.5	1,530.6
Total Assets	8,315.9	2,420.5
Total Current Liabilities	466.6	1,019.5
Long-Term Debt	n.a.	n.a.
Stockholders' Equity	7,849.3	1,401.0
Performance & Financial Condition		
Return on Total Revenues %	-71.03	-113.74
Return on Avg Stockholders' Equity %	-37.61	-95.00
Return on Average Assets %	-32.40	-68.67
Current Ratio	12.09	0.58
Debt / Equity %	n.a.	n.a.

Compound Growth %'s	EPS % n.a.	Net Income % n.a.	Total Revenues % 84.38

Comments

All amounts are in Canadian dollars. The primary aim of the Company is to license its operations to franchisees who will operate under the Pan Smak name. Management estimates a startup cost of $150,000 Canadian for each new location. Single unit profitability was not provided and cannot be determined from the financial statements because of the rapid growth.

Officers	Position	Ownership Information	10/31/95
Stanislaw P. Szary	President, CEO	Number of Shares Outstanding	26,296,882
Jesse Zaniewski	COO	Market Capitalization	$ 21,037,506
C. Blair Wilson	CFO, Secretary	Frequency Of Dividends	n.a.
		Number of Shareholders	Under 500

Other Information

Transfer Agent	Yorkton Securities, Vancouver, B.C.	Where Listed	VSE
Auditor	Ernst & Young LLP	Symbol	PZZ
Market Maker	None	SIC Code	5812
Broker Dealer	Regular Stockbroker	Employees	150

Papnet of Ohio, Inc.

6059 Memorial Drive • Dublin, OH 43017 • Telephone (614)793-9356 • Fax (614)793-9376

Company Description

The Company owns rights to license the Papnet technology. This technology is a computerized scanning, neural network system used to confirm the results of Pap smear diagnostic tests. The Company was formed in 1989 to be the general partner of Papnet Limited Partnership and Papnet Midwest Limited Partnership which had obtained the rights to use the Papnet technology in Ohio, Kentucky and the city of Chicago.

	12/31/95	12/31/94
Per Share Information		
Stock Price	13.50	15.25
Earnings Per Share	0.07	-0.21
Price / Earnings Ratio	192.86	n.a.
Book Value Per Share	0.95	1.06
Price / Book Value %	1,421.10	1,438.70
Dividends Per Share	n.a.	n.a.
Annual Financial Data		
Operating Results (000's)		
Total Revenues	1,030.2	27.8
Costs & Expenses	-570.3	-345.5
Income Before Taxes and Other	459.9	-317.7
Other Items	n.a.	n.a.
Income Tax	n.a.	n.a.
Net Income	459.9	-317.7
Cash Flow From Operations	n.a.	-266.1
Balance Sheet (000's)		
Cash & Equivalents	811.5	535.5
Total Current Assets	938.5	606.1
Fixed Assets, Net	17.3	20.6
Total Assets	8,755.9	1,587.9
Total Current Liabilities	129.2	6.8
Long-Term Debt	n.a.	n.a.
Stockholders' Equity	6,055.0	1,581.1
Performance & Financial Condition		
Return on Total Revenues %	44.64	n.a.
Return on Avg Stockholders' Equity %	12.05	n.a.
Return on Average Assets %	8.89	n.a.
Current Ratio	7.26	88.81
Debt / Equity %	n.a.	n.a.

Compound Growth %'s	EPS % n.a.	Net Income % n.a.	Total Revenues % 3600.87

Comments

The Company has announced a merger with five other companies that each own similar geographically exclusive rights to the Papnet technology. Shareholders of the Company will own 48% of the new company. There have been several stock splits resulting in 8 shares for 1 share since the initial public offering at $10 per share. The compounded growth rate is reflective of the commencement of operations in 1995.

Officers	Position	Ownership Information	12/31/95
David J. Richards	President, CEO	Number of Shares Outstanding	6,400,000
		Market Capitalization	$ 86,400,000
		Frequency Of Dividends	n.a.
		Number of Shareholders	Under 500

Other Information

Transfer Agent	Company Office			Where Listed	OTC-BB
Auditor	Not indicated			Symbol	PPNT
Market Maker	Diversified Capital Markets	Telephone	(614)442-5804	SIC Code	8071
Broker Dealer	Regular Stockbroker			Employees	3

Park-Lexington Company, Inc.

17 E. 47th Street • New York, NY 10017-3808 • Telephone (212)371-7773 • Fax (212)371-7787

Company Description

The Company owns and manages several residential properties in New York City and also manages a portfolio of marketable securities.

	03/31/95	03/31/94	03/31/93	03/31/92
Per Share Information				
Stock Price	300.00	310.00	295.00	295.00
Earnings Per Share	27.33	36.35	29.08	22.69
Price / Earnings Ratio	10.98	8.53	n.a.	n.a.
Book Value Per Share	360.22	344.64	310.28	303.20
Price / Book Value %	83.28	89.95	n.a.	n.a.
Dividends Per Share	23.00	23.00	22.00	22.00
Annual Financial Data				
Operating Results (000's)				
Total Revenues	1,816.4	1,748.5	1,786.6	1,511.4
Costs & Expenses	-760.8	-734.9	-756.3	-713.1
Income Before Taxes and Other	1,055.6	1,013.6	1,030.2	798.3
Other Items	n.a.	212.0	n.a.	n.a.
Income Tax	-390.0	-345.0	-323.0	-243.0
Net Income	665.6	880.6	707.2	555.3
Cash Flow From Operations	514.9	582.1	520.0	605.0
Balance Sheet (000's)				
Cash & Equivalents	101.1	51.0	126.5	175.8
Total Current Assets	3,789.9	5,489.3	5,407.9	5,264.2
Fixed Assets, Net	3,846.2	1,501.3	1,454.3	1,462.0
Total Assets	11,119.9	10,477.6	10,350.2	10,215.8
Total Current Liabilities	405.4	371.1	334.7	360.7
Long-Term Debt	n.a.	n.a.	n.a.	n.a.
Stockholders' Equity	8,576.6	8,205.5	7,887.5	7,719.1
Performance & Financial Condition				
Return on Total Revenues %	36.64	50.36	39.59	36.74
Return on Avg Stockholders' Equity %	7.93	10.94	9.06	n.a.
Return on Average Assets %	6.16	8.46	6.88	n.a.
Current Ratio	9.35	14.79	16.16	14.59
Debt / Equity %	n.a.	n.a.	n.a.	n.a.

Compound Growth %'s	EPS %	6.40	Net Income %	6.22	Total Revenues %	6.32

Comments

1994 results reflect a one-time benefit of $212,000 to comply with GAAP in the recording of deferred income taxes. The underlying value of the real property holdings is worthy of investigation.

Officers	Position	Ownership Information	03/31/95
Howard G. Sloane	President	Number of Shares Outstanding	23,809
		Market Capitalization	$ 7,142,700
		Frequency Of Dividends	Quarterly
		Number of Shareholders	Under 500

Other Information

Transfer Agent	United States Trust Company of New York		Where Listed	OTC-PS
Auditor	Eisner & Lubin		Symbol	PKLX
Market Maker	Forbes, Walsh, Kelly & Co, Inc	Telephone (800)221-3747	SIC Code	6510
Broker Dealer	Regular Stockbroker		Employees	8

Pay-O-Matic Corp.

160 Oak Drive • Syosset, NY 11791 • Telephone (516)496-4900 • Fax (516)469-2282

Company Description

The Company provides a wide array of financial and currency services on both the consumer and business levels including check cashing, bill payment, benefits disbursement, armored transport, coin and currency supply and check processing. The Company was formed in 1950.

	12/31/94	12/31/93	12/31/92
Per Share Information			
Stock Price	7.50	12.25	12.25
Earnings Per Share	0.88	1.54	1.59
Price / Earnings Ratio	8.52	7.95	7.70
Book Value Per Share	20.42	19.42	17.87
Price / Book Value %	36.73	63.08	68.55
Dividends Per Share	n.a.	n.a.	n.a.
Annual Financial Data			
Operating Results (000's)			
Total Revenues	32,725.5	32,133.3	30,290.1
Costs & Expenses	-30,948.8	-29,670.5	-27,884.3
Income Before Taxes and Other	1,444.8	2,179.1	2,172.9
Other Items	n.a.	n.a.	n.a.
Income Tax	-873.3	-1,174.0	-1,128.9
Net Income	571.5	1,005.2	1,044.0
Cash Flow From Operations	3,765.4	1,983.0	5,467.0
Balance Sheet (000's)			
Cash & Equivalents	24,395.4	17,220.6	27,880.9
Total Current Assets	29,273.0	22,529.1	32,304.5
Fixed Assets, Net	7,127.3	6,459.6	6,486.3
Total Assets	37,955.4	30,528.4	40,298.2
Total Current Liabilities	24,373.4	17,425.9	27,892.5
Long-Term Debt	479.2	477.2	785.6
Stockholders' Equity	13,102.8	12,625.3	11,620.1
Performance & Financial Condition			
Return on Total Revenues %	1.75	3.13	3.45
Return on Avg Stockholders' Equity %	4.44	8.29	9.41
Return on Average Assets %	1.67	2.84	2.68
Current Ratio	1.20	1.29	1.16
Debt / Equity %	3.66	3.78	6.76

Compound Growth %'s	EPS %	-25.61	Net Income %	-26.01	Total Revenues %	3.94

Comments

1995 results were not released until after we went to press. For a longer term perspective, we report a steady rise in revenues from the 1988 level of $22 million. The Company reacquired 8,452 of its shares in 1994 at about $11 per share. Compound earnings and earnings per share growth may be misleading because they are based on only three years of data.

Officers	Position	Ownership Information	12/31/95
Michael Barone	Chairman, Vice President	Number of Shares Outstanding	641,736
Antoinette Mustafa	Chairman	Market Capitalization	$ 4,813,020
Rayman Mustafa	President	Frequency Of Dividends	n.a.
Murray Wolf	Secretary	Number of Shareholders	Under 500
Stephen Wolf	Treasurer		

Other Information

Transfer Agent	Registrar & Transfer Company			Where Listed	OTC-PS
Auditor	Rothschild,Topal,Miller&Kraft			Symbol	PAYO
Market Maker	Roney & Co.	Telephone	(800)321-2038	SIC Code	7389
Broker Dealer	Regular Stockbroker			Employees	n.a.

Peckham Industries, Inc.

20 Haarlem Avenue • White Plains, NY 10603 • Telephone (914)949-2000 • Fax (914)949-2075

Company Description

The Company is involved in the production and sale of asphaltic concrete, stone and liquid asphalt used in the construction of roads. In addition, a wholly-owned subidiary engages in the leasing of commercial real estate. All businesses are conducted in New York State. The Company acquired stock in January, 1995, for $115 per share, but claims that this was only because it was a large block. Another 2,100 shares were acquired on March 1, 1994 for $65 per share.

	12/31/94	12/31/93	12/31/92
Per Share Information			
Stock Price	75.00	70.00	60.00
Earnings Per Share	10.00	3.00	1.00
Price / Earnings Ratio	7.50	23.33	60.00
Book Value Per Share	163.60	169.90	164.88
Price / Book Value %	45.84	41.20	36.39
Dividends Per Share	0.20	0.15	0.15
Annual Financial Data			
Operating Results (000's)			
Total Revenues	78,756.0	74,769.0	59,629.0
Costs & Expenses	-76,101.0	-73,585.0	-59,925.0
Income Before Taxes and Other	2,655.0	1,184.0	-296.0
Other Items	n.a.	n.a.	n.a.
Income Tax	-659.0	-302.0	474.0
Net Income	1,996.0	882.0	178.0
Cash Flow From Operations	1,652.0	7,854.0	4,470.0
Balance Sheet (000's)			
Cash & Equivalents	694.0	3,431.0	1,069.0
Total Current Assets	20,088.0	19,796.0	18,622.0
Fixed Assets, Net	32,941.0	34,347.0	36,471.0
Total Assets	54,064.0	55,479.0	56,946.0
Total Current Liabilities	10,587.0	11,425.0	11,189.0
Long-Term Debt	7,066.0	9,070.0	11,277.0
Stockholders' Equity	31,162.0	29,734.0	29,150.0
Performance & Financial Condition			
Return on Total Revenues %	2.53	1.18	0.30
Return on Avg Stockholders' Equity %	6.56	3.00	0.61
Return on Average Assets %	3.64	1.57	0.30
Current Ratio	1.90	1.73	1.66
Debt / Equity %	22.68	30.50	38.69

Compound Growth %'s	EPS %	216.23	Net Income %	234.87	Total Revenues %	14.92

Comments

1995 results were not available when we went to press. Sales to state and local government units and agencies usually represent between 25% and 30% of revenues. Compounded earnings and earnings per share growth can be misleading because only three years of information were available and the Company serves the construction industry which can be affected by economic conditions.

Officers	Position	Ownership Information	12/31/94
Janet G. Peckham	Chairman, CEO	Number of Shares Outstanding	175,000
John R. Peckham	President, COO	Market Capitalization	$ 13,125,000
James V. DeForest	Exec VP	Frequency Of Dividends	Annual
Frank J. Franco	Secretary	Number of Shareholders	Under 500
Joseph V. Kuch	Vice President		

Other Information					
Transfer Agent	Company Office			Where Listed	OTC-PS
Auditor	BDO Seidman			Symbol	PCKH
Market Maker	Chicago Corporation, The	Telephone	(312)855-7664	SIC Code	5032
Broker Dealer	Standard Investment	Tel/Ext	(888)783-4688	Jack	Employees	100

Pekin Life Insurance Company

2505 Court Street • Pekin, IL 61558 • Telephone (309)346-1161 • Fax (309)346-8510

Company Description

The Company underwrites various life, medical, group, disability and other insurance policies as well as annuity and retirement programs. Over 1,000 independent agencies, predominately located in Illinois and surrounding states, write policies for Pekin Life. The Company was founded in 1965. The Farmers Automobile Insurance Association and its subsidiary own approximately 49.3% of the Company. In 1993, shares were split 2 for 1. All per share amounts have been adjusted accordingly.

	12/31/95	12/31/94	12/31/93	12/31/92
Per Share Information				
Stock Price	17.50	12.63	8.63	7.57
Earnings Per Share	1.28	0.98	0.81	0.93
Price / Earnings Ratio	13.67	12.89	10.65	8.14
Book Value Per Share	8.46	7.57	6.86	6.36
Price / Book Value %	206.86	166.84	125.80	119.03
Dividends Per Share	0.17	0.16	0.14	0.13
Annual Financial Data				
Operating Results (000's)				
Total Revenues	145,266.4	146,562.3	130,006.1	116,142.6
Costs & Expenses	-127,130.1	-131,680.9	-118,038.8	-102,058.2
Income Before Taxes and Other	18,136.3	14,881.4	11,967.3	14,084.4
Other Items	n.a.	n.a.	n.a.	n.a.
Income Tax	-6,895.7	-6,221.0	-4,838.3	-5,898.2
Net Income	11,240.6	8,660.3	7,129.0	8,186.2
Cash Flow From Operations	37,404.9	43,729.4	31,950.3	30,074.5
Balance Sheet (000's)				
Cash & Equivalents	13,863.8	2,098.1	2,544.5	3,026.8
Total Current Assets	24,105.0	12,528.3	36,350.0	31,799.3
Fixed Assets, Net	22,020.6	2,113.2	2,294.9	2,476.6
Total Assets	391,849.6	343,263.0	300,874.6	268,092.0
Total Current Liabilities	8,267.7	7,143.1	5,698.7	6,556.7
Long-Term Debt	n.a.	n.a.	n.a.	n.a.
Stockholders' Equity	74,446.4	66,584.5	60,372.3	55,933.1
Performance & Financial Condition				
Return on Total Revenues %	7.74	5.91	5.48	7.05
Return on Avg Stockholders' Equity %	15.94	13.64	12.26	15.45
Return on Average Assets %	3.06	2.69	2.51	3.33
Current Ratio	2.92	1.75	6.38	4.85
Debt / Equity %	n.a.	n.a.	n.a.	n.a.

Compound Growth %'s	EPS % 11.24	Net Income % 11.15	Total Revenues % 7.74

Comments

The increase in earnings during 1995 was attributable to a rise in investment income from the larger asset base. The Company intends to expand geographically, especially with its managed care products.

Officers	Position	Ownership Information	12/31/95
Robert W. Scheffler	President, CEO	Number of Shares Outstanding	8,800,000
Ronnie D. Fry	COO	Market Capitalization	$ 154,000,000
Paul A. Tornatore	Senior VP	Frequency Of Dividends	Quarterly
William E. Tunis	Treasurer, Secretary	Number of Shareholders	1,174
Paul R. Weghorst	VP - Sales		

Other Information				
Transfer Agent	Company Office		Where Listed	OTC-BB
Auditor	Norbert Zabinski & Co.		Symbol	PKIN
Market Maker	Monroe Securities, Inc.	Telephone (800)766-5560	SIC Code	6310
Broker Dealer	Pink sheet specialist		Employees	703

Penn Fuel Gas, Inc.

55 South Third Street • Oxford, PA 19363 • Telephone (610)932-2000 • Fax (610)932-5349

Company Description

The Company provides natural gas distribution, transmission and storage services to 70,000 customers from facilities in Pennsylvania and also sells liquefied petroleum gas and merchandise to 28,300 customers in Pennsylvania, Delaware, and Maryland. The Pennsylvania customers are geographically dispersed, covering over half of the counties in the state. The Company has outstanding a cumulative preferred stock which accounts for $10 million of equity. This has been excluded from book value calculations related to the common stock. Earnings per share are earnings after deducting preferred stock dividends.

	12/31/95	12/31/94	12/31/93	12/31/92
Per Share Information				
Stock Price	59.00	57.00	53.50	52.00
Earnings Per Share	7.07	6.55	5.99	2.73
Price / Earnings Ratio	8.35	8.70	8.93	19.05
Book Value Per Share	86.51	81.44	74.89	68.90
Price / Book Value %	68.20	69.99	71.44	75.47
Dividends Per Share	2.00	n.a.	n.a.	n.a.
Annual Financial Data				
Operating Results (000's)				
Total Revenues	106,749.0	123,410.0	115,997.0	105,631.4
Costs & Expenses	-97,827.0	-114,128.0	-107,090.0	-100,758.8
Income Before Taxes and Other	8,922.0	9,147.0	8,907.0	4,872.5
Other Items	378.0	n.a.	n.a.	n.a.
Income Tax	-3,223.0	-3,442.0	-3,602.0	-1,907.4
Net Income	6,077.0	5,705.0	5,305.0	2,965.1
Cash Flow From Operations	12,371.0	17,927.0	15,152.0	3,579.3
Balance Sheet (000's)				
Cash & Equivalents	5,357.0	11,788.0	5,892.0	1,899.8
Total Current Assets	27,437.0	36,744.0	34,306.0	30,812.8
Fixed Assets, Net	132,602.0	122,897.0	115,237.0	108,368.8
Total Assets	184,277.0	174,367.0	159,236.0	147,607.8
Total Current Liabilities	20,482.0	19,376.0	40,702.0	17,102.8
Long-Term Debt	55,644.0	58,904.0	34,995.0	56,359.6
Stockholders' Equity	72,842.0	69,205.0	64,505.0	60,204.3
Performance & Financial Condition				
Return on Total Revenues %	5.69	4.62	4.57	2.81
Return on Avg Stockholders' Equity %	8.56	8.53	8.51	5.01
Return on Average Assets %	3.39	3.42	3.46	2.06
Current Ratio	1.34	1.90	0.84	1.80
Debt / Equity %	76.39	85.12	54.25	93.61

Compound Growth %'s	EPS %	37.33	Net Income %	27.02	Total Revenues %	0.35

Comments

In January, 1995, the Company filed a request for a $5 million rate increase. Action was received in September when a $2.25 million increase was granted. In February, 1996, The Company filed another rate case requesting an $11 million increase on which action is expected by November, 1996. Earnings per share declined from the 1991 level of $3.77 to a low point in 1992 before rebounding. Therefore, compound growth in earnings and earnings per share are probably misleading.

Officers	Position	Ownership Information	12/31/95
Terry H. Hunt	President, CEO	Number of Shares Outstanding	717,583
George C. Rhodes, Sr.	Senior VP	Market Capitalization	$ 42,337,397
Eleanor R. Ross	Secretary	Frequency Of Dividends	Quarterly
Ronald J. Frederick	Vice President	Number of Shareholders	Under 500
Edward L. McCusker	Vice President, Treasurer		

Other Information				
Transfer Agent	Company Office		Where Listed	OTC-BB
Auditor	KPMG Peat Marwick LLP		Symbol	PFUL
Market Maker	S.J. Wolfe & Co.	Telephone (800)262-2244	SIC Code	4924
Broker Dealer	Regular Stockbroker		Employees	750

Pennate Corporation

320 Lexington Avenue • New York, NY 10016 • Telephone (212)889-7676 • Fax (212)779-1451

Company Description

The Company owns property in Brooklyn, New York, and holds equity investments in companies which it works to support. The two equities held at June 30, 1995, were a 5.79% interest in Ages Health Services Inc., a public company, and a 5% interest in Quality Industries, Inc.

	06/30/95	06/30/94	06/30/93	06/30/92
Per Share Information				
Stock Price	0.39	0.40	0.66	0.34
Earnings Per Share	-0.48	-1.01	-0.56	-0.01
Price / Earnings Ratio	n.a.	n.a.	n.a.	n.a.
Book Value Per Share	0.02	0.49	1.43	1.98
Price / Book Value %	1,950.00	81.63	46.15	17.17
Dividends Per Share	n.a.	n.a.	n.a.	n.a.
Annual Financial Data				
Operating Results (000's)				
Total Revenues	220.8	449.2	400.8	495.1
Costs & Expenses	-191.6	-265.3	-402.4	-494.0
Income Before Taxes and Other	-333.2	-846.2	-471.5	-13.0
Other Items	n.a.	n.a.	n.a.	n.a.
Income Tax	-11.0	117.2	49.2	3.0
Net Income	-344.2	-729.0	-422.3	-10.0
Cash Flow From Operations	23.8	9.7	13.9	108.5
Balance Sheet (000's)				
Cash & Equivalents	24.0	21.8	70.7	248.6
Total Current Assets	339.3	582.9	643.9	757.7
Fixed Assets, Net	107.7	126.2	1,954.8	2,530.7
Total Assets	467.6	725.6	2,686.6	3,357.6
Total Current Liabilities	373.3	258.3	1,599.1	1,847.8
Long-Term Debt	n.a.	n.a.	n.a.	n.a.
Stockholders' Equity	11.1	355.4	1,087.5	1,509.8
Performance & Financial Condition				
Return on Total Revenues %	-155.90	-162.28	-105.37	-2.02
Return on Avg Stockholders' Equity %	-187.83	-101.05	-32.52	-0.66
Return on Average Assets %	-57.70	-42.73	-13.97	-0.29
Current Ratio	0.91	2.26	0.40	0.41
Debt / Equity %	n.a.	n.a.	n.a.	n.a.

Compound Growth %'s	EPS % n.a.	Net Income % n.a.	Total Revenues % -23.60

Comments

The Company has been plagued with problems over recent years. Now, with little cash, the Company is the defendant in certain litigation, has a tenant in default and is severely delinquent on property tax payments. Both equity investments have promise if the Company can survive.

Officers	Position	Ownership Information	06/30/95
Kuno Laren	President	Number of Shares Outstanding	723,200
Inga Lamonaca	Secretary	Market Capitalization	$ 282,048
		Frequency Of Dividends	n.a.
		Number of Shareholders	Under 500

Other Information

Transfer Agent	Registrar & Transfer Company			Where Listed	OTC-BB
Auditor	Jerry Goldberg			Symbol	PNNT
Market Maker	R.A. Mackie & Co., Inc.	Telephone	(800)328-1550	SIC Code	6510
Broker Dealer	Standard Investment	Tel/Ext	(888)783-4688 Jack	Employees	1

Penns Woods Bancorp, Inc.

300 Market Street • Williamsport, PA 17703-0967 • Telephone (717)398-2213 • Fax (717)398-2280

Company Description

Penns Woods Bancorp, Inc. is a bank holding company with three wholly-owned subsidiaries; Jersey Shore State Bank, Woods Real Estate Development Co., Inc. and Woods Investment Company, Inc. Jersey Shore State Bank, the principal subsidiary of the Company, is a full-service commercial bank offering standard commercial and consumer banking services through its seven offices located in Clinton and Lycoming Counties, Pennsylvania. Woods Real Estate Development Co., Inc. engages in real estate transactions on behalf of the Company and the Bank. Woods Investment Company, Inc. is engaged in investment activities. The Bank was formed in 1934.

	12/31/95	12/31/94	12/31/93	12/31/92
Per Share Information				
Stock Price	35.75	32.17	27.34	24.56
Earnings Per Share	3.05	2.66	3.14	2.33
Price / Earnings Ratio	11.72	12.09	8.71	10.54
Book Value Per Share	23.35	18.84	17.40	15.14
Price / Book Value %	153.10	170.75	157.13	162.22
Dividends Per Share	1.00	0.79	0.89	0.56
Annual Financial Data				
Operating Results (000's)				
Net Interest Income	10,902.4	9,980.1	9,421.4	7,177.4
Loan Loss Provision	-300.0	-577.0	-791.0	-545.0
Non-Interest Income	2,215.0	2,137.2	2,941.9	1,586.5
Non-Interest Expense	-7,534.1	-6,997.6	-6,097.2	-4,712.8
Income Before Taxes and Other	5,283.2	4,542.7	5,475.0	3,506.1
Other Items	n.a.	n.a.	n.a.	n.a.
Income Tax	-1,421.2	-1,174.1	-1,496.5	-855.9
Net Income	3,862.0	3,368.6	3,978.5	2,650.2
Balance Sheet (000's)				
Cash & Securities	82,993.1	78,850.9	73,210.8	61,220.7
Loans, Net	151,287.2	149,365.4	106,239.4	100,233.1
Fixed Assets, Net	3,808.9	4,068.9	3,416.5	3,475.6
Total Assets	242,628.6	235,637.8	184,901.7	167,008.3
Deposits	202,257.6	190,838.6	144,741.4	140,584.1
Stockholders' Equity	29,684.8	23,839.2	19,447.4	16,955.0
Performance & Financial Condition				
Net Interest Margin	n.a.	n.a.	n.a.	n.a.
Return on Avg Stockholders' Equity %	14.43	15.56	21.86	14.80
Return on Average Assets %	1.62	1.60	2.26	1.34
Equity to Assets %	12.23	10.12	10.52	10.15
Reserve as a % of Non-Performing Loans	130.72	72.05	72.21	64.64

Compound Growth %'s	EPS %	9.39	Net Income %	13.37	Net Interest Income %	14.95

Comments

During 1995, Lock Haven Savings Bank was merged with and into the Company. 102,111 shares of the Company's common stock were issued in exchange for all of the outstanding stock of Lock Haven Savings Bank. The financial statements have been restated to include the accounts and operations of the bank for all periods prior to the merger, except for the 1992 income statement and the 1992 and 1993 balance sheets. There was a 50% stock dividend in 1995 and a 100% stock dividend in 1993. All per share amounts have been restated accordingly. The Company was incorporated in 1983.

Officers	Position	Ownership Information	12/31/95
Theodore H. Reich	Exec VP, CEO	Number of Shares Outstanding	1,271,339
Sonya E. Hartranft	Secretary, Controller	Market Capitalization	$ 45,450,369
Chris B. Ward	Treasurer	Frequency Of Dividends	Quarterly
Ronald A. Walko	Vice President	Number of Shareholders	774
Hubert A. Valencik	Vice President		

Other Information			
Transfer Agent	Company Office	Where Listed	OTC-BB
Auditor	Parente, Randolph, Orlando	Symbol	PWOD
Market Maker	F.J. Morrissey & Co., Inc.	Telephone (800)842-8928	SIC Code	6020
Broker Dealer	Regular Stockbroker	Employees	110

Pennsylvania Manufacturers Corporation

380 Sentry Parkway • Blue Bell, PA 19422-2328 • Telephone (610)397-5068 • Fax (215)665-5061

Company Description

The Company sells property and casualty insurance and reinsurance as well as workers' compensation and other lines of commercial insurance. The Company operates in the Mid-Atlantic and Southern regions, primarily in Pennsylvania and the six contiguous states. The Company was founded in 1916 and boasts 316 consecutive quarterly dividends.

	12/31/95	12/31/94	12/31/93	12/31/92
Per Share Information				
Stock Price	17.00	16.25	13.25	11.25
Earnings Per Share	0.97	2.32	3.37	1.67
Price / Earnings Ratio	17.53	7.00	3.93	6.74
Book Value Per Share	24.45	21.29	22.23	19.34
Price / Book Value %	69.53	76.33	59.60	58.17
Dividends Per Share	0.36	0.36	0.32	0.28
Annual Financial Data				
Operating Results (000's)				
Total Revenues	661,336.0	656,154.0	772,368.0	935,254.0
Costs & Expenses	-626,423.0	-590,774.0	-682,747.0	-895,159.0
Income Before Taxes and Other	34,913.0	65,380.0	89,621.0	40,095.0
Other Items	n.a.	n.a.	14,119.0	n.a.
Income Tax	-10,783.0	-8,130.0	-21,324.0	671.0
Net Income	24,130.0	57,250.0	82,416.0	40,766.0
Cash Flow From Operations	15,913.0	2,294.0	479.0	-42,294.0
Balance Sheet (000's)				
Cash & Equivalents	9,170.0	13,150.0	1,147.0	7,302.0
Total Current Assets	599,978.0	614,732.0	605,711.0	645,072.0
Fixed Assets, Net	56,649.0	68,071.0	68,792.0	55,953.0
Total Assets	3,258,572.0	3,181,979.0	3,197,909.0	3,142,821.0
Total Current Liabilities	301,465.0	289,026.0	2,358,150.0	2,387,618.0
Long-Term Debt	203,848.0	203,975.0	194,836.0	185,684.0
Stockholders' Equity	609,668.0	524,862.0	534,383.0	468,105.0
Performance & Financial Condition				
Return on Total Revenues %	3.65	8.73	10.67	4.36
Return on Avg Stockholders' Equity %	4.25	10.81	16.44	8.93
Return on Average Assets %	0.75	1.79	2.60	1.33
Current Ratio	1.99	2.13	0.26	0.27
Debt / Equity %	33.44	38.86	36.46	39.67

Compound Growth %'s	EPS %	-16.56	Net Income %	-16.04	Total Revenues %	-10.91

Comments

GAAP requires that the unrealized gains on investments be reflected in shareholders' equity, but not the income statement. Management correctly indicates that equity per share increased $3.16 in 1995 due to the excellent performance of the bond market. 1993 results reflect a nonrecurring benefit of $14 million, or $.58 per share, which is primarily related to GAAP for the reporting of income taxes.

Officers	Position	Ownership Information	12/31/95
Frederick W. Anton III	Chairman, CEO	Number of Shares Outstanding	23,877,248
John W. Smithson	President, COO	Market Capitalization	$ 405,913,216
Francis W. McDonnell	Senior VP, CFO	Frequency Of Dividends	Quarterly
Robert L. Pratter	Secretary	Number of Shareholders	Under 500
Douglas M. Moe	Treasurer		

Other Information				
Transfer Agent	Chemical Mellon Shareholder Services		Where Listed	OTC-BB
Auditor	Coopers & Lybrand LLP		Symbol	PMFRA
Market Maker	Herzog, Heine, Geduld, Inc.	Telephone (800)221-3600	SIC Code	6330
Broker Dealer	Regular Stockbroker		Employees	100

Peoples Savings Bank of Troy

635 South Market Street • Troy, OH 45373 • Telephone (513)339-5000 • Fax (513)339-3297

Company Description

Peoples Savings Bank of Troy primarily makes loans for the purchase, construction and improvement of real estate by using funds from savings deposits made by the general public. It operates three banking offices in Troy, Ohio. During 1994, its wholly owned subsidiary, Peoples Building and Savings Service Corporation, completed its sole activity, the development of a fourteen unit condominium project. Savings Service Corporation had no activity in 1995 and no future activities are planned. The Bank was chartered in 1890 as an Ohio mutual building and savings bank. During 1989, the Bank completed a successful stock conversion, which raised $2.991 million, with 373,943 shares issued at $8 per share.

	06/30/95	06/30/94	06/30/93	06/30/92
Per Share Information				
Stock Price	9.75	7.32	8.17	2.29
Earnings Per Share	1.37	1.44	1.11	0.35
Price / Earnings Ratio	7.12	5.08	7.36	6.54
Book Value Per Share	8.67	7.35	5.92	4.85
Price / Book Value %	112.46	99.59	138.01	47.22
Dividends Per Share	0.04	0.04	0.05	0.03
Annual Financial Data				
Operating Results (000's)				
Net Interest Income	4,615.7	4,483.2	4,099.0	3,531.3
Loan Loss Provision	n.a.	n.a.	-55.0	-312.0
Non-Interest Income	405.4	447.4	428.0	358.0
Non-Interest Expense	-2,587.9	-2,649.8	-2,536.8	-2,805.2
Income Before Taxes and Other	2,433.3	2,280.8	1,935.2	772.1
Other Items	n.a.	250.0	n.a.	n.a.
Income Tax	-747.3	-775.5	-626.0	-363.0
Net Income	1,686.0	1,755.3	1,309.2	409.1
Balance Sheet (000's)				
Cash & Securities	8,837.9	3,513.0	16,112.2	21,124.1
Loans, Net	88,300.4	85,940.3	80,203.5	80,111.3
Fixed Assets, Net	2,931.2	2,741.9	2,847.8	3,062.0
Total Assets	102,162.5	93,825.5	100,792.8	106,650.7
Deposits	85,174.1	81,686.5	89,932.6	99,927.6
Stockholders' Equity	10,396.3	8,711.6	6,988.9	5,715.1
Performance & Financial Condition				
Net Interest Margin	n.a.	n.a.	n.a.	n.a.
Return on Avg Stockholders' Equity %	17.65	22.36	20.61	7.44
Return on Average Assets %	1.72	1.80	1.26	0.38
Equity to Assets %	10.18	9.28	6.93	5.36
Reserve as a % of Non-Performing Loans	393.89	153.27	n.a.	n.a.

Compound Growth %'s	EPS %	57.60	Net Income %	60.33	Net Interest Income %	9.34

Comments

The loan portfolio is heavily concentrated in real estate mortgages which represent 87% of total loans. The returns on equity and returns on assets are some of the highest we have seen. These have been consistent for three years with strong growth rates as well. Compounded earnings and earnings per share growth is excellent but maybe not as good as calculated because of low earnings in 1992, the base year.

Officers	Position	Ownership Information	06/30/95
Ronald B. Scott	President, CEO	Number of Shares Outstanding	1,199,092
William B. Whidden	Senior VP, Treasurer	Market Capitalization	$ 11,691,147
Mark A. Douglas	Vice President, Senior Loan Officer	Frequency Of Dividends	Semi-Annual
Bea M. Jones	Vice President, Secretary	Number of Shareholders	604
Richard K. Bender	Vice President		

Other Information

Transfer Agent	Company Office		Where Listed	OTC-BB
Auditor	KPMG Peat Marwick LLP		Symbol	PESV
Market Maker	S.J. Wolfe & Co.	Telephone (513)273-1626	SIC Code	6020
Broker Dealer	Regular Stockbroker		Employees	41

Performance Nutrition, Inc.

3230 Commander Drive • Carrollton, TX 75006 • Telephone (214)250-2274 • Fax (214)931-0203

Company Description

The Company is in the business of designing and marketing high performance nutritional supplements to the athletic, health and wellness markets. The Company's customers consist of professional, college, and high school sports teams as well as physicians, health professionals and regional retailers.

	09/30/95	09/30/94	09/30/93
Per Share Information			
Stock Price	3.00	1.15	2.75
Earnings Per Share	0.12	-0.14	-0.02
Price / Earnings Ratio	25.00	n.a.	n.a.
Book Value Per Share	n.a.	0.04	-0.01
Price / Book Value %	n.a.	2,875.00	n.a.
Dividends Per Share	n.a.	n.a.	n.a.
Annual Financial Data			
Operating Results (000's)			
Total Revenues	4,211.1	2,709.2	762.5
Costs & Expenses	-3,186.2	-3,884.7	-935.8
Income Before Taxes and Other	1,025.0	-1,175.5	-173.2
Other Items	n.a.	n.a.	n.a.
Income Tax	n.a.	n.a.	n.a.
Net Income	1,025.0	-1,175.5	-173.2
Cash Flow From Operations	n.a.	-992.9	-19.6
Balance Sheet (000's)			
Cash & Equivalents	n.a.	235.4	3.5
Total Current Assets	n.a.	515.9	95.2
Fixed Assets, Net	n.a.	698.4	19.3
Total Assets	n.a.	1,476.5	240.4
Total Current Liabilities	n.a.	657.5	316.5
Long-Term Debt	n.a.	440.1	n.a.
Stockholders' Equity	n.a.	378.9	-76.1
Performance & Financial Condition			
Return on Total Revenues %	24.34	-43.39	-22.72
Return on Avg Stockholders' Equity %	n.a.	-776.28	n.a.
Return on Average Assets %	n.a.	-136.93	n.a.
Current Ratio	n.a.	0.78	0.30
Debt / Equity %	n.a.	116.15	n.a.

Compound Growth %'s	EPS % n.a.	Net Income % n.a.	Total Revenues % 135.00

Comments

Fast growth enabled the Company to show a profit in the most recent full year and management projects earnings of $.34 per share for the current year. The Company continues to expand on its product lines. However, none of the financial statements were audited according to the Company's spokesperson. Furthermore, there was not a balance sheet as of the year ended September 30, 1995, available for distribution even though earnings were already released.

Officers	Position	Ownership Information	09/30/95
Gary V. ewellyn	Chairman, President	Number of Shares Outstanding	n.a.
Tamra A. Halling	Secretary, Treasurer	Market Capitalization	n.a.
Robert Corliss	Director	Frequency Of Dividends	n.a.
W. Durwood Gordon, Jr.	Director	Number of Shareholders	Under 500
Rudy D. Beck	Director		

Other Information

Transfer Agent	American Registrar and Transfer Company			Where Listed	OTC-BB
Auditor	Not indicated			Symbol	PFNT
Market Maker	Coastal Securities Ltd.	Telephone	(214)979-0600	SIC Code	2833
Broker Dealer	Regular stockbroker			Employees	20

Petaluma, Bank of

1321 Commerce, Suite G • Petaluma, CA 94954 • Telephone (707)765-2222 • Fax (707)765-4568

Company Description

Bank of Petaluma commenced business as a state-chartered commercial bank in 1987. It is primarily locally owned and serves the banking needs in the Northern California community of Petaluma and surrounding areas. Local businesses include retailing, professional service organizations, real estate, vineyards and the dairy and poultry industries.

	12/31/95	12/31/94	12/31/93	12/31/92
Per Share Information				
Stock Price	14.00	12.00	10.75	10.75
Earnings Per Share	1.76	0.86	0.76	1.05
Price / Earnings Ratio	7.95	13.95	14.14	10.24
Book Value Per Share	15.28	12.84	12.25	11.48
Price / Book Value %	91.62	93.46	87.76	93.64
Dividends Per Share	0.15	0.10	n.a.	n.a.
Annual Financial Data				
Operating Results (000's)				
Net Interest Income	4,834.7	3,637.8	2,768.3	2,528.8
Loan Loss Provision	-312.9	-246.9	-120.0	-120.0
Non-Interest Income	941.4	517.6	433.6	323.3
Non-Interest Expense	-4,194.4	-3,452.5	-2,704.5	-2,085.0
Income Before Taxes and Other	1,268.8	456.0	377.4	647.1
Other Items	n.a.	n.a.	n.a.	n.a.
Income Tax	-281.0	-4.6	-25.0	-158.1
Net Income	987.8	451.4	352.4	489.0
Balance Sheet (000's)				
Cash & Securities	49,331.0	41,779.0	21,602.5	21,167.6
Loans, Net	56,903.0	48,186.7	40,512.0	31,108.8
Fixed Assets, Net	1,720.4	1,727.6	1,183.2	384.0
Total Assets	111,866.4	95,683.6	65,764.9	54,880.8
Deposits	91,137.9	82,767.7	57,763.4	47,394.0
Stockholders' Equity	8,583.8	7,210.1	5,665.8	5,313.4
Performance & Financial Condition				
Net Interest Margin	5.49	5.57	5.57	5.61
Return on Avg Stockholders' Equity %	12.51	7.01	6.42	9.65
Return on Average Assets %	0.95	0.56	0.58	0.97
Equity to Assets %	7.67	7.54	8.62	9.68
Reserve as a % of Non-Performing Loans	1041.67	317.52	95.82	112.78

Compound Growth %'s	EPS %	18.79	Net Income %	26.41	Net Interest Income %	24.11

Comments

The Bank's loan portfolio is made up primarily of real estate and commercial loans, totalling 57% and 26%, respectively. The 1993 dip in earnings was never explained in the annual reports. There was branch acquisition activity at the time that might have accounted for a portion of the decline. 1995 results showed a strong rebound and a double-digit return on equity.

Officers	Position	Ownership Information	12/31/95
Daniel G. Libarle	Chairman	Number of Shares Outstanding	561,738
Walter E. Bragdon	President, CEO	Market Capitalization	$ 7,864,332
Donald J. Morris	Exec VP, Other	Frequency Of Dividends	Irregular
Arlene A. Brians	Senior VP, COO	Number of Shareholders	672
Pat Wasik	Secretary		

Other Information

Transfer Agent	U.S. Stock Transfer Corporation			Where Listed	OTC-BB
Auditor	Richardson & Company			Symbol	BPLU
Market Maker	Hoefer & Arnett, Inc.	Telephone	(415)362-7111	SIC Code	6020
Broker Dealer	Regular Stockbroker			Employees	75

Pharmaceutical Laboratories, Inc.

1229 West Corporate Drive • Arlington, TX 76006 • Telephone (817)633-1461 • Fax (817)633-8146

Company Description

The Company develops, produces and markets sublingual (under the tongue) vitamin and nutritional products in liquid form. The Company plans to create, develop and expand new vitamin and nutritional products for national distribution. There was a name change in 1992 from Sublingual Products International to the current name.

	12/31/95	12/31/94	12/31/93
Per Share Information			
Stock Price	1.62	1.00	1.75
Earnings Per Share	0.06	0.06	-0.13
Price / Earnings Ratio	27.00	16.67	n.a.
Book Value Per Share	0.20	n.a.	-0.07
Price / Book Value %	810.00	n.a.	n.a.
Dividends Per Share	n.a.	n.a.	n.a.
Annual Financial Data			
Operating Results (000's)			
Total Revenues	4,578.8	3,365.1	2,807.1
Costs & Expenses	-4,207.2	-2,942.5	-3,701.9
Income Before Taxes and Other	371.7	422.6	-894.7
Other Items	n.a.	n.a.	n.a.
Income Tax	74.8	n.a.	n.a.
Net Income	446.4	422.6	-894.7
Cash Flow From Operations	-633.6	157.3	-317.5
Balance Sheet (000's)			
Cash & Equivalents	63.0	149.0	74.8
Total Current Assets	2,566.9	1,038.5	591.8
Fixed Assets, Net	961.9	113.3	488.6
Total Assets	3,654.0	1,151.8	1,080.4
Total Current Liabilities	1,541.8	1,170.6	1,130.3
Long-Term Debt	592.0	10.2	463.4
Stockholders' Equity	1,508.3	-29.1	-513.4
Performance & Financial Condition			
Return on Total Revenues %	9.75	12.56	-31.87
Return on Avg Stockholders' Equity %	60.36	n.a.	n.a.
Return on Average Assets %	18.58	37.87	-127.82
Current Ratio	1.66	0.89	0.52
Debt / Equity %	39.25	n.a.	n.a.

Compound Growth %'s	EPS % 0.00	Net Income % 5.63	Total Revenues % 27.72

Comments

1994 results marked the first year for a healthy income and positive cash flow. Cash flow pressures were greatly relieved as well. In 1995, positive results continued. The financial ratios were further aided by the conversion of shareholder notes to common stock and the placement of $592,000 of long term debt. During 1995, the Company also acquired real estate and equipment valued at $802,000 by issuing 300,000 shares of restricted common stock and assuming a mortgage obligation of approximately $202,000.

Officers	Position	Ownership Information	12/31/95
Jerry McClure	President, CEO	Number of Shares Outstanding	7,606,100
Dona Efflandt	Secretary	Market Capitalization	$ 12,321,882
		Frequency Of Dividends	n.a.
		Number of Shareholders	Under 500

Other Information			
Transfer Agent	Interwest Transfer Co., Inc.	Where Listed	OTC-BB
Auditor	Weaver and Tidwell	Symbol	PHLB
Market Maker	Frankel (WM.V.) & Co., Inc. Telephone (800)631-3091	SIC Code	2833
Broker Dealer	Regular Stockbroker	Employees	20

Phil-Good Products Incorporated

3500 West Reno Avenue • Oklahoma City, OK 73107-6136 • Telephone (405)942-5527 • Fax (405)942-8002

Company Description

The Company specializes in the manufacture of precision custom molding plastics. The majority of customers are located in the southwest United States with Little Giant Pump Company as a major account. The Company was organized and incorporated in 1959. The Company is buying back stock in an effort to avoid becoming an SEC reporting company.

	06/30/95	06/30/94	06/30/93	06/30/92
Per Share Information				
Stock Price	1.12	0.44	0.31	0.31
Earnings Per Share	0.31	0.18	0.12	0.11
Price / Earnings Ratio	3.61	2.44	2.58	2.82
Book Value Per Share	2.39	1.89	1.56	1.42
Price / Book Value %	46.86	23.28	19.87	21.83
Dividends Per Share	0.10	n.a.	0.10	0.10
Annual Financial Data				
Operating Results (000's)				
Total Revenues	5,056.7	3,939.6	3,678.2	2,986.8
Costs & Expenses	-4,671.0	-3,703.4	-3,512.1	-2,827.6
Income Before Taxes and Other	385.7	236.2	166.1	159.2
Other Items	n.a.	n.a.	n.a.	n.a.
Income Tax	-145.8	-83.9	-54.1	-51.0
Net Income	239.9	152.3	112.0	108.2
Cash Flow From Operations	458.4	90.0	239.4	255.7
Balance Sheet (000's)				
Cash & Equivalents	280.8	177.7	158.8	105.2
Total Current Assets	1,134.7	846.2	705.7	574.1
Fixed Assets, Net	842.9	935.1	484.6	389.4
Total Assets	2,005.2	1,806.2	1,212.9	984.1
Total Current Liabilities	440.9	327.6	368.8	268.3
Long-Term Debt	430.5	598.4	126.9	63.0
Stockholders' Equity	1,133.8	880.2	717.2	652.9
Performance & Financial Condition				
Return on Total Revenues %	4.74	3.87	3.04	3.62
Return on Avg Stockholders' Equity %	23.83	19.07	16.35	17.52
Return on Average Assets %	12.59	10.09	10.20	11.79
Current Ratio	2.57	2.58	1.91	2.14
Debt / Equity %	37.97	67.98	17.70	9.64

Compound Growth %'s	EPS %	41.25	Net Income %	30.42	Total Revenues %	19.18

Comments

The Company, although small, grew at a compound growth rate of over 40% over the last three years. This performance is better than the message to shareholders from the Company's president in which he refers to all supporters of the current Administration as "nincompoops". We cannot comment on the latter but are thankful that the numbers are audited.

Officers	Position	Ownership Information	06/30/95
Walter J. Phillips	President	Number of Shares Outstanding	473,590
Dale H. Roberts	Exec VP	Market Capitalization	$ 530,421
Peggy L. Phillips	Secretary, Treasurer	Frequency Of Dividends	Irregular
Virginia L. Phillips	Vice President	Number of Shareholders	Under 500

Other Information

Transfer Agent	Company Office		Where Listed	OTC-PS
Auditor	William J.Garner, Inc.		Symbol	PHGD
Market Maker	R.A. Mackie & Co., Inc.	Telephone (800)328-1550	SIC Code	3080
Broker Dealer	Regular Stockbroker		Employees	40

Pioneer Communications, Inc.

140 North Monroe • Lancaster, WI 53813 • Telephone (608)723-4140 • Fax (608)723-2410

Company Description

The Company provides telecommunications services to southwestern Grant County, Wisconsin. A telephone directory division publishes directories for various telephone companies throughout Wisconsin, Minnesota and Iowa. The Company was formed in 1987 for the purpose of acquiring and operating communications related companies.

	12/31/95	12/31/94	12/31/93	12/31/92
Per Share Information				
Stock Price	38.50	34.56	31.45	28.02
Earnings Per Share	6.62	6.08	6.42	5.44
Price / Earnings Ratio	5.82	5.68	4.90	5.15
Book Value Per Share	38.52	34.56	31.45	28.02
Price / Book Value %	100.00	100.00	100.00	100.00
Dividends Per Share	3.50	3.25	3.25	3.25
Annual Financial Data				
Operating Results (000's)				
Total Revenues	6,104.2	5,705.6	5,782.6	5,132.0
Costs & Expenses	-4,285.2	-3,864.2	-3,843.2	-3,696.7
Income Before Taxes and Other	1,818.9	1,640.4	1,758.6	1,435.3
Other Items	n.a.	n.a.	n.a.	n.a.
Income Tax	-671.9	-641.0	-703.8	-541.4
Net Income	1,147.0	999.4	1,054.9	893.9
Cash Flow From Operations	2,007.1	n.a.	n.a.	n.a.
Balance Sheet (000's)				
Cash & Equivalents	659.9	1,090.8	832.7	635.9
Total Current Assets	5,155.5	4,211.6	4,331.9	3,020.3
Fixed Assets, Net	5,853.3	6,115.6	5,105.4	5,437.2
Total Assets	11,333.0	10,728.7	9,897.6	8,732.1
Total Current Liabilities	1,003.9	931.5	755.7	735.6
Long-Term Debt	3,453.7	3,609.2	3,551.6	3,106.5
Stockholders' Equity	6,329.6	5,680.1	5,167.8	4,604.9
Performance & Financial Condition				
Return on Total Revenues %	18.79	17.52	18.24	17.42
Return on Avg Stockholders' Equity %	19.10	18.43	21.59	20.31
Return on Average Assets %	10.40	9.69	11.32	10.37
Current Ratio	5.14	4.52	5.73	4.11
Debt / Equity %	54.56	63.54	68.73	67.46

Compound Growth %'s	EPS %	6.76	Net Income %	8.67	Total Revenues %	5.95

Comments

The Company benefits from the size of its divisions, as they are considered to be small telecommunications utilities subject to reduced regulation which allows greater flexibility in regulatory matters. Temporary investments of $2.6 million are included in current assets and are immediately accessible.

Officers	Position	Ownership Information	12/31/95
Douglas Timmerman	President	Number of Shares Outstanding	164,340
G. Burton Bloch	Secretary	Market Capitalization	$ 6,330,377
Edward J. Neckvatal	Treasurer	Frequency Of Dividends	Annual
Mark V. Brickl	Vice President	Number of Shareholders	1,000
Gerald Knapp	Vice President		

Other Information					
Transfer Agent	Company Office			Where Listed	Order Matching Only
Auditor	Kiesling & Associates			Symbol	n.a.
Market Maker	None			SIC Code	4810
Broker Dealer	Standard Investment	Tel/Ext	(888)783-4688 Jack	Employees	40

Pioneer Railcorp

1318 S. Johanson Rd. • Peoria, IL 61607 • Telephone (309)697-1400 • Fax (309)697-1677

Company Description

The Company is the parent company of eight active short-line common carrier railroad operations (the Company's primary business), an equipment leasing company, an aircraft subsidiary, and a service company. The Company and its subsidiaries operate in Alabama, Arkansas, Illinois, Michigan, Minnesota, Mississippi and Tennessee. As of March 26, 1996, officers and directors, as a group, owned 44.3% of the Company's outstanding shares. The Company was incorporated in Iowa in 1986.

	12/31/95	12/31/94	12/31/93	12/31/92
Per Share Information				
Stock Price	2.69	2.71	2.10	n.a.
Earnings Per Share	0.10	0.08	0.04	0.04
Price / Earnings Ratio	26.90	33.88	52.50	n.a.
Book Value Per Share	0.66	0.43	0.28	0.21
Price / Book Value %	407.58	630.23	750.00	n.a.
Dividends Per Share	n.a.	n.a.	n.a.	n.a.
Annual Financial Data				
Operating Results (000's)				
Total Revenues	8,580.4	6,369.7	4,947.1	3,167.4
Costs & Expenses	-7,672.0	-5,509.3	-4,592.4	-3,055.6
Income Before Taxes and Other	1,081.6	914.7	606.3	274.3
Other Items	-124.4	-125.2	-155.0	n.a.
Income Tax	-495.4	-398.5	-207.0	-94.0
Net Income	461.7	390.9	244.3	180.3
Cash Flow From Operations	1,442.1	1,770.5	800.1	214.0
Balance Sheet (000's)				
Cash & Equivalents	276.2	179.4	45.5	166.4
Total Current Assets	2,056.7	1,464.2	1,106.3	1,013.9
Fixed Assets, Net	15,220.2	10,228.4	7,051.9	4,558.1
Total Assets	17,923.9	12,296.8	8,172.5	5,581.8
Total Current Liabilities	2,980.3	2,320.0	1,463.2	1,005.6
Long-Term Debt	9,934.7	6,470.7	4,084.2	2,893.0
Stockholders' Equity	2,970.9	1,806.2	2,344.0	1,642.3
Performance & Financial Condition				
Return on Total Revenues %	5.38	6.14	4.94	5.69
Return on Avg Stockholders' Equity %	19.33	18.84	12.25	14.10
Return on Average Assets %	3.06	3.82	3.55	4.87
Current Ratio	0.69	0.63	0.76	1.01
Debt / Equity %	334.41	358.24	174.24	176.15

Compound Growth %'s	EPS %	12.62	Net Income %	36.82	Total Revenues %	39.40

Comments

A substantial portion of the Company's assets consists of property and equipment. These assets include railcars, locomotives, land and road beds, buildings and equipment and the real property easement rights associated with the railway. In 1995, The Company purchased 30 railcars and six locomotives. Also during 1995, several stock transactions and a 2 for 1 stock split occurred. Per share amounts have been restated to reflect these transactions.

Officers	Position	Ownership Information	12/31/95
Guy L. Brenkman	Chairman, President	Number of Shares Outstanding	4,487,881
Daniel A. LaKemper	Secretary	Market Capitalization	$ 12,072,400
John P. Wolk	Treasurer	Frequency Of Dividends	n.a.
		Number of Shareholders	1,753

Other Information			
Transfer Agent	Company Office	Where Listed	CE
Auditor	McGladrey & Pullen LLP	Symbol	PRR
Market Maker	Paragon Capital Corporation	Telephone (212)785-4700	SIC Code	4013
Broker Dealer	Regular Stockbroker	Employees	70

Pocahontas Bankshares Corporation

P.O.Box 1559 • Bluefield, WV 24701 • Telephone (304)325-8181 • Fax (304)325-3727

Company Description

Pocahontas Bankshares Corporation is a multi-bank, interstate bank holding company, headquartered in Bluefield, West Virginia. Its two subsidiaries, First Century Bank, N.A. and First Century Bank, Virginia, operate eight branches in southern West Virginia and southwestern Virginia. The Bank's primary source of revenue is derived from loans to customers who are predominately small to medium-size businesses and middle income individuals. It began active operations in 1984.

	12/31/95	12/31/94	12/31/93	12/31/92
Per Share Information				
Stock Price	30.88	28.00	21.00	16.25
Earnings Per Share	2.41	2.26	1.55	1.71
Price / Earnings Ratio	12.81	12.39	13.55	9.50
Book Value Per Share	23.19	21.16	20.37	19.65
Price / Book Value %	133.16	132.33	103.09	82.70
Dividends Per Share	1.10	1.00	0.88	0.85
Annual Financial Data				
Operating Results (000's)				
Net Interest Income	11,605.0	10,914.0	9,387.0	9,285.0
Loan Loss Provision	-839.0	-395.0	-459.0	-698.0
Non-Interest Income	1,551.0	1,703.0	1,682.0	1,505.0
Non-Interest Expense	-8,561.0	-8,985.0	-8,600.0	-7,799.0
Income Before Taxes and Other	3,756.0	3,237.0	2,010.0	2,293.0
Other Items	n.a.	n.a.	123.0	n.a.
Income Tax	-1,342.0	-980.0	-586.0	-588.0
Net Income	2,414.0	2,257.0	1,547.0	1,705.0
Balance Sheet (000's)				
Cash & Securities	78,992.0	81,672.0	76,545.0	80,865.0
Loans, Net	175,649.0	169,340.0	175,473.0	156,141.0
Fixed Assets, Net	5,417.0	4,811.0	4,640.0	3,714.0
Total Assets	265,980.0	261,299.0	261,974.0	247,030.0
Deposits	232,172.0	230,882.0	229,451.0	214,716.0
Stockholders' Equity	23,186.0	21,161.0	20,366.0	19,644.0
Performance & Financial Condition				
Net Interest Margin	n.a.	n.a.	n.a.	n.a.
Return on Avg Stockholders' Equity %	10.89	10.87	7.73	8.84
Return on Average Assets %	0.92	0.86	0.61	0.70
Equity to Assets %	8.72	8.10	7.77	7.95
Reserve as a % of Non-Performing Loans	53.96	94.52	87.35	82.57

Compound Growth %'s	EPS % 12.12	Net Income % 12.29	Net Interest Income % 7.72

Comments

All share and per share data has been restated to reflect a 1994 two-for-one stock split. The loan portfolio is concentrated in residential real estate mortgages, which represent 57% of total loans. It is hard to ascertain a reason for the only moderate growth, although we do note the inching up to good return on equity and return on asset ratios. These last few years have generally been very favorable to the banking industry.

Officers	Position	Ownership Information	12/31/95
B. L. Jackson, Jr.	Chairman	Number of Shares Outstanding	1,000,000
R.W. "Buz" Wilkinson	President, CEO	Market Capitalization	$ 30,880,000
Charles A. Peters	Secretary	Frequency Of Dividends	Quarterly
J. Ronald Hypes	Treasurer	Number of Shareholders	593
W. E. Albert	Other		

Other Information			
Transfer Agent	Company Office	Where Listed	OTC-BB
Auditor	Coopers & Lybrand LLP	Symbol	PCHB
Market Maker	Ryan, Beck & Co.	Telephone (800)325-7926	SIC Code	6020
Broker Dealer	Regular Stockbroker	Employees	127

Pocono Hotels Corporation

1209 Orange Street • Wilmington, DE 19801 • Telephone (717)226-4506 • Fax (717)226-4697

Company Description

The Company is a holding company whose subsidiary owns and operates a resort in Skytop, Pennsylvania. The subsidiary also develops and sells cluster homes. The Company was formed in 1925. The occupancy rate, while getting better, was less than 50% for the past several years. There are discussions regarding the possible legalization of gambling in the area. The resort could clearly benefit from this taking place.

	12/31/95	12/31/94	12/31/93	12/31/92
Per Share Information				
Stock Price	95.75	55.00	60.00	45.00
Earnings Per Share	-2.49	3.60	-19.39	16.25
Price / Earnings Ratio	n.a.	15.28	n.a.	2.77
Book Value Per Share	139.68	142.19	132.82	149.33
Price / Book Value %	68.55	38.68	45.17	30.13
Dividends Per Share	n.a.	n.a.	n.a.	n.a.
Annual Financial Data				
Operating Results (000's)				
Total Revenues	9,396.4	9,659.8	9,276.8	9,363.7
Costs & Expenses	-9,294.3	-9,442.1	-9,522.8	-9,409.7
Income Before Taxes and Other	102.1	217.6	-246.0	-46.0
Other Items	n.a.	n.a.	68.4	471.1
Income Tax	-60.6	-116.3	53.2	-199.7
Net Income	41.5	101.3	-124.3	225.4
Cash Flow From Operations	110.2	1,054.6	750.1	257.4
Balance Sheet (000's)				
Cash & Equivalents	222.7	862.3	183.4	790.0
Total Current Assets	1,063.2	1,464.7	830.9	1,474.3
Fixed Assets, Net	3,535.2	3,549.3	3,822.6	3,465.4
Total Assets	5,471.3	5,422.1	5,355.9	6,211.2
Total Current Liabilities	974.8	828.7	763.3	1,482.8
Long-Term Debt	n.a.	n.a.	n.a.	n.a.
Stockholders' Equity	4,362.1	4,443.3	4,408.0	4,570.1
Performance & Financial Condition				
Return on Total Revenues %	0.44	1.05	-1.34	2.41
Return on Avg Stockholders' Equity %	0.94	2.29	-2.77	5.04
Return on Average Assets %	0.76	1.88	-2.15	3.81
Current Ratio	1.09	1.77	1.09	0.99
Debt / Equity %	n.a.	n.a.	n.a.	n.a.

Compound Growth %'s	EPS % n.a.	Net Income % -43.13	Total Revenues % 0.12

Comments

The Company has 9,423 shares of $100 par value, 7% cumulative preferred stock outstanding. Income (loss) per common share is calculated after deducting dividends paid on the preferred stock. Preferred stock dividend arrearage at December 31, 1995, amounted to $2.1 million.

Officers	Position	Ownership Information	12/31/95
Stewart F. Campbell	Chairman, CEO	Number of Shares Outstanding	9,812
John B. Hogan	Secretary	Market Capitalization	$ 939,499
Donald H. Miller	Treasurer	Frequency Of Dividends	n.a.
John B. Campbell	Vice President	Number of Shareholders	9,812
Richard L. Price, Jr.	Vice President		

Other Information

Transfer Agent	Company Office		Where Listed	OTC-BB
Auditor	KPMG Peat Marwick LLP		Symbol	PHTL
Market Maker	Forbes, Walsh, Kelly & Co, Inc	Telephone (800)221-3747	SIC Code	7011
Broker Dealer	Regular Stockbroker		Employees	220

Polaris Aircraft Income Fund II

201 Mission Street, 27th floor • San Francisco, CA 94105 • Telephone (415)284-7440 • Fax (415)284-7450

Company Description

The Partnership owns and leases commercial jet aircraft. Of the 30 aircraft originally acquired, 23 remained at the end of 1995. The Partnership was formed in 1984 and will terminate no later than December, 2010. The officers listed are those of the general partner, Polaris Investment Management Corporation.

	12/31/95	12/31/94	12/31/93	12/31/92
Per Unit Information				
Price Per Unit	58.00	38.00	55.40	n.a.
Earnings Per Unit	9.94	-8.87	-1.91	n.a.
Price / Earnings Ratio	5.84	n.a.	n.a.	n.a.
Book Value Per Unit	215.02	218.82	252.69	n.a.
Price / Book Value %	26.97	17.37	21.92	n.a.
Distributions Per Unit	13.75	25.00	20.00	n.a.
Cash Flow Per Unit	33.43	15.08	19.11	n.a.
Annual Financial Data				
Operating Results (000's)				
Total Revenues	21,093.3	14,443.9	15,558.9	17,990.2
Costs & Expenses	-15,376.3	-17,661.1	-15,510.8	-19,699.2
Operating Income	5,717.1	-3,217.2	48.1	-1,709.0
Other Items	n.a.	n.a.	n.a.	n.a.
Net Income	5,717.1	-3,217.2	48.1	-1,709.0
Cash Flow From Operations	16,712.6	7,541.5	12,139.9	17,781.4
Balance Sheet (000's)				
Cash & Equivalents	25,884.7	14,662.1	97.5	4.8
Total Current Assets	28,623.7	15,802.8	22,482.8	20,224.1
Investments In Aircraft	76,487.4	91,954.4	104,927.6	118,790.8
Total Assets	107,820.3	110,568.4	129,706.5	141,436.9
Total Current Liabilities	179.9	741.5	2,608.6	1,255.5
Long-Term Debt	n.a.	n.a.	n.a.	n.a.
Partners' Capital	106,368.5	108,290.3	125,396.3	136,459.2
Performance & Financial Condition				
Return on Total Revenues %	27.10	-22.27	0.31	-9.50
Return on Average Partners' Capital %	n.a.	n.a.	n.a.	n.a.
Return on Average Assets %	n.a.	n.a.	n.a.	n.a.
Current Ratio	159.14	21.31	8.62	16.11
Debt / Equity %	n.a.	n.a.	n.a.	n.a.

Compound Growth %'s	EPU % n.a.	Net Income % n.a.	Total Revenues % n.a.

Comments

One-fourth of all assets are cash at December 31, 1995. The Partnership's appraised valuation is $219 per unit. The trading price appears to be approximately equal to the cash position. Aircraft leasing is a highly competitive industry and some of the lessees are financially troubled. However, management reports that two years of good traffic growth has reduced the industry supply of available aircraft for lease by about 20%.

Officers	Position	Ownership Information	12/31/95
James W. Linnan	President	Number of Shares Outstanding	499,997
Marc A. Meiches	CFO	Market Capitalization	$ 28,999,826
Norman C. T. Liu	Vice President	Frequency Of Distributions	Quarterly
		Number of Partners	16,426

Other Information					
Transfer Agent	Company Office			Where Listed	Order Matching Only
Auditor	Arthur Andersen LLP			Symbol	n.a.
Market Maker	None			SIC Code	7359
Broker Dealer	Chicago Partnership Board	Tel/Ext	(800)272-6273 690	Employees	None

Polk (R.L) & Co.

1155 Brewery Park Blvd. • Detroit, MI 48207 • Telephone (313)393-0880 • Fax (313)393-2860

Company Description

The Company is an international multi-divisional marketing company. Its' automobile marketing group provides a full line of products and services to U.S. and Canadian auto makers including data processing, target marketing, laser printing, statistical services and full scale marketing programs. The Company's direct marketing group specializes in reaching their database of over 90 million households in the U.S. for a large variety of clients. A separate division publishes over 1,300 city directories covering 6,500 communities. As part of a massive database, the Company records vehicle registration information throughout the United States. The Company also has a separate division that provides marketing services to banks. Founded in 1870, R.L. Polk is the oldest consumer marketing company in America.

	12/31/92	12/31/91
Per Share Information		
Stock Price	100.00	100.00
Earnings Per Share	-3.02	13.13
Price / Earnings Ratio	n.a.	7.62
Book Value Per Share	230.76	243.10
Price / Book Value %	43.34	41.14
Dividends Per Share	6.00	7.00
Annual Financial Data		
Operating Results (000's)		
Total Revenues	310,973.9	295,548.5
Costs & Expenses	-300,148.7	-281,485.0
Income Before Taxes and Other	10,825.2	14,063.5
Other Items	-6,529.7	n.a.
Income Tax	-5,711.0	-6,577.0
Net Income	-1,415.6	7,486.5
Cash Flow From Operations	9,292.9	17,570.7
Balance Sheet (000's)		
Cash & Equivalents	4,102.3	4,111.6
Total Current Assets	122,902.5	119,294.1
Fixed Assets, Net	70,043.6	57,737.6
Total Assets	266,343.3	249,155.3
Total Current Liabilities	61,879.1	53,834.5
Long-Term Debt	61,335.8	50,995.2
Stockholders' Equity	126,645.0	138,910.2
Performance & Financial Condition		
Return on Total Revenues %	-0.46	2.53
Return on Avg Stockholders' Equity %	-1.07	5.67
Return on Average Assets %	-0.55	2.86
Current Ratio	1.99	2.22
Debt / Equity %	48.43	36.71

Compound Growth %'s	EPS % n.a.	Net Income % n.a.	Total Revenues % 5.22

Comments

The Company only releases financial statements to its shareholders. We were able to obtain the 1992 and 1991 reports. 1992 results include a nonrecurring expense of $6,529,716, or $11.89 per share, in connection with the adoption of GAAP in connection with reporting income taxes and postretirement benefits. It was reported to us that 1995 earnings were $13.4 million on revenues of $344.7 million and that the stock traded as low as $50 per share recently.

Officers	Position	Ownership Information	12/31/93
Steven R. Polk	Chairman, CEO	Number of Shares Outstanding	548,792
Robert Tatum	CFO	Market Capitalization	$ 54,879,200
Lee Marx	Secretary	Frequency Of Dividends	Quarterly
		Number of Shareholders	Under 500

Other Information

Transfer Agent	Company Office			Where Listed	OTC-PS
Auditor	Deloitte & Touche LLP			Symbol	POLL
Market Maker	Monroe Securities, Inc.	Telephone	(800)766-5560	SIC Code	2679
Broker Dealer	Pink sheet specialist			Employees	3500

Polyplastex United, Inc.

3671 131st Avenue North • Clearwater, FL 34622 • Telephone (813)573-1881 • Fax (813)572-7865

Company Description

The Company produces large format computer generated graphics, electrostatic printing, hand painting and seaming, primarily for the outdoor advertising industry. This is a change from its former business which was liquidated as a result of continuing losses. The Company was organized as a sole proprietorship in 1943 and became a public company in 1955. A tender offer was proposed by the Company in late 1995 for up to 50,000 shares at $6 per share to be paid in increments over 3 years.

	06/30/95	06/30/94	06/30/93	06/30/92
Per Share Information				
Stock Price	4.50	6.75	6.75	6.75
Earnings Per Share	-2.56	-2.35	-0.60	-0.84
Price / Earnings Ratio	n.a.	n.a.	n.a.	n.a.
Book Value Per Share	4.69	7.32	15.47	11.39
Price / Book Value %	95.95	92.21	43.63	59.26
Dividends Per Share	n.a.	n.a.	n.a.	n.a.
Annual Financial Data				
Operating Results (000's)				
Total Revenues	1,658.8	1,053.0	12,275.5	11,643.7
Costs & Expenses	-3,068.2	-1,200.2	-12,684.3	-12,363.1
Income Before Taxes and Other	-1,527.6	-1,362.0	-419.6	-719.5
Other Items	n.a.	n.a.	n.a.	n.a.
Income Tax	n.a.	n.a.	70.6	234.0
Net Income	-1,527.6	-1,362.0	-349.0	-485.5
Cash Flow From Operations	-73.5	3,341.6	253.5	-324.4
Balance Sheet (000's)				
Cash & Equivalents	1,191.4	510.9	110.7	131.0
Total Current Assets	2,590.2	3,217.7	6,133.6	6,539.4
Fixed Assets, Net	2,321.7	1,721.6	2,659.2	2,841.9
Total Assets	5,811.1	5,958.8	8,946.8	9,574.9
Total Current Liabilities	517.2	525.6	2,539.4	2,591.0
Long-Term Debt	1,317.1	153.9	n.a.	110.0
Stockholders' Equity	2,851.8	4,303.6	6,232.5	6,581.6
Performance & Financial Condition				
Return on Total Revenues %	-92.09	-129.35	-2.84	-4.17
Return on Avg Stockholders' Equity %	-42.70	-25.85	-5.45	n.a.
Return on Average Assets %	-25.96	-18.28	-3.77	n.a.
Current Ratio	5.01	6.12	2.42	2.52
Debt / Equity %	46.19	3.58	n.a.	1.67

Compound Growth %'s	EPS % n.a.	Net Income % n.a.	Total Revenues % -47.77

Comments

Management reports that they believe they have litigation and a number of other problems behind them and can now focus on new business opportunities. The Company has a $3 million tax loss carryforward to offset future profits should there be any.

Officers	Position	Ownership Information	06/30/95
Dennis Peskin	President	Number of Shares Outstanding	608,255
Katherine Rice	Treasurer, Secretary	Market Capitalization	$ 2,737,148
		Frequency Of Dividends	Irregular
		Number of Shareholders	Under 500

Other Information

Transfer Agent	Continental Stock Transfer & Trust Co.			Where Listed	OTC-PS
Auditor	Cherry, Bekaert & Holland, LLP			Symbol	PYPX
Market Maker	A.G. Edwards & Sons, Inc.	Telephone	(800)325-8197	SIC Code	7312
Broker Dealer	Regular Stockbroker			Employees	25

Portland Brewing Company

2730 NW 31st Avenue • Portland, OR 97210 • Telephone (503)226-7623 • Fax (503)226-2702

Company Description

The Company is a regional specialty brewer of lagers and ales with the capacity to brew over 100,000 barrels per year from two breweries. The Company sells its products in twelve western states. The Company also operates a retail establishment known as the Portland Pub which opened for business in 1986. Operations expanded with a new facility in 1993. A public offering in 1995 raised $2.4 million on the sale of 413,177 shares and another offering during the year ended June 30, 1994, raised $2.4 million on the sale of 698,520 shares. The Company has managed its public offerings by itself, proving that not only can they brew a good bottle of beer, but they also know something about corporate finance.

	12/31/95	12/31/94	06/30/94	06/30/93
Per Share Information				
Stock Price	7.00	5.33	4.00	3.33
Earnings Per Share	0.13	0.04	0.05	0.06
Price / Earnings Ratio	53.85	133.25	80.00	55.50
Book Value Per Share	3.47	2.75	2.70	2.12
Price / Book Value %	201.73	193.82	148.15	157.08
Dividends Per Share	n.a.	n.a.	n.a.	n.a.
Annual Financial Data				
Operating Results (000's)				
Total Revenues	11,001.4	3,777.7	4,239.7	2,216.8
Costs & Expenses	-10,626.3	-3,657.1	-4,143.3	-2,176.1
Income Before Taxes and Other	358.0	120.6	96.4	36.2
Other Items	n.a.	n.a.	n.a.	n.a.
Income Tax	-119.2	-48.1	-39.3	11.6
Net Income	238.8	72.5	57.2	47.9
Cash Flow From Operations	296.5	535.5	-106.0	148.0
Balance Sheet (000's)				
Cash & Equivalents	156.5	566.5	1,004.0	107.1
Total Current Assets	2,010.0	1,706.3	1,857.9	572.3
Fixed Assets, Net	6,751.3	3,641.2	2,882.7	1,846.5
Total Assets	8,906.1	5,515.4	4,915.4	2,492.9
Total Current Liabilities	994.5	871.5	394.2	469.1
Long-Term Debt	537.7	n.a.	n.a.	n.a.
Stockholders' Equity	7,184.4	4,574.9	4,470.0	2,023.8
Performance & Financial Condition				
Return on Total Revenues %	2.17	1.92	1.35	2.16
Return on Avg Stockholders' Equity %	4.06	1.60	1.76	3.69
Return on Average Assets %	3.31	1.39	1.54	2.87
Current Ratio	2.02	1.96	4.71	1.22
Debt / Equity %	7.48	n.a.	n.a.	n.a.

Compound Growth %'s	EPS %	29.40	Net Income %	70.87	Total Revenues %	70.57

Comments

During 1994, the Company changed its year end from June 30, to December 31. Accordingly, the operating results for the six months ended December 31, 1994, are not comparable with the other years presented.

Officers	Position	Ownership Information	12/31/95
Charles A. Adams	President, Chairman	Number of Shares Outstanding	2,069,397
Frederick L. Bowman	Vice President	Market Capitalization	$ 14,485,779
Shannon W. Novak	Vice President, Secretary	Frequency Of Dividends	n.a.
Glenmore James	Vice President, Treasurer	Number of Shareholders	3,500
G. Eugene Clark	VP - Sales		

Other Information

Transfer Agent	OTC Stock Transfer, Inc.		Where Listed	Order Matching Only
Auditor	Arthur Andersen LLP		Symbol	n.a.
Market Maker	Company Office	Telephone (800)386-2739	SIC Code	2082
Broker Dealer	Regular Stockbroker		Employees	68

Portsmouth Square, Inc.

2251 San Diego Ave., Ste.A-151 • San Diego, CA 92110-2926 • Telephone (619)298-7201 • Fax (619)298-3418

Company Description

The major asset is a 49.8% interest in Justice Investors, a limited partnership which owns and the Financial District Holiday Inn in San Francisco, California. The Company is both a general partner and a limited partner. Santa Fe Financial Corporation holds 480,757 shares, or 64% of the Company.

	12/31/95	12/31/94	12/31/93	12/31/92
Per Share Information				
Stock Price	17.37	16.37	15.44	n.a.
Earnings Per Share	1.15	1.13	1.11	n.a.
Price / Earnings Ratio	15.10	14.49	13.91	n.a.
Book Value Per Share	2.02	1.57	1.20	n.a.
Price / Book Value %	859.90	1,042.70	1,286.70	n.a.
Dividends Per Share	0.70	0.75	0.90	n.a.
Annual Financial Data				
Operating Results (000's)				
Total Revenues	1,643.4	1,621.1	1,565.2	n.a.
Costs & Expenses	-201.0	-211.9	-172.4	n.a.
Income Before Taxes and Other	1,442.4	1,409.2	1,392.8	n.a.
Other Items	n.a.	n.a.	n.a.	n.a.
Income Tax	-578.3	-564.6	-558.2	n.a.
Net Income	864.1	844.6	834.6	n.a.
Cash Flow From Operations	627.7	425.1	699.2	n.a.
Balance Sheet (000's)				
Cash & Equivalents	1,206.1	1,103.4	1,240.8	n.a.
Total Current Assets	1,269.6	1,147.9	1,284.7	n.a.
Fixed Assets, Net	n.a.	n.a.	n.a.	n.a.
Total Assets	1,635.1	1,217.3	1,287.3	n.a.
Total Current Liabilities	117.3	38.6	146.4	n.a.
Long-Term Debt	n.a.	n.a.	n.a.	n.a.
Stockholders' Equity	1,517.8	1,178.6	896.6	n.a.
Performance & Financial Condition				
Return on Total Revenues %	52.58	52.10	53.32	n.a.
Return on Avg Stockholders' Equity %	64.09	81.40	n.a.	n.a.
Return on Average Assets %	60.59	67.44	n.a.	n.a.
Current Ratio	10.82	29.70	8.77	n.a.
Debt / Equity %	n.a.	n.a.	n.a.	n.a.

Compound Growth %'s	EPS %	1.79	Net Income %	1.75	Total Revenues %	2.47

Comments

The Company recently signed a new lease with Holiday Inn which should boost revenue. It has a term of 10 years with a 5 year option. The property itself may have a value of $40 million to $60 million which, if it is ever realized, would equate to between $23 and $37 per share.

Officers	Position	Ownership Information	12/31/95
R N. Gould	Chairman, President	Number of Shares Outstanding	750,000
Virginia W. Simpson	Secretary, Vice President	Market Capitalization	$ 13,027,500
L. Scott Shields	Treasurer	Frequency Of Dividends	Semi-Annual
Lawrence I. Kramer, Jr.	Vice President	Number of Shareholders	343

Other Information					
Transfer Agent	U.S. Stock Transfer Corporation			Where Listed	OTC-BB
Auditor	Ernst & Young LLP			Symbol	PRSI
Market Maker	Wedbush Morgan Securities, Inc	Telephone	(800)421-0251	SIC Code	6510
Broker Dealer	Regular Stockbroker			Employees	2

Power Test Investors Limited Partnership

125 Jericho Turnpike • Jericho, NY 11753 • Telephone (516)338-6000 • Fax (516)338-6062

Company Description

The Partnership owns and leases 291 gasoline service stations and 5 petroleum distribution terminals all of which are located in the eastern United States. Getty Petroleum Corp. (NYSE) is the sole lessee. The Partnership was formed in 1985 as a limited partnership to invest in the Power Test Realty Company, an operating partnership formed for the purpose of acquiring and leasing back certain assets of Getty Oil Company. The officers listed are officers and employees of CLS General Partnership Corp. which manages the affairs of both this partnership and the operating partnership.

	12/31/95	12/31/94	12/31/93	12/31/92
Per Unit Information				
Price Per Unit	8.50	7.62	8.25	6.12
Earnings Per Unit	1.20	0.90	0.80	0.88
Price / Earnings Ratio	7.08	8.47	10.31	6.95
Book Value Per Unit	0.79	0.34	0.17	0.12
Price / Book Value %	1,076.00	2,241.20	4,852.90	5,100.00
Distributions Per Unit	0.74	0.74	0.74	0.68
Cash Flow Per Unit	0.90	1.05	1.02	1.03
Annual Financial Data				
Operating Results (000's)				
Total Revenues	13,391.4	11,088.3	10,546.6	11,339.2
Costs & Expenses	-5,510.1	-5,168.0	-5,293.7	-5,534.1
Operating Income	7,800.3	5,860.6	5,199.8	5,746.4
Other Items	n.a.	n.a.	n.a.	n.a.
Net Income	7,800.3	5,860.6	5,199.8	5,746.4
Cash Flow From Operations	5,841.4	6,808.7	6,659.4	6,722.7
Balance Sheet (000's)				
Cash & Equivalents	5,754.5	2,523.7	1,983.6	1,679.2
Total Current Assets	5,754.5	2,523.7	1,983.6	1,679.2
Investments In Leases	4,767.1	5,747.2	6,476.3	6,995.9
Total Assets	40,867.2	40,459.5	41,916.3	43,040.4
Total Current Liabilities	277.5	358.4	335.8	357.7
Long-Term Debt	35,456.5	37,908.9	40,440.5	41,927.4
Partners' Capital	5,133.3	2,192.1	1,140.0	755.3
Performance & Financial Condition				
Return on Total Revenues %	58.25	52.85	49.30	50.68
Return on Average Partners' Capital %	212.97	351.76	548.68	n.a.
Return on Average Assets %	19.18	14.23	12.24	13.14
Current Ratio	20.74	7.04	5.91	4.69
Debt / Equity %	690.72	1729.30	3547.30	5550.80

Compound Growth %'s	EPU %	10.89	Net Income %	10.72	Total Revenues %	5.70

Comments

During 1995, the Partnership sold 14 stations to Getty which resulted in a gain of $3.1 million. It sold 5 stations in 1994 for a gain of $658,000.

Officers	Position	Ownership Information	12/31/95
Leo Liebowitz	President, Treasurer	Number of Shares Outstanding	6,501,577
Milton Safenowitz	Exec VP	Market Capitalization	$ 55,263,405
Milton Cooper	Secretary	Frequency Of Distributions	Quarterly
		Number of Partners	593

Other Information

Transfer Agent	Company Office			Where Listed	OTC-BB
Auditor	Coopers & Lybrand LLP			Symbol	POWNZ
Market Maker	Pennsylvania Merchant Group	Telephone	(800)762-8624	SIC Code	6510
Broker Dealer				Employees	n.a.

Prab, Inc.

5944 E. Kilgore Road • Kalamazoo, MI 49003 • Telephone (616)382-8200 • Fax (616)382-7770

Company Description

The Company designs and manufactures metal scrap reclamation systems and bulk material handling equipment. These products are sold around the world and are used in a variety of manufacturing processes to reduce labor cost, increase productivity, improve quality and save materials and energy resources. The Company is a Michigan corporation organized in 1961.

	10/31/95	10/31/94	10/31/93	10/31/92
Per Share Information				
Stock Price	1.38	1.00	0.47	0.38
Earnings Per Share	0.27	0.21	0.01	-0.95
Price / Earnings Ratio	5.11	4.76	47.00	n.a.
Book Value Per Share	0.46	-0.02	-0.35	-0.44
Price / Book Value %	300.00	n.a.	n.a.	n.a.
Dividends Per Share	n.a.	n.a.	n.a.	n.a.
Annual Financial Data				
Operating Results (000's)				
Total Revenues	13,845.4	9,865.7	8,914.7	10,313.5
Costs & Expenses	-12,620.1	-9,275.1	-8,947.1	-12,120.6
Income Before Taxes and Other	1,287.9	533.6	63.5	-1,807.1
Other Items	n.a.	135.3	n.a.	-32.8
Income Tax	n.a.	337.0	n.a.	n.a.
Net Income	1,287.9	1,005.9	63.5	-1,840.0
Cash Flow From Operations	1,338.5	724.9	489.8	n.a.
Balance Sheet (000's)				
Cash & Equivalents	323.3	255.7	372.5	153.0
Total Current Assets	4,269.5	3,640.4	2,878.1	3,244.9
Fixed Assets, Net	961.3	894.1	958.4	1,141.7
Total Assets	5,248.8	4,615.8	4,152.7	4,783.2
Total Current Liabilities	2,049.3	1,709.5	1,033.0	1,261.9
Long-Term Debt	n.a.	985.5	1,842.9	2,644.7
Stockholders' Equity	3,185.6	1,893.1	908.2	805.7
Performance & Financial Condition				
Return on Total Revenues %	9.30	10.20	0.71	-17.84
Return on Avg Stockholders' Equity %	50.72	71.82	7.41	-321.66
Return on Average Assets %	26.11	22.94	1.42	-28.95
Current Ratio	2.08	2.13	2.79	2.57
Debt / Equity %	n.a.	52.06	202.92	328.25

Compound Growth %'s	EPS %	419.62	Net Income %	350.34	Total Revenues %	10.31

Comments

At December 31, 1995, the Company had a net operating loss carryforward of approximately $6.8 million to offset future taxable income. Two series of preferred stock are included in Stockholder's Equity, a convertible and a non-convertible preferred. Both series contain certain liquidation preferences, dividend, and other rights. Per share amounts have been adjusted to reflect the effects of the potential conversion or liquidation of the preferred.

Officers	Position	Ownership Information	10/31/95
John J. Wallace	Chairman	Number of Shares Outstanding	2,647,860
Gary A. Herder	President, CEO	Market Capitalization	$ 3,654,047
Eric V. Brown, Sr.	Secretary	Frequency Of Dividends	n.a.
		Number of Shareholders	1,168

Other Information			
Transfer Agent	Illinois Stock Transfer	Where Listed	OTC-BB
Auditor	Plante & Moran LLP	Symbol	PRAB
Market Maker	First Manhattan Co.	Telephone (212)756-3411	SIC Code	3569
Broker Dealer	Regular Stockbroker	Employees	85

Precision Optics Incorporated

612 Industrial Way West • Eatontown, NJ 07724-2214 • Telephone (908)542-4801 • Fax (908)542-5721

Company Description

The Company manufactures precision optical and laser components for industrial and other customers. In 1995, sales to one customer accounted for 53% of total sales. The Company was founded by current CEO Walter Merkl in 1961 and incorporated in 1966. It went public in 1969. The stock was listed on NASDAQ until 1994.

	06/30/95	06/30/94	06/30/93	06/30/92
Per Share Information				
Stock Price	0.81	1.41	1.87	1.37
Earnings Per Share	0.06	0.09	0.08	0.05
Price / Earnings Ratio	13.50	15.67	23.38	27.40
Book Value Per Share	2.09	2.03	1.96	1.88
Price / Book Value %	38.76	69.46	95.41	72.87
Dividends Per Share	n.a.	n.a.	n.a.	n.a.
Annual Financial Data				
Operating Results (000's)				
Total Revenues	825.2	1,002.3	984.0	970.9
Costs & Expenses	-736.9	-889.5	-878.3	-919.5
Income Before Taxes and Other	86.7	109.5	105.7	51.5
Other Items	n.a.	n.a.	n.a.	n.a.
Income Tax	-35.6	-30.4	-36.3	-11.6
Net Income	51.1	79.1	69.4	39.8
Cash Flow From Operations	50.4	137.8	158.4	85.0
Balance Sheet (000's)				
Cash & Equivalents	228.3	382.8	214.2	332.0
Total Current Assets	1,159.0	1,404.3	1,544.8	1,438.2
Fixed Assets, Net	159.0	184.6	207.3	240.7
Total Assets	1,847.3	1,829.3	1,794.4	1,711.4
Total Current Liabilities	60.1	101.7	120.7	107.2
Long-Term Debt	n.a.	n.a.	n.a.	n.a.
Stockholders' Equity	1,787.2	1,727.6	1,673.7	1,604.3
Performance & Financial Condition				
Return on Total Revenues %	6.19	7.89	7.06	4.10
Return on Avg Stockholders' Equity %	2.91	4.65	4.24	2.53
Return on Average Assets %	2.78	4.36	3.96	2.34
Current Ratio	19.28	13.81	12.80	13.42
Debt / Equity %	n.a.	n.a.	n.a.	n.a.

Compound Growth %'s	EPS %	6.27	Net Income %	8.69	Total Revenues %	-5.28

Comments

Declining sales are attributed to a falloff in business from major customers principally serving the military. Most or all of net income over the last four years is attributable to interest and dividend income. The Company appears to have an excellent liquidation value as compared to its trading value, although there is no indication that management would ever intend to liquidate.

Officers	Position	Ownership Information	06/30/95
Walter A. Merkl	President, Treasurer	Number of Shares Outstanding	852,999
Elfriede M. Lange	Vice President, Secretary	Market Capitalization	$ 690,929
		Frequency Of Dividends	n.a.
		Number of Shareholders	Under 500

Other Information			
Transfer Agent	Registrar & Transfer Company	Where Listed	BE
Auditor	Curchin & Company	Symbol	PREO
Market Maker	M. Rimson & Co., Inc.	Telephone (800)207-3195	SIC Code	5049
Broker Dealer	Regular Stockbroker	Employees	20

Preformed Line Products Company

660 Beta Drive • Cleveland, OH 44143 • Telephone (216)461-5200 • Fax (216)473-9319

Company Description

The Company manufactures and sells high quality cable anchoring and control hardware and systems, overhead and underground splice cases and related products, and fiber optic splicing and communications systems for the power utility, telecommunications and cable television industries.

	12/31/95	12/31/94	12/31/93	12/31/92
Per Share Information				
Stock Price	37.06	36.00	26.00	21.25
Earnings Per Share	3.26	3.15	1.89	2.27
Price / Earnings Ratio	11.37	11.43	13.76	9.36
Book Value Per Share	28.39	25.72	23.05	22.03
Price / Book Value %	130.54	139.97	112.80	96.46
Dividends Per Share	0.88	0.88	0.88	0.88
Annual Financial Data				
Operating Results (000's)				
Total Revenues	159,250.0	145,109.0	112,012.0	111,779.2
Costs & Expenses	-143,851.0	-128,487.0	-102,514.1	-100,654.4
Income Before Taxes and Other	15,399.0	15,509.0	9,220.7	10,752.7
Other Items	n.a.	n.a.	n.a.	-0.8
Income Tax	-5,316.0	-5,779.0	-3,377.2	-3,733.4
Net Income	10,083.0	9,730.0	5,843.5	7,018.5
Cash Flow From Operations	17,309.0	17,309.0	6,981.4	10,792.0
Balance Sheet (000's)				
Cash & Equivalents	6,526.0	6,266.4	3,506.2	8,352.6
Total Current Assets	54,941.0	57,198.6	42,625.1	40,157.4
Fixed Assets, Net	41,849.0	41,205.6	38,668.5	35,594.2
Total Assets	122,895.0	119,532.8	101,074.2	89,825.2
Total Current Liabilities	17,350.0	18,570.8	18,202.6	11,290.0
Long-Term Debt	16,645.0	20,294.0	10,378.8	9,087.3
Stockholders' Equity	87,709.0	79,437.2	71,195.6	68,053.5
Performance & Financial Condition				
Return on Total Revenues %	6.33	6.71	5.22	6.28
Return on Avg Stockholders' Equity %	12.06	12.92	8.39	10.54
Return on Average Assets %	8.32	8.82	6.12	7.92
Current Ratio	3.17	3.08	2.34	3.56
Debt / Equity %	18.98	25.55	14.58	13.35

Compound Growth %'s	EPS %	12.82	Net Income %	12.84	Total Revenues %	12.52

Comments

The Company's financial strength, good current ratio and low debt/equity ratio, should enable management to focus on new opportunities with deregulation of the telecommunications industry and the growing demand for fiber optic cables.

Officers	Position	Ownership Information	12/31/95
Jon R. Ruhlman	President	Number of Shares Outstanding	3,089,024
Robert G. Ruhlman	Exec VP	Market Capitalization	$ 114,479,229
John J. Herda	VP - Finance	Frequency Of Dividends	Quarterly
J. Richard Hamilton	Secretary	Number of Shareholders	Under 500
Jon Barnes	VP - Sales		

Other Information

				Where Listed	OTC-BB
Transfer Agent	National City Bank, Cleveland, OH			Symbol	PLIN
Auditor	Ernst & Young			SIC Code	3699
Market Maker	McDonald & Company Securities	Telephone	(216)413-2350	Employees	150
Broker Dealer	Regular Stockbroker				

Premier Parks, Inc.

11501 Northeast Expressway • Oklahoma City, OK 73131 • Telephone (405)478-2414 • Fax (405)475-2555

Company Description

Formerly known as Tierco Group, Inc., the Company operates six theme parks with 1995 attendance of 4.1 million. They are Adventure World, near Baltimore, MD., Frontier City and Whitewater Bay in Oklahoma City, OK., Geauga Lake near Cleveland, OH., Darien Lake & Camping Resort near Buffalo, NY., and Wyandot Lake in Columbus, OH. The Company is actively pursuing opportunities to acquire additional parks.

	12/31/95	12/31/94	12/31/93	12/31/92
Per Share Information				
Stock Price	2.19	0.88	n.a.	n.a.
Earnings Per Share	-0.09	0.01	0.10	4.03
Price / Earnings Ratio	n.a.	88.00	n.a.	n.a.
Book Value Per Share	1.07	1.08	0.99	0.89
Price / Book Value %	204.67	81.48	n.a.	n.a.
Dividends Per Share	n.a.	n.a.	n.a.	n.a.
Annual Financial Data				
Operating Results (000's)				
Total Revenues	41,496.0	24,908.0	21,866.0	17,432.0
Costs & Expenses	-43,126.0	-24,655.0	-20,279.0	-2,855.0
Income Before Taxes and Other	-1,807.0	170.0	1,445.0	-1,308.0
Other Items	-140.0	n.a.	n.a.	18,396.0
Income Tax	762.0	-68.0	-91.0	-427.0
Net Income	-1,185.0	102.0	1,354.0	16,661.0
Cash Flow From Operations	10,646.0	1,060.0	2,699.0	1,980.0
Balance Sheet (000's)				
Cash & Equivalents	28,787.0	1,366.0	3,026.0	5,919.0
Total Current Assets	35,008.0	4,019.0	5,026.0	7,611.1
Fixed Assets, Net	116,001.0	38,572.0	27,788.0	21,004.0
Total Assets	173,318.0	45,539.0	36,707.0	30,615.1
Total Current Liabilities	11,584.0	3,275.0	2,695.0	3,149.8
Long-Term Debt	93,213.0	22,216.0	20,820.0	15,627.0
Stockholders' Equity	45,911.0	18,134.0	13,192.0	11,838.4
Performance & Financial Condition				
Return on Total Revenues %	-2.86	0.41	6.19	95.58
Return on Avg Stockholders' Equity %	-3.70	0.65	10.82	n.a.
Return on Average Assets %	-1.08	0.25	4.02	31.68
Current Ratio	3.02	1.23	2.20	n.a.
Debt / Equity %	203.03	122.51	157.82	132.01

Compound Growth %'s	EPS % n.a.	Net Income % n.a.	Total Revenues % 33.52

Comments

Net Income for the year ended December 31, 1992, includes an extraordinary gain of $18.4 million. The Company's revenues are derived primarily from the sale of tickets for entrance to its parks (53% in 1995) and the sale of food, merchandise, games and attractions within the parks (47% in 1995). There was no known public trading in the stock of the Company before 1994 and no reliable price quotations. As of March 1, 1996, officers and directors, as a group, owned 80.7% of the outstanding common stock of the Company.

Officers	Position	Ownership Information	12/31/95
Kieran E. Burke	Chairman, CEO	Number of Shares Outstanding	24,287,772
Gary Story	President, COO	Market Capitalization	$ 53,190,221
James F. Dannhauser	CFO	Frequency Of Dividends	n.a.
Richard A. Kipf	Secretary, Treasurer	Number of Shareholders	862

Other Information				
Transfer Agent	Liberty Bank & Trust Co. of Oklahoma Cit		Where Listed	OTC-PS
Auditor	KPMG Peat Marwick LLP		Symbol	PARK
Market Maker	Frankel (WM.V.) & Co., Inc.	Telephone (800)631-3091	SIC Code	7996
Broker Dealer	Regular Stockbroker		Employees	4800

Premis Corporation

15301 Highway 55 West • Plymouth, MN 55447 • Telephone (612)550-1999 • Fax (612)550-2999

Company Description

The Company is in the business of developing and selling computer software for use by the food distribution and retail industries. Prior to March 1994, the Company was only selling systems based on proprietary software applications. At that time, the Company acquired the rights to certain retail inventory management software which has provided substantial growth in sales. The Company was incorporated in Minnesota in 1982.

	03/31/95	03/31/94	03/31/93	03/31/92
Per Share Information				
Stock Price	0.25	n.a.	n.a.	n.a.
Earnings Per Share	0.18	0.06	0.01	n.a.
Price / Earnings Ratio	1.39	n.a.	n.a.	n.a.
Book Value Per Share	0.26	0.08	0.02	0.01
Price / Book Value %	96.15	n.a.	n.a.	n.a.
Dividends Per Share	n.a.	n.a.	n.a.	n.a.
Annual Financial Data				
Operating Results (000's)				
Total Revenues	3,017.6	892.2	606.3	539.5
Costs & Expenses	-2,542.9	-790.3	-569.2	-537.7
Income Before Taxes and Other	474.7	98.9	37.2	1.7
Other Items	n.a.	50.0	n.a.	n.a.
Income Tax	n.a.	n.a.	n.a.	n.a.
Net Income	474.7	148.9	37.2	1.7
Cash Flow From Operations	355.4	76.6	35.3	-4.5
Balance Sheet (000's)				
Cash & Equivalents	427.0	119.2	59.0	38.9
Total Current Assets	1,185.0	239.9	113.3	92.3
Fixed Assets, Net	48.8	61.0	32.1	13.2
Total Assets	1,559.6	351.4	145.3	105.5
Total Current Liabilities	651.5	140.8	80.3	84.2
Long-Term Debt	226.1	3.3	6.6	n.a.
Stockholders' Equity	682.0	207.3	58.4	21.2
Performance & Financial Condition				
Return on Total Revenues %	15.73	16.69	6.13	0.32
Return on Avg Stockholders' Equity %	106.75	112.10	93.31	8.74
Return on Average Assets %	49.68	59.96	29.63	1.57
Current Ratio	1.82	1.70	1.41	1.10
Debt / Equity %	33.15	1.58	11.31	n.a.

Compound Growth %'s	EPS %	324.26	Net Income %	548.94	Total Revenues %	77.51

Comments

Sales and net income for the nine months ended December 31, 1995, amounted to $4.3 million and $602,000 ($.20 per share), as compared to $2.0 million and $327,000 ($.13 per share) for the same period in 1994. The Company's stock price was quoted at $2.00 per share at December 31, 1995. There was no trading activity in the stock prior to March 1995.

Officers	Position	Ownership Information	03/31/95
F.T. Biermeier	President, CEO	Number of Shares Outstanding	2,590,694
Mary Ann Calhoun	Vice President, Secretary	Market Capitalization	$ 647,674
		Frequency Of Dividends	n.a.
		Number of Shareholders	111

Other Information

Transfer Agent	Company Office		Where Listed	OTC-BB
Auditor	Price Waterhouse LLP		Symbol	PMIS
Market Maker	Hanifen, Imhoff, Inc.	Telephone (303)291-5351	SIC Code	7373
Broker Dealer	Regular Stockbroker		Employees	28

Prevent Products, Inc.

1167 Ottawa Avenue • West Saint Paul, MN 55118 • Telephone (612)457-4385

Company Description

The Company manufactures and sells corespun cotton gloves and leg garments under the tradenames Geriglove and Gerileg. These are used primarily by elderly people with fragile skin as protection from possible abrasions. The Company was formed and incorporated in 1986 for the purpose of developing new health care products. As of October 31, 1995, six such products had been developed.

	10/31/95	10/31/94
Per Share Information		
Stock Price	1.50	1.00
Earnings Per Share	0.02	0.01
Price / Earnings Ratio	75.00	100.00
Book Value Per Share	0.15	0.12
Price / Book Value %	1,000.00	833.33
Dividends Per Share	n.a.	n.a.
Annual Financial Data		
Operating Results (000's)		
Total Revenues	582.8	452.2
Costs & Expenses	-540.1	-433.2
Income Before Taxes and Other	42.7	19.0
Other Items	n.a.	n.a.
Income Tax	-10.7	-4.8
Net Income	32.0	14.2
Cash Flow From Operations	5.3	-43.9
Balance Sheet (000's)		
Cash & Equivalents	136.7	87.9
Total Current Assets	295.5	200.9
Fixed Assets, Net	3.6	3.8
Total Assets	299.1	205.8
Total Current Liabilities	33.5	16.5
Long-Term Debt	n.a.	n.a.
Stockholders' Equity	265.6	189.3
Performance & Financial Condition		
Return on Total Revenues %	5.50	3.14
Return on Avg Stockholders' Equity %	14.09	n.a.
Return on Average Assets %	12.69	n.a.
Current Ratio	8.82	12.17
Debt / Equity %	n.a.	n.a.

Compound Growth %'s	EPS %	100.00	Net Income %	125.47	Total Revenues %	28.87

Comments

Two new products will be coming to market. These are the GeriHip, a corespun cotton hip protector, and the Ankle Calf Exerciser, a piece of equipment used in wound care. Although small, the Company has endured the processes of new product development and remains enthusiastic about the future. The compound growth rates are excellent, but are based on only two years of data.

Officers	Position	Ownership Information	10/31/95
Mario C. Garcia, MD,FACP	President	Number of Shares Outstanding	1,825,000
Carol Garcia	CEO	Market Capitalization	$ 2,737,500
Kristofer Lund	Vice President, CFO	Frequency Of Dividends	n.a.
		Number of Shareholders	Under 500

Other Information				
Transfer Agent	United Stock Transfer,Inc.		Where Listed	Order Matching Only
Auditor	Samuel T. Kantos & Associates		Symbol	n.a.
Market Maker	Van Clemens & Co.	Telephone (612)938-5117	SIC Code	3840
Broker Dealer	Gerry Shapiro	Tel/Ext (612)373-2300	Employees	3

Prime Capital Corporation

10275 W Higgins Road • Rosemont, IL 60018 • Telephone (708)294-6000 • Fax (708)294-6070

Company Description

The Company has been a provider of merchant banking financial services since 1977. Products include the leasing and rental of equipment and in some cases the sale of the resulting receivable, financial consulting, private placement of debt and a variety of other types of financing and financial services. At December 31, 1995, officers and directors, as a group owned 61.4% of the Company's outstanding common stock.

	12/31/95	12/31/94	12/31/93	12/31/92
Per Share Information				
Stock Price	1.75	0.94	0.50	0.22
Earnings Per Share	-0.43	-0.47	0.47	0.42
Price / Earnings Ratio	n.a.	n.a.	1.06	0.52
Book Value Per Share	0.65	1.08	1.55	1.08
Price / Book Value %	269.23	87.04	32.26	20.37
Dividends Per Share	n.a.	n.a.	n.a.	n.a.
Annual Financial Data				
Operating Results (000's)				
Total Revenues	7,038.1	4,678.4	7,559.4	10,695.5
Costs & Expenses	-9,049.2	-6,955.7	-5,656.3	-10,555.3
Income Before Taxes and Other	-1,836.2	-1,998.0	2,008.4	-1,485.2
Other Items	n.a.	n.a.	n.a.	3,293.1
Income Tax	n.a.	n.a.	n.a.	n.a.
Net Income	-1,836.2	-1,998.0	2,008.4	1,807.9
Cash Flow From Operations	-2,837.7	-3,801.9	1,200.0	-1,795.1
Balance Sheet (000's)				
Cash & Equivalents	2,001.9	1,945.4	4,060.1	2,088.9
Total Current Assets	63,289.7	21,782.5	9,400.5	8,597.9
Fixed Assets, Net	2,866.6	2,196.8	368.2	535.7
Total Assets	69,954.4	26,941.4	10,650.9	9,137.8
Total Current Liabilities	8,867.3	14,428.8	2,937.5	4,525.0
Long-Term Debt	58,300.3	7,889.5	1,092.3	n.a.
Stockholders' Equity	2,786.9	4,623.1	6,621.1	4,612.8
Performance & Financial Condition				
Return on Total Revenues %	-26.09	-42.71	26.57	16.90
Return on Avg Stockholders' Equity %	-49.56	-35.54	35.76	44.79
Return on Average Assets %	-3.79	-10.63	20.30	4.78
Current Ratio	7.14	1.51	3.20	1.90
Debt / Equity %	2091.90	170.65	16.50	n.a.

Compound Growth %'s	EPS % n.a.	Net Income % n.a.	Total Revenues % -13.02

Comments

During the years 1993, 1994 and 1995, the Company sold equipment loan and lease receivables with an aggregate principal amount totaling $152.9 million. Income received from these sales amounted to $2.0 million in 1995, $632,000 in 1994, and $1.8 million in 1993. In January of 1996, the Company sold a similar pool of receivables for $85.3 million. Income recognized on this transaction amounted to approximately $3.7 million. The Company has net operating and passive loss carryfowards of approximately $8.4 million and investment tax credit carryforwards of $645,000, expiring through 2010.

Officers	Position	Ownership Information	12/31/95
James A. Friedman	President, CEO	Number of Shares Outstanding	4,280,165
Robert C. Benson	Senior VP	Market Capitalization	$ 7,490,289
		Frequency Of Dividends	n.a.
		Number of Shareholders	315

Other Information

Transfer Agent	LaSalle National Trust, N.A.		Where Listed	OTC-BB
Auditor	KPMG Peat Marwick LLP		Symbol	PMPC
Market Maker	Herzog, Heine, Geduld, Inc.	Telephone (800)221-3600	SIC Code	7352
Broker Dealer	Regular Stockbroker		Employees	44

Puroflow Incorporated

16559 Saticoy Street • Van Nuys, CA 91406 • Telephone (818)756-1388 • Fax (818)779-3902

Company Description

The Company, incorporated in Delaware in 1961, specializes in the design and manufacture of automotive airbag filters and other high performance filters. The Company is currently in receivership as a result of a default on its loan agreement in 1995. In addition, there is significant litigation involving several matters all of which the Company believes will not have a significant adverse effect on the Company's financial position. It appears that the Company has improved its operations and has returned to profitability for the latest fiscal year. As of February 1996, the Company had a backlog of orders totaling $5.5 million as compared to $5.2 million in the prior year.

	01/31/96	01/31/95	01/31/94	01/31/93
Per Share Information				
Stock Price	1.00	0.77	1.69	1.51
Earnings Per Share	0.19	-0.53	-0.15	-0.81
Price / Earnings Ratio	5.26	n.a.	n.a.	n.a.
Book Value Per Share	0.24	0.04	0.53	0.54
Price / Book Value %	416.67	1,925.00	318.87	279.63
Dividends Per Share	n.a.	n.a.	n.a.	n.a.
Annual Financial Data				
Operating Results (000's)				
Total Revenues	8,815.9	9,058.8	6,041.1	8,327.3
Costs & Expenses	7,940.8	-9,585.7	-6,796.1	-11,066.1
Income Before Taxes and Other	875.1	-526.8	-754.9	-2,738.9
Other Items	23.0	-1,845.3	189.0	n.a.
Income Tax	n.a.	n.a.	n.a.	64.7
Net Income	898.1	-2,372.2	-565.9	-2,674.2
Cash Flow From Operations	219.3	728.6	-107.2	-2,137.4
Balance Sheet (000's)				
Cash & Equivalents	n.a.	74.4	18.9	180.5
Total Current Assets	2,865.5	3,250.5	5,737.3	6,173.0
Fixed Assets, Net	1,019.4	1,337.3	1,555.8	1,648.5
Total Assets	3,962.0	4,720.8	7,329.1	7,897.0
Total Current Liabilities	2,878.8	4,464.4	4,913.9	6,035.9
Long-Term Debt	n.a.	71.4	108.0	52.5
Stockholders' Equity	1,083.2	185.1	2,307.2	1,780.9
Performance & Financial Condition				
Return on Total Revenues %	10.19	-26.19	-9.37	-32.11
Return on Avg Stockholders' Equity %	141.63	-190.36	-27.69	-98.08
Return on Average Assets %	20.69	-39.37	-7.43	-32.80
Current Ratio	1.00	0.73	1.17	1.02
Debt / Equity %	n.a.	38.58	4.68	2.95

Compound Growth %'s	EPS % n.a.	Net Income % n.a.	Total Revenues % 1.92

Comments

Discontinued operations resulted in a charge of $1.8 million for the year ended January 31, 1995. In March 1996, the Company entered into an agreement with an investment banker to raise between $960,000 and $2.0 million of equity through a private placement of stock. Proceeds of the offering are to be used to reduce bank debt and for operating purposes.

Officers	Position	Ownership Information	01/31/96
Reuben M. Siwek	Chairman	Number of Shares Outstanding	4,578,521
Michael H. Figoff	President, CEO	Market Capitalization	$ 4,578,521
		Frequency Of Dividends	n.a.
		Number of Shareholders	321

Other Information

Transfer Agent	Continental Stock Transfer & Trust Co.		Where Listed	OTC-BB
Auditor	Rose, Snyder & Jacobs		Symbol	PURO
Market Maker	Fahnestock & Co., Inc.	Telephone (212)422-7813	SIC Code	3491
Broker Dealer	Regular Stockbroker		Employees	78

Queen City Investments, Inc.

P.O. Box 1370 • Long Beach, CA 90801-1370 • Telephone (310)437-0011

Company Description

The Company might be best described as an investment company. It's major investments are an interest in Farmers & Merchants Bank of Long Beach, California, and a 27,000 acre ranch in Aroyo Grande, California. The Company also leases 25,000 acres from the U.S. Government and raises cattle on the properties. The Company was formed in 1973.

	12/31/95	12/31/94
Per Share Information		
Stock Price	266.00	255.00
Earnings Per Share	24.77	27.59
Price / Earnings Ratio	10.74	9.24
Book Value Per Share	268.76	242.86
Price / Book Value %	98.97	105.00
Dividends Per Share	n.a.	n.a.
Annual Financial Data		
Operating Results (000's)		
Total Revenues	3,982.4	3,841.1
Costs & Expenses	-2,261.5	-1,911.6
Income Before Taxes and Other	1,720.9	1,929.5
Other Items	n.a.	n.a.
Income Tax	-506.4	-577.1
Net Income	1,214.5	1,352.4
Cash Flow From Operations	n.a.	n.a.
Balance Sheet (000's)		
Cash & Equivalents	185.9	105.6
Total Current Assets	8,864.3	8,143.1
Fixed Assets, Net	2,033.7	1,860.6
Total Assets	15,006.0	15,081.9
Total Current Liabilities	0.0	1,200.1
Long-Term Debt	1,829.3	1,975.0
Stockholders' Equity	13,176.7	11,906.7
Performance & Financial Condition		
Return on Total Revenues %	30.50	35.21
Return on Avg Stockholders' Equity %	9.68	n.a.
Return on Average Assets %	8.07	n.a.
Current Ratio	n.a.	6.79
Debt / Equity %	13.88	16.59

Compound Growth %'s	EPS %	-10.22	Net Income %	-10.20	Total Revenues %	3.68

Comments

The financial statements are not audited. The outside accountants prepare a compiled report using income tax basis reporting. Marketable securities and the investment in land assets are stated at cost. The last trade, before we went to press, was at $290 per share on May 23, 1996. It was handled by Standard Investment in Tustin, California, as broker/dealer.

Officers	Position	Ownership Information	12/31/95
Kenneth Walker	President	Number of Shares Outstanding	49,027
Marisala Tejeda	Secretary	Market Capitalization	$ 13,041,182
Charles Hagan	Vice President	Frequency Of Dividends	n.a.
		Number of Shareholders	Under 500

Other Information

Transfer Agent	Company Office				Where Listed	OTC-BB
Auditor	Windes & McClaughry				Symbol	QUCT
Market Maker	Seidler Companies, Inc., The	Telephone	(800)421-0164		SIC Code	6790
Broker Dealer	Standard Investment	Tel/Ext	(888)783-4688	Jack	Employees	n.a.

RF Industries, LTD

7610 Miramar Road, Bldg. 6000 • San Diego, CA 92126-4202 • Telephone (619)549-6340 • Fax (619)549-6345

Company Description

The Company is engaged in the design, manufacture and distribution of coaxial connectors used in professional radio communication applications. The Company also designs and produces radio frequency links which transmit and receive control signals for the remote operation and monitoring of equipment. As of October 31, 1995, officers and directors, as a group, owned 11.7% of the Company's outstanding common stock. The Company was incorporated in the state of Nevada in 1979 and had its initial public offering of stock in 1984.

	10/31/95	10/31/94	10/31/93	10/31/92
Per Share Information				
Stock Price	1.25	1.22	0.25	0.05
Earnings Per Share	0.07	0.39	0.06	0.01
Price / Earnings Ratio	17.86	3.13	4.17	5.00
Book Value Per Share	1.06	1.01	0.37	0.30
Price / Book Value %	117.92	120.79	67.57	16.67
Dividends Per Share	n.a.	n.a.	n.a.	n.a.
Annual Financial Data				
Operating Results (000's)				
Total Revenues	3,425.9	3,252.8	2,049.6	1,823.9
Costs & Expenses	-3,150.9	-2,480.6	-1,802.1	-1,780.3
Income Before Taxes and Other	274.9	772.2	247.5	43.7
Other Items	n.a.	n.a.	n.a.	n.a.
Income Tax	-103.3	121.0	-24.0	-10.1
Net Income	171.6	893.2	223.5	33.6
Cash Flow From Operations	30.0	459.4	253.0	108.7
Balance Sheet (000's)				
Cash & Equivalents	211.3	862.1	456.6	279.5
Total Current Assets	2,789.8	2,282.0	1,555.0	1,353.2
Fixed Assets, Net	127.1	119.0	133.5	118.7
Total Assets	2,955.0	2,423.5	1,695.0	1,479.3
Total Current Liabilities	245.1	184.9	395.8	391.1
Long-Term Debt	n.a.	n.a.	12.2	24.7
Stockholders' Equity	2,709.9	2,238.7	1,287.0	1,063.5
Performance & Financial Condition				
Return on Total Revenues %	5.01	27.46	10.91	1.84
Return on Avg Stockholders' Equity %	6.94	50.67	19.02	3.21
Return on Average Assets %	6.38	43.37	14.08	2.36
Current Ratio	11.38	12.34	3.93	3.46
Debt / Equity %	n.a.	n.a.	0.94	2.32

Compound Growth %'s	EPS %	91.29	Net Income %	72.26	Total Revenues %	23.38

Comments

The Company has contracted with Hytek International, LTD., a principal shareholder, for technical and marketing services and cash in exchange for shares of the Company's stock at the rate of 200,000 shares per year. This arrangement has two remaining years.

Officers	Position	Ownership Information	10/31/95
Jack A. Benz	Chairman	Number of Shares Outstanding	2,538,547
Howard F. Hill	President, CEO	Market Capitalization	$ 3,173,184
Terry Gross	Secretary	Frequency Of Dividends	n.a.
		Number of Shareholders	783

Other Information

Transfer Agent	Continental Stock Transfer & Trust Co.			Where Listed	OTC-BB
Auditor	J.H. Cohen & Co.			Symbol	RFIL
Market Maker	Paragon Capital Corporation	Telephone	(800)729-7173	SIC Code	3678
Broker Dealer	Regular Stockbroker			Employees	24

RWC, Incorporated

P.O. Box 920 • Bay City, MI 48707-0579 • Telephone (517)684-4030 • Fax (517)684-3960

Company Description

The Company designs, builds and provides parts for special machinery primarily in the automotive and appliance industries. They consider themselves to be specialists in high production automatic assembly and metal fabricating equipment. The Company was formed in 1945. A tender offer to repurchase 60,000 shares, about 10% of issued shares, at $10 per share was submitted to the shareholders in January, 1996.

	10/31/95	10/31/94
Per Share Information		
Stock Price	7.75	7.00
Earnings Per Share	-1.30	-0.67
Price / Earnings Ratio	n.a.	n.a.
Book Value Per Share	7.64	9.23
Price / Book Value %	101.44	75.84
Dividends Per Share	0.35	n.a.
Annual Financial Data		
Operating Results (000's)		
Total Revenues	34,140.7	25,666.5
Costs & Expenses	-31,476.7	-26,272.2
Income Before Taxes and Other	2,664.1	-605.6
Other Items	-2,522.1	n.a.
Income Tax	-945.0	194.0
Net Income	-803.1	-411.6
Cash Flow From Operations	6,428.6	-196.8
Balance Sheet (000's)		
Cash & Equivalents	5,037.2	69.3
Total Current Assets	11,863.6	9,707.2
Fixed Assets, Net	1,906.5	1,738.3
Total Assets	15,263.3	11,796.3
Total Current Liabilities	7,031.8	5,464.3
Long-Term Debt	43.7	516.7
Stockholders' Equity	4,592.9	5,550.1
Performance & Financial Condition		
Return on Total Revenues %	-2.35	-1.60
Return on Avg Stockholders' Equity %	-15.83	n.a.
Return on Average Assets %	-5.94	n.a.
Current Ratio	1.69	1.78
Debt / Equity %	0.95	9.31

Compound Growth %'s	EPS %	n.a.	Net Income %	n.a.	Total Revenues %	33.02

Comments

1995 results reflect a one-time charge of $2.5 million to conform to GAAP for the accrual of postretirement benefits. Without such charge, earnings were $2.79 per share. Management believes there will be opportunities for growth and that their favorable balance sheet will be helpful in the coming years. We were unable to obtain 1993 and 1992 financial information.

Officers	Position	Ownership Information	10/31/95
Ricard W. Glenn	President, CEO	Number of Shares Outstanding	601,239
William G. Perlberg	Secretary, Treasurer	Market Capitalization	$ 4,659,602
		Frequency Of Dividends	Annual
		Number of Shareholders	Under 500

Other Information					
Transfer Agent	Company Office			Where Listed	OTC-PS
Auditor	Weinlander, Fitzhugh et al			Symbol	RWCI
Market Maker	Hill, Thompson, Magid & Co.Inc	Telephone	(800)631-3083	SIC Code	3599
Broker Dealer	Regular Stockbroker			Employees	220

Radio Frequency Company, Inc.

150 Dover Road • Millis, MA 02054-0158 • Telephone (617)762-4900 • Fax (617)762-4952

Company Description

The Company operates in a single segment within the electronics industry. The Company designs, manufactures and sells advanced technology, high frequency heat processing systems for the industrial market.

	03/30/96	03/25/95	03/26/94	03/27/93
Per Share Information				
Stock Price	3.25	3.25	3.00	4.00
Earnings Per Share	0.06	0.10	0.07	-0.24
Price / Earnings Ratio	54.17	32.50	42.86	n.a.
Book Value Per Share	3.64	2.52	2.58	3.82
Price / Book Value %	89.29	128.97	116.28	104.71
Dividends Per Share	0.16	0.16	0.16	0.16
Annual Financial Data				
Operating Results (000's)				
Total Revenues	3,594.0	3,375.9	3,734.4	3,076.9
Costs & Expenses	3,523.2	-3,240.0	-3,701.6	-3,405.0
Income Before Taxes and Other	70.8	135.8	32.9	-328.1
Other Items	n.a.	n.a.	43.9	n.a.
Income Tax	12.0	-44.3	-11.3	111.7
Net Income	58.8	91.5	65.5	-216.4
Cash Flow From Operations	152.1	942.3	288.6	605.3
Balance Sheet (000's)				
Cash & Equivalents	1,217.9	1,415.4	1,534.4	1,386.8
Total Current Assets	4,288.1	3,966.0	3,481.7	3,595.7
Fixed Assets, Net	575.1	604.2	499.2	624.3
Total Assets	5,237.0	4,871.2	4,023.8	4,370.3
Total Current Liabilities	1,902.3	1,467.6	609.2	890.9
Long-Term Debt	n.a.	n.a.	n.a.	n.a.
Stockholders' Equity	3,306.5	3,392.2	3,414.6	3,479.5
Performance & Financial Condition				
Return on Total Revenues %	1.64	2.71	1.75	-7.03
Return on Avg Stockholders' Equity %	1.76	2.69	1.90	-5.90
Return on Average Assets %	1.16	2.06	1.56	-4.68
Current Ratio	2.25	2.70	5.72	4.04
Debt / Equity %	n.a.	n.a.	n.a.	n.a.

Compound Growth %'s	EPS % -7.42	Net Income % -5.25	Total Revenues % 4.08

Comments

Although the Company has liquidity and no debt, operations have not provided a reasonable return on equity. Management is focused on new product development. The Company's research and development expenses exceeded plan because of unforeseen technical obstacles in developing new high powered systems for equipment in the rapidly expanding ceramic and bulk material drying categories. Management reports a $1 million increase in orders at the end of fiscal 1995 over the previous year end and is quite confident about 1996.

Officers	Position	Ownership Information	03/30/96
Thomas W. James	President, CEO	Number of Shares Outstanding	909,425
Melvyn H. Harris, M.D.	Treasurer	Market Capitalization	$ 2,955,631
Wallace J. Ross	Vice President	Frequency Of Dividends	Annual
		Number of Shareholders	Under 500

Other Information			
Transfer Agent	American Stock Transfer & Trust Company	Where Listed	OTC-PS
Auditor	Andrew K. Baxter, CPA	Symbol	RFRQ
Market Maker	H.C. Wainwright & Co., Inc. Telephone (800)225-6790	SIC Code	5084
Broker Dealer	Regular Stockbroker	Employees	33

Radva Corporation

301 First Street • Radford, VA 24143 • Telephone (540)639-2458 • Fax (540)731-3731

Company Description

The Company produces and sells molded and fabricated expanded polystyrene foam products such as packaging materials and containers and has also developed and patented housing construction panels utilizing polystyrene foam reinforced with steel. In addition, they build and sell machinery used to manufacture the panels, along with the licensing rights to market the panels. The Company's facilities are located in Radford and Portsmouth, Virginia.

	12/31/95	12/31/94	12/31/93	12/31/92
Per Share Information				
Stock Price	1.06	1.06	0.38	0.69
Earnings Per Share	0.13	0.14	0.02	0.14
Price / Earnings Ratio	8.15	7.57	19.00	4.93
Book Value Per Share	0.77	0.63	0.49	0.47
Price / Book Value %	137.66	168.25	77.55	146.81
Dividends Per Share	n.a.	n.a.	n.a.	n.a.
Annual Financial Data				
Operating Results (000's)				
Total Revenues	10,793.0	11,687.3	10,453.2	10,997.7
Costs & Expenses	-10,231.8	-11,153.4	-10,360.6	-10,483.9
Income Before Taxes and Other	519.9	533.9	92.6	513.8
Other Items	-27.6	n.a.	n.a.	174.7
Income Tax	-10.4	-9.7	n.a.	-174.7
Net Income	482.0	524.2	92.6	513.8
Cash Flow From Operations	334.5	631.4	209.9	1,055.7
Balance Sheet (000's)				
Cash & Equivalents	349.9	189.1	7.3	175.1
Total Current Assets	4,135.4	3,084.7	2,500.0	3,234.2
Fixed Assets, Net	2,307.8	3,567.3	2,899.7	2,846.6
Total Assets	7,997.5	8,317.6	7,206.1	7,503.0
Total Current Liabilities	1,984.9	3,950.0	4,305.1	4,624.0
Long-Term Debt	2,833.2	2,010.2	793.6	864.2
Stockholders' Equity	3,179.4	2,357.4	1,833.2	1,740.6
Performance & Financial Condition				
Return on Total Revenues %	4.47	4.49	0.89	4.67
Return on Avg Stockholders' Equity %	17.41	25.02	5.18	34.62
Return on Average Assets %	5.91	6.75	1.26	7.24
Current Ratio	2.08	0.78	0.58	0.70
Debt / Equity %	89.11	85.27	43.29	49.65

Compound Growth %'s	EPS %	-2.44	Net Income %	-2.11	Total Revenues %	-0.62

Comments

Included in revenues for 1995, is a gain of $1.0 million relating to the sale of an 80% interest in its wholly owned subsidiary. The Company has net operating loss carryforwards and investment tax credit carryforwards of $1.9 million and $213,000, respectively, expiring through 2005 and 2000. The Company has a 31% interest in a joint venture in Russia. The facility, which produces building panels, has not yet had results significant to the Company's financial statements.

Officers	Position	Ownership Information	12/31/95
Luther I. Dickens	President	Number of Shares Outstanding	4,104,727
James M. Hylton	Secretary, Treasurer	Market Capitalization	$ 4,351,011
William F. Fry	Vice President, Controller	Frequency Of Dividends	n.a.
Stephen L. Dickens	Vice President	Number of Shareholders	318

Other Information

Transfer Agent	American Transfer & Trust Company		Where Listed	OTC-BB
Auditor	Persinger & Company LLP		Symbol	RDVA
Market Maker	Ernst & Company	Telephone (800)845-4330	SIC Code	3086
Broker Dealer	Regular Stockbroker		Employees	180

Ragar Corp.

33 Whitehall Street • New York, NY 10004 • Telephone (212)898-8888 • Fax (212)898-8800

Company Description

The Company sells and installs floor coverings for the residential housing market in Nevada. The Company was organized in the state of New York in 1988, to seek out a suitable business for acquisition or merger. An initial public offering was completed in 1990. In June, 1995, the Company acquired all of the outstanding stock of Carpet Barn Holdings, Inc., in exchange for 13,217,750 shares of its common stock.

	12/31/95	06/01/95	12/31/94	12/31/93
Per Share Information				
Stock Price	3.88	n.a.	n.a.	n.a.
Earnings Per Share	0.02	n.a.	n.a.	n.a.
Price / Earnings Ratio	194.00	n.a.	n.a.	n.a.
Book Value Per Share	0.24	n.a.	n.a.	n.a.
Price / Book Value %	1,616.70	n.a.	n.a.	n.a.
Dividends Per Share	n.a.	n.a.	n.a.	n.a.
Annual Financial Data				
Operating Results (000's)				
Total Revenues	23,999.9	16,382.6	42,551.7	34,572.9
Costs & Expenses	-23,255.9	-12,645.5	-36,975.6	-33,451.6
Income Before Taxes and Other	744.0	3,737.1	4,888.3	1,113.8
Other Items	n.a.	n.a.	n.a.	n.a.
Income Tax	-254.6	-1,270.6	-1,662.0	-378.7
Net Income	489.4	2,466.5	3,226.3	735.1
Cash Flow From Operations	3,460.6	1,762.5	6,074.4	1,185.9
Balance Sheet (000's)				
Cash & Equivalents	693.4	n.a.	n.a.	n.a.
Total Current Assets	4,993.4	n.a.	n.a.	n.a.
Fixed Assets, Net	415.7	n.a.	n.a.	n.a.
Total Assets	24,084.5	n.a.	n.a.	n.a.
Total Current Liabilities	8,750.0	n.a.	n.a.	n.a.
Long-Term Debt	8,811.6	n.a.	n.a.	n.a.
Stockholders' Equity	6,487.3	n.a.	n.a.	n.a.
Performance & Financial Condition				
Return on Total Revenues %	2.04	n.a.	n.a.	n.a.
Return on Avg Stockholders' Equity %	n.a.	n.a.	n.a.	n.a.
Return on Average Assets %	n.a.	n.a.	n.a.	n.a.
Current Ratio	0.57	n.a.	n.a.	n.a.
Debt / Equity %	135.83	n.a.	n.a.	n.a.

Compound Growth %'s	EPS %	n.a.	Net Income %	-12.68	Total Revenues %	-11.46

Comments

1995 operating results include the seven months ended December 31, 1995 (under new ownership) and the five months ended June 1, 1995 (under former management). The years ended December 31, 1994 and 1993 are as a predecessor company. The results of operations are not comparable to the predecessor operations due to the amortization of intangible assets and interest expense incurred on the acquisition debt. Balance sheets, per share information and statistics are not presented prior to 1995, due to lack of comparability. Stay tuned for next year when there should be some meaningful comparisons.

Officers	Position	Ownership Information	12/31/95
Philip A. Herman	President	Number of Shares Outstanding	14,932,142
Steven Chesin	Senior VP, COO	Market Capitalization	$ 57,936,711
Mark Szporka	CFO	Frequency Of Dividends	n.a.
Gary Peiffer	Secretary	Number of Shareholders	312
Jeffrey Wiens	Controller		

Other Information

Transfer Agent	Corporate Stock Transfer, Inc.		Where Listed	OTC-BB
Auditor	McGladrey & Pullen LLP		Symbol	RAGC
Market Maker	A.J. Michaels & Co.	Telephone (516)231-3686	SIC Code	5713
Broker Dealer	Regular Stockbroker		Employees	110

Ramsay Managed Care, Inc.

639 Loyola Avenue, Suite 1725 • New Orleans, LA 70113 • Telephone (504)585-0515 • Fax (504)585-0505

Company Description

The Company provides mental health and substance abuse services provided by both independent and affiliated providers on behalf of its clients, insurance carriers, HMO's and self-insured employers. The Company also provides HMO services and provides prepaid health services to its members. The Company was incorporated in Delaware in 1993, and began operations in October 1993, as a result of the acquisition of Florida Psychiatric Management, Inc. The Company became publically traded in April, 1995.

	06/30/95	06/30/94
Per Share Information		
Stock Price	2.88	n.a.
Earnings Per Share	-0.41	0.03
Price / Earnings Ratio	n.a.	n.a.
Book Value Per Share	0.88	0.23
Price / Book Value %	327.27	n.a.
Dividends Per Share	n.a.	n.a.
Annual Financial Data		
Operating Results (000's)		
Total Revenues	16,214.0	5,849.0
Costs & Expenses	-17,977.0	-5,626.0
Income Before Taxes and Other	-1,763.0	223.0
Other Items	n.a.	n.a.
Income Tax	192.0	-155.0
Net Income	-1,571.0	68.0
Cash Flow From Operations	2,570.0	506.0
Balance Sheet (000's)		
Cash & Equivalents	4,314.0	763.0
Total Current Assets	6,044.0	1,610.0
Fixed Assets, Net	1,196.0	572.0
Total Assets	20,848.0	13,288.0
Total Current Liabilities	6,524.0	2,827.0
Long-Term Debt	7,820.0	2,209.0
Stockholders' Equity	5,584.0	1,194.0
Performance & Financial Condition		
Return on Total Revenues %	-9.69	1.16
Return on Avg Stockholders' Equity %	-46.36	n.a.
Return on Average Assets %	-9.20	n.a.
Current Ratio	0.93	0.57
Debt / Equity %	140.04	185.01

Compound Growth %'s	EPS %	n.a.	Net Income %	n.a.	Total Revenues %	177.21

Comments

Comparisons of operations between 1995 and 1994 are not meaningful due to the startup nature of the business. For the six months ended December 31, 1995, the Company had revenues of $10.5 million, and a net loss of $1.5 million, as compared to revenues of $6.3 million and a net loss of $2,000, for the same period in 1994. In March, 1996, the Company announced the agreement to sell its HMO operation to an investor group for approximately $4.5 million.

Officers	Position	Ownership Information	06/30/95
Paul J. Ramsay	Chairman	Number of Shares Outstanding	6,370,909
Martin Lazoritz	Exec VP	Market Capitalization	$ 18,348,218
Parveez A. Oliaii	Exec VP	Frequency Of Dividends	n.a.
Warwick D. Syphers	CFO, Secretary	Number of Shareholders	615
Philip G. Symon	Treasurer		

Other Information					
Transfer Agent	First Union National Bank of NC			Where Listed	OTC-BB
Auditor	Ernst & Young LLP			Symbol	RMCR
Market Maker	Herzog, Heine, Geduld, Inc.	Telephone	(800)221-3600	SIC Code	8099
Broker Dealer	Regular Stockbroker			Employees	180

Rand McNally

8255 North Central Park Avenue • Skokie, IL 60076-2908 • Telephone (847)329-8100 • Fax (847)673-0813

Company Description

The Company publishes, prints, manufactures and distributes geographic information products. It also has a number of other businesses related to its core business and the travel industry. Formed in 1856, the Company has long set the world standard in geographic information. The Company claims they are a private company even though shares are traded freely in the over-the-counter market. Please enjoy our vignette of their wonderful history.

	12/31/95	12/31/94	12/31/93
Per Share Information			
Stock Price	345.00	154.00	150.00
Earnings Per Share	11.42	13.07	6.62
Price / Earnings Ratio	30.21	11.78	22.66
Book Value Per Share	108.13	103.24	93.39
Price / Book Value %	319.06	149.17	160.62
Dividends Per Share	4.60	4.40	4.20
Annual Financial Data			
Operating Results (000's)			
Total Revenues	468,899.0	438,525.0	395,288.0
Costs & Expenses	-454,305.0	-410,989.0	-376,177.0
Income Before Taxes and Other	18,066.0	25,124.0	7,797.0
Other Items	n.a.	n.a.	1,487.0
Income Tax	-5,431.0	-10,870.0	-1,894.0
Net Income	12,635.0	14,254.0	7,390.0
Cash Flow From Operations	n.a.	n.a.	n.a.
Balance Sheet (000's)			
Cash & Equivalents	7,556.0	30,010.0	28,750.0
Total Current Assets	176,173.0	182,039.0	153,200.0
Fixed Assets, Net	96,754.0	100,491.0	101,950.0
Total Assets	314,232.0	315,716.0	291,100.0
Total Current Liabilities	75,987.0	84,584.0	62,150.0
Long-Term Debt	66,735.0	67,452.0	70,850.0
Stockholders' Equity	119,639.0	112,592.0	104,350.0
Performance & Financial Condition			
Return on Total Revenues %	n.a.	3.25	1.87
Return on Avg Stockholders' Equity %	10.88	13.14	n.a.
Return on Average Assets %	4.01	4.70	n.a.
Current Ratio	2.32	2.15	2.47
Debt / Equity %	55.78	59.91	67.90

Compound Growth %'s	EPS %	31.34	Net Income %	30.76	Total Revenues %	8.91

Comments

There is no indication in the shareholder's report that these numbers have been audited nor are the financial statements as complete as what are traditionally found. Based on nonrecurring gains and the reversal of a 1994 writeoff, it appears that the decline in earnings per share from operations was really more like a drop from $13.74 a share in 1994 to $8.28 a share in 1995. Even this is speculation because the full detail of what is referred to as "unusual items" is not provided.

Officers	Position	Ownership Information	12/31/95
Andrew McNally IV	Chairman, CEO	Number of Shares Outstanding	1,106,392
John S. Bakalar	President, COO	Market Capitalization	$ 381,705,240
Edward C. McNally	Secretary	Frequency Of Dividends	Quarterly
		Number of Shareholders	n.a.

Other Information			
Transfer Agent	First Trust of Illinois, N.A., Chicago	Where Listed	OTC-BB
Auditor	Not indicated in report	Symbol	RNMC
Market Maker	Howe Barnes Investments, Inc.	Telephone (800)621-2364	SIC Code	2740
Broker Dealer	Regular Stockbroker	Employees	5000

Map Making

William Rand and Andrew McNally opened their first print shop on Chicago's Lake Street in 1856, five years before the beginning of the American Civil War. Recognizing that Chicago had become a booming rail center, Messrs. Rand and McNally decided to produce railroad tickets, timetables and other transportation related items. Their business grew and prospered, even side stepping the worst of the Great Chicago Fire of 1871 which put them out of business for only three days. The next year saw the production of Rand McNally's first map, and in 1880 they began to manufacture globes and maps for schools.

The Company had grown to 675 employees by 1899 when, after forty-three years in business with his co-founder, William Rand sold his share of the Company to Andrew McNally. By 1905, both of the founders had passed away (within a year of each other), leaving their heirs to carry on.

And this they did. Within two years, the Company was producing the first *photo-auto guides*, predecessors to modern road maps. These included written directions and photographs of landmarks found along routes covered by the map. Andrew McNally II even managed to supply some of the photos used to illustrate the Chicago-Milwaukee guide while on his honeymoon!

The age of the automobile had obviously arrived, but road maps were still quite cumbersome to use, relying on long road names and difficult graphics to identify highways. The development in 1917 of a system for numbering highways was a welcome enhancement of Rand McNally's product and undoubtedly helped popularize automobile touring in America. Gulf Oil teamed up with the Company to this end as well, distributing Rand McNally maps at its service stations.

While the rise of the automobile greatly augmented the demand for Rand McNally products, other markets existed for their maps as well. Charles Lindbergh even put the Company's product to use, navigating the land portion of his famed trans-Atlantic flight of 1927 with Rand McNally maps at his side. By World War II and Germany's invasion of Poland, public demand for European maps had reached such a pitch that the Company's presses operated overtime for the war's duration.

Today, Rand McNally continues in its business of providing diversified products and services. The Company still supplies transportation tickets and related items for ground and now air travel through its Docu-Systems segment. In addition, they now have three other segments, including Book Services, related to book manufacture; Publishing, which provides complete global geographic information; and Media Services, a provider of digital packaging solutions. As the twentieth century draws to a close, they are well prepared, it seems, to enter into the third century in which they will be doing business.

Randall Bearings, Inc.

Greenlawn Ave. and Lake St. • Lima, OH 45802-1258 • Telephone (419)223-1075 • Fax (419)228-0200

Company Description

The Company manufactures various types of bearings. It was organized in 1918 and went public in 1946 with an offering of 100,000 shares at $3.50 per share. The Company last repurchased its own shares during 1991 at which time 23,406 shares were acquired for $117,030.

	12/31/95	12/31/94	12/31/93	12/31/92
Per Share Information				
Stock Price	8.69	4.75	4.75	4.75
Earnings Per Share	1.07	1.10	0.80	0.68
Price / Earnings Ratio	8.12	3.86	5.00	6.99
Book Value Per Share	13.77	12.93	12.03	11.43
Price / Book Value %	63.11	32.87	33.25	41.56
Dividends Per Share	0.23	0.20	0.20	0.20
Annual Financial Data				
Operating Results (000's)				
Total Revenues	8,655.2	7,600.4	6,430.8	6,221.7
Costs & Expenses	-7,751.5	-6,709.1	-5,784.2	-5,783.1
Income Before Taxes and Other	753.0	752.6	526.7	438.6
Other Items	n.a.	n.a.	n.a.	n.a.
Income Tax	-277.6	-266.4	-167.7	-139.4
Net Income	475.4	486.1	359.0	299.2
Cash Flow From Operations	n.a.	n.a.	n.a.	n.a.
Balance Sheet (000's)				
Cash & Equivalents	757.2	909.4	1,083.6	374.6
Total Current Assets	4,699.7	4,531.4	4,046.9	3,707.9
Fixed Assets, Net	2,565.4	2,480.5	2,255.9	2,422.6
Total Assets	7,309.8	7,053.7	6,368.5	6,222.1
Total Current Liabilities	773.4	876.7	690.9	696.2
Long-Term Debt	112.2	183.0	132.1	261.7
Stockholders' Equity	6,121.2	5,748.1	5,350.9	5,080.8
Performance & Financial Condition				
Return on Total Revenues %	5.49	6.40	5.58	4.81
Return on Avg Stockholders' Equity %	8.01	8.76	6.88	6.01
Return on Average Assets %	6.62	7.24	5.70	5.02
Current Ratio	6.08	5.17	5.86	5.33
Debt / Equity %	1.83	3.18	2.47	5.15

Compound Growth %'s	EPS %	16.31	Net Income %	16.69	Total Revenues %	11.63

Comments

Inventory is stated at LIFO. The accumulative LIFO reserve was about $500,000 at December 31, 1995. The Company is in excellent financial condition and has strong growth over the years for which we have reports. With the stock trading at below book value, it is clear that low visibility has a real impact on the pricing of a security.

Officers	Position	Ownership Information	12/31/95
B G. Dickerson	Chairman, President	Number of Shares Outstanding	44,453
K C. Harrod	Exec VP	Market Capitalization	$ 386,297
R R. Harris	Secretary, Treasurer	Frequency Of Dividends	Quarterly
W R. Buchanan	VP - Manufacturing	Number of Shareholders	Under 500

Other Information

Transfer Agent	The First National Bank of Chicago		Where Listed	OTC-PS
Auditor	Rea & Associates Inc.		Symbol	RBRG
Market Maker	Robotti & Eng, Incorporated	Telephone (212)986-4800	SIC Code	3490
Broker Dealer	Regular Stockbroker		Employees	65

Ravens Metal Products, Inc.

861 East Tallmadge Avenue • Akron, OH 44310 • Telephone (216)630-4528 • Fax (216)630-4535

Company Description

The Company designs, manufactures, and sells aluminum truck trailers and bodies, including dump trailers and bodies and flatbed trailers used in the transportation industry. These products are sold direct to customers and through a nationwide network of dealerships. The Company also sells a variety of after-market parts for trucks and trailers. The Company was incorporated in the state of West Virginia in 1956 and reincorporated in the state of Delaware in 1986.

	03/31/95	03/31/94	03/31/93	03/31/92
Per Share Information				
Stock Price	2.13	2.13	n.a.	n.a.
Earnings Per Share	0.23	0.26	0.53	-0.65
Price / Earnings Ratio	9.26	8.19	n.a.	n.a.
Book Value Per Share	0.42	0.18	-0.06	-1.67
Price / Book Value %	507.14	1,183.30	n.a.	n.a.
Dividends Per Share	n.a.	n.a.	n.a.	n.a.
Annual Financial Data				
Operating Results (000's)				
Total Revenues	42,160.6	25,797.6	20,038.9	14,685.7
Costs & Expenses	-39,398.6	-24,191.7	-19,354.9	-15,325.7
Income Before Taxes and Other	2,762.0	1,605.9	684.0	-640.0
Other Items	n.a.	n.a.	531.0	n.a.
Income Tax	-960.8	423.2	-284.0	n.a.
Net Income	1,801.2	2,029.1	931.0	-640.0
Cash Flow From Operations	685.3	1,235.5	193.7	n.a.
Balance Sheet (000's)				
Cash & Equivalents	394.0	606.1	587.7	433.8
Total Current Assets	9,773.3	6,040.2	4,825.1	3,292.7
Fixed Assets, Net	5,896.8	2,195.6	2,246.5	2,098.7
Total Assets	19,405.2	8,420.3	7,168.7	5,477.6
Total Current Liabilities	6,090.4	3,471.3	3,400.7	6,842.9
Long-Term Debt	9,716.1	3,129.4	3,921.6	1,012.7
Stockholders' Equity	3,267.1	1,373.3	-496.4	-2,948.2
Performance & Financial Condition				
Return on Total Revenues %	4.27	7.87	4.65	-4.36
Return on Avg Stockholders' Equity %	77.63	462.79	-54.06	23.23
Return on Average Assets %	12.95	26.03	14.72	-11.58
Current Ratio	1.60	1.74	1.42	0.48
Debt / Equity %	297.40	227.87	n.a.	n.a.

Compound Growth %'s	EPS %	33.01	Net Income %	39.09	Total Revenues %	42.13

Comments

During the year ended March 31, 1994, the Company realized a gain of $565,000 on the settlement of disputes and collection of life insurance proceeds relating to a previous chairman of the Company. Officers and directors, as a group, owned 89.6% of the Company's outstanding common shares at June 21, 1995. There has been little trading activity in the Company's stock. The Company's market maker maintains a bid of between $.10 and $.25, although we do not know of any sellers at that price. A few trades took place at between $1.50 and $2.75 per share. For the nine months ended December 31, 1995, the Company had sales of $28.4 million and a net loss of $29,000 as compared to $30.3 million and Net Income of $1.2 million in 1994.

Officers	Position	Ownership Information	03/31/95
Lowell P. Morgan	President	Number of Shares Outstanding	7,769,392
Jacob Pollock	CEO, Treasurer	Market Capitalization	$ 16,548,805
Nicholas T. George	Secretary	Frequency Of Dividends	n.a.
John J. Stitz	Vice President, CFO	Number of Shareholders	4,100

Other Information				
Transfer Agent	Company Office		Where Listed	OTC-PS
Auditor	Coopers & Lybrand LLP		Symbol	RAMPA
Market Maker	Chicago Corporation, The	Telephone (800)621-1674	SIC Code	3715
Broker Dealer	Regular Stockbroker		Employees	250

Real Estate Income Partners III Ltd Partnership

27611 La Paz Road • Laguna Niquel, CA 92607-0009 • Telephone (714)643-7490

Company Description

The Partnership owns real estate properties which it acquired for cash shortly after formation. The properties include shopping centers, office buildings, research and development buildings, and a combination office and warehouse building. They are geographically dispersed around the United States. The Partnership was formed in 1985 and raised $63.5 million in a private placement at that time.

	12/31/95	12/31/94	12/31/93	12/31/92
Per Unit Information				
Price Per Unit	323.00	245.00	166.00	209.38
Earnings Per Unit	-10.17	-23.86	7.44	-74.45
Price / Earnings Ratio	n.a.	n.a.	22.31	n.a.
Book Value Per Unit	544.70	586.95	635.90	662.81
Price / Book Value %	59.30	41.74	26.10	31.59
Distributions Per Unit	32.08	27.37	32.08	32.88
Cash Flow Per Unit	37.73	28.96	28.38	32.60
Annual Financial Data				
Operating Results (000's)				
Total Revenues	5,191.0	4,718.0	5,125.0	5,208.0
Costs & Expenses	-4,397.0	-4,349.0	-4,647.0	-4,286.0
Operating Income	-653.0	-1,531.0	478.0	-4,778.0
Other Items	n.a.	n.a.	n.a.	n.a.
Net Income	-653.0	-1,531.0	478.0	-4,778.0
Cash Flow From Operations	2,397.0	1,840.0	1,803.0	2,071.0
Balance Sheet (000's)				
Cash & Equivalents	980.0	1,085.0	1,056.0	1,389.0
Total Current Assets	2,477.0	2,585.0	1,859.0	2,139.0
Investments In Real Estate	32,373.0	34,920.0	38,085.0	39,444.0
Total Assets	34,850.0	37,505.0	40,825.0	42,470.0
Total Current Liabilities	448.0	391.0	423.0	487.0
Long-Term Debt	n.a.	n.a.	n.a.	n.a.
Partners' Capital	34,402.0	37,114.0	40,402.0	41,983.0
Performance & Financial Condition				
Return on Total Revenues %	-12.58	-32.45	9.33	-91.74
Return on Average Partners' Capital %	n.a.	n.a.	n.a.	n.a.
Return on Average Assets %	-1.80	-3.91	1.15	-10.86
Current Ratio	5.53	6.61	4.39	4.39
Debt / Equity %	n.a.	n.a.	n.a.	n.a.

Compound Growth %'s	EPU % n.a.	Net Income % n.a.	Total Revenues % -0.11

Comments

Although the initial intent was to hold properties for a long term, the partners now wish to proceed with an orderly liquidation of the Partnership. The general partner has examined several alternative methods and is expected to proceed at the appropriate time. An appraiser was asked by the general partner to value the properties at December 31, 1995, under the assumption that all properties would be sold over the next four years. The unit valuation, as reported by the general partner, was $532.90. 1992 results include a $4.9 million writedown of the property value.

Officers	Position	Ownership Information	12/31/95
Brent R. Donaldson	Other	Number of Shares Outstanding	63,534
Robert M. Anderson	Other	Market Capitalization	$ 20,521,482
Arthur B. Birtcher	Other	Frequency Of Distributions	Quarterly
Ronald E. Birtcher	Other	Number of Partners	7,498
Richard G. Wollack	Other		

Other Information

Transfer Agent	Company Office				Where Listed	Order Matching Only
Auditor	KPMG Peat Marwick				Symbol	n.a.
Market Maker	None				SIC Code	6510
Broker Dealer	Chicago Partnership Board	Tel/Ext	(800)272-6273	690	Employees	None

Real Goods Trading Corporation

555 Leslie Lane • Ukiah, CA 95482-5507 • Telephone (707)468-9292 • Fax (707)468-9394

Company Description

The Company sells alternative energy and conservation products through mail order catalogs and its three retail stores located in Hopland, California, Amherst, Wisconsin and Eugene, Oregon. The Company was incorporated in California in 1990.

	03/31/95	03/31/94	03/31/93	03/31/92
Per Share Information				
Stock Price	8.94	6.75	5.50	n.a.
Earnings Per Share	0.01	0.05	0.02	n.a.
Price / Earnings Ratio	894.00	135.00	275.00	n.a.
Book Value Per Share	1.32	1.29	0.41	0.34
Price / Book Value %	677.27	523.26	1,341.50	n.a.
Dividends Per Share	n.a.	n.a.	n.a.	n.a.
Annual Financial Data				
Operating Results (000's)				
Total Revenues	16,403.0	11,944.0	7,790.5	6,191.8
Costs & Expenses	-16,368.0	-11,570.0	-7,721.3	-6,181.8
Income Before Taxes and Other	35.0	316.0	69.3	10.0
Other Items	n.a.	n.a.	n.a.	n.a.
Income Tax	-14.0	-163.0	-25.8	-4.4
Net Income	21.0	153.0	43.5	5.6
Cash Flow From Operations	-788.0	106.0	-89.4	-152.2
Balance Sheet (000's)				
Cash & Equivalents	832.0	2,605.0	344.2	309.7
Total Current Assets	3,897.0	4,647.0	1,741.4	1,234.9
Fixed Assets, Net	1,668.0	768.0	164.3	127.4
Total Assets	5,734.0	5,589.0	1,920.4	1,370.4
Total Current Liabilities	1,174.0	1,116.0	765.8	415.5
Long-Term Debt	41.0	61.0	n.a.	n.a.
Stockholders' Equity	4,519.0	4,412.0	1,154.7	954.9
Performance & Financial Condition				
Return on Total Revenues %	0.13	1.28	0.56	0.09
Return on Avg Stockholders' Equity %	0.47	5.50	4.12	n.a.
Return on Average Assets %	0.37	4.07	2.64	n.a.
Current Ratio	3.32	4.16	2.27	2.97
Debt / Equity %	0.91	1.38	n.a.	n.a.

Compound Growth %'s	EPS %	-29.29	Net Income %	-30.52	Total Revenues %	38.37

Comments

In 1991 and 1993, the Company sold, without the use of brokers, agents or dealers, 200,000 shares of its common stock at $5.00 per share. During February, 1993, the Company commenced a direct public offering (under Regulation A of the Securities and Exchange Act of 1934) of 600,000 shares of its common stock at $6.00 per share. Within six months, and with only limited use of selling agents, the Company sold all the shares, realizing gross proceeds of $3.6 million. Sales and Net Income for the nine months ended December 31, 1995, amounted to $12.7 million and $27,000, respectively, as compared to $13.3 million and $110,000 for the comparable period in 1994.

Officers	Position	Ownership Information	03/31/95
John Schaeffer	President, CEO	Number of Shares Outstanding	3,421,674
James T. Robello	Controller, CFO	Market Capitalization	$ 30,589,766
		Frequency Of Dividends	n.a.
		Number of Shareholders	4,216

Other Information					
Transfer Agent	U.S. Stock Transfer Corporation			Where Listed	PSE
Auditor	Deloitte & Touche LLP			Symbol	RGT
Market Maker	n.a.			SIC Code	5961
Broker Dealer	A.G. Edwards & Sons, Inc.	Tel/Ext	(707)528-2332	Employees	111

Real Silk Investments, Incorporated

445 N. Pennsylvania St.,Ste500 • Indianapolis, IN 46204-1800 • Telephone (317)632-7359 • Fax (317)632-5104

Company Description

The Company is a regulated investment company and, except for certain gains accruing before this election, is not taxed on its income. Investments are predominently a diversified portfolio of common stocks in approximately 55 different companies.

	12/31/95	12/31/94	12/31/93	12/31/92
Per Share Information				
Stock Price	380.00	300.00	300.00	300.00
Earnings Per Share	85.18	-12.10	73.45	73.57
Price / Earnings Ratio	4.46	n.a.	4.08	4.08
Book Value Per Share	575.03	505.13	531.15	470.95
Price / Book Value %	66.08	59.39	56.48	63.70
Dividends Per Share	15.28	13.92	13.15	12.00
Annual Financial Data				
Operating Results (000's)				
Total Revenues	14,414.6	-2,794.5	n.a.	n.a.
Costs & Expenses	-357.3	-317.1	n.a.	n.a.
Income Before Taxes and Other	14,057.3	-3,111.6	n.a.	n.a.
Other Items	n.a.	n.a.	n.a.	n.a.
Income Tax	-29.7	1,118.8	n.a.	n.a.
Net Income	14,027.6	-1,992.8	n.a.	n.a.
Cash Flow From Operations	n.a.	n.a.	n.a.	n.a.
Balance Sheet (000's)				
Cash & Equivalents	10.4	52.1	n.a.	n.a.
Total Current Assets	107,501.8	95,988.3	n.a.	n.a.
Fixed Assets, Net	44.7	50.6	n.a.	n.a.
Total Assets	107,555.7	96,038.9	n.a.	n.a.
Total Current Liabilities	10.5	34.7	n.a.	n.a.
Long-Term Debt	n.a.	n.a.	n.a.	n.a.
Stockholders' Equity	94,697.9	83,186.7	n.a.	n.a.
Performance & Financial Condition				
Return on Total Revenues %	97.32	71.31	n.a.	n.a.
Return on Avg Stockholders' Equity %	15.77	n.a.	n.a.	n.a.
Return on Average Assets %	13.78	n.a.	n.a.	n.a.
Current Ratio	n.a.	2764.10	n.a.	n.a.
Debt / Equity %	n.a.	n.a.	n.a.	n.a.

Compound Growth %'s	EPS %	5.01	Net Income %	n.a.	Total Revenues %	n.a.

Comments

Operating expenses are less than 0.4% of net assets, an admirable rate for even the simplest of mutual funds. If you like the stocks they buy and hold, you could have a piece of it at a discount from current value.

Officers	Position	Ownership Information	12/31/95
Daniel R. Efroymson	President, Treasurer	Number of Shares Outstanding	164,683
L A. Cox	Secretary	Market Capitalization	$ 62,579,540
Loralei M. Efroymson	Vice President	Frequency Of Dividends	Quarterly
M A. Singer	Other	Number of Shareholders	Under 500
J D. Hagan	Other		

Other Information

Transfer Agent	Chemical Mellon Shareholder Services			Where Listed	OTC-PS
Auditor	KPMG Peat Marwick LLP			Symbol	RSHM
Market Maker	McDonald & Company Securities	Telephone	(216)443-2350	SIC Code	6799
Broker Dealer	Standard Investment	Tel/Ext	(888)783-4688 Jack	Employees	10

Red Rose Collection, Inc.

42 Adrian Court • Burlingame, CA 94010 • Telephone (415)692-4500 • Fax (415)692-1750

Company Description

The Company markets and distributes products which emphasize personal growth and development. It conducts business through its nationwide mail order catalog, its wholesale distribution network, its bimonthly magazine, and a single retail store in San Francisco, California. Major product lines are gifts, stationery, books, clothing and products that assist people in becoming more aware of their human potential.

	05/31/95	05/31/94
Per Share Information		
Stock Price	3.00	3.00
Earnings Per Share	-0.06	-0.40
Price / Earnings Ratio	n.a.	n.a.
Book Value Per Share	-0.85	-0.83
Price / Book Value %	n.a.	n.a.
Dividends Per Share	n.a.	n.a.
Annual Financial Data		
Operating Results (000's)		
Total Revenues	13,682.6	13,774.4
Costs & Expenses	-13,871.0	-15,046.9
Income Before Taxes and Other	-188.3	-1,272.5
Other Items	n.a.	n.a.
Income Tax	n.a.	n.a.
Net Income	-188.3	-1,272.5
Cash Flow From Operations	-311.7	-340.7
Balance Sheet (000's)		
Cash & Equivalents	97.0	68.3
Total Current Assets	2,040.4	2,319.2
Fixed Assets, Net	831.6	575.4
Total Assets	2,876.2	2,914.9
Total Current Liabilities	2,102.8	1,999.0
Long-Term Debt	3,500.2	3,546.4
Stockholders' Equity	-2,726.9	-2,630.5
Performance & Financial Condition		
Return on Total Revenues %	-1.38	-9.24
Return on Avg Stockholders' Equity %	7.03	n.a.
Return on Average Assets %	-6.50	n.a.
Current Ratio	0.97	1.16
Debt / Equity %	n.a.	n.a.

Compound Growth %'s	EPS %	n.a.	Net Income %	n.a.	Total Revenues %	-0.67

Comments

Through May, 1995, the Company has relied on equity infusions from its shareholders and certain other financing including a SCOR stock offering. Management believed it would generate sufficient cash from operations in fiscal 1996. The Company is about to begin a Regulation A stock offering for up to 250,000 of new shares at $10 per share. The Company hopes it will be able to list the stock on the Pacific Stock Exchange's SCOR Marketplace, which is accessible through American Online, after the offering. The proceeds would be used to pay off indebtedness and provide working capital.

Officers	Position	Ownership Information	05/31/95
Rinaldo S. Brutoco	President, CEO	Number of Shares Outstanding	3,204,514
Lalla Shanna Brutoco	Senior VP, Secretary	Market Capitalization	$ 9,613,542
James Gala	Treasurer, CFO	Frequency Of Dividends	n.a.
Rebecca Spencer	Vice President	Number of Shareholders	Under 500
Patricia Ogata	Vice President		

Other Information			
Transfer Agent	Company Office	Where Listed	Order Matching Only
Auditor	Deloitte & Touche LLP	Symbol	n.a.
Market Maker	Company Office	SIC Code	5961
Broker Dealer	None	Employees	n.a.

Reflectix, Inc.

P.O. Box 108 • Markleville, IN 46056 • Telephone (317)533-4332 • Fax (317)533-2327

Company Description

The Company is engaged in the manufacture and sale of reflective insulation products which include insulation for attics, crawl spaces, basement walls, heat ducts, water pipes and wall insulation. The market is the do-it-yourself market, agriculture market and OEM manufacturers nationwide. The Company was founded in 1980. They will soon be relocating the corporate headquarters, which are now located in Utah, to be next to the manufacturing facilities in Indiana.

	06/30/95	06/30/94	06/30/93	06/30/92
Per Share Information				
Stock Price	0.47	0.94	0.57	0.50
Earnings Per Share	0.06	0.07	0.09	0.07
Price / Earnings Ratio	7.83	13.43	6.33	7.14
Book Value Per Share	0.26	0.20	0.20	0.11
Price / Book Value %	180.77	470.00	285.00	454.55
Dividends Per Share	n.a.	n.a.	n.a.	n.a.
Annual Financial Data				
Operating Results (000's)				
Total Revenues	7,766.2	7,032.3	6,939.3	6,257.7
Costs & Expenses	-7,244.6	-6,357.0	-6,353.8	-5,757.5
Income Before Taxes and Other	497.2	669.3	585.4	500.2
Other Items	n.a.	n.a.	52.0	n.a.
Income Tax	-174.0	-233.8	-215.6	-160.0
Net Income	323.2	435.5	421.8	340.2
Cash Flow From Operations	421.9	504.2	453.7	n.a.
Balance Sheet (000's)				
Cash & Equivalents	235.1	151.3	125.4	n.a.
Total Current Assets	1,807.3	1,261.8	1,041.1	n.a.
Fixed Assets, Net	1,963.5	1,390.1	942.3	n.a.
Total Assets	3,780.9	2,651.9	1,983.4	n.a.
Total Current Liabilities	1,630.0	685.5	798.0	n.a.
Long-Term Debt	563.1	746.6	210.6	n.a.
Stockholders' Equity	1,587.7	1,196.4	974.8	n.a.
Performance & Financial Condition				
Return on Total Revenues %	4.16	6.19	6.08	5.44
Return on Avg Stockholders' Equity %	23.21	40.12	55.23	n.a.
Return on Average Assets %	10.05	18.79	20.09	n.a.
Current Ratio	1.11	1.84	1.30	n.a.
Debt / Equity %	35.47	62.41	21.61	n.a.

Compound Growth %'s	EPS %	-5.01	Net Income %	-1.70	Total Revenues %	7.46

Comments

Management reports a number of new products in development as well as the introduction of a new state-of-the-art production machine. Although there are a lot of shares outstanding, which forces this stock to trade at a low price, it should be noted that compounded revenue growth over the last 8 years is approximately 26%.

Officers	Position	Ownership Information	06/30/95
Stephen C. Painter	President	Number of Shares Outstanding	6,026,053
Richard Grant	Vice President, Treasurer	Market Capitalization	$ 2,832,245
Arlan H. Landey	VP - Sales	Frequency Of Dividends	n.a.
Charles E. Painter	Other	Number of Shareholders	Under 500

Other Information

Transfer Agent	Western States Transfer & Registrar,Inc.	Where Listed	OTC-BB
Auditor	Geo. S. Olive & Co. LLC	Symbol	RECT
Market Maker	Alpine Securities Corporation	Telephone (800)521-5588	SIC Code	3990
Broker Dealer	Regular Stockbroker	Employees	55

Reo Plastics, Inc.

11850-93rd Avenue North • Maple Grove, MN 55369-3633 • Telephone (612)425-4171 • Fax (612)425-0735

Company Description

The Company's operations principally involve the custom injection molding, decorating, and assembling of thermoplastics for customers in various industries nationwide.

	04/30/95	04/30/94	04/30/93	04/30/92
Per Share Information				
Stock Price	11.50	9.25	9.25	6.50
Earnings Per Share	1.49	1.44	1.10	0.99
Price / Earnings Ratio	7.72	6.42	8.41	6.57
Book Value Per Share	13.11	11.62	10.18	9.07
Price / Book Value %	87.72	79.60	90.86	71.66
Dividends Per Share	n.a.	n.a.	n.a.	n.a.
Annual Financial Data				
Operating Results (000's)				
Total Revenues	14,268.1	12,253.0	10,888.5	10,719.3
Costs & Expenses	-12,996.0	-11,050.8	-9,963.9	-9,858.5
Income Before Taxes and Other	1,272.0	1,202.2	924.6	860.8
Other Items	n.a.	n.a.	n.a.	n.a.
Income Tax	-479.0	-435.0	-337.0	-332.0
Net Income	793.0	767.2	587.6	528.8
Cash Flow From Operations	-215.4	2,121.2	214.0	32.0
Balance Sheet (000's)				
Cash & Equivalents	77.4	746.5	98.5	84.5
Total Current Assets	7,647.8	5,575.2	5,546.1	4,393.4
Fixed Assets, Net	4,858.1	2,754.9	2,684.6	3,048.0
Total Assets	12,543.9	8,430.1	8,420.7	7,721.4
Total Current Liabilities	5,110.0	1,756.2	2,490.0	1,818.4
Long-Term Debt	200.0	200.0	200.0	715.8
Stockholders' Equity	6,979.0	6,185.9	5,418.7	4,831.1
Performance & Financial Condition				
Return on Total Revenues %	5.56	6.26	5.40	4.93
Return on Avg Stockholders' Equity %	12.05	13.22	11.47	11.58
Return on Average Assets %	7.56	9.11	7.28	7.30
Current Ratio	1.50	3.17	2.23	2.42
Debt / Equity %	2.87	3.23	3.69	14.82

Compound Growth %'s	EPS % 14.60	Net Income % 14.46	Total Revenues % 10.00

Comments

For the first six months of fiscal 1996, sales were $9.1 million as compared to $6.6 in the same period last year, a 37% increase. Profits were off slightly. Compounded growth percentages are also favorable for this company that trades below book value.

Officers	Position	Ownership Information	04/30/95
Earl A. Patch	President	Number of Shares Outstanding	532,500
		Market Capitalization	$ 6,123,750
		Frequency Of Dividends	n.a.
		Number of Shareholders	Under 500

Other Information

				Where Listed	OTC-BB
Transfer Agent	Northwestern Bank, North Wilkesboro, NC			Symbol	REOP
Auditor	McGladrey & Pullen, LLP			SIC Code	3089
Market Maker	R.J. Steichen & Co.	Telephone	(800)328-8217	Employees	200
Broker Dealer	Regular Stockbroker				

Reserve Petroleum Company (The)

6801 N. Broadway, Suite 300 • Oklahoma City, OK 73116-9092 • Telephone (405)848-7551 • Fax (405)848-7888

Company Description

The Company is engaged principally in the exploration for and the development of oil and natural gas properties. The Company owns mineral interests in approximately 94,627 net acres located in nine states with 57,880 acres being in Texas and Oklahoma. As a result of its mineral ownership the Company has royalty interests in 10 producing gas wells. Officers and directors, as a group, own approximately 33% of the Company's outstanding shares. The Company was organized under the laws of the state of Delaware in 1911.

	12/31/95	12/31/94	12/31/93	12/31/92
Per Share Information				
Stock Price	21.94	22.07	21.00	20.50
Earnings Per Share	3.50	0.65	1.34	0.96
Price / Earnings Ratio	6.27	33.95	15.67	21.35
Book Value Per Share	34.47	32.11	32.35	31.90
Price / Book Value %	63.65	68.73	64.91	64.26
Dividends Per Share	1.00	1.00	1.00	1.00
Annual Financial Data				
Operating Results (000's)				
Total Revenues	2,021.9	1,643.4	1,561.3	1,642.1
Costs & Expenses	-1,477.1	-1,541.3	-1,399.9	-1,392.3
Income Before Taxes and Other	544.8	102.2	161.4	249.7
Other Items	n.a.	n.a.	55.9	n.a.
Income Tax	48.3	8.6	10.7	-84.5
Net Income	593.0	110.8	228.0	165.3
Cash Flow From Operations	786.9	710.9	485.9	776.8
Balance Sheet (000's)				
Cash & Equivalents	175.0	112.6	98.6	307.3
Total Current Assets	3,399.9	3,086.9	3,337.9	3,426.8
Fixed Assets, Net	2,026.3	1,998.7	1,959.3	1,808.4
Total Assets	6,200.1	5,798.1	5,947.0	5,865.1
Total Current Liabilities	165.9	119.5	205.1	89.9
Long-Term Debt	n.a.	n.a.	n.a.	n.a.
Stockholders' Equity	5,860.0	5,444.2	5,509.0	5,474.1
Performance & Financial Condition				
Return on Total Revenues %	29.33	6.74	14.60	10.07
Return on Avg Stockholders' Equity %	10.49	2.02	4.15	3.04
Return on Average Assets %	9.89	1.89	3.86	2.84
Current Ratio	20.49	25.82	16.27	38.12
Debt / Equity %	n.a.	n.a.	n.a.	n.a.

Compound Growth %'s	EPS %	53.91	Net Income %	53.09	Total Revenues %	7.18

Comments

The Company has filed an action in a Texas court to quiet title on an interest it has in mineral rights associated with two producing oil and gas wells. If the Company is successful in this action which is set for trial in August 1996, it should receive approximately $850,000 of production revenues held in suspense by the wells' operator.

Officers	Position	Ownership Information	12/31/95
Mason McLain	President	Number of Shares Outstanding	169,997
Jerry L. Crow	Treasurer, Secretary	Market Capitalization	$ 3,729,734
Robert T. McLain	Vice President	Frequency Of Dividends	Annual
		Number of Shareholders	1,445

Other Information

Transfer Agent	Company Office			Where Listed	OTC-BB
Auditor	Grant Thornton LLP			Symbol	RSRV
Market Maker	Hill, Thompson, Magid & Co.Inc	Telephone	(800)631-3083	SIC Code	6792
Broker Dealer	Regular Stockbroker			Employees	8

Rhinelander Telecommunications, Inc.

53 North Stevens Street • Rhinelander, WI 54501-0340 • Telephone (715)369-4641 • Fax (715)369-1274

Company Description

The Company provides local and long distance telephone access to 22,000 access lines for Rhinelander and surrounding communities in Wisconsin.

	12/31/95	12/31/94	12/31/93	12/31/92
Per Share Information				
Stock Price	22.50	21.50	22.75	12.50
Earnings Per Share	1.14	1.40	1.23	1.34
Price / Earnings Ratio	19.74	15.36	18.50	9.33
Book Value Per Share	12.77	11.59	10.64	9.84
Price / Book Value %	176.19	185.50	213.82	127.03
Dividends Per Share	0.46	0.44	0.42	0.40
Annual Financial Data				
Operating Results (000's)				
Total Revenues	15,575.6	15,232.7	11,587.9	11,073.0
Costs & Expenses	-12,101.2	-11,241.0	-8,202.1	-7,321.7
Income Before Taxes and Other	3,474.4	3,984.5	3,374.9	3,733.9
Other Items	n.a.	n.a.	n.a.	n.a.
Income Tax	-1,419.6	-1,544.4	-1,234.9	-1,394.1
Net Income	2,054.8	2,440.1	2,140.0	2,339.7
Cash Flow From Operations	5,995.1	4,273.5	4,119.7	3,840.7
Balance Sheet (000's)				
Cash & Equivalents	2,639.2	1,297.7	1,489.1	1,488.2
Total Current Assets	6,254.8	4,226.8	4,005.0	3,711.4
Fixed Assets, Net	34,094.8	32,290.0	31,562.9	23,190.0
Total Assets	49,036.5	41,622.9	40,678.1	27,460.7
Total Current Liabilities	4,601.8	2,459.8	3,261.2	2,403.3
Long-Term Debt	15,898.3	13,372.7	13,644.9	4,207.7
Stockholders' Equity	22,629.2	20,239.6	18,576.6	17,178.7
Performance & Financial Condition				
Return on Total Revenues %	13.19	16.02	18.47	21.13
Return on Avg Stockholders' Equity %	9.59	12.57	11.97	13.72
Return on Average Assets %	4.53	5.93	6.28	7.80
Current Ratio	1.36	1.72	1.23	1.54
Debt / Equity %	70.26	66.07	73.45	24.49

Compound Growth %'s	EPS %	-5.25	Net Income %	-4.24	Total Revenues %	12.05

Comments

The Company acquired Crandon Telephone in the last quarter of 1993 which accounts for a portion of the growth. Management says that 1994 revenues would have grown 16% without the addition. In late 1995, Rib Lake Telephone Company was acquired which brings in some new management, increases the customer base, provides entry into the cable industry and increases the Company's wireless position.

Officers	Position	Ownership Information	12/31/95
Donald A. Anklam	President	Number of Shares Outstanding	1,772,377
Kirby H. Roen	Secretary, Treasurer	Market Capitalization	$ 39,878,483
Dexter C. Defnet	Vice President	Frequency Of Dividends	Quarterly
Lee A. Lappin	Other	Number of Shareholders	356

Other Information				
Transfer Agent	Company Office		Where Listed	OTC-BB
Auditor	Kiesling Associates		Symbol	RLND
Market Maker	Gabelli & Company, Inc.	Telephone (914)921-5153	SIC Code	4810
Broker Dealer	Regular Stockbroker		Employees	83

Ridgewood Properties, Inc.

2859 Paces Ferry Rd., Ste. 700 • Atlanta, GA 30339 • Telephone (770)434-3670 • Fax (770)433-8935

Company Description

The Company acquires, develops, operates and sells real estate in the Southeast and "Sunbelt" areas. Additionally, through its investment in a limited partnership, it is engaged in acquiring and managing hotel properties in the Southeast. The Company's president is the owner of approximately 42% of the outstanding common shares. The Triton Group, Ltd. is the owner of all 450,000 shares of covertible redeemable preferred stock (liquidation preference of $3.6 million). The Company was incorporated in the state of Delaware in 1985.

	08/31/95	08/31/94	08/31/93	08/31/92
Per Share Information				
Stock Price	2.06	2.75	n.a.	n.a.
Earnings Per Share	-1.77	-0.64	-0.32	-0.76
Price / Earnings Ratio	n.a.	n.a.	n.a.	n.a.
Book Value Per Share	2.08	3.98	3.50	3.82
Price / Book Value %	99.04	69.10	n.a.	n.a.
Dividends Per Share	n.a.	n.a.	n.a.	n.a.
Annual Financial Data				
Operating Results (000's)				
Total Revenues	8,675.0	30,082.0	18,619.0	16,667.0
Costs & Expenses	-10,293.0	-33,713.0	-20,479.0	-21,127.0
Income Before Taxes and Other	-1,618.0	-3,631.0	-1,860.0	-4,460.0
Other Items	n.a.	n.a.	n.a.	n.a.
Income Tax	-38.0	n.a.	n.a.	n.a.
Net Income	-1,656.0	-3,631.0	-1,860.0	-4,460.0
Cash Flow From Operations	-1,483.0	-1,307.0	-1,883.0	-1,776.0
Balance Sheet (000's)				
Cash & Equivalents	1,880.0	2,804.0	2,142.0	1,749.0
Total Current Assets	2,532.0	3,622.0	2,142.0	1,749.0
Fixed Assets, Net	6,909.0	10,729.0	29,830.0	34,394.0
Total Assets	9,673.0	14,351.0	34,655.0	38,857.0
Total Current Liabilities	1,265.0	1,496.0	2,748.0	2,245.0
Long-Term Debt	2,796.0	5,415.0	11,343.0	14,188.0
Stockholders' Equity	5,612.0	7,440.0	20,564.0	22,424.0
Performance & Financial Condition				
Return on Total Revenues %	-19.09	-12.07	-9.99	-26.76
Return on Avg Stockholders' Equity %	-25.38	-25.93	-8.65	-18.09
Return on Average Assets %	-13.79	-14.82	-5.06	-10.69
Current Ratio	2.00	2.42	0.78	0.78
Debt / Equity %	49.82	72.78	55.16	63.27

Compound Growth %'s	EPS % n.a.	Net Income % n.a.	Total Revenues % -19.56

Comments

Since the Company is not generating sufficient operating cash flow to cover overhead and debt service, it must continue to sell real estate, seek alternative financing or recapitalize the Company. These are options it is currently reviewing. With the stock price at less than 50% of book value at August 31, 1995, and significant holdings of real estate, potential investors need to investigate the market values of the properties held. No reliable stock price quotes were available for fiscal years 1993 and 1992.

Officers	Position	Ownership Information	08/31/95
N. Russell Walden	President	Number of Shares Outstanding	963,480
Karen S. Hughes	Secretary, CFO	Market Capitalization	$ 1,984,769
Byron T. Cooper	Vice President	Frequency Of Dividends	n.a.
		Number of Shareholders	300

Other Information			
Transfer Agent	Society National Bank	Where Listed	OTC-PS
Auditor	Price Waterhouse LLP	Symbol	RWPI
Market Maker	Carr Securities Corporation	Telephone (800)221-2243	SIC Code	6513
Broker Dealer	Regular Stockbroker	Employees	500

Riviera Holdings Corporation

2901 Las Vegas Blvd. South • Las Vegas, NV 89109 • Telephone (702)734-5110 • Fax (702)794-9527

Company Description

The Company operates the Riviera Hotel & Casino in Las Vegas, Nevada. The hotel and casino complex is located on the heavily traveled Las Vegas Strip. The complex consists of approximately 1.7 million square feet which includes 2,100 hotel rooms, five restaurants, a 105,000 square foot casino, a 100,000 square foot convention center, four showrooms, an entertainment lounge and 44 food and retail concessions. The Company was incorporated in Nevada during January, 1993, to acquire the assets of Riviera, Inc. Casino-Hotel Division on June 30, 1993, pursuant to a plan of reorganization. On June 30, 1993, as part of reorganization, the Company issued to the existing holders of secured debt, 4.8 million shares of its common stock and $100 million of mortgage notes, due in 2002, in exchange for $126 million of existing debt plus accrued interest of $15.2 million.

	12/31/95	12/31/94	12/31/93
Per Share Information			
Stock Price	8.50	2.82	n.a.
Earnings Per Share	1.26	1.00	0.54
Price / Earnings Ratio	6.75	2.82	n.a.
Book Value Per Share	5.48	4.15	3.16
Price / Book Value %	155.11	67.95	n.a.
Dividends Per Share	n.a.	n.a.	n.a.
Annual Financial Data			
Operating Results (000's)			
Total Revenues	151,895.9	154,431.0	76,442.3
Costs & Expenses	-142,220.4	-146,766.2	-73,835.4
Income Before Taxes and Other	9,675.5	7,664.7	2,606.9
Other Items	n.a.	n.a.	n.a.
Income Tax	-3,332.0	-2,875.0	n.a.
Net Income	6,343.5	4,789.7	2,606.9
Cash Flow From Operations	16,738.2	16,372.3	765.9
Balance Sheet (000's)			
Cash & Equivalents	21,962.0	16,425.4	13,187.7
Total Current Assets	31,084.4	26,168.3	22,120.4
Fixed Assets, Net	121,049.4	120,024.3	116,765.2
Total Assets	157,931.5	151,925.4	143,704.1
Total Current Liabilities	20,377.3	19,805.5	17,012.3
Long-Term Debt	108,249.3	110,171.1	111,543.2
Stockholders' Equity	26,281.9	19,938.4	15,148.6
Performance & Financial Condition			
Return on Total Revenues %	4.18	3.10	3.41
Return on Avg Stockholders' Equity %	27.45	27.30	n.a.
Return on Average Assets %	4.09	3.24	n.a.
Current Ratio	1.53	1.32	1.30
Debt / Equity %	411.88	552.56	736.32

Compound Growth %'s	EPS %	26.00	Net Income %	32.44	Total Revenues %	-1.64

Comments

The results of operations for the period ended December 31, 1993 are for a six month period, and accordingly, are not comparable to those for the years ended December 31, 1994 and 1995. All share information has been adjusted for the 4 for 1 stock split which took place in November, 1995.

Officers	Position	Ownership Information	12/31/95
William L. Westerman	President, CEO	Number of Shares Outstanding	4,800,000
John Wishon	Secretary	Market Capitalization	$ 40,800,000
Duane Krohn	Treasurer, CFO	Frequency Of Dividends	n.a.
		Number of Shareholders	240

Other Information				
Transfer Agent	American Stock Transfer & Trust Company		Where Listed	OTC-PS
Auditor	Deloitte & Touche LLP		Symbol	RVHC
Market Maker	Koonce Securities, Inc.	Telephone (800)368-2802	SIC Code	7011
Broker Dealer	Regular Stockbroker		Employees	2100

Robroy Industries, Inc.

River Road • Verona, PA 15147-0097 • Telephone (412)838-2100 • Fax (412)828-3952

Company Description

The Company manufactures a variety of conduit, tubing and other enclosure products. The Company was formed in 1905. Shares were split 2.5 to 1 in September, 1994. All per share amounts for earlier years have been restated.

	06/30/95	06/30/94	06/30/93	06/30/92
Per Share Information				
Stock Price	17.50	19.00	19.00	12.60
Earnings Per Share	0.68	1.84	1.80	1.76
Price / Earnings Ratio	25.74	10.33	10.56	7.16
Book Value Per Share	16.45	15.94	16.39	12.75
Price / Book Value %	106.38	119.20	115.92	98.82
Dividends Per Share	0.24	0.21	0.19	n.a.
Annual Financial Data				
Operating Results (000's)				
Total Revenues	111,005.1	104,199.6	94,328.6	73,277.8
Costs & Expenses	-102,053.9	-93,902.2	-84,287.9	-63,745.0
Income Before Taxes and Other	3,836.5	10,297.4	10,040.8	9,532.7
Other Items	n.a.	n.a.	n.a.	n.a.
Income Tax	-1,520.8	-3,840.0	-3,731.7	-3,365.8
Net Income	2,315.7	6,457.5	6,309.1	6,166.9
Cash Flow From Operations	4,463.5	8,046.8	4,301.3	7,199.1
Balance Sheet (000's)				
Cash & Equivalents	7,449.3	2,940.1	3,475.0	2,333.0
Total Current Assets	43,725.0	35,301.3	33,140.9	23,155.9
Fixed Assets, Net	16,688.9	14,247.9	13,922.2	11,174.7
Total Assets	75,021.0	72,496.6	68,630.2	51,096.5
Total Current Liabilities	14,721.0	10,098.7	9,511.8	5,541.7
Long-Term Debt	3,250.0	5,363.3	7,797.7	n.a.
Stockholders' Equity	56,340.1	55,851.8	49,974.9	44,676.0
Performance & Financial Condition				
Return on Total Revenues %	2.09	6.20	6.69	8.42
Return on Avg Stockholders' Equity %	4.13	12.20	13.33	14.72
Return on Average Assets %	3.14	9.15	10.54	12.54
Current Ratio	2.97	3.50	3.48	4.18
Debt / Equity %	5.77	9.60	15.60	n.a.

Compound Growth %'s	EPS %	-27.17	Net Income %	-27.85	Total Revenues %	14.85

Comments

1995 included a restructuring charge of $3.5 million, or $1.02 per share. Restructuring included the relocation of the Verona plant, the closure and sale of other facilities, and the acquistion of certain companies and product lines. This nonrecurring item significantly increases the negative compounded earnings decline.

Officers	Position	Ownership Information	06/30/95
Peter McIlroy II	Chairman, President	Number of Shares Outstanding	3,425,780
Louis J. Kirchner	Exec VP, CFO	Market Capitalization	$ 59,951,150
John R. Brown	Vice President	Frequency Of Dividends	Quarterly
		Number of Shareholders	Under 500

Other Information			
Transfer Agent	Mellon Securities Trust Company	Where Listed	OTC-BB
Auditor	Deloitte & Touche LLP	Symbol	RROYA
Market Maker	Legg Mason Wood Walker, Inc.	Telephone (800)732-1229	SIC Code	5063
Broker Dealer	Regular Stockbroker	Employees	999

Rochester & Pittsburgh Coal Company

655 Church Street • Indiana, PA 15701 • Telephone (412)349-5800 • Fax (412)349-5460

Company Description

The Company has been mining bituminous steam coal in western Pennsylvania since 1882. Substantially all sales are made, under long-term supply contracts, to electricity generating plants located adjacent or near to the Company's mines. In 1992, the Company acquired coal properties in southwest Pennsylvania. The Company is developing these properties and it expects development to be complete in 1997. This mine will allow the Company to access the general eastern utility coal market and should constitute a major part of the Company's operations.

	12/31/95	12/31/94	12/31/93	12/31/92
Per Share Information				
Stock Price	29.32	34.25	39.38	39.50
Earnings Per Share	-1.03	0.72	2.06	4.11
Price / Earnings Ratio	n.a.	47.57	19.12	9.61
Book Value Per Share	59.06	60.33	61.31	60.84
Price / Book Value %	49.64	56.77	64.23	64.92
Dividends Per Share	0.75	1.50	1.50	1.50
Annual Financial Data				
Operating Results (000's)				
Total Revenues	225,879.0	196,773.0	161,941.0	198,502.0
Costs & Expenses	-228,127.0	-191,294.0	-153,893.0	-179,853.0
Income Before Taxes and Other	-3,872.0	4,304.0	3,876.0	18,649.0
Other Items	n.a.	n.a.	4,709.0	n.a.
Income Tax	337.0	-1,838.0	-1,502.0	-4,459.0
Net Income	-3,535.0	2,466.0	7,083.0	14,190.0
Cash Flow From Operations	27,615.0	15,844.0	13,049.0	20,078.0
Balance Sheet (000's)				
Cash & Equivalents	27,437.0	30,656.0	23,737.0	27,400.0
Total Current Assets	109,024.0	129,614.0	101,600.0	121,101.0
Fixed Assets, Net	322,363.0	230,169.0	183,009.0	144,974.0
Total Assets	491,407.0	410,994.0	356,884.0	327,579.0
Total Current Liabilities	33,601.0	32,631.0	27,844.0	25,037.0
Long-Term Debt	120,784.0	75,693.0	29,455.0	13,203.0
Stockholders' Equity	203,114.0	207,450.0	210,794.0	209,401.0
Performance & Financial Condition				
Return on Total Revenues %	-1.57	1.25	4.37	7.15
Return on Avg Stockholders' Equity %	-1.72	1.18	3.37	6.86
Return on Average Assets %	-0.78	0.64	2.07	4.51
Current Ratio	3.24	3.97	3.65	4.84
Debt / Equity %	59.47	36.49	13.97	6.31

Compound Growth %'s	EPS %	n.a.	Net Income %	n.a.	Total Revenues %	4.40

Comments

At December 31, 1995, the Company had an accrued liability of approximately $133 million as a reserve for workers' compensation benefits, mine closings, postretirement benefits and health benefits. Operating results were severely impacted by a seven-month-long mine workers strike. Depreciation, depletion and amortization amounted to $13.2 million for 1995, and slightly less for earlier years. Note the resulting significant amount cash flow from operations.

Officers	Position	Ownership Information	12/31/95
Thomas W. Garges, Jr.	President, CEO	Number of Shares Outstanding	3,439,275
Peter Iselin	VP - Finance, Secretary	Market Capitalization	$ 100,839,543
W. Joseph Engler, Jr.	Vice President	Frequency Of Dividends	Quarterly
George M. Evans	Vice President, Treasurer	Number of Shareholders	750
Thomas M. Majcher	Vice President		

Other Information

Transfer Agent	First Chicago Trust Company of New York			Where Listed	OTC-BB
Auditor	Ernst & Young LLP			Symbol	DRAE
Market Maker	Pennsylvania Merchant Group	Telephone	(800)762-8624	SIC Code	1221
Broker Dealer	Regular Stockbroker			Employees	1670

Rocky Mount Mills

P.O. Box 1240 • Rocky Mount, NC 27802-1240 • Telephone (919)442-0197 • Fax (919)442-9309

Company Description

The Company has spun yarns since 1818 and was incorporated in 1874. It sufferred from an industry decline in the 1980's and increased competition. In 1991, it was reported to shareholders that management was considering alternatives such as sale, merger or liquidation. A redirection away from supplying the apparel markets to home furnishing items and specialy products was contemplated. When we called the Company in May, we were advised that they will be closing their doors on June 22, 1996.

	09/26/93	09/26/92
Per Share Information		
Stock Price	18.00	18.00
Earnings Per Share	1.59	2.04
Price / Earnings Ratio	11.32	8.82
Book Value Per Share	50.70	49.12
Price / Book Value %	35.50	36.64
Dividends Per Share	n.a.	n.a.
Annual Financial Data		
Operating Results (000's)		
Total Revenues	n.a.	n.a.
Costs & Expenses	n.a.	n.a.
Income Before Taxes and Other	n.a.	n.a.
Other Items	n.a.	n.a.
Income Tax	n.a.	n.a.
Net Income	n.a.	n.a.
Cash Flow From Operations	n.a.	n.a.
Balance Sheet (000's)		
Cash & Equivalents	289.6	183.5
Total Current Assets	5,237.1	5,780.2
Fixed Assets, Net	6,638.1	5,956.8
Total Assets	12,239.0	12,125.0
Total Current Liabilities	2,938.1	3,549.2
Long-Term Debt	3,162.4	2,423.1
Stockholders' Equity	6,084.1	5,893.8
Performance & Financial Condition		
Return on Total Revenues %	n.a.	n.a.
Return on Avg Stockholders' Equity %	n.a.	n.a.
Return on Average Assets %	n.a.	n.a.
Current Ratio	1.78	1.63
Debt / Equity %	51.98	41.11

Compound Growth %'s	EPS % -22.06	Net Income % n.a.	Total Revenues % n.a.

Comments

The financial information is not audited. Regretfully, we did not have more current data. This may be an interesting investment but it requires investigation into the potential value of the property in liquidation and managements' ability to execute a plan. Management had engaged the consulting firm of Ernst & Young to work with them in planning the direction of the Company and possibly the liquidation.

Officers	Position	Ownership Information	09/26/93
Thomas B. Battle	President	Number of Shares Outstanding	120,000
John M. Mebane, Jr.	Exec VP	Market Capitalization	$ 2,160,000
		Frequency Of Dividends	n.a.
		Number of Shareholders	Under 500

Other Information				
Transfer Agent	Company Office		Where Listed	OTC-BB
Auditor	None indicated		Symbol	RKYM
Market Maker	Hill, Thompson, Magid & Co.	Telephone (800)631-3083	SIC Code	2281
Broker Dealer	Pink sheet specialist		Employees	150

Roseville Telephone Company

211 Lincoln Street • Roseville, CA 95678-2614 • Telephone (916)786-6141 • Fax (916)786-1225

Company Description

The Company provides local and toll telephone service and network access services in an 83 square mile area in Placer and Sacramento Counties in California. Currently, no other telephone company operates in the area served by the Company and the area has experienced substantial growth in recent years as a surburban area to the city of Sacramento, the capitol of the State of California. The Company was incorporated in the state of California in 1914.

	12/31/95	12/31/94	12/31/93	12/31/92
Per Share Information				
Stock Price	25.00	24.00	35.50	28.38
Earnings Per Share	1.24	1.39	1.55	1.63
Price / Earnings Ratio	20.16	17.27	22.90	17.41
Book Value Per Share	11.69	11.37	10.67	10.04
Price / Book Value %	213.86	211.08	332.71	282.67
Dividends Per Share	0.58	0.55	0.53	0.55
Annual Financial Data				
Operating Results (000's)				
Total Revenues	111,068.0	106,258.0	100,000.0	93,142.0
Costs & Expenses	-73,017.0	-67,537.0	-60,479.0	-55,239.0
Income Before Taxes and Other	31,141.0	34,221.0	37,902.0	36,268.0
Other Items	n.a.	n.a.	n.a.	n.a.
Income Tax	-12,634.0	-13,866.0	-15,384.0	-14,452.0
Net Income	18,507.0	20,355.0	22,518.0	21,816.0
Cash Flow From Operations	32,785.0	36,731.0	36,647.0	31,378.0
Balance Sheet (000's)				
Cash & Equivalents	24,854.0	21,282.0	9,847.0	11,200.0
Total Current Assets	54,126.0	53,379.0	38,498.0	29,386.0
Fixed Assets, Net	178,225.0	173,359.0	168,571.0	144,685.0
Total Assets	256,889.0	246,808.0	226,459.0	190,760.0
Total Current Liabilities	21,638.0	20,322.0	19,143.0	16,152.0
Long-Term Debt	33,750.0	37,321.0	40,000.0	25,000.0
Stockholders' Equity	174,393.0	164,675.0	142,921.0	128,159.0
Performance & Financial Condition				
Return on Total Revenues %	16.66	19.16	22.52	23.42
Return on Avg Stockholders' Equity %	10.92	13.23	16.61	18.04
Return on Average Assets %	7.35	8.60	10.79	12.42
Current Ratio	2.50	2.63	2.01	1.82
Debt / Equity %	19.35	22.66	27.99	19.51

Compound Growth %'s	EPS %	-8.71	Net Income %	-5.34	Total Revenues %	6.04

Comments

Significant growth in total revenues has not translated into improvements in earnings per share performance. The Company, in the past, has focused on providing traditional communications services. It is now actively evaluating other opportunities in long-distance and wireless communications as well as in the cable television industry.

Officers	Position	Ownership Information	12/31/95
Robert L. Doyle	Chairman	Number of Shares Outstanding	14,915,424
Brian H. Strom	President, CEO	Market Capitalization	$ 372,885,600
Michael D. Campbell	Vice President, CFO	Frequency Of Dividends	Quarterly
		Number of Shareholders	9,600

Other Information			
Transfer Agent	Company Office	Where Listed	Other
Auditor	Ernst & Young LLP	Symbol	RVTL
Market Maker	Gabelli & Company, Inc.	Telephone (914)921-5154	SIC Code	4813
Broker Dealer	Regular Stockbroker	Employees	501

Ross Industries, Inc.

P.O. Box 70 • Midland, VA 22728 • Telephone (540)439-3271 • Fax (540)439-2740

Company Description

The Company, incorporated in Virginia, manufactures and sells machines used in the food processing and packaging industries. Products include, mechanical meat tenderizers, meat and fish block presses, slicers and form, fill, and seal packaging machinery.

	06/30/95	06/30/94	06/30/93	06/30/92
Per Share Information				
Stock Price	0.12	0.10	0.16	0.24
Earnings Per Share	0.02	-0.01	0.11	-1.08
Price / Earnings Ratio	6.00	n.a.	1.45	n.a.
Book Value Per Share	0.37	0.36	1.13	1.03
Price / Book Value %	32.43	27.78	14.16	23.30
Dividends Per Share	n.a.	n.a.	n.a.	n.a.
Annual Financial Data				
Operating Results (000's)				
Total Revenues	12,963.8	10,698.5	7,830.3	7,621.3
Costs & Expenses	-12,865.4	-10,758.9	-7,699.3	-8,931.8
Income Before Taxes and Other	98.4	-60.5	131.0	-1,310.5
Other Items	n.a.	n.a.	50.0	n.a.
Income Tax	n.a.	n.a.	-50.0	n.a.
Net Income	98.4	-60.5	131.0	-1,310.5
Cash Flow From Operations	336.6	33.4	744.1	-1,240.4
Balance Sheet (000's)				
Cash & Equivalents	137.9	124.0	242.2	n.a.
Total Current Assets	5,578.0	6,607.6	5,037.4	n.a.
Fixed Assets, Net	1,216.1	1,317.0	1,438.3	n.a.
Total Assets	6,801.8	7,933.9	6,475.7	n.a.
Total Current Liabilities	3,509.4	4,746.0	3,827.8	n.a.
Long-Term Debt	6.2	n.a.	1,265.5	n.a.
Stockholders' Equity	3,286.3	3,187.9	1,382.4	n.a.
Performance & Financial Condition				
Return on Total Revenues %	0.76	-0.57	1.67	-17.19
Return on Avg Stockholders' Equity %	3.04	-2.65	n.a.	n.a.
Return on Average Assets %	1.34	-0.84	n.a.	n.a.
Current Ratio	1.59	1.39	1.32	n.a.
Debt / Equity %	0.19	n.a.	91.54	n.a.

Compound Growth %'s	EPS %	-57.36	Net Income %	-13.36	Total Revenues %	19.37

Comments

The Company's majority stockholders converted $1.2 million in notes plus interest to 5,291,140 shares of the Company's common stock and purchased another 1,708,860 shares for cash of $427,000, in August, 1993. Sales to a distributor owned by the majority stockholders totaled $4.5 million during fiscal 1995. The Company is currently, and has been since 1990, in default of its loan obligations with the FDIC, who assumed the obligations when they took over the Company's lending institution in 1990. The Company is currently in discussions with the FDIC (sounds like they have been for awhile) and believe that, until a refinancing occurs, existing cash flow is adequate to cover operations.

Officers	Position	Ownership Information	06/30/95
Timothy Puvogel	President	Number of Shares Outstanding	8,896,153
James T. McFarland	VP - Finance	Market Capitalization	$ 1,067,538
Richard W. Brown	VP - Sales	Frequency Of Dividends	n.a.
		Number of Shareholders	255

Other Information					
Transfer Agent	Company Office			Where Listed	OTC-BB
Auditor	Deloitte & Touche LLP			Symbol	ROSX
Market Maker	Wachtel & Company	Telephone	(202)898-1018	SIC Code	3556
Broker Dealer	Regular Stockbroker			Employees	100

Rudy's Restaurant Group, Inc.

11900 Biscayne Blvd, Ste 806 • Miami, FL 33181 • Telephone (305)895-7200 • Fax (305)895-2881

Company Description

The Company, through two subsidiaries, owns and operates six Japanese steak and seafood restaurants which were acquired in 1985. The restaurants are located in Pittsburgh, Cleveland, Cincinnati, Minneapolis, Miami and Washington, D.C.

	10/01/95	10/02/94	10/03/93	09/27/92
Per Share Information				
Stock Price	0.80	0.54	0.32	0.14
Earnings Per Share	0.26	0.12	0.18	0.07
Price / Earnings Ratio	3.08	4.50	1.78	2.00
Book Value Per Share	1.03	0.75	0.62	0.44
Price / Book Value %	77.67	72.00	51.61	31.82
Dividends Per Share	n.a.	n.a.	n.a.	n.a.
Annual Financial Data				
Operating Results (000's)				
Total Revenues	11,090.9	9,721.2	8,298.7	10,876.4
Costs & Expenses	-10,002.6	-8,888.6	-7,803.0	-9,871.3
Income Before Taxes and Other	1,037.7	516.9	485.8	515.2
Other Items	n.a.	n.a.	374.1	-129.1
Income Tax	-46.0	-65.0	-207.2	-112.2
Net Income	991.7	451.9	652.7	273.9
Cash Flow From Operations	1,424.5	696.4	1,017.8	52.9
Balance Sheet (000's)				
Cash & Equivalents	1,476.7	341.5	927.7	199.5
Total Current Assets	1,753.2	606.6	1,936.7	1,588.2
Fixed Assets, Net	2,094.8	2,076.4	1,050.2	860.7
Total Assets	4,582.5	3,438.1	3,730.6	4,035.7
Total Current Liabilities	945.4	792.8	1,397.3	1,889.2
Long-Term Debt	n.a.	n.a.	n.a.	510.7
Stockholders' Equity	3,637.0	2,645.3	2,193.3	1,540.6
Performance & Financial Condition				
Return on Total Revenues %	8.94	4.65	7.87	2.52
Return on Avg Stockholders' Equity %	31.57	18.68	34.96	19.51
Return on Average Assets %	24.73	12.61	16.81	6.48
Current Ratio	1.85	0.77	1.39	0.84
Debt / Equity %	n.a.	n.a.	n.a.	33.15

Compound Growth %'s	EPS %	54.87	Net Income %	53.56	Total Revenues %	0.65

Comments

The Company maintains its books on a 52/53 week per year basis. As of December 31, 1995, officers and directors of the Company, as a group, owned 59% of the Company's outstanding shares. Total revenues for the twelve weeks ended December 24, 1995, were $2.5 million and Net Income was $240,000 ($.06 per share) as compared to $2.5 million and $150,000 ($.04 per share) for the same period in 1994. During December, 1995, the Company entered into an agreement to purchase four restaurants for a total of $2.4 million.

Officers	Position	Ownership Information	10/01/95
Douglas M. Rudolph	President, CEO	Number of Shares Outstanding	3,520,000
Marie G. Peterson	CFO, COO	Market Capitalization	$ 2,816,000
		Frequency Of Dividends	n.a.
		Number of Shareholders	380

Other Information

			Where Listed	OTC-BB
Transfer Agent	Chemical Mellon Shareholder Services		Symbol	RUDY
Auditor	Deloitte & Touche LLP		SIC Code	5812
Market Maker	Carr Securities Corporation	Telephone (800)221-2243		
Broker Dealer	Regular Stockbroker		Employees	270

SBC Financial Corporation

101 Falls Boulevard • Chittenango, NY 13037 • Telephone (315)687-3921 • Fax (315)687-3728

Company Description

SBC Financial Corporation is the holding company for its wholly owned subsidiary, the State Bank of Chittenango. The Bank provides a variety of consumer and commercial banking services from its sole branch in Chittenango, New York.

	12/31/95	12/31/94	12/31/93	12/31/92
Per Share Information				
Stock Price	33.00	27.50	27.25	25.00
Earnings Per Share	3.25	2.70	2.25	1.86
Price / Earnings Ratio	10.15	10.19	12.11	13.44
Book Value Per Share	35.24	29.92	30.84	29.19
Price / Book Value %	93.64	91.91	88.36	85.65
Dividends Per Share	0.85	0.70	0.60	0.55
Annual Financial Data				
Operating Results (000's)				
Net Interest Income	2,045.0	2,019.5	1,963.6	1,823.0
Loan Loss Provision	-200.0	-95.0	-60.0	-182.5
Non-Interest Income	324.5	314.0	293.6	308.9
Non-Interest Expense	-1,632.6	-1,746.5	-1,868.2	-1,632.9
Income Before Taxes and Other	536.9	492.0	328.9	316.4
Other Items	n.a.	n.a.	27.0	n.a.
Income Tax	-139.0	-161.0	-80.6	-89.0
Net Income	397.9	331.0	275.4	227.4
Balance Sheet (000's)				
Cash & Securities	18,601.8	15,131.8	13,354.7	13,202.8
Loans, Net	27,593.2	26,726.3	25,686.0	26,423.5
Fixed Assets, Net	1,054.9	1,110.9	1,190.8	1,266.1
Total Assets	47,973.7	43,819.0	41,093.4	41,595.9
Deposits	42,954.9	39,580.0	36,597.4	37,336.3
Stockholders' Equity	4,313.2	3,661.9	3,775.0	3,573.0
Performance & Financial Condition				
Net Interest Margin	n.a.	n.a.	n.a.	n.a.
Return on Avg Stockholders' Equity %	9.98	8.90	7.49	6.51
Return on Average Assets %	0.87	0.78	0.67	0.57
Equity to Assets %	8.99	8.36	9.19	8.59
Reserve as a % of Non-Performing Loans	70.56	87.52	154.96	93.93

Compound Growth %'s	EPS %	20.45	Net Income %	20.51	Net Interest Income %	3.91

Comments

Over half of the Bank's loan portfolio is from real estate mortages. The balance is split between installment loans and commercial/other loans at 25% and 24%, respectively. 1995 marked the fourth consecutive year in which earnings growth exceeded 20%. There has also been a steady improvement in earnings as a percentage of assets and equity.

Officers	Position	Ownership Information	12/31/95
William W. Cassell	Chairman	Number of Shares Outstanding	122,400
Thomas S. Bielicki	President, CEO	Market Capitalization	$ 4,039,200
Susan J. Taylor	CFO, Treasurer	Frequency Of Dividends	Quarterly
Ronald A. Emhoff	Head Cashier, Secretary	Number of Shareholders	325

Other Information			
Transfer Agent	Company Office	Where Listed	OTC-BB
Auditor	Fust, Charles, Chambers & Har.	Symbol	SBCF
Market Maker	Ryan, Beck & Co.	SIC Code	6020
Broker Dealer	Regular Stockbroker	Telephone (800)325-7926	Employees	23

Salient Systems, Inc.

4330 Tuller Road • Dublin, OH 43017-5008 • Telephone (614)792-5800 • Fax (614)792-5888

Company Description

The Company is engaged in the manufacturing of wheel impact load detectors and other products for the railroad industry. The Company was formed in 1984. It completed a secondary stock offering in early 1996, raising $931,500 on the placement of 162,000 shares. $571,501 had been received by December 31, 1995.

	12/31/95	12/31/94	12/31/93
Per Share Information			
Stock Price	5.50	5.50	5.12
Earnings Per Share	0.04	0.04	0.06
Price / Earnings Ratio	137.50	137.50	85.33
Book Value Per Share	0.49	0.29	0.24
Price / Book Value %	1,122.50	1,896.60	2,133.30
Dividends Per Share	n.a.	n.a.	n.a.
Annual Financial Data			
Operating Results (000's)			
Total Revenues	1,979.8	1,572.2	1,863.0
Costs & Expenses	-1,781.2	-1,420.4	-1,665.6
Income Before Taxes and Other	191.7	151.8	197.4
Other Items	n.a.	n.a.	68.8
Income Tax	-54.6	-31.7	-63.8
Net Income	137.1	120.1	202.4
Cash Flow From Operations	508.2	-268.6	715.9
Balance Sheet (000's)			
Cash & Equivalents	737.3	539.6	906.3
Total Current Assets	1,962.2	1,207.3	1,623.0
Fixed Assets, Net	289.8	107.0	131.9
Total Assets	2,256.3	1,322.6	1,763.4
Total Current Liabilities	567.0	353.4	868.4
Long-Term Debt	n.a.	n.a.	118.1
Stockholders' Equity	1,689.3	969.2	776.8
Performance & Financial Condition			
Return on Total Revenues %	6.92	7.64	10.87
Return on Avg Stockholders' Equity %	10.31	13.76	37.21
Return on Average Assets %	7.66	7.78	n.a.
Current Ratio	3.46	3.42	1.87
Debt / Equity %	n.a.	n.a.	15.21

Compound Growth %'s	EPS %	-18.35	Net Income %	-17.71	Total Revenues %	3.09

Comments

Sales of wheel impact load detectors have dropped as a percentage of total sales, largely as a result of product expansion in other areas. Much focus has been on developing and marketing state-of-the-art data management and measurement/detection systems. The Company is developing several new products that it hopes to introduce in late 1996.

Officers	Position	Ownership Information	12/31/95
Harold D. Harrison	CEO	Number of Shares Outstanding	3,463,240
Sharron A. Harrison	Secretary, Treasurer	Market Capitalization	$ 19,047,820
		Frequency Of Dividends	n.a.
		Number of Shareholders	Under 500

Other Information				
Transfer Agent	Oxford Transfer & Registry Agency, Inc.		Where Listed	OTC-BB
Auditor	Groner, Boyle & Quillin, PLL		Symbol	SLTS
Market Maker	Paragon Capital Corporation	Telephone (800)345-0505	SIC Code	8731
Broker Dealer	Regular Stockbroker		Employees	15

San Joaquin Bank

1301 17th Street • Bakersfield, CA 93301 • Telephone (805)395-1610 • Fax (805)395-1098

Company Description

San Joaquin Bank offers standard banking services at its two branches in Bakersfield, California, which is in the heart of the San Joaquin Valley. In 1987, the Bank formed a subsidiary, Kern Island Company, to acquire, develop, sell or operate commercial and residential real property. In 1983, the Bank formed a limited partnership, Farmersville Village Grove Associates, to acquire and operate low-income housing projects.

	12/31/95	12/31/94	12/31/93	12/31/92
Per Share Information				
Stock Price	18.00	13.25	11.00	10.50
Earnings Per Share	1.56	1.21	0.94	0.81
Price / Earnings Ratio	11.54	10.95	11.70	12.96
Book Value Per Share	12.68	10.77	9.38	8.43
Price / Book Value %	141.96	123.03	117.27	124.56
Dividends Per Share	n.a.	n.a.	n.a.	n.a.
Annual Financial Data				
Operating Results (000's)				
Net Interest Income	6,425.0	5,650.0	4,708.0	4,282.0
Loan Loss Provision	-475.0	-320.0	-80.0	-75.0
Non-Interest Income	990.0	866.0	854.0	725.0
Non-Interest Expense	-4,437.0	-4,245.0	-3,883.0	-3,619.0
Income Before Taxes and Other	2,503.0	1,951.0	1,599.0	1,313.0
Other Items	n.a.	n.a.	n.a.	n.a.
Income Tax	-983.0	-773.0	-689.0	-522.0
Net Income	1,520.0	1,178.0	910.0	791.0
Balance Sheet (000's)				
Cash & Securities	59,242.0	43,994.0	42,750.0	28,530.0
Loans, Net	66,599.0	67,504.0	60,833.0	61,807.0
Fixed Assets, Net	705.0	727.0	867.0	1,051.0
Total Assets	129,725.0	114,435.0	107,082.0	94,157.0
Deposits	117,435.0	104,030.0	97,743.0	85,411.0
Stockholders' Equity	11,001.0	9,467.0	8,289.0	7,369.0
Performance & Financial Condition				
Net Interest Margin	n.a.	n.a.	n.a.	n.a.
Return on Avg Stockholders' Equity %	14.85	13.27	11.62	11.36
Return on Average Assets %	1.25	1.06	0.90	0.87
Equity to Assets %	8.48	8.27	7.74	7.83
Reserve as a % of Non-Performing Loans	149.60	254.51	232.53	n.a.

Compound Growth %'s	EPS %	24.42	Net Income %	24.32	Net Interest Income %	14.48

Comments

All per share amounts are restated to adjust for 10% stock dividends issued in 1992, 1993, 1994 and 1995. The Bank primarily makes commercial and real estate loans, representing 60% and 32% of total loans, respectively. Even though there have been no cash dividends, shareholders have little reason to complain. With return on equity above 14% in 1995, management is wise to keep cash in the Company. The Bank was formed in 1980.

Officers	Position	Ownership Information	12/31/95
Bruce Maclin	Chairman	Number of Shares Outstanding	986,900
Bart Hill	President, CEO	Market Capitalization	$ 17,764,200
John W. Ivy, Sr.	Vice President, Sr Loan Officer	Frequency Of Dividends	Irregular
Stephen M. Annis, Sr.	Head Cashier, CFO	Number of Shareholders	275

Other Information				
Transfer Agent	Company Office		Where Listed	OTC-BB
Auditor	Brown Armstrong Randall Reyes		Symbol	SJQN
Market Maker	Hoefer & Arnett, Inc.	Telephone (415)362-7111	SIC Code	6020
Broker Dealer	Regular Stockbroker		Employees	72

Santa Clara, Bank of

2027 El Camino Real • Santa Clara, CA 95052 • Telephone (408)249-5900 • Fax (408)987-9580

Company Description

The Bank of Santa Clara operates eight branches in northern California, mostly in the area in and surrounding San Jose. This area, also referred to as Silicon Valley, is home to many high technology businesses. Loans are made to individuals and to small and medium sized businesses. The Bank was formed 23 years ago and has been able to capitalize on the explosive business and population growth of the area.

	12/31/95	12/31/94	12/31/93	12/31/92
Per Share Information				
Stock Price	11.00	9.29	7.27	6.00
Earnings Per Share	1.46	1.36	1.32	1.04
Price / Earnings Ratio	7.53	6.83	5.51	5.77
Book Value Per Share	10.44	10.08	8.66	7.56
Price / Book Value %	105.36	92.16	83.95	79.37
Dividends Per Share	0.45	0.43	0.24	0.19
Annual Financial Data				
Operating Results (000's)				
Net Interest Income	11,948.9	11,504.2	10,461.6	9,093.4
Loan Loss Provision	-475.0	-660.0	-450.0	-340.0
Non-Interest Income	2,474.0	2,436.9	2,157.7	1,713.7
Non-Interest Expense	-9,878.1	-9,602.5	-9,047.8	-7,851.1
Income Before Taxes and Other	4,069.8	3,678.6	3,121.5	2,615.9
Other Items	n.a.	n.a.	n.a.	n.a.
Income Tax	-1,334.0	-1,216.0	-856.0	-707.5
Net Income	2,735.8	2,462.6	2,265.5	1,908.4
Balance Sheet (000's)				
Cash & Securities	85,981.0	60,340.1	57,771.0	43,607.0
Loans, Net	134,418.5	126,242.8	120,212.7	102,729.4
Fixed Assets, Net	2,167.0	1,598.8	2,095.2	2,151.3
Total Assets	226,606.8	193,604.5	183,438.8	150,851.7
Deposits	206,331.4	175,853.9	167,494.8	137,118.8
Stockholders' Equity	19,361.1	16,818.4	14,830.5	12,945.8
Performance & Financial Condition				
Net Interest Margin	n.a.	n.a.	n.a.	n.a.
Return on Avg Stockholders' Equity %	15.12	15.56	16.31	15.79
Return on Average Assets %	1.30	1.31	1.36	1.23
Equity to Assets %	8.54	8.69	8.08	8.58
Reserve as a % of Non-Performing Loans	85.48	39.36	n.a.	n.a.

Compound Growth %'s	EPS %	11.97	Net Income %	12.76	Net Interest Income %	9.53

Comments

During 1995 the Bank declared a 2 for 1 stock split and had stock dividends in 1995, 1994 and 1993. All share and per share information has been restated. Also during 1995, the Bank purchased land for $1,040,000 on which it plans to build a new main office facility. The loan portfolio is diversified between real estate, commercial and installment loans, which represent 42%, 22% and 35% of total loans, respectively. The Bank has consistently had outstanding returns on assets and equity.

Officers	Position	Ownership Information	12/31/95
Ronald D. Reinartz	CEO	Number of Shares Outstanding	1,854,562
Lawrence S. Santa Maria	Senior VP, COO	Market Capitalization	$ 20,400,182
Judith J. Reinartz	Senior VP	Frequency Of Dividends	Semi-Annual
James C. Audibert	Senior VP	Number of Shareholders	430
Gene Maxwell	Sr Loan Officer		

Other Information				
Transfer Agent	Company Office		Where Listed	OTC-BB
Auditor	Grant Thornton		Symbol	BKSL
Market Maker	Ryan, Beck & Co.	Telephone (800)325-7926	SIC Code	6020
Broker Dealer	Regular Stockbroker		Employees	131

Santa Maria, Bank of

P.O.Box 6090 • Santa Maria, CA 93456 • Telephone (805)937-8551 • Fax (805)937-6582

Company Description

Bank of Santa Maria is a community bank serving the central coast of California with ten branches. It has 17 straight years of increases in both total assets and profits. Management's stated goal is to serve the entire central coast area. In pursuit of this plan, Templeton National Bank was acquired in 1995 and Citizens Bank of Paso Robles was acquired in 1996.

	12/31/95	12/31/94	12/31/93	12/31/92
Per Share Information				
Stock Price	14.00	12.50	11.25	10.25
Earnings Per Share	1.15	0.96	0.81	0.78
Price / Earnings Ratio	12.17	13.02	13.89	13.14
Book Value Per Share	10.01	8.96	8.20	7.36
Price / Book Value %	139.86	139.51	137.20	139.27
Dividends Per Share	0.11	0.08	0.05	0.05
Annual Financial Data				
Operating Results (000's)				
Net Interest Income	14,248.0	12,790.0	11,814.9	10,864.7
Loan Loss Provision	-700.0	-250.0	-601.8	-907.0
Non-Interest Income	2,592.3	2,357.9	2,460.2	2,132.4
Non-Interest Expense	-11,112.0	-10,808.2	-10,307.5	-8,900.1
Income Before Taxes and Other	5,028.3	4,089.8	3,365.8	3,190.0
Other Items	n.a.	n.a.	n.a.	n.a.
Income Tax	-1,878.9	-1,529.0	-1,245.7	-1,239.0
Net Income	3,149.4	2,560.8	2,120.1	1,951.0
Balance Sheet (000's)				
Cash & Securities	99,738.7	82,399.0	65,689.4	52,315.7
Loans, Net	148,690.5	146,533.5	129,189.1	137,934.0
Fixed Assets, Net	10,212.6	10,586.6	8,471.1	8,285.1
Total Assets	263,577.3	244,135.5	208,087.2	201,695.2
Deposits	234,054.4	218,594.8	188,786.8	184,230.2
Stockholders' Equity	27,503.6	23,973.8	17,928.9	16,004.7
Performance & Financial Condition				
Net Interest Margin	6.53	6.15	5.97	6.35
Return on Avg Stockholders' Equity %	12.24	12.22	12.50	12.95
Return on Average Assets %	1.24	1.13	1.03	0.99
Equity to Assets %	10.43	9.82	8.62	7.94
Reserve as a % of Non-Performing Loans	1730.46	169.15	86.14	58.99

Compound Growth %'s	EPS %	13.82	Net Income %	17.31	Net Interest Income %	9.46

Comments

The loan portfolio of the Bank is well diversified throughout industries, with real estate related loans accounted for approximately 60% of total loans at December 31, 1995. In addition to registering fine returns on assets and equity, they are equally as proud of their "Santa Maria Style", greeting each customer with a smile and a cup of coffee.

Officers	Position	Ownership Information	12/31/95
William A. Hares	President, Chairman of the Board	Number of Shares Outstanding	2,748,261
David Verhelst	Exec VP	Market Capitalization	$ 38,475,654
F. Dean Fletcher	Exec VP, CFO	Frequency Of Dividends	Annual
Carol Bradfield	Senior VP	Number of Shareholders	1,071
Douglas Bradley	Senior VP, COO		

Other Information			
Transfer Agent	Chemical Mellon Shareholder Services	Where Listed	OTC-BB
Auditor	Dayton and Associates	Symbol	BSMR
Market Maker	Maguire Investments	Telephone (805)922-6901	SIC Code	6020
Broker Dealer	Regular Stockbroker	Employees	178

Sarnia Corporation

6850 Versar Center • Springfield, VA 22151 • Telephone (703)642-6800 • Fax (703)642-6825

Company Description

The Company owns and operates two four-story office buildings, known as Versar Center, on 18.3 acres in Springfield, Virginia. The Company was incorporated in 1982 to acquire the property from its then parent, Versar, Inc. On June 30, 1994, Versar spun-off the Company to Versar's shareholders and the Company began to be publicly traded. Versar rents about 36% of the Company's space.

	06/30/95	06/30/94	06/30/93	06/30/92
Per Share Information				
Stock Price	0.25	0.19	n.a.	n.a.
Earnings Per Share	-0.06	-0.25	-0.14	n.a.
Price / Earnings Ratio	n.a.	n.a.	n.a.	n.a.
Book Value Per Share	-0.28	-0.22	-0.43	n.a.
Price / Book Value %	n.a.	n.a.	n.a.	n.a.
Dividends Per Share	n.a.	n.a.	n.a.	n.a.
Annual Financial Data				
Operating Results (000's)				
Total Revenues	2,676.0	2,446.0	2,504.0	3,110.0
Costs & Expenses	-2,946.0	-2,990.0	-3,254.0	-3,418.0
Income Before Taxes and Other	-270.0	-544.0	-750.0	-308.0
Other Items	n.a.	-440.0	86.0	27.0
Income Tax	n.a.	-140.0	n.a.	n.a.
Net Income	-270.0	-1,124.0	-664.0	-281.0
Cash Flow From Operations	435.0	692.0	-210.0	69.0
Balance Sheet (000's)				
Cash & Equivalents	3.0	3.0	3.0	3.0
Total Current Assets	434.0	357.0	371.0	3.0
Fixed Assets, Net	12,871.0	13,005.0	13,428.0	17,231.0
Total Assets	13,305.0	13,362.0	13,799.0	17,234.0
Total Current Liabilities	765.0	211.0	311.0	6,216.0
Long-Term Debt	12,062.0	12,403.0	14,292.0	10,743.0
Stockholders' Equity	-1,278.0	-1,008.0	-1,980.0	-1,316.0
Performance & Financial Condition				
Return on Total Revenues %	-10.09	-45.95	-26.52	-9.04
Return on Avg Stockholders' Equity %	23.62	75.23	40.29	23.90
Return on Average Assets %	-2.02	-8.28	-4.28	-1.51
Current Ratio	0.57	1.69	1.19	n.a.
Debt / Equity %	n.a.	n.a.	n.a.	n.a.

Compound Growth %'s	EPS % n.a.	Net Income % n.a.	Total Revenues % -4.89

Comments

Springfield is located about 14.5 miles southwest of downtown Washington, D.C. The two buildings have about 228,500 square feet of leasable space and are occupied 100% and 93% at June 30, 1995. The Company can build an additional 168,000 square feet under existing zoning regulations and an additional 391,000 square feet by special exception.

Officers	Position	Ownership Information	06/30/95
Charles I. Judkins, Jr.	President, CEO	Number of Shares Outstanding	4,572,545
Lawrence W. Sinnott	Treasurer	Market Capitalization	$ 1,143,136
William G. Denbo	Vice President, General Manager	Frequency Of Dividends	n.a.
		Number of Shareholders	832

Other Information

Transfer Agent	Bank of New York			Where Listed	OTC-BB
Auditor	Price Waterhouse LLP			Symbol	SARN
Market Maker	Gabelli & Company, Inc.	Telephone	(914)921-5154	SIC Code	6512
Broker Dealer	Regular Stockbroker			Employees	6

Scientific Industries, Inc.

70 Orville Drive • Bohemia, NY 11716 • Telephone (516)567-4700 • Fax (516)567-5896

Company Description

The Company manufactures and sells laboratory equipment, including mixers, timers, rotators and pumps. The products are used by hospital, clinic and research laboratories, pharmaceutical and medical device manufacturers and other industries. Officers and directors, as a group, owned 48.9% of the Company's outstanding common stock at September 30, 1995. The Company was incorporated in Delaware in 1954.

	06/30/95	06/30/94	06/30/93	06/30/92
Per Share Information				
Stock Price	1.06	0.47	0.63	0.16
Earnings Per Share	0.22	0.26	0.30	0.19
Price / Earnings Ratio	4.82	1.81	2.10	0.84
Book Value Per Share	1.77	1.52	1.23	0.91
Price / Book Value %	59.89	30.92	51.22	17.58
Dividends Per Share	n.a.	n.a.	n.a.	n.a.
Annual Financial Data				
Operating Results (000's)				
Total Revenues	2,713.3	2,559.2	2,538.5	2,194.9
Costs & Expenses	-2,414.0	-2,212.7	-2,229.4	-2,027.2
Income Before Taxes and Other	299.3	346.5	309.1	167.7
Other Items	n.a.	28.5	56.9	45.6
Income Tax	-93.0	-131.3	-92.2	-58.4
Net Income	206.3	243.7	273.8	154.9
Cash Flow From Operations	149.1	329.3	335.3	187.2
Balance Sheet (000's)				
Cash & Equivalents	315.6	318.3	565.9	224.9
Total Current Assets	1,570.4	1,473.5	1,210.6	863.0
Fixed Assets, Net	107.5	69.3	31.5	37.6
Total Assets	1,779.3	1,618.3	1,286.9	934.1
Total Current Liabilities	265.7	317.8	243.9	200.8
Long-Term Debt	n.a.	n.a.	n.a.	n.a.
Stockholders' Equity	1,463.3	1,259.1	1,015.5	733.3
Performance & Financial Condition				
Return on Total Revenues %	7.60	9.52	10.79	7.06
Return on Avg Stockholders' Equity %	15.16	21.43	31.31	23.62
Return on Average Assets %	12.14	16.78	24.66	18.38
Current Ratio	5.91	4.64	4.96	4.30
Debt / Equity %	n.a.	n.a.	n.a.	n.a.

Compound Growth %'s	EPS %	5.01	Net Income %	10.02	Total Revenues %	7.32

Comments

For the six months ended December 31, 1995, the Company had sales of $1.3 million and net income of $87,000 ($.09 per share) as compared to $1.3 million and $134,000 ($.14 per share) for the same period in 1994. The Company's stock price at December 31, 1995, was quoted at an average bid/ask price of $1.38.

Officers	Position	Ownership Information		06/30/95
Lowell A. Kleiman	President, Treasurer	Number of Shares Outstanding		826,239
Cathy Pulver	Vice President, Secretary	Market Capitalization	$	875,813
Helena R. Santos	Controller	Frequency Of Dividends		n.a.
		Number of Shareholders		994

Other Information				
Transfer Agent	Continental Stock Transfer & Trust Co.		Where Listed	OTC-BB
Auditor	Nussbaum Yates & Wolpow		Symbol	SCND
Market Maker	Paragon Capital Corporation	Telephone (800)521-8877	SIC Code	3821
Broker Dealer	Regular Stockbroker		Employees	17

Scioto Downs, Inc.

6000 South High Street • Columbus, OH 43207 • Telephone (614)491-2515 • Fax (614)491-4626

Company Description

The Company's sole business is the ownership and operation of a harness horse racing facility in Columbus, Ohio, where it has conducted racing since 1959. Revenues are earned from commissions on pari-mutuel wagering and various other related operations, including admissions, concessions and parking.

	10/31/95	10/31/94	10/31/93	10/31/92
Per Share Information				
Stock Price	13.75	13.00	15.94	20.63
Earnings Per Share	-0.22	-0.33	-0.31	-0.20
Price / Earnings Ratio	n.a.	n.a.	n.a.	n.a.
Book Value Per Share	8.18	8.49	8.99	9.41
Price / Book Value %	168.09	153.12	177.31	219.23
Dividends Per Share	0.10	0.10	0.10	0.10
Annual Financial Data				
Operating Results (000's)				
Total Revenues	6,332.7	6,053.3	6,050.7	6,147.1
Costs & Expenses	-6,568.5	-6,396.5	-6,327.9	-6,324.5
Income Before Taxes and Other	-235.9	-343.1	-277.2	-177.4
Other Items	n.a.	41.0	n.a.	n.a.
Income Tax	106.0	104.0	90.0	56.0
Net Income	-129.9	-198.1	-187.2	-121.4
Cash Flow From Operations	478.4	484.7	602.6	638.0
Balance Sheet (000's)				
Cash & Equivalents	787.8	685.1	669.1	599.8
Total Current Assets	995.9	879.4	817.4	827.2
Fixed Assets, Net	7,799.9	8,293.2	8,804.3	9,134.3
Total Assets	8,795.8	9,172.6	9,621.8	9,961.6
Total Current Liabilities	3,665.2	493.2	428.1	381.4
Long-Term Debt	n.a.	3,263.2	3,369.3	3,475.2
Stockholders' Equity	4,871.2	5,059.0	5,357.7	5,604.5
Performance & Financial Condition				
Return on Total Revenues %	-2.05	-3.27	-3.09	-1.97
Return on Avg Stockholders' Equity %	-2.62	-3.80	-3.42	-2.13
Return on Average Assets %	-1.45	-2.11	-1.91	-1.21
Current Ratio	0.27	1.78	1.91	2.17
Debt / Equity %	n.a.	64.50	62.89	62.01

Compound Growth %'s	EPS % n.a.	Net Income % n.a.	Total Revenues % 1.00

Comments

At December 27, 1995, officers and directors, as a group, owned 39% of the Company's outstanding common stock.

Officers	Position	Ownership Information	10/31/95
Robert S. Steele	President, COO	Number of Shares Outstanding	595,767
Roderick H. Willcox	Secretary	Market Capitalization	$ 8,191,796
William C. Heer	Treasurer	Frequency Of Dividends	Semi-Annual
Laverne A. Hill	Vice President	Number of Shareholders	1,759
Timothy V. Luther	Controller		

Other Information

Transfer Agent	Company Office		Where Listed	OTC-BB
Auditor	Coopers & Lybrand LLP		Symbol	SCDO
Market Maker	Advest, Inc.	Telephone (800)998-9834	SIC Code	7948
Broker Dealer	Regular Stockbroker		Employees	350

Sea Pines Associates, Inc.

32 Greenwood Drive • Hilton Head Island, SC 29938 • Telephone (803)785-3333 • Fax (803)842-1927

Company Description

The Company owns and operates a full-service resort in Sea Pines Plantation on Hilton Head, Island, South Carolina. The resort consists of three golf courses, tennis and various other recreational facilities, home and villa rentals and food and beverage services. The Company also is involved in real estate brokerage, country club operations and the development of a retirement community.

The Company was incorporated in 1987.

	10/31/95	10/31/94	10/31/93	10/31/92
Per Share Information				
Stock Price	5,400.00	5,250.00	5,250.00	5,250.00
Earnings Per Share	-118.84	367.93	209.20	258.84
Price / Earnings Ratio	n.a.	14.27	25.10	20.28
Book Value Per Share	4,068.00	4,548.00	4,541.77	4,693.59
Price / Book Value %	132.74	115.44	115.59	111.85
Dividends Per Share	361.00	361.00	361.00	361.00
Annual Financial Data				
Operating Results (000's)				
Total Revenues	33,105.0	34,428.0	35,577.0	35,645.0
Costs & Expenses	-33,522.0	-33,197.0	-34,753.0	-34,635.0
Income Before Taxes and Other	-417.0	1,193.0	824.0	1,010.0
Other Items	n.a.	n.a.	n.a.	n.a.
Income Tax	125.0	-289.0	-310.0	-374.0
Net Income	-292.0	904.0	514.0	636.0
Cash Flow From Operations	1,708.0	2,542.0	2,090.0	2,438.0
Balance Sheet (000's)				
Cash & Equivalents	1,968.0	1,847.0	1,687.0	2,715.0
Total Current Assets	5,249.0	5,190.0	5,539.0	6,716.0
Fixed Assets, Net	40,954.0	35,998.0	36,132.0	34,086.0
Total Assets	51,706.0	45,161.0	44,601.0	43,418.0
Total Current Liabilities	6,631.0	5,992.0	5,836.0	6,086.0
Long-Term Debt	17,902.0	14,115.0	14,515.0	14,062.0
Stockholders' Equity	9,996.0	11,175.0	11,158.0	11,531.0
Performance & Financial Condition				
Return on Total Revenues %	-0.88	2.63	1.44	1.78
Return on Avg Stockholders' Equity %	-2.76	8.10	4.53	5.46
Return on Average Assets %	-0.60	2.01	1.17	1.51
Current Ratio	0.79	0.87	0.95	1.10
Debt / Equity %	179.09	126.31	130.09	121.95

Compound Growth %'s	EPS % n.a.	Net Income % n.a.	Total Revenues % -2.43

Comments

The Company's capital stock was originally issued in units consisting of 500 shares of preferred stock and 750 shares of common stock. Virtually all stock transactions have been in units as originally issued. All share and per share amounts are converted to units. The preferred stock has a liquidation preference of $7.60 per share ($3,800 per unit) and annual dividends per share of $.72 per share ($361 per unit).

Officers	Position	Ownership Information	10/31/95
Francis S. Webster	Chairman	Number of Shares Outstanding	2,457
Angus Cotton	Secretary	Market Capitalization	$ 13,267,800
Thomas C. Morton	Treasurer	Frequency Of Dividends	Quarterly
Arthur P. Sundry	Other	Number of Shareholders	697

Other Information				
Transfer Agent	Wachovia Bank of North Carolina		Where Listed	OTC-BB
Auditor	Ernst & Young LLP		Symbol	SPSU
Market Maker	Robinson-Humphrey Company Inc.	Telephone (800)241-0445	SIC Code	7997
Broker Dealer	Dean Witter	Tel/Ext (212)392-3790	Employees	265

Seaboard Automotive, Inc.

721 Blackhorse Pike • Blackwood, NJ 08012 • Telephone (609)227-4397 • Fax (609)232-3322

Company Description

The Company distributes automotive aftermarket parts to over 200 independent jobber/retailers in eastern and central Pennsylvania and southern New Jersey. Products such as brake parts, exhaust systems, chassis parts, shock absorbers and other undercar, high wear items are the Company's speciality. The Company, founded in Delaware in 1991, acquired all of the stock of Seaboard Automotive in 1993 and assumed its name. Seaboard was founded in 1972. Two private placements in 1994 raised approximately $844,000.

	06/30/95	06/30/94	06/30/93	06/30/92
Per Share Information				
Stock Price	2.75	5.50	2.75	2.75
Earnings Per Share	0.05	0.09	0.05	0.05
Price / Earnings Ratio	55.00	61.11	55.00	55.00
Book Value Per Share	0.56	0.52	0.31	0.25
Price / Book Value %	491.07	1,057.70	887.10	1,100.00
Dividends Per Share	n.a.	n.a.	n.a.	n.a.
Annual Financial Data				
Operating Results (000's)				
Total Revenues	23,310.2	22,445.9	21,551.4	21,864.8
Costs & Expenses	-22,853.9	-21,826.5	-21,147.0	-21,474.8
Income Before Taxes and Other	456.3	619.4	404.4	389.9
Other Items	n.a.	n.a.	n.a.	n.a.
Income Tax	-193.8	-216.2	-179.5	-164.1
Net Income	262.4	403.2	224.9	225.8
Cash Flow From Operations	-155.0	-1,730.9	-154.5	-123.7
Balance Sheet (000's)				
Cash & Equivalents	20.9	31.0	3.6	21.2
Total Current Assets	8,659.1	8,252.5	6,033.7	5,712.6
Fixed Assets, Net	1,468.2	1,212.5	763.8	635.8
Total Assets	10,243.0	9,525.2	6,830.2	6,367.5
Total Current Liabilities	6,418.1	6,315.6	5,084.1	5,024.0
Long-Term Debt	989.9	654.5	438.5	260.8
Stockholders' Equity	2,774.8	2,555.1	1,307.6	1,082.7
Performance & Financial Condition				
Return on Total Revenues %	1.13	1.80	1.04	1.03
Return on Avg Stockholders' Equity %	9.85	20.88	18.82	n.a.
Return on Average Assets %	2.65	4.93	3.41	n.a.
Current Ratio	1.35	1.31	1.19	1.14
Debt / Equity %	35.68	25.62	33.54	24.09

Compound Growth %'s	EPS %	n.a.	Net Income %	5.13	Total Revenues %	2.16

Comments

As of September 1, 1995, officers and directors, as a group, owned 54.6% of the Company's outstanding common stock.

Officers	Position	Ownership Information	06/30/95
James R. Coulter	Chairman	Number of Shares Outstanding	4,917,709
Joseph P. Coulter	President	Market Capitalization	$ 13,523,700
Stephen M. Coulter	Exec VP	Frequency Of Dividends	n.a.
John T. Coulter	Vice President	Number of Shareholders	323
Christopher P. Coulter	VP - Sales		

Other Information				
Transfer Agent	Continental Stock Transfer & Trust Co.		Where Listed	OTC-PS
Auditor	Coopers & Lybrand LLP		Symbol	SEAB
Market Maker	Havkit Corp. NY	Telephone (212)233-1800	SIC Code	5013
Broker Dealer	Regular Stockbroker		Employees	177

Sel-Drum International, Inc.

601 Amherst Street • Buffalo, NY 14207-2925 • Telephone (800)263-9356 • Fax (800)563-3192

Company Description

The Company's primary business is the distribution of high mortality copier replacement parts, toners and drums and the manufacture of drums. The Company markets its products in both the U.S. and Canada. The Company was incorporated in Colorado in 1993 and became an operating company in 1995, when it acquired all the outstanding shares of a privately-held Canadian company in exchange for 6.1 million of its shares.

	07/31/95	07/31/94
Per Share Information		
Stock Price	1.50	n.a.
Earnings Per Share	0.08	n.a.
Price / Earnings Ratio	18.75	n.a.
Book Value Per Share	-0.18	n.a.
Price / Book Value %	n.a.	n.a.
Dividends Per Share	n.a.	n.a.
Annual Financial Data		
Operating Results (000's)		
Total Revenues	14,178.3	13,381.8
Costs & Expenses	-13,224.5	-12,480.4
Income Before Taxes and Other	911.0	901.4
Other Items	n.a.	n.a.
Income Tax	-297.1	-318.4
Net Income	613.9	583.0
Cash Flow From Operations	52.5	688.1
Balance Sheet (000's)		
Cash & Equivalents	166.0	18.4
Total Current Assets	5,104.2	4,713.8
Fixed Assets, Net	1,104.3	1,096.1
Total Assets	6,405.2	5,919.6
Total Current Liabilities	2,627.8	2,671.3
Long-Term Debt	n.a.	373.7
Stockholders' Equity	3,454.5	-838.9
Performance & Financial Condition		
Return on Total Revenues %	4.33	n.a.
Return on Avg Stockholders' Equity %	46.94	n.a.
Return on Average Assets %	9.96	n.a.
Current Ratio	1.94	n.a.
Debt / Equity %	n.a.	n.a.

Compound Growth %'s	EPS %	n.a.	Net Income %	5.30	Total Revenues %	5.95

Comments

Included in Stockholders' Equity at July 31, 1995, is $4.8 million of preferred stock. Trading in the Company's common stock began in June, 1995. The balance sheet and operating results for the year ended July 31, 1994, are pro forma and are presented for comparative purposes. For the three months ended January 31, 1996, the Company had sales of $3.5 million and Net Income of $184,000 as compared to $3.7 million and $97,000, respectively, for the same period in the prior fiscal year.

Officers	Position	Ownership Information	07/31/95
Brian Turnbull	President, CEO	Number of Shares Outstanding	7,622,000
Brien Murtagh	Exec VP	Market Capitalization	$ 11,433,000
Stephen Dadson	Secretary	Frequency Of Dividends	n.a.
Gerald Maunder	Vice President	Number of Shareholders	390
Al Green	Other		

Other Information

Transfer Agent	U.S. Stock Transfer Corporation			Where Listed	OTC-BB
Auditor	Mengel, Metsger, Barr & Co.			Symbol	SDUM
Market Maker	Paragon Capital Corporation	Telephone	(800)521-8877	SIC Code	3861
Broker Dealer	Regular Stockbroker			Employees	70

Seven J Stock Farm, Inc.

808 Travis St., Ste. 1353 • Houston, TX 77002-5701 • Telephone (713)228-8900 • Fax (713)228-8913

Company Description

The principal operations of the Company consist of producing and selling field crops, leasing pastures, and gathering and transporting natural gas through pipelines. The Company also receives oil and gas royalties on the 11,140 acres of land it owns in Houston County, Texas. The Company was incorporated in the state of Texas in 1948.

	10/31/95	10/31/94	10/31/93	10/31/92
Per Share Information				
Stock Price	3.50	3.50	2.75	2.50
Earnings Per Share	0.11	0.12	0.10	0.15
Price / Earnings Ratio	31.82	29.17	27.50	16.67
Book Value Per Share	1.06	0.95	0.83	0.72
Price / Book Value %	330.19	368.42	331.33	n.a.
Dividends Per Share	n.a.	n.a.	n.a.	n.a.
Annual Financial Data				
Operating Results (000's)				
Total Revenues	686.0	600.0	546.0	652.0
Costs & Expenses	-459.0	-385.0	-358.0	-380.0
Income Before Taxes and Other	227.0	215.0	188.0	272.0
Other Items	n.a.	n.a.	n.a.	n.a.
Income Tax	-65.0	-34.0	-39.0	-51.0
Net Income	162.0	181.0	149.0	221.0
Cash Flow From Operations	299.0	158.0	345.0	215.0
Balance Sheet (000's)				
Cash & Equivalents	487.0	376.0	86.0	181.0
Total Current Assets	631.0	525.0	594.0	619.0
Fixed Assets, Net	1,168.0	1,046.0	853.0	777.0
Total Assets	1,807.0	1,579.0	1,455.0	1,402.0
Total Current Liabilities	176.0	132.0	184.0	227.0
Long-Term Debt	n.a.	n.a.	n.a.	n.a.
Stockholders' Equity	1,541.0	1,379.0	1,198.0	1,049.0
Performance & Financial Condition				
Return on Total Revenues %	23.62	30.17	27.29	33.90
Return on Avg Stockholders' Equity %	11.10	14.05	13.26	22.95
Return on Average Assets %	9.57	11.93	10.43	14.82
Current Ratio	3.59	3.98	3.23	2.73
Debt / Equity %	n.a.	n.a.	n.a.	n.a.

Compound Growth %'s	EPS %	-9.82	Net Income %	-9.83	Total Revenues %	1.71

Comments

Total Revenues for 1995 of $686,000 were broken down as follows: farm produce sales 38%, pipeline operations 29%, ranch leases 17%, and oil and gas royalties 16%. The Company's land is stated at a cost of $303,000.

Officers	Position	Ownership Information	10/31/95
John R. Parten	Chairman, President	Number of Shares Outstanding	1,451,000
Valerie Coulter	Secretary	Market Capitalization	$ 5,078,500
R.F. Pratka	Vice President, Treasurer	Frequency Of Dividends	n.a.
		Number of Shareholders	866

Other Information				
Transfer Agent	Company Office		Where Listed	OTC-BB
Auditor	Mattison and Riquelmy		Symbol	SEVJ
Market Maker	Carr Securities Corporation	Telephone (800)221-2243	SIC Code	6792
Broker Dealer	Regular Stockbroker		Employees	10

Shenandoah Telecommunications Company

124 South Main Street • Edinburg, VA 22824 • Telephone (540)984-4141 • Fax (540)984-1892

Company Description

The Company is a holding company that through its subsidiaries provides local and long distance telephone, cable TV, mobile communications and unregulated communications services, as well as other communications related products and services, to the Shenandoah Valley area of Virginia. The Company was founded in the state of Virginia in 1902.

	12/31/95	12/31/94	12/31/93	12/31/92
Per Share Information				
Stock Price	24.50	22.00	20.38	25.75
Earnings Per Share	1.66	1.29	1.22	1.07
Price / Earnings Ratio	14.76	17.05	16.70	24.07
Book Value Per Share	10.44	9.21	8.28	7.37
Price / Book Value %	234.67	238.87	246.14	349.39
Dividends Per Share	0.48	0.38	0.30	0.28
Annual Financial Data				
Operating Results (000's)				
Total Revenues	22,910.4	20,531.6	18,245.0	17,521.1
Costs & Expenses	-13,713.4	-12,709.6	-12,077.1	-11,342.3
Income Before Taxes and Other	10,338.3	7,822.0	7,153.9	6,178.7
Other Items	-534.7	-393.3	-69.5	26.2
Income Tax	-3,573.0	-2,577.6	-2,481.8	-2,189.7
Net Income	6,230.7	4,851.0	4,602.6	4,015.3
Cash Flow From Operations	8,161.3	7,281.6	6,634.1	7,253.9
Balance Sheet (000's)				
Cash & Equivalents	7,348.7	9,505.5	8,410.8	2,635.0
Total Current Assets	15,308.9	15,165.0	13,629.4	10,011.3
Fixed Assets, Net	36,826.2	31,896.2	31,503.9	30,652.6
Total Assets	59,897.0	52,464.2	49,652.1	44,839.5
Total Current Liabilities	4,258.8	2,386.2	3,854.6	2,709.6
Long-Term Debt	10,097.0	9,517.9	9,051.9	8,500.2
Stockholders' Equity	39,271.3	34,616.7	31,176.0	27,701.6
Performance & Financial Condition				
Return on Total Revenues %	27.20	23.63	25.23	22.92
Return on Avg Stockholders' Equity %	16.87	14.75	15.63	15.32
Return on Average Assets %	11.09	9.50	9.74	9.23
Current Ratio	3.59	6.36	3.54	3.69
Debt / Equity %	25.71	27.50	29.03	30.68

Compound Growth %'s	EPS %	15.76	Net Income %	15.77	Total Revenues %	9.35

Comments

At December 31,1995, the Company had certificates of deposit of $1.2 million and investments in securities totaling $10 million. During 1995, a gain on sale of investments of $1.1 million was realized.

Officers	Position	Ownership Information	12/31/95
Christopher E. French	President	Number of Shares Outstanding	3,760,760
Harold Morrison, Jr.	Secretary	Market Capitalization	$ 92,138,620
Dick D. Bowman	Treasurer	Frequency Of Dividends	Annual
Noel M. Borden	Vice President	Number of Shareholders	3,226
Zane Neff	Other		

Other Information				
Transfer Agent	Company Office		Where Listed	OTC-BB
Auditor	McGladrey & Pullen LLP		Symbol	SHET
Market Maker	Carr Securities Corporation	Telephone (800)221-2243	SIC Code	4813
Broker Dealer	Regular Stockbroker		Employees	140

Shopsmith, Inc.

6530 Poe Avenue • Dayton, OH 45414 • Telephone (513)898-6070 • Fax (513)890-5197

Company Description

The Company produces and markets quality woodworking tools and other woodworking products. Products are distributed directly to consumers through demonstration and mail selling channels. The name "Shopsmith" is a registered trademark which the Company applies to the majority of its products.

	04/01/95	04/02/94	04/03/93	03/31/92
Per Share Information				
Stock Price	1.19	1.44	2.75	4.88
Earnings Per Share	0.56	-3.58	-0.59	-0.35
Price / Earnings Ratio	2.13	n.a.	n.a.	n.a.
Book Value Per Share	-0.46	-1.17	2.43	3.05
Price / Book Value %	n.a.	n.a.	113.17	160.00
Dividends Per Share	n.a.	n.a.	n.a.	n.a.
Annual Financial Data				
Operating Results (000's)				
Total Revenues	17,728.9	48,045.6	51,113.0	53,237.1
Costs & Expenses	-16,391.6	-56,538.5	-52,686.5	-54,461.0
Income Before Taxes and Other	1,420.7	-8,675.0	-1,573.5	-1,223.9
Other Items	n.a.	19.0	n.a.	n.a.
Income Tax	n.a.	n.a.	185.0	407.0
Net Income	1,420.7	-8,656.0	-1,388.5	-816.9
Cash Flow From Operations	2,041.2	923.6	-504.4	490.3
Balance Sheet (000's)				
Cash & Equivalents	360.9	749.3	202.9	913.7
Total Current Assets	3,799.2	6,058.1	12,026.9	12,212.6
Fixed Assets, Net	613.0	932.8	4,161.6	3,678.4
Total Assets	4,415.3	7,032.5	16,380.2	16,215.1
Total Current Liabilities	4,717.0	8,191.3	8,894.6	7,062.6
Long-Term Debt	426.4	n.a.	1,742.3	2,127.6
Stockholders' Equity	-1,224.7	-2,802.8	5,743.3	7,024.9
Performance & Financial Condition				
Return on Total Revenues %	8.01	-18.02	-2.72	-1.53
Return on Avg Stockholders' Equity %	n.a.	-588.75	-21.75	-11.02
Return on Average Assets %	24.82	-73.94	-8.52	-5.18
Current Ratio	0.81	0.74	1.35	1.73
Debt / Equity %	n.a.	n.a.	30.34	30.29

Compound Growth %'s	EPS % n.a.	Net Income % n.a.	Total Revenues % -30.69

Comments

Prior to the year ended April 1, 1995, the Company had experienced several years of losses and accumulated a deficiency in equity and working capital. In fiscal year 1994, the Company began an intense restructuring effort to stem the losses and regain profitability. Included in the loss for 1994 is $4.3 million for discontinued operations and restructuring. As a result of its restructuring efforts, the Company showed a profit in fiscal year 1995. For the nine months ended December 30, 1995, the Company had sales of $11.6 million and Net Income of $2.3 million ($.87 per share), as compared to $11.8 million and $983,000 ($.39 per share) for the same period in 1994. The stock was trading for about $2 per share on December 31, 1995.

Officers	Position	Ownership Information	04/01/95
John R. Folkerth	President, CEO	Number of Shares Outstanding	2,654,566
William C. Becker	VP - Finance, Treasurer	Market Capitalization	$ 3,158,934
Lawrence R. Jones	Vice President	Frequency Of Dividends	n.a.
		Number of Shareholders	1,321

Other Information

Transfer Agent	Huntington National Bank			Where Listed	OTC-BB
Auditor	Crowe, Chizek & Co.			Symbol	SHOP
Market Maker	Wedbush Morgan Securities, Inc	Telephone	(800)421-0251	SIC Code	3550
Broker Dealer	Regular Stockbroker			Employees	122

Sierra Monitor Corporation

1991 Tarob Court • Milpitas, CA 95035 • Telephone (408)262-6611 • Fax (408)262-9042

Company Description

The Company designs and develops hazardous gas monitoring devices for the protection of personnel and facilities in industrial work places. Products are sold primarily to oil, gas and chemical companies, waste-water treatment plants, parking garages and landfill projects. The Company was incorporated in California in 1978.

	12/31/95	12/31/94	12/31/93	12/31/92
Per Share Information				
Stock Price	0.38	0.25	0.27	0.12
Earnings Per Share	n.a.	0.05	0.08	n.a.
Price / Earnings Ratio	n.a.	5.00	3.38	n.a.
Book Value Per Share	0.21	0.21	0.16	0.08
Price / Book Value %	180.95	119.05	168.75	150.00
Dividends Per Share	n.a.	n.a.	n.a.	n.a.
Annual Financial Data				
Operating Results (000's)				
Total Revenues	4,803.9	5,839.8	4,922.1	3,475.5
Costs & Expenses	-4,773.4	-5,178.4	-4,385.5	-3,454.5
Income Before Taxes and Other	30.5	661.5	536.6	21.0
Other Items	n.a.	n.a.	n.a.	n.a.
Income Tax	-12.5	-145.0	213.0	n.a.
Net Income	18.0	516.5	749.6	21.0
Cash Flow From Operations	13.3	810.0	352.7	10.2
Balance Sheet (000's)				
Cash & Equivalents	310.6	990.9	230.0	85.0
Total Current Assets	2,619.9	2,475.7	1,970.8	1,306.1
Fixed Assets, Net	101.5	143.5	109.2	79.2
Total Assets	2,800.3	2,665.1	2,137.1	1,455.6
Total Current Liabilities	605.7	493.7	575.7	649.9
Long-Term Debt	n.a.	n.a.	n.a.	n.a.
Stockholders' Equity	2,194.5	2,171.4	1,561.3	805.7
Performance & Financial Condition				
Return on Total Revenues %	0.38	8.84	15.23	0.60
Return on Avg Stockholders' Equity %	0.83	27.67	63.34	2.64
Return on Average Assets %	0.66	21.51	41.73	1.53
Current Ratio	4.33	5.01	3.42	2.01
Debt / Equity %	n.a.	n.a.	n.a.	n.a.

Compound Growth %'s	EPS %	-37.50	Net Income %	-4.99	Total Revenues %	11.39

Comments

Revenues were up significantly in 1995 resulting primarily from work on a Navy contract. However, this contract has lower than normal margins and consequently the overall profit margin suffered. Trading in the Company's stock was sporadic prior to 1993.

Officers	Position	Ownership Information	12/31/95
Gordon R. Arnold	CEO, President	Number of Shares Outstanding	10,276,888
Michael C. Farr	Vice President	Market Capitalization	$ 3,905,217
Stephen R. Ferree	Vice President	Frequency Of Dividends	n.a.
		Number of Shareholders	361

Other Information

Transfer Agent	U.S. Stock Transfer Corporation			Where Listed	OTC-BB
Auditor	KPMG Peat Marwick LLP			Symbol	SRMC
Market Maker	Herzog, Heine, Geduld, Inc.	Telephone	(800)221-3600	SIC Code	3829
Broker Dealer	Regular Stockbroker			Employees	33

Sierra, Bank of the

P.O.Box 1930 • Porterville, CA 93258 • Telephone (209)782-4900 • Fax (209)782-4999

Company Description

Bank of the Sierra is a California state-chartered commercial bank which commenced operations in 1978. The Bank now has seven branches, plus two Real Estate Centers, two Agricultural Service Centers, a Bank Card Center, and a wholly owned real estate development corporation, Valley Foothill Funding, Inc. The Bank serves the central part of the San Joaquin Valley and the south central section of the Sierra Nevada mountain range.

	12/31/95	12/31/94	12/31/93	12/31/92
Per Share Information				
Stock Price	24.00	13.00	10.00	7.33
Earnings Per Share	1.53	1.52	1.28	1.08
Price / Earnings Ratio	15.69	8.55	7.81	6.79
Book Value Per Share	9.24	5.04	6.75	5.36
Price / Book Value %	259.74	257.94	148.15	136.75
Dividends Per Share	0.22	0.13	0.11	0.09
Annual Financial Data				
Operating Results (000's)				
Net Interest Income	16,162.0	14,109.0	12,147.0	11,274.0
Loan Loss Provision	-1,607.0	-450.0	-1,300.0	-1,025.0
Non-Interest Income	3,386.0	3,349.0	3,457.0	3,619.0
Non-Interest Expense	-12,560.0	-11,644.0	-9,754.0	-9,907.0
Income Before Taxes and Other	5,381.0	5,364.0	4,550.0	3,961.0
Other Items	n.a.	n.a.	n.a.	n.a.
Income Tax	-1,860.0	-1,869.0	-1,601.0	-1,466.0
Net Income	3,521.0	3,495.0	2,949.0	2,495.0
Balance Sheet (000's)				
Cash & Securities	84,614.0	64,377.0	70,591.0	38,522.0
Loans, Net	204,291.0	194,309.0	155,701.0	150,358.0
Fixed Assets, Net	7,231.0	6,870.0	6,113.0	3,650.0
Total Assets	304,607.0	271,664.0	236,757.0	196,381.0
Deposits	280,313.0	244,382.0	219,748.0	180,433.0
Stockholders' Equity	21,274.0	17,585.0	15,539.0	12,345.0
Performance & Financial Condition				
Net Interest Margin	n.a.	n.a.	n.a.	n.a.
Return on Avg Stockholders' Equity %	18.12	21.10	21.15	22.28
Return on Average Assets %	1.22	1.37	1.36	1.36
Equity to Assets %	6.98	6.47	6.56	6.29
Reserve as a % of Non-Performing Loans	77.61	79.27	1712.50	1371.43

Compound Growth %'s	EPS %	12.31	Net Income %	12.17	Net Interest Income %	12.76

Comments

The Bank maintains a diversified loan portfolio comprised of commercial, installment, real estate construction and mortgage loans. Real estate related loans account for approximately 53% of total loans. 1995 results were flat because, in management's estimation, the area's economy continued to be recessionary, characterized by a stagnant housing market and a high unemployment rate. However, the Bank still had excellent returns on assets and equity.

Officers	Position	Ownership Information	12/31/95
James C. Holly	President, CEO	Number of Shares Outstanding	2,303,070
Kenneth E. Goodwin	Exec VP, COO	Market Capitalization	$ 55,273,680
Jack B. Buchold	Senior VP, CFO	Frequency Of Dividends	Annual
Charlie C. Glenn	Senior VP	Number of Shareholders	471
Richard W. Vorreyer	Vice President		

Other Information			
Transfer Agent	Chemical Mellon Shareholder Services	Where Listed	OTC-BB
Auditor	McGladrey & Pullen, LLP	Symbol	BSRR
Market Maker	J. Alexander Securities, Inc.	Telephone (213)687-8400	SIC Code	6020
Broker Dealer	Regular Stockbroker	Employees	201

Sims-Agricultural Products, Inc.

3795 County Road 29 • Mt. Gilead, OH 43338 • Telephone (419)946-2015 • Fax (419)946-6571

Company Description

The Company is primarily in the business of manufacturing and marketing a complete line of micronutrients and granular nitrogen sulfate used in agriculture. It also is involved in the conversion of zinc filter cake into granulated and powdered finished products. The Company was founded in January, 1991, and went public in October, 1993, at $5 per share.

	06/30/95	06/30/94	06/30/93	06/30/92
Per Share Information				
Stock Price	6.00	5.00	n.a.	n.a.
Earnings Per Share	0.23	0.22	n.a.	n.a.
Price / Earnings Ratio	26.09	22.73	n.a.	n.a.
Book Value Per Share	1.49	1.23	n.a.	n.a.
Price / Book Value %	402.68	406.50	n.a.	n.a.
Dividends Per Share	n.a.	n.a.	n.a.	n.a.
Annual Financial Data				
Operating Results (000's)				
Total Revenues	5,476.3	3,965.0	3,453.7	3,428.4
Costs & Expenses	-5,057.5	-3,643.1	-3,264.6	-3,726.5
Income Before Taxes and Other	379.6	306.2	109.9	-484.2
Other Items	n.a.	n.a.	n.a.	n.a.
Income Tax	-133.4	-114.0	n.a.	n.a.
Net Income	246.1	192.2	109.9	-484.2
Cash Flow From Operations	51.4	-78.4	-9.7	-14.1
Balance Sheet (000's)				
Cash & Equivalents	5.5	11.8	20.3	1.3
Total Current Assets	1,817.0	1,746.6	1,040.5	661.2
Fixed Assets, Net	3,048.0	2,092.1	1,653.3	1,455.7
Total Assets	5,042.6	4,057.1	2,933.6	2,356.8
Total Current Liabilities	1,787.5	1,046.7	928.0	1,767.1
Long-Term Debt	1,255.9	1,347.5	1,461.2	1,036.4
Stockholders' Equity	1,830.3	1,542.0	544.5	-446.7
Performance & Financial Condition				
Return on Total Revenues %	4.49	4.85	n.a.	n.a.
Return on Avg Stockholders' Equity %	14.60	18.42	224.67	n.a.
Return on Average Assets %	5.41	5.50	4.15	n.a.
Current Ratio	1.02	1.67	n.a.	n.a.
Debt / Equity %	68.62	87.38	n.a.	n.a.

Compound Growth %'s	EPS %	n.a.	Net Income %	49.65	Total Revenues %	16.90

Comments

1994 results were reviewed, but not audited by an independent CPA firm. The stock price was floating around its offering price until June, 1995. We believe the recent rise to $18 ($9 after a 2 for 1 split in April, 1996) was a least partly attributable to press coverage.

Officers	Position	Ownership Information	06/30/95
Dallas Paul	President	Number of Shares Outstanding	1,030,300
John Bowen	Secretary, Treasurer	Market Capitalization	$ 6,181,800
		Frequency Of Dividends	n.a.
		Number of Shareholders	Under 500

Other Information

Transfer Agent	Company Office		Where Listed	OTC-BB
Auditor	Robert J. LeHew & Associates		Symbol	SAGG
Market Maker	Wien Securities Corp.	Telephone (800)624-0050	SIC Code	2873
Broker Dealer	Regular Stockbroker		Employees	35

Sivyer Steel Corporation

225 South 33 Street • Bettendorf, IA 52722 • Telephone (319)355-1811 • Fax (319)355-3946

Company Description

The Company manufactures steel castings for the construction, mining, railroad, transportation, valve, oil field, demolition equipment, scrap and solid waste recycling industries. It's facilities are located in Bettendorf, Iowa, and Moline, Illinois. The corporate office is in Milwaukee, Wisconsin. The Company was organized in Wisconsin in 1909 (also the first year of Walker's Manual). It went public in 1930.

	11/27/94	11/28/93	11/27/92
Per Share Information			
Stock Price	60.00	45.00	42.00
Earnings Per Share	17.10	4.50	0.24
Price / Earnings Ratio	3.51	10.00	175.00
Book Value Per Share	57.53	39.38	37.49
Price / Book Value %	104.29	114.27	112.03
Dividends Per Share	n.a.	n.a.	n.a.
Annual Financial Data			
Operating Results (000's)			
Total Revenues	23,912.7	21,384.3	73,277.8
Costs & Expenses	-22,899.7	-20,857.2	-63,745.0
Income Before Taxes and Other	1,013.0	527.2	9,532.7
Other Items	1,305.0	n.a.	n.a.
Income Tax	-336.0	-8.2	-3,365.8
Net Income	1,982.0	518.9	6,166.9
Cash Flow From Operations	2,193.2	514.2	7,199.1
Balance Sheet (000's)			
Cash & Equivalents	2,130.2	942.5	n.a.
Total Current Assets	8,397.8	6,357.3	6,389.0
Fixed Assets, Net	3,051.8	2,715.5	2,457.0
Total Assets	12,282.3	9,073.4	8,846.0
Total Current Liabilities	4,090.2	3,017.3	3,345.0
Long-Term Debt	36.8	57.6	1,174.0
Stockholders' Equity	6,639.0	4,544.9	4,327.0
Performance & Financial Condition			
Return on Total Revenues %	8.29	2.43	0.14
Return on Avg Stockholders' Equity %	35.44	11.70	0.66
Return on Average Assets %	18.56	5.79	0.31
Current Ratio	2.05	2.11	1.91
Debt / Equity %	0.55	1.27	27.13

Compound Growth %'s	EPS %	744.10	Net Income %	741.35	Total Revenues %	11.15

Comments

1994 results include a one-time benefit of $1.3 million, $1.13 per share, due to the likelihood of recognizing the benefit of certain tax carryovers as a reduction to future income taxes. Compound growth rates arc misleading because of the poor results in 1992, the base year, as well as the nonrecurring item in 1994. The Company continues to experience growth and has placed considerable attention to the global marketplace. 1995 revenues were not yet available but were forecast by management in the prior annual report to increase 24% with a significant increase in net income.

Officers	Position	Ownership Information	11/27/94
Everett G. Smith	Chairman	Number of Shares Outstanding	115,402
Claude D. Robinson	President, CEO	Market Capitalization	$ 6,924,120
Thomas Clasen	Secretary	Frequency Of Dividends	n.a.
Patricia M. Adrian	Treasurer	Number of Shareholders	Under 500
Patrick J. Comparin	Vice President		

Other Information

				Where Listed	OTC-PS
Transfer Agent	Company Office			Symbol	SIVS
Auditor	n.a.			SIC Code	3499
Market Maker	Hill, Thompson, Magid & Co.Inc	Telephone	(800)631-3083	Employees	275
Broker Dealer	Standard Investment	Tel/Ext	(888)783-4688	Jack	

Slippery Rock Financial Corporation

100 South Main Street • Slippery Rock, PA 16057-1245 • Telephone (412)794-2210 • Fax (412)794-2259

Company Description

Slippery Rock Financial Corporation is a one bank holding company for its wholly-owned subsidiary The First National Bank of Slippery Rock. The Bank operates in and around Slippery Rock, Pennsylvania and has five locations.

	12/31/95	12/31/94	12/31/93	12/31/92
Per Share Information				
Stock Price	76.00	56.00	54.00	50.00
Earnings Per Share	7.25	6.58	6.41	5.16
Price / Earnings Ratio	10.48	8.51	8.42	9.69
Book Value Per Share	53.15	47.40	42.78	37.76
Price / Book Value %	142.99	118.14	126.23	132.42
Dividends Per Share	1.91	1.57	1.36	1.10
Annual Financial Data				
Operating Results (000's)				
Net Interest Income	7,608.4	6,993.0	6,370.7	5,855.7
Loan Loss Provision	-275.0	-162.5	-250.0	-275.0
Non-Interest Income	902.1	809.1	916.7	755.0
Non-Interest Expense	-4,679.6	-4,533.8	-4,080.1	-3,955.2
Income Before Taxes and Other	3,555.8	3,105.8	2,957.3	2,380.5
Other Items	n.a.	n.a.	n.a.	n.a.
Income Tax	-1,056.3	-839.5	-748.0	-602.0
Net Income	2,499.5	2,266.3	2,209.3	1,778.5
Balance Sheet (000's)				
Cash & Securities	32,901.6	30,131.4	33,687.6	30,662.7
Loans, Net	121,648.3	111,575.6	98,864.6	91,000.2
Fixed Assets, Net	3,700.5	3,259.2	2,713.4	1,774.7
Total Assets	162,011.3	147,373.9	141,267.7	126,783.4
Deposits	140,664.4	129,321.8	124,470.7	112,114.6
Stockholders' Equity	18,313.4	16,329.9	14,739.1	13,008.2
Performance & Financial Condition				
Net Interest Margin	n.a.	n.a.	n.a.	n.a.
Return on Avg Stockholders' Equity %	14.43	14.59	15.92	14.47
Return on Average Assets %	1.62	1.57	1.65	1.44
Equity to Assets %	11.30	11.08	10.43	10.26
Reserve as a % of Non-Performing Loans	109.88	n.a.	115.36	210.25

Compound Growth %'s	EPS %	12.00	Net Income %	12.01	Net Interest Income %	9.12

Comments

The Bank's loan portfolio is made up primarily of real estate loans and loans to individuals, comprising 69% and 20% of total loans, respectively. On March 19, 1996, the Bank agreed to acquire certain deposit liabilities of the Harrisville, Pennsylvania office of Mellon Bank, N.A. The Bank will assume deposit liabilities of approximately $26 million and acquire the land, building, and equipment presently occupied by Mellon. In September, 1995, the stock became listed on the NASD Electronic Bulletin Board which makes trading easier for anyone who wants to buy or sell shares. It may also account for some or all of the sharp 35% jump in share price for the year.

Officers	Position	Ownership Information	12/31/95
William C. Sonntag	President, CEO	Number of Shares Outstanding	344,531
Dale R. Wimer	Exec VP	Market Capitalization	$ 26,184,356
Doris R. Blackwood	Secretary	Frequency Of Dividends	Semi-Annual
Eleanor L. Cress	Vice President	Number of Shareholders	536
Mark A. Volponi	Controller, Treasurer		

Other Information				
Transfer Agent	Company Office		Where Listed	OTC-BB
Auditor	Snodgrass		Symbol	SRCK
Market Maker	Legg Mason Wood Walker, Inc.	Telephone (212)429-4949	SIC Code	6020
Broker Dealer	Regular Stockbroker		Employees	96

Smith Investment Company

11270 West Park Place • Milwaukee, WI 53223-0976 • Telephone (414)359-4030 • Fax (414)359-4198

Company Description

The Company is involved in a wide range of industries including automotive products, water heaters, electric motors, fiberglass piping, feed storage systems, ceramic coating, barber and beauty salon furniture and fixtures, commercial warehousing and packaging, and multicolor printing. The Company is currently exempt from SEC reporting requirements.

	12/31/95	12/31/94	12/31/93	12/31/92
Per Share Information				
Stock Price	63.00	52.50	49.00	19.62
Earnings Per Share	11.81	10.15	5.77	-7.40
Price / Earnings Ratio	5.33	5.17	8.49	n.a.
Book Value Per Share	76.99	64.28	56.39	53.94
Price / Book Value %	81.83	81.67	86.89	36.37
Dividends Per Share	1.10	1.00	1.00	1.00
Annual Financial Data				
Operating Results (000's)				
Total Revenues	136,240.0	127,735.0	104,147.0	80,011.0
Costs & Expenses	-112,816.0	-107,125.0	-92,233.0	-82,010.0
Income Before Taxes and Other	21,046.0	17,883.0	8,887.0	-4,000.0
Other Items	n.a.	n.a.	n.a.	-9,127.0
Income Tax	-1,354.0	-959.0	727.0	793.0
Net Income	19,692.0	16,924.0	9,614.0	-12,334.0
Cash Flow From Operations	10,318.0	6,193.0	4,528.0	-2,491.0
Balance Sheet (000's)				
Cash & Equivalents	199.0	394.0	185.0	418.0
Total Current Assets	31,003.0	30,468.0	23,224.0	20,603.0
Fixed Assets, Net	44,080.0	42,526.0	41,742.0	42,722.0
Total Assets	194,108.0	175,641.0	157,987.0	152,565.0
Total Current Liabilities	43,551.0	37,378.0	32,005.0	43,074.0
Long-Term Debt	17,622.0	26,894.0	27,914.0	15,601.0
Stockholders' Equity	127,690.0	107,195.0	94,033.0	89,952.0
Performance & Financial Condition				
Return on Total Revenues %	0.97	13.25	9.23	-15.42
Return on Avg Stockholders' Equity %	16.77	16.82	10.45	-12.49
Return on Average Assets %	10.65	10.15	6.19	-7.54
Current Ratio	0.71	0.82	0.73	0.48
Debt / Equity %	13.80	25.09	29.69	17.34

Compound Growth %'s	EPS %	43.07	Net Income %	43.12	Total Revenues %	19.41

Comments

Other assets include a 30.7% equity interest in the A.O. Smith Corporation. At December 31, 1995, the fair market value of that investment was $131 million and it was recorded on the books as $114 million. Management believes that the improved financial condition arising over the last couple of years will allow it the opportunity to pursue attractive growth opportunities that may arise.

Officers	Position	Ownership Information	12/31/95
Arthur O. Smith	Chairman, CEO	Number of Shares Outstanding	1,658,533
Bruce M. Smith	President	Market Capitalization	$ 104,487,579
Glen R. Bomberger	VP - Finance	Frequency Of Dividends	Quarterly
Wesley A. Ulrich	Secretary, Treasurer	Number of Shareholders	Under 500

Other Information				
Transfer Agent	Firstar Trust Company, Milwaukee, WI		Where Listed	OTC-BB
Auditor	Ernst & Young LLP		Symbol	SMIC
Market Maker	Robert W. Baird & Co.	Telephone (800)562-2288	SIC Code	3621
Broker Dealer	Regular Stockbroker		Employees	5

Snow Summit Ski Corporation

880 Summit Boulevard • Big Bear Lake, CA 92315 • Telephone (909)866-5766 • Fax (909)866-3201

Company Description

The Company is the owner and operator of Snow Summit ski area and Summit ski area in Southern California. The Company has been granted the right to use National Forest Service land as the sites for its ski operations, but these permits have expiration dates.

	04/30/95	04/30/94	04/30/93	04/30/92
Per Share Information				
Stock Price	170.00	170.00	165.00	150.00
Earnings Per Share	17.37	12.31	2.17	17.31
Price / Earnings Ratio	9.79	13.81	76.04	8.67
Book Value Per Share	134.43	118.05	105.74	105.16
Price / Book Value %	126.46	144.01	156.04	142.64
Dividends Per Share	1.00	n.a.	1.00	n.a.
Annual Financial Data				
Operating Results (000's)				
Total Revenues	24,665.2	23,894.1	21,231.9	23,059.6
Costs & Expenses	-22,639.6	-22,521.1	-20,942.4	-21,084.9
Income Before Taxes and Other	2,025.6	1,373.0	289.5	1,974.6
Other Items	n.a.	n.a.	n.a.	n.a.
Income Tax	-841.7	-534.0	-141.8	-795.3
Net Income	1,183.9	839.0	147.8	1,179.4
Cash Flow From Operations	3,440.1	3,381.7	1,028.2	2,287.8
Balance Sheet (000's)				
Cash & Equivalents	1,338.5	1,619.1	643.7	771.1
Total Current Assets	3,616.2	4,002.0	2,776.9	2,883.0
Fixed Assets, Net	15,220.3	14,865.2	16,155.9	13,968.0
Total Assets	20,145.7	20,214.9	20,319.1	18,275.8
Total Current Liabilities	1,309.4	4,454.8	3,561.0	4,457.5
Long-Term Debt	5,769.4	7,046.5	8,704.2	5,634.4
Stockholders' Equity	9,161.1	8,045.4	7,206.3	7,126.7
Performance & Financial Condition				
Return on Total Revenues %	4.80	3.51	0.70	5.11
Return on Avg Stockholders' Equity %	13.76	11.00	2.06	21.54
Return on Average Assets %	5.87	4.14	0.77	6.64
Current Ratio	2.76	0.90	0.78	0.65
Debt / Equity %	62.98	87.59	120.79	79.06

Compound Growth %'s	EPS %	0.12	Net Income %	0.13	Total Revenues %	2.27

Comments

Despite being subject to the forces of Mother Nature, the Company has consistently returned a profit and is constantly looking for ways to improve operations. After three years of intense negotiations, management has concluded a lease/purchase agreement for 2.7 acres of property adjacent to the Snow Summit base area. Plans are in the works to expand and provide a large number of new and improved services intended to greatly enhance Snow Summit.

Officers	Position	Ownership Information	04/30/95
richard C. Kun	President	Number of Shares Outstanding	68,150
Steven Trainor	VP - Finance	Market Capitalization	$ 11,585,500
Thomas Banish	Vice President	Frequency Of Dividends	Quarterly
greg Ralph	VP - Sales	Number of Shareholders	Under 500
Robert Tarras	Controller		

Other Information						
Transfer Agent	U.S. Stock Transfer Corporation			Where Listed	OTC-BB
Auditor	Grant Thornton			Symbol	n.a.
Market Maker	Seidler Companies, Inc., The	Telephone	(800)421-0164	SIC Code	7999
Broker Dealer	Standard Investment	Tel/Ext	(888)783-4688	Jack	Employees	n.a.

Solid Controls, Inc.

820 South Fifth Street • Hopkins, MN 55343 • Telephone (612)933-9053 • Fax (612)933-8961

Company Description

The Company designs and manufactures a diversified line of integrated machine controls, providing modern technology to the plastic machine industry.

	03/31/95	03/31/94	03/31/93	03/31/92
Per Share Information				
Stock Price	2.19	2.37	2.50	1.87
Earnings Per Share	-0.07	0.04	0.09	0.04
Price / Earnings Ratio	n.a.	59.25	27.78	46.75
Book Value Per Share	2.33	2.55	2.59	2.63
Price / Book Value %	93.99	92.94	96.53	71.10
Dividends Per Share	0.13	0.13	0.13	0.13
Annual Financial Data				
Operating Results (000's)				
Total Revenues	3,381.2	2,864.2	3,179.8	2,647.0
Costs & Expenses	-3,490.0	-2,804.2	-3,038.6	-2,565.3
Income Before Taxes and Other	-108.8	60.0	141.2	81.7
Other Items	n.a.	n.a.	n.a.	n.a.
Income Tax	20.0	-9.0	-40.4	-29.5
Net Income	-88.8	51.0	100.8	52.2
Cash Flow From Operations	166.0	-45.3	268.4	0.4
Balance Sheet (000's)				
Cash & Equivalents	1,217.0	1,222.6	1,369.2	1,276.4
Total Current Assets	2,509.9	2,694.2	2,777.5	2,774.2
Fixed Assets, Net	44.4	59.3	59.8	65.6
Total Assets	2,902.1	3,166.7	3,283.2	3,379.0
Total Current Liabilities	132.1	126.4	179.2	203.1
Long-Term Debt	n.a.	n.a.	n.a.	n.a.
Stockholders' Equity	2,768.5	3,020.2	3,065.4	3,118.7
Performance & Financial Condition				
Return on Total Revenues %	-2.63	1.78	3.17	1.97
Return on Avg Stockholders' Equity %	-3.07	1.68	3.26	1.65
Return on Average Assets %	-2.93	1.58	3.03	1.53
Current Ratio	19.01	21.31	15.50	13.66
Debt / Equity %	n.a.	n.a.	n.a.	n.a.

Compound Growth %'s	EPS % n.a.	Net Income % n.a.	Total Revenues % 8.50

Comments

The first six months of fiscal 1996 show a return to profitability with $50,000 in net earnings at $.04 per share. The balance sheet is free from long term debt and the current ratio is about 19 to 1. This doesn't count another $190,000 in marketable securities classified as a long term asset. The real question is whether the Company is seeking growth opportunities with all that money just sitting around.

Officers	Position	Ownership Information	03/31/95
Ronald A. Kokesh	President	Number of Shares Outstanding	1,185,804
A. Larry Katz	Secretary	Market Capitalization	$ 2,596,911
Kevin R. Kokesh	VP - Sales	Frequency Of Dividends	n.a.
Alan E. Wenker	Controller	Number of Shareholders	Under 500

Other Information			
Transfer Agent	Mellon Securities Trust Company	Where Listed	OTC-BB
Auditor	Deloitte & Touche LLP	Symbol	SLDC
Market Maker	Monroe Securities, Inc.	Telephone (800)766-5560	SIC Code	5063
Broker Dealer	Regular Stockbroker	Employees	n.a.

Sound One Corporation

1619 Broadway • New York, NY 10019 • Telephone (212)765-4757 • Fax (212)708-7802

Company Description

The Company is engaged in the business of providing sound and editing services to the motion picture and television industries. Most of the business is conducted on the East Coast. The Digital Audio Division (DAD) commenced operations in July of 1994. The Company has been public since 1972. The Company bought and retired 686,849 shares of its stock in 1993 and 1994 which amounted to 30.8% of all shares.

	12/31/94	12/31/93	12/31/92
Per Share Information			
Stock Price	2.43	4.37	1.87
Earnings Per Share	0.24	-0.71	0.09
Price / Earnings Ratio	10.13	n.a.	20.78
Book Value Per Share	2.12	1.34	2.76
Price / Book Value %	114.62	326.12	67.75
Dividends Per Share	n.a.	n.a.	n.a.
Annual Financial Data			
Operating Results (000's)			
Total Revenues	10,920.1	10,204.6	9,057.5
Costs & Expenses	-10,651.1	-10,141.6	-8,837.1
Income Before Taxes and Other	269.0	-1,399.9	220.3
Other Items	n.a.	n.a.	n.a.
Income Tax	20.4	219.9	-66.5
Net Income	289.4	-1,180.0	153.8
Cash Flow From Operations	586.4	1,092.7	1,568.1
Balance Sheet (000's)			
Cash & Equivalents	764.4	233.0	1,470.0
Total Current Assets	2,741.3	1,580.9	2,557.4
Fixed Assets, Net	6,911.2	7,557.8	6,098.1
Total Assets	9,652.6	9,157.7	8,675.6
Total Current Liabilities	1,926.9	1,742.0	1,307.6
Long-Term Debt	3,687.9	3,511.9	603.4
Stockholders' Equity	3,310.6	3,021.3	5,572.8
Performance & Financial Condition			
Return on Total Revenues %	2.65	-11.56	1.70
Return on Avg Stockholders' Equity %	9.14	-27.46	2.75
Return on Average Assets %	3.08	-13.23	1.88
Current Ratio	1.42	0.91	1.96
Debt / Equity %	111.40	116.24	10.83

Compound Growth %'s	EPS %	63.30	Net Income %	37.16	Total Revenues %	9.80

Comments

The 1995 results will be released at the shareholders' meeting in August. 1993 results reflect two nonrecurring expenses. One was the abandonment of fixed assets to enable the installation of DAD which amounted to $1,191,458. The other was a litigation settlement with the former president of the Company which amounted to $271,503.

Officers	Position	Ownership Information	12/31/94
Elisha Birnbaum	Chairman	Number of Shares Outstanding	1,562,554
Jeremy Koch	President, CEO	Market Capitalization	$ 3,797,006
Gaetano Spera	Secretary, Treasurer	Frequency Of Dividends	n.a.
		Number of Shareholders	Under 500

Other Information

Transfer Agent	Continental Stock Transfer & Trust Co.			Where Listed	OTC-BB
Auditor	Arthur Yorkes & Company			Symbol	SOUD
Market Maker	Forbes, Walsh, Kelly & Co, Inc	Telephone	(800)221-3747	SIC Code	7810
Broker Dealer	Regular Stockbroker			Employees	n.a.

Southern Michigan Bancorp, Inc.

51 West Pearl Street • Coldwater, MI 49036 • Telephone (517)279-5500 • Fax (517)279-7986

Company Description

Southern Michigan Bancorp, Inc. is a bank holding company with one subsidiary, Southern Michigan Bank & Trust. The Bank provides banking services within three counties of southwestern Michigan: Branch, Hillsdale and Calhoun.

	12/31/95	12/31/94	12/31/93	12/31/92
Per Share Information				
Stock Price	29.00	21.44	19.50	15.38
Earnings Per Share	2.82	2.21	1.79	1.69
Price / Earnings Ratio	10.28	9.70	10.89	9.10
Book Value Per Share	21.56	19.85	18.67	17.56
Price / Book Value %	134.51	108.01	104.45	87.59
Dividends Per Share	0.99	0.75	0.70	0.64
Annual Financial Data				
Operating Results (000's)				
Net Interest Income	9,096.3	7,737.5	6,702.4	7,194.0
Loan Loss Provision	-222.0	-180.0	n.a.	-480.0
Non-Interest Income	1,528.8	1,427.2	1,580.8	1,418.7
Non-Interest Expense	-6,953.2	-6,366.6	-6,156.7	-6,244.8
Income Before Taxes and Other	3,450.0	2,618.0	2,126.6	1,887.9
Other Items	n.a.	n.a.	-36.5	n.a.
Income Tax	-835.0	-600.0	-500.0	-422.0
Net Income	2,615.0	2,018.0	1,590.1	1,465.9
Balance Sheet (000's)				
Cash & Securities	77,033.1	67,208.1	58,786.0	52,160.0
Loans, Net	121,627.3	118,840.8	111,149.8	114,123.0
Fixed Assets, Net	3,962.2	3,287.3	3,029.6	3,035.0
Total Assets	209,977.1	195,624.9	178,452.9	172,477.1
Deposits	185,524.1	174,071.4	158,956.1	154,256.3
Stockholders' Equity	18,497.1	16,855.2	16,801.0	15,436.0
Performance & Financial Condition				
Net Interest Margin	5.20	4.90	5.00	5.35
Return on Avg Stockholders' Equity %	14.79	11.99	9.86	9.89
Return on Average Assets %	1.29	1.08	0.91	0.86
Equity to Assets %	8.81	8.62	9.41	8.95
Reserve as a % of Non-Performing Loans	914.44	918.86	151.27	148.22

Compound Growth %'s	EPS %	18.61	Net Income %	21.28	Net Interest Income %	8.14

Comments

The Bank's loan portfolio is fairly well diversified. Commercial, financial and agricultural loans, real estate mortgages, and loans to individual consumers represent 42%, 33%, and 25%, respectively, of total loans. All per share amounts have been adjusted to reflect a 2 for 1 split in 1995.

Officers	Position	Ownership Information	12/31/95
Jerry L. Towns	Chairman, CEO	Number of Shares Outstanding	857,984
James T. Grohalski	Exec VP, CFO	Market Capitalization	$ 24,881,536
Michael R. Madden	Senior VP	Frequency Of Dividends	Quarterly
James R. Cole	Senior VP	Number of Shareholders	466
Julie A. Waterbury	Vice President, Controller		

Other Information				
Transfer Agent	Company Office		Where Listed	OTC-BB
Auditor	Crowe, Chizek and Company LLP		Symbol	SOMC
Market Maker	First Michigan Corporation	Telephone (517)278-7189	SIC Code	6020
Broker Dealer	Regular Stockbroker		Employees	102

Southern Scottish Inns, Inc.

1726 Montreal Circle • Tucker, GA 30084 • Telephone (770)938-5966 • Fax (770)938-6382

Company Description

The Company franchises, finances, owns and leases motels as well as restaurants in association with the motels. At December 31,1995, the Company held fanchises on 343 motels, including Passport Inns, Red Carpet Inns, Scottish Inns and Master Hosts Inns. The motels are located in the southern United States.

	09/30/95	12/31/94	12/31/93	12/31/92
Per Share Information				
Stock Price	1.50	1.32	1.07	1.01
Earnings Per Share	0.51	0.18	0.12	0.16
Price / Earnings Ratio	n.a.	7.33	8.92	6.31
Book Value Per Share	4.31	3.45	3.26	3.37
Price / Book Value %	34.80	38.26	32.82	29.97
Dividends Per Share	n.a.	n.a.	n.a.	n.a.
Annual Financial Data				
Operating Results (000's)				
Total Revenues	4,684.0	4,986.6	4,151.3	3,982.9
Costs & Expenses	-3,503.2	-4,134.9	-3,591.2	-3,607.1
Income Before Taxes and Other	1,180.8	851.6	560.1	375.9
Other Items	n.a.	-172.1	-191.6	60.0
Income Tax	n.a.	-256.8	-96.5	-75.8
Net Income	1,180.8	422.7	272.0	360.0
Cash Flow From Operations	n.a.	550.3	182.9	399.0
Balance Sheet (000's)				
Cash & Equivalents	137.5	83.4	148.2	112.1
Total Current Assets	1,724.4	1,382.0	1,260.0	1,080.4
Fixed Assets, Net	3,912.5	4,089.2	3,794.3	3,998.8
Total Assets	16,343.8	14,344.4	13,915.5	13,928.2
Total Current Liabilities	1,690.4	2,142.4	1,979.7	1,614.8
Long-Term Debt	3,057.7	2,125.0	2,356.5	2,853.7
Stockholders' Equity	9,184.1	8,003.3	7,580.6	7,797.4
Performance & Financial Condition				
Return on Total Revenues %	25.21	8.48	6.55	9.04
Return on Avg Stockholders' Equity %	13.74	5.43	3.54	4.55
Return on Average Assets %	7.70	2.99	1.95	2.55
Current Ratio	1.02	0.65	0.64	0.67
Debt / Equity %	33.29	26.55	31.09	36.60

Compound Growth %'s	EPS %	63.00	Net Income %	63.00	Total Revenues %	16.00

Comments

The Company's financial statements are not yet available as we go to press. Therefore, the results shown for 1995 are for the nine months ended September 30, 1995. Officers and directors, as a group, owned 56.7% of the Company's outstanding shares at September 30, 1995. Compound growth percentages are estimates by us under the assumption that the last quarter of 1995 was similar to the first three quarters of the year.

Officers	Position	Ownership Information	09/30/95
Harry C. McIntire	Chairman	Number of Shares Outstanding	2,322,466
Jack M. Dubard	President	Market Capitalization	$ 3,483,699
Bobby E. Guimbellot	CEO	Frequency Of Dividends	n.a.
		Number of Shareholders	910

Other Information

Transfer Agent	First National Bank of Commerce			Where Listed	OTC-BB
Auditor	Robert J. Clark			Symbol	SOHS
Market Maker	Morgan Keegan & Company, Inc.	Telephone	(800)238-7533	SIC Code	6794
Broker Dealer	Regular Stockbroker			Employees	144

Southland National Insurance Corporation

1812 University Boulevard • Tuscaloosa, AL 35401 • Telephone (205)345-7410 • Fax (205)752-6020

Company Description

The Company, incorporated in Alabama in 1969, is principally engaged in the life insurance business, offering a variety of life insurance products. The Company is licensed in Alabama, Florida, Georgia, Louisiana, Mississippi and Tennessee, with license applications pending in Arkansas and North Carolina. As of March 15, 1996, officers and directors, as a group, owned 29% of the Company's outstanding common stock.

	12/31/95	12/31/94	12/31/93	12/31/92
Per Share Information				
Stock Price	15.75	13.00	11.25	10.75
Earnings Per Share	3.72	2.84	4.45	2.39
Price / Earnings Ratio	4.23	4.58	2.53	4.50
Book Value Per Share	33.34	22.04	23.50	19.38
Price / Book Value %	47.24	58.98	47.87	55.47
Dividends Per Share	0.09	0.16	n.a.	n.a.
Annual Financial Data				
Operating Results (000's)				
Total Revenues	9,350.2	7,307.9	7,291.7	6,968.7
Costs & Expenses	-8,214.7	-6,437.5	-5,954.5	-6,274.3
Income Before Taxes and Other	1,135.5	870.4	1,337.2	694.3
Other Items	n.a.	n.a.	3.7	15.8
Income Tax	-203.0	-158.2	-224.5	-113.7
Net Income	932.6	712.2	1,116.4	596.4
Cash Flow From Operations	3,536.9	1,859.0	1,814.6	1,961.3
Balance Sheet (000's)				
Cash & Equivalents	870.2	990.0	694.8	453.9
Total Current Assets	1,587.2	1,628.0	1,077.0	792.1
Fixed Assets, Net	584.0	643.0	706.6	729.2
Total Assets	32,511.7	25,994.0	23,649.6	20,903.0
Total Current Liabilities	301.9	275.0	498.7	606.2
Long-Term Debt	n.a.	n.a.	n.a.	n.a.
Stockholders' Equity	8,351.3	5,520.0	5,885.1	4,823.3
Performance & Financial Condition				
Return on Total Revenues %	9.97	9.75	15.31	8.56
Return on Avg Stockholders' Equity %	13.45	12.49	20.85	13.07
Return on Average Assets %	3.19	2.87	5.01	3.06
Current Ratio	5.26	5.92	2.16	1.31
Debt / Equity %	n.a.	n.a.	n.a.	n.a.

Compound Growth %'s	EPS %	15.89	Net Income %	16.07	Total Revenues %	10.30

Comments

The Company's principal assets and liabilities are investments and policy liabilities. At December 31, 1995, investments totaled $27.7 million and consisted of fixed maturities of $21.7 million, equity securities of $4.0 million, and miscellaneous investments of $2.0 million. Policy liabilities at December 31, 1995, totaled $22.8 million and consisted almost entirely of accrued policy benefits.

Officers	Position	Ownership Information	12/31/95
William H. Lanford	President, CEO	Number of Shares Outstanding	250,453
Ronald J. Koch	Secretary, Treasurer	Market Capitalization	$ 3,944,635
Jo A. Mansfield	Vice President	Frequency Of Dividends	Irregular
Dennis E. Painter	Vice President	Number of Shareholders	5,146
Robert H. Rust	Vice President		

Other Information				
Transfer Agent	Company Office		Where Listed	OTC-BB
Auditor	Coopers & Lybrand LLP		Symbol	DSAY
Market Maker	Hill, Thompson, Magid & Co.Inc	Telephone (800)631-3083	SIC Code	6311
Broker Dealer	Regular Stockbroker		Employees	52

Southside Bank

P.O.Box 1005 • Tappahannock, VA 22560 • Telephone (804)443-4333 • Fax (804)443-1271

Company Description

Southside Bank is a state chartered bank with seven locations serving several counties in the Tappahannock area of Virginia.

	12/31/95	12/31/94	12/31/93	12/31/92
Per Share Information				
Stock Price	27.00	23.50	21.75	21.00
Earnings Per Share	2.10	2.03	1.81	1.60
Price / Earnings Ratio	12.86	11.58	12.02	13.13
Book Value Per Share	14.91	13.18	12.33	21.80
Price / Book Value %	181.09	178.30	176.40	96.33
Dividends Per Share	0.71	0.70	0.68	1.25
Annual Financial Data				
Operating Results (000's)				
Net Interest Income	6,712.6	6,723.8	6,284.4	5,609.0
Loan Loss Provision	-324.0	-480.0	-671.8	-821.8
Non-Interest Income	1,019.6	799.1	891.3	805.9
Non-Interest Expense	-4,494.4	-4,208.4	-3,977.1	-3,378.6
Income Before Taxes and Other	2,913.8	2,834.5	2,526.8	2,214.5
Other Items	n.a.	n.a.	n.a.	n.a.
Income Tax	-774.6	-768.3	-680.6	-583.6
Net Income	2,139.1	2,066.3	1,846.2	1,630.9
Balance Sheet (000's)				
Cash & Securities	39,725.5	33,115.1	37,676.6	37,631.6
Loans, Net	117,447.3	111,830.0	97,471.4	87,573.8
Fixed Assets, Net	3,333.7	3,242.5	2,334.8	2,293.8
Total Assets	164,321.2	151,307.5	140,398.4	129,768.3
Deposits	147,283.1	136,004.9	126,334.0	116,949.4
Stockholders' Equity	15,265.8	13,447.6	12,574.6	11,119.9
Performance & Financial Condition				
Net Interest Margin	n.a.	n.a.	n.a.	n.a.
Return on Avg Stockholders' Equity %	14.90	15.88	15.58	15.35
Return on Average Assets %	1.36	1.42	1.37	1.34
Equity to Assets %	9.29	8.89	8.96	8.57
Reserve as a % of Non-Performing Loans	68.19	89.83	108.17	n.a.

Compound Growth %'s EPS % 9.49 Net Income % 9.46 Net Interest Income % 6.17

Comments

The Bank's loan portfolio is made up primarily of real estate loans and loans to individuals, representing 70% and 23% of total loans, respectively. In May, 1995, a new branch opened in eastern Hanover County. Unfortunately, the stock is not listed on the Electronic Bulletin Board. Therefore, a little more work is involved in becoming a shareholder, although it shouldn't be too hard with over 1,000 shareholders and more than one million shares outstanding.

Officers	Position	Ownership Information	12/31/95
F.Y. Hundley	Chairman	Number of Shares Outstanding	1,023,596
T. M. Boyd	President, CEO	Market Capitalization	$ 27,637,092
Ned Stephenson	CFO, Vice President	Frequency Of Dividends	Semi-Annual
Dennis Elmore	Vice President	Number of Shareholders	1,100
C. Tony Hudson	Vice President, Senior Loan Officer		

Other Information				
Transfer Agent	Company Office		Where Listed	Order Matching Only
Auditor	Deloitte & Touche LLP		Symbol	n.a.
Market Maker	None - Company Office	Telephone (804)443-4333	SIC Code	6020
Broker Dealer	None		Employees	70

Spartan Mills

463 Howard Street • Spartanburg, SC 29303 • Telephone (803)574-0211 • Fax (803)587-0291

Company Description

The Company produces fabrics. Approximately 254,000 shares, 19% of the Company, are owned by an employee stock ownership plan. The Company does not release an annual income statement but does distribute an audited balance sheet.

	12/03/94	11/27/93	11/27/92
Per Share Information			
Stock Price	88.00	87.00	91.00
Earnings Per Share	-3.82	8.80	n.a.
Price / Earnings Ratio	n.a.	0.10	n.a.
Book Value Per Share	137.56	139.05	128.22
Price / Book Value %	63.97	0.57	70.97
Dividends Per Share	1.00	1.00	1.00
Annual Financial Data			
Operating Results (000's)			
Total Revenues	n.a.	n.a.	n.a.
Costs & Expenses	n.a.	n.a.	n.a.
Income Before Taxes and Other	n.a.	n.a.	n.a.
Other Items	n.a.	n.a.	n.a.
Income Tax	n.a.	n.a.	n.a.
Net Income	-6,544.0	10,716.0	n.a.
Cash Flow From Operations	n.a.	n.a.	n.a.
Balance Sheet (000's)			
Cash & Equivalents	313.0	2,339.0	1,211.8
Total Current Assets	136,740.0	137,047.0	144,795.7
Fixed Assets, Net	144,291.0	145,256.0	147,439.5
Total Assets	293,376.0	293,024.0	299,593.9
Total Current Liabilities	57,915.0	43,869.0	57,422.5
Long-Term Debt	23,901.0	27,714.0	35,893.2
Stockholders' Equity	186,603.0	190,837.0	177,863.2
Performance & Financial Condition			
Return on Total Revenues %	n.a.	n.a.	n.a.
Return on Avg Stockholders' Equity %	-3.47	5.81	n.a.
Return on Average Assets %	-2.23	3.62	n.a.
Current Ratio	2.36	3.12	2.52
Debt / Equity %	12.81	14.52	20.18

Compound Growth %'s	EPS %	n.a.	Net Income %	n.a.	Total Revenues %	n.a.

Comments

Since December 2, 1989, equity (after the payment of dividends) has grown from $175 million to $186 million in 1994, a compounded annual growth rate of just slightly over 1%. No wonder the income statement is not attached. They also take a long time to release the results. The November, 1995 year end statement was expected to be released some time in June, 1996, which was after we went to press. Net income for the years shown was estimated by us by looking at the change in retained earnings. Other items could have affected that as well. The balance sheet numbers are the only firm numbers available. LIFO is used to calculate inventory. At the November, 1994 year end, inventory was valued $31.7 million lower than FIFO values.

Officers	Position	Ownership Information	12/03/94
Walter S. Montgomery	President, CEO	Number of Shares Outstanding	1,356,485
Perry Conley	CFO	Market Capitalization	$ 119,370,680
		Frequency Of Dividends	n.a.
		Number of Shareholders	Under 500

Other Information

Transfer Agent	Company Office			Where Listed	OTC-PS
Auditor	Ernst & Young			Symbol	SNML
Market Maker	Roney & Co.	Telephone	(800)321-2038	SIC Code	2200
Broker Dealer	Regular Stockbroker			Employees	n.a.

Sportsman's Guide, Inc. (The)

411 Farewell Ave., South • St. Paul, MN 55075 • Telephone (612)451-3030 • Fax (612)450-6130

Company Description

The Company is an outdoor consumer catalog marketer, offering a variety of merchandise such as apparel, footwear, hunting and shooting accessories, fishing and camping goods, optics, collectibles, and a variety of gift items. Operations are conducted from one facility in South St. Paul, Minnesota, with catalogs being distributed throughout the United States. Over 1.1 million customers purchased from the Company's catalogs during 1995. Approximately 54 million catalogs were mailed to existing and prospective customers during that year. The Company was incorporated in Minnesota in 1977.

	12/29/95	12/30/94	12/31/93	01/01/93
Per Share Information				
Stock Price	0.20	0.91	0.21	0.16
Earnings Per Share	-0.07	0.10	-0.02	0.02
Price / Earnings Ratio	n.a.	9.10	n.a.	8.00
Book Value Per Share	0.07	0.14	0.02	0.04
Price / Book Value %	285.71	650.00	1,050.00	400.00
Dividends Per Share	n.a.	n.a.	n.a.	n.a.
Annual Financial Data				
Operating Results (000's)				
Total Revenues	101,905.0	96,398.0	60,191.0	43,199.5
Costs & Expenses	-104,004.0	-93,248.0	-60,654.0	-42,688.7
Income Before Taxes and Other	-2,099.0	3,107.0	-478.0	510.8
Other Items	n.a.	n.a.	n.a.	n.a.
Income Tax	355.0	-385.0	n.a.	n.a.
Net Income	-1,744.0	2,722.0	-478.0	510.8
Cash Flow From Operations	1,276.0	-125.0	1,120.0	39.3
Balance Sheet (000's)				
Cash & Equivalents	n.a.	653.0	n.a.	n.a.
Total Current Assets	19,411.0	17,891.0	12,851.5	8,029.4
Fixed Assets, Net	4,298.0	3,288.0	1,808.5	593.6
Total Assets	23,709.0	21,179.0	14,660.0	8,623.0
Total Current Liabilities	21,874.0	13,940.0	11,554.4	6,028.0
Long-Term Debt	220.0	3,773.0	1,774.0	708.4
Stockholders' Equity	1,548.0	3,292.0	570.0	1,048.1
Performance & Financial Condition				
Return on Total Revenues %	-1.71	2.82	-0.79	1.18
Return on Avg Stockholders' Equity %	-72.07	140.96	-59.08	95.07
Return on Average Assets %	-7.77	15.19	-4.11	9.75
Current Ratio	0.89	1.28	1.11	1.33
Debt / Equity %	14.21	114.61	311.22	67.59

Compound Growth %'s	EPS % n.a.	Net Income % n.a.	Total Revenues % 33.12

Comments

The Company maintains a 52/53 week fiscal year. Net operating losses totaling approximately $3.8 million are available and expire in the year 2010. As of March 19, 1996, officers and directors, as a group, owned 42.5% and 55%, of the Company's outstanding common and preferred stock, respectively. The Company has entered in to an agreement to merge with a subsidiary of Vista 2000, Inc. The merger has not yet taken place because, according to management, of recent announcements regarding operational problems at Vista.

Officers	Position	Ownership Information	12/29/95
Gary Olen	President, CEO	Number of Shares Outstanding	23,335,833
Gregory Binkley	Senior VP, COO	Market Capitalization	$ 4,667,167
Charles B. Lingen	CFO, Treasurer	Frequency Of Dividends	n.a.
William G. Luth	Vice President	Number of Shareholders	300
Larry Popps	Vice President		

Other Information

Transfer Agent	Norwest Bank		Where Listed	OTC-BB
Auditor	Grant Thornton LLP		Symbol	GIDE
Market Maker	Van Clemens & Co.	Telephone (800)325-8865	SIC Code	5961
Broker Dealer	Regular Stockbroker		Employees	750

Spring Street Brewing Company, Inc.

113 University Place, 11th FL • New York, NY 10003 • Telephone (212)228-5787 • Fax (212)228-7093

Company Description

The Company produces and markets Wit and Amber Wit, hand-crafted Belgian recipe beers, and plans on developing additional beers. The products are currently sold through distributors in fifteen states. The Company raised more than $2.2 million through a direct public offering in 1995. Even more notable than their products might be the fact that an order matching service to buy or sell shares of the Company stock has been established on the internet: http://www.interport.net/witbeer.

	09/30/95	09/30/94
Per Share Information		
Stock Price	1.85	0.56
Earnings Per Share	-0.07	-0.07
Price / Earnings Ratio	n.a.	n.a.
Book Value Per Share	0.13	0.05
Price / Book Value %	1,423.10	1,120.00
Dividends Per Share	n.a.	n.a.
Annual Financial Data		
Operating Results (000's)		
Total Revenues	419.1	330.8
Costs & Expenses	-903.0	-788.5
Income Before Taxes and Other	-528.4	-488.0
Other Items	17.3	n.a.
Income Tax	n.a.	n.a.
Net Income	-511.1	-488.0
Cash Flow From Operations	-345.8	-345.8
Balance Sheet (000's)		
Cash & Equivalents	644.8	200.8
Total Current Assets	985.3	414.9
Fixed Assets, Net	39.2	35.2
Total Assets	1,029.4	455.3
Total Current Liabilities	352.2	165.7
Long-Term Debt	n.a.	n.a.
Stockholders' Equity	611.8	289.6
Performance & Financial Condition		
Return on Total Revenues %	-121.96	-147.51
Return on Avg Stockholders' Equity %	-113.40	n.a.
Return on Average Assets %	-68.85	n.a.
Current Ratio	2.80	2.50
Debt / Equity %	n.a.	n.a.

Compound Growth %'s	EPS %	n.a.	Net Income %	n.a.	Total Revenues %	26.68

Comments

The Company contracts for production space, thereby avoiding large capital outlays. As more capital is needed, the Company was continuing with their stock offering into fiscal 1996.

Officers	Position	Ownership Information	09/30/95
Andrew D. Klein	President, CEO	Number of Shares Outstanding	7,926,637
Margaritte L. Malfy	Senior VP	Market Capitalization	$ 14,664,278
Kenneth Harootunian	Vice President	Frequency Of Dividends	n.a.
		Number of Shareholders	Under 500

Other Information				
Transfer Agent	Company Office		Where Listed	Order Matching Only
Auditor	Arthur Andersen LLP		Symbol	n.a.
Market Maker	www.interport.net/witbeer		SIC Code	2082
Broker Dealer	None		Employees	n.a.

434

St. Louis Steel Casting Inc.

2300 Falling Springs Road • Sauget, IL 62206-1102 • Telephone (314)353-5800 • Fax (618)337-2277

Company Description

The Company is engaged in the foundry industry, specifically in the production of carbon, low alloy steel castings. Hydraulic Press Brick Company, a 56% owned subsidiary, produces expanded shale aggregate which is used principally in the construction industry in the components of walls, floors and structural elements.

	09/30/95	09/30/94	09/30/93	09/30/92
Per Share Information				
Stock Price	23.00	17.50	12.50	11.50
Earnings Per Share	5.50	6.26	1.93	1.63
Price / Earnings Ratio	4.18	2.80	6.48	7.06
Book Value Per Share	30.98	26.24	20.50	18.97
Price / Book Value %	74.24	66.69	60.98	60.62
Dividends Per Share	0.75	0.52	0.40	0.40
Annual Financial Data				
Operating Results (000's)				
Total Revenues	26,820.0	21,334.0	12,945.0	12,744.0
Costs & Expenses	-23,150.0	-17,901.0	-11,878.0	-11,786.0
Income Before Taxes and Other	3,556.0	3,401.0	1,051.0	936.0
Other Items	-502.0	-336.0	-106.0	-167.0
Income Tax	-1,414.0	-1,199.0	-369.0	-282.0
Net Income	1,640.0	1,866.0	576.0	487.0
Cash Flow From Operations	2,393.0	3,995.0	705.0	1,369.0
Balance Sheet (000's)				
Cash & Equivalents	1,368.0	2,576.0	1,238.0	1,420.0
Total Current Assets	9,550.0	8,384.0	6,148.0	5,459.0
Fixed Assets, Net	5,036.0	4,506.0	3,481.0	3,258.0
Total Assets	14,998.0	13,511.0	9,767.0	8,900.0
Total Current Liabilities	2,352.0	2,032.0	1,327.0	1,126.0
Long-Term Debt	n.a.	726.0	58.0	109.0
Stockholders' Equity	9,239.0	7,824.0	6,115.0	5,658.0
Performance & Financial Condition				
Return on Total Revenues %	6.11	8.75	4.45	3.82
Return on Avg Stockholders' Equity %	19.22	26.77	9.79	8.88
Return on Average Assets %	11.51	16.03	6.17	5.58
Current Ratio	4.06	4.13	4.63	4.85
Debt / Equity %	n.a.	9.28	0.95	1.93

Compound Growth %'s	EPS %	49.99	Net Income %	49.89	Total Revenues %	28.15

Comments

1995 results include approximately $767,000 of gain from property transactions. 1994 and 1993 results include income from the receipt of insurance proceeds of $1,284,000 and $282,000, respectively. Officers and directors and their families own 48% of the Company. First quarter 1996 results were $.69 per share as compared to $1.38 per share in the same period last year. No explanation was provided.

Officers	Position	Ownership Information	09/30/95
Christian B. Peper, Jr.	Chairman	Number of Shares Outstanding	298,225
Earl J. Bewig	President, COO	Market Capitalization	$ 6,859,175
Robert H. Schnellbacher	Secretary	Frequency Of Dividends	Quarterly
Robert N. Stewart	Treasurer	Number of Shareholders	212
Gregory D. Fore	VP - Sales		

Other Information			
Transfer Agent	KeyCorp Shareholder Services, Inc.	Where Listed	OTC-BB
Auditor	Kerber, Eck & Braeckel	Symbol	STLO
Market Maker	Burns, Pauli & Co., Inc.	SIC Code	3320
Broker Dealer	Regular Stockbroker	Employees	75

Telephone (800)325-3373

Standard Electronics, Inc.

215 John Glenn Drive • Amherst, NY 14228-2227 • Telephone (716)691-3061 • Fax (716)691-3170

Company Description

The Company is a wholesale distributor of electronic parts and equipment primarily to retailers located in Western New York. It is also the Sony franchisee for its geographic area. The Company buys back shares of stock even in bad times. The $6 per share that it pays is well below book value. The 1995 repurchase was at $5 per share.

	06/30/95	06/30/94	06/30/93	06/30/92
Per Share Information				
Stock Price	5.00	6.00	6.00	6.00
Earnings Per Share	0.01	1.26	-3.59	-1.56
Price / Earnings Ratio	500.00	4.76	n.a.	n.a.
Book Value Per Share	11.88	11.86	10.58	14.15
Price / Book Value %	42.09	50.59	56.71	42.40
Dividends Per Share	n.a.	n.a.	n.a.	n.a.
Annual Financial Data				
Operating Results (000's)				
Total Revenues	10,285.4	10,503.6	11,422.5	14,512.2
Costs & Expenses	-10,283.7	-10,431.7	-12,031.1	-14,830.1
Income Before Taxes and Other	1.7	71.9	-610.8	-317.9
Other Items	n.a.	n.a.	n.a.	n.a.
Income Tax	n.a.	116.0	74.0	84.0
Net Income	1.7	187.9	-536.8	-233.9
Cash Flow From Operations	234.7	588.5	-368.7	-146.3
Balance Sheet (000's)				
Cash & Equivalents	18.6	66.7	14.3	n.a.
Total Current Assets	3,332.0	3,128.5	3,273.0	3,729.1
Fixed Assets, Net	780.0	903.7	966.5	1,000.0
Total Assets	4,833.3	4,682.8	4,835.5	5,329.1
Total Current Liabilities	2,587.4	2,359.4	2,625.2	2,496.3
Long-Term Debt	481.4	559.6	631.5	697.6
Stockholders' Equity	1,764.4	1,763.7	1,578.8	2,119.2
Performance & Financial Condition				
Return on Total Revenues %	0.02	1.79	-4.70	-1.61
Return on Avg Stockholders' Equity %	0.09	11.24	-29.03	-10.45
Return on Average Assets %	0.03	3.95	-10.56	-4.36
Current Ratio	1.29	1.33	1.25	1.49
Debt / Equity %	27.29	31.73	40.00	32.92

Compound Growth %'s	EPS %	-99.21	Net Income %	-99.11	Total Revenues %	-10.84

Comments

1994 results include a nonoperating benefit of $116,000 arising from the accounting for income taxes. The Company has stabilized after losses in 1991, 1992 and 1993. We did not have access to 1993 results. The compounded income growth and EPS growth are only calculated from 1994 to 1995 because of the earlier losses.

Officers	Position	Ownership Information	06/30/95
Not Available		Number of Shares Outstanding	148,483
		Market Capitalization	$ 742,415
		Frequency Of Dividends	n.a.
		Number of Shareholders	Under 500

Other Information

Transfer Agent	Manufacturers & Traders Trust Co.			Where Listed	OTC-PS
Auditor	BDO Seidman, LLP			Symbol	SDEL
Market Maker	Hill, Thompson, Magid & Co.Inc	Telephone	(800)631-3083	SIC Code	5065
Broker Dealer	Standard Investment	Tel/Ext	(888)783-4688 Jack	Employees	40

Standard Industries, Inc.

P.O. Box 27500 • San Antonio, TX 78227 • Telephone (210)623-3131 • Fax (210)623-4461

Company Description

The Company's operations consist primarily of the manufacture and sale of batteries and related automotive products and wholesale and retail distribution to customers throughout the United States. The Company changed its name in 1978 from Standard Electric Company.

	12/31/94	12/31/93	12/31/92
Per Share Information			
Stock Price	4.00	4.00	4.00
Earnings Per Share	-17.39	-5.00	-42.08
Price / Earnings Ratio	n.a.	n.a.	n.a.
Book Value Per Share	15.89	33.16	36.31
Price / Book Value %	25.17	12.06	11.02
Dividends Per Share	n.a.	n.a.	n.a.
Annual Financial Data			
Operating Results (000's)			
Total Revenues	21,548.0	21,588.0	21,002.4
Costs & Expenses	-22,284.9	-21,528.8	-21,708.5
Income Before Taxes and Other	-824.1	-232.9	-2,013.6
Other Items	n.a.	n.a.	n.a.
Income Tax	n.a.	n.a.	n.a.
Net Income	-824.1	-232.9	-2,013.6
Cash Flow From Operations	-14.1	180.1	879.6
Balance Sheet (000's)			
Cash & Equivalents	157.2	138.0	549.0
Total Current Assets	5,712.5	5,520.0	5,404.7
Fixed Assets, Net	4,293.8	4,612.8	5,278.8
Total Assets	10,239.8	10,378.3	10,960.8
Total Current Liabilities	8,868.3	4,665.0	4,685.9
Long-Term Debt	613.1	4,130.8	4,459.4
Stockholders' Equity	758.4	1,582.6	1,815.4
Performance & Financial Condition			
Return on Total Revenues %	-3.82	-1.08	-9.59
Return on Avg Stockholders' Equity %	-70.41	-13.71	-71.35
Return on Average Assets %	-7.99	-2.18	-15.64
Current Ratio	0.64	1.18	1.15
Debt / Equity %	80.84	261.02	245.64

Compound Growth %'s	EPS % n.a.	Net Income % n.a.	Total Revenues % 1.29

Comments

Losses in recent years have caused the Company to be in default on certain of its debt. The auditors have issued a going concern qualification. There are also litigation matters relating to both environmental issues and worker's compensation claims. The 1995 report was not available when we went to press.

Officers	Position	Ownership Information	12/31/94
Steven A. Dubinski	Secretary, Treasurer	Number of Shares Outstanding	47,720
		Market Capitalization	$ 190,880
		Frequency Of Dividends	Quarterly
		Number of Shareholders	Under 500

Other Information

Transfer Agent	Frost National Bank, San Antonio, TX			Where Listed	OTC-BB
Auditor	Carneiro, Chumney & Co.,L.C.			Symbol	STIT
Market Maker	Carr Securities Corporation	Telephone	(800)221-2243	SIC Code	3692
Broker Dealer	Standard Investment	Tel/Ext	(888)783-4688 Jack	Employees	75

Stearns & Lehman, Inc.

52 Surrey Road • Mansfield, OH 44901 • Telephone (419)522-2722 • Fax (419)522-1152

Company Description

The Company manufactures, markets and sells specialty food products, including extracts, flavorings, liquid spices, Italian syrups, and candy oils. The Company has recently issued $300,000 of subordinated convertible notes which bear interest at 9% and are due on March 1, 1997. These notes are convertible into common stock at the rate of 182 shares for each $1000 of principal.

	04/30/95	04/30/94	11/30/93	11/30/92
Per Share Information				
Stock Price	6.50	n.a.	n.a.	n.a.
Earnings Per Share	0.06	-0.01	0.02	-0.05
Price / Earnings Ratio	108.33	n.a.	n.a.	n.a.
Book Value Per Share	1.05	0.70	0.52	0.43
Price / Book Value %	619.05	n.a.	n.a.	n.a.
Dividends Per Share	n.a.	n.a.	n.a.	n.a.
Annual Financial Data				
Operating Results (000's)				
Total Revenues	5,558.8	802.3	1,705.3	1,312.0
Costs & Expenses	-5,350.3	-914.2	-1,657.8	-1,412.4
Income Before Taxes and Other	206.6	-113.4	44.3	-103.3
Other Items	n.a.	42.4	n.a.	n.a.
Income Tax	-49.9	38.5	n.a.	n.a.
Net Income	156.7	-32.4	44.3	-103.3
Cash Flow From Operations	-335.3	13.8	-140.0	-257.7
Balance Sheet (000's)				
Cash & Equivalents	640.7	81.5	47.0	147.5
Total Current Assets	2,567.6	1,156.8	830.5	596.3
Fixed Assets, Net	1,016.8	907.4	737.9	598.7
Total Assets	4,212.0	2,735.0	1,611.2	1,238.9
Total Current Liabilities	924.4	820.8	364.7	232.8
Long-Term Debt	63.9	210.0	104.6	81.5
Stockholders' Equity	2,879.2	1,679.3	1,142.0	924.6
Performance & Financial Condition				
Return on Total Revenues %	2.82	-4.04	2.60	-7.87
Return on Avg Stockholders' Equity %	6.88	-2.30	4.29	n.a.
Return on Average Assets %	4.51	-1.49	3.11	n.a.
Current Ratio	2.78	1.41	2.28	2.56
Debt / Equity %	2.22	12.50	9.16	8.81

Compound Growth %'s	EPS %	73.21	Net Income %	88.04	Total Revenues %	61.81

Comments

1994 results are for a short period of 5 months and include a one-time benefit of adopting GAAP for the reporting of income taxes. However, revenue has increased substantially and the Company closed the last year with a good current ratio and $640,000 of cash.

Officers	Position	Ownership Information	04/30/95
John Chuprinko	CFO	Number of Shares Outstanding	2,744,308
		Market Capitalization	$ 17,838,002
		Frequency Of Dividends	n.a.
		Number of Shareholders	Under 500

Other Information

Transfer Agent	Company Office			Where Listed	OTC-PS
Auditor	Coopers & Lybrand LLP			Symbol	n.a.
Market Maker	Diversified Capital Markets	Telephone	(614)442-5804	SIC Code	2087
Broker Dealer	Regular Stockbroker			Employees	40

Steelcase Inc. and Subsidiaries

P.O. Box 1967 • Grand Rapids, MI 49501-1967 • Telephone (616)247-2710 • Fax (616)247-2295

Company Description

Steelcase Inc. is the world's leading designer and manufacturer of office furniture and entire furniture systems. They operate under a multitude of divisions, ventures and partnerships. There are approximately twenty manufacturing plants worldwide and 18,400 employees. The Company was founded in Grand Rapids, Michigan in 1912. The Company is extremely sensitive to the display of their corporate financial information and has requested that it not be reproduced. However, we will provide you certain information in this specially tailored format.

Revenue and Earnings

A number of sources estimate revenue to be approximately $2.3 billion, although the Company claims that $2.5 billion in revenues was attained in 1995. The differences may arise out of inconsistencies in the placement of joint venture operations.

Earnings have been inconsistent due to problems with international joint ventures. For the year ended February 28, 1996, earnings are reported to have exceeded $100 million and approximated $500 per share.

Shares, Price Range and Stockholders Equity

There are approximately 238,000 common shares outstanding as well as two classes of preferred stock. In 1992, the Company had a 1 for 100 reverse split designed to eliminate many of the non-family shareholders.

$7,000 - $8,500 is the reported price range per share over the last five years.
Book Value per Share is estimated by us to be about $5,800.

Market and Other Information

Shares are not traded on any established exchange.
Shares may be highly illiquid.

Broker Dealer	Jack Norberg, Standard Investment, Telephone (888)783-4688
Market Maker	None
SIC code	2520
Market Capitalization	$1.85 billion (estimate only)

Officers and Directors

Robert C. Pew	Chairman of the Board
Peter M. Wege	Vice-Chairman of the Board
James P. Hackett	President and Chief Executive Officer

Stein Industries, Inc.

26 North Fifth Street • Minneapolis, MN 55403-1602 • Telephone (612)375-1606 • Fax (612)375-1905

Company Description

The Company's primary businesses are the manufacture and sale of display fixtures and materials to a wide range of store retailers throughout the U.S. and the marketing of electronic components, primarily switches, to national and international manufacturers. The Company was founded in 1907 in Wisconsin and assumed its present name in 1971.

	12/31/95	12/31/94	12/31/93	12/31/92
Per Share Information				
Stock Price	4.00	3.50	4.00	n.a.
Earnings Per Share	1.42	1.13	0.93	1.53
Price / Earnings Ratio	2.82	3.10	4.30	n.a.
Book Value Per Share	7.05	5.63	4.50	3.40
Price / Book Value %	56.74	62.17	n.a.	n.a.
Dividends Per Share	n.a.	n.a.	n.a.	n.a.
Annual Financial Data				
Operating Results (000's)				
Total Revenues	23,669.2	18,343.6	13,364.6	13,543.4
Costs & Expenses	-21,665.3	-16,585.1	-11,960.9	-11,444.8
Income Before Taxes and Other	1,805.8	1,549.7	1,239.0	1,898.6
Other Items	n.a.	n.a.	n.a.	n.a.
Income Tax	-630.1	-610.9	-464.3	-534.1
Net Income	1,175.7	938.7	774.7	1,364.5
Cash Flow From Operations	760.6	-241.6	359.3	1,445.0
Balance Sheet (000's)				
Cash & Equivalents	1,172.4	451.2	903.5	1,094.6
Total Current Assets	7,858.3	6,175.9	4,942.2	4,333.8
Fixed Assets, Net	315.7	305.6	221.9	212.5
Total Assets	8,217.0	6,493.0	5,188.2	4,644.1
Total Current Liabilities	2,272.1	1,763.7	1,414.1	1,569.0
Long-Term Debt	86.9	55.9	41.5	46.3
Stockholders' Equity	5,838.0	4,662.3	3,723.6	3,028.8
Performance & Financial Condition				
Return on Total Revenues %	4.97	5.12	5.80	10.07
Return on Avg Stockholders' Equity %	22.39	22.39	22.95	58.15
Return on Average Assets %	15.99	16.07	15.76	32.69
Current Ratio	3.46	3.50	3.50	2.76
Debt / Equity %	1.49	1.20	1.12	1.53

Compound Growth %'s	EPS %	-2.46	Net Income %	-4.84	Total Revenues %	20.45

Comments

Although profits have actually declined since 1992, the Company has demonstrated good growth in revenues and has been around for a long time. A healthy balance sheet adds reason to take a sharp look at this company.

Officers	Position	Ownership Information	12/31/95
Norman R. Stein	Chairman	Number of Shares Outstanding	827,893
James H. Lear	President, CEO	Market Capitalization	$ 3,311,572
Michael J. Stein	COO	Frequency Of Dividends	n.a.
Philip B. Halverson	Treasurer, CFO	Number of Shareholders	Under 500

Other Information

Transfer Agent	Mellon Securities Trust Company			Where Listed	OTC-BB
Auditor	Abdo, Abdo & Eick			Symbol	SNND
Market Maker	Koonce Securities, Inc.	Telephone	(800)368-2802	SIC Code	2540
Broker Dealer	Pink sheet specialist			Employees	110

Steritek, Inc.

121 Moonachie Avenue • Moonachie, NJ 07074 • Telephone (201)460-0500 • Fax (201)507-1016

Company Description

The Company currently provides contract packaging services and promotional materials assembly for manufacturers of products in the pharmaceutical, medical, personal health and beauty industries. The Company also provides certain health care companies and others a means of communicating with physicians via fax. Until October, 1995, the Company's primary business was the distribution of its proprietary pressure monitors and the manufacturing and distribution of products used in conjuncton with electron microscopes. This business was sold in October, 1995.

	06/30/95	06/30/94	06/30/93	06/30/92
Per Share Information				
Stock Price	0.50	0.50	2.25	1.50
Earnings Per Share	0.04	-0.29	0.12	0.53
Price / Earnings Ratio	12.50	n.a.	18.75	2.83
Book Value Per Share	0.47	0.43	0.72	0.60
Price / Book Value %	106.38	116.28	312.50	250.00
Dividends Per Share	n.a.	n.a.	n.a.	n.a.
Annual Financial Data				
Operating Results (000's)				
Total Revenues	5,954.2	4,283.4	6,489.0	6,988.8
Costs & Expenses	-5,624.0	-5,109.1	-5,689.0	-5,093.4
Income Before Taxes and Other	330.3	-825.6	800.0	1,895.4
Other Items	n.a.	n.a.	n.a.	n.a.
Income Tax	-184.9	-214.5	-371.5	n.a.
Net Income	145.4	-1,040.1	428.5	1,895.4
Cash Flow From Operations	666.1	-761.7	416.7	n.a.
Balance Sheet (000's)				
Cash & Equivalents	263.7	402.3	929.0	705.1
Total Current Assets	1,639.5	1,825.2	2,340.0	2,424.9
Fixed Assets, Net	1,192.7	858.6	866.2	574.3
Total Assets	3,059.8	3,015.7	4,001.7	3,383.7
Total Current Liabilities	945.5	1,172.9	877.1	1,179.1
Long-Term Debt	291.7	300.0	571.7	86.7
Stockholders' Equity	1,688.2	1,542.8	2,552.9	2,117.9
Performance & Financial Condition				
Return on Total Revenues %	2.44	-24.28	6.60	27.12
Return on Avg Stockholders' Equity %	9.00	-50.79	18.35	n.a.
Return on Average Assets %	4.79	-29.64	11.60	n.a.
Current Ratio	1.73	1.56	2.67	2.06
Debt / Equity %	17.28	19.45	22.39	4.09

Compound Growth %'s	EPS %	-57.74	Net Income %	-57.51	Total Revenues %	-5.20

Comments

The Company's contract packaging operations accounted for 86% of total sales for the year ended June 30, 1995. As of June 30, 1995, the Company has available, net operating loss carryforwards totaling $2.2 million, expiring through 2006. Trading in the Company's stock was very sporadic during the two years ended June 30, 1995. The prices presented are estimates based on SEC reporting information. For the six months ended December 31, 1995, the Company had sales of $3.0 million, and net income of $307,000 (.08 per share) as compared to $2.6 million, and $109,000 ($.03 per share) for the same period in 1994.

Officers	Position	Ownership Information	06/30/95
Albert J. Wozniak	President, CEO	Number of Shares Outstanding	3,586,285
James K. Wozniak	Vice President, Secretary	Market Capitalization	$ 1,793,143
		Frequency Of Dividends	n.a.
		Number of Shareholders	138

Other Information

Transfer Agent	Midlantic Bank, N.A.		Where Listed	OTC-PS
Auditor	M.R. Weiser & Co.		Symbol	DSNN
Market Maker	Paragon Capital Corp.	Telephone (800)521-8877	SIC Code	7389
Broker Dealer	Regular Stockbroker		Employees	135

Sterling Sugars, Inc.

P.O. Box 572 • Franklin, LA 70538 • Telephone (318)828-0620 • Fax (318)838-1757

Company Description

The Company is a grower and processor of sugarcane from which it produces raw sugar and molasses. The Company's raw sugar factory is located on 65 acres of land outside the city of Franklin, Louisana. Farming acreage includes 11,607 acres of owned land and 1,560 acres of leased land. The Company also leases oil and gas rights and has two producing wells on its property from which it receives royalties. The Company is incorporated in the state of Delaware and has been growing and processing sugarcane in Louisana since 1807.

	01/31/96	01/31/95	01/31/94	01/31/93
Per Share Information				
Stock Price	5.63	4.94	3.94	3.50
Earnings Per Share	0.85	0.30	-0.40	-0.23
Price / Earnings Ratio	6.62	16.47	n.a.	n.a.
Book Value Per Share	5.45	4.63	4.33	4.73
Price / Book Value %	103.30	106.70	90.99	74.00
Dividends Per Share	n.a.	n.a.	n.a.	n.a.
Annual Financial Data				
Operating Results (000's)				
Total Revenues	29,644.6	34,250.6	13,932.8	19,006.7
Costs & Expenses	26,429.9	-32,952.7	-15,831.1	-19,869.5
Income Before Taxes and Other	3,214.6	1,297.9	-1,898.3	-862.8
Other Items	n.a.		n.a.	200.0
Income Tax	1,095.0	-555.5	715.0	310.0
Net Income	2,119.6	742.4	-983.3	-552.8
Cash Flow From Operations	-1,136.0	8,508.7	-3,829.4	-3,727.8
Balance Sheet (000's)				
Cash & Equivalents	134.1	623.2	544.0	377.8
Total Current Assets	14,794.6	8,827.5	14,290.5	9,960.1
Fixed Assets, Net	11,980.5	11,027.2	11,926.6	10,580.8
Total Assets	27,969.6	20,879.6	26,513.3	20,887.2
Total Current Liabilities	9,625.6	4,333.8	11,168.9	4,119.2
Long-Term Debt	4,017.5	4,371.4	4,694.2	4,390.7
Stockholders' Equity	13,628.5	11,346.4	10,604.0	11,587.3
Performance & Financial Condition				
Return on Total Revenues %	7.15	2.17	-7.06	-2.91
Return on Avg Stockholders' Equity %	16.97	6.76	-8.86	-4.66
Return on Average Assets %	8.68	3.13	-4.15	-2.88
Current Ratio	1.54	2.04	1.28	2.42
Debt / Equity %	29.48	38.53	44.27	37.89

Compound Growth %'s	EPS %	183.33	Net Income %	185.51	Total Revenues %	14.45

Comments

Land is recorded at a cost of $1.8 million which amounts to approximately $156 per acre and at December 31, 1995, the Company's stock was selling at close to book value. A worthwhile excercise for potential investors would be to estimate the fair market value of the Company's properties.

Officers	Position	Ownership Information	01/31/96
Craig P. Caillier	President, CEO	Number of Shares Outstanding	2,500,000
Stanley H. Pipes	Vice President, Treasurer	Market Capitalization	$ 14,075,000
		Frequency Of Dividends	n.a.
		Number of Shareholders	745

Other Information

Transfer Agent	Whitney National Bank of New Orleans		Where Listed	OTC-BB
Auditor	LeGlue & Company		Symbol	SSUG
Market Maker	S.J. Wolfe & Co.	Telephone (800)262-2244	SIC Code	2060
Broker Dealer	Regular Stockbroker		Employees	223

© 1996 Walker's Manual, LLC   All rights reserved.   No part of this information may be reproduced without written permission.   (510) 283-9993

Stonecutter Mills Corporation

P.O. Box 157 • Spindale, NC 28160 • Telephone (704)286-2341 • Fax (704)287-7280

Company Description

The Company manufactures high grade fabrics and has a number of other businesses including wood products, trucking and warehousing. It has manufacturing facilities in both Spindale and Mill Spring, North Carolina. The history of the Company proudly dates back to 1920. Please enjoy our one page summary.

	07/01/95	07/02/94	07/01/93	06/30/92
Per Share Information				
Stock Price	276.00	83.00	79.00	66.00
Earnings Per Share	71.07	61.07	42.28	30.21
Price / Earnings Ratio	3.88	1.36	1.87	2.18
Book Value Per Share	389.27	330.75	274.93	238.84
Price / Book Value %	70.90	25.09	28.73	27.63
Dividends Per Share	12.60	7.80	6.20	6.10
Annual Financial Data				
Operating Results (000's)				
Total Revenues	n.a.	n.a.	n.a.	n.a.
Costs & Expenses	n.a.	n.a.	n.a.	n.a.
Income Before Taxes and Other	n.a.	n.a.	n.a.	n.a.
Other Items	n.a.	n.a.	n.a.	n.a.
Income Tax	n.a.	n.a.	n.a.	n.a.
Net Income	9,577.2	8,230.3	5,698.5	4,071.2
Cash Flow From Operations	n.a.	n.a.	n.a.	n.a.
Balance Sheet (000's)				
Cash & Equivalents	10,301.6	7,965.8	376.8	375.6
Total Current Assets	45,379.3	40,145.7	34,983.8	27,776.5
Fixed Assets, Net	20,750.6	16,655.4	16,759.0	19,040.1
Total Assets	66,536.5	57,305.2	52,182.7	47,119.8
Total Current Liabilities	13,026.9	10,552.9	11,575.7	9,704.9
Long-Term Debt	1,052.0	2,180.2	3,557.9	5,228.6
Stockholders' Equity	52,457.7	44,572.1	37,049.2	32,186.2
Performance & Financial Condition				
Return on Total Revenues %	n.a.	n.a.	n.a.	n.a.
Return on Avg Stockholders' Equity %	19.74	20.17	16.46	13.94
Return on Average Assets %	15.47	15.03	11.48	8.95
Current Ratio	3.48	3.80	3.02	2.86
Debt / Equity %	2.01	4.89	9.60	16.24

Compound Growth %'s	EPS %	33.00	Net Income %	33.00	Total Revenues %	33.00

Comments

The Company does not provide a detailed income statement although we doubt that any of the shareholders would complain. We calculated earnings growth at 33%, the same as revenue growth. Inside ownership is not available.

Officers	Position	Ownership Information	07/01/95
James R. Cowan	Chairman, President	Number of Shares Outstanding	134,760
Dan Briscoe	Senior VP	Market Capitalization	$ 37,193,760
Gerald N. Rodelli	Senior VP	Frequency Of Dividends	Quarterly
T P. Walker	Secretary	Number of Shareholders	Under 500
James M. Perry	Treasurer		

Other Information

Transfer Agent	Company Office			Where Listed	OTC-BB
Auditor	Dixon, Odom & Co., LLP			Symbol	STCMA
Market Maker	A.G. Edwards & Sons, Inc.	Telephone	(800)325-8197	SIC Code	2399
Broker Dealer	Regular Stockbroker			Employees	1000

Textiles

In the mid-nineteenth century, large scale mechanization of the textile industry launched the Industrial Revolution in Europe. It was then that textiles migrated from a cottage industry to factory production. In America, this transition naturally began in areas located close to the cotton fields. Stonecutter's founder, Kenneth Tanner, is credited with the transformation of one of these areas, Spindale, North Carolina, from an agrarian economy to a textile complex.

Stonecutter is named after a nearby creek bearing the same name. It was originally constructed on a hill making it a highly visible landmark in the surrounding rural landscape. Mr. Tanner's vision for the area extended far beyond his first mill and encompassed a completely modern village, replete with electric lights, water, sewerage, baths, landscape design, a movie theater, a dairy, a steam laundry and other public buildings. He founded his new company in 1920 with $1,250,000 of stock subscriptions and proceeded to move dirt with mules and drag pans to prepare the site.

Before Stonecutter was established, Spindale had been a quiet rural outpost with people either living and working on their farms or cutting timber for local companies. Cash resources were for the most part minimal. People grew their own food and an informal barter system existed for the procurement of other goods. Stonecutter changed all of this, and Spindale became an industrial center where people could work for wages and improve their standard of living.

Tanner began his enterprise by looming cotton; rayon followed five years later. It wasn't long, unfortunately, before America fell into the Great Depression. The Company only survived this difficult era because of attributes that also account for its long-term success: conservatism, determination and a commitment to quality. They continued to keep pace with new technologies and at the same time to prize their employees, focusing on a supportive workplace and ongoing training. A testimony to this commitment was the establishment in 1943 of a profit sharing plan in recognition of employees' contributions to the Company's ongoing success.

One day in 1950, twenty-five years after the first rayon came off Stonecutter's looms, employees were surprised, but perhaps delighted as well to find that their weekly wages had been delivered in the form of small pouches sewn of rayon and filled with silver coins! Can you imagine the three tons of coins it took to fulfill this obligation arriving from the Federal Reserve under armed guard and the commotion it must have caused in Spindale?

In 1996, after seventy-six years in business, Stonecutter is not only viable, but has become a fully integrated and successful operation that includes fabric manufacture, retail sales of cloth and timber products and a trucking company. The Company has truly succeeded in living up to Kenneth Tanner's vision.

Summit Bancorp, Inc.

P.O.Box 5480 • Johnstown, PA 15904 • Telephone (814)269-3451 • Fax (814)269-4612

Company Description

Summit Bancorp, Inc., a one bank holding company, was formed in 1990. Its wholly-owned subsidiaries are Summit Bank and Cambria Thrift Consumer Discount Company (Cambria). The Bank has eight branch offices and Cambria Thrift has two offices, all in Pennsylvania. Cambria was acquired in 1995 to create a different customer base and the opportunity to market existing Bank products to them.

	12/31/95	12/31/94	12/31/93	12/31/92
Per Share Information				
Stock Price	46.00	42.00	39.00	35.00
Earnings Per Share	5.38	5.13	4.65	3.65
Price / Earnings Ratio	8.55	8.19	8.39	9.59
Book Value Per Share	47.49	39.14	38.02	34.55
Price / Book Value %	96.86	107.31	102.58	101.30
Dividends Per Share	1.32	1.24	1.20	1.10
Annual Financial Data				
Operating Results (000's)				
Net Interest Income	5,251.4	4,963.1	4,692.0	4,314.5
Loan Loss Provision	-174.5	-197.0	-222.0	-364.0
Non-Interest Income	688.2	664.7	639.4	582.4
Non-Interest Expense	-3,902.9	-3,839.1	-3,513.2	-3,424.9
Income Before Taxes and Other	1,862.2	1,591.8	1,596.3	1,108.0
Other Items	n.a.	n.a.	-111.9	n.a.
Income Tax	-446.6	-346.1	-403.0	-265.0
Net Income	1,415.5	1,245.6	1,081.4	843.0
Balance Sheet (000's)				
Cash & Securities	50,804.9	38,862.9	37,636.9	35,233.3
Loans, Net	88,785.5	85,725.5	76,649.3	71,607.4
Fixed Assets, Net	2,020.4	1,993.9	1,993.1	1,866.4
Total Assets	142,942.3	128,400.0	117,410.2	109,895.2
Deposits	126,354.6	113,657.3	104,398.9	100,191.5
Stockholders' Equity	12,537.8	10,269.7	8,861.1	8,002.9
Performance & Financial Condition				
Net Interest Margin	n.a.	n.a.	n.a.	n.a.
Return on Avg Stockholders' Equity %	12.41	13.02	12.82	10.95
Return on Average Assets %	1.04	1.01	0.95	0.79
Equity to Assets %	8.77	8.00	7.55	7.28
Reserve as a % of Non-Performing Loans	285.98	141.02	439.53	258.75

Compound Growth %'s	EPS %	13.81	Net Income %	18.86	Net Interest Income %	6.77

Comments

Management anticipates either purchasing other finance companies or opening other offices of Cambria in order to expand this segment of the business. Approximately 71% of the bank's loan portfolio is made up of real estate mortgage loans. Management reports that non-performing loans were less than one-half of 1% of total loans and that several new products and services will be added in 1996. The Company very generously facilitates stock trading by introducing buyers to sellers without charge.

Officers	Position	Ownership Information	12/31/95
Elmer C. Laslo	President	Number of Shares Outstanding	264,034
William F. McQuaide	CEO, Chairman of the Board	Market Capitalization	$ 12,145,564
William G. McKelvey	Senior VP	Frequency Of Dividends	Semi-Annual
William J. Smith	Senior VP, Treasurer	Number of Shareholders	n.a.
Thomas G. Fetsko	Senior VP		

Other Information				
Transfer Agent	Company Office		Where Listed	Order Matching Only
Auditor	S.R. Snodgrass, A.C.		Symbol	n.a.
Market Maker	None - Company Office	Telephone (814)269-3451	SIC Code	6020
Broker Dealer	None		Employees	100

Summit Bank Corporation

4360 Chamblee-Dunwoody Rd. • Atlanta, GA 30341 • Telephone (404)454-0400 • Fax (404)457-5531

Company Description

The Company was organized in 1986 to become the parent bank-holding company of Summit National Bank upon its formation. The initial marketing was to individuals and small to medium sized businesses in northeast metropolitan Atlanta, Asian-Americans located throughout Atlanta and clients requiring international transaction services.

	12/31/95	12/31/94	12/31/93	12/31/92
Per Share Information				
Stock Price	10.63	8.37	7.67	5.50
Earnings Per Share	1.33	1.37	1.18	0.73
Price / Earnings Ratio	7.99	6.11	6.50	7.53
Book Value Per Share	10.95	9.43	8.13	6.95
Price / Book Value %	97.08	88.76	94.34	79.14
Dividends Per Share	0.28	n.a.	n.a.	n.a.
Annual Financial Data				
Operating Results (000's)				
Net Interest Income	6,469.0	5,745.0	4,099.0	3,565.0
Loan Loss Provision	-397.0	-430.0	-611.0	-711.0
Non-Interest Income	2,873.0	2,660.0	2,299.0	2,717.0
Non-Interest Expense	-5,802.0	-5,209.0	-4,211.0	-4,525.0
Income Before Taxes and Other	3,143.0	2,766.0	1,576.0	1,046.0
Other Items	n.a.	n.a.	n.a.	n.a.
Income Tax	-1,042.0	-838.0	82.0	-25.0
Net Income	2,101.0	1,928.0	1,658.0	1,021.0
Balance Sheet (000's)				
Cash & Securities	42,915.0	28,576.0	27,331.0	17,529.0
Loans, Net	76,491.0	72,198.0	71,416.0	56,803.0
Fixed Assets, Net	2,932.0	2,500.0	1,097.0	351.0
Total Assets	130,076.0	108,146.0	104,410.0	78,119.0
Deposits	109,816.0	90,639.0	88,376.0	65,275.0
Stockholders' Equity	15,413.0	13,273.0	11,441.0	9,783.0
Performance & Financial Condition				
Net Interest Margin	5.90	5.79	5.25	n.a.
Return on Avg Stockholders' Equity %	14.65	15.60	15.62	11.01
Return on Average Assets %	1.76	1.81	1.82	1.37
Equity to Assets %	11.85	12.27	10.96	12.52
Reserve as a % of Non-Performing Loans	136.74	656.97	335.98	148.19

Compound Growth %'s	EPS %	22.14	Net Income %	27.19	Net Interest Income %	21.97

Comments

An Asian Banking Center was opened in September, 1994, and has shown excellent growth. 1995 revenues from international banking services grew by 23%. The Bank just opened its fourth Atlanta office in May, 1996, and has additional expansion goals for three additional counties that had, previous to July, 1996, been subject to state restrictions in branch banking.

Officers	Position	Ownership Information	12/31/95
David Yu	President, CEO	Number of Shares Outstanding	1,407,688
Pin Pin Chau	Exec VP	Market Capitalization	$ 14,963,723
H. A. Dudley, Jr.	Exec VP	Frequency Of Dividends	Irregular
Gary K. McClung	Secretary, CFO	Number of Shareholders	403

Other Information			
Transfer Agent	Sun Trust Bank	Where Listed	OTC-BB
Auditor	KPMG Peat Marwick LLP	Symbol	SBGA
Market Maker	Robinson-Humphrey Company Inc.	Telephone (800)241-0445	SIC Code	6020
Broker Dealer	Regular Stockbroker	Employees	78

Sutter Basin Corporation, Ltd.

10982 Knights Road • Robbins, CA 95676 • Telephone (916)738-4456

Company Description

The Company is a diversified agricultural operation which provides custom farming services, raises various crops and provides drying and storage services. The property is located in California's Sacramento Valley. There are only 2,077 shares outstanding.

	12/31/95	12/31/94
Per Share Information		
Stock Price	62.00	60.00
Earnings Per Share	8.11	2.20
Price / Earnings Ratio	7.64	27.27
Book Value Per Share	80.72	72.62
Price / Book Value %	76.81	82.62
Dividends Per Share	n.a.	n.a.
Annual Financial Data		
Operating Results (000's)		
Total Revenues	770.2	866.5
Costs & Expenses	-751.8	-859.9
Income Before Taxes and Other	18.3	5.8
Other Items	n.a.	n.a.
Income Tax	-1.4	-1.3
Net Income	16.8	4.6
Cash Flow From Operations	-67.1	19.4
Balance Sheet (000's)		
Cash & Equivalents	22.3	27.3
Total Current Assets	28.3	37.6
Fixed Assets, Net	339.9	181.2
Total Assets	368.9	222.0
Total Current Liabilities	16.3	70.7
Long-Term Debt	185.0	0.5
Stockholders' Equity	167.7	150.8
Performance & Financial Condition		
Return on Total Revenues %	2.19	0.53
Return on Avg Stockholders' Equity %	10.57	n.a.
Return on Average Assets %	5.70	n.a.
Current Ratio	1.74	0.53
Debt / Equity %	110.34	0.32

Compound Growth %'s	EPS %	268.64	Net Income %	269.09	Total Revenues %	-11.12

Comments

It is possible that the remaining property has substantial appreciation. The Company will not comment. However, we did determine that fully-depreciated equipment with an original cost of $242,000 was sold during 1995 for cash at a gain of $68,150, or $32.81 per share. A more difficult task may be finding shares available for sale. Compounded growth rates are misleading because only two years were available for the calculation.

Officers	Position	Ownership Information	12/31/95
Luther C. Anderson	Chairman	Number of Shares Outstanding	2,077
Thomas A. Butler	President	Market Capitalization	$ 128,774
N H. Bruggman	Secretary	Frequency Of Dividends	n.a.
		Number of Shareholders	Under 500

Other Information

Transfer Agent	Company Office			Where Listed	OTC-BB
Auditor	Tenney and Company			Symbol	SUBC
Market Maker	Chicago Corporation, The	Telephone	(800)621-1674	SIC Code	0700
Broker Dealer	Pink sheet specialist			Employees	n.a.

TIF Instruments, Inc.

9101 N.W. 7th Avenue • Miami, FL 33150 • Telephone (305)757-8811 • Fax (305)757-3105

Company Description

The Company is in the business of manufacturing electronic testing and measurement equipment primarily for the automotive, airconditioning and refrigeration industries. The Company also deals directly with the needs of contractors and wholesalers. The Company went public in 1960.

	06/30/95	06/30/94
Per Share Information		
Stock Price	32.00	29.50
Earnings Per Share	8.42	4.81
Price / Earnings Ratio	3.80	6.13
Book Value Per Share	52.38	52.38
Price / Book Value %	61.09	56.32
Dividends Per Share	n.a.	n.a.
Annual Financial Data		
Operating Results (000's)		
Total Revenues	25,302.8	21,312.5
Costs & Expenses	-21,703.6	-19,253.7
Income Before Taxes and Other	3,599.2	2,058.8
Other Items	n.a.	n.a.
Income Tax	-1,360.3	-779.8
Net Income	2,238.9	1,279.0
Cash Flow From Operations	n.a.	n.a.
Balance Sheet (000's)		
Cash & Equivalents	7,166.3	5,675.4
Total Current Assets	19,589.5	16,643.4
Fixed Assets, Net	340.5	335.4
Total Assets	19,930.0	16,978.8
Total Current Liabilities	2,451.4	1,994.6
Long-Term Debt	n.a.	n.a.
Stockholders' Equity	16,199.2	13,928.3
Performance & Financial Condition		
Return on Total Revenues %	8.85	6.00
Return on Avg Stockholders' Equity %	14.86	n.a.
Return on Average Assets %	12.13	n.a.
Current Ratio	7.99	8.34
Debt / Equity %	n.a.	n.a.

Compound Growth %'s	EPS %	75.05	Net Income %	75.05	Total Revenues %	18.72

Comments

Substantial growth is supported by a very strong balance sheet showing no long term debt and a current ratio of about 8 to 1. The Company does not release the full financial statements to its shareholders, but instead prepares a one page condensed version from the audited statements. Compound growth rates are misleading because only two years are reported.

Officers	Position	Ownership Information	06/30/95
Thomas Gerard	President	Number of Shares Outstanding	265,904
Jamie Gerard	Treasurer	Market Capitalization	$ 8,508,928
Elliot Gerard	VP - Manufacturing	Frequency Of Dividends	n.a.
Thomas Wolff	VP - Sales	Number of Shareholders	Under 500

Other Information					
Transfer Agent	Sun Trust Bank, Atlanta, GA			Where Listed	OTC-BB
Auditor	Not indicated			Symbol	TIFS
Market Maker	Monroe Securities, Inc.	Telephone	(800)766-5560	SIC Code	3820
Broker Dealer	Regular Stockbroker			Employees	400

TMS, Inc.

206 West 6th Avenue • Stillwater, OK 74074 • Telephone (405)377-0880 • Fax (405)377-0452

Company Description

The Company performs research, development, selling and licensing of computer software and high technology computer-related products. The Company's products are geared toward two segments of the computer software business: electronic image management and the storage and retrieval of large databases that are searchable on personal computers. The Company was incorporated in the state of Oklahoma in 1981.

	08/31/95	08/31/94	08/31/93	08/31/92
Per Share Information				
Stock Price	0.66	0.26	0.22	0.10
Earnings Per Share	0.08	0.04	0.05	-0.04
Price / Earnings Ratio	8.25	6.50	4.40	n.a.
Book Value Per Share	0.27	0.18	0.13	0.06
Price / Book Value %	244.44	144.44	169.23	166.67
Dividends Per Share	n.a.	n.a.	n.a.	n.a.
Annual Financial Data				
Operating Results (000's)				
Total Revenues	4,221.1	3,436.8	2,800.9	2,123.9
Costs & Expenses	-3,796.6	-3,098.1	-2,383.7	-2,444.3
Income Before Taxes and Other	455.6	352.3	434.1	-316.2
Other Items	n.a.	n.a.	n.a.	n.a.
Income Tax	315.8	-1.7	-4.0	n.a.
Net Income	771.5	350.6	430.1	-316.2
Cash Flow From Operations	622.2	419.3	565.7	134.6
Balance Sheet (000's)				
Cash & Equivalents	114.2	240.0	166.9	88.1
Total Current Assets	1,326.0	1,109.4	821.8	581.8
Fixed Assets, Net	1,446.8	602.7	376.9	319.4
Total Assets	3,131.7	1,782.2	1,310.2	1,039.1
Total Current Liabilities	499.0	325.6	241.7	358.4
Long-Term Debt	378.3	n.a.	n.a.	181.3
Stockholders' Equity	2,254.4	1,456.6	1,068.5	499.5
Performance & Financial Condition				
Return on Total Revenues %	18.28	10.20	15.35	-14.89
Return on Avg Stockholders' Equity %	41.58	27.77	54.85	-53.23
Return on Average Assets %	31.40	22.68	36.61	-28.11
Current Ratio	2.66	3.41	3.40	1.62
Debt / Equity %	16.78	n.a.	n.a.	36.29

Compound Growth %'s	EPS %	26.49	Net Income %	33.94	Total Revenues %	25.73

Comments

Revenues are comprised mostly of software license fees and royalties, making up 55% to 80% of revenues in the years presented. For the six months ended February 29, 1996, the Company had revenues of $2.5 million and Net Income of $419,000 ($.04 per share), as compared to $2.0 million and $620,000 ($.07 per share) for the same period in the prior year. On March 15, 1996, a merger between the Company and Sequoia Data Corporation was consummated. The Company issued approximately 3.6 million of its shares for all the outstanding shares of Sequoia.

Officers	Position	Ownership Information	08/31/95
J. Richard Phillips	Chairman, CEO	Number of Shares Outstanding	8,404,947
Maxwell Steinhardt	President, COO	Market Capitalization	$ 5,547,265
Art Crotzer	Senior VP	Frequency Of Dividends	n.a.
Dale May	VP - Finance, Treasurer	Number of Shareholders	725
Rick Scanlan	Vice President		

Other Information

Transfer Agent	American Securities Transfer, Inc.			Where Listed	OTC-BB
Auditor	KPMG Peat Marwick LLP			Symbol	TMSS
Market Maker	Herzog, Heine, Geduld, Inc.	Telephone	(800)221-3600	SIC Code	7372
Broker Dealer	Regular Stockbroker			Employees	64

TNR Technical, Inc.

279 Douglas Ave., Ste., 1112 • Altamonte Springs, FL 32714 • Telephone (407)682-4311 • Fax (407)682-4469

Company Description

The Company is an authorized distributor for several battery manufacturers, including Sanyo, Eveready, Duracell, and Sony, and stocks one of the largest battery inventories in the southeastern United States. In addition, the Company designs and builds custom battery pack assemblies. The Company was incorporated in New York and has been in business since 1979.

	07/31/95	07/31/94	07/31/93	07/31/92
Per Share Information				
Stock Price	3.25	1.63	1.75	1.00
Earnings Per Share	1.67	0.56	0.50	0.39
Price / Earnings Ratio	1.95	2.91	3.50	2.56
Book Value Per Share	6.69	5.02	4.45	3.96
Price / Book Value %	48.58	32.47	39.33	25.25
Dividends Per Share	n.a.	n.a.	n.a.	n.a.
Annual Financial Data				
Operating Results (000's)				
Total Revenues	3,745.3	3,605.2	2,821.5	2,411.9
Costs & Expenses	-3,546.3	-3,449.5	-2,691.6	-2,310.8
Income Before Taxes and Other	199.0	155.7	130.0	101.1
Other Items	n.a.	n.a.	n.a.	n.a.
Income Tax	239.0	-7.5	n.a.	n.a.
Net Income	438.0	148.2	130.0	101.1
Cash Flow From Operations	-83.0	51.5	122.7	2.4
Balance Sheet (000's)				
Cash & Equivalents	100.3	353.8	362.6	230.2
Total Current Assets	1,709.7	1,488.7	1,325.4	1,181.5
Fixed Assets, Net	56.9	37.5	33.0	38.9
Total Assets	2,022.6	1,532.2	1,364.3	1,226.4
Total Current Liabilities	268.2	215.8	196.1	188.2
Long-Term Debt	n.a.	n.a.	n.a.	n.a.
Stockholders' Equity	1,754.4	1,316.4	1,168.2	1,038.2
Performance & Financial Condition				
Return on Total Revenues %	11.69	4.11	4.61	4.19
Return on Avg Stockholders' Equity %	28.53	11.93	11.78	10.23
Return on Average Assets %	24.64	10.24	10.03	8.71
Current Ratio	6.38	6.90	6.76	6.28
Debt / Equity %	n.a.	n.a.	n.a.	n.a.

Compound Growth %'s	EPS %	62.39	Net Income %	63.03	Total Revenues %	15.80

Comments

Net Income for 1995 includes a credit of $239,000 resulting from a change in accounting method for income taxes. For the six months ended January 31, 1996, the Company had Total Revenues and Net Income of $1.9 million and $85,000 ($.32 per share) as compared to $1.7 million and $32,000 ($.12 per share) for the same period in the prior fiscal year. At December 31,1995, the stock was trading at an average bid/ask price of $3.88 per share with a book value per share of $7.00.

Officers	Position	Ownership Information		07/31/95
Jerrold Lazarus	Chairman, CEO	Number of Shares Outstanding		262,422
Wayne Thaw	President, COO	Market Capitalization	$	852,872
		Frequency Of Dividends		n.a.
		Number of Shareholders		1,622

Other Information

Transfer Agent	American Stock Transfer & Trust Company			Where Listed	OTC-BB
Auditor	Burton R. Abrams			Symbol	TNRK
Market Maker	Mayer & Schweitzer, Inc.	Telephone	(800)631-3094	SIC Code	3691
Broker Dealer	Regular Stockbroker			Employees	21

Tangram Enterprise Solutions, Inc.

5511 Capital Ctr. Dr. Ste. 400 • Raleigh, NC 27606-3365 • Telephone (919)851-6000 • Fax (919)851-6004

Company Description

The Company develops and markets information technology and software distribution products and services. The Company's leading product, AM:PM, provides asset management solutions across heterogeneous networks, accomplishing such tasks as software distribution, asset tracking, data distribution, data collection and remote resource management. The Company is the result of a merger between two companies in 1993 that were majority owned by Safeguard Scientifics, Inc., a $1.5 billion NYSE company. Safeguard continues to own approximately 72% of the Company.

	12/31/95	12/31/94	12/31/93	12/31/92
Per Share Information				
Stock Price	1.75	1.16	2.32	1.13
Earnings Per Share	-0.08	-0.04	-0.06	0.04
Price / Earnings Ratio	n.a.	n.a.	n.a.	28.25
Book Value Per Share	0.57	0.65	0.70	0.09
Price / Book Value %	307.02	178.46	331.43	1,255.60
Dividends Per Share	n.a.	n.a.	n.a.	n.a.
Annual Financial Data				
Operating Results (000's)				
Total Revenues	12,538.0	12,778.0	13,733.0	16,767.0
Costs & Expenses	-12,845.0	-13,361.0	-14,592.0	-15,189.0
Income Before Taxes and Other	-307.0	-583.0	-859.0	1,578.0
Other Items	n.a.	n.a.	n.a.	n.a.
Income Tax	-878.0	-16.0	633.0	-307.0
Net Income	-1,185.0	-599.0	-226.0	1,271.0
Cash Flow From Operations	2,123.0	3,034.0	4,631.0	2,878.0
Balance Sheet (000's)				
Cash & Equivalents	92.0	614.0	752.0	240.0
Total Current Assets	3,202.0	5,060.0	5,228.0	6,485.0
Fixed Assets, Net	278.0	500.0	956.0	3,299.2
Total Assets	12,829.0	15,048.0	15,787.0	15,181.0
Total Current Liabilities	4,581.0	5,085.0	3,660.0	6,390.0
Long-Term Debt	n.a.	500.0	n.a.	6,594.0
Stockholders' Equity	8,246.0	9,368.0	10,715.0	2,197.0
Performance & Financial Condition				
Return on Total Revenues %	-9.45	-4.69	-1.65	7.58
Return on Avg Stockholders' Equity %	-13.46	-5.97	-3.50	81.47
Return on Average Assets %	-8.50	-3.89	-1.46	8.68
Current Ratio	0.70	1.00	1.43	1.01
Debt / Equity %	n.a.	5.34	n.a.	300.14

Compound Growth %'s	EPS % n.a.	Net Income % n.a.	Total Revenues % -9.23

Comments

Included in assets at December 31, 1995, is goodwill of $5.9 million relating to the originating merger in 1993. In March of 1996, the Company sold the assets and liabilities of one of its divisions in exchange for the cancellation of $850,000 of debt relating to the original purchase of the division.

Officers	Position	Ownership Information	12/31/95
W. Christopher Jesse	President, CEO	Number of Shares Outstanding	14,527,876
Nancy M. Dunn	CFO, VP - Finance	Market Capitalization	$ 25,423,783
Steven F. Kuekes	Vice President	Frequency Of Dividends	n.a.
		Number of Shareholders	3,000

Other Information			
Transfer Agent	Chemical Mellon Shareholder Services	Where Listed	OTC-PS
Auditor	Ernst & Young LLP	Symbol	TESI
Market Maker	Frankel (WM.V.) & Co., Inc. Telephone (800)631-3091	SIC Code	7372
Broker Dealer	Regular Stockbroker	Employees	98

Tech Electro Industries, Inc.

430 Wiley Post Road • Dallas, TX 75244-2131 • Telephone (214)239-7151 • Fax (214)661-3746

Company Description

The Company imports, distributes and sells electronics components used in the manufacture and assembly of high-technology products such as computers, oilfield test equipment, medical instrumentation and uninterruptable power supply systems. The Company also sells batteries and battery related products. In January of 1992, the Company was formed in the state of Texas to acquire 100% of the outstanding common stock of an existing privately held company which had been in business since 1968.

	12/31/95	12/31/94	12/31/93	12/31/92
Per Share Information				
Stock Price	2.13	4.50	3.42	2.25
Earnings Per Share	0.03	0.01	-0.06	-0.12
Price / Earnings Ratio	71.00	450.00	n.a.	n.a.
Book Value Per Share	0.92	0.74	0.72	0.93
Price / Book Value %	231.52	608.11	475.00	241.94
Dividends Per Share	n.a.	n.a.	n.a.	n.a.
Annual Financial Data				
Operating Results (000's)				
Total Revenues	3,550.2	3,670.9	3,443.9	2,516.7
Costs & Expenses	-3,509.8	-3,644.2	-3,557.5	-2,636.5
Income Before Taxes and Other	40.5	26.7	-113.6	-119.9
Other Items	n.a.	n.a.	n.a.	n.a.
Income Tax	-13.0	-13.6	51.8	27.0
Net Income	27.5	13.1	-61.8	-92.9
Cash Flow From Operations	97.6	185.1	-149.0	n.a.
Balance Sheet (000's)				
Cash & Equivalents	139.8	120.1	6.0	29.1
Total Current Assets	1,846.4	1,965.2	1,976.8	1,702.2
Fixed Assets, Net	136.9	96.1	100.3	56.1
Total Assets	2,211.3	2,089.0	2,107.5	2,132.5
Total Current Liabilities	447.3	1,005.9	1,071.9	940.6
Long-Term Debt	445.0	279.0	244.6	59.0
Stockholders' Equity	1,219.3	704.5	691.4	1,033.2
Performance & Financial Condition				
Return on Total Revenues %	0.77	0.36	-1.80	-3.69
Return on Avg Stockholders' Equity %	2.86	1.88	-7.17	n.a.
Return on Average Assets %	1.28	0.62	-2.92	n.a.
Current Ratio	4.13	1.95	1.84	1.81
Debt / Equity %	36.50	39.61	35.37	5.71

Compound Growth %'s	EPS % 200.00	Net Income % 109.94	Total Revenues % 12.15

Comments

On February 1, 1996, the Company closed on a public offering of its common and preferred stock and related warrants, yielding proceeds to the Company of $2.1 million. As we go to press, the Company's securities are now traded on the Nasdaq Small Capital Issues Market under the symbol TELE, TELEU, and TELEW. The Company's common shares, which were trading in the last quarter of 1995, at an average of $2.13, are trading at $1.13 per share, as of May 21, 1996. While this decrease in price is not what one would expect to happpen when a company's securities go from the OTC market to a major exchange, it is an example of what can take place. This company is not included in the 500 UNLISTED count.

Officers	Position	Ownership Information	12/31/95
Craig D. La Taste	President	Number of Shares Outstanding	958,275
Julie A. Sansom-Reese	Treasurer	Market Capitalization	$ 2,041,126
David L. Arnold	Vice President, Secretary	Frequency Of Dividends	n.a.
		Number of Shareholders	562

Other Information

Transfer Agent	Securities Transfer Corporation		Where Listed	OTC-BB
Auditor	King, Burns & Company PC		Symbol	TELE
Market Maker	Frankel (WM.V.) & Co., Inc.	Telephone (800)631-3091	SIC Code	5065
Broker Dealer	Regular Stockbroker		Employees	17

Technology 80 Inc.

658 Mendelssohn Ave. North • Minneapolis, MN 55427 • Telephone (612)542-9545 • Fax (612)542-9785

Company Description

The Company designs, manufactures, and markets motion control components and systems for original equipment manufacturers, machine and instrument builders and end users located worldwide. Products are sold through direct sales, manufacturers representatives and distributors. Officers and directors, as a group, owned 53.8% of the Company's outstanding common stock at November 30, 1995. The Company was incorporated in the state of Minnesota during 1980.

	08/31/95	08/31/94	08/31/93	08/31/92
Per Share Information				
Stock Price	1.63	1.50	1.25	0.47
Earnings Per Share	0.37	0.60	0.30	0.21
Price / Earnings Ratio	4.41	2.50	4.17	2.24
Book Value Per Share	2.47	2.01	1.50	1.19
Price / Book Value %	65.99	74.63	83.33	39.50
Dividends Per Share	n.a.	n.a.	n.a.	n.a.
Annual Financial Data				
Operating Results (000's)				
Total Revenues	3,899.3	3,254.8	2,797.7	2,380.5
Costs & Expenses	-2,914.2	-2,603.4	-2,311.7	-2,053.1
Income Before Taxes and Other	985.2	651.3	486.0	327.4
Other Items	n.a.	580.0	n.a.	n.a.
Income Tax	-340.1	-271.1	-5.0	n.a.
Net Income	645.1	960.2	481.0	327.4
Cash Flow From Operations	761.3	377.7	266.2	217.2
Balance Sheet (000's)				
Cash & Equivalents	926.2	458.4	1,199.0	943.7
Total Current Assets	3,233.0	2,959.6	2,474.0	1,868.7
Fixed Assets, Net	90.2	66.4	64.2	65.1
Total Assets	4,195.4	3,392.5	2,538.2	1,933.7
Total Current Liabilities	265.5	278.8	230.9	107.4
Long-Term Debt	n.a.	n.a.	n.a.	n.a.
Stockholders' Equity	3,857.8	3,113.6	2,307.3	1,826.3
Performance & Financial Condition				
Return on Total Revenues %	16.54	29.50	17.19	13.75
Return on Avg Stockholders' Equity %	18.51	35.43	23.27	19.69
Return on Average Assets %	17.00	32.38	21.51	18.28
Current Ratio	12.18	10.61	10.72	17.40
Debt / Equity %	n.a.	n.a.	n.a.	n.a.

Compound Growth %'s	EPS %	20.78	Net Income %	25.37	Total Revenues %	17.88

Comments

During the year ended August 31, 1994, the Company changed its method of accounting for income taxes to conform to the new standards. The result was a charge to operations of $580,000 during that year. For the three months ended November 30, 1995, the Company had sales of $872,000 and Net Income of $90,000 ($.05 per share) as compared to $798,000 and $125,000 ($.08 per share) for the same period in 1994.

Officers	Position	Ownership Information	08/31/95
Duane A. Markus	President, CEO	Number of Shares Outstanding	1,561,670
James A. Burkett	COO	Market Capitalization	$ 2,545,522
Thomas L. Gould	Secretary	Frequency Of Dividends	n.a.
		Number of Shareholders	196

Other Information

Transfer Agent	First National Bank of Minneapolis			Where Listed	OTC-BB
Auditor	Lurie, Besikof et. al.			Symbol	TKAT
Market Maker	R.J. Steichen & Co.	Telephone	(612)341-6200	SIC Code	3679
Broker Dealer	Regular Stockbroker			Employees	24

Tehama County Bank

P.O.Box 890 • Red Bluff, CA 96080 • Telephone (916)529-0436 • Fax (916)529-0908

Company Description

Tehama County Bank is a community bank serving the Northern California area with four branch offices in and around Red Bluff, the home of Mt. Shasta. Recreation, farming and lumber are the main industries in these communities.

	12/31/95	12/31/94	12/31/93	12/31/92
Per Share Information				
Stock Price	13.88	11.88	9.96	9.00
Earnings Per Share	1.23	1.19	1.10	0.84
Price / Earnings Ratio	11.28	9.98	18.07	21.43
Book Value Per Share	9.02	7.61	6.45	5.16
Price / Book Value %	153.88	156.11	308.22	348.84
Dividends Per Share	n.a.	n.a.	n.a.	n.a.
Annual Financial Data				
Operating Results (000's)				
Net Interest Income	5,545.2	4,426.7	3,520.6	2,929.1
Loan Loss Provision	-330.0	-180.0	-182.5	-125.0
Non-Interest Income	1,775.1	1,654.9	1,382.3	1,005.7
Non-Interest Expense	-4,102.7	-3,335.1	-2,491.9	-2,120.3
Income Before Taxes and Other	2,887.7	2,566.4	2,228.6	1,689.6
Other Items	n.a.	n.a.	n.a.	n.a.
Income Tax	-1,039.0	-890.7	-708.0	-557.8
Net Income	1,848.7	1,675.7	1,520.6	1,131.8
Balance Sheet (000's)				
Cash & Securities	42,408.5	28,087.3	26,492.8	29,366.3
Loans, Net	80,582.2	73,423.4	58,320.7	41,691.9
Fixed Assets, Net	1,137.9	1,182.9	430.0	215.8
Total Assets	127,826.5	106,390.2	88,690.9	72,961.5
Deposits	113,586.7	94,645.8	78,925.7	65,333.8
Stockholders' Equity	13,085.9	10,758.0	8,862.2	6,927.6
Performance & Financial Condition				
Net Interest Margin	n.a.	n.a.	n.a.	n.a.
Return on Avg Stockholders' Equity %	15.51	17.08	19.26	17.86
Return on Average Assets %	1.58	1.72	1.88	1.71
Equity to Assets %	10.24	10.11	9.99	9.49
Reserve as a % of Non-Performing Loans	595.30	279.29	81.63	425.22

Compound Growth %'s	EPS %	13.56	Net Income %	17.77	Net Interest Income %	23.71

Comments

The loan portfolio is fairly well diversified. Real estate mortgage loans and installment loans comprise approximately 68% of total loans. The shares split 2 for 1 in 1994. All per share amounts have been adjusted accordingly. The Bank completed a management transition in 1995 with former president and CEO Dan Cargile retiring after serving eleven years at the helm.

Officers	Position	Ownership Information	12/31/95
William P. Ellison	President, CEO	Number of Shares Outstanding	1,450,621
Helen M. McIntosh	COO	Market Capitalization	$ 20,134,619
W. Steven Gilman	Senior VP, COO	Frequency Of Dividends	Irregular
Frank S. Onions	Senior VP, CFO	Number of Shareholders	975
David L. Roberts	Senior VP, Senior Loan Officer		

Other Information				
Transfer Agent	U.S. Stock Transfer Corporation		Where Listed	OTC-BB
Auditor	Perry-Smith & Co.		Symbol	THMC
Market Maker	Hoefer & Arnett, Inc.	Telephone (415)362-7160	SIC Code	6020
Broker Dealer	Regular Stockbroker		Employees	57

Tel-Instrument Electronics Corp.

728 Garden Street • Carlstadt, NJ 07072 • Telephone (201)933-1600 • Fax (201)933-7340

Company Description

The Company designs and manufactures avionic test equipment for the civil aviation industry and avionic testing and electronic equipment for the military. The Company's products are used to test navigation and communications equipment installed in aircraft and range in price from $5,000 to $13,000 per unit.

	03/31/95	03/31/94	03/31/93	03/31/92
Per Share Information				
Stock Price	0.19	0.02	0.13	0.56
Earnings Per Share	0.01	-0.09	-0.14	0.03
Price / Earnings Ratio	19.00	n.a.	n.a.	18.67
Book Value Per Share	-0.74	-0.74	-0.64	-0.50
Price / Book Value %	n.a.	n.a.	n.a.	n.a.
Dividends Per Share	n.a.	n.a.	n.a.	n.a.
Annual Financial Data				
Operating Results (000's)				
Total Revenues	1,865.5	1,317.4	1,430.9	2,199.7
Costs & Expenses	-1,855.0	-1,436.6	-1,631.5	-2,115.4
Income Before Taxes and Other	10.5	-119.1	-200.6	84.3
Other Items	12.0	n.a.	n.a.	n.a.
Income Tax	n.a.	n.a.	n.a.	n.a.
Net Income	22.5	-119.1	-200.6	84.3
Cash Flow From Operations	103.3	-26.8	29.6	141.5
Balance Sheet (000's)				
Cash & Equivalents	38.8	16.0	53.7	47.4
Total Current Assets	795.6	704.2	565.3	760.2
Fixed Assets, Net	40.2	26.2	33.4	49.0
Total Assets	872.4	780.8	640.4	825.9
Total Current Liabilities	1,314.8	1,210.7	951.2	936.0
Long-Term Debt	165.0	200.0	200.0	200.0
Stockholders' Equity	-1,184.0	-1,176.5	-1,027.4	-796.8
Performance & Financial Condition				
Return on Total Revenues %	1.20	-9.04	-14.02	3.83
Return on Avg Stockholders' Equity %	n.a.	n.a.	n.a.	n.a.
Return on Average Assets %	2.72	-16.77	-27.36	8.39
Current Ratio	0.61	0.58	0.59	0.81
Debt / Equity %	n.a.	n.a.	n.a.	n.a.

Compound Growth %'s	EPS % -30.66	Net Income % -35.64	Total Revenues % -5.34

Comments

Sales to the U.S. and Canadian Governments amounted to 32%, 17% and 21% of sales for the fiscal years ended March 31, 1995, 1994 and 1993, respectively. For the year ended March 31, 1995, the Company's auditors issued a going concern opinion on the financial statements. Operations appear to be improving; for the nine months ended December 31, 1995, the Company had sales of $1.7 million and Net Income of $133,000 ($.08 per share) as compared to $1.3 million and a loss of $39,000 ($.04) for the same period in 1994. The Company's stock price was quoted at an average bid/ask price of $1.25 at December 31,1995.

Officers	Position	Ownership Information	03/31/95
Harold K. Fletcher	President, CEO	Number of Shares Outstanding	1,603,806
Robert H. Walker	Exec VP	Market Capitalization	$ 304,723
Richard J. Wixson	VP - Manufacturing	Frequency Of Dividends	n.a.
George J. Leon	General Manager	Number of Shareholders	689

Other Information			
Transfer Agent	Registrar & Transfer Company	Where Listed	OTC-BB
Auditor	Coopers & Lybrand LLP	Symbol	TINE
Market Maker	Herzog, Heine, Geduld, Inc.	Telephone (800)221-3600	SIC Code	3825
Broker Dealer	Regular Stockbroker	Employees	15

Telebyte Technology, Inc.

270 Pulaski Road • Greenlawn, NY 11740 • Telephone (800)835-3298 • Fax (516)385-8184

Company Description

The Company designs, manufactures and markets electronic data communications products. The products are sold to end users, dealers, distributors and original equipment manufacturers. As of December 31, 1995, officers and directors, as a group, owned 38% of the Company's outstanding common stock. The Company was incorporated in New York in 1983 and reincorporated in Nevada in 1987. The Company can be reached via the internet at http://telebyteusa.com. or E-Mail at invest@telebyteusa.com.

	12/31/95	12/31/94	12/31/93	12/31/92
Per Share Information				
Stock Price	0.94	0.63	1.25	0.38
Earnings Per Share	0.07	0.18	0.15	0.09
Price / Earnings Ratio	13.43	3.50	8.33	4.22
Book Value Per Share	1.39	1.32	1.13	0.98
Price / Book Value %	67.63	47.73	110.62	38.78
Dividends Per Share	n.a.	n.a.	n.a.	n.a.
Annual Financial Data				
Operating Results (000's)				
Total Revenues	3,827.5	3,838.6	3,901.5	3,304.7
Costs & Expenses	-3,723.9	-3,631.7	-3,659.8	-3,159.4
Income Before Taxes and Other	103.6	207.0	241.7	145.3
Other Items	n.a.	n.a.	n.a.	49.5
Income Tax	-2.0	75.0	-12.0	-55.5
Net Income	101.6	282.0	229.7	139.3
Cash Flow From Operations	320.1	25.0	163.5	159.9
Balance Sheet (000's)				
Cash & Equivalents	609.5	439.4	545.5	447.8
Total Current Assets	2,205.4	2,129.1	1,981.5	1,804.3
Fixed Assets, Net	1,198.5	1,158.3	1,128.1	1,128.8
Total Assets	3,451.4	3,339.1	3,165.8	2,994.7
Total Current Liabilities	313.6	251.6	303.1	335.1
Long-Term Debt	1,046.3	1,089.3	1,123.8	1,150.4
Stockholders' Equity	2,091.5	1,998.2	1,738.9	1,509.2
Performance & Financial Condition				
Return on Total Revenues %	2.65	7.35	5.89	4.22
Return on Avg Stockholders' Equity %	4.97	15.09	14.14	9.68
Return on Average Assets %	2.99	8.67	7.46	4.75
Current Ratio	7.03	8.46	6.54	5.38
Debt / Equity %	50.03	54.52	64.63	76.23

Compound Growth %'s	EPS %	-8.04	Net Income %	-9.99	Total Revenues %	5.02

Comments

During 1995, the Company increased its spending on R&D, hired additional sales people and invested in capital improvements. At December 31, 1995, the Company had net operating loss carryforwards of approximately $1.1 million expiring from 2001 through 2006.

Officers	Position	Ownership Information	12/31/95
Joel A. Kramer	Chairman, President	Number of Shares Outstanding	1,501,566
Kenneth S. Schneider	Senior VP, Treasurer	Market Capitalization	$ 1,411,472
		Frequency Of Dividends	n.a.
		Number of Shareholders	339

Other Information

Transfer Agent	American Stock Transfer & Trust Company			Where Listed	OTC-BB
Auditor	Grant Thornton LLP			Symbol	TBTI
Market Maker	Paragon Capital Corporation	Telephone	(800)521-8877	SIC Code	3669
Broker Dealer	Regular Stockbroker			Employees	35

Telecomm Industries Corp.

9310 Progress Parkway • Mentor, OH 44060 • Telephone (216)639-0090 • Fax (216)639-6660

Company Description

The Company is a distributor of telecommunication services in Ohio and Michigan for Ameritech Corporation. The Company also sells and services equipment and provides installation, maintenance and repair services. The Company was incorporated as Scotco Data Leasing in 1967. It was inactive from 1984 to 1993.

	09/30/95	12/31/94	12/31/93	12/31/92
Per Share Information				
Stock Price	2.38	0.44	0.50	n.a.
Earnings Per Share	0.03	0.05	0.03	0.07
Price / Earnings Ratio	n.a.	8.80	16.67	n.a.
Book Value Per Share	0.14	0.10	0.05	0.09
Price / Book Value %	1,700.00	440.00	1,000.00	n.a.
Dividends Per Share	n.a.	n.a.	n.a.	n.a.
Annual Financial Data				
Operating Results (000's)				
Total Revenues	3,506.9	1,870.3	1,504.9	895.4
Costs & Expenses	-3,174.4	-1,734.4	-1,230.1	-464.0
Income Before Taxes and Other	332.3	112.1	224.9	431.3
Other Items	n.a.	295.2	n.a.	n.a.
Income Tax	-116.0	-40.0	-38.0	n.a.
Net Income	216.2	367.3	186.9	431.3
Cash Flow From Operations	-216.2	153.1	447.5	333.5
Balance Sheet (000's)				
Cash & Equivalents	173.9	85.8	37.5	62.0
Total Current Assets	1,582.5	703.3	341.2	506.7
Fixed Assets, Net	251.3	43.9	188.6	162.5
Total Assets	2,222.5	1,262.9	541.2	680.7
Total Current Liabilities	730.7	287.8	175.0	82.8
Long-Term Debt	155.4	100.7	48.1	54.4
Stockholders' Equity	1,232.6	695.5	318.2	543.5
Performance & Financial Condition				
Return on Total Revenues %	6.17	19.64	12.42	48.17
Return on Avg Stockholders' Equity %	22.43	72.46	43.37	105.61
Return on Average Assets %	12.41	40.72	30.59	n.a.
Current Ratio	2.17	2.44	1.95	6.12
Debt / Equity %	12.61	14.47	15.10	10.00

Compound Growth %'s	EPS %	n.a.	Net Income %	n.a.	Total Revenues %	73.00

Comments

The Company has not yet completed its reporting for 1995. The most current information is for the nine months ended September 30, 1995. As of March 31, 1995, officers and directors, as a group, owned 75.7%, of the Company's outstanding common stock. During 1995, the Company pursued corporate acquisitions to increase its distributorship of Ameritech products. The compound growth rate in revenues was estimated by us by annualizing the first nine months of 1995.

Officers	Position	Ownership Information	09/30/95
Steven W. Smith	President, CEO	Number of Shares Outstanding	8,522,791
Raymond W. Sheets, Jr.	Treasurer, Secretary	Market Capitalization	$ 20,284,243
		Frequency Of Dividends	n.a.
		Number of Shareholders	380

Other Information

Transfer Agent	Continental Stock Transfer & Trust Co.			Where Listed	OTC-BB
Auditor	Deimling Forbes & Associates			Symbol	TCMM
Market Maker	Carr Securities Corporation	Telephone	(800)221-2243	SIC Code	4813
Broker Dealer	Regular Stockbroker			Employees	33

Temco Service Industries, Inc.

One Park Avenue • New York, NY 10016-5802 • Telephone (212)889-6353 • Fax (212)213-9854

Company Description

The Company provides total building maintenance services including cleaning, gardening, pest control, mechanical maintenance, security and indoor air quality consulting. The Company was founded in 1917 and is now international in scope.

	09/30/95	09/30/94	09/30/93	09/30/92
Per Share Information				
Stock Price	36.00	27.00	21.50	17.00
Earnings Per Share	1.89	2.67	2.12	6.48
Price / Earnings Ratio	19.05	10.11	10.14	2.62
Book Value Per Share	38.83	34.75	29.93	32.24
Price / Book Value %	92.71	77.70	71.83	52.73
Dividends Per Share	n.a.	n.a.	n.a.	n.a.
Annual Financial Data				
Operating Results (000's)				
Total Revenues	175,348.2	135,539.4	129,151.1	134,183.1
Costs & Expenses	-173,101.4	-133,376.2	-126,501.2	-130,645.7
Income Before Taxes and Other	2,246.7	2,163.2	2,296.2	2,850.7
Other Items	n.a.	531.7	n.a.	2,246.0
Income Tax	-1,196.2	-1,212.4	-1,131.4	-1,607.1
Net Income	1,050.5	1,482.5	1,164.8	3,489.6
Cash Flow From Operations	-3,367.6	5,204.5	4,449.0	7,928.0
Balance Sheet (000's)				
Cash & Equivalents	3,531.1	9,980.1	7,976.6	7,492.2
Total Current Assets	35,479.4	32,034.5	29,414.4	28,730.0
Fixed Assets, Net	16,008.8	14,441.3	12,364.6	15,136.7
Total Assets	57,645.3	52,013.6	46,294.3	50,804.5
Total Current Liabilities	23,400.4	19,721.5	19,850.0	20,295.4
Long-Term Debt	4,173.0	5,375.6	4,120.0	7,207.0
Stockholders' Equity	21,586.6	19,318.1	16,640.8	17,362.6
Performance & Financial Condition				
Return on Total Revenues %	0.60	1.09	0.90	2.60
Return on Avg Stockholders' Equity %	5.14	8.25	6.85	23.59
Return on Average Assets %	1.92	3.02	2.40	7.14
Current Ratio	1.52	1.62	1.48	1.42
Debt / Equity %	19.33	27.83	24.76	41.51

Compound Growth %'s	EPS %	-33.68	Net Income %	-32.98	Total Revenues %	9.33

Comments

1994 results include a nonrecurring benefit of $531,700 from adopting GAAP reporting of income taxes. 1992 results include a nonrecurring gain of $2,246,029 on sale of discontinued operations. 1995 showed a sharp increase in revenue of $40 million, a 29% increase over the prior year.

Officers	Position	Ownership Information	09/30/95
Herman J. Hellman	Chairman, CEO	Number of Shares Outstanding	555,902
Harvey Newman	Exec VP	Market Capitalization	$ 20,012,472
Edward Valenti	Secretary, Treasurer	Frequency Of Dividends	Irregular
Joseph Bailey	Vice President	Number of Shareholders	Under 500
Ann M. McVey	Controller		

Other Information				
Transfer Agent	American Stock Transfer & Trust Company		Where Listed	OTC-BB
Auditor	KPMG Peat Marwick LLP		Symbol	TMCS
Market Maker	Herzog, Heine, Geduld, Inc.	Telephone (800)221-3600	SIC Code	7349
Broker Dealer	Regular Stockbroker		Employees	7000

Terre Aux Boeufs Land Co., Inc.

c/o PH Stiges, P.O. Box 61260 • New Orleans, LA 70161-1260

Company Description

The Company holds U.S. Government securities and certain property rights off of the New Orleans coast. Shares trade infrequently, but a number of market makers are registered for this security.

	12/31/95	12/31/94	12/31/93	12/31/92
Per Share Information				
Stock Price	20.00	22.00	22.00	25.00
Earnings Per Share	0.47	0.25	-0.03	-0.32
Price / Earnings Ratio	42.55	88.00	n.a.	n.a.
Book Value Per Share	31.16	30.69	30.44	30.47
Price / Book Value %	64.18	71.68	72.27	82.05
Dividends Per Share	n.a.	n.a.	n.a.	n.a.
Annual Financial Data				
Operating Results (000's)				
Total Revenues	39.8	26.8	20.9	24.3
Costs & Expenses	-27.4	-23.3	-23.8	-32.5
Income Before Taxes and Other	12.4	3.4	-2.9	-8.2
Other Items	n.a.	n.a.	n.a.	n.a.
Income Tax	-2.1	2.0	2.3	1.2
Net Income	10.3	5.4	-0.6	-7.0
Cash Flow From Operations	8.5	6.7	-8.1	-7.5
Balance Sheet (000's)				
Cash & Equivalents	22.2	20.6	10.3	13.4
Total Current Assets	362.1	661.4	656.0	656.6
Fixed Assets, Net	9.9	9.9	9.9	9.9
Total Assets	681.6	671.3	665.9	666.5
Total Current Liabilities	n.a.	n.a.	n.a.	n.a.
Long-Term Debt	n.a.	n.a.	n.a.	n.a.
Stockholders' Equity	681.6	671.3	665.9	666.5
Performance & Financial Condition				
Return on Total Revenues %	25.78	20.18	-2.81	-28.82
Return on Avg Stockholders' Equity %	1.52	0.81	-0.09	-1.05
Return on Average Assets %	1.52	0.81	-0.09	-1.05
Current Ratio	n.a.	n.a.	n.a.	n.a.
Debt / Equity %	n.a.	n.a.	n.a.	n.a.

Compound Growth %'s	EPS %	88.00	Net Income %	89.94	Total Revenues %	17.88

Comments

The property rights are of an unknown value. Land is on the books at $9,925 but annual property taxes of an almost equal amount are paid. A little research here may yield a big reward. Compounded earnings and earnings per share growth rates are misleading because only two years entered the calculation.

Officers	Position	Ownership Information	12/31/95
Not Available		Number of Shares Outstanding	21,875
		Market Capitalization	$ 437,500
		Frequency Of Dividends	n.a.
		Number of Shareholders	Under 500

Other Information			
Transfer Agent	Company Office	Where Listed	OTC-BB
Auditor	Doody and Doody	Symbol	TAUX
Market Maker	Hill, Thompson, Magid & Co.Inc	Telephone (800)631-3083 SIC Code	6790
Broker Dealer	Pink sheet specialist	Employees	n.a.

Thomas Edison Inns, Inc.

40 Pearl Street N.W. • Grand Rapids, MI 49503 • Telephone (616)776-2600 • Fax (616)776-2776

Company Description

The Company is engaged in the hospitality business including the operation of hotels and restaurants. The Company owns the Thomas Edison Inn, the St. Clair Inn and the Spring Lake Holiday Inn, all in Michigan. In September, 1995, the Company issued 1,500,000 shares of common stock to the Meritage Capital Corp. in exchange for a note receivable in the amount of $10.5 million. In January 1996, the Meritage Capital Corp. acquired control of the Company and the name will soon be changed to the Meritage Hospitality Group.

	11/30/95	11/30/94	11/30/93	11/30/92
Per Share Information				
Stock Price	6.63	7.50	7.50	7.13
Earnings Per Share	-1.13	-0.02	0.15	0.20
Price / Earnings Ratio	n.a.	n.a.	50.00	35.65
Book Value Per Share	2.01	3.44	3.46	3.30
Price / Book Value %	329.85	218.02	216.76	216.06
Dividends Per Share	n.a.	n.a.	n.a.	n.a.
Annual Financial Data				
Operating Results (000's)				
Total Revenues	15,069.8	15,458.8	14,639.5	14,543.7
Costs & Expenses	-17,840.3	-15,256.7	-14,244.0	-14,019.4
Income Before Taxes and Other	-2,770.5	202.1	395.5	524.4
Other Items	n.a.	-117.3	n.a.	n.a.
Income Tax	721.4	-112.0	-165.1	-225.2
Net Income	-2,049.1	-27.2	230.4	299.2
Cash Flow From Operations	425.3	989.9	1,056.1	1,687.1
Balance Sheet (000's)				
Cash & Equivalents	1,336.9	621.8	450.7	756.5
Total Current Assets	3,014.9	1,969.2	1,531.0	2,311.4
Fixed Assets, Net	13,218.3	13,645.0	14,068.6	14,866.9
Total Assets	17,983.5	19,688.4	20,004.0	20,144.6
Total Current Liabilities	2,971.3	1,562.9	1,981.1	6,740.8
Long-Term Debt	11,204.9	12,251.7	12,240.2	7,871.4
Stockholders' Equity	3,055.4	5,225.1	5,252.2	5,021.8
Performance & Financial Condition				
Return on Total Revenues %	-13.60	-0.18	1.57	2.06
Return on Avg Stockholders' Equity %	-49.49	-0.52	4.49	6.14
Return on Average Assets %	-10.88	-0.14	1.15	1.46
Current Ratio	1.01	1.26	0.77	0.34
Debt / Equity %	366.73	234.48	233.05	156.74

Compound Growth %'s	EPS % n.a.	Net Income % n.a.	Total Revenues % 1.19

Comments

During 1995, substantial legal expenses associated with the change in control of the Company were incurred and, according to management, were the primary reason for the fiscal year loss. On March 28, 1996, officers and directors, as a group, owned 28.8% of the Company's outstanding common stock.

Officers	Position	Ownership Information	11/30/95
Christopher B. Hewett	President, CEO	Number of Shares Outstanding	1,520,150
Robert E. Schermer, Jr.	Senior VP, Treasurer	Market Capitalization	$ 10,078,595
Gerard Belisle, Jr.	Senior VP	Frequency Of Dividends	n.a.
James R. Saalfeld	Vice President, Secretary	Number of Shareholders	350

Other Information				
Transfer Agent	Mellon Securities Trust Company		Where Listed	OTC-BB
Auditor	Grant Thornton LLP		Symbol	TEIR
Market Maker	Stifel, Nicolaus & Co.	Telephone (800)776-6821	SIC Code	7011
Broker Dealer	Regular Stockbroker		Employees	142

Tidewater, Bank of

P.O.Box 3368 • Virginia Beach, VA 23454 • Telephone (804)422-0000 • Fax (804)491-6303

Company Description

Bank of Tidewater is a community bank serving the communities of Virginia Beach, Virginia and surrounding areas. The bank has five locations, four of which are located in Virginia Beach. A sixth branch is expected to open during the second half of 1996. The Bank's primary emphasis is developing loan and deposit relationships with individuals and small businesses.

	12/31/95	12/31/94	12/31/93	12/31/92
Per Share Information				
Stock Price	16.25	16.63	16.50	9.38
Earnings Per Share	1.34	1.25	0.95	1.00
Price / Earnings Ratio	12.13	13.30	17.37	9.38
Book Value Per Share	9.95	9.89	9.36	8.84
Price / Book Value %	163.32	168.15	176.28	106.11
Dividends Per Share	1.80	0.60	0.44	0.34
Annual Financial Data				
Operating Results (000's)				
Net Interest Income	6,760.6	6,214.8	5,087.3	4,769.3
Loan Loss Provision	-180.0	-188.0	-190.0	-395.0
Non-Interest Income	2,307.5	2,081.8	1,826.9	1,722.4
Non-Interest Expense	-6,063.7	-5,598.2	-4,840.6	-4,483.4
Income Before Taxes and Other	2,824.4	2,510.4	1,883.5	1,613.2
Other Items	n.a.	n.a.	26.7	n.a.
Income Tax	-976.0	-817.5	-644.3	-322.6
Net Income	1,848.4	1,692.9	1,265.9	1,290.6
Balance Sheet (000's)				
Cash & Securities	50,275.3	37,367.0	55,572.0	46,726.6
Loans, Net	86,923.5	75,101.4	62,369.7	54,387.1
Fixed Assets, Net	3,248.7	2,964.1	2,835.0	2,992.2
Total Assets	141,950.1	117,320.6	122,392.2	106,162.0
Deposits	126,390.1	102,934.5	109,634.3	94,495.1
Stockholders' Equity	13,528.3	12,983.9	12,176.5	11,184.8
Performance & Financial Condition				
Net Interest Margin	5.87	5.58	4.95	4.81
Return on Avg Stockholders' Equity %	13.94	13.46	10.84	12.89
Return on Average Assets %	1.43	1.41	1.11	1.29
Equity to Assets %	9.53	11.07	9.95	10.54
Reserve as a % of Non-Performing Loans	414.18	486.60	321.43	115.00

Compound Growth %'s	EPS %	10.25	Net Income %	12.72	Net Interest Income %	12.33

Comments

The bank's loan portfolio consists primarily of commercial and consumer loans, representing 61% and 21% of total loans, respectively. In 1995, the shareholders were paid a special dividend of $1 per share in addition to the regular dividend because of the Bank's high capital position. At the end of 1995, nonperforming loans comprised only 0.2% of total assets.

Officers	Position	Ownership Information	12/31/95
Elizabeth A. Duke	President, CEO	Number of Shares Outstanding	1,359,156
Larry G. Harcum	Exec VP, COO	Market Capitalization	$ 22,086,285
W. Kevin King	Exec VP, Senior Loan Officer	Frequency Of Dividends	Quarterly
Neal A. Petrovich	Exec VP, CFO	Number of Shareholders	921
Patty Bedrosian	Senior VP		

Other Information

Transfer Agent	Company Office			Where Listed	OTC-BB
Auditor	KPMG Peat Marwick LLP			Symbol	BKTI
Market Maker	Wheat, First Securities, Inc.	Telephone	(800)446-1016	SIC Code	6020
Broker Dealer	Regular Stockbroker			Employees	87

Tork, Inc.

1 Grove Street • Mount Vernon, NY 10550 • Telephone (914)664-3542 • Fax (914)664-5052

Company Description

The Company manufactures electronic and electromechanical time switches, photoelectric controls, and occupancy sensors to control the demand and use of energy. It also manufactures horns, bells, strobes, etc. for visible and audible signaling. These products are used in commercial and industrial buildings. Subsequent to the last year end, the Company repurchased 80,632 shares of stock at $10 per share.

	07/31/95	07/31/94	07/31/93	07/31/92
Per Share Information				
Stock Price	11.12	6.50	6.25	6.25
Earnings Per Share	0.79	0.97	0.66	0.65
Price / Earnings Ratio	14.08	6.70	9.47	9.62
Book Value Per Share	12.21	12.11	11.26	10.70
Price / Book Value %	91.07	53.67	55.51	58.41
Dividends Per Share	n.a.	n.a.	n.a.	n.a.
Annual Financial Data				
Operating Results (000's)				
Total Revenues	15,290.8	15,826.0	14,831.8	14,743.4
Costs & Expenses	-14,502.7	-14,902.5	-14,208.0	-14,125.8
Income Before Taxes and Other	788.1	903.8	582.5	585.3
Other Items	n.a.	n.a.	n.a.	n.a.
Income Tax	-298.0	-298.9	-172.7	-179.1
Net Income	490.1	604.9	409.9	406.2
Cash Flow From Operations	5.9	911.2	-98.9	789.1
Balance Sheet (000's)				
Cash & Equivalents	2,467.7	2,719.1	1,659.7	2,154.0
Total Current Assets	8,015.3	8,042.4	6,698.2	6,958.5
Fixed Assets, Net	880.9	1,057.5	949.5	1,063.6
Total Assets	9,965.4	10,055.2	8,864.5	8,883.6
Total Current Liabilities	2,463.5	2,537.8	1,855.1	2,221.9
Long-Term Debt	n.a.	n.a.	n.a.	n.a.
Stockholders' Equity	7,501.8	7,517.4	7,009.4	6,661.6
Performance & Financial Condition				
Return on Total Revenues %	3.20	3.82	2.76	2.76
Return on Avg Stockholders' Equity %	6.53	8.33	6.00	6.28
Return on Average Assets %	4.90	6.39	4.62	4.86
Current Ratio	3.25	3.17	3.61	3.13
Debt / Equity %	n.a.	n.a.	n.a.	n.a.

Compound Growth %'s	EPS %	6.72	Net Income %	6.45	Total Revenues %	1.22

Comments

1995 results were negatively affected by the Company's Mexican subsidiary which was hurt by the devaluation of the peso. This devaluation also resulted in a reduction of assets and equity (net profit and loss statement) of $494,917. The current ratio would even be better than reported if the extra cash tucked away in stock mutual funds of $662,000 were reported as a current asset.

Officers	Position	Ownership Information	07/31/95
Dorset White	Chairman, CEO	Number of Shares Outstanding	614,554
R. Sam Shankar	President, COO	Market Capitalization	$ 6,833,840
Carmen Caputo	VP - Finance, Treasurer	Frequency Of Dividends	n.a.
Michael Bizzoco	VP - Sales	Number of Shareholders	Under 500

Other Information				
Transfer Agent	Registrar & Transfer Company		Where Listed	OTC-BB
Auditor	KPMG Peat Marwick LLP		Symbol	TORK
Market Maker	Wachtel & Co., Inc.	Telephone (202)898-1018	SIC Code	5063
Broker Dealer	Regular Stockbroker		Employees	120

Torrington Water Company

110 Prospect Street • Torrington, CT 06790-0867 • Telephone (203)489-4149 • Fax (860)496-7889

Company Description

The Company provides water to residential and business customers in Torrington, Connecticut, and surrounding communities. In 1992, the Company split the shares 2 for 1. All per share amounts have been adjusted accordingly.

	12/31/93	12/31/92
Per Share Information		
Stock Price	80.00	80.00
Earnings Per Share	9.92	4.90
Price / Earnings Ratio	8.06	16.33
Book Value Per Share	47.19	47.34
Price / Book Value %	169.53	168.99
Dividends Per Share	2.08	2.02
Annual Financial Data		
Operating Results (000's)		
Total Revenues	2,720.0	2,387.2
Costs & Expenses	-1,867.1	-1,797.1
Income Before Taxes and Other	852.9	590.1
Other Items	169.6	n.a.
Income Tax	-308.1	-226.4
Net Income	714.4	363.7
Cash Flow From Operations	843.7	832.9
Balance Sheet (000's)		
Cash & Equivalents	38.5	28.2
Total Current Assets	755.0	742.0
Fixed Assets, Net	12,312.4	11,578.0
Total Assets	14,324.1	13,252.0
Total Current Liabilities	1,234.7	2,075.9
Long-Term Debt	2,128.0	1,140.0
Stockholders' Equity	3,973.4	3,408.8
Performance & Financial Condition		
Return on Total Revenues %	26.26	15.23
Return on Avg Stockholders' Equity %	19.35	11.02
Return on Average Assets %	5.18	2.80
Current Ratio	0.61	0.36
Debt / Equity %	53.56	33.44

Compound Growth %'s	EPS %	102.45	Net Income %	96.44	Total Revenues %	13.94

Comments

1993 results include a one-time benefit of $169,627, or $2.35 per share, for the adoption of GAAP for the accounting of income taxes. We were unable to obtain a more current report but will keep trying. The bid price on December 31, 1995, was $70.50 per share. The compound earnings per share and net income growth rates are misleading because it only includes two years of data and the most recent year has a nonrecurring gain.

Officers	Position	Ownership Information	12/31/93
Richard D. Calhoun	President	Number of Shares Outstanding	72,000
Mary J. Day	Treasurer	Market Capitalization	$ 5,760,000
Thomas K. Hubbard	Vice President, Secretary	Frequency Of Dividends	Quarterly
Catherine C. Roscello	Controller	Number of Shareholders	Under 500

Other Information				
Transfer Agent	Company Office		Where Listed	OTC-PS
Auditor	David R. Daggett		Symbol	TORW
Market Maker	Folger Nolan Fleming Douglas	Telephone (800)326-3633	SIC Code	4940
Broker Dealer	Regular Stockbroker		Employees	16

Tower Bancorp Inc.

P.O.Box 8 • Greencastle, PA 17225 • Telephone (717)597-2137 • Fax (717)597-5033

Company Description

Tower Bancorp Inc. is the parent company of The First National Bank of Greencastle, which is engaged in providing banking and bank related services in southcentral Pennsylvania through its five locations. The Bank has a proud history that dates back to its formation in 1864. In fact, it has occupied the same location on Center Square in Greencastle ever since.

	12/31/95	12/31/94	12/31/93	12/31/92
Per Share Information				
Stock Price	45.00	45.00	36.25	30.50
Earnings Per Share	5.67	5.52	4.37	3.87
Price / Earnings Ratio	7.94	8.15	8.30	7.88
Book Value Per Share	40.10	34.80	31.92	28.62
Price / Book Value %	112.22	129.31	113.57	106.57
Dividends Per Share	1.22	1.08	0.95	0.87
Annual Financial Data				
Operating Results (000's)				
Net Interest Income	6,299.0	6,005.0	5,449.0	5,283.0
Loan Loss Provision	n.a.	-13.0	-235.0	-290.0
Non-Interest Income	719.0	697.0	735.0	809.0
Non-Interest Expense	-3,921.0	-3,824.0	-3,576.0	-3,836.0
Income Before Taxes and Other	3,097.0	2,865.0	2,373.0	1,966.0
Other Items	n.a.	n.a.	n.a.	n.a.
Income Tax	-812.0	-748.0	-684.0	-473.0
Net Income	2,285.0	2,117.0	1,689.0	1,493.0
Balance Sheet (000's)				
Cash & Securities	38,353.0	35,441.0	35,613.0	38,666.0
Loans, Net	93,905.0	93,282.0	84,750.0	77,048.0
Fixed Assets, Net	1,830.0	1,972.0	1,951.0	2,026.0
Total Assets	139,182.0	135,378.0	125,495.0	120,435.0
Deposits	119,760.0	114,214.0	109,284.0	106,893.0
Stockholders' Equity	16,148.0	13,343.0	12,319.0	11,029.0
Performance & Financial Condition				
Net Interest Margin	n.a.	n.a.	n.a.	n.a.
Return on Avg Stockholders' Equity %	15.50	16.50	14.47	14.27
Return on Average Assets %	1.66	1.62	1.37	1.29
Equity to Assets %	11.60	9.86	9.82	9.16
Reserve as a % of Non-Performing Loans	3601.85	n.a.	252.02	n.a.

Compound Growth %'s	EPS %	13.58	Net Income %	15.24	Net Interest Income %	6.04

Comments

The Bank's loan portfolio consists primarily of real estate mortgages which represent 80% of total loans. Return on equity and return on assets were extremely impressive over the last four years. Management states their intent to remain an independent corporate entity.

Officers	Position	Ownership Information	12/31/95
Jeff B. Shank	President, CEO	Number of Shares Outstanding	423,485
John H. McDowell, Sr.	Exec VP	Market Capitalization	$ 19,056,825
Donald Chlebowski, Jr.	Vice President, Head Cashier	Frequency Of Dividends	Semi-Annual
Darlene D. Niswander	Vice President	Number of Shareholders	865
Donald G. Kunkle	Vice President		

Other Information				
Transfer Agent	Company Office		Where Listed	OTC-BB
Auditor	Smith Elliott Kearns & Company		Symbol	TOBC
Market Maker	Ferris, Baker Watts Inc. Inv.	Telephone (800)344-4413	SIC Code	6020
Broker Dealer	Regular Stockbroker		Employees	70

Tower Properties Company

911 Main Street • Kansas City, MO 64105 • Telephone (816)421-8255 • Fax (816)374-0611

Company Description

The Company owns, develops, leases and manages real property in the Kansas City metropolitan area. The improved real estate owned by the Company consists of 15 properties which include office buildings, apartment complexes, a warehouse/office facility and automobile parking lots and garages. The Company was originally incorporated in Missouri in 1971.

	12/31/95	12/31/94	12/31/93	12/31/92
Per Share Information				
Stock Price	75.00	65.00	65.00	65.00
Earnings Per Share	8.84	4.75	2.90	1.58
Price / Earnings Ratio	8.48	13.68	22.41	41.14
Book Value Per Share	120.66	108.90	101.43	98.57
Price / Book Value %	62.16	59.69	64.08	65.94
Dividends Per Share	n.a.	n.a.	n.a.	n.a.
Annual Financial Data				
Operating Results (000's)				
Total Revenues	13,152.9	11,697.1	9,870.7	8,913.5
Costs & Expenses	-10,787.9	-10,402.7	-9,316.4	-8,471.4
Income Before Taxes and Other	2,365.0	1,294.4	554.3	442.0
Other Items	-27.0	-28.7	135.2	-21.8
Income Tax	-827.8	-453.9	-194.0	-148.0
Net Income	1,510.2	811.8	495.5	272.2
Cash Flow From Operations	3,982.0	2,778.3	2,341.8	2,069.4
Balance Sheet (000's)				
Cash & Equivalents	5.6	23.2	18.7	523.3
Total Current Assets	1,400.6	772.5	817.7	2,256.8
Fixed Assets, Net	45,102.4	35,918.1	30,982.7	29,629.7
Total Assets	56,504.1	42,497.9	36,669.5	32,939.0
Total Current Liabilities	1,355.4	957.2	832.7	1,282.3
Long-Term Debt	19,300.9	17,820.5	10,313.2	13,617.5
Stockholders' Equity	20,635.3	18,618.0	17,327.2	16,818.9
Performance & Financial Condition				
Return on Total Revenues %	11.48	6.94	5.02	3.05
Return on Avg Stockholders' Equity %	7.69	4.52	2.90	1.62
Return on Average Assets %	3.05	2.05	1.42	0.96
Current Ratio	1.03	0.81	0.98	1.76
Debt / Equity %	93.53	95.72	59.52	80.97

Compound Growth %'s	EPS %	77.53	Net Income %	77.03	Total Revenues %	13.85

Comments

Included in Total Assets at December 31,1995, is an investment in the common stock of a bank of $2.4 million. Included in Total Liabilities are borrowings from that same bank of $13.9 million.

Officers	Position	Ownership Information	12/31/95
James M. Kemper, Jr.	President, CEO	Number of Shares Outstanding	171,014
Benjamin F. Bryan	Exec VP	Market Capitalization	$ 12,826,050
Chester A. Wittwer, Jr.	Vice President, Secretary	Frequency Of Dividends	n.a.
Margaret V. Allinder	Other	Number of Shareholders	571

Other Information

Transfer Agent	UMB Bank		Where Listed	OTC-BB
Auditor	Arthur Andersen LLP		Symbol	TPOP
Market Maker	George K. Baum & Company	Telephone (816)474-1100	SIC Code	6512
Broker Dealer	Regular Stockbroker		Employees	45

Transnational Industries, Inc.

P.O. Box 198, U.S. Route 1 • Chadds Ford, PA 19317 • Telephone (610)459-5200 • Fax (610)459-3830

Company Description

Through its subsidiary, the Company produces astronomical simulation equipment (planetariums) and simulation domes. The Company also services such equipment under maintenance contracts. Its principal customers are domestic and international museums, educational facilities, defense contractors, and the entertainment industry. The Company was incorporated in Delaware in 1985, and in 1986 it acquired Spitz Space Systems, Inc., which was founded in 1944. Officers and directors, as a group, owned 71.9% of the Company's outstanding common stock at April 18, 1996.

	01/31/96	01/31/95	01/31/94	01/31/93
Per Share Information				
Stock Price	2.32	3.10	3.00	3.20
Earnings Per Share	0.39	29.18	-8.00	-17.77
Price / Earnings Ratio	5.95	0.11	n.a.	n.a.
Book Value Per Share	4.78	4.11	-68.92	-17.80
Price / Book Value %	48.54	75.43	n.a.	n.a.
Dividends Per Share	n.a.	n.a.	n.a.	n.a.
Annual Financial Data				
Operating Results (000's)				
Total Revenues	5,761.0	5,310.0	5,713.0	7,611.0
Costs & Expenses	5,545.0	-5,041.0	-5,705.0	-7,022.0
Income Before Taxes and Other	216.0	269.0	8.0	589.0
Other Items	n.a.	8,767.0	-832.0	-2,445.0
Income Tax	n.a.	-7.0	-23.0	-276.0
Net Income	216.0	9,029.0	-847.0	-2,132.0
Cash Flow From Operations	-299.0	491.0	240.0	630.0
Balance Sheet (000's)				
Cash & Equivalents	339.0	670.0	524.0	97.0
Total Current Assets	2,825.0	2,790.0	2,472.0	3,325.0
Fixed Assets, Net	584.0	545.0	869.0	968.0
Total Assets	5,842.0	5,891.0	5,790.0	8,734.0
Total Current Liabilities	1,872.0	2,078.0	1,962.0	17,481.0
Long-Term Debt	1,734.0	1,793.0	11,148.0	261.0
Stockholders' Equity	2,236.0	2,020.0	-7,320.0	-9,008.0
Performance & Financial Condition				
Return on Total Revenues %	3.75	170.04	-14.83	-28.01
Return on Avg Stockholders' Equity %	10.15	n.a.	n.a.	n.a.
Return on Average Assets %	3.68	154.59	-11.66	n.a.
Current Ratio	1.51	1.34	1.26	0.19
Debt / Equity %	77.55	88.76	n.a.	n.a.

Compound Growth %'s	EPS %	-98.66	Net Income %	-97.61	Total Revenues %	-8.86

Comments

During 1994, the Company completed a comprehensive debt and equity restructuring and for the fiscal year ended January 31, 1995, recognized a gain on the elimination of debt of $8.8 million. Also, in conjunction with the restructuring, the Company issued warrants, purchased and repurchased certain preferred and common stock, implemented a reverse 20 to 1 stock split and made other changes to its equity structure. Preferred stock has liquidation preference and dividend requirements. Unpaid preferred dividends at January 31, 1996, totaled $252,000.

Officers	Position	Ownership Information	01/31/96
Charles H. Holmes, Jr.	President, CEO	Number of Shares Outstanding	324,220
Paul L. Dailey, Jr.	CFO	Market Capitalization	$ 752,190
		Frequency Of Dividends	n.a.
		Number of Shareholders	100

Other Information

Transfer Agent	American Stock Transfer & Trust Company		Where Listed	OTC-BB
Auditor	Stockton Bates & Company		Symbol	TRSN
Market Maker	Carr Securities Corporation	Telephone (800)212-243	SIC Code	3699
Broker Dealer	Regular Stockbroker		Employees	52

This page left intentionally blank.

Tremont Advisors, Inc.

555 Theodore Fremd Avenue • Rye, NY 10580 • Telephone (914)921-3400 • Fax (914)921-3499

Company Description

The Company is a holding company which, through its subsidiaries, renders consulting and specialized investment services to investment funds, investment managers, institutional investors, and high net worth individuals, with respect to the organization and management of their investment portfolios or programs, as well as sponsoring its own multi- manager funds. In addition, the Company offers marketing and business development consulting services to investment management firms and to individual investment advisors.

	12/31/95	12/31/94	12/31/93	12/31/92
Per Share Information				
Stock Price	0.94	1.34	0.50	0.45
Earnings Per Share	n.a.	-0.04	0.03	n.a.
Price / Earnings Ratio	n.a.	n.a.	16.67	n.a.
Book Value Per Share	0.38	0.38	0.03	0.10
Price / Book Value %	247.37	352.63	1,666.70	450.00
Dividends Per Share	n.a.	n.a.	n.a.	n.a.
Annual Financial Data				
Operating Results (000's)				
Total Revenues	3,462.8	3,826.3	1,690.8	1,196.5
Costs & Expenses	-3,452.7	-4,019.1	-1,559.3	-1,192.7
Income Before Taxes and Other	10.1	-197.9	127.8	3.8
Other Items	n.a.	n.a.	n.a.	n.a.
Income Tax	-2.3	29.7	-44.6	-2.8
Net Income	7.8	-168.2	83.2	1.0
Cash Flow From Operations	-135.3	123.8	215.2	-190.3
Balance Sheet (000's)				
Cash & Equivalents	455.1	901.1	65.5	123.1
Total Current Assets	1,208.0	1,437.4	498.0	405.1
Fixed Assets, Net	231.8	233.8	56.5	44.0
Total Assets	2,202.1	2,172.0	637.1	478.4
Total Current Liabilities	745.6	723.3	524.5	137.6
Long-Term Debt	n.a.	n.a.	n.a.	n.a.
Stockholders' Equity	1,456.5	1,448.7	112.6	339.9
Performance & Financial Condition				
Return on Total Revenues %	0.23	-4.40	4.92	0.08
Return on Avg Stockholders' Equity %	0.54	-21.55	36.77	n.a.
Return on Average Assets %	0.36	-11.98	14.92	0.28
Current Ratio	1.62	1.99	0.95	2.94
Debt / Equity %	n.a.	n.a.	n.a.	n.a.

Compound Growth %'s	EPS % n.a.	Net Income % 100.01	Total Revenues % 42.51

Comments

The operating results for 1995, 1994, and 1993, include revenues from a foreign subsidiary, located in Bermuda, of $1.5 million, $2.8 million, and $872,000, respectively. Operating profits relating to this subsidiary for the same period were $42,000, $837,000, and $7,000, respectively. At December 31, 1995, the Company has two classes of common stock with shares outstanding, one class of preferred stock with no shares outstanding and several stock option plans with a total of 325,000 options outstanding.

Officers	Position	Ownership Information	12/31/95
Sandra L. Manzke	Chairman, CEO	Number of Shares Outstanding	3,844,457
Robert I. Schulman	President, COO	Market Capitalization	$ 3,613,790
Stephen T. Clayton	CFO	Frequency Of Dividends	n.a.
Suzanne S. Hammond	Secretary, Treasurer	Number of Shareholders	170

Other Information

Transfer Agent	Chemical Mellon Shareholder Services			Where Listed	OTC-BB
Auditor	Ernst & Young LLP			Symbol	TMAVA
Market Maker	Gabelli & Company	Telephone	(914)921-5154	SIC Code	6282
Broker Dealer	Regular Stockbroker			Employees	20

Troy Mills, Inc.

30 Monadnock Street • Troy, NH 03465-1000 • Telephone (603)242-7711 • Fax (603)242-6896

Company Description

The Company, which was founded in 1865, now makes parts for the automobile industry including filters, insulation, mats, fabric parts and liners, panel trim, and seating. Most employees are part of an employee stock ownership plan sponsored by the Company. The Company has a glorious history, part of which we tried to capture on the next page.

	10/28/95	10/29/94	10/30/93	10/31/92
Per Share Information				
Stock Price	2.12	6.00	7.00	6.00
Earnings Per Share	-2.65	0.26	0.97	0.95
Price / Earnings Ratio	n.a.	23.08	7.22	6.32
Book Value Per Share	8.38	10.30	10.99	9.54
Price / Book Value %	25.30	58.25	63.69	62.89
Dividends Per Share	n.a.	0.22	0.25	0.10
Annual Financial Data				
Operating Results (000's)				
Total Revenues	42,030.9	45,831.5	44,152.0	39,908.2
Costs & Expenses	-44,412.9	-47,145.7	-42,799.6	-38,652.5
Income Before Taxes and Other	-2,670.8	-1,364.1	1,244.8	1,216.1
Other Items	n.a.	1,085.0	n.a.	n.a.
Income Tax	650.1	479.6	-503.8	-490.7
Net Income	-2,020.7	200.5	740.9	725.4
Cash Flow From Operations	1,267.3	1,048.8	2,430.4	983.8
Balance Sheet (000's)				
Cash & Equivalents	5,904.2	6,326.0	663.0	275.0
Total Current Assets	10,603.1	11,734.9	11,124.4	9,554.8
Fixed Assets, Net	11,397.3	11,409.0	8,644.8	7,744.7
Total Assets	22,478.9	23,863.6	20,378.8	17,347.3
Total Current Liabilities	6,137.7	5,454.4	4,072.9	3,126.3
Long-Term Debt	7,312.7	7,134.5	6,284.0	4,944.7
Stockholders' Equity	6,387.5	8,408.2	8,379.2	7,798.3
Performance & Financial Condition				
Return on Total Revenues %	-4.81	0.44	1.68	1.82
Return on Avg Stockholders' Equity %	-27.32	2.39	9.16	9.73
Return on Average Assets %	-8.72	0.91	3.93	4.17
Current Ratio	1.73	2.15	2.73	3.06
Debt / Equity %	114.49	84.85	74.99	63.41

Compound Growth %'s	EPS % n.a.	Net Income % n.a.	Total Revenues % 1.74

Comments

1994 results include a one-time benefit of $1.1 million, or $1.42 per share, created by retroactively changing depreciation methods to slower methods. Having experienced two difficult years, management restructured in 1995 with a major emphasis on reducing product costs. In 1995, $2.5 million was spent on equipment for increased capacity. $1.7 million is planned as a capital investment in 1996 which will mainly support cost reduction and facility needs.

Officers	Position	Ownership Information	10/28/95
Barrett F. Ripley	President, CEO	Number of Shares Outstanding	762,201
John S. Goodnow	Secretary	Market Capitalization	$ 1,615,866
Martin W. Ballen	Vice President	Frequency Of Dividends	Quarterly
Frederick W. MacMillan	Vice President, CFO	Number of Shareholders	Under 500
James A. Cuddy	VP - Manufacturing		

Other Information			
Transfer Agent	John R. Goodnow & Co., Keene, NH 03465	Where Listed	OTC-BB
Auditor	Coopers & Lybrand, LLP	Symbol	TMIL
Market Maker	Folger Nolan Fleming Douglas	Telephone (800)326-3633	SIC Code	5199
Broker Dealer	Regular Stockbroker	Employees	402

Horses to Automobiles

Troy Mills has the distinction of holding the New Hampshire state record for continuity of family ownership in the textile industry and is third overall in the United States. Five generations of the Ripley family have been at the helm, beginning with Barrett Ripley in 1865. But Troy's history actually starts even a few years earlier than that.

An immigrant from Yorkshire County, England, Thomas Goodall had an idea in 1857 for an improved and more economical horse blanket. Historically, horse blankets had been square in shape, woolen, imported, and expensive. Functionally, it was difficult to keep a square blanket on a horse, so Mr. Goodall improved the design by tapering the blanket. He also made it more affordable to purchase by loom-weaving a combination of cotton and wool into an inexpensive fabric. Horse blankets were then a basic necessity, so these cheaper ones found a ready market in 1857 despite the poor economy.

Goodall's mill was located in Troy, New Hampshire. This site had evolved early on from eighteenth century settlers' needs for a variety of milled products, including those made from textiles. The Ripley family legacy began when Barrett Ripley formed a partnership to acquire Mr. Goodall's mill. He renamed it the Troy Blanket Mill and began to run the manufacturing operation. In those days, before the advent of *horseless* carriages, a farmer was judged by his horse team and the way in which he cared for his animals. Thus it came to pass that having a well-fitting, colorful plaid or patterned Troy blanket for one's horse was a status symbol.

As modes of transportation have changed, Troy has evolved and diversified as well. Having once simply supplied the textile needs of horses, the Company now markets its synthetic fabrics to many and diverse industries. Chief among them, however, is the automotive industry. Troy allows automobile manufacturers to define specific product requirements, to color match under multiple lighting conditions and to test color fastness of their fabrics, thereby ensuring the customer's satisfaction with their product. In the meantime, certain clothing fads have positively impacted the Company as well. A few years ago you may have noticed colorfully lined denim and cotton work jackets popularized by rap singers. It was Troy that made the linings for these jackets. Earlier on, when western wear was quite popular, Troy's business in imitation sheepskin was strong. These fleeting fashions boost Troy's sales and demonstrate their versatility, but do not impair the emphasis on their main customer, the automotive industry. Troy Mills remains loyal to the transportation industry, and after more than 130 years of being in business has not waivered in its focus.

We are indebted to Mr. Fuller Ripley for the information provided by his book, *The Fabric Of Troy*, published by Troy Mills, Inc., 1986

Turbotville National Bancorp, Inc.

P.O.Box 37 • Turbotville, PA 17772 • Telephone (717)649-5118 • Fax (717)649-5788

Company Description

Turbotville National Bancorp, Inc. is a Pennsylvania corporation organized as the holding company of Turbotville National Bank. The Bank provides standard banking services at its one location in Turbotville, Pennsylvania.

	12/31/95	12/31/94	12/31/93	12/31/92
Per Share Information				
Stock Price	315.00	315.00	310.00	295.00
Earnings Per Share	52.55	54.16	50.73	47.78
Price / Earnings Ratio	5.99	5.82	6.11	6.17
Book Value Per Share	488.28	431.84	403.93	364.94
Price / Book Value %	64.51	72.94	76.75	80.84
Dividends Per Share	14.00	14.00	13.25	13.00
Annual Financial Data				
Operating Results (000's)				
Net Interest Income	1,910.6	1,990.2	1,890.1	1,890.1
Loan Loss Provision	-42.0	-82.0	-140.0	-140.0
Non-Interest Income	180.2	163.3	163.1	163.1
Non-Interest Expense	-1,158.0	-1,192.0	-1,095.2	-1,095.2
Income Before Taxes and Other	890.8	879.6	818.0	818.0
Other Items	n.a.	n.a.	n.a.	n.a.
Income Tax	-239.1	-208.0	-226.2	-226.2
Net Income	651.7	671.6	591.8	591.8
Balance Sheet (000's)				
Cash & Securities	16,043.3	14,863.0	17,609.5	18,318.7
Loans, Net	35,687.3	33,779.1	31,533.4	29,096.9
Fixed Assets, Net	338.8	347.7	322.9	362.2
Total Assets	52,536.2	49,521.8	50,104.3	48,299.2
Deposits	46,022.0	43,765.4	44,870.9	43,555.9
Stockholders' Equity	6,054.6	5,354.9	5,008.7	4,525.3
Performance & Financial Condition				
Net Interest Margin	n.a.	n.a.	n.a.	n.a.
Return on Avg Stockholders' Equity %	11.42	12.96	12.41	13.76
Return on Average Assets %	1.28	1.35	1.20	1.28
Equity to Assets %	11.52	10.81	10.00	9.37
Reserve as a % of Non-Performing Loans	373.97	307.91	132.54	130.12

Compound Growth %'s	EPS %	3.22	Net Income %	3.27	Net Interest Income %	0.36

Comments

The bank's loan portfolio is made up largely of real estate loans, totalling 80% of total loans, with consumer loans comprising 19%. Shares trade infrequently and are best acquired using a bank stock specialist or pink sheet specialist. Although growth ratios are not high, the Bank continues to have favorable earnings when expressed as a percentage of total assets or equity.

Officers	Position	Ownership Information	12/31/95
James W. Foust	Chairman	Number of Shares Outstanding	12,400
P. Thomas Yoder, Jr.	President, CEO	Market Capitalization	$ 3,906,000
Charles A. Wright	Secretary, Head Cashier	Frequency Of Dividends	Irregular
Paul R. Ranck	Vice President	Number of Shareholders	235
Brentha J. Snyder	Other		

Other Information				
Transfer Agent	Company Office		Where Listed	OTC-BB
Auditor	Larson, Kellett & Associates		Symbol	TVNB
Market Maker	F.J. Morrissey & Co., Inc.	Telephone (800)842-8928	SIC Code	6020
Broker Dealer	Pink sheet specialist		Employees	21

UCI Medical Affiliates, Inc.

6168 St. Andrews Road • Columbia, SC 29212 • Telephone (803)772-8840 • Fax (803)772-8406

Company Description

The Company owns and operates a network of 25 freestanding medical centers located throughout South Carolina. The centers, which are typically open for extended hours and out-patient care only, are staffed by physicians, other healthcare providers, and administrative staff. The Company acts as the primary care provider for injured workers of firms insured through Companion Insurance Company. Companion owns 45% of the Company's common stock. The most recent capital transactions have been a 1 for 5 reverse stock split in 1994, and the acquisition during 1993, 1994, and 1995, by Companion Insurance Company of a total of 1,679171 shares of the Company's common stock for a total of $3.4 million (of this 218,180 shares were acquired in November 1996).

	09/30/95	09/30/94	09/30/93	09/30/92
Per Share Information				
Stock Price	2.50	2.43	0.80	0.80
Earnings Per Share	-0.43	0.28	0.21	n.a.
Price / Earnings Ratio	n.a.	8.68	3.81	n.a.
Book Value Per Share	0.93	0.93	0.23	0.03
Price / Book Value %	268.82	261.29	347.83	2,666.70
Dividends Per Share	n.a.	n.a.	n.a.	n.a.
Annual Financial Data				
Operating Results (000's)				
Total Revenues	17,992.6	12,540.0	9,799.4	8,330.4
Costs & Expenses	-19,352.4	-12,438.9	-9,392.8	-8,327.5
Income Before Taxes and Other	-1,359.7	32.2	406.6	2.9
Other Items	n.a.	n.a.	138.2	n.a.
Income Tax	n.a.	612.2	-138.2	n.a.
Net Income	-1,359.7	644.4	406.6	2.9
Cash Flow From Operations	-460.0	-744.2	289.7	189.2
Balance Sheet (000's)				
Cash & Equivalents	76.5	210.3	23.9	8.4
Total Current Assets	3,458.5	2,538.6	1,320.2	979.0
Fixed Assets, Net	2,795.4	1,098.3	487.1	267.6
Total Assets	10,215.7	6,674.3	2,940.3	2,452.2
Total Current Liabilities	3,841.5	1,776.3	2,164.8	1,899.8
Long-Term Debt	3,121.1	2,295.2	168.5	400.6
Stockholders' Equity	3,253.0	2,602.8	457.0	49.4
Performance & Financial Condition				
Return on Total Revenues %	-7.56	5.14	4.15	0.04
Return on Avg Stockholders' Equity %	-46.44	42.12	160.58	1.12
Return on Average Assets %	-16.10	13.40	15.08	0.11
Current Ratio	0.90	1.43	0.61	0.52
Debt / Equity %	95.94	88.18	36.87	810.84

Compound Growth %'s	EPS % n.a.	Net Income % n.a.	Total Revenues % 29.26

Comments

Earnings and Net Income (loss) for the three months ended December 31, 1995, were $5.2 million and $134,000 ($.04 per share) as compared to $3.6 million and a loss of $186,000 (-$.07 per share) for the same period in 1994.

Officers	Position	Ownership Information	09/30/95
M.F. McFarland, III	President, CEO	Number of Shares Outstanding	3,508,164
Stephen S. Seeling	COO, Secretary	Market Capitalization	$ 8,770,410
Jerry F. Wells, Jr.	CFO	Frequency Of Dividends	n.a.
D. Michael Stout	Vice President	Number of Shareholders	698
Jitendra S. Mehta	Vice President		

Other Information

Transfer Agent	American Stock Transfer & Trust Company		Where Listed	OTC-BB
Auditor	Price Waterhouse LLP		Symbol	UCIM
Market Maker	Carr Securities Corporation	Telephone (800)221-2243	SIC Code	8093
Broker Dealer	Regular Stockbroker		Employees	301

USANA, Inc.

4550 So. Main Street • Salt Lake City, UT 84107 • Telephone (801)288-2290 • Fax (801)288-2285

Company Description

The Company develops, manufactures, packages and markets its own line of nutritional, antioxidant and non-toxic skin care products. The products are distributed through a network marketing organization with approximately 50,000 distributors in all 50 states, Puerto Rico and Canada. As of March 31, 1996, officers and directors, as a group, owned 64% of the Company's outstanding common stock. The Company was incorporated in Utah during 1992 as a wholly-owned subsidiary of Gull Laboratories, Inc. In January,1993, the Company was spun off from Gull as a separate corporation.

	12/31/95	12/31/94	12/31/93
Per Share Information			
Stock Price	10.50	1.06	0.31
Earnings Per Share	0.41	0.06	-0.06
Price / Earnings Ratio	25.61	17.67	n.a.
Book Value Per Share	1.04	0.32	n.a.
Price / Book Value %	1,009.60	331.25	n.a.
Dividends Per Share	n.a.	n.a.	n.a.
Annual Financial Data			
Operating Results (000's)			
Total Revenues	24,734.5	7,326.9	3,869.2
Costs & Expenses	-21,007.3	-6,923.1	-4,153.9
Income Before Taxes and Other	3,727.2	351.3	-350.6
Other Items	n.a.	n.a.	n.a.
Income Tax	-1,422.0	-26.0	38.7
Net Income	2,305.2	325.3	-311.9
Cash Flow From Operations	3,871.1	522.7	258.4
Balance Sheet (000's)			
Cash & Equivalents	2,976.4	646.9	287.9
Total Current Assets	5,360.7	1,839.5	756.2
Fixed Assets, Net	4,576.1	847.0	1,093.1
Total Assets	10,173.6	2,789.6	1,889.7
Total Current Liabilities	3,566.2	994.0	478.4
Long-Term Debt	3.9	7.0	15.2
Stockholders' Equity	6,554.5	1,721.5	1,396.2
Performance & Financial Condition			
Return on Total Revenues %	9.32	4.44	-8.06
Return on Avg Stockholders' Equity %	55.71	20.87	n.a.
Return on Average Assets %	35.57	13.91	n.a.
Current Ratio	1.50	1.85	1.58
Debt / Equity %	0.06	0.40	1.09

Compound Growth %'s	EPS %	583.33	Net Income %	608.57	Total Revenues %	152.84

Comments

Included in Costs & Expenses are distributor incentives of $10.8 and $3.1 million in 1995 and 1994, respectively. The Company has two stock option plans under which 1,000,000 shares of its stock are reserved.

Officers	Position	Ownership Information	12/31/95
Myron W. Wentz	Chairman, President	Number of Shares Outstanding	6,280,119
David A. Wentz	Exec VP	Market Capitalization	$ 65,941,250
John B. McCandless IV	Other	Frequency Of Dividends	n.a.
		Number of Shareholders	321

Other Information

Transfer Agent	Progressive Transfer Company		Where Listed	OTC-BB
Auditor	Grant Thornton LLP		Symbol	USNA
Market Maker	Wilson-Davis & Co., Inc.	Telephone (801)532-1313	SIC Code	2834
Broker Dealer	Regular Stockbroker		Employees	135

Union Bankshares, Inc.

P.O.Box 667 • Morrisville, VT 05661 • Telephone (802)888-6600 • Fax (802)888-7697

Company Description

Union Bankshares, Inc. is a one bank holding company located in Morrisville, Vermont. Its subsidiary, Union Bank, is a commercial bank which grants commercial, residential, agribusiness, consumer and municipal loans primarily to customers in northern Vermont.

	12/31/95	12/31/94	12/31/93	12/31/92
Per Share Information				
Stock Price	18.00	17.50	16.75	14.00
Earnings Per Share	2.92	2.26	2.39	1.76
Price / Earnings Ratio	6.16	7.74	7.01	7.95
Book Value Per Share	15.84	13.97	12.88	11.40
Price / Book Value %	113.64	125.27	130.05	122.81
Dividends Per Share	1.24	1.10	0.90	0.80
Annual Financial Data				
Operating Results (000's)				
Net Interest Income	8,608.4	7,745.0	7,313.5	6,635.0
Loan Loss Provision	-450.0	-200.0	-135.0	-249.0
Non-Interest Income	1,877.9	1,381.8	1,333.8	1,242.3
Non-Interest Expense	-5,642.9	-5,500.5	-5,495.0	-5,110.5
Income Before Taxes and Other	4,393.4	3,426.3	3,017.2	2,517.8
Other Items	n.a.	n.a.	423.6	n.a.
Income Tax	-1,327.8	-1,026.0	-879.5	-631.3
Net Income	3,065.6	2,400.3	2,561.3	1,886.5
Balance Sheet (000's)				
Cash & Securities	34,486.6	23,119.2	31,475.2	31,409.3
Loans, Net	118,827.2	114,473.3	99,988.2	92,169.2
Fixed Assets, Net	2,438.3	2,536.1	2,364.5	2,155.9
Total Assets	160,235.4	144,840.3	137,730.7	129,137.1
Deposits	139,208.8	126,071.4	121,759.2	114,747.3
Stockholders' Equity	16,593.4	14,809.6	13,799.4	12,226.6
Performance & Financial Condition				
Net Interest Margin	n.a.	n.a.	n.a.	n.a.
Return on Avg Stockholders' Equity %	19.52	16.78	19.68	15.40
Return on Average Assets %	2.01	1.70	1.92	1.45
Equity to Assets %	10.36	10.22	10.02	9.47
Reserve as a % of Non-Performing Loans	243.90	83.37	141.73	59.11

Compound Growth %'s	EPS %	18.38	Net Income %	17.57	Net Interest Income %	9.07

Comments

During 1994 and 1995 the Bank repurchased 25,399 shares of their own stock and are currently holding 80,299 shares of treasury stock. This factor combined with the outstanding operational results and growth rates make the Company worthy of investigation.

Officers	Position	Ownership Information	12/31/95
Kenneth D. Gibbons	President	Number of Shares Outstanding	1,047,601
Peter Haslam	Secretary	Market Capitalization	$ 18,856,818
Marcia M. Mongeon	Treasurer	Frequency Of Dividends	Quarterly
Cynthia D. Borck	Vice President	Number of Shareholders	302

Other Information					
Transfer Agent	Company Office			Where Listed	OTC-PS
Auditor	A.M. Peisch & Company			Symbol	NSR
Market Maker	First Albany Corporation	Telephone	(800)541-5061	SIC Code	6020
Broker Dealer	Regular Stockbroker			Employees	93

Union National Bancorp, Inc.

117 East Main Street • Westminster, MD 21157 • Telephone (410)848-7200 • Fax (410)840-9919

Company Description

Union National Bancorp, Inc. is the one-bank holding company of Union National Bank which provides a full range of banking services to individuals and businesses through its main office and six branches in Caroll County, Maryland.

	12/31/95	12/31/94	12/31/93	12/31/92
Per Share Information				
Stock Price	30.00	26.00	21.37	18.62
Earnings Per Share	2.15	2.40	2.44	2.43
Price / Earnings Ratio	13.95	10.83	8.76	7.66
Book Value Per Share	19.83	16.72	16.86	14.54
Price / Book Value %	151.29	155.50	126.75	128.06
Dividends Per Share	0.52	0.50	0.46	0.38
Annual Financial Data				
Operating Results (000's)				
Net Interest Income	8,999.3	8,820.0	8,619.0	7,836.9
Loan Loss Provision	-212.0	-342.0	-425.0	-470.0
Non-Interest Income	977.6	1,315.0	1,028.0	874.8
Non-Interest Expense	-7,058.6	-6,799.0	-6,179.0	-5,594.7
Income Before Taxes and Other	2,706.2	2,994.0	3,043.0	2,647.0
Other Items	n.a.	n.a.	n.a.	248.3
Income Tax	-911.9	-990.0	-1,009.0	-866.9
Net Income	1,794.2	2,004.0	2,034.0	2,028.3
Balance Sheet (000's)				
Cash & Securities	66,061.8	61,535.7	59,018.9	43,772.4
Loans, Net	145,052.5	138,059.0	126,994.6	126,286.7
Fixed Assets, Net	3,850.9	3,281.1	3,355.0	2,633.2
Total Assets	218,816.1	207,226.2	192,290.0	175,511.3
Deposits	193,461.8	182,533.1	172,816.4	160,367.0
Stockholders' Equity	16,540.0	13,948.4	14,060.9	12,124.9
Performance & Financial Condition				
Net Interest Margin	4.56	4.82	5.12	5.13
Return on Avg Stockholders' Equity %	11.77	14.31	15.54	18.00
Return on Average Assets %	0.84	1.00	1.11	1.22
Equity to Assets %	7.56	6.73	7.31	6.91
Reserve as a % of Non-Performing Loans	322.48	n.a.	n.a.	n.a.

Compound Growth %'s	EPS %	-4.00	Net Income %	-4.01	Net Interest Income %	4.72

Comments

The Bank's loan portfolio is made up primarily of real estate and commercial loans at 63% and 20% of total loans, respectively. On October 27, 1995, the Company entered into a definitive agreement to acquire Maryland Permanent Bank & Trust Co. of Owlings, Maryland. The Company will pay $22.74 per share for all of Maryland Permanent's 340,328 shares. At December 31, 1995, total assets of Maryland Permanent were $39,338,649. In early 1996, Joseph H. Beaver, Jr. retired from the office of president.

Officers	Position	Ownership Information	12/31/95
K. Wayne Lockard	Chairman	Number of Shares Outstanding	834,000
Virginia W. Smith	President	Market Capitalization	$ 25,020,000
Denise L. Owings	Secretary	Frequency Of Dividends	Annual
Thomas F. See	Treasurer	Number of Shareholders	442
Dominic F. Pagio	Vice President		

Other Information

Transfer Agent	Company Office			Where Listed	OTC-BB
Auditor	Stegman & Company			Symbol	UBMD
Market Maker	Legg Mason Wood Walker, Inc.	Telephone	(212)428-4949	SIC Code	6020
Broker Dealer	Regular Stockbroker			Employees	113

Union Pump Company

87 Capitol Avenue S.W. • Battle Creek, MI 49014 • Telephone (616)966-4600 • Fax (616)962-7549

Company Description

The Company manufactures and sells industrial pumps for use in the oil and gas processing industries. Their manufacturing facilities are in Battle Creek, Michigan, and Burlington, Ontario, Canada. Domestic export sales accounted for 30% and 25% of total sales in 1994 and 1993, respectively.

	12/31/94	12/31/93	12/31/92
Per Share Information			
Stock Price	425.00	500.00	240.00
Earnings Per Share	62.23	32.06	83.52
Price / Earnings Ratio	6.83	15.60	2.87
Book Value Per Share	556.43	513.75	486.61
Price / Book Value %	76.38	97.32	49.32
Dividends Per Share	5.00	5.00	5.00
Annual Financial Data			
Operating Results (000's)			
Total Revenues	66,771.0	60,900.0	69,536.0
Costs & Expenses	-63,578.0	-58,814.0	-65,806.0
Income Before Taxes and Other	2,305.0	1,741.0	3,730.0
Other Items	n.a.	n.a.	n.a.
Income Tax	-798.0	-781.0	-1,042.0
Net Income	1,507.0	960.0	2,688.0
Cash Flow From Operations	1,102.0	2,211.0	n.a.
Balance Sheet (000's)			
Cash & Equivalents	36.0	45.0	n.a.
Total Current Assets	19,008.0	17,195.0	n.a.
Fixed Assets, Net	17,129.0	16,130.0	n.a.
Total Assets	36,959.0	34,032.0	32,689.0
Total Current Liabilities	19,512.0	14,850.0	n.a.
Long-Term Debt	3,487.0	2,916.0	n.a.
Stockholders' Equity	12,276.0	14,791.0	14,939.0
Performance & Financial Condition			
Return on Total Revenues %	2.26	1.58	3.87
Return on Avg Stockholders' Equity %	11.14	6.46	n.a.
Return on Average Assets %	4.25	2.88	n.a.
Current Ratio	0.97	1.16	n.a.
Debt / Equity %	28.41	19.71	n.a.

Compound Growth %'s	EPS %	-13.68	Net Income %	-25.12	Total Revenues %	-2.01

Comments

The Company executed a 1 for 12 reverse split in 1996 that reduced outstanding shares from 21,662 to about 1,791. This now prices the stock at about $5,000 per share. This follows other reverse splits of the past. Management claims that the reason for the reverse split was to reduce broker commission expense for any shareholder selling shares in the future. The logic of this, if you choose to believe it, is that a single share sold at $425 may have a 10% commission but a single share at $5,000 would most certainly have less than a 10% commission. Often, reverse splits are used to reduce the number of stockholders and to reduce trading activity. 1995 reports had not been issued when we went to press.

Officers	Position	Ownership Information	12/31/94
Peter Ordway	President, CEO	Number of Shares Outstanding	22,062
Patricia Spiess	Vice President, Secretary	Market Capitalization	$ 9,376,350
		Frequency Of Dividends	Quarterly
		Number of Shareholders	Under 500

Other Information

Transfer Agent	Company Office			Where Listed	OTC-PS
Auditor	BDO Seidman			Symbol	UPUM
Market Maker	Carr Securities Corporation	Telephone	(800)221-2243	SIC Code	5084
Broker Dealer	Pink sheet specialist			Employees	n.a.

Uniprop Manufactured Housing Communities Income II

280 Daines Street, 3rd floor • Birmingham, MI 48009-6250 • Telephone (810)645-9261 • Fax (810)645-2154

Company Description

The Partnership acquired, maintains, operates and will ultimately dispose of income producing residential real properties consisting of nine manufactured housing communities located in Florida, Michigan, Nevada and Minnesota. The Partnership was formed in 1986. $66 million was raised with a public offering of units at $20 each. The officers listed are those of Uniprop, Inc., the original general partner.

	12/31/95	12/31/94	12/31/93
Per Unit Information			
Price Per Unit	6.50	7.90	6.60
Earnings Per Unit	0.16	0.43	0.85
Price / Earnings Ratio	40.63	18.37	7.76
Book Value Per Unit	7.08	7.58	14.80
Price / Book Value %	91.81	104.22	44.59
Distributions Per Unit	0.66	7.60	1.40
Cash Flow Per Unit	0.59	0.72	1.45
Annual Financial Data			
Operating Results (000's)			
Total Revenues	11,210.5	11,302.2	10,114.1
Costs & Expenses	-10,670.4	-9,857.4	-7,261.4
Operating Income	540.2	1,444.9	2,852.6
Other Items	n.a.	n.a.	n.a.
Net Income	540.2	1,444.9	2,852.6
Cash Flow From Operations	1,953.2	2,387.2	4,776.8
Balance Sheet (000's)			
Cash & Equivalents	388.3	1,373.2	n.a.
Total Current Assets	1,345.1	2,373.2	n.a.
Investments In Real Estate	49,136.1	50,096.5	n.a.
Total Assets	54,472.2	56,093.9	n.a.
Total Current Liabilities	154.7	239.9	n.a.
Long-Term Debt	29,894.6	29,786.0	n.a.
Partners' Capital	23,595.5	25,251.1	n.a.
Performance & Financial Condition			
Return on Total Revenues %	4.82	12.78	28.20
Return on Average Partners' Capital %	n.a.	n.a.	n.a.
Return on Average Assets %	n.a.	n.a.	n.a.
Current Ratio	8.69	9.89	n.a.
Debt / Equity %	126.70	117.96	n.a.

Compound Growth %'s	EPU % n.a.	Net Income % n.a.	Total Revenues % n.a.

Comments

The properties were originally acquired for cash. A mortgage loan was obtained in 1993, which accounts for the large cash distribution to partners in 1994. The most recent valuation provided by the general partner was $11.92 per unit.

Officers	Position	Ownership Information	12/31/95
Paul M. Zlotoff	President	Number of Shares Outstanding	3,303,387
Gloria Koster	CFO	Market Capitalization	$ 21,472,016
Andrew Feuereisen	Controller	Frequency Of Distributions	Quarterly
		Number of Partners	4,850

Other Information						
Transfer Agent	Company Office				Where Listed	Order Matching Only
Auditor	BDO Seidman LLP				Symbol	n.a.
Market Maker	None				SIC Code	6510
Broker Dealer	Chicago Partnership Board	Tel/Ext	(800)272-6273	690	Employees	3

United Coasts Corporation

233 Main Street • New Britain, CT 06050-2350 • Telephone (203)223-5000 • Fax (860)229-1111

Company Description

The Company is an insurance holding company whose wholly-owned subsidiary, United Coastal Insurance Company, operates as an excess and surplus lines property and casualty insurer in 46 states. The Company was formed in 1985. ACMAT Corporation owns 84% of the common stock.

	12/31/94	12/31/93
Per Share Information		
Stock Price	4.75	5.00
Earnings Per Share	0.78	0.74
Price / Earnings Ratio	6.09	6.76
Book Value Per Share	7.30	6.68
Price / Book Value %	65.07	74.85
Dividends Per Share	n.a.	n.a.
Annual Financial Data		
Operating Results (000's)		
Total Revenues	25,058.0	23,526.0
Costs & Expenses	-14,191.4	-12,997.5
Income Before Taxes and Other	10,866.5	10,528.5
Other Items	n.a.	n.a.
Income Tax	-2,913.4	-2,876.8
Net Income	7,953.1	7,651.7
Cash Flow From Operations	965.5	8,390.1
Balance Sheet (000's)		
Cash & Equivalents	4,607.1	4,865.5
Total Current Assets	16,697.0	8,791.5
Fixed Assets, Net	302.9	348.9
Total Assets	118,606.4	112,146.8
Total Current Liabilities	764.7	461.7
Long-Term Debt	n.a.	3,065.0
Stockholders' Equity	74,408.7	68,096.3
Performance & Financial Condition		
Return on Total Revenues %	31.74	32.52
Return on Avg Stockholders' Equity %	11.16	n.a.
Return on Average Assets %	6.89	n.a.
Current Ratio	21.83	19.04
Debt / Equity %	n.a.	4.50

Compound Growth %'s	EPS %	5.41	Net Income %	3.94	Total Revenues %	6.51

Comments

1995 results were not available when we went to press. We are interested in following the growth in revenues, as well as earnings, and the overall soundness of the balance sheet.

Officers	Position	Ownership Information	12/31/94
Henry W. Nozko, Sr.	Chairman	Number of Shares Outstanding	10,187,189
Henry W. Nozko, Jr.	President, Treasurer	Market Capitalization	$ 48,389,148
Joseph D. Scollo, Jr.	Senior VP	Frequency Of Dividends	n.a.
Robert H. Frazer	Vice President, Secretary	Number of Shareholders	Under 500

Other Information

Transfer Agent	American Stock Transfer & Trust Company			Where Listed	OTC-BB
Auditor	KPMG Peat Marwick, LLP			Symbol	UCOA
Market Maker	Sherwood Securities Corp.	Telephone	(800)435-1235	SIC Code	6330
Broker Dealer	Regular Stockbroker			Employees	15

United Screw and Bolt Corporation

24950 Great Northern Corp Ctr. • North Olmsted, OH 44070-5333 • Telephone (216)979-0909 • Fax (216)979-0599

Company Description

The Company manufactures and markets injection-molded plastic products, metal stampings, and other key precision components approximately 69% and 75% of which were provided to the automotive industry in 1995 and 1994, respectively. Sales to one customer accounted for 48% of revenue in both 1995 and 1994. There was a 3 for 1 stock split in 1993. All per share amounts have been adjusted accordingly.

	12/31/95	12/31/94	12/31/93	12/31/92
Per Share Information				
Stock Price	69.00	48.00	35.00	26.33
Earnings Per Share	7.53	4.19	5.73	4.28
Price / Earnings Ratio	9.16	11.46	6.11	6.15
Book Value Per Share	55.29	49.22	45.49	40.95
Price / Book Value %	124.80	97.52	76.94	64.30
Dividends Per Share	1.00	0.96	0.95	0.87
Annual Financial Data				
Operating Results (000's)				
Total Revenues	119,826.3	95,114.3	102,666.6	91,687.5
Costs & Expenses	-108,352.8	-88,262.2	-93,188.4	-84,983.4
Income Before Taxes and Other	11,473.5	6,852.1	9,478.2	6,704.1
Other Items	n.a.	n.a.	n.a.	193.6
Income Tax	-4,277.6	-2,557.4	-3,564.1	-2,477.3
Net Income	7,195.9	4,294.7	5,914.1	4,420.4
Cash Flow From Operations	3,571.5	6,971.8	6,722.9	9,739.6
Balance Sheet (000's)				
Cash & Equivalents	1,631.2	5,561.2	6,234.2	12,231.1
Total Current Assets	35,706.3	32,907.6	32,314.9	32,623.5
Fixed Assets, Net	29,028.0	24,436.2	25,326.7	24,800.8
Total Assets	68,059.1	59,989.2	59,905.6	58,384.5
Total Current Liabilities	12,727.3	7,518.8	8,269.6	10,550.2
Long-Term Debt	322.8	277.8	555.6	2,033.3
Stockholders' Equity	52,051.4	48,096.7	47,138.7	42,018.4
Performance & Financial Condition				
Return on Total Revenues %	6.01	4.52	5.76	4.61
Return on Avg Stockholders' Equity %	14.37	9.02	13.27	10.95
Return on Average Assets %	11.24	7.16	10.00	7.76
Current Ratio	2.81	4.38	3.91	3.09
Debt / Equity %	0.62	0.58	1.18	4.84

Compound Growth %'s	EPS %	20.72	Net Income %	17.64	Total Revenues %	9.33

Comments

The Company recovered nicely from the 1994 slow down in record growth and is well positioned to seek new opportunities. Available cash and marketable securities with virtually no debt makes the balance sheet favorable.

Officers	Position	Ownership Information	12/31/95
Rex A. Ogg	President, CEO	Number of Shares Outstanding	941,416
Frank M. Rasmussen	Secretary	Market Capitalization	$ 64,957,704
Randall V. Gaj	Treasurer	Frequency Of Dividends	Quarterly
Paul A. Funtash, Jr.	Controller, CFO	Number of Shareholders	Under 500

Other Information				
Transfer Agent	National City Bank, Cleveland, Ohio		Where Listed	OTC-BB
Auditor	KPMG Peat Marwick LLP		Symbol	USWB
Market Maker	Parker/Hunter Incorporated	Telephone (412)562-8025	SIC Code	3469
Broker Dealer	Standard Investment	Tel/Ext (888)783-4688 Jack	Employees	1100

Universal Metals & Machinery, Inc.

5906 Armour Drive • Houston, TX 77020-8104 • Telephone (713)675-6361 • Fax (713)675-7819

Company Description

The Company is in the business of wholesale distribution of industrial machinery and equipment. In 1993, the Company entered into a 50-50 joint venture with Dynamic Products, Inc. to acquire stainless steel inventory from a third party.

	06/30/95	06/30/94	06/30/93	06/30/92
Per Share Information				
Stock Price	2.25	2.19	2.12	2.25
Earnings Per Share	0.33	0.15	0.22	-0.52
Price / Earnings Ratio	6.82	14.60	9.64	n.a.
Book Value Per Share	9.37	9.05	8.90	8.68
Price / Book Value %	24.01	24.20	23.82	25.92
Dividends Per Share	n.a.	n.a.	n.a.	n.a.
Annual Financial Data				
Operating Results (000's)				
Total Revenues	11,520.8	8,351.4	7,692.6	7,647.9
Costs & Expenses	-11,215.9	-8,243.6	-7,522.9	-7,970.1
Income Before Taxes and Other	305.0	107.8	169.8	-322.3
Other Items	n.a.	n.a.	10.0	n.a.
Income Tax	-152.4	-38.2	-77.8	78.4
Net Income	152.6	69.5	102.0	-243.9
Cash Flow From Operations	-559.3	70.4	34.5	-197.2
Balance Sheet (000's)				
Cash & Equivalents	124.2	139.1	128.9	43.9
Total Current Assets	6,973.5	6,123.7	5,866.8	5,537.4
Fixed Assets, Net	871.8	805.5	866.7	900.5
Total Assets	8,423.6	7,698.7	6,952.8	6,655.6
Total Current Liabilities	3,565.9	2,995.4	2,754.4	2,052.5
Long-Term Debt	464.6	462.7	27.4	534.2
Stockholders' Equity	4,393.1	4,240.5	4,171.0	4,069.0
Performance & Financial Condition				
Return on Total Revenues %	1.32	0.83	1.33	-3.19
Return on Avg Stockholders' Equity %	3.53	1.65	2.48	-5.82
Return on Average Assets %	1.89	0.95	1.50	-3.59
Current Ratio	1.96	2.04	2.13	2.70
Debt / Equity %	10.58	10.91	0.66	13.13

Compound Growth %'s	EPS %	22.47	Net Income %	22.31	Total Revenues %	14.63

Comments

1995 results include a nonrecurring gain of $178,516 from the sale of a building. Pre-tax earnings from the joint venture were $142,876 and $82,682 for the years 1995 and 1994, respectively, which is substantially all Net Income before nonrecurring items.

Officers	Position	Ownership Information	06/30/95
Not Available		Number of Shares Outstanding	468,720
		Market Capitalization	$ 1,054,620
		Frequency Of Dividends	n.a.
		Number of Shareholders	Under 500

Other Information

Transfer Agent	Chemical Mellon Shareholder Services			Where Listed	OTC-PS
Auditor	Coopers & Lybrand LLP			Symbol	UVMM
Market Maker	Newby & Company	Telephone	(800)456-3992	SIC Code	5084
Broker Dealer	Regular Stockbroker			Employees	30

Utz Engineering, Inc.

101 Industrial East • Clifton, NJ 07012-1707 • Telephone (201)778-4560 • Fax (201)778-4239

Company Description

The Company offers products and services to the hybrid electronics and circuit board industries. The principal products include solder printing stencils, thick-film printing screens, metal masks, computer artwork generation, and custom photo-plotting. The Company was formed in 1971 in New Jersey. The name was changed from Donald Utz Engineering, Inc. It had its first public stock offering in 1985.

	03/31/95	03/31/94	03/31/93	03/31/92
Per Share Information				
Stock Price	2.00	2.00	2.00	1.50
Earnings Per Share	0.40	0.43	0.21	0.37
Price / Earnings Ratio	5.00	4.65	9.52	4.05
Book Value Per Share	2.65	2.41	2.11	1.53
Price / Book Value %	75.47	82.99	94.79	98.04
Dividends Per Share	0.15	0.10	n.a.	n.a.
Annual Financial Data				
Operating Results (000's)				
Total Revenues	6,143.2	5,403.7	4,712.1	4,639.8
Costs & Expenses	-5,447.3	-4,649.6	-4,335.4	-4,083.2
Income Before Taxes and Other	694.3	735.2	376.7	539.4
Other Items	n.a.	-9.0	n.a.	n.a.
Income Tax	-301.5	-307.3	-177.7	-187.4
Net Income	392.8	418.9	199.0	352.0
Cash Flow From Operations	601.5	449.5	316.2	605.0
Balance Sheet (000's)				
Cash & Equivalents	694.3	286.5	444.4	499.2
Total Current Assets	2,230.8	2,049.4	1,658.1	1,471.7
Fixed Assets, Net	504.0	524.5	696.5	762.7
Total Assets	2,771.5	2,605.1	2,396.0	2,277.1
Total Current Liabilities	157.0	202.6	246.2	294.5
Long-Term Debt	17.8	39.9	60.2	78.8
Stockholders' Equity	2,596.7	2,362.6	2,065.4	1,841.5
Performance & Financial Condition				
Return on Total Revenues %	6.39	7.75	4.22	7.59
Return on Avg Stockholders' Equity %	15.84	18.92	10.19	21.30
Return on Average Assets %	14.61	16.75	8.52	17.50
Current Ratio	14.21	10.12	6.73	5.00
Debt / Equity %	0.69	1.69	2.91	4.28

Compound Growth %'s	EPS %	2.63	Net Income %	3.72	Total Revenues %	9.81

Comments

Although small, the Company continues to demonstrate solid growth and is financially well positioned to benefit from the explosion of the new communication superhighway. Current assets include cash and marketable securities of $1.1 million as of March 31, 1995. 1996 results should now be obtainable from the Company as they were not available in time for this edition.

Officers	Position	Ownership Information	03/31/95
Donald L. Utz	Chairman, Treasurer	Number of Shares Outstanding	980,000
Frank Colonese	President, CEO	Market Capitalization	$ 1,960,000
Raynal W. Andrews, III	VP - Manufacturing	Frequency Of Dividends	n.a.
		Number of Shareholders	Under 500

Other Information

Transfer Agent	Jersey Transfer, Verona, NJ			Where Listed	OTC-BB
Auditor	Fallon & Fallon			Symbol	DONU
Market Maker	Pars Securities, Inc.	Telephone	(201)670-0700	SIC Code	3679
Broker Dealer	Regular Stockbroker			Employees	62

Valley Fair Corporation (The)

260 Bergen Turnpike • Little Ferry, NJ 07643 • Telephone (201)440-4000 • Fax (201)807-0043

Company Description

The Company operates two discount stores under the name "Valley Fair" in the state of New Jersey. The stores sell hard and soft goods as well as health and beauty aids and groceries. Through its wholly-owned subsidiary, L.F. Widmann, Inc., the Company operates 128 retail drug and health and beauty aid stores, primarily in Pennsylvania and also 11 other Mid-Atlantic and Mid-Western states.

	01/29/95	01/30/94	01/31/93
Per Share Information			
Stock Price	26.00	26.00	28.50
Earnings Per Share	0.07	1.97	1.71
Price / Earnings Ratio	371.43	13.20	16.67
Book Value Per Share	50.18	50.10	48.12
Price / Book Value %	51.81	51.90	59.23
Dividends Per Share	n.a.	n.a.	n.a.
Annual Financial Data			
Operating Results (000's)			
Total Revenues	75,562.6	74,530.5	71,759.0
Costs & Expenses	-75,552.6	-73,228.1	-70,672.5
Income Before Taxes and Other	10.0	1,302.5	1,086.5
Other Items	n.a.	n.a.	n.a.
Income Tax	16.0	-577.4	-455.0
Net Income	26.0	725.1	631.5
Cash Flow From Operations	184.4	-140.3	2,389.7
Balance Sheet (000's)			
Cash & Equivalents	3,652.6	4,977.5	4,432.2
Total Current Assets	30,908.3	31,637.7	28,873.8
Fixed Assets, Net	4,579.3	4,991.0	5,307.1
Total Assets	35,784.2	36,889.0	34,512.6
Total Current Liabilities	16,062.9	6,409.5	6,026.2
Long-Term Debt	701.9	11,098.9	9,766.8
Stockholders' Equity	18,469.0	18,447.4	17,728.1
Performance & Financial Condition			
Return on Total Revenues %	0.03	0.97	0.88
Return on Avg Stockholders' Equity %	0.14	4.01	n.a.
Return on Average Assets %	0.07	2.03	n.a.
Current Ratio	1.92	4.94	4.79
Debt / Equity %	3.80	60.17	55.09

Compound Growth %'s	EPS %	-79.77	Net Income %	-79.71	Total Revenues %	2.62

Comments

The Company operates on the basis of a 52/53 week year. As we go to print, the operating results for the year ended January 31, 1996, are not avaliable. For the thirty-nine weeks ended October 29, 1995, the Company had revenues of $51.5 million, and net income of $130,000 ($.35 per share), as compared to $49.2 million and a loss $76,000 (-$.21 per share) for the same period in 1994.

Officers	Position	Ownership Information	01/29/95
Edwin Lehr	President, CEO	Number of Shares Outstanding	368,053
Thomas R. Ketteler	Secretary	Market Capitalization	$ 9,569,378
Ross N. Alfieri	Treasurer, CFO	Frequency Of Dividends	n.a.
Saul S. Schottenstein	Vice President	Number of Shareholders	1,161
Philip J. Ganguzza	Vice President		

Other Information

Transfer Agent	Registrar & Transfer Company			Where Listed	OTC-BB
Auditor	Alpern, Rosenthal & Co.			Symbol	VALL
Market Maker	Macallaster Pitfield Mackay	Telephone	(212)422-9366	SIC Code	5411
Broker Dealer	Regular Stockbroker			Employees	690

Vasco Corp.

1919 S. Highland Avenue • Lombard, IL 60148 • Telephone (708)495-0755 • Fax (708)495-0279

Company Description

The Company manufactures and sells a variety of products related to security, including hand-held tokens, smart cards, and biometrics. Computer related products include extended end user authentication and virus protection for financial institutions, industry and government. The Company holds patents on a number of these products. The primary market for these products is Europe. The Company also offers consulting services in implementing new software applications in a variety of areas. These services are targeted towards domestic companies. The Company went public in 1985 and has since raised additional capital by issuing preferred stock.

	12/31/95	12/31/94	12/31/93	12/31/92
Per Share Information				
Stock Price	6.87	0.37	0.50	0.25
Earnings Per Share	-0.03	0.01	n.a.	0.02
Price / Earnings Ratio	n.a.	37.00	n.a.	12.50
Book Value Per Share	0.08	0.08	0.02	0.01
Price / Book Value %	8,587.50	462.50	2,500.00	2,500.00
Dividends Per Share	n.a.	n.a.	n.a.	n.a.
Annual Financial Data				
Operating Results (000's)				
Total Revenues	3,800.1	2,751.2	2,199.3	2,302.0
Costs & Expenses	-4,408.2	-2,526.5	-2,118.9	-1,802.8
Income Before Taxes and Other	-608.0	224.7	80.4	499.1
Other Items	n.a.	n.a.	n.a.	-16.1
Income Tax	251.0	-87.0	-30.0	-193.9
Net Income	-357.0	137.7	50.4	289.1
Cash Flow From Operations	58.7	-436.1	453.8	318.7
Balance Sheet (000's)				
Cash & Equivalents	744.6	38.1	209.2	2.8
Total Current Assets	2,213.8	1,429.8	917.5	913.9
Fixed Assets, Net	123.3	79.1	104.0	63.6
Total Assets	2,494.5	2,111.0	1,521.8	1,339.7
Total Current Liabilities	1,059.6	665.9	403.8	434.9
Long-Term Debt	7.3	60.0	745.9	512.3
Stockholders' Equity	1,416.9	1,363.7	340.0	242.8
Performance & Financial Condition				
Return on Total Revenues %	-9.40	5.00	2.29	12.56
Return on Avg Stockholders' Equity %	-25.68	16.16	17.28	243.52
Return on Average Assets %	-15.50	7.58	3.52	22.55
Current Ratio	2.09	2.15	2.27	2.10
Debt / Equity %	0.51	4.40	219.39	210.97

Compound Growth %'s	EPS % n.a.	Net Income % n.a.	Total Revenues % 18.19

Comments

Although technically a penny stock, this Company appears financially sound. There has been steady growth and market penetration while maintaining a reasonable balance sheet. However, there are a lot of shares outstanding. Our calculations were made assuming full conversion of the preferred shares.

Officers	Position	Ownership Information	12/31/95
John C. Haggard	President	Number of Shares Outstanding	17,638,539
Ken Hunt	CEO	Market Capitalization	$ 121,176,763
Michael B. Wiggen	Vice President, CFO	Frequency Of Dividends	n.a.
		Number of Shareholders	Under 500

Other Information

Transfer Agent	Fidelity Transfer Co., Salt Lake City		Where Listed	OTC-BB
Auditor	Price Waterhouse LLP		Symbol	VASC
Market Maker	Paragon Capital Corporation	Telephone (800)521-8877	SIC Code	3695
Broker Dealer	Regular Stockbroker		Employees	20

Versatech Industries, Inc.

210 Bartor Road • Toronto, Ontario M9M 2W6 Canada • Telephone (416)745-2424 • Fax (416)745-0436

Company Description

The Company is engaged in the engineering, systems integration and manufacturing of reusable, returnable and recyclable plastic packaging and plastic products. The automotive industry is a major focus of the Company. In addition, a division is in the business of selling, leasing and servicing materials handling equipment. Most of the business is conducted in Canada. The Company has a convertible preferred stock in addition to its common.

	12/31/94	12/31/93	12/31/92
Per Share Information			
Stock Price	3.00	1.00	n.a.
Earnings Per Share	0.15	-0.22	n.a.
Price / Earnings Ratio	20.00	n.a.	n.a.
Book Value Per Share	0.52	0.27	n.a.
Price / Book Value %	576.92	370.37	n.a.
Dividends Per Share	n.a.	n.a.	n.a.
Annual Financial Data			
Operating Results (000's)			
Total Revenues	7,348.4	3,252.7	1,718.8
Costs & Expenses	-7,024.9	-3,540.0	-1,420.1
Income Before Taxes and Other	323.5	-287.3	298.7
Other Items	n.a.	n.a.	n.a.
Income Tax	-95.0	n.a.	n.a.
Net Income	228.5	-287.3	298.7
Cash Flow From Operations	-10.9	-689.0	39.9
Balance Sheet (000's)			
Cash & Equivalents	n.a.	n.a.	n.a.
Total Current Assets	2,130.3	1,643.9	962.2
Fixed Assets, Net	851.5	834.1	462.1
Total Assets	2,981.8	2,508.0	1,442.0
Total Current Liabilities	1,990.7	1,738.7	1,015.9
Long-Term Debt	157.1	159.9	30.4
Stockholders' Equity	809.7	344.4	40.1
Performance & Financial Condition			
Return on Total Revenues %	n.a.	-8.83	n.a.
Return on Avg Stockholders' Equity %	39.60	-149.43	n.a.
Return on Average Assets %	8.33	-14.55	n.a.
Current Ratio	1.07	0.95	n.a.
Debt / Equity %	19.40	46.42	n.a.

Compound Growth %'s	EPS % n.a.	Net Income % -12.53	Total Revenues % 106.77

Comments

All amounts reported are in U.S. dollars. The Company is active in acquiring and merging related businesses. For purposes of per share calculations, we assumed a conversion of the preferred stock. The 1995 reports will not be available until June, 1996, but are important to review in light of the acquisitions.

Officers	Position	Ownership Information	12/31/94
Jack S. Lee	President	Number of Shares Outstanding	1,557,546
Michael E. Matson	VP - Finance	Market Capitalization	$ 4,672,638
J. Rob Lee	Vice President	Frequency Of Dividends	n.a.
Robert Syme	VP - Research	Number of Shareholders	Under 500
Frank Principe	VP - Sales		

Other Information

Transfer Agent	Interwest Transfer Co., Inc.		Where Listed	OTC-BB
Auditor	KPMG Peat Marwick Thorne		Symbol	VERS
Market Maker	Frankel (WM.V.) & Co., Inc.	Telephone (800)631-3091	SIC Code	3080
Broker Dealer	Regular Stockbroker		Employees	n.a.

Vicon Fiber Optics Corp.

90 Secor Lane • Pelham Manor, NY 10803 • Telephone (914)738-5006 • Fax (914)738-6920

Company Description

The Company manufactures fiber optic illuminating systems and components for use in conjunction with dental equipment and instruments utilizing fiber optic elements. The Company believes that it is one of the leading domestic manufacturers of fiber optic components and systems for use in the dental industry. The Company was incorporated in Delaware in 1969.

	12/31/95	12/31/94	12/31/93	12/31/92
Per Share Information				
Stock Price	0.94	0.19	0.30	0.32
Earnings Per Share	0.06	0.03	0.03	0.22
Price / Earnings Ratio	15.67	6.33	10.00	1.45
Book Value Per Share	0.26	0.19	0.16	0.03
Price / Book Value %	361.54	100.00	187.50	1,066.70
Dividends Per Share	n.a.	n.a.	n.a.	n.a.
Annual Financial Data				
Operating Results (000's)				
Total Revenues	2,825.9	1,998.0	1,940.9	1,866.2
Costs & Expenses	-2,151.1	-1,528.7	-1,498.8	-1,445.8
Income Before Taxes and Other	674.8	469.4	442.1	420.4
Other Items	126.7	n.a.	n.a.	1,006.6
Income Tax	-236.9	-195.2	-197.0	-187.6
Net Income	564.6	274.1	245.1	1,239.5
Cash Flow From Operations	274.1	290.0	515.9	281.1
Balance Sheet (000's)				
Cash & Equivalents	858.7	1,020.9	926.7	414.1
Total Current Assets	2,169.3	1,819.1	1,523.0	1,102.4
Fixed Assets, Net	95.8	103.2	72.2	92.8
Total Assets	2,836.7	2,699.1	2,548.4	1,545.0
Total Current Liabilities	257.4	303.6	397.6	309.4
Long-Term Debt	424.2	805.1	834.5	874.1
Stockholders' Equity	2,155.1	1,590.4	1,316.3	279.1
Performance & Financial Condition				
Return on Total Revenues %	19.98	13.72	12.63	66.42
Return on Avg Stockholders' Equity %	30.15	18.86	30.72	n.a.
Return on Average Assets %	20.40	10.45	11.97	93.06
Current Ratio	8.43	5.99	3.83	3.56
Debt / Equity %	19.68	50.62	63.40	313.17

Compound Growth %'s	EPS %	-35.15	Net Income %	-23.06	Total Revenues %	14.83

Comments

The Company entered into a joint venture agreement with Anshon Fiber Optic Products, Ltd., a China corporation, in 1992. Anshon manufactures certain of the Company's products. During the year ended December 31, 1995, three customers accounted for 65% of the Company's sales. As of December 31, 1995, officers and directors, as a group, owned 14.6% of the Company's outstanding common stock.

Officers	Position	Ownership Information	12/31/95
Leonard Scrivo	President, CEO	Number of Shares Outstanding	8,340,636
Les Wasser	Secretary, Controller	Market Capitalization	$ 7,840,198
		Frequency Of Dividends	n.a.
		Number of Shareholders	1,038

Other Information

Transfer Agent	Continental Stock Transfer & Trust Co.			Where Listed	OTC-BB
Auditor	Sheft Kahn & Company LLP			Symbol	VFOX
Market Maker	Meyerson & Co.	Telephone	(800)333-3113	SIC Code	3845
Broker Dealer	Regular Stockbroker			Employees	25

Virginia Hot Springs, Incorporated

c/o The Homestead • Hot Springs, VA 24445 • Telephone (540)839-5500 • Fax (540)839-7656

Company Description

The Company was owner and operator of The Homestead, a famous resort in Hot Springs, Virginia. Because of operational difficulties, it transferred the resort to a new management company operated and financed by Club Corporation International (ClubCorp.). The Company owns an 80% interest in the new venture and various parcels of land. The directors, as a group, own 38.4% of the Company. It is the stated intention of management to have an orderly liquidation of the Company over the next ten years or so.

	12/31/95	12/31/94
Per Share Information		
Stock Price	9.50	15.00
Earnings Per Share	0.59	-0.02
Price / Earnings Ratio	16.10	n.a.
Book Value Per Share	3.55	3.08
Price / Book Value %	267.61	487.01
Dividends Per Share	n.a.	n.a.
Annual Financial Data		
Operating Results (000's)		
Total Revenues	428.9	271.5
Costs & Expenses	-155.9	-281.2
Income Before Taxes and Other	272.9	-12.9
Other Items	n.a.	n.a.
Income Tax	n.a.	n.a.
Net Income	272.9	-12.9
Cash Flow From Operations	n.a.	n.a.
Balance Sheet (000's)		
Cash & Equivalents	285.1	11.3
Total Current Assets	285.1	11.3
Fixed Assets, Net	1,752.5	1,753.3
Total Assets	2,088.8	1,815.9
Total Current Liabilities	n.a.	n.a.
Long-Term Debt	n.a.	n.a.
Stockholders' Equity	2,078.8	1,805.9
Performance & Financial Condition		
Return on Total Revenues %	63.62	-4.75
Return on Avg Stockholders' Equity %	14.05	n.a.
Return on Average Assets %	13.98	n.a.
Current Ratio	n.a.	n.a.
Debt / Equity %	n.a.	n.a.

Compound Growth %'s	EPS % n.a.	Net Income % n.a.	Total Revenues % 57.98

Comments

1994 results are for 9 months. Financial reports were compiled but not audited. The agreement with ClubCorp. calls for the mandatory buyout of the Company's interest in The Homestead in 1999. A formula has been established in setting the price and is generally based on a multiple of operating cash flow in the fifth year of the agreement with certain additional provisions should the calculated amount be less than $15 million. Compounded revenue growth is misleading because only two years were available for the calculation.

Officers	Position	Ownership Information	12/31/95
Daniel H. H. Ingalls	President	Number of Shares Outstanding	585,390
Pasco H.Merrill	Secretary	Market Capitalization	$ 5,561,205
Abbie I. Calder	Director	Frequency Of Dividends	n.a.
Hebert E. Jones	Director	Number of Shareholders	Under 500
Truman T. Semans	Director		

Other Information

Transfer Agent	Company Office			Where Listed	OTC-BB
Auditor	Pannell Kerr Forster PC			Symbol	VHSI
Market Maker	Scott & Stringfellow, Inc.	Telephone	(800)446-7074	SIC Code	6790
Broker Dealer	Regular Stockbroker			Employees	n.a.

Viskon-Aire Corporation

410 Winfield Avenue • Salisbury, MD 21801 • Telephone (410)543-8800 • Fax (410)860-5894

Company Description

The Company manufactures and sells about a dozen different lines of air filters. Distribution is throughout the United States. The Company was formed in 1979 and was distributed to shareholders of Drico Industrial Corp. in their liquidation in 1983. The Company has been buying back its shares at about $9 per share which is higher than the published prices of about $5 per share.

	12/31/95	12/31/94	12/31/93	12/31/92
Per Share Information				
Stock Price	9.00	9.00	9.00	9.00
Earnings Per Share	-0.84	-0.59	0.77	0.28
Price / Earnings Ratio	n.a.	n.a.	11.69	32.14
Book Value Per Share	12.13	12.97	12.38	13.16
Price / Book Value %	74.20	69.39	72.70	68.39
Dividends Per Share	n.a.	n.a.	n.a.	n.a.
Annual Financial Data				
Operating Results (000's)				
Total Revenues	6,884.3	7,099.1	6,785.5	6,006.3
Costs & Expenses	-7,101.6	-6,955.2	-6,592.1	-5,713.5
Income Before Taxes and Other	-217.3	143.9	193.4	292.8
Other Items	n.a.	n.a.	n.a.	n.a.
Income Tax	87.3	-52.6	-64.2	-108.9
Net Income	-129.9	91.3	129.2	183.9
Cash Flow From Operations	88.2	234.3	45.6	269.6
Balance Sheet (000's)				
Cash & Equivalents	121.6	292.4	159.8	475.0
Total Current Assets	2,052.8	2,066.6	1,974.7	2,135.1
Fixed Assets, Net	1,363.8	1,140.2	1,159.8	1,164.4
Total Assets	3,511.3	3,298.0	3,225.0	3,374.8
Total Current Liabilities	811.6	390.8	390.8	396.2
Long-Term Debt	819.2	896.8	915.1	938.9
Stockholders' Equity	1,880.5	2,010.4	1,919.1	2,039.7
Performance & Financial Condition				
Return on Total Revenues %	-1.89	1.29	1.90	3.06
Return on Avg Stockholders' Equity %	-6.68	4.65	6.53	9.20
Return on Average Assets %	-3.82	2.80	3.92	5.66
Current Ratio	2.53	5.29	5.05	5.39
Debt / Equity %	43.57	44.61	47.68	46.03

Compound Growth %'s	EPS % n.a.	Net Income % n.a.	Total Revenues %	4.65

Comments

Sales in 1985 were $3,331,756, which would compute to a 7.75% compounded revenue growth over the last 10 years. The Company uses the LIFO method in accounting for inventory. The LIFO reserve at December 31, 1995, was $219,119.

Officers	Position	Ownership Information	12/31/95
Henry Zenzie	President	Number of Shares Outstanding	154,987
Stephen M. Mulinos	Exec VP, Treasurer	Market Capitalization	$ 1,394,883
Mary Rowin	Secretary	Frequency Of Dividends	n.a.
George C. Alpaugh	Other	Number of Shareholders	Under 500

Other Information

Transfer Agent	American Stock Transfer & Trust Company			Where Listed	OTC-BB
Auditor	Twilley, Rommel & Moore, P.A.			Symbol	VIAI
Market Maker	Tweedy Browne Company L.P.	Telephone	(212)916-0606	SIC Code	3990
Broker Dealer	Regular Stockbroker			Employees	50

Wailuku Agribusiness Co., Inc.

P.O. Box 520 • Wailuku, HI 96793 • Telephone (808)244-9570 • Fax (808)242-7068

Company Description

The Company grows and sells macadamia nuts and owns agricultural properties on the island of Maui, Hawaii. It is also a 36.83% general partner in The Hawaii Tropical Plantation, a tourist operation for people to visit the different fields of tropical fruits, plants and trees with a final stop at the retail store. C. Brewer and Company, Limited, a subsidiary of Buyco, Inc., owns an 87.7% interest in the Company. The Company has been in existence since 1875.

	12/25/94	12/26/93	12/27/92
Per Share Information			
Stock Price	515.00	450.00	389.00
Earnings Per Share	35.52	2.79	38.57
Price / Earnings Ratio	14.50	161.29	10.09
Book Value Per Share	431.15	398.79	365.29
Price / Book Value %	119.45	112.84	106.49
Dividends Per Share	5.00	3.00	3.00
Annual Financial Data			
Operating Results (000's)			
Total Revenues	11,293.5	8,498.8	11,385.3
Costs & Expenses	-3,258.8	-3,152.2	-3,866.5
Income Before Taxes and Other	8,034.7	2,269.3	7,518.8
Other Items	n.a.	n.a.	n.a.
Income Tax	-2,706.7	-1,794.5	-1,733.6
Net Income	5,328.0	474.7	5,785.3
Cash Flow From Operations	5,029.1	2,600.9	11,371.9
Balance Sheet (000's)			
Cash & Equivalents	0.7	0.7	0.7
Total Current Assets	60,225.1	56,653.6	54,493.1
Fixed Assets, Net	13,205.2	13,933.8	13,116.7
Total Assets	74,564.2	71,605.1	68,623.5
Total Current Liabilities	4,337.0	5,042.1	5,953.3
Long-Term Debt	n.a.	n.a.	n.a.
Stockholders' Equity	64,672.8	59,818.0	54,793.2
Performance & Financial Condition			
Return on Total Revenues %	47.18	5.59	50.81
Return on Avg Stockholders' Equity %	8.56	0.83	11.10
Return on Average Assets %	7.29	0.68	8.80
Current Ratio	13.89	11.24	9.15
Debt / Equity %	n.a.	n.a.	n.a.

Compound Growth %'s	EPS %	-4.04	Net Income %	-4.03	Total Revenues %	-0.40

Comments

1993 results reflect the cost of discontinuing pineapple operations at $3,077,397, or $20.52 per share. Financial results are not sent to the shareholders until after the shareholders meeting in November or December.

Officers	Position	Ownership Information	12/25/94
Avery B. Chumbley	President	Number of Shares Outstanding	150,000
Kathleen F. Oshiro	Secretary	Market Capitalization	$ 77,250,000
Brad S. Baker	Treasurer	Frequency Of Dividends	Quarterly
James S. Andrasick	Vice President	Number of Shareholders	Under 500
Kent T. Lucien	Vice President		

Other Information

					Where Listed	OTC-PS
Transfer Agent	C. Brewer and Co., Ltd., Honolulu, HI				Symbol	WKUA
Auditor	Coopers and Lybrand LLP				SIC Code	0173
Market Maker	Abel-Behnke Corp.	Telephone	(808)536-2341		Employees	35
Broker Dealer	Standard Investment	Tel/Ext	(888)783-4688	Jack		

Walker International Industries, Inc.

4 Ken-Anthony Pl.,S.Lake Blvd. • Mahopac, NY 10541 • Telephone (999)999-9999

Company Description

The Company is engaged in various aspects of the photography business including film processing and maintaining a portrait studio. Approximately 25% of sales are generated through the portrait studio which is operated under a licensing agreement with a national retailer.

	11/30/95	11/30/94	11/30/93
Per Share Information			
Stock Price	2.20	1.62	0.87
Earnings Per Share	0.23	0.05	-0.34
Price / Earnings Ratio	9.57	32.40	n.a.
Book Value Per Share	3.69	3.39	3.16
Price / Book Value %	59.62	47.79	27.53
Dividends Per Share	n.a.	n.a.	n.a.
Annual Financial Data			
Operating Results (000's)			
Total Revenues	1,550.1	1,400.4	1,506.7
Costs & Expenses	-1,489.4	-1,383.6	-1,628.0
Income Before Taxes and Other	60.7	16.7	-121.2
Other Items	10.3	n.a.	n.a.
Income Tax	-2.0	n.a.	n.a.
Net Income	69.0	16.7	-121.2
Cash Flow From Operations	96.4	71.9	n.a.
Balance Sheet (000's)			
Cash & Equivalents	332.5	n.a.	n.a.
Total Current Assets	1,015.5	1,116.0	1,140.1
Fixed Assets, Net	203.8	151.5	167.7
Total Assets	1,320.6	1,267.5	1,307.9
Total Current Liabilities	220.4	135.3	182.9
Long-Term Debt	n.a.	n.a.	n.a.
Stockholders' Equity	1,100.3	1,132.3	1,125.0
Performance & Financial Condition			
Return on Total Revenues %	4.45	1.19	n.a.
Return on Avg Stockholders' Equity %	6.18	1.48	n.a.
Return on Average Assets %	5.33	1.30	n.a.
Current Ratio	4.61	n.a.	n.a.
Debt / Equity %	n.a.	n.a.	n.a.

Compound Growth %'s	EPS %	360.00	Net Income %	312.05	Total Revenues %	1.43

Comments

The Company is highly liquid with total cash and investments of $1.02 million, or $3.42 per share. This may explain why the Company has been buying back shares over recent years at prices below book value. However, management maintains that it is continuing to investigate other potentially profitable opportunities. Compound growth rates are probably not meaningful because they are computed on only two years of data.

Officers	Position	Ownership Information	11/30/95
Peter Walker	Chairman, President	Number of Shares Outstanding	298,081
Richard Norris	Secretary, Treasurer	Market Capitalization	$ 655,778
Ronald Whitworth	General Manager	Frequency Of Dividends	n.a.
Mona Schwartz	General Manager	Number of Shareholders	n.a.
Charles Snow	Director		

Other Information				
Transfer Agent	American Stock Transfer & Trust Company		Where Listed	OTC-BB
Auditor	Kofler, Levenstein, Romanotto		Symbol	WINT
Market Maker	M.H. Meyerson & Co., Inc.	Telephone (800)333-3113	SIC Code	7220
Broker Dealer	Regular Stockbroker		Employees	n.a.

Warwick Valley Telephone Co.

49 Main Street • Warwick, NY 10990 • Telephone (201)764-8181 • Fax (914)386-3299

Company Description

The Company is an independent telephone company providing telephone service to customers in the towns of Warwick and Goshen, New York and the townships of Vernon and West Milford, New Jersey. The Company provides local telephone service to residential and business customers, access and billing and collection services to interexchange carriers and the sale and leasing of telecommunications equipment. The Company was established in 1907.

	12/31/95	12/31/94	12/31/93	12/31/92
Per Share Information				
Stock Price	48.50	47.50	40.25	32.00
Earnings Per Share	3.45	2.82	2.66	2.27
Price / Earnings Ratio	14.06	16.84	15.13	14.10
Book Value Per Share	23.01	21.19	19.94	18.83
Price / Book Value %	210.78	224.16	201.86	169.94
Dividends Per Share	1.74	1.68	1.64	1.60
Annual Financial Data				
Operating Results (000's)				
Total Revenues	13,561.2	12,579.2	11,393.2	10,524.6
Costs & Expenses	-9,862.6	-9,494.2	-8,409.4	-7,730.0
Income Before Taxes and Other	2,737.8	2,062.0	2,018.9	1,927.5
Other Items	n.a.	n.a.	n.a.	n.a.
Income Tax	-584.5	-312.5	-376.2	-525.7
Net Income	2,153.4	1,749.5	1,642.6	1,401.8
Cash Flow From Operations	3,264.3	2,818.8	2,726.7	2,471.9
Balance Sheet (000's)				
Cash & Equivalents	482.0	422.0	1,529.5	753.4
Total Current Assets	5,975.5	4,690.0	5,324.6	4,330.8
Fixed Assets, Net	21,940.4	21,983.4	19,641.8	17,868.9
Total Assets	29,418.0	27,657.6	25,792.7	23,010.8
Total Current Liabilities	4,720.2	3,801.7	2,663.4	4,373.4
Long-Term Debt	7,000.0	7,370.0	7,490.0	3,610.0
Stockholders' Equity	14,744.2	13,499.2	12,636.3	11,859.8
Performance & Financial Condition				
Return on Total Revenues %	15.88	13.91	14.42	13.32
Return on Avg Stockholders' Equity %	15.25	13.39	13.41	12.03
Return on Average Assets %	7.55	6.55	6.73	6.29
Current Ratio	1.27	1.23	2.00	0.99
Debt / Equity %	47.48	54.60	59.27	30.44

Compound Growth %'s	EPS % 14.97	Net Income % 15.38	Total Revenues % 8.82

Comments

Revenues during the year ended December 31, 1995, consisted of local network service 20%, network access and long distance service 56%, and miscellaneous 24%. The Company has developed new services during the past two years, including an internet online service for which they have 1,600 customers. Revenue, net income, dividends and book value are all at new highs.

Officers	Position	Ownership Information	12/31/95
Howard Conklin, Jr.	Chairman	Number of Shares Outstanding	618,957
Fred M. Knipp	President, CEO	Market Capitalization	$ 30,019,415
Philip P. Demarest	Secretary, Treasurer	Frequency Of Dividends	Quarterly
Herbert Gareiss, Jr.	Vice President	Number of Shareholders	607
Henry L. Nielsen, Jr.	Other		

Other Information

Transfer Agent	Company Office		Where Listed	OTC-BB
Auditor	Bush & Germain, P.C.		Symbol	WWVY
Market Maker	Legg Mason Wood Walker, Inc.	Telephone (212)428-4949	SIC Code	4813
Broker Dealer	Regular Stockbroker		Employees	92

Washington Life Insurance Company of America

214 Jefferson Street • Lafayette, LA 70502-3468 • Telephone (318)233-0230 • Fax (318)237-2652

Company Description

The Company provides a variety of life insurance products. The Company had a 3 for 2 split of its shares in 1993. All per share amounts have been adjusted accordingly. In 1995, there was a purchase offer from a limited partnership group for up to 934,226 shares at $2.75 per share.

	12/31/95	12/31/94	12/31/93	12/31/92
Per Share Information				
Stock Price	2.75	2.75	1.75	1.91
Earnings Per Share	0.05	0.20	-0.26	0.01
Price / Earnings Ratio	55.00	13.75	n.a.	191.00
Book Value Per Share	2.29	2.04	2.04	2.30
Price / Book Value %	120.09	134.80	85.78	83.04
Dividends Per Share	n.a.	n.a.	n.a.	0.08
Annual Financial Data				
Operating Results (000's)				
Total Revenues	5,039.9	5,225.3	5,903.7	7,279.3
Costs & Expenses	-4,901.3	-4,760.2	-6,208.7	-7,098.9
Income Before Taxes and Other	77.2	303.2	-391.4	3.8
Other Items	n.a.	n.a.	n.a.	n.a.
Income Tax	-9.2	n.a.	n.a.	n.a.
Net Income	68.0	303.2	-391.4	3.8
Cash Flow From Operations	n.a.	n.a.	n.a.	n.a.
Balance Sheet (000's)				
Cash & Equivalents	937.7	515.5	871.1	1,723.1
Total Current Assets	937.7	515.5	871.1	1,723.1
Fixed Assets, Net	3,117.9	3,191.7	3,278.2	3,382.1
Total Assets	37,169.6	37,423.8	37,533.6	39,555.7
Total Current Liabilities	89.5	173.9	251.2	299.1
Long-Term Debt	n.a.	n.a.	n.a.	n.a.
Stockholders' Equity	3,429.6	3,361.6	3,058.4	3,449.8
Performance & Financial Condition				
Return on Total Revenues %	1.35	5.80	-6.63	0.05
Return on Avg Stockholders' Equity %	2.00	9.45	-12.03	0.13
Return on Average Assets %	0.18	0.81	-1.02	0.01
Current Ratio	10.48	2.97	3.47	5.76
Debt / Equity %	n.a.	n.a.	n.a.	n.a.

Compound Growth %'s	EPS %	7.00	Net Income %	161.73	Total Revenues %	-11.53

Comments

The financial statements are prepared using regulatory rules and probably are not in accordance with GAAP. We have also used the "net change in capital and surplus" as the bottom line results, which reflects changes in certain reserves and the unrealized value of capital gains and losses. Therefore, compounded earnings and earnings per share amounts are misleading as overall trends.

Officers	Position	Ownership Information	12/31/95
Not Available		Number of Shares Outstanding	1,500,000
		Market Capitalization	$ 4,125,000
		Frequency Of Dividends	n.a.
		Number of Shareholders	Under 500

Other Information

Transfer Agent	Company Office		Where Listed	OTC-BB
Auditor	Not indicated		Symbol	WLIA
Market Maker	Morgan Keegan & Company, Inc.	Telephone (800)289-5019	SIC Code	6310
Broker Dealer	Regular Stockbroker		Employees	14

Waste Recovery, Inc.

309 S. Pearl Expressway • Dallas, TX 75201 • Telephone (214)741-3865 • Fax (214)741-8965

Company Description

The Company is in the tire recovery business, specializing in the processing of scrap tires into a refined fuel supplement referred to as tire-derived fuel. Income is generated from the sale of this fuel and fees charged for the disposal of tires. More than 12 million tires were received for processing at the Company's four plants in Oregon, Texas, Georgia and Pennsylvania. Through its subsidiary Domino Salvage and a partnership interest, it also has operations in Illinois and the Northeast. Domino was acquired in 1995 for approximately $900,000. The Company was organized in Texas in 1982.

	12/31/95	12/31/94	12/31/93	12/31/92
Per Share Information				
Stock Price	1.27	1.27	1.72	0.68
Earnings Per Share	-0.12	0.06	-0.08	0.02
Price / Earnings Ratio	n.a.	21.17	n.a.	34.00
Book Value Per Share	0.01	-0.22	-0.72	-0.70
Price / Book Value %	n.a.	n.a.	n.a.	n.a.
Dividends Per Share	n.a.	n.a.	n.a.	n.a.
Annual Financial Data				
Operating Results (000's)				
Total Revenues	14,580.8	12,622.6	8,822.8	8,329.9
Costs & Expenses	-15,185.0	-12,253.1	-8,930.8	-7,722.1
Income Before Taxes and Other	-926.8	163.0	-108.0	607.8
Other Items	n.a.	447.5	-87.6	-260.8
Income Tax	n.a.	n.a.	n.a.	-100.0
Net Income	-926.8	610.6	-195.6	247.0
Cash Flow From Operations	487.6	400.2	907.8	818.8
Balance Sheet (000's)				
Cash & Equivalents	726.6	261.1	140.0	79.1
Total Current Assets	3,415.3	4,422.1	1,842.6	1,276.1
Fixed Assets, Net	4,859.4	3,339.0	3,264.4	3,389.7
Total Assets	10,732.4	8,745.1	5,876.1	5,394.8
Total Current Liabilities	3,177.8	3,483.7	5,038.9	4,617.5
Long-Term Debt	4,409.2	4,002.6	359.2	122.4
Stockholders' Equity	2,899.0	1,258.8	-362.9	-225.0
Performance & Financial Condition				
Return on Total Revenues %	-6.36	4.84	-2.22	2.97
Return on Avg Stockholders' Equity %	-44.58	136.30	66.54	-69.71
Return on Average Assets %	-9.52	8.35	-3.47	4.64
Current Ratio	1.07	1.27	0.37	0.28
Debt / Equity %	152.10	317.96	n.a.	n.a.

Compound Growth %'s	EPS % n.a.	Net Income % n.a.	Total Revenues % 20.52

Comments

Included in stockholder's equity is 203,580 shares of cumulative preferred stock with a total liquidation preference of $2.8 million. Undeclared cumulative preferred stock dividends of $143,000 per year are used in determining earnings (loss) per share. In conjunction with a rights offering during 1995, the Company raised approximately $2.2 millon and issued 3,238,857 shares of its common stock. In April, 1996, the Company announced that it had been awarded a $2 million contract to clean up an abandoned tire pile in Washington State.

Officers	Position	Ownership Information	12/31/95
Allan Shivers, Jr.	Chairman	Number of Shares Outstanding	10,726,410
Thomas L. Earnshaw	President, CEO	Market Capitalization	$ 13,622,541
Robert L. Thelen	Exec VP	Frequency Of Dividends	n.a.
Sharon K. Price	VP - Finance, CFO	Number of Shareholders	444
Andrew J. Sabia	Vice President		

Other Information				
Transfer Agent	Securities Transfer Corporation		Where Listed	OTC-BB
Auditor	Price Waterhouse LLP		Symbol	WRII
Market Maker	Paragon Capital Corporation	Telephone (800)521-8877	SIC Code	4953
Broker Dealer	Regular Stockbroker		Employees	200

Watchdog Patrols, Inc.

99 Powerhouse Road • Roslyn Heights, NY 11577-2082 • Telephone (516)484-0850 • Fax (516)484-2819

Company Description

The Company provides a variety of security services in the State of New York including uniformed guards, trained guard dogs, motorized patrol and inspection, electronic protective systems and confidential security analyses.

	12/31/95	12/31/94	12/31/93	12/31/92
Per Share Information				
Stock Price	1.31	1.56	1.87	1.50
Earnings Per Share	0.08	0.10	0.27	0.19
Price / Earnings Ratio	16.38	15.60	6.93	7.89
Book Value Per Share	2.00	1.98	1.93	1.71
Price / Book Value %	65.50	78.79	96.89	87.72
Dividends Per Share	0.06	0.05	0.05	0.05
Annual Financial Data				
Operating Results (000's)				
Total Revenues	7,301.2	7,815.7	7,919.6	6,023.4
Costs & Expenses	-7,105.6	-7,495.7	-7,119.6	-5,463.1
Income Before Taxes and Other	195.5	284.9	800.0	560.3
Other Items	n.a.	n.a.	n.a.	n.a.
Income Tax	-58.7	-118.7	-349.4	-251.2
Net Income	136.9	166.3	450.6	309.1
Cash Flow From Operations	41.9	15.4	295.9	-12.9
Balance Sheet (000's)				
Cash & Equivalents	1,711.6	1,816.4	1,906.7	1,720.4
Total Current Assets	3,575.5	3,492.0	3,569.3	3,001.8
Fixed Assets, Net	64.9	50.6	57.6	64.6
Total Assets	3,705.2	3,546.6	3,628.4	3,067.5
Total Current Liabilities	355.5	233.3	397.6	203.7
Long-Term Debt	n.a.	n.a.	n.a.	n.a.
Stockholders' Equity	3,349.7	3,313.3	3,230.7	2,863.8
Performance & Financial Condition				
Return on Total Revenues %	1.87	2.13	5.69	5.13
Return on Avg Stockholders' Equity %	4.11	5.08	14.79	11.23
Return on Average Assets %	3.77	4.63	13.46	10.30
Current Ratio	10.06	14.97	8.98	14.74
Debt / Equity %	n.a.	n.a.	n.a.	n.a.

Compound Growth %'s	EPS %	-25.05	Net Income %	-23.78	Total Revenues %	6.62

Comments

The Company has not shown significant growth, and maybe none after an inflation adjustment. Half of current assets, or $1.7 million, is cash. Management does not report on any specific plans other than to maintain control over costs, keep services competitive, and service customers more effectively. No details are provided in the annual shareholder report.

Officers	Position	Ownership Information	12/31/95
Phyllis Berger	Chairman	Number of Shares Outstanding	1,674,000
Earl Smith	President	Market Capitalization	$ 2,192,940
George Jaffee	Other	Frequency Of Dividends	Annual
		Number of Shareholders	Under 500

Other Information

Transfer Agent	American Stock Transfer & Trust Company		Where Listed	OTC-BB
Auditor	George S. Goldberg & Co.		Symbol	WDGT
Market Maker	Frankel (WM.V.) & Co., Inc.	Telephone (800)631-3091	SIC Code	7382
Broker Dealer	Regular Stockbroker		Employees	400

Watson Industries Inc.

P.O. Box 11250 • Pittsburgh, PA 15238 • Telephone (412)362-8300 • Fax (412)274-5770

Company Description

The Company manufactures and sells paint and other coatings for industrial use. The container and closure industry is the primary market for these products. The Company has recently announced that it will buy back its shares for $80 per share, which was slightly higher than the trading level before the announcement.

	11/30/95	11/30/94	11/30/93
Per Share Information			
Stock Price	80.00	n.a.	58.00
Earnings Per Share	9.10	n.a.	14.80
Price / Earnings Ratio	8.79	n.a.	3.92
Book Value Per Share	141.40	n.a.	96.27
Price / Book Value %	56.58	n.a.	60.25
Dividends Per Share	42.00	n.a.	3.75
Annual Financial Data			
Operating Results (000's)			
Total Revenues	6,404.0	n.a.	5,328.5
Costs & Expenses	-4,703.4	n.a.	-3,023.6
Income Before Taxes and Other	1,420.0	n.a.	2,304.8
Other Items	n.a.	n.a.	n.a.
Income Tax	-501.5	n.a.	-807.2
Net Income	918.5	n.a.	1,497.6
Cash Flow From Operations	2,386.8	n.a.	2,177.7
Balance Sheet (000's)			
Cash & Equivalents	220.9	n.a.	670.7
Total Current Assets	10,417.2	n.a.	9,324.0
Fixed Assets, Net	3,756.4	n.a.	3,721.9
Total Assets	15,953.8	n.a.	14,618.5
Total Current Liabilities	1,386.3	n.a.	1,708.2
Long-Term Debt	30.5	n.a.	49.8
Stockholders' Equity	14,314.5	n.a.	12,645.2
Performance & Financial Condition			
Return on Total Revenues %	14.34	n.a.	28.11
Return on Avg Stockholders' Equity %	n.a.	n.a.	n.a.
Return on Average Assets %	n.a.	n.a.	n.a.
Current Ratio	7.51	n.a.	5.46
Debt / Equity %	0.21	n.a.	0.39

Compound Growth %'s	EPS % n.a.	Net Income % n.a.	Total Revenues % n.a.

Comments

The Company does not report total sales, but instead reports gross profit on sales (sales less cost of goods sold). Because of this, it receives a qualified opinion. Only 1995 and 1993 results were available. To provide you with a slighly longer term view, 1991, 1987 and 1973 gross profit on sales were $4.2 million, $4.4 million and $1.8 million, respectively.

Officers	Position	Ownership Information	11/30/95
H. Knox Watson	President	Number of Shares Outstanding	99,177
Michael A. Caruso, Jr.	Exec VP	Market Capitalization	$ 7,934,160
Joseph S. Wilkoski	Secretary, Treasurer	Frequency Of Dividends	Quarterly
James E. Lore	Vice President	Number of Shareholders	Under 500
Gary E. Silke	Vice President		

Other Information						
Transfer Agent	Company Office			Where Listed	OTC-PS	
Auditor	S.R.Snodgrass, A.C.			Symbol	n.a.	
Market Maker	Legg Mason Wood Walker, Inc.	Telephone	(212)428-4949	SIC Code	2851	
Broker Dealer	Standard Investment	Tel/Ext	(888)783-4688	Jack	Employees	75

Watson Land Company

22010 South Wilmington Avenue • Carson, CA 90745 • Telephone (310)952-6400 • Fax (310)522-8788

Company Description

The Company is engaged in the construction and leasing of industrial commercial properties in the southern California area. As a real estate investment trust (REIT) it is exempt from federal tax. The Company bought back 106,000 shares of its stock in 1995 for $26 per share.

	12/31/95	12/31/94	12/31/93	12/31/92
Per Share Information				
Stock Price	26.00	26.00	26.00	25.00
Earnings Per Share	1.37	1.60	1.40	1.54
Price / Earnings Ratio	18.98	16.25	18.57	16.23
Book Value Per Share	2.20	2.52	2.82	2.98
Price / Book Value %	1,181.80	1,031.80	921.99	838.93
Dividends Per Share	1.37	1.70	1.24	1.52
Annual Financial Data				
Operating Results (000's)				
Total Revenues	43,046.9	45,228.7	43,913.9	43,412.5
Costs & Expenses	-31,987.9	-32,123.2	-32,421.5	-30,624.2
Income Before Taxes and Other	11,059.0	13,105.5	11,492.4	12,788.3
Other Items	n.a.	n.a.	n.a.	n.a.
Income Tax	-264.4	-310.0	-125.0	-200.0
Net Income	10,794.6	12,795.5	11,367.4	12,588.3
Cash Flow From Operations	16,553.0	19,403.9	16,977.1	19,994.6
Balance Sheet (000's)				
Cash & Equivalents	2,898.3	4,019.7	3,905.3	3,119.4
Total Current Assets	10,605.8	9,346.1	7,320.5	6,517.9
Fixed Assets, Net	147,597.5	150,730.4	155,645.5	159,549.9
Total Assets	171,393.7	174,000.5	176,901.6	179,178.1
Total Current Liabilities	6,010.9	6,035.6	5,959.5	7,341.9
Long-Term Debt	139,025.5	143,203.8	143,256.4	135,773.5
Stockholders' Equity	17,315.6	20,073.0	22,653.0	24,296.5
Performance & Financial Condition				
Return on Total Revenues %	25.08	28.29	25.89	29.00
Return on Avg Stockholders' Equity %	57.74	59.90	48.42	50.01
Return on Average Assets %	6.25	7.29	6.38	7.14
Current Ratio	1.76	1.55	1.23	0.89
Debt / Equity %	802.89	713.42	632.40	558.82

Compound Growth %'s	EPS %	-3.82	Net Income %	-4.99	Total Revenues %	-0.28

Comments

A weakness in the real estate markets, particularly in southern California, has caused a dissappointing year for management although they remain optimistic.

Officers	Position	Ownership Information	12/31/95
William T. Huston	Chairman	Number of Shares Outstanding	7,859,192
Richard M. Cannon	President, CEO	Market Capitalization	$ 204,338,992
Bradley D. Frazier	Secretary	Frequency Of Dividends	Quarterly
		Number of Shareholders	Under 500

Other Information

Transfer Agent	Company Office				Where Listed	Other
Auditor	Coopers & Lybrand LLP				Symbol	n.a.
Market Maker	None				SIC Code	6510
Broker Dealer	Standard Investment	Tel/Ext	(888)783-4688	Jack	Employees	30

West Virginia-American Water Company

500 Summers Street • Charleston, WV 25327-1906 • Telephone (304)340-2007 • Fax (304)340-2076

Company Description

The Company provides water to both residential and business customers in the State of West Virginia. Although there are other water providers in the State, the Company is aggressively seeking to expand markets through acquistion and normal growth. In early 1996, the Company offered to buy back the shares of a shareholder for book value of $39.51 per share. We heard a report that the Company has now frozen the buy back price as a disincentive to continuing ownership to the remaining outside shareholders.

	12/31/95	12/31/94	12/31/93
Per Share Information			
Stock Price	39.51	38.35	37.20
Earnings Per Share	4.22	3.61	3.21
Price / Earnings Ratio	9.36	10.62	11.59
Book Value Per Share	39.51	38.35	37.20
Price / Book Value %	100.00	100.00	100.00
Dividends Per Share	2.90	2.47	2.53
Annual Financial Data			
Operating Results (000's)			
Total Revenues	58,360.5	56,322.6	52,550.7
Costs & Expenses	-47,067.0	-46,999.9	-44,284.2
Income Before Taxes and Other	11,096.4	9,206.9	8,143.6
Other Items	n.a.	n.a.	n.a.
Income Tax	-4,134.5	-3,613.3	-3,101.0
Net Income	6,961.9	5,593.7	5,042.6
Cash Flow From Operations	11,491.0	11,032.5	8,488.5
Balance Sheet (000's)			
Cash & Equivalents	235.3	382.5	5,637.1
Total Current Assets	10,443.5	9,995.1	14,787.0
Fixed Assets, Net	205,082.4	181,737.2	167,297.9
Total Assets	249,323.5	219,081.7	208,697.6
Total Current Liabilities	28,998.2	19,966.5	10,529.3
Long-Term Debt	85,364.9	77,966.1	82,187.4
Stockholders' Equity	66,078.2	59,399.3	58,070.9
Performance & Financial Condition			
Return on Total Revenues %	11.93	9.93	9.60
Return on Avg Stockholders' Equity %	11.10	9.52	9.21
Return on Average Assets %	2.97	2.62	2.68
Current Ratio	0.36	0.50	1.40
Debt / Equity %	129.19	131.26	141.53

Compound Growth %'s	EPS %	14.66	Net Income %	17.50	Total Revenues %	5.38

Comments

Management reports the implementation of a $2.4 million rate increase in early 1996, as well as other favorable regulatory developments. Approvals have also been obtained for the first public/private partnership, the Boone County Regional Water Project, whereby property taxes from the private sector will be used to pay for debt service on the public sector portion of the project. The Company hopes it can use this as a model for other regional water projects within the state. Beware of possibly not having a market for this stock other than by redemption by the Company.

Officers	Position	Ownership Information	12/31/95
C E. Jarrett	President	Number of Shares Outstanding	1,563,057
Stephen N. Chamber	Secretary	Market Capitalization	$ 61,756,382
D K. Carr	Vice President	Frequency Of Dividends	n.a.
M A. Miller	Vice President, Treasurer	Number of Shareholders	Under 500
T R. Bailey	Controller		

Other Information					
Transfer Agent	United National Bank, Charleston, WV			Where Listed	OTC-PS
Auditor	Price Waterhouse LLP			Symbol	WVAW
Market Maker	Chicago Corporation, The	Telephone	(312)855-7664	SIC Code	4940
Broker Dealer	Standard Investment	Tel/Ext	(888)783-4688 Jack	Employees	368

Westbrook-Thompson Agency

c/o NationsBank, P.O. Box 1317 • Fort Worth, TX 73101-1317

Company Description

The Agency collects and distributes, to its unit holders, royalty payments from producing oil and gas properties, after deducting from such receipts amounts to satisfy taxes and other expenses. The Agency was formed upon the dissolution of Westbrook-Thompson Holding Corp. in 1966.

	12/31/95	12/31/94	12/31/93
Per Share Information			
Stock Price	15.00	14.25	14.00
Earnings Per Share	3.57	2.79	2.71
Price / Earnings Ratio	4.20	5.11	5.17
Book Value Per Share	0.01	0.01	0.01
Price / Book Value %	150,000.00	142,500.00	140,000.00
Dividends Per Share	3.57	2.79	2.71
Annual Financial Data			
Operating Results (000's)			
Total Revenues	756.3	609.7	602.7
Costs & Expenses	-100.9	-96.8	-104.6
Income Before Taxes and Other	655.4	512.9	498.1
Other Items	n.a.	n.a.	n.a.
Income Tax	n.a.	n.a.	n.a.
Net Income	655.4	512.9	498.1
Cash Flow From Operations	655.4	512.9	498.1
Balance Sheet (000's)			
Cash & Equivalents	348.8	269.8	252.6
Total Current Assets	348.8	269.8	252.6
Fixed Assets, Net	n.a.	n.a.	n.a.
Total Assets	348.8	269.9	252.6
Total Current Liabilities	348.8	269.8	252.6
Long-Term Debt	n.a.	n.a.	n.a.
Stockholders' Equity	0.1	0.1	0.1
Performance & Financial Condition			
Return on Total Revenues %	86.66	84.12	82.64
Return on Avg Stockholders' Equity %	n.a.	n.a.	n.a.
Return on Average Assets %	211.88	196.31	n.a.
Current Ratio	1.00	1.00	1.00
Debt / Equity %	n.a.	n.a.	n.a.

Compound Growth %'s	EPS %	14.78	Net Income %	14.72	Total Revenues %	12.02

Comments

Unitholders generally receive approximately a 20% annual return on current unit price. This fluctuates with both production levels and oil and gas prices. There are also some tax advantages in the depletion deduction allowed unit holders.

Officers	Position	Ownership Information	12/31/95
Not Available		Number of Shares Outstanding	183,510
		Market Capitalization	$ 2,752,650
		Frequency Of Dividends	Quarterly
		Number of Shareholders	Under 500

Other Information

Transfer Agent	NationsBank, Fort Worth, TX			Where Listed	OTC-BB
Auditor	Deloitte & Touche LLP			Symbol	WBTMU
Market Maker	Monroe Securities, Inc.	Telephone	(800)766-5560	SIC Code	1300
Broker Dealer	Regular Stockbroker			Employees	n.a.

Westminster Capital, Inc.

9665 Wilshire Blvd., M-10 • Beverly Hills, CA 90212 • Telephone (310)278-1930 • Fax (310)271-6274

Company Description

Until 1991, the Company's business consisted primarily of the operations of its subsidiary FarWest S & L Association. In 1991, the S & L was taken over by the Resolution Trust Company (RTC) and the Company's interest terminated. Since RTC's take over of FarWest, the Company's significant continuing operations and assets consist of cash, marketable securities, an interest in a telephone company, a loan portfolio secured by automobile leases and a convertible debenture. The Company continues to seek an investment in or acquisition of one or more businesses. The Company was formed in Delaware in 1959.

	12/31/95	12/31/94	12/31/93	12/31/92
Per Share Information				
Stock Price	2.16	1.31	1.34	0.30
Earnings Per Share	0.17	-0.21	1.59	-0.39
Price / Earnings Ratio	12.71	n.a.	0.84	n.a.
Book Value Per Share	2.96	2.74	2.98	1.39
Price / Book Value %	72.97	47.81	44.97	21.58
Dividends Per Share	n.a.	n.a.	n.a.	n.a.
Annual Financial Data				
Operating Results (000's)				
Total Revenues	4,596.0	6,706.0	17,236.0	319.0
Costs & Expenses	-2,819.0	-6,422.0	-705.0	-1,237.0
Income Before Taxes and Other	1,777.0	284.0	16,531.0	-918.0
Other Items	-49.0	-114.0	-410.0	-151.0
Income Tax	-420.0	-1,778.0	-3,687.0	-1,956.0
Net Income	1,308.0	-1,608.0	12,434.0	-3,025.0
Cash Flow From Operations	-1,734.0	4,058.0	13,998.0	480.0
Balance Sheet (000's)				
Cash & Equivalents	1,715.0	800.0	n.a.	n.a.
Total Current Assets	22,805.0	26,200.0	27,045.0	28,767.0
Fixed Assets, Net	1,378.0	1,500.0	56.0	49.0
Total Assets	28,199.0	29,400.0	27,171.0	29,058.0
Total Current Liabilities	4,634.0	7,435.0	3,875.0	2,689.0
Long-Term Debt	n.a.	n.a.	n.a.	15,507.0
Stockholders' Equity	23,100.0	21,500.0	23,296.0	10,862.0
Performance & Financial Condition				
Return on Total Revenues %	28.46	-23.98	72.14	-948.28
Return on Avg Stockholders' Equity %	5.87	-7.18	72.80	-24.45
Return on Average Assets %	4.54	-5.68	44.23	-13.72
Current Ratio	4.92	3.52	6.98	10.70
Debt / Equity %	n.a.	n.a.	n.a.	142.76

Compound Growth %'s	EPS %	-67.30	Net Income %	-67.57	Total Revenues %	143.33

Comments

Income for 1995, 1994 and 1993, includes $1,209,000, $3,528,000 and $16,819,000, respectively, for the settlement of a lawsuit against Drexel Burnham and Michael Milken.

Officers	Position	Ownership Information	12/31/95
William Belzberg	Chairman, CEO	Number of Shares Outstanding	7,815,000
Philip J. Gitzinger	Exec VP, CFO	Market Capitalization	$ 16,880,400
		Frequency Of Dividends	n.a.
		Number of Shareholders	1,085

Other Information

Transfer Agent	Boston EquiServe			Where Listed	PSE
Auditor	KPMG Peat Marwick LLP			Symbol	WI
Market Maker	Paragon Securities Corp.	Telephone	(212)785-4700	SIC Code	6799
Broker Dealer	Regular Stockbroker			Employees	13

Westwood Incorporated

Mill Street • Southbridge, MA 01550 • Telephone (508)764-3252 • Fax (508)764-6586

Company Description

The Company manufactures cloth for clothing and upholstery through its own weaving division and also finishes cotton that comes from other companies. The Company went public in 1969, but has generally refused to issue financial statements, even to its shareholders, since 1983. In 1984, the Company offered to buy back all outstanding shares at $3 per share. Currently, it informally offers any shareholder $4 per share and occasionally does acquire shares in this manner.

	10/01/94	10/02/93	10/03/92
Per Share Information			
Stock Price	4.00	4.20	4.75
Earnings Per Share	0.38	1.08	0.86
Price / Earnings Ratio	10.53	3.89	5.52
Book Value Per Share	13.10	12.70	11.25
Price / Book Value %	30.53	33.07	42.22
Dividends Per Share	n.a.	n.a.	n.a.
Annual Financial Data			
Operating Results (000's)			
Total Revenues	59,776.5	55,931.3	44,801.1
Costs & Expenses	-58,901.3	-54,316.3	-43,293.9
Income Before Taxes and Other	875.2	1,615.0	1,507.2
Other Items	-29.8	-66.7	-32.5
Income Tax	-512.8	-580.3	-692.8
Net Income	332.6	967.9	781.9
Cash Flow From Operations	-9.6	812.8	79.9
Balance Sheet (000's)			
Cash & Equivalents	501.2	615.2	n.a.
Total Current Assets	18,365.6	16,665.4	n.a.
Fixed Assets, Net	819.2	891.0	n.a.
Total Assets	19,360.2	17,723.2	n.a.
Total Current Liabilities	7,656.7	6,408.0	n.a.
Long-Term Debt	n.a.	n.a.	n.a.
Stockholders' Equity	11,486.6	11,138.2	n.a.
Performance & Financial Condition			
Return on Total Revenues %	0.56	1.73	1.75
Return on Avg Stockholders' Equity %	2.94	9.02	7.88
Return on Average Assets %	1.79	n.a.	n.a.
Current Ratio	2.40	2.60	n.a.
Debt / Equity %	n.a.	n.a.	n.a.

Compound Growth %'s	EPS %	-33.53	Net Income %	-34.78	Total Revenues %	15.51

Comments

Recent strength may be a result of having growing customers like WalMart. Fixed assets are almost fully depreciated, but are said to be in excellent condition. The president is 74 years old and not active in the business. The CEO and major shareholder (60% of shares) is 72 years old and has no family in the business. A number of employees also own shares. Compounded growth rates can be misleading because they are only based on two years.

Officers	Position	Ownership Information	10/01/94
Howard Olian	Chairman, CEO	Number of Shares Outstanding	876,927
Louis C. Broughton	President	Market Capitalization	$ 3,507,708
Jerome T. Kocur	Secretary, Treasurer	Frequency Of Dividends	n.a.
		Number of Shareholders	Under 500

Other Information

Transfer Agent	Company Office				Where Listed	OTC-BB
Auditor	Cole, Roberts & Herbert				Symbol	WWOD
Market Maker	Tweedy Browne Company L.P.	Telephone	(212)916-0606		SIC Code	2290
Broker Dealer	Standard Investment	Tel/Ext	(888)783-4688	Jack	Employees	80

Wichita National Life Insurance Company

711 D Avenue • Lawton, OK 73502-1709 • Telephone (405)353-5776 • Fax (405)353-6482

Company Description

The Company underwrites life, accident and health insurance.

	12/31/95	12/31/94	12/31/93
Per Share Information			
Stock Price	5.50	4.00	4.00
Earnings Per Share	0.16	-0.27	0.27
Price / Earnings Ratio	34.38	n.a.	14.81
Book Value Per Share	4.90	5.21	5.54
Price / Book Value %	112.24	76.78	72.20
Dividends Per Share	0.15	0.10	0.10
Annual Financial Data			
Operating Results (000's)			
Total Revenues	6,164.8	5,214.6	5,078.2
Costs & Expenses	-5,907.0	-5,574.0	-4,634.1
Income Before Taxes and Other	257.8	-359.4	444.1
Other Items	n.a.	n.a.	n.a.
Income Tax	-54.5	21.0	-103.2
Net Income	203.3	-338.4	340.9
Cash Flow From Operations	n.a.	n.a.	n.a.
Balance Sheet (000's)			
Cash & Equivalents	10,750.2	10,262.8	9,671.7
Total Current Assets	12,124.5	11,766.7	11,210.3
Fixed Assets, Net	470.2	460.6	490.8
Total Assets	13,924.4	13,501.1	12,995.6
Total Current Liabilities	513.2	506.0	373.5
Long-Term Debt	n.a.	n.a.	n.a.
Stockholders' Equity	6,163.9	6,560.8	6,977.1
Performance & Financial Condition			
Return on Total Revenues %	3.30	-6.49	6.71
Return on Avg Stockholders' Equity %	3.19	-5.00	n.a.
Return on Average Assets %	1.48	-2.55	n.a.
Current Ratio	23.62	23.25	30.02
Debt / Equity %	n.a.	n.a.	n.a.

Compound Growth %'s	EPS %	-23.02	Net Income %	-22.78	Total Revenues %	10.18

Comments

There is no indication that the financial statements have been audited. The 1996 dividend was increased to 20 cents per share.

Officers	Position	Ownership Information	12/31/95
L B. McClung	Chairman	Number of Shares Outstanding	1,259,226
Randy B. Gilliland	President	Market Capitalization	$ 6,925,743
Ronnie J. Denham	Secretary, Treasurer	Frequency Of Dividends	n.a.
Myron G. McChurin	Vice President	Number of Shareholders	Under 500
Eldon J. Proctor	Vice President		

Other Information					
Transfer Agent	Company Office			Where Listed	OTC-PS
Auditor	n.a.			Symbol	n.a.
Market Maker	J.B. Ricards Securities Corp.	Telephone	(800)621-5253	SIC Code	6310
Broker Dealer	Regular Stockbroker			Employees	11

Winthrop Partners 81 LTD Partnership

One International Place • Boston, MA 02110 • Telephone (617)330-8600 • Fax (617)330-7969

Company Description

The Partnership's business is the owning, leasing and the eventual disposition of real estate assets. Two properties are still owned. They are a warehouse/distribution facility and a retail nursery and crafts store, both in Columbus, Ohio. A third property was sold during 1995. The Company was formed in 1981 and raised capital through a public offering of units. It raised $12.5 million at that time and used the funds to acquire the properties. The officers listed are those of the general partners.

	12/31/95	12/31/94	12/31/93	12/31/92
Per Unit Information				
Price Per Unit	69.95	40.00	279.00	248.19
Earnings Per Unit	10.02	5.11	16.71	37.17
Price / Earnings Ratio	6.98	7.83	16.70	6.68
Book Value Per Unit	84.39	202.62	209.14	231.19
Price / Book Value %	82.89	19.74	133.40	107.35
Distributions Per Unit	128.25	11.62	38.76	81.26
Cash Flow Per Unit	128.43	16.17	41.34	86.27
Annual Financial Data				
Operating Results (000's)				
Total Revenues	376.4	501.5	892.3	1,343.4
Costs & Expenses	-104.1	-362.1	-286.0	-356.7
Operating Income	272.4	139.4	468.0	986.7
Other Items	n.a.	n.a.	n.a.	n.a.
Net Income	272.4	139.4	468.0	986.7
Cash Flow From Operations	3,224.6	406.0	1,038.1	2,166.1
Balance Sheet (000's)				
Cash & Equivalents	233.9	179.3	172.1	273.6
Total Current Assets	235.3	179.3	172.1	273.6
Investments In Real Estate	1,671.4	4,639.3	4,890.3	5,515.9
Total Assets	1,906.7	4,820.8	5,070.5	5,790.1
Total Current Liabilities	86.7	52.9	150.2	311.0
Long-Term Debt	n.a.	n.a.	n.a.	n.a.
Partners' Capital	1,820.1	4,767.9	4,920.3	5,479.0
Performance & Financial Condition				
Return on Total Revenues %	72.36	27.80	52.45	73.45
Return on Average Partners' Capital %	n.a.	n.a.	n.a.	n.a.
Return on Average Assets %	8.10	2.82	8.62	15.55
Current Ratio	2.72	3.39	1.15	0.88
Debt / Equity %	n.a.	n.a.	n.a.	n.a.

Compound Growth %'s	EPU %	-35.40	Net Income %	-34.89	Total Revenues %	-34.56

Comments

Although the larger of the three properties was sold, the remaining two are under lease until dates in 1997 and 1998. Management intends to continue to distribute cash flow to the partners. No independent appraisal has been provided by the general partner. The declining growth rates are reflective of the sale of one of the three original properties. Cash flow from operations and cash flow per unit include proceeds from the sale of assets.

Officers	Position	Ownership Information	12/31/95
Richard J. McCready	President	Number of Shares Outstanding	25,109
Michael L. Ashner	CEO	Market Capitalization	$ 1,756,375
Jeffrey Furber	Exec VP	Frequency Of Distributions	Quarterly
Anthony R. Page	CFO	Number of Partners	1,258
Ronald Kravit	Other		

Other Information					
Transfer Agent	Company Office		Where Listed	Order Matching Only
Auditor	Arthur Andersen LLP		Symbol	n.a.
Market Maker	None		SIC Code	6510
Broker Dealer	Chicago Partnership Board	Tel/Ext (800)272-6273 690	Employees	None

Wisconsin Fuel & Light Company

211 Forest Street • Wausau, WI 54402-1627 • Telephone (715)845-2141 • Fax (715)847-6208

Company Description

The Company is a public utility engaged in the distribution of natural gas to a diversified base of residential, commercial and industrial customers, primarily in the communities of Manitowac and Wausau, Wisconsin. In 1994, the Company issued $2 million of redeemable preferred stock through a private placement.

	12/31/95	12/31/94	12/31/93	12/31/92
Per Share Information				
Stock Price	40.00	36.00	38.00	35.00
Earnings Per Share	3.31	2.41	3.82	3.97
Price / Earnings Ratio	12.08	14.94	9.95	8.82
Book Value Per Share	26.34	25.35	25.35	23.85
Price / Book Value %	151.86	142.01	149.90	146.75
Dividends Per Share	2.32	2.32	2.30	2.16
Annual Financial Data				
Operating Results (000's)				
Total Revenues	45,915.3	47,702.3	51,397.6	45,795.8
Costs & Expenses	-43,146.3	-45,870.3	-48,478.1	-42,846.0
Income Before Taxes and Other	2,768.9	1,832.0	2,888.0	2,930.4
Other Items	n.a.	n.a.	n.a.	n.a.
Income Tax	-1,025.2	-572.5	-1,027.0	-1,004.6
Net Income	1,743.7	1,259.5	1,861.0	1,925.9
Cash Flow From Operations	4,914.9	4,083.2	-1,445.6	3,128.7
Balance Sheet (000's)				
Cash & Equivalents	213.7	34.9	252.2	815.5
Total Current Assets	12,287.0	11,264.2	13,820.6	11,441.7
Fixed Assets, Net	25,566.1	24,630.8	23,180.2	21,581.4
Total Assets	43,476.4	44,518.4	46,626.5	39,082.6
Total Current Liabilities	10,697.2	8,366.1	10,417.6	13,448.8
Long-Term Debt	11,650.0	12,720.0	13,290.0	7,860.0
Stockholders' Equity	14,905.9	14,418.9	12,391.8	11,599.9
Performance & Financial Condition				
Return on Total Revenues %	3.80	2.64	3.62	4.21
Return on Avg Stockholders' Equity %	11.89	9.40	15.51	17.27
Return on Average Assets %	3.96	2.76	4.34	5.14
Current Ratio	1.15	1.35	1.33	0.85
Debt / Equity %	78.16	88.22	107.25	67.76

Compound Growth %'s	EPS %	-5.88	Net Income %	-3.26	Total Revenues %	0.09

Comments

The Company has paid a dividend for 41 straight years and boasts of the fact that it has never been reduced. It has also been seeking regulatory approval for a new design in the way it bills its customers. This would be a fairly high monthly charge and a lower unit energy charge. Timing of such a change, if approved, is uncertain.

Officers	Position	Ownership Information	12/31/95
Mark T. Maranger	President, CEO	Number of Shares Outstanding	489,985
Hugh H. Bell	Secretary	Market Capitalization	$ 19,599,400
Paul C. Baird	Treasurer	Frequency Of Dividends	Quarterly
Edward C. Vallis	Vice President	Number of Shareholders	Under 500
Monte K. Gehring	Vice President		

Other Information				
Transfer Agent	Firstar Trust Company, Milwaukee, WI		Where Listed	OTC-BB
Auditor	Arthur Andersen LLP		Symbol	WIFL
Market Maker	B.C. Ziegler and Company	Telephone (414)258-3244	SIC Code	4920
Broker Dealer	Regular Stockbroker		Employees	160

Woodbury Telephone Company (The)

299 Main Street South • Woodbury, CT 06798 • Telephone (203)263-2121 • Fax (203)263-2770

Company Description

The Company furnishes local and long distance telephone services and sells telephone equipment in the towns of Woodbury, Southbury, and Bethlehem, Connecticut and portions of the towns of Oxford and Roxbury Connecticut. The Company is a Connecticut Corporation which commenced business in 1899.

	12/31/95	12/31/94	12/31/93	12/31/92
Per Share Information				
Stock Price	25.00	24.00	26.00	25.00
Earnings Per Share	2.38	2.11	1.69	1.98
Price / Earnings Ratio	10.50	11.37	15.38	12.63
Book Value Per Share	16.64	15.78	15.01	14.55
Price / Book Value %	150.24	152.09	173.22	171.82
Dividends Per Share	1.52	1.52	1.52	1.52
Annual Financial Data				
Operating Results (000's)				
Total Revenues	13,080.8	12,337.5	11,715.1	11,554.3
Costs & Expenses	-10,073.2	-9,720.6	-9,710.8	-9,203.0
Income Before Taxes and Other	3,007.5	2,616.9	2,004.3	2,351.2
Other Items	n.a.	n.a.	n.a.	n.a.
Income Tax	-1,175.7	-992.7	-701.8	-825.2
Net Income	1,831.8	1,624.2	1,302.5	1,526.0
Cash Flow From Operations	3,540.6	4,493.0	3,569.2	3,362.4
Balance Sheet (000's)				
Cash & Equivalents	2,238.8	1,942.9	2,154.5	1,794.8
Total Current Assets	5,555.3	5,541.2	5,326.8	4,993.4
Fixed Assets, Net	20,398.8	20,971.4	19,893.8	20,170.7
Total Assets	27,323.2	28,083.9	26,994.3	26,609.5
Total Current Liabilities	1,938.7	2,915.2	1,953.4	1,998.6
Long-Term Debt	9,000.0	9,000.0	9,000.0	9,000.0
Stockholders' Equity	12,801.7	12,139.0	11,683.8	11,550.4
Performance & Financial Condition				
Return on Total Revenues %	14.00	13.16	11.12	13.21
Return on Avg Stockholders' Equity %	14.69	13.64	11.21	13.42
Return on Average Assets %	6.61	5.90	4.86	5.81
Current Ratio	2.87	1.90	2.73	2.50
Debt / Equity %	70.30	74.14	77.03	77.92

Compound Growth %'s	EPS %	6.33	Net Income %	6.28	Total Revenues %	4.22

Comments

Increases in Total Revenues in 1995 and 1994 resulted primarily from increases in the customer base and increased usage of long distance. Expenditures for telephone plant and equipment totaled approximately $8.5 million over the four years ended December 31, 1995.

Officers	Position	Ownership Information	12/31/95
J. Garry Mitchell	Chairman	Number of Shares Outstanding	769,107
Donald E. Porter	President, CEO	Market Capitalization	$ 19,227,675
Harmon L. Andrews	Secretary	Frequency Of Dividends	Quarterly
		Number of Shareholders	710

Other Information			
Transfer Agent	Company Office	Where Listed	OTC-BB
Auditor	Ernst & Young LLP	Symbol	WBTL
Market Maker	Chicago Corporation, The	Telephone (312)855-7664	SIC Code	4813
Broker Dealer	Regular Stockbroker	Employees	73

Woodward Governor Company

5001 North Second Street • Rockford, IL 61125 • Telephone (815)877-7441 • Fax (815)636-6033

Company Description

The Company designs and manufactures engine fuel delivery and engine control systems, subsystems and components. Products range from devices that are used on diesel engines, steam turbines, industrial and aircraft gas turbines and hydraulic turbines. The Company sells directly to OEM's, service providers and equipment users world wide. The Company was established in 1870 and incorporated in the state of Delaware.

	09/30/95	09/30/94	09/30/93	09/30/92
Per Share Information				
Stock Price	63.50	82.00	69.50	82.00
Earnings Per Share	4.11	-1.11	-1.36	7.23
Price / Earnings Ratio	15.45	n.a.	n.a.	11.34
Book Value Per Share	68.21	66.29	69.42	73.90
Price / Book Value %	93.09	123.70	100.12	110.96
Dividends Per Share	3.72	3.72	3.72	3.70
Annual Financial Data				
Operating Results (000's)				
Total Revenues	379,736.0	333,207.0	331,156.0	374,173.0
Costs & Expenses	-348,462.0	-311,337.0	-301,535.0	-341,197.0
Income Before Taxes and Other	20,183.0	-5,195.0	23,084.0	32,976.0
Other Items	n.a.	n.a.	-17,417.0	n.a.
Income Tax	-8,247.0	1,922.0	-9,695.0	-12,764.0
Net Income	11,936.0	-3,273.0	-4,028.0	20,212.0
Cash Flow From Operations	31,321.0	35,805.0	37,222.0	54,127.0
Balance Sheet (000's)				
Cash & Equivalents	12,451.0	10,272.0	10,497.0	7,633.0
Total Current Assets	209,015.0	181,279.0	170,168.0	173,928.0
Fixed Assets, Net	118,066.0	122,911.0	144,016.0	151,126.0
Total Assets	349,599.0	323,318.0	332,461.0	331,653.0
Total Current Liabilities	92,651.0	67,528.0	62,359.0	70,110.0
Long-Term Debt	27,796.0	32,665.0	36,246.0	40,135.0
Stockholders' Equity	197,903.0	193,846.0	206,222.0	219,690.0
Performance & Financial Condition				
Return on Total Revenues %	3.14	-0.98	-1.22	5.40
Return on Avg Stockholders' Equity %	6.09	-1.64	-1.89	9.44
Return on Average Assets %	3.55	-1.00	-1.21	6.33
Current Ratio	2.26	2.68	2.73	2.48
Debt / Equity %	14.05	16.85	17.58	18.27

Compound Growth %'s	EPS %	-17.16	Net Income %	-16.10	Total Revenues %	0.49

Comments

To address a changing market for its products, the Company has made significant changes to its operations. Restructuring expenses amounted to $6.0, $32.7, and $3.5 million during fiscal years 1995, 1994 and 1993, respectively. For the three months ended December 31, 1995, the Company had total revenues of $88.1 million and Net Income of $4.2 million ($1.44 per share) as compared to $90.4 million and $3.2 million ($1.10 per share) for same quarter in 1994.

Officers	Position	Ownership Information	09/30/95
John A. Halbrook	Chairman, CEO	Number of Shares Outstanding	2,901,212
Vern H. Cassens	CFO, Treasurer	Market Capitalization	$ 184,226,962
Carol J. Manning	Secretary	Frequency Of Dividends	Quarterly
Ronald E. Fulkrod	Vice President	Number of Shareholders	2,179
Peter A. Gomm	Vice President		

Other Information				
Transfer Agent	Wachovia Bank of North Carolina		Where Listed	OTC-BB
Auditor	Coopers & Lybrand		Symbol	WGOV
Market Maker	A.G. Edwards & Sons, Inc.	Telephone (314)289-3000	SIC Code	3625
Broker Dealer	Regular Stockbroker		Employees	3071

Workforce Systems Corp.

269 Cusick Road, Ste. C-2 • Alcoa, TN 37701 • Telephone (615)681-6034 • Fax (615)681-6147

Company Description

The Company, through several subsidiaries, provides specialized labor services on a contract basis to businesses, also manufactures thawing trays for another company and provides certain fabrication services. The Company was formed during August, 1992, and was incorporated in the state of Florida. During 1993, the Company completed a public offering of stock and began to seek acquisition candidates. During 1994 and 1995, the Company acquired a controlling interest in three companies for which it exchanged shares of its common and preferred stock.

	06/30/95	06/30/94
Per Share Information		
Stock Price	8.25	8.25
Earnings Per Share	0.33	0.15
Price / Earnings Ratio	25.00	55.00
Book Value Per Share	2.93	0.22
Price / Book Value %	281.57	3,750.00
Dividends Per Share	n.a.	n.a.
Annual Financial Data		
Operating Results (000's)		
Total Revenues	2,825.0	1,840.1
Costs & Expenses	-2,192.6	-1,551.6
Income Before Taxes and Other	632.5	288.6
Other Items	45.0	-26.9
Income Tax	-239.4	-99.4
Net Income	438.1	162.3
Cash Flow From Operations	-528.8	153.1
Balance Sheet (000's)		
Cash & Equivalents	91.7	11.3
Total Current Assets	1,992.9	116.4
Fixed Assets, Net	2,027.4	1.7
Total Assets	7,366.2	528.4
Total Current Liabilities	1,123.3	200.6
Long-Term Debt	720.5	n.a.
Stockholders' Equity	4,409.4	327.8
Performance & Financial Condition		
Return on Total Revenues %	15.51	8.82
Return on Avg Stockholders' Equity %	18.50	n.a.
Return on Average Assets %	11.10	n.a.
Current Ratio	1.77	0.58
Debt / Equity %	16.34	n.a.

Compound Growth %'s	EPS %	120.00	Net Income %	169.93	Total Revenues %	53.52

Comments

The Company changed its year end from January 31, to June 30 during 1994. Accordingly, the statement of operations for the period ended June 30, 1994, is for a 17 month period. Operations prior to that period were not significant. For the six months ended December 31, 1995, the Company had total revenues of $2.2 million and Net Income of $300,000, as compared to $880,000 and $179,000, for the same period in 1994.

Officers	Position	Ownership Information	06/30/95
Ella B. Chesnutt	President	Number of Shares Outstanding	1,503,724
Jayme Dorrough	Vice President, Secretary	Market Capitalization	$ 12,405,723
		Frequency Of Dividends	n.a.
		Number of Shareholders	51

Other Information				
Transfer Agent	Florida Atlantic Stock Transfer		Where Listed	OTC-BB
Auditor	Lyle h. Cooper		Symbol	WFSC
Market Maker	Grady and Hatch & Co.	Telephone (800)541-1291	SIC Code	7363
Broker Dealer	Regular Stockbroker		Employees	40

World Wide Limited

West Wind Building, Box 1380 • Cayman Islands, British W.I. • Telephone (809)949-4122 • Fax (809)945-2956

Company Description

The Company's main activity is the rental of real estate in the Cayman Islands where the Company has its executive offices. It was incorporated in the Commonwealth of the Bahamas where there are no income or capital gains taxes.

	01/31/95	01/31/94	01/31/93	01/31/92
Per Share Information				
Stock Price	8.00	14.00	14.50	14.50
Earnings Per Share	1.18	1.60	2.58	1.74
Price / Earnings Ratio	6.78	8.75	5.62	8.33
Book Value Per Share	18.30	18.63	19.28	18.44
Price / Book Value %	43.72	75.15	75.21	78.63
Dividends Per Share	1.50	2.25	1.75	2.00
Annual Financial Data				
Operating Results (000's)				
Total Revenues	1,623.2	1,801.1	2,317.6	1,730.1
Costs & Expenses	-928.1	-855.5	-788.4	-703.0
Income Before Taxes and Other	695.1	945.6	1,529.2	1,027.1
Other Items	n.a.	n.a.	n.a.	n.a.
Income Tax	n.a.	n.a.	n.a.	n.a.
Net Income	695.1	945.6	1,529.2	1,027.1
Cash Flow From Operations	809.3	1,116.6	1,274.8	1,173.2
Balance Sheet (000's)				
Cash & Equivalents	1,938.2	2,070.1	1,819.4	1,280.8
Total Current Assets	2,833.3	2,209.4	2,880.0	1,718.8
Fixed Assets, Net	7,194.5	7,342.0	7,408.1	9,233.3
Total Assets	10,837.5	11,038.2	11,423.7	12,006.8
Total Current Liabilities	10.6	19.6	20.6	56.3
Long-Term Debt	n.a.	n.a.	n.a.	n.a.
Stockholders' Equity	10,826.9	11,018.5	11,403.1	10,908.4
Performance & Financial Condition				
Return on Total Revenues %	42.82	52.50	65.98	59.37
Return on Avg Stockholders' Equity %	6.36	8.43	13.71	9.35
Return on Average Assets %	6.36	8.42	13.05	8.50
Current Ratio	267.27	112.66	139.94	30.52
Debt / Equity %	n.a.	n.a.	n.a.	n.a.

Compound Growth %'s	EPS %	-12.14	Net Income %	-12.20	Total Revenues %	-2.10

Comments

The Company lost one major client in 1995, resulting in a decline in profits. The Company has no debt and, until the most current year, maintained fairly consistent cash flow. Aside from visiting the beautiful Cayman Islands to inspect your investment, we are not sure if any other ownership benefits go along with being a shareholder. No current published quotes were available but a principal of the Company indicated that he believed trades would take place at around $8.00 per share.

Officers	Position	Ownership Information	01/31/95
H B. Armstrong	Chairman	Number of Shares Outstanding	591,480
Arni L. Sumarlidason	President	Market Capitalization	$ 4,731,840
William M. Christie	Secretary	Frequency Of Dividends	Annual
		Number of Shareholders	Under 500

Other Information

Transfer Agent	Registrar & Transfer Company		Where Listed	Other
Auditor	Deloitte & Touche LLP		Symbol	n.a.
Market Maker	Company Office	Telephone (809)949-4122	SIC Code	6519
Broker Dealer	None		Employees	7

Wright (G.F.) Steel & Wire Company

243 Stafford Street • Worcester, MA 01603-0045 • Telephone (508)854-6824 • Fax (508)755-3243

Company Description

The Company is engaged in the business of steel fabrication and manufactures products such as runners for sliding doors. It was reported to us that the stock has caused a variety of problems for the investment community because of restrictions related to the Company's employee stock ownership plan. We do not have the details as to those restrictions.

	09/30/94	09/30/93
Per Share Information		
Stock Price	7.00	7.00
Earnings Per Share	-7.62	-1.49
Price / Earnings Ratio	n.a.	n.a.
Book Value Per Share	60.40	68.01
Price / Book Value %	11.59	10.29
Dividends Per Share	n.a.	n.a.
Annual Financial Data		
Operating Results (000's)		
Total Revenues	11,482.0	11,921.0
Costs & Expenses	-12,137.0	-12,049.0
Income Before Taxes and Other	-655.0	-128.0
Other Items	n.a.	n.a.
Income Tax	n.a.	n.a.
Net Income	-655.0	-128.0
Cash Flow From Operations	n.a.	n.a.
Balance Sheet (000's)		
Cash & Equivalents	n.a.	n.a.
Total Current Assets	3,088.0	2,855.0
Fixed Assets, Net	3,088.0	2,855.0
Total Assets	8,598.0	8,311.0
Total Current Liabilities	1,279.0	3,117.0
Long-Term Debt	n.a.	n.a.
Stockholders' Equity	5,849.0	5,194.0
Performance & Financial Condition		
Return on Total Revenues %	-5.70	-1.07
Return on Avg Stockholders' Equity %	-11.86	n.a.
Return on Average Assets %	-7.75	n.a.
Current Ratio	2.41	0.92
Debt / Equity %	n.a.	n.a.

Compound Growth %'s	EPS % n.a.	Net Income % n.a.	Total Revenues % -3.68

Comments

There has not been any revenue growth over the last ten years. We have no information regarding managements' plans. The 1995 results were not available when we went to press.

Officers	Position	Ownership Information	09/30/94
Michael E. Keegan	President, CEO	Number of Shares Outstanding	86,000
		Market Capitalization	$ 602,000
		Frequency Of Dividends	n.a.
		Number of Shareholders	Under 500

Other Information

					Where Listed	OTC-BB
Transfer Agent	First National Bank, Boston, MA				Symbol	WRGF
Auditor	KPMG Peat Marwick LLP				SIC Code	3497
Market Maker	Carr Securities Corporation	Telephone	(800)221-2243		Employees	n.a.
Broker Dealer	Standard Investment	Tel/Ext	(888)783-4688	Jack		

Writer Corporation (The)

27 Inverness Drive East • Englewood, CO 80112 • Telephone (303)790-2870 • Fax (303)792-3286

Company Description

The Company is a developer and builder of planned residential communities in the metropolitan Denver, Colorado area. The homes are marketed to a broad spectrum of middle and upper middle income buyers. Home prices range from $135,000 to 325,000. The Company has sold a total 9,026 homes in 28 communities since its inception. Officers and directors, as a group, owned 55% of the Company's outstanding common stock at March 1, 1996.

	12/31/95	12/31/94	12/31/93	12/31/92
Per Share Information				
Stock Price	1.38	1.82	1.75	1.25
Earnings Per Share	0.17	0.20	-0.08	1.50
Price / Earnings Ratio	8.12	9.10	n.a.	0.83
Book Value Per Share	1.73	1.60	1.38	1.45
Price / Book Value %	79.77	113.75	126.81	86.21
Dividends Per Share	n.a.	n.a.	n.a.	n.a.
Annual Financial Data				
Operating Results (000's)				
Total Revenues	32,129.0	36,489.0	27,047.0	13,688.0
Costs & Expenses	-33,159.0	-35,321.0	-27,931.0	-14,613.0
Income Before Taxes and Other	-1,030.0	1,168.0	-884.0	-925.0
Other Items	1,437.0	n.a.	276.0	8,191.0
Income Tax	714.0	65.0	220.0	n.a.
Net Income	1,121.0	1,233.0	-388.0	7,266.0
Cash Flow From Operations	-592.0	-5,614.0	-5,200.0	-1,988.0
Balance Sheet (000's)				
Cash & Equivalents	1,409.0	1,305.0	2,736.0	723.0
Total Current Assets	39,665.0	40,062.0	35,504.0	27,217.0
Fixed Assets, Net	649.0	423.0	404.0	368.0
Total Assets	41,070.0	41,851.0	36,637.0	43,474.0
Total Current Liabilities	28,006.0	32,293.0	28,415.0	21,993.0
Long-Term Debt	n.a.	n.a.	n.a.	14,358.0
Stockholders' Equity	12,537.0	9,116.0	7,868.0	7,123.0
Performance & Financial Condition				
Return on Total Revenues %	3.49	3.38	-1.43	53.08
Return on Avg Stockholders' Equity %	10.35	14.52	-5.18	n.a.
Return on Average Assets %	2.70	3.14	-0.97	n.a.
Current Ratio	1.42	1.24	1.25	1.24
Debt / Equity %	n.a.	n.a.	n.a.	201.57

Compound Growth %'s	EPS %	-51.61	Net Income %	-46.37	Total Revenues %	32.90

Comments

The Company's inventory of real estate held for sale, $38 million in 1995, has been included in Current Assets and the related debt included in Current Liabilities ($22.4 million in 1995), which is consistent with earlier years. As a result of the Company restructuring its debt arrangements, it recognized a gain on the extinguishment of debt of $1.4 million in 1995 and $8.2 million in 1992. During 1995, the Company issued, through a private placement, 1,530,003 shares of its common stock at a price of $1.50 per share. Another 107,513 shares were issued in 1996 in conjunction with the same private placement.

Officers	Position	Ownership Information	12/31/95
George S. Writer, Jr.	President, CEO	Number of Shares Outstanding	7,247,100
Robert R. Reid	Senior VP	Market Capitalization	$ 10,000,998
Daniel J. Nickless	Senior VP, CFO	Frequency Of Dividends	n.a.
Christopher H. Fellows	Senior VP	Number of Shareholders	400
Derrell Schreiner	Vice President		

Other Information

Transfer Agent	KeyCorp Shareholder Services, Inc.		Where Listed	OTC-BB
Auditor	Deloitte & Touche LLP		Symbol	WRTC
Market Maker	Herzog, Heine, Geduld, Inc.	Telephone (800)221-3600	SIC Code	1531
Broker Dealer	Regular Stockbroker		Employees	77

Wundies Industries, Inc.

1501 West Third Street • Williamsport, PA 17701 • Telephone (717)326-2451 • Fax (717)326-9332

Company Description

The Company is a wholesaler and distributor of womens and childrens clothing with its main facilities located in Williamsport, Pennsylvania. Shares were issued in 1985 to all the shareholders of Panex Industries, Inc. The Company has since issued a cumulative preferred stock that accrues a dividend at the annual rate of 13.25%.

	10/01/95	10/02/94	10/03/93
Per Share Information			
Stock Price	2.82	5.00	6.87
Earnings Per Share	0.38	1.29	0.82
Price / Earnings Ratio	7.42	3.88	8.38
Book Value Per Share	3.43	3.06	1.83
Price / Book Value %	82.22	163.40	375.41
Dividends Per Share	n.a.	n.a.	n.a.
Annual Financial Data			
Operating Results (000's)			
Total Revenues	82,292.0	84,555.0	83,647.0
Costs & Expenses	-79,537.0	-78,779.0	-79,285.0
Income Before Taxes and Other	2,755.0	5,776.0	4,362.0
Other Items	n.a.	n.a.	n.a.
Income Tax	-1,207.0	-2,339.0	-1,891.0
Net Income	1,548.0	3,437.0	2,471.0
Cash Flow From Operations	-3,614.0	12,166.0	-2,988.0
Balance Sheet (000's)			
Cash & Equivalents	145.0	159.0	233.0
Total Current Assets	41,520.0	35,001.0	42,070.0
Fixed Assets, Net	6,591.0	6,246.0	6,566.0
Total Assets	49,667.0	42,488.0	50,072.0
Total Current Liabilities	28,742.0	20,449.0	27,995.0
Long-Term Debt	2,978.0	5,980.0	9,750.0
Stockholders' Equity	16,250.0	14,713.0	11,380.0
Performance & Financial Condition			
Return on Total Revenues %	1.88	4.06	2.95
Return on Avg Stockholders' Equity %	10.00	26.34	23.81
Return on Average Assets %	3.36	7.43	5.20
Current Ratio	1.44	1.71	1.50
Debt / Equity %	18.33	40.64	85.68

Compound Growth %'s	EPS %	-31.93	Net Income %	-20.85	Total Revenues %	-0.81

Comments

Cumulative dividends on the preferred stock totalled $5,847,000 at the last year end which does not appear as a balance sheet liability. We have subtracted these year end amounts in arriving at book value per common share.

Officers	Position	Ownership Information	10/01/95
Not Available		Number of Shares Outstanding	2,082,168
		Market Capitalization	$ 5,871,714
		Frequency Of Dividends	n.a.
		Number of Shareholders	Under 500

Other Information

Transfer Agent	Trust Co. of New Jersey			Where Listed	OTC-BB
Auditor	Ernst & Young LLP			Symbol	WUDS
Market Maker	Gruntal & Co., Incorporated	Telephone	(800)223-7632	SIC Code	5137
Broker Dealer	Regular Stockbroker			Employees	n.a.

Xedar Corporation

2500 Central Avenue • Boulder, CO 80301 • Telephone (303)443-6441 • Fax (303)443-6444

Company Description

The Company's principal business is the design, development, fabrication and sale of high technology electro-optical equipment and related electrical equipment including cameras, video systems, image systems and electrical test equipment. The Company was organized as a Colorado corporation in 1974.

	12/31/95	12/31/94	12/31/93	12/31/92
Per Share Information				
Stock Price	1.00	1.25	1.13	1.13
Earnings Per Share	0.10	0.08	0.22	0.09
Price / Earnings Ratio	10.00	15.63	5.14	12.56
Book Value Per Share	0.97	0.87	0.80	0.57
Price / Book Value %	103.09	143.68	141.25	198.25
Dividends Per Share	n.a.	n.a.	n.a.	n.a.
Annual Financial Data				
Operating Results (000's)				
Total Revenues	1,333.4	1,179.8	1,452.3	751.9
Costs & Expenses	-1,026.6	-982.1	-947.9	-597.3
Income Before Taxes and Other	306.8	197.6	504.5	154.6
Other Items	n.a.	n.a.	n.a.	48.8
Income Tax	-122.0	-46.0	-96.0	-48.8
Net Income	184.8	151.6	408.5	154.6
Cash Flow From Operations	325.5	-51.1	447.3	15.2
Balance Sheet (000's)				
Cash & Equivalents	1,209.3	920.4	974.4	554.0
Total Current Assets	1,652.9	1,474.3	1,426.5	859.8
Fixed Assets, Net	37.9	33.7	34.3	16.3
Total Assets	1,890.2	1,709.0	1,685.6	1,114.7
Total Current Liabilities	106.3	109.9	245.7	83.2
Long-Term Debt	n.a.	n.a.	n.a.	n.a.
Stockholders' Equity	1,783.9	1,599.1	1,439.9	1,031.5
Performance & Financial Condition				
Return on Total Revenues %	13.86	12.85	28.12	20.56
Return on Avg Stockholders' Equity %	10.93	9.98	33.05	16.22
Return on Average Assets %	10.27	8.93	29.17	14.79
Current Ratio	15.55	13.41	5.81	10.34
Debt / Equity %	n.a.	n.a.	n.a.	n.a.

Compound Growth %'s	EPS %	3.57	Net Income %	6.14	Total Revenues %	21.04

Comments

The Company has a strong balance sheet and dedicates a significant effort to research and devlopment which should allow it to continue to grow and remain competitive.

Officers	Position	Ownership Information	12/31/95
Hans R. Bucher	President, Treasurer	Number of Shares Outstanding	1,837,224
Marlis Bucher	Secretary	Market Capitalization	$ 1,837,224
		Frequency Of Dividends	n.a.
		Number of Shareholders	150

Other Information

Transfer Agent	Society National Bank			Where Listed	OTC-BB
Auditor	KPMG Peat Marwick			Symbol	XEDR
Market Maker	Wilson-Davis & Co., Inc.	Telephone	(800)453-5735	SIC Code	3861
Broker Dealer	Regular Stockbroker			Employees	8

York Corrugating Co.

P.O. Box 1192 • York, PA 17405-1192 • Telephone (717)845-3511 • Fax (717)854-0193

Company Description

The Company is a distributor of plumbing, heating and sheet metal supplies and a manufacturer of metal stampings with two warehouses in Pennsylvania. The Company has been repurchasing its shares at $70 per share, slightly higher than the traded price.

	12/31/95	12/31/94	12/31/93	12/31/92
Per Share Information				
Stock Price	58.50	51.00	50.50	44.00
Earnings Per Share	15.00	9.96	-11.99	-1.97
Price / Earnings Ratio	3.90	5.12	n.a.	n.a.
Book Value Per Share	161.81	144.34	132.50	144.94
Price / Book Value %	36.15	35.33	38.11	30.36
Dividends Per Share	1.00	0.56	0.45	0.60
Annual Financial Data				
Operating Results (000's)				
Total Revenues	18,230.3	16,787.0	15,826.4	16,541.4
Costs & Expenses	-17,301.5	-16,349.2	-16,331.7	-16,673.0
Income Before Taxes and Other	928.9	437.8	-505.2	-131.7
Other Items	n.a.	n.a.	n.a.	n.a.
Income Tax	-333.4	-23.8	-12.8	46.5
Net Income	595.5	414.0	-518.0	-85.2
Cash Flow From Operations	564.9	601.8	-363.5	191.5
Balance Sheet (000's)				
Cash & Equivalents	955.8	472.5	249.7	709.4
Total Current Assets	6,520.9	6,258.1	5,597.4	5,903.2
Fixed Assets, Net	1,272.7	1,280.6	1,138.7	1,274.3
Total Assets	7,928.5	7,685.7	6,948.4	7,378.5
Total Current Liabilities	1,402.0	1,591.3	1,083.4	977.5
Long-Term Debt	n.a.	n.a.	n.a.	n.a.
Stockholders' Equity	6,425.7	6,000.2	5,723.2	6,260.6
Performance & Financial Condition				
Return on Total Revenues %	3.27	2.47	-3.27	-0.51
Return on Avg Stockholders' Equity %	9.58	7.06	-8.64	-1.35
Return on Average Assets %	7.63	5.66	-7.23	-1.15
Current Ratio	4.65	3.93	5.17	6.04
Debt / Equity %	n.a.	n.a.	n.a.	n.a.

Compound Growth %'s	EPS %	50.60	Net Income %	43.83	Total Revenues %	3.29

Comments

After losses in 1991, 1992 and 1993, the Company appears to have restabilized itself. The Company sold its Maryland warehouse in 1995, producing nonrecurring income of approximately $400,000, approximately $10 per share, further strengthening the balance sheet. Compounded growth rates in Earnings Per Share and Net Income are misleading because of only two years in the calculation and the nonrecurring income in 1995.

Officers	**Position**	**Ownership Information**	**12/31/95**
K P. Raub	President, Treasurer	Number of Shares Outstanding	39,711
J E. Hovis	Secretary	Market Capitalization	$ 2,323,094
T R. Miller	Vice President	Frequency Of Dividends	Quarterly
		Number of Shareholders	Under 500

Other Information

Transfer Agent	Company Office				Where Listed	OTC-BB
Auditor	Philip R. Friedman and Associa				Symbol	YCRG
Market Maker	A.G. Edwards & Sons, Inc.	Telephone	(314)289-3000		SIC Code	5074
Broker Dealer	Standard Investment	Tel/Ext	(888)783-4688	Jack	Employees	116

York Water Company (The)

130 East Market Street • York, PA 17405 • Telephone (717)845-3601 • Fax (717)852-0058

Company Description

The business of the Company is to impound, purify and distribute water within its franchised territory located in York County, Pennsylvania. The Company's operations, which service a population of approximately 140,000, are subject to regulation by the Pennsylvania Public Utility Commission. The Company has been in business since 1816.

	12/31/95	12/31/94	12/31/93	12/31/92
Per Share Information				
Stock Price	66.00	62.00	57.75	56.00
Earnings Per Share	3.66	3.91	4.13	3.71
Price / Earnings Ratio	18.03	15.86	13.98	15.09
Book Value Per Share	34.16	33.75	33.12	32.31
Price / Book Value %	193.21	183.70	174.37	173.32
Dividends Per Share	3.60	3.60	3.60	3.68
Annual Financial Data				
Operating Results (000's)				
Total Revenues	15,449.3	14,755.7	14,201.8	13,216.7
Costs & Expenses	-11,130.4	-10,815.2	-10,786.8	-9,662.2
Income Before Taxes and Other	3,732.2	3,500.1	3,836.7	2,933.4
Other Items	n.a.	n.a.	n.a.	n.a.
Income Tax	-1,419.9	-1,055.4	-1,285.8	-765.3
Net Income	2,312.2	2,444.7	2,550.9	2,168.1
Cash Flow From Operations	3,000.0	3,754.2	3,673.0	3,296.5
Balance Sheet (000's)				
Cash & Equivalents	n.a.	n.a.	42.6	n.a.
Total Current Assets	3,015.7	2,685.8	3,065.1	4,653.3
Fixed Assets, Net	77,245.7	73,537.3	68,338.8	63,653.5
Total Assets	90,459.7	86,967.3	84,738.2	80,330.0
Total Current Liabilities	7,002.6	4,829.6	3,560.4	4,428.3
Long-Term Debt	32,000.0	32,000.0	32,000.0	34,966.3
Stockholders' Equity	21,771.8	21,251.9	20,597.4	19,832.1
Performance & Financial Condition				
Return on Total Revenues %	14.97	16.57	17.96	16.40
Return on Avg Stockholders' Equity %	10.75	11.68	12.62	11.87
Return on Average Assets %	2.61	2.85	3.09	2.89
Current Ratio	0.43	0.56	0.86	1.05
Debt / Equity %	146.98	150.57	155.36	176.31

Compound Growth %'s	EPS %	-0.45	Net Income %	2.17	Total Revenues %	5.34

Comments

Increases in Total Revenues have resulted primarily from increases in water rates.

Officers	Position	Ownership Information	12/31/95
William T. Morris	President, CEO	Number of Shares Outstanding	637,374
Jeffrey S. Osman	VP - Finance, Secretary	Market Capitalization	$ 42,066,684
Duane R. Close	Vice President	Frequency Of Dividends	Quarterly
Jeffrey R. Hines	Vice President	Number of Shareholders	1,217
Albert J. Shultz	Vice President		

Other Information

Transfer Agent	Company Office			Where Listed	OTC-BB
Auditor	KPMG Peat Marwick LLP			Symbol	YORW
Market Maker	Legg Mason Wood Walker, Inc.	Telephone	(212)428-4949	SIC Code	4941
Broker Dealer	Regular Stockbroker			Employees	91

Zevex International, Inc.

5175 Greenpine Drive • Salt lake City, UT 84123 • Telephone (201)264-1001 • Fax (801)264-1051

Company Description

The Company designs, manufactures, and sells custom and standard products utilizing ultrasonic transducers and related signal processing instrumentation. Products are sold primarily to original equipment manufacturers serving the medical, industrial and aerospace instrumentation markets. As of February 15, 1996, officers and directors and directors, as a group, owned approximately 49% of the Company's outstanding common stock. The Company was incorporated in Nevada in 1987. An issuance of 200,000 units of common stock and warrants in 1993 netted the Company $1.0 million. The units consist of one share of common stock and one warrant to purchase the common at a specific price. At December 31, 1995, the units were trading at a slight premium ($3.73 per share) over the common.

	12/31/95	12/31/94	12/31/93	12/31/92
Per Share Information				
Stock Price	3.63	2.63	5.25	5.80
Earnings Per Share	0.24	-0.02	0.36	0.20
Price / Earnings Ratio	15.13	n.a.	14.58	29.00
Book Value Per Share	2.12	2.26	2.28	1.31
Price / Book Value %	171.23	116.37	230.26	442.75
Dividends Per Share	n.a.	n.a.	n.a.	n.a.
Annual Financial Data				
Operating Results (000's)				
Total Revenues	5,336.6	3,368.6	3,153.0	2,452.9
Costs & Expenses	-4,892.6	-3,459.9	-2,574.6	-2,181.2
Income Before Taxes and Other	443.9	-91.4	578.3	271.6
Other Items	n.a.	n.a.	n.a.	n.a.
Income Tax	-127.1	66.7	-196.9	-81.5
Net Income	316.8	-24.7	381.4	190.1
Cash Flow From Operations	214.4	-461.7	110.3	121.3
Balance Sheet (000's)				
Cash & Equivalents	870.3	864.3	1,462.8	602.9
Total Current Assets	2,874.9	2,543.7	2,642.1	1,287.4
Fixed Assets, Net	363.8	276.2	268.1	120.5
Total Assets	3,247.4	2,824.0	2,912.1	1,409.8
Total Current Liabilities	346.5	273.7	337.1	178.2
Long-Term Debt	n.a.	n.a.	n.a.	4.8
Stockholders' Equity	2,900.9	2,550.3	2,575.0	1,226.7
Performance & Financial Condition				
Return on Total Revenues %	5.94	-0.73	12.10	7.75
Return on Avg Stockholders' Equity %	11.62	-0.96	20.06	16.79
Return on Average Assets %	10.44	-0.86	17.65	13.88
Current Ratio	8.30	9.29	7.84	7.22
Debt / Equity %	n.a.	n.a.	n.a.	0.39

Compound Growth %'s	EPS %	6.27	Net Income %	18.56	Total Revenues %	29.58

Comments

During 1995, the Company increased the size of its facilities and added to its production and testing equipment. Management believes that these and other improvements to operations will allow the Company to continue its profitable growth trend.

Officers	Position	Ownership Information	12/31/95
Dean G. Constantine	President, CEO	Number of Shares Outstanding	1,365,716
Phillip L. McStotts	Secretary, Treasurer	Market Capitalization	$ 4,957,549
David J. McNally	Vice President	Frequency Of Dividends	n.a.
		Number of Shareholders	580

Other Information				
Transfer Agent	Colonial Stock Transfer		Where Listed	OTC-BB
Auditor	Nielsen, Grimmett & Co.		Symbol	ZVXI
Market Maker	Alpine Securities Corporation	Telephone (800)521-5588	SIC Code	3845
Broker Dealer	Regular Stockbroker		Employees	73

Zions Cooperative Mercantile Institution

2200 South 900 West • Salt Lake City, UT 84137 • Telephone (801)579-6179 • Fax (801)579-6275

Company Description

The Company was organized in 1868 and was the first full-line department store in the United States. Their retail lines of business include both full-line conventional department stores and men's and women's ready-to-wear specialty stores and outlet stores. Stores are located in the Salt Lake City and Ogden, Utah, areas and in Pocatello and Idaho Falls, Idaho.

	02/03/96	01/28/95	01/29/94	01/31/93
Per Share Information				
Stock Price	11.00	9.82	9.38	8.00
Earnings Per Share	0.27	1.69	1.46	0.13
Price / Earnings Ratio	40.74	5.81	6.42	61.54
Book Value Per Share	23.64	24.91	23.92	22.79
Price / Book Value %	46.53	39.42	39.21	35.10
Dividends Per Share	0.60	0.60	0.60	0.60
Annual Financial Data				
Operating Results (000's)				
Total Revenues	254,371.3	244,923.6	235,318.9	221,830.2
Costs & Expenses	253,588.9	-240,630.0	-228,281.2	-216,839.0
Income Before Taxes and Other	782.4	4,293.6	5,137.7	391.2
Other Items	n.a.	1,373.7	n.a.	n.a.
Income Tax	200.8	-2,043.0	-1,984.8	-100.2
Net Income	581.6	3,624.3	3,152.9	291.0
Cash Flow From Operations	1,571.0	-3,874.6	-1,237.2	10,504.5
Balance Sheet (000's)				
Cash & Equivalents	2,698.1	2,698.9	5,315.5	3,204.7
Total Current Assets	102,633.2	105,840.3	99,971.6	92,167.6
Fixed Assets, Net	33,273.9	38,191.7	35,332.3	35,775.7
Total Assets	136,504.9	144,629.9	135,947.2	128,634.8
Total Current Liabilities	24,856.1	35,646.9	40,171.9	27,633.7
Long-Term Debt	56,406.3	50,974.2	40,367.7	47,214.4
Stockholders' Equity	51,062.1	53,570.7	51,092.8	49,435.6
Performance & Financial Condition				
Return on Total Revenues %	0.23	1.48	1.34	0.13
Return on Avg Stockholders' Equity %	1.11	6.93	6.27	0.58
Return on Average Assets %	0.41	2.58	2.38	0.23
Current Ratio	4.13	2.97	2.49	3.34
Debt / Equity %	110.47	95.15	79.01	95.51

Compound Growth %'s	EPS %	27.59	Net Income %	25.96	Total Revenues %	4.67

Comments

Management was opposed to a shareholder proposal to be listed on NASDAQ for nonconcise reasons. Earnings are not consistent, probably because of the cyclical nature of the business. Therefore, compound earnings and earnings per share growth rates can be misleading. The balance sheet is reasonably strong for the retail industry. During 1995, management recorded a nonrecurring expense of $1.9 million directly to retained earnings (not an income statement item) to properly reflect unfunded pension liabilities.

Officers	Position	Ownership Information	01/28/96
L. Tom Perry	Chairman	Number of Shares Outstanding	2,159,745
Richard H. Madsen	President, CEO	Market Capitalization	$ 23,757,195
Keith C. Saunders	Exec VP, CFO	Frequency Of Dividends	Quarterly
R. Barry Arnold	Vice President	Number of Shareholders	n.a.
Darrell L. Robinette	Vice President		

Other Information				
Transfer Agent	Company Office		Where Listed	OTC-BB
Auditor	Deloitte & Touche LLP		Symbol	ZNCO
Market Maker	Macallaster Pitfield Mackay	Telephone (212)422-9366	SIC Code	5311
Broker Dealer	Regular Stockbroker		Employees	2602

Indices

This page left intentionally blank.

4000 - 4999
Transportation & Public Utilities

5000 - 5199
Wholesale Trade

5200 - 5999
Retail Trade

6000 - 6299
Banking

This page left intentionally blank.

Over $100,000,000

Steelcase, Inc. and Subsidiaries . . . . . . approx.	2,300,000,000
Kohler Co. . . . . approx.	1,800,000,000
Crowley Maritime Corporation	1,111,158,000
King Kullen Grocery Co., Inc.	702,780,000
Pennsylvania Manufacturers Corporation	661,336,000
Central Steel and Wire Company	628,700,000
Benjamin Moore & Co.	564,211,376
Rand McNally	468,899,000
Cowles Media Company	455,657,000
Ash Grove Cement Company	407,745,251
Woodward Governor Company	379,736,000
Bozzuto's Incorporated	372,437,961
Polk (R.L.) & Co. . . . . approx.	320,000,000
Finch, Pruyn & Company, Incorporated	268,965,000
Houlihan's Restaurant Group, Inc.	267,622,000
Zions Cooperative Mercantile Institution	254,371,323
Irex Corporation	244,532,000
Americold Corporation	234,783,000
Davey Tree Expert Co.	230,101,000
Rochester & Pittsburgh Coal Company	225,879,000
Boswell (J.G.) Company	224,232,000
Fisher Companies Inc.	220,365,878
Computer Integration, Corp.	209,225,759
Harriet & Henderson Yarns, Inc.	203,669,302
Carolina Mills, Inc. . . . . approx.	190,000,000
Temco Service Industries, Inc.	175,348,164
Lady Baltimore Foods, Inc.	166,696,921
Central Investment Corporation	164,792,259
ConBraCo Industries, Inc.	162,633,228
Preformed Line Products Company	159,250,000
Riviera Holdings Corporation	151,895,871
Burnham Corporation	148,730,000
Pekin Life Insurance Company	145,266,398
Smith Investment Company	136,240,000
Amelco Corporation	126,611,000
NCC Industries, Inc.	125,987,326
Maui Land & Pineapple Company, Inc.	125,577,000
United Screw and Bolt Corporation	119,826,303
Louisville Bedding Company	119,487,432
Best Lock Corporation	118,546,487
Roseville Telephone Company	111,068,000
Robroy Industries, Inc.	111,005,132
Bulova Corporation	109,223,000
Continental Resources, Inc.	107,740,700
Penn Fuel Gas, Inc.	106,749,000
Lexington Precision Corporation	104,939,000
Sportsman's Guide, Inc. (The)	101,905,000

$100,000,000 - $50,000,000

Nichols (J.C.) Company	99,305,000
Bovar Inc.	98,304,000
Labor Ready, Inc.	94,361,629
Anderson-Tully Company	84,224,290
International Speedway Corporation	83,893,000
Wundies Industries, Inc.	82,292,000
Monarch Cement Company (The)	81,666,838
Hammett (J.L.) Co. . . . . approx.	80,000,000
Peckham Industries, Inc	78,756,000
Erie Family Life Insurance Company	78,349,951
Cochrane Furniture Company, Inc.	77,310,397
Blue Diamond Coal Company	77,253,589
Valley Fair Corporation (The)	75,562,646

Empire Gas Corporation	74,640,000
Hershey Creamery Company	74,166,114
Bollinger Industries, Inc.	73,159,258
Broughton Foods Company	72,384,540
Investors Insurance Holding Corp.	69,058,000
Exolon-Esk Company	68,592,000
Jamaica Water Supply Company	63,547,000
First of Michigan Capital Corporation	62,864,914
Case, Pomeroy & Company, Inc.	62,541,000
Westwood Incorporated	59,776,524
West Virginia-American Water Company	58,360,474
CT Communications, Inc.	56,018,843
Continental Health Affiliates, Inc.	54,378,000
Investment Properties Associates	53,988,364
North Pittsburgh Systems, Inc.	53,822,458
Allstar Inns, Inc.	52,424,000
Burke-Parsons-Bowlby Corporation	52,132,928
International American Homes, Inc.	51,225,000
Boston Sand & Gravel Co.	50,869,749
Keller Manufacturing Company, Inc.	50,329,631

$49,999,999 - $20,000,000

MLH Income Realty Partnership V	49,451,000
All For A Dollar, Inc.	47,345,417
Kentucky River Coal Corporation	46,428,000
CBR Brewing Company, Inc.	45,964,978
Adrian Steel Company	45,947,177
Wisconsin Fuel & Light Company	45,915,262
Meteor Industries, Inc.	45,372,928
Fall River Gas Company	45,190,483
Investors Heritage Life Insurance Company	44,076,406
Kentucky Investors, Inc.	44,004,611
Cloverleaf Kennel Club	43,556,649
B.B. Walker Company	43,453,000
Watson Land Company	43,046,900
Justiss Oil Co., Inc.	42,495,293
Ravens Metal Products, Inc.	42,160,625
Troy Mills, Inc.	42,030,942
Premier Parks, Inc.	41,496,000
Latshaw Enterprises, Inc.	41,277,000
Denver and Ephrata Telephone and Telegraph Co. . . .	40,810,858
Michigan Rivet Corporation	40,352,238
Computer Services, Inc.	36,222,474
Chillicothe Telephone Company	34,700,823
RWC, Incorporated	34,140,741
Bresler & Reiner, Inc.	33,824,000
Sea Pines Associates, Inc.	33,105,000
CUSA Technologies, Inc.	32,621,070
Pay-O-Matic Corp.	32,596,961
Writer Corporation (The)	32,129,000
Industrial Services of America, Inc.	30,604,106
Brake Headquarters U.S.A., Inc.	30,466,546
Auric Corporation	29,994,732
Sterling Sugars, Inc.	29,644,559
EMC Corporation	29,574,641
Hilliard Corporation	28,861,452
American Consumers, Inc.	28,834,871
Cornet Stores	28,419,689
American Public Life Insurance Company	28,096,297
AFA Protective Systems, Inc.	27,817,803
St. Louis Steel Casting Inc.	26,820,000
LAACO, Ltd.	26,790,000
AVCOM International, Inc.	26,737,000
Fireplace Manufacturers, Incorporated	26,718,906

Life Insurance Company of Alabama	26,014,787
United Coasts Corporation . . . . approx.	26,000,000
Homasote Company	25,733,495
TIF Instruments, Inc.	25,302,800
Biochem International Inc.	25,207,274
USANA, Inc.	24,734,539
Snow Summit Ski Corporation	24,665,163
Mid-Plains Telephone, Inc.	24,605,000
Optical Specialties, Inc.	24,188,000
Ragar Corp.	23,999,903
Crown City Plating Co.	23,927,327
Sivyer Steel Corporation	23,912,712
Stein Industries, Inc.	23,669,245
Seaboard Automotive, Inc.	23,310,167
Shenandoah Telecommunications Company	22,910,352
Artesian Resources Corporation	22,863,379
Du Art Film Laboratories, Inc.	22,592,428
Decker Manufacturing Corporation	22,199,941
Lexington Telephone Company . . . . . . approx.	22,000,000
Standard Industries, Inc.	21,547,978
Polaris Aircraft Income Fund II	21,093,341
Kansas Bankers Surety Company	20,359,083

$19,999,999 - $10,000,000

JMB Income Properties LTD X	19,780,519
Market America, Inc.	19,615,602
Corning Natural Gas Corporation	18,697,358
York Corrugating Co.	18,230,329
UCI Medical Affiliates, Inc.	17,992,640
Shopsmith, Inc.	17,728,890
Bryan Steam Corporation	17,727,561
Pacific Northwest Development Corporation	17,534,406
Bowles Fluidics Corporation	17,071,469
Momed Holding Co.	16,686,755
Real Goods Trading Corporation	16,403,000
Ramsay Managed Care, Inc.	16,214,000
Makepeace (A.D.) Company	15,992,190
Information Analysis Incorporated	15,704,450
Rhinelander Telecommunications, Inc.	15,575,600
DHB Capital Group Inc.	15,519,028
Accuhealth, Inc.	15,468,402
York Water Company (The)	15,449,296
Meda, Inc.	15,319,845
Tork, Inc.	15,290,789
North Carolina Railroad Company	15,132,553
Thomas Edison Inns, Inc.	15,069,765
Old Fashion Foods, Inc.	14,977,056
Goodheart-Willcox Company, Inc., (The)	14,968,000
Waste Recovery, Inc.	14,580,773
HIA, Inc.	14,528,709
Alleghany Pharmacal Corporation	14,433,040
Real Silk Investments, Incorporated	14,414,589
Reo Plastics, Inc.	14,268,080
Mercom, Inc.	14,217,000
Sel-Drum International, Inc.	14,178,254
Firecom, Inc.	14,089,000
North Coast Life Insurance Co.	14,054,541
Prab, Inc.	13,845,432
Ellensburg Telephone Company	13,742,600
Red Rose Collection, Inc.	13,682,611
Bell National Corporation	13,653,000
Warwick Valley Telephone Co.	13,561,185
Monroe Title Insurance Corporation	13,436,323
Power Test Investors Limited Partnership	13,391,419

Aircraft Income Partners, L.P.	13,374,206
First Real Estate Investment Trust of New Jersey	13,250,000
Tower Properties Company	13,152,882
Woodbury Telephone Company (The)	13,080,779
Detroit Legal News Company	13,060,433
Alpha Pro Tech, Ltd.	13,041,000
Ross Industries, Inc.	12,963,759
Mt. Carmel Public Utility Co.	12,752,293
Tangram Enterprise Solutions, Inc.	12,538,000
Fairmount Chemical Co., Inc.	12,403,000
Blue Ridge Real Estate Company	12,327,446
Finance Company of Pennsylvania	12,304,529
Hunter Manufacturing Corp.	12,187,491
Alaska Power & Telephone Company	11,895,630
Moyco Technologies, Inc.	11,880,186
Buffalo Valley Telephone Company	11,725,495
AMCOR Capital Corporation	11,721,755
Bismarck Hotel Company	11,604,033
Universal Metals & Machinery, Inc.	11,520,844
Wright (G.F.) Steel & Wire Company . . . . approx.	11,500,000
Micropac Industries, Inc.	11,445,000
Uniprop Manufactured Housing Communities Income II	11,210,541
Rudy's Restaurant Group, Inc.	11,090,876
Portland Brewing Company	11,001,396
Sound One Corporation . . . . approx.	11,000,000
Radva Corporation	10,793,005
Ogden Telephone Company	10,353,516
CompuDyne Corporation	10,308,000
Standard Electronics, Inc.	10,285,404
Naturade, Inc.	10,096,556
Balcor Current Income Fund 85	10,007,275

Under $10,000,000

Hydraulic Press Brick Company	9,993,000
George Risk Industries, Inc.	9,769,000
Auto-Graphics, Inc.	9,612,926
Network Data Processing Corporation	9,607,291
Stonecutter Mills Corporation	9,577,221
New Ulm Telecom, Inc.	9,544,835
Components Specialties, Inc.	9,443,182
Atlas Environmental, Inc.	9,416,820
Pocono Hotels Corporation	9,396,395
Southland National Insurance Corporation	9,350,195
Mod U Kraf Homes, Inc.	9,275,504
Crystal Mountain, Inc.	9,272,000
Citizens' Electric Company	9,253,601
American Consolidated Laboratories, Inc.	9,003,229
LogiMetrics, Inc.	8,905,618
Puroflow Incorporated	8,815,889
CMP Industries, Inc.	8,699,167
Ridgewood Properties, Inc.	8,675,000
Randall Bearings, Inc.	8,655,220
Pioneer Railcorp	8,580,426
Gateway Energy Corporation	8,460,000
ATS Money Systems, Inc.	8,438,729
Arrow-Magnolia International, Inc.	8,420,495
Esco Transportation Co.	8,296,207
Logan Clay Products Company	8,217,151
Henry County Plywood Corporation	8,171,277
M.H. Rhodes, Inc.	8,083,744
Benthos, Inc.	8,014,416
Ainslie Corporation	7,987,012
CSM Environmental Systems, Inc.	7,966,236
Mid-State Raceway, Inc.	7,880,440

Reflectix, Inc.	7,766,178
Century Realty Trust	7,761,464
Bolt Technology Corporation	7,707,000
Audio Communications Network, Inc.	7,690,379
Blue Fish Clothing, Inc.	7,651,688
Cable Link, Inc.	7,650,356
Health International, Inc.	7,639,927
Chromaline Corporation	7,583,818
Kiewit Royalty Trust	7,581,124
Watchdog Patrols, Inc.	7,301,238
Lamcor, Incorporated	7,163,817
Health Insurance Company of Vermont, Inc.	7,062,375
Florafax International, Inc.	7,046,000
Prime Capital Corporation	7,038,063
Immudyne, Inc.	7,036,967
Viskon-Aire Corporation	6,884,330
Boonton Electronics Corporation	6,859,019
Goddard Industries, Inc.	6,818,082
Avesis Incorporated	6,529,125
Watson Industries Inc.	6,403,990
Scioto Downs, Inc.	6,332,666
Equisure Financial Network Inc.	6,311,216
Chambersburg Engineering Company	6,291,836
Cagy Industries, Inc.	6,288,066
Southern Scottish Inns, Inc. approx.	6,245,320
Wichita National Life Insurance Company	6,164,790
Utz Engineering, Inc.	6,143,223
Community Service Communications, Inc.	6,130,582
Pioneer Communications, Inc.	6,104,157
Optimumcare Corporation	6,035,863
Keweenaw Land Association, Limited	6,027,432
Steritek, Inc.	5,954,236
Dale System, Inc.	5,939,124
Transnational Industries, Inc.	5,761,000
Cardiac Control Systems, Inc.	5,743,469
Christian Brothers, Inc.	5,721,647
Cherokee Equity Corporation	5,707,318
Carco Electronics	5,582,836
Stearns & Lehman, Inc.	5,558,781
Sims-Agricultural Products, Inc.	5,476,347
Hytek Microsystems, Inc.	5,412,270
Zevex International, Inc.	5,336,591
Dover Investments Corporation	5,312,000
AM Communications, Inc.	5,290,000
Real Estate Income Partners III Ltd Partnership	5,191,000
Big Sky Transportation Co.	5,184,584
Fifty Associates	5,112,451
IEA Income Fund XI, L.P.	5,065,426
Phil-Good Products Incorporated	5,056,724
Jetstream LP	5,052,489
Washington Life Insurance Company of America	5,039,868
Image Systems Corporation	5,026,936
Indiana Natural Gas Corporation	4,930,594
National Stock Yards Company	4,811,609
Sierra Monitor Corporation	4,803,943
Networks Electronic Corp.	4,711,082
PagePrompt USA	4,702,544
Telecomm Industries Corp. approx.	4,676,000
Westminster Capital, Inc.	4,596,000
Pharmaceutical Laboratories, Inc.	4,578,815
Batterymarch Trust	4,573,293
Lannett Company, Inc.	4,354,583
TMS, Inc.	4,221,120

Performance Nutrition, Inc.	4,211,121
Great Lakes Realty Corp.	4,011,701
Queen City Investments, Inc.	3,982,443
First Carolina Investors, Inc.	3,927,330
Damson Birtcher Realty Income Fund II	3,905,000
Technology 80 Inc.	3,899,331
Farm Fish, Inc.	3,847,173
Telebyte Technology, Inc.	3,827,500
Vasco Corp.	3,800,133
TNR Technical, Inc.	3,745,288
Mendocino Brewing Company, Inc.	3,714,100
Garden City Company	3,685,806
Daedalus Enterprises, Inc.	3,624,371
Tech Electro Industries, Inc.	3,550,219
Acacia Research Corporation	3,517,711
Radio Frequency Company, Inc.	3,468,637
Tremont Advisors, Inc.	3,462,828
Datamark Holding, Inc.	3,447,086
RF Industries, LTD	3,425,895
Connohio, Inc.	3,411,714
Solid Controls, Inc.	3,381,171
National Properties Corporation	3,334,944
Glengate Apparel, Inc.	3,330,318
Million Dollar Saloon, Inc.	3,270,552
Biddeford and Saco Water Company	3,201,183
Carc, Inc.	3,031,410
Capital Properties, Inc.	3,020,000
Premis Corporation	3,017,568
Lake Charles Naval Stores Co., Inc.	2,899,482
Original Sixteen to One Mine, Inc.	2,836,705
Vicon Fiber Optics Corp.	2,825,930
Workforce Systems Corp.	2,825,030
Megatech Corporation	2,824,952
Del Paint Corporation	2,776,871
Scientific Industries, Inc.	2,713,300
Hosoi Garden Mortuary, Inc.	2,690,971
Market Guide, Inc.	2,687,950
Sarnia Corporation	2,676,000
Hamburg Industries, Inc.	2,659,406
Oak Tree Medical Systems ,Inc.	2,652,889
Interactive Gaming & Communications Corp.	2,627,286
Coal Creek Mining and Manufacturing Company	2,607,373
Heartland Group of Companies, Inc.	2,589,021
Central Coal & Coke Corporation	2,560,363
Ojai Oil Company	2,495,833
American Electromedics Corp.	2,456,000
Pan Smak Pizza Inc.	2,448,875
Buck Hill Falls Company	2,218,139
Genetic Laboratories Wound Care, Inc.	2,217,852
Ophthalmic Publishing Company	2,045,610
Reserve Petroleum Company (The)	2,021,881
Salient Systems, Inc.	1,979,809
KnowledgeBroker, Inc.	1,974,832
Medical Advisory Systems, Inc.	1,953,062
Tel-Instrument Electronics Corp.	1,865,492
Congress Rotisserie, Inc.	1,851,821
Bonal International, Inc.	1,816,990
Park-Lexington Company, Inc.	1,816,418
Pace Medical, Inc.	1,784,939
Polyplastex United, Inc.	1,658,766
Portsmouth Square, Inc.	1,643,418
World Wide Limited	1,623,182
California Almond Investors I	1,590,977

Walker International Industries, Inc.	1,550,142
Discus Acquisition Corporation	1,535,000
DK Investors Inc.	1,389,659
Call Now, Inc.	1,376,343
Xedar Corporation	1,333,441
Chesapeake Investors, Inc.	1,294,353
New York and Harlem Railroad Company	1,290,830
Mills Music Trust	1,268,400
Limco Del Mar, Ltd.	1,115,160
Papnet of Ohio, Inc.	1,030,247
California Orchard Company	946,034
Danbury Industrial Corporation	895,130
Cimetrix Incorporated	836,929
Precision Optics Incorporated	825,208
Sutter Basin Corporation, Ltd.	770,199
Westbrook-Thompson Agency	756,308
Oakridge Energy, Inc.	721,267
Seven J Stock Farm, Inc.	686,000
Prevent Products, Inc.	582,776
Mexco Energy Corporation	573,921
Alaska Northwest Properties, Inc.	521,508
Belle Isle Net Profit Units	446,861
Virginia Hot Springs, Incorporated	428,908
Spring Street Brewing Company, Inc.	419,062
Winthrop Partners 81 LTD Partnership	376,441
Avoca, Incorporated	289,902
Golden Cycle Gold Corporation	273,109
Pennate Corporation	220,791
Cass County Iron Company	193,295
Citizens Growth Properties	129,000
Biloxi Marsh Lands Corporation	110,639
Inmark Enterprises, Inc.	50,346
Terre Aux Boeufs Land Co., Inc.	39,794
Alden Lee Company, Inc.	10,840

Over $10,000,000

Broadway Bancshares Inc.	34,256,000
Mahoning National Bancorp, Inc.	30,952,000
Midland Bancorporation, Inc.	19,187,000
Pacific Capital Bancorp	18,816,000
Anchor Financial Corporation	16,671,288
Sierra, Bank of the	16,162,000
Ames National Corporation	15,644,737
Carolina First BancShares, Inc.	15,460,178
Central Coast Bancorp	14,957,000
Lakeland Bancorp, Inc.	14,733,509
Santa Maria, Bank of	14,247,967
Community Bank of South Florida, Inc.	12,319,000
Santa Clara, Bank of	11,948,918
Pocahontas Bankshares Corporation	11,605,000
First National Community Bank	11,286,463
Penns Woods Bancorp, Inc.	10,902,365
PAB Bankshares, Inc.	10,291,092

$10,000,000 - $5,000,000

Borel Bank and Trust Company	9,939,551
Iowa First Bancshares Corp.	9,891,000
Berlin City Bank, The	9,684,000
Central Bancorporation	9,409,000
Charter National Bancorp, Inc.	9,343,000
Southern Michigan Bancorp, Inc.	9,096,347
First National Bank Holding Company	9,038,826
Union National Bancorp, Inc.	8,999,263
Union Bankshares, Inc.	8,608,375
BWC Financial Corp.	8,081,000
Slippery Rock Financial Corporation	7,608,369
Northwest Bank & Trust Company	7,579,000
Northern Empire Bancshares	7,565,000
American River Holdings	7,195,000
Emergent Group, Inc.	7,112,000
Tidewater, Bank of	6,760,563
First International Bancorp	6,732,227
Southside Bank	6,712,567
Summit Bank Corporation	6,469,000
San Joaquin Bank	6,425,000
Commercial Bancshares Incorporated	6,381,012
Tower Bancorp Inc.	6,299,000
Orrstown Financial Services, Inc.	6,287,000
Franklin Credit Management Corp	6,176,274
Farmers National Bancorp, Inc.	6,156,432
Tehama County Bank	5,545,211
Bay Area Bancshares	5,284,000
Summit Bancorp, Inc.	5,251,412
Cardinal Bancorp, Inc.	5,243,420

Under $5,000,000

Delaware Bancshares, Inc.	4,875,000
Petaluma, Bank of	4,834,700
Peoples Savings Bank of Troy	4,615,714
Central Sierra Bank	4,565,945
Gloucester Bank & Trust Company	4,203,000
Mid Valley Bank	4,127,155
Community Bank, The (NC)	4,058,859
Fairbanco Holding Company, Inc.	3,901,687
Amador, Bank of	3,893,938
Grange National Banc Corp.	3,740,773
McIntosh Bancshares, Inc.	3,554,029
Capital Directions, Inc.	3,299,000
American Bancorp, Inc.	3,064,579
North State National Bank	2,949,045
Damariscotta Bankshares, Inc.	2,764,458
Nicholas Financial, Inc.	2,619,554
Oak Valley Community Bank	2,444,893
National Union Bank of Kinderhook, The	2,120,418
SBC Financial Corporation	2,045,046
Turbotville National Bancorp, Inc.	1,910,614
Lancaster National Bank, The	1,883,824
GNB Financial Services, Inc.	1,656,955

This page left intentionally blank.

Over $100,000,000

Steelcase Inc. and Subsidiaries . . . . . . approx.	1,850,000,000
Kohler Co.	680,760,000
Benjamin Moore & Co.	676,954,350
Ash Grove Cement Company	445,495,120
Pennsylvania Manufacturers Corporation	405,913,216
International Speedway Corporation	403,579,440
Rand McNally	381,705,240
Roseville Telephone Company	372,885,600
North Pittsburgh Systems, Inc.	342,160,000
Cowles Media Company	326,286,596
Fisher Companies Inc.	325,219,365
Boswell (J.G.) Company	246,283,205
Kentucky River Coal Corporation	210,667,500
Watson Land Company	204,338,992
ConBraCo Industries, Inc.	203,155,150
Case, Pomeroy & Company, Inc.	200,489,850
Erie Family Life Insurance Company	185,850,000
Woodward Governor Company	184,226,962
Central Steel and Wire Company	165,555,000
CT Communications, Inc.	158,683,140
Pekin Life Insurance Company	154,000,000
Denver and Ephrata Telephone and Telegraph Co. . . .	139,604,172
Cimetrix Incorporated	134,914,113
Crowley Maritime Corporation	133,025,000
MLH Income Realty Partnership V	127,178,018
Vasco Corp.	121,176,763
North Carolina Railroad Company	117,795,425
Preformed Line Products Company	114,479,229
Mahoning National Bancorp, Inc.	108,675,000
Nichols (J.C.) Company	104,629,875
Smith Investment Company	104,487,579
Rochester & Pittsburgh Coal Company	100,839,543

$100,000,000 - $50,000,000

Anderson-Tully Company	98,940,000
Bovar Inc.	97,479,361
Broadway Bancshares Inc.	95,123,424
Labor Ready, Inc.	92,596,345
Shenandoah Telecommunications Company	92,138,620
Papnet of Ohio, Inc.	86,400,000
Carolina Mills, Inc.	80,512,766
Mid-Plains Telephone, Inc.	79,318,400
Kiewit Royalty Trust	78,958,950
Wailuku Agribusiness Co., Inc.	77,250,000
Ames National Corporation	76,758,108
Finch, Pruyn & Company, Incorporated	74,780,980
Maui Land & Pineapple Company, Inc.	73,682,125
USANA, Inc.	65,941,250
Kansas Bankers Surety Company	65,600,000
United Screw and Bolt Corporation	64,957,704
Hershey Creamery Company	64,822,098
Real Silk Investments, Incorporated	62,579,540
Computer Services, Inc.	61,881,960
West Virginia-American Water Company	61,756,382
Robroy Industries, Inc.	59,951,150
Davey Tree Expert Co.	59,567,533
Lakeland Bancorp, Inc.	59,256,911
Houlihan's Restaurant Group, Inc.	58,188,430
Buffalo Valley Telephone Company	57,995,433
Ragar Corp.	57,936,711
Pacific Capital Bancorp	57,857,303
Burnham Corporation	56,775,295

Harcourt Companies	56,446,250
Biochem International Inc.	56,388,954
DHB Capital Group Inc.	55,365,304
Sierra, Bank of the	55,273,680
Power Test Investors Limited Partnership	55,263,405
Polk (R.L.) & Co.	54,879,200
AM Communications, Inc.	53,796,016
Monarch Cement Company (The)	53,542,233
Premier Parks, Inc.	53,190,221

$49,999,999 - $25,000,000

Anchor Financial Corporation	48,913,961
Americold Corporation	48,609,340
United Coasts Corporation	48,389,148
LAACO, Ltd.	48,286,472
Best Lock Corporation	47,444,670
King Kullen Grocery Co., Inc.	45,455,508
Penns Woods Bancorp, Inc.	45,450,369
Jamaica Water Supply Company	43,906,494
Market America, Inc.	43,690,500
Fall River Gas Company	43,623,279
Bollinger Industries, Inc.	43,570,058
Penn Fuel Gas, Inc.	42,337,397
Makepeace (A.D.) Company	42,138,000
York Water Company (The)	42,066,684
Riviera Holdings Corporation	40,800,000
Carolina First BancShares, Inc.	40,697,178
Rhinelander Telecommunications, Inc.	39,878,483
Harriet & Henderson Yarns, Inc.	38,972,400
Central Investment Corporation	38,741,851
Investors Insurance Holding Corp.	38,633,442
Santa Maria, Bank of	38,475,654
Ellensburg Telephone Company	38,368,624
KnowledgeBroker, Inc.	37,627,865
Stonecutter Mills Corporation	37,193,760
Finance Company of Pennsylvania	36,946,313
Central Coast Bancorp	35,721,982
EMC Corporation	35,668,710
NCC Industries, Inc.	35,003,936
First Carolina Investors, Inc.	34,913,761
Alpha Pro Tech, Ltd.	34,844,478
Adrian Steel Company	34,751,394
First Real Estate Investment Trust of New Jersey . . .	34,705,283
Midland Bancorporation, Inc.	34,705,068
Emergent Group, Inc.	33,586,739
PAB Bankshares, Inc.	32,799,318
Equisure Financial Network Inc.	31,462,045
Pocahontas Bankshares Corporation	30,880,000
Real Goods Trading Corporation	30,589,766
Aircraft Income Partners, L.P.	30,440,015
Atlas Environmental, Inc.	30,073,750
Warwick Valley Telephone Co.	30,019,415
Iowa First Bancshares Corp.	30,000,000
Investment Properties Associates	29,421,600
Orrstown Financial Services, Inc.	29,305,890
Justiss Oil Co., Inc.	29,069,892
Polaris Aircraft Income Fund II	28,999,826
Lexington Telephone Company	28,807,800
Keweenaw Land Association, Limited	28,638,370
Bresler & Reiner, Inc.	28,624,693
IEA Income Fund XI, L.P.	28,437,327
McIntosh Bancshares, Inc.	27,802,650
Southside Bank	27,637,092
Chillicothe Telephone Company	27,624,102

Keller Manufacturing Company, Inc.	26,960,216
First of Michigan Capital Corporation	26,708,699
JMB Income Properties LTD X	26,250,875
Slippery Rock Financial Corporation	26,184,356
Community Bank of South Florida, Inc.	26,078,332
First National Community Bank	25,779,104
CUSA Technologies, Inc.	25,528,548
Tangram Enterprise Solutions, Inc.	25,423,783
Decker Manufacturing Corporation	25,199,831
Mercom, Inc.	25,132,065
Union National Bancorp, Inc.	25,020,000

$24,999,999 - $10,000,000

Southern Michigan Bancorp, Inc.	24,881,536
Northwest Bank & Trust Company	24,225,000
Allstar Inns, Inc.	24,125,395
Investors Heritage Life Insurance Company	24,091,665
Zions Cooperative Mercantile Institution	23,757,195
AFA Protective Systems, Inc.	23,280,158
Fifty Associates	22,999,025
Tidewater, Bank of	22,086,285
Heartland Group of Companies, Inc.	22,028,929
Central Bancorporation	21,813,148
Boston Sand & Gravel Co.	21,721,235
Immudyne, Inc.	21,675,016
Uniprop Manufac Housing Communities Income II	21,472,016
First National Bank Holding Company	21,100,000
Pan Smak Pizza Inc.	21,037,506
CBR Brewing Company, Inc.	20,560,033
Real Estate Income Partners III Ltd Partnership	20,521,482
Borel Bank and Trust Company	20,427,066
Santa Clara, Bank of	20,400,182
Telecomm Industries Corp.	20,284,243
Tehama County Bank	20,134,619
Datamark Holding, Inc.	20,110,029
Temco Service Industries, Inc.	20,012,472
Delaware Bancshares, Inc.	19,844,150
Lady Baltimore Foods, Inc.	19,733,688
Wisconsin Fuel & Light Company	19,599,400
Limoneira Company	19,459,464
Woodbury Telephone Company (The)	19,227,675
Tower Bancorp Inc.	19,056,825
Salient Systems, Inc.	19,047,820
Bulova Corporation	18,993,870
Union Bankshares, Inc.	18,856,818
Damson Birtcher Realty Income Fund II	18,668,740
Ramsay Managed Care, Inc.	18,348,218
Farmers National Bancorp, Inc.	18,186,691
Balcor Current Income Fund 85	17,978,310
Stearns & Lehman, Inc.	17,838,002
Bozzuto's Incorporated	17,820,891
Alaska Power & Telephone Company	17,803,304
San Joaquin Bank	17,764,200
Mendocino Brewing Company, Inc.	17,555,998
New York and Harlem Railroad Company	17,312,100
Berlin City Bank, The	17,091,270
Million Dollar Saloon, Inc.	16,899,970
Westminster Capital, Inc.	16,880,400
Louisville Bedding Company	16,788,894
Ravens Metal Products, Inc.	16,548,805
Cardinal Bancorp, Inc.	16,488,450
Commercial Bancshares Incorporated	16,129,162
Ogden Telephone Company	16,117,920

Interactive Gaming & Communications Corp.	15,757,295
BWC Financial Corp.	15,676,442
Acacia Research Corporation	15,620,212
Auric Corporation	15,474,666
Nicholas Financial, Inc.	15,187,038
Original Sixteen to One Mine, Inc.	15,141,297
Artesian Resources Corporation	15,043,663
Summit Bank Corporation	14,963,723
Brake Headquarters U.S.A., Inc.	14,860,457
Spring Street Brewing Company, Inc.	14,664,278
New Ulm Telecom, Inc.	14,581,496
Portland Brewing Company	14,485,779
Charter National Bancorp, Inc.	14,427,558
Sterling Sugars, Inc.	14,075,000
Waste Recovery, Inc.	13,622,541
Seaboard Automotive, Inc.	13,523,700
AVCOM International, Inc.	13,372,117
Blue Diamond Coal Company	13,326,885
Sea Pines Associates, Inc.	13,267,800
Lexington Precision Corporation	13,233,753
Batterymarch Trust	13,223,600
Golden Cycle Gold Corporation	13,182,159
Peckham Industries, Inc.	13,125,000
Health International, Inc.	13,092,268
Gateway Energy Corporation	13,068,041
Queen City Investments, Inc.	13,041,182
Portsmouth Square, Inc.	13,027,500
Glengate Apparel, Inc.	12,946,276
Tower Properties Company	12,826,050
Century Realty Trust	12,806,102
Northern Empire Bancshares	12,772,866
Workforce Systems Corp.	12,405,723
Franklin Credit Management Corp	12,383,766
Pharmaceutical Laboratories, Inc.	12,321,882
Coal Creek Mining and Manufacturing Company	12,316,409
Megatech Corporation	12,227,339
DK Investors Inc.	12,191,636
Image Systems Corporation	12,176,354
Summit Bancorp, Inc.	12,145,564
Pioneer Railcorp	12,072,400
American River Holdings	12,015,000
Goodheart-Willcox Company, Inc., (The)	11,986,350
Chesapeake Investors, Inc.	11,805,955
Peoples Savings Bank of Troy	11,691,147
PagePrompt USA	11,669,055
Snow Summit Ski Corporation	11,585,500
Bowles Fluidics Corporation	11,475,110
Sel-Drum International, Inc.	11,433,000
Central Coal & Coke Corporation	11,214,900
Market Guide, Inc.	11,186,566
National Properties Corporation	11,168,104
Mills Music Trust	11,108,480
Monroe Title Insurance Corporation	10,944,000
Amador, Bank of	10,870,627
Call Now, Inc.	10,865,550
Jetstream LP	10,817,961
Corning Natural Gas Corporation	10,810,000
Continental Health Affiliates, Inc.	10,805,481
Blue Ridge Real Estate Company	10,781,595
Kentucky Investors, Inc.	10,747,446
Grange National Banc Corp.	10,463,220
Industrial Services of America, Inc.	10,377,600
First International Bancorp	10,273,619

Lannett Company, Inc.	10,099,888
Guaranty Corporation	10,096,000
Thomas Edison Inns, Inc.	10,078,595
Du Art Film Laboratories, Inc.	10,056,486
Community Bank, The (NC)	10,010,220
Writer Corporation (The)	10,000,998

$9,999,999 - $7,500,000

Oakridge Energy, Inc.	9,908,448
Garden City Company	9,897,689
Exolon-Esk Company	9,794,138
Red Rose Collection, Inc.	9,613,542
Valley Fair Corporation (The)	9,569,378
Bay Area Bancshares	9,557,871
Capital Directions, Inc.	9,368,982
AMCOR Capital Corporation	9,298,159
Hosoi Garden Mortuary, Inc.	9,197,050
Crystal Mountain, Inc.	8,878,675
Bryan Steam Corporation	8,799,064
UCI Medical Affiliates, Inc.	8,770,410
TIF Instruments, Inc.	8,508,928
Capital Properties, Inc.	8,500,000
Moyco Technologies, Inc.	8,271,722
Scioto Downs, Inc.	8,191,796
Alden Lee Company, Inc.	7,968,600
Watson Industries Inc.	7,934,160
Petaluma, Bank of	7,864,332
Beaver Coal Company, Ltd.	7,861,448
Vicon Fiber Optics Corp.	7,840,198
American Public Life Insurance Company	7,785,195
Homasote Company	7,737,746
Central Sierra Bank	7,650,753
Damariscotta Bankshares, Inc.	7,513,920

$7,499,999 - $5,000,000

Prime Capital Corporation	7,490,289
Irex Corporation	7,337,556
Cornet Stores	7,273,155
Park-Lexington Company, Inc.	7,142,700
Cherokee Equity Corporation	6,956,898
GNB Financial Services, Inc.	6,926,000
Wichita National Life Insurance Company	6,925,743
Sivyer Steel Corporation	6,924,120
Discus Acquisition Corporation	6,909,932
Alaska Northwest Properties, Inc.	6,908,163
Mid Valley Bank	6,907,956
St. Louis Steel Casting Inc.	6,859,175
Tork, Inc.	6,833,840
Health Insurance Company of Vermont, Inc.	6,726,414
Hytek Microsystems, Inc.	6,691,192
Gloucester Bank & Trust Company	6,677,679
Dover Investments Corporation	6,582,900
Community Service Communications, Inc.	6,466,020
Pioneer Communications, Inc.	6,330,377
ATS Money Systems, Inc.	6,309,373
Optimumcare Corporation	6,302,092
Sims-Agricultural Products, Inc.	6,181,800
Oak Tree Medical Systems ,Inc.	6,140,907
Reo Plastics, Inc.	6,123,750
National Union Bank of Kinderhook, The	6,120,000
Cochrane Furniture Company, Inc.	6,057,623
American Atlantic Company	5,996,625
Burke-Parsons-Bowlby Corporation	5,957,423
Hilliard Corporation	5,880,884

Wundies Industries, Inc.	5,871,714
American Consolidated Laboratories, Inc.	5,812,374
Hammett (J.L.) Co.	5,702,700
North State National Bank	5,675,119
Virginia Hot Springs, Incorporated	5,561,205
TMS, Inc.	5,547,265
Broughton Foods Company	5,467,224
Chromaline Corporation	5,266,697
Arrow-Magnolia International, Inc.	5,209,200
Optical Specialties, Inc.	5,203,681
Bolt Technology Corporation	5,120,574
Avoca, Incorporated	5,090,965
Seven J Stock Farm, Inc.	5,078,500
American Industrial Loan Association	5,053,440
American Electromedics Corp.	5,038,883
Accuhealth, Inc.	5,037,500

$4,999,999 - $2,500,000

Zevex International, Inc.	4,957,549
Biddeford and Saco Water Company	4,933,836
Fairbanco Holding Company, Inc.	4,891,924
All For A Dollar, Inc.	4,865,133
Avesis Incorporated	4,849,750
Pay-O-Matic Corp.	4,813,020
George Risk Industries, Inc.	4,758,878
Mid-State Raceway, Inc.	4,757,334
Empire Gas Corporation	4,739,871
World Wide Limited	4,731,840
Hydraulic Press Brick Company	4,728,276
Sportsman's Guide, Inc. (The)	4,667,167
RWC, Incorporated	4,659,602
Ophthalmic Publishing Company	4,657,052
Naturade, Inc.	4,594,614
Puroflow Incorporated	4,578,521
Lamcor, Incorporated	4,534,412
Oak Valley Community Bank	4,404,589
Radva Corporation	4,351,011
Continental Resources, Inc.	4,291,170
CMP Industries, Inc.	4,261,824
Benthos, Inc.	4,228,027
Washington Life Insurance Company of America . . .	4,125,000
Cagy Industries, Inc.	4,040,695
SBC Financial Corporation	4,039,200
Mt. Carmel Public Utility Co.	4,000,000
Southland National Insurance Corporation	3,944,635
Turbotville National Bancorp, Inc.	3,906,000
Sierra Monitor Corporation	3,905,217
Sound One Corporation	3,797,006
Latshaw Enterprises, Inc.	3,764,813
Indiana Natural Gas Corporation	3,747,755
Reserve Petroleum Company (The)	3,729,734
Cardiac Control Systems, Inc.	3,692,752
Prab, Inc.	3,654,047
Micropac Industries, Inc.	3,627,151
Tremont Advisors, Inc.	3,613,790
Amelco Corporation	3,608,855
Citizens' Electric Company	3,585,972
Audio Communications Network, Inc.	3,522,799
Westwood Incorporated	3,507,708
Southern Scottish Inns, Inc.	3,483,699
Boonton Electronics Corporation	3,475,223
Biloxi Marsh Lands Corporation	3,465,520
B.B. Walker Company	3,453,070

Network Data Processing Corporation	3,394,152
Pace Medical, Inc.	3,380,850
Stein Industries, Inc.	3,311,572
Logan Clay Products Company	3,306,699
Mod U Kraf Homes, Inc.	3,302,596
Firecom, Inc.	3,211,544
Meteor Industries, Inc.	3,182,258
RF Industries, LTD	3,173,184
Limco Del Mar, Ltd.	3,163,050
Shopsmith, Inc.	3,158,934
Congress Rotisserie, Inc.	3,128,496
Cloverleaf Kennel Club	3,128,496
Detroit Legal News Company	3,066,320
National Stock Yards Company	3,031,034
California Almond Investors I	3,019,750
Carco Electronics	3,012,825
Old Fashion Foods, Inc.	2,979,441
Christian Brothers, Inc.	2,964,803
Radio Frequency Company, Inc.	2,955,631
Florafax International, Inc.	2,885,437
Reflectix, Inc.	2,832,245
Rudy's Restaurant Group, Inc.	2,816,000
Genetic Laboratories Wound Care, Inc.	2,768,059
Westbrook-Thompson Agency	2,752,650
Ojai Oil Company	2,738,862
Prevent Products, Inc.	2,737,500
Polyplastex United, Inc.	2,737,148
American Bancorp, Inc.	2,700,000
Farm Fish, Inc.	2,688,605
Carc, Inc.	2,680,000
Pacific Northwest Development Corporation	2,627,000
Life Insurance Company of Alabama	2,600,496
Solid Controls, Inc.	2,596,911
Technology 80 Inc.	2,545,522

Under $2,500,000

CompuDyne Corporation	2,414,478
International American Homes, Inc.	2,397,468
CSM Environmental Systems, Inc.	2,375,426
Mexco Energy Corporation	2,346,458
York Corrugating Co.	2,323,094
Watchdog Patrols, Inc.	2,192,940
Buck Hill Falls Company	2,169,342
Auto-Graphics, Inc.	2,125,299
Michigan Rivet Corporation	2,075,206
Tech Electro Industries, Inc.	2,041,126
Columbia Water Company	2,016,000
Lancaster National Bank, The	2,002,500
Ridgewood Properties, Inc.	1,984,769
Belle Isle Net Profit Units	1,961,000
Utz Engineering, Inc.	1,960,000
Fairmount Chemical Co., Inc.	1,907,359
HIA, Inc.	1,888,091
Crown City Plating Co.	1,885,223
Alleghany Pharmacal Corporation	1,872,596
Information Analysis Incorporated	1,868,212
Xedar Corporation	1,837,224
LogiMetrics, Inc.	1,802,179
Steritek, Inc.	1,793,143
Inmark Enterprises, Inc.	1,792,245
Winthrop Partners 81 LTD Partnership	1,756,375
Momed Holding Co.	1,680,135
Northfield Precision Instrument Corporation	1,639,659

Troy Mills, Inc.	1,615,866
Bismarck Hotel Company	1,486,520
Telebyte Technology, Inc.	1,411,472
Lake Charles Naval Stores Co., Inc.	1,408,680
Viskon-Aire Corporation	1,394,883
North Coast Life Insurance Co.	1,375,530
Danbury Industrial Corporation	1,371,075
Great Lakes Realty Corp.	1,330,826
Citizens Growth Properties	1,319,004
Connohio, Inc.	1,316,946
California-Michigan Land and Water Company	1,302,600
Ainslie Corporation	1,243,950
California Orchard Company	1,237,644
Henry County Plywood Corporation	1,212,058
Big Sky Transportation Co.	1,167,609
Chambersburg Engineering Company	1,167,100
Daedalus Enterprises, Inc.	1,158,554
Sarnia Corporation	1,143,136
Esco Transportation Co.	1,125,456
M.H. Rhodes, Inc.	1,114,295
Cable Link, Inc.	1,104,535
Ross Industries, Inc.	1,067,538
Universal Metals & Machinery, Inc.	1,054,620
Components Specialties, Inc.	1,004,089
Mortgage Oil Company	943,690
Pocono Hotels Corporation	939,499
Hamburg Industries, Inc.	921,803
Goddard Industries, Inc.	894,434
Scientific Industries, Inc.	875,813
Cass County Iron Company	852,872
Fireplace Manufacturers, Incorporated	781,550
Transnational Industries, Inc.	752,190
Standard Electronics, Inc.	742,415
Hunter Manufacturing Corp.	728,203
Bonal International, Inc.	720,326
Precision Optics Incorporated	690,929
Bell National Corporation	686,805
Walker International Industries, Inc.	655,778
Premis Corporation	647,674
Medical Advisory Systems, Inc.	610,709
Wright (G.F.) Steel & Wire Company	602,000
Networks Electronic Corp.	542,715
Phil-Good Products Incorporated	530,421
Meda, Inc.	515,011
Del Paint Corporation	490,853
American Consumers, Inc.	463,722
Terre Aux Boeufs Land Co., Inc.	437,500
Randall Bearings, Inc.	386,297
Tel-Instrument Electronics Corp.	304,723
Pennate Corporation	282,048
Dale System, Inc.	238,550
Sutter Basin Corporation, Ltd.	128,774
Standard Industries, Inc.	190,880

Under 10	
Chambersburg Engineering Company	0.68
Lake Charles Naval Stores Co., Inc.	0.81
Michigan Rivet Corporation	1.27
North Coast Life Insurance Co.	1.39
Premis Corporation	1.39
Hunter Manufacturing Corp.	1.43
Fireplace Manufacturers, Incorporated	1.69
TNR Technical, Inc.	1.95
Goddard Industries, Inc.	2.10
Shopsmith, Inc.	2.13
Firecom, Inc.	2.13
International American Homes, Inc.	2.20
Medical Advisory Systems, Inc.	2.29
Hilliard Corporation	2.63
Bolt Technology Corporation	2.71
American Consumers, Inc.	2.78
American Bancorp, Inc.	2.80
Stein Industries, Inc.	2.82
Continental Resources, Inc.	2.87
Finch, Pruyn & Company, Incorporated	2.89
First Carolina Investors, Inc.	3.04
Rudy's Restaurant Group, Inc.	3.08
Alleghany Pharmacal Corporation	3.13
Finance Company of Pennsylvania	3.27
Life Insurance Company of Alabama	3.44
Cardiac Control Systems, Inc.	3.48
Crown City Plating Co.	3.57
Amelco Corporation	3.57
Blue Diamond Coal Company	3.59
Phil-Good Products Incorporated	3.61
TIF Instruments, Inc.	3.80
Stonecutter Mills Corporation	3.88
George Risk Industries, Inc.	3.89
York Corrugating Co.	3.90
Lancaster National Bank, The	3.99
Network Data Processing Corporation	4.05
Hydraulic Press Brick Company	4.13
Bonal International, Inc.	4.14
Florafax International, Inc.	4.17
St. Louis Steel Casting Inc.	4.18
Westbrook-Thompson Agency	4.20
Southland National Insurance Corporation	4.23
Burke-Parsons-Bowlby Corporation	4.39
Technology 80 Inc.	4.41
Belle Isle Net Profit Units	4.42
Real Silk Investments, Incorporated	4.46
Components Specialties, Inc.	4.52
Bresler & Reiner, Inc.	4.70
Batterymarch Trust	4.75
Scientific Industries, Inc.	4.82
Utz Engineering, Inc.	5.00
Ainslie Corporation	5.00
Jamaica Water Supply Company	5.01
First International Bancorp	5.08
Prab, Inc.	5.11
Latshaw Enterprises, Inc.	5.17
Puroflow Incorporated	5.26
Smith Investment Company	5.33
Fairbanco Holding Company, Inc.	5.33
Farm Fish, Inc.	5.56
Limco Del Mar, Ltd.	5.77
Audio Communications Network, Inc.	5.81

Pioneer Communications, Inc.	5.82
Polaris Aircraft Income Fund II	5.84
Charter National Bancorp, Inc.	5.85
Exolon-Esk Company	5.91
Turbotville National Bancorp, Inc.	5.99
HIA, Inc.	6.00
Ross Industries, Inc.	6.00
Investment Properties Associates	6.14
Union Bankshares, Inc.	6.16
Auric Corporation	6.27
Reserve Petroleum Company (The)	6.27
Lexington Precision Corporation	6.39
New Ulm Telecom, Inc.	6.47
Gloucester Bank & Trust Company	6.52
Sterling Sugars, Inc.	6.62
Keller Manufacturing Company, Inc.	6.64
LAACO, Ltd.	6.72
Riviera Holdings Corporation	6.75
World Wide Limited	6.78
Universal Metals & Machinery, Inc.	6.82
Monarch Cement Company (The)	6.98
Winthrop Partners 81 LTD Partnership	6.98
Crowley Maritime Corporation	7.03
First National Community Bank	7.07
Power Test Investors Limited Partnership	7.08
Mid Valley Bank	7.11
Peoples Savings Bank of Troy	7.12
Central Sierra Bank	7.18
Northern Empire Bancshares	7.24
Bulova Corporation	7.25
American River Holdings	7.31
Southern Scottish Inns, Inc.	7.33
Berlin City Bank, The	7.36
Arrow-Magnolia International, Inc.	7.38
Community Service Communications, Inc.	7.40
First National Bank Holding Company	7.40
Wundies Industries, Inc.	7.42
Burnham Corporation	7.45
Du Art Film Laboratories, Inc.	7.47
Santa Clara, Bank of	7.53
Citizens' Electric Company	7.54
Goodheart-Willcox Company, Inc., (The)	7.59
Sutter Basin Corporation, Ltd.	7.64
Fairmount Chemical Co., Inc.	7.67
Community Bank, The (NC)	7.69
Broadway Bancshares Inc.	7.69
Oak Valley Community Bank	7.71
Reo Plastics, Inc.	7.72
CBR Brewing Company, Inc.	7.79
Community Bank of South Florida, Inc.	7.82
Reflectix, Inc.	7.83
Midland Bancorporation, Inc.	7.89
Tower Bancorp Inc.	7.94
Petaluma, Bank of	7.95
Detroit Legal News Company	7.97
Summit Bank Corporation	7.99
North State National Bank	8.01
Randall Bearings, Inc.	8.12
Writer Corporation (The)	8.12
Radva Corporation	8.15
Louisville Bedding Company	8.21
TMS, Inc.	8.25
Bowles Fluidics Corporation	8.27

Cass County Iron Company	8.29
Chillicothe Telephone Company	8.33
Immudyne, Inc.	8.33
Micropac Industries, Inc.	8.33
Penn Fuel Gas, Inc.	8.35
Kentucky River Coal Corporation	8.37
Farmers National Bancorp, Inc.	8.43
Tower Properties Company	8.48
Garden City Company	8.49
CMP Industries, Inc.	8.52
Summit Bancorp, Inc.	8.55
Cloverleaf Kennel Club	8.70
Mod U Kraf Homes, Inc.	8.70
Central Bancorporation	8.74
Watson Industries Inc.	8.79
Grange National Banc Corp.	8.80
Telecomm Industries Corp.	8.80
Ash Grove Cement Company	8.84
Bay Area Bancshares	8.88
Capital Directions, Inc.	8.92
Borel Bank and Trust Company	8.92
Fifty Associates	8.93
AMCOR Capital Corporation	9.00
Mills Music Trust	9.05
United Screw and Bolt Corporation	9.16
Ojai Oil Company	9.18
Pacific Northwest Development Corporation	9.21
Bovar Inc.	9.23
Ravens Metal Products, Inc.	9.26
Irex Corporation	9.27
Decker Manufacturing Corporation	9.29
Amador, Bank of	9.34
West Virginia-American Water Company	9.36
Boston Sand & Gravel Co.	9.41
Alaska Power & Telephone Company	9.41
Cherokee Equity Corporation	9.42
Bryan Steam Corporation	9.48
Central Investment Corporation	9.49
Cardinal Bancorp, Inc.	9.49
Carolina First BancShares, Inc.	9.55
Central Steel and Wire Company	9.55
Commercial Bancshares Incorporated	9.56
Walker International Industries, Inc.	9.57
Davey Tree Expert Co.	9.71
Iowa First Bancshares Corp.	9.78
Snow Summit Ski Corporation	9.79
Damariscotta Bankshares, Inc.	9.85

10 - 20

Homasote Company	10.00
Xedar Corporation	10.00
Central Coast Bancorp	10.02
Chesapeake Investors, Inc.	10.06
SBC Financial Corporation	10.15
BWC Financial Corp.	10.21
Southern Michigan Bancorp, Inc.	10.28
Bozzuto's Incorporated	10.35
Erie Family Life Insurance Company	10.39
Adrian Steel Company	10.41
Kiewit Royalty Trust	10.42
Chromaline Corporation	10.48
Slippery Rock Financial Corporation	10.48
Acacia Research Corporation	10.49

Woodbury Telephone Company (The)	10.50
LogiMetrics, Inc.	10.50
King Kullen Grocery Co., Inc.	10.51
Delaware Bancshares, Inc.	10.60
Ellensburg Telephone Company	10.63
National Union Bank of Kinderhook, The	10.63
Queen City Investments, Inc.	10.74
Mahoning National Bancorp, Inc.	10.78
Kansas Bankers Surety Company	10.90
Park-Lexington Company, Inc.	10.98
Tehama County Bank	11.28
PAB Bankshares, Inc.	11.30
Preformed Line Products Company	11.37
IEA Income Fund XI, L.P.	11.38
GNB Financial Services, Inc.	11.50
Indiana Natural Gas Corporation	11.53
San Joaquin Bank	11.54
Lady Baltimore Foods, Inc.	11.55
Penns Woods Bancorp, Inc.	11.72
Auto-Graphics, Inc.	11.75
MLH Income Realty Partnership V	11.80
Hershey Creamery Company	11.90
Carc, Inc.	11.90
Pacific Capital Bancorp	11.95
Northwest Bank & Trust Company	11.97
Ogden Telephone Company	12.00
Wisconsin Fuel & Light Company	12.08
Tidewater, Bank of	12.13
Santa Maria, Bank of	12.17
CT Communications, Inc.	12.24
Lakeland Bancorp, Inc.	12.25
AVCOM International, Inc.	12.27
Ames National Corporation	12.36
California Almond Investors I	12.36
Biddeford and Saco Water Company	12.43
First Real Estate Investment Trust of New Jersey	12.43
National Properties Corporation	12.44
Steritek, Inc.	12.50
New York and Harlem Railroad Company	12.52
NCC Industries, Inc.	12.70
Westminster Capital, Inc.	12.71
Pocahontas Bankshares Corporation	12.81
Southside Bank	12.86
Naturade, Inc.	12.93
Coal Creek Mining and Manufacturing Company	12.97
Bell National Corporation	13.00
Anderson-Tully Company	13.14
Hytek Microsystems, Inc.	13.22
North Carolina Railroad Company	13.29
Telebyte Technology, Inc.	13.43
Biochem International Inc.	13.47
Precision Optics Incorporated	13.50
Central Coal & Coke Corporation	13.51
Houlihan's Restaurant Group, Inc.	13.53
Accuhealth, Inc.	13.54
Case, Pomeroy & Company, Inc.	13.65
Pekin Life Insurance Company	13.67
Artesian Resources Corporation	13.68
Anchor Financial Corporation	13.85
Makepeace (A.D.) Company	13.91
Union National Bancorp, Inc.	13.95
Warwick Valley Telephone Co.	14.06
Tork, Inc.	14.08

Pace Medical, Inc.	14.29
Fisher Companies Inc.	14.33
Cowles Media Company	14.60
Industrial Services of America, Inc.	14.63
Orrstown Financial Services, Inc.	14.63
Old Fashion Foods, Inc.	14.65
Century Realty Trust	14.70
Esco Transportation Co.	14.71
Shenandoah Telecommunications Company	14.76
Moyco Technologies, Inc.	15.00
Portsmouth Square, Inc.	15.10
Zevex International, Inc.	15.13
Boonton Electronics Corporation	15.24
California Orchard Company	15.27
Lamcor, Incorporated	15.36
Woodward Governor Company	15.45
Vicon Fiber Optics Corp.	15.67
Sierra, Bank of the	15.69
EMC Corporation	15.71
Dover Investments Corporation	15.79
Virginia Hot Springs, Incorporated	16.10
Watchdog Patrols, Inc.	16.38
Monroe Title Insurance Corporation	17.21
Great Lakes Realty Corp.	17.29
Corning Natural Gas Corporation	17.41
Pennsylvania Manufacturers Corporation	17.53
AFA Protective Systems, Inc.	17.54
Keweenaw Land Association, Limited	17.79
RF Industries, LTD	17.86
York Water Company (The)	18.03
American Public Life Insurance Company	18.06
Computer Services, Inc.	18.29
ATS Money Systems, Inc.	18.33
Citizens Growth Properties	18.55
Kentucky Investors, Inc.	18.66
Boswell (J.G.) Company	18.73
Sel-Drum International, Inc.	18.75
Watson Land Company	18.98
Tel-Instrument Electronics Corp.	19.00
Temco Service Industries, Inc.	19.05
ConBraCo Industries, Inc.	19.21
Rhinelander Telecommunications, Inc.	19.74
Genetic Laboratories Wound Care, Inc.	19.83

Over 20

Roseville Telephone Company	20.16
Original Sixteen to One Mine, Inc.	20.52
Meteor Industries, Inc.	20.83
American Electromedics Corp.	21.50
International Speedway Corporation	21.97
Big Sky Transportation Co.	22.00
Mexco Energy Corporation	22.22
Benjamin Moore & Co.	22.41
Aircraft Income Partners, L.P.	22.61
McIntosh Bancshares, Inc.	22.83
Mid-Plains Telephone, Inc.	23.12
Hosoi Garden Mortuary, Inc.	23.81
Workforce Systems Corp.	25.00
Performance Nutrition, Inc.	25.00
USANA, Inc.	25.61
Robroy Industries, Inc.	25.74
Buffalo Valley Telephone Company	25.80
Sims-Agricultural Products, Inc.	26.09

Investors Heritage Life Insurance Company	26.23
Benthos, Inc.	26.39
Pioneer Railcorp	26.90
Fall River Gas Company	26.92
Pharmaceutical Laboratories, Inc.	27.00
Oak Tree Medical Systems ,Inc.	27.27
Rand McNally	30.21
Seven J Stock Farm, Inc.	31.82
North Pittsburgh Systems, Inc.	32.04
Avoca, Incorporated	32.26
Mercom, Inc.	32.81
Nicholas Financial, Inc.	32.88
Market Guide, Inc.	34.00
Wichita National Life Insurance Company	34.38
Health Insurance Company of Vermont, Inc.	35.00
Image Systems Corporation	35.13
Heartland Group of Companies, Inc.	35.25
CUSA Technologies, Inc.	37.50
JMB Income Properties LTD X	39.33
Equisure Financial Network Inc.	40.00
Uniprop Manufactured Housing Communities Income II	40.63
Zions Cooperative Mercantile Institution	40.74
Denver and Ephrata Telephone and Telegraph Co.	41.62
Terre Aux Boeufs Land Co., Inc.	42.55
Labor Ready, Inc.	46.32
Emergent Group, Inc.	52.50
Portland Brewing Company	53.85
Radio Frequency Company, Inc.	54.17
Market America, Inc.	54.75
Seaboard Automotive, Inc.	55.00
Washington Life Insurance Company of America	55.00
Health International, Inc.	59.38
Avesis Incorporated	59.50
Danbury Industrial Corporation	64.33
Lannett Company, Inc.	64.67
Tech Electro Industries, Inc.	71.00
Interactive Gaming & Communications Corp.	72.00
Prevent Products, Inc.	75.00
National Stock Yards Company	77.22
Congress Rotisserie, Inc.	80.00
Million Dollar Saloon, Inc.	84.50
Cagy Industries, Inc.	84.50
Mendocino Brewing Company, Inc.	94.50
Capital Properties, Inc.	106.25
Stearns & Lehman, Inc.	108.33
AM Communications, Inc.	109.50
Hamburg Industries, Inc.	112.50
Franklin Credit Management Corp	112.50
DK Investors Inc.	129.63
Salient Systems, Inc.	137.50
Papnet of Ohio, Inc.	192.86
Ragar Corp.	194.00
DHB Capital Group Inc.	200.00
First of Michigan Capital Corporation	237.50
Cochrane Furniture Company, Inc.	260.00
CSM Environmental Systems, Inc.	269.00
Valley Fair Corporation (The)	371.43
Biloxi Marsh Lands Corporation	500.00
Standard Electronics, Inc.	500.00
Mt. Carmel Public Utility Co.	500.00
Bollinger Industries, Inc.	587.50
Real Goods Trading Corporation	894.00

This page left intentionally blank.

Under 50 %	
Hunter Manufacturing Corp.	15.56
Universal Metals & Machinery, Inc.	24.01
Amelco Corporation	24.44
Troy Mills, Inc.	25.30
Polaris Aircraft Income Fund II	26.97
Michigan Rivet Corporation	28.24
National Stock Yards Company	28.92
Bulova Corporation	29.02
Crown City Plating Co.	30.81
Ross Industries, Inc.	32.43
Latshaw Enterprises, Inc.	32.48
Dover Investments Corporation	33.62
Goddard Industries, Inc.	33.85
Southern Scottish Inns, Inc.	34.80
Continental Resources, Inc.	34.83
York Corrugating Co.	36.15
Cornet Stores	36.23
Cherokee Equity Corporation	37.36
All For A Dollar, Inc.	37.84
Ainslie Corporation	38.64
Precision Optics Incorporated	38.76
American Bancorp, Inc.	39.79
B.B. Walker Company	40.73
Chambersburg Engineering Company	41.17
Old Fashion Foods, Inc.	41.20
Finch, Pruyn & Company, Incorporated	41.66
Standard Electronics, Inc.	42.09
Bell National Corporation	43.33
M.H. Rhodes, Inc.	43.44
International American Homes, Inc.	43.56
Kentucky Investors, Inc.	43.61
World Wide Limited	43.72
Fireplace Manufacturers, Incorporated	44.00
Lake Charles Naval Stores Co., Inc.	45.65
Life Insurance Company of Alabama	45.69
Logan Clay Products Company	45.98
Zions Cooperative Mercantile Institution	46.53
Phil-Good Products Incorporated	46.86
Medical Advisory Systems, Inc.	47.06
Southland National Insurance Corporation	47.24
Pacific Northwest Development Corporation	47.51
Daedalus Enterprises, Inc.	48.49
Transnational Industries, Inc.	48.54
TNR Technical, Inc.	48.58
Bresler & Reiner, Inc.	49.37
Rochester & Pittsburgh Coal Company	49.64

50 - 100 %	
Aircraft Income Partners, L.P.	50.14
Danbury Industrial Corporation	50.48
Valley Fair Corporation (The)	51.81
Cochrane Furniture Company, Inc.	52.61
Henry County Plywood Corporation	52.85
Hilliard Corporation	52.95
Blue Diamond Coal Company	53.17
Watson Industries Inc.	56.58
Stein Industries, Inc.	56.74
JMB Income Properties LTD X	56.81
Lancaster National Bank, The	57.08
Jetstream LP	59.09
Real Estate Income Partners III Ltd Partnership	59.30
Citizens Growth Properties	59.52

Walker International Industries, Inc.	59.62
Boston Sand & Gravel Co.	59.82
Scientific Industries, Inc.	59.89
TIF Instruments, Inc.	61.09
Harriet & Henderson Yarns, Inc.	61.10
Tower Properties Company	62.16
Investors Heritage Life Insurance Company	62.31
Randall Bearings, Inc.	63.11
Central Investment Corporation	63.18
Detroit Legal News Company	63.40
Reserve Petroleum Company (The)	63.65
Capital Properties, Inc.	63.67
Terre Aux Boeufs Land Co., Inc.	64.18
Turbotville National Bancorp, Inc.	64.51
Jamaica Water Supply Company	64.65
Damson Birtcher Realty Income Fund II	65.29
Mt. Carmel Public Utility Co.	65.49
Watchdog Patrols, Inc.	65.50
Technology 80 Inc.	65.99
Real Silk Investments, Incorporated	66.08
Citizens' Electric Company	67.32
Justiss Oil Co., Inc.	67.54
Telebyte Technology, Inc.	67.63
LogiMetrics, Inc.	67.74
Penn Fuel Gas, Inc.	68.20
Pocono Hotels Corporation	68.55
Burke-Parsons-Bowlby Corporation	69.38
Pennsylvania Manufacturers Corporation	69.53
California Almond Investors I	70.07
Alleghany Pharmacal Corporation	70.85
Stonecutter Mills Corporation	70.90
Micropac Industries, Inc.	71.43
Mod U Kraf Homes, Inc.	72.07
Bryan Steam Corporation	72.08
Charter National Bancorp, Inc.	72.12
First Carolina Investors, Inc.	72.27
Irex Corporation	72.80
Westminster Capital, Inc.	72.97
Alaska Northwest Properties, Inc.	73.64
Viskon-Aire Corporation	74.20
St. Louis Steel Casting Inc.	74.24
CMP Industries, Inc.	74.30
Chesapeake Investors, Inc.	74.46
Broughton Foods Company	74.61
Cagy Industries, Inc.	74.61
Crowley Maritime Corporation	74.85
Utz Engineering, Inc.	75.47
Louisville Bedding Company	75.68
Sutter Basin Corporation, Ltd.	76.81
Health Insurance Company of Vermont, Inc.	77.29
Farm Fish, Inc.	77.52
Rudy's Restaurant Group, Inc.	77.67
Components Specialties, Inc.	77.74
Batterymarch Trust	78.44
Del Paint Corporation	78.57
Cass County Iron Company	78.80
Hydraulic Press Brick Company	79.07
DK Investors Inc.	79.52
Writer Corporation (The)	79.77
Lady Baltimore Foods, Inc.	80.04
American Public Life Insurance Company	80.40
Fairbanco Holding Company, Inc.	80.43
Investors Insurance Holding Corp.	81.26

101 - 150 %

151 - 200 %

Over 200 %

Optimumcare Corporation 412.90
Puroflow Incorporated 416.67
Mendocino Brewing Company, Inc. 417.68
American Electromedics Corp. 430.00
DHB Capital Group Inc. 465.12
International Speedway Corporation 473.37
Hytek Microsystems, Inc. 476.00
Seaboard Automotive, Inc. 491.07
Original Sixteen to One Mine, Inc. 501.16
Ravens Metal Products, Inc. 507.14
Naturade, Inc. 517.14
Biochem International Inc. 559.74
Avesis Incorporated 566.67
Industrial Services of America, Inc. 588.24
Market Guide, Inc. 618.18
Stearns & Lehman, Inc. 619.05
Immudyne, Inc. 625.00
Million Dollar Saloon, Inc. 662.75
North Pittsburgh Systems, Inc. 664.23
Cowles Media Company 673.35
Nicholas Financial, Inc. 674.36
Real Goods Trading Corporation 677.27
North Carolina Railroad Company 685.79
Health International, Inc. 766.13
Image Systems Corporation 780.56
Pharmaceutical Laboratories, Inc. 810.00
Portsmouth Square, Inc. 859.90
Prevent Products, Inc. 1000.00
USANA, Inc. 1009.60
Power Test Investors Limited Partnership 1076.00
Glengate Apparel, Inc. 1084.20
Alden Lee Company, Inc. 1111.10
Salient Systems, Inc. 1122.50
Alpha Pro Tech, Ltd. 1166.70
Watson Land Company 1181.80
Labor Ready, Inc. 1202.30
Papnet of Ohio, Inc. 1421.10
Spring Street Brewing Company, Inc. 1423.10
Cimetrix Incorporated 1491.80
Ragar Corp. 1616.70
Telecomm Industries Corp. 1700.00
Megatech Corporation 1710.50
Pennate Corporation 1950.00
Datamark Holding, Inc. 2016.70
Golden Cycle Gold Corporation 2539.40
Market America, Inc. 4380.00
Interactive Gaming & Communications Corp. 4800.00
American Consolidated Laboratories, Inc. 6550.00
KnowledgeBroker, Inc. 6766.70
Vasco Corp. 8587.50

Based on the years presented

Over 25 %	
Market America, Inc.	285.22
Computer Integration, Corp.	177.68
DHB Capital Group Inc.	166.83
Lannett Company, Inc.	159.55
USANA, Inc.	152.84
Performance Nutrition, Inc.	135.00
Labor Ready, Inc.	123.75
Golden Cycle Gold Corporation	123.61
Versatech Industries, Inc.	106.77
Industrial Services of America, Inc.	104.65
KnowledgeBroker, Inc.	95.29
Equisure Financial Network Inc.	90.46
Nicholas Financial, Inc.	88.55
Pan Smak Pizza Inc.	84.38
Immudyne, Inc.	84.02
Premis Corporation	77.51
Annie's Homegrown, Inc.	74.40
Telecomm Industries Corp. approx.	73.00
Portland Brewing Company	70.57
Stearns & Lehman, Inc.	61.81
International American Homes, Inc.	59.81
Bollinger Industries, Inc.	59.67
AVCOM International, Inc.	55.90
Oak Valley Community Bank	54.88
Workforce Systems Corp.	53.52
Limoneira Company	52.61
Finance Company of Pennsylvania	50.98
Image Systems Corporation	50.78
Optical Specialties, Inc.	50.32
Franklin Credit Management Corp	50.21
Emergent Group, Inc.	45.50
Tremont Advisors, Inc.	42.51
Gateway Energy Corporation	42.41
Ravens Metal Products, Inc.	42.13
Call Now, Inc.	40.33
Pioneer Railcorp	39.40
Real Goods Trading Corporation	38.37
Optimumcare Corporation	37.64
AM Communications, Inc.	37.16
First Carolina Investors, Inc.	36.55
Central Coal & Coke Corporation	36.44
Network Data Processing Corporation	36.39
Cimetrix Incorporated	36.11
Biochem International Inc.	35.88
ATS Money Systems, Inc.	35.34
Premier Parks, Inc.	33.52
Sportsman's Guide, Inc. (The)	33.12
RWC, Incorporated	33.02
Stonecutter Mills Corporation	33.00
Writer Corporation (The)	32.90
Century Realty Trust	30.89
Lamcor, Incorporated	30.89
American River Holdings	30.56
Brake Headquarters U.S.A., Inc.	30.46
Limco Del Mar, Ltd.	30.06
Zevex International, Inc.	29.58
UCI Medical Affiliates, Inc.	29.26
Market Guide, Inc.	29.25
Prevent Products, Inc.	28.87

St. Louis Steel Casting Inc.	28.15
Pharmaceutical Laboratories, Inc.	27.72
Adrian Steel Company	26.88
Components Specialties, Inc.	26.68
Spring Street Brewing Company, Inc.	26.68
Bovar Inc.	26.31
AMCOR Capital Corporation	25.95
TMS, Inc.	25.73
American Consolidated Laboratories, Inc.	25.13

25 - 10 %	
PAB Bankshares, Inc.	24.91
Health International, Inc.	24.73
Foremost Industries, Inc.	24.37
Petaluma, Bank of	24.11
Tehama County Bank	23.71
RF Industries, LTD	23.38
Computer Services, Inc.	23.19
Hilliard Corporation	23.19
Continental Resources, Inc.	22.98
First International Bancorp	22.54
Original Sixteen to One Mine, Inc.	22.21
Summit Bank Corporation	21.97
PagePrompt USA	21.95
Mexco Energy Corporation	21.91
Xedar Corporation	21.04
Firecom, Inc.	20.86
Waste Recovery, Inc.	20.52
Stein Industries, Inc.	20.45
Cable Link, Inc.	19.50
Bowles Fluidics Corporation	19.46
Smith Investment Company	19.41
Bonal International, Inc.	19.37
Ross Industries, Inc.	19.37
Beaver Coal Company, Ltd.	19.21
Phil-Good Products Incorporated	19.18
George Risk Industries, Inc.	19.14
Fireplace Manufacturers, Incorporated	18.92
TIF Instruments, Inc.	18.72
Anchor Financial Corporation	18.66
Central Bancorporation	18.62
Investors Insurance Holding Corp.	18.57
Vasco Corp.	18.19
Technology 80 Inc.	17.88
Terre Aux Boeufs Land Co., Inc.	17.88
Pacific Northwest Development Corporation	17.84
Columbian Rope Company	17.66
Keweenaw Land Association, Limited	17.60
Chromaline Corporation	17.52
Case, Pomeroy & Company, Inc.	17.39
Lexington Precision Corporation	17.19
Alleghany Pharmacal Corporation	17.11
Alpha Pro Tech, Ltd.	17.06
Sims-Agricultural Products, Inc.	16.90
HIA, Inc.	16.56
Hytek Microsystems, Inc.	16.35
International Speedway Corporation	16.19
Central Coast Bancorp	16.18
First Real Estate Investment Trust of New Jersey	16.11
Southern Scottish Inns, Inc. approx.	16.00
Meteor Industries, Inc.	15.87
TNR Technical, Inc.	15.80
EMC Corporation	15.64

10 - 0 %

Hammett (J.L.) Co.	7.48
Reflectix, Inc.	7.46
Scientific Industries, Inc.	7.32
Megatech Corporation	7.31
Fall River Gas Company	7.27
Reserve Petroleum Company (The)	7.18
Bay Area Bancshares	7.15
Cherokee Equity Corporation	6.99
ConBraCo Industries, Inc.	6.92
Summit Bancorp, Inc.	6.77
Henry County Plywood Corporation	6.65
Watchdog Patrols, Inc.	6.62
Midland Bancorporation, Inc.	6.56
United Coasts Corporation	6.51
Hayward Industries, Inc.	6.50
Pace Medical, Inc.	6.48
Kentucky River Coal Corporation	6.35
Park-Lexington Company, Inc.	6.32
Mortgage Oil Company	6.26
Mahoning National Bancorp, Inc.	6.22
Datamark Holding, Inc.	6.20
Southside Bank	6.17
Hunter Manufacturing Corp.	6.08
Roseville Telephone Company	6.04
Tower Bancorp Inc.	6.04
Burnham Corporation	6.02
Pioneer Communications, Inc.	5.95
Sel-Drum International, Inc.	5.95
NCC Industries, Inc.	5.73
Power Test Investors Limited Partnership	5.70
Corning Natural Gas Corporation	5.68
Central Investment Corporation	5.64
Lady Baltimore Foods, Inc.	5.55
Exolon-Esk Company	5.52
Life Insurance Company of Alabama	5.44
West Virginia-American Water Company	5.38
York Water Company (The)	5.34
Mercom, Inc.	5.28
Hershey Creamery Company	5.22
Polk (R.L) & Co.	5.22
Genetic Laboratories Wound Care, Inc.	5.21
Capital Properties, Inc.	5.20
Benjamin Moore & Co.	5.18
GNB Financial Services, Inc.	5.12
Telebyte Technology, Inc.	5.02
Crown City Plating Co.	4.91
Buffalo Valley Telephone Company	4.83
Union National Bancorp, Inc.	4.72
Mendocino Brewing Company, Inc.	4.68
Zions Cooperative Mercantile Institution	4.67
Lexington Telephone Company	4.66
Viskon-Aire Corporation	4.65
AFA Protective Systems, Inc.	4.58
Garden City Company	4.52
Blue Diamond Coal Company	4.51
Ellensburg Telephone Company	4.49
Rochester & Pittsburgh Coal Company	4.40
Crystal Mountain, Inc.	4.28
Northfield Precision Instrument Corporation	4.25
Woodbury Telephone Company (The)	4.22
Information Analysis Incorporated	4.16
National Union Bank of Kinderhook, The	4.10
Radio Frequency Company, Inc.	4.08
Pay-O-Matic Corp.	3.94
SBC Financial Corporation	3.91
Community Bank of South Florida, Inc.	3.88
Queen City Investments, Inc.	3.68
Momed Holding Co.	3.59
LAACO, Ltd.	3.58
Carc, Inc.	3.56
Biddeford and Saco Water Company	3.42
Boston Sand & Gravel Co.	3.40
Bulova Corporation	3.39
CompuDyne Corporation	3.38
York Corrugating Co.	3.29
Louisville Bedding Company	3.26
Iowa First Bancshares Corp.	3.25
Connohio, Inc.	3.21
Balcor Current Income Fund 85	3.17
Broughton Foods Company	3.10
Salient Systems, Inc.	3.09
Great Lakes Realty Corp.	3.04
Bryan Steam Corporation	2.99
Homasote Company	2.95
Ogden Telephone Company	2.79
Makepeace (A.D.) Company	2.75
MLH Income Realty Partnership V	2.75
Jamaica Water Supply Company	2.67
Valley Fair Corporation (The)	2.62
Chambersburg Engineering Company	2.61
Davey Tree Expert Co.	2.59
Farmers National Bancorp, Inc.	2.58
Delaware Bancshares, Inc.	2.54
North Coast Life Insurance Co.	2.50
Ames National Corporation	2.48
Portsmouth Square, Inc.	2.47
Broadway Bancshares Inc.	2.29
Snow Summit Ski Corporation	2.27
LogiMetrics, Inc.	2.25
Cardinal Bancorp, Inc.	2.20
Irex Corporation	2.20
Seaboard Automotive, Inc.	2.16
Central Sierra Bank	2.14
CMP Industries, Inc.	2.12
Buck Hill Falls Company	2.07
Puroflow Incorporated	1.92
Kiewit Royalty Trust	1.78
Troy Mills, Inc.	1.74
Seven J Stock Farm, Inc.	1.71
First of Michigan Capital Corporation	1.64
Logan Clay Products Company	1.61
Boonton Electronics Corporation	1.46
Walker International Industries, Inc.	1.43
Lipe-Rollway Corporation	1.39
Hamburg Industries, Inc.	1.33
Standard Industries, Inc.	1.29
Barnstable Holding Co., Inc.	1.28
Cornet Stores	1.28
CSM Environmental Systems, Inc.	1.24
Tork, Inc.	1.22
Thomas Edison Inns, Inc.	1.19
Crowley Maritime Corporation	1.06
Scioto Downs, Inc.	1.00
Auto-Graphics, Inc.	0.88
Rudy's Restaurant Group, Inc.	0.65
Heartland Group of Companies, Inc.	0.63

Merchants' National Properties, Inc.	0.63
Capital Directions, Inc.	0.60
Accuhealth, Inc.	0.57
California Orchard Company	0.54
Woodward Governor Company	0.49
Ojai Oil Company	0.40
Turbotville National Bancorp, Inc.	0.36
Penn Fuel Gas, Inc.	0.35
Houlihan's Restaurant Group, Inc.	0.14
Pocono Hotels Corporation	0.12
Del Paint Corporation	0.10
Wisconsin Fuel & Light Company	0.09
King Kullen Grocery Co., Inc.	0.04
Florafax International, Inc.	0.02

0 - (10) %

Mt. Carmel Public Utility Co.	-0.02
Real Estate Income Partners III Ltd Partnership	-0.11
Bresler & Reiner, Inc.	-0.26
Watson Land Company	-0.28
Wailuku Agribusiness Co., Inc.	-0.40
Cagy Industries, Inc.	-0.50
Northwest Bank & Trust Company	-0.51
Radva Corporation	-0.62
Citizens' Electric Company	-0.63
Red Rose Collection, Inc.	-0.67
Wundies Industries, Inc.	-0.81
Bell National Corporation	-0.88
Boswell (J.G.) Company	-1.03
Ophthalmic Publishing Company	-1.06
Medical Advisory Systems, Inc.	-1.08
Investors Heritage Life Insurance Company	-1.10
Kentucky Investors, Inc.	-1.16
Mid-State Raceway, Inc.	-1.41
Alaska Northwest Properties, Inc.	-1.67
Big Sky Transportation Co.	-1.77
National Stock Yards Company	-1.78
Fifty Associates	-1.85
Union Pump Company	-2.01
World Wide Limited	-2.10
Cloverleaf Kennel Club	-2.16
Detroit Legal News Company	-2.25
Investment Properties Associates	-2.37
Sea Pines Associates, Inc.	-2.43
California Almond Investors I	-2.58
Damson Birtcher Realty Income Fund II	-2.58
Danbury Industrial Corporation	-2.88
American Consumers, Inc.	-2.93
B.B. Walker Company	-3.23
Carolina Mills Inc.	-3.36
Wright (G.F.) Steel & Wire Company	-3.68
Harriet & Henderson Yarns, Inc.	-3.70
Blue Ridge Real Estate Company	-3.75
Interactive Gaming & Communications Corp.	-3.87
Dale System, Inc.	-3.95
Nichols (J.C.) Company	-4.09
Sarnia Corporation	-4.89
Maui Land & Pineapple Company, Inc.	-5.13
Steritek, Inc.	-5.20
Chesapeake Investors, Inc.	-5.26
Precision Optics Incorporated	-5.28
Tel-Instrument Electronics Corp.	-5.34
IEA Income Fund XI, L.P.	-5.71

Kansas Bankers Surety Company	-6.12
All For A Dollar, Inc.	-6.81
Christian Brothers, Inc.	-7.29
Old Fashion Foods, Inc.	-7.38
American Industrial Loan Association	-7.81
Belle Isle Net Profit Units	-7.82
Benthos, Inc.	-8.32
M.H. Rhodes, Inc.	-8.85
Transnational Industries, Inc.	-8.86
Radio Frequency Company, Inc.	-9.16
Tangram Enterprise Solutions, Inc.	-9.23
Coal Creek Mining and Manufacturing Company	-9.35

(10) - (25) %

Networks Electronic Corp.	-10.74
Standard Electronics, Inc.	-10.84
Pennsylvania Manufacturers Corporation	-10.91
Sutter Basin Corporation, Ltd.	-11.12
Ragar Corp.	-11.46
Washington Life Insurance Company of America	-11.53
Community Service Communications, Inc.	-11.56
Avoca, Incorporated	-11.62
JMB Income Properties LTD X	-11.71
Empire Gas Corporation	-12.67
Prime Capital Corporation	-13.02
Jetstream LP	-13.67
Carco Electronics	-14.15
Aircraft Income Partners, L.P.	-14.43
Daedalus Enterprises, Inc.	-15.47
Biloxi Marsh Lands Corporation	-15.99
Monroe Title Insurance Corporation	-17.59
Justiss Oil Co., Inc.	-17.63
American Atlantic Company	-18.46
Ridgewood Properties, Inc.	-19.56
Continental Health Affiliates, Inc.	-21.93
Inmark Enterprises, Inc.	-23.59
Pennate Corporation	-23.60

Over (25) %

Shopsmith, Inc.	-30.69
Citizens Growth Properties	-33.30
Discus Acquisition Corporation	-34.20
Winthrop Partners 81 LTD Partnership	-34.56
Polyplastex United, Inc.	-47.77
Oakridge Energy, Inc.	-49.35
New York and Harlem Railroad Company	-66.15

Based on the years presented

Over 25 %	
Premis Corporation	548.94
Guaranty Corporation	520.04
Prab, Inc.	350.34
Naturade, Inc.	315.72
Walker International Industries, Inc.	312.05
Computer Integration, Corp.	303.20
Firecom, Inc.	252.97
Gateway Energy Corporation	236.47
First Carolina Investors, Inc.	235.75
Columbian Rope Company	220.26
Million Dollar Saloon, Inc.	198.46
Northfield Precision Instrument Corporation	187.43
Sterling Sugars, Inc.	185.51
Workforce Systems Corp.	169.93
Nicholas Financial, Inc.	167.22
First International Bancorp	165.78
Washington Life Insurance Company of America	161.73
Ainslie Corporation	149.35
Bovar Inc.	141.03
Fireplace Manufacturers, Incorporated	136.01
Labor Ready, Inc.	134.88
Prevent Products, Inc.	125.47
Industrial Services of America, Inc.	117.98
Tech Electro Industries, Inc.	109.94
Immudyne, Inc.	109.74
Blue Diamond Coal Company	108.89
Ash Grove Cement Company	106.36
Heartland Group of Companies, Inc.	100.73
AM Communications, Inc.	100.26
Tremont Advisors, Inc.	100.01
Components Specialties, Inc.	98.62
Torrington Water Company	96.44
Mexco Energy Corporation	91.76
Auto-Graphics, Inc.	91.73
Stearns & Lehman, Inc.	88.04
Anderson-Tully Company	84.61
AMCOR Capital Corporation	83.84
Gloucester Bank & Trust Company	81.25
Pace Medical, Inc.	81.17
Bresler & Reiner, Inc.	80.38
Community Bank, The (NC)	79.97
Network Data Processing Corporation	78.75
Tower Properties Company	77.03
Central Steel and Wire Company	76.27
TIF Instruments, Inc.	75.05
RF Industries, LTD	72.26
Portland Brewing Company	70.87
Bolt Technology Corporation	69.37
Country-Wide Insurance Company	68.58
ATS Money Systems, Inc.	65.55
Burke-Parsons-Bowlby Corporation	64.06
Lexington Precision Corporation	63.97
TNR Technical, Inc.	63.03
Southern Scottish Inns, Inc. approx.	63.00
Arrow-Magnolia International, Inc.	62.99
Limco Del Mar, Ltd.	62.65
Equisure Financial Network Inc.	60.66
Peoples Savings Bank of Troy	60.33
Fairmount Chemical Co., Inc.	60.26

Biochem International Inc.	58.91
Audio Communications Network, Inc.	58.68
Chromaline Corporation	57.38
Riviera Holdings Corporation	55.99
Real Goods Trading Corporation	55.33
Lancaster National Bank, The	54.64
Hytek Microsystems, Inc.	53.88
Rudy's Restaurant Group, Inc.	53.56
Reserve Petroleum Company (The)	53.09
Finance Company of Pennsylvania	52.17
Oak Valley Community Bank	51.34
George Risk Industries, Inc.	50.99
Oak Tree Medical Systems ,Inc.	50.17
St. Louis Steel Casting Inc.	49.89
Sims-Agricultural Products, Inc.	49.65
Hunter Manufacturing Corp.	49.59
Market Guide, Inc.	47.47
Momed Holding Co.	45.67
Boston Sand & Gravel Co.	44.89
Exolon-Esk Company	44.53
Hydraulic Press Brick Company	44.52
Continental Resources, Inc.	43.97
Smith Investment Company	43.12
Alleghany Pharmacal Corporation	41.68
Carolina First BancShares, Inc.	40.84
Borel Bank and Trust Company	39.73
Ravens Metal Products, Inc.	39.09
Sound One Corporation	37.16
Pioneer Railcorp	36.82
All For A Dollar, Inc.	36.59
Midland Bancorporation, Inc.	36.28
Keller Manufacturing Company, Inc.	35.78
Cherokee Equity Corporation	34.96
TMS, Inc.	33.94
Monarch Cement Company (The)	33.85
Fisher Companies Inc.	33.10
Stonecutter Mills Corporation	33.00
EMC Corporation	32.28
Homasote Company	32.13
Image Systems Corporation	31.67
PAB Bankshares, Inc.	31.27
Rand McNally	30.76
Phil-Good Products Incorporated	30.42
Cowles Media Company	30.04
American River Holdings	29.36
Bonal International, Inc.	29.34
Goodheart-Willcox Company, Inc., (The)	28.98
Cardinal Bancorp, Inc.	28.71
Finch, Pruyn & Company, Incorporated	27.51
Summit Bank Corporation	27.19
Penn Fuel Gas, Inc.	27.02
Beaver Coal Company, Ltd.	26.94
Anchor Financial Corporation	26.54
Petaluma, Bank of	26.41
Ogden Telephone Company	26.17
BWC Financial Corp.	25.99
Zions Cooperative Mercantile Institution	25.96
Technology 80 Inc.	25.37
Micropac Industries, Inc.	25.34
Fifty Associates	25.32

25 - 10 %	
Congress Rotisserie, Inc.	24.83
San Joaquin Bank	24.32
Bell National Corporation	24.29
Lakeland Bancorp, Inc.	24.09
Case, Pomeroy & Company, Inc.	23.15
Lamcor, Incorporated	23.11
Louisville Bedding Company	22.41
Universal Metals & Machinery, Inc.	22.31
North State National Bank	21.63
Southern Michigan Bancorp, Inc.	21.28
Mahoning National Bancorp, Inc.	21.14
Life Insurance Company of Alabama	20.74
First National Community Bank	20.57
SBC Financial Corporation	20.51
Central Coast Bancorp	20.50
Kohler Co.	20.29
Farm Fish, Inc.	20.15
Irex Corporation	20.11
Bay Area Bancshares	19.99
Pacific Capital Bancorp	19.89
Bowles Fluidics Corporation	19.68
Du Art Film Laboratories, Inc.	19.28
Central Coal & Coke Corporation	19.26
CT Communications, Inc.	19.13
Decker Manufacturing Corporation	19.05
Summit Bancorp, Inc.	18.86
Zevex International, Inc.	18.56
Original Sixteen to One Mine, Inc.	18.36
Health International, Inc.	18.07
First National Bank Holding Company	18.02
Goddard Industries, Inc.	17.92
Tehama County Bank	17.77
United Screw and Bolt Corporation	17.64
Union Bankshares, Inc.	17.57
West Virginia-American Water Company	17.50
King Kullen Grocery Co., Inc.	17.47
Fairbanco Holding Company, Inc.	17.31
Santa Maria, Bank of	17.31
Columbia Water Company	17.25
Amador, Bank of	17.21
Randall Bearings, Inc.	16.69
Artesian Resources Corporation	16.38
International Speedway Corporation	16.23
Northern Empire Bancshares	16.10
Southland National Insurance Corporation	16.07
DHB Capital Group Inc.	15.86
Shenandoah Telecommunications Company	15.77
Adrian Steel Company	15.54
Warwick Valley Telephone Co.	15.38
Tower Bancorp Inc.	15.24
Moyco Technologies, Inc.	15.20
Grange National Banc Corp.	14.89
Crown City Plating Co.	14.80
Westbrook-Thompson Agency	14.72
Alaska Power & Telephone Company	14.70
Emergent Group, Inc.	14.47
Reo Plastics, Inc.	14.46
Mod U Kraf Homes, Inc.	14.43
Berlin City Bank, The	14.28
Pacific Northwest Development Corporation	14.28
Bryan Steam Corporation	14.00

Central Bancorporation	13.64
Orrstown Financial Services, Inc.	13.45
Hayward Industries, Inc.	13.42
Penns Woods Bancorp, Inc.	13.37
Amelco Corporation	13.19
McIntosh Bancshares, Inc.	12.97
Denver and Ephrata Telephone and Telegraph Co.	12.92
Preformed Line Products Company	12.84
Santa Clara, Bank of	12.76
Community Bank of South Florida, Inc.	12.75
Tidewater, Bank of	12.72
Mortgage Oil Company	12.62
Dover Investments Corporation	12.36
Hosoi Garden Mortuary, Inc.	12.31
Pocahontas Bankshares Corporation	12.29
Sierra, Bank of the	12.17
Crowley Maritime Corporation	12.15
Central Sierra Bank	12.01
Slippery Rock Financial Corporation	12.01
Mendocino Brewing Company, Inc.	11.82
Community Service Communications, Inc.	11.77
Computer Services, Inc.	11.41
Commercial Bancshares Incorporated	11.25
Pekin Life Insurance Company	11.15
Old Fashion Foods, Inc.	11.12
Jamaica Water Supply Company	11.02
Mid Valley Bank	10.88
Charter National Bancorp, Inc.	10.82
Power Test Investors Limited Partnership	10.72
Iowa First Bancshares Corp.	10.67
Carc, Inc.	10.63
National Union Bank of Kinderhook, The	10.49
Mills Music Trust	10.40
GNB Financial Services, Inc.	10.31
Garden City Company	10.14
Scientific Industries, Inc.	10.02

10 - 0 %	
North Pittsburgh Systems, Inc.	9.84
Damariscotta Bankshares, Inc.	9.65
New Ulm Telecom, Inc.	9.53
Southside Bank	9.46
Auric Corporation	9.08
Hershey Creamery Company	9.06
Cass County Iron Company	8.77
Precision Optics Incorporated	8.69
Pioneer Communications, Inc.	8.67
Mid-Plains Telephone, Inc.	8.52
Burnham Corporation	8.32
Genetic Laboratories Wound Care, Inc.	8.17
Ojai Oil Company	8.16
Capital Directions, Inc.	7.94
CMP Industries, Inc.	7.66
AVCOM International, Inc.	7.30
National Properties Corporation	7.20
Kentucky River Coal Corporation	7.01
Esco Transportation Co.	7.01
Corning Natural Gas Corporation	6.93
Broadway Bancshares Inc.	6.47
Tork, Inc.	6.45
Woodbury Telephone Company (The)	6.28
Park-Lexington Company, Inc.	6.22
Xedar Corporation	6.14

American Bancorp, Inc.	5.98
Ames National Corporation	5.91
Latshaw Enterprises, Inc.	5.68
Pharmaceutical Laboratories, Inc.	5.63
Sel-Drum International, Inc.	5.30
Seaboard Automotive, Inc.	5.13
Delaware Bancshares, Inc.	5.05
Biddeford and Saco Water Company	4.72
First Real Estate Investment Trust of New Jersey	4.55
Ellensburg Telephone Company	4.27
Erie Family Life Insurance Company	4.00
United Coasts Corporation	3.94
Utz Engineering, Inc.	3.72
LAACO, Ltd.	3.48
Turbotville National Bancorp, Inc.	3.27
Lexington Telephone Company	2.65
Davey Tree Expert Co.	2.58
Kentucky Investors, Inc.	2.48
Northwest Bank & Trust Company	2.46
Bulova Corporation	2.32
York Water Company (The)	2.17
Kiewit Royalty Trust	1.91
Portsmouth Square, Inc.	1.75
AFA Protective Systems, Inc.	1.46
Investment Properties Associates	1.39
Farmers National Bancorp, Inc.	1.03
Citizens' Electric Company	0.84
Lady Baltimore Foods, Inc.	0.63
Detroit Legal News Company	0.43
Snow Summit Ski Corporation	0.13
Investors Heritage Life Insurance Company	0.07

0 - (10) %

Indiana Natural Gas Corporation	-0.54
Century Realty Trust	-0.80
Keweenaw Land Association, Limited	-0.86
American Consumers, Inc.	-0.87
Avoca, Incorporated	-1.56
Merchants' National Properties, Inc.	-1.65
Reflectix, Inc.	-1.70
Radva Corporation	-2.11
Chillicothe Telephone Company	-2.15
Kansas Bankers Surety Company	-2.23
HIA, Inc.	-2.73
Wisconsin Fuel & Light Company	-3.26
Fall River Gas Company	-3.88
Union National Bancorp, Inc.	-4.01
Wailuku Agribusiness Co., Inc.	-4.03
Rhinelander Telecommunications, Inc.	-4.24
Bozzuto's Incorporated	-4.40
Makepeace (A.D.) Company	-4.55
Stein Industries, Inc.	-4.84
Watson Land Company	-4.99
Sierra Monitor Corporation	-4.99
Buffalo Valley Telephone Company	-5.02
Radio Frequency Company, Inc.	-5.25
Roseville Telephone Company	-5.34
Chesapeake Investors, Inc.	-5.65
Benjamin Moore & Co.	-5.69
Cloverleaf Kennel Club	-6.17
MLH Income Realty Partnership V	-7.14
California Orchard Company	-7.15
Belle Isle Net Profit Units	-7.82

LogiMetrics, Inc.	-7.84
Benthos, Inc.	-8.12
Boswell (J.G.) Company	-9.08
IEA Income Fund XI, L.P.	-9.25
Seven J Stock Farm, Inc.	-9.83
Telebyte Technology, Inc.	-9.99

(10) - (25) %

Queen City Investments, Inc.	-10.20
Connohio, Inc.	-11.08
Central Investment Corporation	-11.57
World Wide Limited	-12.20
Versatech Industries, Inc.	-12.53
Ragar Corp.	-12.68
Ross Industries, Inc.	-13.36
Pennsylvania Manufacturers Corporation	-16.04
Woodward Governor Company	-16.10
ConBraCo Industries, Inc.	-16.20
Coal Creek Mining and Manufacturing Company	-17.27
Salient Systems, Inc.	-17.71
Wundies Industries, Inc.	-20.85
California Almond Investors I	-21.66
Wichita National Life Insurance Company	-22.78
Barnstable Holding Co., Inc.	-23.06
Vicon Fiber Optics Corp.	-23.06
Cochrane Furniture Company, Inc.	-23.63
Watchdog Patrols, Inc.	-23.78
NCC Industries, Inc.	-23.78
American Industrial Loan Association	-24.68

Over (25) %

Union Pump Company	-25.12
Pay-O-Matic Corp.	-26.01
Robroy Industries, Inc.	-27.85
Carolina Mills Inc.	-28.89
Interactive Gaming & Communications Corp.	-29.98
Medical Advisory Systems, Inc.	-30.17
New York and Harlem Railroad Company	-30.44
Real Goods Trading Company	-30.52
American Public Life Insurance Company	-32.35
Temco Service Industries, Inc.	-32.98
Franklin Credit Management Corp	-33.34
American Electromedics Corp.	-34.34
Westwood Incorporated	-34.78
Winthrop Partners 81 LTD Partnership	-34.89
Health Insurance Company of Vermont, Inc.	-35.62
Tel-Instrument Electronics Corp.	-35.64
Foremost Industries, Inc.	-36.56
Big Sky Transportation Co.	-41.23
Citizens Growth Properties	-41.87
Pocono Hotels Corporation	-43.13
Houlihan's Restaurant Group, Inc.	-44.90
Writer Corporation (The)	-46.37
Biloxi Marsh Lands Corporation	-46.54
Cagy Industries, Inc.	-46.82
Monroe Title Insurance Corporation	-53.05
National Stock Yards Company	-53.94
Danbury Industrial Corporation	-54.02
American Atlantic Company	-54.03
Steritek, Inc.	-57.51
Bollinger Industries, Inc.	-58.80
International American Homes, Inc.	-59.25
Capital Properties, Inc.	-59.59

Over 5,000	
MLH Income Realty Partnership V	80,362
Polaris Aircraft Income Fund II	16,426
Aircraft Income Partners, L.P.	15,100
JMB Income Properties LTD X	14,815
Pocono Hotels Corporation	9,812
Roseville Telephone Company	9,600
Real Estate Income Partners III Ltd Partnership	7,498
Jetstream LP	7,482
Southland National Insurance Corporation	5,146

5,000 - 1,001	
Uniprop Manufactured Housing Communities Income II	4,850
Real Goods Trading Corporation	4,216
Ravens Metal Products, Inc.	4,100
Century Realty Trust	3,700
Portland Brewing Company	3,500
Gateway Energy Corporation	3,500
Carolina First BancShares, Inc.	3,300
IEA Income Fund XI, L.P.	3,288
Shenandoah Telecommunications Company	3,226
Tangram Enterprise Solutions, Inc.	3,000
Investors Heritage Life Insurance Company	2,941
North Pittsburgh Systems, Inc.	2,845
International American Homes, Inc.	2,790
Kentucky Investors, Inc.	2,593
Mendocino Brewing Company, Inc.	2,534
Franklin Credit Management Corp	2,382
Mid-Plains Telephone, Inc.	2,281
Florafax International, Inc.	2,200
Woodward Governor Company	2,179
CompuDyne Corporation	2,011
George Risk Industries, Inc.	2,000
HIA, Inc.	2,000
Mercom, Inc.	1,934
Lakeland Bancorp, Inc.	1,921
Farm Fish, Inc.	1,866
Anchor Financial Corporation	1,807
Benjamin Moore & Co.	1,775
Scioto Downs, Inc.	1,759
Pioneer Railcorp	1,753
Hosoi Garden Mortuary, Inc.	1,752
Davey Tree Expert Co.	1,632
TNR Technical, Inc.	1,622
Pacific Capital Bancorp	1,602
Mexco Energy Corporation	1,514
Bulova Corporation	1,500
Mahoning National Bancorp, Inc.	1,470
Reserve Petroleum Company (The)	1,445
Orrstown Financial Services, Inc.	1,422
Community Bank, The (NC)	1,412
Berlin City Bank, The	1,400
CT Communications, Inc.	1,375
International Speedway Corporation	1,373
Naturade, Inc.	1,368
Shopsmith, Inc.	1,321
Commercial Bancshares Incorporated	1,300
Meda, Inc.	1,300
Emergent Group, Inc.	1,296
Golden Cycle Gold Corporation	1,263
Winthrop Partners 81 LTD Partnership	1,258
B.B. Walker Company	1,229
York Water Company (The)	1,217

AMCOR Capital Corporation	1,211
Cimetrix Incorporated	1,200
Pekin Life Insurance Company	1,174
Prab, Inc.	1,168
Valley Fair Corporation (The)	1,161
Erie Family Life Insurance Company	1,145
Genetic Laboratories Wound Care, Inc.	1,100
Lexington Precision Corporation	1,100
Southside Bank	1,100
Northwest Bank & Trust Company	1,100
AM Communications, Inc.	1,090
Westminster Capital, Inc.	1,085
Bell National Corporation	1,075
Santa Maria, Bank of	1,071
PAB Bankshares, Inc.	1,042
Vicon Fiber Optics Corp.	1,038

1,000 - 500	
Pioneer Communications, Inc.	1,000
American Consolidated Laboratories, Inc.	1,000
Bryan Steam Corporation	996
Scientific Industries, Inc.	994
Networks Electronic Corp.	984
Market Guide, Inc.	981
Tehama County Bank	975
Fireplace Manufacturers, Incorporated	956
American Consumers, Inc.	951
Goddard Industries, Inc.	938
Tidewater, Bank of	921
Central Coast Bancorp	886
First National Community Bank	886
National Properties Corporation	882
Heartland Group of Companies	870
Fall River Gas Company	866
Seven J Stock Farm, Inc.	866
Tower Bancorp Inc.	865
New Ulm Telecom, Inc.	864
Premier Parks, Inc.	862
Blue Ridge Real Estate Company	855
Avoca, Incorporated	848
Denver and Ephrata Telephone and Telegraph Co.	845
Megatech Corporation	839
Datamark Holding, Inc.	834
Sarnia Corporation	832
Kiewit Royalty Trust	802
Biochem International Inc.	800
DHB Capital Group Inc.	800
RF Industries, LTD	783
Dover Investments Corporation	777
Penns Woods Bancorp, Inc.	774
Artesian Resources Corporation	758
North Carolina Railroad Company	752
Rochester & Pittsburgh Coal Company	750
Optical Specialties, Inc.	750
Sterling Sugars, Inc.	745
Original Sixteen to One Mine, Inc.	731
TMS, Inc.	725
Alaska Northwest Properties, Inc.	724
Grange National Banc Corp.	720
Woodbury Telephone Company (The)	710
Boonton Electronics Corporation	709
Moyco Technologies, Inc.	701
Monarch Cement Company (The)	700

UCI Medical Affiliates, Inc.	698
Sea Pines Associates, Inc.	697
Allstar Inns, Inc.	692
Tel-Instrument Electronics Corp.	689
Farmers National Bancorp, Inc.	687
Oakridge Energy, Inc.	674
Petaluma, Bank of	672
M.H. Rhodes, Inc.	667
Labor Ready, Inc.	655
Investment Properties Associates	648
Micropac Industries, Inc.	645
Borel Bank and Trust Company	638
Cardiac Control Systems, Inc.	628
Alpha Pro Tech, Ltd.	625
Audio Communications Network, Inc.	618
Ramsay Managed Care, Inc.	615
Warwick Valley Telephone Co.	607
Peoples Savings Bank of Troy	604
Interactive Gaming & Communications Corp.	600
Power Test Investors Limited Partnership	593
Pocahontas Bankshares Corporation	593
First Carolina Investors, Inc.	590
Zevex International, Inc.	580
American Bancorp, Inc.	572
Tower Properties Company	571
Tech Electro Industries, Inc.	562
Mid-State Raceway, Inc.	555
Lannett Company, Inc.	554
Slippery Rock Financial Corporation	536
Carc, Inc.	536
KnowledgeBroker, Inc.	536
Brake Headquarters U.S.A., Inc.	531
Central Coal & Coke Corporation	530
BWC Financial Corp.	511
Health Insurance Company of Vermont, Inc.	510
Buck Hill Falls Company	509
Capital Properties, Inc.	507
Blue Diamond Coal Company	500

Under 500

AFA Protective Systems, Inc.
ATS Money Systems, Inc.
AVCOM International, Inc.
Acacia Research Corporation
Accuhealth, Inc.
Adrian Steel Company
Ainslie Corporation
Alaska Power & Telephone Company
Alden Lee Company, Inc.
All For A Dollar, Inc.
Alleghany Pharmacal Corporation
Amador, Bank of
Amelco Corporation
American Electromedics Corp.
American Public Life Insurance Company
American River Holdings
Americold Corporation
Ames National Corporation
Anderson-Tully Company
Arrow-Magnolia International, Inc.
Ash Grove Cement Company
Atlas Environmental, Inc.
Auric Corporation

Auto-Graphics, Inc.
Avesis Incorporated
Batterymarch Trust
Bay Area Bancshares
Belle Isle Net Profit Units
Benthos, Inc.
Best Lock Corporation
Biddeford and Saco Water Company
Biloxi Marsh Lands Corporation
Bismarck Hotel Company
Blue Fish Clothing, Inc.
Bollinger Industries, Inc.
Bolt Technology Corporation
Bonal International, Inc.
Boston Sand & Gravel Co.
Boswell (J.G.) Company
Bovar Inc.
Bowles Fluidics Corporation
Bozzuto's Incorporated
Bresler & Reiner, Inc.
Broadway Bancshares Inc.
Broughton Foods Company
Buffalo Valley Telephone Company
Burke-Parsons-Bowlby Corporation
Burnham Corporation
CBR Brewing Company, Inc.
CMP Industries, Inc.
CSM Environmental Systems, Inc.
CUSA Technologies, Inc.
Cable Link, Inc.
Cagy Industries, Inc.
California Orchard Company
Call Now, Inc.
Capital Directions, Inc.
Carco Electronics
Cardinal Bancorp, Inc.
Case, Pomeroy & Company, Inc.
Cass County Iron Company
Central Bancorporation
Central Investment Corporation
Central Sierra Bank
Central Steel and Wire Company
Chambersburg Engineering Company
Charter National Bancorp, Inc.
Cherokee Equity Corporation
Chesapeake Investors, Inc.
Chillicothe Telephone Company
Christian Brothers, Inc.
Chromaline Corporation
Citizens Growth Properties
Citizens' Electric Company
Cloverleaf Kennel Club
Coal Creek Mining and Manufacturing Company
Cochrane Furniture Company, Inc.
Community Bank of South Florida, Inc.
Community Service Communications, Inc.
Components Specialties, Inc.
Computer Integration, Corp.
Computer Services, Inc.
ConBraCo Industries, Inc.
Congress Rotisserie, Inc.
Connohio, Inc.
Continental Health Affiliates, Inc.

Premis Corporation
Prevent Products, Inc.
Prime Capital Corporation
Puroflow Incorporated
Queen City Investments, Inc.
RWC, Incorporated
Radio Frequency Company, Inc.
Radva Corporation
Ragar Corp.
Randall Bearings, Inc.
Real Silk Investments, Incorporated
Red Rose Collection, Inc.
Reflectix, Inc.
Reo Plastics, Inc.
Rhinelander Telecommunications, Inc.
Ridgewood Properties, Inc.
Riviera Holdings Corporation
Robroy Industries, Inc.
Rocky Mount Mills
Ross Industries, Inc.
Rudy's Restaurant Group, Inc.
SBC Financial Corporation
Salient Systems, Inc.
San Joaquin Bank
Santa Clara, Bank of
Seaboard Automotive, Inc.
Sel-Drum International, Inc.
Sierra Monitor Corporation
Sierra, Bank of the
Sims-Agricultural Products, Inc.
Smith Investment Company
Snow Summit Ski Corporation
Solid Controls, Inc.
Southern Michigan Bancorp, Inc.
Sportsman's Guide, Inc. (The)
Spring Street Brewing Company, Inc.
St. Louis Steel Casting Inc.
Standard Electronics, Inc.
Stearns & Lehman, Inc.
Stein Industries, Inc.
Steritek, Inc.
Stonecutter Mills Corporation
Summit Bancorp, Inc.
Summit Bank Corporation
Sutter Basin Corporation, Ltd.
TIF Instruments, Inc.
Technology 80 Inc.
Telebyte Technology, Inc.
Telecomm Industries Corp.
Temco Service Industries, Inc.
Terre Aux Boeufs Land Co., Inc.
Thomas Edison Inns, Inc.
Tork, Inc.
Transnational Industries, Inc.
Tremont Advisors, Inc.
Troy Mills, Inc.
Turbotville National Bancorp, Inc.
USANA, Inc.
Union Bankshares, Inc.
Union National Bancorp, Inc.
United Screw and Bolt Corporation
Universal Metals & Machinery, Inc.
Utz Engineering, Inc.

Vasco Corp.
Versatech Industries, Inc.
Virginia Hot Springs, Incorporated
Viskon-Aire Corporation
Washington Life Insurance Company of America
Waste Recovery, Inc.
Watchdog Patrols, Inc.
Watson Industries Inc.
Watson Land Company
West Virginia-American Water Company
Westbrook-Thompson Agency
Wichita National Life Insurance Company
Wisconsin Fuel & Light Company
Workforce Systems Corp.
World Wide Limited
Writer Corporation (The)
Wundies Industries, Inc.
Xedar Corporation
York Corrugating Co.

Notes

MAY WE HAVE YOUR FEEDBACK?

How is our coverage of:	Like	Dislike	Don't Care
Regular Companies	☐	☐	☐
Banks	☐	☐	☐
Partnerships	☐	☐	☐
Foreign Corporations	☐	☐	☐

Comments:

_____
_____
_____
_____
_____

HAVE WE OVERLOOKED YOUR COMPANY?

Please let us know and we will consider your company or a company that you know about for our next edition.

Company Name _____
Street Address _____
City _____ State _____ Zipcode_____
Telephone (____) _____ Country _____

Your Name / Relationship (If Any) _____

Comments:

_____
_____
_____

CAN WE PLACE YOUR ORDER?

Please send me ____ hard cover copies at $75 each (CA residents add 7.5 % sales tax)

Name _____ Title _____
Company Name _____
Street Address _____
City _____ State _____ Zipcode_____
Telephone (____) _____ Country _____

Check one:

☐   Check Enclosed
☐   Charge My Credit Card: ☐ Amex   ☐ VISA   ☐ MC   ☐ Discover

Account # _____ Signature_____

Mail us this card, or for faster service PHONE or FAX your order:

Telephone   (800) 932-2922 *OR* (510) 283-9993
Fax   (510) 283-9513

WINDOW TECH
MAIN POST OFFICE
2070 N BROADWAY
WALNUT CREEK CA 94596-9998
(510) 935-2611
MON thru FRI 8:30am to 5:00pm

NO POSTAGE
NECESSARY
IF MAILED
IN THE
UNITED STATES

BUSINESS REPLY MAIL

FIRST-CLASS MAIL PERMIT NO. 39 WALNUT CREEK CA

POSTAGE WILL BE PAID BY ADDRESSEE

WALKER'S MANUAL, LLC
3650 MT DIABLO BLVD., SUITE 240
LAFAYETTE, CA 94549-9957

WINDOW TECH
MAIN POST OFFICE
2070 N BROADWAY
WALNUT CREEK CA 94596-9998
(510) 935-2611
MON thru FRI 8:30am to 5:00pm

NO POSTAGE
NECESSARY
IF MAILED
IN THE
UNITED STATES

BUSINESS REPLY MAIL

FIRST-CLASS MAIL PERMIT NO. 39 WALNUT CREEK CA

POSTAGE WILL BE PAID BY ADDRESSEE

WALKER'S MANUAL, LLC
3650 MT DIABLO BLVD., SUITE 240
LAFAYETTE, CA 94549-9957

WINDOW TECH
MAIN POST OFFICE
2070 N BROADWAY
WALNUT CREEK CA 94596-9998
(510) 935-2611
MON thru FRI 8:30am to 5:00pm

NO POSTAGE
NECESSARY
IF MAILED
IN THE
UNITED STATES

BUSINESS REPLY MAIL

FIRST-CLASS MAIL PERMIT NO. 39 WALNUT CREEK CA

POSTAGE WILL BE PAID BY ADDRESSEE

WALKER'S MANUAL, LLC
3650 MT DIABLO BLVD., SUITE 240
LAFAYETTE, CA 94549-9957